DANGEROUS INSTINCTS

DANGEROUS INSTINCTS

How Gut Feelings Betray Us

Mary Ellen O'Toole, Ph.D.
and Alisa Bowman

Hudson Street Press

HUDSON STREET PRESS
Published by Penguin Group
Penguin Group (USA) Inc., 375 Hudson Street, New York, New York 10014, U.S.A. • Penguin Group (Canada), 90 Eglinton Avenue East, Suite 700, Toronto, Ontario, Canada M4P 2Y3 (a division of Pearson Penguin Canada Inc.) • Penguin Books Ltd., 80 Strand, London WC2R 0RL, England • Penguin Ireland, 25 St. Stephen's Green, Dublin 2, Ireland (a division of Penguin Books Ltd.) • Penguin Group (Australia), 250 Camberwell Road, Camberwell, Victoria 3124, Australia (a division of Pearson Australia Group Pty. Ltd.) • Penguin Books India Pvt. Ltd., 11 Community Centre, Panchsheel Park, New Delhi – 110 017, India • Penguin Books (NZ), 67 Apollo Drive, Rosedale, Auckland 0632, New Zealand (a division of Pearson New Zealand Ltd.) • Penguin Books (South Africa) (Pty.) Ltd., 24 Sturdee Avenue, Rosebank, Johannesburg 2196, South Africa

Penguin Books Ltd., Registered Offices: 80 Strand, London WC2R 0RL, England

First published by Hudson Street Press, a member of Penguin Group (USA) Inc.

First Printing, October 2011
10 9 8 7 6 5 4 3 2 1

LIBRARY OF CONGRESS CATALOGING-IN-PUBLICATION DATA

O'Toole, Mary Ellen.
Dangerous instincts : how gut feelings lead us astray / Mary Ellen O'Toole and Alisa Bowman.
p. cm.
Includes bibliographical references and index.
ISBN 978-1-59463-083-5 (alk. paper)
1. Criminal behavior, Prediction of. 2. Criminal psychology. I. Bowman, Alisa. II. Title.
HV8073.5.O86 2011
364.3--dc22 2011015663

Printed in the United States of America

PUBLISHER'S NOTE
Penguin is committed to publishing works of quality and integrity. In that spirit, we are proud to offer this book to our readers; however, the story, the experiences, and the words are the authors' alone. The views expressed in this book are those of the authors and not those of Penguin or the FBI. Some names and identifying characteristics have been changed to protect the privacy of the individuals involved.

While the author has made every effort to provide accurate telephone numbers and Internet addresses at the time of publication, neither the publisher nor the author assumes any responsibility for errors, or for changes that occur after publication. Further, the publisher does not have any control over and does not assume any responsibility for author or third-party Web sites or their content.

This book is printed on acid-free paper. ∞

For everyone who has encountered a dangerous or threatening person and has a story to tell

Contents

Acknowledgments

We were thrilled when Caroline Sutton and her team at Hudson Street Press expressed such strong enthusiasm for this book. From the moment we walked in Caroline's office for our first meeting, we knew we were about to join forces with the best possible support team any author could have. In particular, we're grateful for Meghan Stevenson's skilled editing. She helped sharpen the copy, better focus the book, and remove extraneous details that could have bogged down the reading. She not only edited the book; she applied its lessons to her daily life. She couldn't have been any more committed to the cause. We're also thankful that Elizabeth Keenan and Courtney Nobile shepherded us through the publicity process and so expertly helped to get the word out. And we of course were delighted that Hudson Street as a whole provided us with so much support and worked tirelessly to make this book a success.

Michael Harriot, our literary agent at Folio, realized that Mary Ellen should write a book long before Mary Ellen did. He also realized that we would make a great team. He's an excellent matchmaker. This project truly would never have happened if it were not for his ideas and guidance.

We also thank the many gracious people who so generously allowed us to tell their stories in this book so that others might learn from them.

Mary Ellen

I have many people to thank who, because of their support and belief in me, allowed me to accept this wonderful opportunity to write a book about my passion—human behavior. Sadly some of these special people are no longer here, but their influence in my life is present every day. They include my mother, Isabelle Murphy O'Toole, and my aunts and uncles: Ann, Tom, John, and Alice Murphy. They all had a part in raising me. I had my own little village, and I know I am the better for it.

I want to thank my incredible family. Thank you to my sister, Ann O'Toole Caster, and my brother, Michael Regan O'Toole. We were parentless for most of our lives, but we remained a strong and supportive family unit for one another. I would not be who I am today if it were not for my siblings and their families: Andy, Tom, Peter, and Emily Caster; and Nancy, Megan, Olivia, Harlowe, and Mary Beth O'Toole.

Meeting Dr. Robert Hare remains the highlight of my twenty-eight-year FBI career. I tell the story this way: When I first met Dr. Hare at a conference in Seattle, I felt like I was meeting my Dr. Sigmund Freud. I still do. I am so grateful for his professional guidance and help, all the teaching and research he shared with me, and his confidence and trust in me to "spread the word" about psychopathy and its impact on society. To Dr. Hare and his wonderful wife, Averil, I say thank you so much. I am honored to have you as two of my dearest friends.

For years, I have had the privilege of working side by side with some of the most amazing and talented behaviorists in the world—men and women who were willing to share their expertise and support me in developing my own: Alice Casey, FBI Behavioral Analysis Unit (BAU); Marie Dyson, FBI BAU (retired); Matt Logan, Ph.D., Royal Canadian Mounted Police, Behavioral Sciences Unit (BSU) (retired); Tom Neer, FBI BAU (retired); Anthony Pinizzotto, Ph.D., FBI BSU (retired); Robert Ressler, FBI BSU (retired); Sharon Smith, Ph.D., FBI BSU (retired); Mark Safarik, FBI BAU (retired); Ronald Tunkel, ATF BAU.

My very dear friend Special Agent Ann Todd, of the FBI's National Press Office, taught me so much about how to work with the media and how to improve my communication skills in a venue that can be quite brutal. Her support, guidance, and faith in me helped me to get through some tough times and some very challenging interviews. She was so excited about the prospect of me writing this book and told me it would be a success. That was the encouragement I needed.

To my friend the renowned author Alan Jacobson, I want to say thank you. You told me to go for it when I called you and said I was scared and uncertain about whether I had what it took to write a book.

I want to thank all the agencies that over the years gave me the opportunity and privilege to work with their officers, detectives, and prosecutors on such important cases. I also want to say to all the FBI profile coordinators located in FBI field offices throughout the United States that it was an honor to work with you. You brought me into cases that allowed me to broaden my understanding of human behavior and to be impressed every day with the incredible work that you tirelessly do.

To the Texas Tower Heroes, the surviving victims and family members I lovingly call "My Austin Group," thank you for sharing all your time, your information, and mostly yourselves so I could understand what really happened on that hot August day in 1966 on top of the University of Texas tower. Charles Whitman started the carnage, but you ended it and walked into history with your astonishing courage and bravery.

I lost my beloved dog Buddy toward the end of our writing this book. Buddy would wait so patiently during the many hours that my coauthor kept me on the phone, and he kept me company as I edited many pages of this book. Buddy would listen for the sound of the desk lamp as I clicked it off for the day, and he would jump up because he knew it was time for us to take our long walk along the Potomac River. It's not the same without him.

Mike Harriot and Alisa seemed to know there was a book here. I was not so sure about it. They believed in the project and they believed in me. They were so wonderful to work with. I remain in awe of Alisa's talents every day, and I will always be grateful to Mike for putting our team together. He had a vision and he was right.

Alisa

When I first met Mary Ellen, she asked me, "Do you keep your doors locked?" I said, "We lock them at night." She asked, "But not during the day?" She looked at me quizzically, in the way people sometimes look when they know something that you don't. I came home that day and started locking my doors 24-7. This often meant that I accidentally locked out my husband, because he was not used to taking a key with him when he took out the trash. There were also many nights when, due to what I was writing about in this book, I was too scared to be home alone. Oh, and I heard strange noises. And, yes, I had nightmares. I thank him for graciously putting up with me.

He and our daughter, Kaarina, generously shared me with this book. The writing deadline happened to coincide with the winter holidays. I thank them both for forgiving me.

I am also thankful for the many people who listened with rapt attention as I talked about this book. Your questions helped me figure out what did and did not belong in its pages.

I would never have become the writer I am today if it were not for my parents, Marilyn and Don Bauman, who have read every word I have ever written, even the dreadfully boring reports I wrote in high school and college. My great aunt (now deceased) always told me I was brilliant and that I could become anything. I think of her whenever I feel as if I'm staring at a brick wall that I can't scale, and it helps. My high school journalism teacher, Anna Hayden, planted a love of words in my soul. Various writers and mentors talked me into staying in the business many times when I thought about quitting. They know who they are. My literary agent, Michael Harriot, discovered me and told me that I was more valuable than I realized.

And Mary Ellen O'Toole was not only a joy to work with but also had an incredible book inside of her. I'm honored to have had the opportunity to work on it.

Introduction

Not long after I retired from the FBI, I hired Paul, a carpenter, to replace the drywall in my bathroom. He'd originally been referred to me by a close friend, someone who'd known him for some time.

Paul was decorated with tattoos from head to foot, and he wore his hair in a ponytail. I knew that there were plenty of people—perhaps you are one of them—who would think that Paul looked scary.

My friend had also told me that Paul had been a member of a gang many years before. This piece of information concerned me, so I asked Paul about it.

He did not attempt to hide his past. He talked about it openly. "I threw down the colors," he said, implying that he no longer lived that lifestyle.

After talking for a while, I could tell, based on how he'd answered my questions and the referral from my friend, that Paul was a conscientious, hard worker. He was a true craftsman. I could tell from his behavior that he was really a gentle soul. I didn't want to exclude him just because of something he might have been involved in twenty years ago. I based my decision to hire him on the behavior and the personality of the man he is today. I gave him the benefit of the doubt. I hired him to replace the drywall in my bathroom.

When he showed up for work, however, Paul brought along his cousin

Jack. The friend who'd recommended Paul had not mentioned a cousin. Paul had not told me about his cousin. I had not interviewed Jack before, and I had no references for him. I knew absolutely nothing about him.

Normally I did not allow people into my house before asking them a few questions. It comes with the job.

I'd spent more than fourteen years with the FBI's Behavioral Analysis Unit (BAU). The BAU—the focus of the hit television crime drama *Criminal Minds*—consults with law enforcement all over the world to help it understand and solve some of the most violent and complex crimes ever committed.

I'd interviewed some of the world's most prolific serial killers. I'd walked through their lairs. I'd seen what they'd done to their victims. I'd glimpsed the worst examples of man's inhumanity to man.

I've seen what can happen when someone lets the wrong person through her front door.

Should I break this safety rule just this once and allow this other person into my home?

Paul introduced us. We talked briefly. Jack seemed likable, polite, and certainly nonthreatening.

I knew that Paul wanted to mentor someone in the business. I knew he wanted to pass on his master craftsman's skills. We'd talked about this before, and I'd thought it was a nice thing for Paul to want to do.

And since Jack was his cousin, I assumed Paul knew Jack well—well enough to know whether it was a good idea to bring him into the home of an FBI agent. I let them in. Paul supervised Jack the entire time. Neither one gave me any cause for concern. They replaced my drywall, and then they left.

I could see that Paul took great care with his work. He did a quality job. As a result, I hired Paul several times after that. Sometimes Jack came with him. Sometimes he didn't.

I later heard that Jack had been arrested for attempting to hire a contract killer to murder his girlfriend. Then I heard that he'd tried to take out contracts on additional people from his jail cell.

And I'd opened my door and allowed him into my home, even though I had not checked him out, because my gut instinct had told me that he was safe.

Danger Is Not Instinctual

Of all people, I know not to trust gut feelings. Based on what I saw and experienced on the job as an FBI behavioral analyst, I know that you can't decide whether a person or a situation is dangerous based only on whether you feel fearful.

In my work as an FBI agent and an FBI profiler for many years, I've interviewed countless victims who told me that they "never saw it coming." Their feelings did not alert them that danger was in their midst. The instincts and intuition they thought they could trust had let them down and caused them, at times, to willingly walk into harm's way. Over and over again, I saw people unwittingly bring the same sorts of issues and problems into their lives. They:

- didn't know how to get people to open up, do what they wanted, or provide the information they sought
- did not seem to have the ability to recognize the risks they were about to walk into
- consistently made poor decisions that resulted in years of regret
- were not able to recognize individuals who posed a real threat to them or their family

Dangerous Instincts teaches you how to go beyond the gut feelings that get so many people into trouble. In this book you'll find a simple analytical process that will help you to more accurately detect danger, deceit, evasiveness, and more. You'll learn about dangerous behavior, risky situations, high-risk decision making, interpersonal communication, and even psychopaths—individuals without consciences who are stunningly callous and lacking in empathy for others. This book shows you how to peel back human behavior in an illustrative way so you can use that information to make better decisions, size up people more accurately, assess potentially threatening situations, minimize threats in your everyday life, and conduct better "interviews" with people in everyday life situations—both at work and at home.

Do You Go with Your Gut?

We tend to trust our bodily sensations: hair pricking on the backs of our necks, shivers down our spines, racing heartbeats, and sinking gut feelings. We've been taught to read such sensations as signs of trouble and their absence as signs of safety. Yet over and over again, I've seen gut feelings lead people to ignore very rational signs that all is *not* okay and to instead open the door to danger.

It's these gut sensations that cause smart people to do seemingly unwise things, to engage in risky behaviors that earn them the kind of fame no one wants. They become the victims of identity theft, phishing schemes, bad investments, and physical harm. They suffer needless regret and heartache.

Their false security about their ability to judge someone's personality and intentions causes them to trust the very people they should not—con men, pedophiles, serial rapists, murderers, stalkers, spouse abusers, and psychopaths.

Indeed it was very likely just these sorts of "dangerous instincts" that caused investors to trust Bernie Madoff with their money. It's tempting to think that you would not have been tricked by Madoff—that something in your gut would have alerted you that he was up to no good. But are you sure about that? Madoff swindled many highly educated, powerful people over a period of ten to twenty years. Did all of those people ignore their gut instincts when they agreed to those investments? Did they sense fear, trickery, suspicion, and uncertainty, and then push them aside?

Their behavior would suggest otherwise. They followed through with investing their money with him. These investors were not naive. They were not of low intelligence. They were not lacking in common sense.

Investors trusted Madoff precisely because he knew how to manipulate their gut feelings. He disarmed them with his charm. He impressed them with his career accomplishments. He lulled them with glowing recommendations from other investors who were also unknowingly being conned. He was incredibly successful, wealthy, and respected. He had been in business for years. He knew people in high places, and he himself was at the top.

Madoff knew how to make investors feel good about him and about his scheme. He created a sanctuary of false safety. People trusted him. They liked him.

As a result, they gave him their money.

We all like to think of ourselves as smarter and less naive than the typical crime victim. We like to think that we somehow possess instincts that would alert us when a dangerous person is in our midst.

I've found, however, that few if any of us have instincts that are so accurate and perceptive that we should ever rely on them when making important decisions, especially when those decisions involve our safety or the safety of our families, workplaces, or finances.

In reality, our instincts lead us to read people incorrectly. They cause us to overlook or ignore the dangerousness of some people and situations. They cause us to make poor and, at times, unwise and unsafe decisions about whom to trust to:

- manage our money
- watch our children
- clean or repair our homes
- lock up our businesses at night
- work at our companies
- friend us on Facebook
- share our information on Twitter
- help us pass the time as we sit in an airport or wait for a train
- give us or our children a ride
- date and marry

Do You Really Know Your Neighbors?

Frequently when I lecture, someone will raise a hand and claim to be a phenomenally good judge of personality and to have flawless instincts.

Perhaps you feel the same way.

That's why I want you to think about these questions:

1. How do you know that others around you are not dangerous? For instance, how do you decide who to rent a room to, whether it's okay to allow your child to sleep over at a neighbor's house, or whether to give your neighbor the key to yours?

2. How safe is it to allow your child to drive with another teen or parents from the neighborhood?

3. How do you know that your next-door neighbor isn't a dangerous psychopath, a sex offender, or an arsonist?

4. Based on your gut feelings, which of those three types of criminals (arsonist, psychopath, or sex offender) do you think would be worse to have living next door?

If you are like most people, then you probably don't put much thought into whether it's safe for your child to sleep at a neighbor's home or whether it's safe to invite those neighbors to your home for dinner. That's because your instincts tell you that your neighbor is trustworthy, and your instincts tell you this because your neighbor does normal things that other normal, well-adjusted people do. For instance, he's probably married and has kids. He might walk his dog each morning or grow vegetables in a backyard garden. Maybe he dresses up in a suit, gets in a car, and goes to work every day. He probably looks normal, too, and so do his house and yard. The grass is well groomed. The shutters are freshly painted. There's a basketball hoop over the garage door.

He's friendly and polite. He waves when he sees you. He asks you about your day and about your kids. He tells you about his. He makes eye contact. He shakes your hand. He smiles. He's even done generous favors for you, like shovel your sidewalks and driveway when you've been out of town.

All of those seemingly normal characteristics are precisely why park ranger David Parker Ray easily blended into his Elephant Butte Lake neighborhood in New Mexico. His neighbors described him as a "regular guy." None had any idea that he was a sexual sadist who was using a small trailer in his backyard as a torture chamber. It was there that he repeatedly shocked, beat, and terrorized an unknown number of women over a period of many years.

His neighbors thought he was a normal guy and, after I interviewed David Parker Ray, I could understand why. He took my hand and cupped it in both of his. He said, "How are you? It's nice to meet you." He politely answered my questions. He cracked jokes. He was charming and gracious. He seemed as if he was a sixty-year-old man who respected and admired women. I had to continually tell myself, "Don't forget what you know, Mary Ellen. You just came from that toy box." (The "toy box" was David's term for the room where he stored his whips, chains, pulleys, straps, clamps, blades, saws, sex toys, and other devices that he used to torture women. It's where he kept women for hours and days as he tortured them, became sexually aroused, and recorded all his deviant sexual behavior so he could watch it and enjoy it later on.)

I knew what David had done and I knew what David was—a criminal sexual sadist. He was sexually aroused by the victim's response to his infliction of physical and emotional pain. He had kidnapped his victims, drugged them, and kept them in his home and in the toy box for his sexual pleasure.

"It might not seem as if this man is capable of doing that," I reminded myself. "But you know that a victim was found running out of his home, naked, wearing only a chain around her neck and telling police she had been physically tortured, repeatedly, by Ray and a female friend for several days following his kidnapping her."

Indeed, outside his toy box David Parker Ray did not seem anything other than perfectly normal. Inside it, he was anything but.

Our upbringings and our media consumption have trained us to believe numerous myths that cause us to overlook the David Parker Rays in our midst. One of these myths is that of the straggly haired stranger. This is the guy who roams the world, committing heinous crimes, never gets caught, and just keeps on getting away with his horrible behavior. The myth of the straggly haired stranger is one of several I will explore in this book—myths that cause many of us to let our guard down at precisely the wrong moment and to keep it up when we otherwise don't have to.

For instance, you'll learn the following:

- That our instincts often lead us to trust people based on superficial details—details that generally have little to do with true normalcy. In fact, dangerous people can be masters at appearing normal. They dress nicely and keep their houses presentable. They usually don't look out of place. They don't seem threatening, and our underlying belief is that if we are nice to them they will be nice to us.

- We generally distrust people based on superficial details too. This is why we often assume that straggly haired strangers—especially the ones who are socially inept, off-putting, and shifty eyed—pose the greatest threat to us. In reality, some of the most dangerous of people fit right in. They can be outgoing, charming, and exceptionally good at making eye contact and putting us at ease.

In reality, you can't tell whether one of your neighbors is a sex offender, psychopath, or arsonist just by giving him or her the once-over. You also can't tell—based on the type of car he or she owns—if your neighbor is a responsible driver who does not text while behind the wheel or has serious anger-management issues that result in frequent road rage. Knowing that your neighbor is married or has children tells you, for instance, nothing about the massive gun collection in his home, one he keeps loaded and ready to be used at a moment's notice. You don't know if those guns are stored where curious children can access them, or if he uses them to threaten his family when he has had too much to drink after a bad day at the office.

I'm guessing that there's a lot you don't know about your neighbors, but by the end of this book you'll realize what you don't know, why those details are important, and how to fill in those blanks.

As for what's worse, a sex offender, an arsonist, or a psychopath—it depends. A psychopath might be a violent serial killer. That's scary. I wouldn't want someone like that living next door to me! Yet not all psychopaths are violent. In fact, most are not. A sex offender could be a serial rapist or someone with fantasies about abducting and holding adolescent children. For instance, it could be someone like John Esposito, the man who abducted ten-year-old Katie Beers—a child he knew because he was friendly with her family—and for sixteen days confined her in a two-by-three-foot bunker he'd built in his suburban home. Or the sex offender might be someone who was convicted of statutory rape because he'd had sex with a consenting sixteen-year-old when he was eighteen. There's a big difference between those two extremes. The arsonist could be someone like John Leonard Orr, a fire captain and one of the most highly regarded arson investigators in California, who was convicted of setting deadly fires in crowded, public places. Or it could be someone who played with matches when he was twelve, accidentally burned down a family shed, and ended up being labeled an arsonist even though he never set another fire.

"Psychopath," "arsonist," and "sex offender" are all labels. To truly understand whether someone is dangerous, you must look behind the label and study that person's behavior. This book will show you how.

What Profilers Know

I am always asked, "What does a profiler do? How do you analyze behavior? What do you look for?"

TV programs like *Criminal Minds* and *CSI*, along with hundreds of Hollywood movies and books, attempt to capture the essence of the profiler's "process," but they get it wrong a lot of the time. Profiling is not magic. Profilers do not walk into a room, glance at the suit someone is wearing, and proclaim, "You're the killer. I can tell by your body language and that one book on your bookshelf."

No, we're not psychic or mind readers and we don't rely on crystal balls. Instead we are observers of behavior. We take into account what we observe at a crime scene and also consider the behaviors that are absent from a crime scene. We add that to other pertinent information, like forensics (blood-spatter patterns, ballistics, and wound pathology), autopsy reports, investigative reports, and more. We use that information to develop a "criminal investigative analysis" (a profile), investigative and interview strategies, and strategies for the prosecution during court procedures.

For years, as an FBI profiler, I studied human behavior—the behavior of the offender, the behavior of the victim, and the behavior of other people who surrounded both.

It wasn't until after I'd retired that I realized what I'd learned as a profiler could be very useful to others. That is what this book is about. It captures the process of an FBI profiler and applies that process to everyday life. It teaches you how to read behavior so you can assess the dangerousness of situations; make the kinds of decisions that, though all of us make them regularly, have a far-reaching impact on our lives; and effectively communicate with people, especially when strong interviewing skills are essential.

You will probably never find yourself in a position where you have to track down a dangerous criminal. It is not likely you will ever interview a serial killer, a kidnapper, a bank robber, a politician who has taken thousands in bribes, or the victim of a violent crime.

You will, however, be able to learn from a profiler's expertise and apply that expertise to your life. For instance, some of the communication skills I successfully relied on in hundreds of interviews with dangerous criminals can make a big difference in the success of your interpersonal communication with the people around you—family, friends, colleagues, and even strangers.

Normally information about how to stay safe focuses on what to do if you are, for example, tossed into the trunk of a car or abducted at knife- or gunpoint—both of which are incredibly rare situations that the vast majority of people will never find themselves in. Here you will learn how to make the kinds of serious and stressful decisions that confront all of us, all the time. Decisions like the following:

- whether to hand your car keys over to your teen or allow him or her to catch a ride from a friend
- how to respond when a coworker spreads lies about you and tries to malign you at work or on the Internet
- who to hire to manage your finances, fix your computer, babysit your child, or clean your home
- whether it's a good idea to place a personal ad online, what it

should say, and how you will screen the people who respond to it
- what to do when a friend or family member asks to move in with you
- how to handle a bullying incident at your child's school
- how to respond when your college-age daughter accidentally lets it slip that her boyfriend might have anger-management issues

Think about the important decisions you make. Can you trust your housekeeper with a key to your home? Is it safe to let your child's coach give him a ride home from practice? Should you make this financial investment with someone recommended to you? Is it okay to bring the guy you are dating home with you for the night? Should you give your Social Security number and other sensitive information to this financial adviser? Should you confront that neighbor about a problem you are having with him?

Such decisions and how you handle them can pose serious, long-term ramifications. They can result in lost sleep and worry. And in some cases the wrong decision, the wrong actions, or the wrong communication style can put you in a situation where the consequences are stunning and might even result in death or dire legal, financial, or career problems.

Wouldn't you like to know that you are making the best and safest decision in such cases? Wouldn't you want to know how to see signs of danger and do something about it? Wouldn't you like to be able to spot problem behavior before it's too late to respond?

Dangerous Instincts will help you to do all of that and more.

The Secret of SMART Decision Making

While at the FBI, I used a logical, step-by-step process to make important decisions. I used it when deciding how to interview suspects, when doing threat and dangerousness assessments of individuals, and when creating investigative and interview strategies that would lead to the identification of a suspect or cause one to open up and talk about his crimes. This process, however, works for *all* important decisions and can be used by any person. You don't need a background in psychology or criminology to use it.

This book will teach you this process. I call it SMART, an acronym that stands for "sound method of assessing and recognizing trouble." You'll learn more about it in chapter 2. For now, know that this process will show you how to assess other people for signs of potentially dangerous behavioral characteristics. You'll find out how to get people to open up and give you the information you seek—even people like stonewalling spouses, cagey job applicants, and threatening neighbors. You'll even find out how to tell if someone is lying or being evasive—and what to do about it.

Dangerous Instincts will help you minimize your decision-making risk and be safer overall. You will feel more confident and self-assured that you have weighed all your options, done a thorough risk assessment, and made the smartest decision possible.

DANGEROUS INSTINCTS

Chapter 1

Test Your Instincts

Would you date a rapist? Would you get into a drunk driver's car? Would you ask a thief to invest your money? Would you allow your child to sleep over at a pedophile's house? Would you let a serial killer into your home? Would you ignore behavior that warns that someone will likely shoot up a school, college classroom, or a workplace?

Most people answer all of those questions with a loud and confident "No!" I'm guessing you would as well. Like most people, you might assume that you would sense if someone were about to con or hurt you. Perhaps you think that you would get an "all is not right" sensation in your gut, heart, or somewhere else.

Unless you are highly unusual, however, you probably wouldn't sense such danger at all. If more people could sense deceit or danger, a lot fewer people would become victims of violent crime, identity theft, pyramid schemes, and investment fraud.

When I talk with people about the unfortunate events that have taken place over their lives, I hear expressions like "It just came out of nowhere," "I never saw that one coming," and "I can't believe something like this could have happened to me."

Such expressions are telling. They mean that these folks were not forewarned by any gut feelings at all. They did not sense fear. They did not sense deceit. They did not have a premonition of something bad about to happen.

Their instincts and intuition let them down. Have yours let you down too? Later in this book, we'll walk through some of the decisions you've made in the past, and we'll analyze them to see what type of an assessment process you used, how well it's working for you, and whether it can be improved upon.

For now, let's have a little fun. Consider the scenarios in the following pages. Think carefully about what you would do in each. How would you assess the situation? What information would you factor into your decision? What information would you deem not important? Then consult the answer that follows each question to find out just how dangerous your instincts really are.

The Test

1. Jane is widowed and in her early fifties. It's been a few years since her spouse passed away and now she is ready to meet someone. Her friends, however, do not know any bachelors her age, and she's been unable to meet any at church or through her various hobbies. Her friends have been telling her to try online dating. She's resisted for a long time, assuming that she would only meet undesirable men that way. She's also been a little embarrassed to think she might have to resort to this in order to meet a man. And she's wondered if there's something wrong with her that she can't meet someone the old-fashioned way. Maybe she's too old, not attractive anymore, or too set in her ways?

Having exhausted her other options, Jane decides to give online dating a try. She joins an online dating site and reads a bunch of ads on it. Most of the descriptions seem like outright lies or just pathetic. She is about ready to give up hope when she comes across this ad placed by Kevin, a fifty-eight-year-old man:

I am looking for that special someone who will love and care for me and always be there for me as I will be there for her. I'm not into play-

ing games. I'm financially independent and recently retired from running my own company for many years. I've traveled the world. I am physically fit and good-looking. I'm ready to settle down with the perfect soul mate. I will treat you with respect, kindness, caring, understanding, trust, honesty, compassion, love, and joy.

What, if anything, can Jane tell from this ad that will help her to determine whether to get in touch with Kevin? What types of questions might she ask him to determine whether he's someone she would like to date? And what should she tell him about herself?

Should Jane hop on this one quick before someone else snatches up this great catch of a guy? I'm not so sure about that. Before I get into why I think Jane should be wary of this gentleman, let's take a closer look at the potential pros and cons of this decision. On the positive side, Kevin might be the perfect catch, someone who will serve as a wonderful companion for Jane. But I'm a retired FBI profiler who chased bad guys for most of my career, so of course one of the first thoughts that pops into my head is that Kevin could also be a serial killer, rapist, or con man. Con artists have been known to comb dating sites in search of victims. For instance, William Michael Barber (also known as the Don Juan of Con) allegedly lured several of his victims via Internet dating sites. He married them, cleaned out their bank accounts, and then fled.

Romance fraud is one of the top five ruses used by Internet scam artists. In such "sweetheart scams" the con artist usually claims to live in another country. He might tell you that he is blown away by your photo and feels a strong bond and can't wait to meet you in person. Alas, he doesn't have enough money for airfare. Will you send him money for a ticket?

Can you see where this is headed?

But even if Kevin isn't a murderer or a con man, he might have a drinking problem, mental-health issues, or serious anger-management problems. Jane would not want to take on those kinds of problems. He might be someone who gets involved in one dead-end relationship after another. He may have stalked or harassed other women who broke up with him. If he's *not* the perfect catch, it's a waste of Jane's time and might prevent her from finding the right man. More important, dating him could lead to emotional pain and suffering, financial loss, or even physical harm.

Because of all of this, Jane will want to be very careful. If she misreads him and fails to spot danger signs ahead of time, the potential risk to her is quite high. Now let's take a closer look at what Kevin wrote in his ad:

- *I am looking for that special someone who will love and care for me and always be there for me as I will be there for her.* This is what he's looking for. He wants a woman who will always be there for him. So far, so good, although the word "always" should give Jane pause. This could be a sign that Kevin might see the world in black-and-white terms—a world of absolutes—which could suggest a certain amount of rigidness. He writes that he wants someone who would love and care for him. That's asking for a lot. In return, he "will be there for her." That sounds a little inequitable—as if he's not offering as much as he's asking for. He could be using linguistic flattery to lure a woman into having contact with him. His words could be more seductive than truthful.

- *I'm not into playing games.* Whenever someone offers unsolicited information about what they are *not*, it stands out as a red flag. When I see the phrase "I'm not into playing games," I wonder if someone has accused him of playing games in the past. Otherwise, why bring it up?

  It's similar to someone saying, "I don't want to hurt your feelings but . . ." In other words, they don't want to hurt my feelings but are going to go ahead and do it anyway. These kinds of phrases are indicators of deception. They don't necessarily guarantee that someone is trying to deceive you, but they are indicators that they might be. Such phrases should make you pause so you can consider the other person's true motives.

- *I'm financially independent and recently retired from running my own company for many years.* He's implying that he is financially stable. This might be a good thing for Jane.

• *I've traveled the world.* He's worldly. This is possibly another plus in Kevin's favor.

• *I am physically fit and good-looking.* Although this might sound like a plus, I would counsel Jane to think about the kind of person who would boast about being good-looking. Whether he's easy on the eyes or not, most nonnarcissistic people do not describe themselves as "good-looking." Does Jane want to date someone who is self-absorbed? More important, does she want to date someone who might be dangerous? Psychopaths tend to be narcissistic and grandiose—they are precisely the type of people who would brag about owning their own companies, of being good-looking, and of traveling the world.

• *I'm ready to settle down with the perfect soul mate.* This line initially might make Kevin seem like a man who is ready to commit. I, however, would counsel Jane to take a closer look at the word "perfect." No woman is perfect. Is he searching for something that is not real? Will he hold Jane up to standards that she can't possibly meet? It's likely, especially when you add the word "perfect" to the word "always" from a few sentences before.

Now let's consider the term "soul mate." A friend of mine often says, "Soul mates are like unicorns. Neither one exists." I subscribe to that notion. If Kevin is looking for a unicorn, he's setting himself—and Jane—up for disappointment. Jane is only human after all.

He also might be using this phrase and others because he wants to impress women and persuade them to lower their guard. If this man is a psychopath, then he will say anything about himself—true or not—if he thinks it will help him achieve his goal. He will have read that women want a "soul mate," so he will use that term as a lure. It may have helped him to lure women in the past.

• *I will treat you with respect, kindness, caring, understanding, trust, honesty, compassion, love, and joy.* This line certainly makes Kevin sound like a great guy. After all, who wouldn't want to be treated this way? That's precisely why I would counsel Jane to be wary. There are too many positive nouns in this sentence. It's over the top. It's a little too good to be true.

Let's assume for a moment that I'm overanalyzing the ad and that this Kevin is a good guy who just wants to meet a good woman. Maybe, for argument's sake, Kevin asked his granddaughter for help with the ad, and that's why it has so many flowery and over-the-top descriptions.

Even if that's the case, Jane has no way of knowing, from the ad alone, what Kevin is really like. If I were Jane's life coach, I would recommend that she e-mail Kevin a number of open-ended questions that will help her to learn more about him and determine what kind of person he is:

- How do you feel about online dating and the type of people you meet?
- What are your biggest concerns about meeting someone online?
- What do you think are the risks?
- When you've had good dating experiences, how did those experiences go?
- When you've had bad dating experiences, what made those experiences bad?

In his answers, she will want to look for verification that what he said in the ad is true. Here are a few things she could look for and what they mean:

- *He blames all his past failed relationships on the women involved.* He might not be as understanding as he claims to be.

- *He writes numerous "I" and "me" statements.* He could be too self-absorbed for Jane's tastes.

- *He evades her questions.* Rather than directly answering, he says, "Let me get back to you on that" or "I don't know about that but . . ." Or he might pretend he never got the question at all, or he might change the topic. Any of this might mean that there's something he'd rather Jane didn't know.

- *He responds defensively*. He asks, "Why would you ask me something like that?" This, too, could mean that the question has hit a nerve and that he's got something to hide.

- *He continually talks about how great he is*. He might be trying to overcompensate for something Jane might perceive as a negative. He also might be incredibly arrogant and self-centered.

- *He is fearless and disregards any risks*. He might be the type of person who would not be able to understand the feelings of others. If he is a thrill seeker who does not think through his decisions, he might be too willing to take risks involving Jane, her life, her money, her investments, and her feelings, and that could create serious problems for her.

You'll learn more about how to interview people and interpret the answers they provide in chapter 8.

2. Dr. James works in human resources at a major university and will be part of a team interviewing potential candidates for an associate professor position in the English department. He is concerned about the incidents of school and campus shootings, as well as other incidents of workplace violence, throughout the country. What information do you think will be important for Dr. James when he and his team interview an applicant to ensure that the person does not one day threaten violence or act out violently at the university?

Did this question stump you? It stumps most people. And it does because most people assume either that people who are likely to become violent in the workplace have a certain look about them—they are easy to spot—or that it's impossible to spot someone who is likely to become violent until the day that person acts out. They assume that violent people snap, and there's no predicting who will snap and who won't until the day it happens.

Neither of these assumptions is true. People who commit workplace violence don't dress a certain way, have a specific hairstyle, or share any other visual characteristic. They are not necessarily all loners with poor social skills who live alone in a disheveled home with a cat. (This stereotype gives a bad name to those of us who live alone, own a cat, and are very happy and a risk to no one!)

A good interviewer, however, can spot someone who is likely to commit workplace violence.

For example, people who are predisposed to workplace violence are likely to have anger issues, a preoccupation with violence, and are "injustice collectors" (more on injustice collectors on page 186). That means they are easily offended, and they do not forgive or forget. They ruminate about real or imagined insults and blame others for their failures.[1] Of course, Dr. James can't ask, "Are you an injustice collector?" during an interview, but he can ask the following questions:

- How do you feel about the tenure process? What do you think the university administration should take into account when granting or not granting tenure?
- In the past, when management hasn't handled things to your liking, what have you done?
- What type of coworkers have you had problems with in the past and how have you resolved those problems?
- What type of feedback, both negative and positive have you received in your prior positions, and how did you address the negative feedback?

As he listens to a candidate answer these questions, Dr. James will be looking for information that the candidate might accidentally leak out. For instance, does the candidate blame others for conflicts and criticism or take ownership of his other mistakes? Someone who blames others might, at best, not be a joy to work with. At worst, he could be an injustice collector who harbors violent fantasies, resents others for their success, broods about perceived mistreatment at work, and who one day decides to act out violently against his bosses and coworkers.

Dr. James will also want to listen for times when the candidate might have disagreed with a policy and then just ignored it and broke the rules. That could be a red flag. You'll learn more about how to screen people for threatening violent behavior later in this book.

3. A new family has moved into Shannon's neighborhood. They have a son about her son's age, and the children have hit it off. Shannon briefly met the new family on the day they moved in. They seemed pleasant and normal enough. Their son, Kyle, wants her son, Max, to sleep over for the night. What types of things should Shannon make sure she knows before agreeing to allow her son to spend the night?

In my experience, I saw more people willing to let their children go with others they don't know well than to lend their cars to a good friend. If you are a parent and you are being honest with yourself, then you can probably think of times when you've allowed your child to sleep over at another child's house without a second thought. You may have done it without even meeting the other child's parents.

Or if you did know the parents and you did ask some questions, chances are the questions centered on basic things like what time they put the kids to bed and whether dinner would be served.

You did so because your instincts told you that these neighbors were safe, and they probably caused you to think so for these reasons:

- You assume that dangerous people don't have spouses and children, and that they either live alone or live in someone else's neighborhood.
- You assume that no parent could ever hurt a child. You think all parents possess an instinctual empathy that causes them to want to protect any child.
- You assume that people who look normal *are* normal, and your neighbors all look normal.

- Your children attend the same school, and you assume the school would have spotted something and done something about it if there were a problem.

Yet all of these reasons are false, and you'll learn more about why later in this book. Even if Shannon's new neighbors are not pedophiles or murderers, there are still many questions that she has not yet considered:

- Are there loaded guns in the house and, if so, is it possible for the children to access them?
- Does this couple own porn or violent videos that Shannon doesn't want her son to see?
- Does either parent drink excessively or do drugs, including abusing over-the-counter drugs?
- Is either parent verbally or physically abusive?
- Do any members of the family have anger-management issues?
- Does anyone in the family engage in sexually inappropriate behavior?
- Are there animals in the house? If so, are they child-friendly?
- Are hazardous substances like cleaning fluids, pest-control chemicals, and flammables kept out of reach and safely stored?
- Is either parent careless about smoking, cooking, baking, or the proper use of space heaters and likely to accidentally start a fire?
- Do they lock their doors at night?
- Are there other children in the home? If so, what is their disposition? Are any of them likely to bully, abuse, or threaten Shannon's son?
- Who else comes into the home? Who else has access to the children?
- Does either parent have criminal records and for what? Do they associate with people who have criminal records and, if so, for what?

- Have these new neighbors had problems with families in neighborhoods where they've previously lived?

Are you thinking, "Who could ask such questions? My neighbors would think I'm a paranoid freak if I asked such things!" You have a point. These are not the kinds of questions that Shannon can ask in rapid fire while standing on her neighbor's front porch. They could be interpreted as offensive, and the neighbors might become defensive. If they had something to hide, they would make sure to hide it.

I would counsel Shannon to explain that this is not a good night for a sleepover. This is a stalling tactic, designed to provide Shannon with more time to gather important information. Shannon should definitely go online and check to see if these neighbors are registered sex offenders and whether there have been any police reports that mention their names. For instance, if they have a dangerous dog that has bitten someone, there will probably be a police report on the incident or their addresses might be listed on a dangerous-dog registry. Shannon will be able to find any of this publicly available information on the Internet. While she's at it, she might Google the names of all the family members, just to see what comes up. Is either parent writing a blog? If so, what is it about? Are they on Facebook, Myspace, or another social networking site? If so, what types of things do they post?

Do you think this is excessive? Consider that Phillip Garrido, the man accused of kidnapping and holding Jaycee Dugard for eighteen years, was a registered sex offender. His neighbors thought he was an okay guy. One of them spotted a young girl in Garrido's backyard soon after Dugard's disappearance, but he thought nothing of it. Had that neighbor checked up on Garrido and discovered that Garrido was a registered sex offender who was barred by law from spending time with children, he might have thought to call the police.

But let's say everything checks out: Shannon's neighbors are not registered sex offenders, they have a squeaky-clean police record, and a Google search reveals nothing out of the ordinary. Does the absence of information mean that problem behavior is absent? Not necessarily.

Next she might meet with her neighbors in different social settings.

She might visit them for a chat. While in their home, she might see objects that will allow her to ask important questions in a polite way. For instance, if she sees mounted deer heads, she could ask, "Do you hunt?" The answer to that question will allow her to politely ask other questions that help her to determine whether there are guns in the house and where and how they are stored.

She might also have the neighbors over for dinner, during which she can more easily ask many questions and listen carefully to the information they provide. She might, for instance, observe the mother and father. How do they interact? Does the father seem to control the mother and tell her what to do and say? Do they fight a little too openly, as if aggressive arguing is commonplace for them? Do they drink too much? Do they trash everyone they know? How do they treat their children? Are they domineering? Are they on top of things? Or do they ignore their kids?

Over time, as Shannon gets to know this family better, she'll be able to make a better decision about whether it's safe for her child to sleep in their home.

4. A telephone repairman comes to your door. He's dressed in a uniform. He shows you his identification and tells you he is working on lines that were damaged during a recent storm. He tells you his work will be limited to the outside, but he will need access to your phone line inside the house at some point. He is believable, seems trustworthy, his story makes sense, and he is polite and professional. How do you decide whether to let him in?

Perhaps you've let such a person into your home before. Maybe it was someone who wanted to test your water. Maybe it was a salesperson who wanted to give you a free estimate for replacing your windows. Maybe it was a census worker. Whoever it was, you did a quick once-over and assumed that the person did not look dangerous. Anyway, he or she would not be there very long.

You were fortunate.

Several women in the Midwest who opened their doors to Anthony

Joe LaRette were not. He was dressed in a telephone repairman's uniform. Because of this, these women did not perceive him as a threat. They let him into their homes. Then he sexually assaulted and/or murdered them.

Dangerous people are quite adept at seeming harmless and at spinning lies that lead you to trust them. Based on what I've witnessed during my career with the FBI, I can tell you this with conviction: We can't tell if someone is dangerous just by giving them a quick look up and down. I'm trained to detect psychopathic traits in people. Even I wouldn't trust myself to be able to tell—just by looking at someone—if it was safe to let a stranger inside. Psychopathy, the most dangerous of personality disorders, cannot be assessed simply by looking at someone. Most of the time, neither can other types of dangerousness.

You might be thinking that people like Anthony Joe LaRette are rare. That's true. The likelihood of you opening your door to a serial killer is roughly one in 8.7 million. You are more likely to get struck by lightning.

It is more likely, however, that you might be facing someone who is casing your home (in order to burglarize it later) or who has intentions of scamming you.

I recommend that you consider the following before making a decision to open the door:

- Are you expecting someone?
- How easy would it be for the person on the other side of the door to overpower you and force his or her way in? (Note: It's a lot easier for someone to push his or her way in than most people think.)
- Are you alone? If you are not alone, would someone be able to get help or fend off a potential attacker? Is there someone home who is even more vulnerable than you are, making it even more important to not allow a stranger into your home?
- Can you verify the identity of the person on the other side of the door without making yourself vulnerable to an attack?

Can you see who it is through a window or peephole, or talk to the person through the door? Can you call the company to make sure the service person is there legitimately, on company business?

- Does he have anything on him or in his hands that could be used as a weapon against you?

You might say that these are all basic precautions, yet I see people ignore them every day. I have neighbors, for instance, who never lock their doors—day or night. And I know many parents who assume that their latchkey children know better than to open the door whenever someone knocks and no adults are home. I can't tell you how many grieving parents I have comforted who told me, "But she knows not to open the door. I told her never to open the door to a stranger." In my experience, children always open the door.

Later in this book, you'll create your own assessment process for detecting trouble at the front door. For now, however, if you are not expecting someone, you are vulnerable, and you cannot verify the identity of the person at the door, I would recommend not answering the door at all. Anyone with a legitimate reason to be there will leave a note or follow up with a phone call. Although this might seem rude, consider that your safety is more important than whether the company gets the job done that day.

5. Larry is one of many professionals who commutes to work in the D.C. area, where drivers can only travel in the commuter lane—and avoid the worst of the rush-hour traffic—if they have a passenger in their car. For this reason, "slugging" has become a common practice. Sluggers gather at park and ride lots and catch rides with other commuters, usually people they've just met. Larry is such a slugger.

Larry's wife doesn't like that he does this. She worries that it is dangerous and has warned him that he's eventually going to get into a serial killer's car. Larry has assured her that slugging is perfectly safe. No one has ever been murdered as a result of it.

"Serial killers might prey on hitchhikers and prostitutes, but they don't prey on commuters," he tells her. "Anyway, I can fight off anyone. No one is going to overpower me."

Today Larry has a choice between two drivers. One is a woman in a Mercedes. He peers in her window. He sees a child's car seat in the back. The driver is alone. She's dressed in a professional pants suit and seems friendly. It looks like she's got the AC going, and it's a hot day.

The other driver is a man in an old sedan that is missing its hubcaps. He's dressed in jeans and a T-shirt. He has two other passengers. The windows are down. Larry can't tell for sure, but he suspects that this car does not have AC.

Larry decides to go with the woman. He figures the ride will be a lot more pleasant, that few Mercedes-driving mothers are dangerous, and that he could overpower her if it became necessary.

What is wrong with Larry's decision?

Did you just do a set of mental calculations, trying to figure out which car would be safer for Larry? Maybe, like Larry, you thought the woman in the Mercedes was the best bet for the following reasons:

- She's a woman and therefore less of a physical threat.
- She has kids (based on the car seat in the back).
- She's in a luxury car.

Or maybe you thought the other car was a safer bet because the presence of other passengers would provide safety in numbers.

Both decisions, however, are flawed.

First let's talk about the woman in the Mercedes. Beyond taking into account how it might perform in an accident, the type of car means very little in terms of personal safety. So does the presence of the child's car seat.

The fact that she's a woman could possibly make her slightly safer than the other driver, but not for the reasons that you or my hypothetical Larry probably think. If he thinks he can fight her off because he's bigger than she is, he's wrong. If she has a gun, his body size and physical strength will mean very little. She's safer than the other driver because women are three times less likely to die in car accidents than men are. According to the 2009 Traffic Safety Culture Index, men are also more likely to speed, run red lights, tailgate, and drive while fatigued.

But none of this means it's safe to get in her car. I'll elaborate on why in a couple of paragraphs.

First let's consider the other car. The problem with assuming safety in numbers is this: You don't know if the other passengers are innocent commuters like Larry or if they are accomplices planning to work with the driver in order to steal from or even murder Larry. Even if the driver is harmless, you don't know if all the passengers are, too, and vice versa.

But Larry's biggest lapse in judgment is this: He thinks he can look at a driver and tell if he or she is safe. He can't. Even I can't do that, and I'm trained to assess whether someone is a psychopath!

I'm guessing you might not believe me, so let me tell you a story. Colleen Stan also thought she could tell whether someone was dangerous. As she hitchhiked her way from Eugene, Oregon, to Westwood, California, she checked out each person who offered her a ride, trying to calculate the likelihood that the driver might be dangerous. She even passed up two rides because something seemed off about the drivers.

But when a Dodge Colt stopped and she saw a man, woman, and baby inside, she relaxed. They looked like a clean-cut, friendly family. She got in.

The driver was Cameron Hooker. He drove to a remote location, pulled out a knife, threatened to slash Colleen's throat, and then handcuffed, blindfolded, bound, and gagged her. He kept her as a sex slave for the next seven years—torturing her and keeping her locked in small box stored under his bed.

You just can't tell whether someone is dangerous by looking at them or at the type of car they drive or at what's in that car.

It would be exceedingly unlikely for Larry to step inside the car of a serial sexual sadist, but not for him to get in the car with someone who is a high-risk driver. You cannot look at someone and evaluate whether they are a skilled driver. You also cannot look at someone and tell whether they:

- text and drive or practice other dangerous or distracting driving behaviors
- have insurance that's up to date
- have drugs in the car that could get pinned on you if discovered by the police
- are operating a reliable vehicle, with airbags, seat belts and other safety features that are working properly
- have a neurological condition such as Alzheimer's disease that could impair their response time in breaking, swerving to avoid an accident, or taking other actions needed to drive a car safely
- drank alcohol or took drugs—legal or illegal—that morning
- have a bad driving record or prior incidents of aggressive driving or receiving multiple tickets or warnings
- own the car they are in

It doesn't matter how strong of a guy Larry is. If he steps into a car with a bad driver and that driver gets into a terrible accident, Larry is going to get hurt. These potential consequences of slugging won't make the front page of the newspaper, but they can have a serious and lasting negative impact on a person and their family's life.

Larry doesn't know any of these things about either driver. He never even thought of them. That means Larry doesn't have enough information to make a safe decision. More important, his ability to get those answers while standing in the middle of a park and ride lot are slim to none. Larry's wife is correct: Slugging could be dangerous. Eventually there is a good chance it will get him into trouble.

6. Mary works in corporate security for a major bank. She is deciding what the bank should do about Caroline Miller, a twenty-one-year-old teller who has worked at the bank for one year. Caroline's supervisor and a consultant from human resources are worried that Caroline's twenty-four-year-old husband, Jim Miller, may attempt to come into the bank to threaten or hurt his wife.

In the past, Caroline has come to work with bruises and cuts,

and she's explained them away by saying that she fell or was in a car accident. Now, however, Caroline has filed for divorce, and she has told the HR consultant that her husband is abusive.

According to Caroline, Jim has threatened to come to the bank and confront another employee, Peter Jones, because he thinks Caroline is having an affair with him. Since their separation, Jim and Caroline have been seen, by one of her coworkers, sitting in their car and arguing.

Within the last month, Caroline applied for a bank loan in order to purchase a new motorcycle. The loan was declined because of a poor credit rating.

When Caroline initially applied for her position with the bank, Jim also submitted an application for employment and was interviewed but not hired. His employment record was incomplete, and during the interview he admitted that he had a prior felony conviction for possession of drugs and illegal possession of a firearm. He explained that the conviction was a huge misunderstanding and that he was pursuing legal means to have his record "expunged." The woman who interviewed Jim for employment described him as being charming but egotistical. During the interview, the way Jim looked at her made her so uncomfortable that she had to look away. His eyes were like a snake's. It unnerved her.

About nine months ago, an unidentified man robbed the branch of the bank where Caroline works, pointing a gun at her and demanding all the money from her drawer. She complied. The same person is believed to be responsible for at least two other robberies at different banks in the area.

What do you think is going on here? What else does Mary need to know in order to make a decision about how to resolve the situation? Are these isolated events? Or do they all tie together?

I have used this scenario when I train corporate security and human resources personnel. It usually stumps most of the people in the room.

Some people might reason that Jim's charm, incomplete employment record, and attempt to explain away his criminal record as a "misunderstanding" are signs that he might be a psychopath.

I usually have a few people in the room who suspect that Jim might have been the person who robbed the bank.

Never, however, has anyone come up with the following questions for Mary to consider:

1. Is Caroline really a domestic abuse victim? Are the signs of domestic abuse a ruse to distract bank employees from something else?
2. If Jim robbed the bank, did Caroline hand over the money because she was scared or did she do it because she was complicit in his scheme?
3. What was really going on in the car when the coworker saw Jim and Caroline? Were they really fighting over the divorce? Was he making threats that she has not told the bank about? Is his violence escalating?
4. Will he come back to the bank and kill his wife and others because he is paranoid and jealous and suspects Caroline of having an affair?

We've been conditioned to sympathize with and trust people who appear like victims. For instance, a few years ago, when a woman accused three Duke University lacrosse players of rape, most people vehemently took the alleged victim's side. When I heard about the details of that case, however, I was pretty sure that the woman's story was fabricated. False allegations of rape are extremely rare, but this woman said and did several things that caused me to doubt her story.

When I mentioned this to some of my family or friends, they told me that I did not know what I was talking about. Some even became angry with me, saying things like "Who would ever lie about something like that?" The alleged victim's story, however, was eventually proven false, and the lacrosse players were vindicated.

Our natural inclination is to put ourselves in someone else's shoes. We forget, however, that other people do not necessarily wear the same types of shoes we do. They do not necessarily share our behavior, personality, and values. Just because you or I would never falsely accuse someone else of a serious crime like rape doesn't mean that no one else would do such a thing. The same is true in this bank scenario. Looks can be deceiving, and things are not always what they appear to be. If Mary trusts her instinct to protect Caroline, without considering all the facts, she and others at the bank, including customers, might very well end up victims themselves.

7. Graham writes a motivational blog that offers career and life tips. For several months, he's been getting a lot of mail from Lisa, who describes herself as "his biggest fan." This admirer e-mails Graham positive comments once every other week, like clockwork. Graham tries to interact with all his fans and to answer every single e-mail. That way they will continue to come back and tell others about his blog. For this reason, Graham has been responding to Lisa with a quick e-mail that says, "Thank you for reading!" or "Thanks for your kind words!"

Over time Graham has learned that Lisa lives overseas and that she reads his blog because she is currently unemployed and searching for a new job.

Recently Graham posted a photo of himself. That day Lisa e-mailed the following:

I am, of course, your biggest fan, but I would like to offer you a constructive critique. You need to wear your blue suit when you have your photo taken. It goes with your eyes. I suggest wearing it with your red tie, for contrast. You also should cut your hair shorter. This will make you look more self-confident and more polished, like the sexy man I know you to be.

Graham doesn't know what to make of this. Initially he was annoyed, thinking, "How dare she tell me how to dress and cut my hair?" He doesn't respond right away, however, because he can't think of what to write.

A few days go by. Graham gets busy and forgets about the e-mail.

A week later he gets this e-mail from Lisa:

Why didn't you respond to my e-mail? I need to hear from you. I'm not trying to harass you, but I just cannot believe you would be so insensitive and irresponsible as to not respond to your e-mails like this.

A few hours later, he gets yet another e-mail from Lisa. It says:

You apparently are not the person I thought you were. In fact, you seem to have some real flaws in your character. You are obviously very immature, arrogant, and way too self-absorbed. You don't understand the importance of responding immediately to the very people who made this amateur blog even halfway enjoyable. I am done with you, and I intend to make sure you know exactly what I mean. You should not be in a position to influence other people through your worthless blog and advice. I really do hate you.

Then Graham logs on to Facebook, where he finds that Lisa has written several statements on his wall that demonize and insult him.

What about this exchange should give Graham cause for concern? What about it should cause Graham to rest easy?

Do you think that Lisa is a harmless fan? After all, she's a woman who lives overseas. How much of a threat could she possibly pose to Graham? Perhaps Graham should just e-mail a quick "sorry," set the record straight, explain that there's been a misunderstanding, that he's really a good person, and that he was just busy?

Or do you think that Lisa is the kind of Internet nuisance who should be put in her place? Perhaps Graham should fire off an angry e-mail that teaches her some politeness and manners? Perhaps Graham should share Lisa's e-mail address with all of his friends and have them respond with some derogatory comments of their own?

Or do you think Lisa is dangerous and that Graham should send her a curt e-mail asking her to not contact him ever again?

All of these tactics are the opposite of what Graham should do.

In reality, Lisa's gender has little to do with the potential threat she poses to Graham. That she lives overseas *might* be cause for relief, assuming she really does live overseas.

Indeed, Graham may falsely assume he knows more about Lisa than he really does. He's relying on what she's told him, but he doesn't know if any of that information is truthful or factual. Graham is underestimating Internet fabrication, which happens all the time. For all Graham knows, Lisa lives near him and has been following him around for weeks and months without him noticing her. That she knows he owns a blue suit and a red tie suggests as much.

For that matter, Graham can't even know for sure if Lisa is really a woman. It's possible that her entire Internet persona has been fabricated. She might really be a teenage Internet troll who finds enjoyment in wasting people's time online. She might be a convicted felon. For all Graham knows, she might even be his next-door neighbor.

Lisa is behaving like a cyberstalker, and it's very likely that she is one. Three details give this away: She's described herself as Graham's "biggest fan," which puts Graham up on a pedestal. She's sexualized Graham. Then, when she didn't get the response she wanted, she went from adulation to demonization, and her behavior appears to be escalating.

Many people think of cyberstalkers as mere annoyances. Yet cyberstalkers can be potentially very dangerous. These stalkers tend to target victims through Internet chat rooms, discussion boards, social networking sites, blogs, and e-mail. They've been known to steal their victims' identities, send viruses to their victims' computers, bully their victims online, and defame and malign their victims' reputations.

Lisa might physically lash out at Graham's family, too. Often the person most at risk in a stalking case isn't the person being stalked. Rather it's the person or people the stalker sees standing in the way between them and their target.

Not all stalkers escalate to violent behavior. Many of them are only a constant yet annoying presence in someone's life. Lisa's recent e-mail, however, is cause for concern. She's gone from e-mailing once every other week to several times in one week, and the tone and content of the e-mails have dramatically changed as well. This could be a sign that Lisa's behavior is becoming worse, more threatening, and that she might eventually turn physically violent or destructive in other ways. For instance, Lisa has already tried to damage Graham's reputation online. She might show up at his place of employment or even his residence.

If Graham continues to communicate with Lisa in *any* way, he'll only encourage her advances. Negative communication is still communication. If he argues with her, he'll incite her, causing her to become even more obsessed. If he's nice, he'll still increase her obsession. And if he asks her to leave him alone, she won't.

His best strategy is to mitigate or reduce the risk that Lisa will evolve from a nuisance into someone who is set on harming him physically, emotionally, financially, or professionally. He will want to cut off all contact and save copies of all communication from her. If Lisa escalates—by contacting him by phone, leaving handwritten notes at his home, threatening him, mailing him gifts, increasing the frequency of her contact, contacting him by multiple methods (phone, text, e-mail, fax), or revealing that she's somehow gathered more personal information about him—he should contact an intervening resource for help. He might consult law enforcement for a restraining order, or a lawyer, private investigator, or legal consultant. If Lisa begins marring his reputation online, he might consult a firm that specializes in repairing online reputations. He also might contact his Internet service provider and see if they will take up the cause.

How did you do? Did you get a perfect score? Or did you call some of them right and some of them wrong? Most people, if they are being honest, tell me that they guessed correctly on some, and not so correctly on others. You might be the same. That's because gut feelings can be right sometimes—and they can be wrong a lot more often. When it comes to your personal safety and well-being, however, wouldn't you want to use a method that has a better track record? By the end of this book, you will know that method, and you will be able to put it to work for you in your life.

CHAPTER 1 RAP SHEET

- You can't tell if people are dangerous just by looking at them.
- You can't always take people at their word.
- Dangerous people are good at blending in.
- If you ask the right questions, you can learn how someone is likely to behave by listening to his or her answers.
- You can't walk a mile in a dangerous person's shoes because dangerous people wear a different kind of shoe—one that doesn't fit you.

Chapter 2

The Dangers of Relying on Instincts and Intuition

My coauthor knows a woman who believes that all her problems stem from bad luck. She's a single mother who earns not much more than the minimum wage. Her car doesn't always start and her babysitters don't always show up, preventing her from getting to work. She's lost quite a few jobs because of undependable cars and babysitters.

These job losses have led to her not paying bills on time, which has led to her phone, power, or Internet being cut off. She's been evicted from apartments.

If you met this woman and listened to her tale of woe, you would probably think, "The poor thing. She just can't get a break. One person should not have so much bad luck. Life really isn't fair. I really feel sorry for her."

In reality, though, this woman probably isn't any less lucky than you are or I am. Her problems don't stem from bad luck. They stem from decisions that resulted in a lifelong trickle effect.

Let's take a closer look at some of her decisions and the resulting consequences:

- She got angry and decided to take it out on another student. Consequently she was expelled from college.

- She decided to have unprotected intercourse with a man she did not know very well. Consequently she got pregnant, even though she did not have the financial resources or lifestyle to support a baby.
- She decided to take advantage of various people in her life—demanding they give her money and other types of support. Consequently, friends, family members, and even Good Samaritan acquaintances stopped supporting her.
- She became angry with the father of her child for not giving her enough money, so she decided to teach him a lesson. She went to court and severed his paternal rights. Consequently he was no longer available to watch their child while she was at work—causing her to rely on a string of undependable babysitters. Eventually she lost her jobs.

If this woman learned how to accurately assess people and situations for danger and to make thoughtful, analytical decisions rather than impulsive, emotion-driven ones, she'd feel in control of her life and she would stop feeling like a victim of bad luck.

Why Luck Is Dangerous

"Luck" is a nebulous term that means different things to different people. It's not something you can define or quantify. How can you know whether your luck is any worse or better than anyone else's? How can you know if it's getting better or worse? How can you come up with strategies to change it?

Perhaps most problematic is the way people use the concept of luck as a way to avoid taking ownership of their lives. If you see every outcome as a result of luck, you have no motivation to change your decision-making process. Flawed assessment and decision-making processes are what tend to get many people into trouble and bring them disappointment, resentment, failure, and severe negative consequences.

Throughout this book, you will learn an analytical process that will help you to go beyond luck. As a result, you will feel more in control of your life and less like a victim of bad luck.

Why Intuition Is Dangerous

Many books encourage people to trust their intuition; they claim that fear will guide you away from danger and that your sense of happiness will bring good fortune.

According to such books, we are all supposed to have a magical inner radar that allows us to acquire knowledge without thinking or reasoning. For instance, highly intuitive people are thought to be able to feel out whether a person is dangerous. They are supposed to be able to foresee, before they step on board, whether a plane will go down. They are thought to be able to sense danger before danger happens. They are almost psychic.

Yet there is little science to back any of this up. Do you believe in intuition? Do you rely on it when making decisions?

Let's for a moment assume that you answered yes and that intuition plays a huge role in how your conduct your life. If so, I'd like you to think about a few additional questions.

- Do you believe in your powers of intuition so much that you would trust them to tell when to pull a parachute cord after jumping from an airplane, even if you never skydived before?
- Do you believe in intuition so much that you would put your entire life's savings on a number on a roulette wheel that gave you a good feeling?
- Do you believe in it so much that you would trust it to help you drive a car while blindfolded?
- If your son, daughter, brother, or sister told you they were going to abandon their life and family to move across the world to follow a religious charlatan, would you accept the explanation that they "just feel good about him"?

- Would you willingly step foot into the lions' enclosure at a zoo and use your intuition to decide the best way to interact with these dangerous wild animals?

I'm guessing that you would not want to rely on your powers of intuition to do any of these things.

In high-risk situations—situations that could have dire long-term consequences including physical harm or death—it seems reckless to rely on intuition, doesn't it? It sure does to me.

Like luck, intuition is not quantifiable. It's not measurable either. There is no known way to hone or improve it. And we don't even know where it is. Do you feel intuition in your stomach? Your chest? Your head?

Our intuitive read on a given person or situation will be influenced by a range of variables such as our upbringing, culture, and religion. How well rested we are and even whether we are under the influence of drugs or alcohol will affect how we feel about people and situations. Even if you have intuition, your ability to feel out a situation will be dulled by some of the following factors:

- Stress
- Fear
- Lack of experience
- Drugs or alcohol
- Fatigue
- Emotional and/or psychological needs and problems

Note that in a high-risk situation, you will likely be feeling plenty of stress and fear, and you will probably be out of your element too. When you are under stress, your emotions and sensations tend to be even less trustworthy than when you are relaxed. Many people tell me that they have decided against doing something based on a bad feeling they had in their gut. What I've wondered is this: Was that bad feeling a sign that they should not buy the car or take the job, or just a sign that they were nervous or scared? Were they really relying on this mysterious thing known as intuition, or were they simply caving under the pressure of stress?

Think back over your life and about the many different decisions you've made—and especially about the ones you *felt* your way through. How many serious relationships did you get into because you felt a strong connection to someone, only to later realize the person was a jerk? How many business transactions have you made because you had a "good feeling" about something, only to learn later you'd just lost your shirt? How often have you trusted someone because you liked him or her, only to have this person abuse that trust or otherwise hurt you?

If these are things that tend to happen over and over again in your life, your powers of intuition may not be as strong as you believe.

When making important decisions about safety and well-being, do you really want to be relying on something that has proven in the past to be faulty? Do you really want to rely solely on intuition—which can be affected by fatigue, stress, arrogance, ignorance, emotional attraction, and physical or psychological needs—rather than use analytical reasoning, which involves the same process no matter what?

Why Instincts Are Dangerous

Although some people use the two terms interchangeably, "instincts" are not the same thing as "intuition."

Scientists define instincts as inborn behavioral patterns that we exhibit in response to a specific stimulus. For instance, salmon have a spawning instinct that leads them to swim upstream to lay their eggs. Similarly, many birds instinctually fly south in the winter. They do so even though they've never been taught to do it. They are born knowing to do it.

It's obvious that human babies are born with some instincts, because they do many things that no one taught them to do. For instance, they cry when they are hungry or pull away from something that is painful.

Even as adults we engage in more instinctual behavior than we realize, and some of this behavior can harm us more than it helps.

For instance, we have a survival instinct that causes us to fear death and situations that could lead to it. Yet this survival instinct is not necessarily going to keep us out of harm's way. It doesn't prevent danger, and it doesn't teach us how to react to it. Our survival instinct says, "Yes, I want to live!" But it doesn't tell us precisely how to stay alive.

Your survival instinct will probably kick in, for example, if you are ever to find yourself on fire. That instinct, however, will not necessarily tell you what to do to put out the fire. If anything, your natural inclination might be to run. That's why we teach children to stop, drop, and roll. If they haven't been trained via constant repetition and practice, most people will not drop and roll when they are on fire. They will run, which does not put out the fire and may even make it worse.

This is why businesses and schools have earthquake and fire drills—to help people practice the correct response over and over again so that it becomes ingrained.

Let's look at another situation where survival instincts might kick in but not necessarily tell us what to do. Have you ever started to skid after hitting an icy patch on the road, seen a big fat tree ahead and reflexively hit the brake? What happened? Did you end up hitting the tree? Chances are you did.

Indeed, the correct way to steer out of a skid goes against our survival instinct. Our instincts scream, "Hit the brake! Hit the brake!" because we want the car to stop to avoid hitting the tree, but braking won't slow a car when its tires are moving over ice. Rather, it causes the tires to lose traction. End result: You lose control of the car and can't steer out of the skid.

The correct way to steer out of a skid is to turn the wheel in the direction you want to go—away from the tree—and to gently accelerate to encourage the tires to grip the road.

It goes against your body's natural inclinations. This is referred to as being counterintuitive.

Here are a few other situations in which our survival instinct can cause us to do the opposite of what we need to do to be safe:

- Do you remember when John F. Kennedy Jr. crashed his plane into the Atlantic? He was trying to land his plane in the dark. It was foggy, and he could not see the horizon. Therefore he couldn't tell just by looking whether his plane was parallel or perpendicular to the ocean. The plane's instruments told him that it was in a nosedive, but

Kennedy's inner ear told him that the plane was horizontal. He trusted his inner ear and his eyes, and he brought the plane into a nosedive into the ocean. As pilot Eric Nolte wrote of the incident, "Our feelings, indulged without examination, will kill us."

- I lived in San Francisco for many years, so I can tell you firsthand how strong the urge to run outside is after the shaking of an earthquake starts. Yet during the severe earthquakes, people died when they ran outside and were killed by falling debris. The greatest dangers are objects just outside a structure, such as a utility pole or something else that could fall. If you are indoors, the best strategy may not be to run outside but rather to get underneath something sturdy that will cushion you from falling debris, such as a bed or a doorframe.

- Think about what people often do when caught in a riptide. Most people feel an urge to swim against the tide, which allows the tide to pull them farther and farther into the ocean. They eventually get tired and drown. The right thing to do is swim, not away from, but parallel to the current until you escape it, but your instincts won't tell you to do that.

- Sadly, I've seen that in cases of school violence, students' instinct is to hide under their desks rather than to run out of the building. Their survival instincts are telling them two things: "Hide" and

The Dangerous Truth

Many people tell me that they would scream bloody murder if someone attempted to assault or kidnap them. What I've learned from interviewing the victims of violent crime, however, is that your natural reaction to a threat is not necessarily predictable. Some people are mute through an entire encounter. Their fear incapacitates them. Others have told me that they kicked and screamed, cried uncontrollably, or repeatedly asked the offender, "Who are you and why are you doing this?" I've learned that different people react to fear in different ways and that your reaction is unpredictable unless you plan and practice in advance.

"Put something solid between me and the threat." Yet desks do not provide adequate protection from flying bullets, and students who hide under desks or tables become stationary targets.

The Dangers of Instinctlike Habits

Survival instincts are inborn. You don't learn them. They are present from the day you take your first breath.

You can, however, repeatedly practice a behavior until it becomes habitual and as a result instinctlike. For instance, in the FBI we never pick up spent casings during shooting practice because we don't want to habitually bend down and start picking up spent casings in the middle of a real shoot-out, when even the slightest hesitation could get us killed. If we picked up the casings over and over again during practice, that's exactly what we would do in a real-life situation. That's why we practice, practice, and practice the reaction we want to have during an actual shoot-out.

We also practice shooting to hit a target in the torso or head. We don't practice shooting at the kneecaps or the arms. What do you think is going to happen during a real-life shoot-out? We're going to aim for the heart or head—without thinking about it.

The Dangerous Truth

Some home owners like to have a handgun for protection. Initially this might seem like a smart decision. But if you do not train yourself to use a handgun for that specific purpose, then you can't know precisely what you will do if you are ever in the position of facing down an intruder. It's likely that the intruder will be much more skilled at handling and shooting a gun than you are. If you are walking into a face-off for the very first time in your life, your risk of physical harm is very high. If you want to keep a gun in the home, I highly recommend becoming familiar with the gun by doing frequent target practice.

In real life, we automatically default to what we've trained ourselves to do. We lean on instinctlike habits.

And these instinctlike habits can be acquired, trained, and strengthened. The problem, of course, is that you can't practice for every single situation in life before it happens. You might be able to rely on learned instincts in some situations. For instance, if you are a lifeguard, you will probably be able to rescue a drowning victim based on your learned instincts. If you are a lawyer, you can probably negotiate based on learned instincts. And as a profiler who has studied human behavior, I probably make more than a few decisions based on learned instincts.

That's because in each case the person has trained for the situation over and over again, so that their brain and body can operate on autopilot whenever they find themselves in it.

Your ability to think critically also depends on how much practice you've had in making the same sort of decision. But what do you do when you are in a situation that puts you out of your area of practice? If you rely only on untrained, unrehearsed, or raw instincts that you have not honed for that situation, how can you possibly react correctly?

The Dangers of Rigid Rules

If you live in a city or a neighborhood where there is noted criminal activity, you have likely picked up a few tactics that help you to stay safe in that setting. Those tactics have probably worked for you too. Most of them probably involve minimizing contact with people you don't know. For instance, you might be wary whenever a stranger asks you a question or takes an unusual interest in you.

But the complete avoidance of strangers is not really a strategy. It's a lifestyle, and it's what people resort to when they don't know how to do risk assessments. Some strangers are not a threat to you. You may avoid them, however, because you don't have a process in place that helps you to sort out the harmful strangers from the harmless ones. You may default to an interpersonal style of distancing yourself and of being unfriendly and uncommunicative toward anyone you don't know. If you only have one tool in your assessment toolbox, that's the one you will use all the time.

For instance, let's say there's a knock at your front door. How do you decide whether to open the door? You might say that you have a policy: You never open the door when you are not expecting someone. This strategy might have kept you safe in the past, and it's certainly prevented annoying solicitors from getting a piece of your time. But what if the person on the other side of the door is your neighbor, knocking to tell you that the house two doors down is on fire? What if the person on the other side of the door is a motorist who is there to tell you that she thinks she just hit your dog, who is still alive but in dire need of veterinary care? What if the person on the other side of the door is a police officer who is there to tell you about some burglaries in the neighborhood and offer some advice on how you can avoid being a victim? Wouldn't you want to answer your door? Can you see how it would be helpful to have an assessment process that helps you quickly determine when to open the door and when not to?

More important, strangers are not the only people who pose a threat to you. If staying away from strangers is your primary safety strategy, how will you stay safe around all the other people in your life who are not strangers to you? How will you protect your best interests at work, in romantic relationships, and with the various people you hire (housekeepers, contractors, lawn servicers, and so on)? What happens when you find yourself in a situation that falls outside your rigid safety rules? How will you protect yourself?

As you will soon learn, strangers generally pose less of a potential threat to you than others closer to you who you probably openly allow into your comfort zone. It's just as important—if not more important—to be able to assess the threat of people close to you as it is to be able to assess the threat of strangers.

For all of these reasons and more, it's important to have an assessment process you can use to protect yourself physically, emotionally, psychologically, financially, professionally, and legally no matter where you find yourself and no matter who you find yourself with. Without a well-honed and well-practiced assessment process in place, you will find yourself relying on instincts and intuition whenever you are in an unfamiliar situation.

#99 08-07-2019 10:05AM
Item(s) checked out to p11050524.

TITLE: Dangerous instincts : how gut fee
BARCODE: 3 1986 04918 1673
DUE DATE: 08-28-19

Once you learn how to make your own risk assessments, your life will not be so limiting. Rather than feeling paranoid and overly protective, you will realize the power you have to be in charge of your life, your circumstances, and relationships. Decision making will not be so overwhelming, stressful, and uncertain. While life will continue to be challenging, you can anticipate and manage these challenges in a much more effective way.

The SMART Model

In this book you will learn a decision-making and risk-assessment process that does not rely on instinct or intuition. Rather, it relies on experience, practice, and training.

When you make decisions based on instinct or intuition, you *feel* your way through, basing your decisions on gut feelings and emotions. When you make decisions based on the SMART model, you *think* them through. Yes, there might be some emotion and feeling involved. There will be times when you have no other choice than to make a decision despite the fear, sadness, frustration, or other emotion you might be experiencing.

But you will not be making decisions *because* of your emotions. You will learn how to keep feelings of helplessness, confusion, and desperation from nudging you into decisions that could potentially result in calamity. Instead you will make decisions by using an analytical assessment process that is always the same no matter what emotion you might be experiencing.

I call this process the SMART model. As mentioned, it's SMART because it's a:

S = sound
M = method of
A = assessing and
R = recognizing
T = trouble

This method will help you to determine the risk involved in making a decision and avoid making decisions that you will come to regret. It will help you to overcome the weaknesses that could cloud your judgment—weaknesses like inherent biases, stress you might be under, strong emotions, pressure from others, or skills you currently lack. How many times have you felt overwhelmed, desperate, or lost but had to make a decision anyway? The SMART model will be particularly helpful in situations where there is a lot of emotion.

This process will also help you to determine the true risk that any given situation poses. You will know, based on the SMART model, whether the given situation really is safe or whether there are unseen or unanticipated threats that should cause you concern. And you will also be able to assess the risk in trusting other people—with your heart, money, children, livelihood, reputation, or life. Finally, the SMART model will help you determine the best way to interview someone, so you can persuade them to open up and provide you with the information you need to make your decision or to resolve a conflict or problem.

Whenever faced with a dilemma, our goal is for you to ask yourself, "Am I making a SMART decision?" Later on you'll learn how. In the next few chapters, however, let's first look more closely at why this model is so important.

CHAPTER 2 RAP SHEET

- You do not have to feel that you are a victim of bad luck or random circumstances. By learning how to make SMART decisions, you can change your circumstances for the better.
- You probably regret decisions that you made spontaneously, impulsively, and based on your emotions. You are less likely to regret decisions that are thoughtful, careful, and made with your long-term future in mind.
- Many people who believe in intuition in theory would never rely on it during a life-or-death situation because they intuitively know just how unreliable it is.

- Your survival instinct might guide you to safety some of the time, but it's just as likely to guide you into danger.
- You can train your instincts to react to some situations, but you cannot train them to react to all situations.
- The SMART model is a "sound method of assessing and recognizing trouble."

Chapter 3

Personality: It's What Makes People Tick

I'd been working a child-abduction case for months, and I suspected that Tom, a close friend of the victim's mother, might have had something to do with the child's disappearance. Tom had proven difficult to deal with. When I'd tried to ask him questions about the child's disappearance, he'd been uncooperative and suspicious of where the investigation was headed. He was arrogant and confrontational, and he seemed to have a side of himself that he kept secret.

I knew that Tom didn't like me, but I wanted to know more about him and the kind of person he was. So I'd been talking to a number of his friends and acquaintances, and Tom didn't like that. I asked one of them, Allan, if he wouldn't mind coming to the FBI office to talk with me. He agreed.

Tom drove Allan to the office and waited outside for him to finish.

When Allan walked into the interview room, he seemed uncomfortable and nervous. I thought his nervousness was odd. He was not a suspect in the case, and I'm a low-key interviewer. I'm not the type of person who gets someone to talk by pushing my weight around and making threats. Instead I usually get people to open up by being sincere, serious, nonjudgmental, and by listening intently to what they are saying. (More on why this approach works in chapter 8.) I've interviewed many, many people, and my presence doesn't usually make them nervous. In fact, most people open up to me and tell me things they would never tell someone else.

I took a look at Allan. He was dressed casually but had too much clothing on for the mild California weather.

"Are you wired? Do you have a tape recorder on you?" I asked. This was not usually my opening line.

"Yes," he said. He sheepishly pulled a tape recorder from under his shirt and handed it to me.

When I walked out of the interview room that day, the other agents marveled. "Are you psychic?"

The answer to that question is no. I'm not psychic. I suspected that Allan might attempt to tape the interview. And as you keep reading this chapter, you'll understand how I came to that conclusion.

It's Not Mind Reading

What happened with Allan that day was a made-for-TV moment. On television shows such as *Criminal Minds* and *The Mentalist*, the investigators seem to have the ability to read minds and predict human behavior. In one episode of *The Mentalist*, for instance, Patrick Jane (a former psychic con man who now serves as a police consultant) walks into a room and notices that a man in a suit is patting his jacket pocket a few too many times.

He asks to see the drugs the man has hidden in his pocket.

Apparently, according to this show, anyone who pats their jacket pocket must have drugs in it.

It's not that simple.

And while real-life behavioral analysts like me may—at times—seem to be able to read minds or see into the future, we can't. What we are really doing is reading people's behavior for insights into their personality. Once we understand someone's personality, we have a really good idea of what that person is likely to do in a given situation.

For instance, in the example of my interview with Allan, I already knew that Tom was dominant and controlling. I also knew that Tom was extremely concerned about what might be said during the interview. And I knew that Tom was not a rule follower. It's a crime to tape an FBI interview without consent, but that's not the sort of thing that would concern Tom.

It is, however, the kind of thing that would concern Allan, who was a rule follower, for the most part. I knew that Allan had the type of personality that could easily be persuaded to do something. He was intimidated by Tom. Tom had told Allan that he was being harassed by the FBI, and Allan had believed him. Allan was naive, and I was concerned that he was being used by Tom and didn't even realize it.

Allan was willing to commit a federal crime because his friend had told him to do it, but it made him uncomfortable—and it showed. Also he was dressed in an outfit that would have allowed him to hide something.

I'm not psychic, and I can't read minds. I just happened to do a good assessment based on my knowledge of Tom and Allan and what I knew about their behavior and personalities.

Why Feelings Are Unreliable Assessment Tools

When most people try to get a read on someone—whether it's a potential date, employee, babysitter, or stranger—they usually rely on how they feel. If they have a good feeling when they are around the person, they put them in a "positive" category. If they have a bad feeling, they sort them into a "negative" category.

This is where we get the expression "feeling someone out." It's also where we get the expressions "we just click," "we have great chemistry," "I have a good feeling about this one," and "there's just something about him."

The problem with this is that we tend to feel good about people based on superficial characteristics that have very little to do with how innocent or dangerous they really are. The clothes someone wears, the smile on their face, or the warmth of their hug can all make us feel good about a person—even if that person is about to con or hurt us.

As it turns out, it's really easy to manipulate feelings, and dangerous people know how to do just that. They know how to disarm you, get you to feel comfortable, and create the sense that the two of you have a special bond. They do it through impression management. They compliment you, pay attention to you, and spin lies that allow you to believe that the two of you have something in common. That's why they are so successful at conning and manipulating people.

Several other factors can throw off your feelings, too, making them more reliable assessment tools in some situations and a lot less reliable in others. Your feelings can change depending on your internal state. Stress changes how you feel. Alcohol and various medications (both prescription and over-the-counter) will change how you feel. A good night's sleep will change how you feel.

Have you ever gone to bed thinking that your spouse was a despicable human being, only to wake the next morning wondering what you were so angry about the night before? Indeed lack of sleep tends to make us feel more negative. So can stress. And alcohol and some medications can do the opposite, causing us to feel good about people who would usually cause us to have our guard up.

Your feelings about someone can change from moment to moment and day to day. Yet the person in question has not changed at all. You might feel better, but the person in question might be just as dangerous as ever.

Relying on feelings to read people can also cause you to miss or ignore important information that would contradict whatever feelings you have. For instance, early in a new relationship, your feelings of affection for someone could cause you to overlook any number of dangerous details, such as a man's controlling nature or a woman's constant need for attention.

For these reasons, feeling someone out is not an accurate way to assess whether they are a good fit for your company, a good caregiver for your child, or even a good friend or lover.

Why Personality Is So Important

Your personality is the motor that drives all your behavior, decisions, and choices. It conditions how you view the world, how you view others, and how you think others view you. It determines how you cope with stressors and situations. It affects how you act and react to what's going on around you and how you interact with others. It's who you are.

Once you understand someone's personality, you can do a much better job of predicting how that person will react in various situations. You'll be more effective and successful in dealing with others because you will begin to understand their behavior. You will know what makes them tick.

For instance, students tend to threaten violence quite often, but fortunately most of those threats will never be carried out. Still, the seriousness of the threat cannot be determined solely by words. A student may say, "I am going to shoot up the school," but one student might just be saying it, while another may very well do it. That's why I'm often called in to sort out the seriousness of the threat and help determine if a student really will bring a gun to school or set off a bomb. I do this by finding out as much as I can about the student who made the threat, including his unique biological, psychological, and social factors. (This is known as the biopsychosocial model.) I look into his family life, his social life, his academic life, and more. I find out everything I can about his behavior over time. That gives me a sense of his personality, and it helps me to determine whether he is likely to act out in a violent or threatening way.

It's for this reason that signs in airports caution you not to joke about bringing bombs or unauthorized items onto an airplane. The folks in Homeland Security take every single one of those statements seriously because they know nothing about the personalities behind them. You might be a harmless person who says a dumb thing because you are in the middle of a very stressful moment, but the folks in Homeland Security don't know whether you are a harmless, frustrated passenger or a mission-oriented terrorist who just leaked his intentions.

Homeland Security officials can't get a read on your personality just from the outfit you happened to wear to the airport that day or by the expression on your face. If the only words they hear come out of your mouth are, "I want this plane to go down," they are going to take that very seriously.

To be able to tease out whether someone could be dangerous, you must have insight into that person's personality, and you'll gain those insights by observing and learning about that person's behavior over time.

The more you practice reading people, the better you'll get at it and the more accurate your assessments of various people will become. Unlike intuition—which cannot be trained or tested—this step-by-step process of reading behavior and assessing personality can be honed and improved. This is in large part what I did as an FBI profiler. There were no smoke and mirrors. It came down to observing and interpreting behavior, and then understanding the personality that produced that behavior.

You'll learn more about how to read someone else's behavior and know more about their personality later in this book. For now, though, I'd like to go into a few misconceptions about personality.

Myth 1: Adults can have significant changes in their personalities.

More than a hundred years ago, a man named Phineas Gage was in a railroad accident during which an iron rod punctured his cheek and was driven into the frontal lobe of his brain.

Amazingly, he survived the accident and went on to live twelve more years, but he was forever changed. The spike had damaged the part of his brain responsible for weighing future consequences. The iron rod changed the once smart and likable Gage into an impulsive, hostile, and volatile man.

There are only a few things that will cause a radical change in personality. Having an iron rod puncture your frontal lobe is one of them. Others include diseases, trauma, and medications that affect that same area of the brain.

Barring those circumstances, most adults' personalities don't change all that much. As Albert Einstein once famously said, "Women marry men hoping they will change. Men marry women hoping they will not. So each is inevitably disappointed."

The problem with marrying someone with the expectation that he will change is this: Your personality is pretty much formed by your late twenties. Sometime after age thirty, it becomes less and less likely to change and you will take that personality with you into old age.

Personality development is a very complex, dynamic, and interactive process. One's personality is determined by both genetics (nature) and environment. The latter is commonly referred to as the "nurture" part of the equation. Indicators of a person's personality traits begin to emerge at an early age. Then the personality continues to develop and evolve until it becomes hardwired. After that, it's questionable whether a change in one's personality is possible. Researchers from the University of California, Riverside, compared teachers' personality ratings of 2,400 elementary school children from the 1960s with videotaped interviews of those same individuals forty years later. They found that many personality attributes both remained unchanged and affected their behavior as adults. For instance, children with "verbally fluent" personalities (defined as unrestrained talkativeness) spoke fluently, displayed a high degree of intelligence, and were interested in intellectual matters as adults. Children with low verbal fluency tended to give up when faced with obstacles and had an awkward interpersonal style as adults.[2]

Once the personality becomes hardwired, significant changes are not likely. If someone is emotionally distant at age thirty, chances are he will still be emotionally distant years from now too. If your adult friend has always been self-centered and self-focused, it is likely that she will continue to be.

Yes, you can communicate and compromise, and people can successfully modify specific behaviors. They can stop smoking, for instance, or overcome a fear of heights (acrophobia) or a fear of dogs (cynophobia). But those are not hardwired personality traits. Rather, they are acquired fears (phobias) or addictions that can respond to therapy, especially cognitive behavioral therapies.

Adult personality traits, such as extroversion and introversion, do not tend to change, or at least do not change with any significance. So if you marry someone who is reserved, quiet, and low-key—someone who requires less social interaction with others—it's not likely that you will be able to turn that person into someone who is permanently the life of the party and who is energized by involvement with others. Likewise, an adult who is described as disagreeable—always seeing life's glass as half-empty, and with little interest in the well-being of others—is not likely to permanently morph into someone who is compassionate or less antagonistic or who has an overall optimistic or positive view of the world. If you marry someone whose outlook on life is negative despite all the good things that happen to him or her, who is impersonal, suspicious, and lacking in empathy, you will likely live the rest of your life in great frustration and hurt or eventually get divorced.

That's why it's so important to understand a person's personality before allowing a relationship with them to become too intimate. You can never fully get into someone's head, but you can gain insights into their personality by observing their behavior in a variety of situations and over a period of time. The key is to look for a pattern of behavior. The more you observe the person, the better. From time to time, we all engage in behavior that is selfish, strange, and even out of character. Maybe, for instance, you are essentially calm and easygoing but quick to become angry when tired. If someone observes you only when you are fatigued, he might come away with the false notion that you have a short fuse. But if that person sees you in many situations, over a period of time, he or she will have a more accurate view of your personality.

Myth 2: You can leave your personality at the door.

Supervisors often ask employees to leave their personalities at the door, to walk into the conference room, for example, without their conflicts or differences. But employees can't leave their personality at the door any more easily than they can leave a body part at the door. Their personality is who they are. It influences how they communicate, how they interact with others, and how they believe others see them and judge them. It's what makes them unique as a person. An employee who is quick to anger and impulsive cannot change those personality traits just by walking out of one room and into another. Personality is hardwired.

The only ways to prevent someone's seriously problematic personality from showing up at a meeting are either to not invite that person to the meeting or to not hire such a person in the first place.

Myth 3: Some people have Jekyll-and-Hyde personalities.

In Robert Louis Stevenson's novella *The Strange Case of Dr. Jekyll and Mr. Hyde*, Dr. Jekyll takes drugs that release his evil side and slowly turn him into the violent and unstable Mr. Hyde. In real life, many people seem to believe that such seismic personality shifts are possible, even without the magic potion. That's why, when someone commits a horrible act of violence, friends, relatives, and loved ones will remark, "I never saw that side of him" or "He just snapped."

For instance, very few battered spouses ever say, "I knew he was going to abuse me from the moment I first laid eyes on him." If they knew that, they wouldn't have dated and eventually married these men. So when the boyfriend or husband becomes abusive, they frequently see it as a change in personality from good to bad. They will remark, "He's not the person I married" or "Something changed in him."

Yes, normal people do lose their tempers and get angry from time to time. Yes, sometimes when people are under enormous pressure they behave in ways that are aberrant for them. And, yes, certain diseases can erode parts of the brain that are responsible for helping people determine the difference between right and wrong—causing huge shifts in their behavior as a result.

But I am not talking about those sorts of situations here. I'm talking about regular people, who do not "snap" at all. In such people, the potential to act out violently is always there. It's just not noticed, recognized, or interpreted correctly. In such cases, what usually happens is one, or both, of the following:

1. People who are dangerous, abusive, or threatening frequently manifest behaviors that are engaging, charming, and nonthreatening. Someone who is prone to violence, angry outbursts, and aggressiveness, for instance, doesn't usually behave in a concerning way all day long. So loved ones, coworkers, and friends often see what they want

to see and ignore what they don't want to see or what they don't know how to interpret. A woman who is dating a man who is abusive might initially ignore and explain away his jealousy, thinking, "He loves me so much." When that jealousy results in physical abuse, however, she incorrectly thinks he's become a different man.

2. Dangerous people can be very good at impression management and at hiding the concerning aspects of their personalities. A wife abuser, for instance, will turn on the charm early in the relationship, until he knows he's got the woman lured in. Then slowly, over time, he'll reveal his true nature.

Impression management may be one reason why Colonel Russell Williams of the Royal Canadian Air Force was able to escape detection for so many years. He pled guilty to eighty-eight charges, including two counts of first-degree murder. The crimes took place over several years. They started with voyeurism and progressed to breaking into homes, stealing lingerie, and masturbating on women's beds. From there, he progressed to sexually assaulting women and then to rape and murder. His crimes were extreme, but Williams was so adept at seeming normal that no one suspected he could ever be capable of such behavior. He lived a double life. In one part of his life, he was a highly respected and successful air force commander. In another, he was a sexual deviant and a predator.

Myth 4: Quiet people have no personality.

Sometimes, when describing someone else, a person will say, "He has no personality" or "She has zero personality." Unless the person they are describing is no longer in the land of the living, this just isn't the case. There is no such thing as having no personality. We all have a personality.

What people really mean is that the person is shy, reserved, introverted, and not particularly social.

Another mistake people tend to make is to link shyness either with dangerousness or harmlessness. For instance, they might decide that someone who is very shy and socially awkward must be "weird" and therefore "creepy." Or they might think that someone who is a little reticent is "sensitive" and "deep" and therefore "harmless." Yet being outgoing or reserved has no correlation with how dangerous or harmless a person is. Both extroverts and introverts are equally capable of behaving dangerously.

Myth 5: A mood disorder is more concerning than a personality disorder.

A Hollywood celebrity was much in the news as this book was being written. In one story, sources remarked that it was good news that this person didn't have bipolar disorder but rather seemed to *only* have a *common* personality disorder.

What the media didn't quite understand as it reported this story is that a mood disorder, such as bipolar disease, can be very successfully managed with medications and therapy. Many personality disorders are less successfully treated by standard therapies, and certain types of personality disorders can be more problematic than most mood disorders. Although some personality disorders might respond positively to standard therapies, others do not.

Myth 6: You can have a "nice" or "good" personality.

Whenever I hear someone describe a person as "nice" or "good," I always think, "What a cop-out." That description tells me nothing about the personality. It is vanilla; it says nothing about the person's unique makeup. When I hear someone describe a person as "nice," it tells me that the describer is a fencer, someone who doesn't want to say anything negative because they are afraid of being seen as judgmental. They also might not know the person all that well or worry that what they say will get back to this "nice" person. No one is just nice or good. People's personalities are far more complex and dynamic than a one-word adjective can cover. When I ask what someone is like, I want to know about the patterns of behavior he exhibits in interactions with others, his view of the world, his perception of himself, and his perception of how others view him.

CHAPTER 3 RAP SHEET

- You can't read people's minds, but you can—by observing their behavior and listening to what they say—get a read on their personalities. Doing so will allow you to predict how they might react in a given situation.
- Your feelings about someone can be easily manipulated by flattery, impression management, and more. For these reasons, feelings or gut instincts are usually not an accurate way to gauge the dangerousness or trustworthiness of another person.
- Once you understand someone's personality, you can more accurately anticipate, and even predict, how that person will react in various situations.

Chapter 4

What Makes People Dangerous

I watched Gary Leon Ridgway—better known as the Green River Killer—walk down the prison hallway and into the interview room. He thrust his chest out, swayed his shoulders, and walked with an incredible swagger for a guy who was handcuffed and flanked by highly trained and physically fit guards. The men and women in Gary's tactical detail were larger than him and they outnumbered him.

Yet Gary did not walk like a subdued convict. No, if anything, he walked and acted as if this tactical team was really his protective detail. It was as if—in Gary's mind—he was a VIP and these people were sent to follow him around for his protection.

Gary did not walk with shame. No, everything about him seemed to be saying, "I'm Gary Ridgway, and I am proud to be the Green River Killer."

Gary had spent more than two decades kidnapping women off the streets of Seattle, Washington, then killing and burying them in cluster graves in nearby areas. Now he had agreed to plead guilty to these murders and to be interviewed by law enforcement in exchange for not being executed. Part of the agreement involved him assisting the King County Sheriff's Office to identify and locate the bodies of what turned out to be his forty-eight victims.

I joined a team of awesome detectives and incredible interviewers who met with Gary over six months. We couldn't just take Gary's word for what he had done. Serial sexual killers are notorious for bragging about how many people they've murdered. We wanted to find the bodies of his victims so families could finally know what had happened to their loved ones and who was responsible for their deaths. We also needed to know the full extent of Gary Ridgway's damage.

Gary was difficult to interview. He was not consistent with his information, and he was more helpful on some days than others. Sometimes he was interactive and responsive, but on other days, getting information out of Gary was like pulling teeth. One day he would confess to killing a young woman. The next he'd deny it. To pin him down, we had to know every detail about every victim that we suspected he murdered.

It was my role to interview Gary about his personality, family, upbringing, and crime from a behavioral perspective. Using my understanding of psychopathy (a subject you'll learn more about later in this chapter), I crafted a number of questions designed to sort through Gary's lies and evasiveness and to determine whether he felt any remorse for his victims or the crimes he had committed.

On the first day, I walked into the interview room and sat next to him. He turned his head to stare at me. I looked back at him. He was a normal-looking sixty-year-old man with glasses. He was in good shape, with strong, muscled arms. He was polite, quiet, and smiled appropriately. He was actually nice. I expected that he would be.

"Gary, I don't have a lot of time," I said. "I need to get up to Canada to work on this other serial murder case, but there's one thing I'd really like to find out before I go. I want to study only the best serial killers. How good of a serial killer are you? Where would you put yourself on a scale comparing yourself to other serial killers?"

His responses implied that he thought he would be at the top. He thought he was one of the best, if not *the* best serial killer. This is something you might expect a star athlete, renowned scientist, or movie star to say. But a serial killer?

On another occasion he commented that the video camera being used to record all the interviews was not focused on his face, as it should be. Gary appeared to really like being videotaped. It allowed him to be the center of attention and talk about what he loved doing. He believed being taped would make him more famous, and it did.

He openly talked to me and other investigators about his necrophiliac behavior (having sex with the women's lifeless bodies) as if it were completely normal.

I asked Gary if he felt remorse for his victims and his crimes. He responded that he felt bad about them. "What does feeling bad feel like for you?" I asked. If you or I had committed the types of crimes Gary had, we would probably answer such a question by saying that we felt horrible about taking these women's lives and ruining the lives of their loved ones. Gary, however, could not articulate what "feeling bad" meant to him. I pressed him. Eventually he explained that he felt bad about the evidence that was left at the scenes.

Whenever I tell these stories about Gary, people are incredulous. "How can someone be so proud of such violent behavior?" they ask. Most people can't wrap their minds around it.

And that's just it. They can't possibly instinctually understand the personality of a serial sexual killer because it is the complete opposite of their own. They believe someone like this has to be crazy, evil, or a monster, but those are only labels and have no investigative value. Such words have no clinical meaning.

Gary is a serial sexual killer. He killed women for sexual reasons. He liked it, and he was good at it. He had sex with the bodies of dead women because it was sexually gratifying to him. This pathological behavior made Gary feel powerful and omnipotent, and he craved those feelings.

Because I'd spent my career studying and interviewing people just like him, I understood Gary's personality. I knew, before I ever walked into that interview room, what would happen if I told Gary that I was in a hurry to investigate another series of crimes committed by another serial sexual killer that Gary was aware of due to news reports. I knew Gary would be annoyed if I acted like another killer was more successful, more interesting, and more notorious. He would attempt to impress me and get me to understand his point of view.

I knew that killing was probably the one thing that Gary was most proud of. It was the one thing he was exceptionally good at.

He wasn't particularly successful in a lot of areas of his life, but he was one of the most prolific sexual predators ever recorded in the United States. His crimes spanned more than three decades.

Gary hunted human beings. He conned, manipulated, strangled, and murdered one woman after another. He stole their belongings and had sex with their lifeless bodies. Killing was a passion for him. He enjoyed it. He found it exciting and thrilling, and it gave him a sense of power and control. It's what got him out of bed in the morning, and it put him to sleep at night.

He called his encounters with these women "dates."

Gary thought of the women he killed as possessions, and their bodies were a treasured collection for him—a collection that he drove past and visited often.

Gary had kept all of this secret for more than twenty-five years. He'd

The Dangerous Truth

Serial sexual predators like Gary Ridgway are able to lure their victims through impression management and by taking steps to look and behave as normally as possible. Gary hunted street-smart prostitutes who had worked the same strip for years. These were women who understood street survival, and they were aware that there was a killer operating in their neighborhood. They were cognizant that there was danger out there, yet he was able to convince them—through charm and using props he kept in the car with him—that he was not a threat. There were times when he even took his young son with him as he hunted for prostitutes. Those who got into his car saw his son as a sign of safety. They assumed a father with a small boy could not be a serial murderer. In reality, however, a father who is callous enough to take a small child with him while he cruises the strip for a prostitute might also be callous enough to commit murder. That Gary had his son in the car with him said more about how dangerous and mission-oriented he was than about how harmless he might be.

never had the opportunity to talk about the one thing he was most accomplished at and proud of—until these interviews.

So for nearly six months, as these interviews were going on, he boasted about his murderous exploits.

You Can't Walk a Mile in a Criminal's Shoes

It's my hope that by the end of this chapter you will come to understand what motivates dangerous criminals like Gary. It's important to understand the motivations and personalities of people whose behavior is so extreme. Behavior falls along a continuum. Your behavior and the behavior of your friends and family might fall more toward the opposite, more law-abiding end of the continuum. Still, if you understand extremely dangerous behavior, you'll have a framework to use and understand human behavior in general, and yours specifically.

Serial sexual killers like Gary are rare, and they generally prey on highly vulnerable people who live high-risk lifestyles—people like prostitutes, runaways, and the homeless. In my work with the FBI, these victims were particularly compelling for me. Their lives and lifestyles were hard for them to maintain. Most had families who loved them dearly and wanted them home. Their vulnerabilities were often brought about by hardships in life they couldn't avoid, and the vulnerabilities of their lifestyles exposed them to dangerous people such as Gary.

You probably don't live that kind of lifestyle, so the likelihood of you ever meeting someone like Gary is quite small. But chances are you *will* meet a psychopath (more on what a psychopath is in just a few pages). In addition to psychopaths, you will probably, over the course of your life, meet many people who could be dangerous to you in other ways. It's important to be able to assess people's dangerousness. That way you can avoid people who are likely to hurt you financially, psychologically, emotionally, physically, professionally, legally, and in other ways. In this chapter you will learn to dispel fourteen myths that tend to get in the way of spotting dangerous behaviors.

What Blinds You to Danger

Your instincts and intuition are clouded by your own perceptions—based on your own personality and experiences—of what is normal behavior and what is not. You would never con or harm someone, so your gut feelings lead you to believe that your friends, coworkers, and neighbors—who all seem as normal as you—wouldn't either.

But your friends, coworkers, and neighbors aren't you, and they don't share your personality traits and characteristics, your background, your family influence, and more. What stresses them out, worries them, excites them, or saddens them is different from what stresses you out, worries you, excites you, or saddens you.

Your personality isn't the only thing that may bias you and influence your judgment when trying to get inside the head of a potentially dangerous individual. Years of misinformation—fed to you by TV crime dramas, news reports, self-defense courses, and forwarded e-mails—have probably made your ability to judge people even less trustworthy. For instance, on many popular TV programs, most of the psychopathic serial sexual killers start their killing sprees after a life stressor has caused them to "snap" and thus act out in a very aggressive way. As you'll learn later in this chapter, this is rarely the case. This kind of behavior evolves over time. It is not the result of snapping in the course of a twenty-four-hour period.

Television dramas are not the only sources of misinformation. Some of these myths about dangerous people have even been spread by individuals who call themselves experts in psychopathy and serial murder but who are not experts at all. I can't tell you how often I've cringed as I've listened to a television reporter interview someone who claims to be an expert but who has little to no on-the-job training when it comes to dealing with dangerous people, especially psychopaths. In one sentence these so-called experts call someone a psychopathic killer and in the very next refer to them as "a monster" or as having "snapped." Those are giveaways that the person being interviewed knows little to nothing about psychopaths.

In the following pages, we'll take a closer look at some of this misinformation and how it clouds your judgment when deciding whether to put your trust in someone else, be it a friend, romantic partner, employee, coworker, business partner, or hired help. Let's start with myths about psychopaths.

The Dangerous Truth

Many people think that serial sexual killers prefer a specific type of victim and that they will not deviate from that preference. For instance, people often assumed that Ted Bundy, a notorious serial sexual killer operating during the 1970s and early 1980s, preferred to murder women with brown hair parted down the middle. However, when, following his conviction, he was asked about his victim-selection process and victim preference, Bundy replied that hair parted down the middle was simply the style in the seventies. He wasn't necessarily picking victims because of their hairstyle. He was picking victims that he deemed worthy enough (attractive, middle or upper middle class, educated, and so on) to be killed by him.

In reality, the victim selection process that a serial killer uses can be a lot more complex and a lot less rigid than most people think. For Gary Ridgway, it revolved around the victim who was most accessible. Gary was infatuated with prostitutes. He picked women up on a regular basis to have sex with them. He would "date" the same woman over and over, and he would not murder every prostitute he picked up. Their ages varied, they came from different racial and cultural backgrounds, but he picked them because of their lifestyle.

I believe that Gary's choice of victims was the result of his desire to hunt a lot of victims to satiate his paraphiliac interests and predatory instincts. His victims were women who would engage in a wide variety of sexual behaviors in exchange for money. Gary knew that other people they interacted with would be considered suspects in their disappearances. He also knew that these women did not maintain regular schedules and that because of their erratic patterns they could be missing for days, weeks, or months before their families would realize it and report them missing. This gave Gary the opportunity to put a great deal of time and distance between him and his victims.

What Makes a Psychopath Tick?

The word "psychopath" is probably one of the most misunderstood words in the English language, and it is often used to describe people who are not psychopaths at all.

Psychopaths are classically referred to as people without a conscience. It's likely that in your lifetime you will encounter a psychopath and not realize it. He or she might be a neighbor, acquaintance, coworker, friend, or love interest. It might be someone you meet casually, such as a store clerk or a cab driver. It might be the person who works in the next cubicle. It might even be a family member.

My colleague and dear friend Robert D. Hare, Ph.D.—considered the world's foremost expert in psychopathy—estimates that 1 percent of the general population and 10 percent of the prison population is psychopathic. Psychopaths exist in all cultures and races and have existed over time and throughout history.

Although psychopathy is more common in men, psychopaths can be male or female. They can be married and have children. They can be quite smart or of average intelligence. They are not out of touch with reality and they know right from wrong. They look as normal as we do. They can blend in well with the society in which they are living. Most psychopaths are not violent, but because of their cluster of very specific personality traits and characteristics, they live life on the edge. They con and manipulate people. They take risks but take no responsibility for their actions. They lie pathologically, have a profound lack of empathy for others, and are stunningly callous in their interactions with people, even those who should be close to them. They live a life where rules are for the unwashed masses and not for someone as special as they are. They take what they want, when they want it. They are parasitic users of people regardless of the consequences to their victims, and they possess a remarkable ability to walk away from the havoc they wreak with a skip in their step, a smile on their face, and a dark predatory look in their eyes as they spot their next victim.

Psychopathy is a devastating personality disorder (an enduring pattern of thoughts and behaviors that differs from cultural expectations; is pervasive, inflexible, and stable over time; and leads to distress or impairment). It includes a cluster of the following traits, characteristics, and behaviors:

- Glib, superficial charm
- Grandiose sense of self-worth
- Pathological lying
- Cunning and manipulative
- Lack of remorse or guilt
- Shallow emotions
- Callousness and lack of empathy
- Failure to accept responsibility for one's actions
- Stimulation seeking
- Parasitic orientation
- Lack of realistic goals
- Impulsivity
- Irresponsibility
- Poor behavior controls
- Juvenile delinquency
- Early behavior problems
- Criminal versatility[3]

You might recognize some of these traits in yourself or someone you know. That doesn't mean that you are a psychopath. Someone is considered a psychopath when these traits and characteristics are consistently present in every aspect of the person's life, throughout his or her life.

Psychopathy is not an either/or disorder but rather is dimensional. It's a pattern. It emerges at a young age and it becomes fixed. You don't turn psychopathy on and off at will. And psychopaths don't believe there is anything wrong with them, so they don't seek out counseling unless it is in their best interest. For example, in a prison setting many psychopaths will only participate in therapy groups in order to make a better appearance before the parole board.

Not all psychopaths share equal amounts of every single trait, but it is the affective traits that distinguish this personality disorder from all the others: lack of remorse or guilt, shallow emotions, callous lack of empathy for others, and failure to accept responsibility. This lack of remorse and empathy is what allows psychopathic serial sexual killers to sleep next to their wives after having just killed someone. It's also what allows white-collar offenders to risk and lose the retirement savings of their clients and then put all the blame on their clients for agreeing to the investment in the first place. It's what allows certain types of sex offenders to kidnap, sexually assault, and murder children, and then play games of cat and mouse with law enforcement. It's what causes these sex offenders to become empowered by the excitement and thrill of what they just did and at being so clever at getting away with it. It's what allows some politicians or religious or world leaders to egregiously abuse their power and destroy other people around them, especially when their reign of power is coming to an end.

A psychopath feels about as guilty about destroying your peace of mind, reputation, financial livelihood, and life as you do when you blow your nose into a tissue and toss it in the trash. After you discard the tissue, do you worry about it? Do you think about it? Does it bother you that it's there in the trash, feeling discarded and used?

No, it doesn't. And psychopaths feel as emotionally attached to their victims as you feel to that tissue.

It's their lack of remorse and their callous lack of empathy that makes psychopaths so dangerous. For instance, pedophilia is a paraphiliac behavior that is defined as involving fantasies about, sexual attraction to, and illegal sexual interaction with a child or children. Not all pedophiles are psychopaths, and the nonpsychopathic pedophiles can feel remorse and guilt for their behavior. A psychopathic pedophile, however, is someone who is sexually attracted to children, victimizes children, and feels no remorse about this behavior. They will take greater risks to access a child in order to make the crime more exciting, will disregard the consequences of their behavior, will not accept responsibility even when caught, and are more likely to recidivate if the opportunity presents itself.

An arsonist sets fires for a variety of reasons. If someone is hurt or killed, some arsonists are capable of feeling remorse and/or guilt. A psychopathic arsonist, however, would feel no remorse or guilt about property damage or lost lives due to the fires he sets. His concerns would be for himself, about not wanting to be caught or to go to prison.

The psychopathic pedophile and arsonist are also more likely to incorporate thrill and excitement into their crimes to make them even more satisfying for them. They will even modify their behaviors so each time they commit a crime they get better and better at it in order to evade detection and apprehension.

Because of this, when a psychopath engages in criminal behavior he can be one of the most dangerous of criminals.

Psychopaths also have shallow or prototypical emotions. They have learned to pretend, sometimes with precision, how to emulate emotions they see in others around them. Superficially, psychopaths can attempt to show emotions by crying or saying the right words, like "I love you." The emotional landscape of a psychopath, however, lacks depth and breadth. It is barren.[4]

Because of this, psychopaths have to mime feelings and make them up. Asking a psychopath what remorse or guilt feels like is like asking a man what it feels like to be pregnant. It is an experience they have never had. In order to answer the question, they can only resort to what others have told them about this experience and what they have observed in people around them. They cannot speak from personal experience. Psychopaths can describe feelings, but they have no personal experience with them. Their description is based on what they have observed in others, but when you dig a little deeper, you will find that they have a very difficult time describing emotions in an appropriate context, which can frustrate them or even make them angry.

You might assume that, due to their lack of emotion, psychopaths may come off as odd and robotic. Although some do, many are extremely good at impression management. They might not know what remorse *feels* like, but they know what it looks like. They watch TV and observe the people around them. This is why some of them break down and cry in the courtroom. Are they crying because they really feel remorse about what they've done? I doubt it. I've seen killers turn on the tears when they thought they would help them accomplish a goal, and then turn them right back off again. They are actors who know how to pretend to be remorseful because it makes them appear like the people around them.

For instance, Dennis Rader, known as the BTK killer (Bind Torture Kill killer), calmly and dispassionately detailed every aspect of his murders in one of his initial courtroom appearances, and he did so without shedding a tear. He related how the members of the Otero family—including two children—did not die right away when he strangled them. "I had never strangled anyone before, so I really didn't know how much pressure you had to put on a person or how long it would take," he said.

He referred to his victims as "projects." He seemed detached and aloof.

After that day, his attorneys must have explained to him that a little remorse might help him when it came to sentencing. The next time he came to court he appeared, when it was in his best interest, to display more emotion.

However, psychopaths can become angry. For instance, several times when I asked Gary Ridgway about souvenirs he took from his victims, he narrowed his eyes. They became cold and reptilian. I realized that these were the eyes his victims would have seen when he was killing them. Gary was angry that I seemed to think of him as an average serial killer who would take souvenirs. He saw himself as better than that, denied taking souvenirs, and was quite annoyed that I didn't believe him.

Psychopaths are also predatory and manipulative. They don't think the rules apply to them. They are grandiose thrill seekers who take no responsibility for their behavior and have a view of the world in which they dominate and can take whatever they want, when they want it.

"Living on the edge" is a phrase frequently used to describe the psychopathic lifestyle. If they are involved in criminal behavior, their crimes will most likely have a certain quality to them that satisfies their need for thrill and sensation, even if it puts them at a greater risk of being caught. For example, Gary Ridgway drove around with a dead body in his car. This is very high-risk behavior. If he got stopped for a traffic violation or was involved in an accident and the body was found, he would have immediately been arrested and charged.

The Dangerous Truth

Some people think that they can spot a psychopath when he or she walks into the room. But you just can't look at someone and tell whether they have traits of psychopathy. If you meet a psychopath casually, you won't realize what he is. If you know one more intimately, you will eventually feel used and manipulated. You will realize how insignificant you and your feelings are to him. His grandiosity will be apparent in every aspect of his life. You will get worn out dealing with him, and he will blame you for why the marriage or relationship fails. It will never be his fault. You will absolutely know something is wrong, but you may blame it on yourself, seek therapy, try harder, and constantly be afraid.

Myth 1: You are either a psychopath or you aren't.

To assess for psychopathy, we use a clinical instrument called the Psychopathy Checklist-Revised (PCL-R). It consists of twenty items, each scored on a scale of 0–2. This assessment must be done by a highly trained professional. Researched and designed by Dr. Robert Hare, the PCL-R is considered the gold standard for the assessment of this personality disorder.

A person must score 30 out of a possible 40 to be assessed as a psychopath. However, a score in the mid to high twenties indicates that an individual manifests many of the traits and characteristics. Not all psychopaths share equal amounts of every trait in the psychopathic cluster, and some psychopaths score higher on some traits than others. Labeling someone a psychopath is a very serious matter and should not be done casually or recklessly. It has tremendous implications, so the diagnosis should only be made after a proper assessment.

Dr. Hare compares psychopathy to blood pressure. Like blood pressure, everyone has some traits of psychopathy, but some people test much higher in certain traits than others. It's the affective traits of psychopathy (lack of empathy, lack of remorse, and shallow emotions) that are the hallmarks of this disorder.

Myth 2: The words "sociopath" and "psychopath" are interchangeable.

People toss the terms "sociopath" and "psychopath" around on TV as if they mean the same thing, but they don't. The empirical research suggests that there is a neurological difference between psychopaths and nonpsychopaths, and this neurological difference is manifested by the traits and characteristics I listed earlier. Ongoing research suggests there are four types of psychopaths. The type of psychopath someone is depends on how that person manifests the traits and characteristics of the disorder.

"Sociopath," on the other hand, is a term generally used to refer to individuals who have grown up in an environment where being criminally antisocial is the norm. It is a learned behavior. A sociopath's emotional deficits are more likely to be the result of their environment. They may not be neurological. For example, people who grow up with gang violence or some other type of organized crime environment may learn the importance of being antisocial (breaking the law) as a way of life. But they are still capable of feeling a greater range of more normal emotions in some areas of their life, for example, with families and loved ones.

Myth 3: Psychopaths are psychotic.

Usually, when people call someone "a psycho" they really mean "crazy," or out of touch with reality. Psychopaths are not crazy—even if some of the crimes they commit are bizarre and heinous.

For instance, Gary Ridgway was not hearing voices when he revisited the dumpsites and had postmortem sex with the prostitutes he killed. Gary would pull maggots off their vaginal areas. He would break the women's leg bones so he could shove their stiffened legs apart. This is pathological behavior, but it was also the behavior of a man who was completely in touch with reality.

What Gary did may very well be bizarre, but it was not a result of psychosis or impaired judgment. People who are psychotic are out of touch with reality because they suffer from a debilitating mental illness. They can hallucinate and hear voices that tell them to do things that are strange or even illegal.

Gary Ridgway did not hallucinate or hear voices. He had no trouble holding down a job. He blended in with his community and projected a normal persona. He was married, with children and grandchildren. He shopped and ate at neighborhood restaurants, went on vacations, and interacted with other normal people all the time. He did not live a life of erratic, aberrant, or unpredictable behavior. This is why he flew under law enforcement's radar screen for so many years. He maintained a facade of normalcy.

Gary was methodical and calculated. He killed because he enjoyed it, not because he was out of touch with reality.

I've interviewed numerous killers, some of whom practiced cannibalism and necrophilia. Their refrain was similar. They killed because it was thrilling and arousing. Their crimes gave them feelings of power and control over their victims and their victims' lives. They felt omnipotent, and that was a feeling they craved. They didn't do it because they were out of touch with reality or told to do it by voices in their head.

It is important to keep in mind that people who are mentally ill with a psychosis are less likely to act out violently than psychopaths are, and they are far less likely to be able to carry out a well-planned, cold-blooded,

Dangerous Truth

According to a survey done for the Screen Actors Guild, 60 percent of mentally ill characters were portrayed as criminals or as violent offenders, and 70 percent of stories that depict mental illness revolve around a theme of violence.[5] TV and movies are one of our biggest sources of information about violence and deviant behavior, and yet this source routinely provides an inaccurate portrayal of who is and who is not violent. Psychopathy is a personality disorder, one that should not be confused or linked with mental illness.

predatory act of mission-oriented violence. The vast majority of people who are mentally ill are not violent at all, and they are far more likely to become victims of violent crime than they are to be perpetrators of it.

Myth 4: Psychopaths don't know right from wrong.

They do know right from wrong. They know what the laws are, but they don't believe those laws apply to them. They know that killing, raping, stealing, and other actions are crimes and are against the law—and they choose to do those things anyway.

Myth 5: Brain tumors and brain trauma turn law-abiding citizens into psychopaths.

Psychopathy is the result of a person's genetics and environment; you don't snap into being a psychopath as the result of a brain tumor or other neurological injury.

Even Charles Whitman, who shot and killed fourteen people at the University of Texas at Austin, and who was, after an autopsy, determined to have been suffering from a brain tumor, didn't go up in the tower that day because of a tumor. Whether he had a brain tumor or not, his violence was well planned, predatory, cold-blooded, and purposeful, which are all indicators of psychopathy.

I was able to identify warning behaviors in Whitman's life going back to his days in the military, a full six years before the shooting. It was then that he wrote about preparing for a military siege. He wrote about the necessary supplies he would need and how to keep a door from being breached. (In the tower on August 1, 1966, he followed this plan to delay police officers from getting to him.) Five months before the tower shooting, he told his psychiatrist that he fantasized about killing people from the top of the University of Texas tower. The psychiatrist later admitted that he dismissed this revelation because Whitman seemed like "an all-American boy" and didn't look like a psychopath.

Myth 6: Most psychopaths were violently abused as children, their parents made them into what they've become, and most practiced cruelty to animals.

Some psychopaths may have been abused as children. For instance, I've interviewed Joseph Paul Franklin, who attempted to kill adult-magazine publisher Larry Flynt and was convicted of several murders. During that interview, Franklin claimed that his parents had yelled at him, beat him, and starved him. According to Franklin, his mother was a sadist and he once watched her physically abuse a stray dog that he'd brought home. He said that this abuse by his parents had turned him into a cold-blooded killer.[6]

Although people like Franklin may very well have been abused, many other people are abused as children and they do not turn into psychopaths or serial killers. Similarly, some psychopaths might have engaged in cruelty to animals, but not all of them have. And children who do engage in this behavior don't all become psychopaths. It is not a predictive behavior for psychopathy. It is certainly concerning behavior, and when parents see it, it should be addressed immediately with the assistance of trained mental-health professionals.

We know that heredity and environment together contribute to the development of psychopathy. The degree to which each contributes, however, is still uncertain, and very likely varies on an individual basis.

Myth 7: Psychopaths are capable of being in love.

Although in news reports I often read that a psychopath was "really in love with his wife," this is an emotion that they do not feel deeply or at all. Whenever I ask psychopathic serial killers why they did not kill their wives or children, they tell me that it's because they would immediately become a suspect in the murder of someone so close to them. Sometimes psychopathic serial killers will claim to love their wives or children. If I ask, "When was the first time you thought about killing your wife, girlfriend, or mother?" most will then tell me about all the ways they fantasized about doing their wives or girlfriends in.

Myth 8: Most psychopaths are violent.

When you hear the word "psychopath," the first thing that probably comes to mind is a serial killer like Ted Bundy. But most psychopaths are not serial killers. In fact, serial killing is rare and most psychopaths are not violent.

Psychopaths live on the edge by taking advantage of people. They manipulate people and lie to get what they want. But they don't necessarily end up in jail as a result of acting violently. They are not rule followers by nature, but many live right on the edge.

Myth 9: Psychopaths don't work in white-collar professions.

Many people think that psychopathy is a disorder that debilitates people to such a degree that they cannot go on to get an advanced degree or move up the corporate ladder. This just isn't true. Many of them excel in high-stress, high-risk professions. They are stockbrokers, ER physicians, bankers, lawyers, politicians, and even law enforcement officers. These professions are thrilling and provide psychopaths with the power that they seek. Paul Babiak's research into white-collar psychopaths even found that these individuals not only manage successfully in corporate America, but their glibness and charm, and risk-taking and sensation-seeking traits, are viewed as desirable assets despite poor performance appraisals. [7]

A psychopath can cause problems in the workplace. The white-collar psychopath will charm people initially. He or she will do this to win over fellow employees and bosses that they eventually manipulate to accomplish their objectives. These objectives could be anything from embezzlement to taking significant risks with company property (cars, money, investments) to sexual conquests.

Once white-collar psychopaths have people where they want them, they can become the company bully. They can stir up trouble. They can take credit for others' work, blame others for problems, prey on coworkers (through harassment or sexually inappropriate behavior), and create an atmosphere that pits employees against one another.

They can use and manipulate people to climb the corporate ladder or shine as the star of the company. People are in the organization for them to use. Their loyalty is to themselves, and they will betray the corporation if it serves their needs. They can cheat, embezzle, lie, take extraordinary risks, sabotage projects, and violate confidentiality issues while experiencing little if any remorse or feelings of guilt as they do so. They are not team players, but rather live by the philosophy that every man is out for himself. In a corporate culture, however, the need to be covert—"to fly under the radar screen"—is important for psychopaths to achieve their goals. Their calculated use and abuse of the company and its employees can be subtle and/or come out incrementally and selectively so as not to jeopardize their own employment.[8]

Myth 10: Psychopaths are smarter than the average person.

It's easy to mistake a psychopath for being brilliant, because of his or her inflated sense of self-worth (he or she will tell you of their brilliance) and the glib nature that enables them to engage with others on many different topics, albeit on a superficial level.

But psychopaths reflect the intelligence of the general population. There have been some exceptionally bright serial killers, such as Edmund Emil Kemper, whose IQ is thought to be around 160. Kemper, who I've interviewed several times, is rumored to have memorized the Minnesota Multiphasic Personality Inventory (MMPI). The test is used to evaluate the presence of mental illness. It has five hundred items on it, and Kemper knew precisely how to answer each of those items to support his insanity plea. He is one of the smartest killers I've ever interviewed.

On the other end of the spectrum, however, is Billy, whose last name I will not use out of consideration for his living family members. He was never tested for IQ, but he only had a fifth-grade education. When I interviewed him, he talked in one- and two-word answers such as "yup" and "nope." The most he ever said was when I asked him if he had heard of the word "psychopathy." I assumed he would say no, but he told me that he had.

"Really?" I asked. "How do you know about psychopathy?"

"I looked it up in the dictionary," he said. "Do you think I am one?"

"I think it's more important to know if you think you are one," I said. "What do you think?"

"Yes, and I think it's a good thing." He smiled and his eyes sparkled.

That was his most talkative moment. Billy is in prison for serial sexual murder.

Myth 11: People just snap.

As we've already discussed, after a crime is committed the criminal's friends frequently say, "I don't know what happened. He just snapped." They describe someone who was pushed to the brink by life stressors, and then morphed into a madman.

I call this "snap theory," and it comes up again and again and again when a human being behaves in a way that others find inhumane, bizarre, or violent.

Yet people usually don't snap. What happens is that their concerning behavior goes unnoticed. For instance, let's take a look at Andrew Kehoe, the man responsible for the worst school violence in U.S. history. Kehoe was a well-respected member of the Bath, Michigan, community and the treasurer of the board of the Bath Consolidated School. Did he snap when, in 1927, he blew up his property and later himself and a school, killing forty-five people and injuring fifty-eight? No, he didn't.

Kehoe was an injustice collector and was having financial difficulties. He blamed those difficulties on a number of people, including his wife (who had tuberculosis and was in and out of the hospital, racking up a lot of medical bills). He also blamed a property tax levy that was designed to raise money to upgrade the school.

Because Kehoe was trusted and well respected—a member of the board—he was allowed access to the school. For many months, he brought small amounts of dynamite to the school and stored it in various locations. Eventually he had stored hundreds of pounds of it there.

Meanwhile neighbors did notice strange behavior. He was bringing hay into a tool shed, for instance, and they could not figure out why any-one would need hay in a tool shed. None of them suspected, however, that he would later use it to set fire to the shed and other buildings on his property. They also heard him detonating dynamite on his property, but they accepted his explanation that he had just been testing it.

On the day of the incident, he blew up and set fire to his property, killing his wife. He even wired and blew up his remaining farm animals. He then drove to the school in his "machine," a truck he filled with explosives. It was likely the first car bomb ever to be seen in the United States. Using a timer, he detonated the truck shortly after he detonated the explosives at the school. He killed himself and at least forty-five children that day.

People were stunned when this happened, but there were many indicators ahead of time that Kehoe was prone to violence and planning to commit violent acts. He didn't "snap" at all. He planned every detail of his attack months ahead of time.

Similarly, Eric Harris and Dylan Klebold did not just snap. They planned the Columbine High School shooting for months. They meticulously and slowly gathered explosives and firearms. They planned the shooting down to the last detail. For weeks before the incident, they taped each other discussing how they would carry it out.

Dan White—who was convicted of shooting San Francisco mayor George Moscone and supervisor Harvey Milk—didn't just fall into a depression, start eating a lot of junk food, snap, and then murder two people while in a dazed state, as his attorney claimed in his so-called Twinkie defense.

I worked for the San Francisco District Attorney's Office during White's trial and my brother, Michael O'Toole, was the media officer and spokesperson for the San Francisco Police Department during the same time. Michael was there in City Hall when Supervisor Milk's body was found. I paid close attention to the case and sat in on the trial.

Yes, White may have been suffering from depression, but the depression was not the reason he snuck through a basement window and then shot Moscone and Milk. White had resigned from the board of supervisors and he wanted his job back. The mayor would not reinstate him, and White felt that Milk had influenced the mayor's decision.

White, a San Francisco native and a respected family man, was a former firefighter and police officer with an impressive career and pedigree. This made him a compelling defendant. Those who knew him said there were no warning signs of future violence. At the time, our knowledge of threat assessment, risk assessment, and warning behaviors for future violence was still in its infancy. This might be why his Twinkie defense helped to sway the jury to convict him of manslaughter rather than first-degree murder, even though he was predatory and mission-oriented when he committed the attack.

Your usual well-adjusted, law-abiding citizen doesn't "snap" and become a mass murderer or cold-blooded serial killer. There are usually warning signs that these people have the potential to become violent and are planning to carry out a violent act, but those signs often go unrecognized for a number of reasons:

1. We don't like to believe that the people we know—neighbors, teachers, school board members, spouses, and so on—can be plotting and planning violence.

2. People who are prone to violence can be quite good at hiding their plans from others.

3. Signs that someone might become violent are usually mixed with normal behavior. Some potentially violent people seem like normal, caring individuals at times. At other times they seem like angry, vengeful people. These characteristics are mixed together into a big soup, and sometimes it can be difficult to spot the indicators of violence until it's too late.

Kehoe, White, and others thought about their crimes ahead of time, and they exhibited a number of behaviors that indicated that they were contemplating violence. These warning signs, however, went unrecognized, or were misinterpreted or ignored until it was too late.

Myth 12: The maternal instinct protects children.

The mythical maternal instinct is somehow supposed to help mothers keep their children safe at all times. And all moms are supposed to have it.

It's quite possible that most mothers have such an instinct. But after seeing what I've seen during my time with the FBI, I can say that the maternal instinct is not a universal phenomenon.

For instance, when officials were negotiating with David Koresh, the leader of the Branch Davidian religious sect in Waco, Texas, some of them commented that the maternal instincts of the women in the cult would eventually "kick in." They anticipated that, as a result of these instincts, the women would send their young children off the compound and to safety. These instincts would cause the women to take whatever steps were necessary to keep their children safe.

But I wondered, "What maternal instincts?" Some of these women were already living in a situation where David Koresh separated mothers from children. Some of the mothers had already exposed their children to physical, emotional, and sexual danger. Now they were suddenly supposed to develop an instinct that would help to protect their children?

Belief in these so-called maternal instincts is what causes so many people to assume that strangers pose the biggest kidnapping threat to children. Part of this assumption, no doubt, is fed by the media, which has sensationalized the abductions of Adam Walsh, Polly Klaas, Jaycee Dugard, Elizabeth Smart, and many others. Another part of it, though, stems from a flawed belief that no parent—especially a mother—could hurt her own child.

Yet children are a lot more likely to be harmed by family members, caregivers, or others who are close to them than by strangers. Parents commit 34 percent of the sexual assaults on children; strangers carry out only 7 percent of them.

Parents hurt their children for many reasons that some of us find hard to understand. Sometimes it's intentional. Sometimes it is done out of rage. Sometimes it's an accident that the parents cover up. Sometimes it's out of convenience. For instance, for Diane Downs and Susan Smith, their children were in the way, preventing these women from getting what they wanted—romantic partners. They saw their children as objects that could be used, manipulated, and even discarded in order to accomplish their personal goals.

And if parents can hurt their *own* children, what leads you to believe a parent could not hurt *your* child?

The Dangerous Truth

Paraphilias are mental disorders that are defined as involving sexual urges, fantasies, and behaviors that fall into three categories:

1. Nonhuman objects
2. Children or other nonconsenting persons
3. Suffering and/or humiliation

Pedophilia—a specific paraphiliac behavior—involves sexual attraction to, and involvement with, children. Necrophilia involves sexual attraction to corpses. Sexual cannibals become aroused when they consume another human's flesh, and sexual sadists become aroused by their victim's response as the sadist inflicts physical and emotional pain.

Psychopathy and paraphiliac behaviors can manifest together in the same individual, creating a potentially very dangerous person. For instance, Canadian colonel Russell Williams engaged in voyeurism (a paraphiliac behavior) and residential burglaries during which he stole women's lingerie, which he later cataloged and photographed himself wearing. He engaged in these behaviors for years, eventually progressing to sexual assault and murder.

Myth 13: All strangers are dangerous.

A few years ago, I was asked to help Louisiana police investigate the disappearance of Melissa, a twelve-year-old girl. It was suspected that Melissa had run away. Yet she had disappeared from an area where we knew a serial killer had been hunting some of his victims, and I had been working intensely on this serial murder case.

The police wanted my opinion on whether Melissa was a runaway or might be the victim of this serial killer or of something else. I asked them to send me everything they had on the case. As I read the statement made by Carl, the girl's stepfather, I became suspicious. When I saw his arrest record, criminal history, and background, I knew the first step was to see if we could eliminate Carl as a person of interest.

So I asked the police to send me any video footage that had been taken of him. As it turned out, Carl had been interviewed by television reporters while handing out flyers about the missing girl. As I watched these videos, I saw that he was good-looking, articulate, and seemed normal. He expressed concern and worry over the disappearance of his stepdaughter. He seemed comfortable on camera. He appeared to be glib and charming and certainly didn't look dangerous.

Most grieving parents appear on camera out of obligation—in order to help find their children. But they usually seem sad, nervous, and stressed. They are scared and even in shock. This stepfather, however, seemed to enjoy being in the limelight.

I asked the police about his background. I learned that he'd recently been released from prison, where he had served time for a series of rapes of adult women.

I told them, "This is your suspect, right here." I flew down with two of my Behavioral Analysis Unit partners. As I drove to the crime scene, I was listening to the radio and heard a news report about another young woman's body being found in Louisiana. I would subsequently learn that this young woman was a victim of the serial killer I was already looking for.

I met up with the FBI agent on Melissa's case. We talked about Carl and his concerning behavior, and we identified personality issues that would be key to getting him to confess to us. Then we interviewed Carl. I knew that control was important to him, so I said, "You have a lot more control than you think you have." I reminded him that he could control his side of the story. He could say it in his own words and using his own narrative. I explained that he could choose to not take that opportunity, but if he did so others would tell his story for him, and they might make assumptions that could be right or wrong. Carl wanted to be in control, and he wanted to set the story straight. He ultimately took us to the girl's body. Carl was tried and convicted and sent to death row in a cell close to that of the man who was convicted for killing the woman whose body was being uncovered the night my plane had landed.

It might have seemed natural, in that case, to assume that Melissa was also a victim of a serial killer. After all, he was following women to their homes, going inside, and either killing them there or taking them to another location and then killing them.

In reality, however, I knew that Melissa was a lot more likely to be harmed by someone she knew than by someone she didn't.

The same is true of you.

When we think about taking steps to increase our personal safely, our most dangerous instinct is to stay away from the people we don't know and to place our trust in people we know more intimately—family, friends, coworkers, and neighbors.

For instance, if you were a young woman working late at the office, you might ask another employee to walk you to your car—just in case a dangerous stranger was lurking somewhere in the parking lot. The now famous crime writer Ann Rule did just that, years ago when she worked at a suicide hotline with a handsome young man whom she knew well and had befriended. He often walked her to her car at night and asked her to be careful. His name was Ted Bundy.

We are conditioned over and over again in life to fear strangers. We are not conditioned to fear people we know. And all too often, we use inductive reasoning to conclude that someone we have met casually and had a superficial conversation with is safe and poses no threat to us. Yet just as children are more likely to be harmed by their own parents than by strangers, you are much more likely to be harmed by someone you know than by someone you don't know. Consider that of 14,000 murders in the United States in 2008, only 1,742 were committed by strangers. Nearly four times more were committed by people who knew the victim.

And the more intimately you know someone, the more potentially dangerous the relationship is. Most of us generally do not invite strangers into our comfort zone—such as our homes or our cars. Most of us do not hand sensitive information—our Social Security numbers, credit card information, the password to our PayPal account—to people we don't know either.

No, we only trust such information with people we think we know quite well, which is why the people closest to us pose the biggest threat to us.

Myth 14: Dangerous people look scary.

I've interviewed many different neighbors, coworkers, friends, and family members during my career. No matter what a criminal has looked like or how a criminal has behaved in their presence, nearly all of them have told me that they had sized this person up and were shocked at his arrest, whether it was for murder, sexual assault, child abduction, espionage, or other crimes of violence. They said things like:

"I am so surprised. He's such a nice guy."

"We've worked together for years. How could I not have seen this coming?"

"He's been over to my house. Our kids are in the same class. He doesn't seem dangerous."

"He's my next-door neighbor. He says hello every morning when he walks his dog. He seemed so normal."

"I would have noticed something different or strange about him, because I am a good judge of character. I am shocked. He must have just snapped."

I'm guessing that, if I were called to investigate a crime that took place on your block, you'd probably tell me something similar. You would because no one taught you how to read people and assess them for dangerousness.

As a result, when you try to rely on instincts or intuition in order to get a read on someone, chances are you are not getting an accurate read at all.

Terms like "scary looking" and "creepy" are frequently used to describe people, but these terms are not synonymous with what makes someone dangerous. Many people think that dangerous people have a certain look about them. As a result, they think they have the ability to give someone a look up and down and tell whether he or she is dangerous. They bank on this ability whenever they open their front doors without knowing who is on the other side.

Let me tell you, I've spent my career studying the criminal mind and criminal behavior. I've interviewed some of the world's most prolific serial killers and other dangerous offenders. I've made it my business to know all there is to know about them.

I do not have the ability to look at someone and tell for certain if that person is dangerous. And neither do you. No one does.

Ann Rule, the author and former policewoman whom I mentioned earlier, writes in *The Stranger Beside Me* about her experiences working with and knowing the infamous serial killer Ted Bundy. She remained friendly with him for years, and she thought he was a handsome, empathetic, gentle, brilliant young man. There was nothing about him that made her think, "He's dangerous."

Even years later when she saw an artist's rendering of the man who was suspected of killing several young women in her area and noticed that the picture looked a lot like her friend Ted, she doubted herself. She didn't think the Ted she knew could ever be capable of such crimes.

She continued to doubt herself after his capture, and even after he was convicted of kidnapping.

Similarly, some of the women who met Derrick Todd Lee—now known as the Baton Rouge Serial Killer—thought he looked harmless. They described him to me as "incredibly good-looking" with a "beautiful complexion." They said he was clean-cut and soft-spoken—a gentleman for the short period of time it took him to assess the situation and decide to act out violently.

This inability to size up danger goes beyond killers. People lined up to give their money to Bernie Madoff. They voted Rod Blagojevich into office as governor. Plenty of tourists in the 1800s bought the Brooklyn Bridge from George Parker, even though the bridge was not his to sell. He sold it to unsuspecting tourists roughly twice a week for years. Frank Abagnale Jr. posed, before he was even thirty, as an airline pilot, a doctor, and a lawyer before his arrest by the FBI. He was considered one of this country's ultimate con men.

We like to think of the victims of such people as naive. We tell ourselves that we would notice something or that our intuition would tell us something that these victims didn't see. Yet not a single person who watched *The Dating Game* on the day, during the 1970s, when Rodney Alcala was on it thought, "He looks like a serial killer." Thousands of people watched the show that day. If it is so easy to spot a serial killer based on appearance or first impression, don't you think someone who watched that episode would have called the police?

As I mentioned earlier, Charles Whitman was so all-American and clean-cut looking that his psychiatrist did not think that he would carry out his threat to shoot people from the tower, even as Whitman was telling him about his homicidal fantasies.

Robert Hanssen is recognized as one of the most dangerous spies in U.S. history. The fact that he was able to engage in espionage activity while employed as an FBI agent was stunning, not only to the FBI, but to the entire counterintelligence field. What behavior was overlooked or not recognized? How was he able to pull it off for such a long time? If dangerous people actually look dangerous, would he have gotten away with it for as long as he did?

Dangerous people generally don't look any different from regular, everyday people. They don't have a certain look in their eyes. They don't smile a certain way, and they don't wear a uniform or a certain haircut. If they did, we would run away or avoid them.

Sure, some dangerous individuals might look like the shifty-eyed, straggly haired stranger that television dramas have conditioned us to expect, but many of them don't.

CHAPTER 4 RAP SHEET

- Dangerous people can be so good at impression management that your gut feelings will tell you that they are safe and "good guys" when they are anything but.
- Psychopaths lack empathy and remorse. They do not feel guilt about the lives they've ruined.
- People capable of hurting others can look very normal and come across as charming and nonthreatening.
- You and your loved ones are more likely to be harmed by someone you know than by a stranger.
- Dangerous people do not necessarily stand out in a crowd. They don't look different from other people.
- Dangerous people usually don't snap. They exhibit red flags that warn that they might become threatening or violent.

Chapter 5

Why We Miss the Details That Matter

Many years ago the FBI sent me to help find a teenage girl. Julie had walked away from her grandmother's home. She was one of a series of girls who had gone missing in California over a period of time.

When I arrived at the command center, the pressure was on to broadcast the disappearance on every media outlet and to call in every type of support available—helicopters, rescue teams, bloodhounds, evidence response teams, and lots of human power.

Doing so, though, would likely cause some degree of public panic and could even impact the local economy. We were walking a fine line. Underinvestigating the girl's disappearance might allow the kidnapper enough time to escape detection and possibly kill her and dispose of the body. But ratcheting up the investigation and classifying the case as a kidnapping when there was no factual basis for that assumption had its own problems. It could trigger a media frenzy, involve lots of human power, time, and money, and could even involve the apprehension of people as suspects in a crime that never occurred.

What was the right course of action?

As I listened to the detectives at the briefing, I read through diaries and journals that local authorities had gathered from Julie's home. I attempted to develop a victimology (a study of the victim, her personality, habits, interests, thoughts, fantasies, experiences, reactions, perceptions of life, and her fears).

She was a prolific writer. I had a lot to read and only a short time to do it. Time was of the essence. Law enforcement wanted to develop a strategy and wanted my assessment of what I thought had happened as soon as possible. I had only a few hours to hear what they were saying, visit Julie's home, and find out as much as I could about her and surmise what had happened.

I went to the condo where Julie had been staying with her grandmother for the summer. She'd recently arrived there from the Midwest.

From her grandmother, I learned that Julie seemed lonely. I thought she was more than lonely: She was sad. She had no friends in California, was on the quiet side, and didn't have a boyfriend but really wanted one. She had also been spending less and less time with her grandmother, but her grandmother didn't know why. Julie's grandmother had been fairly lenient and had not kept track of her every movement.

From what I'd already read in the journals, and from talking with her grandmother and visiting her home, I could see that Julie was not your typical high-risk victim. She was not an out-of-control child. Rather, she was introverted. She appeared to be a responsible, caring, and loving girl with a heavy dose of teenage insecurity. I also knew that she would not purposefully do something to hurt her grandmother or her family.

The singular theme throughout her journals was her loneliness and her desire for a boyfriend. This loneliness was so pervasive that I felt sad for her as I read about it. She wrote extensively about wanting to find a boyfriend, using phrases like "I want to have someone in my life" and "I wish I had a boyfriend" over and over again.

It was as though she'd made it a mission to find a boyfriend once she got to California.

I went through her bedroom and her closet. There I found a dress that her grandmother had purchased for her. It looked like a wedding dress. I asked her grandmother about it. She told me that she was not thrilled with the dress and didn't know why her granddaughter needed or wanted one like it.

I had my own suspicions about that.

Soon I was back at the command center. "So what is your assessment?" the head of the task force asked.

My opinion was one that would likely be met with skepticism and perhaps even some anger. If I was right about my assessment, we would eventually find the girl and she would be safe. If I was wrong, I risked losing credibility as a profiler and feeling horrible if something happened to her because we had not been aggressive enough from the beginning.

"My opinion is that she came out to California to find a boyfriend, that she met someone, and that she's with that person. She has not been kidnapped, and now she is probably frightened to come home," I said. "This is a situation that snowballed before she could stop it."

I'd come to this conclusion by adding up what we in law enforcement call "the totality of the circumstances." The circumstances were these: This was a low-risk victim in a low-crime area. She had a lot of freedom to go wherever she pleased and had little supervision. She was shy, lonely, insecure, and in search of a boyfriend. She had a wedding dress in her closet. Based on those details, it was my opinion that she had run off either to meet a boyfriend or to find one, and that she might come home on her own if she thought that neither she nor the boyfriend would get in trouble.

I suggested that we tone down the media coverage of the disappearance as much as possible. We asked the media to broadcast that Julie should come home with her new friend, and that she would be loved and welcomed.

Her parents arrived from the Midwest. They were scared and upset. I'm sure they were thinking the worst. Two days later I was sitting with the girl's father. I was going over Elisabeth Kübler-Ross's five stages of grief. He was kind and he held on to my every word as he sat shaking at the kitchen table. I could tell he was depending on me to take care of him, his family, and his daughter. I felt like there was nothing I wouldn't do to help him.

"In the next couple of days, you will find yourself angry with me," I said. "That's normal, if anything can be considered normal during a missing-child investigation. Most parents of missing children feel angry at this point in the investigation, but this is when I am going to need your help the most."

As I said those words, the front door opened and in walked Julie.

Her father fell to his knees and wept. He grabbed her, hugged her, and sobbed uncontrollably.

Julie had been staying with a boy who was about four years older than she was. She hadn't come home one night, and then she'd stayed subsequent nights with him at his family's home. She did know that her grandmother would worry about her, but she didn't realize things had gotten so out of control. She'd never thought that her grandmother would suspect that she had been kidnapped, that her photo would end up on the news, or that her parents would fly in.

A short while later, I left the kitchen, got in a car, and drove away. I never saw Julie or her father again. I wonder what their lives are like now. I hope they are well.

It would have been easy to get caught up in the wrong details that day. I could have fixated on the fact that other girls had gone missing and come to the conclusion that Julie was probably also abducted by a stranger. Had I done so, and had we conducted a full media blitz about Julie and her alleged kidnapper, Julie may have left the area or the state, thinking that the problem was insurmountable. The time, effort, and expense of trying to find her would have been enormous.

Underestimating Risks, Overestimating Benefits

When making critical decisions, most of us weigh the pros and cons. For instance, when deciding whether to take a new job, you might list the points in its favor, such as a bigger salary, a better job title, and job responsibilities that are a better fit for your interests. The negative considerations might include the need to move to a new location, the learning curve, leaving behind your support network, and so forth. There are some people who just don't like change, so any change is a real con for them.

I've found, however, that most people overestimate the potential benefits of various decisions and greatly underestimate the risks. Many of us have suffered from the "shiny ball" syndrome at one time or another in our lives. The new job, the new car, the new house seems to shine, and we want that shiny new ball, so we suspend the good judgment that would be based on an in-depth risk assessment.

In a marriage, for instance, a new bride might notice how her husband dotes on her, but she might ignore his controlling, dominating behavior or his jealousy and suspiciousness. She might even see them as a plus. Perhaps she feels special: She must really be something to have a guy be so jealous over her. Years later, however, his controlling personality really bothers her. She tells people that he's changed: He's not the same man she married.

In reality, he hasn't changed, but she has. She's finally taken in the whole picture. She realized that what at first seemed controlling is in fact dominating. What she initially saw as her husband's jealousy is actually suspicious and threatening behavior. Her husband's personality has not changed. She has taken off her rose-colored glasses and finally seen his behavior for what it really is.

Similarly, when an employee starts a new job she might notice the friendly coworkers and the flirtatious charm of one of her new colleagues, who she even considers sweet. It's not until the sweet, charming, flirtatious guy begins sending inappropriate e-mails and leaving inappropriate gifts on her desk that she realizes she has a problem. Yet his behavior was present all along. She just didn't put it all together at first.

The Riskiest Blind Spot

We don't just underestimate the risks of various decisions; we sometimes don't see the risks at all. And the risks we fail to see are often the very ones that are likeliest to hurt us the most.

For instance, many parents in the suburbs take their children to indoor amusement centers. These places offer lots of fun for the kids: climbing walls, bowling alleys, laser tag, bumper cars, sliding boards, and more. Many also include entertainment for the parents, such as a bar or gambling games.

The benefits of going to such a place? If you are a parent, you can probably rattle them off for me. Your kids get to run around and have fun. They burn off excess energy and get some exercise, and you get to relax.

The obvious cons, however, include the price tag. Such places are also loud and overstimulating, which means the kids might be crabbier later on.

But there are two risks that many parents probably just don't think of.

Risk 1: Physical harm to your child

How safe is the equipment, and how well-trained is the staff? Most people assume that such places are safe simply because they are open for business. They assume that some state agency regulates such places and therefore kids can't get hurt. But these places are not necessarily safe. In Indianapolis, for instance, a five-year-old boy was critically injured on a mini-teacup ride at an Xscape entertainment center that state officials later realized never had a permit to operate. The injuries were caused by a ride that was not properly maintained, and because of that, it jerked so abruptly that the child fractured his skull in two places.

Risk 2: Child molestation and/or abduction

As I've mentioned, kidnappings by strangers are rare, but think about how easy it would be for another adult to walk out with one of your children while you are relaxing at the bar. Incidents of child molestation are much more common and are frequently underreported. Pedophiles and other predators are drawn to places where they know children will be.

Consult the chart on the next page to see a number of other similar decisions and the risky blind spots associated with them.

The Decision	Benefits	Risks	The Blind Spot
You allow a person to rent an apartment or room from you.	Income, the place is not sitting vacant, and it will be maintained.	The tenant loses his job, falls behind on the rent, and then you have to go through an eviction process.	You know little about the tenant's background, behavior, whom he will bring to the house, and if he poses a danger to you or your family if you have to evict him.
A colleague offers to drive you to and from the airport.	You don't have to pay for a cab or a shuttle.	Your colleague might expect a similar favor later on. Your colleague might show up late and you'll miss your flight.	The colleague uses a medication like Xanax that affects his alertness and as a result gets you both into an accident.
You're at a bar. A handsome guy chats you up. You have great chemistry. You decide to go home with him.	He might be the one.	He could have an STD.	He might have a serious anger-management problem that is exacerbated when he drinks. It's rare, but he also might be a rapist and this is how he cons his victims.
Your son comes home and says he heard one of the kids in his class say he was going to bring a gun to school. Your son tells you that this boy is angry at the assistant principal because she suspended him for making verbal threats to a teacher when he was only joking around. Your son asks you not to say anything because he worries the friend will retaliate if he finds out that he tattled. You are considering keeping the secret.	Your child might not be bullied as a result of him sharing this information with you. He won't be blamed for going to his parents about the threat.	This other student brings a gun to school and shows it to some of the other kids.	School counselors and mental-health experts are unaware of this student's new threat (called "leakage") to bring a gun to school. He might escalate to acting out violently, and others at the school could be hurt, including your son.

Why We Are Blind to Risk

In the last chapter I mentioned a number of myths that tend to get in the way of us noticing dangerous people. In addition to those myths, six factors tend to cloud our observations of others and of situations.

Our first impressions: We tend to form a first impression of someone else within minutes, and this impression is often shaped by superficial details: what the person looks like, how they are dressed, their political or religious affiliations, a facial expression, body language, and tone of voice. If our first impression is a positive one, we will likely look for details that support this positive view and filter out details that do not.

Similarly, if the first impression is negative, we look for details that support the negative view and filter out details that support a positive one.

Sometimes we size up other people just to compare them to ourselves. Are they smarter? Are they prettier? Rather than assess them, we compare them.

This is a particularly dangerous blind spot because dangerous people—especially psychopaths—can be masters at impression management. They know precisely how to make a good first impression and win your unwavering trust. They can be charming and glib and seem like the life of the party. At the very least, they seem harmless.

Recommendations from others: Perhaps even before meeting someone, we already have an impression because friends, family, and coworkers have referred to this person as a "good person" or "nice guy." Then, as with first impressions, we filter out the negative and focus on the positive. We assume that they've been prescreened and there's no more work necessary.

Superficial details of normalcy: We trust people who seem normal and distrust people who seem abnormal. As a result, we trust those who fit in—they have a well-groomed front yard, 2.5 kids, an easy smile, and a job. We trust people who do what everyone else does, who look like everyone else, and whose houses and yards look like everyone else's.

For these reasons, initially, many people were duped by Susan Smith, who tearfully went on television asking for the safe rescue and return of her children. She certainly didn't *look* like the type of person who would drown two little boys. No one could imagine that any mother would be capable of doing such a thing.

In reality, however, if a criminal or dangerous person is intent on you *not* knowing what is really going on behind his or her front door, he or she is going to make a concerted effort to look normal. His front lawn will be well manicured. He will dress nicely. He will go to work every day, and he will wave and smile as he drives by. He will even marry and have children because that's what normal people do. Yet you don't know what he is doing to that seemingly perfect family behind closed doors. He could be abusive mentally and physically. He could be engaging in high-risk behaviors that put his family and even his neighbors at risk.

Personal biases: Various biases may cause you to unfairly and incorrectly sort entire groups of people into "dangerous" and "safe" categories. For instance, many people have a bias that causes them to categorize all monks with shaved heads and brown robes as safe. The same goes for most religious clergy and also for many people who attend religious services regularly. For instance, think about how often you've heard the line, "He's a good guy. He's really active in the church." Yet this is a false bias. Little about someone's religious affiliation offers any indication as to whether that person is dangerous or safe. More important, dangerous individuals know about this bias and will mention that they are religious or fans of gospel music just to disarm you.

You may have other biases that cause you to unfairly sort others into dangerous categories. You might do this with people of a certain race, ethnicity, gender, socioeconomic status, or sexual orientation. Think about your natural reaction when you see a Latino youth with tattoos, a do-rag, and loose-fitting jeans that allow his boxers to show. He might be the nicest, most innocent kid around, but your instant reaction may be fear.

Our own personalities: Your personality affects how you view other people. If you are opinionated and rigid, you might sort people into black-and-white categories and have a hard time seeing the gray area in between. If you are selfless and naturally optimistic, you might frequently let down your guard (or never put it up in the first place) because you tend to see the good in people, even the ones who pose a threat to you.

Past experiences: Negative past experiences with certain types of people can cause you to erroneously sort people into good and bad categories. For instance, children of alcoholics might see anyone who takes a drink as having a drinking problem.

How Blind Spots Persist

In late summer 2010, a fifteen-year-old girl, her thirteen-year-old friend, and his eleven-year-old brother pooled some babysitting money, took a cab to the airport, bought three airline tickets, waltzed through security, and boarded a plane. They flew from Jacksonville, Florida, to Nashville, Tennessee—all without their parents' knowledge. Their destination was Dollywood.

When they realized the Nashville airport was two hundred miles from the theme park, they called home and asked for help.

When this story broke, people kept asking the same question: "How do three children walk through an airport and get on a plane without anyone noticing?"

I'm guessing that at least a few people—ranging from the employees who sold the children the tickets to TSA officials to other passengers to flight attendants—did notice. And these folks probably did, initially, wonder where the kids' parents or guardians were but immediately concluded that the adults must be nearby—probably in the restroom or grabbing a cup of coffee.

But they asked few if any questions because they rationalized and normalized the risk away. The airlines were quoted as saying that employees asked no questions because of a company policy that allows children age twelve and older to travel alone without a parent. They said the eleven-year-old was okay because he was with older companions.

TSA officials have commented that they asked no questions because children under age eighteen do not need identification to go through airport security.

I'm guessing that various passengers thought, "Well, the flight attendants are not saying anything, so it must be okay," and the flight attendants probably thought, "They got through security and they have tickets, so it must be okay."

Some other people probably suspected that these kids were not supposed to be on the plane, but they opted to believe that their parents must be somewhere.

Five Ways People Misinterpret Details

The airline incident illustrates how a blind spot can persist. Many times people see behaviors that are odd or even suspicious, and even though they might be skeptical about what is going on, they frequently assign these details into the most logical or ordinary scenario. If these suspicious details are misinterpreted, either purposefully or inadvertently, it is usually for one of the following reasons.

Normalizing: When you normalize, you find a normal explanation for what at first seemed to be a risky behavior or situation. Whenever you put too much emphasis on *superficial indicators of normalcy* and too little emphasis on other telling details, you normalize the situation. For instance, maybe your daughter's boyfriend has complained about how he has been treated at work. You don't know him very well, but there were a few times when you thought he got angry with a neighbor over an unimportant situation in a way that felt a little scary. You might have heard from your daughter that he is spending a lot of money and time going to gun shows, that he just bought a membership in another gun club, and that he never seems to have the money or time to take her out to dinner. Yet you normalize these hints by reminding yourself that he looks like a regular guy; your daughter seems to care about him; and although you are not around him a lot, he does seem to be respectful most of the time. You tell yourself that he's just a guy who is caught up in a bad work situation and his interest in firearms is his way of relaxing. It's his only release. He's normal, therefore his hobby is normal. This normalizing may prevent you from seeing the very real threat that your daughter's boyfriend might be an injustice collector who plans to use some of those guns against his coworkers and bosses or even your daughter.

Similarly, if you've ever worked in a secure building that required you to swipe an access card to get in, you've probably normalized potentially dangerous situations numerous times. Did you ever hold the door for the person behind you, even though you didn't know that person? If so, you probably told yourself that the person must be an employee. See? He's got a cup of coffee in his hand. Who else would he be but an employee? In reality, thieves commonly gain access on the coattails of employees in just this way, and then roam the building.

Similarly, let's say you notice a strange car parked in front of your home and see a man sitting inside that car. You keep glancing out the window. Ten minutes pass. Twenty minutes pass. Finally he leaves. The man's behavior is unusual and concerning, but, instead of calling the police, you normalize the behavior by telling yourself, "Maybe he's just waiting for someone," or "Maybe he's eating his lunch." You don't tell yourself, "Maybe he's casing the neighborhood," do you? Yet that is a very real possibility.

Rationalizing: When you rationalize a situation, you doubt your ability to properly interpret risk, and you mentally talk yourself out of doing something about the very real risk in front of you. For instance, going back to the strange car parked outside your home, you might talk yourself out of calling the police because "The police officer is going to think that I am overreacting," or "I'm going to get that guy in trouble and he isn't doing anything wrong."

Parents sometimes rationalize allowing their children to do dangerous things—such as walking to school by themselves—by telling themselves, "If I don't let him do this, he will never grow up," or "I shouldn't be such a helicopter parent." At other times they rationalize risky behavior by telling themselves that their kids are "good." For example, I can't tell you how many mothers have told me that their daughters were "good parents," even if their daughter was heavily involved in the use of illegal drugs and engaged in high-risk behaviors like prostitution and completely neglectful of her children.

People also tend to rationalize risky behavior because they are too scared to get involved. For instance, you might see a parent lose it in a store and scream at her kids and possibly even swat them on their bottoms. You might find the parent's behavior concerning, but you rationalize it by telling yourself, "She probably just had a really bad day. I'm sure she doesn't act like this all the time. I remember when my children were little, and I know what it feels like to be exasperated." In reality, the frightening issue is what this woman does at home when no one else is watching.

Explaining it away: People often explain away a telling detail by focusing on other details that seem to tell a different story. For instance, in a child-abduction case I worked on years ago, the parents turned the missing child's bedroom into a home office, and they did it within days of the child disappearing. This was concerning behavior. Yet many of the investigators were already convinced that the parents were not involved, so they explained away this behavior with comments like "The house is really small, and they need this space to serve as a command center where flyers can be created." This child has never been found.

Ignoring: Ignoring is a type of magical thinking, pretending that a situation, circumstance, or person is not what it appears to be. People often resort to ignoring when all of the evidence is saying otherwise, but they want—for various reasons—to hold on to their positive view of a person or situation. The mother of a rapist or murderer, for instance, might ignore all the evidence presented against him at trial. The owners of a vicious but beloved dog might ignore all the people who complain of feeling threatened by the dog. A parent might ignore the warning signs of a brooding son who is an injustice collector and has recently been suspended from school. They might even ignore his recent purchase of bomb-making materials.

Icon intimidation: We tend to ignore risky details if someone is iconic; that is, in a position of great power, status, or fame. For instance, many people trusted Bernie Madoff with their money, in part, because he used to be a nonexecutive chair of the NASDAQ stock exchange. How could someone with such an impressive title be a crook?

Whenever I worked a case and was told, "We've got to be careful here," I knew icon intimidation was going to be a factor. Investigators only used that phrase if a suspect had hired a high-profile attorney and they were intimidated by that attorney, if the suspect came from a prominent family, or if the suspect had a powerful job with a powerful title.

We automatically put more trust in CEOs and other successful business leaders, and we tend to discount signs of their wrongdoing for a longer period of time than we would with people of lesser status. We do the same with people who hold positions of trust, such as religious figures, law enforcement officers, and doctors. For instance, would you trust someone who worked for the FBI? I would, and I did. I worked down the hall from Earl Edwin Pitts, the FBI agent who was later charged with spying for the Soviet Union and Russia. We all assumed that the lengthy background investigation, interviews, and application process involved in getting a job with the FBI ensured that the folks we worked with were trustworthy. It didn't occur to anyone—not even me—that Pitts was a spy. His position also allowed him to gain access to the country's secrets and all of us to overlook the initial warning signs.

The status of someone's family can play a role in icon intimidation too. The arrest of Kevin Coe—known as the South Hill Rapist—left Spokane, Washington, residents reeling because he came from such a "fine" family. His father, managing editor of the *Spokane Chronicle*, and mother, Ruth, were considered upstanding citizens. His family was very well-known and well-respected. They were considered leaders of the community.

Now that you know how details tend to get misinterpreted, let's take a fun look at a few hypothetical situations and see how they can be interpreted correctly or incorrectly.

Secret Profiler Tricks

In the popular crime shows, profilers famously walk into a room, look around, and then, based on one small detail—usually a family photo—spout off a litany of conclusions that they've reached about the person who lives in that house. For instance, based on a tiny detail, a TV profiler might conclude that the father has been molesting his daughter for years or that the mother has a drug addiction.

In real life, it just doesn't work that way. FBI behavioral analysts (known colloquially as profilers) don't take one small detail and hang an entire profile, or even a definite conclusion, on it.

For instance, let's take a look at how a TV profiler and real-life profiler (me) would interpret the following details differently.

Detail 1: An Armani suit

TV profiler: The wearer is a company CEO who likes to flaunt his self-importance by wearing expensive clothes and buying expensive things. He has a narcissistic personality disorder. He may even be a malignant narcissistic who feels so grandiose and entitled that he abuses his wife without any concern for her welfare or feelings and has multiple extramarital affairs because he is so handsome and successful.

Mary Ellen says: Expensive clothes don't tell us whether someone is honest or dishonest. Does the rest of him fit with the picture? Does he have a cheap watch and unshined shoes? Or is he wearing an expensive watch and expensive shoes that go with the expensive suit? If the whole look is good, then maybe appearances are important to him.

How does he talk? Is it all about him? Does he constantly seek attention by talking loudly and dominating the conversation? If so, then perhaps he is a narcissist. If not—let's say he asks questions about others around him, behaves graciously or humbly, and is more reserved and quiet—probably not. The Armani suit by itself offers little insight into his personality. His behavior, however, shows a lot more.

Detail 2: A neat and tidy living room with no photos on the walls

TV profiler: The woman of the house is a "clean freak" who is controlling and rigid. She doesn't have photos because they collect too much dust. She has an obsessive-compulsive disorder. If you look in her dresser, you'll find that she color codes her underwear.

Mary Ellen says: What does the rest of the house look like? Is it possible that the living room is the only neat and tidy room in the house? Maybe it's neat and tidy because the owners never use it.

Or maybe the woman of the house is like me and keeps her living room neat and tidy because that's the room where she entertains guests and she wants to have a pleasant and nice place for them to relax and feel comfortable. I can assure you that if were you to walk into my garage, you would not find it to be neat and tidy.

I, too, do not have photos on my living room walls. Yet I own plenty of photos. They are not on the wall because I've never gotten around to hanging them.

Detail 3: An office adorned with framed plaques, degrees, and awards

TV profiler: This guy should ditch his wife and marry himself instead. The guy is in love with himself.

Mary Ellen says: Yes, it could mean that the man is a raging narcissist, but the plaques also could mean that he is proud of his work and loves what he does. It's possible that he's created a special work space that he enjoys coming to every day.

It's also possible that he lives in a small home with no office space. In a very selfless move, he's given all of the wall space at home to the family so they can display their photos and artwork. The only place he can hang his treasured mementos is in his office.

Detail 4: Someone with her arms crossed over her chest

TV profiler: This woman is clearly defensive and has something to hide.

Mary Ellen says: Yes, that's possible, but it's also possible that the gal is cold, isn't wearing an outfit with pockets (and therefore has nowhere else to rest her hands), is trying to cover up a ketchup stain on her shirt, or just stands that way routinely because she's comfortable that way.

Detail 5: A guy who looks away as he says something

TV profiler: This guy is lying, and I don't need a polygraph to prove it.

Mary Ellen says: We assume that people who look down, away, or who seem shifty-eyed are either lying or hiding something. This might be the case. But it could also be true that the person is just shy and his or her interpersonal skills are lacking. People often assume that someone who is guilty will not be able to make eye contact, but this isn't true. Psychopaths are exceptionally good at making eye contact, even when they are telling one lie after another.

Detail 6: Her bookshelf is loaded with books about psychopathy, serial killers, and sex offenders

TV profiler: She's married to someone she's suspicious of. She thinks her husband might be a violent offender, and she's reading these books so she can better understand what makes him tick.

Mary Ellen says: Maybe she's writing a book called *Dangerous Instincts* and these are books she's reading for background.

As we were working on this book, my coauthor had the following titles on her desk:

- *The Biology of Violence*
- *Snakes in Suits*
- *Without Conscience*
- *The Psychopath*
- *The Psychopath: Emotion and the Brain*
- *The Stranger Beside Me*

She was using the books for research. Yet it would be easy for someone to see those books and assume something else. She also has about thirty diet books on her bookshelf. Someone might see all those titles and assume that she has an eating disorder or a weight problem. In reality, she's collaborated on about fifteen diet books. The ones on her bookshelf are either books she's written or books she's consulted for research purposes.

Look at the Totality of the Circumstances

When you sum up a person or a situation based on just one detail, it's like trying to get a sense of what a book is about by reading just one page.

Later I'll show you specifically how to assess risk and make decisions based on the totality of the circumstances. Rather than taking isolated pieces of information—such as someone's body language or a snippet of their conversation—you will learn how to read people and situations and to make smarter decisions as a result. Once you start assessing the behavior of those around you, rather than isolated pieces of information, you will have a better understanding of who people really are and whether they pose a threat to you.

CHAPTER 5 RAP SHEET

- When weighing pros and cons, we tend to underestimate the cons and overlook the biggest risks of all.
- We assume that we can tell at a glance whether someone is dangerous, but even the best FBI behavioral analysts cannot do this. Dangerous people can look about as normal or abnormal as everyone else.
- If a first impression is a good one, we will tend to filter out negative information we notice later on in favor of details that support our first impression.
- Positive recommendations from others can bias our judgment and keep us from noticing danger.
- We tend to become disarmed by superficial indicators of normalcy, even though there is nothing to stop someone who seems normal from also being dangerous.
- We tend to normalize, rationalize, explain away, and ignore risky details.
- If you take one detail and focus on it without taking other details into account, you will likely come to an incorrect conclusion or form a poor decision.

Chapter 6

How to Improve Your Judgment

I was in Baton Rouge trying to help local authorities track down a serial killer.

Eyewitnesses had thought they'd seen a white man with some of the victims either just before they disappeared or around the areas where they had been killed. Still, I knew that the serial killer could be of any race since the races of the victims varied. To learn more about this killer, I had been encouraging local authorities to study assaults that had happened long before, looking for possible survivors from the days when this serial killer was still perfecting his technique.

Eventually authorities traced the incidents back a full year and uncovered three reports from various women who might have been approached or assaulted by the killer, but all of whom had survived. All three women described him as an African American male.

This description, however, did not fit with the eyewitness accounts.

Now investigators faced many perplexing questions. Had the eyewitnesses been mistaken? Was their information flawed? Or were we looking at two separate offenders?

I was sent to see what was similar and what was different about the respective patterns of behavior and to reach a conclusion. As I readied to leave to interview the three women, Pat Englade, the head of the Baton Rouge serial murder task force, pulled me aside. I had built a rapport with him, and I had come to admire him greatly. He'd taken an unfair beating by the media and from the public for not catching this serial killer more quickly. This was an extremely high-profile case, one that had already drawn lots of criticism from armchair profilers. Some of them—retired FBI agents and homicide detectives—were very proactive, even to the point of coming in and trying to take over the investigation.

Still, Englade did not attempt to micromanage our progress. He gave all the investigators the freedom to do their jobs. He trusted us and gave us positive feedback and credit for our work.

"Mary Ellen," he said. "Don't come out of these interviews and tell me that this rapist is a person of interest, because I can't do bullshit with that. That's not helpful. If you don't know if this is our guy, then you don't know. If it's not connected, it's not connected. If it's not him, fine. But tell me straight." I promised I would.

I interviewed all three women extensively. I asked them how this man had approached them, what he had said, and about other details that they might have noticed. I went to each of the locations where the offender first contacted the women. I walked through each scene with the women and made note of every detail. I focused much of my attention on the last victim, who had spent the most time with the offender. Through her eyes and ears, I studied his behavior and learned about his personality.

Then I spoke with Englade.

"Mary Ellen," he said, "I will do what you tell me to do here. I need you to tell me whether this man is the same person we are looking for in connection with the murders in Baton Rouge. Don't give me any BS. Are they connected or not?"

I felt tremendous pressure to get it right. The forward progress of the investigation hinged on my opinion.

If I was wrong, I not only risked slowing down the investigation, I also risked maligning my entire profession. I knew that whatever I told the chief would be broadcast to the media. I might eventually have to testify in court about how I came to my conclusions.

I would have to live with this decision for the rest of my life.

I took a deep breath. Was I the right person to make this decision? Was I ready to make it? Yes and yes.

I knew my craft. I'd been profiling crime scenes and assessing personalities for years. My assessments had helped law enforcement catch rapists, murderers, and child abductors.

I knew what I was doing.

I also had interviewed the three victims extensively. I had considered every piece of new evidence. The offender had approached Diane, one of the victims, at her front door in a nonthreatening manner. She described him as charming, pleasant, polite, and very good-looking. He'd told her that he liked the Christian music that she was playing inside her home. He'd claimed to be lost, and he'd asked for directions to find a job site and to use her phone. I knew phones had gone missing from the homes of other victims. His asking to use her phone was a telling detail.

Then, when Diane handed him the phone, he'd asked if her husband was home. When Diane answered no, he quickly shifted from a polite and charming man and into a brutal killer. He pushed his way through the door, got inside the home, and attacked her. Had her son not come home and scared him away, the attacker might have strangled her to death.

The two other women had described a similar man: good-looking, beautiful skin, hair that was well coiffed, charming, and polite. He'd approached one of them at home too. He'd also asked to use the phone because he "needed directions." As the second survivor retrieved her phone, he walked inside and began looking around at her family photos and asking questions about the people in her life. That's when she'd ordered him out of the home. Fortunately for her, he'd left.

The third woman had caught his eye when she'd been walking to her car in a parking lot. He'd followed her from the lot and then across the street to a restaurant. He parked and asked her to walk over to his car. She thought he was very handsome, had beautiful skin, and hair that was well coiffed. Intrigued, she approached him. That's when she noticed his stunning behavior: He was masturbating in his car. She said, "You are too good-looking to have to do that."

These women were all independently describing the same cluster of behaviors, and those behaviors—high risk and sensation seeking as well as impulsive—were consistent with the other murders we'd been investigating. These women also described a charming man. That explained why the murder victims did not have defensive injuries. This was a man who used his good looks and charm to con women into thinking he was not a threat to them. That charming, nice-guy style, however, dissipated once he was in their comfort zone and could take control, which happened in only a matter of minutes.

"The guy who did these things is the Baton Rouge Serial Killer," I said. I briefed Englade on what I thought he should tell the media and the public so that someone, somewhere, would think, "That describes a guy I know."

Englade held a press conference. He held up an artist's rendering, based on the description Diane had given of her attacker, as he delivered the information I'd suggested. He said that we were looking for a man who was glib, charming, and good-looking—a man who could approach women in a way that was endearing and disarming. Englade said that this man would be a risk taker, and that he'd likely entered other people's homes before when he hadn't committed a murder. People who knew him might have discovered him snooping around their bedrooms, for instance. He also said the man was of African American descent.

Before the conference was over, someone called the task force hotline and said, "The person you are looking for is Derrick Todd Lee." Derrick Todd Lee was later convicted and sentenced to death.

If I had told Englade that the murders were not connected, the Baton Rouge serial murder task force would not have continued to unravel these sexual assaults. A more accurate composite sketch would not have been drawn. A buccal swab (obtained by swabbing the inside of the cheek) had been obtained from Lee several months before, but a judge later determined that it had been obtained in violation of his constitutional rights. At the trial, the judge ruled that the DNA was not admissible evidence in court. Then the judge later readmitted the DNA findings based on the "inevitable discovery exception to the exclusionary rule." This exception allows evidence (DNA) to be admitted back into a legal proceeding even though it was seized in violation of the Constitution based on the presumption that the evidence would have eventually been discovered and lawfully obtained using other investigative techniques. It was the judge's ruling that police would have eventually arrested and gotten a warrant to obtain Lee's DNA because of the behavioral work of the FBI and the task force that resulted in the identification of Lee following the press conference.

If someone had not come forward after Englade's press conference and fingered him as the suspect, Lee would have gone on to kill more women before getting caught, and he may not have been convicted at trial after his arrest if the DNA was permanently excluded as evidence.

Why Your Decision-Making Style Matters

I could have waffled on the day I made that decision. I was tremendously stressed and had a knot in my stomach, but I had to make an informed, analytical decision. How was I able to make such a definitive decision when I was under so much pressure? How was I able to be so confident about my conclusion?

I was able to do so, in part, because I had developed an effective decision-making style for this type of high-stress situation and had extensive experience in making similar decisions. Those factors allowed me and the FBI's BAU to complete an analysis that helped to lead to the conclusion that eventually allowed the task force to catch the killer.

Your level of experience in making high-risk or stressful decisions, as well as your personal biases and your emotional state at the time you make them, will all affect your ability to make a SMART decision. In other words, more effective decision making starts with you. In particular, it depends on your ability to understand your:

- emotions, especially knowing when not to make a decision because of them or in spite of them
- experience and information, especially knowing when you don't know quite enough to make a decision
- resources, especially knowing when and whom to seek out for help

In this chapter you will find self-assessments and reflective questions that will help you to test how well you make decisions and to see what might be clouding your judgment. These exercises will help you to do the following:

Make SMART decisions. People think decision making is a talent you are born with, but that's not necessarily the case. Yes, some people are naturally better at choosing correctly. Still, decision making is a skill that you can learn and improve with practice. When you learn how to make SMART decisions, you will feel more in control of your life. When risky situations come up, they won't feel overwhelming because you will have a system to follow that will help you to make the decision on your own or consult the opinions of others.

When you use the SMART model to make decisions, you do not feel as if you are flipping a coin, picking an option, and then hoping for the best. You will know that you've made a decision that will keep you and your loved ones as safe as possible.

Track your progress at making safer decisions. In a few pages, I will ask you to assess your current decision-making effectiveness. This will allow you to reassess your decision-making effectiveness later on so you can see if you are getting better.

Know your decision-making weaknesses and strengths. Most of us are pretty good at making decisions in some areas of our life and not so good at making them in others. For instance, I'm strong when it comes to deciding whether someone's behavior is problematic or threatening. I'm much weaker when it comes to deciding whether a new computer meets my needs. Purchasing the wrong computer for my needs can result in a significant financial loss as well as long-term problems and frustration. I know this is a weak area for me and that I lack the knowledge and experience others have. As a result, I take my time in deciding whether to purchase a computer, and I will likely consult with other people for insight and information.

Procrastinate less and reason more. Procrastination is a problematic decision-making style that some of us resort to when we feel overwhelmed. Rather than taking ownership of a situation and choosing a course of action, procrastinators continually put it off and remain passive. The SMART model will help you to move beyond procrastination. You will know the difference between indecision—the inability to make a decision because you don't know what to do or how to do it—and a slow, reasoned, careful decision. You will know when the time is right to make a decision and when it's appropriate to wait before making a decision.

How Effective Are Your Decisions?

Let's evaluate the effectiveness of your current decision-making skills. This exercise is not designed to humble you. Rather, I'd like you to complete this exercise so you can learn more about yourself, and so, after some practice, you can take it again to see just how much progress you've made. I encourage you to participate as you read. Go get a notebook or open a file on your computer. Jot down notes and date your entry. Then you can take the test again later and use your first set of notes to see how much progress you've made.

I'd like you to think about three different types of decisions.

Category 1: Rare decisions

What they are: Rare decisions are the ones you make only a few times in your life.

Why they can be dangerous: Rare decisions can affect you for years to come. For instance, the decision to marry the right person could lead to years of happiness. The decision to marry the wrong person could lead to years of misery, painful divorce, and possibly financial devastation. Because you don't make these decisions often, you will feel out of your comfort zone. You may lack important skills or the knowledge needed to make such decisions. You will probably need to consult friends, experts, consultants, or other resources before making a rare decision. Many rare decisions generate a lot of emotion, both positive and negative, which can cloud your judgment.

Types of rare decisions:

- Whether to get married or divorced or to break off a relationship
- Whether to initiate an intervention for a family member or friend
- Whether to buy or sell a house
- Where to attend college
- Whether to get pregnant, adopt, or have more children
- Whether to relocate
- Whether to change jobs or careers
- How to respond to someone who seriously maligns you professionally
- To fire someone (if you rarely do this)
- Whether to purchase or give away a pet
- Whether to seek medical treatment for a friend or loved one

Category 2: Occasional decisions

What they are: You make occasional decisions every so often—perhaps once a year or so.

Why they can be dangerous: While you do have some experience making these kinds of decisions, it's not a skill that you've developed and honed. You might feel more familiar with these kinds of decisions, but if you don't have a good decision-making system in place, you are not likely to be any better at making these than you are at making rare decisions. Because you feel more familiar, though, you might be more cavalier when making an occasional decision.

Types of occasional decisions:

- What car to buy
- Whether to tell family friends something intimate
- Whether to hire (or fire) an employee or household help
- Whether to make a financial investment
- Whether and how to confront a supervisor or a colleague

- Whether to go out with someone you just met online
- Whether and how to ask for a raise
- Where, when, and with whom to travel
- Whether to buy your teenager or preteen a laptop, cell phone, or other expensive piece of equipment
- Whether to report someone or something to law enforcement
- Whether to allow your child to associate with new friends you know little about

Category 3: Frequent decisions

What they are: You make frequent decisions as often as several times a day.

Why they can be dangerous: There is a desensitization that sets in when you make a decision over and over again. You make these decisions so often that you may not even be aware that you are making a decision at all. Also, frequent decisions often lull people into a false sense of safety, especially when they don't, at first, result in negative consequences.

This desensitization can result in everything from reckless or hasty decisions to decisions based on flawed or partially flawed data. As soon as a decision becomes routine, you will need to ensure you give that decision specialized attention to avoid making mistakes due to this desensitization.

Types of frequent decisions:

- Whether to hand over your car keys to your teen or tell your teen that it's okay to catch a ride with a friend
- Allowing your children to walk to school alone
- Allowing your children unmonitored use of a laptop, cell phone, or credit card
- Whether to get into a car with someone who has just had two drinks
- To open your front door when someone knocks without looking through the peephole first

- Agreeing to carpool with someone who has a poor driving record
- Continuing to associate with a friend or associate who displays all of the dangerous behavioral characteristics mentioned in chapter 9
- Not to lock your doors
- To walk alone at night

Think about your life. Come up with examples of a rare, occasional, and very frequent decision you've made. Jot them down in your notebook. Then ponder the following questions and write some notes next to each decision accordingly:

1. **How did your decision turn out?** What was good about it? And what was bad about it? Did it cost you money, time, stress, worry, a damaged relationship, health problems, or peace of mind? Don't assume a decision was "good" because everything turned out okay. For instance, you might have pulled off texting while driving without getting into an accident. That doesn't mean the decision was a good one.

2. **Who helped you make the decision?** With whom, if anyone, did you consult?

3. **How would you decide differently?** If you could go back in time and do it over, what would you change about your decision and why?

4. **If the decision did not result in a good outcome, what happened?** What led to this outcome?

5. **Was this outcome fixable?** If so, what did you do to try to fix the situation? And how did that work for you?

6. **What factors influenced how you made the decision?** Were you emotional, under pressure, or lacking in important information? Did you fail to do something that led you to make a poor decision?

7. Would you make the same decision today? If not, what are the factors that would make you decide differently? What would you now do instead? What was it that caused you to make that decision in the first place? Who would you consult and why?

8. What did you learn about yourself because of this decision? Do you default to flipping-a-coin-style decisions when you are tired or under stress? Do you tend to get lulled into a false sense of safety when making very frequent decisions? Do you get frustrated and say, "Lets just go for it"? Do you use magical thinking, telling yourself, "It will be fine. It will be okay"? Do you default to groupthink, telling yourself, "Everybody else does it"? Or do you use the Scarlett O'Hara of the epic *Gone with the Wind* philosophy of "I will worry about it tomorrow"?

Look over your notes. What have you learned about yourself and about how you make decisions? Don't be too hard on yourself. Even if the majority of your decisions did not turn out well, that only means you have room to learn, practice, and improve. Use this exercise to learn about yourself and your past mistakes. Evaluating what influenced past decisions will help you to avoid allowing those factors to influence your decisions in the future.

On the flip side, try not to get overly confident if most or all of your decisions turned out well. Chances are you still have some room to learn and grow too.

I encourage you to take this assessment every six months to see how your decision-making skills are improving. Give it to your family members, too, especially your children.

How Do People Make Flawed Decisions?

Most people take part in risky behavior from time to time. For instance, many people text while driving, even though they know about the dangers of doing so. Others might get into a car with someone who has had a few drinks, even though they know that alcohol impairs driving ability. I see plenty of people jogging in remote areas in the dark and while wearing headphones. I also know many people who routinely leave their doors and windows unlocked.

Yet these folks are not bad people. They are not sinister, and they don't have a death wish either. Their risky behavior is, however, the result of a flawed decision-making style.

Any regretful decisions you identified in the previous exercise were probably based on a flawed system of decision making as well. Look over your notes and think about what led you to make those decisions. What factors came into play? For instance, did you make the regretful decision because you did any of the following?

Caved under pressure. Have you ever made a purchase because a salesperson talked you into it, only to regret that purchase later? Have you ever decided to do or not do something solely because you didn't want to upset someone? Think about decisions you regret. You caved under pressure if you've made the decision because:

- you worried you would inconvenience someone else
- you didn't want to upset someone else
- you felt pressured to do it
- you wanted to be polite
- you were influenced by your own strong feelings, negative or positive

Were lulled into a false sense of safety. We get lulled into a false sense of safety in a few ways.

1. When everyone else is doing the same thing. If you live in a neighborhood where no one locks their doors, you might think it must be safe to leave your doors unlocked, even if it's not. If all of your friends are piling into a car with a driver who has had a few drinks, you might get in, too, even if under any other circumstances you never would feel safe driving with someone who has had a few drinks. One of the reasons motorists in the Washington, D.C., area feel safe when they are "slugging" (carpooling with strangers they meet in park and ride lots) is because lots of other people are doing the same thing.

2. You've done it before. The more often you practice a dangerous behavior and get away with it, the safer that behavior will feel to you, even though it's not safer at all. The probability of something unfortunate befalling a slugger is the same every single time that slugger accepts a ride from someone he or she doesn't know.

3. Your biases lead you to deem someone harmless when you really don't have enough information to make that judgment. This happens most often when the person in question seemingly shares something in common with you. Perhaps you are members of the same church, alumni of the same school, or volunteers for the same charity. It also tends to happen when someone belongs to an organization or group that you have deemed good, trustworthy, or virtuous. For instance, many people automatically trust anyone who is dressed as a Buddhist monk or Catholic nun. They also trust people who are in positions of authority, such as police officers, members of the military, security officers, or bouncers. Sometimes people blindly trust those who are elderly because they think of them as physically less threatening or less imposing or because of the stereotype of wisdom and weakness coming with age.

Talked yourself into it with rationalizing statements. Rationalizing statements give you a reason to do what you want to do, despite the risks. You might talk yourself into taking a dangerous risk with rationalizing statements like the following:

- It will make my life easier.
- It will save time.
- It will save money.
- It will be much more inconvenient if I don't do it.
- I'm doing it because I love my family.
- You have to trust your child sometime.
- I don't want to get involved. It's someone else's problem.

Didn't have all of the information. The problem with lack of information is this: If you don't know you are missing a key fact, how can you know if you should include it or exclude it from your decision-making process? For instance, if you are buying a house and don't know there will be future problems with the basement when there is an unprecedented amount of rain, how can you factor that possibility into your decision? This is why it's so important to ask yourself, "What is it that I don't know?" It's also a reason to consult others who may know more about this type of decision than you do. They can fill you in on all of the information that you should gather before committing to the decision.

Think about how often you've made a similar decision. If you have made them rarely, then it's a good idea to consult with an expert who can help walk you through the steps and help ensure that you have all the information you need.

Discounted some of the information. This is when you choose to focus on the positive side of a decision and fail to adequately consider potential negative consequences. For instance, many parents allow teens to travel overseas with friends or with school-sponsored trips. They focus on all the positives: what their children will learn, the great opportunity, the affordable price, and so on. They push the negatives out of their minds. For instance, that their home country's law enforcement may not be able to help if they get into trouble in another country. And what happens if they get sick? Does the country they're visiting have a good healthcare system in place? How would they get home in an emergency? Does the family have enough money to medevac them or to pay for shelter or food if they get stranded for days, or longer, and can't get out? What if their friends get arrested for an alleged crime? Who would the family contact if they inexplicably stopped communicating? Will there be enough or any parental supervision? What if there is a natural disaster and there is no communication with that part of the world for hours, days, or even weeks?

Didn't have all of the information because you were too timid to ask for it. This might happen if, for instance, you fail to ask the salesperson about a car's accident record. It could happen if you are about to sleep with a new sexual partner and you can't bring yourself to ask for medical reports showing that he or she does not have an STD. It could happen if you take a new job and realize that it will eventually require multiple moves that your new spouse refuses to make.

Were emotional when you made the decision. Fear, anger, sadness, and other strong emotions can cloud your judgment and cause you to overlook potential future consequences. Strong needs can do the same, like a need for revenge, security, money, prestige, acceptance, etc. For instance, have you ever sent an angry e-mail to someone only to later regret having pressed the send button? Have you ever said something during the heat of an argument that changed your family dynamics forever? What would you do to be able to take those words back?

Even positive emotions can cloud your judgment. For instance, many people have rushed into flawed decisions because they've been in love with someone or have loved an idea or a material item.

You may not be able to keep your emotions in check 100 percent of the time, but you can do the following:

- Think about your emotional state before committing to a decision. Ask yourself, "Am I too stressed, sleep deprived, in love, sad, angry, or out of sorts to make this decision right now?"
- Slow down whenever you notice yourself thinking or saying things that begin with "I just want" or "I just need." For example: "I just need some peace in my life . . ." "I just need to get that . . ." "I just want to get this over with." "I just want to show her/him . . ." "I just want to teach her/him . . ." "This is all I've ever wanted."
- Put off making a decision until you are feeling less emotional and less conflicted.
- Make a point of saying, "I'll think about that and get back to you" whenever anyone presses you to make a decision.
- If possible, give yourself some time and distance before making a decision. The greater the consequences, the more time you should take.
- Talk over potential decisions with a level-headed friend and ask questions like "Do you think I'm too emotional to make

this decision right now?" "If you were me, what would you do?" "What am I missing here?" "What factors am I not taking into consideration?"

Didn't consider the long-term consequences. Flawed decisions are often made with the short term in mind. Try to remember to weigh the long-term consequences too. Ask yourself the following:

- Will I still be able to live with this decision tomorrow or next week?
- Will I still be able to live with this decision six months from now?
- Will I still be able to live with this decision a year from now or even for the rest of my life?

Didn't consider what would happen if you got caught. We've all watched as any number of politicians' and other prominent figures' hopes and dreams were dashed by decisions they'd made in the past because they assumed they would never get caught. Gary Hart, Bill Clinton, Tiger Woods, John Edwards, and the infamous sexting congressman Anthony Weiner all come to mind.

Many people cheat on their spouses because they assume they will never get caught. Many people cheat on their taxes for the same reason. If "not getting caught" or "no one finding out" is an important factor when making a decision, it's probably a good idea to reassesses whether that decision is a SMART one. Will you still be able to live with that decision if you do get caught or if people do find out? Have you thought about how you will deal with this decision if everything does go bad?

Allowed personal biases to overshadow rational judgment. As I was writing this book, the suicide of Rutgers University student Tyler Clementi was in the news. He jumped off the George Washington Bridge after his roommate allegedly secretly videotaped him having sex with a male student and then broadcast it on the Internet. News of the incident resulted in a public outcry. Various people began wearing purple in support of bullied gay and lesbian youths. Then a school board member in northern Arkansas did something stunning. He reportedly posted on Facebook that the only way he would ever wear purple would be if "they all committed suicide."

Word of his posting spread through the Internet. Soon people were calling for his resignation, and he eventually stepped down from the school board and apologized for his "unfortunate" remark.

I'm guessing that this school board member did not think very far into the future as he posted that remark. He probably did not think of the long-term repercussions or foresee that the posting would eventually result in his resignation from the school board. His bias against gays clouded his judgment. His remarks made him look as if he had no empathy for others.

You don't have to be racist, sexist, homophobic, classist, ageist, or anti-Semitic to dehumanize someone. You might dehumanize a person during a moment of anger. You might do it because they are faceless—someone you are interacting with on the Internet or a driver in another car on the freeway.

The Dangerous Truth

Negative biases cause you to put a group of people in the "bad" category and dehumanize them. Positive biases cause you to put them in the "good" category, and once you do that you are a lot less likely to perform a critical risk assessment on them. You might have a positive bias toward members of your class or your religion or those who share your political views. Yet just because you have something in common with someone doesn't mean that person is not dangerous or could not pose a threat to you.

How to Know If You Are Ready to Decide

To ensure that your choice is truly SMART, ask yourself the following questions before rushing into any decision:

1. What is the key decision I am trying to make? (For example, am I deciding to buy a house?)

2. What are the possible long-term and short-term consequences, good and bad? Once I make this decision, how am I likely to feel?

3. What is my past experience in handling this problem or situation?

4. How often do I make decisions about situations like this? Do I make them rarely, occasionally, or frequently? Have I taken steps to overcome my lack of experience in making this type of decision? Have I taken steps to overcome the problems I have encountered when I made this type of decision in the past?

5. What is influencing this decision? Am I feeling pressure to make it? What factors are causing me to feel pressure? Am I in the right state of mind to make this decision? What are my emotions?

6. What is my decision-making style and how does it help or hurt me in handling this problem?

7. Do I have all the information I need to make the decision? Is this information reliable? Am I relying only on the Internet to make this decision? Do I have all the information I need to make a strong decision? If not, or I'm not sure, have I consulted with a person or resource who does know what information I will need to make a good decision?

8. What are the long-term effects of this decision on me, my family, my friends and colleagues, and my place of employment? Have I thought about the consequences, not only in the short term, but also in six months or a year or more down the road?

CHAPTER 6 RAP SHEET

- When you use the SMART model to make decisions, you reduce your risk of negative consequences and gain a sense of control over your life.
- Your ability to make SMART decisions can be honed with practice.
- Rare decisions can be risky because they put you out of your comfort zone and force you to lean on others for help.
- Very frequent decisions can be risky because than can lull you into a false sense of safety.
- Regretful decisions are usually influenced by pressure, a false sense of safety, rationalizing statements, lack of information, strong negative or positive emotions, failure to consider the long-term consequences, failure to consider what would happen if you got caught, or personal biases.

Chapter 7

How to Assess and Mitigate Risk

While we were putting together this book, my coauthor traveled to Italy with a close friend. One evening the two were walking from a restaurant back to their hotel. It was around 11:00 p.m., but they didn't have far to go. It was only a ten-minute walk at the most. The streets they would traverse were well populated, well lit, and lined with shops that were still open.

You'll soon learn how to evaluate the risk of any given situation as low, medium, or high. Since you have not learned how to do that just yet, I'll tell you that my coauthor's risk was medium. It wasn't high, because she was not in a life-or-death situation. But it also wasn't low, because she was in a foreign country where she didn't know the language and she was walking the streets after dark. She also was missing key pieces of information. For instance, she didn't know what sort of crime problems there were where she and her friend were walking.

One's risk is quite dynamic, and it can change quickly. My coauthor's risk was quickly moving up, and her exposure to physical injury was increasing. The farther she walked from the restaurant the higher her risk became as she got deeper and deeper into unfamiliar territory. She and her friend probably stood out as foreigners, making them easy targets for thieves and pickpockets who prey on people from out of town. Because of that, we'd have to upgrade this situation from medium to high, and it could have ultimately become a life-or-death one.

My coauthor and her friend attempted to take a shortcut, one that led them to a busy road that was not well lit. Now their risk was very high. Before reading on, can you think of why?

They were about to walk down the road in the direction of the hotel when my coauthor said, "You know, there are cars whizzing past. There's a blind curve up ahead. It's 11:00 p.m., which means the probability of some of these drivers being drunk is high, and I'm dressed from head to toe in black, which means the drivers can't see me."

She and her friend decided to turn around, backtrack, and take the long way back to the hotel. This decision required that they walk back up a very steep hill. It added another ten minutes to their walk. They were anxious and jittery when they got back to the hotel, but they were also both alive.

What had initially seemed like a benign situation had quickly become a risky one. In hindsight, my coauthor says she would have tried to get more information about the crime problems in the area. She would have asked locals about the best and safest routes to walk at night. She would have found out—before embarking on the walk—who to call and where to go for help if needed. All of this would have taken only a few minutes, but it would have been a few minutes that could have saved her from a lot of potential trouble.

Why the Situation Matters

The nature of the specific situation in which you find yourself affects two aspects of your decision making.

1. How much time and effort you will want to put into a given decision. For instance, in a low-risk situation, the possible consequences of a bad decision are minimal, so it might be okay to rely on quick judgments. But in a high-risk situation the outcome of a bad decision might be physical injury or even death. In such a situation, you will want to assess the risk factors, look ahead, consider the most likely consequences, and then craft your options.

For these reasons, you probably can make a swifter decision when ordering a pizza than when hiring a cleaning person. The consequences of ordering a pizza are minimal. Even if the delivery person is a dangerous character, the exchange is made at the front door and not inside your house. Also, the delivery person must interact with dozens of customers every day. If there's a problem, it will be reported back to the pizza company sooner rather than later. The pizza place creates a built-in danger filter. If this delivery person had created problems for customers, it's likely he would have been filtered out, because customers would have complained.

On the other hand, a cleaning person will be coming into your home, where you are much more vulnerable. Most cleaning people work for themselves. So even if there have been hundreds of complaints, you'd never know it. The potential consequences of hiring the wrong house cleaner could be theft of your belongings, damage to your property, or even identity theft.

Conversely, the cleaning person, Realtor, or service person who willingly walks into a variety of homes and interacts with numerous strangers every day is at an even greater risk. The person she works for could refuse

The Dangerous Truth

Not long ago, a bank was robbed near where my coauthor lives in Emmaus, Pennsylvania. The police chased the robbers, first by car and then on foot. The robbers shot at the police. Other police responded from nearby areas, and the state police and FBI got involved too.

What do you think many of the residents and storekeepers of this small town did when they heard scores of police sirens roaring down Main Street?

They went outside to see what was going on.

By doing so, they greatly increased their risk of getting hurt. Of course, none of them knew that the robbers were on foot, and were armed, dangerous, and willing to take hostages and shoot civilians. That's why the safest thing to do when you hear sirens is the response that is least instinctual: Stay inside and lock your door.

to pay her or write her bad checks. Much worse, she could face down an unfamiliar or dangerous pet. A home owner could falsely accuse her of stealing, assault her, or even attempt to murder her. There could be aspects of the home that might cause her physical injury, such as deteriorating steps, toxic mold, cigarette smoke, or pet feces.

The higher the risk, the more careful your assessment needs to be.

2. Whether you take steps to mitigate the risk. Again, in a low-risk situation you might not take steps to mitigate the risk at all. But in a high-risk situation, you will want to take every precaution possible, and in medium-risk situations, you want to take precautions that will prevent the risk from becoming higher.

You'll learn how to mitigate the risk of any given situation later in this chapter. For now, let's talk about how to determine the level of risk in the first place.

How to Assess Risk

You can use the following scale to determine the level of risk.

> **High risk:** The likelihood of your decision resulting in mental, physical, emotional, or financial harm is high. The consequences are serious to extreme. A flawed decision in a high-risk situation could result in job loss, prolonged legal problems, a marred reputation, harm or loss of a loved one, debt, physical injury, and even death.
>
> **Medium risk:** These situations have potential to escalate (and become high risk) or subside (and become low risk). For instance, having a teen driver in the home leads to dozens of medium-risk decisions every day. If your teen is a good driver and follows all the rules of the road and does as she or he is told, the risk could drop to low. If your teen texts and drives or is operating an old car that is likely to break down as he is driving home from school or work at night, the risk could swing high.
>
> Note that sometimes you will rate a decision as medium risk because you don't have enough information to deem it high

or low, and these unknown factors can easily swing a medium-risk situation into the high-risk category. For instance, my co-author didn't know about the crime problems in the town where she was walking in Italy. If she was in a low-crime area, the risk would have been low. If it was a high-crime area, the risk would have been high. She didn't know the nature of the local crime problems, so the risk was medium.

Low risk: Low-risk decisions result in minimal consequences to your health, livelihood, and loved ones. These decisions include, for instance, what to cook for dinner and whether to buy the shoes that you see on sale. Don't sweat these decisions. Even if you flip a coin and make a flawed decision based on the result, it's not a big deal. Choosing poorly in a low-risk situation won't result in years of regret.

Your level of risk in a given situation is dynamic. It can shift back and forth, from low to medium to high and back down again, based on where you are, what you are doing, and the variables in your environment. Sometimes these shifts are subtle and sometimes they are seismic.

You'll face different types of risky situations. Many people think only of their risk of physical harm when it comes to staying safe and avoiding problems, but there are many types of risky situations, all of which are dynamic and changing. Factors that can quickly turn a low- or medium-risk situation into a high-risk one include the following:

Physical risk: Personal harm due to severe weather events (floods, mudslides, hurricanes, snowstorms, tornadoes, and so on) and harm that results from unstable or unsafe surroundings (earthquakes, dilapidated or poor construction, fires, avalanches, and so on), as well as car accidents, sudden falls, and crime.

Health risk: Food poisoning, flu outbreaks, a new diagnosis (cancer, heart disease, diabetes).

Social or emotional risk: Loss of a loved one, a loved one develops sudden and serious health issues, a loved one moves farther away.

Professional risk: Backbiting coworkers, unfair supervisors, poor company performance that eventually results in layoffs.

Financial risk: Stock market or real estate crashes, identity theft, job loss, robbery.

When trying to decide if a situation is low, medium, or high risk, consider how many different areas of your life the situation affects (professional, personal, financial, health, and social). Think about what might cause the risk to move up and down, and keep in mind these important factors:

1. What are the possible ramifications of this decision six months or a year from now for you and others around you? If the ramifications are high and a lot of people are impacted, you will want to spend more time making the decision.

2. What are the worst possible outcomes of this decision? Are those outcomes serious to extreme? Then the risk is high. Is it minimal? Then the risk is probably low. Does it depend on a number of factors? Then the risk is probably medium and you need more information.

3. How do your physical surroundings factor into the risk involved in this decision? Are your surroundings safe (I'm in my home with the doors locked in a low-crime neighborhood) or not so safe (I'm looking for my car in a deserted parking lot in a big city with lots of crime)? What is going on in your surroundings that could prevent you or someone else from being and staying safe? If the surroundings are safe, the risk might be low. If the surroundings are unsafe, the risk might be high. If you don't know the safety of your surroundings, the risk is medium and more information is needed.

4. Are you about to move into or out of a safety zone? For instance, if you are walking from your place of employment (a safe zone) into a poorly lit, unattended parking garage (unsafe zone), your situation has moved from low to possibly high.

5. Are you about to allow someone you don't know well or at all into a comfort zone? Your home and your car are your comfort zones. Whenever you invite someone into these places, your risk level goes up. Conversely, are you going into a comfort zone of someone you don't know?

Test Your Risk Assessment Smarts

Use the following chart to get a sense of the risk zone into which some decisions fall. Think over the various situations and the reasons you think I ranked them as low, medium, or high.

Situation	Risk	Why
A friend you know very well invites you out for the evening and offers to drive.	Low (Physical risk)	You know the friend well. That means you know she doesn't drink and drive, that she's a safe driver, that she maintains her car, and that she is responsible and won't leave you stranded if she meets someone while you are both out. (Note: If you don't know these details about your friend, your risk level goes up.)
Your cousin asks if she and her two young children can move in with you because she's going through a divorce and financial hardships and needs to pull herself together.	Medium (Financial and physical risk)	You don't know enough about the reasons for her divorce and specifically about her soon-to-be ex-husband. Do you know whether he has threatened her? Is he likely to come to your home and try to hurt her? You also don't know about her disciplinary practices with her children, and you might not know about her personal habits. Does she drink or do recreational drugs? Is she a closet smoker who tends to fall asleep with a cigarette in her hand? You also may not be aware of possible behavior problems that her children might have, and you may not know if she makes a habit of living with others. What if she is parasitic and moves into your home anticipating that you will support her and her children?
You are traveling abroad with a friend. She wants to avoid hotels in the interest of saving money and to look online to see if there are any local families willing to put you both up.	Medium (Financial and physical risk)	There is a lot about this situation that you do not know. You don't know which sites this friend is looking at online. You don't know about their reputation. You don't know if they screen host families. You don't know about the kinds of families who advertise on the sites this friend is considering. You don't know their background, the living conditions of their homes, or their personalities. You also don't know about their previous experiences when hosting international travelers or the experiences of other travelers who have stayed with them.

Situation	Risk	Why
Your fifteen-year-old daughter wants her own computer in her bedroom.	High (Physical risk to both you and your family)	If the computer is in her room, you will have no way to oversee her computer habits. Online predators target young children and teens with unsupervised computer access, and your teen is not old enough to be able to effectively screen who is a threat to her online and who is not. In some families, the son or daughter exercises exclusive rights to their room, their computer, and other possessions. When the parents allow this behavior, or even inadvertently encourage it, they need to understand that they may be encouraging behavior that could evolve into a serious threat to their child's well-being. Parents also need to understand that they inadvertently put their children at risk whenever they allow them to make major decisions about their lives and well-being. Children and teens do not have the maturity or emotional ability to spot Internet predators.

How to Minimize Risk

In the movie *The Blind Side*, Sandra Bullock plays Leigh Anne Tuohy, an upper-class mom who takes in Michael Oher (played by Quinton Aaron), a homeless and traumatized boy who later becomes an all-American football player and first-round NFL draft pick.

In the movie, Oher becomes upset and runs away from the Tuohys' home, which is located in an exclusive area of Memphis, Tennessee. Tuohy decides to look for him and, in the process, drives to a dangerous part of Memphis.

In the movie, Tuohy knows she is driving into an area with a high crime rate. She knows that, as white women in an expensive SUV, she would be noticeable and stick out.

But she doesn't feel she has any other choice. She loves Oher and cannot wait at home while he possibly gets into trouble.

She does, however, take some precautions. She goes to this part of town during the day. She doesn't stay long. She travels in a reliable car that she knows will not break down. She has a cell phone with her. But she gets out of her car to confront members of a gang regarding Oher's whereabouts, and that one action catapults her risk level from medium to high.

She could have taken additional precautions. For instance, she could have called the police and told them where she was headed. She could have gone there with someone else.

Tuohy made a choice that many parents would probably make. No amount of danger will get in the way of the desire many parents have to protect their children. This is why parents are known to run into burning houses. They would rather die than stand back and do nothing while their children perish or are hurt.

This is understandable, of course. Just because a situation poses a great deal of risk doesn't mean you won't willingly find yourself in the middle of it. But you can, as Tuohy did, take steps to minimize your risk. Let's walk through some hypothetical situations and minimize the risk together.

Situation 1

Your college-age daughter calls on her cell phone to tell you she has a flat tire and had to pull over. She is two states away from you.

The possible negative consequences: It's dark, which means other motorists might not be able to see her if she attempts to change the flat. It also means she is easy prey for any predators who happen to be passing by.

The risk level: High.

How to minimize her risk: Stay on the phone with her and have her describe her location, giving you as many landmarks as possible.

Keep her on the phone with you. Use another phone to call 911 and let the police know about her situation. If a cruiser is nearby, an officer can park behind her car to provide a safe buffer while she changes the tire. You might worry that you are being a nuisance by calling the police about her flat tire, but trust me. It's a lot more convenient for one police cruiser to aid your daughter while she fixes a flat than to dispatch the entire police and fire department because a passing motorist hit her car and then proceeded to cause a ten-car pileup.

- Tell her to stay in the car with the widows up and doors locked, even if someone stops and offers to help.
- If she needs a tow, stay on the phone with her the entire time. Ask to be put on speakerphone when she's in the cab of the tow truck. You can also call a taxi or shuttle service to arrange for her to be picked up.
- Advise your daughter not to accept a ride with a stranger even if he looks normal and appears to be willing to provide assistance.

Situation 2

Jenny is a college student. She's recently met another group of students, and they invite her to join them at a local pub.

The possible negative consequences: Jenny doesn't know much about any of these students. She doesn't know if they are the type of people who will look out for her if she gets into trouble with another bar patron. If there are men in the group, she doesn't know if they have anger-management problems that get worse when they drink. She doesn't know if there have been problems at the pub. For example, there may have been recent incidents of men slipping women flunitrazepam, the date-rape drug. She also doesn't know much about the employees at the pub. Do any of them have a criminal record and, if so, what for? Will any of them prey on her if she compromises her judgment and ability to think quickly by drinking too much?

The risk level: High.

How to minimize the risk: Many people attempt to minimize the risk of a situation like this by assigning someone to be a designated driver, but the risks posed by this situation call for much more than that. Jenny will be with unfamiliar people in an unfamiliar setting. She needs her wits about her because she might need to make a quick decision. Drugs and alcohol will compromise her ability to think strategically. She doesn't want to slow her thinking and her reaction time with alcohol. She could search online to see if there have been any reports filed for criminal or suspicious activities at the bar, such as women being harassed or assaulted. Prior to leaving, Jenny should absolutely tell someone where she is going and who she will be with.

Situation 3

Another student is bullying your eleventh grader, who tells you that the student bragged about having access to a gun and said he was going to take it to school and "hurt a few people who deserve it."

The possible negative consequences: There are many unknowns here. You don't know if this student was bluffing. You don't know if he really has access to weapons. And, unlike me and other FBI behavioral analysts, you don't have expert knowledge of the behavior and personalities of people who are likely to commit school violence. Most kids who threaten to shoot do not carry it out. That's a good thing. Still, there is no way—without having a trained expert do a threat assessment—for you to know if this person is serious.

As a result, you do not have the ability to decide—without outside help—if this student is making statements only to scare fellow students or if he is a serious menace. If he is serious, then many students could potentially be harmed or lose their lives if he decides to bring a gun to school.

The risk level: Medium.

How to minimize the risk: Tell a school official what this bully told your son. You want school officials to do a threat assessment or bring in outside help to do one.

When a threat like this comes in, there is usually a protocol already in place to address it. These days most schools do not use just one strategy to respond to a threat, whether it is serious or benign. Over the past decade, most schools have created threat-assessment programs with behavioral assessment and intervention teams. These teams are trained to assess the threat and consider different levels of intervention based on the seriousness of the threat.

This threat should not go unreported out of fear—fear of reprisals, fear of antagonizing the bully, and so on. Your failure to act would enable the bully to continue his behavior unchecked.

Situation 4

Your next-door neighbors create a lot of problems in your neighborhood. The wife, in particular, seems to target neighbors with passive-aggressive behaviors like playing music loud late at night and cluttering her yard with "crap" that has become an eyesore. This woman has been known to call the police on neighbors who are not doing anything out of the ordinary and to scream and yell across the street for no reason. You have seen her and her friends drinking in the yard. Her behavior seems to get worse at these times. She's recently filed a police report about a theft in her home, and now she is accusing your child of the theft.

The possible negative consequences: You know that this woman is volatile, but you don't know where her line is. Will she be able to manage her behavior, or will she escalate to worse and more threatening and harmful behaviors? If you do not handle this situation correctly, the threat could increase even more. She could focus her aggression on you and your family.

The risk level: High.

How to minimize the risk: The natural inclination of many people is to fight fire with fire and retaliate, but that is the opposite of the way to minimize risk in this situation. What you want to do is defuse the situation and keep it from getting worse. Make an effort to stay away from her, her family, and her property. You want to avoid continuing this battle on personal terms. You want to refer the matter to an entity (such as a home-owners' association or the local police) and let her fight it with them. They will have procedures in place to handle these problems. They have both the power and the legal and financial resources to enforce appropriate rules and regulations. They are the best entities to address her behavior, particularly if it begins to escalate. Deferring the problem to one of these entities also puts a buffer between you and her, which is critical.

Situation 5

There is a serial burglar operating in your area, and he's hit all the houses around you. You worry that yours might be next, but you have a guard dog and you work out of your home during the day. Maybe that's enough?

The possible negative consequences: You fear that sooner or later this burglar is going think about breaking into your home. What you don't know is (1) whether the police might catch him before he does, (2) whether your dog is enough of a deterrent to persuade the burglar to stay away, and (3) what the burglar will do if he does manage to break into your home. Will he only take some of your property? Will he also destroy and vandalize your home? Will he hurt your beloved dog? Is it possible the he might break in while you are home and harm you or your family? Is he watching your home right now, and if so, how is he doing it? How has he managed to be successful so far? Why hasn't anyone seen him in your neighborhood?

The risk level: High.

How to minimize the risk: There are many things you can do to make your home harder to break into, and I'll get to those in a little bit. First, however, let's talk about catching this burglar before he or she takes an interest in your home.

This person has been able to gain access to many homes over time. He or she has gotten away with this time and time again. Think about why that might be. Could it be that this person is very normal looking—perhaps someone who does not look like the type of person who would burglarize a house? Could it be that this person has not been caught because he or she blends in? You and your neighbors may very well have seen this person in the neighborhood but didn't think anything of it. Maybe your eyes skipped right past this person because he or she was so good at blending in and creating a facade of normalcy.

To catch this burglar, you and your neighbors will want to be aware of people who might be casing homes. Burglars do not stand in front of a home wearing a mask and holding a laundry bag. They do things that allow them to blend in. This person might walk a dog, jog, or ride a bicycle through the neighborhood. He or she might sit in a car while it is off or idling and appear to be on the phone or texting. Perhaps he or she goes door to door under the pretense of selling something, dropping off flyers, or asking for directions. Chances are you are not looking for someone who appears suspicious. You are looking for someone who does *not* look suspicious. If he looked suspicious or out of place, he probably would have been caught already.

Keep notes on what and who you notice in your neighborhood and compare those notes with your neighbors.

In addition to keeping watch over the neighborhood, do everything possible to make it seem as if you are always home: Keep lights on, keep the shades drawn, and keep a radio or the TV on when you are not home. Make sure your yard is well lit so it's harder for someone to break in without being seen. Make your house harder to break into: Keep the doors and windows locked. Consider getting an alarm system. Talk to your local police about the break-ins and ask them what you should look out for. Make sure you have the local police on your phone's speed dial, and make sure your phones are easy to access.

Brief family members about answering the door or giving out information about your home. Change your routine. Come and go at different times. Change your parking habits so it's not obvious that you are not home when there's no car in front of the home. Show that it is not easy to assume that you are, or are not, at home by making the signs of your presence less predictable. Finally, consider starting a neighborhood watch. Ask police to come in for a public briefing on best practices.

What to Do When the Risk Is Too High

When I was in graduate school, I moved into a small apartment in another town and lived by myself. One night, during my first week there, someone knocked at my door. It was the landlord. I let him in. He proceeded to tell me that he found me attractive and suggested that we have a romantic relationship.

I felt uncomfortable, and I thought he was forward and rude, but it didn't occur to me, at that time in my life, to think any more of it.

Then I called my mother. I told her what had happened and ended the story with "Can you believe he did that?" I was living alone for the first time in my life. I had sized up the situation as low risk, but my mother sized it as high. I was viewing it through the lens of a twenty-year-old who did not have a lot of experience at assessing risk.

My mother told me to start packing. She then called an uncle who lived nearby and asked him to drive over and help me move out. She saw the situation for what it was: extremely high risk. Here I was, a young, vulnerable woman living alone. I had a landlord who was both interested in me and rude and impulsive enough to tell me so. He was in a position of power, and he had a key to my apartment.

My mother didn't leave any room for mitigating that risk. She got me out of there. Within days, I was living in a new apartment.

There will be times when you will want to do the same. You will want to abruptly pull yourself or someone else out of a risky situation, or you will want to avoid getting into a bad situation in the first place. Here are some reasons why you would want to get out of a situation:

1. There isn't enough time to mitigate the risk. There is potential for danger or even imminent danger to yourself and/or others.
2. Even if you take steps to mitigate it, the risk is still very high.
3. No matter how creatively you think, you can't come up with a way to mitigate the risk.

Some examples of times when you would want to pull out or ignore rather than attempt to mitigate the risk include:

- domestic physical or emotional abuse
- a group dynamic in which the group leader is suggesting that everyone do something dangerous (bullying someone else, drinking and driving, texting and driving, engaging in character assassination of a colleague, etc.)
- someone poses a threat to himself and others

In the next chapter, you will learn how to gather information so you can use that information to mitigate risk and make better decisions.

CHAPTER 7 RAP SHEET

- Take more time when making decisions that are high and medium risk.
- High-risk situations can have extreme consequences. Medium-risk situations can swing high or low, depending on the circumstances. Low-risk situations threaten only minimal consequences.
- Try to mitigate as much risk as you can in high- and medium-risk situations.
- Some situations cannot be mitigated. In these cases, the best strategy may be to extricate yourself or others from the situation.

Chapter 8

How to Uncover Information

Many years ago I was interviewing Tina, the spouse of an alleged serial killer. As I read Tina her Miranda rights, she started to cry. She fell out of her chair, onto the floor, and sobbed.

It's common for people to break down during an interview, especially when they are facing possible prison time. It's possible that Tina was both terrified at the possibility of being charged as an accomplice to her husband's crimes and remorseful for potentially ignoring telling signs that he might be terrorizing and murdering women.

I felt for her, and I was concerned, too. She was a rather large woman, and she was heaving so intensely that I worried that she might suffer a health problem as a result.

Still, I had to read her the rights. The interview could not move forward without me doing so, and we wanted to get her side of the story. I'm a compassionate interviewer, but I know better than to stop an interview over a few tears.

I calmly got out of my chair and I knelt next to her. Then I continued to read her rights: "You have the right to remain silent. Anything you say can and will be used against you in a court of law . . ."

As I neared the end, she abruptly stopped crying, sat up, composed herself, and lost all of her symptoms of sadness. She looked at me and said, "It always worked with James."

I was floored, and so were all the detectives, FBI agents, and profilers watching the interview through a two-way mirror. I'd watched people pretend to fall asleep to evade an interview. I'd listened to them as they'd threatened me and other agents with bodily harm. I'd seen a lot of people attempt to evade my questions in many creative ways.

And I'd even seen people turn on the tears, but I'd never seen someone behave in such a manipulative way as Tina had. Her display of emotion was the most convincing display of emotion I'd ever seen. She was a phenomenal actress. She'd been malingering: faking her sadness, fear, and distress for personal gain. She'd put on the show in order to get me to stop the interview and stop reading her the rights, to push me away and refocus the interview so I'd feel sorry for her. She thought her tears would end the interview before it started. They didn't.

How to Conduct an Interview

In this chapter, you will learn how to interview people (including your coworkers, neighbors, family members, and friends) in order to persuade them to tell you what you need to know. You will find out how to put people at ease so they are more likely to reveal important details. You will discover how to tell if someone is lying or being evasive. And you will find out how to observe someone's behavior so you can gain access to critical information about what is going on with them.

An interview is a situation in which you are attempting to obtain information. The word "interview" may sound quite formal, but I think it helps to think in those terms. If you think of this sort of conversation as an interview, it will keep you focused on information, both giving it and receiving it. If you call it something else, it will be easier to lose focus.

An interview is *not* the following:

1. A *confrontation* involving lots of emotion and battle lines being drawn.
2. An *accusation* that involves you telling someone what he or she did or did not do and not allowing this person room to explain his or her position.

3. An *intervention* that involves you telling someone else what his or her problem is and how you are going to fix it.
4. A *lecture* or *sermon* during which you do all of the talking. (Unless you are a preacher, don't preach.)

Confrontations, accusations, interventions, and lectures are all examples of communication styles in which you come at someone from a position of superiority and dominance. There is a time and a place for lecturing, confronting, and so on, but you want to be aware of when and why you are using these confrontational styles, along with the likely consequences.

During an interview, you do not want to act as if you are the person in power. Rather, you want to do everything possible to put your interviewee at ease, to listen, and to ask questions that will get you the information you seek. Ripping someone's head off might allow you to feel better if you are very angry, but it will not get you to your goal. As soon as you walk in and start taking your interviewee down a peg, you will cause that interviewee to shut down, reject what you are saying, resent you, become angry with you, and avoid further communication with you.

The more judgmental, opinionated, accusatory, or angry you are during an interview, the less the person you are interviewing is likely to reveal.

The Dangerous Truth

On TV and in movies, suspect interviews include lots of shouting and even some bodily harm. Foreheads are banged against tabletops. Backs are thrown up against walls. Threats are made, and the suspect is called any number of names. All of this eventually breaks the suspect, reducing him or her to tears and a full confession.

This overly aggressive method of interviewing is not how modern law enforcement, including the FBI, conducts interviews. The best way to get someone to shut up and shut down is to get in his or her face and start yelling.

Do This Before the Interview

To conduct an effective interview, you'll want to prepare for it and put some thought into your strategy before you ever ask a question. I would suggest the following:

Set some goals. What do you want to accomplish during the interview? What are your goals for this interview? What is your objective? What do you hope to find out? Keep in mind that most people do not open up and tell all in just one interview. It might take several interviews for you to pull the full story out of your sullen teen or stonewalling spouse. Make sure your goals are realistic and not intentionally cruel or harmful.

Calm down. The angrier or more aggressive you are, the less effective your interview will be. If you are thinking any of the following phrases, you are probably emotional and now may not be the best time to conduct an interview:

- I've just had it!
- If I don't do this now, I'll never do it.
- I just can't take this anymore.
- That does it!
- I have had it with him.

If needed, take a break and calm down before asking a single question. Again, if you are feeling emotional it's probably not the best time to try to get the information you seek.

Think about how your interviewee will react to the interview. What kind of a person are you dealing with? What will this person likely do if he or she does not want to give you the information you seek? Is he or she likely to cry, shut down, change the subject, walk out of the room, or something else? Think about past conversations and interactions you've had with this person, especially those that might be similar to the one you wish to have now. How did he or she react then? Take what you know about this person's personality and behavior into account and craft your questions and interview style around what you know.

If you worry you'll lose your cool, write a script to follow. Without a doubt, one of the most memorable cases I ever worked on involved the kidnapping, for ransom, of a wealthy and very high-profile computer executive. Such a crime of violence rocked the foundation of his family. For six days, this man was kept by his kidnappers who taunted the family with regular phone calls to dictate the terms of the ransom. The kidnappers had given strict instructions that the FBI was not to be contacted, so I determined that Kathy, the daughter, would be the best person to communicate with them.

Kathy was only in her early twenties and had absolutely no experience with criminal behavior, "bad guys," or the FBI. Kathy was frightened for her dad's safety and worried about what this whole situation was doing to her mom, who already had health problems. She was also very angry that this was happening to her father—to their family. I didn't want Kathy to be blindsided by anything they said to her, or for her to lose control, so I wrote her a script—questions for her to ask the kidnappers. I also wrote out a variety of responses she could provide them, depending on their comments or questions. Before each call, she and I practiced, and I told her how she was going to feel during the calls. I told her they would say things to her that would scare her about what they would do to her father if she didn't follow their demands. I told her they would say things like "kill your father" and "you will never see him again" and that they would try to push her buttons to get a reaction from her. I counseled her on keeping her cool and how to not get angry, demanding, or too emotional.

Every time the phone rang, Kathy and I both jumped, and I know her heart must have been pounding, because mine was too. She would pick up the receiver while I listened in on the other line. I stood right next to Kathy and held on to her as she braved her way through the kidnapper's cruel comments and questions. I would point to the script throughout the call, so she would know what to say. When Kathy started to get angry or emotional, I would tighten my grip on her and point to my long list of directions: "Don't get angry. Don't yell. Don't call them names." Following these phone calls, Kathy would sometimes shake or break down in tears. But she did an incredible job. We eventually found her father and brought him home safely, and the kidnappers were arrested and convicted.

I hope you will never find yourself having to conduct such a high-risk interview. But, if you know there is a lot at stake, and that emotions will run high, prepare a script. Write down what you want to communicate and how you will want to respond to the questions you might expect. Anticipate how your buttons will be pushed. Refer to your script when you find yourself getting upset or off point. Also, practice ahead of time.

Decide where you will conduct the interview. I didn't do much undercover work while in the FBI. Working as an undercover agent requires a special talent that I just didn't think I had. But one time I went undercover to keep an eye on a white-collar suspect who was believed to be offering bribes to other bankers in return for favoritism. The suspect wanted to do business with the bank where I supposedly was working, and he asked for a meeting at a restaurant during lunchtime. I was wired to record our conversation. Obviously this was a pretty important conversation and I wanted it to go well. However, it was loud, hot, and crowded in the restaurant. Other people's conversations were drowning out ours, and I didn't think the recorder was picking up the conversation. I tried to sit closer to the suspect while maintaining some decorum. The waiters, who had no idea what was going on, would come over to the table at the most critical times to fill water glasses or ask if we needed anything. It broke our rhythm. Every once in a while, I would look over to the table where the other agents were sitting, just to make sure they could still see me, but there were too many people around to have a clear view of them. It really was not the best place to have a sensitive conversation.

Another time, when I was not undercover, I went to interview a murder suspect. I wanted it to be somewhere he was comfortable so he would be more likely to open up and talk. I knew an interview room at the precinct was not such a location. He would just clam up if I took him there. On the other hand, we knew he often visited a graveyard late at night, so I suggested the cemetery as a meeting spot. I normally don't interview people while sitting on a grave, but I knew it was the best way to get him to talk, and it worked.

Think about the type of environment that will be the most conducive to your reaching your goal. If your conversation could result in you or the other person crying or having some other emotional response, pick a place that affords both of you privacy and respect. Also think about distractions that could stall the interview—a ringing phone, a blaring television, a bleeping text message, a crying baby, and other people—and try to minimize them if possible.

Decide when to conduct the interview. If possible, find out what is going on in your interviewee's life that might complicate the interview. Check his or her emotional vitals. Stress, depression, grief, anger, and other strong emotions will make it tougher for your interviewee to pay attention, open up, and talk.

For instance, let's say your teen just found out that he was not selected for the varsity football team. He's sullen and has spent much of the afternoon in his room with the door closed. You want to talk to him about his girlfriend who has been practically living in your home, the negative influence she's having on your family's life, and how you want her out. But today is not the best day to talk about his girlfriend. Save it for a better day, when he's not so troubled.

Occasionally you might have no other choice than to interview people during inconvenient times. You might need to do it in an emergency, when time is of the essence and you need to gather information as soon as possible. In such situations, incorporate the problematic timing into your initial delivery so the interviewee will buy into the urgency. For instance, you might say, "I wish I could pick a better time to talk with you about this. I can tell what happened today will make it tough for you to talk with me. I want to make sure you know that I am sensitive to what is going on with you, but this other situation we need to discuss is really urgent."

Decide how you will conduct the interview. Whenever possible, interview someone face-to-face. Face-to-face interviewing allows you to observe behavior. If you cannot interview someone in person, then the phone is your next best option. E-mail and texting are the least desirable because these mediums are so impersonal. They raise the risk of your interviewee misinterpreting your questions, motives, and feelings and of you misinterpreting the interviewee's answers, feelings, and motives.

Some people prefer to handle tough conversations by phone or by text, but I would encourage you to counter any tendency you might have to do such a thing. When you attempt to have a tough conversation in these manners, you are unintentionally broadcasting a message that says, "You are not important enough to me to do this in person." It can leave the other person feeling insignificant, hurt, marginalized, resentful, and unimportant.

Do an assessment of your own style. Use the information you learned about yourself in chapter 6. Also think about how interviews and important conversations have gone for you in the past. Do you tend to become angry? Are you more of a talker than a listener? (See "Are You a Good Listener?" on page 159.)

Do you tend to lecture or become accusatory? For instance, do you tend to say things like "I just tell it like it is," or "I'm just brutally honest," or "I don't have time to figure out what to say—I just say it," or "I don't have time for all that warm-and-fuzzy crap." These are all statements used to justify insensitive and bullying behavior. You might not think of yourself as a bully, but whenever you try to exert power over someone else and shove your opinion down his or her throat, you are bullying, and it most likely feels like bullying to the other person. Once you move into a bullying state, you become dominant and controlling and a lot less likely to get the person you are interviewing to open up.

Think about what adjustments you might want to make to your interviewing style. How might you adapt your natural style to the person you are interviewing? How have interactions between you and this person gone in the past? If things have not gone well, how might you adapt your interview style so things can go better this time around? In my thirty-two years in law enforcement, this is one of the most important concepts I learned. If you are the interviewer, you are in a leadership role and it is up to you to make the necessary changes, modifications, and adjustments to help guide the person you are interviewing to give you the information you are seeking.

The First Five Minutes of the Interview

The first five minutes of the interview can be the most important. During this time you will want to do the following:

Set up your physical surroundings. Limit distractions. Turn off the TV. Put your phone on vibrate or, better, turn it off entirely. Create an atmosphere that will make you and your interviewee comfortable.

For instance, whenever someone comes to my home—whether it's a neighbor, a friend, or hired help—I offer them a refreshment. I say, "I'm going to make some coffee, would you like some?" If they stay longer, I might offer them something to eat too. It's a way of extending an olive branch.

Now let's say you offer the olive branch, and the person you wish to interview says, "No, let's get on with it." Well, then it's best to get on with the interview. The interviewee is already annoyed and doesn't want to be there. No amount of coffee is going to change that. Someone like this is going to be impatient. Forgo the comfort and get right to the point. You might say, "Okay, it sounds as if you want to get right into this conversation and so do I."

Make introductions. If you already know the interviewee, then this might be as simple as saying hello. If you do not know this person, you'll want to introduce yourself and explain who you are. Keep your introduction to just a few sentences. Try not to go on and on and on, listing your credentials or use stalling phrases like "I hate to bring this up," or I'm not sure how to say this," or "I'm not comfortable with this."

Here are examples of effective and not-so-effective ways to introduce yourself.

Say this: "Hi, I'm Jane—I'm Tyler's mom. Your son and my son go to the same school and they ride together on the bus. We live across the street."

Don't say this: "Hi, I'm Jane, your neighbor. I've lived here for twenty years and my house is on the historic registry. I work as a lawyer and am one of the most respected attorneys in the state. My son, Tyler, is on the honor roll and the captain of the football team . . ."

Build rapport. When you build rapport, you are creating a connection that puts your interviewee at ease, making him or her more likely to open up. There are two situations in which this doesn't work. First, rapport building does not work with psychopaths because they do not have the same feelings of empathy as you do. They do not bond on an emotional level with other people. Instead, they feel superior to you and any connection with you is meaningless.

Second, it's important to note that you don't want to spend much, if any, time building rapport if you are in an adversarial situation and your interviewee has already asked you to "get this over with already." This person has his or her mind made up and is impatient for you to finish talking. In this case, do not ramble. Just give the person quick bullet points and come to your conclusion quickly.

But in all other situations rapport building can help get the answers you need. Here are a few ways to build rapport:

1. Explain how much you care about the person or the outcome. For instance, if you are interviewing a family member, you might say, "Because I really care about you," or "Because you are so important to me," or "Because I don't want anything bad to happen to you." Just make sure your comments are sincere. When someone I hardly know starts off a conversation by saying, "I really care about you, Mary Ellen," I think, "If you lied to me about that, what else are you going to lie about?" Insincerity leaks out your pores.

2. Say that you need help. Adults like to give opinions and to fix things. (This isn't necessarily the case with children, who usually just want to be listened to.) When you give adults the opportunity to state their opinions, they will often open up. When you take that opportunity away from them, they will often shut down. To get a person talking, give him an opportunity to help you. Ask questions like these:

- What do you see as the problem here?
- Could you help me with this?
- I would really love your advice about this. Do you mind helping me?
- How would you resolve this if you were me?
- How do we fix this?
- How do you view this situation? What do you think is going on here?

- What do you think I should do?
- How do you think I feel about this?
- What is your perception of this?

You can also make statements like "I don't know how best to handle this. I could really use your help or advice," or "I could really use your assistance. I am not sure how to handle this situation."

This tactic works especially well with people who are reticent to offer advice, ideas, or suggestions. For instance, not long ago, three workers came to repair my roof. One of them was a young woman who seemed very reserved and shy. I also think she may have felt a little intimidated after she learned that I had been an FBI agent. She and the others were at my home for most of the day, and she didn't say more than a few words the entire time. I offered them lunch, which they accepted. As they were eating, I said, "You probably have noticed these color swatches on my wall. I've been planning to paint this room, but I can't seem to make a decision about the color. I am not very good at this."

I turned to the young woman and asked, "Which one do you like?" Well, her face just lit right up. She picked a color. I asked her, "Why do you like that one?" That's when she opened up like a flower. "This is a warm color and you are a warm person. This color speaks to your personality." She went on and on and on. I was just stunned. As it turned out, she was studying interior decorating. Had I not made the effort to draw her out, I would never have gotten the benefit of her expert opinion and insights about decorating.

3. Chat about a common interest. I'm an animal lover, so whenever I interview someone who has dogs or cats, I might say something like "Oh, I see you have cats. I have three feral cats that I feed." If your children are the same age, you could build rapport by talking about your children. Or perhaps you share a similar hobby or political views.

4. Reveal personal information—with caution. By briefly telling your interviewee that you are not perfect and you know it, you help them to relax and they will be more likely to see you as less threatening and less intimidating.

Of course you don't want to tell someone something off-putting. It's probably not a good idea to mention the time you spent in a mental hos-

The Dangerous Truth

Probably the most common way people bring up a potentially tense conversation is by saying, "We need to talk." As a general rule, however, this phrase comes across as quite threatening to people. It forecasts problems, pending doom, and ultimatums. Your loved ones probably have a history of hearing those words and of the resulting conversation not going well. As a result, those words might trigger someone to prepare for battle rather than relax and talk easily.

Even in a serious situation, you don't want to start off this way. For instance, let's say you suspect your boyfriend or spouse of cheating. Try not to go into this type of interview fueled by very strong negative emotions and thoughts such as these:

- I will kill him if he is cheating on me.
- I am so angry.
- That SOB! How dare he?
- He has ruined my life.
- I want to ruin him.

Have goals in mind before approaching your partner. If your goal is to uncover the truth, the advice in this chapter will help. If your goal is to accuse or unload or verbally abuse, this book can't help you. Just keep in mind that words are not retractable. The damage is done forever.

Also remember that emotionally laden interviews can escalate and lead to serious problems. You can evolve into an emotional and verbal abuser. If this happens, you are going to look bad. If your partner is thinking strategically, you will give him more and more reasons to stop the relationship. In the worst-case scenario, the conversation will turn physically abusive and the police could get involved.

pital or a past drug problem. But you might say, "I'm a little nervous right now," or "I'm thinking I might be a bit rough around the edges with this interviewing process, so please bear with me."

5. Introduce the goals of the conversations. Briefly state what you hope to achieve. For instance, you might say, "I hope by the time we are done talking we can reach an agreement on how best to handle this." This is an important piece of the conversation because it forces you to focus on your objective and it helps to prevent you from launching into an accusatory rant. It also tells your interviewee what to expect from the interview. Surprising someone with information may be necessary and, in some cases, part of a well-thought-out strategy, but it can also be very off-putting if used as a weapon to catch someone off guard or box him or her into a corner.

When you introduce the goals of the conversation, try to be as nonconfrontational as possible. For instance, let's say you want to talk to your husband about why he doesn't want to install an alarm system in your home. The factor motivating you is the recent spate of burglaries in your neighborhood, which has pushed this topic to a level of greater significance. Here are examples of how, and how not, to approach the subject.

Say this: "I know you've worked all day and are probably pretty tired. I bet the last thing you want is to sit down with me. You've been really patient, and I appreciate it. I'd like to talk with you about your concerns about getting an alarm installed. I'd like to understand your views on the matter."

Don't say this: "We need to talk about this alarm and why you don't want it."

How to Ask More Effective Questions

For the rest of the interview, you want to ask questions and listen and observe the interviewee as he or she answers, or doesn't answer, them. If you are interviewing someone who is reserved or uncomfortable opening up, intersperse different kinds of questions. Some questions should be focused on how he or she feels ("How did you feel when your boss told you that you were not getting that raise?"), and others should focus on what your interviewee actually did or observed ("What did you tell your boss?"). If you alternate "feelings" questions with "behavior" questions, you will not only get more facts but you will also hear more about emotions, motives, and perceptions.

Listen to what your interviewee is saying as you notice how he or she is saying it. Is this person slumped over and hanging her head on her chest while she talks quietly? Or is she animated and enthusiastic? Is he becoming more and more angry and responding in a combative and defensive manor? All of this is interpersonal intelligence. It gives you information about what your interviewee is thinking and feeling, and how she is reacting to you.

Periodically paraphrase what you've heard the person say. This validates your interviewee, assures her that you've been listening, and will encourage her to open up even more.

Here are some additional pointers that will help you to improve your interview and disarm your interviewee so he feels more comfortable and less defensive:

Offer a few compliments. Even if you are interviewing someone you find contemptuous, you can find a way to give a compliment here and there. You might say, "You are doing a really good job of explaining this," or "Thank you so much for taking the time to talk to me. I know you are very busy and your time is very important."

Ask open-ended questions. These are more likely to get someone talking and to soften up the conversation. Instead of questions that generate one-word answers, ask questions that allow the person to talk and explain. Usually these questions start with "what," "how," or "why."

Slow down your line of questioning. Avoid making your questions come off like machine-gun fire. You don't want to sound like the stereotypical cop from the 1960s crime drama *Dragnet*: "Where were you? Who were you with? Why were you there? What were you doing? Just the facts ma'am. Just the facts."

Such a line of questioning generally makes even the best of people nervous and uncomfortable. It causes many people to shut down, become evasive or angry, or start denying everything.

Use silence to your advantage. Many people become uncomfortable when there is a period of silence in a conversation, and this discomfort causes them to talk in an effort to fill the silence. Give your interviewee ample time to think about and answer every question, and allow a period of silence at the end, giving him or her ample opportunity to say more.

Resist the temptation to fill the silence yourself. If you patiently wait it out and allow a pause, your interviewee just might say a little more.

Acknowledge someone whenever he or she provides you with an honest and sincere answer. Give periodic positive feedback during the entire time the person is talking. You might say, "I appreciate you telling me that," or "I know that was difficult for you. Thank you for opening up."

Don't allow emotion to get them off the hook. Like the woman I mentioned earlier, who cried during the interview, some people will use emotion to stall the conversation. Even if the emotion is authentic, stepping in and catering to the emotion will derail your interview. It's okay to gently put a hand on someone's back or make another conciliatory gesture (as I did when I kneeled next to the woman I was interviewing), but do so with caution. Also keep in mind that crying during an interview can be cathartic and positive, which is why it has always been my practice to allow people to cry. I just pause and let the person cry, without handing them a tissue or gently touching their arm. A touch, a gesture at that point, could cause them to prematurely stop crying.

When a person becomes angry during an interview, I let them have their angry outburst too. I will sit quietly and let them yell, even rant. Once they calm down, I continue. If their anger moves toward aggression, however, it becomes a safety issue, and it will become necessary to terminate the interview and reschedule it for another time.

Reflect back what they say. Summarize what you think your interviewee has said, to make sure that you've got it correct. As you do, acknowledge his or her feelings, especially if those feelings are obvious. For instance, you might say, "It seems like this is a very tough topic for you to talk about. I appreciate you taking the time to talk with me about it."

What Not to Do

As we were working on this book, my coauthor was worried about her daughter, who'd said a little boy in her first-grade class was bending her fingers back until she said uncle. Obviously this concerned her. But it was also a sensitive situation. If she handled it poorly, she risked alienating herself and her daughter from the first-grade teacher. She also risked having the behavior escalate.

She wasn't sure of the right course of action. She needed advice and information. So she called the school principal. She explained the issue and said, "I don't know what to do. I could really use your advice. I'm not sure how to handle this. This is the first time I've ever encountered this problem, but I'm guessing you've dealt with problems like this hundreds of times. Could you tell me what you think I should do?"

The principal did one better. She offered to talk to my coauthor's child and to the little boy in question, get to the bottom of the story, and then do something about it if needed.

As it turned out, my coauthor's daughter was not entirely innocent! The little boy had come up with the idea of bending her fingers back until she said uncle, but she had done it back to him too. The principal gently talked to them both and explained that this was not acceptable behavior.

The situation was resolved.

This might have gone much differently, though. My coauthor could have called the principal and chewed her out for allowing such bullying to go on under her watch. She could have insisted that the little boy be punished or even expelled from school. She could have told everyone in the school what she thought of them and what she thought they should do about this situation. She could have been demanding, threatening, and insulting, which would have gotten her negative results.

She would have derailed the interview, and she would not have gotten what she wanted. There are other ways to derail interviews. Here are some examples.

Don't hijack the conversation. You hijack a conversation whenever you interrupt the person talking and bring the topic back to yourself. For instance, whenever I go to social gatherings, people generally ask me what I do for a living. Usually after I say that I am a retired FBI profiler, the person hijacks the conversation like this:

> Oh, really? That is so cool. Well, you know, I just love watching *Criminal Minds*. That is my favorite TV show of all time. I always wanted to be a profiler. I am really good at reading people. You know, people say that I've got this special gift that allows me to get inside somebody's head. I'm really not sure how to go about doing that because maybe I am too old to be an FBI agent, but I think I could be really good at it . . .

And then for ten minutes or so the person continues to talk about him- or herself. Because I'm never asked another follow-up question, I shut down and just let them go on and on. I provide them with no other information. This person who was so interested in FBI profiling goes home that evening with no more information about me or my work.

If you make the interview all about you, you will turn off the other person and shut that person down. Conversation hijacking embarrasses interviewees. It can make them feel that whatever they were talking about is not important to you. It can make them less likely to bring it up again. They might resent you for being rude, self-focused, and self-absorbed. Every time you do this during an interview, it will be tougher and tougher for you to keep your interviewee talking and on point. You'll also have a tougher time getting this person to communicate with you in the future.

Frequently I will ask people about specifics of a conversation they have had with a friend or a family member. They often tell me that they don't know what their friend or family member said about topic A or B. I ask them why they don't know. They tell me that they didn't ask in-depth questions because they weren't really interested in what the other person had to say. I am always floored by this. An "I don't care attitude" is hard to hide. The person you are talking to will see that attitude on your face and in your behavior, and it will negatively impact your communication with them.

Unless it's vitally important, don't cut off the person with statements like "Oh, hold on one second while I grab this phone call," or "Oh, that reminds me of something," or "Hey, did you see that beautiful house we just passed?" Save those thoughts for later. If you interrupt the interview with such passing thoughts, you are broadcasting one thing and one thing only: "I just asked you a question, but I really don't care about your answer. I am not listening. This conversation is not important to me."

That is not the message you want to send during an interview, particularly a really important interview. If you send that message, the person you are interviewing is probably going to shut down.

Are you a serial interrupter?

You might be a serial interrupter if you:

- check for calls or texts or e-mails during a conversation with another person
- change the topic midstream and pull it back to something you remember in the past
- hoard the conversation
- go off on tangents that only relate to you and your areas of interest or preference
- say things like "Let me stop you here" or "Let me just say this"
- look away and act as if you are not engaged

Don't jump in and fix someone's problems. Many adults are fixers, and many adults are also insulted when someone tries to fix their problems. When fixers hear about a problem, they immediately want to give advice. Are you a fixer? If you are, you will want to hold back your desire to fix during your interview. If someone really just wants to be heard and you jump in to fix things, your interviewee can end up feeling insulted, as if you are treating him or her like a child. This person might feel as if you think he or she is insignificant, incapable, or unintelligent. Most adults know how to fix their own problems. When they come to you with an issue or a problem, ask yourself, "Does this person want to be fixed or does he or she just want someone to listen?"

Don't talk for more than 15 percent of the time. If you are talking this much, then you are not getting the information you seek because you are not listening.

Don't note your displeasure at what the other person is saying. Don't sigh loudly. Don't roll your eyes. Don't make sounds like "pfft."

Don't threaten, manipulate, or bully. For many of us, it's our natural reaction to raise our voices, become argumentative, or become inappropriately forceful or confrontational. Yet these tactics rarely—if ever—get us what we want, especially during an interview. If you don't believe me, think about the one person in your life who you just can't stand because of the way he or she has treated you in the past. Now imagine telling this person the most intimate detail of your life. Would you do it? Hell no. Now think about the people in your life with whom you feel most comfortable sharing your most intimate details. Chances are these people do not talk down to you, bully you, shout at you, or threaten you. If you make someone not like you during an interview, chances are they will not tell you what you want and further conversations with them will become more and more difficult.

Don't tell the other person how he or she should feel. Just as certain things are likely to put a dog in the "red zone" and lead to an attack, certain topics will generate strong emotions or reactions from humans. For instance, laying someone off from a job, breaking up with someone, or informing someone that they or a loved one has a serious health issue are "red zone" topics.

When you are discussing such a topic, your natural reaction might be to tell the other person to not get emotional. Don't do that. For instance, try to not use phrases like "Now, don't get emotional," "Don't get upset," "Don't take it personally," "I don't want you to feel bad," or "Just calm down." These are all attempts to push emotion back down someone's throat, and they don't work. If anything, they will make your interviewee even more emotional. If someone becomes angry, yells, cries, or rants without any move toward physical aggression, you can let that person emote until he or she calms down. If there is a move toward physical aggression, whether against you or self-directed, you need to immediately terminate the interview, attempt to de-escalate the situation, and move to another location if you continue to feel threatened.

Don't blame. Phrases like "You never . . ." or "You always hurt me" or "It's your fault" or "You are a . . ." will likely push your interviewee toward the red zone and derail your interview.

Don't daydream or multitask. Paying close attention to what your interviewee is or is not saying—and how he or she is saying it—will require every ounce of your attention. If you try to multitask by checking e-mail or straightening up the house, you will miss important, telling details and you won't end up with all the information you need.

More important, you'll annoy the person you are interviewing. Think about how you feel when you are talking to someone and her cell phone rings. She looks at the caller ID, and she says, "I've got to take this one." When she finishes the call, she'll say, "I am sorry about that" and you'll say, "That's okay." But is it really okay?

Chances are it's not. Chances are you're annoyed. You're annoyed because this person just subtly told you, "You are less important to me than this call." Answering a cell, sending a text, or checking e-mail while you are having a conversation sabotages that conversation. Don't multitask. Don't check your e-mail, glance at your phone, sort the mail, or flip through a magazine. Being a good listener and multitasking are not compatible.

Don't get emotional. It's important to stay in touch with your emotional state. Getting emotional really limits the outcome of your interview. As soon as you become emotional, you change the direction of your interview and the goals become more about winning, beating up on the other person, and getting your point across than about conducting an interview. If you feel any of this happening, take it as a warning sign.

The more uncomfortable or upset you become, the less effectively you will be able to observe and listen and the more likely it is that the conversation will evolve away from being an interview and become a confrontation. And, at the other end of the spectrum, remember that if you are bored, it's a sign that the person you are interviewing is bored too.

Don't accuse or confront the other person. As I mentioned earlier, you will be asking people to reveal personal information about themselves or something they did. They will not do this if they feel threatened, judged, insulted, or put down by you. These approaches cause people to shut down.

Never call the person you are interviewing derogatory or insulting names. Don't assassinate that person's character by making statements like these:

- You are such a jerk. You don't care about me!
- You're such an ungrateful child!
- What kind of a friend are you to do that behind my back?
- You play favorites with people all the time. You should never be in your position!
- I hate you so much, I am going to call your employer and tell them how you have been abusing me!
- You are just like [your mother, father, or person you both dislike]

I am sure when you read these phrases you can feel the sting in them. What would you feel if you were on the receiving end of them? Would you feel the environment was safe for you to talk and open up? I don't think so. For the same reason, avoid "always" and "never" accusations as well, such as "you always do this" and "you never listen to my side of the story." Phrases like this paint people with a broad brush of previous failures. Their reactions will be varied, but they will most likely be negative. The person will become immediately defensive and try to argue that your perception of them is wrong. Their anger—and yours—will escalate and possibly move into the red zone. If this happens, both of your risk levels go up as well.

To keep the lines of communication open, keep the focus off you and on them. Use statements that do not blame the other person. If you want to tell someone how his or her behavior has impacted you, reference the behavior, not the person. Here are some examples:

- I felt hurt when this happened.
- I did what I did because at the time I thought it was the best choice.

- I am so hurt by all of this. I need to walk away and think before I say something too cruel and hurtful.
- I know that expecting great things from you is exactly how I should feel. I know you want to work to your potential as well. Let's talk about some of the issues you think are getting in your way of doing that.

Don't filibuster. Albert Einstein has been quoted as defining insanity as "doing the same thing over and over again and expecting different results." Yet many people do just that during an interview. They ask a question. They don't get the response they want. So they ask the same question again and again and again. Or they repeatedly say, "Just answer the question. Just answer the question. Just answer the question." Sometimes people will just keep talking louder and louder, without stopping, and they will refuse to be interrupted or halted.

This style of communication goes nowhere and is certain to shut down meaningful discussion.

Are You a Verbal Abuser?

If you use words as weapons to hurt, stun, shock, insult, overwhelm, and overpower, you might be a verbal abuser. Keep in mind that the damage your words inflict may be permanent and irreversible. You can't rescind words communicated in interviews, conversations, e-mails, texts, or letters. You can apologize and say you are sorry, but the original words are there forever. Words can ruin a relationship forever. And they have. So when you hear, "Choose your words wisely," there is a reason for this caution. If you have a tendency to say things that are harsh, critical, and judgmental, don't delude yourself by saying that it is up to the other person to interpret the words correctly or to take what she or he had coming. If you want positive results, change your delivery style from negative to positive.

Are You a Good Listener?

You just learned about many ways to derail an interview, including poor listening skills. How effective of a listener are you? To find out, think about how you would answer the following questions. Also, for a reality check, ask a couple of close and honest friends and/or family members to rate you as well.

1. Typically, how emotional do I get when I am attempting to interview someone? Rate this on a scale of 1–3, where:
   1 = very emotional (angry, sad, frustrated)
   2 = nonemotional and detached
   3 = I remain interested and tempered

2. Typically, how often do I interrupt?
   1 = several times during a conversation
   2 = just once or twice during a conversation
   3 = almost never

3. Do I say things like "What? You've got to be kidding me," or "That reminds of me of the time I . . . ," or "You think that's bad, let me tell you about . . ."
   1 = frequently
   2 = sometimes
   3 = rarely

4. Do I roll my eyes, put my head down, shake my head back and forth, throw myself back in my chair, turn away, get up and walk away, show signs of anger or threatening behavior, or otherwise display that I am not paying attention or do not like what the other person is saying?
   1 = frequently
   2 = sometimes
   3 = rarely

5. Do I fidget until people stop talking and then immediately respond without considering what they've said?

1 = frequently
2 = sometimes
3 = rarely

6. Do I let my mind wander to all the other things on my "to do" list and keep thinking that I just don't have the time for this?
1 = frequently
2 = sometimes
3 = rarely

7. Do I wait until the nanosecond when the speaker goes to take a breath to pounce on him or her with my opinion?
1 = frequently
2 = sometimes
3 = rarely

8. Do I hijack the conversation? For instance by saying something like "Look we've been over this a million times. Your ideas are just not going to work. This is what we are going to do"?
1 = frequently
2 = sometimes
3 = rarely

9. I reflect the person's thoughts and feelings back to the person I am listening to.
1 = frequently
2 = sometimes
3 = rarely

10. I ask open-ended questions to encourage the other person to talk.
1 = frequently
2 = sometimes
3 = rarely

Although this is not a scientific test, it can give you a gauge of where you stand. The higher your score, the better your listening skills. If you scored 8 or less, your listening skills are below average. Make sure to read the next section carefully for ways to practice and improve your listening skills.

How to Be a Better Listener

Years ago I was traveling to a city with some colleagues. One of them was a young, inexperienced agent. On the way to this city, this young agent talked about himself for nearly the entire trip. He didn't ask me or another agent a single question. It was all about him and his exploits, opinions, suggestions, and observations.

On the way home, he did the same thing. As we neared our destination, I said, "If you listen more and talk less, you will learn so much more about people." He readily agreed that listening was important and that he would work on it.

I watched the clock.

Roughly five minutes later, he began talking about himself yet again. He even began boasting that he could talk forever without running out of things to say.

The other agent and I just gave each other a look, and then we tuned him out. I wondered, "How in the world is this guy ever going to conduct an interview with a suspect if he does this much talking?"

This young agent thought that he was blessed with the gift of gab—a natural comedian. As it turned out, his so-called gift was really his downfall. He suffered from "the arrogance of ignorance." He was ignorant of his own arrogance and how it affected his job performance.

During an interview, you want to be listening and observing most of the time. You communicate so much when you sit quietly and just listen and watch. This is the behavior that will create an atmosphere of empathy and sensitivity. This will encourage your friend, child, peer, or spouse to trust you and open up.

Chances are this amount of listening might be difficult for you at first. For years and years, you may have been practicing and strengthening poor communication habits. You can't just reverse them overnight. It will take some practice. It took years and years to develop these poor habits. It will take some time and effort before you learn a new communication style. Interpersonal skills such as listening are perishable and require practice to stay sharp.

To improve your communication habits, practice interviewing a few people in your life—friends, family members, acquaintances. Ask them open-ended questions designed to elicit information. These practice interviews are just for fun—and for you to improve your skills. As you practice interviewing, see if you can craft questions and conversations that allow you to do the following:

1. Create a nonjudgmental environment in which people will become comfortable physically, mentally, and emotionally and open up as a result.

2. Help them to identify and talk about their feelings (happiness, sadness, elation, excitement, anger, frustration, guilt, remorse).

3. Help them evaluate their own behavior and its consequences.

The Dangerous Truth

Many people attempt to fake the appearance of listening by saying "uh-huh" a lot and nodding their heads. It's important to know that if you look like a bobblehead and say "uh-huh" at the wrong moment, it will broadcast to the other person that you are not listening at all. This type of behavior is distracting at best and an interview derailer at worst. I can't tell you how many times I have had conversations with people during which I've watched their heads bobble up and down. I was never sure what they were agreeing with or what they were hearing. When you are listening to someone, your nonverbal behavior must appear genuine and consistent with your words and your feelings. It also cannot be distracting. Others will know if you are being disingenuous, just like a bobblehead doll—mechanical and without empathy.

4. Help them see the implications of their behavior and/or decisions in the future.

5. Help them redesign their strategy and reassess their decisions or conclusions.

6. Communicate your willingness to be supportive.

How to Listen Between the Lines

As you listen, you want to pick up on more than just the content of what is being said. This is why listening requires all of your attention and practice. You want to listen for the following:

1. What they say. What is the person telling you? Do they accidentally let anything slip?

2. What the person doesn't talk about. What *isn't* the person telling you? Is there a pink elephant in the conversation? If yes, it is okay to say that you feel he or she is avoiding the main issue. Your interviewee will let you know if you are off base.

3. How they say it. What emotions does the person seem to be experiencing? Base this on both verbal and nonverbal behavior.

For instance, many years ago I interviewed a serial killer who had already confessed to more than a dozen murders. At the time of the interviews, he was on death row, and I was trying to get more information from him, before his execution, about other murders he may have committed.

I was accompanied by another homicide detective, named Pat, who was a phenomenal interviewer. She was also pretty and petite. Dave, the convicted serial killer, liked Pat a lot and, as a result, had opened up to her.

Dave was talkative but also cagey, dominant, and macho. He attempted to gain control of the interview by making threats. For instance, he casually mentioned how easy it would be for him to reach across the table and strangle us—that he could do it so quickly that the guards would not be able to get to the room and intervene before it was too late.

Still, he talked about the murders he wanted us to know about and was vague on those he didn't want to discuss. He would shift from memories that were crystal clear to memories that were vague, sketchy, and incomplete. He played games with us to let us know that he was in charge.

We had no specific case information about child murders, but I knew it was a possibility that he could have killed a child, even though he had insisted, up to that point, that all of his victims had been adult females. I knew that serial sexual killers evolve into their psychopathy and sexual deviancy. As they develop and learn their preferences for victims, killing, and ways to evade detection, they tend to go through a period of trial and error when they will kill various people around them, even close to them. It is in this period of time that they will make many mistakes and will experiment on victims of different ages, genders, races, and cultures. Because of this, it made sense for me to ask Dave a general question about whether he had ever killed a child.

When I did, he became dark, defensive, and angry. He was adamant about never victimizing children. He used phrases like "How dare you accuse me" and "What do you think I am? A pervert?"

I strongly suspected that he had a psychopathic personality, and I knew that psychopaths have no moral compass or code of ethnics. They don't draw lines in the sand about whom they will or will not victimize based on society's rules of right and wrong. So when he aggressively denied ever abusing children, it told me a lot.

His sudden change in demeanor—from glib and charming to defensive and angry—convinced me that he probably had victimized a child at some point in his past. The proof wasn't in what the man said. It was in what he didn't say and in the change in his behavior.

You might think that this convicted killer had nothing to lose. He was on death row after all. Why not admit to every single murder, including the murder of a child? At that time, he was thought to have only killed women. If he admitted to killing a young child, he would likely have had problems with some of the other inmates in the prison. He wouldn't want to be known as a child killer, since they tend to fall at the bottom of the pecking order in prisons.

Shortly thereafter Pat and I interviewed Dave's estranged wife. She told us a very interesting and chilling story. She said a boy had gone missing in their neighborhood years before. She described Dave as showing a great deal of interest and excitement in the media coverage of the case. He followed the investigation closely, and he'd often ask her to look at the articles in the paper with him. Then, one day, he took her for a drive so he could point out the last route this boy had taken on his bicycle before he was kidnapped and murdered. The case was still unsolved at that time.

It wasn't what Dave had told us that led us to look for this kind of information. It was what he refused to tell us.

This is one of many examples I could give you that shows just how important it is to listen for what isn't being said. Here's just one more.

A friend of mine, Cindy, was at a gas station filling up her car when a man approached her. He was on foot and asked her about the location of a shopping center that was about fifteen miles south of the filling station.

"Are you walking?" she asked.

"Yes," he said. "My car broke down at that shopping center and I need to get back there."

"You are going to be walking all day," she said.

She was in a hurry to get to my house, and the shopping center was in the wrong direction. He seemed helpless and innocent. She said, "I wanted to help him. I feel badly about not helping him. He was a young man, close to my son's age."

"Stop feeling so guilty," I said. "He might not be as helpless and innocent as you think."

Why do you think I came to that conclusion? What was it about what he didn't say that would have led me to conclude that his intentions were not pure? Think about it, and then read on.

He didn't say how he got to where he was. If his car had broken down fifteen miles away, how did he get to the gas station to begin with? Why did he travel more than fifteen miles away from his car, on foot, if getting his car repaired was his primary intention? And if he'd walked from the shopping center, wouldn't he know the way back to the shopping center?

It was what he didn't say that was most important.

It's also what he didn't do. There were many workmen in the area who had vehicles and would have likely been headed in the direction where his car was supposedly located. Cindy noted that he had approached her but none of the men.

As it turns out, there's a police station across the street from this particular gas station where my friend happened to be pumping gas that day. It was eight in the morning. What this person probably didn't want her to know was that he'd been arrested the night before and had spent the night in jail. Cindy could have increased her risk level if she offered to give him a ride to his car.

When listening to your interviewee, it's incredibly important to listen between the lines.

In particular, listen for leakage—information the interviewee may accidentally or purposely allow to slip out. These details are usually collateral to the questions you are asking. For instance, let's say you are interviewing a job candidate about how he views himself working on a team, and you get this answer:

> I think working with teams . . . Well, here's the thing. With the kind of work I've done in the past I've had tight deadlines and meetings with clients and bosses several times a day. It just didn't lend itself to working with others. It would have really slowed down the project.

If you take this person at his word, it sounds as if he's given you a good answer. In reality, however, he hasn't. What he's done is completely evade the question, and he's indirectly told you that, no, he's not a team player at all. He tells you about deadlines, about being responsive to clients, about working hard, and about being independent. You didn't ask about any of those things. The one thing you asked about is the one thing he didn't mention.

Let's look at another situation. Let's say you are considering carpooling with another parent to take your kids and hers to and from soccer practice. You don't want your child being driven around by an unsafe driver, however, so you want to make sure she doesn't have unsafe habits like texting and driving. You have asked her questions like "What do you do when you have a carful of screaming kids and you get an important call? Do you ever have problems with that?" She's given you this answer:

> Oh, you know, I just tune the kids out. When I'm driving the kids around, I just turn up the radio and I let them sit back there and have their fun. I'm one of those parents who is so used to being around kids that I can just tune them out. I don't answer my cell phone unless it's an emergency. As far as texting—not really . . . I used to text, but, no, I don't do that anymore, and, no, I don't really have any problems when I'm driving a bunch of loud kids in my car.

What did she accidentally allow to leak out? Think about it and try to spot all the leakage in her statement. Then read on.

This is what I'm seeing leak out: She just tunes the kids out. Sometimes she texts. And she talks on her cell phone while driving.

This means she's not focused on what the kids are doing and saying. She's not attentive. She tunes out. You didn't ask her if she tunes out, but now you know. She accidentally told you.

She accidentally told you something else too. She does use her cell phone while she drives. She might not use it very much, but she does use it. Her use of the phrase "not really" is also problematic. You'll find out why later in this chapter. But for now, just know that her "not really" probably means that she does text while driving. What constitutes an emergency call for this woman? Is it a call from the hospital? From her client? Her boss? Her husband? Even if it is true that she will only talk on her cell phone if it is a true emergency, it is even more frightening. Driving a group of children while you are distracted by a crisis you are trying to handle via phone is going to put all of you at an even greater risk for something bad happening.

The important point, though, is this: Just from the leakage, you have all of the information you need to make a decision to *not* carpool with this mother. You don't need to follow up with a hard line of questioning to find out just how often and under what circumstances she takes calls and texts while she drives. Instead you can just say, "No thanks," and either drive your child all the time yourself or make plans to carpool with a different parent.

How to Observe Behavior

When you interview someone, you are not just listening. You are also watching. In particular, you should take notice of the following behaviors.

Tuning out: Is your interviewee doing something else? Does your interviewee seem interested in you, or is he or she losing interest quickly? Maybe he or she is watching television, checking his or her

The Dangerous Truth

Many people attempt to read body language as if it were a black-and-white science. For instance, if someone has his or her arms crossed, they say it's a sign of defensiveness. Yet some people with big barrel chests stand with their arms crossed simply because it's comfortable. Other people do it because they are cold. To know if such body language really is a sign of defensiveness, you must observe the behavior over a period of time and listen to the words the person is saying. Does this person usually stand this way? Or does he suddenly start standing this way in response to a particular line of questioning? A sudden change in body language is much more telling than the body language itself. In order to know if someone's behavior is out of the ordinary or inconsistent, you have to have a baseline by which to gauge his or her behavior. In other words, you want to know what their normal behavior is. You can't call behavior unusual, deceptive, or out of the ordinary if you don't know what is ordinary.

smartphone, or obsessively grooming (stroking his beard, putting on her lipstick, picking lint off his slacks, brushing her hair). Or maybe he just appears bored with you. One of the things I learned while doing graduate training in counseling is that if the interviewer feels bored during the interview, the interviewee is probably feeling the same way.

If your interviewee is bored, you will need to find ways to shake up the interview. For instance, I was once less than an hour into an interview with a murderer on death row in Louisiana when the defense attorney walked me outside and told me that the inmate was bored. She was right. Sam was bored, and I had to change things if the interview was going to be successful. I knew I was not likely to get the information I sought if I continued to conduct the interview in the same way, so I changed the approach. Rather than continue to interview him myself, we switched interviewers. We would go from one interviewer to another to another. We changed the questions too. The constant change added variety to the interview, and it kept Sam engaged and interested. He talked with us for nearly eight hours.

Avoidance: Is your interviewee trying to stall the conversation? Maybe he or she answers the phone or invents a reason why he or she has to call someone right now. Other avoidance behaviors include the following:

- Repeated or long bathroom breaks
- Falling asleep or appearing to doze off
- Walking away
- Retreating to a different room
- Sudden displays of emotion (as with the woman I mentioned at the beginning of this chapter who broke down and sobbed)
- Derailing the interview by changing the topic and getting off track
- Blaming you or someone else for the problem
- Clamming up
- Reading a book or newspaper or watching TV or a movie and not responding
- Staring straight ahead or downward and being unresponsive

Hijacking: Does this person take over the interview and steer it into a completely different direction? If this happens, he is trying to take the conversation off track, deflect the heat, or take control of the interview. He is telling you that this conversation is now on his turf and that he is in charge.

Inappropriate emotional response: Does your interviewee show the appropriate emotion for the interview topic? For instance, if you are talking about a sick relative, does the interviewee seem somber or does he or she seem nonplussed? Does the person have a smirk on his face? Does he shake his head at you as if you are wrong and he is dismissing you and what you are saying? Does the person become angry in a way that's disproportionate to what you are saying? Does the person start crying before the interview has really begun? This could mean he is hiding something and doesn't want to talk about it.

Signs of strong, negative emotions: Does your interviewee get angry or red in the face? Do you see veins in his head start to pulsate? Are her fists clenched and pounding the table? Has he raised his voice? Is she swearing and pointing her finger in your face? These are all signs of imminent danger. You have to de-escalate the conversation, and you must do it quickly, especially if other variables like drugs and/or alcohol are involved. Drugs and alcohol could exacerbate the situation and even push the person into his red zone.

Addressing Deceitfulness

Deceitful people require you to use special interviewing skills. In order to get around their deceit, you must be able to spot the dishonesty and also understand why they are being deceitful. Here are some ways a person can deceive you.

Lying or distorting the truth: Your interviewee might give you some truthful information but also a few pieces of false information designed to throw you off track. Or maybe your interviewee is a compulsive liar and everything he or she says is a lie, even the inconsequential details.

Withholding the truth: Your interviewee might give you some information but then refuse to talk about certain topics or begin to filter the information he or she provides.

Evading: Your interviewee might continually change the topic or otherwise try to take the conversation in a different direction.

People engage in deceitful behaviors for a number of reasons. Possible reasons might be that he or she:

- is afraid of the consequences of being open and honest
- is afraid of your reaction
- doesn't want to be judged by you
- doesn't trust you
- doesn't like you
- doesn't want to get other people in trouble
- doesn't want you in his or her business

If your interviewee feels strongly that you are going to judge her harshly, and feels this way because you've judged harshly in the past, it

The Dangerous Truth

You may have read that you can tell someone is lying if he avoids eye contact or looks away when answering a question, if he touches or scratches his face while answering a question, or if his facial expressions are out of sync with his words (for instance frowning when he says, "I'm so happy to see you!").

Although all of this *may* be true, using body language alone to evaluate whether someone is lying is like navigating a ship by only looking at the stars. Very few people have the experience and knowledge to do it correctly. Reading body language and facial expressions is an art form that is a lot more complicated than most people realize. For instance, you can't always assume that a lack of eye contact means someone is lying. It could be that you are dealing with a person who lacks social skills and doesn't make eye contact whether she is telling the truth *or* telling a lie.

will be very difficult for you to get her to open up. You'll want to remove as many barriers as you can. You don't get people to tell the truth by bullying them (by shouting, "Just tell the truth! Just tell the truth! Just tell the truth!"). You do it by making them feel safe enough to reveal the information you seek. If you can address your interviewee's reason for not giving you the information, you've removed the barrier that is preventing her from opening up.

To tell if someone is being deceitful, think about whether any of the following factors are present.

There's no denial. When you ask someone a yes-or-no question and they don't give you a yes-or-no answer, you may have reason to believe that they are hiding something. For instance, if you ask your spouse, "Are you cheating on me?" and you get any of the following answers, you probably are not getting the whole story.

1. **"Not really."** When an answer is qualified by "not really," the respondent is not denying your accusation, and there's usually more to the story. To get the whole story, ask a follow-up question such as, "What do you mean when you say you are 'not really' cheating on me?"

2. **A question.** Instead of a yes or no, you instead get, "Why do you think I would do something like that?" or "Why would you ask me a question like that?"

3. **Protests.** Instead of a yes or no, you hear, "How could I do that? You know I love you," or "How could I do that? I'm too busy to have an affair."

4. **Defensiveness.** Instead of answering your question, he or she is overly sensitive about accusations, innuendo, criticism, and questions about his or her behavior.

5. **Counterattacks.** The person attacks you, your words, your behavior, and anything else about you. This can be a form of hijacking the conversation.

6. **Change of topic.** Instead of answering the question, he or she asks you a question about something else or starts talking about something else.

7. Hair splitting. The most famous example of this is when President Clinton said, "I did not have intercourse with that woman." When a person splits hairs, he or she does not directly answer your question with a yes or no. Instead he or she changes the question slightly to match their answer. For instance, you might ask, "Are you cheating on me?" and he or she might answer, "I am not having an affair."

There's too much denial. In investigations, we would become suspicious if we asked a person about a murder and he answered with a question: "How do you even know she's dead? You can't prove she's dead."

In nonpolice matters, this type of deception might come up if you are confronting your spouse about porn you found on his computer and he says, "There's no porn on that computer." Or maybe you have brought up some charges made to the credit card bill and your spouse says, "There aren't any strange charges on that bill."

The story doesn't add up. If you continually ask open-ended questions and keep your interviewee talking, you can look for places where the story just doesn't make sense. For instance, let's say you are talking to a man you are considering dating. He tells you a sad story about how his wife died of cancer just three years before. A little later on he mentions that he just broke up with his girlfriend of two and a half years. And then he tells you about several other women he has dated recently. Do you see anything wrong with the story? I do. If his wife died three years ago and he had a girlfriend for two and a half, when did he have time to date all of those other women? Did he do it in the past six months? Or was he cheating on his wife and his girlfriend? He is unable to stay on top of his own story.

It's important to note that you might not be able to pull the entire story out of someone. For instance, a pathological liar will lie about every single detail, even about what he or she ate for breakfast. These people have used lies and deception their whole lives and can be masters at it. It's easy for them and almost automatic. You don't need to dig down to the ultimate truth with such a person, and you probably will never be able to. All you need to know is that this person lies about everything and that you should walk away from the relationship. This is a person who will only bring heartache, pain, and many problems to your life.

Similarly, you might not be able to find out all the details of a partner's affair, but you might find out enough to know that his or her story doesn't add up or is improbable. You might not be able to get your teen to tell you about all his reckless driving behaviors, but you might be able to get him to tell you about some or just one of them—enough for you to know that it's time to revoke his car privileges.

How to Interview a Child or Teen

Sometimes as you attempt to interview or have a conversation with a child—especially your own and especially about a sensitive topic—he or she will throw up a brick wall that you just can't jump over. Frequently this brick wall comes in the form of "always" and "never" statements like these:

- You are always accusing me of things I didn't do.
- You never trust me.
- You always treat me like I'm three years old.
- You never let me do anything.
- You never listen to my side of the story.

It's important to be prepared for such comebacks because they can be emotional triggers for you. If you are prepared for them, it's less likely that they will trigger you to switch to bullying or some other nonproductive tactic.

As you address such statements, consider using these pointers:

- Try to not respond to them with an "always" or "never" statement of your own. Try to throw absolute words such as "always," "never," "should," "need to," and "must" out of your vocabulary. They indicate that life is black or white, with no gray area. Real life is not black and white.

• Consider whether there's any truth to the statement. If so, acknowledge it. For instance, if your child says, "You never give me a chance to talk," you might say, "That may be true and I am working on that. I'm sorry that has been my reaction in the past. Let's start fresh. I want to hear what you have to say."

• If there is no basis to the allegations made by your child, resist arguing and having the conversation default to an "I say–you say" standoff. Move beyond these types of barriers or communication blockers. Instead say something like "When are the times you felt comfortable about talking with me or another adult?" or "Let's take a break and take a walk or watch a movie" or "Let's go to our rooms and reconvene in an hour."

Now that you know how to get the information you want out of someone else, it's time to learn what to do with that information. Learn how to size people up and assess them for dangerousness in the next chapter.

CHAPTER 8 RAP SHEET

- Be willing to suspend old habits and communication styles and to develop new and more effective ones to help your interpersonal communications, sharpen your listening skills, and enhance your ability to make better and more sound decisions.
- Interviews require care, consideration, and compassion for others and the ability to show people that you care about them, their circumstances, their feelings, and their future.
- Listen when you'd rather give advice, interrupt, or offer a quick opinion. Look and listen for emotions and learn to recognize them accurately.

Chapter 9

How to Size Someone Up

Years ago I worked on a case involving a nanny. She had told the police that she feared for her life. She said she had been the victim of satanic ritual abuse while growing up and that a relative and former member of this satanic cult had plans to assault and kill her.

We attempted to corroborate her story of prior ritual abuse but were unable to do so. Likewise we could not locate any family members who were planning to travel to where she lived and attempt to hurt her. Nonetheless, this young, soft-spoken, educated woman insisted that her allegations were true. I asked her about the cuts and scratches I noticed on her arms. She told me a stranger had inflicted them.

Although the nanny's story might sound bizarre and unusual, this was not the first time I'd heard such allegations. I'd interviewed other men and women who said they had been victims of ritual childhood abuse. We could never corroborate these stories. We could not find physical evidence, and we couldn't uncover human remains either. We couldn't find graves. We couldn't find evidence of murder, torture, human sacrifices, or cannibalism. When we told these victims that we could find no evidence to support their claims, their responses were hauntingly always the same. They explained that their abusers were masters at covering their tracks and destroying evidence. They had destroyed or consumed all the evidence, and no one in the group would talk.

It was always a perfect conspiracy.

Let me tell you that in all of my years in law enforcement I have never seen a perfect conspiracy. When more than two people know about a crime, the chances of someone talking about it go up exponentially.

Based on all of this, I seriously doubted the nanny's story. Still, I was astounded by her commitment to it and her willingness to accuse family members of such a serious crime despite the absence of any physical evidence.

I asked the nanny to come into my office for one final interview to make sure I had all the details. Clearly there was something wrong in her life, and I wanted to find out what it was.

She walked into my office slowly and cautiously, as though she were in a great deal of pain. I noticed blood on her legs but none on her socks. I asked her what had happened, and she implied that she had just been attacked. She asked to use the restroom. I went with her. In the restroom, she began crying and saying she was in pain. I asked her if she had purposefully done something to hurt herself. After a lot of reassurance from me, she eventually admitted that she had inserted a razor blade inside herself. We called the paramedics and she was rushed to the hospital.

You probably agree with me that this young woman posed a danger to herself and others. She was involved in self-destructive cutting behavior, and her current injuries were serious. Her willingness to implicate a relative in a crime that had never occurred indicated that she was willing to file false charges against people despite the possible criminal implications and consequences.

And she worked as a nanny. When she was released from the hospital, her employers—who now knew about her false allegations and cutting behavior—welcomed her back into their home to care for their young children. They didn't even ask her to undergo a mental-health assessment or intervention.

You might think that this family is an anomaly—that they were either more naive or trusting than most. I don't believe they were anomalies, though. I believe many people would have made the same flawed decision.

Let me tell you about a similar case. Paula (not her real name) met

Dave, a man serving a long prison sentence for serial sexual assault. Although this might seem unusual, women frequently meet men who are serving time. Sometimes they meet them when they are visiting another prisoner, perhaps a relative. Other times they follow the case and get to know the prisoner by writing letters back and forth.

Once Dave was paroled, he and Paula continued their romantic relationship and ultimately married. Dave moved into Paula's home with her young daughters. Not much later there were allegations of sexual molestation involving one of the girls. Then, a short time later, one of the girls went missing. Dave eventually confessed to the murder.

Whenever I tell this story, people look incredulous. They can't understand how Paula could have thought that a man convicted of serial sexual assault was a safe person to date, let alone marry, and to live in the same home with her daughters. But Paula and the parents I mentioned earlier were bright, educated people who cared dearly about their families and children. They were not stupid. They were not naive. And they were not cavalier.

They just didn't know how to tell if someone posed a threat to them or their families. I've seen people make the same kinds of mistakes so many times. They misread others, ignore dangerous behaviors, normalize those behaviors, and delude themselves into believing that dangerous people will automatically stop being dangerous without any kind of intervention.

In this chapter you'll learn how to overcome these common mistakes. You'll find out how to gather and interpret information so you can more effectively spot and understand three types of problematic behavior:

- *Concerning* behavior
- *Threatening* behavior
- *Dangerous* behavior

CTD behaviors, as we'll call them, are all problematic and important to spot and understand, but some are more serious than others. Think of problematic behavior as falling along a continuum. Concerning behavior falls toward the less serious end of the continuum. Dangerous behavior falls toward the most serious end. Threatening behavior falls in the middle. Behavior is dynamic. It is fluid and can change rapidly, so concerning or threatening behaviors can quickly become dangerous.

Like other skills, recognizing and correctly interpreting CTD behaviors will take practice. But once you learn this skill, and practice it, you will be less likely to be duped into believing that someone has "changed" or "snapped." You will no longer misread people and be fooled by them. You will not be surprised or blindsided down the road. You will see trouble early and be able to respond to it before it gets out of control.

This process will free you from black-and-white rules that you may have leaned on in the past, rules like "Don't talk to strangers" and "Don't trust people you don't know." You'll also be able to go beyond meaningless descriptions like "He's a nice guy," "She's harmless," "He's acting out of character," and "That was in the past and people change." Rather, you'll really and truly get a sense for whether someone could manifest CTD behaviors and pose a threat to you, your possessions, your loved ones, your career, or your financial livelihood.

What Makes People Dangerous

Many people ask me how to get "inside someone's head." In reality, you can't. You will never be able to read a person's thoughts, or know their inner world completely, or know with certainty the motives for their behavior. You will never be a mind reader, and neither will I.

You can, however, gain a sense of someone's personality by studying and understanding his or her behavior. Behavior is an expression of a person's personality traits and characteristics. One personality trait does not produce one specific behavior. It's a lot more complicated than that. Personality traits cluster together to form patterns of behavior that can become hardwired for life.[9]

In the pages that follow, you will learn about many possible CTD behaviors and the personalities behind them. The key is to recognize clusters of behaviors and interpret those patterns correctly. Don't take one isolated behavior out of context and use it to form an opinion about what someone must be like. But also don't ignore it, rationalize it, explain it away, or delude yourself into thinking that a person who is dangerous or violent toward someone else "will never turn on me." Try to identify the whole behavior picture, and assess it correctly.

The following is not an exhaustive list of CTD behaviors. Rather, this is a list of behaviors that I have seen over and over in my years of investigating and profiling violent crimes and in studying the people who engage in these behaviors. I will briefly explain many CTD behaviors here. Then, in the section that follows, I'll go into the five CTD behaviors that I think are most important for you to understand, recognize, and interpret in greater depth.

Impulsivity: Behaving with little if any regard for long-term or short-term consequences to self and others.

Inappropriate or out-of-control anger: Repeated eruptions of anger in a variety of situations where anger is not appropriate or warranted. People with inappropriate anger are either unable or unwilling to control their anger. They have a controlled and systemic undercurrent of anger.

Narcissism: Acting self-centered, arrogant, and grandiose, with little or no insight or concern for others. People who behave narcissistically have a sense of entitlement and superiority over others, and an expectation of special treatment and consideration. They believe they are special, unique, and superior to others.

Lack of empathy: Inability and unwillingness to understand the feelings, concerns, and opinions of others. People without empathy lack compassion for others.

Injustice collecting: Injustice collectors do just that: They collect injustices—real or imagined—over their lifetimes. They respond to them in ways that are extraordinarily disproportionate to the perceived injustice.

Objectification of others: Dehumanizing others and not seeing them as humans. People with this behavior may view others as nonpersons or possessions and treat them accordingly.

Blaming others for failures and problems: Seeing oneself as a victim and refusing to accept responsibility for one's life problems. It's always someone else's fault.

Paranoia: Suspicious of the motives and intentions of others.

Rule breaking: The life philosophy that the rules of society do not apply to you.

Use of violence: A history of committing dangerous or violent behavior, including assault, abuse, intimidation, road rage, and more.

Thoughts and fantasies of violence: Suicidal, homicidal, and nihilistic thinking. The manifestation of these behaviors requires immediate intervention by mental-health professionals or law enforcement.

Drug and/or alcohol problems: The use and/or abuse of drugs and/or alcohol that exacerbates other CTD behaviors.

Poor coping skills: Inability to deal with stressors, disappointments, problems, and/or everyday life problems

Equal-opportunity hatred: Dislike for and/or hatred of other people or groups because of real or imagined wrongs or other beliefs and opinions.

Thrill seeking: A pathological or extreme need for thrill, excitement, and/or attention from others, despite the harm or worry it causes.

Problem Behaviors in Depth

To help you better spot and understand some of the most problematic CTD behaviors, I've explained five of them in more detail in the pages that follow.

Problem 1: Impulsive behaviors

When you act impulsively, you tend to consider only momentarily—if at all—the possible consequences of your actions, and then disregard the consequences of your actions. Impulsivity can range from occasional and minor impulsive acts to regular and serious impulsive acts.

We're all impulsive from time to time. Most of us have impulsively run a red light in order to get somewhere more quickly. Or we have occasionally made an impulsive purchase because something was on sale.

People who are routinely impulsive, however, do it often and in every area of their lives. They might quit their jobs because of a momentary hassle they just had with their supervisors. They might repeatedly call in sick at the last minute so they can take a vacation. They might drink too much at parties and then decide to drive home. They might buy a home on a whim, because they "loved" it, but fail to take the time to find out they cannot afford it. They will marry someone whom they don't really know.

Impulsivity becomes a CTD behavior when it is a pattern evident in many aspects of a person's life—at home, at work, while driving a car, from relationship to relationship, and so on—and the behavior compromises their safety and welfare and that of others around them. When it is compounded by the use of drugs and/or alcohol, it can really create problems and increase the likelihood of financial ruin, social problems, and even violence.

Problem 2: Angry behaviors

Some people have a long fuse, whereas others have a very short one. People with a short fuse can become enraged or even explosive over things that the rest of us think of as quite minor. Like impulsivity, anger is something we are all familiar with. We all lose our temper every once in a while. Anger becomes dangerous when it is disproportionate to the events that trigger it; becomes out of control and excessive; results in physical harm or threats of physical harm to others; cannot be easily, quickly, or voluntarily brought under control; and occurs on a regular basis.

For instance, a few years ago it was reported that a disgruntled husband shot and killed his wife and four others because of how his wife cooked his eggs. Clearly there was more to this violence than poorly cooked eggs. It is not unusual, however, for such a minor precipitator to be the trigger that sets into motion a disproportionate response in people with anger-management problems. Someone who wasn't so quick to anger might have sighed loudly about his undercooked eggs rather than pull out a shotgun.

People who are quick to anger often get into trouble when driving. They become easily irate at other drivers and retaliate by cutting them off, tailgating, or throwing objects at their vehicles. You can tell a lot about someone's personality by the way he or she drives a car, and people who are constantly peeling out, driving recklessly, tailgating, and traveling well above the speed limit very likely have problems with anger in other areas of their life.

People who are quick to anger tend to have interpersonal problems with others, too, and these interpersonal problems can erupt over seemingly minor things. For instance, they are the people who will ream out a waitress for bringing them a steak that's well done instead of medium rare. They are the people who will shout at hospital staff when they show up after visiting hours and are not allowed entrance to the hospital. The bagger at the grocery store, for instance, might mix their meat in with their vegetables and the customer will end up telling off the store manager over it.

Drugs or alcohol will exacerbate anger, but someone with a CTD anger problem will become angry without the influence of either.

In addition to the explosively angry individual, there are others who maintain an undercurrent of anger all the time. The anger is right below the surface. Their anger seems controlled, cognitive, and less likely to erupt. These individuals can be quickly frustrated, verbally abusive, and quick to judge or malign others. They maintain strong negative opinions of others without apparent reason or justification and even with evidence to the contrary. They are quick to damage interpersonal relationships.

Problem 3: Narcissism

The word "narcissist" is in vogue right now and is often tossed around to describe people who are somewhat self-absorbed. Those are not the types of people I'm referring to here. I am describing someone who views him- or herself as the center of the universe. Narcissists tend to be elitist and arrogant and see themselves as special and above everyone else. They have a sense of entitlement, a grandiose sense of their own importance, and an unrealistic expectation of favorable treatment. Narcissists are always searching for attention and admiration.

People who are narcissistic will do the following:

- Make choices that meet their needs, ignoring the needs of others.
- Talk endlessly about themselves but want to know little if anything about you.
- Hijack conversations. You will say a line or two about yourself and a narcissistic individual will interrupt and say something like "Let me tell you about me and my opinions." (After all, their opinions are the only ones that matter and therefore more important than anyone else's.)
- Make inappropriate remarks because they don't realize and don't care about how they affect or impact others. They will talk about how great they are, for instance.
- Take credit for an entire project, even if other employees helped get it done. Everything they do is one of a kind, special, unique, and superior to anyone else's work. In reality their work is a mess.
- Not accept blame or failure in a work or personal situation.

In a marital relationship, everything will be about making the narcissistic individual shine. For instance, a narcissistic individual will expect his wife to dress a certain way because how she looks affects how others perceive him. Narcissistic individuals will seek accolades and recognition in everything they do. They will exaggerate, lie, brag, and do whatever they think is appropriate to get what they want, because it is all about them.

Problem 4: Lack of empathy

Some people are exceptionally good at sensing the feelings of others and of anticipating their needs. They are sensitive and compassionate toward others and display this empathy in their words and actions. Other people are more callous, and it's much harder for them to understand the feelings of others. They can't easily walk a mile in someone else's shoes. Sometimes they can't do it at all.

Someone with an inability to empathize will be a poor listener (because he or she doesn't care about you or your problems and feelings). If you have a problem and really need someone to talk to, they may give you a few minutes. Then they will turn you off quickly, respond to you harshly or coldly, or change the topic as quickly as possible. If you try to have an ongoing relationship with someone who lacks empathy, you will feel cheated in the relationship. You will become the listener and never the one who is listened to. You will feel used and taken advantage of.

Problem 5: Injustice collecting

I coined this term back in the late nineties when I was the FBI's lead researcher in school and campus violence. At that time I saw a pattern of behavior in students who seemed to maintain an ongoing pattern of collecting and never forgetting real or imagined injustices. Despite the amount of time that passed, these individuals never forgot. They frequently blew injustices way out of proportion and would never forgive the person they felt had wronged them. They use words like "wronged," "persecuted," and "destroyed" to describe the injustices others have inflicted on them.

Injustice collectors occur in all age groups and in all professions. These individuals do not forgive easily and cannot move on. They take offense easily and hold on to grudges for years. They can even feel slighted by events that never occurred the way they claimed they occurred. They see personal and professional injustices wherever they go.

Injustice collectors might feel slighted if an employee accidentally parks in their space, and they will never forget the day it happened, the time it happened, and the response of the human resources department when they filed a complaint about the incident.

If injustice collectors are passed over for a promotion because someone else was far more qualified, they will see it very differently and perceive it as a major personal and professional insult to them that has ruined their life.

They will still remember and feel slighted about the anniversary a spouse forgot ten years ago.

They are still mad at their mother for things that happened during childhood, even if their mother died years before.

Themes of vengeance are common in the thinking of an injustice collector. An injustice collector will have a long list of grievances about a long list of people. They may even maintain a "hit list." They will tell you about their mean siblings, disloyal friends, backbiting coworkers, good-for-nothing spouses, and terrible mothers.

Injustice collectors begin to move toward CTD behaviors if their response is significantly disproportional to the perceived or real injustice. For example, most people who feel they are being singled out at the workplace for a poor performance rating, or are terminated because of their performance, will go home and cry or have a drink with a friend. An injustice collector who has shifted toward CTD behavior might decide to go back to work with a gun and attempt to harm his former bosses and coworkers. Obviously this reaction is completely disproportionate to the action of the company.

As CTD behaviors cluster together and form a pattern, they can become more and more problematic. Here are some tips for using the information I just provided so you can accurately assess the people in your life.

Screen the people who matter most. You won't have to screen for CTD behaviors in every single person you meet. Don't worry about the waitress who serves you at the diner, or about the pizza delivery person. But you definitely want to screen for concerning, threatening, and dangerous behaviors in your close and intimate relationships. And you'll want to assess someone before granting them access to your intimate life details—such as your Social Security number, the key to your house, and so on.

Look for clusters, not for just one trait. It's when these traits and behaviors cluster together to form a pattern that an individual can move along the behavioral continuum toward becoming dangerous. Someone who is only impulsive, for instance, isn't nearly as threatening as someone who is impulsive, angry, narcissistic, and an injustice collector with homicidal and suicidal thoughts. Many CTD traits can be clustered with narcissism, and when this happens it can create the perfect storm. Narcissism means "it's all about me," which means the narcissist's needs and well-being and future are going to be paramount to yours. It exacerbates other CTD traits.

Don't judge someone based on just one action. Accurately assessing someone's behavior requires establishing a baseline. You want to know how that person typically behaves most of the time. Ideally you want to observe someone in a variety of circumstances, over a period of time, and with a variety of people.

Put it all into context. You also want to be aware of the context in which these behaviors occur so you can assess not only degree of the threat but its long-term and short-term implications.

Where Are Your Danger Zones?

Now that you understand some of the traits, characteristics, and behaviors that can cause people to become dangerous, it's time to find out which types of people are most important for you to take the time to assess. If you know people with many of these traits and behaviors but they are only on the periphery of your life, it might not be a big deal because you do not have very much involvement with them. On the other hand, if someone is a close friend, family member, or a boss or coworker, it can be a much bigger problem.

As I mentioned earlier in the book, many of us are conditioned to fear and be wary of strangers, but strangers are not the only dangerous people in our lives. Often they may pose a much lower threat than people you feel closest to.

The following chart lists the "danger zones" for relationships we have with people on a regular basis. All of us have problems in at least one of these danger zones. If you are a city person, you might make great decisions when you are in zone 1 because you are well practiced at dealing with strangers and casual acquaintances. But how adept are you in the higher zones? How well do you make decisions about coworkers or friends or love interests? Have you trusted someone and allowed someone to get close to you only to later realize that you'd been manipulated or had? If so, then you have had trouble in the higher zones.

And it's in these higher zones where a bad decision can really put you in a very dangerous situation. As you get closer to the "intimate" category, it gets harder and harder to undo a bad decision. The person you've decided to trust has too much information. Too often I've seen that the biggest mistake a victim made was to put someone in the intimate category too soon.

As you look at each danger zone, think about the following questions: Where am I weakest? Where I am most at risk? Where is my family most vulnerable? Where are my finances most vulnerable?

Think about how successfully you are able to navigate each category. Which zone is most dangerous for you?

Zone 1: Strangers and quasi-strangers

This zone includes people you don't know at all (such as the person sitting next to you on the bus or on a flight) as well as people you know little about, such as someone you've met online or through a minor transaction. It includes the person who rings up your groceries, people who frequent the same coffee shop as you, the person who delivers your mail, and other peripheral people in your life who do not enter your comfort zone (your home, your car, your office, etc.).

Zone 2: Acquaintances

This zone includes people you know slightly or superficially. You have only a limited knowledge of them and vice versa. You are friendly with them, but you are not close enough to be considered friends. This might include your neighbors, the people who work in the same building as you do, and people you see occasionally at the gym, church, or your child's school.

Zone 3: Casual friends

This zone includes people you know virtually or see on a regular basis and who know some things about you and your patterns of behavior.

Zone 4: Close friends

This zone includes people you've known for a long time and who you know on a deeper level. It might include your close, long-term friends, your in-laws, your siblings, and some neighbors you feel very close to and who have lived near you for years.

Zone 5: Intimates

This zone includes the people you live with or are close to. It might include romantic partners, your best friend, and your children. It also can include people who know a lot about you—especially sensitive information that you would not want shared with others. For instance, your financial planner and accountant would be considered intimate since both have access to your Social Security number and other personal financial information. Similarly, your doctor would be considered intimate since he or she has access to your potentially sensitive medical information. A therapist or member of the clergy might be intimate if you've shared details about yourself that you would not want broadcast to the public. This zone could also include people who have access to your comfort zone, such as a cleaning person, landlord, contractor, or a computer expert.

When thinking about your danger zones, consider the following two pointers.

Don't spend too much time sorting the people in your life into these categories. It's not as important for you to understand which zone someone falls into as it is for you to understand that the threat someone poses to you goes up with each zone. Despite popular belief, people in zone 1 usually pose the least threat to you. Although the possibility of danger is present in each zone, you don't necessarily need to assess your dry cleaner, for instance, for dangerousness. It's very important to assess your new boyfriend, however, especially if you have young children at home and you are thinking of asking him to move in with you.

It's important to know when the people in your life are moving

from one zone to another. For instance, let's say a casual person you see occasionally at your gym takes an unusual interest in you. He or she fixates on you, posts things about you online, and seems to constantly be watching you and your home. Suddenly this zone 1 or 2 person has become a zone 3 or 4 person and a much greater threat to you.

How to Interview for Dangerousness

So now you know about the personality traits and behaviors that can be CTD, and about the danger zones that make it even more important for you to assess for those traits.

Now, let's talk about how to uncover the information you need to decide if someone manifests concerning, threatening, or dangerous behaviors. Your assessment might involve an interview with just one person, or it might involve gathering information from several people—others who know the person in question through various parts of his or her life.

We all show more of ourselves to some people and less to others, and the people around us do the same. There are five aspects of oneself that are important to understand and think about when trying to decide if someone is concerning, threatening, or dangerous to you. Once you understand these aspects of yourself, you will more easily be able to identify different people to talk to in order to obtain the information you seek.

Aspect 1: Public self

This is the part of yourself that you show to the public. Your acquaintances see this part of you. Your public self, for instance, is the persona you show to the checkout person who sees what you buy at the grocery store each week and gains insights from those products. The people who work at my grocery store, for instance, probably knew that I had a dog. They didn't know it because I'd shared this information with them. Rather, they knew it because I shopped there twice a week and purchased Frosty Paws each time.

Aspect 2: Professional self

This is the self you show at work. The people you work with probably know if you are married or single, a parent or not a parent, where you went to school and what you studied, and where you grew up. They might know your political views, if you've shared them. They are aware of casual information that you've been willing to share. They will also infer information about you during the eight hours a day that you spend with them. For example, they can draw conclusions about you based on whether you go out with "the group" for lunch, the friendships you form, what time you come to work and what time you leave, your interpersonal skills, your work habits, and so on. Some of these inferences might be right and some may be quite incorrect. But they can add up to how your coworkers view you.

Aspect 3: Personal self

This is the self that you normally would only show to friends. It's the part of yourself that you keep somewhat guarded and may include your personal schedule and activities, health problems, financial issues, and the location of the secret key you use to get into your house when you are locked out.

The Dangerous Truth

With the advent of social media such as Facebook, Myspace, and Twitter, details that were once considered "personal" are now often broadcast publicly to anyone who wants them. It's commonplace for people to post their current location, what they own and where they keep it in the house, their daily schedule, and other often very personal details. When you put private and personal details out in the public domain, you risk having strangers find something out about you that you wish they did not know. Putting this information on the Internet allows it to go out to thousands, and even millions, of people. You can never take it back.

Aspect 4: Private self

This is the area of your life and personality that you show only to your immediate family and very close friends. This might include serious health or mental-health issues, family problems, financial issues, legal issues, sexual issues, personal idiosyncrasies, and other details and information that you feel protective about and would not want broadcast to the general public.

Aspect 5: Secret self

This is the area of your life and personality that only you know about and that you do not share with anyone if you can help it, not even your spouse, partner, parent, or best friend. Your secret life might include behavior that embarrasses you, past dalliances, and behavior that would cause severe embarrassment or professional problems if others knew about it. It could include sexual fantasies or obsessions, suicidal fantasizes, or violent fantasies. It could include a shopping, alcohol, or gambling addiction. It might include an affinity for online porn.

You won't be able to find out everything about every single person you wish to assess. When assessing someone for CTD behaviors, think about the following questions.

1. How intimate is your relationship potentially going to become? The more intimate the relationship, the more you want to know about someone. The less intimate the relationship, the less you will likely need to know. For instance, you will want to do a thorough and complete assessment on someone you are planning to marry. Your assessment can be less thorough for peripheral people in your life.

2. What parts of this person's life could possibly affect you and your loved ones? For instance, you probably don't care about the online habits of someone you might hire to paint your house or repair your car. This behavior probably has no impact on how effectively your mechanic replaces your brake pads. On the other hand, if you are an employer, the significance of these habits becomes more important. And certainly if your relationship with someone becomes intimate, knowing a great deal more about these habits will be critical.

3. What's the risk level of this situation? In an extremely high-risk situation, you will want to know more about the person you are assessing than you would need to know in a low-risk situation. For instance, a school principal who is trying to assess whether a given student is planning to carry out an act of targeted violence will need to obtain a lot of information immediately. The school's behavioral intervention team will likely interview the student's parents and ask sensitive and uncomfortable questions such as "Has your child ever indicated that he has suicidal or homicidal thoughts?" "Does your child have access to weapons, including guns?" "What has your child recently posted on the Internet that might be indicative of plans to act out violently, including videos, photos, and violent rhetoric?"

Depending on how you answer the previous three questions, you might only need to find out a little bit. For instance, if you are interviewing someone you wish to hire to do some work in your home, you not only don't need to know about his or her secret side, you also would most likely offend that person by asking about it. It's really okay for your handyman to keep his private ideas and thoughts to himself.

On the other hand, if you are talking with a family member because you are worried that he or she has a drug problem or is entertaining thoughts of suicide, you will want to delve into his or her secret side and bring in mental-health experts to do an assessment. Similarly, if you are dating someone and thinking about becoming a lot more intimate, you will want to find out as much as you possibly can about every single area of that person's life. In these instances, not only do you absolutely need this information, you also will likely have an easier time accessing that information because your relationship puts you in a position to observe the person and the behaviors in question over a period of time and in different contexts and to ask a lot more personal questions.

There are no black-and-white rules about how deep to dig (see the next section), but you'll want to think about the different aspects of a person's life whenever you are dealing with someone you want to know more about. Whether it's a neighbor, a coworker, a friend, or someone else, think about which parts of that person's life might affect you and about what you want and need to know in order to make a decision about your next course of action.

How to Dig Deep

Depending on whom you are assessing and why, you might interview friends, coworkers, family members, and even consult with others such as clergypersons, mental-health professionals, or even a private investigator. And you may interview the person directly about their life, relationships with others, habits, practices, finances, and physical health.

These interviews do not have to be formal. For instance, if you are dating someone, you probably don't want to sit down with his or her mother and say, "Now, I'm trying to assess Jake to make sure he's a trustworthy guy and someone I would like to get close to. What can you tell me about him?"

But you do want to ask questions that will help you go beyond meaningless qualifiers like "She's nice" and "He's a good guy" that tell you little to nothing about someone's behavior or personality.

Ask questions designed to help you make sure the person will not cause problems for you. For instance, if you are planning on hiring someone who will be coming into your home to do work, you want to know if this person is likely to steal, damage your home, or act in a way that makes you feel uncomfortable or threatened. To determine this information, you will want to interview people who have hired this person in the past, and you want to go beyond questions like "What did you think of him?" and "What kind of a job did he do?" You will want to ask questions like these:

- Has this person caused any problems for you when he's worked in your home?
- Did he ever do or say anything that made you feel uncomfortable? If so, why?

- Did you ever find him roaming your home with no explanation as to why he was in a room he wasn't supposed to be in?
- Have you ever asked him to change some aspect of his work? If so, how did he respond to your feedback?
- Were you afraid to fire him?

You'll want to think of all the details you want to check out, and you'll want to write those details down. That way you'll be less likely to forget to ask an important question. You can look at your list as you interview people. To help you practice coming up with interview questions for various situations, I've included a number of sample assessments in the next chapter.

But first you need the final piece of the SMART model—how to use all of these techniques and information to make a decision. The next chapter will show you how.

CHAPTER 9 RAP SHEET

- CTD behaviors are the result of personality traits and characteristics that cluster together and can form a lifetime pattern of behavior.
- The people closest to you probably pose a greater threat to you than strangers.
- When assessing someone for CTD behaviors, think about the following aspects of your own, as well as his or her, life: public, professional, personal, private, and secret.

Chapter 10

How to Make a Decision

When criminal profilers like me go to a crime scene and attempt to draw a conclusion, we review all the information we can. We study witness statements, lists of all the evidence recovered from the scene, the forensic analysis of that evidence, police reports, investigative reports, neighborhood investigations, weather reports, crime scene photos, autopsy reports, the victimology (a study of the victim), and much more.

We look for the smallest details and nuances. We analyze how everything is interconnected, in order to look at the totality of the circumstances (see page 99). We do not identify one variable and give that piece disproportionate importance compared with all the other pieces. No, we look at how all the details interact, affect each other, connect, and evolve. And then we use those details to create a behavioral blueprint of the crime scene, a comprehensive understanding of the victim, the offender, and their interaction with one another.

For instance, we can frequently determine—from the totality of the circumstances—the unique personality of the offender, including their motivations, mental disorders, sexual disorders and habits, emotional versus chronological age (some people behave much younger than their physical age), gender, occupation, work history, social history, and much more.

We look for behavior that is present at the scene and, equally as important, behavior that is absent. For instance, if the victim in a bloody crime scene appears to have tried to fight off her attacker, we would expect to find evidence of their struggle with each other. This would include defensive injuries on the victim; body hairs from either the offender or the victim; fibers from clothing, carpets, and other items; DNA recovered from blood; semen; or contact DNA. When we don't find physical evidence indicative of such a struggle, we wonder why. Does it mean that someone tried to clean up the crime scene before he or she left? If so, what does that say about the attacker? It could mean the offender is evidence conscious and knows that if certain evidence is recovered it could lead to his being identified. It could also suggest that the person responsible is known to the victim, and will logically come up in an investigation, so he needs to destroy evidence that associates him with the crime.

When you make a decision, you'll go through a very similar process. Just like a profiler, you will gather lots of evidence and information. You will evaluate it. You will not allow one piece of information to overshadow another. You will look at the totality of everything you've been able to uncover.

The information a profiler uses to draw conclusions is based on a comprehensive review of a wide range of information. Your clues will be based on:

- information you've gathered through your interviews (see chapter 8)
- what you know about the situation (see chapter 7)
- what you know about yourself (see chapter 6)
- your own observations
- what you've learned through other resources, including a quick Internet search

You will take all that information and look at its *totality*. It helps to write it all down to make sure you are properly weighing all the clues. That is what I do. Once you have everything on paper, it will be easier for you to see where additional information or research is necessary. Writing it down also helps to ensure that you don't pay too much attention to isolated or sensational pieces of information and ignore other pieces altogether.

When analyzing your information, I would suggest the following approach.

Do not be swayed by superficial indicators of normalcy. As I wrote earlier, you cannot get an accurate read on someone by the way he or she looks or by how friendly he or she seems. Check yourself. Have you been swayed by any of the following faulty evaluations?

- The person you are evaluating seems "nice" or "friendly."
- The person you are evaluating is highly respected or comes from a good family.
- The person you are evaluating looks harmless.
- The person you are evaluating is religious, went to the same college as you, belongs to the same fraternal organization or charity, or in some other way shares something in common with you that lures you into a false sense of safety.
- The person you are evaluating has the trappings of a normal life: a house, a yard, a dog, a marriage, and one or more children.
- The person you are evaluating seems important: graduated from an important school, is wearing an expensive suit, is driving an expensive car, and otherwise lulls you with impressive titles or monikers.

Make sure you've screened for CTD behaviors. Make sure you have assessed whether the people involved in your particular situation have exhibited any of the dangerous or threatening behaviors described in chapter 9: anger problems, impulsive behavior, injustice collecting, signs of lack of empathy and callousness.

Depending on the type of decision you are making, you also might want to assess people for other characteristics that are important to that decision. For instance, you might not want to hire a financial planner who is a risk taker or a babysitter who is easily frustrated, exhibits poor coping behaviors, is emotionally immature, and shows a pattern of making poor decisions. In some hiring situations, you may not mind employees who are not team players. But in others it may be essential. Think about all the behavioral characteristics that are important for this particular decision and make sure you've gathered enough information to assess the various people involved.

Know the totality of the circumstances before making any decision: Don't make decisions based solely on one detail. Ask yourself some questions.

- Is there any information that I've overlooked or neglected to gather?
- Have I considered all the variables in the situation?
- Have I looked at all aspects of each person involved?
- Have I dug deep enough into their personal, family, work, private, and secret lives? Do I understand what makes them tick?
- What is the primary motivator for this behavior? What are the likely benefits and consequences?
- Is there something else I need to know but don't have time to find out?

Know when to stop digging and start deciding. Keep in mind that you probably won't be able to find out everything you want to know about a situation or person. Even in law enforcement, we have crime scenes where the physical evidence recovered yielded little if any forensic value. Similarly, you might find that you could not get as much information as you wanted about a person or that some information was too risky to gather.

You may never feel that you have everything you need, and you might have to make a decision when less is known than you would like.

Writing down the information you've gathered and comparing it to the information you wish you had will help you determine if you have enough information to make a thoughtful and prudent decision.

Consider your personal biases: Have you interpreted all this information correctly? Have your personal biases swayed you in one direction or another? Have you failed to gather key information because you are too timid, scared, or stressed?

Assuming you have all the information, know everything you need to know about the various people involved, and have interpreted the information correctly, then it's time for you to draw a conclusion based on what you know. When coming to a conclusion, think about the following:

- Does all of the information fit together? If not, why not?
- Am I seeing a pattern of behavior?
- Am I seeing one or more problems?
- Does my assessment tell me what to decide and how to prioritize the actions I will need to take to handle the situation?
- What are the risks? Where are the land mines?

Once you know the answers to some of these questions, you will be able to decide on a better, safer, and more effective course of action.

When forming a decision, remember to think about the possible benefits and negative ramifications of your decision not only today but a week from today, six months from today, a year from today, and three years from today. Ask yourself the following:

- Do I feel pressured to make this decision?
- Am I making this decision because I feel stressed, overwhelmed, rushed, frightened, bored, emotionally high, or in love?
- Am I making excuses in an attempt to justify my decision?
- What regrets might this decision lead to down the road?
- What potential problems might this decision cause for me six months from now, a year from now, and three years from now?
- What am I gaining by making this decision? What am I losing? What might I leave behind? What new problems will I encounter?

- How will my decision affect other people in my life who are important to me? How will it affect them in six months, one year, and three years?
- If others know about my decision or it becomes public, how would I feel and would it cause damage to me, my family, or others close to me?

Do a litmus test on your emotional state. If you are feeling shaky, emotional, or pressured, it might help to consult someone else. A therapist, arbitrator, friend, life coach, member of the clergy, or someone else you trust might help you sort through the decision and stay balanced.

Sample Assessments and Decisions

You are now familiar with every step in the SMART model. You know how to evaluate your judgment and avoid common pitfalls that could cloud it. You also know how to mitigate risk, conduct interviews, assess for CTD behaviors, and how to use all of that information to make a better decision.

Now let's get a little practice. It will help you to hone the process so you can better use it in real life.

In the following pages, I'm going to walk you through several situations and show you how I would complete the steps of this decision-making process. As we walk through each assessment and decision, I'll point out the factors that might cloud your judgment. I'll show you how I would weigh the pros and cons and take the potential long-term consequences into account. By doing so, I hope you will be able to see how the SMART model works in specific situations. It's also my hope that this will provide you with some practice and begin to sharpen your skills.

Sample Assessment

Is This Handyman Dangerous?

The situation: You are looking for someone to paint the inside of your house. You know the job will take almost a week. You want someone you can trust. What should you do to screen potential painters? What questions should you ask? What information will be important in making your decision?

Think about your answer, and then read on.

The Assessment

Usually, when we hire anyone, we want to know "How much is it going to cost?" "Is he or she competent?" and "Have they done good work for other clients?" That's why typical interview questions are as follows:

- What do you charge?
- How long have you been doing this?
- Do you have any references?
- Are materials included in the price?
- How long will it take you to finish?

We usually want to hire someone who is nice and friendly too. So if the person smiles a lot and seems pleasant, we give them a high score in our assessment process. Yet, as you've already learned, how nice or how pleasant a person appears usually has little to do with how dangerous they really are.

Rarely if ever does anyone think to ask if the person has a criminal record. Yet whether he or she has been arrested may be the most important detail for you to know about the person who will be coming into your home. This is a high-risk decision, as your home is your comfort zone. Your home is where you go to feel safe.

You do not want to hire someone who will:

- be searching for the location where you hide your secret key
- be casing your house and looking for where you keep your valuables so he or she can break in later and steal them
- steal items that he or she thinks you won't miss until many weeks later
- give your information to someone else who is unsafe
- attack you

- disrespect your property
- behave inappropriately—for instance by making sexual advances toward you or a family member

You don't just want to know if he has a criminal record. You also want to know what that record was for. Just because a person has a criminal record does not mean that you can't trust them. Find out as much as you can about the crime and then think about how that crime applies to the job at hand. For instance, someone who was convicted of doing drugs twenty years ago, went to rehab, got clean, and has stayed clean since is probably not a threat to you and may well be capable of doing an excellent job of providing you a service. Someone who was convicted of stealing just a year ago, however, poses a much higher risk to you and your personal property. And someone who has convictions for assault should be screened very carefully. If the behavior is recent and/or reoccurring, this person could pose a threat to you if a situation arises where there is a dispute between you.

It's important to note that the absence of a criminal record does not necessarily mean that criminal or dangerous behavior is not present. You will need to find out more than just this information in order to assess the people you wish to hire.

Are you thinking that you could never be so rude as to ask someone if they have been arrested? Consider that a person without a criminal record won't mind being asked this question because she or he has nothing to hide. Think about how you would feel if someone asked you this question. Would you be put off, or would you empathize with the home owner who is worrying about his or her safety? I'm guessing that you would empathize, which is how any truly nonthreatening person will react.

You also might be thinking that it's so easy for people to lie and answer such a question with a no. That's true, but you learned how to detect deceit in chapter 8. Use those skills.

For instance, I recently interviewed a number of house painters. One painter came to me at the recommendation of a friend, someone who happened to also work in law enforcement. I asked this painter whether he would be bringing others into the house to help him paint. He answered that question by telling me how long he had been painting houses and how good he was at what he did. I noticed that he evaded my question. That made me suspicious.

I told him that I was a retired FBI agent, and I asked him if he or any of his coworkers had a criminal record. He stuttered, looked away, and then began talking quickly about the success of his business and about how he's never gotten any complaints. I hadn't asked him whether he'd gotten any complaints. Since he volunteered this, it made me assume that he had. More important, he had again evaded my question, making me even more suspicious. He never called me back with a quote.

I went with a different painter who did a wonderful job.

I ask everyone I wish to hire whether they have a record. I assure you that it would frighten you to know just how many times my "do you have a criminal record?" question has tipped me off that someone might not be so harmless after all.

In addition to asking about the criminal record, you might want to go even deeper, depending on the job you are hiring for. How thoroughly you screen your hired home help will depend on a few factors:

1. **If they've already been prescreened.** If the person you are hiring works for an established company, then a screening process may already be in place. For instance, if your insurance company sends someone to repair your roof, they will likely send a roofer they have used in the past. If this roofer were problematic, other home owners would likely have complained to your insurance company about him or her. As a result, it's likely that your insurance company would have filtered out any workers who have caused problems in the past.

2. **How much access this worker will have to your home.** If the person will be working outside the home or will be coming in and leaving while you are home, your screening process can be less intensive. On the other hand, if you are hiring someone who will have long-term unsupervised access to your home, you will want to screen more thoroughly. For instance, you'd want to screen a babysitter, nanny, or au pair much more thoroughly than the person who delivers and installs your satellite dish.

3. How regularly the person will have access to your home. You will want to screen people more thoroughly if you are going to have an ongoing relationship with them, and maybe less thoroughly if it's just a short-term, quick, one-time-only job. For long-term, regular relationships, you'll want to continuously update your dangerousness assessment as you get to know more and more about the person. Keep in mind, however, that someone can come into your home just one time and acquire enough information about you and/or your family to hurt you, then or later on.

If the painter will have unsupervised access to your home, you'll want to screen thoroughly. That means you'll want to find out if your house painter exhibits one or more of the five dangerous behaviors (described on pages 182–186). To do so, you will want to ask questions that will give you information about whether they possess any of those dangerous qualities. You'll want to ask emotion-laden questions, most of which will start with phrases like "How did you feel when" and "How would you feel if." As various painters answer these questions, observe their comfort level. Do they struggle with the question? Do they provide evasive answers? Do they seem uncomfortable? If so, why?

Listen to the answers. Notice if a painter continually blames others, focuses on real or imagined slights that he mentions have victimized him over his lifetime, and fails to accept responsibility for problems in his life. Here are some questions you might ask:

- Can you tell me about conflicts you've had in the past with home owners or colleagues and how you've handled them?
- In the past, when a home owner experienced a problem that stalled a project—for instance a sudden financial stressor or a death in the family—how did you feel? How did you handle it?

You'll also want to talk with other people who know this person, and you'll want to ask questions designed to help you go beyond "He's a nice guy" and help you get at what you really want to know. Depending on the worker you are hiring, those questions might be:

- What issues came up on your job and how did Mr. X handle them?
- What were you most impressed with? Where could you recommend improvement?
- Have you or anyone in your family ever felt uncomfortable around him or her?
- What did your children say about him?
- How did he and his coworkers treat your pets?
- When you brought up issues or problems regarding his work, how did Mr. X take that criticism/feedback?
- How did you feel about Mr. X when the job was finally done?

Sample Decision

Should you go on this bargain cruise with some other women from church?

The situation: A woman you know from church is organizing a cruise and she's asked you to come along. You'll be spending five days and four nights in the Caribbean. This is enticing to you because it has been a hard, cold winter. A few days of warmth and sunshine are just what your mood needs. Plus, at only $450 for the whole trip, this is a bargain. The price even includes meals. You don't know the organizer that well, but she has always been nice, outgoing, and friendly to you in the past. If you decide to go, you will be traveling with her and five of her good friends and sharing a cabin with one other woman.

Think about how you would make this decision. Then read on.

The Decision

To make this decision, you'll want to counteract your excitement about the cruise. Remind yourself that this trip will have you traveling for a full week with a group of women you do not know very well at all—and you'll be sharing a room with one of them. You know little to nothing about the habits, values, personalities, or behaviors of this group of women and about your potential roommate in particular. What should you find out about these women? What unknown factors about them, their behaviors, and their personalities could cause problems for you on the cruise?

Think about all the potential negative consequences of going on this cruise. They might include the following:

- Since this cruise is being organized by another woman—who is potentially the leader of this circle of friends—you could easily find yourself outnumbered and feeling like an outsider. If you don't fit into the group or do not agree with their habits and values, this could potentially be a miserable experience for you.
- Will you and your roommate be going to sleep around the same time? What will you do if you are an early-to-bed person and she is a night owl?
- Will this group of women want to party when you prefer not to, and then try to coerce you into going along with their plans?
- Will they want you to go with them on expensive land excursions that you can't afford?
- Will you feel as if you must hang out with them the entire time, even if you would rather be alone or do your own thing?
- What will you do if they react to your personality or behavior in a negative way?
- What if your cabin mate is one of those people who takes over the cabin, causing you to feel uncomfortable and unwelcome there?
- What if one or more of the women tends to get out of control and needs you and others to keep her from getting herself into trouble when she drinks?
- Are any of the women demanding, controlling, moody, or sulky to the point that their problems could be significantly disruptive to the others?

Any of those factors could cause serious problems for you during this cruise—problems that will make this so-called vacation seem more like a nightmare.

If I were making this decision, I would not want this trip to be the first time I'd ever socialized with this group of women. I would create opportunities to go out with them socially so I could get to know them better and observe their behavior. I would also ask the person organizing the trip a lot of questions—questions designed to help me determine how likely any of the potential consequences are to arise. For instance, I would ask questions like these:

- Tell me about the woman I will be rooming with. What is she like? What are some of her unique habits?
- Tell me more about the other women going on the cruise. What are they like? Have you cruised with them before? If so, tell me about some of your experiences.
- Will we be hanging out as a group the entire time?
- Will we be meeting one another for meals or social time?
- What kinds of social activities do you think will be involved?
- What kinds of side trips might we be taking?
- How much drinking does the group like to do?
- What happens if, at the last minute, I decide not to go?
- Do you cruise a lot? If so, what have those experiences been like?

You also will want to assess this group of women. Find out more about the leader of the group and what she is like. Every group has a leader, even within friends. Does the same person generally lead the group at all times or does the leadership role shift from one woman to another depending on what is going on? Is the organizer of the cruise the leader of the group? Is there friction in the group? Are there historical problems in the group that will follow these women onto the cruise ship?

Once you determine who the leader is, you'll want to assess her leadership style and ability, her decision-making skills, and her ability to be a role model. Make sure she is the type of person you will feel comfortable traveling with. I know that this sounds like a lot of work just to decide whether to go on a short vacation, but even a little assessment of the people you will be traveling with can go a long way in helping you to make the best decision, and it is not just about the money. Remember, you will be away from home and your support group, living in very small quarters, and most likely outside of the United States or your home country in a place where the enforcement of laws will be very different. If you pick the wrong travel partners and there is a problem, or several problems, you will find yourself dependent on people you might not like or are even afraid of, and you will have limited options for making alternative plans. Do your homework.

Sample Decision

Is it the time right to introduce your new boyfriend to your children?

The situation: You are a single parent and have met someone you care about very much. You want to bring this man home and introduce him to your two young children. He is anxious to meet your children, and you are anxious to have someone in your life. Your goal is to get remarried.

Think about how you would make this decision, and then read on.

The Decision

You might have a tendency to want to rush into and solidify this new relationship, but this is a decision that you will want to take a lot of time and thought with, as you are not the only person affected by it. Your children will be affected as well.

Even though you care about this man and have come to feel close to him, it's important to remind yourself that you still do not know him in each of the six areas of his life (see chapter 9). You probably have not had ample time to observe his behavior in a wide range of circumstances. Early in a relationship, most people make an attempt to impress each other. They hide and downplay their unfavorable qualities. It will take time before you know this man fully enough to be able to answer important questions like these:

- How is he with children?
- Is he someone your children can respect and grow fond of?
- Will he respect your parenting style? What are his parenting style and philosophies?
- Does he have behaviors or habits that you would not want your children exposed to?
- What are his relationships like with others in his family, including his own children?
- Is he potentially dangerous? For instance, is he dating you to gain access to your children? What are his intentions regarding your children?

That last question is chilling, and it's also something that many women don't want to think about. Still, it happens, and it's something that you want to guard your children against.

Because this is a relationship that will, over time, potentially become more and more intimate, you will want to observe this boyfriend as much as possible and learn as much as you can about him, and you will want to do this in several different situations.

Before introducing him to your children, you will want to do a danger assessment on him—screening him for behaviors that could suggest long-term problems (see chapter 9).

Over time you might notice what he says about other people and about his place of employment. For instance, does he often blame others for his problems? (A sign of injustice collecting.)

Notice how he drives his car. Is he prone to road rage? (A sign of anger.) Does he run red lights, change lanes excessively, tailgate, drink and drive, or fill the car with cigarette smoke? (Possible signs of impulsiveness, anger problems, and immaturity.) How would you feel with your children in the car with him?

How does he talk to and about other people? Is he rude? Does he interrupt a lot? Does he talk down to people? Does he act like a bully? (Possible signs of arrogance, lack of empathy, and callousness.) Would you want your children on the receiving end of that kind of interpersonal communication style?

How well does he listen? Does he tend to dominate the conversation? How does he take criticism—real or imagined? Does he take responsibility for his own actions or blame others? (These could be signs of someone who can be dominating and controlling, as well as someone who is a blamer.)

Does he regularly sulk? Does he go through periods of time when his mood becomes dark and unresponsive or has he had outbursts of anger? (These are possible signs that he has problems with anger, injustice collecting, or serious mental-health issues.)

Is he jealous without cause, checking up on you, your whereabouts, and who you are with? Has he unexpectedly showed up at places where you have been? Is he becoming demanding of your time and attention to the exclusion of contact with your friends and family? Has he been unfaithful to you during your relationship? (These are possible signs of narcissism and of someone who is dangerously jealous, possessive, and suspicious.)

Who are his friends and what are they like? Are his friendships short term? Are his long-term friendships few or nonexistent? (If he has problems developing and maintaining friendships, this could be indicative of poor interpersonal communication and relationship skills.)

Does he ever cause you to feel unsafe or threatened? How does he treat your pets? (Signs of anger, impulsivity, or lack of empathy.)

Does he drink and drive? Use illegal drugs or abuse OTC drugs? (These are possible signs of impulsivity, a "rules don't apply" philosophy, immaturity, anger problems, and lack of empathy and/or concern for others and their welfare.)

You will also want to notice signs that he has a personality that is not compatible with long-term intimacy. For instance, does he lie, withhold information, or overstate claims? Has he boasted about getting away with lying to others? If he lies to others, what will stop him from lying to you?

Is he exceedingly frugal and does he expect you to pay most of the time? If so, what will stop him from moving in and becoming a parasite who lives off your paychecks?

Is he already talking about getting married, even though you've known each other for just a few months? An affirmative answer to this final question could be a big red flag. Many people assume that someone like this is a great catch. They might think, "Finally! I met a man who does not have a fear of commitment!" Yet you want to carefully consider why he is in such a hurry. Why is he pushing things forward? What is his main motivation? Is he really in love, or is some other reason motivating him to tie the knot?

Maybe he is a parasite who will do with you what he has done in his other relationships: move in with you, quit his job, and live off your paychecks. Worse, maybe he's a pedophile.

What do your friends think of him? Use the eyes and ears of others for feedback and include these details in your assessment.

Once you've done a danger assessment, you will want to introduce him to your children slowly and gradually. Try to avoid inadvertently sharing your opinions with your children up front, which will influence their own thinking or inhibit them from giving you their true opinion. For example, comments like "He's a great guy" or "I know you will love him—he is really nice" can communicate how you feel about him. It can be very intimidating to a child to attempt to form a different conclusion.

You might first introduce him to your children in a neutral location outside the home, and you might do it for a short period of time. During this first encounter, you will be watching what he does, listening to what he says, and noticing how he interacts with your kids and how they interact with him. Afterward, you'll want to ask your children what they thought, and you will want to spend time listening closely to what they say rather than talking to them about their experience with this new person. Here are some examples of some questions that might help you get started. Notice that these are open-ended questions rather than questions that require a yes-or-no answer. They are also questions that focus on your child's feelings, insights and experiences, and not on yours.

- What did you notice about him?
- What did you think about him?
- How did you feel about meeting him?
- Was there anything that made you feel uncomfortable?
- What are your feelings about him becoming more a part of this family?

Some children are likely to be resentful of a new man who comes into their mother's life, but be careful to not ignore the information your children give you about this man. If they are afraid of or intimidated by him, ask yourself what it is about him that caused their fear or concern. Was it something he said or did—something that is a sign of danger?

Sample Assessment

Is it too risky to open the front door?

The situation: It's 9:30 p.m. Your doorbell rings. You are at home with your small children, who are asleep. Your spouse is not home. You are not expecting anyone. You look through the peephole and do not recognize the person on the other side of the door. Do you answer the door?

Think about your answer, and then read on.

The Assessment

This very situation happened to my coauthor as we were working on this book. She was fearful of answering the door because there had been a series of home invasions in her neighborhood, some of which had taken place while the homeowners were asleep. Yet she was afraid of not answering the door for precisely the same reason.

If she opened the door, she might allow a burglar to gain access to her home. If she didn't open the door, she might inadvertently cause a burglar to assume that the house was empty, causing him to look for a way to break in.

She quickly thought of ways she could mitigate the risk of a potential burglar breaking in and harming her and her daughter. She:

- called her husband and left a message asking him to come home
- turned on the porch light, so the person standing on the porch would know that someone was home
- dialed 911 on her phone and put her finger on the call button, ready to press it if need be

Then she opened the door. A Plexiglas storm door now separated her from the man on her porch. As it turned out, it was one of her neighbors. He was concerned about a strange car parked on the street.

My coauthor took a few actions to minimize her risk, but there is at least one more action she could have taken. She could have shouted through the door, without opening it, and asked the man on the other side who he was and what he wanted. This would have prevented her from having to open the door—and making herself and her daughter more vulnerable—to gain the same information.

When assessing whether to open your door, you will want to consider the following:

- The time of day. Is it late at night or the middle of the night? If it's dark, that raises the risk of danger.
- Who else is home with you? Is there someone there who could call 911 or help you defend yourself? That would lower the risk of danger. Are you home alone with small children that you would want to protect? This would raise the risk of danger.
- Whether you are expecting someone. If you are expecting someone, this lowers the risk. If you are not, it raises it.
- The purpose for the person being on the other side of the door. If you ask the person, through a shut door, who he is and what he wants and he doesn't give you a good reason or a logical or believable explanation, there's no reason for you to open your door.

Sample Assessment

What should you do if you suspect that your daughter's boyfriend is abusive?

The situation: You've overheard your college-age daughter's boyfriend talking down to her, ordering her around, and calling her what you think are derogatory names. You interpret his interpersonal style as abusive and you worry about physical abuse as well.

Think about how you would find out whether your suspicions are valid, and then read on.

The Assessment

This is a delicate situation, one that will probably take every ounce of your self-control. If you are like most parents, you will be tempted to swoop in and unleash Armageddon on this boyfriend and/or to forbid your daughter from seeing him again. That might not result in a favorable outcome, however. First, it could trigger his abusive behavior to escalate. Second, it might cause your daughter to shut down and become evasive, sneaking around to see him and no longer confiding in you about what is going on. Even worse, it could result in your daughter putting emotional, even physical, distance between her and you and the rest of the family.

Here are some suggestions for how to learn as much as you can about what is going in with your daughter and her relationship and how to develop a course of action:

- Think about what you know and what you don't. You might be tempted to rush in and interpret what you overheard. Hold back. You don't know all the details just yet. To determine how much of a threat this young man poses to your daughter, you will need additional information, and some of it may not be easy to obtain. Some information about the boyfriend will have to come from your daughter, through her eyes.

- Think about your personal style and how that might cause her to react. How have conversations with your daughter gone in the past? When you've asked your daughter important, probing questions, has she shut down? Gotten defensive? Become argumentative? What about your interview style caused those reactions in her? It's very important to think about this now—before you ask a single question. You want to adjust your interview style so you can put her at ease and get her to open up. If your line of questioning has caused an undesirable result in the past, think about what triggered it and adjust accordingly.

Perhaps most important, think about whether you are the best person to gather this information. Will you become too emotional? Are you so enmeshed with your daughter that you will not be able to listen calmly? Does she usually confide in you? Or is she more likely to confide in someone else—perhaps a sibling or an aunt? Is your style or tendency to lecture, threaten, problem solve, or yell? If you answer yes, then understand that if you do not change this style it is likely it will impede your ability to get the information you critically need.

- Plan the interview. Where will you do it? Since she might become emotional, a crowded public venue is probably not the best location. Since she might be tempted to run, hide, and lock the door behind her, your home might not be ideal either. Perhaps a calming, sparsely populated neutral location would work best—such as a nearby park where you can talk while you walk. Think about the pros and cons of when, where, how, and who. When will you do it? Who else will be there? What is your strategy? Where will you talk with her? What is the best environment to help your daughter to open up?

- Conduct the interview. The toughest part will probably be the beginning, when you first bring up the topic. Try to stay away from a tension-provoking introduction like "I don't like him!" or "You need to break up with him!" That might come later, but it will kill your interview if you start with it. She may feel defensive of him and resentful, even embarrassed that you feel she is not capable of handling her own problems. To prevent her from shutting down, you'll want to ask open-ended questions that do not sound judgmental of him or her. You will also want to keep the focus on her, how she feels, and her overall safety, not on what you want. For instance, you might want to introduce the discussion by saying something like this:

> I am concerned about Joe because I heard how he spoke to you. It sounded scary to me. It's important for me to hear from you what you think of him and that behavior.

Then you might follow up with questions like these:

- Tell me about Joe. What is he like?
- Have you ever been frightened of him? Can you tell me about those times?
- Have there been times when you thought he could have hurt you or someone else?
- Have there been times when you and/or others have had to "talk him down" from his becoming angry with others?
- What would your friends tell me about him and his behavior?
- Are there times he has threatened you or been physical with you?

As she answers, look for signs of evasiveness. For instance, notice if she answers your yes-or-no questions with a "not really." You will want to follow up on all occurrences of "not really" and get to the bottom of what that means for her. Ask, "What do you mean you have 'not really' been frightened?" "Not really frightened" of him most likely means that she has been frightened at some time in the past.

As a mother you will probably want to rush in and protect her. You might be tempted to tell her what to do or to give her a lecture. Instead give her the opportunity to talk. Listen. You want to hear how she describes the situation and how she feels.

Be prepared, however, for her to shut down. This will be very difficult for her to talk about. In that case, you might say, "Just so you know, your not talking with me is not going to prevent me from making sure that you are safe. By not talking with me you may leave me no choice but to talk with others about this young man. I understand that you are embarrassed or not comfortable talking to me about this. I understand that. But I am worried about you, and I will find out about this in other ways if I have to because this is a situation where you could get hurt."

- Don't expect a one-time dump of information. Note that this might take several discussions. Try not to exhaust her with too many questions. She probably won't break down and tell you everything during just one talk. You might want to say, "We've talked enough for today. You can even set aside a day and time when you will talk again.

• Interpret the information you've gathered. Based on what she told you, do you think this is a one-time incident (not likely) or a disturbing pattern of behavior that will escalate (likely)? Use others, such as trustworthy friends or parents who have been through similar situations, to help you evaluate the information and the behavior. Although you might be able to call school officials and make them aware of a possible problem, note that most probably will not openly share information with you due to legal concerns about privacy.

• Decide on a course of action. This could be a dangerous situation, one that will likely get worse if you do nothing. And of course the age of your daughter will be a major factor in how aggressive you will want to be, should be, or can be. If your daughter is of legal age, by law she can make her own decisions, and you can only advise, unless she poses a danger to herself or others. Have a discussion with your daughter about what you plan to do. Your plans might include calling up the school and asking officials to help you ensure that he stays away from her. They might include getting law enforcement involved and getting a restraining order.

Often in cases like this, parents just want their daughters to be out of the relationship and for the young man to get help. More serious steps, like going to the school or law enforcement, are seen as too severe because of the negative consequences. However, if the behavior is egregious and dangerous enough, it may not be sufficient to handle it on your own. Getting professional help may be essential to keep him from revictimizing her or someone else.

• Be prepared for your daughter to stick up for him and to tell you that she doesn't want to get him in trouble. Be prepared for her to worry that he will become angry and really hurt her if you intervene. Be prepared for her to worry about other kids in school gossiping about her, teasing her, or worse.

Educate your daughter and help her get in front of her choices six months or even a year in the future, so she can realize the long-term consequences of her decisions on her life.

Sample Assessment

How do you assess a problem employee?

The situation: An employee has made veiled threats to another employee in his unit. This is an ongoing pattern of behavior that you have documented in your position as a human resources person. But you are concerned about retaliation if you terminate him. You have also had some incidents of anonymous nuisance situations on the job, including some vandalism and minor property damage. You have no evidence that this employee is responsible, but you suspect him. He has recently been passed over for a promotion that was given to a younger person with less time on the job. You are concerned about his behavior escalating.

Think about how you would go about addressing this problem, and then read on.

The Assessment

When I was at the FBI BAU, I often got calls about individuals and their potential for workplace violence. I sometimes learned that the person had been a problem for a long time, his behavior had escalated, and now there were plans to terminate him because there was concern of his behavior becoming violent. I would then be asked for my assessment of the person and to factor in a strategy for terminating his or her employment.

These are some of the questions I would ask about the employee and the situation, and the answers I received.

You've been worried about this employee for a while?

Yes, we have.

So it's almost Christmas Eve (or some other holiday or significant date for the employee) and you want to let this employee go right away?

Yes, we do.

Several times I was tempted to respond, "You've got to be kidding me," but I didn't. The only way they could possibly make this situation any worse would be to make sure every single employee at the company was present on the day of the firing and then do the equivalent of a perp walk as they very publicly escorted the problem employee out of the building.

I knew they'd already made the decision to fire. They didn't want my opinion about whether to let the problem employee go. What they wanted to know was this: how best to handle the termination to minimize a negative response by the employee at that time or at some time in the future.

Let's walk through how you might decide to develop a strategy for the successful and safe termination of a problem employee.

- Decide on your goal. In this case it's to safely terminate an employee while mitigating the risk of this employee harming the company or its employees now or in the future.

- Know as much as possible about this employee, his job performance, and his personality, and problems he has had in the past with managers and coworkers. Be knowledgeable about the current precipitating issues.

You also want to find out everything you can about what might be going on in other areas of this person's life that might exacerbate how he views his termination. Does he go home to a loving family? Does he live alone? Did his wife just leave him? Has this employee talked to coworkers or his supervisor about stressful problems in his life? Is he an injustice collector? Has he ever acted out in the past? How important is his job to him? Is he quick to anger? Does he have access to weapons? What will his support network be like once he leaves the company?

Termination from one's job can be extremely stressful and embarrassing for a person. It is also mentally and emotionally debilitating, particularly for someone who is heavily or pathologically invested in his or her job. For someone whose coping skills are dysfunctional and/or weak, the loss of a job can have a devastating impact, particularly if his or her social or family network is weak or even nonexistent. Severing someone's ties to his or her employment or school might be severing the one social and interpersonal attachment he or she has left. As an employer, you need to know this. Losing that attachment can be extremely problematic for the person and result in a desperate response.

Decide who will terminate the employee. If you are planning on doing it, consider how you are viewed by this person. Does he consider you the source of his problems or blame you for his current situation? If he does view you in this light, you do not want to be the person in charge of terminating him. This could significantly increase his feelings of a personal vendetta.

Also, have you terminated employees in the past? How did those terminations go? Did they go well? Or did the employees become angry? If the employees became angry, are you sure you have the skills needed to terminate a problem employee who might become violent? If so, what will you do differently to prevent this problem employee from becoming angry? If not, who can you call on to help you terminate this employee? If you are a small business, is there an association or arbitration group you can call for assistance?

Think of ways you can mitigate the risk of this employee turning violent or destructive toward himself or others—both at the present time as well as in the future. First and foremost, you will want to give this person some dignity by showing appropriate empathy. The last thing you want to do is walk this employee out in front of his or her coworkers.

1. Do not do the firing when there is an audience or others around. Give the person some dignity.

2. If the employee is mad at or has a grudge against certain supervisors, they should not be present during the firing. Have a neutral person do the termination.
3. Make this employee feel cared for. Give him severance, even if it's not part of the company policy. Pay out all his vacation. Set him up with a job-finding service. Make it about how you will help him readjust.
4. When explaining the reasons for termination, do not blame the employee. Blame his behavior instead. For instance, you could word it like this: "Many employees are frightened. Some of the e-mails that you've sent have caused them to feel threatened." Remind him that your concern is not just for the company but for his welfare too.
5. Be willing to say, "I am sorry," if appropriate, and show appropriate empathy. For instance, say, "I'm sorry it turned out like this," and "I know this must be hard on you."
6. If the employee needs to gather up some possessions (and there is a concern over allowing him to return to his office and computer), have a neutral party (the head of security or human resources) deliver his personal belongings to him. This will also allow you to monitor his behavior and reaction to the termination.
7. Follow up with the employee, particularly if there is a concern for safety. If company policies permit, meet for coffee or lunch for some time after the termination. This will allow you to monitor the employee to find out how he is handling the termination. Always have neutral parties meet with the former employee and never anyone the employee held a grudge against. For safety, send two people rather than one and let the police know where and when the meeting is taking place, if warranted.
8. Stay in touch over a period of time. This not only causes the employee to feel cared for, it also allows you to see if his mood or behavior is deteriorating as result of the loss of his job and the potential for revenge or displaced violence is increasing.

Bonus Advice for Home Owners

If you are a home owner and you need to let go of hired help, you may be tempted to get it over with just to get them out of your life. You also might be tempted to unload on them about their awful work and creepy presence in your home. This, however, could easily backfire and result in the person having a vendetta against you.

Keep your goal in mind. It is to get this person out of your home and out of your life. To ensure that this happens, you will have to use a little psychology. Avoid arguing, insulting, or threatening them. Don't "hold on to" their tools or equipment to "teach them a lesson." Pay for the work that's been done to date, even if the job is half-finished and even if you will lose money and have to hire someone to fix mistakes. While in some extreme cases you may have no alternative but to withhold payment or even file a legal claim, realize that these actions will perpetuate a relationship with this person. If he or she is potentially dangerous, such actions can cause you and your family all types of problems.

To give you an example, I once hired someone to cut my grass. After finishing mowing my lawn, he drove over and crushed my yard ornaments. Then he broke my expensive landscape lights.

And then he committed the ultimate violation. He left my fence gate open. Buddy, my beloved new rescue dog, got out, which frightened me because I worried that he would get hit by a car. I eventually tracked down Buddy and got him home safe, but then I definitely wanted to let this guy have it for leaving the gate open. I thought about the condescending way he'd spoken to me in the past and how arrogant he'd been.

But then I took an emotional step back and thought about this man's personality. That arrogance and the anger that I found so off-putting were red flags—ones that I knew to pay attention to.

Instead of letting him have it, I telephoned him and casually said, "Look, the gate was open when I got home and my dog ran off. I am such a fanatic about this dog. I am just over-the-top about him. If anything happened to him, I don't know what I would do. I know I'm overly sensitive about the fence gate, and I'm sorry about that. But I'm thinking that it might be best if I cut the grass myself since I know I will always remember to keep the gate closed."

Then I wrote him a check for the work he'd done, along with a note thanking him. I even suggested that I would keep him in mind for future work. I have never had contact with him since.

Sample Decision

What should you do about the guy who pays too much attention to you at the gym?

The situation: You belong to an expensive gym and have paid for an entire year's membership in order to get a discount. Lately, however, you have not been enjoying your workouts because a man has been taking too much interest in you. Initially he just seemed to be politely chatting, but soon he was annoyingly pointing out what you were doing right and wrong. Eventually he began commenting on your choice of outfits, your makeup, and your hairstyle. At first you thought he must be harmless. After all, the gym is expensive and he's a lawyer. But it has reached the point where he seems to find you as soon as you walk in, and then dominates your time while you are there. He continually asks you questions about your personal life, especially about whether you are dating someone. Even when he's not right there talking to you, he stares at you and turns his head as you walk by.

He's made you so uncomfortable that you even stopped going to the gym for a while. Then when you showed up again, he seemed angry and made a snide comment about how you are slacking off on your workouts and it shows.

Think about how you would handle this situation, and then read on.

The Decision

Many factors might affect your judgment as you attempt to make this decision. Maybe you don't want to hurt the guy's feelings or you feel uncomfortable confronting the situation. Maybe you have been swayed by the fact that he's a lawyer who works out at a gym catering to successful professionals. Maybe you worry that you are not reading the situation correctly. Perhaps the guy is harmless and you are being overly sensitive.

Consider what you don't know about this situation. Do a behavior assessment on the man and consider how your risk level could go up or down depending on how you handle the situation.

It is important to keep the situation in perspective. Right now the man is a nuisance, and he has crossed a boundary with you by saying things that are inappropriate. At the moment, however, you have no evidence that he is either a stalker or a follower. Understand that incorrectly labeling people—even casually—is, at the very least, insensitive and, at the extreme, could be grounds for a defamation lawsuit. There are different types of stalkers, and it takes a great deal of expertise to do a professional threat assessment on one. A simple and reliable way to do a behavioral assessment for a novice, however, is to look at whether his behavior is escalating.

Nuisance behavior becomes concerning when it begins to escalate and becomes intrusive and more threatening. A behavior is escalating if it increases in frequency (he's attempting to contact you more often) or intensity (he's starting to threaten you or become highly critical or insulting). It's also escalating if he seems to be learning from his mistakes. For instance, if you start to go to the gym at a different time, he realizes what's going on, and he starts going to the gym at that time, too, he's escalating. The more aggressive he becomes and the more risks he is willing to take to make contact, the more worried you should be about his behavior.

To figure out what to do about this situation, consider the following:

- Think about your goal. What do you want? Many women would probably walk away from a situation like this. They'd give up an entire year's worth of membership dues in order to avoid feeling so uncomfortable and having to confront the situation. There's no absolute right or wrong here, but when you take the time to think about what you want, you will probably find that you want to be able to get in a workout in peace, without having some annoying man chatting you up the whole time. You also want to feel safe, and you want to know that this man hasn't somehow followed you home or otherwise taken his interest in you beyond the gym. Stopping going to the gym will not get you to any of those goals.

• Consider other possible options that might get you closer to what you want. You could try a few options incrementally:

1. Talk with a gym manager. Explain the situation. Ask if there have been other complaints about this man bothering women. Ask for the manager's advice or request that the manager handle the situation.
2. The next time this man comes over to you, explain that you feel uncomfortable. You might say, "Look, I am not comfortable with all of this attention. I really want to focus on my workout," and then make it very clear that you are not going to engage in a conversation.
3. Always come to the gym with a partner and work out with that person. This will make it more difficult for this man to intercede.
4. Ask a gym employee or another patron to walk you to your car.
5. If this man's behavior escalates (for instance, he starts leaving notes on your car), make a formal complaint to the gym. If that does not help, ask the gym for a refund.
6. If it still continues to escalate (he's calling you at home), consider contacting law enforcement and getting a restraining order. Make sure to find out what restraining orders are all about, how they can be enforced, and how they can be violated. Do not engage with him at all. Any type of communication—positive or negative—can encourage someone like this. Just answering the phone and telling

him to stop calling or to go away can cause him to continue or even escalate. Do not call him to give him a piece of your mind, and do not talk to him out of politeness. Ignore his every advance.

As I mentioned, there is no one right way to handle this. Once you weigh all your options, you may very well decide to stop going to this gym. You might walk away from the money and you might join a different gym or stop exercising altogether. That's your choice to make. But just know that you have options and that each option affects your risk level differently.

Sample Decision

You just learned that the father of your child's friend is a registered sex offender. What should you do?

The situation: You just found out through the rumor mill that the fifty-year-old father of your son's good friend is a registered sex offender. At first you didn't think it could possibly be true. After all, you've known this family for a long time. But then you checked the sex-offender registry for your county and found that he was convicted in federal court ten years ago for the possession of child pornography. Now this father is offering to give your son and other members of the team rides home from soccer practice.

Think about what you would do about this situation, and then read on.

The Decision

You have many unanswered questions. What does this conviction really mean? Is this just something harmless—something he got caught for many years ago and then never did again? If he never abused a child, does that make him less dangerous than someone who was actually charged and convicted of assaulting a child?

What are the important issues for you to consider as you make your assessment and subsequent decision?

To sort out what this conviction means, you might research reliable sites online (such as the frequently asked questions area of the sex-offender registry itself), or you may want to seek information from law enforcement.

Since I already know what information you need, I will fill you in. A federal conviction for this type of crime is a big deal. Federal prosecutors only take on a limited number of cases. When federal prosecutors decide to get involved, you can bet that a case is quite extensive. Otherwise the feds would likely defer the prosecution to the state.

The second critical and concerning issue is the conviction itself. If this father is looking at child pornography, that suggests he is fueling his own sexual fantasies about children. If these sexual fantasies began during his adolescence and continued into adulthood (he was forty when convicted), this increases the probability that his behavior is paraphiliac and not just harmless curiosity.

Paraphiliac behavior involves the need for unusual or bizarre imagery or acts for sexual arousal. Examples of some of the more common paraphiliac behaviors include pedophilia (sexual attraction to children), voyeurism (sexual attraction to watching unwitting people in the act of disrobing or naked or engaged in sexual activities), and exhibitionism (exposing one's genitals to unsuspecting strangers for the purpose of being sexually aroused). Most people who exhibit paraphiliac behavior tend to exhibit more than one of them. This is incredibly concerning.

The third major issue is this father's age. He is fifty. How likely is it that this man has been "satisfied" with only viewing child pornography over his lifetime? Is it likely that he has never attempted to act out sexually with a child? The absence of a criminal record for acting out against a child does not mean the behavior is absent. He may never have gotten caught or the child might never have told anyone. If a parent is the abuser, the child might never report it and the abuse can continue for years.

If this father has acted out or attempted to act out his sexual fantasies on a child, he could be classified as a pedophile. Pedophilia is difficult to treat and rarely cured.

You may never know for sure whether this father acted out his sexual fantasies involving children, but that is a gray area that I personally would not want my child caught up in. This is not a father you want around your son when other adults are not present.

Here are some other factors to keep in mind:

- You don't have all the information regarding this father's potential threat to your child, and you probably never will. Your assessment and decision of how to handle the situation must err on the side of extreme caution.

- You might feel empathy for the father and particularly for his son. You might feel the father has paid his dues and that his son, who apparently has done nothing wrong, should not be penalized because of his father's actions. Your assessment of the situation and your decision about how to handle matters can take into consideration your sensitivity toward both father and son. It is critical, however, that you understand the larger ramifications of what your son could go through for years and years were this father to abuse him under your watch. If you and your son want him to have an ongoing relationship with his friend, you will need to appreciate the potential for problems and be willing to be vigilant in monitoring your son's well-being.

- You or your spouse might be tempted to give this father a piece of your mind. Perhaps you want to tell him to stay away from your child if he knows what's good for him. Keep in mind that it's illegal to harass someone just because his name is listed on the sex-offender registry. If you do this, you very well might find yourself on the wrong side of the law.

- The whole situation might make you feel so uncomfortable that your initial reaction is to ignore it and try not to deal with it at all. Or you might be tempted to have some magical thinking. Perhaps your son has been under the care of this family before and nothing bad has happened. You might tell yourself that if nothing bad happened in the past, nothing bad will happen in the future. You also might tell yourself that the father is probably attracted to females, so the boys are probably "safe." Although some pedophiles do have gender preferences, it would be naive to think that one would never violate his own gender preference during a moment of opportunity. There is a definite possibility your son could be victimized by this father, so close and ongoing monitoring of his affiliation with the family is essential.

- Think about how you will protect your child. You obviously do not want a situation where your child might be alone with this father. To accomplish this goal, you need to politely decline his offer. You can say, "Thanks, but I enjoy watching soccer practice and don't mind driving him myself."

- Decide what you want to do with this information. Your child is not the only child at risk. Do other parents know that he's a registered sex offender? Is it up to you to tell them? Or is the responsibility of each parent to be vigilant about finding background information on their children's friends' parents?

- If this information gets out, what will happen to your son's friend? Will he become ostracized or bullied? And more distressing, is this boy being abused by his own father? You may or may not consider whether it's your moral responsibility to do something about these issues. You can consider talking to school officials. Let them know what you've learned and what you are worried about. Counseling and mental-health professionals at your child's school are trained and experienced in handling delicate situations like this in the most effective and sensitive ways. They are a great resource in this type of situation.

You are now well on your way to mastering the SMART model. You might even be finding that you are already thinking differently and changing the way you make decisions. You now know how to spot and outsmart dangerous people and how to avoid becoming one of their victims. In the final chapter of this book, you'll find out how to avoid becoming the object of their attention in the first place.

CHAPTER 10 RAP SHEET

- SMART decisions are not based on just one detail. They are based on the totality of the circumstances.
- Write down all the details to make sure you are weighing and interpreting them properly.
- Look for holes and blind spots. What might you have missed? What might you have overlooked?
- Before making any decision, carefully consider its long-term ramifications. Can you live with all the possible negative consequences of this decision?

Chapter 11

The *Dangerous Instincts* Safety Guide

In the typical movie or television suspense thriller, a tiny woman wakes in the middle of the night. She hears noises and suspects someone is in her home. She gets out of bed, goes to the kitchen, grabs a knife, and slowly proceeds to tiptoe through the house, in search of the intruder, with an expression of horror and fear on her face.

Now that you've read most of this book, I'd like you to think about that scenario and about what's wrong with it. If you were awakened in the middle of the night, what would you do? Would you run to the kitchen to look for a knife? Would you grab a handgun you have never used before or practiced with? Or would you do something else?

It's my hope, after reading this book, that you would do something else. It's my hope that you would think about the best ways to mitigate your risk of being attacked by the person or people in your home. Will you be mitigating your risk of attack by grabbing a knife and walking through the house in search of the intruder? It's not likely. Here are some examples of what's more likely to occur in that scenario, and then some suggestions of what you might do instead:

1. You become startled by your teenager, who happens to be sneaking back in through his bedroom window, and possibly injure him or her in the process. (In other words, there

is no intruder. The strange noise you heard was made by a family member.)

2. You become startled by a real intruder, who probably knows how to handle a knife (or a gun) much better than you do. This person might also be bigger and stronger than you and have enough strength and adrenaline running through their body to get the knife away from you and use it against you.

You see, going for the knife and then in search of the intruder is actually one way to *increase* the risk. To decrease it you might do the following:

- Grab the phone and call for help. Okay, the phone line has been cut (as always seems to be the case in movies). So pick up your cell phone instead.
- If you and your family members can't run outside, lock your bedroom door. If you have small children in the house, get them all in the same room and lock and barricade the door.
- If someone tries to break down the locked bedroom door, climb out the window (if possible). Yell, scream, holler, and make noise to alert others around your home that you are in danger.

As I hope you can see, what you've already learned throughout this book is what to do to assess your situation, your thinking, and others in order to stay safe. I could provide you with a long list of tips to memorize. For instance, I could tell you what to do if you ever get tossed into the trunk of a car or what to do if someone tries to abduct you at gunpoint. But fortunately it's not likely you will ever find yourself in the trunk of a car, and it's not likely that you will ever find yourself staring down the barrel of a handgun either. What is likely are hundreds if not thousands of possible other scenarios—scenarios that cannot be navigated with an instruction manual because you'd never be able to memorize all the instructions.

You can't memorize how to avoid all the specific problems in life that involve dangerous situations and dangerous people. The possibilities are infinite. But you can do five things that will help you to avoid danger, minimize your risk, and make better decisions that can impact your life and the lives of your family members for years to come.

1. Fine-tune your decision-making skills (chapter 6).
2. Mitigate risks (chapter 7).
3. Identify the critical and relevant information you need and interpret that information based on the totality of the circumstances (chapters 5 and 8).
4. Develop your listening and interview skills to obtain critical and relevant information (chapter 8).
5. Assess for dangerousness and threatening behavior in others (chapter 9).

The skills you develop in these five areas will help you figure out your best course of action in nearly any situation that could be dangerous or threatening or concerning to you. You won't need someone like me to tell you what to do. You'll be able to stay safe on your own. It's for that reason that this chapter does not contain a list of ways to burglarproof your home, get free from bindings, or disarm an attacker. Instead, in this chapter you're going to learn a process to make yourself and your loved ones less vulnerable—so you will be less likely to get into a threatening situation in the first place.

What Makes You Vulnerable

Dangerous people often seek out vulnerable people—people who are most likely to fall for their schemes. Because of this, one of the ways you can make yourself and everyone around you safer is to think about your vulnerabilities. What would make you more likely to fall for a con? What would make you more likely to allow a dangerous person to get close to you? Where are your vulnerable areas? Think about these questions for yourself, and think about them for your family members.

For instance, at different times in your life you might be emotionally vulnerable. The following states are usually accompanied by emotional vulnerability:

- Low self-esteem
- Insecurity
- Loneliness
- Sadness
- Fear

Being emotionally vulnerable can cause most people to seek comfort, answers, and help. And it's during these times in our lives that many of us let down our guard or are too ready to trust someone we should not trust. If a dangerous person happens to walk into your life when you are experiencing a moment of desperation, he or she could seem like a savior to you. You might embrace this person and feel thankful that he or she has walked into your life at precisely the right time.

In reality, the dangerous person has probably read you much better than you read them. He may have even targeted you because he recognized your low self-esteem, insecurity, loneliness, neediness, or sadness and knew he could exploit or use you because of it. This dangerous person knew that you—more so than someone else—would respond to flattery, companionship, and easy fixes. He knew that you felt broken and that you were searching for a solution. All he had to do was make you think that he had the solution you wanted.

It's for these reasons that con artists prey on the elderly, particularly shut-ins or widows. They know they are lonely. So they call and offer them the antidote to loneliness. They chat with them over the phone and keep them company. Eventually they ask for money or something else.

It's also for these reasons that dangerous men prey on women who are getting over a breakup or divorce. It's why they prey on children whose parents have recently gone through a divorce.

And it's why they prey on people with chronic or terminal illnesses.

It's for all of these reasons that you will want to take steps to overcome these vulnerabilities, and you'll want to help your family members do the same.

You will also want to think about other factors that might make your family members vulnerable. If you have children, for instance, you'll want to remember that their ability to assess risk is not as good as that of most adults. They lack the judgment and experience of someone older. This is why you don't want to leave it up to them to decide, for instance, if they should answer the direct message they got on Facebook from a person who isn't in their inner circle of friends. This is why you don't want their computers in their rooms, where you cannot monitor their activities. It's why you want them in a common area, where you can see what they are doing and monitor who they are interacting with and what they are communicating about.

It's also why you want to do your own danger or threat assessments on their friends, and especially on the friend who emerges as the leader of the social circle. Is the leader domineering, a bully, impulsive, or someone with anger problems or who is likely to influence others to engage in behavior that is high risk, dangerous, or even illegal?

If your child is a more introverted and shy person who is more of a follower than a leader, he or she could be pulled along by such a person and end up getting involved in risky behavior, behavior that could result in long-term problems.

Your children are not yet capable of making these assessments. They need your help.

I recommend that you assess the following areas of your life and for your family members. Ask yourself if you have taken all available precautions to mitigate risk in these areas. Think about what problems could develop in these areas. How could you get hurt? What can you do to reduce the following?

- Professional risk
- Financial risk
- Physical risk
- Emotional risk

Don't wait until there's a crisis to reduce your vulnerabilities. Do it now, so you can avert a crisis in the future.

Make Yourself Less Attractive to Dangerous People

I just mentioned many ways people leave themselves emotionally open to being victimized. There are also a few ways that some people physically broadcast "I'm an easy mark."

The primary one: They are just too nice. Someone who is intent on harming you will probably watch you for a while without your knowledge. If you are unusually kind, this person will notice. If you tend to answer any question someone asks, this person will notice. If you have a hard time saying no, this person will notice.

I'm not suggesting that you turn yourself into a cold, heartless individual who never talks about herself and keeps all her information private. I am suggesting, however, that you pay close attention to what types of information you transmit and how someone with impure motives might interpret that information or possibly use it against you. Think twice before giving someone your address and other contact information. When someone pays too much attention to you, wonder why, especially if that person asks you personal questions about where you live and who you live with. If someone invades your personal space and causes you to feel uncomfortable, don't think, "I don't want to hurt his feelings." Take care of yourself and put up a boundary instead.

In the beginning this might feel foreign to you. Over time, as you pay more attention to your vulnerabilities, it will become second nature.

The same is true for the SMART model. Using it is a skill, one you

The Dangerous Truth

It's estimated that 35 percent of students have been threatened while they were online. Your professional reputation is also at risk. Anyone can find what you post, and what goes online stays online forever. As a general rule of thumb, if you wouldn't want it on a billboard in print large enough for random passing motorists to see, you don't want it online either.

can hone with practice. You are now familiar with the method. It's time to start putting it to work. Every time you use it, you will sharpen your skills. Keep practicing. Using the SMART model is a perishable skill. If you stop, you'll backslide.

The more you use and practice what you've learned in this book, the better you will get. To ensure that you put in that practice, I encourage you to find a *Dangerous Instincts* buddy or to form a group. Consult this friend or group of people regularly. Meet once a month or so and talk over what's going on in your lives and how the SMART model might apply. Whenever you are about to make an important decision, consult your friend or the group. You can go through the book together and consider what action is best for each situation that comes up in your lives.

You will know the SMART model is working because you will see the evidence in your decisions. You will feel more in control of your life, and you will experience a lot less regret. You will feel less insecure.

You will no longer feel conflicted, wondering, "What should I do?" You will know what to do. You'll make a SMART decision, and you'll feel more and more in control every time you do so.

CHAPTER 11 RAP SHEET

- Your SMART skills will help you make safer decisions in any situation you find yourself.
- Emotional vulnerabilities such as loneliness, grief, and low self-esteem can make you more likely to let down your guard at the wrong moment.
- Dangerous people know how to use your emotional vulnerabilities against you.
- It's important to do a danger assessment for your children, because they are not yet able to do this assessment on their own.
- Try to reduce your professional, financial, physical, and emotional vulnerabilities now so you are a less attractive target for someone trying to take advantage of you or your family.

Appendix

The *Dangerous Instincts* Resource List

Interviewing, decision making, and risk assessment all require a certain amount of information gathering. For instance, before interviewing someone you'll want to know as much as you can about that person. Before making a decision, you'll want to know all the potential consequences. To mitigate risk in any given situation, you'll want to fully understand all the circumstances involved.

You can't always find out what you need to know from other people. Some questions are too rude or too intrusive to ask. For instance, you probably don't feel comfortable knocking on your neighbor's door and asking, "Are there any dangerous people who reside in or visit your home?"

Fortunately a lot of the information you will need in order to make decisions and assessments and to conduct interviews can be gathered—at least in part—from public sources. In this chapter, you'll find a list of resources that will help you do just that.

How to Research Local Crime Problems

Go to the local police department and ask for summary crime reports and news and press releases about crime rates in neighborhoods. Archives of the local newspaper will also contain crime-related information. You can check any or all of the following Web resources too:

- The websites for local, regional, state, and federal law enforcement agencies: Many law enforcement agencies have their own websites where they post a variety of information, including crime activity and their responses to those problems.

- CrimeMapping.com: This free Web service allows you to click on a state and find the latest information on reported crimes in many of its areas.

- CrimeReports.com: Similar to CrimeMapping, this free service allows you to type in an address, and then it will show you on a map the reported crimes and sex-offender data for that area.

- Ucrdatatool.gov: The U.S. Department of Justice's Uniform Crime Reporting (UCR) Program allows you to see state and national crime statistics.

- FBI.gov/stats-services/crimestats/crime_statistics: Here you'll find reports you can download about specific crimes. You can also research the FBI's UCR database.

Information You Might Want to Know Before You Move

In addition to researching local crime problems (mentioned earlier), you might want to ask your Realtor about access to public transportation, possible traffic issues (when and where rush hour is an issue), the location of grocery stores and other types of essential shopping, whether there's a home owners' association and how effectively it functions, and whether you will be responsible for snow removal and street upkeep. You'll also want to find out about the municipality or incorporated area. What kinds of emergency services are available? Are the firefighters salaried professionals or volunteers? Must you pay dues to benefit from emergency services? How large are the local police and fire services, what geographic area do they cover, and how fast or slow is their usual response time? Are there hydrants in the neighborhood, or must water be pumped or trucked in to fight a fire? Can you register to get alerts by phone, text, or e-mail when there is a local Amber Alert or another emergency?

Here are some resources to check out:

- Access to food delivery: This could be important if you have a medical emergency. You can check to see if Meals On Wheels (mowaa.org) or MANNA (mannapa.org) operate in the area.

- The quality of the school system: Psk12.com, School Data Direct (schooldatadirect.org), SchoolMatters.com, and *U.S. News & World Report* offer rankings of public schools, high schools, and colleges. If you plan to homeschool or you have a child with special needs, you'll want to check with the state and local school district to find out about support, resources, and accreditation and registration requirements.

- The quality of local utilities: Ask your Realtor whether cable, DSL, and other utilities are available, especially if you are considering moving to a rural area. Find out what type of heating (natural gas, propane, electric) the house uses and whether the electricity is reliable (does it go out frequently during storms?).

- The quality of local hospitals: Various Internet sites offer hospital report cards and accreditation ratings. Examples include ipro.org/hospitals, ConsumerReportsHealth.org, and HealthGrades (healthgrades.com).

- Whether the home is in a flood zone: FloodSmart.gov is a site run by the National Flood Insurance Program that will help you determine whether a home is in a flood area. It also helps you find agents who sell supplemental flood insurance.

Information You Might Want to Know About Another Person

You can find out a lot about a person just by searching online. For instance, you can learn the following:

- If there's a dangerous dog in the house: Virginia has a dangerous-dog registry (virginia.gov/vdacs_dd/public/cgi-bin/public.cgi). Other states may follow Virginia's lead. Check to see if your state has.

- If any of your neighbors are convicted sex offenders: Every state has a sex-offender registry. You can find links to each of these registries through the FBI's site: fbi.gov/scams-safety/registry.

- If he or she has abused animals: Suffolk County, New York, started a registry of animal offenders, and some other states might follow suit. Check to see if your state has such as registry.

- What types of information someone has been posting online: Do an Internet search to see what someone has posted on Twitter, blogs, and other publicly accessible online forums.

Information You Might Want Before You Travel

Gathering the right knowledge before you travel can help you avoid certain types of problems and be better prepared to handle others. Here are some resources you might find particularly helpful:

- The U.S. Centers for Disease Control and Prevention (cdc.gov) offers information on flu outbreaks and other health issues. This information might allow you to avoid areas where certain diseases are common or severe, or to take steps to prevent catching them.

- The U.S. Department of Homeland Security (dhs.gov) has a security-advisory system on its site. This system gives you a color-coded national threat level and detailed and up-to-date information about what is and is not allowed on airlines.

- The U.S. Department of State (state.gov) issues travel warnings and alerts. It also lists helpful information such as the location of U.S. embassies in various countries. You can also find crime and security information on various countries and details about the quality of their medical systems. And you can register with them when you travel.

• You can find information on weather conditions (such as an approaching hurricane) at weather.com or, within the United States, at the National Weather Service site (weather.gov).

How to Be a Better Myth Buster

Throughout this book, you've learned about many common myths that tend to get people into trouble. The best way to avoid becoming a victim of misinformation is to arm yourself with credible information. I've listed some resources here to help you do just that:

- National Institutes of Health (nih.gov): For all types of health information, and specifically information about mental-health and personality disorders.
- Centers for Disease Control and Prevention (cdc.gov): For all types of health information.
- WebWiseKids.org: For information about cybersafety and Internet bullying.
- National Behavioral Intervention Team Association (nabita.org): For details on how to enroll your workplace, school, or campus in its program.
- National Center for Missing and Exploited Children (missingkids.com): For all types of information about missing children.
- America's Missing: Broadcast Emergency Response (amberalert.gov): For all types of information about missing children.

Notes

1. U.S. Department of Justice, Federal Bureau of Investigation. *Workplace Violence: Issues in Response*. Washington, D.C., 2004.
2. C. S. Nave, R. A. Sherman, D. C. Funder, S. E. Hampson, and L. R. Goldberg, "On the Contextual Independence of Personality: Teacher's Assessments Predict Directly Observed Behavior After Four Decades," *Social Psychological and Personality Science* 1 (2010): 327–34.
3. R. Hare, *Without Conscience: The Disturbing World of the Psychopaths Among Us*. New York: Guilford Press, 1999.
4. J. Reid Meloy, *Violent Attachments* (Northvale, NJ: Jason Aronson Inc., 1992).
5. Mental Health America, *American Opinions on Mental Health Issues* (Alexandria, VA: NMHA, 1999).
6. Reference approved by MSNBC, which taped this interview for use in *Criminal Mindscape*.
7. P. Babiak, C. Neumann, R. Hare, "Corporate Psychopathy: Talking the Walk," *Behavioral Science and the Law* 28 (2010): 174–93.
8. Paul Babiak, *Snakes in Suits* (New York: ReganBooks, 2006).
9. Mary Ellen O'Toole, *The School Shooter: A Threat Assessment Perspective* (Quantico, VA: FBI Academy, 2000).

Index

Table of Contents

CHAPTER 1

Scope and Overview

CHAPTER 2

Preconception Stage: Established Law

CHAPTER 3

Preconception Stage: Emerging Theories of Liability

II. WRONGFUL CONCEPTION AND WRONGFUL PREGNANCY

CHAPTER 4

CONCEPTION STAGE

CHAPTER 6

Prenatal Stage: Emerging Theories of Liability

CHAPTER 1

Scope and Overview

I. [§1.1] SCOPE

This text is a compilation of important legal issues and theories associated with cases arising from the process of human procreation. The coverage of the subject matter focuses primarily on the legal aspects of birth actions, but it also treats medically related considerations in these actions.

The treatment of relevant legal issues and theories are organized according to the chronological stages in the birth process: preconception; conception; and prenatal. This organization format was chosen for the text because it allows the practitioner to isolate the stage of procreation in which the case arose, turn to the pertinent chronological medical-legal portion of the text, and identify the significant issues and theories involved. The principal question the practitioner needs to ask in considering birth and pregnancy cases, therefore, is at what stage of development did the case arise.

Moreover, the chronological steps of the birth process are further divided into treatments of *established law* and *emerging theories*. The established law portions of the text consider birth and pregnancy issues that have received significant legal attention, whereas the emerging theory portions discuss new theories of recovery, and novel, but soon to be everyday, legal issues relating to the procreation process.

The treatment of the title subject is related to the birth and pregnancy processes, and therefore a number of subjects fall outside the scope of the book. Issues dealing with the actual event of the child leaving the mother's womb, as well as neonatal subjects have been excluded except to the extent that they have an impact on issues relating to the preconception, conception, and prenatal stages of development.

II. [§1.2] SUMMARY

There are three major stages in the process of human procreation: (1) *preconception*, the time frame up to, but not including, the actual conception of the new human life; (2) *conception*, the time frame when fertilization takes place and the decisions are made regarding whether to seek fertilization; and (3) *prenatal*, the time frame from post-conception to the time at which the child actually leaves the mother's body. Because of the significance and chronological importance of these physiological steps, this text has been organized to coincide with these steps. This textual organization is logical because it focuses attention on issues a practitioner will encounter in handling a birth case, and it allows the practitioner to turn directly to the chronological stage of the procreation process at which the case arose. Moreover, within each segment of the text, the legal subjects are divided into the respective headings or chapters of established law or emerging theories.

The treatment of the preconception stage of development considers in detail the established law and emerging theories relating to preconception cases. Preconception established law, Chapter 2, focuses on cases and theories that have been developed and defined, but which arise in the narrow legal area, relating to birth, that centers on factual situations preceding the conception stage.

Subjects treated within Chapter 2 include surgical sterilization and contraception. Both issues are significant since the United States Supreme Court has held that a person has a constitutional right to control his or her reproductive functions and system. There is textual consideration of liability for surgical sterilization and the sterilization of incompetent persons is also discussed. Under the contraception division of Chapter 2, the liabilities of the manufacturer or seller of the contraceptive and the prescribing physician are considered, and the limitation on actions issue is covered. Finally, Chapter 2 includes a sample complaint/petition for the initiation of a suit based on injury caused by a contraceptive.

The emerging theories of liability portion of the preconception stage, found in Chapter 3, focuses attention on new theories of action. The Chapter begins with treatment of preconception torts, and discusses various bases of liability associated with preconception torts. In addition, the subjects of wrongful conception and wrongful pregnancy, recently defined theories of liability involving unsuccessful sterilization or contraceptive procedures which result in the birth of an unplanned child, are discussed in detail. These new theories of liability are considered in terms of tort and contract actions, and what types of damages can be recovered. In addition, Chapter 3 contains a discussion of relevant limitation on actions issues arising in wrongful conception and wrongful pregnancy cases, and a sample wrongful conception complaint.

The next stage of human development is the conception stage, discussed in Chapter 4. The Chapter divides the conception stage into three main topics beginning with artificial insemination. Artificial insemination is the instrumental injection of semen into the uterus to induce pregnancy. This division treats the subjects of the rights and obligations of the particular parties involved, medical considerations, and legislative considerations. The second main division focuses on *in vitro*, or test tube, fertilization. Issues discussed within this division are relevant constitutional considerations and civil liability for the destruction of a test tube conceptus. Finally, Chapter 4 has a division centering on surrogate motherhood. Surrogate motherhood is the legal process by which an infertile person, or couple, hires a fertile woman to carry the first party's fetus to term, and then to give the child to the first party, generally in consideration for monetary payment. The surrogate motherhood division also includes a sample surrogate mother contract that details specifically how to frame a contract between the respective parties.

The prenatal stage of development considers established law and emerging theories of liability. The established law chapter, Chapter 5, focuses on the topics of abortion and feticide, prenatal injury actions, and miscellaneous rights and entitlements of the fetus. The abortion division considers consent issues, the roles played by physicians, hospitals, and abortion clinics, the effect of Medicaid, and liability for feticide. The prenatal injury division discusses causes of action for prenatal injuries to the fetus, injury to the parents caused by the potential harm to the fetus, and the wrongful death of the fetus. Finally, various miscellaneous rights and entitlements regarding the fetus are treated including whether the fetus is a person under the Civil Rights Act, 42 USC §1983, and the Fourteenth Amendment, and the right of the fetus to medical services or treatment.

The emerging theories discussion in Chapter 6 covers four emerging theories of liability: wrongful birth, an action brought by the parents of an unhealthy child caused by the negligence of the defendant; wrongful life, an action brought by an unhealthy child for its birth caused by the negligence of the defendant; dissatisfied life, an action brought by an illegitimate child for damages relating to its status as a bastard; and diethylstilbestrol related liability. Within the wrongful birth division, topics such as the elements of the cause of action, damages and a sample complaint are covered. Regarding wrongful life, Chapter 6 discusses questions regarding the recognition of the cause of action and presents example complaints. The dissatisfied life division covers policy considerations relating to whether to allow the action, the nature of the injury, and damages sought. The diethylstilbestrol related liability division covers the background of these actions, the causation-in-fact manufacturer identity issue, limitation on actions issues, and contains an example complaint.

III. [§1.3] BACKGROUND

Within the past few decades there has been a significant growth in the body of law surrounding the processes of birth and pregnancy, and the time period associated with these processes. It is no longer unusual to have legal actions that involve birth and pregnancy and the attendant preconception, conception, and prenatal issues.

There are a number of reasons for the growing legal attention to the subjects of birth and pregnancy. First, social mores of American society have changed in recent years. Subjects such as birth control, abortion, and the prenatal condition of the unborn are widely discussed. The mass media have made the subjects less mysterious and more understandable. In addition, recent advances in medical science have brought about significant changes to the physiological aspects of the birth process. For example, the procedure of artificial insemination is routinely being used by many couples heretofore unable to conceive a child. By means of genetic testing and counseling, parents have a better idea than ever before about the health of their prenatal infant, and sterilization operations are being performed on many men and women. In short, the advances in medical science have reshaped the way American society thinks about birth.

But along with the changing mores and the changes in medical science, many legal controversies have arisen about the birth process and the steps leading up to a child actually leaving the mother's womb. These controversies began to show up in the legal system during the 1960s and early 1970s. In the last few years, more cases than ever before have been litigated on birth and pregnancy issues, and the legal system has begun to be faced with new and novel causes of action associated with these cases.

At the preconception stage of procreation there have been numerous cases involving defective sterilization operations. Typically the facts are that the parents agree to limit the size of their family. One consents to be sterilized, and both spouses assume the sterilization has been done correctly. However, at some future time the wife becomes pregnant, and the couple is faced with an unplanned child. Traditionally, the courts would not allow recovery under such circumstances because the joy of having a child was deemed to outweigh any damage there might be. Today, this is not always the ruling, and some courts have allowed a new cause of action called wrongful conception to be pursued. Under this theory the parents assert that they should be compensated for the unplanned child. Finally, a few cases have been decided that focus on the issue of stating a cause of action for preconception torts. In these cases, an injury to the mother has later caused injury to an unborn child who was not conceived at the time of the original injury. Some courts recognize this cause of action, while others do not. Nonetheless, this is an issue that will continue to receive considerable court attention.

The conception stage of procreation has also been the subject of increasing legal consideration. Subjects such as the legal consequences of artificial insemination, *in vitro* fertilization, and surrogate motherhood are regularly receiving judicial and legislative consideration.

There has been significant litigation on cases that find their beginning in the prenatal stage of development. For example, courts have recently begun to recognize two new causes of action involving planned, but unhealthy children. Here what typically happens is that either a doctor fails to diagnose a deformed or diseased unborn infant when he has the ability to do so, or a genetic test is negligently performed or mistakenly interpreted. The result is a planned, but unhealthy infant. This is called either wrongful birth or wrongful life. In a wrongful birth action, the parents of the baby bring suit for damages caused by a negligent third party. A growing number of courts have recognized this cause of action. However, there is a wide divergence among the courts that have recognized the cause of action as to the appropriate amount of damages to be awarded in such cases. In a wrongful life action, the unhealthy infant brings the action for his or her damages.

In addition, there are other significant pregnancy and birth issues that involve established law. These subjects include surgical sterilization and the liability for the negligent performance thereof, and liability relating to injury caused by the use of contraceptives.

In short, the growing number of birth and pregnancy cases is causing judicial consideration of new and novel causes of action, while established legal issues in this area continue to be litigated. The law in this area is far from being settled; it is just beginning to develop.

CHAPTER 2

Preconception Stage: Established Law

I. SURGICAL STERILIZATION

I. SURGICAL STERILIZATION

A. In General

1. [§2.1] Definitions: Contraceptive, Eugenic, and Therapeutic Sterilizations

Sterilization operations may be broadly classified as contraceptive, eugenic, or therapeutic. Contraceptive sterilizations are usually elective medical procedures which are primarily performed to prevent further childbearing, often for socio-economic reasons. Such operations normally take the form of a tubal ligation in the female or a vasectomy in the male. Eugenic sterilizations, also described as negative eugenics, purport to limit the population of physically and mentally impaired individuals. EUGENIC STERILIZATION STATUTES: A CONSTITUTIONAL RE-EVALUATION, 14 Journal of Family Law 280 (1975). Eugenic sterilizations may be mandated by statute. See, for example, *Buck v Bell*, 274 US 200, 47 SCt 584, 74 LE 1000

(1927), where the United States Supreme Court upheld a state's compulsory, eugenic sterilization statute as applied to an institutionalized mentally defective adult female. Sterilizations on eugenic grounds may, however, be performed without statutory authority or mandate on the consent of the parents or guardians of incompetent persons. [See §§2.22-2.26.] Therapeutic sterilizations, like the contraceptive ones, are voluntary in nature and are performed for reasons of the physical or mental health of the persons to be sterilized. [As to the constitutional permissibility of sterilization procedures, see §2.2.]

Cases involving the alleged negligent performance of a sterilization operation which result in the birth of an unplanned child are discussed in §§3.8-3.51, regarding wrongful pregnancy or wrongful conception. In these cases the plaintiff-parents seek recovery for damages including the costs of the pregnancy and birth and the costs of raising the unplanned child.

2. [§2.2] Background and Constitutionality

The advent of substantial statutory and case law involving *voluntary* surgical sterilizations is a recent development. Only in the last few decades have voluntary sterilizations been performed in large numbers. In an early Minnesota case, *Christensen v Thornby*, 192 Mn 123, 255 NW 620 (1934), the state Supreme Court expressly held that surgical sterilizations were not contrary to public policy and that an action, if properly pleaded, could be maintained against a physician for the improper or negligent performance of such an operation. In addition, in *Shaheen v Knight*, 11 PaDC2d 41 (1957), a Pennsylvania county court held that a contract between a physician and a patient calling for the physician to sterilize the patient for contraceptive reasons was not void by reason of public policy. Beginning with these initial cases, courts have held that voluntary sterilization operations for contraceptive and/or therapeutic reasons are not against public policy, and that liability can be assessed against a proper defendant, under the appropriate facts, for the negligent performance or non-performance of a sterilization operation for contraceptive or therapeutic purposes. See also *Jessin v Cty of Shasta*, 79 CaR 359, 274 CaA2d 737 (1969). [For definitions of contraceptive or therapeutic sterilizations, see §2.1.]

The history of involuntary, eugenic sterilizations [defined in §2.1] dates back to the 19th century, when the only known surgical procedure therefor was castration. Statutes commonly subjected various types of criminals to compulsory sterilization. EUGENIC STERILIZATION STATUTES: A CONSTITUTIONAL RE-EVALUATION, 14 Journal of Family Law 280 (1975). [For a compilation of state eugenic sterilization statutes, see §2.3.] In *State v*

Feilen, 70 Wa 65, 126 P 75 (1912), the Washington Supreme Court rejected a challenge to a criminal sterilization statute under the Eighth Amendment and held that it did not constitute a cruel and unusual punishment. A federal district court, however, interpreted a similar state statute, requiring the sterilization of certain criminals, as being violative of the Eighth Amendment. *Davis v Berry*, 216 F 413 (SD Ia 1914). In a civil context, the United States Supreme Court, in *Buck v Bell*, 274 US 200, 47 SCt 584, 74 LE 1000 (1927), upheld a state statute authorizing the compulsory, eugenic sterilization of an institutionalized mentally impaired adult female whose mother and daughter were also described by the Court as feeble-minded. The Court rejected due process and equal protection challenges to the state's sterilization order, entered pursuant to a judgment of the state Supreme Court [143 Va 310, 130 SE 516 (1926)], and, in the words of Mr. Justice Holmes, held that "Three generations of imbeciles are enough." 274 US at 207. However, at least one court has said that compulsory, eugenic sterilization would have to overcome a much higher constitutional hurdle today. See *In re Grady*, 85 NJ 235, 426 A2d 474 (1981). Specifically, it has been suggested that compulsory, eugenic sterilization statutes encroach upon the individual's fundamental right of procreation and must therefore be held to the standard of satisfying a compelling state interest; otherwise, they may be considered constitutionally infirm. 14 Journal of Family Law 280. *See generally* R. K. Sherlock and R. D. Sherlock, STERILIZING THE RETARDED: CONSTITUTIONAL, STATUTORY AND POLICY ALTERNATIVES, 60 North Carolina LR 943 (1982); STERILIZATION, RETARDATION AND PARENTAL AUTHORITY, 1978 Brigham Young LR 380.

The surgical sterilization of incompetent persons based on the consent of their parents or guardians, and by order of a proper court, is considered in §§2.22—2.26.

3. [§2.3] Survey of State Sterilization Statutes

Twenty-four states have statutes providing for compulsory, eugenic sterilization. The eugenic sterilization statutes are: ALA. CODE tit. 45, §243 (1958); ARIZ. REV. STAT. ANN. §§36-531 to 540 (1956); CAL. PENAL CODE §§645, 2670 (West 1970); CAL. WELF. & INST'NS CODE §7254 (West 1972); CONN. GEN. STAT. ANN. §17-19 (1973 P. P.); DEL. CODE ANN. tit. 16, §§5701-5705 (1953); IDAHO CODE §§39-3901 to -3910 (1961); IND. ANN. STAT. §§22-1601 to -1618 (Burns 1964); IOWA CODE ANN. §§145.1-.22 (1972); ME. REV. STAT. ANN. tit. 34, §§2461-2468 (1965); MICH. COMP. LAWS ANN. §§720.301-.310 (1968); MINN. STAT. ANN. §§256.07-.10 (1971); MISS. CODE ANN. §§41-95-1 to -19 (1972); MONT. REV. STAT. ANN. §§69-6401 to -6406 (1970); N. H. REV. STAT. ANN. §174:1 (Supp. 1973); N. H. REV. STAT. ANN. §§174:2-:14 (1964); N. C. GEN. STAT. §§35-36 to -49, -51 to -52, -54, -56 (Cum. Supp.

1973); N. C. GEN. STAT. §§35.40.1, -43, -45, -47, -49, -51 to -56 (1966); OKLA. STAT. ANN. tit. 43A, §§341-346 (1954); ORE. REV. STAT. §§436.010-.150 (1973); S. C. CODE ANN. §§32-671 to -680 (1968); S. D. COMPILED LAWS ANN. §§27-11-1 to 06, -17-1 to -34 (1967); UTAH CODE ANN. §§64-10-1 to -7 (1968); VT. STAT. ANN. tit. 18, §§8701-8704 (1968); VA. CODE ANN. §§37.1-156 to -171 (1970); W. VA. CODE ANN. §§27-16-1 to -5 (Cum. Supp. 1974); and WIS. STAT. ANN. §46.12 (1957).

The following table provides a detailed analysis of the various state compulsory, eugenic sterilization statutes.

State	Basis For Statute			Persons Subject						Type Of Proceeding			Who Initiates Proceeding	
	Genetic	Environmental	Criminal	Mental Defective	Mentally Ill	Epileptic	Other	Institutionalized	At Large	Court	Board Hearing	Examination	Superintendent	Other
AL[2]								X					X	
AZ	X	X		X	X	X	X	X			X		X	
CA	X		X[3]	X	X			X			X		X	
CN		X						X		X			X	
DE			X	X	X	X		X	X		X			X[10]
ID		X		X[11]				X		X				X[12]
IN	X	X		X	X	X		X			X		X	
IA	X	X	X	X	X	X	X[13]	X			X		X	X[14]
ME	X			X	X			X			X[17]	X[17]		X[18]
MI	X	X	X	X	X	X	X[20]	X	X	X[21]		X[21]	X	X[22]
MN				X	X			X				X[24]	X	
MS	X	X		X	X	X		X			X		X	
MT	X	X		X				X	X		X		X	X[26]
NH	X	X		X	X			X			X		X	
NC	X	X		X	X			X	X		X		X	X[28]
OK	X	X	X	X	X	X		X			X		X	
OR	X	X	X	X	X			X	X		X			X[31]
SC	X	X	X	X	X	X		X			X		X	
SD	X[34]	X[34]		X	X		X[13]	X	X[35]		X[36]	X[34]	X[37]	X[37]
UT		X	X[41]	X	X	X		X			X		X	
VT	X	X		X	X							X[42]		X[43]
VA	X	X		X	X			X			X			
WV	X	X		X	X			X	X	X				X[45]
WS			X	X	X			X					X[46]	X

State		Notice						Consent			Type Of Operation			
	SUBJECT PRESENT	Subject	Kin	Guardian	RIGHT TO COUNSEL	RIGHT TO APPEAL	COMPULSORY	Subject	Kin	Guardian	Vasectomy	Salpingectomy	Asexualization	CASTRATION PROHIBITED
AL							X							
AZ	X			X	X	X	X				X	X		X
CA	X[4]	X	X	X		X	X	X[5]	X[5]	X[5]	X	X	X[6]	
CN			X[7]	X[7]					X[8]	X[8]	X	X[9]		
DE			X	X			X							
ID	X		X	X	X	X			X	X				X
IN	X	X	X	X	X	X	X				X	X		
IA	X	X	X[15]	X[15]	X	X	X	X[16]	X[16]	X[16]				X
ME		X	X	X	X[19]	X	X	X[16]	X[16]	X[16]	X	X[9]		
MI	X	X	X	X	X	X	X	X[23]	X[23]	X[23]	X	X		
MN	X							X[25]	X[25]	X[25]	X	X[9]		
MS	X	X	X	X		X	X				X	X		X
MT	X	X	X	X				X[27]	X[27]	X[27]				
NH	X	X		X		X	X				X	X		X
NC	X	X	X	X		X	X		X[29]	X[29]			X[30]	
OK	X	X		X	X	X	X				X	X		X
OR	X	X		X[32]	X	X		X[33]	X[33]	X[33]				
SC	X	X	X	X	X	X	X							X
SD	X[38]	X	X	X	X[39]	X		X[40]	X[40]	X[40]				
UT	X	X		X	X	X	X				X	X	X[30]	
VT	X							X[44]	X[44]	X[44]	X	X		
VA	X	X		X		X	X				X	X		X
WV	X	X			X	X	X							X
WS			X	X			X							

NOTES TO TABLE

[1] The references, above, are summaries of the present eugenic sterilization statutes. If a category is not marked for a particular statute, it means that either the statute specifically excludes the category or no mention of it is made.

[2] *In re Opinion of the Justices*, 230 Ala. 543, 162 So. 123 (1935) (advisory opinion), declared the statute, ALA. CODE tit. 45, §243 (1958), unconstitutional. It has, however, never been repealed.

[3] One convicted of carnal abuse of a female under the age of 10 years is subject to sterilization in the punitive sense. CAL. PENAL CODE §645 (West 1970).

[4] One who is classified as a moral or sexual degenerate, and is a recidivist for two sex crimes or any three other crimes, has no right to attend the proceeding. CAL. PENAL CODE §2670 (West 1970).

[5] Anyone given notice may consent, but the statute is compulsory in the absence of consent. CAL. PENAL CODE §2670 (West 1970).

[6] One who is classified as a criminal and recidivist for two sex crimes or any three other crimes, provided he is a moral or sexual degenerate, is subject to asexualization. CAL. PENAL CODE §2670 (West 1970).

[7] If there is no next of kin or guardian to be given notice, the notice is given to the board of trustees of the institution where the subject is confined. CONN. GEN. STAT. ANN. §17-19 (1973 P.P.).

[8] If no legal guardian or next of kin can be found, the board of trustees of the institution in which the subject is confined may consent. CONN. GEN. STAT. ANN. §17-19 (1973 P.P.).

[9] The female sterilization surgical procedure called for is similar to the salpingectomy. It results in an interruption of the passage of the ova through the fallopian tubes to the uterus. CONN. GEN. STAT. ANN. §17-19 (1973 P.P.) (tubal surgery); ME. REV. STAT. ANN. tit. 34, §2461 (1965) (fallectomy); MINN. STAT. ANN. §256.08 (1971) (tubectomy).

[10] If the subject is institutionalized, the board of control of the institution initiates the proceeding. If the subject is at large, the State Board of Trustees of the Delaware State Hospital initiates the proceeding. DEL. CODE ANN. tit. 16, §§5701-5702 (1953).

[11] The classifications used by the statute are "mental and organical retardates". IDAHO CODE §39-3901 (1961).

[12] A parent or guardian of the subject or an administrator of the state board of health may file the petition for sterilization. IDAHO CODE §39-3903 (1961).

[13] Syphilitic. IOWA CODE ANN. §145.2 (1972); S.D. COMPILED LAWS ANN. §27-11-2 (1967).

[14] A member of the state board of eugenics may initiate the proceeding. IOWA CODE ANN. §145.2 (1972).

[15] If the subject is found to be incompetent then notice is given to the next of kin or guardian. IOWA CODE ANN. §145.11 (1972).

[16] If the subject is found to be competent he may consent, if not, the next of kin or guardian may consent. IOWA CODE ANN. §145.14 (1972); ME. REV. STAT. ANN. tit. 34, §2461 (1965). If there is no consent the statute is compulsory. IOWA CODE ANN. §145.9 (1972); ME. REV. STAT. ANN. tit. 34, §2462 (1965).

[17] If there is consent to the sterilization then a council of physicians may order the operation. If there is no consent then a hearing is held by the Department of Health. ME. REV. STAT. ANN. tit. 34, §§2461, 2463 (1965).

[18] The medical staff of the institution containing the subject initiates the proceeding. ME. REV. STAT. ANN. tit. 34, §2462 (1965).

[19] If there is no next of kin or guardian, then an attorney will be appointed. ME. REV. STAT. ANN. tit. 34, §2464 (1965).

[20] Sexual perverts. MICH. COMP. LAWS ANN. §720.301 (1968).

[21] If there is no consent, there is a court proceeding. MICH. COMP. LAWS ANN. §720.303 (1968). If there is consent, then only a medical examination is necessary. MICH. COMP. LAWS ANN. §720.304 (1968).

[22] The next of kin or legal guardian may initiate the proceeding. MICH. COMP. LAWS ANN. §720.305 (1968).

[23] The subject may consent if competent. If he is not, then he still must give written consent, but along with a guardian. If there is no consent the statute is compulsory. MICH. COMP. LAWS ANN. §720.304 (1968).

[24] An examination is conducted by the superintendent, physician and psychologists. MINN. STAT. ANN. §256.08 (1971).

[25] The subject and next of kin or guardian must consent if the subject is insane. MINN. STAT. ANN. §256.08 (1971). If the subject is feeble-minded, the next of kin or guardian may consent. MINN. STAT. ANN. §256.07 (1971).

[26] An application for sterilization may be made by or on behalf of the subject. MONT. REV. CODES ANN. §69-6403 (1970).

[27] The subject and his parents or guardian must consent. MONT. REV. CODES ANN. §69-6404 (1970).

[28] If the subject is at large or institutionalized his next of kin or guardian may consent. N.C. GEN. STAT. §35-39 (Cum. Supp. 1973).

[29] The next of kin or legal guardian may consent, but if there is no consent the statute is compulsory. N.C. GEN. STAT. §35-39 (Cum. Supp. 1973).

[30] The statute provides for sterilization by vasectomy, salpingectomy, or asexualization. N.C. GEN. STAT. §35-44 (Cum. Supp. 1973); UTAH CODE ANN. §64-10-7 (1968).

[31] Any two persons or any licensed physician may initiate the proceeding. ORE. REV. STAT. §436.025 (1973).

[32] Notice is given to the subject's public defender. ORE. REV. STAT. §436.041 (1973).

[33] The subject may consent if competent. If incompetent, the subject still must consent, but with the consent of his next of kin or legal guardian also. ORE. REV. STAT. §436.110 (1973).

[34] If the subject is afflicted with an inheritable form of mental illness, the applicable statute has a genetic basis. S.D. COMPILED LAWS ANN. §27-11-7 (1967). If the subject is retarded, the applicable statute has an environmental basis. S.D. COMPILED LAWS ANN. §27-17-4 (1967).

[35] The statute applies to retardates at large. S.D. COMPILED LAWS ANN. §27-11-2 (1967).

[36] If the subject is mentally ill and institutionalized the sterilization may be performed on the decision of the superintendent with the support of the medical staff. S.D. COMPILED LAWS ANN. §27-11-3 (1967). If the subject is retarded, institutionalized or not, a hearing is held by the County Commission for the Mentally Retarded. S.D. COMPILED LAWS ANN. §27-17-3 (1967).

[37] If the subject is mentally ill and institutionalized the superintendent initiates the proceeding. S.D. COMPILED LAWS ANN. §27-11-3 (1967). If the subject is retarded any resident of the state may initiate the proceeding. S.D. COMPILED LAWS ANN. §27-17-4 (1967).

[38] Only a retardate may attend the proceeding. S.D. COMPILED LAWS ANN. §27-17-10 (1967).

[39] Only a retardate is provided with counsel. S.D. COMPILED LAWS ANN. §27-17-10 (1967).

[40] Consent is required by the subject and his next of kin or guardian, but if no next of kin or guardian can be located, the subject's consent alone is sufficient. S.D. COMPILED LAWS ANN. §§27-11-1, 27-17-2 (1967).

[41] This classification includes only criminals with degenerate sexual tendencies. UTAH CODE ANN. §64-10-1 (1968).

[42] An examination by two physicians or surgeons is required. VT. STAT. ANN. §8702 (1968).

[43] If the subject is found competent enough to consent to the sterilization he may initiate the proceeding; if not competent, then his next of kin or guardian may initiate the proceeding. VT. STAT. ANN. §8702 (1968).

[44] If the subject is competent enough to consent, he may do so; if not competent, then his next of kin or guardian must consent, but the subject must still voluntarily submit to the operation. VT. STAT. ANN. §8702 (1968).

[45] The parent, guardian, committee, or authority responsible for the subject may initiate the proceeding. W.VA. CODE ANN. §27-16-1 (Cum. Supp. 1974).

[46] An examination by a surgeon and psychiatrists is required to determine if sterilization is needed. WIS. STAT. ANN. §46.12 (1957).

The statutory survey and analytical tables appearing in this section were reprinted, by permission, from EUGENIC STERILIZATION STATUTES: A CONSTITUTIONAL RE-EVALUATION, 14 Journal of Family Law 280 (1975).

One should distinguish eugenic sterilization statutes from those sterilization statutes which are wholly voluntary in nature and which are essentially contraceptive and therapeutic, and not eugenic in nature. A number of states have voluntary sterilization statutes. A representative sample of these statutes follows.

North Carolina has two voluntary sterilization statutes. One is entitled "Operation lawful upon request of married person or person over 18," found at N.C. GEN. STAT. §90-271 (1981), which reads as follows:

> It shall be lawful for any physician or surgeon licensed by this State when so requested by any person 18 years of age or over, or less than 18 years of age if legally married, to perform upon such person a surgical interruption of vas deferens or Fallopian tubes, as the case may be, provided a request in writing is made by such person prior to the performance of such surgical operation, and provided, further, that prior to or at the time of such request a full and reasonable medical explanation is given by such physician or surgeon to such person as to the meaning and consequences of such operation; and provided, further, that the surgical interruption of Fallopian tubes is performed in a hospital or ambulatory surgical facility licensed by the Department of Human Resources. (1963, c. 600; 1965, cc. 108, 941; 1971, c. 1231, s. 1; 1973, c. 476, s. 152; c. 998, s. 1; 1977, c. 7; 1979, c. 728.)

The second North Carolina voluntary sterilization statute, located at N.C. GEN. STAT. §90-272 (1981), provides for "Operation on unmarried minor." It states:

> Any such physician or surgeon may perform a surgical interruption of vas deferens or Fallopian tubes upon any unmarried person under the age of 18 years when so requested in writing by such minor and in accordance with the conditions and requirements set forth in G.S. 90-271, provided that the juvenile court of the county wherein such minor resides, upon petition of the parent or parents, if they be living, or the guardian or next friend of such minor, shall determine that the operation is in the best interest of such minor and shall enter an order authorizing the physician or surgeon to perform such operation. (1963, c. 600; 1971, c. 1231, s. 1.)

New Mexico has two statutes which relate to voluntary sterilizations. The first, "Sterilization — Consent of abandoning spouse unnecessary," is located at N.M. GEN. STAT. §12-3-43 (1978). It states:

> Any person, otherwise capable of consenting to medical treatment, need not obtain the consent of his spouse for his voluntary medical sterilization if such person has been abandoned by his spouse. History: Laws 1971, ch. 14, §3; 1973, ch. 266, §1.

The other New Mexico statute, "Special qualifications prohibited," at N.M. GEN. STAT. §12-34-14 (1978), states:

> No hospital which permits any operation that results in sterilization to be performed therein or medical staff of such hospital shall require any person upon whom a sterilization operation is to be performed to meet any special qualifications which are not imposed on individuals seeking other types of operations in the hospital. History: Laws 1973, ch. 359, §14.

Oregon has one statutory section dealing with voluntary sterilizations. This statute, entitled "Voluntary sterilization authorized," is located at ORE. REV. STAT. §435.305, and states:

> (1) A person may be sterilized by appropriate means upon his request and upon the advice of a physician licensed by the State Board of Medical Examiners.
>
> (2) No physician or hospital may be held liable for performing a sterilization without obtaining the consent of the spouse of the person sterilized.
>
> (3) Free clinics to sterilize males under subsection (1) of this section may be conducted as a part of the program provided for in ORS 435.205. (1967 c. 441 §15; 1969 c. 31 §1; 1973 c. 479 §1; 1975 c. 591 §1.)

Virginia has two statutes concerning voluntary sterilizations. The first, VA. CODE ANN. §54-325.9 (Cum. Supp. 1981), "Sterilization operations for persons eighteen years or older capable of informed consent," states:

> It shall be lawful for any physician licensed by the State Board of Medicine to perform a vasectomy, salpingectomy, or other surgical sexual sterilization procedure on any person eighteen years of age or older, who has the capacity to give informed consent, when so requested in writing by such person. Prior to or at the time of such request, a full, reasonable, and comprehensible medical explanation as to the meaning and consequences of such an operation and as to alternative methods or contraception shall be given by the

> physician to the person requesting the operation. No such operation shall be performed prior to thirty days from the date of the written request therefor upon a person who has not previously become the natural or adoptive parent of a child. (1981, c. 454.)

The second statute, VA. CODE ANN. §54-325.14 (Cum. Supp. 1981), "No liability for non-negligent performance of operation," states:

> Subject to the rules of law applicable generally to negligence, no physician licensed by the State Board of Medicine shall be either civilly or criminally liable by reason of having performed a vasectomy, salpingectomy, or other surgical sexual sterilization procedure upon any person in this Commonwealth as authorized by §§54-325.9 through 54-325.11. (1981, c. 454.)

B. Liability for Surgical Sterilization

1. Consent

a. [§2.4] Necessity for Consent

A physician performing a surgical sterilization is no more free to act without the patient's consent than in any other medical context [see *Davidson v Shirley*, 616 F2d 224 (5th Cir 1980); *Kelton v District of Columbia*, 413 A2d 919 (DC 1980)], unless the sterilization surgery is authorized pursuant to a statute or court order for compulsory, eugenic sterilization, [see §§2.1, 2.3], or a medical emergency requires immediate surgical treatment [see §2.5]. A surgeon who performs an operation without the consent of the patient, or the consent of another authorized person, commits a trespass on the body of the patient in the nature of a battery and may therefore be subject to liability for damages. *Beck v Lovell*, 361 So2d 245 (La 1978). Moreover, the often irreversible consequences of surgical sterilization make the patient's consent particularly important. See, e.g.,*Hundley v St Francis Hosp*, 161 CaA2d 800, 327 P2d 131 (1958); *Rogers v Lumbermen's Mutual Casualty Co*, 119 So2d 649 (La 1960); *Sutter v Biggs,* 377 Mi 80, 139 NW2d 684 (1966); *Rothe v Hull*, 352 Mo 926, 180 SW2d 7 (1944).

Physicians undertaking to surgically sterilize an individual must first take special care to obtain the patient's informed, intelligent consent to the operation and all of its potential effects. [As to informed consent, see §2.8.] There are circumstances in which a patient's consent may be held implied [see §2.12], but the clearly preferable course is for the physician to obtain advance specific consent to the surgical sterilization, whether the effect of sterility is intended or only a reasonably likely incident of the surgery.

Generally, the patient must be legally capable of giving the required consent [see §2.6], or the person acting on the patient's behalf must be fully authorized to do so [see §§2.5, 2.6], and the scope of the consent given must extend to the particular surgical procedure performed [see §2.10]. Failure to meet these criteria may subject the physician to liability even if the operation itself is performed with the requisite degree of skill and care. See, e.g., *Beck v Lovell*, 361 So2d 245 (La 1978), where the court held that a physician was liable for a tubal ligation performed without the patient's express or implied consent, notwithstanding the skillful performance of the operation. And see *Rogers v Lumbermen's Mutual Casualty Co*, 119 So2d 649 (La 1960), where a physician was held liable in damages for the performance of a total hysterectomy and a bilateral salpingopherectomy. The court, in *Rogers*, found that the plaintiff had consented only to an appendectomy and that the additional procedures which resulted in sterility, and for which liability was imposed, were different in nature from the procedure authorized by the patient and involved risks and results not contemplated by the patient's original consent. The consent of the person to be sterilized is therefore an absolute condition precedent to the legal performance of the procedure, absent statutory authority for compulsory, eugenic sterilization. And even in the latter situation, strict procedural safeguards must be carefully observed. [As to the constitutional aspects of compulsory, eugenic sterilization, see §2.2.]

The consent need not be reduced to a signed writing in the absence of a statutory requirement therefor, since obtaining signed authorizations on a formal instrument is usually only a rule of professional custom [*Maercklein v Smith*, 129 Co 72, 266 P2d 1095 (1954)], although obtaining written and signed consent forms is the most common and prudent practice. The claim of plaintiffs, a husband and wife, that a physician was negligent as a matter of law for failing to obtain a *written* consent to the performance of a vasectomy on the husband went more to the question of the *scope* of the written consent that the physician did obtain relating to the performance of a cystoscopy to relieve prostatitis and hypertrophy of the prostate. See *Pomush v McGroarty*, 285 NW2d 91 (Mi 1979) [claim dismissed for failure to raise issue at trial].

b. [§2.5] Emergency Exception

The advent of an *emergency* requiring immediate action for the preservation of the patient's life or health is a widely recognized exception to the requirement for express or implied consent to a surgical procedure. *Kritzer v Citron*, 101 CaA2d 33, 224 P2d 808 (1950). In an emergency situation the physician is in effect *privileged* to proceed with the necessary surgery without the patient's consent. The emergency defense to a lack of consent is therefore distinct from the defense of *implied* consent. *Kritzer*, above. It is necessary, however, that the emergency arise under conditions that render it impossible or impracticable to obtain the patient's consent or the consent of anyone authorized to act for the patient. *Kelton v District of Columbia*, 413 A2d 919 (DC 1980); *Beck v Lovell*, 361 So2d 245 (La 1978); *Rogers v Lumbermen's Mutual Casualty Co*, 119 So2d 649 (La 1960). In the absence of evidence that the patient's medical problem was immediate and life-threatening, the emergency defense may be rejected on the grounds that no true emergency existed. *Tabor v Scobee*, 254 SW2d 474 (Ky 1951).

c. [§2.6] Capacity to Consent

In order for a patient's consent to sterilization surgery to be legally valid and effective, the patient giving the consent must be *competent* to do so. Otherwise, it is necessary that consent be obtained from someone who is competent and authorized to act on the patient's behalf. *Bang v Charles T Miller Hosp*, 251 Mn 427, 88 NW2d 186 (1958). [For a discussion of consent by a parent or guardian for the sterilization of an incompetent person, see §2.23.] Questions of a person's competence to consent to the performance of a sterilization operation may arise, for example, in connection with the person's mental capacity [see, e.g., *Petro v McCullough*, 385 NE2d 1195 (In 1979)], the effect of drugs, particularly sedatives [see, e.g., *Wheeler v Barker*, 208 P2d 68 (Ca 1949)], or the person's age. Although minors generally are held to be incompetent to consent to surgery, there may be circumstances under which a person who is not of legal age may effectively consent to performance of a sterilization operation. In *Smith v Seibly*, 431 P2d 719 (Wa 1967), an 18-year-old minor, who was married and the head of a family, was held to have validly consented to the performance of a vasectomy. In addition to his head-of-family status, the minor was a high school graduate, earned his own living, and maintained his own home. The court viewed the minor as being an emancipated person for the purpose of consenting to the operation, provided the physician fully disclosed the ramifications, implications, and probable consequences of a vasectomy in terms that were fully comprehensible to a person of the minor's age. Thus, factors other than age, including intelligence, maturity, training, experience, economic independence, behavior as an adult, and freedom from parental control, may be relevant in determining the validity of a minor's consent to a sterilization operation. [For illustrative cases, see §2.7.] [As to the necessity and validity of a representative's consent to the sterilization of an incompetent person, see §2.23.]

d. [§2.7] —Illustrative Cases

The following cases are illustrative of the general principles governing questions of persons' competency to consent to surgical sterilization [generally, see §2.6] and the application of those principles by courts in particular situations:

In *Petro v McCullough*, 385 NE2d 1195 (In 1979), a plaintiff sought damages from her physician on the grounds that he had performed a sterilization procedure on the plaintiff, a tubal ligation, to which the plaintiff could not have validly consented by reason of her mental incompetence. While hospitalized as an expectant mother, the plaintiff was encouraged to submit to a tubal ligation which was subsequently performed by the defendant-physician. The plaintiff, however, alleged, as the basis for the defendant's liability, that the defendant knew or should have known of the plaintiff's legal disability at the time when the consent to the sterilization surgery was procured. It appeared that the plaintiff had been judicially committed to a mental institution four years prior to the disputed surgery and that in the interim she had been released and recommitted several times. The defendant also admitted that the plaintiff had been diagnosed as mildly unstable and mildly retarded. Nevertheless, the trial court granted summary judgment to the defendant on the grounds that the plaintiff had freely and voluntarily consented to the sterilization and that she had not been so incapacitated as to be legally adjudged incompetent. On appeal, the summary judgment for the defendant-physician was reversed when the appellate court found that the trial court had actually resolved questions of fact bearing on the plaintiff's legal competency to consent rather than merely determining whether any questions of fact existed. The appellate court held that the plaintiff should be given the opportunity to present and litigate the issue of her mental capacity to execute the disputed consent to sterilization.

In *Smith v Seibly*, 72 Wa2d 16, 431 P2d 719 (1967), the litigation arose from a vasectomy operation performed on the plaintiff, a minor, by the defendant-physician. At the time of the operation the plaintiff was 18-years-old, married, and the father of a child. He was employed, supported his family, and maintained a home for himself, his wife, and his child. However, he was afflicted with a progressive muscular disease, myasthenia gravis, described as chronic and incurable, which would possibly affect his future earning capacity and ability to support his family. Under these circumstances the plaintiff and his wife decided to limit the size of their family by having the plaintiff sterilized. Their family doctor refused to perform the operation because of the plaintiff's age and the doctor's knowledge of the instability of the marriage. At that point, the plaintiff and his wife sought the services of another doctor, the defendant, and visited the defendant's offices requesting that he perform a vasectomy. The plaintiff represented that the sterilization was desired because of his affliction with the disease. The defendant illustrated the operation with a diagram and explained that it would result in permanent sterilization. There was a factual dispute as to whether the plaintiff represented to the defendant that he was of legal age, but it did appear that the defendant read aloud and presented the following statement to the plaintiff and his wife: "TO WHOM IT MAY CONCERN: we, the undersigned, hereby consent to the sterilization operation to be performed on the husband, having been told that the operation is a permanent thing, that there is no chance for a reestablishment of a viable sperm in the semen." The defendant then told the plaintiff and his wife to think about the operation and, if they still wished it performed, to sign the statement and return it to his office. Twelve days later, the plaintiff returned, presented the consent statement signed by himself and his wife, and the defendant performed the operation. Subsequently, the plaintiff brought an action against the defendant alleging that the defendant was negligent in performing the vasectomy on the plaintiff, was negligent in failing to explain to the plaintiff the permanent consequences of the surgery, and that the surgery was performed without valid permission. The plaintiff asked damages in the amount of $52,000. The defendant's answer denied the allegations of negligence and liability and alleged that the plaintiff was barred from recovery because he had signed a consent to the operation. Although the complaint contained allegations based on a theory of negligence, the parties agreed that the trial court properly submitted the case to the jury on an assault theory. One of the instructions read in part: ". . . the vasectomy is an assault and battery if surgery was performed without valid consent." The plaintiff's theory was that a minor could not give a valid consent to such a surgery. The defendant's view, adopted by the trial court, was that under some conditions a minor may be emancipated for the purpose of giving consent to surgery. The jury returned a verdict for the defendant and judgment was entered. On appeal, the plaintiff contended, in part, that the trial court had erred in its instructions relating to the consent issue. The exceptions taken to the trial court's action on the consent instructions were all based on the ground that the plaintiff, being a minor, could not give consent to the operation, that his consent was void, and that parental consent was necessary to prevent the defendant from being liable. The state Supreme Court noted that it had long been recognized that, for certain purposes, emancipation of minors might occur even in the absence of a statute. The defendant had contended that the plaintiff was emancipated for the purpose of giving consent to the operation, or, at least, that a jury question was presented on this issue. The court concluded that a married minor, 18-years-of-age, who has successfully completed high school and is the head of his own family, who earns his own living and maintains his own home, is emancipated for the purpose of giving a valid consent to surgery if a full disclosure of the ramifications, implications, and probable consequences of the surgery has been made by the doctor in terms which are fully comprehensible to the minor. Thus, age, intelligence, maturity, training, experience, economic independence or lack thereof, general conduct as an adult, and freedom from the control of the parents are all factors to be considered in such a case. The court noted that the plaintiff was married, and independent of parental control and financial support, and that it was for the jury to decide if he was sufficiently intelligent, educated, and knowledgeable to make a legally binding decision.

In *Wheeler v Barker*, 92 CaA2d 776, 208 P2d 68 (1949), the plaintiff brought action to recover damages for a technical assault and battery arising from the performance by the defendant-physician of an allegedly unauthorized hysterotomy. For several months before the operation the plaintiff had been treated by the defendant for continued vaginal bleeding. In January 1946, the defendant made a pelvic examination and found what appeared to be a small fibroid tumor on the interior surface of the uterus. In succeeding months other examinations revealed that the mass was in the right ovarian region. During July 1946, the plaintiff consulted other physicians, one of whom diagnosed her symptom as an ovarian cyst; the other physician indicated a growth on the uterus. Both recommended immediate surgery. On August 1, 1946, the plaintiff was again examined by the defendant and he again advised surgery. After the plaintiff had telephoned her husband, she consented to an operation, but she testified that she consented only to the removal of her right ovary and nothing more. The defendant and his nurse testified that the plaintiff was told it might be necessary to remove the right ovary or the uterus, depending on the condition found during surgery, and that the defendant promised not to remove both ovaries, consistent with the only limitation requested by the plaintiff. On August 4, the plaintiff went to the hospital where she signed a consent to "whatever anesthetic and operation which may be decided to be necessary or advisable." A registered nurse signed as a witness. The plaintiff however, contended that she had no recollection of ever having signed such a release and that she did not sign it before she had taken a sedative. The nurse who signed the consent as a witness testified that the plaintiff signed the release during the afternoon while she was awake and before any sedative had been administered. In the course of the surgery the defendant opened the plaintiff's abdomen and found that her ovaries were not diseased. Instead, the defendant found that the mass which had been felt on examination was a large tumor attached to the uterus adjacent to the right ovary, and that the uterian wall was filled with multiple fibroid tumors. The attending surgeons, consulted about the condition, agreed that a subtotal hysterotomy was necessary, and proceeded with that operation. On completion of the surgery the plaintiff's husband was told what had been done, and when the effects of the anesthetic subsided the plaintiff was told. Neither of them expressed any dissatisfaction. The postoperative course was normal. The first difficulty between the parties arose when the defendant refused to give the plaintiff sleeping pills which she requested. She became angry and ceased to be the defendant's patient. The defendant, his assistant surgeon, and another local physician all testified that the operation was necessary and in accordance with the standards of practice in the community to preserve the plaintiff's health, and that she would have continued to suffer from the bleeding had the uterus not been removed. The court noted that the consent document was general in its terms and contained a consent to whatever operation might be found necessary or advisable. Furthermore, the court noted that the purpose of the operation was to stop the vaginal bleeding that had continued for several months and to remove the growth on the female organs. In the court's view, it was the defendant's duty to do whatever was necessary to effect a cure, and in exercising his best judgment as to the proper course to pursue he was performing a professional service for which he had been employed. The court observed that when a surgeon is confronted with an emergency or an unanticipated condition, where immediate action is necessary for the preservation of the life or health of the patient and where it is impracticable to obtain express, informed consent to an operation which he deems to be immediately necessary, it is the surgeon's duty to do what the occasion demands consistent with the usual and customary practice among physicians and surgeons in the same or similar localities, and the surgeon is justified in extending the operation and in removing and overcoming the condition without the express consent of the patient. However, the court noted that, notwithstanding the plaintiff's admission of the genuineness and due execution of the consent, she had a right at trial to offer evidence to the effect that her signature was secured through fraud or duress, or while she was under the influence of a sedative, or that for any other reason she did not know what she was signing. The plaintiff had in fact testified without objection that she was not aware of what she was signing and that she signed the consent document after a sedative had been administered. But in both of these particulars she was contradicted by the nurse who signed the consent form as a witness to the plaintiff's signature. In view of the conflict, the implied finding of the jury against the plaintiff's contentions was not disturbed by the reviewing court.

e. [§2.8] Informed Consent

Under the general doctrine of informed consent to surgery, a physician has the duty to disclose to a patient the nature of a proposed course of treatment, the probable consequences of such treatment, and the possible risks or dangers which may reasonably be anticipated. *Funke v Feldman*, 512 P2d 539 (Ks 1973); *Bang v Charles T Miller Hosp*, 251 Mn 427, 88

NW2d 186 (1958). The physician must also inform the patient of alternative methods of treatment and their attendant risks and consequences. *Zeleznik v Jewish Chronic Disease Hosp*, 366 NYS2d 163 (1975). These disclosures are necessary in order for the patient to form the basis for an intelligent and valid consent. In the absence of adequate disclosure, the patient's consent will be considered invalid and ineffective to authorize the surgical procedure and therefore will not afford the physician protection from liability for his or her performance of the surgery. [As to the necessity of consent and the surgeon's liability in the absence thereof, see §2.4.]

Certain surgical procedures, not specifically characterized as sterilization procedures, have the potential for rendering the person on whom they are performed sterile or otherwise unable to procreate. In order for the patient's consent to such procedures to be effective, the physician must make it clear that sterility is a possible consequence. The patient then will be able to make an intelligent decision whether to consent to the procedure or to elect some other course of treatment. *Bang v Charles T Miller Hosp*, 251 Mn 427, 88 NW2d 186 (1958). As also recognizing the duty of a physician to disclose that a surgical procedure might result in an inability to procreate, as well as the duty to inform a patient of alternative methods of treatment, see *Fontenelle v United States*, 327 FSupp 801 (SD NY 1971), and *Thornton v Annest*, 19 WaA 174, 574 P2d 1199 (1978). [For illustrative cases, see §2.9.]

The validity of a patient's consent to surgical sterilization, in terms of whether the consent can be fairly considered intelligent and informed, may also depend on whether the primary surgical procedure, to which sterilization was an incident, is actually performed. In *Kritzer v Citron*, 101 CaA2d 33, 224 P2d 808 (1950), for example, the plaintiff-patient had consented to sterilization as part of the delivery of her child by cesarean section. When the child was delivered spontaneously, however, without the necessity for the cesarean procedure, an issue arose as to whether the physician was privileged to perform the sterilization even though the birth was normal. The court resolved the controversy on grounds other than informed consent, when it found that the plaintiff had either expressly or impliedly consented to the sterilization in a conversation with her physician following the delivery of the child.

f. [§2.9] —Illustrative Cases

The following cases are illustrative of the general principles governing questions of persons' informed consent to surgical sterilizations [generally, see §2.8], and the application of those principles by courts in particular situations:

In *Bang v Charles T Miller Hosp*, 251 Mn 427, 88 NW2d 186 (1958), the court held that a physician had the duty to inform a patient with an enlarged prostate gland that severance of the spermatic cords in connection with a prostate operation would result in sterility and that failure to take such action might result in an infection which would be dangerous to the patient's health. The plaintiff began having urinary trouble and consulted a doctor who sent him to the hospital for a cystoscopic examination. The plaintiff testified that the examining physicians informed him of an enlargement of the prostate gland and bladder soreness and recommended that some of the tissue should be removed from the gland to overcome the problem. The plaintiff then consulted the defendant and after the initial examination, the defendant informed the plaintiff that he wished to make a cystoscopic examination and suggested that the plaintiff be admitted to the hospital. After further examination, the defendant operated on the plaintiff and in the course of the operation severed the plaintiff's spermatic cords. The plaintiff admitted that he did not expect to tell the doctor what to do, and that he had faith in the doctor. He expected that the doctor would operate and do whatever was necessary to cure his condition. He did not ask the doctor what he intended to do and left it up to the doctor to do the right thing. At the trial the defendant acknowledged that the operation he performed, a transurethral prostatic resection, involved the severing of the spermatic cords. The court was of the opinion that under the record the question as to whether the plaintiff consented to the severance of his spermatic cords was a fact question for the jury. Regarding the consent issue, the court said that, if in the course of the operation to which the patient consented, the surgeon discovered conditions not anticipated before the operation was commenced, which if not removed would endanger the life or health of the patient, the surgeon would be justified in extending the operation to remove and overcome those conditions even though no express consent was obtained or given by the patient. The court noted that it had no desire to hamper the medical profession in the progress it had made and continued to make in connection with the study and solution of health and disease problems, but that it was the court's opinion that it was reasonable to require that, where a physician or surgeon can ascertain alternatives in advance of an operation, and where no immediate emergency exists, a patient should be informed of the alternative possibilities and given a chance to decide among them before the doctor proceeds with the operation. Applying the rule to the case, the court found that, when no immediate emergency exists, a patient should be informed before such an operation that the severance of his spermatic cords would result in his sterilization, but that if they were not severed there would be a possibility of an infection which could have serious consequences. Under the circumstances, the patient should at least have had the opportunity of deciding whether he wanted to take the chance of a possible infection if the operation was performed in one manner or to become sterile if performed in another.

In *Thornton v Annest*, 19 WaA 174, 574 P2d 199 (1978), the court affirmed a jury verdict in favor of the defendant-physician in a case involving the alleged failure of the defendant to secure the plaintiff's informed consent to a surgical sterilization. On November 16, 1973, the defendant-physician removed the fallopian tubes and appendix of the 29-year-old plaintiff, Joyce Thornton. Subsequently, the plaintiff brought an action against the defendant alleging that the removal of her tubes and the resulting sterilization was unnecessary. In support of her appeal from a jury verdict in favor of the defendant, the plaintiff assigned error, in part, to the denial of her motion for a partial directed verdict on the issue of whether an informed consent was given. On November 14, 1973, the plaintiff experienced pain in the pelvic area and nausea. On November 16, 1973, the defendant performed an exploratory surgery on the plaintiff for the purpose of determining the cause of her symptoms. During the surgery the defendant discovered that the plaintiff's appendix was acutely inflammed, and that both of her fallopian tubes were afflicted acutely and chronically with pelvic inflammatory disease. In the course of the operation, the defendant removed the plaintiff's fallopian tubes. The defendant testified that prior to surgery he told the plaintiff that he felt her problem was recurrent pelvic inflammatory disease, and that he wanted to conduct an exploratory operation to better ascertain her condition. He further testified that he told the plaintiff that if the disease was extensive it would necessitate the removal of her tubes and uterus, and that he would remove anything necessary to alleviate her abdominal problem. He testified that the plaintiff consented to the surgery and that she said she wanted him to do everything proper for her. Moreover, the record contained a written consent form signed by the plaintiff for an exploratory laparotomy and for such other procedures which the doctor might consider necessary or advisable in the course of the operation. The plaintiff, however, claimed that the defendant failed to inform her before the surgery of certain alternatives which were feasible methods of treatment. Specifically, the plaintiff presented evidence of four possible alternative courses of action: antibiotic treatment; surgical aspiration of pus; hysterosalpingogran x-ray test; and consultation with a gynecologist. The court noted, however, that whether an alternative treatment was feasible in relation to the physical condition of a particular patient, so as to require the doctor to disclose such an alternative to the patient, was a question of fact for the jury. Under the physical conditions described in the case, the court found that the jury was entitled to believe that the disease was chronic, rather than acute, and not susceptible to either antibiotic treatment or surgical aspiration. The x-ray tests, or consultation with a gynecologist, were not established as alternatives for treating the disease, but were merely alternatives in diagnosing its extent. The jury was therefore entitled to believe the testimony of the defendant, and the experts called on his behalf, that he complied with the proper standard of medical care in performing the exploratory surgery as a method of diagnosing the plaintiff's symptoms. Accepting that the extent of the disease was properly disclosed by the surgery, the jury was then within its province to ascertain whether the defendant complied with the requisite standard of care in removing the tubes.

The decision in *Lewis v Shaver*, 236 NC 510, 73 SE2d 320 (1953), concerned a damages action against a defendant-physician who performed an operation on the plaintiff in which he removed an ovary and tied her fallopian tubes. The Supreme Court of North Carolina noted that the evidence tended to show that the plaintiff went to the hospital for the removal of a cyst on one of her ovaries, that she was not informed that her ovary was to be removed or her fallopian tubes tied, and that she never consented to the operation. The plaintiff consulted several other physicians after leaving the hospital about pains in her side and inquired as to why she could not have any more children. Another physician performed a second surgery on the plaintiff and discovered that one of her tubes had been removed and that her tubes were blocked. This discovery prompted the plaintiff to bring the suit to recover damages resulting from the unauthorized aspects of the first operation.

In *Fontenelle v United States*, 327 FSupp 801 (SD NY 1971), the plaintiff instituted an action pursuant to the Federal Tort Claims Act stating that he was admitted to a United States public health service hospital where he underwent genital-urinary surgery and alleging that while he gave his consent to the named surgical procedures, it was not an informed consent because he was not told of the possible consequences of the surgery, including incontinence and impotence. The defendant moved to dismiss the complaint on the ground that the court lacked jurisdiction over the subject matter. The government's position was that if the plaintiff gave his consent, he had no cause of action for the consequences of the surgery, and that if he did not give his consent, the surgery was an assault and battery and hence a claim excluded from the operation of the Federal Tort Claims Act. The court held that the issue presented in the case was whether the plaintiff was informed as to the consequences of his operation at the time he gave his consent and whether, if he was not so informed, such failure constituted negligence on the part of the defendant's agents, giving the plaintiff a right to recover for malpractice. These factual issues could only be resolved at trial, the court concluded, and therefore the court denied the defendant's motion to dismiss the complaint on jurisdictional grounds.

g. [§2.10] Scope of Consent

It is the general practice of physicians and hospitals to require persons who are about to undergo surgery to sign written consent forms. [As to the necessity of signed, written consent forms, see §2.4.] The general rule prohibiting the performance of surgical operations without the patient's consent extends to surgical procedures different in nature from that for which consent is given, and to procedures involving risks and results not contemplated at the time consent to the procedures is given. *Rogers v Lumbermen's Mutual Casualty Co*, 119 So2d 649 (La 1960). If the consent forms do not specifically refer to sterilization as a consequence of the operation to be performed, a question may arise whether the patient's consent is effective to authorize procedures which result in sterility. The scope of the consent actually given will depend on the language of the consent form, the patient's intent, and the circumstances under which the form is executed. *Davidson v Shirley*, 616 F2d 224 (5th Cir 1980); *Kelton v District of Columbia*, 413 A2d 919 (DC 1980); *Hundley v St Francis Hosp*, 161 CaA2d 800, 327 P2d 131 (1958). [For illustrative cases, see §2.11.]

h. [§2.11] —Illustrative Cases

The following cases are illustrative of the general principles governing questions of the scope of persons' consent to surgical procedures as encompassing surgical sterilization [generally, see §2.10], and the application of those principles by courts in particular situations.

In *Davidson v Shirley*, 616 F2d 224 (5th Cir 1980), the court held that consent forms executed prior to a cesarean section delivery and an anticipated tubal ligation were effective to manifest consent to the removal of the patient's uterus, as well as constituting consent to the removal of her right ovary and fallopian tube. In consultation with the patient's physician, the patient and her husband agreed to a cesarean section delivery and requested that a tubal ligation be performed during the delivery for the purpose of rendering the patient sterile. The patient signed a consent form authorizing both procedures and also authorizing "such additional operations or procedures as are considered therapeutically necessary on the basis of findings during the course of said operation." In addition, the patient and her husband executed a "permit for sterilization" which authorized sterilization as well as "any operation" deemed advisable by her physician. They also executed a statement to the physician requesting and consenting to sterilization. During the course of delivery by cesarean section, the physician discovered and removed a large ovarian tumor which, in combination with the delivery, resulted in significant blood loss. In order to halt the flow of blood, the physician determined that removal of the patient's uterus was necessary. The court reasoned that the language of the consent form authorizing such additional operations or procedures as were considered "therapeutically necessary" established the patient's consent to removal of her uterus, where removal of the uterus was shown by the evidence to be "therapeutically necessary" and thus within the scope of the consent given.

But, in *Kelton v District of Columbia*, 413 A2d 919 (DC 1980), a standard surgical consent form for delivery of a child by cesarean section was held not sufficient to authorize surgical sterilization of the mother by tubal ligation, absent any signs of an emergency need therefor. For other decisions finding that forms executed by patients to consent to surgical procedures also authorized additional procedures which resulted in sterility, see, e.g., *Danielson v Roche*, 241 P2d 1028 (Ca 1952) ["all and any singular treatments or operations which may now or during the contemplated services be deemed advisable or necessary"]; *Wheeler v Barker*, 208 P2d 68 (Ca 1949) ["whatever anesthetic and operation which may be decided to be necessary or advisable"]. However, in *Rogers v Lumbermen's Mutual Casualty Co*, 119 So2d 649 (La 1960), the court held that a consent form signed by a patient prior to undergoing an appendectomy was ineffective to authorize a hysterectomy, which the operating physician testified he performed as a precautionary measure. The consent form, which was termed an "authority to operate," purported to authorize the physician in charge to "administer such treatment and . . . such anesthetics as found necessary to perform this operation which is advisable in the treatment of this patient." The court described the consent form as being so ambiguous that it was worthless, particularly since it failed to designate the nature of the operation for which consent was given. The court said that the record abundantly substantiated the patient's contention that she never at any time gave her consent to any operation except one for the removal of her appendix, and, furthermore, that she was ignorant of any possibility that the operation could result in the removal of her reproductive organs. Moreover, the court reasoned that the alleged defense of emergency, or of the necessity for the operation as one performed in the interest of the health of the patient, was destroyed by the testimony of the surgeon that no emergency existed and that he removed the female organs as a precautionary measure and because he felt that to do so was good surgical procedure.

In *Beck v Lovell*, 361 So2d 245 (La 1978), the plaintiff appealed from a lower court judgment rejecting her claim against her physician, the hospital, and the physician's insurer for alleged medical malpractice consisting of ligation of the plaintiff's fallopian tubes without the plaintiff's consent. The court of appeals reversed in part and rendered judgment in favor of the plaintiff against her physician. The plaintiff, attended by her physician, entered the hospital in premature labor for the birth of her third child. With the plaintiff's consent, she was scheduled for a possible cesarean section delivery. During either the plaintiff's first or second pregnancy, her doctor had suggested a hysterectomy because of a blood incompatibility between the plaintiff and her husband, which condition posed a successively greater threat to each conceived child. The plaintiff, however, had rejected that suggestion. It was conceded that on numerous occasions the plaintiff and her doctor had discussed the possibility of tubal ligation, but the plaintiff maintained that she had never consented expressly or impliedly to the ligation. Instead, in every instance she claimed to have told the doctor that she would think about it and let him know. Conversely, the doctor contended that these discussions led him to believe that the plaintiff desired to have her tubes tied following delivery of the third child. Based on his belief that the plaintiff had consented to ligation during a visit early in the third pregnancy, he wrote "C-Section, T L" in large letters on the face of his record to indicate that the plaintiff desired to have her tubes tied after the birth of the third child. About two or three hours before the delivery in question, the plaintiff was requested by the admitting nurse at the hospital to sign a form for "consent to operation, anesthetics and other medical services," provided by the hospital. The form contained, among other things, the following provision: "I am aware that sterility may result from this operation. I know that a sterile person is incapable of becoming a parent." This provision, at the plaintiff's insistence, was stricken from the form. The record did not show conclusively whether the plaintiff or the admitting nurse marked out the provision. As thus altered, the form accompanied the plaintiff's chart into the operating room and was present there during the surgical procedure. After the delivery, an assisting surgeon asked the plaintiff's doctor whether the patient's tubes would be tied. The question of consent then arose and was discussed by the physicians. Because the patient was under anesthesia and no hospital tubal ligation consent form was found on the patient's chart, the plaintiff's doctor sent one of the attending nurses into the hall where the full form was presented to and signed by the plaintiff's husband. The nurse then presented the signed form to the plaintiff's doctor who performed the ligation. In substance, the plaintiff's doctor testified that he was certain that the plaintiff desired tubal ligation, and that he would not have ligated her tubes without her consent. The defendants maintained that they did not rely on the husband's written consent, but contended that the plaintiff gave her express or implied consent. The plaintiff's husband testified that he was of the opinion that his wife was opposed to ligation, that he told the doctor that he thought his wife was opposed, and that if the doctor would go back into the operating room and obtain his wife's consent that he would sign the consent form. Shortly after the doctor returned to the operating room, according to the husband, a nurse returned with a consent form and reported that the plaintiff had consented; the husband then signed the form. The plaintiff sought to have liability imposed on the hospital, under respondeat superior, for the actions of its nurses in failing to obtain a signed tubal ligation consent form provided. It was also contended that the nurses were negligent in not advising the surgeon that no such form was signed by the patient. Finally, it was argued that the hospital was liable for the doctor's action in proceeding without authorization. The court noted that it was clear that attention of the surgeon was directed to the fact that no tubal ligation consent form had been signed by the patient. When this was done, the surgeon, who was in undisputed charge of the operating room, directed an attending nurse to seek the consent of the plaintiff's husband. The nurse, acting on the doctor's orders, did as requested. Under the circumstances, the court found no negligence on the part of the admitting nurse, who attached the form signed by the plaintiff to the plaintiff's chart which accompanied the plaintiff into the operating room. The court also found that the record was totally devoid of evidence to support the claim that the hospital was responsible for the surgeon's actions under the doctrine of respondeat superior. The court concluded that it was not shown that the hospital had any control whatsoever over the surgeon or the manner in which he conducted the surgery. However, after viewing the record in light of the applicable rules of law, the court found that the surgeon did not have express or implied permission or consent from the plaintiff to ligate her tubes. The court acknowledged that there was conflict of testimony on the issue of consent. However, the court said it could not escape the conclusion that the surgeon entertained some doubt as to whether the plaintiff had consented. Although there was no evidence that he was aware of the deletion made on the form signed by the plaintiff on admission, the form was in the operating room and was available to the surgeon. Had he consulted the chart and noted the deletion, this should have caused him to question whether the plaintiff desired ligation, and should have alerted him to the possibility that even if the plaintiff had previously given such consent, she had changed her mind. Additionally, if the surgeon was certain that the plaintiff had given express verbal consent, as he contended, there would have been no need to acquire the husband's consent. The court therefore concluded that the surgeon and his insurer were liable in damages for a tubal ligation performed on the plaintiff without her express or implied consent, notwithstanding that the operation was skillfully performed.

i. [§2.12] Implied Consent

Despite the fact that express consent may not have been given, under some circumstances a patient's implied consent to the performance of a surgical procedure resulting in sterility may be presumed. Frequently, where a patient has given express consent to a particular surgical procedure, the physician, in the course of performing that surgery, discovers an unanticipated condition, perhaps requiring emergency treatment. Because of the condition of the patient, it is impossible to obtain the patient's express consent. It may, however, be possible to find that the patient impliedly consented to such further emergency or necessary treatment. Implied consent to surgical treatment resulting in sterility has been found, for example, where patients expressly consented to procedures such as the removal of a single ovary [*Wheeler v Barker*, 208 P2d 68 (Ca 1949)] or exploratory surgery to determine the cause of pelvic inflammation [*Thornton v Annest*, 574 P2d 199 (Wa 1978)], and the subsequent discovery of other conditions, such as the presence of fibroid tumors or acutely inflammed fallopian tubes, has necessitated the additional treatment which resulted in sterility [*Davidson v Shirley*, 616 F2d 224 (5th Cir 1980); *Rothe v Hull*, 352 Mo 926, 180 SW2d 7 (1944)].

Implied consent may be manifested by acts or conduct; consent need not necessarily be shown by a writing or by express words. The argument that consent may be implied only in the face of an emergency overlooks the fact that in an emergency situation the physician is in effect privileged to proceed with necessary surgery without the patient's consent. In other words, emergency and consent are two distinct defenses. *Kritzer v Citron*, 101 CaA2d 33, 224 P2d 808 (1950). However, express consent to a nonsterilizing surgical procedure was not taken as implied consent to sterilization when emergency conditions did not exist and when sterilization was not medically necessary. See, e.g., *Rogers v Lumbermen's Mutual Casualty Co*, 119 So2d 649 (La 1960), where the court held that consent to a hysterectomy could not be implied where the patient had expressly consented to an appendectomy only and where the operating physician testified that no emergency existed and that the hysterectomy was performed as a precautionary measure only. For an example of consent to a sterilization operation implied from the actions of the patient, see *Kritzer v Citron*, 101 CaA2d 33, 224 P2d 808 (1950), holding that a woman and her husband manifested consent to a sterilization operation, where the woman submitted to the operation without objection and her husband voiced no objection when he was informed that the operation had been performed. The operation was to have been done in conjunction with a delivery by cesarean section. However, the birth occurred spontaneously and the operation was performed as an independent procedure after delivery. The woman and her husband claimed unsuccessfully that their original consent to the sterilization operation was without effect because the operation was not performed as originally planned.

j. [§2.13] Spousal Consent

The existence of a marital relationship between two persons as husband and wife does not ordinarily confer authority on one spouse to consent to the performance of sterilization surgery on the other spouse, absent a medical emergency. *Beck v Lovell*, 361 So2d 245 (La 1978). See *Haywood v Allen*, 406 SW2d 721 (Ky 1966), where a husband's consent was considered alone sufficient authority for a surgeon's having tied-off the patient-wife's fallopian tubes in the course of performing a delivery by cesarean section. Aside from the validity of interspousal consent, however, questions may also arise concerning the necessity of joint consent by both spouses to the sterilization of one of them. In other words, when a sterilization operation is performed on a married person, must the physician obtain the consent of the nonpatient as well as the consent of the patient spouse? Although it is in the physician's interest to obtain the spouse's consent when possible, the courts have held that spousal consent is not necessary provided the consent of the patient has been obtained. *Kritzer v Citron*, 101 CaA2d 33, 224 P2d 808 (1950); *Ponter v Ponter*, 135 NJ Super 50, 342 A2d 574 (1975); *Murray v VanDevander*, 522 P2d 302 (Ok 1974).

A New Jersey court has taken the position that a woman has a constitutional right to be sterilized without her husband's consent. *Ponter v Ponter*, 135 NJ Super 50, 342 A2d 574 (1975). Relying on the position taken by the United States Supreme Court in *Doe v Bolton*, 410 US 179, 93 SCt 739, 35 LE2d 201 (1973), and *Roe v Wade*, 410 US 113, 93 SCt 705, 35 LE2d 147 (1973), which the New Jersey court described as standing for the proposition that a woman has the right in most circumstances to control her reproductive functions, the court said that a woman's right to determine whether or not to bear children takes precedence over any contrary interests which her husband might have. A married woman's right to voluntary sterilization on her own consent was therefore considered a natural and logical corollaryof her right to procure an abortion without her husband's consent. [For a discussion of abortion, see §§5.1-5.48.] Protection of this right, in the court's view, was available in the form of a proscription against state action that would deny the right. The court also refused to recognize the existence of a cause of action by the nonsterilized spouse against the physician who performed the sterilization procedure. And in *Murray v VanDevander*, 522 P2d 302 (Ok 1974), the court affirmed a judgment in favor of a physician in an action in which the husband of a woman on whom the physician performed a hysterectomy without the husband's consent alleged that the physician had interfered with his marital rights and those of his wife. Noting that the woman had consented to the operation, the court said that the natural right of a married woman to her health is not qualified by requiring that she have her husband's consent in order to receive surgical care from a physician. The court added that there was no necessity for the physician to obtain the husband's consent. Nor did the physician breach any duty by performing the operation without such consent. The court rejected the husband's contention that he had a right, as an incident to marriage, to a wife who was capable of bearing children. The court said that it was neither prepared to create a right of a husband to have a fertile wife nor to allow recovery for damage to such a right. In summary, the court reasoned that the right of a person who is capable of competent consent to control his or her own body is paramount. In addition, the court noted that there was no allegation in the petition that the plaintiff's wife was of diminished capacity or otherwise incapable of consent. The plaintiff husband also contended that the defendant had secured the patient's consent by means of overreaching, and that the use of the defendant's confidential and professional position to obtain the consent of the plaintiff's wife rendered the consent void. The court, however, was of the opinion that the plaintiff's wife, rather than the plaintiff, would be the proper party to complain of such behavior by the physician.

2. Negligence

a. [§2.14] Generally

Surgically performed sterilization operations may cause personal injury to the patient, aside from the intended result of sterilization. In situations where this occurs, the question of professional negligence or medical malpractice goes to the manner in which the sterilization procedure was performed. See, e.g., *Fernon v Itkin*, 476 FSupp 1 (MD Fl 1977) [pain associated with vasectomy]; *Bathke v Rahn*, 46 CaA 694, 116 P2d 640 (1941) [pain and nervous disorder as result of vasectomy]; *Rach v Wise*, 46 MiA 729, 208 NW2d 570 (1973) [partial impotency as result of vasectomy]; *Pump v Fox*, 172 OhSt 371, 177 NE2d 520 (1961) [incontinence as result of hysterotomy]; *McCoy v Stevens*, 182 Wa 55, 44 P2d 799 (1935) [burns from x-ray as contraceptive procedure].

Aside from the manner in which a surgical sterilization procedure is performed, however, questions of medical malpractice may also arise regarding the fact that the procedure was performed at all. The issues in this type of action concern whether the physician properly diagnosed the patient's problem and whether the physician prescribed the sterilization surgery as the correct treatment. In other words, the sterilization procedure, regardless of how it was performed, may have been the result of negligence. *Hundley v St Francis Hosp*, 161 CaA 800, 327 P2d 131 (1958) [unnecessary removal of uterus, fallopian tube, and one ovary, all without pathological abnormality]; *Pearson v Boines*, 367 A2d 653 (De 1976), affd, 386 A2d 651 (De 1978) [tubal ligation not required on diagnosis of multiple sclerosis]; *Young v Clement*, 367 So2d 828 (La 1979) [unnecessary removal of fallopian tubes and ovaries].

Also actionable are those cases where the patient and physician have agreed on one type of surgical procedure and, instead, the patient is actually subjected to a different operation resulting in undesired sterility or other untoward consequences. See, e.g., *Hill v Stewart*, 209 So2d 809 (Ms 1968). Actions falling into any of these categories are, despite the fact that they arise in the context of surgical sterilization procedures, essentially typical medical malpractice actions. The elements to be established for a prima facie case are the same as in any other type of medical malpractice action. The plaintiff, in order to recover, must plead and prove that the physician failed to use due care, as measured against the standards of the medical profession in the community, in the prescription and/or performance of the surgical procedure, which failure caused the plaintiff's injuries. See, e.g., *Pierce v Smith*, 301 So2d 805 (Fl 1974), and other cases cited above. [For illustrative cases, see §2.15.]

It should be noted that in these cases no child is conceived and born as a result of the physician's malpractice; rather, the injured party is the patient. By contrast, if a child is conceived and born following the unsuccessful performance of a sterilization operation, and the parent sues for damages caused by the unexpected or unplanned child, the action is referred to as one for wrongful conception or wrongful pregnancy. This cause of action, which is an emerging theory of recovery, is discussed in detail at §§3.8-3.51.

b. [§2.15] Illustrative Cases

The following cases are illustrative of the general principles governing liability for the negligent performance of surgical sterilization procedures [generally, see §2.14], where the result of the physician's negligence is other than pregnancy and birth [see §3.8], and the application of those principles to particular situations:

Whether a cause of action is stated when it is alleged that a sterilization operation was negligently performed will depend on the specific facts of the case. For example, in *Pierce v Smith*, 301 So2d 805 (Fl 1974), a man sued his physician and the physician's insurance carrier for malpractice based on complications resulting from the performance of a bilateral vasectomy. The patient had a prior history of bleeding of which the physician was aware. According to the patient, he was allowed to leave the physician's office after the operation while he was still bleeding. He returned two days later in a swollen condition. The bleeding continued. The patient said the physician recommended the application of ice packs and prescribed an antibiotic. Several physicians who testified for the defendant physician admitted that the patient's ultimate loss of a testicle was caused by the continued excessive bleeding. The court did not directly address the issue of the cause of action, but held that under the circumstances the jury had the right to conclude that the physician had failed to take appropriate precautions to control the bleeding. And in *Maercklein v Smith*, 129 Co 72, 266 P2d 1095 (1954), the court apparently found that a cause of action had been stated for the alleged wrongful performance of a vasectomy. The patient asserted that he and the physician had agreed upon the performance of a circumcision operation. However, a sterilization operation was actually performed. The patient alleged that he had been damaged by the physician's negligence. The court noted that for the patient to prevail he would need to prove the contract and the negligence. In *Pritchard v Neal*, 139 GaA 512, 229 SE2d 18 (1976), the plaintiff was found to have stated a cause of action for a surgeon's negligent performance of a tubal ligation which resulted in the mother's subsequent pregnancy, the death of the fetus, and the decomposition of the fetus in the mother's womb.

In *Church v Adler*, 350 IlA 471, 113 NE2d 327 (1953), the appellate court reversed and remanded a decision by the trial court which had found that the plaintiff failed to state a cause of action regarding the alleged negligent performance of a sterilization operation. The plaintiff's pleading alleged, in various forms, malpractice on the part of the defendant, a physician and surgeon, allegedly employed by the plaintiff to treat her illness. The plaintiff employed the defendant to treat her for diseased ovaries and the defendant did so treat her for about 90 days. The plaintiff however alleged that the defendant was unskillful and negligent in his care for her, and that, as the result of his alleged malfeasances and misfeasances, she became sick, sore, lame, and disordered, and would remain so for the rest of her life, and that she became unable to become successfully pregnant and give birth to children. The plaintiff acknowledged that the defendant informed her that he had removed her diseased ovaries, and that she could bear no more children. However, the plaintiff asserted that she continued to suffer from the same illness after the operation and that thereafter the defendant refused the plaintiff's demand to treat her further for her disorders, for which he had been paid, and which he had stated he had remedied. The plaintiff alleged that by reason of the alleged events she was compelled to consult another surgeon who correctly diagnosed her illness as diseased ovaries and performed an operation to remove the ovaries, and that thereafter the plaintiff regained her health. The plaintiff sought damages in the amount of $22,000. On appeal, the court held that sufficient facts were set forth to spell out a cause of action so as to require the defendant to answer. Moreover, the court said that if the plaintiff succeeded in proving her allegations, that as a result of the defendant's negligent care she suffered damages, she would be entitled to recover.

In *Iverson v Lancaster*, 158 NW2d 507 (ND 1968), the plaintiffs, husband and wife, brought actions against the defendant-physician and defendant-medical partnership for damages allegedly caused by the physician's negligent diagnosis of the plaintiff-wife's condition, which negligence resulted in the performance of an unnecessary sterilization operation. The plaintiffs alleged that the physician negligently failed to diagnose the condition of hypertension, commonly known as high blood pressure, as due to coarctation of the aorta. Moreover, they alleged that he advised that, because of hypertension, the wife should not become pregnant. Acting on this advice, she underwent a hysterectomy which prevented her from bearing further children. Subsequently, the physician discovered that the plaintiff-wife had coarctation of the aorta and recommended corrective surgery which resulted in the elimination of her hypertension. The two causes of action, one brought by the wife and the other brought by her husband, were consolidated for trial. When the plaintiffs rested their cases at the completion of the submission of their evidence, the defendants moved for a dismissal with prejudice as to each of the causes of their actions and, in the alternative, for a directed verdict. The trial court granted the motion for dismissal. On appeal, the Supreme Court of North Dakota reversed and remanded the cases for new trial. The plaintiffs successfully argued that the trial court erred in sustaining an objection to the plaintiffs' cross-examination of the defendant-physician directed toward establishing the standard of skill and care ordinarily exercised by doctors in the community.

In *Rache v Wise*, 46 MiA 729, 208 NW2d 570 (1973), the plaintiffs alleged that an agreement was entered into with the defendant to perform a vasectomy on the plaintiff-husband and to render necessary postoperative care. In addition, the plaintiffs alleged that the defendant represented that a vasectomy was simple surgery, involving no danger of complications, and that the plaintiff-husband would be able to resume his occupation and family life within 48 hours following the surgery. The plaintiffs alleged that the defendant did not perform the vasectomy in a professional manner and that, as a result, the husband's left testicle was permanently injured and eventually atrophied, that the plaintiff-husband was subjected to intense pain and suffering for four months, that he was confined to his home and unable to return to work for six weeks, that he was required to receive periodic injections of hormones to replace the hormones normally produced by the left testicle, that he was permanently partially incapacitated in the performance of normal conjugal relations with his wife, and that he would continue to suffer periodic pain and continuous mental anguish. The plaintiffs sought damages in the amount of $85,000.

In *Hundley v St Francis Hosp*, 161 CaA 800, 327 P2d 131 (1958), the plaintiff brought action against the defendant-physician for the alleged unnecessary performance of an operation which resulted in her sterilization. The plaintiff's complaint alleged in part that the defendant-physician treated her in an unnecessary, careless, and negligent manner. The court noted that the evidence made clear that the plaintiff's complaint relied on the claimed negligent and careless manner of the operation, as well as the allegation that the surgery performed was unnecessary. The court noted that the condition requiring surgery was a dropping of the uterus, and that there was also evidence of a pre-operative diagnosis of rectocele and cystocele. The operation removed the body of the uterus, a fallopian tube, and an ovary (one tube and ovary had previously been removed). There was evidence that the plaintiff did not consent to these excisions, that pathological examination of the excised tissues revealed them to be normal, and the court believed that there was evidence from which the jury could find that it was not accepted surgical practice to remove such organs when there were no pathological abnormalities. The defendant in defense, offered testimony that clinical, as distinguished from pathological, findings could warrant such removal. However, the evidence of two medical witnesses was subject to a contrary view and, still further, the jury could view the testimony of the physician's witnesses as being insufficient to show the claimed clinical necessity, the court believed.

In *Pearson v Boines*, 367 A2d 653 (De 1976), affd, 386 A2d 651 (De 1978), a specialist in multiple sclerosis had examined the plaintiff and concluded that she was suffering from the disease. He advised her that she should have no more children and went on to recommend that she have something done to prevent pregnancy. The plaintiff signed a consent to have a sterilization operation performed by another doctor, a specialist in obstetrics and gynecology. Two days later, the first doctor wrote the second doctor confirming a diagnosis of multiple sclerosis and suggested a tubal ligation as an absolute medical necessity. The plaintiff further alleged that she was led to believe the operation was of extreme importance. Subsequently, the operation was successfully performed. However, two years later a third physician allegedly told the plaintiff that she did *not* have multiple sclerosis and never had. The plaintiff argued that it was at this point that she learned the sterilization had not been necessary. The plaintiff sought to maintain an action for negligence in the performance of the allegedly unnecessary sterilization surgery, but the cause was held barred by the applicable statute of limitations. Similarly, in *Young v Clement*, 367 So2d 828 (La 1979), the plaintiffs brought an action against the defendant-physician following the removal of the plaintiff-wife's fallopian tubes and ovaries, which the plaintiffs claimed were healthy. Also, an errant stitch had blocked a ureter and required additional corrective surgery. The suit alleged a course of surgical procedures which followed a persistent uterine infection during pregnancy, the failure to diagnose and treat properly, and, specifically, the negligent suturing of the ureter during the removal of the ovaries. An amending petition was filed specifying that the removal of the tubes and ovaries was an unwarranted procedure because they were neither inflammed, infected, nor malignant. Another supplemental petition was filed alleging that the hospital knew or should have known that the surgeon improperly performed unwarranted surgery and wrongfully permitted him to operate in the hospital without proper supervision. The action was held properly maintainable.

3. Limitation on Actions

a. [§2.16] Generally

Limitations issues are often dispositive in actions involving unauthorized or negligently prescribed or performed surgical sterilization procedures. In many such cases, the patients cannot, or do not, know at the time of the wrongful acts or omissions, that they have been injured. This raises the question of when the applicable limitation periods begins to run. Several approaches may be taken by the courts—some favorable to plaintiffs' maintenance of their actions, and others less so. The "discovery rule," as it is frequently termed, delays the running of limitation periods until the injured parties have knowledge of, or, by acting with due diligence, reasonably should have knowledge of their injuries and the most probable cause thereof. A less favorable rule, at least from the plaintiff's point of view, is that the limitation periods run from the time when the wrongful act or omission occurred, regardless of whether the plaintiff should have or could have known of the injury or damage at that time. [For a discussion of when causes of action accrue for purposes of medical malpractice actions, see §2.17.] In addition, the limitations issue can be affected by the tolling of the statute of limitations. A statute will be tolled, for example, where an injury has been concealed by the defendant. See *Taylor v Wilmington Medical Center, Inc*, 538 FSupp 339 (DC De 1982). [For a discussion of the tolling of the statute of limitations in a medical malpractice action involving a sterilization operation, see §2.18.]

b. [§2.17] Accrual of Cause

Generally, the accrual of a cause of action begins the running of the statute of limitations. Moreover, the right of action must be established before the statute begins to run. However, there are contrasting rules regarding when the statute begins to run. One rule provides that the statute begins to run from the time of the wrongful act or omission. Thus, in *Pearson v Boines*, 386 A2d 651 (De 1978), the court held that the statute began to run when the sterilization was performed. A woman was sterilized because a physician determined she had multiple sclerosis. However, two years later, she was told by another physician that she never had the disease and even if she had, sterilization probably was unnecessary. But by that time two years had passed, which was the limitations period generally applied to malpractice claims. The court held that its earlier decision in *Layton v Allen*, 246 A2d 794 (De 1968), which held that the statute of limitations did not begin to run in medical malpractice actions in which the injury was inherently unknowable and the plaintiff blamelessly ignorant, did not apply because an error-in-diagnosis-case is not one involving an inherently unknowable injury to a blameless ignorant plaintiff.

By contrast, there is authority for another rule that defines the beginning of the running of the statute of limitations as the time the plaintiff discovers, or by reasonable diligence should discover, the injury. For example, in *Iverson v Lancaster*, 158 NW2d 507 (ND 1968), the court held that the limitations period begins to run in a malpractice action from the time the act of malpractice with resulting injury is, or by reasonable diligence could be, discovered. The plaintiff alleged that the physician had failed to diagnose her condition of hypertension as due to coarctation of the aorta and, based on the negligent diagnosis, advised her to undergo a sterilization operation since she should not become pregnant. The physician contended that the action accrued when the sterilization operation took place, and because 2 years had passed since that date, the action was barred. However, the court held that the statute did not begin to run until the woman and her husband were advised that she had coarctation of the aorta. Moreover, the court said the woman and her husband did not discover, nor could they by reasonable diligence have discovered, the physician's alleged negligence until they were informed of the coarctation of the woman's aorta and of the remedial effect which would be obtained by means of corrective surgery.

And, in *Young v Clement*, 367 So2d 828 (La 1979), the court held that prescription does not run against persons who are ignorant of the existence of facts that would entitle them to bring a malpractice action, as long as such ignorance is not willful and does not result from their neglect. The patient, in *Young*, had undergone an operation that resulted in the removal of her fallopian tubes and ovaries. Subsequently, she was shown a pathologist's report that discussed the removal of the tubes and ovaries. More than 3 years after the operation the patient and her husband amended an earlier filed petition in the case and alleged that the removal of the tubes and ovaries was unwarranted. The court held that the prescription did not run, and reasoned that the patient and her husband could not be held to a superior ability to interpret the pathologist's report to mean that he was wrong, and that they needed to sue within a year or lose their right. And, in *Hundley v St Francis Hosp*, 327 P2d 131 (Ca 1958), the court said that in malpractice actions, while the physician-patient relation continues, the plaintiff is not ordinarily put on notice of the negligent conduct of the physician upon whose skill, judgment, and advice the patient continues to rely. Thus, the court said, in the absence of the actual discovery of the negligence, the statute does not begin to run during such period, and this is true even though the condition itself is known to the plaintiff, so long as its negligent cause and deleterious effect is not discovered.

c. [§2.18] Tolling

In some situations involving actions based on sterilization operations the courts have held that the running of the statute of limitations should be tolled. For example, the tolling of a statute can be appropriate when an injury has been concealed. Thus, in *Taylor v Wilmington Medical Ctr, Inc*, 538 FSupp 339 (D De 1982), the court held that the fraudulent concealment of a cause of action may toll the statute of limitations. Moreover, the court said that in order for the tolling to occur there must be both fraud and concealment and there must be actual subjective knowledge by the defendant of the wrong done. In *Taylor*, a husband and wife alleged that they were advised that a birth defective baby was due to a genetic malady, and that, based on that information, the husband had undergone a vasectomy. Later, however, after the statute had run, they discovered that the defect was not necessarily genetically inherited.

C. Liability for Refusal to Perform Surgical Sterilization — 42 USC §1983

1. [§2.19] Color of State Law Requirement

Under 42 USC §1983, persons who are deprived of rights, privileges, or immunities "secured by the Constitution and laws" of the United States are entitled to bring an action for damages and injunctive relief against individuals and governmental bodies who are responsible for the deprivation. In order to establish a prima facie §1983 cause of action, §1983 requires that the challenged conduct be "under color of law." The "color of law" requirement limits the scope of §1983 to regulation of state and local governmental conduct, as distinct from purely private conduct. Moreover, the requirement means that state action is a condition precedent to stating a §1983 claim. [For a detailed guide to actions under §1983, see Nahmod, Civil Rights and Civil Liberties Litigation – A Guide to §1983 (Shepard's/McGraw-Hill 1979).]

For various reasons, hospitals may refuse to permit their facilities to be used for the performance of sterilization procedures. This is particularly true in the case of religiously affiliated hospitals. In a number of instances, persons who have been denied the use of hospital facilities for sterilization procedures have brought §1983 actions alleging violation of federal constitutional rights under color of state law. While some of these actions have involved public hospitals [see *McCabe v Nassau Cty Medical Center*, 453 F2d 698 (2d Cir 1971); *Hathaway v Worcester City Hosp*, 341 FSupp 1385 (D Ma 1972)], most have been brought against private institutions. Whether the defendant is a public or private hospital, however, it is necessary for the plaintiff to prove that the hospital was acting under color of state law when it denied the use of its facilities for the purpose sought.

Whether there is state action for the purpose of a §1983 action depends on the particular circumstances of each case, and therfore must be determined on a case-by-case basis. *Burton v Wilmington Parking Auth*, 365 US 715, 81 SCt 865, 6 LE2d 45 (1961). State action has been found to exist, or at least to have been sufficiently alleged to withstand a motion to dismiss, where the hospital was a county medical center, a public facility which was funded, regulated, and controlled, wholly or in part, by the state and county in which it was located. *McCabe v Nassau Cty Medical Center*, 453 F2d 698 (2d Cir 1971). The court said that the complaint, which sought injunctive and declaratory relief and damages based on the medical center's refusal to permit a sterilization operation to be performed on a woman, sufficiently alleged that the hospital was vested with power "possessed by virtue of state law," and that its conduct was "supported by state action." In *McCabe*, the defendant-hospital had declined to allow the contraceptive sterilization of the plaintiff to take place because of regulations promulgated by the hospital that women between the ages of 25 and 29 years of age would not be sterilized unless they had five living children. In this case the plaintiff had only four living children at the time she sought the sterilization operation. And, in *Downs v Sawtelle*, 574 F2d 1 (1st Cir 1978), it was determined that a community hospital was engaged in state action for purposes of the color of state law requirement in a case involving an alleged conspiracy to sterilize the plaintiff. The involvement of the state in the operation of the defendant-hospital was multi-faceted. Thirty percent or more of its operating budget resulted from Medicare funds. The hospital was also subject to significant governmental regulation. Any profits earned by the hospital were to be distributed to the town of Milo where the hospital was located. If the hospital should be dissolved, all assets after payment of debts reverted to the town of Milo, and the Milo Selectmen had the authority to appoint the hospital's board of directors.

Mere state regulation, funding, or subsidization of an otherwise private entity is not, however, sufficient to render that entity's conduct state action. See, e.g., *Jackson v Metropolitan Edison Co*, 419 US 345, 95 SCt 449, 42 LE2d 477 (1974). Thus, the fact that a private hospital is entitled to a partial exemption from the payment of state taxes, is subject to state regulation, or receives government funding, either directly or as compensation for services rendered to patients under state and federal Welfare, Medicare, and Medicaid programs, has been held to be insufficient to establish that the hospital acted under color of state law when it denied the use of its facilities for sterilization operations. *Chrisman v Sisters of St Joseph of Peace*, 506 F2d 308 (9th Cir 1974); *Ham v Holy Rosary Hosp*, 165 Mt 391, 529 P2d 361 (1974). For example, in *Ham*, above, the defendant-hospital was subject to state regulation and control in accordance with the laws of Montana and was licensed annually by the state of Montana. In addition, the hospital was subject to the regulations for hospitals and related institutions promulgated by the Montana Department of Health and Environmental Sciences. The hospital had had the benefit of general exemptions from taxation for nonprofit corporations organized for charitable, scientific, religious, or educational purposes. The hospital had also been paid with public funds for services rendered to eligible patients under state and federal Welfare, Medicare, and Medicaid programs. And, in *Chrisman*, above, the defendant had received federal Hill-Burton construction funds, enjoyed state tax exemption and was generally under state regulation. However, the court noted that the Congress had acted to prohibit courts from using the receipt of Hill-Burton funds as the basis for compelling an individual or hospital to perform any sterilization procedure if the performance of such procedure was prohibited by the hospital on the basis of religious belief or moral convictions. The court acknowledged that there was no formula for determining the threshold at which the reception of aid or regulation by the state cloaked private actions with the color of state law. However the court believed that the involvement of the state in the actions of these defendants did not rise to the level of significance required to state a cause of action under §1983. Here, the defendants had received since 1961 approximately 13 per cent of their construction funds from the state and from federal agencies. Additionally, they were licensed by the state but were not compelled by state regulations to perform sterilizations on request. In another case, the fact that a partially tax-exempt and government-funded hospital had the only maternity ward in a city, and therefore was the only hospital where a woman could obtain a tubal ligation in connection with a delivery by cesarean section, has been held not to render the hospital's refusal to permit performance of the sterilization procedure state action. *Taylor v St Vincent's Hosp*, 523 F2d 75 (9th Cir 1975), cert den, 424 US 948 (1975).

2. [§2.20] Mootness

In a number of cases, persons who have been denied the use of hospital facilities for the performance of sterilization procedures have brought suit against the hospitals under 42 USC §1983, alleging violation of their constitutional rights based on the refusal of the hospital to permit the use of its facilities for sterilization procedures. [As to issues regarding the "color of state law" requirement of 42 USC §1983, see §2.19.]

What is the effect on such a suit if the person succeeds in being sterilized while the suit is pending? Ordinarily, sterility following a sterilization operation is a permanent condition. Thus, there rarely is any reason or necessity for repeating the operation. Because of this fact, a number of courts have held that there is no viable controversy susceptible of judicial resolution and relief when the person bringing suit seeks injunctive relief or a declaratory judgment against the hospital which denied the use of its facilities. Such suits have been held to be moot. See, e.g., *Chrisman v Sisters of St Joseph of Peace*, 506 F2d 308 (9th Cir 1974); *Allan v Sisters of St Joseph*, 490 F2d 81 (5th Cir 1974). For example, in *Allan*, the plaintiff asked only for injunctive relief, seeking to make the defendant provide facilities for sterilization, and for general relief. There was no specific claim for damages, nor did the plaintiff initiate the suit as a class action. This was merely an action brought by an individual plaintiff who asked for a sterilization that she had already obtained. The court noted that even if it was inclined to grant an injunction requiring the defendant to provide facilities for the surgery, it would make no difference to the plaintiff because she had already been sterilized. The court noted its awareness that there were limitations restricting the scope of the mootness doctrine, including that a controversy is considered viable and not moot when the consequences of the activity at issue might adversely affect the complainant. Additionally, an issue that is capable of repetition, yet evading review, is not considered moot because of the underlying controversy that continues to exist between the parties. However, the court concluded that the issue was moot and said that while a pregnancy is normally capable of repetition with regard to the individual plaintiff, giving rise to a subsequent claim for an abortion, a sterilization completely terminates any possibility of the controversy recurring.

The result has been different, however, when damages were sought in addition to injunctive relief, or when suit was brought as a class action. Subsequent sterilization of the plaintiff has been held not to render such actions moot. *Taylor v St Vincent's Hosp*, 523 F2d 75 (9th Cir 1975), cert den, 424 US 948 (1976); *Chrisman v Sisters of St Joseph of Peace*, 506 F2d 308 (9th Cir 1974); *McCabe v Nassau Cty Medical Center*, 453 F2d 698 (2d Cir 1971). For example, in *McCabe*, the court said although the request for injunctive relief was moot and academic, the claim for damages was not. The court noted that the plaintiff had sought $250,000 in damages because she had been in constant fear of becoming pregnant during the period when the sterilization operation was not available. Moreover, the court noted the plaintiff's action was not mooted merely because she no longer needed equitable relief, and that the claim for damages was not nominal.

3. [§2.21] Constitutional Rights Violated

Because of the difficulty of demonstrating state action by hospitals in connection with their refusal to allow hospital facilities to be used for sterilization operations [see §2.19], in actions under 42 USC §1983 the courts only rarely have reached the question whether such action by a hospital amounts to a violation of constitutionally protected rights. In one such case, *Hathaway v Worcester City Hosp*, 341 FSupp 1385 (D Ma 1972), it was held that the refusal of a city hospital to permit its facilities to be used for sterilization operations did not violate the constitutional rights of a woman who sought to have her fallopian tubes severed in order to prevent further conception. The hospital routinely refused to permit the performance of sterilization operations on the basis of the legal opinion of the city solicitor that such operations were of doubtful legality under a controlling state statute. The court said that no constitutional right is violated by a governmental entity's general and nondiscriminatory refusal to perform a particular type of operation, particularly where the person desiring the operation is unable to establish a financial inability to pay for the operation at some other hospital.

Similarly, in *Padin v Fordham Hosp*, 392 FSupp 447 (SD NY 1975), the court held that a woman's constitutional rights were not violated when a tubal ligation was not performed on the woman on the scheduled date. The woman was admitted to the hospital, which was a publicly funded and controlled institution, for a delivery by cesarean section, in connection with which the tubal ligation was to be performed. However, the sterilization procedure was not done at the time of delivery because of the anesthesiologist's refusal, on religious grounds, to assist in such an operation. Approximately three months later, the woman was readmitted to the hospital and the tubal ligation was performed. The court said that it was the hospital's prerogative to schedule sterilization operations at times when appropriate personnel would be available, so long as scheduling did not operate to effectively establish a policy of not permitting such operations. The woman made no claim that the hospital or its officials followed a policy of assigning tubal ligation operations to physicians in such a way that the hospital effectively refused to permit its facilities to be used for the performance of such procedures.

D. Sterilization of Incompetent Persons

1. [§2.22] Generally

The severely limited ability of some mentally retarded or impaired persons to understand the nature and consequences of sexual activity and to exercise judgment about such activity has constituted the major reason for considering the contraceptive sterilization of these persons. See *Matter of Guardianship of Eberhardy*, 102 Wi2d 539, 307 NW2d 881 (1981). The potentially tragic consequences of pregnancy for an individual who neither understands his or her condition nor is capable of taking responsibility for a child may, in some cases, necessitate considering the alternative of preventing procreation as early as the onset of fertility. See *Matter of A W*, 637 P2d 366 (Co 1981).

This type of sterilization has been characterized as being neither compulsory nor voluntary. The term compulsory refers to a sterilization that the state imposes despite objections by the person to be sterilized or one who represents his or her interests. See *In re Grady*, 85 NJ 235, 426 A2d 467 (1981). Eugenic sterilizations are compulsory and are aimed at limiting the population of physically and mentally impaired individuals. [As to a discussion of eugenic sterilizations in general, see §2.1.] Moreover, the term voluntary is equally inappropriate since the person involved is without the capacity to give informed consent, and any explanation of the proposed sterilization could only mislead the person. [As to a statutory survey of voluntary sterilization statutes, see §2.3.]

Thus, what is proposed for such a person is best described neither as compulsory nor voluntary, but as lacking personal consent because of a legal disability. See *In re Grady*, 85 NJ 235, 426 A2d 467 (1981). The immense ramifications of these types of sterilization operations, however, have led to judicial consideration of the subject of sterilizations and whether they should be performed on mentally impaired persons. Sterilizations may be said to destroy an important part of a person's social and biological identity — the ability to reproduce. It affects not only the health and welfare of the individual but the well being of all society. See *In re Grady*, 85 NJ 235, 426 A2d 467 (1981). Any legal discussion of sterilization must, therefore, acknowledge that the right to procreate is fundamental to the very existence and survival of the race. See *Skinner v Oklahoma*, 316 US 535, 62 SCt 1110, 86 LE 1655 (1942). Additionally, there is a "penumbral" substantive right of privacy in marriage which bars the intrusion of the state into decisions involving contraception. See *Griswold v Connecticut*, 381 US 479, 85 SCt 1678, 14 LE2d 510 (1965). In *Eisenstadt v Baird*, 405 US 438, 92 SCt 1029, 31 LE2d 349 (1972), the United States Supreme Court extended the *Griswold* rationale to unmarried persons and stated that if the right to privacy means anything, it is the right of the individual, married or single, to be free from unwarranted governmental intrusion into matters so fundamentally affecting a person as the decision to bear or beget a child. *Doe v Bolton*, 410 US 179, 93 SCt 739, 35 LE2d 201 (1973); *Roe v Wade*, 410 US 113, 93 SCt 705, 35 LE2d 147 (1973). Reading these cases in conjunction with *Skinner* leads to the conclusion that an individual has a fundamental right not only to bear a child, but to decide not to be the source of another life. The cases invalidating restrictions on abortion absent a compelling state interest also have as their basis the constitutional right of individual control over procreative decisions. *See* DEVELOPMENTS IN THE LAW: THE CONSTITUTION AND THE FAMILY, 93 Harvard LR 1159 (1980).

The complementary rights of procreation and sterilization imply as well the right to choose between the alternatives. The procreative alternatives available to competent adults must also extend where possible to individuals who are not mentally competent to make the choice for themselves. The inability to choose competently should not result in the loss of a person's constitutional interests. If the decision whether or not to procreate is a valuable incident to a person's right of privacy, then it should not be discarded solely because the person's mental condition prevents the conscious exercise of the choice. See *In re Grady*, 85 NJ 235, 426 A2d 467 (1981).

Because the decision to be sterilized is a permanent one, it should be delayed whenever possible to see if the person becomes competent to make a decision in the future. See *Matter of A W*, 637 P2d 366 (Co 1981).

The types of mental impairments that have led to requests by others for a person's sterilization have included a person afflicted with Down's Syndrome [see, e.g., *Matter of C D M*, 627 P2d 607 (Ak 1981); *In re Grady*, 85 NJ 235, 426 A2d 467 (1981)], and severely retarded persons [see *Matter of A W*, 637 P2d 366 (Co 1981); *Wentzel v Montgomery Gen Hosp, Inc*, 293 Md 685, 447 A2d 1244 (1982); *Matter of Guardianship of Hayes*, 93 Wa 228, 608 P2d 635 (1980)]. In addition, concern for a female's inability to cope with menstruation [see *Matter of A W*, 637 P2d 366 (Co 1981)], pain in connection with menstruation [see *Wentzel v Montgomery Gen Hosp, Inc*, 293 Md 685, 447 A2d 1244 (1982)], and possibly of becoming pregnant in the future [see *Matter of C D M*, 627 P2d 607 (Ak 1981); *Matter of A W*, 637 P2d 366 (Co 1981); *Matter of Guardianship of Hayes*, 93 Wa 228, 608 P2d 635 (1980)], have been specific reasons others have sought the sterilization of the person.

This type of sterilization has been sought in the case of minors [see *Wentzel v Montgomery Gen Hosp, Inc*, 293 Md 685, 447 A2d 1244 (1982) (13-years-old); *Matter of A W*, 637 P2d 366 (Co 1981) (15-years-old); *Matter of Guardianship of Hayes*, 93 Wa 228, 608 P2d 635 (1980) (16-years-old)], and older persons [see, e.g., *Matter of C D M*, 627 P2d 607 (Ak 1981) (19-years-old), *In re Grady*, 85 NJ 235, 426 A2d 467 (1981) (19-years-old)].

When the parents of a mentally impaired person have sought to have the person sterilized under these circumstances, their consent has been generally ruled ineffective without a court order. See *A L v G R H*, 325 NE2d 501 (In 1975). [As to the issue of consent, generally, in the sterilization of mentally impaired persons, see §2.23.] Therefore, parents have sought court ordered sterilizations in these cases. Before the courts have considered the merits of the parents' contentions, however, they have sought to resolve the issue of whether jurisdiction exists for the granting of such an order. In some instances, it has been held that the court needs specific statutory authority to grant such an order. See *Interest of M K R*, 515 SW2d 467 (Mo 1974). In addition, grants of general jurisdictional authority have been held not to confer jurisdiction in these cases. See *Holmes v Power*, 439 SW2d 579 (Ky 1968). However, there is authority now that courts of general jurisdiction have authority to order or approve the sterilization of mentally impaired persons. See *Matter of C D M*, 627 P2d 607 (Ak 1981). [As to question of jurisdiction to grant orders authorizing sterilization of mentally impaired persons, see §2.24.]

In some instances where jurisdiction has been recognized, specific procedures and standards have been established for the handling of cases involving the sterilization of mentally impaired persons. These standards include the appointment of a guardian ad litem to represent the person whose sterilization is sought in determining whether alternative methods of contraception would be satisfactory, and whether sterilization is in the impaired person's best interests. See *Matter of C D M*, 627 P2d 607 (Ak 1981). [As to standards for authorization of sterilization of mentally impaired persons, see §2.25.]

In addition, there are some state statutes that mandate the definition of mentally incompetent persons, and the procedures to be followed in seeking to have these persons sterilized. See, *e.g.*, GA. CODE ANN. §84-930 et seq. [As to a more detailed description of these statutory provisions, see §2.26.]

In some instances, where a person who is not competent to consent to a sterilization operation is sterilized at the request of government authorities, or with court approval, the person's constitutional rights may be violated. In these cases, persons have brought actions under 28 USC §1983 for the denial of their constitutional rights. [As to discussion of liability in connection with wrongfully performed sterilization actions on mentally impaired persons, see §2.27.]

2. [§2.23] Consent and Authorization

When the sterilization of a mentally incompetent person is sought, an important issue is who can consent to, or authorize the procedure. A person who is mentally incompetent does not have the legal capacity to consent to anything. See *Holmes v Powers*, 439 SW2d 579 (Ky 1968). With certain limited exceptions, a parent has authority to consent on behalf of his or her child to medical treatment of the child. A parent's authority in this area derives from the duty to protect and care for his or her children. Does this authority extend to consenting to the performance of a sterilization operation on a child who is mentally incapable of giving consent? The answer apparently is that the parent's consent is ineffective without an accompanying court order. See *Matter of A W*, 637 P2d 366 (Co 1981).

Consent by parents to the sterilization of their mentally retarded offspring has a history of abuse which indicates that parents, at least in this limited context, cannot be presumed to have an identity of interests with their children. The inconvenience of caring for the incompetent child, coupled with fears of sexual promiscuity or exploitation, may lead parents to seek a solution which infringes their offspring's fundamental procreative rights. See *Matter of A W*, 637 P2d 366 (Co 1981). For example, in *A L v G R H*, 163 InA 636, 325 NE2d 501 (1975), cert den, 425 US 936, 96 SCt 1669,

48 LE2d 178 (1976), an action in which a parent sought a declaration of her right under the common law to have her 15 year-old mentally defective son sterilized, the court held that the common law does not invest parents with such power even though they sincerely believe that sterilization is in their child's best interests. Nor do the parents of a non-minor mentally defective child have authority to consent to the child's sterilization since, by reason of the child's emancipation, the parents no longer have any control over the child's person or property. *Holmes v Powers*, 439 SW2d 579 (Ky 1968). In the absence of specific statutory authority, the guardian of a mentally defective person lacks the power to consent to the sterilization of his or her ward without court approval. See *Ruby v Massey*, 452 FSupp 361 (1978); *Matter of A W*, 637 P2d 366 (Co 1981); *A L v G R H*, 163 InA 636, 325 NE2d 501 (1975), cert den, 425 US 936, 96 SCt 1669, 48 LE2d 178 (1976); *In the Matter of Mary Moe*, 385 Ma 555, 432 NE2d 712 (1982); *In re Penny N*, 120 NH 269, 414 A2d 541 (1980).

Moreover, to simply allow the parents or guardians of a mentally retarded person to substitute their decision and consent to sterilization for that of the incompetent person is not an adequate solution. The decision to sterilize is more complex and more reflective of public policy considerations than the decision whether to terminate treatment of a person terminally ill. See *Matter of A W*, 637 P2d 366 (Co 1981). Because of the past abuses involving the consent of parents or guardians to perform sterilization on mentally impaired persons, courts have reasoned that they, the courts, must be the final arbiter on this matter. See *Matter of A W*, above. Since the sterilization decision involves a variety of factors well suited to rational development in judicial proceedings, a court can take cognizance of these factors and reach a fair decision of what is the incompetent's best interest. See *In re Grady*, 85 NJ 235, 426 A2d 467 (1981).

One court has stated that an incompetent person has the same constitutional right of privacy as anyone else to choose whether or not to undergo sterilization. Unfortunately, the incompetent person lacks the ability to make that choice for himself or herself. It is not pretended that the choice of the person's parents, the person's guardian ad litem, or the court is the person's own choice. But it is a genuine choice nevertheless, one designed to further the same interests the person might have pursued had the person had the ability to decide for himself or herself. Having the choice made in the person's behalf produces a more just and compassionate result than leaving the person with no way of exercising a constitutional right. The court should accept the responsibility of providing the person with a choice to compensate for the person's inability to exercise personally an important constitutional right. See *In re Grady*, 85 NJ 235, 426 A2d 467 (1981). [As to a more detailed discussion of standards for court authorization of the sterilization of mentally impaired people, see §2.25.]

3. [§2.24] Jurisdiction of the Court

Until recently, courts generally have concluded that, in the absence of specific statutory authority for the sterilization of mentally incompetent persons, they lacked jurisdiction to authorize, order, or approve the sterilization of such persons. The reasoning on which this conclusion is based is clear. Because of the irreversible physical consequences of sterilization, which permanently deprives a person of the right to beget or bear children, specific statutory authorization has been viewed as an essential prerequisite to jurisdiction. See, e.g, *Hudson v Hudson*, 373 So2d 310 (Al 1979); *Interest of M K R*, 515 SW2d 467 (Mo 1974). Statutory grants of general jurisdictional authority, and even specific grants of authority in matters involving the affairs of incompetent persons, have been held not to confer jurisdiction to order sterilization of persons who are mentally incompetent. See, e.g., *Wade v Bethesda Hosp*, 337 FSupp 671 (SD Oh 1971) [construing Ohio statute]; *Hudson v Hudson*, 373 So2d 310 (Al 1979); *Guardianship of Tulley*, 83 CaA3d 698, 145 CaR 266 (1978), cert den, 440 US 967 (1979); *Guardianship of Kemp*, 118 CaR 64, 43 CaA3d 758 (1974); *Matter of S C E*, 378 A2d 144 (De 1977); *Holmes v Powers*, 439 SW2d 579 (Ky 1968); *Interest of M K R*, 515 SW2d 467 (Mo 1974); *Matter of D D*, 64 AD2d 898, 408 NYS2d 104, affd, 49 NY2d 879, 427 NYS2d 990 (1978); *Frazier v Levi*, 440 SW2d 393 (Tx 1969). But see *Matter of Sallmaier*, 85 Misc2d 295, 378 NYS2d 689 (1976); *In re Simpson*, 180 NE2d 206 (Oh 1962), discussed below.

In *Hudson v Hudson*, 373 So2d 310 (Al 1979), the court was faced with a case of first impression involving the equity powers of the circuit court to order sterilization of a mentally deficient minor, absent legislative authority. The court said it was reluctant to act in this field absent specific statutory authorization. The inherent equity power of the circuit court over both incompetents and minors did not include the power to order a surgical sterilization under the circumstances of the case, absent specific legislative authorization. The profound nature of the constitutional and social issues raised by the case, and the irreversible character of the physical consequences of the requested relief, precluded judicial resolution absent legislative action. And, in *Interest of M K R*, 515 SW2d 467 (Mo 1974), the court noted that although the Missouri Statutes provided that the juvenile code be liberally construed so as to provide such care as is necessary to the child's welfare, such construction could not be utilized to give the juvenile court jurisdiction and powers not conferred upon it by statute. The court concluded that the provisions of none of the sections of the juvenile code conferred on the juvenile court the jurisdiction and power to order or authorize the sterilization of a child. The courts were not faced in this case with a prayer for a judgment authorizing ordinary medical treatment, or radical surgery necessary to preserve the life of a child. Rather, the case was one which involved a request for sanction by the state of an operation which would irreversibly deny to a human being a fundamental right, the right to bear or beget a child. Jurisdiction of the juvenile court to exercise the awesome power of denying that right could not be inferred from the general language of the sections of the code. Such jurisdiction could be conferred by specific statute, the court said. Whatever might be the merits of permanently depriving a child of this right, the juvenile court could not do so without statutory authority which provided guidelines and adequate legal safeguards determined by the people's elected representatives to be necessary after full consideration of the constitutional rights of the individual and the general welfare of the people.

In recent years, however, a number of courts have recognized the existence of jurisdiction to authorize, order, or approve the sterilization of mental incompetents, despite the absence of specific statutory authority. In *Stump v Sparkman*, 436 US 951, 98 SCt 1099, 55 LE2d 331 (1978), an action was brought under 42 USC §1983 based on an alleged violation of the constitutional rights of a mentally retarded minor whose sterilization was authorized by an Indiana Circuit Court judge acting on the petition of the child's mother. The United States Supreme Court said that it could not agree with the conclusion of the Seventh Circuit Court of Appeals that there was a "clear absence of all jurisdiction" in the state circuit court to consider the petition. The Court pointed out that, by statute, Indiana Circuit Courts had original exclusive subject matter jurisdiction in all cases at law and in equity, jurisdiction over the settlement of estates and guardianships, appellate jurisdiction as conferred by law, and jurisdiction over "all other causes, matters, and proceedings where exclusive jurisdiction thereof is not conferred by law upon some other court, board or officer." The Court emphasized that neither statute nor case law had circumscribed this "broad" grant of jurisdiction to foreclose consideration of a petition for authorization of a minor's sterilization.

Moreover, where a court is one of general jurisdiction it has traditionally been regarded as having the power to hear all controversies which may be brought before the court within the legal bounds of rights or remedies, except insofar as has been expressly and unequivocably denied by the state's constitution or statutes. This has been particularly true with respect to the jurisdiction of courts of equity over incompetents. It is a universal rule of equity that where persons are not equal to protecting themselves in particular cases, the courts will protect them. As part of the inherent power of equity, a court of equity has full and complete jurisdiction over the persons of those who labor under any legal disability and also over their property. Where legal disability of the individual is shown, the jurisdiction of the court is plenary and potent to afford whatever relief may be necessary to protect the person's interests and preserve his or her estates. While this is indeed a special exercise of equity jurisdiction, it is beyond question that by virtue thereof the court may pass upon purely personal rights. See *Matter of C D M*, 627 P2d 607 (Ak 1981). As also taking the position that courts of general jurisdiction have authority to order, authorize, or approve the sterilization of mental incompetents, see *Matter of A W*, 627 P2d 366 (Co 1982); *In the Matter of Mary Moe*, 385 Ma 555, 432 NE2d 712 (1982); *In re Simpson*, 180 NE2d 206 (Oh 1962) [but see *Wade v Bethesda Hosp*, 337 FSupp 671 (SD Oh 1971) (interpreting Ohio statute)]; *Matter of Guardianship of Eberhardy*, 102 Wi2d 539, 307 NW2d 881 (1981).

Several courts have concluded that jurisdiction exists by reason of the doctrine of parens patriae, under which a court has authority to hear matters involving the welfare of incompetent persons. The inherent parens patriae jurisdiction is broad enough to encompass the decision whether consent for sterilization should be given by a court on behalf of persons who lack the capacity to give or withhold consent for themselves. The parens patriae power derives from the inherent equitable authority of the sovereign to protect those persons within the state who cannot protect themselves because of an innate legal disability. While traditionally used to protect the economic and property interests of the legally disabled, it has also been invoked to protect personal rights. *In re Grady*, 85 NJ 235, 426 A2d 467 (1981). See also *Matter of C D M*, 627 P2d 607 (Ak 1981); *Wentzel v Montgomery Gen Hosp, Inc*, 293 Md 685, 447 A2d 1244 (1982); *Matter of Sallmaier*, 85 Misc2d 295, 378 NYS2d 689 (1976). *See generally*, West, PARENS PATRIAE: JUDICIAL AUTHORITY TO ORDER THE STERILIZATION OF MENTAL INCOMPETENTS, 2 J of Legal Medicine 523 (Dec 1981).

Clearly, there is jurisdiction when a statute specifically authorizes a court to approve the sterilization of an incapacitated person. See, *e.g.*, *In re Penny N*, 120 NH 269, 414 A2d 541 (1980).

However, there is authority for the proposition that even if jurisdiction is present, the sterilization should not be ordered by the court because of the complexities of the public policy consideration involved. Instead the legislature should have the opportunity to conduct hearings and undertake fact finding which could lead to the declaration of public policy and legislative guidelines for the exercise of the court's plenary jurisdiction. It would be inappropriate to either permit the sterilization of an incompetent person where there has been no determination by the legislature of the state's public policy defining what is in the person's best interests, or attempt to set forth guidelines when the preferred branch of government to enunciate general rules of public policy is the legislature. The only guideline available to courts faced with this issue appears to be the best interests of the person to be sterilized. But no one who has dealt with this standard has expressed complete satisfaction with it. It is not an objective test and it is not intended to be. The substantial workability of the test rests upon the informed fact finding and the wise exercise of discretion by trial courts engendered by long experience with the standard. However, sterilization as understood by the medical sciences is substantially irreversible, and thus the sterilization of any person pursuant to an order in the exercise of judicial discretion must be considered irreversible. The vague, although frequently useful, best interest analysis appears to be inadequate unless there is an authoritative declaration of public policy to guide the exercise of that irreversible discretionary act. Courts, even by taking judicial notice of medical treatises, know very little of the techniques or efficacy of contraceptive methods or of thwarting the ability to procreate by methods short of sterilization. While courts are always dependent upon the opinions of expert witnesses, it would appear that the exercise of judicial discretion unguided by well thought-out policy determinations, reflecting the interest of society, as well as of the person to be sterilized, is hazardous indeed. A properly thought-out public policy on sterilization or alternative contraceptive methods could well facilitate the entry of these persons into a more nearly normal relationship with society. A court has been held not an appropriate forum for making policy in such a sensitive area. See *Matter of Guardianship of Eberhardy*, 102 Wi2d 539, 307 NW2d 881 (1981).

4. [§2.25] Standards for Authorization

Recognizing that sterilization ordinarily is irreversible and that the consequence of sterilization is permanent termination of the basic right to procreate, courts in a number of states have gone to great lengths to delineate the standards which should govern a decision whether to authorize, order, or approve the sterilization of mentally incompetent persons. Basic due process considerations require that a guardian ad litem be appointed to represent the person whose sterilization is sought [see, e.g., *In re Penny N*, 414 A2d 541 (NH 1980); *In re Grady*, 85 NJ 235, 426 Ad 467 (1981)], that an evidentiary hearing be held [see, e.g., *Matter of C D M*, 627 P2d 607 (Ak 1981); *In the Matter of Mary Moe*, 385 Ma 555, 432 NE2d 712 (1982)], and that the evidence establish that sterilization is in the person's best interests [see, e.g., *Wentzel v Montgomery Gen Hosp, Inc*, 293 Md 685, 447 A2d 1244 (1982)]. The person's best interest has been defined as whether the person could have a richer and more active life only if the risk of pregnancy was permanently eliminated. See *In re Grady*, 85 NJ 235, 426 A2d 474 (1981). Moreover, it has been noted that a person's best interest in this context can also be defined as the sterilization being necessary for the person's medical or mental health. For example, in *Wentzel v Montgomery Gen Hosp, Inc*, 293 Md 685, 447 A2d 1244 (1982), the court believed the evidence failed to disclose that sterilization was in the incompetent person's best interest as being necessary for the person's medical or mental health. Manifestly, the fact that the person experienced pain and irritation during her menstrual cycle, which she did not understand and with which she had difficulty in coping, did not in itself provide any basis for authorizing a hysterectomy. Nor did the mere fact that she could become pregnant and give birth to a child, for whom she could not care, provide justification to authorize the operation.

In the absence of any legislative determination to the contrary, the clear and convincing standard of proof should apply in this kind of case. Preponderance of the evidence, as a standard of proof, does not sufficiently protect the person's interest in preserving his or her physical integrity. On the other hand, the beyond a reasonable doubt standard is overprotective. That standard would be inappropriate in a proceeding in which the overriding consideration is the incapacitated person's best interest, and in which no loss of liberty or stigmatization will result. See *In re Penny N*, 414 A2d 541 (NH 1980).

A number of courts have established specific rules and procedures relating to court orders for the sterilization of incompetent persons. Typically, these procedures are detailed and specific. For example, in *Matter of C D M*, 627 P2d 607 (Ak 1981), the court held that a court considering a petition for sterilization of a mentally incompetent person must decide:

> (1) whether the person is legally incompetent to decide whether or not to be sterilized; (2) whether the person is capable of reproduction; (3) whether the person would be unable to adequately care and provide for a child; (4) whether alternative methods of contraception would be satisfactory or whether sterilization is the only practicable means of contraception; (5) whether, to the extent it is possbile to make such a determination, the person understands the consequences of sterilization and desires to be sterilized; and (6) whether those persons petitioning for sterilization are motivated by a genuine concern for the person or by convenience.

In order for the petition to be granted, it must be established by clear and convincing evidence that sterilization is in the person's best interests.

Similarly, in *In the Matter of Mary Moe*, 385 Ma 555, 432 NE2d 712 (1982), the court held that the doctrine of substituted judgment should be applied by a court whose approval is sought for the sterilization of a mentally incompetent person. Under this doctrine, it is the responsibility of the court to decide what choice would be made by the incompetent person if he or she were capable of deciding. Evidence must be offered and the court must make findings on the following matters:

> (1) whether the person, despite being mentally incompetent, is able to make an informed decision as to the need for and desirability of sterilization; (2) whether the person is physically able to

procreate; (3) whether the person is likely to engage in sexual activity; (4) whether the person would be unable to care for a child; (5) whether the use of less obtrusive means of birth control is feasible and whether such means of contraception would be effective; (6) whether sterilization is medically necessary, *i.e.*, whether the possibility of pregnancy would endanger the physical or mental health of the person; and (7) whether a sterilization operation would cause health risks, trauma, or psychological damage to the person.

To the extent possible, the court must elicit testimony from the person concerning his or her understanding of and desire for sterilization.

Similar standards governing judicial authorization of sterilization of mentally incompetent persons are stated in *Matter of A W*, 637 P2d 366 (1981); *Wentzel v Montgomery Gen Hosp, Inc*, 293 Md 685, 447 A2d 1244 (1982); *In re Grady*, 85 NJ 235, 426 A2d 474 (1981); *Matter of Guardianship of Hayes*, 93 Wa 228, 608 P2d 635 (1980).

In addition, other requirements have been established to protect the rights of the incompetent person. To ensure that adequate evidence will be presented at the judicial hearing, a court may appoint one or more experts in the field of mental retardation to examine the mentally retarded person and to testify at the hearing about the person's mental and physical condition and any other relevant factors. Also, while the mentally retarded person need not testify or be present at the proceedings if the person's presence would serve no useful purpose, the trial judge should talk with the person and observe the person's physical and mental condition. The wishes of the person, although not conclusive, are relevant, and a strong indication that the person does not wish to be sterilized must weigh heavily against authorizing the procedure. See *Matter of A W*, 637 P2d 366 (Co 1981).

5. [§2.26] Survey of State Incompetent Persons' Sterilization Statutes

A number of states have statutes providing for the sterilization of mentally incompetent people. These statutes provide jurisdiction for the court to order the sterilization of mentally incompetent persons, establish procedures for obtaining the consent for the operation, and set out specific standards for court authorized sterilizations.

For example, the Georgia statutory scheme, which begins at GA. CODE ANN. §84-930 et seq. (1979), states when it shall be lawful to authorize such a sterilization [see GA. CODE ANN. §84-932 (1979)], the prerequisites to the performance thereof [see GA. CODE ANN. §84-933 (1979)], who may perform the operations pursuant to this act [see GA. CODE ANN. §84-935 (1979)], and civil and criminal liability under the act [see GA. CODE ANN. §84-935 (1979)]. The entire Georgia law reads as follows:

84-931. Voluntary Sterilization Act; short title of law. This law [§§84-931 through 84-935.2] shall be known as and may be defined as the "Voluntary Sterilization Act." (Acts 1970, p. 683.)

84-932. Same; sterilization lawful under certain conditions. It shall be lawful for any physician duly licensed without restriction to practice medicine and surgery pursuant to the provisions of this Chapter or Chapter 84-12, establishing a State Board of Medical Examiners and providing for the issuance of licenses to practice medicine and acting in collaboration or consultation with at least one other physician also so licensed, and so requested by any person 21 years of age or over, or less than 21 years of age if legally married, to perform upon such person a sterilization procedure, provided a request in writing is made by such person and by his or her spouse, if married and if such spouse can be found after reasonable effort, and provided, further, that prior to or at the time of such request a full and reasonable medical explanation is given by such physician to such person as to the meaning and consequence of such operation. (Acts 1970, p. 683.)

84-933. Same; finding of need; definitions; prerequisites to performance; performance of sterilization procedure.

(a) Finding of need. The General Assembly of Georgia finds that the present laws of Georgia provided no way for the performance of sterilization procedures as hereinafter defined upon persons, whether or not 21 years of age, who, because of mental retardation, brain damage, or both, are irreversibly and incurably mentally incompetent to the degree that such persons with or without economic aid (charitable or otherwise) from others could not provide care and support for one or more children procreated by them in such a way that such children could reasonably be expected to survive to the age of 21 years without suffering or sustaining serious mental or physical harm.

(b) Definitions. For all purposes of this section the following words and terms shall have the meanings hereinafter stated:

(i) "Person subject to this section:" A person, whether or not 21 years of age, who, because of mental retardation, brain damage, or both, is irreversibly and incurably mentally incompetent to the degree that such person, with or without economic aid (charitable or otherwise) from others could not provide care and support for one or more children procreated by such person in such a way that such children could reasonably be expected to survive to the age of 21 without suffering or sustaining serious mental or physical harm, when there has been, according to the procedures of this section as hereinafter stated, the required findings that the condition of such person is irreversible and incurable;

(ii) "Physician:" A person duly licensed to practice medicine and surgery in Georgia without restriction pursuant to the laws of Georgia;

(iii) "Accredited hospital:" A hospital licensed by the State Board of Health of Georgia and accredited by the Joint Commission of Accreditation of Hospitals;

(iv) "Sterilization procedure:" Any procedure or operation performed by a physician which is designed or intended to prevent conception and which is not designed or intended to unsex the patient by removing the ovaries or testicles.

(c) Prerequisites to performing a sterilization procedure on a person subject to this section. A sterilization procedure may be performed by a physician on a person subject to this section pursuant to subsection (d) of this section only after satisfaction of all of the following conditions precedent:

(i) A petition shall be filed by one or more of the parent or parents or legal guardian or next-of-kin of the person alleged to be subject to this section, or by the Chairman of the State Board of Health, or by the director of any county board of health, or of the Director of the State Department of Family and Children Services (or the county director of any county departments thereof) in the probate court in the county of residence of such person alleged to be subject to this section stating the reasons why such person is alleged to be subject to this section and containing the written consent of the parent or parents not filing the petition, if such parents are surviving, can be found after reasonable effort, and are mentally competent, and if no such parent or parents survive, or can be found after reasonable effort, or if such parent or parents are mentally incompetent, the written consent of a guardian ad litem who shall be appointed by the probate court and who shall make investigation and report to the probate court before the hearing shall commence, provided that such guardian ad litem shall be a duly qualified and licensed member of the State Bar of Georgia. The written consent of any parent shall not be required if such parent has not within six months of the date of the filing of said petition provided any support or maintenance to the person subject to this section and said parent does not reside within the same household as said person.

(ii) The judge of the probate court shall appoint two physicians, neither of whom is the physician who proposes to perform the sterilization procedure on the person alleged to be subject to this section and neither of whom is a member of the committee of the accredited hospital described in subsection (iii) hereof, who shall make an investigation and report to the court before the hearing shall commence that they have examined the person alleged to be subject to this section and whether or not they find such person to be a person subject to this section and that the condition of such person is irreversible and incurable in their opinion.

(iii) Prior to the hearing on the application, evidence shall be presented to the court that a sterilization procedure has been approved for the person alleged to be subject to this section by a committee of the medical staff of the accredited hospital in which the operation is to be performed. Such committee shall be one established and maintained in accordance with the standards promulgated by the Joint Commission on the Accreditation of Hospitals, and its approval must be by a majority vote of a membership of not less than three members of the hospital staff, the physician proposing to perform the sterilization procedure on the person alleged to be subject to this section and not being counted as a member of the committee for this purpose. The approval of such committee as above specified shall be based upon a finding that the person alleged to be subject to this section and that the condition of such person is irreversible and incurable in the opinion of the majority of the committee as above specified.

(iv) After hearing, if the judge of the probate court shall find by a legal preponderance of all of the evidence above specified that the person alleged to be subject to this section is a person subject to this section and that the condition of such person is irreversible and incurable, he shall enter an order and judgment authorizing the physician to perform such sterilization procedure in accordance with the provisions of subsection (d) of this section.

(v) An appeal to the superior court may be had by the applicant person alleged to be subject to this section or any other interested party on such judgment in the probate court as in other cases made and provided by the laws of this State. The proceedings before the superior court shall constitute a trial de novo, and upon application of either party shall be heard before a jury; any decision of the superior court, or of any court, in such cases may be appealed to the higher courts of this State as in other civil cases; the cost of appeal, if any, to the superior and higher courts, shall be taxed as in other civil cases; and the pendency of any appeal shall stay the proceedings in the probate court until the appeal be finally determined. Pauper's affidavits regarding court costs and costs of appeal may be filed as in other cases made and provided by the laws of this State.

(vi) The person alleged to be subject to the provisions of this section shall have the right to counsel at all stages of the proceedings provided for herein.

(d) Performance of sterilization procedure. After judgment of the court in accordance with the preceding subsections of this section shall have become final to the effect that such sterilization shall be performed upon such person subject to this section, a sterilization procedure may be performed by a physician upon such person subject to this section in an accredited hospital. (Acts 1970, pp. 683, 684; 1971, p. 869.)

84-934. Same; "sterilization procedure" defined. Wherever used in this law [§§84-931 through 84-935.2] the words "sterilization procedure" shall include and authorize the performance by the physician of any procedure or operation which is designed or intended to prevent conception and which is not designed or intended to unsex the patient by removing the ovaries or testicles. (Acts 1970, pp. 683, 687.)

84-935. Same; who may perform operations. No operation under this law [§§84-931 through 84-935.2] shall be performed by any person other than a physician duly licensed without restriction to practice medicine and surgery in this State pursuant to this Chapter. (Acts 1970, pp. 683, 687.)

84-935.1. Same; civil and criminal liability; intent of law. When an operation shall have been performed in compliance with the provisions of this law [§§84-931 through 84-935.2], no physician duly licensed without restriction to practice medicine and surgery in this state or other person legally participating in the execution of the provisions of this law shall be liable civilly or to criminal prosecution on account of such operation or participation therein, except in the case of negligence in the performance of said procedures. Nothing in this law shall be construed so as to require compliance with this law or to prevent the medical or surgical treatment for sound therapeutic purposes of any person in this State by a physician duly licensed without restriction to practice medicine and surgery in this State, which treatment may involve the nullification or destruction of the reproductive functions at the same time that it serves such sound therapeutic purposes. (Acts 1970, pp. 683, 687.)

84-935.2. Same; exemptions. Nothing in this law [§§84-931 through 84-935.2] shall require a hospital to admit any patient under the provisions hereof for the purpose of performing a sterilization procedure, nor shall any hospital be required to appoint a

> committee such as contemplated under section 84-933(c) (iii). A physician, or any other person who is a member of or associated with the staff of a hospital, or any employee of a hospital in which a sterilization procedure has been authorized, who shall object to such sterilization procedure on moral or religious grounds shall not be required to participate in the medical procedures or the committee procedures leading to such sterilization procedure, and the refusal of any such person to participate therein shall not form the basis of any claim for damages on account of such refusal or for any disciplinary or recriminatory action against such person. (Acts 1970, pp. 683, 688.) . . .

In addition, Virginia has established statutory guidelines for the sterilization of children incapable of informed consent [see VA. CODE ANN. §54-325.10 (Cum. Supp. 1981)] and for certain adults incapable of informed consent [see VA. CODE ANN. §54-325.11 (Cum. Supp. 1981)]. Moreover, standards for court-authorized sterilization of these persons has also been set up. See VA. CODE ANN. §54-325.12 (Cum. Supp. 1981). These statutory provisions read as follows:

> §54-325.10. VA. CODE ANN. (Cum. Supp. 1981) Sterilization operations for certain children incapable of informed consent. —It shall be lawful for any physician licensed by the State Board of Medicine to perform a vasectomy, salpingectomy, or other surgical sexual sterilization procedure on a person fourteen years of age or older and less than eighteen years of age when:
>
> 1. A petition has been filed in the circuit court of the county or city wherein the child resides by the parent or parents having custody of the child or by the child's guardian, spouse, or next friend requesting that the operation be performed;
> 2. The court has made the child a party defendant, served the child, the child's guardian, if any, the child's spouse, if any, and the child's parent who has custody of the child with notice of the proceedings and appointed for the child an attorney-at-law to represent and protect the child's interests;
> 3. The court has determined that a full, reasonable, and comprehensible medical explanation as to the meaning, consequences, and risks of the sterilization operation to be performed and as to alternative methods of contraception has been given by the physician to the child upon whom the operation is to be performed, to the child's guardian, if any, to the child's spouse, if any, and, if there is no spouse, to the parent who has custody of the child;

4. The court has determined by clear and convincing evidence that the child's mental abilities are so impaired that the child is incapable of making his or her own decision about sterilization and is unlikely to develop mentally to a sufficient degree to make an informed judgment about sterilization in the foreseeable future;

5. The court, to the greatest extent possible, has elicited and taken into account the views of the child concerning the sterilization, giving the views of the child such weight in its decision as the court deems appropriate;

6. The court has complied with the requirements of §54-325.12; and

7. The court has entered an order authorizing a qualified physician to perform the operation not earlier than thirty days after the date of the entry of the order, and thirty days have elapsed. The court order shall state the date on and after which the sterilization operation may be performed. (1981, c. 454.)

§54-325.11. Sterilization operations for certain adults incapable of informed consent. — It shall be lawful for any physician licensed by the State Board of Medicine to perform a vasectomy, salpingectomy, or other surgical sexual sterilization procedure on a person eighteen years of age or older, who does not have the capacity to give informed consent to such an operation, when:

1. A petition has been filed in the circuit court of the county or city wherein the person resides by the person's parent or parents, guardian, committee, spouse, or next friend requesting that the operation be performed;

2. The court has made the person a party defendant, served the person, the person's guardian, if any, the person's spouse, if any, and if there is no spouse, the person's parent with notice of the proceedings and appointed for the person an attorney-at-law to represent and protect the person's interests;

3. The court has determined that a full, reasonable, and comprehensible medical explanation as to the meaning, consequences, and risks of the sterilization operation to be performed and as to alternative methods of contraception has been given by the physician to the person upon whom the operation is to be performed, to the person's guardian, if any, to the person's spouse, if any, and, if there is no spouse, to the parent;

4. The court has determined (i) that the person has been adjudicated incompetent in accordance with §37.1-128.02, has previously been adjudicated incapacitated for the purposes of

consenting to a sterilization operation in accordance with §37.1-128.1 or has been adjudicated in the proceeding specified in this section to be incapacitated for the purposes of consenting to a sterilization operation in accordance with §37.1-128.1, and (ii) that the person is unlikely to develop mentally to a sufficient degree to make an informed judgment about sterilization in the foreseeable future;

5. The court, to the greatest extent possible, has elicited and taken into account the views of the person concerning the sterilization, giving the views of the person such weight in its decision as the court deems appropriate;

6. The court has complied with the requirements of §54-325.12; and

7. The court had entered an order authorizing a qualified physician to perform the operation not earlier than thirty days after the date of the entry of the order, and thirty days have elapsed. The court order shall state the date on and after which the sterilization operation may be performed. (1981, c. 454.)

§54-325.12. Standards for court-authorized sterilization of certain persons. — A. In order for the circuit court to authorize the sterilization of a person in accordance with §54-325.10 or §54-325.11, it must be proven by clear and convincing evidence that:

1. There is a need for contraception. The court shall find that the person is engaging in sexual activity at the present time or is likely to engage in sexual activity in the near future and that pregnancy would not usually be intended by such person if such person were competent and engaging in sexual activity under similar circumstances;

2. There is no reasonable alternative method of contraception to sterilization;

3. The proposed method of sterilization conforms with standard medical practice, and the treatment can be carried out without unreasonable risk to the life and health of the person; and

4. The nature and extent of the person's mental disability renders the person permanently incapable of caring for and raising a child. The court shall base this finding on empirical evidence and not solely on standardized tests.

B. The criteria set out in subsection A of this section shall be established for the court by independent evidence based on a medical, social, and psychological evaluation of the person upon whom the sterilization operation is to be performed. (1981, c. 454.)

6. [§2.27] Liability

When a hospital refuses to permit its facilities to be used for a sterilization operation and state action is implicated, the person who sought the operation may have a cause of action under 42 USC §1983 for a deprivation of constitutional rights. [For a more detailed discussion of §1983 actions, see §2.19.] Similarly, when a person who is not competent to consent to a sterilization operation is sterilized on the initiative of government authorities or with court approval, the circumstances may be such as to violate the person's constitutional rights and also to provide the basis for a §1983 action. [As to the sterilization of mentally incompetent persons, generally see §2.22.] And when a person undergoes a sterilization operation based on a negligent medical diagnosis, liability may result based on a denial of the person's constitutional rights.

In view of the absolute immunity of judges from liability for damages under §1983, a judge who authorizes the sterilization of an incompetent person cannot be held liable unless the act was clearly outside the judge's "judicial jurisdiction." In other words, unless there is a "clear absence of all jurisdiction" over the subject matter, a judge is immune from liability for judicial acts. *Pierson v Ray*, 386 US 547, 87 SCt 1213, 18 LE2d 288 (1967). Immunity is the rule even if the judge acts in "excess of jurisdiction." [For a detailed discussion on judicial immunity from liability for damages under §1983, see Nahmod, CIVIL RIGHTS AND CIVIL LIBERTIES LITIGATION — A GUIDE TO §1983, §§7.06-7.09 (Shepard's/McGraw-Hill 1979).]

The scope of a judge's immunity from liability for ordering the sterilization of a 15-year-old mentally retarded girl was considered by the United States Supreme Court in *Stump v Sparkman*, 435 US 349, 98 SCt 1099, 55 LE2d 331 (1978). The petition of the girl's mother to have a tubal ligation performed on her daughter was approved by the judge of the Circuit Court of DeKalb County, Indiana, following an ex parte proceeding in which no guardian ad litem was appointed to represent the child's interests and no hearing was held. In a subsequent suit under §1983, the girl and her husband sought to have the judge held liable in damages for violation of her constitutional rights. By statute, the Circuit Court of DeKalb County had "original, exclusive jurisdiction in all cases at law and in equity." Pointing to this broad grant of jurisdictional authority and noting that there was no Indiana statute or case law prohibiting a Circuit Court judge from considering a sterilization petition, the Supreme Court reasoned that the judge did not act in the clear absence of subject matter jurisdiction. Consequently, he was immune from liability.

A different result as to the scope of a judge's immunity was reached in *Wade v Bethesda Hosp*, 337 FSupp 671 (SD Oh 1971), also involving a §1983 action against a judge who ordered the sterilization of a mentally retarded person. The district court concluded that the judge's action was not within the scope of his jurisdiction and that he therefore was not immune from liability. In view of the decision in the *Stump* case, there is at least a question as to the continuing validity of the analysis in *Wade*. [See, as questioning the correctness of the decision in *Wade*, Nahmod, CIVIL RIGHTS AND CIVIL LIBERTIES LITIGATION — A GUIDE TO §1983, §7.07 (Shepard's/McGraw-Hill 1979).]

Although §1983 damages actions against judges will be unsuccessful unless it can be established that the judge acted in the clear absence of jurisdiction in ordering the sterilization of a person who was not competent to give consent, other potential defendants should not be ignored. See, e.g., *Downs v Sawtelle*, 574 F2d 1 (1st Cir 1978) [action under §1983 against a community hospital at which an alleged wrongful sterilization operation was performed on a deaf-mute of borderline or dull normal intelligence]. Involuntary sterilization of persons who are not competent to give consent may also give rise to a cause of action in malpractice. See, *e.g.*, *Gooley v Moss*, 398 NE2d 1314 (In 1979) [malpractice action by a woman who alleged that she was wrongfully sterilized while institutionalized in a state hospital].

A liability action arising from the negligent misdiagnosis of sickle cell trait was the basis for a §1983 suit in *Avery v County of Burke*, 660 F2d 111 (4th Cir 1981). The plaintiff maintained that the county, its board of health and social services and several individuals wrongfully caused her sterilization after informing her that she had sickle cell trait. The plaintiff became pregnant and sought prenatal care at a clinic operated by the Burke County Health Department. Following a blood test, nurses at the clinic told the plaintiff that she had sickle cell trait. The nurses urged the plaintiff to consider sterilization, and told her that because she had sickle cell trait, childbirth would either immediately endanger her life or take two or three years off her life. They also advised her that a woman with the sickle cell trait is unable to take birth control pills. Employees of the defendant recommended the sterilization after warning that pregnant women with sickle cell trait are more susceptible to numerous diseases. Based on these representations, the plaintiff and her mother consented to the sterilization. Subsequently, after the sterilization had been performed, the plaintiff discovered that she did not have sickle cell trait. The plaintiff brought suit for deprivation of her rights of privacy and procreation in violation of the Fourteenth Amendment. Read in the light most favorable to the plaintiff, the court said the evidence disclosed that a trier of fact could reasonably find that the Boards did not adequately discharge their statutory duties. Burke County had a substantial black population, and the sickle cell trait effects approximately 10 per cent of the black people in the United States. Nonetheless, prior to the plaintiff's sterilization, neither board adopted policies, rules, or regulations for counseling and sterilizing persons believed to have sickle cell trait. These activities were by custom left solely to the discretion of the individual employees.

II. CONTRACEPTION

A. [§2.28] In General

The use of contraceptives is a protected constitutional right. It falls within the "penumbral" right of privacy in marriage which prohibits the intrusion of government into decisions involving contraception. See *Griswold v Connecticut*, 381 US 479, 85 SCt 1678, 14 LE2d 510 (1965). Moreover, the *Griswold* rationale has been held to also apply to unmarried persons, as well. If the right to privacy has any meaning, it is the right of the individual, regardless of marital status, to be free from unwarranted state intrusion into matters so fundamentally personal as the decision to bear or beget a child. See *Eisenstadt v Baird*, 405 US 438, 925 SCt 1029, 31 LE2d 349 (1972); *Doe v Bolton*, 410 US 179, 93 SCt 739, 35 LE2d 201 (1973); *Roe v Wade*, 410 US 113, 93 SCt 705, 35 LE2d 147 (1973).

Today, contraceptives are widely used in the United States, and it has been estimated that eight and one-half million women use oral contraceptives alone. *See* Barrett, PRODUCT LIABILITY AND THE PILL, 19 Cleveland State LR 468 (1970). In addition, it was also estimated in 1970 that more than three million women in the United States were using intrauterine contraceptive devices (IUD) as their method of birth control. *See* Van Dyke, THE DALKON SHIELD: A "PRIMER" IN IUD LIABILITY, 6 Western State LR 1 (1978).

The rationale behind using these contraceptive devices is to prevent conception and pregnancy for medical, psychological and social reasons. However, paralleling the growth in the use of these devices has been an increasing number of personal injuries arising from the use of contraceptives. A study compiled in the mid 1970's indicated that, of the total number of users of oral contraceptives, one female in 66,000 under age 35, and one female in 25,000 over age 35, would die each year from abnormal bloodclotting. This rate is almost eight times that of women not taking the pill. Moreover, the risk of heart attack is greater in users of the pill, and the risk of stroke is higher in pill users. *See* Frey, THE PILL AND THE CODE, 15 Journal of Family Law 1 (1976-77). The use of IUD's has also been associated with perforation of the uterus, sterility, cancer, ectopic gestation and pelvis inflammatory disease. *See* Food and Drug Administration Advisory Committee, REPORT ON INTRAUTERINE CONTRACEPTIVE DEVICES (1968).

Generally speaking, the two primary types of contraceptives that have engendered litigation have been oral contraceptives [see, e.g., *Oresman v G*

D Searle & Co, 321 FSupp 449 (D RI 1971); *Goldstein v G D Searle & Co*, 62 IlA3d 344, 378 NE2d 1141 (1978); *Leibowitz v Ortho Pharmaceutical Corp*, 224 Pa Super 418, 307 A2d 449 (1973)], and intrauterine devices [see, e.g., *Du Jardin v Ventura County General Hosp*, 60 CaA3d 350, 138 CaR 20 (1977); *Jones v Sportelli*, 166 NJ Super 383, 399 A2d 1047 (1979); *Terhune v A H Robins*, 90 Wa2d 9, 577 P2d 975 (1978)].

Most of the substantive and procedural litigation in the area of contraceptives has involved oral contraceptives. Hundreds of cases involving IUD's have been filed, but there are few appellate court decisions on the merits of these actions. Most of the actions involving IUD's have been consolidated under the Federal Multiple District Litigation Rules. See, e.g., *A H Robins, Inc, "Dalkon Shield" Liability Litigation*, 406 FSupp 540 (1975); *In re A H Robins Co, Inc, "Dalkon Shield", etc*, 419 FSupp 710 (1976); *In re A H Robins Co, Inc*, 438 FSupp 942 (1977); *In re Ortho Pharmaceutical Corp "Lippes Loop" Products Liability Litigation*, 447 FSupp 1073 (1978); *In re A H Robins, Inc*, 453 FSupp 108 (1978); *In re G D Searle & Co "Copper-Seven" IUD Products Liability Litigation*, 483 FSupp 1343 (1980); *In re A H Robins, Inc*, 505 FSupp 221 (1981).] The IUD cases have been consolidated because the actions involve common questions of fact, and consolidated pretrial proceedings pursuant to 28 USC §1407, the statute establishing the judicial panel on multi-district litigation, best serves the convenience of the parties and witnesses in the action. See *A H Robins Co, Inc, "Dalkon Shield" Liability Litigation*, 406 FSupp 540 (1975). In the vast majority of these actions, the plaintiffs have sought substantial sums and punitive damages. Through the fall of 1981, some 1,573 suits involving claims for compensatory damages well over $500,000,000, and claimed punitive damages in excess of $2.3 billion dollars, were pending against A. H. Robins, according to an affidavit of the secretary and assistant general counsel for A. H. Robins Company dated June 19, 1981. See *In re Northern District of California "Dalkon Shield" IUD Prods*, 526 FSupp 887 (ND Ca 1981). The plaintiffs have sought recovery against various IUD defendants on theories of negligence, strict products liability, breach of warranty, conspiracy and fraud. See *Van Dyke*, above. In addition, it has been held that there is no reason to justify excluding the role of an IUD from the purview of a state consumer fraud act. In *Jones v Sportelli*, 166 NJ Super 383, 399 A2d 1047 (1979), the defendant argued that as a matter of law the proscriptions of the state consumer fraud act were inapplicable to the sale of an IUD, principally because such an item is a prescription-legend product not directly available to members of the general public and obtainable only by, on, or through the order of a licensed physician. However, the court said there was no reason justifying the exclusion of the sale of an IUD from the act's coverage.

It should also be noted that a class action suit against the manufacturer of the Dalkon Shield has been decertified. The decertification order was filed in *In re Northern District of California "Dalkon Shield" IUD Products Liability Litigation: Abed v A H Robins & Co*, Nos. 81-4656 (9th Cir July 15, 1982). The court held the requirements of typicality, adequacy of representation, and commonality were not met by the punitive damages class. In part, the court said FED. R. CIV. P. 23(6)(1)(B) certification is proper only when separate punitive damage claims necessarily will affect later claims. Two classes had been previously certified by the U.S. District Court for the Northern District of California. One class was made up of nationwide plaintiffs bringing punitive damages actions. The other class was based on a California class action on the issue of liability. The district court erred by ordering certification without sufficient evidence of, or even a preliminary fact-finding inquiry concerning Robins' actual assets, insurance, settlement experience, and continuing exposure. The court's other consideration for certifying was that the punitive damage issue was a nationwide class action was to insure that Robins would be punished only once. The court noted that no rule of law limits the amount of punitive damages a jury may award. A class action, however, is not the only way to protect a defendant from unreasonable punitive damages. Given the difficulties in complying with the requirements of FED. R. CIV. P. 23(b)(1)(B) in this case, it was error to certify a nationwide class of punitive damages claimants. In addition, the court said the California class action should not have been certified either. In part, the court said in products liability actions individual issues may outnumber common issues. No single happening or accident occurs to cause similar types of physical harm or property damage. No one set of operative facts establishes liability. No single proximate cause applies equally to each potential class member and defendant. Furthermore, the alleged tortfeasor's affirmative defenses may depend on facts peculiar to each plaintiff's case. From the large California class the court may be able to find plaintiffs whose claims are fairly representative of the varying injuries. In proving liability under a negligence theory, however, the plaintiffs have to prove not only their injuries, but that Robins and each defendant owed them a duty of care and also what those different standards of care were, if they were breached, and if the breaches proximately caused the plaintiff's varying injuries. To prove liability under a breach of warranty theory, representative plaintiffs must exist for each type of warranty, assurance, or medical advice each plaintiff received. The difficulty of meeting the typicality requirement seems obvious.

In cases involving contraceptives, plaintiffs have typically brought suit against the manufacturer of the contraceptive [see e.g., *Dunkin v Syntex Laboratories*, 443 FSupp 121 (WD Tn 1977); *Whittington v Eli Lilly & Co*, 333 FSupp 98 (SD WV 1971); *Leibowitz v Ortho Pharmaceutical Corp*, 224 Pa Super 418, 307 A2d 449 (1973)], and the prescribing physician [see, e.g., *Hamilton v Hardy*, 549 P2d 1099 (Co 1976); *Green v Lilliewood*, 249 SE2d 910 (SC 1978); *Godard v Ridgway*, 445 P2d 757 (Wy 1968)].

One of the theories of recovery in actions against manufacturers or sellers has centered on breach of warranty. It is alleged that the defendant's product was not fit for the purpose for which it was sold, and thus that the defendant has breached an express or implied warranty of merchantability. In the context of contraceptives such a breach has been alleged where use of the contraceptive allegedly resulted in the plaintiff suffering a stroke [see *Dunkin v Syntex Laboratories, Inc*, 443 FSupp 121 (WD Tn 1977)] [for a more detailed discussion of the liability of manufacturers and sellers of contraceptives generally, see §2.29], and where the contraceptive did not prevent pregnancy [see *Whittington v Eli Lilly & Co*, 333 FSupp 98 (SD WV 1971)] [for a more detailed discussion of liability relating to warranty of a contraceptive's effectiveness, see §2.30].

Actions have also been brought against manufacturers and sellers of contraceptives based on a defect in the design of the contraceptive. See *Brochu v Ortho Pharmaceutical*, 642 F2d 652 (1st Cir 1981). The plaintiff alleges that under RESTATEMENT (SECOND) OF TORTS §402A liability attaches if there is a defective condition in a product sold to a consumer. Design defects are those which result from improper planning, testing, and design. [For a more detailed discussion of the liability of manufacturers or sellers based on defective design, see §2.31.]

Actions against the sellers and manufacturers of contraceptives have been based on defective warnings. See *McEwen v Ortho Pharmaceutical Corp*, 270 Or 375, 507 P2d 653 (1973). It is the duty of the manufacturer of a prescription drug to make timely and adequate warnings of any dangerous side effects which the manufacturer knows, or in the exercise of reasonable care, should know about. See *Stevens v Parke, Davis & Co*, 107 CaR 45, 9 Ca3d 51, 507 P2d 653 (1973). Moreover, the warning that is required must be adequate. If the warning is adequate, the defendant will be relieved from liability. See *Lawson v G D Searle & Co*, 64 Il2d 543, 356 NE2d 779 (1976). [For a more detailed discussion of adequacy of warning in cases involving contraceptives, see §2.33.] Finally, if the cause of action is based on the inadequacy of the warning, reliance by the plaintiff must be proven. If it can be shown that the injury resulting from the use of the product would not have been prevented even had adequate warnings been given, the defendant will not be held liable. *See* Sherman, PRODUCTS LIABILITY, §7.13 (Shepard's/McGraw-Hill 1981). [For a more detailed discussion of the element of reliance in actions based on inadequacy of warning, see §2.34.]

In same instances, actions have been brought against physicians in conjunction with injury from the use of a contraceptive. The theory in these actions is based on the physician's supervision of the contraceptive's use by the plaintiff. See *Hamilton v Hardy*, 549 P2d 1099 (Co 1976). For example, the failure of a physician to warn a patient of subsequently discovered risks may provide the basis for an action sounding in negligence. See *Tresemer v Barke*, 150 CaR 384, 86 CaA3d 656 (1978). [For a more detailed discussion of the liability of a physician in cases involving contraceptives and personal injury, see §2.35.]

The issue of the accrual, running, and tolling of the statute of limitations may also be important in the context of personal injury actions relating to contraceptives. The important factor in these cases is that the side effect that has been caused by the contraceptive may not manifest itself immediately. Therefore, the question becomes one of when the limitations period began to run and whether it was tolled. In some jurisdictions, the injury marks the accrual of the cause of action. See, e.g., *Doyle v Planned Parenthood of Seattle-King County*, 31 WaA 126, 639 P2d 240 (1982). However, in other jurisdictions, the limitations period will not accrue until the injury has been discovered. See, e.g., *Goodman v Meade Johnson & Co*, 388 FSupp 1070 (D NJ 1974), affd in part, rev in part on other grds, 534 F2d 566 (3d Cir 1976). [For a more detailed discussion of limitations issues that arise in the context of personal injury-contraceptive cases, see §2.36.]

B. Liability of Manufacturer or Seller of Contraceptive

1. Breach of Warranty

a. [§2.29] Generally

As with any other drug, the possibility exists that oral contraceptives will not have the desired effect or will cause undesirable side effects. What is the liability, if any, of the manufacturer or seller of an oral contraceptive if a woman becomes pregnant or develops certain conditions caused by her use of the drug? In a number of cases, women who have become pregnant despite their use of oral contraceptives and women who have suffered physical injuries allegedly as a result of the use of such drugs have sought to have the manufacturer held liable on a breach of warranty theory. If there is no warranty either implied or express, the plaintiff cannot recover in a breach of warranty action. For example, in *Whittington v Eli Lilly & Co*, 333 FSupp 98 (SD WV 1971), the plaintiff became pregnant, and gave birth to a child, although she was taking an oral contraceptive. When the contraceptive was prescribed, the physician allegedly told the plaintiff that he had prescribed the pill hundreds of times and had not had a failure. At that time, the physician furnished the plaintiff with a booklet concerning the contraceptive, and the plaintiff also received an instruction pamphlet with each packet of that contraceptive. But the plaintiff was never told that the contraceptive was absolutely fool-proof and positively effective. The plaintiff premised her cause of action on alleged breach of an implied warranty of fitness for the purpose for which the drug was intended, alleging that the defendant warranted absolute efficacy of the pill. However, the court noted that according to the plaintiff's deposition she talked with no one who claimed to be representing Eli Lilly and Company about the contraceptive and its effectiveness. There was no warranty, either express or implied, made to the plaintiff that the contraceptive would absolutely prevent pregnancy. According to the plaintiff's own deposition, the pamphlet furnished her by the doctor stated that it was only "virtually" 100 per cent effective, and "virtually" is clearly not synonymous with absolutely. Moreover, the test by the manufacturer revealed that there existed a certain minimal percentage of individuals who would not be afforded absolute protection by the pill and could become pregnant. Manufacturers of products are not liable under a breach of warranty theory to persons, who, having taken or received drugs, contract that which the drug was designed to prevent where brochures published by the manufacturer to be used by physicians and furnished to individual takers in connection with administration of the drug contained no warranty, either expressed or implied, as to the absolute effectiveness of the drug. And a manufacturer cannot be required, under a theory of breach of implied warranty, to insure against the susceptibility of a particular individual. Its duty is to reasonably guard against probabilities, not possibilities. See *Chambers v G D Searle & Co*, 441 FSupp 377 (D Md 1975).

In addition, under the Uniform Commercial Code there is mandated a warranty of merchantability that requires goods to be fit for the ordinary purpose for which such goods are used. See generally UCC §2-314. In the context of birth control pill cases, in which the plaintiff-woman has suffered personal injury by use of the pill, it has been held that the potential for adverse side effects, such as strokes, in some users does not make the pills unfit for ordinary purposes. As a matter of law, where a prescription drug is sold by a drug manufacturer which has warned the medical community of the specific risks associated with the use of the drug, the warranty of merchantability is not breached if a particular user suffers the adverse side effect which the warning identified. To hold otherwise would make the drug manufacturer an insurer of the drug user's health. See *Dunkin v Syntex Laboratories, Inc*, 443 FSupp 121 (WD Tn 1977).

Under the Uniform Commercial Code, there is an implied warranty of merchantability whenever goods are the subject of a sales transaction. In the absence of a sale, however, an implied warranty of merchantability does not necessarily arise. Thus, in *Allen v Ortho Pharmaceutical Corp*, 387 FSupp 364 (SD Tx 1974), it was held that since there was no sale of an oral contraceptive, the manufacturer was entitled to summary judgment in an action by a woman who claimed that the manufacturer was liable on a breach of warranty theory for personal injuries she suffered when a bloodclot developed, allegedly as a result of her use of the drug. A sample of the drug was provided free of charge by the manufacturer to the woman's physician, who in turn provided it to the woman. Although the court acknowledged that the manufacturer may well have dispensed the sample in the expectation of future profits, it refused to conclude that such an expectation was sufficient consideration to characterize the transaction as a sale within the meaning of the applicable provision of the Texas Business and Commerce Code, which defined a sale as the "passing of title from the seller to the buyer for a price." It was not clear, the court said, that the woman or her physician promised anything to the manufacturer in exchange for the sample. Any benefit to the manufacturer was merely fortuitous. Nor was there any evidence that by accepting the sample, the woman suffered any legal detriment.

In an action predicated on breach of an implied warranty, the UCC §2-607 requires that the plaintiff, a non-purchaser, give notice of the breach to the defendant, a remote manufacturer, as a prerequisite to maintain the action. See *Goldstein v G D Searle & Co*, 62 IlA3d 344, 378 NE2d 1141 (1978). However, where there is proper warning, a manufacturer of a prescription drug cannot be held liable on a breach of warranty theory. Because of the desirability of permitting drugs of proven value to be marketed despite known or suspected risks in the drugs, a drug labeled with appropriate warning, properly tested and approved by the federal Food and Drug Administration, and marketed properly under federal regulation is, as a matter of law, a reasonably safe product. See *Leibowitz v Ortho Pharmaceutical Corp*, 224 Pa Super 418, 307 A2d 449 (1973). [As to defective warnings in general, see §2.32.]

b. [§2.30] Warranty of Effectiveness

Where a woman who is not satisfied with the performance of an oral contraceptive seeks to have the manufacturer held liable on a breach of warranty theory, it must be established that there was a warranty. Under the Uniform Commercial Code, an implied warranty of merchantability arises whenever the seller is a merchant with respect to goods of the kind sold. UCC §2-314(a). A warranty of fitness for a particular purpose is implied whenever the seller is aware of a particular purpose for which goods are to be used and that the buyer is relying on the seller's skill or judgment to provide suitable goods. UCC §2-315.

Where information furnished by a drug manufacturer for dissemination to persons taking a drug contains no warranty, either express or implied, as to the absolute effectiveness of the drug, the manufacturer is not liable to persons who, despite their proper use of the drug, develop the condition which the drug was intended to prevent. *Whittington v Eli Lilly & Co*, 333 FSupp 98 (SD WV 1971). In *Whittington*, the court held that Eli Lilly and Company did not warrant the absolute effectiveness of its oral contraceptive "C-Quens." It accordingly ordered summary judgment in favor of Lilly in a breach of warranty action by a woman who became pregnant despite her use of "C-Quens." A pamphlet provided to the woman when "C-Quens" pills were prescribed for her use stated that, when taken as directed, the pills offered "virtually 100% protection." Although the physician who prescribed the pills allegedly told the woman he had given "C-Quens" to hundreds of women without a failure, none of the informational literature furnished by Lilly to the general public and prescribing physicians contained any assertions that "C-Quens" was a totally effective method of preventing conception.

The fact that a woman who uses an oral contraceptive is unusually susceptible to injury from use of the drug does not render the manufacturer liable on a theory of breach of warranty, either an implied warranty of merchantability or fitness for a particular purpose, where the drug manufacturer has warned the medical community of specific risks or side effects associated with use of the drug. *Dunkin v Syntex Laboratories, Inc*, 443 FSupp 121 (WD Tn 1977) [woman sought unsuccessfully to recover from drug manufacturer for stroke allegedly suffered as result of use of birth control pills]. The manufacturer cannot be required to insure against the susceptibility of a particular person. The manufacturer's duty is to reasonably guard against probabilities, not possibilities. *Chambers v G D Searle & Co*, 441 FSupp 377 (D Md 1975) [unsuccessful suit to recover on breach of warranty theory for stroke injuries allegedly caused by use of oral contraceptive.] See also *Leibowitz v Ortho Pharmaceutical Corp*, 224 Pa Super 418, 307 A2d 449 (1973).

Typically, birth control pills are purchased by consumers from retailers, usually drug stores or pharmacies, which obtain the pills from drug companies or wholesalers. In order to hold a seller of goods liable on a breach of warranty theory, the Uniform Commercial Code requires the buyer to give the seller reasonable notice of any breach. UCC §2-607(3)(1). Must the buyer give notice to the manufacturer when seeking to hold the manufacturer as well as the seller liable? In a case involving an alleged breach of warranty in connection with the sale and use of an oral contraceptive, the court held that the buyer must give notice of breach to the retailer only, not to the manufacturer. *Goldstein v G D Searle & Co*, 62 IlA3d 344, 378 NE2d 1141 (1978). It can reasonably be expected, the court said, that a retailer receiving notice from a buyer will give similar notice to the manufacturer in order to preserve any right of action for breach of warranty against the manufacturer. And see *Fischer v Mead Johnson Laboratories*, 41 AD2d 737, 341 NYS2d 257 (1973), holding that notice to the manufacturer of birth control pills was not a prerequisite to a suit for breach of warranty because notice is not required when goods are sold for human consumption.

2. [§2.31] Defective Design

RESTATEMENT (SECOND) OF TORTS §402A states that strict liability will attach if there is a "defective condition" in a product sold to a user or consumer. The concept of strict liability is applied to design defects as well as manufacturing defects. Design defects are those which result from improper planning, design, product analysis, or testing, and which result in a product that is identical to that contemplated by the manufacturer, but which is unsafe or dangerous in some way because of error in planning, design, or testing. It has been said that the basic test of whether a design defect exists is whether the manufacturer knew or should have known that the product resulting from the planning process would be unfit for use by the ordinary consumer. Sherman, PRODUCTS LIABILITY, §7.12 (Shepard's/McGraw-Hill 1981).

A cause of action in strict liability may be made out by a claim that a design defect inheres in a birth control pill because of the quantative composition of its ingredients. *Brochu v Ortho Pharmaceutical Corp*, 642 F2d 652 (1st Cir 1981). In the *Brochu* case, a woman who suffered a cerebral thrombosis allegedly caused by birth control pills she was taking sued the manufacturer of the pills on a strict liability theory. Although the manufacturer described the design defect argument as a "semantic ploy," the court said that it was unwilling to conclude that, under New Hampshire law, no drug could ever be classified as unreasonably dangerous because of its design. The court also noted that a jury finding of liability was supported by the evidence, including testimony that the pills, which contained an amount of synthetic estrogen (100 mcg.), posed greater health risks than pills with lower estrogen levels, that all the manufacturer's birth control pills were equally effective in preventing conception, no matter what level of estrogen they contained, and that the increased health risks from the higher level of estrogen outweighed whatever advantage, if any, the pills had in preventing conception. In other words, it was possible to conclude that the pills were unreasonably dangerous because of their design.

3. Defective Warning

a. [§2.32] Duty to Warn

The failure to provide adequate warning of the foreseeable risks from the use of a product may result in the manufacturer's liability, under either a negligence or a strict liability theory. When it comes to prescription drugs, it is the duty of the manufacturer to make timely and adequate warnings of any dangerous side effects which the manufacturer knows, or in the exercise of reasonable care should know to exist. *Stevens v Parke, Davis & Co*, 107 CaR 45, 9 Ca3d 51, 507 P2d 653 (1973); *McEwen v Ortho Pharmaceutical Corp*, 270 Or 375, 528 P2d 522 (1974). This rule applies to oral contraceptive drugs. See, e.g., *Lindsay v Ortho Pharmaceutical Corp*, 637 F2d 87 (2d Cir 1980); *Seley v G D Searle & Co*, 67 OhSt2d 192, 423 NE2d 831 (1981).

In the case of prescription drugs, the duty to warn generally is satisfied if the manufacturer provides adequate warning to the medical profession. *McCue v Norwich Pharmacal Co*, 453 F2d 1033 (1st Cir 1972); *Timm v Upjohn Co*, 624 F2d 536 (5th Cir 1980). Warnings to the medical profession are sufficient because prescription drugs can be obtained only through the authorization of a physician, who is responsible for supervising their use. When the prescription drug in question is an oral contraceptive, the manufacturer's duty to warn generally is satisfied if physicians are given adequate warning of the drug's side effects. *Goodson v Searle Laboratories*, 471 FSupp 546 (D Cn 1978); *Chambers v G D Searle & Co*, 441 FSupp 377 (D Md 1975); *Dunkin v Syntex Laboratories, Inc*, 443 FSupp 121 (WD Tn 1977); *Mahr v G D Searle & Co*, 28 Il Dec 624, 390 NE2d 1214 (1979); *Ortho Pharmaceutical Corp v Chapman*, 388 NE2d 541 (In 1979); *McEwen v Ortho Pharmaceutical Corp*, 270 Or 375, 528 P2d 522 (1974). See also *Terhune v A H Robins Co*, 90 Wa2d 9, 577 P2d 975 (1978) [intrauterine device].

However, the failure of the manufacturer to give similar warnings to women using birth control pills may expose the manufacturer to liability for injuries suffered as the result of their use. Regulations adopted in implementation of the Federal Food, Drug and Cosmetic Act require that inserts be placed in packages of oral contraceptives warning women of the harmful side effects associated with the use of such drugs. 21 CFR §310.501. Part of the rationale for enacting the package insert regulations was to make women using oral contraceptives more aware of the possible side effects of the drugs and to enable them to identify drug-related problems which might otherwise go unnoticed. *Pharmaceutical Manufacturers Assn v Food & Drug Admin*, 484 FSupp 1179 (D De 1980). Where violation of a statute or regulation having the force of a statute is considered to be negligence per se, a drug manufacturer's violation of the package insert regulations will relieve the plaintiff in a products liability case involving oral contraceptives from proving specific acts of negligence on the part of the manufacturer. *Lukaszewicz v Ortho Pharmaceutical Corp*, 510 FSupp 961 (ED Wi 1981).

b. [§2.33] Adequacy of Warning

Whether the manufacturer of oral contraceptive drugs fulfills its duty to warn of risks and dangerous side effects from the use of such drugs depends, assuming a warning is given, on its adequacy. If the warning is adequate, the manufacturer will be relieved of liability, either in negligence or on a strict liability theory, for injuries resulting from the use of the drug, assuming it is not contaminated or impure and is not defectively designed or produced. See Comment k to §402A of the RESTATEMENT (SECOND) OF TORTS, which states that the seller of unavoidably unsafe products, including new or experimental drugs, cannot be held strictly liable for unfortunate consequences attending their use, provided they are properly prepared and marketed and proper warning is given. A manufacturer is required to give reasonable warning of the risks and dangers that are foreseeable from the use of a product. *See* Sherman, PRODUCTS LIABILITY, §§1.10, 7.13 (Shepard's/McGraw-Hill 1981). The adequacy of the warning may be the central issue in determining whether a product such as an oral contraceptive drug is unreasonably dangerous under the doctrine of strict liability as set forth in §402A. *Lawson v G D Searle & Co*, 64 Il2d 543, 356 NE2d 779 (1976).

The scope of the warning given depends largely on the judgment of the manufacturer. It has been held that a warning in connection with the use of an oral contraceptive is adequate when it reasonably discloses to the medical profession all inherent risks which the manufacturer knew, or should have known to exist. *Seley v G D Searle*, 67 OhSt2d 192, 423 NE2d 381 (1981).

The adequacy of a warning depends on its factual content, its expression of the facts, and the method by which the warning is conveyed. *Ortho Pharmaceutical Corp v Chapman*, 388 NE2d 541 (In 1979); *Seley v G D Searle*, 67 OhSt2d 192, 423 NE2d 381 (1981). Thus, a warning may be inadequate if it does not sufficiently indicate the scope of the danger or if it does not clearly bring the danger to the attention of the proper person. Sherman, PRODUCTS LIABILITY, §7.13 (Shepard's/McGraw-Hill 1981).

Warnings given by manufacturers of oral contraceptives have been held adequate where the risks and possible side effects associated with the use of particular birth control pills were disclosed in the PHYSICIAN'S DESK REFERENCE, in direct warnings to the medical profession, and in package inserts and leaflets directed to women using the drugs. See, e.g., *Goodson v Searle Laboratories*, 471 FSupp 546 (D Cn 1978); *Chambers v G D Searle & Co*, 441 FSupp 377 (D Md 1975), affd, 567 F2d 264 (4th Cir 1977); *Dunkin v Syntex Laboratories, Inc*, 443 FSupp 121 (WD Tn 1977); *Lawson v G D Searle & Co*, 64 Il2d 543, 356 NE2d 779 (1976); *Leibowitz v Ortho Pharmaceutical Corp*, 224 Pa Super 418, 307 A2d 449 (1973).

On the other hand, warnings have been held inadequate where the package insert failed to disclose the existence of a positive correlation between the risk of cerebral thrombosis and the level of estrogen in an oral contraceptive [see *Brochu v Ortho Pharmaceutical Corp*, 642 F2d 652 (1st Cir 1981)]; where the manufacturer failed to take reasonable measures to alert treating physicians to the risks associated with use of birth control pills [see *Lindsay v Ortho Pharmaceutical Corp*, 481 FSupp 314 (ED NY 1979)]; and where the manufacturer issued no warnings to physicians or other persons concerning the possible risks associated with the use of certain birth control pills by women who smoke [see *Skill v Martinez*, 91 FRD 498 (D NY 1981)]. As also holding warnings to be inadequate, see *Hamilton v Hardy*, 549 P2d 1099 (Co 1976); *Mahr v G D Searle & Co*, 28 Il Dec 624, 390

NE2d 1214 (1979); *Ortho Pharmaceutical Corp v Chapman*, 388 NE2d 541 (In 1979); *McEwen v Ortho Pharmaceutical Corp*, 528 P2d 522 (Or 1974).

c. [§2.34] Reliance

Reliance is an element of a cause of action based on the inadequacy of the warning given by the manufacturer of a product. It has been held that a manufacturer cannot be held liable on a defective warning theory if it can be shown that the injury resulting from use of the manufacturer's product would not have been prevented even had an adequate warning been given. *See* Sherman, PRODUCTS LIABILITY, §7.13 (Shepard's/McGraw-Hill 1981). Thus, where it is demonstrated that adequate warnings of the risks or side effects associated with the use of oral contraceptives would not have made a difference in a physician's decision to prescribe birth control pills for a patient, there can be no reliance on the warnings as given and no liability on the part of the manufacturer. See, e.g., *Chambers v G D Searle & Co*, 441 FSupp 377 (D Md 1975), affd, 567 F2d 269 (4th Cir 1977); *Vaughn v G D Searle & Co*, 272 Or 367, 536 P2d 1247 (1975), cert den, 423 US 1054 (1976). However, where the evidence establishes that, had adequate warnings been given, the physician would have recommended that the patient not use or cease the use of birth control pills, reliance on the warnings is demonstrated. See, e.g., *Skill v Martinez*, 91 FRD 498 (D NJ 1981); *McEwen v Ortho Pharmaceutical Corp*, 528 P2d 522 (Or 1974). Some courts have concluded that the question of reliance is really one of causation and have reasoned that in the absence of any warning at all, or in the absence of an adequate warning, there is a rebuttable presumption that failure to warn was a proximate cause of the patient's use of the drug. *Seley v G D Searle & Co*, 67 OhSt2d 192, 423 NE2d 831 (1981).

C. [§2.35] Liability of Physician

Since birth control pills and contraceptive devices are obtained on the prescription of a physician and are used under a physician's supervision, physicians may be liable for injury resulting from their use. Typically, liability is sought to be imposed on a negligence theory. See, e.g., *Hamilton v Hardy*, 549 P2d 1099 (Co 1976); *Batiste v American Home Prods Corp*, 32 NC App 1, 231 SE2d 269 (1977) [alleged negligent prescription of oral contraceptives]; *Godard v Ridgway*, 445 P2d 757 (Wy 1968) [alleged improper positioning of an intrauterine device]; *Killebrew v Johnson*, 404 NE2d 1194 (In 1980); *Green v Lilliewood*, 249 SE2d 910 (SC 1978) [alleged negligent failure to remove IUD].

The failure of a physician to warn a women of subsequently discovered risks from the use of contraceptive devices may provide the basis for a negligence action. In *Tresemer v Barke*, 150 CaR 384, 86 CaA3d 656 (1978), a woman who had used a Dalkon Shield intrauterine device alleged that the physician who prescribed the device was negligent in failing to warn her of certain dangerous side effects associated with its use. Although the physician had been unaware of the potential side effects at the time he prescribed the device, he later learned of the possible hazards associated with use of the device, but did not inform the woman. The court reasoned that the confidential-patient relationship gave rise to a duty to warn and that the woman's allegations consequently stated a cause of action against the physician. See also *Gugino v Harvard Community Health Plan*, 403 NE2d 1166 (Ma 1980) [recognizing that physician had a continuing obligation to warn a woman of subsequently discovered risks from the use of a Dalkon Shield].

Actions in which physicians have been sought to be held liable on theories other than negligence generally have not been successful. In *Batiste v American Home Prods Corp*, 32 NC App 1, 231 SE2d 269 (1977), for example, a woman who suffered a severe stroke allegedly as the result of taking Ovral, an oral contraceptive, brought a breach of warranty action against the doctor who prescribed the drug. She claimed that the doctor breached implied warranties of fitness and merchantability in prescribing the drug, which allegedly was defective, dangerous, unsafe for human consumption, and unfit for its intended purpose. The woman reasoned that a physician who provides a prescription for a drug is a "seller" within the meaning of the Uniform Commercial Code and consequently may be liable for breach of warranty. The court held, however, that dismissal of the action was proper. It said that persons who, for a fee, provide professional medical services for the guidance and assistance of others cannot be held liable in the absence of negligence or intentional misconduct.

D. [§2.36] Limitation on Actions

Women who use birth control pills or contraceptive devices, particularly intrauterine devices, may experience certain side effects. Typically, the symptoms of these side effects do not manifest themselves immediately. Because of the lapse of time between use of birth control pills or contraceptive devices and manifestation of side effects from their use, statute of limitations problems often arise in tort actions against physicians who prescribed the pills or devices or drug companies which manufactured them.

If the jurisdiction in which the action is brought adheres to the rule that the statute of limitations begins to run when the wrongful act is committed or the injury occurs, the action will be time-barred if it is not brought within the applicable limitations period, even if the plaintiff was unaware of her injury or the commission of a wrongful act until after the limitations period has expired. See, e.g., *Doyle v Planned Parenthood of Seattle-King Cty, Inc*, 31 WaA 126, 639 P2d 240 (1982). If the jurisdiction adheres to the discovery rule, the statute of limitations does not begin to run until the injury and its probable cause are discovered or reasonably should have been discovered. See, e.g., *Raymond v Eli Lilly & Co*, 371 A2d 170 (NH 1977) [statute of limitations did not begin to run until woman who became blind allegedly as result of use of birth control pills became aware that she had a possible claim against the manufacturer of the pills]. As also taking the position that the discovery rule applies in tort actions arising out of the use of birth control pills or other contraceptive devices, see *Ballew v A H Robins Co*, 688 F2d 1325 (11th Cir 1982); *In re Northern District of California*, 503 FSupp 194 (ND Ca 1980); *Goodman v Meade Johnson & Co*, 388 FSupp 1070 (D NJ 1974), affd in part, rev in part on other grds, 534 F2d 566 (3d Cir 1976); *Tresemer v Barke*, 86 CaA3d 656, 150 CaR 384 (1979); *Witherell v Weimer*, 77 IlA3d 582, 396 NE2d 268 (1979); *Ooft v City of New York*, 104 Misc2d 879, 429 NYS2d 376 (1980) [statute of limitations does not begin to run until patient can reasonably discover foreign object, including intrauterine device]. Where the defendant fraudulently conceals the existence of a cause of action, the running of the statute of limitations will be tolled until the cause of action is discovered. *Merrill v Reville*, 380 A2d 96 (Vt 1977).

In some instances, plaintiffs have alleged that a defendant should be equitably estopped from pleading the running of the statute of limitations so as to bar an action. For example, in *Knaysi v A H Robins Co*, CCH Products Liability Reporter ¶9332 (1982), the plaintiffs brought suit against the defendant-manufacturer of an intrauterine device (IUD). The plaintiff-wife had become pregnant after insertion of the device and in the first trimester suffered a spontaneous septic abortion. The plaintiffs sought to prove that the defendant was aware from test results that the effectiveness of the device in preventing pregnancy was lower than it advertised, and that, from both test results and the reports of physicians, spontaneous abortions often occurred in connection with its use. They alleged that, despite this adverse information, the defendant concealed these reports and continued to issue false advertising to the medical community and the public as to the superior efficacy and safety of its contraceptive. The court held that summary judgment based on the running of the statute of limitations should not have been granted to the manufacturer of an IUD because there existed a triable issue of fact regarding the plaintiff's theory that the manufacturer should be equitably estopped by its conduct from raising the bar of statute of limitations. The court noted that for the doctrine to apply the defendant must have control and superior, or exclusive, knowledge of the facts necessary for the plaintiff to make out a cause of action, and that the defendant by affirmative misstatements conceals these essential facts from the plaintiff. Here, the court noted, the plaintiff alleged that she relied on information about the product from the manufacturer, and that the manufacturer provided information about the device that it knew was false. Therefore the court held that the facts alleged, if proved, could estop the defendant from pleading the bar of the statute of limitations.

Under the Uniform Commercial Code, actions for breach of warranty must be brought within four years from the tender or delivery of goods. UCC §2-725. Consequently, an action under the Code against a manufacturer of birth control pills for injuries resulting from an alleged breach of warranty must be brought within four years or be time-barred. *Raymond v Eli Lilly & Co*, 412 FSupp 1392 (D NH 1976), affd, 556 F2d 628 (1st Cir 1977); *Redfield v Mead, Johnson & Co*, 512 P2d 776 (Or 1973).

E. [§2.37] Sample Complaint/Petition

The increased use of oral contraceptives has resulted, in part, in numerous allegations made by plaintiffs that ingestion of an oral contraceptive by the plaintiff-woman resulted in some form of physical ailment or disability. In many of these instances the plaintiff-woman, and her husband if she is married, will bring an action against her physician. See, e.g., *Batiste v American Home Prods Corp*, 32 NC App 1, 231 SE2d 269 (1977). [As to the liability of a physician in cases involving contraceptives, see §2.35.] However, more typically, the plaintiff-woman, and her husband, will bring an action against the manufacturer or seller of the contraceptive. See, e.g., *Whittington v Eli Lilly & Co*, 333 FSupp 98 (SD WV 1971). [As to the liability of manufacturers or sellers of contraceptives generally, see §2.29.] The following sample complaint and demand for jury trial suggests one way to draft the initial pleading in an oral contraceptive case based on theories of negligence, strict liability, fraudulent misrepresentation and negligent misrepresentation by the defendant-manufacturer of the oral contraceptive. The injury complained of in the complaint is a stroke, the action is filed in federal district court, and the basis for the court's jurisdiction is diversity of citizenship. The plaintiffs are a woman who ingested the oral contraceptive, and her husband. The sample complaint states:

COMPLAINT AND DEMAND
FOR JURY TRIAL

FIRST CAUSE OF ACTION

1. Plaintiffs, [______________________________] husband and wife, are citizens of the State of [______________________________] and reside at [______________] in [______________

_______________]. Defendant, [name of manufacturer], is a corporation incorporated under the laws of the state of [__________] and has a place of business on [__________] in [__________________] and no place of business in [______________]. The amount in controversy, exclusive of interest and costs, exceeds the sum of Ten Thousand Dollars ($10,000.00).

2. [Manufacturer] has been since [__________] and is a manufactuer of and has been since [________] and is engaged in the business of selling drugs, including the following birth control pills: [trade name of pills.]

3. Plaintiff, [wife], consumed [trade name of pill] for the purpose of general contraception pursuant to the prescription of her physician from about [__________] through [__________] and as the direct and proximate cause of its consumption suffered serious bodily injury including an occlusion of her right middle cerebral artery on [__________], numerous cerebral seizures since that date, continuing paralysis of the left side of her body, and other permanent physical and mental injuries.

4. [Manufacturer] was negligent in the testing, manufacturing, labeling, marketing and promoting of [trade name of pill] and was also negligent in obtaining and retaining permission from the United States Government to market the drug for purposes of general contraception, in failing to heed warnings that came to it from others about the dangerous properties of [trade name of pill], in failing to give adequate warnings about these properties and to give adequate instruction in the use of [trade name of pill] to [wife] and to her prescribing physician, in failing to heed warnings and to give adequate warnings to [wife] and to her prescribing physician about the increased risk of thromboembolic disease associated with the consumption of higher dosages of [__________] such as [trade name of pill.]

5. [Manufacturer] violated the Federal Food, Drug and Cosmetics Act and drug, health and safety laws of the State of [__________] in the testing, manufacturing, labeling, marketing, and promoting [trade name of pill] for purposes of general contraception and in obtaining and retaining permission from the United States Government to market the drug for purposes of general contraception.

6. The injuries sustained by [wife] were caused by the above-described negligence of [________] with no fault or lack of care on the part of [wife] contributing thereto.

7. By reason of the foregoing, plaintiff [wife] has suffered and will continue to suffer great physical and mental pain and loss of the

full use of her body, and has incurred and will continue to incur medical expenses attendant thereto and has lost and will continue to lose earnings and the power to earn.

SECOND CAUSE OF ACTION

8. Plaintiff repeats and realleges each and every allegation contained in paragraphs 1 through 3, inclusive, and paragraph 7 of this complaint, and incorporates the same herein by reference as if they were fully set forth.

9. [Trade name of pill] was expected to and did reach the plaintiff consumer [wife] without substantial change in the condition in which it was sold. [Trade name of pill] was sold to [wife] in a defective condition unreasonably dangerous to her because, among other things, (1) it contained unreasonably high levels of [injury causing ingredient] and (2) [manufacturer] failed to accompany its product with proper directions and warnings to [wife] and to her prescribing physician.

THIRD CAUSE OF ACTION

10. Plaintiff repeats and realleges each and every allegation contained in paragraphs 1 through 3, inclusive, and paragraph 7 of this complaint, and incorporates the same herein by reference as if they were fully set forth.

11. [Name of manufacturer] fraudulently misrepresented to plaintiff [wife] and her prescribing physician material facts about [trade name of drug] knowing its representations to be false or incomplete or at least knowing that it was ignorant of the truth of its representations, with the intent that plaintiff [wife] and her prescribing physician rely upon these representations. [Wife] and her prescribing physician did rely on [manufacturer] representations in ignorance of their falsity and in reliance upon these representations [wife] did consume [trade name of drug.]

12. If [manufacturer] was not aware of the falsity or incompleteness of its statements, it made such statements negligently in disregard of the dangerous nature of [trade name of drug.]

FOURTH CAUSE OF ACTION

13. Plaintiff [husband] alleges and realleges each and every allegation contained in paragraphs 1 through 6, inclusive, and paragraphs 9, 11 and 12 of this complaint, and incorporates the same herein by reference as if they were fully set forth.

14. As a result of the liability pleaded in the first three causes of action, plaintiff [husband] has been and will continue to be deprived of the full consortium of his wife and has been obligated and will in

the future be obligated to incur expenses because of his wife's injuries.

Wherefore, plaintiff [wife] demands a judgment for money damages against defendant [manufacturer] in the sum of [amount of claimed damages] on the First, Second and Third Causes of Action and plaintiff [husband] demands a judgment for money damages in the sum of [amount of claimed damages] on the Fourth Cause of Action, together with interest and costs.

DEMAND FOR JURY TRIAL

Please take notice that plaintiffs demand a trial by jury of all issues in this action.

[Wife]
[Husband]
By Their Attorneys
[Date] [Name of Attorneys]

CHAPTER 3

Preconception Stage: Emerging Theories of Liability

I. PRECONCEPTION TORTS

A. In General

1. [§3.1] Generally; Definitions

Preconception torts are those committed against an unborn infant's mother before the infant is conceived, but which affect the mother in such a manner that the infant, either when conception takes place or during the period of gestation, is injured and is born in an unhealthy condition. The preconception tort action is generally brought by, or on behalf of, the child for injuries suffered and damages resulting from the commission of the tort. See, e.g., *Bergstreser v Mitchell*, 577 F2d 22 (8th Cir 1978); *Jorgensen v Meade Johnson Laboratories, Inc*, 483 F2d 237 (10th Cir 1973); *Morgan v United States*, 143 FSupp 580 (D NJ 1956). However, preconception tort actions can be brought by the parents of a child injured by the wrongful action of the defendant prior to conception. In such a case the plaintiff-parents allege that they have suffered a loss by virtue of the birth of the child in an unhealthy condition. See *Olson v St Croix Valley Memorial Hosp*, 55 Wi2d 628, 201 NW2d 63 (1972).

Judicial consideration of actions involving preconception torts has taken place only in recent years. Historically, courts have been hesitant to recognize legal rights for unborn children in actions involving personal injury [see e.g., *Dietrich v North Hampton*, 138 Ma 14 (1884)], much less preconception tort actions. There is, however, modern authority for the proposition that an action can be recognized for preconception tort injuries. See, e.g., *Jorgensen v Meade Johnson Laboratories*, 483 F2d 237 (10th Cir 1973). [For a more detailed discussion of the background of Preconception Torts, see §3.2.]

A threshold issue in determining whether to recognize actions based on preconception injuries has centered on the policy considerations involved. It has been recognized that duty is not a static concept and may exist to one foreseeably harmed although he or she be unknown and remote in time and place. See *Renslow v Mennonite Hosp*, 67 Il2d 348, 10 Il Dec 484, 367 NE2d 1250 (1977). The contrary view is that recognition of a cause of action for preconception injury would require the extension of traditional tort concepts beyond manageable bounds. See *Albala v City of New York*, 54 NY2d 269, 445 NYS2d 108 (1981). Therefore, the issue of whether policy considerations should allow or disallow a cause of action for preconception torts is unresolved and, in most jurisdictions, has not been considered. [As to a more detailed discussion of the policy considerations involved in preconception torts, see §3.3.]

Liability can be sought for preconception torts in a number of different factual situations including medical malpractice [see, e.g., *Albala v City of New York*, 54 NY2d 269, 445 NYS2d 108 (1981)], radiation injuries (which often involve the Federal Tort Claims Act) [see, e.g., *Monaco v United States*, 661 F2d 129 (9th Cir 1981)], and products liability [see, e.g., *Jorgensen v Meade Johnson Laboratories, Inc*, 483 F2d 237 (10th Cir 1973); *In re Agent Orange Products Liability Litigation*, 506 FSupp 762 (ED NY 1980)]. Preconception torts are to be distinguished from cases in which preconception events result in a birth of a planned or unplanned infant, *i.e.,* wrongful birth, wrongful life, or wrongful conception, because, in preconception tort cases, had the alleged negligence not occurred the plaintiff-infant would have in all likelihood been born normal. In preconception tort cases the defendant's negligence makes the difference between life in an impaired state and life in a healthy state. By contrast, in wrongful birth, wrongful life, and wrongful conception cases the negligence of the defendant makes the difference between life in an impaired state and nonexistence. [As to a more detailed discussion of the definition and background of wrongful conception, see §§3.8, 3.9; as to a more detailed discussion of the definition and background of wrongful birth, see §§6.1, 6.2; as to a more detailed discussion of the definition and background of wrongful life, see §§6.13, 6.14.]

2. [§3.2] Background

Historically, courts have been reluctant to recognize legal rights for unborn children in cases involving personal injury. See, e.g., *Dietrich v North Hampton*, 138 Ma 14 (1884). Therefore, before any courts recognized the right of an infant, or of his or her parents to sue on the infant's behalf, for a preconception tort, the courts had to deal with the issue of whether to recognize a right of action for a prenatal injury. [As to prenatal personal injuries generally, see §5.1.] The distinguishing factor between preconception injuries and prenatal injuries is the time at which the injury happened. Preconception injuries happen, as the name suggests, before conception takes place; prenatal injuries take place after an infant has been conceived and before the infant is born. The reversal in the *Dietrich* case, above, came in 1946 in *Bonbrest v Kotz*, 65 FSupp 138 (D DC 1946), in which a physician was held liable in a tort action brought by a child, after his birth, for injuries suffered from acts committed by the physician while the unborn child was a viable fetus. The court reasoned that a viable unborn fetus, although residing in its mother's womb, is capable of extrauterine life and, while dependent for its continued development on sustenance derived from its mother, is not a part of the mother as that term is generally understood. If a right of action is denied to the child it will be compelled, without any fault on its part, to go through life carrying the seal of another's fault and bearing a very heavy burden of infirmity and inconvenience without any compensation therefor, the court said. Therefore, the court reasoned that it is but natural justice that a child, if born alive and viable should be allowed to maintain an action in the courts for injuries wrongfully committed upon its person while in the womb of its mother. That there was no precedent for the court's decision did not concern the court because it said the absence of precedent should afford no refuge to those who by their wrongful act have invaded the right of an individual in their professional capacities. What right is more inherent, and more sacrosanct, than that of individuals in the possession and enjoyment of their lives, their limbs and their bodies, the court asked. [For a more detailed discussion of the background of prenatal personal injury actions brought by or on behalf of the child, see §5.2.]

The first court decision to discuss the possibility of a preconception cause of action was *Zepeda v Zepeda*, 41 IlA2d 240, 190 NE2d 849 (1963), cert den, 379 US 945, 85 SCt 444, 13 LE2d 545 (1964). In *Zepeda*, which involved an action brought on behalf of an illegitimate infant for damages against his father arising from the infant's status as a bastard, sometimes referred to as an action for dissatisfied life [as to a more detailed discussion of dissatisfied life, see §6.22], the court posed a hypothetical question asking what if wrongful conduct takes place before conception. The court concluded that the defendant could be held accountable if his or her act was completed before the plaintiff was conceived. It is possible to incur a conditional prospective liability in tort to one not yet in being, the court said. It makes no difference how much time elapses between a wrongful act and a resulting injury if there is a causal relation between them, the court reasoned. The first case to recognize that a cause of action could be brought for a preconception tort was *Jorgensen v Meade Johnson Laboratories, Inc*, 483 F2d 237 (10th Cir 1973). In *Jorgensen*, a case involving an alleged preconception injury caused by an oral contraceptive, the court said that Oklahoma courts would treat the problem of the injuries alleged in the case as one of causation and proximate cause to be determined by competent medical proof. Since the *Jorgensen* decision, a number of courts have addressed the issue of whether to allow a cause of action for a preconception injury. Some courts have allowed the plaintiff to pursue such a cause of action [see, e.g., *Renslow v Mennonite Hosp*, 67 Il2d 348, 10 Il Dec 484, 367 NE2d 1250 (Il 1977)], while others have denied the cause of action [see *Albala v City of New York*, 54 NY2d 269, 445 NYS2d 108 (1981)]. [For a more detailed discussion of the policy considerations involved in the recognition of a preconception injury action, see §3.3.]

3. [§3.3] Policy Considerations; Recognition of Cause of Action

There are fundamental policy questions that arise when considering whether a cause of action for a preconception tort [as to the definition and background of preconception torts, see §§3.1, 3.2] is cognizable. For example, it has been considered whether a defendant owes a duty to an unconceived person, whether the need for an end to responsibility, short of perpetual liability for a single wrongful act, dictates that a duty for preconception torts not be imposed [see *Renslow v Mennonite Hosp*, 67 Il2d 348, 10 Il Dec 484, 367 NE2d 1250 (1977)], and whether the perimeter of liability in cases involving preconception torts can be judicially established in a reasonable and practical manner [see *Albala v City of New York*, 54 NY2d 269, 445 NYS2d 108 (1981)].

There is authority for the proposition that policy considerations favor the extension of tort liability to preconception injuries that culminate in the birth of an unhealthy child. One court has held that duty is not a static concept, and a duty may exist to one foreseeably harmed though he or she be unknown and remote in time and place. A defendant, therefore, may be held liable to a person whose existence is not apparent at the time of the defendant's act. See *Renslow v Mennonite Hosp*, 67 Il2d 348, 10 Il Dec 484, 367 NE2d 1250 (1977). Moreover, it has been noted that where an action is recognized for prenatal injuries to a child [as to prenatal personal injuries generally, see §5.1] an action for preconception injuries to the child should also be recognized. See, e.g., *Bergstreser v Mitchell*, 577 F2d 22 (8th Cir 1978); *Renslow v Mennonite Hosp*, 67 Il2d 348, 10 Il Dec 484, 367 NE2d 1250 (1977). It is illogical, in the view of some courts, to bar relief for an act done prior to conception where the defendant would be liable for the same conduct had the child, unbeknownst to the defendant, been conceived prior to the defendant's act. See *Renslow v Mennonite Hosp*, 67 Il2d 348, 10 Il Dec 484, 367 NE2d 1250 (1977).

In addition, issues centering on perpetual liability have been considered. In a case involving a single tort committed against the child's mother it was said that, while there may be potential for perpetual claims arising from chemical accidents or long term radiation exposure, a one-time tort is not, by its nature, self perpetuating, nor is the plaintiff a remote descendant. When such a case is presented, the judiciary will exercise its traditional role of drawing rationale distinctions, consonant with current perceptions of justice, between harms which are not compensable and those which are. See *Renslow v Mennonite Hosp*, 67 Il2d 348, 10 Il Dec 484, 367 NE2d 1250 (1977). If the view prevailed that tortious conduct occurring prior to conception is not actionable in behalf of an infant ultimately injured by the wrong, then an infant suffering personal injury from a defective food product, manufactured before his conception, would be without a remedy. See *Jorgensen v Meade Johnson Laboratories, Inc*, 483 F2d 237 (10th Cir 1973).

By contrast, there is authority for the proposition that such a claim should not be recognized. In the view of some courts, the perimeters of liability, although a proper legislative concern in cases such as these, cannot be judicially established in a reasonable and practical manner. The recognition of a cause of action for a preconception tort would require the extension of traditional tort concepts beyond manageable bounds. There would be staggering implications associated with any proposition that would honor claims assuming the breach of an identifiable duty for less than a perfect birth. When faced with a novel cause of action, it has been held that sentiment should be put aside and the law must establish the rules ascribing liability in a manner which avoids the drawing of artificial and arbitrary boundaries. Moreover, the foreseeability of a mother having a child in the future (after an alleged preconception tort) does not alone establish a duty to the plaintiff on the part of the defendant. Foreseeability alone is not the hallmark of legal duty, for, if foreseeability was the sole test, there would be no logical confining of the extension of liability. If liability was established in such a case, could liability be logically precluded in a case where a negligent motorist collides with another vehicle containing a female passenger who sustains a punctured uterus as a result of the accident and subsequently gives birth to a deformed child. Finally, the recognition of a cause of action under preconception circumstances would, under this view, have the undesirable impact of encouraging the practice of "defensive medicine". A physician faced with the alternative of saving a patient's life by administering a treatment involving the possibility of adverse consequences to after conceived offspring of that patient would, if exposed to liability of great magnitude, undoubtedly be inclined to advise against the treatment rather than risk the possibility of having to recompense a child born with a handicap. Accordingly, society as a whole would bear the cost of the court's placing physicians in a direct conflict between their moral duty to patients and the proposed legal duty to those hypothetical future generations outside the immediate zone of danger. See *Albala v City of New York*, 54 NY2d 269, 445 NYS2d 108 (1981).

B. Bases of Liability

1. [§3.4] Medical Malpractice

The types of medical malpractice cases involving preconception torts in which plaintiffs have sought recovery have included the negligent transfusion of blood into the mother that results in sensitization of the mother's blood and injury to the fetus during gestation [see, e.g., *Morgan v United States*, 143 FSupp 580 (D NJ 1956); *Renslow v Mennonite Hosp*, 67 Il2d 348, 10 Il Dec 484, 367 NE2d 1250 (1977); *Olson v St Croix Valley Memorial Hosp*, 55 Wi2d 628, 201 NW2d 63 (1972)], the negligent performance of a cesarean section on the infant's mother that results in a rupture of the uterus during the infant's gestation [see, *Bergstreser v Mitchell*, 577 F2d 22 (8th Cir 1978)], and the negligent perforation of the infant's mother's uterus during an abortion procedure [see *Albala v City of New York*, 54 NY2d 269, 445 NYS2d 108 (1981)].

A duty to the as yet unconceived infant has been found to exist. Duty is not a static concept. A duty may exist to one foreseeably harmed though he or she be unknown and remote in time and place. A defendant may be held liable to a person whose existence was not apparent at the time of his act. See *Renslow v Mennonite Hosp*, 67 Il2d 348, 10 Il Dec 484, 367 NE2d 1250 (1977). However, it has also been held that the foreseeability that a woman would again conceive a child after an abortion, and that the health of the child born thereafter would be adversely affected by damage to the mother's uterus, would not alone establish a duty to the infant-plaintiff on the part of the defendant. Foreseeability alone is not the hallmark of legal duty because, if it was the sole test, the extension of liability could not be logically confined. See *Albala v City of New York*, 46 NY2d 401, 413 NYS2d 895, 386 NE2d 807 (1979). [As to policy considerations in general in preconception torts, see §3.3.]

2. [§3.5] Products Liability

Under the doctrine of products liability, a manufacturer is required to be reasonably careful to prevent dangerous conditions in its products, and to use reasonable care and skill in designing the products so that they are reasonably safe for the purposes for which they are intended, and for other uses which are foreseeable. This duty is commensurate with the danger involved. In determining what precautions, if any, are required under the circumstances, the likelihood of harm, and the gravity of the harm if it happens, must be balanced against the burden of the precaution which would be effective to avoid the harm. See, e.g., *Putnsen v Clay Adams, Inc*, 12 CaA3d 1062, 91 CaR 319 (1970). Moreover, the manufacturer of a product has a duty to warn consumers of potential dangers from the product when it knows or should know they exist. See, e.g., *Tayar v Roux Laboratories, Inc*, 460 F2d 494 (10th Cir 1972).

Courts that have considered cases centering on preconception injury alleged to have been caused by a product have come to differing conclusions regarding the recognition of the cause of action. [As to the general policy considerations involved in recognizing preconception torts, see §3.3.] For example, in *Jorgensen v Meade Johnson Laboratories, Inc*, 483 F2d 237 (10th Cir 1973), the plaintiff alleged that the defendant's oral contraceptive product altered the chromosome structure within the body of the plaintiff's wife, and as a result thereof, a mongoloid deformity was created within the viable fetus of the minor plaintiff during the period of development prior to birth. The court said that, regardless of allegations as to when or how the effects developed, the case should not be viewed from the standpoint of alleged effects on the mother, but from that of the twins and the injuries allegedly inflicted on them. The court reasoned that if the view prevailed that tortious conduct occurring prior to conception is not actionable on behalf of an infant ultimately injured by the wrong, then an infant suffering personal injury from a defective food product, manufactured before his or her conception, would be without remedy. The court believed the problem of the injuries alleged was one of causation and proximate cause, to be determined by competent medical proof. Moreover, it did not appear to the court beyond doubt that the plaintiff could prove no set of facts in support of his claims which would entitle him to relief.

However, in a suit against the federal government for alleged preconception tort injuries, the court said the injuries were suffered incident to or arising out of service and could not be recompensed in an action maintained directly against the government. In *In re "Agent Orange" Product Liability Litigation*, 506 FSupp 762 (ED NY 1980), the children of Vietnam veterans alleged that they had suffered genetic and somatic injury as a result of a parent having been exposed to Agent Orange. Therefore, the court considered the question of whether the injuries suffered by these children, who were not and never were members of the military, were derivative injuries suffered incident to or arising out of military service, or whether they were direct injuries independent of those of their parents. The court noted that pursuant to the United States Supreme Court decision in *Feres v United States*, 340 US 135, 71 SCt 153, 95 LE 152 (1950), the Federal Tort Claims Act did not waive sovereign immunity with respect to claims of servicemen arising out of activities incident to or arising out of their military service. The court said the children's claims of genetic and physical harm were indirect because they arose only as the result of injuries to their veteran parents. The injuries alleged by the children had their genesis in the exposure of their parents and, assuming that Agent Orange could produce the genetic changes alleged, the injuries were inflicted on the servicemen at the time of the exposure. Thus, although Agent Orange may ultimately be found to have caused injuries in subsequently conceived children, those injuries arose out of and were incident to the service of the parent, the court said, and to hold otherwise might open the door for governmental liability to countless generations of claimants having ever diminishing genetic relationship to the person actually injured. Therefore, the children's claims for genetic injuries and birth defects from Agent Orange exposure of their veteran parents could not be recompensed in an action maintained directly against the government.

Practitioners in New York state should be aware of a statute, NY Civ Prac §214b, that extends the filing time for alleged Agent Orange injuries suffered while the plaintiff was in the service in the Armed Forces of the United States and Indo-China. The law provides that anyone who served in Indo-China between January 1, 1962, and May 7, 1975, may commence an action for damages within two years from the date of the discovery of the injury, or within two years from the date when through the exercise of reasonable diligence the cause of such injury should have been discovered, whichever is later. The New York legislature's findings which accompanied the original passage of this measure in 1981 took note of the fact that more than 600,000 New York residents served in Indo-China, and a large number of these were exposed to Agent Orange. [For a discussion of preconception tort cases involving radiation-related injuries, but arising under the Federal Tort Claims Act, see §3.6.].

3. [§3.6] Radiation Injuries; Federal Tort Claims Act

There is scientific evidence that radiation may cause genetic damage, and therefore have a deleterious effect on unborn children. This knowledge has acquired legal significance in federal regulations that set radiation exposure levels for the general public and workers. Estep & Forgotson, LEGAL LIABILITY FOR GENETIC INJURIES FROM RADIATION, 24 Louisiana LR 1 (1963). Moreover, with a growing national dependence on nuclear energy, and the continued exposure of many people to radiation, it would appear that questions regarding radiation, its adverse effect on humans, and the possibility of infants born with defects allegedly attributable to the radiation, will increase in number. Moore, RADIATION AND PRECONCEPTION INJURIES: SOME INTERESTING PROBLEMS IN TORT LAW, 28 Southwestern LJ 414 (1974). Thus far the cases that have been filed alleging preconception injury resulting from radiation have been filed against the United States by members of the Armed Forces. Therefore, the cases arising from a factual setting involving alleged radiation related preconception torts have been brought under the Federal Tort Claims Act (FTCA). The act is designed primarily to remove the sovereign immunity of the United States from suits in tort and, with certain specific exceptions, to render the government liable in tort as a private individual would be in like circumstances.

The FTCA is codified essentially in Title 28 of the United States Code, sections 1346 and 2671-2680. Jurisdiction of the federal district courts over actions brought under the FTCA is provided in 28 USC §1346(b), which states that the district courts "shall have jurisdiction of civil actions against the United States for money damages . . . for injury or loss of property, or personal injury or death caused by the negligent or wrongful act or omission of any employee of the government while acting within the scope of his office of employment, under circumstances where the United States, if a private person, would be liable to the claimant in accordance with the law of the place where the act or omission occurred." *Brooks v United States*, 337 US 49, 69 SCt 918, 93 LE 1200 (1948); *Feres v United States*, 340 US 135, 71 SCt 153, 95 LE 152 (1950); *United States v Brown*, 348 US 110, 75 SCt 141, 99 LE 139 (1954). Application of the *Feres* doctrine has been held to bar a suit brought on behalf of an infant-plaintiff for a birth defect allegedly caused by a genetic change in her father that developed when he was exposed to radiation while serving in the Armed Forces. In *Monaco v United States*, 661 F2d 129 (9th Cir 1981), the court noted that while the *Feres* doctrine had been applied broadly, the exception does not extend to all instances in which an injury is remotely related to activities incident to military service. The infant-plaintiff argued that her injury was not the result of an in-service injury because the chromosomal change in her father which induced her injury was not an injury. Whether the child's injury occurred when she was born with a birth defect or when her father suffered chromosomal change, the allegedly negligent act drawn into question was performed while her father was in the service, the court noted. Thus, just as her father could not recover on the grounds that his injury was post service, the court said it could not grant the child's recovery on these grounds. In addition, the child argued that the *Feres* doctrine did not block her claims because she was never a member of the Armed Services. The court noted that the child sought relief for an injury to herself, rather than indemnity for losses due to injury to her father, but that this did not change the court's substantive analysis. The court held that it must examine the government's activity in relation to military personnel on active duty. The *Feres* doctrine, in the court's view, stood on shakey ground, with its precise justification somewhat confused. But the doctrine had been applied consistently to avoid examining acts of military personnel which were allegedly negligent with respect to other members of the Armed Forces. While the injuries claimed by the family may well have become manifest long after the father left the service, the court could not rule on either claim without examining acts occurring while the father was in the service. The court said the result in the case disturbed it, particularly with respect to the child. In the child's case, the price of avoiding examination of the events long past, and involving her behavior in no respect, appeared to be complete denial of recovery. The court added that, if developed doctrine did not bind it, it might be inclined to make an exception in cases such as this.

However, in *Hinkie v United States*, 524 FSupp 277 (ED Pa 1981), the court held that the plaintiffs' claims against the United States were not barred by the *Feres* doctrine. The plaintiffs alleged, in part, radiation caused injuries to the father resulted in chromosomal alterations, and that these injuries subsequently manifested themselves as defects at the time of the births of his children. The court noted that there had been two lines of cases regarding recovery by members of a serviceman's family since *Feres*.

Members of a serviceman's family have recovered against the United States for injuries caused directly to them independent of any injury to the serviceman, if they arise from noncombatant activities. However, recovery by family members has been barred under the *Feres* doctrine where the cause of action is ancillary or derivative to the serviceman's action for his own injury. This case did not fall neatly into either line of cases, in the court's view. The court said it rejected applying the theories to bar every action somehow involving an injured serviceman because that result did not follow from the Supreme Court's analysis of *Feres* in *Stencel Aero Engineering Corp v United States*, 431 US 666, 97 SCt 2054, 52 LE2d 665 (1977). The court noted that the Supreme Court, in *Stencel*, had listed three factors justifying the *Feres* doctrine: first, the relationship between the government and members of its armed forces is distinctively federal in character, and it would make little sense to have the government's liability to members of the armed service dependent on the fortuity of where the soldier happened to be stationed at the time of the injury; second, the Veterans' Benefits Act establishes a statutory no-fault compensation scheme which provides pensions to injured servicemen; third, extreme results might develop if suits under the Federal Tort Claims Act were allowed for negligent orders given or negligent acts committed in the course of military duty. Applying these factors to the case at bar, the court said the first factor carried little weight where the plaintiffs are related to the federal government only by the veteran status of the husband or father. The second factor also was discounted since under the act the individual plaintiffs would be receiving nothing for their own physical injuries; rather, they would be recovering only dependents' benefits related to whatever disabling effects the veteran had suffered. The court also found that the third factor would not warrant dismissal since the court found it difficult to see how this lawsuit would adversely affect military discipline. The undermining of discipline, or the refusal to follow orders, presented less of a problem to the court because of the time lapse involved. The court said it was aware of the difficulties of proof facing the plaintiffs, but determined that the *Feres/Stencel* doctrine did not mandate dismissal of the plaintiffs' cause of action. The court pointed out that it had not decided whether other exceptions to the Federal Tort Claims Act, for example, the discretionary function exception, were applicable to the plaintiffs' claims. It only held that the plaintiffs' claims against the United States were not barred by the *Feres* doctrine.

C. [§3.7] Example Complaint

A complaint for an action alleging the commission of a preconception tort [as to definition of preconception torts, see §3.1] needs to be drafted so as to recite the reasons why an injury has been suffered by the plaintiff-infant or -parents. An example of a case in which a preconception tort was alleged and pleaded is *Renslow v Mennonite Hosp*, 67 IlA2d 348, 10 Il Dec 484, 367 NE2d 1250 (1977). In *Renslow*, it was alleged that a negligently performed blood transfusion prior to the conception, gestation and birth of an infant resulted in injury to the infant. The *Renslow* complaint stated, in pertinent part, as follows:

COMPLAINT

COUNT 1

EMMA M. RENSLOW, by her attorneys for cause of action against MENNONITE HOSPITAL, a corporation, states that:

1. On or about October 8, 1965, Defendant hospital owned, operated, managed and maintained and controlled a certain hospital, located in the city of Bloomington, County of McLean, and State of Illinois, wherein it treated persons suffering from various ailments, and provided rooms, laboratories, drugs, and various medical devices and services for patients admitted to said hospital for medical care and treatment in said hospital.

2. On or about October 8, 1965, through and including October 14, 1965, DR. HANS STROINK, Defendant herein, was an agent or employee of said hospital, and was in fact the Director of Laboratories for said hospital, and had under his supervision and control various laboratory technicians who, among other duties, were charged from time to time, and including the period mentioned herein, with the typing of blood for use in transfusion of patients in said hospital.

3. On or about October 8, 1965, the Plaintiff, EMMA M. RENSLOW, then known as EMMA MURPHY, a minor age 13, and born April 16, 1952, was admitted as a patient in said hospital by Dr. Seymour R. Goldberg, a duly licensed physician and surgeon in the State of Illinois, and member of the medical staff of said Defendant hospital.

4. At all times mentioned herein the Plaintiff was in the exercise of all due care and caution for her own personal well being commensurate with her age and experience.

5. On October 8, 1965, pursuant to the order of Dr. Seymour Goldberg, said minor Plaintiff was infused with 500 c.c. of whole blood as part of the care and treatment for her condition of ill-being. Additionally, on or about October 9, 1965, by order of Dr. Seymour Goldberg, an additional 500 c.c. of whole blood was infused in said minor Plaintiff as part of the treatment for her condition of physical ill-being. On both said dates of blood infusion, the Plaintiff was and

still is blood type A RH negative, and the blood infused aforesaid was in fact type A RH positive.

6. On October 8, 1965, said Defendant hospital, acting through its agent or employee, DR. HANS STROINK, as Director of Laboratories, and acting through its agents, certain laboratory technicians, the exact names of whom are not presently known, selected the blood units to be transfused into the Plaintiff, exercised blood typing techniques, and went through procedures to compare the Plaintiff's blood type with the blood types about to be transfused into the Plaintiff, said acts all occurring in the course of care and treatment of the Plaintiff while a patient in Defendant hospital and in the course of the professional supervision and responsibility of the said DR. HANS STROINK and the laboratory technicians aforesaid, all of said persons being agents or employees of Defendant Hospital.

7. As a direct and proximate result of the foregoing the mistyped blood was in fact transfused into the Plaintiff, permanently injuring her by sensitizing her blood.

8. At the time of the transfusions aforesaid up through and including November 15, 1973, the Plaintiff had no adverse reactions known by her to said blood transfusions, had no Knowledge whatsoever of the medical consequences of being transfused with the wrong blood and first became aware of her blood sensitization from said transfusions in December, 1973, as a result of routine antibody screening of her blood during the course of prenatal visitation with Dr. A. K. Patel, a duly licensed physician and surgeon in the State of Illinois specializing in obstetrics and gynecology, who attended the Plaintiff for and during a state of pregnancy at said time.

9. Subsequently, during the course of her pregnancy, the Plaintiff developed increasing medical and blood chemistry signs of sensitization to such an extent that definite jeopardy to her unborn child was diagnosed by the said Dr. A. K. Patel, resulting in the Plaintiff being hospitalized at Brokaw Hospital, Normal, Illinois, on or about March 25, 1974, where labor was induced leading to the live birth of a premature infant female child, now known as LEAH ANN RENSLOW, a minor, who was in fact jaundiced and required an immediate and complete exchange transfusion of her blood at said Brokaw Hospital and subsequent transfer to St. Francis Hospital, Peoria, Illinois, to the premature facility located therein for additional care and treatment as a premature infant, and a second complete exchange transfusion of her blood.

10. The selection, transfusion and management of the infusion of blood in the Plaintiff at MENNONITE HOSPITAL in October of 1965 as aforesaid was exclusively and solely within the control, direction, management and maintenance of said Defendant hospital and its agents or employees, DR. HANS STROINK, and various laboratory technicians as aforesaid.

11. During the selection and typing of the blood aforesaid and the transfusing of same the Plaintiff exercised no control, direction, or management whatsoever over the entire process aforedescribed.

12. During the transfusion of blood aforesaid in October, 1965, the entire process of selection of the blood, typing, comparing and transfusing was exclusively managed and maintained and controlled by Defendant hospital and its agents or employees aforesaid at the time of the injury thereby committed on the Plaintiff.

13. The occurrence speaks for itself; that is, the occurrence would not have taken place in the ordinary course of things if Defendant hospital acting through its agents or employees aforesaid had not negligently failed to use proper care in the selection, typing, comparing, transfusing and other techniques of the blood infused into the Plaintiff aforesaid; and the control, management and maintenance of said transfusion process and blood selection and typing process was at all times under the exclusive control, direction and management of the Defendant hospital, DR. HANS STROINK, as Director of its Laboratories, and the various laboratory technicians involved in the procedure aforesaid.

14. As a direct and proximate result of the aforesaid negligence by the Defendant hospital, acting by and through its agent or employee, Defendant DR. HANS STROINK, and the laboratory technicians aforesaid, the Plaintiff sustained severe and permanent personal injuries by virtue of her blood being sensitized, resulting in the premature birth of her child, LEAH ANN RENSLOW, and will in the future incur difficult and abnormal pregnancies and medical problems with the birth of any subsequent children, arising from any and all subsequent pregnancies.

AND FURTHER, the Plaintiff has expended or become obligated to expend large sums of money for hospital care and treatment, medical bills and drug bills, endeavoring to be cared for as a result of her pregnancy and the premature birth of her child aforesaid, and will in the future incur additional unusual and extra expenses for any medical care and attention and hospitalization from any future pregnancies or birth of any future child borne by the Plaintiff.

AND FURTHER, the Plaintiff has suffered great mental anguish following her diagnosis as a blood sensitized person; and throughout the pregnancy and delivery of her child aforesaid, she suffered great mental anguish for her own well being and for the well being of her child. Additionally, she will in the future suffer great fear for her physical well being and the physical well being of any child in gestation as a result of future pregnancies.

15. At all times mentioned herein, at and subsequent to November, 1973, the Plaintiff is and was the duly married spouse of Steven Renslow, and the child born aforesaid, LEAH ANN RENSLOW, is a product of the marriage of Steven Renslow to the Plaintiff.

WHEREFORE, the Plaintiff, EMMA M. RENSLOW, prays judgment against MENNONITE HOSPITAL, a corporation, in the sum of FIVE HUNDRED THOUSAND DOLLARS ($500,000) plus costs of this suit. . . .

COUNT VI

EMMA M. RENSLOW, as mother and next friend of LEAH ANN RENSLOW, a minor, by her attorneys, LAW OFFICES OF STRODEL & KINGERY, ASSOC., for cause of action against MENNONITE HOSPITAL, a corporation, states that:

1–3. Plaintiff repeats and realleges the allegations contained in paragraphs (1) through (3) of Count I as and for paragraphs (1) and (3) of this Count.

4. At all times mentioned herein, said minor Plaintiff was in the exercise of all care and caution, and due to her age, was incapable in any way of contributing to her own ill-being.

5. On October 8, 1965, pursuant to the order of Dr. Seymour Goldberg, the said minor Plaintiff's mother, then known as EMMA MURPHY, was infused with 500 c.c. of whole blood as part of the care and treatment for her condition of ill-being. Additionally, on or about October 9, 1965, by order of Dr. Seymour Goldberg, the said EMMA MURPHY (RENSLOW) was infused with an additional 500 c.c. of whole blood as part of the treatment for her condition of physical ill-being. On both said dates of blood infusion, EMMA MURPHY (RENSLOW) was and still is blood type A RH negative, and the blood infused aforesaid was in fact type A RH positive.

6. On October 8, 1965, and October 9, 1965, said Defendant hospital, acting through its agency or employee, DR. HANS STROINK, as Director of Laboratories, and acting through its agents, certain laboratory technicians, the exact names of whom are not presently known, selected the blood units to be transfused into

Plaintiff's mother, exercised blood typing techniques and went through procedures to compare the blood type of Plaintiff's mother, said acts all occurring in the course of care and treatment of the Plaintiff's mother while she was a patient in Defendant hospital, and in the course of the professional supervision and responsibility of the said DR. HANS STROINK and the laboratory technicians aforesaid, all of said persons being agents or employees of Defendant Hospital.

7. As a direct and proximate result of the foregoing the mis-typed blood was in fact transfused into the Plaintiff's mother, permanently injuring her by sensitizing her blood.

8. At the time of the transfusions aforesaid up through and including November 15, 1973, the Plaintiff's mother had no adverse reactions known by her to said blood transfusions, had no knowledge whatsoever of the medical consequences of being transfused with the wrong blood and first became aware of her blood sensitization from said transfusions in December, 1973, as a result of routine antibody screening of her blood during the course of prenatal visitation with Dr. A. K. Patel, a duly licensed physician and surgeon in the State of Illinois specializing in obstetrics and gynecology, who attended Plaintiff's mother for and during a state of pregnancy at said time.

9. Subsequently, during the course of said pregnancy, Plaintiff's mother developed increasing medical and blood chemistry signs of sensitization to such an extent that definite jeopardy to this Plaintiff, the unborn child, was diagnosed by the said Dr. A. K. Patel, resulting in EMMA RENSLOW being hospitalized at Brokaw Hospital, Normal, Illinois, on or about March 25, 1974, where labor was induced leading to the live birth of the Plaintiff, LEAH ANN RENSLOW, who was in fact jaundiced and required an immediate and complete exchange transfusion of her blood at said Brokaw Hospital and subsequent transfer to St. Francis Hospital, Peoria, Illinois, to the premature facility located therein for additional care and treatment as a premature infant, and a second complete exchange transfusion of her blood.

10. The selection, transfusion and management of the infusion of blood into EMMA RENSLOW at MENNONITE HOSPITAL in October of 1965 as aforesaid was exclusively and solely within the control, direction, management and maintenance of said Defendant hospital and its agents or employees, DR. HANS STROINK, and various laboratory technicians as aforesaid.

11. During the selection and typing of the blood aforesaid and the transfusing of same EMMA RENSLOW the Plaintiff exercised

no control, direction or management whatsoever over the entire process aforedescribed.

12. During the transfusion of blood aforesaid in October, 1965, the entire process of selection of the blood, typing, comparing and transfusing was exclusively managed and maintained and controlled by Defendant hospital and its agents or employees aforesaid at the time of the injury thereby committed on EMMA RENSLOW.

13. The occurrence speaks for itself; that is, the occurrence would not have taken place in the ordinary course of things if Defendant hospital acting through its agents or employees aforesaid had not negligently failed to use proper care in the selection, typing, comparing, transfusing and other techniques of the blood infused into EMMA RENSLOW as aforesaid; and the control, management and maintenance of said transfusion process and blood selection and typing process was at all times under the exclusive control, direction and management of the Defendant hospital, DR. HANS STROINK, as Director of its Laboratories, and the various laboratory technicians involved in the procedure aforesaid.

14. As a direct and proximate result of the aforesaid negligence by Defendant Hospital as aforedescribed, the minor Plaintiff, while still in gestation, had her life placed in jeopardy due to hemolitic processes occurring within her blood and body, and as a direct and proximate result thereof, her birth was prematurely induced; and further, at the time of her birth she was jaundiced and was suffering from the medical condition of ill-being known as hyperbilirubinemia and required an exchange transfusion immediately subsequent to her birth of all the blood in her body. Additionally, following said exchange transfusion, the minor Plaintiff was transferred to the premature infant facility at St. Francis Hospital, Peoria, Illinois, where she required special medical care and attention, including a second complete exchange transfusion of all the blood in her body. And additionally, as a direct and proximate result of the sensitization of her mother's blood aforedescribed and the occurrence of the hyperbilirubinemia in the minor Plaintiff, the brain of said minor Plaintiff became irritated and the other organs of her body subjected to sensitivities and stresses of an unnatural degree, together with permanent damage to her nervous system and brain.

AND FURTHER, said minor Plaintiff will for the rest of her life suffer from the results of brain damage resulting from the circumstances of her birth aforesaid and will require medical care and attention or therapy of various kinds for the rest of her life.

WHEREFORE, EMMA RENSLOW, as mother and next friend of LEAH ANN RENSLOW, a minor, prays judgment against MENNONITE HOSPITAL, a corporation, in the sum of FIVE HUNDRED THOUSAND DOLLARS ($500,000) plus costs of this suit. . . .

II. WRONGFUL CONCEPTION

A. In General

1. [§3.8] Definitions: Wrongful Conception and Wrongful Pregnancy

If the purpose of a defendant's actions is to prevent conception or pregnancy, a growing number of courts are requiring that the defendant be held legally responsible if in fact the conception or birth is not prevented. See, e.g., *Custodio v Bauer*, 251 CaA2d 303, 59 CaR 463 (1967); *Cockrum v Baumgartner*, 99 IlA3d 271, 425 NE2d 968 (1981); *Troppi v Scarf*, 31 MiA 240, 187 NW2d 511, leave den, 385 Mi 753 (1971); *Bowman v Davis*, 48 OhSt2d 41, 356 NE2d 496 (1976); *Speck v Finegold*, 439 A2d 110 (Pa 1981). Legal actions arising from the negligent failure to prevent conception, or to terminate pregnancy, which results in the birth of an unplanned child are referred to as wrongful conception or wrongful pregnancy actions.

Wrongful conception and wrongful pregnancy cases, although sometimes referred to interchangeably, are distinguishable based on when the alleged injury, which led to the birth of the unplanned child, occurred. For example, when the negligent act did not prevent conception of the unplanned child, the injury takes place at the moment of conception and thus the action is called wrongful conception. Wrongful conception actions typically arise in cases involving negligently performed sterilization operations that are performed to prevent conception, pregnancy, and birth.

The types of sterilization operations that have been the basis of wrongful conception cases have included tubal ligation operations [see, e.g., *White v United States*, 510 FSupp 146 (D Ks 1981); *Custodio v Bauer*, 251 CaA2d 303, 59 CaR 463 (1967); *Clevenger v Haling*, 379 Ma 154, 394 NE2d 1119 (1979); *Sard v Hardy*, 379 A2d 1014 (Md 1977)], laproscopic cauterizations [see *Hartke v McKelway*, 526 FSupp 97 (1981)], and vasectomies [see, e.g., *Hackworth v Hart*, 474 SW2d 377 (Ky 1971); *Sherlock v Stillwater Clinic*, 260 NW2d 169 (Mn 1977); *Speck v Finegold*, 439 A2d 110 (Pa 1981)]. [For a brief description of the surgical procedures for female and male sterilizations and observations concerning the permanence of these operations, see ELECTIVE STERILIZATION, 113 University of Pennsylvania LR 415

(1965).] In addition, liability can result from negligently dispensing tranquilizers rather than birth control pills. See *Troppi v Scarf*, 31 MiA 240, 187 NW2d 511, leave den, 385 Mi 753 (1971).

By contrast, where the fact of conception and pregnancy is known, and the pregnancy is not successfully terminated, or where the fact of pregnancy is not discovered until a time at which an abortion would be unlawful or dangerous to the mother, the action is best described as one for wrongful pregnancy. The types of situations in which wrongful pregnancy cases have developed have included unsuccessfully performed abortions [see, e.g., *Wilczynski v Goodman*, 73 IlA3d 51, 29 Il Dec 216, 391 NE2d 479 (1979); *Speck v Finegold*, 439 A2d 110 (Pa 1981)], and failure to diagnose pregnancy in time to allow for an abortion [see, e.g., *Clapham v Yanga*, 102 MiA 47, 300 NW2d 727 (1981); *Ziemba v Sternberg*, 45 AD2d 230, 357 NYS2d 265 (1974); *Rieck v Medical Protective Co of Fort Wayne, Indiana*, 64 Wi2d 514, 219 NW2d 242 (1974)].

Regardless of how injury arose, however, the common factor in both wrongful conception and wrongful pregnancy cases is that the child is unplanned and unexpected. [As to situations where the child is planned but is born in a defective or diseased condition that can be attributed to negligence on the part of the defendant, see §6.1 on wrongful birth, the parents' action, and see §6.13 on wrongful life, the action brought on behalf of the child.] This cause of action is exclusively that of the parents since it is the parents and not the unplanned child who have sustained both physical and financial injury by the defendant's negligence. See *Sherlock v Stillwater Clinic*, 260 NW2d 169 (Mn 1977). In some wrongful conception or wrongful pregnancy cases the child is born in a healthy, normal condition. See *Custodio v Bauer*, 251 CaA2d 303, 59 CaR 463 (1967); *Clapham v Yanga*, 102 MiA 47, 300 NW2d 727 (1980). But in other instances, the child is born in a diseased or defective condition. See, e.g., *La Point v Shirley*, 409 FSupp 118 (WD Tx 1976); *Speck v Finegold*, 439 A2d 110 (Pa 1981). Nevertheless, the action is still referred to as one for wrongful conception or wrongful pregnancy since the underlying fact is that the child is unplanned.

While some courts have referred to a negligent sterilization case or an unsuccessful abortion procedure as a wrongful birth action [See, e.g., *White v United States*, 510 FSupp 146 (D Ks 1981); *Public Health Trust v Brown*, 388 So2d 1084 (Fl 1980); *M & Wife v Schmid Laboratories, Inc*, 178 NJ Super 122, 428 A2d 515 (1981); *Speck v Finegold*, 439 A2d 110 (Pa 1981)], or a wrongful life action [see, e.g., *Coleman v Garrison*, 327 A2d 757 (De 1974), affd, 349 A2d 8 (De 1975); *Ladies Center of Clearwater, Inc v Reno*, 341 So2d 543 (Fl 1977); *Clegg v Chase*, 89 Misc2d 510, 391 NYS2d 969 (1977); *Bowman v Davis*, 48 OhSt2d 41, 356 NE2d 496 (1976)], it is more properly denominated an action for wrongful conception or wrongful pregnancy, for it is at the point of conception, or the failure to diagnose or the misdiagnosis of pregnancy, that the injury claimed by the parents originates.

Generally, in wrongful conception or wrongful pregnancy cases, damages are sought by the parents of the unplanned child for the parents' losses or injuries, as individuals or as a couple, and for the costs of raising the child to majority. [For a more detailed discussion of damages in general, parents' losses and injuries, and child rearing costs, see §3.27, §3.31, and §3.40.]

Wrongful conception and wrongful pregnancy actions are typically brought in tort and contract. [For a more detailed discussion of tort actions considered and contract actions considered, see §3.10 and §3.22.]

When wrongful conception and wrongful pregnancy actions were initially brought by parents of unplanned children, there were interposed public policy reasons for not allowing recognition of the cause of action. [For a more detailed discussion of the background of wrongful conception and wrongful pregnancy actions, see §3.9.] In more recent times, however, public policy and general malpractice considerations have led many courts to recognize the cause of action for wrongful conception and wrongful pregnancy. [For a more detailed discussion of these public policy and malpractice considerations, see §3.10 and §3.11.]

2. [§3.9] Background

Few courts, prior to 1967, considered the question whether the parents of an unplanned child may maintain an action against a defendant for an improperly performed sterilization operation or abortion procedure, and, if so, the extent to which the compensatory damages are recoverable. The first of what were later to become known as wrongful conception cases was decided in *Christensen v Thornby*, 192 Mn 123, 255 NW 620 (1934), which was a breach of contract action. In *Christensen*, the plaintiff-husband had undergone a vasectomy after his wife had experienced great difficulty in giving birth to her first child. When his wife subsequently became pregnant and delivered her second child, the husband brought suit for his anxiety and expenses incident to the birth, claiming that the physician who had performed the vasectomy had led him to believe that the operation had been successful. On appeal, the court affirmed the trial court's demurrer to the complaint on the ground that the plaintiff had failed to allege that the false representation was made with fraudulent intent sufficient to support his allegation of deceit. Apart from the technical disposition made in this case, however, the court expressly held that sterilizations were not contrary to public policy and that an action, if properly pleaded, could be maintained against a physician for the improper performance of such an operation. The question of damages, once liability on the part of a physician is established, was neither raised nor directly considered. Nevertheless, the *Christensen* opinion was later relied on by other courts to preclude parents from recovering damages for the economic costs of an unplanned child based on dictum that stated that the plaintiff had been blessed with the fatherhood of an additional child. The court said the expenses alleged were remote from the avowed purpose of the operation, and the court posed the question that, if damages were recoverable, might the plaintiff also charge the defendant with the cost of nurturing and educating the child during its minority. Following the *Christensen* decision, several theories were developed by the courts and commentators to support the view that, as a matter of public policy, parents should not be permitted to recover damages for the birth of a healthy child, even though the infant may have been unplanned or unwanted at the time of conception. One of the strongest arguments was that the allowance of damages would be inapposite to the historically conceived purpose of marriage. An early Pennsylvania case, *Shaheen v Knight*, 6 Lyc 19, 11 Pa D & C 2d 41 (1957), stated that the great end of matrimony was not the comfort and convenience of the immediate parties, but the procreation of a progeny having a legal title to maintenance by the father. The court, in *Shaheen*, which was a contract action, was also concerned with the injustice of requiring a negligent physician to pay for all the economic costs of an unplanned child while the parents derived all the joy, affection, and satisfaction from rearing the child. In the court's view, an action for damages should not be countenanced since it would have the effect of reducing the child to an "emotional bastard" when he inevitably learned that his birth was attributable to a doctor's negligence and not his parents' desires. Finally, a number of courts took the position that any damage caused to the parents was more than offset by the intangible benefits gained by the birth of a child. See, e.g., *Gleitman v Cosgrove*, 49 NJ 22, 227 A2d 689 (1967); *Ball v Mudge*, 64 Wa2d 247, 391 P2d 201 (1964). In summary, although most courts recognized that the unwanted birth caused both physical and financial injury to the parents, recovery was denied because of the potential emotional injury to the child, repugnance to social ethics with respect to the family establishment, and the position that the incidental parental burdens were outweighed by the benefits. *See* NOTE, THE BIRTH OF A CHILD FOLLOWING AN INEFFECTIVE STERILIZATION OPERATION AS LEGAL DAMAGE, 9 Utah LR 808 (1965).

The first case to expressly reject these policy arguments, and to hold that the parents of an unplanned normal child could recover all damages proximately caused by a negligently performed sterilization operation, was *Custodio v Bauer*, 251 CaA2d 303, 59 CaR 463 (1967). In *Custodio*, the court allowed as damages not only the expenses immediately incident to the pregnancy and birth, but all the reasonable costs of maintaining and supporting the child during his minority. The court pointed out that the compensation was not for the so-called unwanted child or emotional bastard, but to replenish the family exchequer so that the new arrival would not deprive the other members of the family of what was planned as their just share of the family income. The court acknowledged that some courts had suggested that the better view in these cases would be to deny the claim because of the possibility of causing emotional injury to the child, but the court instead held that the injury could be no greater than that to be found in many families where planned parenthood had not always succeeded. Moreover, the court noted that there was a changing trend in social ethics with respect to the family establishment. City, state, and federal agencies had instituted programs for dispensing contraceptive information with a view toward economic betterment of segments of the population.

Following the *Custodio* decision, a number of courts adopted the view that public policy consideration should not prevent recognition of a cause of action for wrongful conception or wrongful pregnancy. See, e.g., *Jackson v Anderson*, 230 So2d 503 (Fl 1970); *Cockrum v Baumgartner*, 99 IlA3d 271, 425 NE2d 968 (1981); *Speck v Finegold*, 439 A2d 110 (Pa 1981); *Rivera v State*, 94 Misc 2d 157, 404 NYS2d 950 (1978); *Bowman v Davis*, 48 OhSt2d 41, 356 NE2d 496 (1976). [For a more detailed discussion of public policy considerations involved in recognizing a cause of action for wrongful conception and wrongful pregnancy, see §3.10.] In addition, there is also authority that to refuse to recognize a cause of action for the unplanned birth of a child would leave a void in the area of recovery for medical malpractice, and would result in the dilution of the standard of care in this medical area. See, e.g., *Troppi v Scarf*, 31 MiA 240, 187 NW2d 511, leave den, 385 Mi 753 (1971); *Sherlock v Stillwater Clinic*, 260 NW2d 169 (Mn 1977); *Kingsbury v Smith*, 442 A2d 1003 (NH 1982); *Speck v Finegold*, 439 A2d 110 (Pa 1981). [For a more detailed discussion of medical malpractice considerations involved in recognizing a cause of action for wrongful conception or wrongful pregnancy, see §3.11.]

While the courts faced the issue of whether to recognize the cause of action in these cases, they also began to consider what types of damages would be recoverable. In one of the leading cases, *Troppi v Scarf*, 31 MiA 240, 187 NW2d 511, leave den, 385 Mi 753 (1971), the court said it was arguable that the birth of a healthy child conferred so substantial a benefit as to outweigh the expenses of the child's birth and support. In a great majority of instances, the *Troppi* court believed that this was no doubt true. But the court posed the question whether, as a matter of law, a healthy child always conferred such an overriding benefit.

In the years since the *Custodio* and *Troppi* decisions, a growing number of courts have recognized a cause of action for wrongful pregnancy or wrongful conception. See, e.g., *Hartke v McKelway*, 526 FSupp 97 (DC 1981) [applying the law of the District of Columbia]; *Coleman v Garrison*, 327 A2d 757, affd, 349 A2d 8 (De 1974); *Pierce v DeGracia*, 103 IlA3d 511, 59 Il Dec 267, 431 NE2d 768 (1982); *Troppi v Scarf*, 31 MiA 240, 187 NW2d

511 (1974), leave den, 385 Mi 753 (1971); *Kingsbury v Smith*, 442 A2d 1003 (NH 1982). In these courts, the primary issue being litigated now concerns what kinds of elements can be included in assessing damages. [For a more detailed discussion of damages in wrongful conception and wrongful pregnancy cases, and specific elements thereof, see §3.28.] *See generally*, NOTE, LIABILITY FOR FAILURE OF BIRTH CONTROL METHODS, 76 Columbia LR 1187 (1976).

B. Tort Actions Considered

1. [§3.10] Public Policy Considerations

Wrongful conception or wrongful pregnancy actions that are brought in tort typically involve failed contraception [see *Ochs v Borrelli*, 187 Cn 253, 445 A2d 883 (1982); *Troppi v Scarf*, 31 MiA 240, 187 NW2d 511, leave den, 385 Mi 753 (1971)], an unsuccessful abortion [see, e.g., *Speck v Finegold*, 439 A2d 110 (Pa 1981)], or the misdiagnosis, or failure to diagnose, pregnancy which results in a woman's inability to exercise her right to seek an abortion [see *Ziemba v Sternberg*, 45 AD2d 530, 357 NYS2d 265 (1974)]. [For a discussion of wrongful conception and wrongful pregnancy in general, see §3.8, §3.9.] Because these situations involve the issues of contraception and abortion, the question of whether public policy considerations should allow the recognition of a cause of action for wrongful conception or wrongful pregnancy has arisen in a number of these actions. When these actions first emerged, there existed a judicial reluctance to recognize the cause of action based on public policy considerations. See, e.g., *Gleitman v Cosgrove*, 49 NJ 22, 227 A2d 689 (1967). [For a more detailed discussion of the background of this action, see §3.9.] However, the current trend is to recognize the cause of action based in general terms on the acceptance of abortion and contraception. See, e.g., *Custodio v Bauer*, 59 CaR 463, 251 CaA2d 303 (1967); *Troppi v Scarf*, 31 MiA 240, 187 NW2d 511 (1971). Therefore, the public policy objections to the cause have generally been answered in the negative because of these societal and legal changes. For example, a sterilization operation for therapeutic purposes to protect the physical or mental health of the patient or, in the case of a vasectomy, the wife, is not against public policy. See *Custodio v Bauer*, 59 CaR 463, 251 CaA2d 303 (1967).

In addition, it has been suggested that such an operation for the purpose of family limitation, motivated solely by personal or socio-economic considerations, is likewise not antithetical to public policy. See *Shaheen v Knight*, 11 Pa D&C2d 41 (1957). Moreover, a judicial declaration of preemptive public policy should express the will of the people. In the case of contraceptives, where a state's advocacy of family planning is so vigorous as to include payments for contraceptives as part of its welfare program, public policy cannot be said to disfavor contraception. Contraceptives are used to prevent the birth of children, and to say that for reasons of public policy contraceptive failure can result in no damage as a matter of law ignores the fact that millions of persons use contraceptives daily to avoid the very result which the defendants characterize as a benefit (the birth of an unplanned child), and not a detriment. Those millions of persons, by their conduct, express the sense of the community. See *Troppi v Scarf*, 31 MiA 240, 187 NW2d 511, leave den, 385 Mi 753 (1971).

In addition, recent United States Supreme Court decisions regarding a woman's right to seek an abortion have helped to overcome public policy objections to a cause of action for wrongful conception or wrongful pregnancy. The choice not to procreate, as part of one's right to privacy, has become, subject to certain limitations, a constitutional guarantee. See *Griswold v Connecticut*, 381 US 479, 85 SCt 1678, 14 LE2d 510 (1965); *Roe v Wade*, 410 US 113, 93 SCt 705, 35 LE2d 147 (1973); *Doe v Bolton*, 410 US 179, 93 SCt 755, 35 LE2d 147 (1973). A policy that would make physicians liable for the foreseeable consequences of all negligently performed operations, except those involving sterilization, would constitute an impermissible infringement of a fundamental right. See *Bowman v Davis*, 48 OhSt2d 41, 356 NE2d 496 (1976). Where a fundamental right has been violated, the law must provide a remedy. See *Rivera v State*, 94 Misc 2d 157, 404 NYS2d 950 (1978).

Another abortion-related argument against recognizing an action for wrongful conception or wrongful pregnancy is that, because public policy favors birth over abortion, the approval of such a cause of action is in contravention of a legislatively declared policy. However, this argument has not prevailed for a number of reasons. First, recognition of a cause of action in the circumstances of this type of case has no impact on whether abortions are performed; it neither advances nor impedes abortion activity, and therefore cannot be said to be in conflict with a public policy which favors childbirth over abortion. The recognition of such causes of action would merely accord injuries received as a result of negligently performed sterilization or abortion procedures the same legal protections accorded any other negligently performed medical procedure. Second, reliance on the state's public policy favoring birth over abortion to defeat the plaintiff's cause of action cannot succeed because it conflicts with the plaintiff's constitutional right to seek a termination of pregnancy under certain circumstances. Were the plaintiff merely free to seek the abortion, but unable to seek a remedy at law for injuries consequent upon the negligent performance of that abortion, the right would be hollow. See *Speck v Finegold*, 439 A2d 110 (Pa 1981).

It has also been recognized that while most parents hold the sentiment that the birth of a healthy albeit unplanned child is always a benefit, this sentiment should not be raised to the level of public policy. See *Cockrum v*

Baumgartner, 99 IlA3d 271, 425 NE2d 968 (1981). The notion that individuals should be compensated for the negligence of a physician in facilitating the birth of an unwanted child is no more offensive to the belief that life, whether wanted or unwanted, is an ultimate good which can in no sense be regarded as a wrong than is the concept of birth control itself. There are both positive and negative aspects to childbearing. It is no answer to say that a result, which one specifically seeks to avoid, might be regarded as a blessing by someone else. See *Rivera v State*, 94 Misc 2d 157, 404 NYS2d 950 (1978). The plaintiff-parents of an unplanned child, wrongfully conceived and born, suffer a substantial wrong, and an action for this wrong should be permitted in which the usual common-law principles of damage should be applied. See *Speck v Finegold*, 439 A2d 110 (Pa 1981). And, the uniqueness of life is in no way denigrated by a couple's choice not to have a child. Regardless of motivation, a couple has the right to determine whether they will have a child. That right is legally protectable and need not be justified or explained. To provide that the violation of this right would result in no injury would effectively nullify the right. See *Cockrum v Baumgartner*, 99 IlA3d 271, 425 NE2d 968 (1981). It is fundamental that one may seek redress for every substantial wrong, and that a wrongdoer is responsible for the natural and probable consequences of his or her misconduct. See *Speck v Finegold*, 439 A2d 110 (Pa 1981).

Additionally, it has been recognized that a tort action brought by the parents of an unplanned child, conceived as the result of an unsuccessful vasectomy, merely requires the extension of existing principles of tort law to new facts. The determination that parents may bring an action under a tort theory in the circumstances of an unwanted pregnancy or birth recognizes that the defendants owe the plaintiffs a duty of care because the plaintiffs have interests which are entitled to legal protection. See *Speck v Finegold*, 439 A2d 110 (Pa 1981). Finally, if the birth of a normal child precluded recovery on the grounds of public policy, an anomalous situation would result. It is uncontroverted that prior to the normal delivery of a child an action would lie for injury or damage to the parents. Therefore, should the plaintiffs file immediately and push for a final hearing before delivery, or should the court recognize a cause of action defeasible upon the happening of a condition subsequent. The fallacy in the defendant's argument to this effect is that it suggests as vitiating liability a fact which mitigates damages. See *Jackson v Anderson*, 230 So2d 503 (Fl 1970). [As to public policy considerations relating to damage recovery in wrongful conception and wrongful pregnancy actions, see §3.27.]

2. [§3.11] Malpractice Considerations

Assuming that the elements necessary to support an action for medical malpractice are present, some courts have permitted actions for wrongful pregnancy or wrongful conception based on the theory that nonrecognition of a cause of action for wrongful conception or wrongful pregnancy [as to wrongful conception and wrongful pregnancy in general, see §3.8] would leave a void in the area of recovery for medical malpractice and would dilute the standard of professional conduct and expertise in the area of family planning. See, *Kingsbury v Smith*, 442 A2d 1003 (NH 1982). [As to the public policy considerations involved in recognition of a cause of action for wrongful conception or wrongful pregnancy, see §3.10.] There is no viable reason for exempting a physician from liability when his negligence proximately and wrongfully causes a patient to become pregnant. See *Boone v Mullendore*, 416 So2d 718 (Al 1982). Fundamental tort principles would be frustrated if there were no duty of care imposed upon physicians who negligently performed sterilization or abortion procedures which resulted in the birth of an unplanned child. The prophylactic factor of preventing future harm has been important in the development of tort law, and the concern is not only with compensation of the victim but with admonition of the wrongdoer. When defendants realize they may be held liable, there is a strong incentive to prevent reoccurrence of the harm. See *Speck v Finegold*, 439 A2d 110 (Pa 1981). In a case involving the negligent filling of a birth control prescription which led to an unexpected pregnancy, the court said public policy favors a tort scheme which encourages pharmacists to exercise care in filling prescriptions. To absolve the defendant of liability would be to remove one deterrent against the negligent dispensing of drugs. See *Troppi v Scarf*, 31 MiA 240, 187 NW2d 511, leave den, 385 Mi 753 (1971).

Moreover, it has been recognized that analytically a cause of action for the unplanned birth of a child following an unsuccessful sterilization operation or an unsuccessful abortion procedure is indistinguishable from an ordinary medical malpractice action. The essential elements of tort liability are alleged. According to traditional tort principles, once allegations of duty, breach of duty, and proximate cause are proven, the tortfeasor is liable for all damages which ordinarily and in the natural cause of things flow from the commission of the tort. See *Cockrum v Baumgartner*, 99 IlA3d 271, 54 Il Dec 751, 425 NE2d 968 (1981).

3. [§3.12] Illustrative Cases, Generally

Wrongful conception and wrongful pregnancy actions based in tort have arisen in a number of different factual settings. [As to wrongful conception and wrongful pregnancy tort actions in general, see §3.10.] The common denominator in these cases is that an unplanned child is born following the negligent performance of a medical procedure to prevent conception or the continuation of a pregnancy. Examples of fact situations that have led to the initiation of wrongful conception actions have included unsuccessful sterilization or contraception procedures. [For a more detailed discussion of these cases, see §3.13.] Factual settings that have resulted in wrongful pregnancy actions have included unsuccessful abortion procedures and failures to diagnose pregnancy. [For a more detailed discussion of unsuccessful abortion procedures and failures to diagnose pregnancies, see §§3.14, 3.15.]

a. [§3.13] Unsuccessful Sterilization or Contraception

Often, for a variety of reasons, parents choose not to have children at all, or to limit the number of children in their family. In order to carry out this desire one of the parents will undergo a surgical sterilization operation to prevent him or her from being able to procreate. The choice to undergo the operation is voluntary, and in many instances the operation is successful. However, at times, the operation is not successful, the person is still able to successfully procreate, and, without the knowledge that he or she is still fertile, other forms of contraception are not used and a pregnancy ensues. After the child is born, the parents allege that but for the improper performance of the operation the unplanned child would not have been conceived and born. The duty to mitigate damages by seeking an abortion has been held not to exist. See e.g., *Troppi v Scarf*, 31 MiA 240, 187 NW2d 511, leave den, 385 Mi 753 (1971). [For a more general discussion of the duty to mitigate, see §3.29.] [As to the public policy and malpractice considerations involved in recognizing a tort action for wrongful conception or wrongful pregnancy, see §§3.10, 3.11.] Generally, the types of sterilization cases that are involved are tubal ligations on women [see, e.g., *Custodio v Bauer*, 251 CaA2d 303, 59 CaR 463 (1967); *Ochs v Borrelli*, 187 Cn 253, 445 A2d 883 (1982); *Sard v Hardy*, 379 A2d 1014 (Md 1977)], and vasectomies on men [see, e.g., *Cockrum v Baumgartner*, 99 IlA3d 271, 425 NE2d 968 (1981); *Speck v Finegold*, 439 A2d 110 (Pa 1981)]; other cases involving contraceptive failures have arisen where a prescription for birth control pills was negligently filled with tranquilizers [see *Troppi v Scarf*, 31 MiA 240, 187 NW2d 511 (1971)], and where a woman read a pamphlet discussing sterilization operations and relied thereon before undergoing an unsuccessful operation [see *Roman v City of New York*, 110 Misc 2d 799, 442 NYS2d 945 (1981)].

The following cases are illustrative of the general tort principles and policy considerations as they have been applied to wrongful conception actions that arose from unsuccessful sterilization or contraceptive procedures:

In *Custodio v Bauer*, 251 CaA2d 303, 59 CaR 463 (1967), the plaintiffs brought an action against a physician to recover damages resulting from the pregnancy of the plaintiff-wife following the failure of an operation undertaken and performed to accomplish her sterilization. The plaintiffs alleged, in part, that the physician was liable for malpractice because the operation was performed in a negligent manner (i.e., that there was an insufficient cutting of the fallopian tubes, that the defendants failed to inform the plaintiff that the operation was not absolute in nature, and that the defendants were negligent in failing to inform the plaintiff of other surgical procedures that would accomplish a complete sterilization). The court said the allegations of the three causes of action for negligence were sufficient to show a failure to use due care with respect to duties owed to the plaintiffs, and to show a possible battery on the plaintiff for lack of effective consent.

In *Cockrum v Baumgartner*, and *Raja v Tulsky*, 99 IlA3d 271, 54 Il Dec 751, 425 NE2d 968 (1981), two cases were consolidated for appeal. In *Cockrum v Baumgartner*, the physician attempted to perform a vasectomy on the plaintiff-father. The father returned for a sperm test one month later and was informed by the physician that the operation was successful. About six weeks later, the plaintiff-wife became pregnant. Then the physician performed another test on the husband and detected the presence of live sperm cells. The Cockrums subsequently became parents of an unplanned child. In *Raja v Tulsky*, Edna Raja alleged that she was negligently advised that she was not pregnant when she was in fact pregnant. Subsequently she gave birth to an unplanned child. The court viewed the actions as analytically indistinguishable from ordinary malpractice actions. The essential elements of tort liability were alleged. The plaintiffs alleged that because of the defendants' breach of duty to properly treat and advise them, they would be required to incur the expenses of rearing the unplanned child. The court said according to traditional tort principles, once these allegations of duty, breach of duty, and proximate cause are proven, the tortfeasor is liable for all damages which ordinarily and in the natural course of things flow from the commission of the tort.

In *Roman v City of New York*, 110 Misc 2d 799, 442 NYS2d 945 (1981), the defendant Planned Parenthood moved for summary judgment in a case involving wrongful conception. The court noted that this case was unique in that the moving defendant was not charged with wrongful treatment or diagnosis, but rather the wrongful act was alleged to be a misstatement contained in a booklet published by the defendant. The plaintiff had attended a lecture concerning sterilization. At the end of this lecture the booklet was distributed. The plaintiff testified that she referred to the booklet and read it both before and after the sterilization operation. The booklet was entitled "Voluntary Sterilization Of Men And Women — The

Surest Way To Avoid Unwanted Pregnancy". The booklet stated, in part, that there was no possibility of pregnancy after the performance of a tubal ligation, and that therefore the use of contraceptives was unnecessary. However, the plaintiff subsequently became pregnant and gave birth to a healthy child. The court noted that the evidence was not clear if the operation was improperly performed or whether there was a spontaneous regeneration of the plaintiff's fallopian tubes. The court, therefore, presumed that the plaintiff's pregnancy resulted from the failure of a properly performed sterilization. The court noted that the pleading was consistent with a cause of action based on negligent misrepresentation, but that a cause of action sounding in negligence requires the establishment of a duty owed by the defendant to the plaintiffs. The court said that not every negligent statement is actionable, and that a defendant will only be held answerable where it is bound by some relational duty arising out of a public calling, contract or other. The court said it did need to decide whether a relational duty would have existed if the plaintiff had sought out Planned Parenthood's advice, because she did not. The evidence was overwhelming that the plaintiff sought the advice of friends and relatives and relied on the knowledge of the physicians and staff at the hospital, the court said. The plaintiff did not go to the defendant and the defendant did not contact her. Their sole relationship was the plaintiff's fortuitous receipt of the defendant's booklet at the hospital. The court noted that one who publishes a text cannot be said to assume liability for all misstatements, said or unsaid, to a potentially unlimited public for a potentially unlimited period. Thus, the court concluded that the relational duties sufficient to give rise to a cause of action in negligent misrepresentation were not present.

In *Speck v Finegold*, 439 A2d 110 (Pa 1981), the court viewed the action for injuries suffered as a result of a negligently performed vasectomy (and a negligently performed abortion) as merely requiring the extension of existing principles of tort law to new facts: damages alleged to result from the birth of an unplanned, unwanted, genetically defective child. The court reasoned that the defendant-physicians owed the plaintiffs a duty of care because the plaintiffs had interests which were entitled to legal protection. It was noted by the court that there is the view that no duty of care should extend from the doctor to the patient in a case involving damages alleged as a result of the birth of an unplanned child. However, the court said that public policy supported the recognition of the action, and if the plaintiffs had been substantially injured by the defendants' negligence, to deny the plaintiffs the opportunity to present their case in court would be to grant an unjustifiable and unfair windfall to the defendants, who would escape liability for the harm resulting from their alleged negligence.

In *Troppi v Scarf*, 31 MiA 240, 187 NW2d 511, leave den, 385 Mi 753 (1971), the plaintiffs, husband and wife, had decided to limit the size of their family. Therefore they consulted a physician who prescribed a birth control pill for the wife. However, instead of filling the prescription, the pharmacist negligently supplied the wife with a mild tranquilizer. Believing that the pills she had purchased were contraceptives, the wife took them on a daily basis. Subsequently, she became pregnant and gave birth to an unplanned child. At issue, the court said, was the extent to which the pharmacist was civilly liable for the consequences of his negligence. The court held that public policy could not be said to disfavor contraception where the state's advocacy of family planning is so vigorous as to include payments for contraceptives as part of the welfare program. Moreover, the court noted that contraception has been held to be within a constitutionally protected zone of privacy that surrounds the marital relationship. The court noted that since the state may not infringe upon the rights of husband and wife to use contraceptives to limit the size of their family, it may not constitutionally denigrate the right by completely denying protection provided as a matter of course to similar rights. The court believed that potential tortfeasors, when faced with the imposition of civil liability, are encouraged to exercise more care in the performance of their duties. The court applied this theory to the case and said public policy favors a tort scheme which encourages pharmacists to exercise great care in filling prescriptions, and reasoned that to absolve the defendant of all liability would be to remove a deterrent against the negligent dispensing of drugs.

Here are examples of other cases in which the actionability of a tort action for wrongful conception or wrongful pregnancy arising from an unsuccessful sterilization procedure is considered:

In *Hartke v McKelway*, 526 FSupp 97 (D DC 1981), court concludes that District of Columbia would be likely to follow the weight of authority and recognize cause of action for wrongful conception.

In *White v United States*, 510 FSupp 146 (D Ks 1981), court holds cause of action stated for medical malpractice involving an unsuccessful sterilization operation.

In *Bishop v Byrne*, 265 FSupp 460 (1967), the court holds that, although no contract action was stated because of lack of express warranty or guarantee of the operation's success, the jury could find the physician had performed the sterilization operation in a negligent manner and thus caused the wife pain and suffering.

In *Bennett v Graves*, 557 SW2d 893 (Ky 1977), summary judgment properly granted to physician who performed a tubal ligation, which the physician thought was best for the plaintiff's health and which he thought would be successful since the procedure involved a low failure rate.

In *Pierce v Piver*, 45 NC App 111, 262 SE2d 320 (1980), the appellate court reverses the trial court's grant of motion to dismiss for failure to state claim upon which relief could be granted; the appellate court says action is one for medical malpractice, sounding in negligence and breach of contract, and that plaintiffs' complaint adequately states claim for relief under legal principles of North Carolina.

In *Sorkin v Lee*, 78 AD2d 180, 434 NYS2d 500 (1980), court holds cause of action exists for the birth of unplanned child if physician's negligence caused it. And, in *Rivera v State*, 94 Misc 2d 157, 404 NYS2d 950 (1978), court holds that the notion that individuals should be compensated for the negligence of a physician in facilitating the birth of an unwanted child is no more offensive to the belief that birth or life, whether wanted or unwanted, is an ultimate good which cannot be regarded as a wrong, than is the concept of birth control itself.

In *Vaughn v Shelton*, 514 SW2d 870 (Tn 1974), the court apparently recognizes cause of action for wrongful conception and says that it could have been concluded from the facts that one or both of the wife's tubes were not closed, and therefore that it was error for the trial court to direct a verdict for the defendant at the conclusion of the plaintiff's evidence.

b. [§3.14] Misdiagnosis or Failure to Diagnose Pregnancy

In order for a woman to exercise her constitutionally protected rights involving abortion she must first be aware that she is pregnant. This knowledge on her part is also necessary before the performance of an abortion may be considered unlawful or a health risk. At times a pregnancy cannot be accurately discovered by the woman and thus she will seek medical assistance and advice regarding her condition. If the medical advice is that she is not pregnant when in fact she is, and if the later discovery of the pregnancy comes too late in the pregnancy to utilize the abortion procedure where the plaintiff would have chosen to use it, the physician may be liable for the inaccurate diagnosis based on the theory that the plaintiff's right to exercise her constitutional rights to choose an abortion was abridged by the physician. In these cases the plaintiff typically alleges that but for the negligent diagnosis, she would have sought the performance of an abortion to prevent the unwanted or unplanned child. Examples of the types of inaccurate diagnoses that have resulted in litigation have included the failure to diagnose pregnancy [see *Ziemba v Sternberg*, 45 AD2d 230, 357 NYS2d 265 (1974)], and the diagnosis of pregnancy as obesity and high blood pressure [see *Clapham v Yanga*, 102 MiA 47, 300 NW2d 727 (1981)].

[As to the public policy and malpractice considerations involved in recognizing a tort action for wrongful conception or wrongful pregnancy, see §§3.10, 3.11.]

The following cases are illustrative of the general principles relating to the issue of actionability in wrongful pregnancy cases arising from a misdiagnosis or failure to diagnose pregnancy:

In *Clapham v Yanga*, 102 MiA 47, 300 NW2d 727 (1981), Loriann Clapham was fourteen-years-old when her mother took her to the defendant-physician for a medical examination. Loriann had been complaining of dizzy spells, fainting, and missed menstrual periods. According to both Loriann and her mother, the defendant said that these symptoms were a manifestation of obesity and low blood pressure. There was testimony that after the defendant was served with the complaint in the case he told his associate that he had suspected pregnancy during Loriann's initial examination. In fact, Loriann was pregnant, and later gave birth to an unplanned child. Loriann testified that had she known she was pregnant, she would have sought an abortion. The court concluded that a jury could find, without specific testimony on the standard of care, that it is negligent not to give a patient who complains of the symptoms experienced by Loriann a pregnancy test. This is particularly true, the court said, in light of the defendant's admission that he suspected from the initial visit that Loriann was pregnant. The court noted that Mrs. Clapham testified she assumed a pregnancy test had been conducted since the probable cause of her daughter's condition was obvious, and when the defendant said nothing about the possibility of pregnancy she did not concern herself with it.

In *Ziemba v Sternberg*, 45 AD2d 230, 357 NYS2d 265 (1974), the court recognized that a negligent failure to diagnose a pregnancy gives rise to a cause of action for malpractice. In *Ziemba*, the plaintiff-wife advised the defendant-physician that she didn't want to have children and requested that he advise her regarding the proper medication to prevent pregnancy. Later, she told the physician that she thought she might be pregnant, but the physician advised her she was not. Subsequently, the plaintiff discovered she was four and one-half months pregnant. The plaintiff alleged that the failure to diagnose her pregnancy was due to the physician's negligence and carelessness in failing to recognize obvious signs and symptoms of pregnancy within a reasonable time when she would have taken the necessary medical steps to terminate her pregnancy. The court viewed the action as one for malpractice which it described as the appropriate remedy by which recovery may be had for damages sustained as the result of a physician's failure to exercise ordinary and reasonable care in the diagnosis or treatment of a patient. The court noted that the United States Supreme Court had articulated the constitutional right of a woman to seek such an abortion in the first trimester of pregnancy. See *Roe v Wade*, 410 US 113, 93

SCt 705, 35 LE2d 147 (1973); *Doe v Bolton*, 410 US 179, 93 SCt 739, 35 LE2d 201 (1973). The court concluded that when, as one of the consequences of the physician's lack of reasonable care, the plaintiff was not advised of her pregnancy so that she could terminate it within a reasonable time, and was subsequently advised by another physician that she was pregnant, the damages sustained by the plaintiff and her husband may be the natural consequences of the physician's malpractice for which recovery would lie.

c. [§3.15] Unsuccessful Abortion

In some instances, after having discovered an unplanned pregnancy, a woman will exercise her constitutional rights and undergo an abortion operation. Her intention is to prevent the birth of an unplanned or unwanted child. The reason the woman has conceived is not the issue, as it is in negligently performed sterilization cases. [For a more detailed discussion of cases arising from unsuccessful sterilization or contraceptive procedures, see §3.13.] Rather the issue is the manner in which the abortion was performed and whether it was performed with due care. Where it is determined that the procedure was performed in a negligent manner, the physician may be held liable for wrongful pregnancy if a child is subsequently born. [As to the public policy and malpractice considerations involved in recognizing a tort action for wrongful conception or wrongful pregnancy, see §§3.10, 3.11.]

The following cases are illustrative of the general principles relating to the issue of actionability in wrongful pregnancy cases arising from the performance of an unsuccessful abortion:

In *Speck v Finegold*, 439 A2d 110 (Pa 1981), the plaintiff-husband suffered from an inherent defect of the genes causing the disease neurofibromatosis. The husband and wife, after having had two children who inherited the defects and the accompanying disease, decided not to have other children for genetic and economic reasons. Therefore, the husband underwent a vasectomy. Later, however, the wife became pregnant because the Specks were unaware that the vasectomy had not been successful. At this point the wife sought the medical assistance of a physician to perform an abortion. The abortion was performed and the Specks were told it was successful. Subsequently, the wife gave birth to an unplanned, and diseased child. The court viewed the action brought by the parents, for injuries suffered as a result of negligently performed abortion and vasectomy procedures, as merely requiring the extension of existing principles of tort law to new facts, and said it is fundamental that one may seek redress for every substantial wrong and that a wrongdoer is responsible for the natural and probable consequences of his or her misconduct. Moreover, the court recognized that, under the circumstances of this case, the parents could bring an action in tort because the defendants owed the plaintiffs a duty of care since the plaintiffs had interests which were entitled to legal protection.

In *Wilczynski v Goodman*, 73 IlA3d 51, 29 Il Dec 216, 391 NE2d 479 (1979), a woman charged a physician with the failure to perform a proper abortion which later led to the birth of an unplanned child. The woman brought the action in counts sounding in negligence, breach of contract, and breach of warranty. The woman alleged the physician was negligent because he failed to possess or exercise the requisite skill and diligence in performing the operation of abortion for which he was engaged to the plaintiff's detriment. The defendant argued that the plaintiff's suit was not cognizable at law, should await legislative sanction, and should not be legitimized by judicial fiat. The court noted that the plaintiff's action could be maintained without contravening the precepts of *Roe v Wade*, 410 US 113, 93 SCt 705, 35 LE2d 147 (1973), *Doe v Bolton*, 410 US 179, 93 SCt 739, 35 LE2d 201 (1973), or the established legislative public policy of Illinois favoring life over abortion. Moreover, the court held that a cognizable cause of action had been stated for the negligent performance of an abortion procedure.

4. [§3.16] Proximate Cause

It is not required that the negligence of the defendant be the sole cause of the plaintiff's injury in order for the plaintiff to recover damages therefor. All that is required is that the negligence in question be a proximate cause of the injury. See *Champion v Bennetts*, 37 Ca2d 815, 236 P2d 155 (1955). In the context of wrongful conception and wrongful pregnancy cases [as to wrongful conception and wrongful pregnancy in general, see §3.8], defendants have contended that the injuries or damages, if any [for a more detailed discussion of damages in wrongful conception and wrongful pregnancy cases, see §3.27], suffered by the plaintiffs, were not the proximate result of any breach of duty on their part because of the intervening sexual relations between the parents. See *Custodio v Bauer*, 59 CaR 463, 251 CaA2d 303 (1967). The general test of whether an independent intervening act, which actively operates to produce an injury, breaks the chain of causation is the foreseeability of that act. See, e.g., *Gill v Epstein*, 62 Ca2d 611, 44 CaR 45, 401 P2d 397 (1965).

However, there is general agreement among the courts that have considered this issue that sexual relations do not act to break the chain of causation because the possibility of conceiving an unplanned child is not unforeseeable. For one court it was difficult to conceive how the very act, the consequences of which the sterilization operation was designed to forestall, could be considered unforeseeable. See *Custodio v Bauer*, 59 CaR 463, 251 CaA2d 303 (1967). Moreover, the part played by a husband in impregnating his wife following an unsuccessful sterilization operation has been held not to be an intervening cause. See *Bishop v Byrne*, 265 FSupp 460 (SD WV 1967). The impregnation by the father is but the physiological cause, and not the legal proximate cause, of the alleged damage. See *Ladies Center of Clearwater, Inc v Reno*, 341 So2d 543 (Fl 1977). And, whether a defendant's negligence in the performance of a sterilization operation, or in failure to warn the plaintiff of its possible temporary nature, or the natural regeneration of a fallopian tube, was the sole proximate cause, or whether each was a concurring cause of the pregnancy, is a matter of proof. See *Custodio v Bauer*, 59 CaR 463, 251 CaA2d 303 (1967).

5. [§3.17] —Illustrative Cases

The following cases are illustrative of the general principles relating to proximate cause [generally, see §3.16] in the context of wrongful conception and wrongful pregnancy actions:

In *Bishop v Byrne*, 265 FSupp 460 (SD WV 1967), the court said that if it could be established that the sterilization operation was negligently performed, and that as a result mental or physical suffering, or both, accompanied it, the victim had been injured. The part played by the husband in bringing about this condition did not amount to an intervening cause.

In *Custodio v Bauer*, 59 CaR 463, 251 CaA2d 303 (1967), the court said the general test of whether an independent intervening act, which actively operates to produce an injury, breaks the chain of causation is the foreseeability of that act. The court found it difficult to conceive how the very act (the birth of a child), the consequences of which the operation was designed to forestall, could be considered unforeseeable. Whether the defendant's negligence and the performance of the operation, or in failure to warn the plaintiffs of its possible temporary nature, or the natural regeneration of a fallopian tube, was the sole proximate cause, or whether each was a concurring cause of pregnancy, is a matter of proof.

In *Ladies Center of Clearwater, Inc v Reno*, 341 So2d 543 (Fl 1977), the plaintiff brought an action for damages resulting from an unsuccessful abortion and birth of a child alleging negligence and breach of contract by the Ladies Center of Clearwater, Incorporated, and a physician. The defendants filed a third-party complaint against the unwed father, alleging that his negligent failure to employ a method of contraception was the legal proximate cause of any injuries or losses suffered by the plaintiff. The court affirmed the findings of the trial judge in which he determined that the impregnation by the third-party defendant was but the physiological cause, and not the legal proximate cause, of the alleged damage. The court believed that the only cause of action against the third-party defendant was one in bastardy, after determining that illegal fornication had not been elevated to tort in the eyes of the law, and having further determined that, as a result, the defendants/third-party plaintiffs had no right of indemnification or contribution from the third-party defendant.

In *Troppi v Scarf*, 31 MiA 240, 187 NW2d 511, leave den, 385 Mi 753 (1971), the court assumed, for the purpose of appraising the correctness of the ruling dismissing the complaint, that the defendant's negligence was a cause in fact of the plaintiff's pregnancy. The possibility that she might become pregnant was certainly a foreseeable consequence of the defendant's failure to fill a prescription for birth control pills, the court said. Therefore, the court held it could not say the defendant's negligence was not a proximate cause of the birth of the child.

In *Roman v City of New York*, 110 Misc 2d 799, 442 NYS2d 945 (1981), the court said it was not prepared to conclude that the harm caused the plaintiff was not reasonably foreseeable. In *Roman*, the plaintiff brought a wrongful conception action against Planned Parenthood which had published a booklet on the topic of sterilization. The booklet said, in part, that following a tubal ligation there is no possibility of pregnancy, and that contraceptives are thereafter not necessary. The plaintiff alleged that she read the booklet before undergoing a sterilization operation, that later she did not use contraceptives, and that she subsequently became pregnant and gave birth to an unplanned child. The complaint charged that the defendant knew, or should have known, that its statement concerning the need for contraceptives was false. The court noted that the pleading was consistent with a cause of action based on negligent representation. The court said the implication in the plaintiff's argument that duty and foreseeability are identical in scope was not altogether correct. The existence of a legal duty is not grounded on the factor of foreseeability alone, the court said. Not every negligent statement is actionable. By contrast, the court noted that a defendant will only be held answerable where it is bound by some relational duty arising out of a public calling, contract or other, and that, therefore, a judge's decision about whether to impose an actionable duty may be conditioned on many factors including the foreseeability factor.

6. [§3.18] Consent Forms/Informed Consent

Patients are typically required to read and sign medical consent forms before undergoing elective surgery. The form generally sets forth the patient's consent to undergo the operation, and, at times, sets forth the possible risks of the procedure. The form is one means of obtaining the informed consent of the patient to undergo the procedure. The doctrine of informed consent follows from the rule that a physician, treating a mentally competent adult under nonemergency circumstances, cannot properly undertake or perform surgery or administer therapy without the prior consent of his patient. See, e.g., *McGlees v Cohen*, 158 Md 60, 148 A 124 (1930). [For a general discussion of the necessity of consent to surgical sterilization procedures, see §2.4.] Moreover, in order for the patient's consent to be effective, it must be an informed consent, one that is given after the patient has received a fair and reasonable explanation of the contemplated treatment or procedure. See, e.g., *Sard v Hardy*, 379 A2d 1014 (Md 1977). The doctrine of informed consent is based on patients' rights to exercise control over their own body, at least when undergoing elective surgery, by deciding for themselves whether to submit to the particular therapy. The doctrine takes account of the probability that unlike the physician, patients are untrained in medical science, and therefore depend completely on the trust and skill of their physician for the information on which they make their decisions. See *Cobbs v Grant*, 8 Ca3d 229, 104 CaR 505, 502 P2d 1 (1972). The duty to explain the procedure to the patient includes the duty to warn the patient of any material risks or dangers inherent in the therapy so as to enable the patient to make an intelligent and informed choice about whether to undergo the treatment. See *Bang v Charles T Miller Hosp*, 251 Mn 427, 88 NW2d 186 (1958). The issue of informed consent can arise in wrongful conceptional cases [as to wrongful conception actions in general, see §3.8], if, following an unsuccessful sterilization operation and the birth of an unplanned child, the plaintiff alleges that the defendant-physician was negligent in failing to advise the plaintiff that the sterilization operation undertaken might not succeed in preventing future pregnancies and in failing to disclose alternative means of achieving the desired result, thereby precluding the plaintiff from giving his or her informed consent.

The types of sterilization cases in which the informed consent issue has arisen have included tubal ligations on women [see *Bowman v Davis*, 48 OhSt2d 41, 356 NE2d 496 (1976)], and vasectomies on men [see *Maggard v McKelvey*, 627 SW2d 44 (Ky 1981)]. In many cases involving informed consent and a sterilization procedure, the issue of the plaintiff's signing of a consent form, and whether this relieved a defendant of liability for negligence, has arisen. See, e.g., *Sard v Hardy*, 379 A2d 1014 (Md 1977); *Bowman v Davis*, 48 OhSt2d 41, 356 NE2d 496 (1976). Where the form is designed to release the hospital and attending physician from the consequences of their negligence, the intent must be set out in clear and unequivocal terms. In the context of a wrongful conception case, where the only result of sterilization described in a medical consent form is the failure to ever again procreate or conceive children, it has been held that the form could be interpreted to apply only to the effects of a successful operation. See *Bowman v Davis*, 48 OhSt2d 41, 356 NE2d 496 (1976).

7. [§3.19] —Illustrative Cases

The following cases are illustrative of the general principles relating to informed consent and consent forms generally [generally, see §3.18]:

In *Bennett v Graves*, 557 SW2d 893 (Ky 1977), the plaintiff expressed her desire not to have any more children to the defendant-physician and they together discussed sterilization procedures. The physician advised against a hysterectomy immediately after the delivery of a child because of the enlargement of the uterus. He advised that the plaintiff have a tubal ligation. The operation was performed, but the plaintiff subsequently became pregnant. The plaintiff asserted that the physician breached his duty to obtain her informed consent because he did not inform her that the operation might not prevent further pregnancy which resulted in injury (the conception and birth of an unplanned child) to her. Before the operation was performed the plaintiff signed a consent to surgery form which provided that she acknowledged that no guarantee or assurance had been given to her as to the results of the operation. The court said it was inconceivable that a woman who knew of her propensity to become pregnant would not have discussed with her doctor the chances of success or failure in the tubal ligation procedure. The physician performed an operation with a very low failure rate, the court noted, which the physician thought was best for the plaintiff's health following delivery of her eighth child, and which he thought would be effective. Because there was no genuine issue as to any material fact, the court affirmed the summary judgment granted by the trial court.

In *Sard v Hardy*, 379 A2d 1014 (Md 1977), the court held that if the information the physician withheld from the patient was material to the patient's decision regarding the type of sterilization operation, the physician would be liable. The plaintiff had entered the hospital for the birth of a child. It was agreed between the plaintiff and her physician that, at the time of the delivery of the child, a tubal ligation would be performed. Some 10 to 15 minutes before being taken into the delivery room the plaintiff was handed a consent form which she signed without reading. It provided that the patient understood what was meant by sterilization, that if the operation was successful the patient would be unable to bear children in the future, but that the patient also understood that such an operation was not successful in all cases. The plaintiff's husband, whose testimony revealed that he was functionally illiterate, had previously signed the form. The court said that the protection of the patient's fundamental right of physical self-determination mandated that the scope of a physician's duty to disclose therapeutic risks and alternatives be governed by the patient's informational needs. Thus, the court said, the appropriate test is not what the physician, in the exercise of his or her medical judgment, thinks a patient should know before acquiescing in a proposed course of treatment; rather, the focus is on what data the patient requires in order to make an intelligent decision. Once the physician has ascertained the risks and alternatives, and has communicated this information to the patient, the court said that it is the patient's exclusive right to weigh these risks, together with individual subjective fears and hopes and to determine whether or not to place his or her body in the hands of the surgeon or physician. Applying this law to the case, the court held a jury could conclude that the effectiveness of the sterilization was of such importance to the plaintiff, or to a reasonably prudent person in her position, that the failure to reveal data about risks of failure and more efficient alternative methods would have induced the plaintiff to consent to the operation, while she would not have done so had adequate disclosure been made.

In *Bowman v Davis*, 48 OhSt2d 41, 356 NE2d 496 (1976), the plaintiffs, husband and wife, signed a "patient sterilization consent form" before the wife underwent a tubal ligation. Subsequently, she became pregnant and gave birth to an unplanned child. The form provided, in part, that those who signed it understood the purpose and effect of the sterilization procedure, and that they voluntarily consented to the operation and absolved the attending physicians and the hospital from responsibility for any untoward or unfavorable results arising from the procedure. The court noted that it had held indemnity agreements purporting to release a party from the consequences of his or her negligence, but failing to express that intent in clear and unequivocal terms, to be unenforceable. Although the hospital consent form was not an indemnity agreement, it appeared to have been designed to release the hospital and attending physicians from the consequences of their negligence. That intent was not, in the court's view, set out in clear and unequivocal terms. Since the only result of sterilization, as described in the form, was the failure to ever again create, conceive, or bear any more children, the form could easily be interpreted to apply only to the effects of a successful operation. Therefore, the court held that the plaintiffs' signatures on the consent form did not relieve the physician and the hospital from liability for negligence.

8. [§3.20] Interspousal Immunity

The doctrine of interspousal immunity provides that, as a matter of law, claims for personal injuries between married persons may not justify a recovery of damages. See, e.g., *Merenoff v Merenoff*, 76 NJ 535, 388 A2d 951 (1978). In jurisdictions where the doctrine has been abrogated, in part or in whole, there may arise issues concerning the effect of the doctrine in its more limited form on actions arising from the conception and birth of an unplanned child. For example, in *M & Wife v Schmid Laboratories, Inc*, 178 NJ Super 122, 428 A2d 515 (1981), an action was brought by a husband and wife against the manufacturer of a contraceptive device (condom), and the retailer of the device, for the birth of an unplanned child, the plaintiffs alleging breach of warranty, negligence, and strict liability. The retailer, in addition to denying liability, filed a counterclaim against the plaintiff-husband alleging negligence in the use of the condom and demanding contribution. The plaintiff-husband argued that he could not be liable to his wife in negligence because of the doctrine of interspousal immunity. The court did not view the retailer's counterclaim as falling within one of the situations where the interspousal immunity doctrine continues to have viability. While some matters or proceedings between a husband and wife within the privacy of the bedroom may remain within the protection of interspousal immunity, the court said that it was clear the plaintiffs had lifted the veil of secrecy by their suit and placed squarely in issue all the facts surrounding their use or misuse of the alleged defective product. The asserted tortious behavior of the husband did not trench upon the privileged or consensual aspects of married life, and disclosure was the unavoidable result of the plaintiffs' lawsuit since, in a products liability action, the details concerning the use or misuse of the product are both relevant and material and may constitute a defense to a claim for damages resulting from harm caused by a defective product. *M & Wife v Schmid Laboratories*, above.

9. [§3.21] Federal Tort Claims Act

In some cases a sterilization operation is performed not by a private doctor, but by a doctor associated with a branch of the armed services. In instances where a service-related doctor performs a sterilization, and later an unplanned child is conceived and born [as to wrongful conception and wrongful pregnancy cases in general, see §3.8], the plaintiffs sue the United States Government under the Federal Tort Claims Act. *See* 28 USC §2671, et seq. Title 28 [28 USC §1346(b)] establishes the jurisdiction of federal district courts to adjudicate cases of governmental tort liability under the Act: "The district courts . . . shall have exclusive jurisdiction of civil actions on claims against the United States, for money damages . . . for injury . . . caused by the negligent or wrongful act or omission of any employee, of the government while acting within the scope of his office or employment under circumstances where the United States, if a private person, would be liable to the claimant in accordance with the law of the place where the act or omission occurred."

In these cases the plaintiff alleges that the operation was performed in a negligent manner which later resulted in an unplanned pregnancy and the birth of a child. In some of the cases the unsuccessful operation is performed on the person in the service [see *Harten v Coons*, 502 F2d 1363 (10th Cir 1974)], while in others it is performed on the spouse of the person in the service [see, e.g., *Grunch v United States*, 538 FSupp 534 (ED Mi 1982); *Herring v Knab*, 458 FSupp 359 (SD Oh 1978)].

However, the government is not liable under the act for injuries to servicemen where the injuries arise out of or in the course of activity incident to service. See *Feres v United States*, 340 US 135, 71 SCt 153, 95 LE 152 (1950). For example, in *Harten v Coons*, 502 F2d 1363 (10th Cir 1974), the court held that the United States was not liable for an alleged negligently performed vasectomy because the surgery, whether elective or required, was "incident to service" when performed upon a serviceman on active duty. The serviceman was taking advantage of medical privileges granted only to service personnel by reason of his status as a serviceman. In addition, where there is an alleged breach of duty to correctly inform a patient concerning the nature and consequences of an operation, but the operation is medically indicated and performed in accordance with the applicable standards of medical care, the breach of the duty to inform is not actionable under the Federal Tort Claims Act. See *Herring v Knab*, 458 FSupp 359 (SD Oh 1978), where the plaintiff alleged that government doctors at a naval hospital performed a tubal ligation in a negligent manner, which resulted in a later pregnancy, and that the government doctors negligently failed to advise their patient of the risks surrounding the tubal ligation and the possibility of future pregnancies.

C. Contract Actions Considered

1. [§3.22] Generally

The basis for a wrongful conception or wrongful pregnancy action [as to the definition of wrongful conception and wrongful pregnancy actions, see §3.8] can emerge from an alleged breach of contract just as it can arise from an alleged tort. [For a more complete discussion of wrongful conception and wrongful pregnancy actions based in tort, see §§3.10, 3.11.] Typically, an action sounding in contract is alleged in conjunction with a tort-related allegation, or is alleged by itself because of problems in complying with the tort statute of limitations. An action based on medical malpractice, the most commonly made allegation in wrongful conception and wrongful pregnancy cases, need not be limited to a tort theory. If a plaintiff can prove that a surgeon has promised a particular result, as distinguished from a mere generalized statement that the result will be good, and that the patient consented to an operation or other procedure in reliance on that promise, there can be recovery on the theory of breach of contract. See, e.g., *Depenbrok v Kaiser Foundation Health Plan, Inc*, 79 CaA3d 167, 144 CaR 724 (1978). However, a plaintiff may not circumvent the statute of limitations merely by pleading an action, which is in substance a tort action, as a contract action. See, e.g., *Christ v Lipsitz*, 99 CaA3d 894, 160 CaR 498 (1979).

As the actions of wrongful conception and wrongful pregnancy have developed, there has been a continuing discussion of the public policy considerations involved in recognizing the actions. Many cases that have considered the theories of recovery in terms of public policy issues have arisen in circumstances involving negligence. See, e.g., *Cockrum v Baumgartner*, 99 IlA3d 271, 54 Il Dec 751, 425 NE2d 968 (1981) [negligent vasectomy, tubal ligation and misdiagnosis of pregnancy]; *Speck v Finegold*, 439 A2d 110 (Pa 1981) [negligently performed vasectomy and abortion procedures]. In addition, these issues have also been discussed in actions alleging both tort and contract bases of liability. See, e.g., *Hackworth v Hart*, 474 SE2d 377 (Ky 1971) [alleged assurance by physician operation would be successful, negligently performed vasectomy];*Sard v Hardy*, 379 A2d 1014 (Md 1977) [alleged breach of an express warranty of therapeutic result that the plaintiff would, after operation, be unable to have more children, failure to advise the possibility in tubal ligation operation]. The courts have not distinguished between contract and tort theories in their policy discussions; rather, they have considered the question of whether to allow the cause of action in an isolated setting and have determined whether the cause of action should be allowed for policy considerations without regard to the theory of liability on which the case is founded.

The trend today is to recognize these causes of action. It has been held that a sterilization operation for therapeutic purposes, to protect the physical or mental health of the patient, or, in the case of a vasectomy, the wife, is not against public policy. See, e.g., *Custodio v Bauer*, 59 CaR 463, 251 CaA2d 303 (1967). In addition, it has been noted that the choice not to procreate, as part of one's right to privacy, has become, subject to certain limitations, a constitutional guaranty. See, e.g., *Bowman v Davis*, 48 OhSt2d 41, 356 NE2d 496 (1976). Another court has said that realistically there are both positive and negative aspects to childbearing, and it is no answer to say that a result, which one specifically seeks to avoid, might be regarded as a blessing by someone else. See, e.g., *Rivera v State*, 94 Misc 2d 157, 404 NYS2d 950 (1978). In addition, it has been noted that if a cause of action for wrongful conception was not recognized, it would leave a void in the area of recovery for medical malpractice and would dilute the standard of professional conduct in the area of family planning. See, e.g., *Kingsbury v Smith*, 442 A2d 1003 (NH 1982). It would appear, then, that the public policy issue is resolved not based on the type of action brought, but rather on the merits of the individual claim and the jurisdiction involved. Therefore, in the proper setting, arguments relating to the public policy issue may be extrapolated from decisions arising from a tort setting and applied to actions arising from a contract setting. [For a more detailed discussion of the public policy and malpractice considerations of wrongful conception and wrongful pregnancy actions sounding in tort, see §3.10, and §3.11.]

In addition to the public policy considerations involved in these actions, there are a number of contract related issues involved. For example, in the absence of a special agreement, a physician or surgeon does not warrant or guarantee a good result or that a cure will be effected. See, e.g., *Eckleberry v Kaiser Foundation Northern Hosps*, 359 P2d 1090 (Or 1961). A physician or surgeon is not an insurer of the success of his or her treatment. See, e.g., *Peters v Gelb*, 303 A2d 685 (De 1973), affd, 314 A2d 901 (De 1974). The theory is that courts generally are hesitant to impose liability based on a physician's therapeutic or hopeful comments. See *Garcia v Von Micsky*, 602 F2d 51 (2d Cir 1979). Therefore, in order to enforce a warranty by a physician, it is necessary for the plaintiff to allege and prove the making of the warranty, the plaintiff's reliance thereon, and a separate consideration. See, e.g., *Rogala v Silva*, 16 IlA3d 63, 305 NE2d 571 (1973). The warranty that must be proved is an express agreement to accomplish a particular result. See *Hackworth v Hart*, 474 SW2d 377 (Ky 1971).

When alleging the existence of an express warranty or guarantee to perform a successful operation, some courts have held that the plaintiff must prove these allegations by clear and convincing evidence rather than the normal preponderance standard applied in other civil actions. This higher burden of proof is required by some courts to insure that the trier of fact does not find liability predicated on a physician's mere opinion. See *Clevenger v Haling*, 379 Ma 154, 394 NE2d 1119 (1979). [For a more detailed discussion of the necessity of an express warranty and the burden of proof necessary to prove the express warranty, see §3.23.]

In addition, the plaintiff must prove that a separate consideration, rather than past consideration, was paid in return for the express warranty for the operation. See *Wilson v Blair*, 65 Mt 155, 211 P 289 (1922). [For a more detailed discussion of the element of the breach of contract action relating to separate consideration, see §3.25.] An express warranty, even if it exists, will not be enforced unless there is separate consideration. See *Coleman v Garrison*, 327 A2d 757 (De 1974), affd, 349 A2d 8 (De 1975).

Once an action sounding in contract for wrongful conception or wrongful pregnancy has been recognized, the next issue is what elements of damage can be recovered. A detailed discussion of damages, with background and policy considerations, is found at §§3.27 et seq.

2. Necessity of Express Warranty

a. [§3.23] Generally; Burden of Proof

Generally, a wrongful conception or wrongful pregnancy action [as to a definition of wrongful conception and wrongful pregnancy actions, see §3.8] is brought against a physician. See, e.g., *Sard v Hardy*, 379 A2d 1014 (Md 1977); *Clevenger v Haling*, 379 Ma 154, 394 NE2d 1119 (1979). A plaintiff alleging a contract theory [as to wrongful conception and wrongful pregnancy actions brought in contract, generally, see §3.22] in a wrongful conception or wrongful pregnancy action, therefore, must allege and prove the making of a warranty, the plaintiff's reliance thereon, and a separate consideration. See, e.g., *Rogala v Silva*, 16 IlA3d 63, 305 NE2d 571 (1973). [As to a more complete discussion of separate consideration, see §3.25.] Courts have been reluctant to find liability in wrongful conception, wrongful pregnancy, and medical malpractice actions generally based on a contract theory without an express warranty to effect a specific result because of the courts' desire not to impose liability on a physician for comments which are therapeutic or hopeful in nature. See, e.g., *Garcia v Von Micsky*, 602 F2d 51 (2d Cir 1979). In addition, there is general agreement that a physician is not a warrantor of cures or required to guarantee results, and so proof of an express contract is required before liability will be imposed. See, e.g., *Custodio v Bauer*, 251 CaA2d 303, 59 CaR 463 (1967). Therefore, to satisfy the express warranty element of the action the plaintiff must prove that the doctor's statement was an express agreement to accomplish a particular result as contrasted with the expression of a professional opinion as to the effectiveness of the procedure. See, e.g., *Hackworth v Hart*, 474 SW2d 377 (Ky 1971).

A collateral issue to the express warranty requirement is the standard or the burden of proof that will be required to substantiate the plaintiff's allegations regarding the promise. There is authority for the proposition that where the plaintiff alleges a breach of contract, he or she must prove the existence of the express warranty by "clear proof" [see, e.g., *Clevenger v Haling*, 379 Ma 155, 394 NE2d 1119 (1979)], or "clear and convincing evidence" [see, e.g., *Sard v Hardy*, 379 A2d 1014 (Md 1977)]. It has been suggested that a burden of proof higher than the burden of proof in typical civil actions is required in these actions to insure that the trier of fact will not adopt a relaxed attitude that might subject a physician to liability for statements aimed at therapeutic reassurance or hopeful expression of opinion. See, e.g., *Clevenger v Haling*, 379 Ma 155, 394 NE2d 1119 (1979); *Sard v Hardy*, 379 A2d 1014 (Md 1977).

b. [§3.24] Illustrative Cases

The following cases are illustrative of the general principles [see generally §3.23] relating to the element of express warranty in wrongful conception and wrongful pregnancy actions sounding in contract:

In *Garcia v Von Micsky*, 602 F2d 51 (2d Cir 1979), it was alleged that a warranty that the plaintiff would not again become pregnant following a sterilization operation was made orally by defendant-physician to the plaintiff five months after the surgery had been performed. There was testimony that the physician told the plaintiff that she had nothing to worry about and that it was impossible for her to have any more children. The court affirmed the district judge's ruling that, as a matter of law, the physician's statement was not a warranty. To hold, as the plaintiffs urged, would have, in the court's view, elevated the deceased doctor's therapeutic reassurance to his patient to the status of a guaranty, made without contract or compensation and at the risk of absolute liability. This, the court held, did not make good sense, either medically or legally.

In *Bishop v Byrne*, 265 FSupp 460 (SD WV 1967), the defendant-physician performed a sterilization operation on the plaintiff-wife, but subsequently she became pregnant. The court noted that a physician does not warrant or insure that a treatment will be successful in the absence of a special contract to that effect. The discovery depositions established that the physician made no express warranty or guaranty of the operation's success. That the parties may have assumed and expected there would be no subsequent pregnancies failed to alter the undisputed fact that no express promise to that effect was given. Nor did such an assumption, under any legal theory known to the court, create an express warranty. Therefore, the court found as a matter of law that the plaintiffs had stated no cause of action on the theory of breach of warranty, and that the defendant's motion for summary as to this aspect of the plaintiffs' case must be granted.

In *Custodio v Bauer*, 251 CaA2d 303, 59 CaR 463 (1967), the plaintiffs and defendants agreed in writing that the latter would sterilize the plaintiff-wife, by an operative procedure, and that she agreed to pay a reasonable fee for that service. Performance by the plaintiffs, other than the wife's submitting to the operation, was not clearly alleged. Failure of performance by defendants and resulting damages were set forth. The court noted that a doctor is not a warrantor of cures or required to guarantee results, but that, where there is proof of an express contract, the physician can be held liable for a promise to effect a cure or a certain result. Therefore, the court said there were sufficient allegations to withstand the general demurrer, or to warrant an opportunity to amend.

In *Rogala v Silva*, 15 IlA3d 973, 305 NE2d 571 (1973), the appellate court found that the trial court was correct in determining that the evidence presented by the plaintiffs failed to establish the existence of any warranty as to the success of a sterilization operation. The plaintiffs' evidence alleged that the defendant-physician told the plaintiff-wife that if the physician were to perform the operation it would be irreversible and that the wife would not be able to have any more children. In the court's opinion this evidence established only that the physician admonished the plaintiff as to the seriousness of the operation that she was requesting and that, in connection with this, he expressed an opinion as to its probable outcome. Such admonitions were both necessary and proper under the circumstances and should not, in the absence of an express undertaking, be elevated to the stature of a warranty. Even in the sphere of commercial transactions, where the parties deal at arm's length, a mere expression of opinion is not sufficient to create a warranty. The application of the ordinary rules dealing with mercantile contracts to a contract entered into between a physician and a patient is not justified. The relationship is a peculiar one inasmuch as the physician cannot, and should not, so terrify the patient by pointing out to him the manifold dangers which are present at any time the slightest surgical operation is performed. There is a difference between so-called therapeutic reassurances that the patient will recover and express promises that the treatment will produce a specific result.

In *Hackworth v Hart*, 474 SW2d 377 (Ky 1971), the defendant-physician performed a vasectomy on the plaintiff-husband. Subsequently, the physician informed the plaintiff that he was sterile but was told by the plaintiff that his wife was pregnant. The plaintiff-husband testified that the physician assured him prior to the operation that the operation was a "sure thing." The court noted that a physician may contract to cure his patient in which case he may be held liable for breach of contract if the cure is unsuccessful. However, the physician, in absence of such an express agreement, does not warrant the outcome of a treatment, and will not be held liable for an honest mistake of judgment where the proper course is open to reasonable doubt. The court reserved judgment as to under what circumstances an express contract to accomplish a particular result would be found and enforced. That question, the court noted, would depend on the evidence and facts of the particular case. The assurance by the physician that the operation was foolproof was taken by the court as the expression of a professional opinion as to the effectiveness of the operation to accomplish sterility. The court thought this evidence, combined with evidence that showed that only one semen test was made for the plaintiff-husband, presented a jury question so that the trial court erred in directing a verdict.

In *Sard v Hardy*, 379 A2d 1014 (Md 1977), the plaintiff testified that the defendant had affirmatively assured her before the operation that she would not be having any more children. Despite this assurance in the performance of the tubal ligation, the wife became pregnant and delivered an unplanned child. The court adopted the rule that although a patient may recover for breach of an express, preoperative warranty to effect a particular result, despite the absence of a separate consideration, he or she may do so only upon proving by clear and convincing evidence that the physician did, in fact, make the alleged warranty. The court said the issue was whether the plaintiff's testimony, standing alone, was sufficient evidence on which to submit to the jury the plaintiff's contract claim that the defendant had expressly warranted that the wife would be sterile following the surgery. The court thought it was not, particularly in light of the requirement that the jury find the existence of the warranty by clear and convincing evidence. The statement attributed to the defendant that the wife would not have any more children did not by itself rise to a level of a guaranty, and beyond a mere hopeful expression of opinion or predication of an expected result. Accordingly, the court said the trial court acted properly in directing a verdict on the express warranty claims.

In *Clevenger v Haling*, 379 Ma 154, 394 NE2d 1119 (1979), the plaintiff testified that before the sterilization operation the defendant-physician said that she would not have any more children after the operation, and that the operation was a permanent thing. The court said the defendant rightly emphasized the significance of a tubal ligation which, according to the testimony, is effective in the overwhelming percentage of the cases where the surgical procedure is carried out with due care. The defendant's words were designed to make sure that the plaintiff knew that the operation was nonreversible in character. The parties did not focus on the question of a promise, nor were the words used promissory in nature. Doubt could be lessened or removed in such a case if the physician were to call the attention to the possibility that the operation might not succeed despite all standard surgical precautions. But the court was persuaded on the whole that the case for liability was not sufficiently demonstrated to warrant submission to the jury.

The following cases are illustrative of the principles relating to the level of proof necessary to establish the existence of an express warranty in wrongful conception and wrongful pregnancy actions sounding in contract:

In *Sard v Hardy*, 379 A2d 1014 (Md 1977), the court said that, in order to strike a balance in protecting both the public and physicians, actions based on an alleged contract must be substantiated by clear proof. Instructions to the jury may well stress this requirement and point to tests of truth, such as the complexity or difficulty of an operation as bearing on the probability that a given result was promised. Therefore, although a patient may recover for breach of an express, preoperative warranty to effect a particular result, despite the absence of a separate consideration, he or she may do so only upon proving by clear and convincing evidence that the physician did, in fact, make the alleged warranty.

In *Clevenger v Haling*, 379 Ma 154, 394 NE2d 1119 (1979), the court said actions based on cases involving claims that a physician had contracted to achieve a particular medical result are allowable but there must be clear proof. Clear proof does not require proof of special consideration for the promise nor does it heighten the burden of proof. What it does require is that the trier of fact give attention to particular factors in deciding whether the physician made a statement which, in the context of the relationship, could have been reasonably interpreted by the patient as a promise that a given result or cure would be achieved. The factors relevant in such an appraisal, and their respective values or weights, will vary with the circumstances of given cases. It should be regarded as a negative factor, although not one in itself determinative, that the physician and patient did not focus on the question whether the physician was undertaking to achieve a given result. The trier of fact should not adopt a relaxed attitude that might subject a physician to liability for making statements reasonably calculated only to reassure a patient or for stating the significant consequences that could be expected to follow upon a successful surgical procedure.

3. Necessity of Consideration

a. [§3.25] Separate Consideration

In order for a plaintiff to prevail in a wrongful conception or wrongful pregnancy action [as to the definition and background of wrongful conception and wrongful pregnancy actions, see §3.8, and §3.9] based on a breach of contract [as to wrongful conception and wrongful pregnancy actions sounding in contract generally, see §3.22] the plaintiff must establish, in most cases, the existence of separate consideration for an express warranty [as to express warranty in general, see §3.23], and reliance on the warranty. See, e.g., *Rogala v Silva*, 16 IlA3d 63, 305 NE2d 571 (1973).

It is generally agreed that where a defendant-physician enters into a special agreement with the plaintiff under the terms of which the defendant increases his responsibility by guaranteeing the results of an operation, in order to make such a special agreement a contract it must be supported by a separate consideration, and the past consideration resulting from the plaintiff's agreement to pay for the sterilization operation is not sufficient. See, e.g., *Wilczynski v Goodman*, 73 IlA3d 51, 29 Il Dec 216, 391 NE2d 479 (1979); *Sard v Hardy*, 379 A2d 1014 (Md 1977); *Clegg v Chase*, 89 Misc 2d 510, 391 NYS2d 966 (1977). If there is no separate consideration to support an alleged express warranty, the warranty, even if it exists, will not be enforceable. See *Coleman v Garrison*, 349 A2d 8 (De 1975).

There is also authority for the proposition that separate consideration is required only where the alleged warranty is made postoperatively. See, e.g.,

Sard v Hardy, 379 A2d 1014 (Md 1977), in which the court said that where the warranty is made prior to the surgery or treatment, the patient may recover in contract by proving breach of an express warranty, and that proof of a separate consideration is not required. Proof of separate consideration is required only where the alleged warranty is made postoperatively.

b. [§3.26] Illustrative Cases

The following cases are illustrative of the general principles [see generally §3.25] relating to the element of separate consideration in wrongful conception and wrongful pregnancy cases sounding in contract:

In *Herrera v Roessing*, 533 P2d 60 (Co 1975), the appellate court said while it is true that there can be a special contract between a physician and patient guarantying successful results from surgery there must be consideration to support such a warranty. In this case the court found there was no evidence of any consideration to the defendant for the alleged contract and warranty entered into after surgery. Shortly after a tubal ligation had been performed on the plaintiff a discussion took place in which the physician told her that he was sure that she would not get pregnant in the future and that she needed no other protection against becoming pregnant. However, the plaintiff did become pregnant and gave birth to an unplanned child. The complaint alleged that at the time the parties discussed the plaintiff's desire to be sterilized, the physician orally agreed and warranted that the operation would absolutely prevent the plaintiff from having any further pregnancies. The court noted that the evidence presented at trial was devoid of any proof of any warranty or conversation on the subject prior to surgery. The court also noted the statement of the trial court that the comments made in the discussion between the parties after surgery about the chances of the plaintiff becoming pregnant again were mere opinions and reassurances of a doctor to a patient, and not a guarantee, and the court agreed. Here, the court said, there was no evidence of any consideration to the defendant for the alleged contract and warranty entered into after surgery.

In *Coleman v Garrison*, 349 A2d 8 (De 1975), the court held that, to be enforceable, a warranty or guarantee of success of an operation must be express and be supported by a separate consideration. Here the only consideration involved was the fee for the operation itself. Therefore, assuming that the promise was made as the plaintiffs contended, there was no consideration to support it and it was not enforceable. Thus, the plaintiffs could not recover on a warranty theory. The plaintiffs had contended that the surgeon entered into an oral contract with them promising that the operation would be 100 per cent successful and that the wife would not become pregnant again. The doctor denied making such a promise.

In *Wilczynski v Goodman*, 73 IlA3d 51, 29 Il Dec 216, 391 NE2d 479 (1979), it was alleged that, after a therapeutic abortion, the defendant-physician warranted to the plaintiff that the operation was successful, upon which warranty the plaintiff relied to her detriment, and that her subsequently continuing condition of pregnancy went undiagnosed until such date as to have made impossible a further attempt at aborting the pregnancy. The alleged warranty carried with it no allegation of consideration at all, except reliance thereon by the plaintiff. No additional separate consideration was pleaded. Assuming, the court said, that the statement attributed to the defendant, promising to terminate the pregnancy in return for payment, could be construed as a warranty, the dismissal of the breach of warranty count was correct since a separate consideration is required to support such a warranty.

In *Sard v Hardy*, 379 A2d 1014 (Md 1977), the court said proof of separate consideration in breach of warranty actions brought against a physician is required only where the alleged warranty is made postoperatively. Where the warranty is made prior to the surgery or treatment the patient may recover in contract by proving breach of an express warranty, in which action even proof of a separate consideration is not required. The plaintiff-wife testified that she had been affirmatively assured by the defendant-physician before the operation that she would not have any more children. But the court did not think that her testimony was sufficient evidence on which to submit to the jury the plaintiffs' contract claim that the defendant had expressly warranted to them that the wife would be sterile following the surgery. Accordingly, the court said, the trial court acted properly in directing a verdict on the express warranty claims.

In *Clegg v Chase*, 89 Misc 2d 510, 391 NYS2d 966 (1977), the plaintiffs' warranty actions were dismissed, since the complaint alleging negligence on the part of the defendant in performing tubal ligation on the plaintiff-mother, which resulted in the birth of an unplanned child, did not allege the existence of a special contract, accompanied by consideration separate and distinct from the fee for the sterilization operation.

D. Damages

1. In General

a. [§3.27] Background; Policy Considerations

In the early stages of wrongful conception and wrongful pregnancy litigation [as to the definition of wrongful conception and wrongful pregnancy actions, see §3.8], an issue often raised was whether the parents of the unplanned child had suffered an injury from which damage could result. [As to wrongful conception and wrongful pregnancy actions sounding in tort, see §3.10; as to wrongful conception and wrongful pregnancy actions sounding in contract, see §3.22.] The defendant would argue that the plaintiff had suffered no damage, and that the birth of the child through a normal delivery process was a gift rather than an injury from which damages would flow. See, e.g., *Christensen v Thornby*, 192 Mn 123, 255 NW 620 (1934); *Shaheen v Knight*, 6 Lyc 19, 11 Pa D & C2d 41 (1957).

In one of the first wrongful conception cases, *Christensen v Thornby*, 192 Mn 123, 255 NW 620 (1934), the court addressed the issue of allowing damages for the economic costs of raising an unplanned child. The plaintiff had undergone a vasectomy after his wife had experienced great difficulty in giving birth to her first child. When his wife subsequently became pregnant and delivered her second child, the plaintiff brought suit for his anxiety and expenses incident to the birth, claiming that the physician who had performed the vasectomy had deceived him into believing that the operation had been successful. The trial court sustained a demurrer to the complaint, and, on appeal, the appellate court affirmed on the ground that the plaintiff had failed to allege that the false representation was made with fraudulent intent sufficient to support his allegation of deceit. Nevertheless, the following dicta from the *Christensen* opinion was later relied on by other courts as authority for precluding parents from recovering damages for the economic costs of an unplanned child:

> . . . [T]he plaintiff has been blessed with the fatherhood of another child. The expenses alleged are incident to the bearing of a child, and their avoidance is remote from the avowed purpose of the operation. As well might the plaintiff charge the defendant with the cost of nurture and education of the child during its minority. 192 Mn 126, 255 NW 622 (1934).

In the years following the *Christensen* case, courts and commentators developed several theories to support the view that, as a matter of public policy, parents should not be permitted to recover damages for the birth of a healthy child, even though the infant may have been unplanned or unwanted at the time of conception. Perhaps the most fundamental argument was that the allowance of damages would be antithetical to the historically conceived purpose of marriage. In *Shaheen v Knight*, 6 Lyc 19, 11 Pa D & C2d 41 (1957), the court ruled that a physician who violated a promise to perform an effective, elective sterilization operation was not liable for the consequences of such a breach of contract. The plaintiff, the father of four children, wanted no more. As a result of an ineffective sterilization, however, the plaintiff remained fertile and was able to impregnate his wife, who delivered a healthy baby. After finding the defendant in breach of the contract, the court said that the plaintiff had suffered no compensable damage. The only damages asked were the expenses of rearing and educating the unwanted child. The court, however, was of the opinion that to allow damages for the normal birth of a normal child was foreign to the universal public sentiment of the people. It was also stated that an action for damages should not be countenanced since it would have the effect of reducing the child to an "emotional bastard" when he or she inevitably learned that the birth was attributable to a doctor's negligence and not his or her parents' desires.

Finally, a number of courts took the position that any damage cost to the parents was more than offset by the intangible benefits gained by the birth of a child. In *Ball v Mudge*, 64 Wa2d 247, 391 P2d 201 (1964), for example, the court said that a jury might well have concluded that the plaintiffs suffered no damage in the birth of a normal, healthy child, whom they dearly loved and would not consider placing for adoption, and that the cost incidental to such a birth was far outweighed by the blessing of a cherished child, albeit an unwanted child at the time of conception and birth.

The first case to expressly reject these policy arguments, and to hold that the parents of an unplanned normal child could recover damages proximately caused by a negligently performed sterilization operation, was *Custodio v Bauer*, 251 CaA2d 303, 59 CaR 463 (1967). The court was careful to point out that the awardable damages were not for the new life but rather for the diminution in the family wealth that necessarily resulted in a hardship to the other members of the family.

The *Custodio* decision was followed by another leading case, *Troppi v Scarf*, 31 MiA 240, 187 NW2d 511 (1971), leave den, 385 Mi 753 (1971), which also rebutted public policy objections to allowing damage recovery in these actions. In *Troppi*, the court said a judicial determination of preemptive public policy should express the manifest will of the people. To say that, for reasons of public policy, contraceptive failure that results in the birth of an unplanned child can mean no damage as a matter of law ignores the fact that tens of millions of persons use contraceptives daily to avoid the very result which the defendant would say is *always* a benefit, never a detriment, the court said. Those tens of millions of persons, by their conduct, express the contrary sense of the community, the court reasoned.

Subsequently, other courts have held that damages can be recovered in wrongful conception and wrongful pregnancy cases because legally cognizable damage has been sustained by the parents from the unplanned conception or unexpected continuance of a pregnancy and the resultant birth of an unplanned child. See, e.g., *Hartke v McKelway*, 526 FSupp 97

(D DC 1981); *White v United States*, 510 FSupp 146 (D Ks 1981); *Boone v Mullendore*, 416 So2d 718 (Al 1982); *Wilbur v Kerr*, 628 SW2d 568 (Ar 1982); *Custodio v Bauer*, 251 CaA2d 303, 59 CaR 463 (1967); *Anonymous v Hospital*, 35 Cn Super 112, 398 A2d 312 (1979); *Coleman v Garrison*, 327 A2d 757 (De 1974), affd, 349 A2d 8 (De 1975); *Public Health Trust v Brown*, 388 So2d 1084 (Fl 1980); *Pierce v De Gracia*, 103 IlA3d 511, 59 Il Dec 267, 431 NE2d 768 (1982); *Cockrum v Baumgartner*, 99 IlA3d 271, 425 NE2d 968 (1981); *Wilczynski v Goodman*, 73 IlA3d 51, 391 NE2d 479 (1979); *Maggard v McKelvey*, 627 SW2d 44 (Ky 1981); *Troppi v Scarf*, 31 MiA 240, 187 NW2d 511 (1971), leave den, 385 Mi 753 (1971); *Clapham v Yanga*, 102 MiA 47, 300 NW2d 727 (1980); *Green v Sudakin*, 81 MiA 545, 265 NW2d 411 (1978); *Sherlock v Stillwater Clinic*, 260 NW2d 169 (Mn 1977); *Kingsbury v Smith*, 442 A2d 1003 (NH 1982); *P v Portadin*, 179 NJ Super 465, 432 A2d 556 (1981); *Sorkin v Lee*, 78 AD2d 180, 434 NYS2d 300 (1980); *Bowman v Davis*, 48 OhSt2d 41, 356 NE2d 496 (1976); *Speck v Finegold*, 439 A2d 110 (Pa 1981); *Garwood v Locke*, 552 SW2d 892 (Tx 1977); *Beardsley v Wierdsma*, 650 P2d 288 (Wy 1982). [As to the definition of wrongful conception and wrongful pregnancy actions, see §3.8; as to elements of damages generally, see §3.28.] *See generally*, Bryan, DAMAGES — THE NOT SO "BLESSED EVENT," 46 North Carolina LR 949 (1968).

b. [§3.28] Elements, Generally

Where an unplanned child is conceived, or a pregnancy is unsuccessfully aborted, with the result that a child is born because of some breach on the part of the defendant, liability can follow. See, e.g., *Speck v Finegold*, 439 A2d 110 (Pa 1981). [As to the definition of wrongful conception and wrongful pregnancy actions, see §3.8.] If liability is proven, damages may be awarded. [As to the background and policy considerations of damage awards in wrongful conception and wrongful pregnancy actions, see §3.27.]

The specific elements of recoverable damages are not always the same and will be defined by the jurisdiction in which the action is brought. However, elements that have been sought and awarded include the injury and losses suffered by the parents [see, e.g., *Hartke v McKelway*, 526 FSupp 97 (D DC 1981); *White v United States*, 510 FSupp 146 (D Ks 1981); *Boone v Mullendore*, 416 So2d 718 (Al 1982); *Wilbur v Kerr*, 628 SW2d 568 (Ar 1982); *Custodio v Bauer*, 251 CaA2d 303, 59 CaR 463 (1967); *Anonymous v Hospital*, 35 Cn Super 112, 398 A2d 312 (1979); *Public Health Trust v Brown*, 388 So2d 1084 (Fl 1980); *Wilczynski v Goodman*, 73 IlA3d 51, 391 NE2d 479 (1979); *Maggard v McKelway*, 627 SW2d 44 (Ky 1981); *Troppi v Scarf*, 31 MiA 240, 187 NW2d 511 (1971), leave den, 385 Mi 753 (1971); *Sherlock v Stillwater Clinic*, 260 NW2d 169 (Mn 1977); *Kingsbury v Smith*, 442 A2d 1003 (NH 1982); *P v Portadin*, 179 NJ Super 465, 432 A2d 556

(1981); *Sorkin v Lee*, 78 AD2d 180, 434 NYS2d 300 (1980); *Speck v Finegold*, 439 A2d 110 (Pa 1981); *Beardsley v Wierdsma*, 650 P2d 288 (Wy 1982)], and losses based on child rearing costs [see, e.g., *Anonymous v Hospital*, (1976-11), 33 Cn Super 126, 306 A2d 204 (1976); *Pierce v De Gracia*, 103 IlA3d 511, 59 Il Dec 267, 431 NE2d 768 (1982); *Cockrum v Baumgartner*, 99 IlA3d 271, 425 NE2d 968 (1981); *Clapham v Yanga*, 102 MiA 47, 300 NW2d 727 (1980); *Troppi v Scarf*, 31 MiA 240, 187 NW2d 511, leave den, 385 Mi 753 (1971); *Sherlock v Stillwater Clinic*, 260 NW2d 169 (Mn 1977); *Bowman v Davis*, 48 OhSt2d 41, 356 NE2d 496 (1976)].

Parental losses or injuries are those directly incurred by either the father or mother of the unplanned child. Examples of recoverable elements of damages flowing from their injuries or losses include recovery for emotional distress [see, e.g., *Hartke v McKelway*, 526 FSupp 97 (D DC 1981); *Custodio v Bauer*, 251 CaA2d 303, 59 CaR 463 (1967)], pain and suffering [see, e.g., *Public Health Trust v Brown*, 388 So2d 1084 (Fl 1980); *Kingsbury v Smith*, 442 A2d 1003 (NH 1982)], lost wages [see, e.g., *Maggard v McKelvey*, 627 SW2d 44 (Ky 1981); *P v Portadin*, 179 NJ Super 467, 432 A2d 556 (1981)], loss of consortium [see, e.g., *Boone v Mullendore*, 416 So2d 718 (Al 1982); *Bowman v Davis*, 48 OhSt2d 41, 356 NE2d 496 (1976)], and general medical expenses [see, e.g., *Wilbur v Kerr*, 628 SW2d 568 (Ar 1982); *Bushman v Burns Clinic Medical Center*, 83 MiA 453, 268 NW2d 683 (1978)].

By contrast, child rearing costs are sought by the parents to recompense them and the family for the costs of raising the unplanned child. The primary issues bearing on recovery for this element of damages are whether this element should even be recognized [see, e.g., *Maggard v McKelway*, 627 SW2d 44 (Ky 1981) (yes); *Rieck v Medical Protective Co of Fort Wayne, Indiana*, 64 Wi2d 514, 219 NW2d 242 (1974) (no)], and, if so, whether full recovery should be granted [see *Cockrum v Baumgartner*, 99 IlA3d 271, 425 NE2d 968 (1971)], or whether the "benefit rule" should be applied to reduce the award [see *Sherlock v Stillwater Clinic*, 260 NW2d 169 (Mn 1977)]. [For a more detailed discussion of parental losses and child rearing losses associated with the birth of an unplanned child, see §3.31, and §3.40, respectively.]

In addition, losses suffered by the siblings of the unplanned child have been sought, but there is general agreement that these losses are not cognizable. See, e.g., *Aronoff v Snider*, 292 So2d 418 (Fl 1974); *Cox v Stretton*, 77 Misc 2d 155, 352 NYS2d 834 (1974). [For a more detailed discussion of losses claimed by siblings of an unplanned child, see §3.48.]

c. [§3.29] Mitigation

One of the damage related issues [as to damages generally, see §3.27] in wrongful conception and wrongful pregnancy cases [as to the definition of wrongful conception and wrongful pregnancy, see §3.8] centers on whether the plaintiff has a duty to *mitigate* damages. The courts that have addressed the issue have agreed that there is no such duty to mitigate damages in this context.

It has been suggested that parents who seek to recover the costs of raising and educating an unplanned child should be required to mitigate damages through abortion or adoption. The theory is that if the child is born the parents should either pay for the child's upbringing themselves or put the child out for adoption, thereby reducing the financial burden on the defendant for the child's maintenance. However, the doctrine which requires a plaintiff to take measures to minimize the financial consequences of a defendant's negligence generally requires only that *reasonable* measures be taken under the circumstances to avoid or minimize the damages. See *Smith v Jones*, 382 Mi 176, 169 NW2d 308 (1969). And these alternatives are uniquely personal choices which cannot be forced upon parents as a means of mitigating damages in cases involving unplanned children. See *Cockrum v Baumgartner*, 99 IlA3d 271, 425 NE2d 968 (1981). If the negligence of a tortfeasor results in conception of a child by a woman whose emotional makeup is inconsistent with aborting or placing the child for adoption, then under the principle that the tortfeasor takes the injured party as the tortfeasor finds her, the tortfeasor cannot complain that the damages that will be assessed are greater than those that would have resulted had the tortfeasor negligently caused the conception of a child by a woman who was willing to abort or place the child for adoption. See *Troppi v Scarf*, 31 MiA 240, 187 NW2d 511, leave den, 385 Mi 753 (1971).

This doctrine has been applied in the context of wrongful conception and wrongful pregnancy cases. See, e.g., *Morris v Frudenfeld*, 185 CaR 76 (1982); *Cockrum v Baumgartner*, 99 IlA3d 271, 425 NE2d 968 (1981); *Clapham v Yanga*, 102 MiA 47, 300 NW2d 727 (1980); *Troppi v Scarf*, 31 MiA 240, 187 NW2d 511, leave den, 385 Mi 753 (1971); *Sherlock v Stillwater Clinic*, 260 NW 169 (Mn 1977); *Rivera v State*, 94 Misc 2d 157, 404 NYS2d 950 (1978). In determining reasonableness, the best interests of the child must be considered. While the reasonableness of a plaintiff's efforts to mitigate is ordinarily to be decided by the trier of fact, one court has held that, as a matter of law, no mother, either wed or unwed, can reasonably be *required* to abort or place her child for adoption. See *Troppi v Scarf*, 31 MiA 240, 187 NW2d 511, leave den, 385 Mi 753 (1971). Another court noted that causation and mitigation are usually fact issues, but that if the jury is to consider in all cases whether the mother could have and should have terminated her pregnancy it might subject the parties to a decision on damages determined by hindsight and greatly influenced by the individual ethical and religious bias of the jurors. Because such situations require difficult decisions which must be resolved by weighing a variety of personal, medical, and social considerations, a defendant's exposure to damages should not depend upon them. See *Sorkin v Lee*, 78 AD2d 180, 434 NYS2d 300 (1980), app dis, 53 NY2d 797 (1981). The decision not to conceive a child is totally distinguishable from the decision to abort or place for adoption a child who is already conceived, and it is not reasonable for a defendant to require the parents of an unplanned child to consider adoption or abortion. See *Cockrum v Baumgartner*, 99 IlA3d 271, 425 NE2d 968 (1981). In addition, unless a decision is between alternatives which ordinary persons would recognize as reasonable, a party is not required to mitigate damages by choosing the course which would be the most efficient means of minimizing damages. See, e.g., *Clapham v Yanga*, 102 MiA 47, 300 NW2d 727 (1980).

Moreover, it has been held that a living child almost universally gives rise to emotional, spiritual bonds which few parents can bring themselves to break. Once a child is born, he or she should be treated with love regardless of whether he or she was wanted when conceived. See *Troppi v Scarf*, 31 MiA 240, 187 NW2d 511, leave den, 385 Mi 753 (1971). There is also authority for the proposition that the right to have an abortion may not automatically be converted into an *obligation* to have one. See *Ziemba v Sternberg*, 45 AD2d 230, 357 NYS2d 265 (1974). The decision to have an abortion or not is for the individual to make, based on whatever religious, philosophical, or moral principles the individual may adhere to, or upon consideration of the medical risks involved. Just as the law may not impose the philosophy of one group upon the public at large, neither may it permit the public to invade the province of the individual in an area as private as sovereignty over one's body. See *Rivera v State*, 94 Misc 2d 157, 404 NYS2d 950 (1978).

d. [§3.30] —Illustrative Cases

The following cases are illustrative of the general principles relating to the issue of mitigation in wrongful conception and wrongful pregnancy cases [generally, see §3.29], and the application of those general principles by courts in specific circumstances. In these cases, courts discuss whether mitigation of damages is reasonable in the context of the birth of an unplanned child and conclude that mitigation is not reasonable:

In *Cockrum v Baumgartner*, 99 IlA3d 271, 425 NE2d 968 (1981), the court said the decision not to conceive a child is totally distinguishable from the decision to abort or place for adoption a child who is already conceived. It is not reasonable for a defendant to require the parents of an unplanned child to consider adoption or abortion. These alternatives are uniquely personal choices which cannot be forced upon parents as a means of mitigating damages.

In *Clapham v Yanga*, 102 MiA 47, 300 NW2d 727 (1980), the court affirmed a judgment for the plaintiff in a suit brought by a minor and her parents against a defendant-physician alleging damages for medical malpractice in the diagnosis and treatment of the minor, whose pregnancy was incorrectly diagnosed as obesity and low blood pressure. Subsequently, an unplanned child was born to the plaintiff-minor. The minor, who was unmarried, cared for her child for a period of 16 months. Thereafter, the minor's parents cared for the child. A portion of the jury verdict in favor of the plaintiffs was allocated to the minor and her expenses in raising her son. Another portion was allocated to the minor's parents for their costs in raising the child. The court held that the minor's parents did not lose their right to receive damages because they voluntarily assumed legal guardianship of their daughter's offspring. Although this burden was voluntarily assumed in a strict legal sense, the court reasoned, it was dubious to argue that the parents had voluntarily assumed the responsibility. Once their 15 year-old daughter proved herself incapable of caring for the infant, the parents had the choice of: (1) acquiescing in the minor's decision to have the infant adopted, an alternative which undoubtedly would have been emotionally and morally wrong for them and most grandparents similarly situated; or (2) caring for the baby themselves. The plaintiffs were not faced with a choice that most ordinary, similarly situated individuals would consider reasonable the court said. The plaintiffs could have chosen not to care for their grandchild and witness the continuing disintegration of their family, or assume guardianship. For most, this would represent no real choice, the court concluded.

In *Troppi v Scarf*, 31 MiA 240, 187 NW2d 511, leave den, 385 Mi 753 (1971), the court said a living child almost universally gives rise to emotional and spiritual bonds which few parents can bring themselves to break. Once a child is born it obviously should be treated with love regardless of whether it was wanted when it was conceived. The court opined that many, perhaps most, persons living today are conceptional accidents in the sense that their parents did not desire that a child result from the particular act of intercourse in which the person was conceived. Nevertheless, when the child is born, most parents accept it with love. The court also noted that, for purposes of mitigation, the standards by which reasonable conduct is determined are less stringent when used to evaluate the subsequent acts of the injured party than when used to evaluate the tortious act itself. In determining reasonableness, the best interest of the child must be considered. The law has long recognized the desirability of permitting a child to be reared by its natural parents. As a matter of personal conscience and choice, parents may wish to keep an initially unwanted child. Further, even though the parents of an unwanted child may not want to rear the child, they may conclude that the psychological impact on them of rejecting the child and placing the child for adoption, never to see the child again, would be such that it is better to rear the child themselves. If the negligence of a tortfeasor results in conception of a child by a woman whose emotional and mental makeup is inconsistent with aborting or placing the child for adoption, then, under the principle that the tortfeasor takes the injured party as he finds him or her, the tortfeasor cannot complain that the damages that will be assessed against him or her are greater than those that would be determined if he or she had negligently caused the conception of a child by a woman who was willing to abort or place the child for adoption. While the reasonableness of a plaintiff's efforts to mitigate is ordinarily to be decided by the trier of fact, the court was persuaded to rule, as a matter of law, that no mother, wed or unwed, can reasonably be required to abort or place her child for adoption. The plaintiffs were held entitled to have the jurors instructed that if they found that the negligence of a defendant was a cause in fact of the plaintiffs' injury, they might not, in computing the amount, if any, of the plaintiffs' damages, take into consideration the fact that the plaintiffs might have aborted the child or placed the child for adoption.

In the following cases, the courts discuss the issue of whether a plaintiff has a duty to abort an unwanted pregnancy, and conclude that no such duty exists:

In *Ziemba v Sternberg*, 45 AD2d 230, 357 NYS2d 265 (1974), the plaintiffs brought action against the defendant-physician alleging that the defendant had been negligent in misdiagnosing the plaintiff-wife's pregnancy. When the pregnancy was discovered, it was too late for the plaintiff-wife to safely seek an abortion. The court noted that it could not agree with the conclusion of a dissenting justice that, since a legal abortion was still available to the plaintiff-wife at the time her pregnancy was discovered, her failure to avail herself of that alternative should have barred her claim for damages. The right to have an abortion, the court held, may not automatically be converted to an obligation to have one. The decision whether to undertake that medical procedure must rest on a number of factors, including the stage to which the pregnancy has progressed, the health and condition of the woman at the time, and professional judgment and counsel received.

In *Rivera v State*, 94 Misc 2d 157, 404 NYS2d 950 (1978), the plaintiffs brought action against the defendants alleging negligence in the defendants' unsuccessful performance of a tubal ligation. The defendants maintained that the plaintiff-wife's failure to terminate her unwanted pregnancy by an abortion precluded recovery. The court said that a rule of law which would require the plaintiff to have an abortion would constitute an invasion of privacy of the grossest and most pernicious kind. The decision to have an abortion or not is for the individual to make, based on whatever religious, philosophical, or moral principles the individual may have, or upon consideration of the medical risks involved.

In *Sorkin v Lee*, 78 AD2d 180, 434 NYS2d 300 (1980), appeal dis, 53 NY2d 797 (1981), the plaintiffs brought a damage action against the defendant-physician alleging the negligent performance of a vasectomy, the consequence of which was the birth of an unplanned child. The court noted the dissent's contention that the mother's failure to abort was a matter of defense to be submitted to the jury for their consideration on the question of damages. The court agreed that causation and mitigation are usually fact issues, but held that, if the jury considered in all such cases whether the mother could have and should have terminated her pregnancy, it would subject the parties to a decision on damages determined by hindsight and heavily influenced by the individual ethical and religious bias of the jurors. Because such situations require difficult decisions which must be resolved by weighing a variety of personal, medical, and social considerations, a defendant's exposure to damages should not, in the court's view, depend on them.

2. Parents' Injury or Loss

a. [§3.31] Generally

It is generally recognized in wrongful conception and wrongful pregnancy cases [as to the definition of wrongful conception and wrongful pregnancy, see §3.8] that one of the elements of damages that can be recovered is that associated with the losses suffered by the parents of the unplanned child. [As to elements of damages in general, see §3.28.]

For example, parents may recover for the emotional distress associated with the conception and birth of the unplanned child. It has been judicially noticed that a period of pregnancy followed by the birth of a child can cause the mother some mental worry and anxiety. See, e.g., *Bishop v Byrne*, 265 FSupp 460 (SD WV 1967). [See generally, §3.32.] Recovery has also been granted for the pain and suffering of the parents' associated with the birth. The time period involved is typically pregnancy through delivery. See *P v Portadin*, 179 NJ Super 465, 432 A2d 556 (1981). [See generally, §3.34.] A mother's loss of wages during the pregnancy and delivery periods has been sought and recovered. See *Kingsbury v Smith*, 442 A2d 1003 (NH 1982). [See generally, §3.36.] A husband's loss of his wife's consortium during the pregnancy and delivery of the unplanned child is an injury for which recovery will lie. See *Boone v Mullendore*, 416 So2d 718 (Al 1982). [See generally, §3.37.] And the medical expenses associated with the failed sterilization [see, e.g., *Bushman v Burns Clinic Medical Center*, 83 MiA 453, 268 NW2d 683 (1978)] and the pregnancy and birth related costs [see, e.g., *Wilczynski v Goodman*, 73 IlA3d 51, 391 NE2d 479 (1979)], are recoverable as an element of damages. [See generally, §3.39.]

These losses are related directly to the parents and are to be distinguished from the losses related to the expense of raising the child. [As to the child raising expenses generally, see §3.40.]

b. [§3.32] Emotional Distress

Recovery for the emotional distress associated with the conception, pregnancy and birth of an unplanned child [as to the definition of wrongful conception and wrongful pregnancy, see §3.8] is one element of damages [as to other elements of damages related directly to the parents, see §3.31] that has been sought by the plaintiffs in wrongful conception and wrongful pregnancy cases. See, e.g., *Hartke v McKelway*, 526 FSupp 97 (D DC 1981); *White v United States*, 510 FSupp 146 (D Ks 1981); *Boone v Mullendore*, 416 So2d 718 (Al 1982); *Anonymous v Hospital*, 35 Cn Super 112, 398 A2d 312 (1971); *Green v Sudakin*, 81 MiA 545, 265 NW2d 411 (1978); *M & Wife v Schmid Laboratories, Inc*, 178 NJ Super 122, 428 A2d 515 (1981); *Sala v Tomlinson*, 73 AD2d 724, 422 NYS2d 506 (1979). [As to elements of damages in wrongful conception and wrongful pregnancy cases in general, see §3.27.] Plaintiffs have alleged that but for the breach or negligence of the defendant the plaintiffs would not have been made to experience the emotional distress associated with the birth of a child. One court took judicial notice that a period of pregnancy followed by the birth of an unplanned child would cause the mother some mental worry and anxiety. See *Bishop v Byrne*, 265 FSupp 460 (SD WV 1967).

This element has been sought by the plaintiff-father for his emotional suffering resulting from observing his wife's pregnancy. See *White v United States*, 510 FSupp 146 (D Ks 1981). Damages for emotional distress have also been sought by the plaintiff-mother for her reaction to pregnancy [see, e.g., *Hartke v McKelway*, 526 FSupp 97 (D DC 1981); *Custodio v Bauer*, 251 CaA2d 303, 59 CaR 463 (1967); *Sala v Tomlinson*, 73 AD2d 724, 422 NYS2d 506 (1979)], and, in the case of an unmarried woman, the woman's embarrassment of being pregnant. See *Morris v Frudenfeld*, 185 CaR 76 (1982). Additionally, it has been held that both parents could recover damages for emotional distress in an action involving the unplanned birth of a defective and diseased child. See *Speck v Finegold*, 439 A2d 110 (Pa 1981).

In actions sounding in tort it has been noted that the alleged injury to the parent must be foreseeable for mental distress damages to be recoverable. See *Speck v Finegold*, 439 A2d 110 (Pa 1981). Moreover, another consideration is whether the plaintiff was put in peril or fear of personal injury, or was physically injured or suffered pecuniary loss. In *White v United States*, 510 FSupp 146 (D Ks 1981), the court said that if mental pain and suffering are not accompanied by physical injury or pecuniary loss, recovery is allowed only if the conduct complained of is malicious, willful, or wanton. And in *Anonymous v Hospital*, 35 Cn Super 112, 398 A2d 312 (1979), the court said a plaintiff cannot generally recover damages for emotional distress caused by witnessing an injury to another, even if the injured party is related to the plaintiff, since the plaintiff was not put in peril or fear of personal injury. Emotional distress is a proper element of damages only when it results from the breach of a duty to the particular plaintiff.

Actions for damages arising from wrongful conception or wrongful pregnancy may be founded in contract. Damages for mental anguish, however, are generally not permitted in breach of contract actions. An exception to this rule has been created where the contract at issue is concerned not with trade and commerce but with life and death, not with profit but with elements of personality, not with pecuniary aggrandizement but with matters of mental concern and solicitude. For example, in *Green v Sudakin*, 81 MiA 545, 265 NW2d 411 (1978), the court said that a breach of duty with respect to such contracts will inevitably and necessarily result in mental anguish and pain, and in such cases the parties may reasonably be said to have contracted with reference to the payment of damages therefor in the event of breach.

However, not all courts have allowed the plaintiff to pursue this element of damages. In *Speck v Finegold*, 268 Pa Super 342, 408 A2d 496 (1979), the court denied damages based on the emotional disturbance and mental stress claimed by the plaintiff-parents due to the birth of a diseased, unplanned child. The court said that unlike the measurability of pecuniary loss to which the plaintiffs were entitled, there is no legal realm of accountability to which the plaintiffs can look for claimed mental and emotional damages arising out of the birth of their child which could factually place them in a more favorable category than parents who generally, in the vicissitudes and vagaries of life, face the everyday potential of pain and suffering in the raising of their children. In the court's view, it was not possible to distinguish the mental and emotional travail which the plaintiffs claimed from the pain and suffering of parents who raise a retarded child or whose infant is born blind or mongoloid or falls victim to one of the countless natural diseases or being healthy becomes permanently injured, disfigured, or handicapped by reason of an accident. The fact that the plaintiffs did not want the infant did not alter the sameness in the quality and nature of pain and suffering experienced by all parents in the everyday work of parenthood. The court held, therefore, that to allow the plaintiffs damages for mental and emotional stress would be to give them a societal advantage not conceivable in other cases of parenthood. [The Pennsylvania Supreme Court at 439 A2d 110 (Pa 1981), reversed the decision in the *Speck* case, cited above, on the issue of recoverability of damages for emotional injury, and in doing so also effectively reversed earlier decisions by the Pennsylvania Superior Court in *Stirbing v de Quevedo*, 288 Pa Super 436, 432 A2d 239 (1980), and *Mason v Western Pennsylvania Hosp*, 286 Pa Super 354, 428 A2d 1366 (1981).]

c. [§3.33] —Illustrative Cases

The following cases are illustrative of the general principles relating to recovery for the parents' emotional distress arising from the birth of an unplanned child. [Generally, see §3.32.] In these cases recovery was permitted:

In *Hartke v McKelway*, 526 FSupp 97 (D DC 1981), the court affirmed the plaintiff's right to collect damages for mental pain, anguish and suffering, following the birth of an unplanned child. The plaintiff had undergone a sterilization operation because she desired to prevent future pregnancies. The jury found in favor of the plaintiff and awarded damages of $100,000 for mental anguish, as well as pain and suffering. The appellate court characterized the $100,000 figure as high, but concluded that it was not so excessive as to require that it be set aside, particularly in view of the plaintiff's testimony concerning her fear of pregnancy. The plaintiff had feared becoming pregnant due to previous problems she had experienced, including an ectopic pregnancy.

In *Custodio v Bauer*, 251 CaA2d 303, 59 CaR 463 (1967), the plaintiff-parents brought an action against the defendant-physicians alleging that the defendants had negligently performed a sterilization operation on plaintiff-wife, and subsequently an unplanned child had been born to the plaintiffs. The court said that if the plaintiffs could show physical complications and mental, physical, and nervous pain and suffering, which the operation was designed to prevent, they should be able to recover. However, the court noted that if the failure of the sterilization operation and the ensuing pregnancy benefited the wife's emotional and nervous makeup, the defendant should be able to offset any damages assessed against them.

In *Green v Sudakin*, 81 MiA 454, 265 NW2d 411 (1978), the plaintiff-parents of an unplanned child brought an action seeking damages from the defendant-physicians for alleged medical malpractice and breach of contract. The defendants performed a tubal ligation on the plaintiff-wife, but subsequently an unplanned child was born to the plaintiffs. In fact, what had happened was that the defendants had failed to perform the agreed upon tubal ligation. The jury determined that the defendants had failed to notify the plaintiffs of this fact, and entered a verdict of $95,000 in favor of the plaintiffs. The defendants contended, in part, on appeal that the trial court had erred in instructing the jury that their verdict could include an award for mental pain and suffering. The court noted that damages for mental anguish are generally not permitted in breach of contract actions. However, an exception to this rule has been created by the courts in cases where the contract at issue is concerned not with trading commerce but with life and death, not with profit but with elements of personality, not with pecuniary aggrandizement but with matters of mental concern and solicitude. Then a breach of duty with respect to such contracts will inevitably and necessarily result in mental anguish, pain and suffering. In such cases the parties may reasonably be said to have contracted with reference to the payment of damages therefor in event of breach. Far from being outside the contemplation of the parties they are an integral and inseparable part of it. The agreement in the instant case is intensely personal in nature. The failure to perform such a contract could foreseeably cause great mental pain and suffering. Therefore, the court found that a damage award for mental anguish is appropriate under the circumstances of this case.

In *M & Wife v Schmid Laboratories*, 178 NJ Super 122, 428 A2d 515 (1981), the court held that in a case involving the alleged failure of a birth control device (condom) that resulted in the birth of two unanticipated children the recoverable damages would be limited to compensation for the mental and emotional anguish resulting from the birth of the children.

In *Speck v Finegold*, 439 A2d 110 (Pa 1981), the plaintiff-parents brought negligence and breach of contract actions against two defendant-physicians for the unsuccessful performances of a vasectomy and an abortion. Subsequently, an unhealthy child was born to the plaintiffs. Since the court believed that the plaintiff-parents had suffered a substantial wrong, it said an action should be permitted in which the usual common-law principles of damages should be applied. Further, since the alleged injury including the mental distress associated with having to be the parent of a defective, diseased child was foreseeable, mental distress damages should be recoverable also.

In the following cases, which are illustrative of the general principles relating to recovery for the parents' emotional suffering associated with the birth of an unplanned child, recovery was denied based on policy considerations or a question of proof.

In *White v United States*, 510 FSupp 146 (DC Ks 1981), the plaintiff-parents brought an action for medical malpractice against the defendant alleging the negligent performance of a sterilization operation on the plaintiff-mother by employees of the defendant. Subsequently, an unplanned child was born to the plaintiffs. The plaintiff-father sought damages for emotional and mental suffering as a result of his wife's pregnancy. The court, applying Georgia law, said that if mental pain and suffering are not accompanied by physical injury or pecuniary loss, recovery is allowed only if the conduct complained of is malicious, willful or wanton. Therefore, the court concluded the plaintiff-husband would recover for his mental and emotional suffering if he proved that the conduct of the defendant was malicious, willful or wanton.

In *Anonymous v Hosp*, 35 Cn Super 112, 398 A2d 312 (1979), the plaintiff-parents of an unplanned child brought a medical malpractice action against the defendant-hospital and a defendant-physician. They alleged that the defendant-physician performed a sterilization operation on the plaintiff-wife in a negligent manner, and subsequently she became pregnant and gave birth to a child. One of the plaintiffs' allegations was that as a result of the carelessness and negligence of the defendants, the plaintiff-husband suffered severe emotional stress and depression, during and after the pregnancy, eventually resulting in a serious psychiatric illness that necessitated his hospitalization, and that he suffered and would continue to suffer in the future from severe emotional stress and depression. The court concluded that no cause of action existed in favor of the plaintiff-husband for his severe emotional stress and depression. Generally a plaintiff cannot recover damages for emotional distress, caused by witnessing an injury to another, even if the injured person is related to the plaintiff, since the plaintiff was not put in peril or fear of personal injury to himself. Emotional distress is a proper element of damages only when it results from the breach of a duty to the particular plaintiff. The plaintiffs' substitute complaint did not contain any allegation that the plaintiff-husband was a witness to any portion of the surgery performed by the defendant-physician upon his wife. The surgical procedure in this case was personal to the wife. The alleged negligence of the defendants was a breach of the duty owed solely and exclusively to her, and not to her husband. Accordingly, the plaintiff-husband was not entitled to recover damages for his claimed emotional stress and depression.

In *Sala v Tomlinson*, 73 AD2d 724, 422 NYS2d 506 (1979), a cause of action for damages for emotional distress and anxiety occasioned by the birth of an unplanned child subsequent to an unsuccessful sterilization operation was not recognized by the court. The court noted that a cause of action for damages for emotional distress and anxiety occasioned by the birth of a child subsequent to an unsuccessful sterilization is not recognized in New York. Such damages are uncertain, contingent, speculative and virtually impossible to measure as against the intangible and complex human benefits of motherhood and fatherhood.

d. [§3.34] Pain and Suffering

Damages for the physical pain and suffering experienced by the mother of an unplanned child [as to actions based on wrongful conception and wrongful pregnancy in general, see §§3.8, 3.9] are recoverable by the parents [as to other recoverable elements of damages associated with injury or loss to the parents, see generally §3.31] if proven. See, e.g., *Hartke v McKelway*, 526 FSupp 97 (D DC 1981); *Boone v Mullendore*, 416 So2d 718 (Al 1982); *Custodio v Bauer*, 251 CaA2d 303, 59 CaR 463 (1967); *Ochs v Borrelli*, 187 Cn 253, 445 A2d 883 (1982); *Public Health Trust v Brown*, 388 So2d 1084 (Fl 1980); *Maggard v McKelvey*, 627 SW2d 44 (Ky 1981); *Troppi v Scarf*, 31 MiA 240, 187 NW2d 511 (1971), leave den 385 Mi 753 (1971); *Sherlock v Stillwater Clinic*, 260 NW2d 169 (Mn 1977); *Kingsbury v Smith*, 442 A2d 1003 (NH 1982); *Sorkin v Lee*, 78 AD2d 180, 434 NYS2d 300 (1980); *Beardsley v Wierdsma*, 650 P2d 288 (Wy 1982). [As to elements of damages in wrongful conception and wrongful pregnancy in general, see §3.28.]

Damages for the mother's pain and suffering are allowed so as to place the injured plaintiff in the position she would have been in had no wrong occurred. See *Sherlock v Stillwater Clinic*, 260 NW2d 169 (Mn 1977). The time period in determining the amount of pain and suffering associated with the birth of the child is typically the period from pregnancy through delivery. See *P v Portadin*, 179 NJ Super 465, 432 A2d 556 (1981). A jury verdict that included damages for a mother relating to the childbirth process has been upheld, [see *Public Health Trust v Brown*, 388 So2d 1084 (Fl 1980)] and it has been noted that pregnancy and its attendant pain and suffering are inextricably related to child bearing. See *Troppi v Scarf*, 31 MiA 240, 187 NW2d 511 (1971), leave den, 385 Mi 753 (1971). Moreover, one court has taken judicial notice that a period of pregnancy followed by birth of an unplanned child would cause the mother some physical injury and some physical pain and suffering. See *Bishop v Byrne*, 265 FSupp 460 (SD WV 1967).

Plaintiffs have based claims of pain and suffering on a mother's fear for her life [see *Bishop v Byrne*, 265 FSupp 460 (SD WV 1967)], the discomfort associated with pregnancy [see, e.g., *Coleman v Garrison*, 327 A2d 757 (De 1974) affd 349 A2d 8 (De 1975); *Bushman v Burns Clinic Medical Center*, 83 MiA 453, 268 NW2d 683 (1978)], the mother's fear of pregnancy [see *Hartke v McKelway*, 526 FSupp 97 (D DC 1981)], the mother's fear the baby would be deformed [see *Ochs v Borrelli*, 187 Cn 253, 445 A2d 883 (1982)], and the mother's discomfort associated with a second sterilization operation and a painful x-ray procedure to verify the success of the second sterilization [see *Ochs v Borrelli*, 187 Cn 253, 445 A2d 883 (1982)].

e. [§3.35] —Illustrative Cases

The following cases are illustrative of the general principles relating to recovery for damages relating to pain and suffering associated with pregnancy and birth of an unplanned child [generally, see §3.34]:

In *Hartke v McKelway*, 526 FSupp 97 (D DC 1981), the trial jury awarded the plaintiff $100,000 for pain, suffering, and mental anguish associated with an unplanned pregnancy and a subsequent unplanned birth. The plaintiff-mother had sought damages from the defendant-physician under the theories of the negligent performance of the sterilization operation, failure to obtain the plaintiff's informed consent to the procedure performed, and breach of warranty. While the damage figure was high, the court concluded that it was not so excessive as to require the court to set it aside, in view of the plaintiff's testimony concerning her fear of pregnancy and the obvious effects which her experiences had on her, which were corroborated by several of the plaintiff's witnesses. The defendant himself, the court noted, admitted that the plaintiff was very frightened about the possibility of pregnancy when she came to him for advice on how best to avoid it. Therefore, the court would not disturb the jury's verdict on this issue.

In *Bishop v Byrne*, 265 FSupp 460 (SD WV 1967), the court was faced with a diversity action in which the amount expended by the plaintiffs for the birth of an unplanned child was only $684. The defendant took the position that that amount in controversy was less than the required amount to sustain federal jurisdiction. Under this pretext the court examined the wife's claim. The court noted that the complaint alleged that she lived in fear of her life and health because of the negligent performance of a sterilization operation by the defendant-physician. The complaint did not affirmatively allege any physical injury to, or pain and suffering by, her. But, the court said, such injuries could fairly be inferred, and the court took judicial notice of that which it characterized as common knowledge, that a period of pregnancy followed by the birth of a child under such circumstances would cause the mother some physical injury, some physical pain and suffering, and some mental worry and anxiety. Damages for physical pain and suffering and mental worry and anxiety, being unliquidated and indeterminate in character, are generally for jury determination. To dismiss the controversy as to the wife for failure of her claim to meet the jurisdictional requirement as to amount would necessitate a determination, as a matter of law, on a subject that time and again has been declared to be in the first instance within the jury's province. Requisite jurisdictional amount, therefore, was found to exist as to the wife's claim.

In *Ochs v Borrelli*, 187 Cn 253, 445 A2d 887 (1982), the plaintiff testified to her anxiety throughout her pregnancy that the unplanned baby would be deformed, her inability to eat or sleep, and such physical complications as a ruptured vein. Several months after the child's birth, the plaintiff underwent a second sterilization operation procedure which she testified caused her four weeks of serious discomfort; she then returned for an x-ray to verify the success of the second sterilization operation. In light of the evidence the court said a jury award of $49,985 for pain and suffering, and medical expenses was not clearly excessive.

In *Public Health Trust v Brown*, 388 So2d 1084 (Fl 1980), the court affirmed a jury award of damages for pain and suffering caused by the undesired pregnancy and the process of child birth. The jury had found that physician-employees of Jackson Memorial Hospital had negligently performed a tubal ligation on the plaintiff, with a result that she became pregnant and delivered her sixth child. She was awarded $10,837 for pain and suffering caused by the undesired pregnancy, medical expenses and lost wages.

In *Troppi v Scarf*, 31 MiA 240, 187 NW2d 511 (1971), leave den, 385 Mi 753 (1971), the court reasoned that since pregnancy and its attendant pain, suffering, and other elements of claimed damages are inextricably related to childbearing, it did not think it would be sound to attempt to separate those segments of damage from the economic cost of the unplanned child and applied the same interest rule. Accordingly, the court said the benefits of the unplanned child may be weighed against all the elements of claimed damages. The plaintiff-parents of an unplanned child had brought suit against the defendant-pharmacist for the negligent filling of a prescription.

In *Sherlock v Stillwater Clinic*, 270 NW2d 169 (Mn 1977), the court ruled that the parents of an unplanned child should at least be entitled to recover all damages immediately incident to pregnancy and birth. The allowance of these damages is wholly consistent with the elementary principle of compensatory damages which seeks to place the injured plaintiffs in the position that they would have been in had no wrong occurred. Incidental damages include such items as pain and suffering incurred by the child's mother.

f. [§3.36] Lost Wages or Income

A plaintiff's pregnancy with and birth of an unplanned child [as to wrongful conception and wrongful pregnancy actions in general, see §§3.8, 3.9] necessarily results in some lost wages and earning potential by the plaintiff-mother. Therefore, the loss of wages during an unexpected pregnancy and subsequent delivery has been sought and recovered by the plaintiff-mother as an element of damage in a wrongful conception or wrongful pregnancy action. See, e.g., *Public Health Trust v Brown*, 388 So2d 1084 (Fl 1980); *Maggard v McKelvey*, 627 SW2d 44 (Ky 1981); *Kingsbury v Smith*, 442 A2d 1003 (NH 1982); *P v Portadin*, 179 NJ Super 465, 432 A2d 556 (1981); *Stribling v de Quevedo*, 288 Pa Super 436, 432 A2d 239 (1980); *Beardsley v Wierdsma*, 650 P2d 288 (Wy 1982). [As to damages in general in wrongful conception and wrongful pregnancy actions, see §3.31.] The period during which these lost wages can be recovered is pregnancy and delivery. See *P v Portadin*, 179 NJ Super 465, 432 A2d 556 (1981).

An example of recovery of this element was in *Public Health Trust v Brown*, 388 So2d 1084 (Fl 1980), where the jury found that the physician-employees of the defendant hospital had negligently performed a tubal ligation on the plaintiff with the result that she became pregnant and gave birth to an unplanned child. The plaintiff was awarded $10,837 for damages which included lost wages caused by the undesired pregnancy and the process of childbirth. On appeal the court did not disturb that finding.

g. [§3.37] Loss of Consortium

When a woman unexpectedly becomes pregnant, or remains pregnant after an unsuccessful abortion, and gives birth to an unexpected child [as to wrongful conception and wrongful pregnancy actions in general, see §§3.8, 3.9] her husband as a consequence is denied, at least temporarily, her comfort, companionship, services and consortium. Therefore, as one element of damages in a wrongful conception or wrongful pregnancy action, a husband may recover for his loss of consortium occasioned by the unplanned pregnancy and birth. See, e.g., *Boone v Mullendore*, 416 So2d 718 (Al 1982); *Coleman v Garrison*, 327 A2d 757 (De 1974), affd, 349 A2d 8 (De 1975); *Maggard v McKelvey*, 627 SW2d 44 (Ky 1981); *Bushman v Burns Clinic Medical Center*, 83 MiA 453, 268 NW2d 683 (1978); *Kingsbury v Smith*, 442 A2d 1003 (NH 1982); *P v Portadin*, 179 NJ Super 465, 432 A2d 556 (1981); *Sorkin v Lee*, 78 AD2d 180, 434 NYS2d 300 (1980); *Bowman v Davis*, 48 OhSt2d 41, 356 NE2d 496 (1976). [As to other elements of damage relating to injury or loss suffered by the parents of an unplanned child, see §3.31.]

However, where both husband and wife claim damages for loss of consortium arising from the pregnancy with and birth of an unplanned child the wife's claim may be denied. See *White v United States*, 510 FSupp 146 (D Ks 1981). Damages for loss of consortium may be recovered for the period from pregnancy to immediately after birth of the child. See, e.g., *Boone v Mullendore*, 416 So2d 718 (Al 1982); *Coleman v Garrison*, 327 A2d 757 (De 1974), affd, 349 A2d 8 (De 1975); *Bushman v Burns Clinic Medical Center*, 83 MiA 453, 268 NW2d 683 (1978). [As to elements of damages in general in wrongful conception and wrongful pregnancy cases, see §3.28.]

h. [§3.38] —Illustrative Cases

The following cases are illustrative of the general principles relating to recovery for injuries associated with the loss of consortium, companionship, and services when the plaintiff-mother becomes or remains pregnant with an unplanned child. [Generally, see §3.37.] In these cases the plaintiff-father seeks recovery for loss of consortium:

In *Coleman v Garrison*, 327 A2d 757 (De 1974), affd, 349 A2d 8 (De 1975), the plaintiff-parents brought a malpractice action against the defendants alleging the improper performance of a sterilization operation on the wife, after which she became pregnant and gave birth to a sixth child. The court found that the plaintiffs may be allowed provable damages for the loss to the plaintiff-husband of the comfort, companionship, services and consortium of the plaintiff-wife. However, the loss of consortium is limited to the loss arising from pregnancy and immediately after birth.

In *Bushman v Burns Clinic Medical Center*, 83 MiA 453, 268 NW2d 683 (1978), the plaintiff-parents filed a complaint against the defendants for damages for medical malpractice and breach of warranty arising out of the allegedly unsuccessful performance of a vasectomy on the plaintiff-husband. After the vasectomy, the wife had become pregnant and later gave birth to an unplanned child. The court found that the plaintiff-husband could be awarded damages for the loss of consortium of the plaintiff-wife, but that the loss was limited to that arising from the pregnancy and birth.

In *Sherlock v Stillwater Clinic*, 260 NW2d 169 (Mn 1977), it was held that the parents of an unplanned child should be entitled to recover all damages immediately incident to pregnancy and birth. The allowance of these damages is wholly consistent with the elementary principle of compensatory damages which seeks to place the injured plaintiffs in the position that they would have been in had no wrong occurred. Incidental damages include such items as the loss of consortium to the extent that it can be proved.

In *Kingsbury v Smith*, 442 A2d 1003 (NH 1982), the court held in a wrongful conception case that because the wife's cause of action sounded in negligence, a separate cause of action for the husband's loss of consortium is permitted by statute.

In *Sorkin v Lee*, 78 AD2d 180, 434 NYS2d 300 (1980), it was held that if the plaintiffs could prove that the wife's pregnancy was the result of medical malpractice, established law would permit the plaintiff-husband to recover damages for the loss of his wife's consortium. The plaintiff-parents brought a negligence action against the defendant-physician alleging that the defendant performed a vasectomy on the plaintiff-husband in a careless manner and as a result the wife became pregnant and gave birth to an unplanned child.

In *Bowman v Davis*, 48 OhSt2d 41, 356 NE2d 496 (1976), the plaintiff-parents sued the defendant-physicians for the unplanned birth of a child following the performance of an allegedly unsuccessful tubal ligation on the plaintiff-mother. At trial, the jury awarded the plaintiff-father $12,500 for the loss of consortium and expenses. That verdict was upheld by the court on appeal. The court was not faced with the damages issue directly, but rather was faced with the issue of whether public policy prohibited the recovery of damages for the unplanned birth of a child following a negligent sterilization procedure. The court concluded that public policy did not prohibit recovery under these circumstances.

In the following wrongful conception action recovery for loss of consortium claimed by the plaintiff-wife was denied:

In *White v United States*, 510 FSupp 146 (D Ks 1981), the plaintiff-parents sought recovery for damages resulting from the birth of an unplanned child. The plaintiffs alleged that the child had been born following the negligent performance of a tubal ligation by government employees. Both plaintiffs sought damages for temporary loss of consortium. Applying Georgia law, the court noted that the action by the spouse for consortium is derivative of the action for damages by the injured spouse. If the injured spouse cannot recover, the other spouse is not entitled to recover. The court noted that the husband would be entitled to recover for loss of consortium if his wife recovered on her claim. However, the wife had no action for loss of consortium because her husband had no claim for injuries. Therefore, a motion by the defendant for summary judgment regarding the wife's claim for temporary loss of consortium was granted.

i. [§3.39] Medical Expenses

In instances where an unplanned child is conceived and subsequently given birth to [as to wrongful conception and wrongful pregnancy actions in general, see §§3.8, 3.9] the parents of the child necessarily suffer some medical expenses. [As to elements of damage directly related to parents of unplanned children, see §3.31]. These general medical expenses are recoverable as an element of damages in a wrongful conception or wrongful pregnancy action. See, e.g., *Hartke v McKelway*, 526 FSupp 97 (D DC 1981); *Public Health Trust v Brown*, 388 So2d 1084 (Fl 1980); *Garwood v Locke*, 552 SW2d 892 (Tx 1977). The allowance of this element of damages has been based on the principle of compensatory damages which seeks to place the injured plaintiff in the position the plaintiff would have been in had no wrong occurred. See *Sherlock v Stillwater Clinic*, 260 NW2d 169 (Mn 1977). Examples of these medical expenses include the costs of the unsuccessful sterilization operation in wrongful conception cases [see, e.g., *Wilbur v Kerr*, 628 SW2d 568 (Ar 1982); *Coleman v Garrison*, 327 A2d 757 (De 1974), affd, 349 A2d 8 (De 1975); *Bushman v Burns Clinic Medical Center*, 83 MiA 453, 268 NW2d 683 (1978); *Kingsbury v Smith*, 442 A2d 1003 (NH 1982); *Beardsley v Wierdsma*, 650 P2d 288 (Wy 1982)], the costs and expenses of pregnancy, [see, e.g., *Boone v Mullendore*, 416 So2d 718 (Al 1982); *Wilbur v Kerr*, 628 SW2d 568 (Ar 1982); *Wilczynski v Goodman*, 73 IlA3d 51, 391 NE2d 479 (1979); *Sherlock v Stillwater Clinic*, 260 NW2d 169 (Mn 1977); *Kingsbury v Smith*, 442 A2d 1003 (NH 1982); *P v Portadin*, 179 NJ Super 465, 432 A2d 556 (1981); *Sorkin v Lee*, 78 AD2d 180, 434 NYS2d 303 (1980)], and hospital and other costs associated with the birth [see, e.g., *Wilczynski v Goodman*, 73 IlA3d 51, 391 NE2d 479 (1979); *Maggard v McKelvey*, 627 SW2d 44 (Ky 1981); *Sherlock v Stillwater Clinic*, 260 NW2d 169 (Mn 1977); *Kingsbury v Smith*, 442 A2d 1003 (NH 1982); *P v Portadin*, 179 NJ Super 465, 432 A2d 556 (1981); *Sorkin v Lee*, 78 AD2d 180, 434 NYS2d 303 (1980); *Beardsley v Wierdsma*, 650 P2d 288 (Wy 1982)].

The argument that these expenses should not be compensable because of public policy factors has been rejected. One court has said that the practical effect of prohibiting recovery for this element of damages would be to allow tortious conduct by a medical practitioner to be totally uncompensable. Unwarranted immunity would thereby be extended to the medical profession if damages ensuing from improper treatment were denied. See *Wilczynski v Goodman*, 73 IlA3d 51, 391 NE2d 479 (1979).

An example of a jury award for medical expenses associated with an unplanned birth is found in *Public Health Trust v Brown*, 388 So2d 1084 (Fl 1980). The plaintiff-mother was awarded $10,835 for injuries including medical expenses caused by the undesired pregnancy and the process of childbirth, and on appeal the award was affirmed. The plaintiff-mother had brought an action against the defendants alleging the negligent performance of a tubal ligation, with the result that the woman became pregnant and gave birth to an unplanned child.

3. Child Rearing Expenses

a. [§3.40] Elements, Generally

One of the elements of damages often sought by plaintiff-parents in wrongful conception and wrongful pregnancy cases [as to wrongful conception and wrongful pregnancy cases in general, see §§3.8, 3.9] is that associated with normal child rearing expenses. [As to other elements of damages sought in wrongful conception and wrongful pregnancy cases, see §3.28.] The specific expenses sought have included the economic costs of raising the child to majority [see, e.g., *Boone v Mullendore*, 416 So2d 718 (Al 1982); *Wilbur v Kerr*, 628 SW2d 568 (Ar 1982); *Ochs v Borrelli*, 187 Cn 253, 445 A2d 883 (1982); *Anonymous v Hospital (1976-11)*, 33 Cn Super

126, 366 A2d 204 (1976); *Coleman v Garrison*, 349 A2d 8 (De Supr 1975); *Public Health Trust v Brown*, 388 So2d 1084 (Fl 1980); *Pierce v De Gracia*, 103 IlA3d 511, 59 Il Dec 267, 431 NE2d 768 (1982); *Cockrum v Baumgartner*, 99 IlA3d 271, 425 NE2d 968 (1981); *Wilczynski v Goodman*, 73 IlA3d 51, 391 NE2d 479 (1979); *Maggard v McKelvey*, 627 SW2d 44 (Ky 1981); *Clapham v Yanga*, 102 MiA 47, 300 NW2d 727 (1980); *Troppi v Scarf*, 31 MiA 240, 187 NW2d 511 (1971), leave den, 385 Mi 753 (1971); *Sherlock v Stillwater Clinic*, 260 NW2d 169 (Mn 1977); *P v Portadin*, 179 NJ Super 465, 432 A2d 556 (1981); *M & Wife v Schmid Laboratories, Inc*, 178 NJ Super 122, 428 A2d 515 (1981); *Sorkin v Lee*, 78 AD2d 180, 434 NYS2d 303 (1980); *Rivera v State*, 95 Misc2d 157, 404 NYS2d 950 (1978); *Bowman v Davis*, 48 OhSt2d 41, 356 NE2d 496 (1976); *Mason v Western Pennsylvania Hosp*, 286 Pa Super 354, 428 A2d 1366 (1981); *Stribling v de Quevedo*, 288 Pa Super 436, 432 A2d 239 (1980); *Terrell v Garcia*, 496 SW2d 124 (Tx 1973); *Rieck v Medical Protective Co of Fort Wayne, Indiana*, 64 Wi2d 514, 219 NW2d 242 (1974)], educating the child [see, e.g., *Cockrum v Baumgartner*, 99 IlA3d 271, 425 NE2d 968 (1981); *Sherlock v Stillwater Clinic*, 260 NW2d 169 (Mn 1977); *M & Wife v Schmid Laboratories, Inc*, 178 NJ Super 122, 428 A2d 515 (1981)], and providing institutional care, nursing, and special attention for an unhealthy child [see, e.g., *Bowman v Davis*, 48 OhSt2d 41, 356 NE2d 496 (1976)]. In one case, the court characterized the plaintiff-parents damages request as one to replenish the family exchequer so that the new arrival would not deprive other members of the family of what was planned for them. See, *Custodio v Bauer*, 251 CaA2d 303, 59 CaR 463 (1967).

The granting of this element of damages has not been universal. Some courts have refused to allow this element of damages for policy reasons. See, e.g., *Rieck v Medical Protective Co of Fort Wayne, Indiana*, 64 Wi2d 514, 219 NW2d 242 (1974). [See generally, §3.41.] However, other courts have considered the policy questions and have resolved them in favor of allowing this element of damages. See, e.g., *Ochs v Borrelli*, 187 Cn 253, 445 A2d 883 (1982). [As to these policy reasons, see §3.43.] When the policy considerations have favored recovery, courts have generally followed one of two theories in assessing the amount for recovery. One of the theories is predicated on allowing the plaintiff complete recovery for the child rearing expenses. See, e.g., *Bowman v Davis*, 48 OhSt2d 41, 356 NE2d 496 (1976). [As to full recovery of all child rearing costs, see §3.44.] The second theory has been based on comparing the "benefit" the plaintiff received from the birth of the child against the costs and responsibilities of raising the child, and reducing the recovery by the amount of the benefit. See, e.g., *Troppi v Scarf*, 31 MiA 240, 187 NW2d 511, leave den, 385 Mi 753 (1971). [As to the application of the benefit rule, see §3.46.] See generally WRONGFUL

CONCEPTION: WHO PAYS FOR BRINGING UP BABY?, 47 Fordham LR 418 (1978).

A peripheral issue that has been raised concerns whether, in these cases, grandparents may recover their expenditures in raising an unplanned child. For example, in *Clapham v Yanga*, 102 MiA 47, 300 NW2d 727 (1980), the court affirmed a jury verdict of $133,700 in favor of the plaintiffs. The plaintiffs were the unplanned infant's mother and the infant's grandparents. The plaintiffs brought suit against the defendant-physician alleging damages for medical malpractice in the diagnosis and treatment of the mother, whose pregnancy was diagnosed as obesity and low blood pressure. Subsequently, an unplanned baby was born to the plaintiff-minor. A portion of the judgment was predicated upon the child rearing expenses to be incurred by the plaintiff-mother and the plaintiff-grandparents. One of the issues before the court was whether grandparents of a minor child's baby may obtain damages where they provide for the infant's care. The court held that such damages were proper. The defendant contended that it was error for the trial court to charge the jury that it could award the grandparents damages to compensate them for the impairment of their life style and costs of raising the mother's son since they voluntarily assumed the duties of guardianship. The court stated that the grandparents did not lose their right to receive damages because they voluntarily assumed legal guardianship of their daughter's baby. Although this burden was voluntarily assumed in a strict legal sense, the court said, it took no legal scholarship to see the dubiousness in the claim of voluntariness. The plaintiff-grandparents could have chosen not to care for their grandchild and witnessed the continuing disintegration of their family, or assumed guardianship. For most people, this would constitute no real choice. Moreover, the court said, it was convinced that allowing the grandparents to receive damages where they had assumed the responsibility of their minor daughter's child fostered important state policy. Michigan law provided that custody decisions are to be made to promote the best interest of the child. Although there was no custody battle in this case, guardianship with the grandparents was a clearly superior placement alternative to adoption. The psychological impact on the child of removing him from his grandparents and mother, who, however immature and unable to cope with parenthood, were a familiar source of comfort and care, and placing him in alien surroundings, could be devastating to the young infant's psyche. To absolutely deprive grandparents of damages in circumstances such as these would weaken the primary state goal in child custody. Grandparents who would prefer to care for a minor daughter's baby, rather than have the child adopted, might be economically forced to allow the latter to occur. Therefore, the court held that the grandparents of a minor child's baby may obtain damages, including those for the cost of rearing the child, as the grandparents provide for the infant's care, just as the baby's parents might have.

b. [§3.41] Policy and Other Considerations Against Award

Recovery of child rearing costs [as to the elements of child rearing costs, see §3.40] as an element of damages [as to elements of damages in general, see §3.28] in wrongful conception and wrongful pregnancy actions [as to wrongful conception and wrongful pregnancy actions in general, see §§3.8, 3.9] has been rejected by some courts based on public policy and general damages considerations. [As to policy and other considerations favoring recovery for child rearing expenses, see §3.43.]

One of the primary public policy considerations against recovery is that to require a physician to provide for the financial cost of the upbringing of the child, while the parents retain the benefits of keeping the child, would be to establish a result that would be entirely out of proportion to the culpability involved. See, e.g., *Coleman v Garrison*, 349 A2d 8 (De 1975); *P v Portadin*, 179 NJ Super 465, 432 A2d 556 (1981); *Sorkin v Lee*, 78 AD2d 180, 434 NYS2d 303 (1980); *Rieck v Medical Protective Co v Fort Wayne, Indiana*, 64 Wi2d 514, 219 NW2d 242 (1974). Moreover, such a recovery against a physician, hospital, or manufacturer of surgical equipment used in an unsuccessful sterilization operation would likely open the way for fraudulent claims. See *Beardsley v Wierdsma*, 650 P2d 288 (Wy 1982). Common sense dictates that it is in society's best interest to hold physicians to a standard of professional competence and impose liability when they are negligent in treating their patients. But to hold a doctor responsible for the support of a mistakenly conceived child takes the doctor well beyond the scope of his duty to his patient as commonly thought of by both the public and medical profession. Public policy can, and in this instance does, cut off the legal responsibility of the physician even though he may have been negligent and the injured are innocent. See, e.g., *Maggard v McKelvey*, 627 SW2d 44 (Ky 1981); *Hickman v Myers*, 632 SW2d 869 (Tx 1982). Even where the chain of causation is complete and direct, recovery may sometimes be denied on grounds of public policy. To permit the parents to keep their child or shift the entire cost of its upbringing to a physician who failed to determine or inform them of the fact of pregnancy would be to create a new category of surrogate parent. See *Rieck v Medical Protective Co of Fort Wayne, Indiana*, 64 Wi2d 514, 219 NW2d 242 (1974). And it has been suggested that the claimed injury is too remote from the alleged negligence to allow recovery of damages for child rearing expenses. See *Beardsley v Wierdsma*, 650 P2d 288 (Wy 1982).

It has also been reasoned that litigation cannot answer every question, that every question cannot be answered in terms of dollars and cents [see, e.g., *Wilbur v Kerr*, 628 SW2d 568 (Ar 1982)], and that there is something distasteful in holding that a child is not worth what it costs to raise it [see, e.g., *Hartke v McKelway*, 526 FSupp 97 (D DC 1981)]. Another court has suggested that it is a matter of universally shared emotion and sentiment that the intangible but all important, incalculable but invaluable benefits of parenthood far outweigh any of the mere monetary burdens involved. See *Public Health Trust v Brown*, 388 So2d 1084 (Fl 1980). And, the satisfaction, joy and companionship which normal parents have in rearing a child make the economic loss associated with the child worthwhile. These intangible benefits, while impossible to value in dollars and cents, are undoubtedly the things that make life worthwhile. See *Terrell v Garcia*, 496 SW2d 124 (Tx 1973).

There is also authority for the proposition that the child might be harmed by learning that he or she not only was not wanted by his or her parents, but was reared by funds supplied by another person. See *Boone v Mullendore*, 416 So2d 718 (Al 1982). This will undermine society's need for a strong and healthy family relationship. Society has not yet become so sophisticated as to dismiss that emotional trauma as nonsense. See *Wilbur v Kerr*, 628 SW2d 568 (Ak 1982).

Courts have also relied on damage related considerations to forestall recovery for child rearing expenses. For example, recovery may not be had for damages which are uncertain or conjectural. After a child is born how can it be said within the ambit of legal predictability that the monetary cost of that life is worth more than its value, courts have asked. See, e.g., *Boone v Mullendore*, 416 So2d 718 (Al 1982); *Coleman v Garrison*, 349 A2d 8 (De 1975). And damages predicated on the cost of rearing the unplanned child are too speculative. See, e.g., *Terrell v Garcia*, 496 SW2d 124 (Tx 1973); *Beardsley v Wierdsma*, 650 P2d 288 (Wy 1982). Furthermore, the public policy which deems precious even potential life while yet in the womb, at such cost and expense as that condition may entail, does not countenance as compensable damage to its parent or parents those additional costs and expenses necessary to sustain and nurture that life once it comes to fruition upon and after a successful birth, another court has reasoned. See *Wilczynski v Goodman*, 73 IlA3d 51, 391 NE2d 479 (1979). Another damages problem that has been considered is what to do if the money is recovered. One court pondered the possibilities of what to do with the money: should the money go directly to the family to use as the parents see fit, should the money be placed in a special trust fund for the child, or should a guardian ad litem be appointed for the benefit of the child to insure the money recovered actually goes to the rearing of the child. See *Boone v Mullendore*, 416 So2d 718 (Al 1982).

It has been recognized that some courts have applied a balancing test which permits the jury to say that a life has been weighed and found wanting. However, this kind of judgment, if appropriate at all, might be applied at the end of life, after it has been lived and when the facts can be identified. But any attempt to apply it at birth can only be an exercise in prophecy, an undertaking not within the speciality of fact finders. See *Coleman v Garrison*, 349 A2d 8 (De 1975).

It has also been suggested that the judiciary is not the proper branch of government to approve the recovery of such an element of damages. If such damages are to be recognized in cases of this character, they should be evaluated first by legislative study, with consideration given to changing professional, economic, social, and moral standards and conditions. See *Wilczynski v Goodman*, 73 IlA3d 51, 391 NE2d 479 (1979).

c. [§3.42] —Illustrative Cases

The following cases are illustrative of the public policy and other considerations [generally see §3.41] that have been relied on to prevent recovery for child rearing expenses, and the application of these considerations by courts in particular cases:

In *Hartke v McKelway*, 526 FSupp 97 (D DC 1981), the plaintiff-mother of an unplanned child brought action against the defendant-physician on theories of negligence in the performance of a sterilization operation upon her, failure to obtain her informed consent to the procedure performed, and breach of a warranty that the plaintiff would not become pregnant. The court, applying District of Columbia law, said that there was something inherently distasteful in holding that a child is not worth what it costs to raise it. Moreover, there is something seemingly unjust about imposing the entire cost of raising the child on the physician. On the other hand, the admitted uncertainty of damages should not work to the plaintiff's disadvantage, as the normal rule is to place the burden of uncertainty on the wrongdoer. However these factors would be balanced in the more difficult case where the plaintiff originally sought sterilization for economic reasons, that is not necessary in this case, the court stated. The evidence was that the plaintiff sought sterilization because she had previously suffered an ectopic pregnancy, and feared for her life should she become pregnant again. There was no evidence to support the view that she sought to avoid the expenses of raising another child. To allow the plaintiff-mother to recover the cost of raising this child would be to give her a windfall, the court concluded.

In *Boone v Mullendore*, 416 So2d 718 (Al 1982), the defendant-physician removed cysts from the plaintiff-wife's fallopian tubes and ovaries. Following the operation the woman was informed that she was sterile. However, she later became pregnant and delivered a healthy child. The plaintiffs sought damages for medical expenses and costs reasonably incurred in the rearing of the unplanned child to its majority. However, on appeal, the court refused to allow these costs as an element of recoverable damages. A normal healthy life should not be the basis for a compensable wrong, the court observed. Any damages of this kind would tend to be extremely speculative in nature, and awarding such damages could have a significant impact on the stability of the family unit and the child. The court asked who could place a price tag on the child's smile or the parental pride in a child's achievement. Another problem the court considered was the possible harm that could be caused to the unwanted child who will one day learn that he or she not only was not wanted by his or her parents, but was reared by funds applied by another person. Some authors, the court said, have referred to such a child as an "emotional bastard" in a realistic, but harsh, attempt to describe the stigma that will attach once he or she learns the true circumstances of his or her upbringing. Another problem the court considered related to what to do with the money recovered. If damages are awarded for the care and maintenance of the child, should the money go directly to the family to use as the parents see fit, should the money be placed in a special trust fund for the child, or should a guardian ad litem be appointed for the benefit of the child to insure that the money recovered actually goes to the rearing of the child, the court asked. The court noted that nothing in its opinion should be construed as addressing, or commenting upon, the measure of damages attendant with a right of action, if any, in favor of the parents of the child, in an action of this type, when the child is born and afflicted with predetermined or readily foreseeable genetic or hereditary defects.

In *Wilbur v Kerr*, 628 SW2d 568 (Ar 1982), the court was persuaded for several reasons to follow those courts which have declined to grant damages for the expense of raising a child. It is a question which meddles with the concept of life and the stability of the family unit, the court said. Litigation cannot answer every question; every question cannot be answered in terms of dollars and cents. The court was also convinced that the damage to the child would be significant; that being an unwanted or "emotional bastard" who will someday learn that his parents did not want it and, in fact, went to court to force someone else to pay for its raising, will be harmful to that child. It will undermine society's need for a strong and healthy family relationship. The court believed that society had not become so sophisticated as to dismiss that emotional trauma as nonsense. The claim requesting the expense of raising an unwanted, healthy child must be denied as against public policy, the court concluded.

In *Coleman v Garrison*, 349 A2d 8 (De Supr 1975), the plaintiff-parents sought damages relative to the costs of raising an unplanned child from the defendants who allegedly performed an improper sterilization operation on the plaintiff-wife. The court held that the plaintiffs' claim that the surgeon should be compelled to assume financial responsibility for raising and educating the unplanned child may not be recovered in a court of law. First, as to the legal concept, it is settled law that recovery may not be had for damages which are speculative or conjectural. After a child is born how can it be said within the ambit of legal predictability that the monetary cost of that life is worth more than its value, the court asked. The court said that it recognized that a few courts, approaching the problem in clinical terms, had applied a balancing test which, presumably, would permit a jury to say that a life has been weighed and found wanting and thus the parents have been damaged. The court said that it seemed that that kind of judgment, if appropriate at all in an American court of law, might be applied at the end of life, after it had been lived and when the facts can be identified. But, any attempt to apply it at birth can only be an exercise in prophecy, an undertaking not within the speciality of the fact finders. Moreover, the court pointed to public policy factors and reasoned that to require the physician to provide for the financial cost of the upbringing of the child, while the parents retained the benefits of keeping their child, would be to establish a result that would be wholly out of proportion to the culpability involved.

In *Public Health Trust v Brown*, 388 So2d 1084 (Fl 1980), the court was faced with the question of whether the cost of raising a previously unwanted but healthy and normal child is a recoverable element of damages following the negligent performance of a tubal ligation. At the trial court level, the final judgment included $19,500 which, in a special verdict, was assessed for the past and discounted future reasonable costs of raising the unplanned child, offset by the value of his love and affection, companionship and other mother-child relationships. The court held that such a claim should not be recognized. The parent cannot be said to have been damaged by the birth and rearing of a normal, healthy child. It is a matter of universally shared emotion and sentiment that the intangible but all important, incalculable but invaluable benefits of parenthood far outweigh any of the mere monetary burdens involved. The court said this may be deemed conclusively presumed by the fact that a prospective parent does not abort or subsequently place the unwanted child for adoption. On a more practical level, the court said, the validity of the principle may be tested simply by asking any parent the purchase price for a particular youngster. Since this is the rule of experience, it should be, the court believed, the appropriate rule of law. It is a rare but happy instance in which a specific judicial decision can be based solely upon a reflection of one of the humane ideals which form the foundation of the legal system. This, the court believed, was just such a case. Therefore, the judgment in favor of plaintiff was reduced by $19,500, the amount which the jury assessed for past and future costs of raising the unplanned child.

In *Wilczynski v Goodman*, 73 IlA3d 51, 391 NE2d 479 (1979), the court held that child rearing costs following the birth of an unplanned child after an unsuccessful abortion were not recoverable. In this case the plaintiff-mother brought action against the defendant-physician alleging that the physician had negligently failed to perform a proper abortion. One of the types of damages the plaintiff sought was that for the costs of raising the unplanned child. The court cited public policy reasons for denying recovery. The court referred to the Illinois Abortion Act of 1975, which it characterized as strongly condemning abortion and supporting the right to life. A public policy which deems precious even potential life while yet in the womb, at such cost and expense as that condition may entail, does not countenance as compensable damage to its parent or parents those additional costs and expenses necessary to sustain and nurture that life once it comes to fruition upon and after a successful birth. The existence of a normal, healthy life is an esteemed right under Illinois laws, rather than a compensable wrong. If such damages are to be recognized in cases of this character, they should be evaluated by legislative study first, with consideration given to changing professional, economic, social, and moral standards and conditions.

In *Maggard v McKelvey*, 627 SW2d 44 (Ky 1981), the court held that damages in a case arising from the birth of an unwanted child could not include costs incurred for the care and maintenance of the child. The plaintiff-husband had gone to the defendant-physician for the performance of a vasectomy. The operation was performed, but subsequently the plaintiff-wife became pregnant and gave birth to an unplanned child. The plaintiffs' complaint stated that had the vasectomy been performed in a careful and skillful manner, which the defendant failed to do, the plaintiff would not have become pregnant. The court asked whether these damages came within the bounds of consequential damages for the negligent conduct of a physician, and concluded that to answer negatively would defy logic and be contrary to the concept of causation and tort as articulated by the Kentucky Supreme Court. The court said it would be illogical to say that the damages claimed were not within the foreseeability of the injury, orbit of risk, or zone of danger. However, these concepts do not set the outer limits on tort damages. The final hurdle to be jumped is that of public policy. The court viewed sanctioning such an expansion of a physician's liability to be a question of public policy, and said that common sense dictates that it is in society's best interest to hold physicians to a standard of professional competence and impose liability when they are negligent in treating their patients. But to hold a doctor responsible for the support of a mistakenly conceived child takes him well beyond the scope of his duty to his patient, as commonly thought of by both the lay public and the medical profession. Public policy can, and in this instance does, cut off the legal responsibility of the physician, even though he or she may be negligent and the injured are innocent. Without a clear expression of public opinion, some indication from the legislature, or an interpretation by the Kentucky Supreme Court to the contrary, the court concluded that Kentucky's public policy prohibits the extension of liability to include these damages.

In *P v Portadin*, 179 NJ Super 465, 432 A2d 556 (1981), the plaintiff-parents of an unplanned child brought a medical malpractice action against the defendants claiming that the defendants had negligently performed an authorized sterilization procedure. As a result, the plaintiffs' alleged that the plaintiff-wife became pregnant and gave birth to a normal child. The plaintiffs sought damages for the future costs of rearing the child. The court refused to recognize this element of damages. The court quoted with approval the case of *Berman v Allan*, 80 NJ 421, 404 A2d 8 (1979), and said that the recovery for the future expenses which the parents may incur in raising, educating and supervising the child are precluded. Quoting the reasoning in the *Berman* decision, the court said that in essence the plaintiffs desire to retain all the benefits relating to the birth of the child, the love and joy they will experience as parents, while saddling the defendants with the enormous expenses attendant on the child's rearing. Under the facts and circumstances alleged in the *Berman* case, the court there found that such an award would be wholly disproportionate to the culpability involved, and that the allowance of such a recovery would both constitute a windfall to the parents and place too unreasonable a financial burden upon physicians. Therefore, the court said it had no hesitancy in concluding that the plaintiffs were precluded from recovering any expenses for raising their child. And in *M & Wife v Schmid Laboratories, Inc*, 178 NJ Super 122, 428 A2d 515 (1981), the plaintiff-parents brought a negligence and products liability action against the defendant manufacturer and retailer of a contraceptive device (condom). The plaintiffs alleged that the condom was defective and caused the wife to become pregnant and give birth to normal, healthy twin daughters. The plaintiffs made a broad claim for compensatory damages resulting from the birth of their children as a result of the alleged defective condom. They contended these damages should include the costs of rearing and educating the children. The court cited with approval the reasoning in the *Berman* case and said that although the *Berman* case could be distinguished from the present case on several grounds the court interpreted the holding of *Berman* as establishing a policy on recoverable damages in cases involving charges of wrongful life and wrongful birth. The court acknowledged that well established principles of proximate cause applicable in negligence cases sanction recovery for all damages proximately flowing from the negligent act. However, by drawing the line where it did and withdrawing from consideration items of damage relating to educating and rearing the child, the court said it had adopted a limited measure of recoverable damages in this type of case. That the defendant in this case was a corporate manufacturer as opposed to an individual practicing physician, or that this action was grounded in strict liability and breach of warranty principles as well as negligence, did not lead the court to conclude that the factual distinctions in the cases warranted its departure from the measure of damages established in *Berman*.

In *Sorkin v Lee*, 78 AD2d 180, 434 NYS2d 303 (1980), the plaintiff-parents of an unplanned child brought an action against the defendant-physician for the allegedly negligent performance of a vasectomy. The plaintiffs sought child rearing costs, but the court denied that element of damages and said to hold the physician responsible for the cost of future care of a healthy normal child based upon the parents' private decision on how to accept the unplanned pregnancy was to inflict a penalty on the defendant that is out of all proportion to his wrong. It is one thing to add the cost of the medical bills and assess damages against a negligent physician for extraordinary unanticipated expenses resulting from the preventable birth of a defective baby, but it is quite another to assess him for the myriad cost of raising a normal, healthy child for some indefinite period in the future, the court said.

In *Terrell v Garcia*, 496 SW2d 124 (Tx 1973), the court said that public sentiment recognizes that the benefits accruing to the parents of an unplanned or unwanted child outweigh their economic loss in rearing and educating a healthy, normal child. The satisfaction, joy and companionship which normal parents have in rearing a child make the economic loss associated with the child worthwhile, the court said. These intangible benefits, while impossible to value in dollars and cents are undoubtedly the things that make life worthwhile, the court said.

In *Rieck v Medical Protective Co of Fort Wayne, Indiana*, 64 Wi2d 514, 219 NW2d 242 (1974), the court said negligence plus an unbroken sequence of events establishing cause in fact does not necessarily lead to a determination that a defendant is liable for the plaintiff's injuries. The plaintiff-parents alleged that a defendant-physician examined the plaintiff-mother, diagnosed her condition as a condition other than pregnancy and prescribed medication for the condition. Later, the plaintiff consulted a second obstetrician who diagnosed her as 17 weeks pregnant. Further, the plaintiffs alleged that had they known of the pregnancy it would have been their intention to have the mother undergo an operation to terminate the pregnancy. However, when the plaintiffs learned of the pregnancy, it was too late for the medical operation because of the dangers involved. The plaintiffs sought damages together with costs and disbursements, for the stresses involved and the extra expenditures of money that they would have to raise and spend in the upbringing of this child. The court noted that recovery, or the determination to impose or not to impose liability, involves public policy considerations. Even where the chain of causation is complete and direct, recovery may sometimes be denied on grounds of public policy. To permit the parents to keep their child and shift the entire cost of its upbringing to a physician who failed to determine or inform them of the fact of pregnancy would be to create a new category of surrogate parent. Every child's smile, every bond of love and affection, every reason for parental pride in a child's achievements, every contribution by the child to the welfare and well being of the family and parents, would remain with the mother and father. For the most part, these are intangible benefits, but they are nonetheless real, the court said. On the other hand, every financial cost or detriment including the cost of food, clothing and education, would be shifted to the physician who allegedly failed to timely diagnose the fact of pregnancy. The court believed that such a result would be wholly out of proportion to the culpability involved, and that the allowance of recovery would place too unreasonable a burden on physicians, under the facts and circumstances alleged in this case.

d. [§3.43] Policy and Other Considerations Favoring Award

In order for a plaintiff to recover child rearing costs [as to the elements of child rearing costs, see §3.40] as an element of damages [as to elements of damages in general, see §3.28] in wrongful conception and wrongful pregnancy actions [as to wrongful conception and wrongful pregnancy actions in general, see §3.8, §3.9], it must first be determined that such an award would not violate public policy or other damage related considerations. [As to policy and other considerations disfavoring recovery for child rearing expenses, see §3.41]. There is authority for the proposition that while most parents hold the sentiment that the birth of a healthy, albeit unplanned, child is always a benefit, this sentiment should not be raised to the level of public policy so as to preclude recovery of these damages. See, e.g., *Ochs v Borrelli*, 187 Cn 253, 445 A2d 883 (1982); *Cockrum v Baumgartner*, 99 IlA3d 271, 425 NE2d 968 (1981). The compensation is not for the so-called unwanted child, but to replenish the family exchequer so that the new arrival will not deprive the other family members of what was planned as their just share of the family income. See *Custodio v Bauer*, 251 CaA2d 303, 59 CaR 463 (1967).

One court has taken judicial notice of the fact that raising a child from birth to maturity is a costly enterprise, and hence injurious, although it is an experience that abundantly recompenses most parents with intangible rewards. There is no affront to public policy in the recognition of these costs and no inconsistency that parental pleasure softens but does not eradicate economic reality. The plaintiffs' testimony confirming their love for an unplanned child should not become a reason for denying them financial relief. See *Ochs v Borrelli*, 187 Cn 253, 445 A2d 883 (1982). It has also been held that the anticipated cost of raising an unplanned child is not too speculative or immeasurable to prevent recovery. Such calculations are made by estate planners, insurance companies and sometimes by private parties incident to support proceedings or matrimonial settlements. See *Rivera v State*, 94 Misc2d 157, 404 NYS2d 950 (1978). And it has been recognized that the costs of rearing a normal, healthy child are a direct financial injury to the parents, no different in immediate effect from the medical expenses resulting from the wrongful conception and birth of the child. Although public sentiment may recognize that to the vast majority of parents the long-term and enduring benefits of parenthood outweigh the economic costs of rearing a healthy child, it is myopic to declare that those benefits exceed the costs as a matter of law. Compensatory damages for the cost of rearing the child would also serve the useful purpose of an added deterrent to the negligent performance of sterilizations. See *Sherlock v Stillwater Clinic*, 260 NW2d 169 (Mn 1977). And public policy cannot support an exception to tort liability when the impact of such an exception would impair the exercise of a constitutionally protected right. It is now clearly established that parents have a constitutionally protected interest located within the zone of privacy created by several fundamental constitutional guarantees to employ contraceptive devices to limit the size of their family. Therefore, the argument that an exception, grounded in public policy, to the normal duty of a tortfeasor to assume liability for all the damages, including child rearing costs, that he has proximately caused is unpersuasive. See *Ochs v Borrelli*, 187 Cn 253, 445 A2d 883 (1982).

When recovery for child rearing costs as an element of damages has been recognized, the amount of the recovery has been based either on the entire amount of the expenses or application of the benefit rule. The full recovery principle provides that the defendant recompense the plaintiff for all child rearing costs, which typically include the costs of education, medicine, and often general child raising costs. See *Cockrum v Baumgartner*, 99 IlA3d 271, 425 NE2d 968 (1981). [As to full recovery, see §3.44.] By contrast, the benefit rule, which applies RESTATEMENT (SECOND) OF TORTS §920 (1977), says that the amount of injury should be calculated by reducing the total damages for child rearing expenses by the benefit received by the plaintiff from the birth of the unplanned child. See, e.g., *Pierce v De Gracia*, 431 NE2d 768 (Il 1982). [As to the benefit rule and its application, see §3.46.]

e. [§3.44] Full Recovery of All Costs

A defendant in a wrongful conception or wrongful pregnancy case [as to wrongful conception and wrongful pregnancy actions in general, see §§3.8, 3.9] may be liable for all costs associated with the rearing of an unplanned child. [As to other elements of damages in wrongful conception and wrongful pregnancy cases, see §3.28.] The allowance of rearing costs is not an aspersion upon the value of the child's life, but is rather a recognition of the importance of the parents' fundamental right to control their reproductivity. See *Cockrum v Baumgartner*, 99 IlA3d 271, 425 NE2d 968 (1981). Moreover, the anticipated cost of raising the unplanned child is not too speculative to permit recovery. Such calculations are made by estate planners, insurance companies and private parties. See, *Rivera v State*, 95 Misc2d 157, 404 NYS2d 950 (1978).

f. [§3.45] —Illustrative Cases

The following cases are illustrative of the general principles relating to questions of full recovery for child rearing expenses [generally, see §3.44], and the application of those principles by courts in particular cases:

In *Cockrum v Baumgartner*, 99 IlA3d 271, 425 NE2d 968 (1981), the court held that the plaintiff-parents could recover damages for the expenses of raising and educating an unplanned child. The decision consolidated two earlier cases, *Cockrum v Baumgartner*, where the plaintiff-parents brought a negligence action alleging medical malpractice by the defendant-physician in the performance of a vasectomy on the father, and *Raja v Tulsky*, where the plaintiff-parents brought suit against a defendant-medical center in which they alleged the medical center had misdiagnosed the mother's pregnancy so as to prevent the plaintiffs from terminating the pregnancy. In both cases, the trial court dismissed the counts seeking compensation for the expenses of raising and educating the child. The defendants argued that public policy deemed the birth of the child a precious gift rather than a compensable wrong. The court said that while it agreed that most parents hold the sentiment that the birth of a healthy, albeit unplanned, child is always a benefit, it was not inclined to raise the sentiment to the level of public policy. The uniqueness of life is in no way denigrated by a couple's choice not to have a child. Regardless of motivation, a couple has the right to determine whether they will have a child. The allowance of rearing costs is not an aspersion upon the value of the child's life. It is instead a recognition of the importance of the parents' fundamental right to control their reproductivity. The court said it could not endorse the view that effectively nullified this right by providing that its violation resulted in no injury. The court noted the reliance other courts had placed on so-called benefit rule found in RESTATEMENT (SECOND) OF TORTS §920 (1977). To the extent that this section has been used to permit the emotional rewards of parenthood to offset its financial costs the court said, it had been misapplied. Section 920 clearly provides that a benefit to the plaintiff caused by the defendant's tortious act may be considered in mitigation of the plaintiff's injury only where the benefit is to the same interest which was harmed. The rewards of parenthood should not be allowed in mitigation of rearing costs because these rewards are emotional in nature and, great though they may be, do nothing whatever to benefit the plaintiff's injured financial interest.

In *Bowman v Davis*, 48 OhSt2d 41, 356 NE2d 496 (1976), the plaintiff-parents sought damages following the allegedly negligent performance of a tubal ligation on plaintiff-wife, and the resulting premature birth of twins, one of whom suffered from such congenital abnormalities as kidney and hip malfunction and mental retardation. At trial the plaintiffs sought damages for a number of items including the economic costs of rearing twins including, in the case of the abnormal twin, the costs of institutionalization, care, nursing, and special attention. The jury awarded the plaintiffs a general verdict in the amount of $450,000. Although the court on appeal did not speak directly to the issue of the recovery of damages for child rearing, it did affirm the judgment and the amount of damages.

g. [§3.46] Benefit Rule; Reduction of Recovery

At times in wrongful conception and wrongful pregnancy cases [as to wrongful conception and wrongful pregnancy actions in general, see §§3.8, 3.9] the benefit rule is applied. The benefit rule, which is set out in RESTATEMENT (SECOND) OF TORTS §920 (1977), provides that where the defendant's conduct causes harm to the plaintiff but also results in a benefit to the plaintiff, the value of the benefit is, where equitable, considered regarding mitigation of damages. In the context of the birth of an unplanned child it is argued that the birth of the child represents a benefit to the plaintiff which must be offset against the harm to the plaintiff. For example, in a case where the rule was applied it was stated that in assessing damages the trier of fact should be allowed to consider the potential benefits of the unplanned child which might accrue to the family interests. See *Pierce v de Gracia*, 103 IlA3d 511, 59 Il Dec 267, 431 NE2d 768 (1982). Family size, family income, age of the parents, and marital status are some, but not all of the factors to be considered in determining the extent to which the birth of a child represents a benefit to the parents. See *Troppi v Scarf*, 31 MiA 240, 187 NW2d 511 (1971), leave den, 385 Mi 753 (1971). Computation of rearing costs must include an assessment of the reasonably foreseeable expenses that will be incurred by the parents. Then the trier of fact is required to reduce these costs by the value of the child's aid, comfort, and society which will benefit the parents for the duration of their lives. While the dollar value of the benefits to be offset is difficult to assess, recovery for the loss of aid, comfort and society in wrongful death actions where similar problems of proof are presented are routinely allowed. See *Sherlock v Stillwater Clinic*, 260 NW2d 169 (Mn 1977). The process of balancing the child rearing expenses against the value of the benefits conferred by the unplanned child is not impermissibly speculative. There is no basis for distinguishing this case from other tort cases in which the trier of fact fixes damages for wrongful death or loss of consortium. See *Ochs v Borrelli*, 187 Cn 253, 445 A2d 883 (1982).

However, not all courts have agreed that application of the benefit rule is appropriate in these cases. The benefit rule places the parent in the win-lose situation that if they admit that the child is a welcome addition and that they love the child and rear it properly, they may get no damages at all. Thus, it would be to their advantage, at least monetarily so, to deny any affection for the child and to emphasize all of the economic problems the child will cause, thus increasing damages and the possibility of emotional trauma in the child at the time he or she learns of the earlier court proceedings. See *Boone v Mullendore*, 416 So2d 718 (Al 1982). Moreover, to the extent the rule is used to permit the emotional rewards of parenthood to affect its financial costs the rule is misapplied. The rule provides that a benefit to the plaintiff caused by the defendant's tortious act may be considered in mitigation of the plaintiff's injury only where the benefit is to the same interest which was harmed. The rewards of parenthood should not be allowed in mitigation of rearing costs because these rewards are emotional in nature and do nothing to benefit the plaintiff's injured financial interest. See *Cockrum v Baumgartner*, 99 IlA3d 271, 425 NE2d 968 (1981). And the benefit or offset concept smacks of condemnation law, where the trier of fact determines the value of land taken by the condemnor. The trier of fact then determines the benefit that results to the landowner, which benefit is deducted from the original value to determine the proper award. If the concept of benefit or offset is applied to actions arising from the birth of an unplanned child following a sterilization operation there could be an incongruous result such as that the benefits could be greater than the damages, in which event someone could argue that the parents owed something to the tortfeasors. A child should not be viewed as a piece of property, with fact finders first assessing the expense and damage incurred because of a child's life, then deducting the value of that child's life. See *Beardsley v Wierdsma*, 650 P2d 288 (Wy 1982).

h. [§3.47] —Illustrative Cases

The following cases are illustrative of the general principles relating to the benefit rule [generally, see §3.46], and the application of the principles by courts in particular cases:

In *Stills v Gratton*, 55 CaA3d 698, 127 CaR 652 (1976), the plaintiff-mother brought a malpractice action against the defendant-physicians alleging the negligent performance of an abortion. As a consequence of the malpractice, an unplanned child was born to her. The court ruled that the plaintiff, in the event the trier of fact found in her favor on the liability issue, should be permitted to recover all the damages to which she would be entitled under ordinary tort principles. However, the court noted, under those same principles the defendants would be allowed to prove any offsets for benefits conferred and amounts chargeable to the plaintiff under her duty to mitigate damages. And in *Custodio v Bauer*, 251 CaA2d 303, 59 CaR 463 (1967), the court cited RESTATEMENT (SECOND) OF TORTS §920 (1977), and said if the alleged failure of the sterilization operation and the ensuing pregnancy benefited the wife's emotional and nervous makeup, or any infirmities relating to her kidney and bladder organs (conditions that had existed prior to the unplanned pregnancy), the defendant should be able to offset it against the damages. In *Custodio* the plaintiff-parents of an unplanned child sought to recover damages resulting from the pregnancy of the plaintiff-wife following the failure of an operation undertaken and performed to accomplish her sterilization. The plaintiffs based their action on negligence, misrepresentation, and contract theories. The court said that one could not categorically say whether the unplanned child would be emotionally upset if he arrived in an environment where each of the other members of the family needed to contribute to his support, or whether he would have a happier and more well adjusted life if he brought with him the wherewithal to make it possible. But the court said that the compensation is not for the so-called unwanted child or emotional bastard, but to replenish the family exchequer so that the new arrival will not deprive the other members of the family of what was planned as their just share of the family income.

In *Anonymous v Hospital (1976-11)*, 33 Cn Super 126, 366 A2d 204 (1976), the plaintiff-parents of an unplanned child brought a malpractice suit charging the defendant hospital and physician with negligence in the performance of a bilateral tubal ligation. One of the elements of damages the plaintiff sought was the costs of raising and bringing up their unplanned child. The defendants demurrered based on the contention that this cause of action was not authorized by statute or common law and was against the public policy of Connecticut. The court, however, disagreed and reasoned that the safer course would be to allow the allegations of the complaint to stand and to permit the defendants to argue in mitigation of damages the satisfaction, joy, and companionship, which normal parents receive in the rearing of a child and which make economic loss worthwhile. Although the specific ascertainment of damages in that area is difficult, that should not prevent their consideration by the trier of fact.

In *Pierce v de Gracia*, 103 IlA3d 511, 59 Il Dec 267, 431 NE2d 768 (1982), the court was faced with the issue of whether the parents of a healthy child born subsequent to an unsuccessful sterilization operation may recover damages for the expense of rearing that child to majority. The court said certainly the costs of rearing an unplanned child to majority are damages which proximately flow from either the tort of medical negligence or the breach of contract by a physician who fails to properly perform a vasectomy. In assessing damages, the court said, the jury should be allowed to consider the potential benefits of the unplanned child which may accrue to the family interests. Parental age, marital status, family income, family size, and health of all family members are factors in this consideration, the court said. The possible benefits do not automatically offset all damages nor are they to be completely ignored by the jury, the court reasoned.

In *Troppi v Scarf*, 31 MiA 240, 187 NW2d 511 (1971), leave den, 385 Mi 753 (1971), the plaintiff-parents of an unplanned child brought a negligence action against the defendant-physician for the defendant's negligent act of supplying tranquilizer pills rather than birth control pills called for by a prescription. The court said that it was arguable that the birth of a healthy child confers so substantial a benefit as to outweigh the expenses of his birth and support. In the great majority of cases, this is no doubt true, or people would not choose to multiply so freely. But, the court asked, could it say as a matter of law that a healthy child always conferred an overriding benefit. The court said that the benefit rule was pertinent to this case and cited RESTATEMENT (SECOND) OF TORTS §920 (1977). If the defendant's tortious conduct conferred a benefit to the same interest which was harmed by his conduct, the dollar value of the benefit is to be subtracted from the dollar value of the injury in arriving at the amount of damages properly awardable. The benefits of the unplanned child may be weighed against all of the elements of the claimed damage. However, the court said the application of the benefit rule to prevent any recovery for the expenses of rearing an unwanted child was unwise. Such a rule would be equivalent to declaring that in every case, as a matter of law, the services and companionship of a child have a dollar equivalent greater than the economic cost of his support, to say nothing of the inhibitions, the restrictions, and the pain and suffering caused by pregnancy and the obligation to rear the child. The court said that the essential point, in the application of the benefit rule, was that the trier of fact must have the power to evaluate the benefit according to all of the circumstances of the case presented. Family size, family income, age of the parents, and marital status are some, but not all, of the factors which the trier must consider in determining the extent to which the birth of a particular child represents a benefit to his or her parents. As to the costs of rearing the child until his majority, this is a computation which is routinely performed in countless cases. It should be clear that ascertainment of gross damages is a routine task. Whatever uncertainty attends the final award arises from application of the benefit rule, which requires the trier of fact to compute the dollar value of the companionship and services of an unwanted child. Placing a dollar value on these segments may well be more difficult than assessing damages for the plaintiff's lost wages. But difficulty in determining the amount to be subtracted from the gross damages does not justify the denying of recovery altogether. Michigan law is clear that there need be only a basis for reasonable ascertainment of the amount of the damages. If the fact of liability is proven, difficulty in determining damages will not bar recovery.

In *Sherlock v Stillwater Clinic*, 260 NW2d 169 (Mn 1977), the court held that one of the elements of damages in a wrongful conception case was the cost of rearing the unplanned child. The plaintiffs brought suit against the defendants claiming that their eighth child's unplanned birth was a direct result of one of the defendant's employee's negligent postoperative care of the plaintiff-husband following the performance of a vasectomy. Ethical and religious considerations aside, the court reasoned, it must be recognized that the costs of rearing a normal, healthy child are a direct financial injury to the parents, no different in immediate effect from the medical expenses resulting from the wrongful conception and birth of the child. Although public sentiment may recognize that to the vast majority of parents the long term and enduring benefits of parenthood outweigh the economic costs of rearing a healthy child, it would seem myopic to declare that those benefits exceed the costs as a matter of law. Compensatory damages for the cost of rearing the child to the age of majority would also serve the useful purpose of an added deterrent to the negligent performance of sterilization operations. Thus, the court concluded, where the parents of an unplanned, healthy child choose to include the costs of child rearing as an item of damages in their claim, the court will permit them to recover the reasonably foreseeable costs of rearing, subject to an offset for the value of the benefits conferred to them by the child. Computation of rearing costs must begin with an assessment of the reasonably foreseeable expenses that will be incurred by the parents to maintain, support, and educate their child. In the case of a normal, healthy child the court anticipated that these expenses would not ordinarily be projected beyond the age of majority. Moreover, in keeping with the same interest limitation of RESTATEMENT (SECOND) OF TORTS §920 (1977), and its underlying purpose to prevent unjust enrichment, the trier of fact will then be required to reduce these costs by the value of the child's aid, comfort, and society which will benefit the parents for the duration of their lives. The court said to assist the jury in measuring the various and complex elements of damage, it would require that all future actions for wrongful conception be submitted to the jury with a special verdict form along with explanatory instructions. Coupled with these precautions should be a strict judicial scrutiny of verdicts to prevent excessive awards, the court said.

4. [§3.48] Siblings' Losses

When an unplanned child is born [as to wrongful conception and wrongful pregnancy actions in general, see §§3.8, 3.9] the child's brothers and sisters are necessarily forced to share the assets of their family. This situation has resulted in actions brought on behalf of the siblings to recover for this diminution in wealth when the unplanned child is the result of an unforeseen conception or pregnancy and an action ensues for wrongful conception or wrongful pregnancy. However, courts that have addressed this issue have been in agreement that such an element of damages, or in some cases a separate cause of action, is not recognizable. See, e.g., *White v United States*, 510 FSupp 146 (D Ks 1981); *Aronoff v Snider*, 292 So2d 418 (Fl 1974); *Cox v Stretton*, 77 Misc2d 155, 352 NYS2d 834 (1974). [As to elements of damages in wrongful conception and wrongful pregnancy cases, see §3.28.]

The siblings of an unplanned infant suffer no damage from the birth of the unplanned child. See *Aronoff v Snider*, 229 So2d 418 (Fl 1974). Moreover, there is no proportional share of their parents' worldly goods to which children are entitled. Infants are not entitled as a matter of right to any specific share of their parents' wealth, much less their care, affection, or training. No duty has been breached, and no fundamental right has been violated. See *Cox v Stretton*, 77 Misc2d 155, 352 NYS2d 834 (1974).

E. Limitations, Discovery Rule Applied

1. [§3.49] Generally

One fact pattern in a wrongful conception cause of action involves the negligent or improper performance of an elective sterilization operation which results in the conception and birth of an unplanned child. [As to wrongful conception causes of action in general, see §§3.8, 3.9.] The issue of when the cause of action accrues is of particular importance in cases arising from improperly performed sterilization operations since, at times, it is difficult or impossible for the plaintiff to know that the operation has not been successful. It is possible that the plaintiff may not realize the operation was not successful until conception has taken place and an unplanned pregnancy has begun. In the context of wrongful conception cases courts have generally applied the discovery rule to the issue of when the cause of action accrued. See, e.g., *Bishop v Byrne*, 265 FSupp 460 (SD WV 1967); *Wilford v Jenkins*, 226 So2d 245 (Fl 1969); *Hackworth v Hart*, 474 SW2d 377 (Ky 1971); *Teeters v Currey*, 518 SW2d 512 (Tn 1974); *Hays v Hall*, 488 SW2d 412 (Tx 1972).

The discovery rule provides that the plaintiff's cause of action accrues when the plaintiff discovers, or in the exercise of reasonable diligence, should have discovered the injury. See *Bishop v Byrne*, 265 FSupp 460 (SD WV 1967). In cases involving unplanned conceptions, accrual of an action has been defined as the time when the plaintiff-mother discovered she was pregnant, or in the exercise of reasonable care, should have discovered the pregnancy [see *Teeters v Currey*, 518 SW2d 512 (Tn 1974)] or, in the case of an unsuccessful vasectomy, when the plaintiff-husband discovered that his wife was pregnant by him [see *Hackworth v Hart*, 474 SW2d 377 (Ky 1971)].

In addition, even when the cause of action has accrued, the running of the statute of limitations will be tolled if the injury has been fraudulently concealed by the defendant. Normally some positive act of concealment must be proven for the plaintiff to succeed in having the statute tolled. However, in a confidential relationship setting, such as exists where a doctor performs a sterilization operation on a patient, mere silence can constitute fraudulent concealment. See *Hardin v Farris*, 87 NM 143, 530 P2d 407 (1974).

2. [§3.50] Illustrative Cases

The following cases are illustrative of the general principles relating to limitation issues in wrongful conception cases, and specifically when an action accrues [generally, see §3.49]:

In *Bishop v Byrne*, 265 FSupp 460 (SD WV 1967), the plaintiffs brought a diversity action against the defendant-physician for alleged negligence and breach of warranty in the performance of a sterilization operation on the wife. The negligent operation complained of was performed on July 20, 1962, but the action was not commenced until June 22, 1965. The defendant asserted that the two-year statute of limitation as a bar to the maintenance of the tort portion of this action. The breach of warranty aspect was governed by a five-year limitation, and thus there was no question that the breach of warranty was not instituted within that period. The court, applying West Virginia law, held that in medical malpractice suits the period of limitation does not commence to run against the plaintiff's cause of action until he or she learns of, or by the exercise of reasonable diligence should have learned of, the defendant's negligent act or omission. Therefore, the court overruled the defendant's motion to invoke the two-year limitation as a bar to the tort portion of this action.

In *Wilford v Jenkins*, 226 So2d 245 (Fl 1969), the parents of an unplanned child brought an action against the defendant-physician for the alleged negligent performance of a sterilization operation on the plaintiff-wife. The operation was performed in December 1961, but the wife became pregnant and subsequently gave birth to a baby on April 10, 1967. The trial judge ruled that the plaintiffs had not filed the actions within the period defined by the statute of limitations, and thus granted a summary judgment for the defendant. However, on appeal the court reversed and remanded the case. The court noted that negligence actions were governed by a four-year statute of limitations. As to the negligence count, the court noted, that the law in Florida is that a statute of limitations begins to run when there has been notice of invasion of the legal rights of the plaintiff, or when he or she has been put on notice of his or her right of action. In this case the plaintiffs were not aware, and could not have been aware, of any right of action sounding in negligence until the plaintiff-wife became pregnant, and the court took judicial notice that this had to have occurred sometime in 1966. The court reasoned that it did not have to be concerned about the exact date of conception since the suit was filed well within two years thereafter, and certainly within the applicable four-year statutory period. Therefore, the negligence action was not barred by the statute of limitation.

In *Hackworth v Hart*, 474 SW2d 377 (Ky 1971), the court was faced with determining when the statute of limitations began to run in a case involving an unsuccessful vasectomy operation. The court ruled that the plaintiffs' cause of action commenced to run at the time the plaintiff-husband discovered or should have discovered that the operation was not successful. The court said that such a discovery would usually be made when it was discovered that one was not sterile and that his wife was pregnant by him. However, the court noted that the question of when a woman discovers or should in the exercise of usual care and curiosity have discovered her pregnancy was a difficult one. Therefore, the court adopted the rule that the cause of action in malpractice cases, where pregnancy is the critical question, commences to run from the time the pregnancy is or should be discovered.

In *Teeters v Currey*, 518 SW2d 512 (Tn 1974), the court was faced with the issue of whether the statute of limitations in a medical malpractice action involving an allegedly negligently performed bilateral tubal ligation began to run from the date of the injury or from the date of the discovery of the injury. On June 5, 1970, the plaintiff gave birth to a normal child. The defendant was the attending physician. Following delivery the defendant performed the sterilization surgery on June 6, 1970. On December 6, 1972, the plaintiff was hospitalized again and discovered that she was pregnant. On March 9, 1973, the plaintiff gave birth to a premature child. The plaintiff instituted suit on November 15, 1973, three years, five months and nine days after the operation, but approximately 11 months after discovering her pregnancy. The plaintiff alleged that during the course of a later surgery it was discovered that the earlier surgery performed by the defendant was negligently and inadequately done and was not performed in accordance with proper standards of care and good medical practice. The defendant's answer pled the statute of limitations and denied that he was guilty of any act of negligence. The trial court granted summary judgment in favor of the defendant without explanation, but the court on appeal said that the real basis for the collapse of this suit in the trial court was the statute of limitations plea. Therefore, the court posed the question of when does the cause of action accrue. The court recognized the discovery doctrine, under which the statute does not begin to run until the negligent injury is, or should have been, discovered. The court said it adopted as the rule of Tennessee the principle that in most classes of cases where medical malpractice is asserted to have occurred through the negligent performance of surgical procedures, the cause of action accrues and the statute of limitations begins to run when the patient discovers, or in the exercise of reasonable care and diligence for his own health and welfare, should have discovered the resulting injury. In *Teeters*, the cause of action accrued when the plaintiff discovered that she was pregnant, or in the exercise of reasonable care and diligence, she should have so discovered.

In *Hays v Hall*, 488 SW2d 412 (Tx 1972), the court held that in malpractice cases arising from vasectomy operations the statute of limitations begins to run on the date of the discovery of the true facts concerning the failure of the operation, or from the date it should, in the exercise of ordinary care and diligence, have been discovered. The plaintiff-wife had given birth to two deformed children, one of whom had died. The plaintiff-husband had a vasectomy operation performed to avoid the possibility of the birth of other deformed children. The defendant performed the surgical operation on the husband on July 28, 1966. Approximately one month after the operation, the husband returned to the defendant to be examined and tested to determine whether the operation was successful. The defendant performed a test and informed the husband that he was sterile. On September 27, 1967, the wife was examined by her physician and was informed that she was pregnant. The wife gave birth to their third child on January 11, 1968. On September 28, 1967, the father had returned to the defendant and informed him of his wife's pregnancy. The defendant performed another test, and informed the husband that there were no live sperm in his semen, and further advised that the wife's pregnancy was caused by sperm cells having been trapped in the seminal tract above the point where the vasectomy incision had been made. In July 1968, the wife was again informed by her physician that she was pregnant. The husband upon being tested a third time by the defendant was again told he was sterile. On February 9, 1969, the wife gave birth to her fourth child. This suit was brought against the defendant on May 16, 1969. In applying the law to this case, the court reversed the lower court's dismissal of the cause of action for the reason that the suit was filed after limitations had run, and remanded the cause of trial on the merits.

The impact of concealment on the running of the statute of limitations was considered in the following case.

In *Hardin v Farris*, 87 NM 143, 530 P2d 407 (1974), the plaintiffs alleged that on June 20, 1969, the defendant-physician performed a tubal ligation operation on the plaintiff-wife for the purpose of making her infertile. Moreover, the plaintiffs alleged that on or about June 21, 1969, a surgical pathological report was placed in the hospital file of the wife which showed that the tubal ligation was not complete, and that defendant failed to tell the plaintiff of that fact after having had knowledge of it. Subsequently, the wife became pregnant and gave birth to an unplanned child. The plaintiffs alleged that the injury was proximately caused by and through the carelessness and negligence of the defendant. The defendant, in his answer, made general denials and affirmatively pled the statute of limitations as a bar to the plaintiffs' complaint. The trial court granted the defendant's motion for judgment on the pleadings, and reasoned that an action for injuries to the person for negligent malpractice must be brought within three years after the accrual of the cause of action. The plaintiffs contended that the running of the statute was tolled by the defendant's fraudulent concealment of the report which indicated that the operation was negligently performed. The court concluded that where a party against whom a cause of action accrues prevents the one entitled to bring the cause from obtaining knowledge thereof by fraudulent concealment, or where the cause is known to the injuring party, but is of such character as to conceal itself from the injured party, the statutory limitation on the time for bringing the action will not begin to run until the right of action is discovered, or, by the exercise of ordinary diligence, could have been discovered. Fraudulent concealment is not restricted to actions in which fraud is the major issue in the action. Neither does it create a new or separate cause of action. It merely tolls the running of a statute of limitations. Normally some positive act of concealment must be shown such as a false representation. However, in a confidential relationship where there exists a duty to speak, such as in a doctor-patient relationship, mere silence constitutes fraudulent concealment. Therefore, the court reversed the trial court's judgment and remanded the case to the trial court with instructions to reinstate it on its trial calendar.

F. [§3.51] Sample Complaint

A pleading initiating a cause of action for wrongful conception or wrongful pregnancy [as to a definition of wrongful conception and wrongful pregnancy, see §3.8] will depend on the facts of the particular case. Nonetheless, the following sample complaint can be referred to when initiating a wrongful conception or wrongful pregnancy action. In this complaint the plaintiffs, husband and wife, allege that they suffered an injury, consisting of the birth of an unplanned child, following the negligent performance of a vasectomy on the plaintiff-husband. The complaint states:

COMPLAINT

Plaintiff [husband] for his complaint against the defendants and each of them states and alleges:

COUNT 1

I

That at all times material hereto, plaintiff [husband] and [wife] were and still are husband and wife.

II

That at all times herein mentioned, defendants were, and still are physicians duly licensed to practice their profession in the State of [________________] and are engaged in their practice in the medical profession, as a partnership.

III

That on or about [date of operation] the [husband] employed [______________________] clinic as physicians to treat the plaintiff professionally for the purpose of performing a vasectomy, so as to accomplish a sterilization that would permanently prevent procreation of a fetus, for which plaintiff [husband] agreed to pay a reasonable sum for said service.

IV

That on [date of operation] at [______________________] clinic, located in [___________________] the defendant [defendant-physician's name] undertook as a physician to perform the vasectomy, so as to accomplish the act of sterilization on plaintiff [husband.]

V

That said [defendant-physician] failed to use reasonable care or skill of a physician in that the surgical procedure was not completely performed and sterilization was not accomplished which resulted in a subsequent conception of a child through sexual intercourse, with plaintiff's wife becoming aware of her pregnancy on or about [date of discovery of pregnancy] at which time plaintiff discovered the negligent actions and conduct of [defendant-physician] which pregnancy resulted in the birth of a baby on [date of birth.]

VI

That by reason of aforesaid, plaintiff-husband has incurred hospital-medical expenses for the birth of said child and sterilization of his wife in the sum of [__________] and the birth of the child will require of plaintiff additional costs to properly care for and raise the said child to the age of maturity; that said cost is estimated to be in the sum of [__________] Dollars over such period of time which constitutes additional special damages to this plaintiff.

VII

That as a further result, plaintiff suffered great pain, anxiety, and loss of sensation from the ineffective surgical procedure performed on him, loss of the consortium and society of his wife, suffered the anxiety of the childbirth and has parental responsibility to raise said child all to his general damage in the sum of [__________] Dollars.

COUNT 2

I

Plaintiff realleges the allegations contained in paragraphs I, II, III, IV and VII of Count 1 and incorporates them herein by reference.

II

That at all times herein mentioned, said defendants and each of them were negligent in failing to inform plaintiff that said surgical procedure and sterilization was not absolute in nature and that a possibility did exist that he could impregnate; that in relying upon defendants' [name of physicians] representations that said operation was not foolproof, plaintiff failed to use protective devices or methods that would have avoided conception of his [number of children] child which was born on [date of child's birth]; that all of said conduct has resulted in damage and injury to this plaintiff as herein set forth.

COUNT 3

I

Plaintiff realleges the allegations contained in paragraphs I, II, III, IV and VII of Count 1 and incorporates them herein by reference.

II

That at all times herein mentioned, said defendants and each of them were negligent in their post-operative care and instruction to plaintiff and they were further negligent on information and belief, on imparting to plaintiff proper information concerning laboratory test of plaintiff's sperm sample or negligent in the analysis of said sample; that all of said conduct has resulted in damage and injury to this plaintiff as herein set forth:

Plaintiff [wife] for her complaint against the defendants and each of them states and alleges:

COUNT 1

I

Realleges paragraphs I, II, III and V of Count 1 and Paragraph II of Count 2 of the complaint of [husband] and incorporates them herein by reference.

II

That plaintiff herein advised defendants that she and her husband had mutually agreed that they could not financially, emotionally or physically afford any more than their seven minor children who comprised their family as of [date of husband's vasectomy.]

III

That following said surgical procedure for sterilization as aforementioned on her husband, plaintiff and her husband resumed sexual relations which resulted in plaintiff becoming pregnant and giving birth to a baby on [date of child's birth] and thereafter, plaintiff also underwent a sterilization type surgery to prevent future conception.

IV

That as a result of defendants' conduct as aforementioned plaintiff endured the anxiety and apprehension of carrying and the delivery of a child, suffered the apprehension and anxiety of undergoing a surgical procedure for sterilization and plaintiff will have continued responsibility of nurturing, guiding, counseling, and educating said child until the child attains majority or is emancipated all to plaintiff's general damage.

Wherefore plaintiff [husband] prays for judgment against the defendants and each of them in the sum of [__________] Dollars.

Wherefore plaintiff [wife] prays for judgment against the defendants and each of them in the sum of [__________] Dollars all together with their costs and disbursements herein.

[Name of Attorneys]

[Date]

CHAPTER 4

Conception Stage

I. ARTIFICIAL INSEMINATION

I. ARTIFICIAL INSEMINATION

A. In General

1. [§4.1] Definition; Overview

Artificial insemination is the instrumental injection of semen into the vagina or uterus to induce pregnancy. It fulfills the insemination process without coitus. Blakiston, GOULD MEDICAL DICTIONARY (McGraw-Hill 4th ed 1979). The procedure of artificial insemination provides a method for a couple who otherwise would be unable to conceive a child because of the husband's infertility or sterility to have a child biologically related to the wife. By contrast where the sterility or infertility problem afflicts the wife, the couple may choose to use a "surrogate mother" to carry the husband's child. [As to surrogate motherhood generally, see §4.25.]

Three types of artificial insemination exist with each being distinguished by the identity of the semen donor. The types are: AIH, homologous insemination, in which semen from the husband is used for insemination;

AIC, in which the semen of a donor and the husband are "confused or combined"; and AID, heterologous insemination, which is artificial insemination usually by an unknown donor. AIH is used in a variety of situations, including where there are physical difficulties suffered by either husband or wife. In these instances, intercourse is sometimes prevented by physical problems. In addition, at times psychological problems exist which render insemination by intercourse useless. When AIC is used, the semen of the husband and a donor is combined and then used for insemination. Most often physiological or psychological reasons are the basis for using AIC. Sometimes the husband suffers from oligozoospermia, poor sperm motility, and thus has a lower than average fertility count. By using this type of insemination, the husband, although not certain that the child is his, is at least comforted in knowing that there is a chance the child might be his. Although AIH and AIC are sometimes used, this division focuses on AID. In instances of AID, semen from someone other than the woman's husband is used for insemination. At times this is necessary because the husband suffers from a condition known as azoospermia, or the absence of all sperm cells. AID is also an alternative where there is concern of possible transmission of genetic defects such as Tay-Sach disorder, sickle cell anemia, hemophilia, or Huntington's chorea to the offspring. Also, AID is used when Rh blood factors are incompatible between the parents or where the woman to be inseminated is single. The success rate of AID is reported to be about 80 per cent. The artificial insemination process is a relatively easy medical procedure. A syringe is inserted into the vagina of the woman and semen is injected toward the opening of the uterus. The procedure is so simple that women have inseminated themselves without professional assistance. At least one news story has suggested that home self-insemination kits may some day be available as over-the-counter products. See generally Shaman, LEGAL ASPECTS OF ARTIFICIAL INSEMINATION, 18 Journal of Family Law 331 (1979-1980); Smith, FOR UNTO US A CHILD IS BORN -LEGALLY, 56 ABAJ 143 (1970); Blakiston, GOULD MEDICAL DICTIONARY, (McGraw-Hill 4th ed 1979); ARTIFICIAL INSEMINATION AND SURROGATE MOTHERHOOD: A NURSERY FULL OF UNRESOLVED QUESTIONS, 17 Willamette LR 913 (1981).

The procedure of artificial insemination has not always been viewed in favorable terms by courts. Some early cases held that artificial insemination was tantamount to adultery [see, e.g., *Doornbos v Doornbos*, 23 USLW 2308 (1954)] and that the child was illegitimate [see, e.g., *Gursky v Gursky*, 39 Misc2d 1083, 242 NYS2d 406 (1963)]. Now, however, there are both statutes [see, e.g., CAL CIV CODE §7005 (West 1980)] and cases [see, e.g., *People v Sorensen*, 66 CaR 7, 437 P2d 495 (1968)] that provide authority for the proposition that the performance of artificial insemination is neither adulterous nor results in the birth of an illegitimate child. [As to the background of artificial insemination see, §4.2.]

The artificial insemination by donor procedure typically involves a number of parties. These parties include the woman to be inseminated (in most instances she is married, but not always), her husband if she is married, the male semen donor and the resulting child who has been conceived by artificial insemination. Because of the diverse interests of these parties, the issues arising from the rights and obligations of the respective parties is of primary interest in situations involving artificial insemination by donor. [As to the rights and obligations of the particular parties, see §§4.3–4.9.] For example, pursuant to many artificial insemination statutes, a married woman must obtain her spouse's consent to the procedure. In most instances both the wife and her husband must request and consent to the performance of artificial insemination by a donor. See, e.g., CAL CIV CODE §7005 (West 1980); N Y DOM REL LAW §73 (McKinney 1977). [As to the requirement of spousal consent, see §4.3.] To fulfill the consent requirement in artificial insemination by donor various forms have been drafted. The forms typically describe the artificial insemination by donor procedure, and in some cases have a provision in which the wife and husband stipulate to counseling on potential side effects of artificial insemination. [As to artificial insemination by donor forms, see §4.4.] The issue of the husband's, as contrasted to the semen donor's, rights and obligations has also received judicial and legislative consideration. Generally, the issues arising in this context relate to the husband's duty to support the child who is conceived not by the husband's semen, but by the semen of a donor. In the typical situation, courts have held that the fact that a child is conceived by artificial insemination rather than the husband's semen does not vitiate the husband's responsibility to support the child. See e.g., *People v Sorensen*, 68 CaA2d 280, 66 CaR 7, 437 P2d 495 (1968). In addition, most statutes relating to artificial insemination appear to provide that the husband is responsible for support of the child if the husband has validly consented to the performance of artificial insemination by donor. These statutes include VA CODE §64.1-7.1 (1974), which provides that any child born to a married woman, which was conceived by artificial insemination performed at the request of and with the consent of the woman and her husband, shall be presumed, for all purposes, the legitimate child of the woman and her husband the same as a natural child not conceived by means of artificial insemination. [As to the husband's rights and obligations in artificial insemination by donor situations, see §4.5.] The rights and obligations of the semen donor have also received attention. Many statutes have sought to define these rights and obligations because biologically the semen donor is the father of the child conceived by artificial insemination, rather than the woman's husband. Therefore, artificial insemination statutes have generally stated that the artificial insemination semen donor is not the offspring's legal father. A typical example of this statute is CONN GEN STAT §45-69 which provides that a donor of sperm used in artificial insemination by donor shall not have any right or interest in any child born as the result of artificial insemination. To make sure the parties understand the donor's rights and obligations, a number of forms have been developed to clarify this issue. [As to the rights and obligations of a semen donor generally, and forms to define these rights and obligations, see §4.6 and §4.7.] In some cases the woman seeking to be inseminated may not be married, but instead may be single. Therefore, the issue of a single woman's rights and obligations regarding the artificial insemination procedure has been raised. For example, only one statute appears to place married and unmarried women on the same footing regarding who may perform artificial insemination and under what circumstances. See OR REV STAT §677.365 (1977). Moreover, one commentator has raised the question whether the right of a single woman to bear a child by artificial insemination is constitutionally protected, and that commentator has concluded that it is. See Kritchevsky, THE UNMARRIED WOMAN'S RIGHT TO ARTIFICIAL INSEMINATION: A CALL FOR AN EXPANDED DEFINITION OF FAMILY, 4 Harvard Women's LJ 1 (1981). [As to the rights and obligations of unmarried females undergoing artificial insemination, see §4.8.] Finally, the status of the child conceived by artificial insemination has received judicial and legislative attention. It is now held that such a child is legitimate [see *In re Adoption of Anonymous*, 74 Misc2d 99, 345 NYS2d 430 (1973)], and there are statutes which provide that a child conceived by means of artificial insemination is the legitimate child of the woman and her husband if both requested and consented to the procedure. See, e.g., FLA STAT ANN §742.11 (1981); MICH COMP LAWS ANN §700.111 (1980). [As to the status and legitimacy of a child conceived by artificial insemination by donor, see §4.9.]

There are also important medical considerations involved prior to and in the performance of the artificial insemination by donor procedure. [Generally, see §4.10.] For example, the issue has been raised regarding who may perform artificial insemination. Artificial insemination statutes usually provide that only licensed physicians, or persons under their control, may perform artificial insemination. See, e.g., GA CODE ANN §74-101.1 (1973); OR REV STAT §677.360 (1977). [As to who may perform artificial insemination, see §4.11.] The issue of donor selection, use, and confidentiality has received attention. One statute provides that only licensed physicians can select semen donors. See OR REV STAT §677.360 (1977). Moreover, a recent medical study has suggested that there exists the possibility that screening of artificial semen donors for genetic diseases is not thorough enough. See Curie-Cohen, Luttrell, Shapiro, CURRENT PRACTICE OF ARTIFICIAL INSEMINATION BY DONOR IN THE UNITED STATES, 300 New England Journal of Medicine 585 (1979). [As to semen donor selection, use and confidentiality, see §4.12.] Medical forms that have been developed to assist physicians in terms of the semen donor appear at §4.13.

Another medical consideration, the selection and management of recipients, has been researched and considered by the American Fertility Society. The Society is composed of members who are engaged in the research and therapy of involuntary infertility. The Society's guidelines regarding the selection and management of recipients are located at §4.14. Moreover, the Society has established suggested procedures for the medical technique of semen cyropreservation. These procedures are located at §4.15. Finally, issues have been raised regarding the possibility of artificial insemination and malpractice. It has been suggested that when these cases arise, the courts will treat the cases similar to blood transfusion cases. See Shaman, LEGAL ASPECTS OF ARTIFICIAL INSEMINATION, 18 Journal of Family Law 331 (1979-1980). [As to malpractice and artificial insemination, see §4.16.]

There have been various legislative approaches to the issues posed by artificial insemination. About one-half of the states now have statutes dealing with artificial insemination. See, e.g., CAL CIV CODE §7005 (West Supp 1980); MD EST & TRUSTS CO DC ANN §1-206(b) (1974). [As to a statutory survey, see §4.17.] Some of the statutes have been modeled after the Uniform Parentage Act's sections which deal with artificial insemination. See, e.g., COLO REV STAT §19-6-106 (1978); WASH REV CODE ANN §26.26.050 (Supp 1980-1981). [As to the model United Parentage Act, see §4.18.] Moreover, The American Fertility Society has drafted model legislation that provides suggestions for sections dealing with the definition of artificial insemination, who are qualified practitioners, and the status of the resulting child. [As to The American Fertility Society's model artificial insemination legislation, see §4.19.]

2. [§4.2] Background

Human artificial insemination [as to the definition and overview of artificial insemination, see §4.1] is not a modern day phenomenon, but rather was first successfully accomplished about 1790. However, the first recorded successful use of artificial insemination in the United States was in 1866. See Shaman, LEGAL ASPECTS OF ARTIFICIAL INSEMINATION, 18 Journal of Family Law 331 (1980). By the early part of the twentieth century artificial insemination was generally accepted in the medical profession as a means to relieve the inability or inadvisability of conception by other means. Only recently, however, has this alternative to childlessness become generally socially acceptable. See COMMENT, ARTIFICIAL INSEMINATION AND SURROGATE MOTHERHOOD - A NURSERY FULL OF UNRESOLVED QUESTIONS, 17 Willamette LR 913 (1981). In the early cases involving artificial insemination by donor (AID), a number of courts held that the performance of the procedure, with or without the husband's consent, was tantamount to adultery. For example, a 1921 Canadian case decided by the Ontario

Supreme Court reasoned that "the essence of the offense of adultery consists, not in the moral turpitude of the act of sexual intercourse, but in the voluntary surrender to another person of the reproductive powers or faculties . . .", and therefore concluded that AID was adulterous. See *Orford v Orford*, 58 D.L.R. 251 (1921). Subsequently, an American court in Illinois held that AID was adulterous. In *Doornbos v Doornbos*, 23 USLW 2308 (1954), the plaintiff-wife, in a divorce action, sought a declaratory judgment that a minor child was not the child of her husband, but rather had been conceived by artificial insemination. Moreover, she asserted that because the child had never been adopted by her husband, the husband had no legal right to the child. A judgment entered by the lower court held that the child was illegitimate, and the appellate court dismissed the appeal. And, in *Gursky v Gursky*, 39 Misc2d 1083, 242 NYS2d 406 (1963), there was testimony adduced at a husband's action for annulment and separation that the parties agreed that the defendant-wife would be artificially inseminated with the semen of a third-party donor. The plaintiff and defendant both signed the consent to have her artificially inseminated. The plaintiff, in addition, promised to pay all the expenses involved to have the procedure performed. A contract was signed by the plaintiff for a waiver of liability and for medical and/or surgical treatments. As a result of the artificial insemination a child was born. It was noted at the trial that the birth certificate listed the defendant as the mother and the plaintiff as the father. Therefore, the court said it was confronted with the problem of determining whether a child conceived by means of artificial insemination of a married woman through the use, with the husband's consent, of semen contributed by a donor other than the husband is legitimate. After reviewing New York statutes dealing with illegitimate children, the court concluded that the child, which was indisputably the offspring of artificial insemination by a third-party donor with the consent of the mother's husband, was not the legitimate issue of the husband. However, a different result, predicated primarily on the ground that there is a strong public policy in favor of legitimacy, was reached in *People v Sorensen*, 66 CaR 7, 437 P2d 495 (1968). In this case the court said that in the absence of legislation prohibiting artificial insemination, the off-spring of the defendant's valid marriage to the child's mother was lawfully begotten and was not the product of an illicit or an adulterous relationship. Moreover, the court noted that adultery is defined as the voluntary sexual intercourse of a married person with a person other than the offender's husband or wife. The court noted that it had been suggested that the doctor and the wife committed adultery by the process of artificial insemination. However, the court said that since the doctor may be a woman, or the husband himself may administer the insemination by a syringe, this theory is patently absurd. To consider it an act of adultery with the donor, who at the time of insemination may be a thousand miles away or even be dead, is equally absurd, the court said. One legal commentator has concluded that it is doubtful that any American court today would hold that AID constitutes adultery. See Shaman, LEGAL ASPECTS OF ARTIFICIAL INSEMINATION, 18 Journal of Family Law 331 (1979-1980).

Artificial insemination has developed because of the numerous obstacles in a marriage that may prevent the parents from conceiving and bearing a child. For example, there may be prolems of sterility, impotence, physiological (genital) impediments, the desire to avoid transmission of inheritable characteristics, and the danger of improperly matched Rh blood factors. Moreover, the other alternatives to childlessness may not be acceptable to the couple. Forced childlessness would necessitate the couple accepting the fact that they cannot conceive or bear children. Another alternative is extramarital conception, but societal pressures tend to discourage this alternative. A third alternative is adoption. This alternative is socially acceptable, but may not satisfy the wife's desire to bear a child biologically related to her. See Smith, THROUGH A TEST TUBE DARKLY: ARTIFICIAL INSEMINATION AND THE LAW, 67 Michigan LR 127 (1968). A fourth alternative, the use of a surrogate mother [generally, see §4.25] is typically used where the female, as contrasted to the male, is sterile or infertile.

The number of births associated with conception brought about by artificial insemination has been estimated to be 1,000-1,200 per year during this century. Smith, *above*. However, another commentator has estimated that the number of artificial insemination births each year is as high as 20,000. Shaman, *above*. And another commentator has suggested that at least 250,000 Americans have been conceived by artificial insemination. Black, LEGAL PROBLEMS OF SURROGATE MOTHERHOOD, 16 New England LR 373 (1981).

B. Rights and Obligations of Particular Parties

1. Relations Between Husband and Wife

a. [§4.3] Spousal Consent

One of the issues relating to the performance of artificial insemination by donor (AID) [generally, see §4.1] on a married woman is whether spousal consent of the husband is necessary. Many of the artificial insemination statutes [as to a survey of state artificial insemination statutes, see §4.17] have provisions dealing with spousal consent. Typically, before the artificial insemination procedure is performed, both the husband and wife must request and consent to the performance of artificial insemination. The request and consent must be in writing and signed by both husband and wife. See, e.g., ALASKA STAT §20.-20.010 (1975); CAL CIV CODE §7005 (West 1980); COLO REV STAT, 19-6-106 (1977); CONN GEN STAT §45-69g(b); FLA

STAT ANN §742.11 (West 1973); KAN STAT ANN §23-128 (1981); MONT REV CODES ANN §40-6-106 (1975); NY DOM REL LAW §73 (McKinney 1977); NC GEN STAT §49a-1 (1976); OKLA STAT tit. 10 §552 (1974); TEX FAM CODE ANN tit. 12 §12.03 (Vernon 1977); VA CODE §64.1-7.1 (1977); WASH REV CODE §26.26.050 (1981); WIS STAT §891.40 (1979-1980); WYO STAT §14-2-103(a) (1978). [As to example consent forms for artificial insemination, see §4.4.] The consent of the husband to the artificial insemination of his wife may be presumed. See MD EST & TRUSTS ANN §1-206(b) (1974). In some instances this spousal consent is to be kept part of the medical records. See, e.g., CAL CIV CODE §7005 (West 1980). In addition, it may be necessary to file the original consent document under the same rules as adoption papers in the district court of the county where the husband and wife reside, [see, e.g., KAN STAT ANN §23-128 (1981)], or to file the husband's consent with the registrar of vital statistics [see, e.g., WASH REV CODE §26.26.050 (1981)]. Where the woman seeking to be artificially inseminated is not married, in some states she must nonetheless submit her request and consent before the operation is performed. See, e.g., OR REV STAT §677.365(1). Spousal consent, in some states, is necessary for the child, conceived by the artificial process, to be considered legitimate. For example, NC GEN STAT §49a-1 (1976), provides that for a child conceived through the process of artificial insemination to be legitimate, the husband and wife must request and consent in writing to the procedure. And TENN CODE ANN §53-446 (1981) states that a child born to a married woman as a result of artificial insemination, with the consent of the woman's husband, shall be deemed legitimate. [Generally, see §4.9.] Consent of the husband may be necessary for the child to be considered as the child of the husband and wife for purposes of intestate succession. See MICH COMP LAWS ANN §700.111 (1980).

A tangential issue in terms of spousal consent to AID procedures is whether consent to AID, once given, continues until pregnancy is accomplished. In *K S v G S*, 182 NJ Super 102, 440 A2d 64 (1981), it was held that consent of the husband, once given, is presumed to be effective at the time when pregnancy occurs, unless the husband establishes by clear and convincing evidence that such consent has been revoked or rescinded. The matter was before the court on the plaintiff-wife's motion for pendente lite support and custody of the infant child, who was born during the course of the plaintiff's marriage to the defendant but was conceived by AID. Several months after their marriage the plaintiff learned of the AID procedure. The defendant stipulated that he gave his verbal consent to the procedure at that time. However, written consent was not obtained from the defendant. A donor was selected and a series of three artificial insemination procedures took place in July 1978. The initial insemination process was successful and the plaintiff was tested positive for pregnancy on August 19, 1978.

However, that pregnancy did not result in a live birth because a spontaneous miscarriage took place in early September 1978. The defendant, after the miscarriage, expressed feelings of sympathy and urged the plaintiff to continue the procedures when she was able to do so. Although the defendant testified to the contrary, the court found that he expressed no reservations to continuing the AID procedures for any reason at that time. During 1978 the parties had several discussions concerning the continuing costs of the AID procedures. The defendant contended he told the plaintiff to stop the AID treatments because of the cost. However, the court said this testimony was not credible and was inconsistent with the plaintiff's convincing testimony that the defendant accompanied the plaintiff to the expert's office for the insemination procedure on several occasions in 1979, including at least one occasion in October 1979. The defendant also admitted, the court noted, he never advised the expert at any time that he had any reservations concerning continuing the AID procedure. Beginning in November 1978, the plaintiff continued with the AID procedures at the rate of approximately three inseminations during her fertile cycles. In October 1979, she became pregnant with the child who was later born. On December 30, 1979, the defendant left the marital premises. In a telephone conversation between the parties shortly after that date the defendant advised the plaintiff he objected to her pregnancy. On October 7, 1980, the plaintiff filed a complaint for divorce seeking support for the child. The court noted that in the absence of a husband's consent to artificial insemination, support obligations may not be imposed upon him. Moreover, the court said that, in the case at bar, the initial consent of the husband was clearly established. The defendant contended he withdrew his consent to the AID procedure prior to conception by informing the plaintiff of his opposition to continuing the inseminations. He further contended that the plaintiff then went ahead with AID procedures surreptitiously, without his knowledge or approval, and in the face of his opposition. The court noted that when the plaintiff finally conceived, it was approximately 15 months after the defendant's initial consent. The court said AID induced pregnancy is equated with naturally induced pregnancy occurring during the course of a marriage for purposes of analysis of questions concerning traditional issues of legitimacy and parental obligations. In legitimacy or paternity cases where pregnancy has been naturally induced, the central issue is often an evidentiary question of access or non-access of the putative father at the time of conception. The court recognized that, from the point of view of the partners involved in artificial insemination, there is a physical and pyschological difference in the manner the pregnancy will be perceived. From the point of view of the female partner, although the child is conceived artificially, from all other aspects it is a natural child, carried to term exactly as if conception had taken place by natural means. For the male partner, the court said, it is quite possible that his perception of the pregnancy will be substantially different. He is not the natural father, as the mother is the natural parent, and must be well aware of that fact. He may experience feelings of inadequacy, resentment, or other negative attitudes toward the pregnancy, as illustrated by the case at bar. Thus, from the male point of view the pregnancy and resulting child is, in many ways, similar to an adoption of the resulting child. The court said public policy considerations seeking to prevent children born as a result of AID procedures from becoming public charges or being bastardized require that a presumption of consent exist and that a strong burden be placed on one seeking to rebut the presumption. The same policy considerations are present whether the question presented is one of initial or continued consent. The absence of any authority limiting the continuing effectiveness of consent also led the court to the conclusion that consent of the husband, in the case of married partners, once given, is presumed to be effective at the time when pregnancy occurs, unless the husband establishes by clear and convincing evidence that such consent has been revoked or rescinded. In this case, the court held that the defendant did not meet that burden.

b. [§4.4] Artificial Insemination Consent Forms

Prior to the performance of artificial insemination by donor [generally, see §4.1] it is advisable for the husband and wife to sign a written document agreeing and consenting to the performance of artificial insemination. The agreement form essentially indicates the parties' understanding of the procedure, and establishes their legal consent to have the procedure performed. [As to spousal consent, see §4.3.] The following forms are examples of how such documents might be drafted, and what items would be included:

AGREEMENT OF UNDERSTANDING

Husband and wife, each of whom desire the wife to be artificially inseminated for the purpose of conceiving a child to be treated in all respects as the natural child of husband and wife, freely and knowingly agree to the terms of this agreement and understand that they are bound by it.

Husband and wife agree and consent that the physician, with the assistance of sperm bank personnel, will obtain the necessary sperm from a donor who shall not be advised of the identity of either husband and wife, nor shall the husband and wife ever be advised of the identity of the donor. The husband and wife shall rely upon the judgment and the discretion of sperm bank personnel to select a donor whose physical and mental characteristics appear compatible with those of husband and wife. It is also agreed that on occasion, donor sperm that have been frozen for purposes of storage may be used.

Husband and wife hereby take cognizance of the fact that within the normal human population a certain percentage of children with physical or mental defects are born. Despite screening of donors for genetic disorders, there is no reason to assume that the incidence of congenital anomalies would be different from that in the general population, and the sperm bank cannot and will not be held responsible for the physical and mental characteristics of any child born as a result of artificial insemination. The husband and wife also take cognizance of the fact that although donors are screened for sexually transmitted disease, there is no way of completely protecting the recipient. The husband and wife, therefore, agree not to take any legal action whatsoever against sperm bank personnel in the event of a physically or mentally deficient child or in the event of the appearance of a sexually transmitted disease.

It is further understood and agreed that the nature of this agreement is such that it must remain confidential. There is no benefit and considerable risk to informing relatives, friends, ministers, and the off-spring of the procedure, and other physicians involved in the care of the recipients need not be informed of the procedure. Therefore, the husband and wife agree that the sole copy of this document will be given to (name of responsible medical doctor or department) and kept in (his, her, departmental) confidential files.

Wife____________________________

Husband __________________________

Physician _________________________

Date____________________________

[Reprinted with the permission of The American Fertility Society.]

AGREEMENT FOR ARTIFICIAL INSEMINATION

We, ____________ and ____________ , being husband and wife and both over the age of 21 years, do hereby request and authorize Dr. ________________________ [treating physician] to inseminate artificially ______________________ [wife], and to use the semen of ________________ [the husband *or* the husband and a donor *or* a donor or donors] for this purpose. We authorize him to employ such assistants as may be necessary for the purpose of accomplishing the artificial insemination.

We represent that we were married at __________________, on ____________________, 19____, and that we have cohabited together as man and wife since that date. We are extremely anxious to have a child and we believe that this artificial insemination will promote our mutual happiness and well-being.

We understand that several attempts at artificial insemination may be necessary and that Dr. ____________________ does not warrant or guarantee that pregnancy or full term pregnancy will result from the artificial insemination.

To induce Dr. ________________ to render the services herein requested, we, and each of us agree that:

1. Under no circumstances shall we require that the name of the donor of the semen be divulged to us or anyone else, and we accordingly forever waive all rights, if any, that we may have as to the name, identity, or any information of any kind concerning the donor. We shall rely on the discretion of Dr. ____________ in the selection of qualified donors.

2. We release Dr. ______________________ from any and all liability and responsibility of any nature whatsoever which may result from complications of childbirth or delivery or from the birth of an infant or infants abnormal in any respect, or from the heredity or hereditary tendencies of such issue, or from any other adverse consequences which may arise in connection with or as a result of the artificial insemination herein authorized.

3. We shall refrain from bringing legal action of any kind, and refrain from aiding or abetting anyone else in bringing legal action for or on account of any matter or thing which might arise out of the artificial insemination herein contemplated.

4. We shall indemnify Dr. __________ for any attorneys' fees, court costs, damages, judgments, or any other losses or expenses incurred by him or for which he may be responsible with respect to any claim, legal action, or defense thereto, arising out of the artificial insemination herein contemplated ________________ [*if appropriate, add:* including any claim of or legal action brought by the child or children resulting from the artificial insemination].

Dated________________, 19_____.

[*Signatures of husband and wife*]

[*Attestation*]

[Reprinted with the permission of The American Medical Association.]

CONSENT TO ARTIFICIAL INSEMINATION

Date: _____________, 19_____, Time: _______ o'clock _____m.

We, _____________ and ____________, being husband and wife and both of legal age, authorize Dr. ___________________________ [treating physician] and such assistants as he may designate to inseminate ____________________ [wife] artificially, and to use the semen of ____________________ [the husband *or* the husband and a donor or donors *or* a donor or donors] for this purpose. We authorize Dr. _______________ to employ such assistants he may desire to assist him.

We understand that even though the insemination may be repeated as often as recommended by Dr. _________, there is no guarantee on his part or assurance that pregnancy or full term pregnancy will result.

We agree to rely upon the sole discretion of Dr. ____________ in the selection of qualified donors and never to seek to discover the identity of any donor. We agree that following the insemination, Dr. ___________________ may destroy all records and information concerning the identity of the donor or donors.

We, and each of us, acknowledge our obligation to care for and support and otherwise treat any child as the result of such artificial insemination in all respects as though it were our natural born child.

We understand that if pregnancy shall result, there is a possibility of complications of childbirth or delivery, or the birth of an abnormal infant or infants, or undesirable hereditary tendencies of such issue, or other adverse consequences.

[*Signatures*]

[*Attestation*]

[Reprinted with the permission of The American Medical Association.]

CONSENT TO ARTIFICIAL INSEMINATION WITH PROVISION FOR STIPULATION REGARDING COUNSELING ON POTENTIAL SIDE EFFECTS AND RELEASE OF PHYSICIAN AND DONOR FROM RESULTING LIABILITY

_____________ and _____________, husband and wife herein, hereby stipulate that Dr. ___________________________ [treating physician] who will perform artificial insemination by donor (AID) procedures on ______________________ [wife], has advised them in the presence of each other that the artificial insemination process may result, despite all precautions in donor selection, in the birth of an abnormal child or children. Husband and wife further stipulate that Dr. ________________ has advised them in the presence of each other as to the potential psychological implications that the birth of a child through the artificial insemination donor (AID) procedure may have on both their marital relationship and the child or children.

Husband and wife specifically release Dr. ______________ and the donor or donors whose semen is finally selected for the artificial insemination of ______________ [wife] from any and all liability and responsibility of any nature whatsoever that may result from the birth of an infant or infants abnormal in any respect, and further specifically release Dr. ______________ and the donor or donors whose semen is finally selected for the artificial insemination of ______________________________ [wife] from any and all liability and responsibility whatsoever for any psychological consequences that the procedure may have on the marital relationship of ________________ [husband] and ________________ [wife]. Such specific releases are not intended in any way to diminish the further releases, general and specific, given by husband and wife in this instrument.

[*Signatures of husband and wife*]

[*Attestation*]

[Reprinted with the permission of The American Medical Association.]

c. [§4.5] Husband's Rights and Obligations

In the context of artificial insemination [generally, see §4.1] there may arise questions about the husband's, as contrasted to the donor's [generally, see §4.6], rights and obligations in terms of the resulting child. The types of questions that have arisen have centered primarily on the husband's duty to provide child support to the child following the husband's separation or divorce from the child's mother, and the husband's visitation rights to the child after separation or divorce.

In the typical child support situation, the courts have held that the fact that the child is conceived by means of artificial insemination does not void a husband's responsibility to provide support for that child provided that the husband's consent [generally, see §4.3] was obtained before the procedure was performed. For example, in *People v Sorenson*, 68 CaA2d 280, 66 CaR 7, 437 P2d 495 (1968), a sterile husband and his wife consented to her artificial insemination, which resulted in the birth of a child. For the following four years they lived together in a normal family relationship. When the husband and wife were divorced, the wife stated that she wanted no child support from her husband. However, under the divorce decree the court retained jurisdiction regarding the possible support obligation of plaintiff in regard to a minor child born to defendant. Later, when the wife became ill and unable to work, she applied for public assistance, which was given to her until she was able to resume work. Although the district attorney demanded child support, her former husband did not support the child. A municipal court found him to be in violation of the state's penal code and placed him on probation on condition that he make certain monthly payments for support. In reaching a decision, the court noted that the determinative factor was whether the relationship of father and child existed. It stated that a child conceived through heterologous artificial insemination does not have a natural father, as that term is commonly used. The anonymous donor of the sperm cannot be considered the natural father, because he is no more responsible for the use made of his sperm than is the donor of blood or a kidney. With the use of frozen semen, the donor may even be dead at the time the semen is used. Moreover, the court stated that one who actively participated and consented to his wife's artificial insemination knew the legal responsibility of fatherhood and criminal responsibility for nonsupport. One who consents to the production of a child cannot create a temporary relation to be assumed and disclaimed at will, but the arrangement must be of such character as to impose an obligation of supporting those for whose existence he is directly responsible. Moreover, the court said that it was safe to assume that without the defendant's active participation and consent, the child would not have been procreated. Therefore, the court noted that it was sufficient to find that the husband was the lawful father of the child to establish the responsibility to support, and that the husband was the lawful father. And in *Gursky v Gursky*, 39 Misc2d 1083, 242 NYS2d 406 (1963), the plaintiff-husband brought an action for annulment, and alleged that there was no issue of the marriage. Testimony adduced at the trial revealed that the parties agreed that the defendant-wife would be artificially inseminated with the semen of a third-party donor. The plaintiff and defendant both signed the consent to have her artificially inseminated. The plaintiff, in addition, promised to pay all expenses involved to perform the procedure. A contract was signed by the plaintiff for a waiver of liability and for medical and/or surgical treatments. As a result of the artificial insemination a child was born. The court concluded that the child, which was indisputably the offspring of artificial insemination by a third-party donor with the consent of the mother's husband, was not the legitimate issue of the husband. However, the court said it did not follow that the husband was thereby free of obligation to furnish support for the child. The husband's declarations and conduct respecting the artificial insemination of this wife by means of a third-party donor, including the husband's written consent to the procedure, implied a promise on his part to furnish support for any offspring resulting from the insemination. This, in the light of the wife's concurrence and submission to artificial insemination, was found by the court to be sufficient to constitute an implied contract. Moreover, the court held that a reading of the document of consent signed by the husband clearly revealed that it constituted more than a mere acquiescence in, or approval of, an agreement to have the procedure of artificial insemination take place. The consent was in its terms a request to the physician to conduct the artificial insemination for the express purpose of providing a child for the mutual happiness of the parties. There was nothing in the record to indicate that the wife would have undergone artificial insemination in the absence of the husband's consent. To relieve the husband of any duty of furnishing support for the child resulting from the artificial insemination of the wife, to which she submitted in reliance of her husband's wishes, would, in the court's view, cause a financial burden on the wife which in equity and conscience should be borne by the husband. The circumstances properly called for the court's invocation and application of the doctrine of equitable estoppel so as to cast upon the husband, as between husband and wife, the primary duty of support for the child here involved. See also *K S v G S*, 182 NJ Super 102, 440 A2d 64 (1980), where the court held the defendant to be the lawful father of a child conceived by artificial insemination, and as such at least partially responsible for the child's support.

Legislation addressing the problem of the paternal duties created by artificial insemination has also apparently conditioned imposition of all such support obligations in a marital context on a husband's valid consent to use of the procedure. For example, VA CODE §64.1-7.1 (1974) states that any child born to a married woman, which is conceived by means of artificial insemination performed at the request of and with the consent in writing of such woman and her husband, shall be presumed, for all purposes, the legitimate natural child of such woman and such husband the same as a natural child not conceived by means of artificial insemination. WASH REV CODE §26.26.050 (1981), states that if, under the supervision of a licensed physician and with the consent of her husband, a wife is inseminated artificially with semen donated by a man not her husband, the husband is treated in law as if he were the natural father of a child thereby conceived. And WIS STAT ANN §891.40 (1979-1980) states that if a woman is artificially inseminated by semen donated by another man, and not her husband, the husband of the mother at the time of conception of the child shall be the natural father of the child conceived. See also CAL CIV CODE §7005 (West 1975); COLO REV STAT §19-6-106 (1977); FLA STAT ANN §742.11 (West 1973); MD EST & TRUSTS CODE ANN §1-206(b) (1975); NY

DOM REL LAW §73 (McKinney 1974); TEX FAM CODE ANN tit. 12, §12.03 (Vernon, 1977).

Moreover, it has been recognized that a father to a child, conceived with the semen of a third party, has visitation rights even though the child biologically is not his offspring. For example, in *Strnad v Strnad*, 190 Misc 786, 78 NYS2d 390 (1948), the court considered a situation where a woman was artificially inseminated by a third-party donor with the consent of her husband. The court held that the husband was entitled to visitation, and also held that the child had been potentially adopted or semi-adopted by the defendant. Moreover, the court said, so far as this defendant was concerned and with particular reference to visitation, he was entitled to the same rights as those acquired by a foster parent who has formally adopted a child, if not the same rights as those to which a natural parent under the circumstances would be entitled. This case arose from a custody proceeding between the husband and wife for visitation rights between the defendant-father and the child, who the court assumed had been conceived by artificial insemination by donor.

In order for a child conceived by artificial insemination to be adopted by a second husband of the child's mother, where the first husband was not the sperm donor, the first husband must have consented to the adoption of the child. In *Adoption of Anonymous*, 74 Misc2d 99, 345 NYS2d 430 (1973), the husband consented to artificial insemination of the wife and was listed as the father on the birth certificate. The couple later separated and were divorced. Both the separation agreement and the divorce decree referred to the child as the "daughter" or "child" of the couple. Support and visitation were awarded and the husband faithfully supported and visited the child. Subsequently, when the wife remarried, her second husband wanted to adopt the child. The proposed adoption was opposed by the first husband. The second husband argued that consent of the first should not be required as he was not the parent of the child. The court noted that New York had a strong policy in favor of legitimacy. In addition, the court held that a child born of consensual artificial insemination by donor during a valid marriage is a legitimate child entitled to the rights and privileges of a naturally conceived child of the same marriage, and that the father of such a child is therefore the parent whose consent is required to the adoption of such child by another. Therefore, the court dismissed the petition for adoption of the child by the wife's second husband.

2. Donor's Rights and Obligations

a. [§4.6] Generally

One type of artificial insemination [generally, see §4.1] uses the sperm of a third-party donor. This process is referred to as artificial insemination by donor (AID). Since the donor is biologically the father of the offspring, and since the donor usually does not desire to be regarded as the offspring's legal father, it has been necessary to statutorily establish the donor's relationship to the offspring. The artificial insemination statutes that have addressed this issue have uniformly stated that the third-party donor is not the offspring's legal father. For example, CAL CIV CODE §7005(b) (West 1980), states that the donor of semen provided for use in artificial insemination of a woman other than the donor's wife is treated in law as if he were not the natural father of the child. And CONN GEN STAT §45-69, states that a donor of sperm used in AID, or any person claiming through him, shall not have any right or interest in any child born as a result of AID. See also TEX FAM CODE tit. 12, §12.03 (1974); WIS STAT §891.40 (1979-1980). However, if the donor and the woman to be artificially inseminated agree in writing that the donor shall be the legal father, then the offspring will be the donor's child. See WASH REV CODE §26.26.050(2) (1981).

In addition, the issue of a sperm donor's visitation rights in terms of a child conceived by the donor's sperm has arisen in case law. In *C M v C C*, 152 NJ Super 160, 377 A2d 821 (1977), C. C. had a child who was conceived through the use of sperm donated by C. M. C.C. testified that she had been discussing with C. M. the possibility of having a child by artificial insemination, inquiring of him whether she should ask one of his friends to supply the sperm. C. M. suggested that he provide it and C. C. agreed to his suggestion. C. M. testified that he and C. C. had been seeing each other for some time and were contemplating marriage. She wanted a child and wanted him to be the father, but did not want to have intercourse with him before their marriage. Therefore, he agreed to provide the sperm. C. C. conceived a child. C. M. testified that until C. C. was about three months pregnant, he assumed he would act toward the child in the same manner as most fathers act toward their children. C. C. denied this, testifying that C. M. was to be only a visitor in her home much the same as any other of her friends. At that point the relationship between C. M. and C. C. ended. Subsequently, C. M. filed an application for visitation rights to the baby. Initially, the juvenile and domestic relations court noted that the natural father is entitled to visitation rights with respect to his illegitimate children in New Jersey. However, the court said the key issue in this case was whether C. M. was the natural father of the child or whether he should be considered not to be such because the sperm used to conceive was transferred to C. C. by other than natural means. The court noted that this was a case of first impression, presenting a unique factual situation with no reported legal precedence directly on point, in New Jersey or any other jurisdiction. The court noted that this case was different from other artificial insemination cases in that there was not a married couple. Moreover, there was no anonymous donor. The issue was whether a man is any less a father because he provides the semen by a method different from that normally used, the court said. The court said it is in a child's best interest to have two parents whenever possible. The court took no position as to the propriety of the use of artificial insemination between unmarried persons, but said it was concerned with the best interests of the child in granting custody or visitation, and for such consideration would not make any distinction between a child conceived naturally or artificially. In this situation, the court noted, a man wanted to take upon himself the responsibility of being a father to a child he was responsible for helping to conceive. The evidence did not support C. C.'s argument that he was unfit, but demonstrated that C. M. attempted to establish a relationship with the child but was thwarted in his attempts by C. C. Moreover, the court said that contrary to C. C.'s argument, C. M. had shown a genuine interest in the child, and was financially capable of contributing to his support. C. C.'s consent and active participation in the procedure leading to conception should place upon him the responsibilities of fatherhood, the court said. Therefore, the court would not deny him the privileges of fatherhood, and granted his motion for the right of visitation.

There are various donor related forms that have been used in the AID process. For example, there are semen donor forms [see §4.7] and statement of understanding forms [see §4.4]. These forms typically explain what the AID process is, under what guidelines the donor is participating, and what obligations the donor has in the donating process.

b. [§4.7] Artificial Insemination Donor Forms

Because artificial insemination by donor [generally, see §4.1] necessarily involves a third-party donor it may be of benefit for the donor to execute a document that sets out the donor's expression of understanding. The document states that the donor understands what his semen will be used for, and consents to participate in the program. The American Fertility Society, a professional organization that researches infertility and its attendant issues, has drafted the following example form for a semen donor:

STATEMENT OF UNDERSTANDING

I understand that the ________[organization]________ collects semen specimens that may at times be used for artificial insemination.

I voluntarily consent to participate in this program by providing semen specimens. I understand that this participation is on a confidential basis; that is, that the recipient will not be informed of my identity and I shall not be informed of the recipient's identity. I also understand that, should I contract any contagious or venereal disease, I must notify the ______________ and decline donating semen until after I have received adequate treatment.

Finally, the nature of this agreement is confidential and the sole copy of this agreement will remain with the office of the ______.

Donor ______________________________

Date________________________________

[Reprinted with the permission of The American Fertility Society.]

3. [§4.8] Unmarried Female Rights and Obligations

One of the results of the development of artificial insemination [generally, see §4.1] has been to create a method by which an unmarried woman may become pregnant without first participating in sexual intercourse. See Kindregan, STATE POWER OVER HUMAN FERTILITY AND INDIVIDUAL LIBERTY, 23 Hastings LJ 1401 (1972). Moreover, it is possible that an unmarried woman may artificially inseminate herself without the assistance of a clinic or physician. See *C M v C C*, 152 NJ Super 160, 377 A2d 821 (1981).

An issue that has arisen in the area of artificial insemination and the unmarried woman is whether the artificial insemination of an unmarried woman is legal. One commentator has suggested that it is legal for an unmarried woman to become pregnant by artificial insemination and for a doctor to provide the service for her. In reaching this conclusion the commentator noted that the right to bear a child, even an illegitimate one, is constitutionally protected. See Kritchevsky, THE UNMARRIED WOMAN'S RIGHT TO ARTIFICIAL INSEMINATION: A CALL FOR AN EXPANDED DEFINITION OF FAMILY, 4 Harvard Women's LJ 1 (1981). Only one state statute appears to address the issue of artificial insemination and the unmarried woman, ORE REV STAT §677.365 (1977), which specifically places married and unmarried women on the same footing regarding who may perform an artificial insemination and under what circumstances. The statute states in part that artificial insemination shall not be performed upon a woman without her prior written consent and, if she is married, the prior written consent of her husband.

The only case concerning artificial insemination and an unmarried woman is *C M v C C*, 152 NJ Super 160, 377 A2d 821 (1977). In this case the court considered an application by C. M. for visitation rights to a child. C. M. had provided the semen that C. C. had used to inseminate herself, but at no time had the two been married. The case developed when C. C. and C. M. discussed the possibility of having a child by artificial insemination. C. M. testified that he and C. C. had been seeing each other for some time and were contemplating marriage. However, C. C. did not want to have intercourse with C. M. before their marriage. Therefore, C. M. agreed to provide the semen. Subsequently, C. C. inseminated herself with C. M.'s semen and became pregnant. Before the child was born, however, C. M. and C. C. broke off their relationship. C. M. testified that until C. C. was about three months pregnant, he had assumed he would act toward the child in the same manner as most fathers act toward their children. C. C. denied this, and testified that C. M. was only to be a visitor in her home, much as any other of her friends. After the child was born, C. M. sought visitation rights to the baby. Initially, the court said that a natural father is entitled to visitation rights with respect to his illegitimate children. The key issue in this case is whether C. M. is the natural father of the child or whether he should be considered not to be such because the semen used to conceive was transferred to C. C. by other than natural means. The court noted that C. C. did not dispute that the semen used to conceive the child was provided by C. M. If the conception had taken place by intercourse, there would be no question that the "donor" would be the father. The issue becomes whether a man is any less a father because he provides the semen by a method different from that normally used, the court said. The courts have consistently shown a policy for favoring the requirement that a child be provided with a father as well as a mother, the court said. In a situation where there is an anonymous donor the courts have required that the person who consents to the use of sperm, not his own, be responsible for fathering the child. In this case, there is a known man who is the donor. There is no husband. If the couple had been married and the husband's sperm was used artificially, he would be considered the father. If a woman conceives a child by intercourse, the donor who is not married to the mother is no less a father than the man who is married to the mother. Likewise, if an umarried woman conceives a child through artificial insemination from semen from a known man, that man cannot be considered to be less a father because he is not married to the woman. The court said it is in a child's best interest to have two parents whenever possible. The court took no position as to the propriety of the use of artificial insemination between unmarried persons, but said it must be concerned with the best interest of the child in the granting of custody or visitation, and for such consideration would not make any distinction between a child conceived naturally or artificially. Therefore, the court would not deny C. M. the privileges of fatherhood, and granted his motion for the right of visitation.

4. [§4.9] Status of Child; Legitimacy

In the early stages of the development of artificial insemination [generally, see §4.1] it was generally held that offspring conceived by artificial insemination, regardless of spousal consent, were illegitimate. For example, in *Gursky v Gursky*, 242 NYS2d 406, 39 Misc2d 1083 (1963), the court held that a child, conceived by artificial insemination involving a third party, was not the legitimate issue of the husband. However, this view was later disputed, and rejected. In *In re Adoption of Anonymous*, 74 Misc 2d 99, 345 NYS2d 430 (1973), the court determined that a child conceived of consentual donor insemination (AID) during a valid marriage is a legitimate child entitled to the rights and privileges of a naturally conceived child of the same marriage. The court reasoned that New York had a strong policy in favor of legitimacy, and that it would seem absurd to hold illegitimate a child born during a valid marriage of parents desiring but unable to conceive a child, and both consenting and agreeing to the impregnation of the mother by a carefully and medically selected anonymous donor. The court noted that there existed moral and religious objections to artificial insemination, but that the policy was stronger against bigamous, incestuous, and adulterous relationships. The court held that, because such objections had not prevented, as a matter of state policy, the legitimation of the children of bigamous, incestuous, and adulterous marriages, it must conclude that New York policy was for the protection of the child, not the parents. It would serve no purpose whatsoever, in the court's view, to stigmatize the AID child, or to compel the parents formally to adopt in order to confer upon the AID child the status and rights of a naturally conceived child.

In addition to cases such as *Adoption of Anonymous*, above, there is also statutory authority that offspring conceived by artificial insemination are legitimate, in relation to the husband of their mother, and enjoy all the rights and privileges of any child conceived through natural means. However, a child conceived through artificial insemination is not considered the legal offspring of the actual semen donor. [Generally, see §4.6.] Most of the statutes that address artificial insemination include provisions legitimatizing a child or children born through means of artificial insemination to a husband and wife who have requested and consented [generally, see §4.3] to the procedure. For example, TENN CODE ANN §53-446 (Michie Supp 1981) states that a child born to a married woman as a result of artificial insemination, with the consent of the husband, shall be deemed to be a legitimate child of the husband and wife. And NY DOM REL LAW §73 (McKinney 1977) says any child born to a married woman by means of artificial insemination performed by a person authorized to practice medicine and with the consent in writing of the woman and her husband shall be deemed the legitimate natural child of the husband and wife for all purposes. See also CAL CIV CODE §7005 (West Supp 1980); FLA STAT ANN §742.11 (1981); GA CODE ANN §74-101.1 (1973); MD EST & TRUSTS CODE ANN §1-206(b) (1974); MICH COMP LAWS ANN §700.11 (1980); NY DOM REL LAW §73 (McKinney 1977); NC GEN STAT §49a-1 (1976); TEX FAM CODE

ANN tit. 12, §12.03 (Vernon 1975); WIS STAT §891.40 (1979-1980). All children born within marriage, or within the usual period of gestation thereafter, who have been conceived by artificial insemination, are irrebuttably presumed legitimate if the husband and wife consented in writing to the use and administration of artificial insemination. See GA CODE ANN §74-101.1 (1973).

C. Medical Considerations

1. [§4.10] Generally

There are a number of medical considerations involved in the performance of artificial insemination [as to artificial insemination in general, see §4.1] by donor procedure. For example, in some states only licensed physicians can perform artificial insemination. See, e.g., OR REV STAT §677.360 (1977); WASH REV CODE §26.26.050 (1981). [As to who may perform artificial inseminations, see §4.11.] In addition, there are in some instances requirements dealing with donor selection, use, and confidentiality. Under OR REV STAT §677.360 (1977), only licensed physicians and persons under their control may select artificial insemination semen donors. And it has been suggested that the genetic screening of semen donors may not be adequate. See Curie-Cohen, Luttrell, Shapiro, CURRENT PRACTICE OF ARTIFICIAL INSEMINATION BY DONOR IN THE UNITED STATES, 300 New England Journal of Medicine 585 (1979). [As to donor selection, use, and confidentiality, see §4.12.] There have also been forms drafted for those involved in semen donations. For example, there are American Medical Association forms for consent of the wife of the semen donor and for an offer to serve as a semen donor. These forms indicate the participants' understanding of the artificial insemination by donor process. [As to donor related medical forms, see §4.13.] Furthermore, guidelines for the selection and management of artificial recipients, and medical techniques associated with semen cryopreservation have been established by The American Fertility Society. The Society is composed of professionals in the infertility medical field. [As to guidelines for the selection and management of recipients, see §4.14; as to guidelines for semen cryopreservation, see §4.15.] Issues of malpractice in the performance of artificial insemination by donor have also been addressed. One statute, GA CODE ANN §74-101.1 (1973), states that a physician shall not be relieved in a civil action from his or her negligent administration or performance of artificial insemination. [As to malpractice and artificial insemination, see §4.16.]

2. [§4.11] Who May Perform Artificial Insemination

One of the medical considerations [generally, see §4.10] involved in artificial insemination [generally, see §4.1] is who may perform artificial insemination. Statutes dealing with artificial insemination typically limit its administration to licensed physicians. For example, OR REV STAT §677.360 (1977) states that only licensed physicians and persons under their supervision may perform artificial insemination. Another artificial insemination statute, GA CODE ANN §74-101.1 (1973) provides that licensed physicians and surgeons shall be the only persons authorized to administer and perform artificial insemination upon any female. The statute further states that any other person or persons who shall attempt to administer or perform, or who shall actually administer or perform, artificial insemination upon any female human being shall be guilty of a felony, and on conviction therefor shall be punished by imprisonment for not less than one year, nor more than five years. See also CAL CIV CODE §7005 (West Supp 1981); CONN GEN STAT §45-69-g(a) (1981); MONT REV CODES ANN §61-306 (1977); NEV REV STAT §126.061 (1979); WASH REV CODE §26.26.050 (1981); WYO STAT §14-2-103 (1980).

There are documented cases where a woman has artificially inseminated herself without medical assistance. See *C M v C C*, 152 NJ Super 160, 377 A2d 821 (1977). The performance of artificial insemination by one not licensed to practice medicine may even, in the absence of an explicit penalty, constitute the unauthorized practice of medicine. See Shaman, LEGAL ASPECTS OF ARTIFICIAL INSEMINATION, 18 Journal of Family Law 331 (1980).

And it has been suggested that there is a possibility, although it is remote, that a doctor who performs artificial insemination in a state where artificial insemination is not allowed would be engaging in the unauthorized practice of medicine. See Shaman, *above* at 347.

3. [§4.12] Donor Selection, Use, and Confidentiality

There are a number of issues involving donor selection, use, and confidentiality that may arise in the context of medical considerations [generally, see §4.10] in the performance of artificial insemination by donor (AID) [generally, see §4.1].

The issue of the selection of the donor has been addressed in OR REV STAT §677.360 (1977), which states that only licensed physicians and persons under their supervision may select artificial insemination donors. Furthermore, OR REV STAT §677.370 (1977) states that no semen shall be donated for use in artificial insemination by any person who has a disease or defect known by him to be transmissible by genes, or knows or has reason to know that he or she has a venereal disease. In addition, NYC DEPT OF HEALTH, HEALTH CODE §§21.01-21.07 (1973) requires that records be kept of donors and recipients and that all potential donors must undergo a physical examination as well as tests for venereal disease and Rh blood facts.

Moreover, it has been suggested that the screening of artificial donors for genetic diseases is inadequate. Recently, a comprehensive study was published in the New England Journal of Medicine regarding artificial insemination by donor, its scope, and current methods. The writers of the article sent questionnaires to physician-members of The American Fertility Society, to authors of recent articles on the subject, and to departments of obstetrics and gynecology in medical schools. The questionnaire dealt with artificial insemination, success rates, methods of donor selection, and a diagnostic testing of recipients. The respondents of the survey accounted for about 3,600 donor births per year. The survey stated that donors in the sample were subjected to little genetic screening. Biochemical tests were not performed on a regular basis, and family histories were typically superficial. Screening was not carried out for many of the traits and afflictions with which would lead to rejection of the donor. For example, while 92 per cent of the respondents said they would reject a donor with a translocation or trisomy, only 12½ per cent examined the donor's karotype to determine if the condition existed. Moreover, while nearly 95 per cent of the respondents said they would reject a carrier of Tay-Sachs disease, only one per cent said they tested donors for that malady. In conclusion the study stated:

> The screening of donors for genetic diseases is inadequate. A list of genetic traits needs to be established that can be used routinely for screening donors. This procedure will ensure that children born through artificial insemination have a minimum number of genetic defects. This screening should be conducted by people trained in recognizing and evaluating genetic traits.
>
> Current practices reflect little concern for the possibility of consanguineous matings or other effects of multiple donor use. Guidelines are needed to limit the number of pregnancies produced by a single donor.
>
> Present records on artificial insemination are woefully deficient. At a minimum, records should be maintained on the outcome of these pregnancies and on paternity. In addition, the procedure needs to be legitimized in most states to dispel fear of keeping written records. [Currie-Cohen, Luttrell, Shapiro, CURRENT PRACTICE OF ARTIFICIAL INSEMINATION BY DONOR IN THE UNITED STATES, 300 New England Journal of Medicine 585 (1979); reprinted with permission of the publisher.]

Another issue in AID cases centers on the confidentiality of records pertaining to AID. This type of artificial insemination is highly secretive so that the donor, in many cases, will remain anonymous. The reasons the donor prefers to remain anonymous are twofold: first, the fact that the donor is anonymous protects the donor, child, and parents from emotional stress; second, the anonymity protects the donor from legal involvement with the child. [Generally, see §4.6.] See Curie-Cohen, Luttrell, Shapiro, *above* at 589. It has been suggested that the confidentiality of AID records presents an issue that could portend significant litigation in the future. There have been no cases to date involving this issue. But because of the recent interest of adopted children in seeking to learn the identity of their biological parents, it would appear to be only a matter of time until AID children begin to bring suits claiming their right to know the identity of their biological fathers. See Shaman, LEGAL ASPECTS OF ARTIFICIAL INSEMINATION, 18 Journal of Family Law 331 (1979-1980).

In addition, The American Fertility Society, which is made up of over 7,000 members who are involved in research and therapy of involuntary infertility, has established the following guidelines regarding selection and management of donors:

SELECTION AND MANAGEMENT OF DONORS

1. OCCUPATION

Medical students and faculty, hospital house staff, or graduate students in the allied health sciences are traditional donors and preferred because of their understanding the biologic need of the program, accessibility, and selection with regard to health and intelligence. For some minorities, students or other convenient groups of donors screened by their choice of occupation as to health and intelligence may have to be recruited.

2. AGE

Preferably under 35 to avoid genetic hazards possibly related to aging.

3. PRIOR FERTILITY

Desired but not required.

4. FAMILY HISTORY

Donor Screening History. Exclusions should include mental retardation, neurologic disorders, unexplained deaths under 30, and significant congenital defects. Recognized and suspected hereditary and familial disorders such as diabetes and hypertension should be noted and avoided when matching the recipient. In rural communities, the residence of donor's family should not be in close proximity to that of the recipient's.

5. MEDICAL HISTORY

There should be nothing suggestive of any recognized or suspected congenital defects or hereditary and familial disease.

6. PHYSICAL EXAMINATION AND REVIEW BY PHYSICIAN

The above information should be reviewed and signed by a physician affiliated with the semen bank or doing the inseminations. At that time, careful note should also be made to the donor's height, weight, color of hair and eyes, complexion, body build, racial and religious background, and blood type.

7. TESTING OF SEMEN

Instructions should be given for correct collection of semen [see §4.15 on cryopreservation]. The criteria for acceptable sperm specimens should be left to the discretion of the physician procuring the donor. In general, motility above 50%, concentration of the motile sperm in the range of 30 to 50 million/ml., and normal oval forms above 60% are commonly used criteria. The first acceptable specimen should be cultured for gonorrhea before anticipated need for the donor. With subsequent specimens, the culture should be repeated if there is any suspicion, based on a significant number of white blood cells in the specimen of an infection. Every specimen should be analyzed before insemination for count, motility (percent and character), and the presence of white blood cells.

8. BLOOD TESTS ON DONORS

Consider the following laboratory examinations: Hepatitis B, syphilis, blood type, and Rh factor. Tay-Sachs should be screened for in Jewish donors, sickle-cell trait should be screened for in black donors. A chromosomal analysis should not be required unless there is a specific indication.

9. LIMITATIONS OF THE USE OF DONORS

A. By avoiding the matching of donors and recipients from the same area of family origin, the risk of consanguinity between offsprings of recipients by the same donor is virtually eliminated. Because of the mobile aspect of most donor pools, the chances of one donor successfully inseminating a large number of recipients is further reduced. In general, a donor should not be used after 15 successful pregnancies.

B. Care should be taken to discontinue the use of semen from donors who fail to produce a conception within a reasonable period of time.

11. RECORDS

The physician performing inseminations, or the sperm bank providing the semen, may consider biannual review and upgrading of donor records, and elimination of out-of-date records.

12. COMPENSATION TO DONORS

Any written agreement between a sperm bank or physician and donor shall indicate that any payment to the donor is to provide for transportation, inconvenience, and other incidental expenses incurred in donating the sample, rather than direct payment for the semen.

[Reprinted with the permission of The American Fertility Society.]

A compilation of artifical insemination donor related forms is located at §4.7.

4. [§4.13] —Forms

The execution of medical related artificial insemination by donor forms may be appropriate in some cases. For example, forms may be beneficial to the semen donor and the donor's wife so as to fully explain the artificial insemination procedure, and what is to be expected of the semen donor. [Generally, see §4.6.] The American Medical Association has drafted two suggested medical forms for use by the semen donor and the donor's wife:

OFFER TO SERVE AS SEMEN DONOR

Date: ______________, 19____ Time: __________o'clock ____.m.
To Dr.______________________ [treating physician]:

1. I offer my services as a donor of semen with the understanding that the identity of any recipient shall not be disclosed to me, nor shall you voluntarily reveal my identity to any recipient.

2. To the best of my knowledge:

(a) I am in good health; I have no communicable disease; and I do not now, nor have I ever suffered, from any physical or mental impairment or disability, whether inherited or as a result of any disease or ailment, except as follows: ________________________.

(b) I am not now nor have I ever been afflicted with syphilis or any other venereal disease, except as follows: ________________.

(c) None of my grandparents, parents, brothers, sisters, or children, if any, nor their lineal descendants, have ever been afflicted with emotional illness or any inherited mental or physical disabilities or disease, except as follows: ________________ .

3. For the purpose of determining whether I am acceptable as a donor of semen, I consent to a physical examination, including the

taking of blood and other body fluids, by you or any other physician whom you may designate.

[*Signature*]

[*Attestation*]

[Reprinted with permission of The American Medical Association.]

CONSENT OF WIFE OF SEMEN DONOR

Date:__________, 19_____
To Dr.____________________ [treating physician]:

1. I have read my husband's offer to serve as a donor of semen and to the best of my knowledge the statements he has made are true.

2. If my husband is accepted as a donor, I understand that it is your intention to use his semen for purposes of artificial insemination, but not with respect to myself.

3. I know that artificial insemination is a medical procedure intended to cause pregnancy through the use of semen introduced by means other than sexual intercourse.

4. I agree that I shall not attempt to discover the identity of any recipient of my husband's semen.

5. In serving as a donor of semen, I know that my husband may become the father of a child or children of which I am not the mother, but I nevertheless consent to the performance of such services by him.

[*Signature*]

[*Attestation*]

[Reprinted with permission of The American Medical Association.]

5. [§4.14] Recipients; Selection and Management

The American Fertility Society has established guidelines for the Society's members regarding the selection and management of artificial insemination recipients. [As to artificial insemination generally, see §4.1.] The Society is made up of professionals who are involved in research and therapy of involuntary infertility. The selection of donors, and use of their semen, is one issue arising in the medical context of artificial insemination by donor. [Generally, see §4.12.] The intent of the guidelines is to provide minimal but feasible guidelines for practitioners who perform artificial insemination using donors. The guidelines are as follows:

SELECTION AND MANAGEMENT OF RECIPIENTS

1. INDICATIONS

A history of infertility of at least one year duration, absence of contributing female factors (after proper evaluation), and abnormal sperm count and quality would be sufficient ground for initiating artificial insemination by donors (AID).

Additionally AID is indicated when any of the following conditions are present in the husband:

A. Sterility;
B. Severe oligospermia or other abnormalities of semen;
C. Known hereditary and genetic disease (i.e. Tay-Sachs, Huntington's disease, hemophilia, chromosomal anomalies, etc.);
D. Rh (or other blood group) incompatibility;
E. Spinal cord injury (i.e., paraplegia);
F. Exposure to environmental mutagens.

Relative indications include:

A. Immunological factors in male;
B. Unexplained infertility.

2. EVALUATION OF THE FEMALE

Evaluation of the female should include:

A. History including genetic screening;
B. Physical examination;
C. Appropriate laboratory tests should be considered: i.e., serologic tests for syphilis, rubella, GC smear, Pap smear, blood type and Rh, and other studies when indicated;
D. Documentation and timing of ovulation. Recommended techniques for timing include BBT, cervical mucus changes (spinnbarkeit, ferning, viscosity determination) and vaginal cytology. Documentation of ovulation in previous cycles also includes endometrial biopsies or plasma progesterone assays;
E. Evaluation of tubal factor: Rubin's test, hysterosalpingography and/or laparoscopy when indicated;
F. Psychological evaluation of the couple: Desirable but not mandatory;
G. Counseling: AID procedure should be explained to the couple and they should be given an opportunity to ask questions;
H. Signing of Agreement of Understanding.

3. TECHNIQUE

Frequency: One to three inseminations per month may be performed. Frequent inseminations will shorten the number of months of exposure.

Timing: Inseminations should be timed as closely as possible prior to the time of ovulation.

Technique: The patient is placed in lithotomy position. A speculum is inserted in the vagina and the cervix can be wiped clean with a dry cotton ball. Two techniques of insemination are described:
(a) Intracervical: Approximately 0.1 ml. of the semen is injected with inseminating polyethylene tube into the cervical mucus, the rest spilling out and collecting in the vaginal pool;
(b) Cervical cap: 0.1 ml. of the semen is injected in the cervical canal and the rest placed in a cervical cap.

4. RECORD KEEPING

Recipient: Usual record maintained, excluding the name of the donor.

Donor: Coded record to be kept and periodically updated.

5. SPECIAL INFORMATION FOR RECIPIENTS

A. Although the donors are screened for sexually transmitted disease, there is no way of completely protecting the recipient.
B. Despite screening of the donors for genetic disorders, there is no reason to assume that the incidence of congenital anomalies would be different from that in the general population.
C. Recipient should be informed of current legal status in the locality where AID is being performed.
D. The general consensus is that there is no benefit and considerable risk to informing the relatives, friends, ministers, and the offspring of the procedure.
E. To preserve confidentiality, other physicians involved in the care of the recipient need not be informed of the procedure.

[Reprinted with permission of The American Fertility Society.]

6. [§4.15] Medical Technique

In typical situations there are two steps before artificial insemination [generally, see §4.1] by donor is accomplished. First, semen from the donor is frozen and stored. This is referred to as semen cryopreservation. Second, the semen must be thawed. At this point the semen is ready for insemination. These are two of the important medical considerations [generally, see §4.10] in the artificial insemination process since they are done in preparation of the actual insemination process. The American Fertility Society, a professional organization composed of practitioners involved in the research and therapy of persons afflicted with infertility, has developed guidelines for their members relative to approved ways of carrying out semen cryopreservation and semen thawing. These guidelines are:

TECHNIQUE OF SEMEN CRYOPRESERVATION

The technique of freezing and storing human semen is quite variable. Therefore, it is recommended that individuals desiring to start a sperm bank should visit one currently in operation. The most common technique employed in freezing human semen samples is described below:

1. Donors collect semen samples by masturbating into clean, well rinsed containers. Any residual detergent or soap film may be toxic to the spermatozoa. Some laboratories employ sterile containers, others do not.
2. As soon as liquefaction has occurred, a small aliquot is removed for analysis of count, motility, morphology and estimate of presence of infection (unusual number of WBC present), and the volume of the ejaculate is measured. At this time other procedures (cultures, etc.) may be performed if desired.
3. Glycerol is added to the remaining ejaculate to a final volume of 5-10 per cent, usually 7.5 per cent. This is a critical step. Glycerol must be added dropwise with constant stirring of the ejaculate since too rapid an addition of glycerol without stirring may be toxic to the spermatozoa.
4. After addition of glycerol, the specimen is allowed to stand for 15 minutes to allow this additive to exert its cryoprotective action.
5. Measured aliquots of the specimen are placed into containers (straws, vials, etc.) and the containers sealed. Labeling should be completed at this time, employing a code to identify those specimens to be used for AID.
6. The labeled containers are suspended in liquid nitrogen vapor above the surface of liquid nitrogen. The rate of freezing is critical because ice crystals may form within the cell and significantly reduce recoverable motility.
7. The samples are then stored under the surface of the liquid nitrogen.

THAWING OF FROZEN SAMPLES

Various temperatures have been employed for the thawing of samples. Most commonly, removal of the sample from storage and allowing it to thaw at room temperature has given results equivalent to thawing at other temperatures. Prior to use, the motility of the specimen should be checked to insure its quality.

In general the recovery of motility after freezing and thawing human semen will correlate directly with the sperm count and motility prior to freezing. Thus, the better the pre-freeze motile sperm count, the better the post-thaw motile sperm count. Occasional ejaculates that appear to be of high quality prior to freezing are found to have unacceptable motility after thawing. Semen samples with sperm count below 40 million/ml. and pre-freeze motility below 60 per cent will likely have so low a post-thaw motility as to be of little or no value for AID. As a general guideline, a semen sample can be expected to lose up to 50 per cent of its original motility after freezing and thawing.

The initial success in the use of normal frozen semen prompted several attempts to freeze and store oligospermic specimens. Unfortunately, these attempts met with little success. At this time frozen sperm banking offers virtually no help to the oligospermic male seeking to improve his fertility potential.

The length of time that human semen samples may be stored in liquid nitrogen remains controversial. Pregnancies have resulted from inseminations with specimens stored as long as 10 years, but evidence has been reported that samples may undergo a gradual decline in recoverable motility after three years in storage in liquid nitrogen.

[Reprinted with permission of The American Fertility Society.]

7. [§4.16] Malpractice

Although no case involving negligent or wrongful artificial insemination [generally, see §4.1] as medical malpractice has yet been reported, the possibility of malpractice and artificial insemination has been considered and one state has provided for this possibility in its artificial insemination statutes. It has been suggested that when malpractice cases involving artificial insemination arise, the courts will treat the cases similar to blood transfusion cases. Legal liability for malpractice may result for doctors who perform artificial insemination by donor (AID) without taking necessary precautions. For example, when the doctor has not adequately tested the AID donor for genetic defects in the donor's background a medical malpractice action might arise. See Shaman, LEGAL ASPECTS OF ARTIFICIAL INSEMINATION, 18 Journal of Family Law 331 (1979-1980). The statute dealing with medical malpractice and artificial insemination is found in GA CODE ANN §74-101.1 (1973). The statute provides that any physician or surgeon who shall obtain a written authorization signed by a husband and wife authorizing him to perform artificial insemination shall be relieved of civil liability to the husband or wife or to any child conceived by artificial insemination for the results of the artificial insemination, provided that the written authorization shall not relieve the physician from any civil liability arising from his or her own negligent administration or performance of artificial insemination. [As to other medical considerations involving artificial insemination, see §4.10.]

D. Legislative Considerations

1. [§4.17] Statutory Survey

About half the states in the United States had statutes relating to artificial insemination in 1982. The first of these statutes was enacted in Georgia in 1964. The Georgia legislation addressed the issue of the legal status of children born by means of artificial insemination and legitimized these children. These statutes are: ALASKA STAT §20.20.010 (1979); ARK STAT ANN §61-141 (1971); CAL CIV CODE §7005 (West 1980); COLO REV STAT §19-6-106 (1978); CONN GEN STAT §45-69-f-n (West Supp 1980); FLA STAT ANN §742.11 (1981); GA CODE ANN tit. 74 §101.1 (1973); KAN STAT ANN §23-128-130 (1981); LA CIV CODE ANN Art. 188 (West Supp 1980); MD EST & TRUSTS CODE ANN §1-206(b) (1974); MICH COMP LAWS ANN §700.111 (West Supp 1980); MINN STAT ANN §257.56 (West Supp 1980); MONT REV CODES ANN §40-6-106 (1979); NEV REV STAT §126.061 (1979); NY DOM REL LAW §73 (McKinney 1977); NC GEN STAT §49A-1 (1976); OKLA STAT ANN tit. 10 §§551-52 (West Supp 1980); OR REV STAT §§109.234, 109.247, 677.355, 677.360, 677.365, 677.379, (1979); TENN CODE ANN §53-446 (Michie Supp 1981); TEX FAM CODE ANN tit. 12 §12.03 (1974); VA CODE §64.1-7.1 (Supp 1979); WASH REV CODE §26.26.050 (1981); WIS STAT ANN §891.40 (1980); WYO STAT §14-2-103 (1978).

The artificial insemination statutes typically provide for spousal request and consent before artificial insemination is performed [see, e.g., ALASKA STAT §20-10.010 (1975); CAL CIV CODE §7005 (West 1980); NY DOM REL LAW §73 (McKinney 1977)], the husband's (as opposed to the semen donor's) rights and obligations [see, e.g., VA CODE §64.1-7.1 (1974); WASH REV CODE §26.26.050 (1981)], and the status of the artificially inseminated conceived child [see, e.g., GA CODE ANN §74-101.1 (1973); TENN CODE ANN §53-446 (Michie 1981)]. In addition, some statutes prescribe who may perform artificial insemination [see, e.g., CAL CIV CODE §7005 (West 1980); OR REV STAT §677.360 (1977)]; and who may select semen donors [see, e.g., OR REV STAT §677.360 (1977)].

An example of a typical artificial insemination statute is CAL CIV CODE §7005 (West 1980), which states:

§7005. Artificial insemination of wife; husband as natural father; donor not natural father

(a) If, under the supervision of a licensed physician and with the consent of her husband, a wife is inseminated artificially with semen donated by a man not her husband, the husband is treated in law as if he were the natural father of a child thereby conceived. The husband's consent must be in writing and signed by him and his wife. The physician shall certify their signatures and the date of the insemination, and . . . retain the husband's consent . . . as part of the medical record, where it shall be kept confidential and in a sealed file. However, the physician's failure to do so does not affect the father and child relationship. All papers and records pertaining to the insemination, whether part of the permanent record of a court or of a file held by the supervising physician or elsewhere, are subject to inspection only upon an order of the court for good cause shown.

(b) The donor of semen provided to a licensed physician for use in artificial insemination of a woman other than the donor's wife is treated in law as if he were not the natural father of a child thereby conceived.

2. [§4.18] Uniform Parentage Act §5 (Artificial Insemination)

The Uniform Parentage Act §5 includes language addressing the issue of artificial insemination by donor. The act provides:

§5 Artificial Insemination

(a) If, under the supervision of a licensed physician and with the consent of her husband, a wife is inseminated artificially with semen donated by a man not her husband, the husband is treated in law as if he were the natural father of a child thereby conceived. The husband's consent must be in writing and signed by him and his wife. The physician shall certify their signatures and the date of the insemination, and file the husband's consent with the [State Department of Health], where it shall be kept confidential and in a sealed file. However, the physician's failure to do so does not affect the father and child relationship. All papers and records pertaining to the record of a court or of a file held by the supervising physician or elsewhere, are subject to inspection only upon an order of the court for good cause shown.

(b) The donor of semen provided to a licensed physician for use in artificial insemination of a married woman other than the donor's wife is treated in law as if he were not the natural father of a child thereby conceived.

The provisions of the Act have been substantially adopted in a number of states including California [see CAL CIV CODE §7005 (West 1980)] and Washington [see WASH REV CODE ANN §26.26.050 (Supp 1980-1981)]. See also, COLO REV STAT §19-6-106 (1978); MONT REV CODES ANN §61-306 (Supp 1977); NEV REV STAT §126.061 (1979); WYO STAT §14-2-103 (1980).

However, it has been suggested that the Act's provision dealing with artificial insemination does not address many complex and serious problems raised by the practice of artificial insemination. See 9A UNIFORM LAWS ANN, UNIFORM PARENTAGE ACT, Commissioner's Comment to §5, at 593 (1979).

3. [§4.19] Model Legislation

The advent of artificial insemination [generally, see §§4.1, 4.2] is relatively recent. Although the first reported successful use of artificial insemination in the United States was in the 1800's, artificial insemination by donor (AID) did not become generally accepted until the 20th Century. Generally, see Shaman, LEGAL ASPECTS OF ARTIFICIAL INSEMINATION, 18 Journal of Family 331 (1980); COMMENT, ARTIFICIAL INSEMINATION AND SURROGATE MOTHERHOOD – A NURSERY FULL OF UNRESOLVED QUESTIONS, 17 Willamette LR 913 (1981). This developing medical speciality evoked an initial judicial response [see, e.g., *Strnad v Strnad*, 190 Misc 786, 78 NYS2d 390 (1948)] and later a legislative response [as to a survey of state statutes dealing with artificial insemination, see §4.17]. In addition, one professional group directly associated with artificial insemination, The American Fertility Society, has recently drafted model legislation in the area of artificial insemination by donor. The Society is composed of members who are actively involved in research and involuntary infertility. The Society's model legislation was designed as a guide to state legislative committees developing legislation in this area. The legislation would give equal protection to the physicians, parents, offspring, and donors. The model legislation for artificial insemination with donor semen was based on the Society's legislative experience in preparing a similar document in the state of Oregon. The model legislation defines artificial insemination by donor, establishes criteria for qualified practitioners and donors, establishes procedures for the practitioner to follow, provides for the status of the resulting child, and states that artificial insemination by donor shall not be the basis for an allegation of adultery on the part of the mother. Specifically, the model legislation provides as follows:

ARTIFICIAL INSEMINATION WITH DONOR SEMEN

Definition

The instillation of semen from a donor into the reproductive tract of a woman who is not the wife of the donor by a physician or health practitioner with the intent of causing pregnancy. No provisions of this act are intended to apply to artificial insemination with husband's semen.

Qualified Practitioners

Artificial insemination with donor semen shall only be performed by:

1. A licensed physician; or
2. A health practitioner under the direct supervision of a licensed physician; which persons shall hereafter be referred to as "practitioners".

Any person performing artificial insemination with donor semen who does not meet the above qualifications shall be subject to a fine of $__________ and a jail sentence of up to ________________. No penalty shall accrue to any other party and the legal status of the parties, including any resultant child, shall not be affected.

Donor

If the donor is a man other than the recipient's husband,

1. The practitioner or sperm bank obtaining the seminal fluid from the potential donor shall:
   a. obtain a family medical history (omitting names and other identifying information);
   b. perform a physical examination; and
   c. screen for sexually transmitted disease. If the results of any of the above indicate a possibility that an infectious or genetically determined disease might be transmitted, the semen from that potential donor would not be used for insemination. If, in the discretion of the practitioner or sperm bank, it is deemed advisable, chromosomal and metabolic studies shall also be performed.

2. The medical history and results of any test performed shall be recorded. No other information concerning the donor shall be revealed.
3. When it has been determined that a donor is qualified, he shall be required to sign a consent form stating that he knows his semen may be used for artificial insemination with donor semen and that his identity will remain confidential.
4. The donor shall have no rights in or liability to any child conceived through artificial insemination with donor semen, whether or not the donor's identity is known to the recipient.

Practitioner

1. Prior to performing artificial insemination with donor semen, the practitioner shall:
   a. fully disclose to the recipient and her spouse, if she has one, all material hazards; and
   b. obtain signed request and consent forms from both the recipient and her spouse, if she has one.

   The burden of disclosing marital status is fully on the recipient. If she fails to inform the practitioner of her marriage, it shall in no way affect the practitioner's liability. If she informs the practitioner that she is married the practitioner shall not perform artificial insemination with donor semen without the consent of the spouse, subject to the same penalties and limitations set forth in section ____________ (qualified practitioners) of this statute.
2. If the practitioner has complied with the provisions of this statute and has carried out a standard level of practice in the selection of donor or sperm bank, and in the processing and administration of the semen, the practitioner shall not be liable to the donor, recipient, her spouse or any resultant child. This includes, but is not limited to, liability for:
   a. any complication of pregnancy;
   b. any defect in the newborn child;
   c. any sexually transmitted disease that develops in the recipient;
   d. "wrongful birth" actions brought by the resultant child;
   e. adultery or accomplice thereto; or
   f. support of the child.

Resultant Child

1. A child conceived through artificial insemination with donor semen of a recipient with the consent of her spouse is the legitimate child of both recipient and spouse. Such child shall

have all the rights of a child conceived by natural means using the spouse's sperm, including but not limited to the rights of inheritance and support.

2. A child conceived through artificial insemination with donor semen is not the child of the donor unless the donor is the husband of the mother.

Recipient and Spouse

Artificial insemination with donor semen with the consent of the spouse shall not be the basis for an allegation of adultery on the part of the mother, and the birth of any resultant child shall give rise to a conclusive presumption that the marriage has been consummated.

[Reprinted with permission of The American Fertility Society.]

II. IN VITRO FERTILIZATION

A. In General

1. [§4.20] Definition

In vitro refers to a process or reaction carried out in a culture dish or test tube. See Blakiston, GOULD MEDICAL DICTIONARY (McGraw-Hill 4th ed 1979). *In vitro* fertilization (IVF) describes a relatively new procedure in which immature ova are removed from a woman, placed in a culture medium, and fertilized with sperm. Subsequently, in a few days, when the product of conception, the conceptus, has grown into the blastocyst stage, it is transplanted into the mother's uterus. See COMMENT, THE "BRAVE NEW BABY" AND THE LAW; FASHIONING REMEDIES FOR THE VICTIMS OF IN VITRO FERTILIZATION, 4 American Journal of Law and Medicine 319 (1978). The woman from whom the ova are taken and the "mother" who actually allows the fetus to develop inside her are most often two different women. In some cases a woman will take hormones to stimulate the production of ova. See Flannery, Weisman, Lispett, Braverman, TEST TUBE BABIES; LEGAL ISSUES RAISED BY IN VITRO FERTILIZATION, 67 Georgetown LJ 1295 (1979).

Conception resulting from *in vitro* fertilization should be distinguished from conception involving artificial insemination [generally, see §4.1] or surrogate motherhood [generally, see §4.25]. *In vitro* fertilization can be used by a woman who cannot conceive normally, is sterile, or can conceive but is not willing to gestate the fetus. In the first case, the woman can furnish the egg for fertilization *in vitro*, and subsequently the conceptus can be implanted and develop through natural gestation in the woman. In the second case, an egg from another woman, a donor, would be necessary, but the conceptus could be implanted in the woman and would gestate naturally. In the final case, another female would allow her body to be used, and then gestation of the *in vitro* fertilized egg would take place inside the other female. By contrast, artificial insemination is typically used when the male is infertile and the female is inseminated with the sperm of a donor. Gestation then takes place within the female. See Shaman, LEGAL ASPECTS OF ARTIFICIAL INSEMINATION, 18 Journal of Family Law 331 (1980). And, where a surrogate mother is used, the female is usually infertile or sterile, and thus the sperm of the male is inseminated into a "surrogate" mother, conception ensues, and the surrogate mother carries the fetus through gestation and birth. See COMMENT, ARTIFICIAL INSEMINATION AND SURROGATE MOTHERHOOD: A NURSERY FULL OF UNRESOLVED QUESTIONS, 17 Willamette LR 913 (1981).

2. [§4.21] Background

The birth of the first baby conceived through *in vitro* fertilization (IVF) [as to the definition of *in vitro* fertilization, see §4.20] was reported to the world on July 26, 1978. See Flannery, Weisman, Lipsett, Braverman, TEST TUBE BABIES: LEGAL ISSUES RAISED BY IN VITRO FERTILIZATION, 67 Georgetown LJ 1295 (1979). The birth of the child marked the culmination of nearly four decades of *in vitro* fertilization experimentation. See COMMENT, THE "BRAVE NEW BABY" AND THE LAW: FASHIONING REMEDIES FOR THE VICTIMS OF IN VITRO FERTILIZATION, 4 American Journal of Law and Medicine 319 (1978). Subsequently, it was reported on August 26, 1982, that the nation's fifth *in vitro* fertilization baby had been born, and that the baby was normal. DENVER POST, August 26, 1982, at 6A (Associated Press report).

Nonetheless, the process of *in vitro* fertilization remains experimental, and there are questions regarding whether children conceived by *in vitro* fertilization might be more likely to suffer birth defects. The procedure by which *in vitro* fertilization is performed is complicated. The first step consists of the extraction of ova from a woman's body. Next the ova are placed in a culture medium where fertilization takes place. There is significant difficulty in finding a medium that is close enough to a woman's body to allow the conception to take place. If conception takes place, the resulting conceptus is transplanted into its mother's body. At this stage, the conceptus must be transplanted at the proper time in the mother's menstrual cycle so the mother's body will understand that she is pregnant. However, the process is not performed without risk. The process necessitates the manipulation of the ova and conceptus before transplantation into the mother, and some experts suggest that this movement could cause an abnormally high number of *in vitro* fertilization children to suffer birth defects. There is hope that with the continued development of amniocentesis and other *in vitro* examination techniques, the availability of abortion, and the fact that a mother's body can spontaneously abort a defective fetus, the number of *in vitro* fertilization children born with defects will be limited. And yet, it is still unclear whether any *in vitro* fertilization children will be born with severe defects. See 4 American Journal of Law and Medicine at 321-323. There are a number of medical clinics studying the process of *in vitro* fertilization including the Eastern Virginia Medical School in Norfolk, Virginia, which has established an *in vitro* fertilization clinic.

In addition, there exists a federal regulation, 45 CFR §46.204 (1981), which addresses the issue of research applications and proposals involving *in vitro* fertilization. The regulation states that the Secretary of the Department of Health and Human Services shall establish one or more advisory boards to address issues relating to *in vitro* fertilization. The members of the board shall be competent to deal with medical, legal, social, ethical, and related issues. The members of the board may include, for example, research scientists, physicians, psychologists, sociologists, educators, lawyers, and ethicists, as well as representatives from the general public. At the request of the Secretary, the Ethical Advisory Board shall advise the Secretary regarding individual applications or proposals. No application or proposal involving human *in vitro* fertilization may be funded by the department, or any component thereof, until the application or proposal has been reviewed by the board, and the board has rendered its advice as to its acceptability from an ethical standpoint.

B. [§4.22] Constitutional Considerations

An issue directly related to *in vitro* fertilization (IVF) [as to the definition of *in vitro* fertilization, see §4.20] is whether the United States Constitution prohibits, or should protect, access to *in vitro* fertilization when the procedure is intended to culminate in the birth of a live child. It is agreed that the government may properly regulate some aspects of medical care if the government can prove a "rational" basis for the regulation. See, e.g., *Wynn v Scott*, 448 FSupp 997 (ND Il), affd sub nom, *Wynn v Carey*, 582 F2d 1375 (7th Cir 1978). However, if the government regulation infringes upon a right protected by the Constitution, the government is required to show a more important reason for imposing the regulation. Regulations imposing a burden on a fundamental right must be justified by compelling state interests, and must be narrowly drawn to express only those interests. See *Carey v Population Serv Internatl*, 431 US 678, 97 SCt 2010, 52 LE2d 675 (1977). Therefore, in order to determine whether a government regulation on procreation by *in vitro* fertilization would survive a constitutional challenge, it is necessary to determine whether a person has a fundamental right to procreation by means of *in vitro* fertilization, and whether, if such a right exists, the government interest underlying the regulation is compelling enough to justify the infringement. The contention that may be made, that persons have a fundamental right to use *in vitro* fertilization as an alternative means of procreation, is likely to be based on the United States Supreme Court's decisions regarding privacy rights. The Supreme Court has held that, in the context of personal privacy, an individual may, without being burdened by unjustified government regulation, make decisions regarding procreation [see, e.g., *Skinner v Oklahoma*, 316 US 535, 62 SCt 1110, 86 LE 1655 (1942)], family relationships [see, e.g., *Prince v Massachusetts*, 321 US 158, 64 SCt 438, 88 LE 645 (1944)], contraception [see, e.g., *Carey v Population Serv Internatl*, 431 US 678, 97 SCt 2010, 52 LE2d 675 (1977)], and whether to bear or beget a child [see, e.g., *Eisenstadt v Baird*, 405 US 438, 92 SCt 1029, 31 LE2d 349 (1972)]. It has been suggested that one of the three zones of privacy may be found to create a similar fundamental interest in using *in vitro* fertilization. The zones are the right to be free from interference by the government with procreative potential, the right of privacy in the marital relationship, and the right to choose whether to bear or beget a child. However, public policy considerations may lead governments or their agencies to prohibit in whole or in part government support of programs related to *in vitro* fertilization. Moreover, some states may choose to prohibit or restrict *in vitro* fertilization. The decisions may be arrived at after consideration is given to the medical technology that is required to produce one successful blastocyst for implantation. Medical technology requires the formation and destruction of numerous blastocysts in order to produce one blastocyst for implantation. This fact may lead a court to conclude that the process of *in vitro* fertilization represents an impermissible destruction of human life and thus should be prohibited. It is possible that prohibition of the use of, or funding for, *in vitro* fertilization based on this rationale would withstand a constitutional challenge under the rational basis standard. See Flannery, Weisman, Lipsett, Braverman, TEST TUBE BABIES: LEGAL ISSUES RAISED BY IN VITRO FERTILIZATION, 67 Georgetown Law Journal 1295 (1979).

C. Civil Liability

1. [§4.23] Tort Action for Destruction of In Vitro Fertilization Conceptus

Civil liability involving *in vitro* fertilization [as to the definition of *in vitro* fertilization, see §4.20] may arise in a number of situations including liability for the destruction of an *in vitro* fertilization conceptus or liability for the birth of a severely defective child. Civil liability involving *in vitro* fertilization (IVF) [as to the background of *in vitro* fertilization, see §4.21] may arise in a number of settings, but it is likely the most common situation may be where an *in vitro* fertilization conceptus is destroyed. For example, the negligence of the experimenter may cause the unintentional destroying of the conceptus. Additionally, the conceptus may be destroyed on purpose where several ova are taken from the woman and fertilized although only one conceptus is implanted. The remaining conceptuses would be destroyed. See COMMENT, THE "BRAVE NEW BABY" AND THE LAW: FASHIONING REMEDIES FOR THE VICTIMS OF IN VITRO FERTILIZATION, 4 American Journal of Law and Medicine, 319 (1978).

The only case addressing this subject is *Del Zio v Presbyterian Hosp*, 74 Civ 3588 (SD NY 1978), where an action was brought by the parents of an *in vitro* fertilization conceived conceptus against the defendants for the alleged unconsented to act by the defendants that destroyed the conceptus. The plaintiffs alleged [as to a copy of the plaintiffs' complaint, see §4.24] that the plaintiff-woman's fallopian tubes were blocked and that she could not conceive a child naturally. Therefore the plaintiffs sought the services of the defendants so that an *in vitro* fertilization could be attempted. An operation was performed and eggs were removed from the plaintiff-woman. The eggs were fertilized with semen from the plaintiff-husband. A culture of the fluid was prepared, put into a culture tube, and placed in an incubator. Subsequently, however, the culture was removed from the incubator and the stopper was removed from the tube thereby destroying its sterile condition. The plaintiffs brought an action seeking $1,000,000 on behalf of the plaintiff-woman, and $500,000 on behalf of the plaintiff-husband. The plaintiffs predicated their action on the theories of intentional infliction of mental and physical anguish and wrongful conversion of the plaintiff-woman's property. In bringing a motion to dismiss, the defendants' contended, in part, that the plaintiffs had failed to set forth a cause of action capable of relief as recognized by federal law or the law of New York due to the patent uncertainty of the *in vitro* fertilization process and the undisputed facts of the case. The defendants asserted that the action was unique in American jurisprudence—one of first impression. They contended the causes of action seeking damages for permanent injuries, emotional distress, and derivative relief were too conjectural and too speculative to form the underlying basis for litigation. They described *in vitro* fertilization as not accepted medical practice, but the creation of life outside the mother. Moreover, the defendants argued that the viability of the destroyed conceptus could not be asserted, and that viability was needed before an action could be stated. The defendants said the plaintiffs sought to place liability for the termination of the experiment at the earliest and most uncertain phases. In addition, the defendants said the speculation presented by the plaintiffs' causes of action was immeasurable. The court was asked to sustain a cause of action for the loss of a dream in a woman who rested her hopes for a child upon an experimental process heretofore unsuccessful upon human subjects, the defendant argued. To sustain the plaintiffs' cause of action would be to invent a brand new ground for suit, the defendants concluded. By contrast, the plaintiffs argued that successful pregnancies had been achieved by *in vitro* fertilization. The plaintiffs said that two weeks after the defendants terminated the plaintiffs' *in vitro* fertilization, a report was published that an Australian medical team had succeeded in implanting a test-tube embryo in a woman. Moreover, the plaintiffs said a British professor had announced the successful birth of three babies conceived by *in vitro* fertilization. Therefore the plaintiffs argued that the defendants' statement that *in vitro* fertilization had never been successfully performed upon human subjects was untrue. The plaintiffs said that is was apparent that the plaintiff-wife would have had some chance of success if the defendant had not wrongfully intervened. The plaintiffs also argued that when the defendant-physician wrongfully interfered with the plaintiffs' *in vitro* fertilization procedure, he assumed all of the duties and liabilities inherent in a physician-patient relationship, and that the jury was entitled to award damages therefor. In addition, the plaintiffs argued that their claim was not speculative and that the causes of action were not unprecedented. It should be the pragmatic determination of the trier of the facts upon a complete analysis of the evidence presented at trial, the plaintiffs said, regarding the issue of speculative damages. And regarding the precedence issue, the plaintiffs said this should not constitute the basis for or require dismissal of the complaint. The law should never allow the suffering of an injury where damage has ensued without providing a remedy for recovery, the plaintiffs argued. The real question in the plaintiffs' view was not whether there was any precedent for this action, since that was not an unscalable barrier, but whether the defendant inflicted such a wrong upon the plaintiffs as resulted in lawful damages. In summary, the plaintiffs said that, by considering the allegations of the complaint to be true (as the court must upon a motion to dismiss), it was clear that: (1) the defendants wrongfully violated the right of the plaintiff-wife and her husband for her to have the *in vitro* implant and thereby committed a tort upon the plaintiffs; (2) the damage and injury inflicted by the defendants upon the plaintiffs was foreseeable; and (3) the plaintiffs' had viable claims for their conscious pain and suffering which were measurable as in any other tort case for such type of claim. The court, in a memorandum decision, 74 Civ 3588 (SD NY 1978) [as to the full text of the decision, see §4.24], denied the defendants' motion to dismiss. The court said the question of the procedure's success went more to the question of damage and liability. Therefore, the court held the plaintiffs were entitled to go to trial on their claim that the defendants wrongfully interfered with the *in vitro* fertilization procedure. After a trial to the jury, the plaintiffs were awarded a $50,000 verdict. See Flannery, Weisman, Lipsett, Braverman, TEST TUBE BABIES: LEGAL ISSUES RAISED BY IN VITRO FERTILIZATION, 67 Georgetown LJ 1295 (1979).

2. [§4.24] Text of Memorandum Decision and Amended Complaint: Del Zio v Presbyterian Hosp, 74 Civ 3588 (SD NY 1978)

The following amended complaint and memorandum decision were part of the record in the case of *Del Zio v Presbyterian Hosp*, 74 Civ 3588 (SD NY 1978) [as to a discussion of tort actions for destruction of an *in vitro* fertilization conceptus, see §4.23]. In *Del Zio*, the plaintiffs brought an action for wrongful conversion of the plaintiff-wife's property and intentional infliction of mental and physical anguish after the defendants destroyed a culture in which eggs from the plaintiff-wife and sperm from the plaintiff-husband had been mixed. Had the culture not been destroyed the resulting conceptus would have been implanted into the plaintiff-wife, the plaintiffs asserted. After the defendants' motion to dismiss the action for failure to state a claim was denied, the case was tried by a jury and the plaintiffs were awarded a $50,000 verdict.

The text of the unreported memorandum decision, dated April 12, 1978, stated:

> STEWART, District Judge:
>
> Plaintiffs, Mr. and Mrs. Del Zio, allege in their complaint that defendants wrongfully and deliberately terminated an in-vitro fertilization procedure involving material obtained from the husband and wife, and did so without the knowledge or consent of plaintiffs. Plaintiffs further allege that they each suffered severe physical and mental pain and other injuries and incurred substantial medical expenses in connection with the wrongfully aborted fertilization procedure. In short, plaintiffs have alleged an intentional tort which was aimed directly at the man and woman who had undertaken the procedure and which caused them compensable damage. Defendants have moved to dismiss for failure to state a cause of action.
>
> We think this case is distinguishable from those relied upon by defendants. It does not involve a claim on behalf of an unborn child, fetus or embryo. Nor does it involve a claim for prenatal injuries to an unborn fetus. It is unlike *Tobin v Grossman*, 24 N.Y.2d 609, 301 N.Y.S.2d 554 (1969); it does not seek damages for injurious acts done to a third person, but rather asserts a claim for damages directly and intentionally inflicted on plaintiffs. See *Johnson v. State*, 37 N.Y.2d 378, 372 N.Y.S.2d 638, 334 N.E.2d 590 (1975).
>
> Defendants also argue that plaintiffs have no cause of action because the possibility of success of the fertilization procedure is highly speculative. We think, however, that this goes to the question of damages and not liability. Accordingly, we conclude that

plaintiffs are entitled to go to trial on their claim that defendants wrongfully interfered with the fertilization procedure.

The motion of defendants is denied.

SO ORDERED.

The text of the plaintiffs' amended complaint stated as follows:

COMPLAINT

Plaintiffs, by their attorney. . . . respectfully allege as follows:

FIRST CLAIM

FIRST: This action is brought by plaintiffs, DORIS DEL ZIO and her husband, JOHN E. DEL ZIO, against defendants for damages for personal injuries and property damage by reason of the unlawful, wrongful, wanton and malicious acts of defendants in the City of New York on or about the 13th day of September 1973. The said unlawful and wrongful acts consisted of the destruction by defendants of a culture used for the in-vitro fertilization of the eggs of plaintiff, DORIS DEL ZIO, by the semen of her husband, plaintiff JOHN E. DEL ZIO.

SECOND: Pursuant to the provisions of 28 USC 1332, this Court has jurisdiction of the action by reason of the amount of damages sought, i.e., One Million ($1,000,000.00) Dollars in the First Claim and Five Hundred Thousand ($500,000.00) Dollars in the Second Claim, and the diversity of citizenship of the parties. Plaintiffs are residents and citizens of the State of Florida. Upon information and belief, defendant RAYMOND L. VANDE WIELE, is a citizen of the State of New York. Defendant, THE PRESBYTERIAN HOSPITAL IN THE CITY OF NEW YORK, hereinafter "Hospital", is a voluntary hospital having its main office and principal place of business in the City, County and State of New York; and, upon information and belief defendant, TRUSTEES OF COLUMBIA UNIVERSITY IN THE CITY OF NEW YORK, reside in the City, County, and State of New York.

THIRD: At all the times herein stated defendant VANDE WIELE was the Director of Service of Obstetrics and Gynecology of the defendant Hospital, and in committing the acts complained of herein, he acted as the agent, servant and employee of the defendant Hospital. At the same times, defendant VANDE WIELE was a professor and Chairman of the Department of Obstetrics and Gynecology at Columbia University and, upon information and belief, in committing the acts complained of herein, he acted as the agent, servant and employee of the defendant TRUSTEES OF COLUMBIA UNIVERSITY IN THE CITY OF NEW YORK.

FOURTH: The medical technique referred to as "in-vitro fertilization" is a procedure wherein follicular fluid containing female eggs and other ovarian matter is extracted by abdominal surgery. The fluid is then mixed with a culture medium to which is added male semen containing spermatozoa. The mixture is kept sterile and in an incubator at body temperature for at least a four-day period, during which time cellular divisions occur. The divided cell is called the blastocyst stage of the embryo. The blastocyst is then implanted into the female by catheterization through the cervix to grow into a full term infant.

FIFTH: The in-vitro fertilization process is well known to the medical profession and has been successfully employed with certain animals and with human beings. It is applicable to women who desire children but cannot become pregnant because of defects or blockage in their fallopian tubes.

SIXTH: Plaintiffs, JOHN E. DEL ZIO and DORIS DEL ZIO, were married on December 22, 1968. In 1970 they moved from the State of New York to the State of Florida where they have resided ever since.

SEVENTH: The marriage was a second one for each of the plaintiffs. But for the blockage of Mrs. Del Zio's fallopian tubes, both were capable of having children as was evidenced by the fact that Mrs. Del Zio had a child by her first marriage and JOHN E. DEL ZIO has had two (2) children by his prior marriage.

EIGHTH: Six (6) weeks after their marriage in December 1968, Mrs. Del Zio developed an ovarian cyst which ruptured and required surgery. After the operation, Mrs. Del Zio's physician placed her on a temperature charting course in order to determine the time of ovulation to aid her in becoming pregnant since plaintiffs desired to have a child as soon as possible.

NINTH: Thereafter, for the next fourteen (14) months no pregnancy occurred, and Mrs. Del Zio's physician performed a hysterosalpingogram which determined that Mrs. Del Zio's fallopian tubes were blocked. This was confirmed by another physician who agreed that the blockage was sufficiently severe to prevent pregnancy in Mrs. Del Zio.

TENTH: Plaintiffs were referred by their physician to Dr. William J. Sweeney at New York Hospital in the City of New York, and in April 1970 Dr. Sweeney performed a dilatation, fractional curettage and laparoscopy upon Mrs. Del Zio. These procedures revealed that Mrs. Del Zio had manifold adhesions involving her ovaries and her fallopian tubes which were completely blocked. In May 1970, Dr. Sweeney performed a laparotomy upon Mrs. Del Zio to remove the blockage. The operation appeared to be successful and Mrs. Del Zio thereafter became pregnant in or about October 1970. In December 1970 she suffered a miscarriage which terminated the pregnancy.

ELEVENTH: In or about June 1971 Dr. Sweeney examined Mrs. Del Zio and a hysterosalpingogram revealed that her fallopian tubes were again blocked. In July 1971 Mrs. Del Zio underwent further surgery to remove the blockage, and she was then placed on a fertility drug called Clomid for a number of months in order to aid her ovulation cycle.

TWELFTH: Notwithstanding the said surgery and medication, Mrs. Del Zio was unable to conceive because of persistent abdominal adhesions and fallopian tubular closures.

THIRTEENTH: In or about August 1972 plaintiffs learned of the in-vitro fertilization procedure whereby pregnancy could occur through by-passing the fallopian tubes. Plaintiffs inquired of Dr. Sweeney and he explained the possible benefits and attendant risks of that procedure and that up to that date no successful human implant was known. Dr. Sweeney further explained that the preparation could be painful for Mrs. Del Zio inasmuch as she would have to take the aforesaid fertility drug, Clomid, which could produce cysts on her ovaries; that if a pregnancy did occur there was no certainty that the child would be normal; and that she would have to undergo abdominal surgery to remove the follicular fluid and eggs from her ovaries. Dr. Sweeney fully informed plaintiffs, who were cognizant of the risks, hazards and expense involved, and they decided to go forward with the medical procedures necessary for Mrs. Del Zio to achieve pregnancy.

FOURTEENTH: The next twelve (12) months were spent in preparation for the required surgery. Mrs. Del Zio was given Clomid, the dosage of which had to be varied because she did not ovulate with certain dosages and other dosages caused large ovarian cysts. Throughout the year her basal body temperatures had to be taken and charted on a regular basis in order to plan the timing of the operation which had to occur at or about the time of ovulation.

FIFTEENTH: Prior thereto, in August 1972, when the plaintiffs and Dr. Sweeney had decided to proceed with the in-vitro process, Dr. Sweeney communicated with Dr. Landrum Shettles, then a physician at the Obstetrics and Gynecology Department at the defendant Hospital, who was a recognized authority in the field, and Dr. Shettles agreed with Dr. Sweeney to perform the laboratory work that would be required for the in-vitro fertilization.

SIXTEENTH: Thereafter, and on or about September 12, 1973, Mrs. Del Zio was admitted to the New York Hospital. There, Mrs. Del Zio underwent abdominal surgery by Dr. Sweeney, who performed a laparotomy to remove ovarian tissue and the fluid from the follicles of each of her ovaries which contained her eggs. The operation was successful and Mrs. Del Zio was returned from the operating room to the recovery room in good condition.

SEVENTEENTH: The fluid and tissue recovered from Mrs. Del Zio were placed in a sterile tube and sealed. Dr. Sweeney called Dr. Shettles at approximately 10:45 A.M. that morning and informed him that Mr. Del Zio was personally going to deliver the tube to him.

EIGHTEENTH: At approximately 11:00 A.M. on the same day, September 12, 1973, plaintiff JOHN E. DEL ZIO delivered the sealed tube to Dr. Shettles at the defendant Hospital and semen was then recovered from Mr. Del Zio. Dr. Shettles prepared a culture of the fluid, ovarian matter and the semen in a sterile culture tube which he stoppered and then placed into an incubator in the laboratory of Dr. Mary Parshley situated at the premises of defendant, Columbia University, which adjoins the defendant Hospital. The culture was to remain for four (4) days so that cell division could occur and a blastocyst would emerge. Preparations for the implantation of the blastocyst into Mrs. Del Zio were made by Dr. Sweeney for September 16, 1973, at New York Hospital.

Thereafter, on the next day, September 13, 1973, at approximately 2:00 P.M. Dr. Shettles was summoned to the office of defendant VANDE WIELE in the defendant Hospital. The tube containing the fertilized in-vitro culture was on defendant VANDE WIELE's desk. The stopper had been removed thereby destroying its sterile condition.

NINETEENTH: Defendant VANDE WIELE asked Dr. Shettles what he had placed in the culture tube and Dr. Shettles informed defendant VANDE WIELE of its contents; of Dr. Sweeney's participation and request, and of the situation and background of plaintiffs, JOHN E. DEL ZIO and DORIS DEL ZIO. Defendant VANDE WIELE then said that the culture was useless; that he, VANDE WIELE, had caused the culture to be removed from the said Dr. Parshely's laboratory incubator in the premises of defendant, Columbia University; and deliberately rendered it useless by removing the stopper therefrom and destroying its sterile condition.

Dr. Shettles asked defendant VANDE WIELE to return the culture tube to him and defendant VANDE WIELE refused to do so.

TWENTIETH: Dr. Shettles left defendant VANDE WIELE's office and immediately called Dr. Sweeney and related to him the acts and statements of defendant VANDE WIELE. Dr. Sweeney thereupon called defendant VANDE WIELE who stated to Dr. Sweeney that he had destroyed the culture because, he alleged, there was a proscription on in-vitro fertilization by the National Institute of Health and that it was therefore necessary for him, defendant VANDE WIELE, to terminate the culture immediately.

TWENTY-FIRST: That the said statement by defendant VANDE WIELE was in fact false, fraudulent, wrongful and malicious; that no such proscription existed and that, in actuality, defendant VANDE WIELE maliciously destroyed the culture, without inquiring as to its origin, ownership and purpose.

TWENTY-SECOND: That, thereafter, inquiry was made of the Department of Health, Education and Welfare, Public Health Service, National Institute of Health, Bethesda, Maryland, as to whether such proscription existed as defendant VANDE WIELE had stated as a purported justification of his wrongful act.

TWENTY-THIRD: By letter dated November 2, 1973, the National Institute of Health responded stating that in-vitro fertilization "is not proscribed by law or by official N.I.H. policy". . . .

TWENTY-EIGHTH: That the defendants' said wrongful actions have caused and are continuing to cause DORIS DEL ZIO, wife of the plaintiff, JOHN E. DEL ZIO, severe physical and mental pain and anguish and other injuries and disabilities which have continued since September 13, 1973, and will continue indefinitely, thereby depriving the plaintiff of the services and consortium of his wife.

TWENTY-NINTH: That the wrongful acts of defendants as herein set forth have caused plaintiff, JOHN E. DEL ZIO, shock, intense pain and suffering, and anguish and money damages, all of which have continued since the 13th day of September 1973 and which will continue indefinitely.

WHEREFORE, plaintiffs seek judgment against the defendants for the following:

ON THE FIRST CLAIM

Damages in favor of plaintiff, DORIS DEL ZIO, against the defendants in the amount of One Million ($1,000,000.00) Dollars.

ON THE SECOND CLAIM

Damages in favor of plaintiff, JOHN E. DEL ZIO, against the defendants in the amount of Five Hundred Thousand ($500,000) Dollars.

[Attorney]

[Date]

III. SURROGATE MOTHERHOOD

A. In General

1. [§4.25] Definition and Background

Surrogate motherhood, or surrogate parenting, describes a legal arrangement in which an individual or couple unable to conceive a child for some reason hires a "surrogate" to take the place of, or substitute for, the "mother". In some instances the party seeking to utilize the services of a surrogate mother is a single person, while in other instances it is a husband and wife. In surrogate motherhood arrangements the sperm of an unrelated male, in the case of an unmarried person, or the husband, in the case of a married couple, is inseminated into the surrogate mother. Typically the surrogate mother is sought because of the wife's infertility or sterility. By contrast, where the husband is infertile or sterile, the couple may choose to utilize artificial insemination, wherein a sperm donor is sought out, the wife is artificially inseminated, and the couple has a child related biologically to the wife. See COMMENT, ARTIFICIAL INSEMINATION AND SURROGATE MOTHERHOOD: A NURSERY FULL OF UNRESOLVED QUESTIONS, 17 Willamette LR 913 (1981). Artificial insemination by donor is the medical procedure used to impregnate the surrogate mother. [As to artificial insemination generally, see §§4.1, 4.2.] Then, in conjunction with an agreement or contract between the surrogate mother and the other party, the conceptus matures into a fetus and continues to develop in the womb of the surrogate. After the child is born, and assuming that no complications have arisen, the child is given by the surrogate to the other party, the party pays the surrogate a fee for her services, the father acknowledges paternity, and the couple adopts the child. See generally Bird, SURROGATE MOTHERHOOD, California Lawyer, February 1982, at 21; Black, LEGAL PROBLEMS OF SURROGATE MOTHERHOOD, 16 New England LR 313 (1981); Keane, LEGAL PROBLEMS OF SURROGATE MOTHERHOOD, 1980 Southern Illinois LJ 201 (1980); COMMENT, ARTIFICIAL INSEMINATION AND SURROGATE MOTHERHOOD – A NURSERY FULL OF UNRESOLVED PROBLEMS, 17 Willamette Law Review 913 (1981); COMMENT, PARENTHOOD BY PROXY: LEGAL IMPLICATIONS OF SURROGATE BIRTH, 67 Iowa LR 385 (1982); SURROGATE MOTHERS: THE LEGAL ISSUES, 7 American

Journal of Law and Medicine 323 (1981). In other words, surrogate parenting, as it most frequently happens, allows a couple in which the wife is infertile to have a child that is related biologically to the husband. Bird, *above.*

Surrogate motherhood arrangements are not new, but they have become increasingly visible in recent years. It has been said that surrogate motherhood is an area of legal practice that did not exist before about 1978. See Handel and Sherwyn, SURROGATE PARENTING, Trial, April 1982, at 57. This development has been caused by a number of factors. It has been estimated that one out of six couples has an infertility problem. Moreover, there are no longer enough children available through adoption. The shortage of adoptable children has developed for a number of reasons. First, contraceptives are being widely used. Second, there are close to two million abortions performed each year. Third, some unwed mothers are now keeping their babies rather than putting them up for adoption. SURROGATE PARENTING, The Surrogate Foundation, Inc. Moreover, the nationwide wait for adoptable babies is three to seven years. Handel and Sherwyn, *above.* Artificial insemination has been used by some couples in an attempt to have children, but this procedure has not worked in cases where the woman is sterile, or for some other medical reason is unable to have children. One alternative to a childless couple who is unable to conceive their own children has been the use of surrogate parenting. Couples may be motivated to hire a surrogate mother for reasons other than necessity. For instance, a woman may choose to seek a more convenient method of bearing a child so as to not interrupt her career. 7 American Journal of Law and Medicine at 324.

It has been predicted that in the 1980's and 1990's more single women will become surrogate mothers for women who cannot have children.Cetron and O'Toole, ENCOUNTERS WITH THE FUTURE: A FORECAST OF LIFE IN THE TWENTY-FIRST CENTURY (McGraw-Hill 1982). The reasons that surrogate mothers offer their services also arise for a variety of reasons. For example, a surrogate mother's primary interest may be financial in nature. In typical cases the surrogate mother receives $5,000 to $10,000, or more, plus expenses. Bird, *above.* In addition, for some surrogate mothers, an interest in helping others, specifically those who cannot conceive and bear a child on their own, serves as the reason for participating in surrogate agreements. 7 American Journal of Law and Medicine at 325.

In conjunction with the activity in the area of surrogate motherhood there have been established various groups to assist in the medical and legal issues relating to the subject. For example, the Surrogate Parent Foundation, a California educational corporation, was formed to provide information to the public and encourage the research and study of surrogate motherhood. The Foundation has an advisory board which includes attorneys and medical doctors.

Another unresolved issue is whether the couple or the doctor can be held liable if the surrogate mother dies or has her health impaired by the pregnancy. It has been suggested that where the contract provides for the surrogate mother and her husband to assume all risks incident to the pregnancy, including death, a negligence action would not be appropriate, since it would be unclear what the father's duty to the surrogate mother would be, and in any event, the surrogate mother would have entered into this arrangement knowing what risks she would be exposed to. If any of the harm done to the surrogate mother was a result of some action by the physician, the surrogate mother could bring a medical malpractice action. If the surrogate mother dies, her family or her estate could bring a wrongful death action against the physician. KY ATTY GEN OP, 7 FLR 2246 (1981).

It has been estimated that by the end of 1981, there were about 100 children born to surrogate mothers and adopted by others. Bird, *above*.

Despite the apparent simplicity and advantages for all of the parties in the surrogate motherhood process, there are still many unresolved issues and problems because of the legal and medical novelty of the processes involved. For example, there are serious ethical considerations involved for attorneys who participate in setting up surrogate mother arrangements, or in drafting surrogate mother-infertile couple contracts. The primary ethical issue centers on the duty of an attorney to not counsel or assist his client in conduct the attorney knows to be illegal. Because the legality of surrogate mother contracts has yet to be established either judicially or legislatively, the ethical issues should be considered by the attorney. [Generally, see §4.26.]

There are also significant constitutional questions regarding whether a state can proscribe surrogate mother contracts. The most important constitutional question is whether a state can proscribe the entering into of a surrogate mother contract even though individuals possess a constitutionally protected right to privacy. See, e.g., *Planned Parenthood of Central Missouri v Danforth*, 428 US 52, 49 LEd2d 752, 96 SCt 2882 (1976). There is authority for the proposition that the state can proscribe such a contractual arrangement based on statutory and public policy reasons [see *Doe v Attorney General*, 106 MiA 169, 307 NW2d 438 (1981)], but some commentators believe that to proscribe such contracts may violate the parties' right to privacy. See Black, LEGAL PROBLEMS OF SURROGATE MOTHERHOOD, !6 New England LR 373 (1981). [Generally, see §4.27.]

Additionally, there exist unresolved issues focusing on contract law considerations. If a surrogate mother contract is held enforceable, there are unique problems with a surrogate mother-personal service contract that make the agreement, in some respects, difficult to enforce. Moreover, there are policy and statutory considerations that have been viewed as militating against the legality of surrogate mother contracts. These considerations have centered on the belief that public policy does not countenance the selling of babies. See *Syrkowski v Applewyard*, 8 FLR 2139 (Mi 1981). [Generally, see §4.28.]

Because existing law does not provide a procedure for judicial recognition of a contract establishing a surrogate mother-infertile couple agreement, a number of proposed legislative measures have been considered in various legislatures. A draft of a proposed Surrogate Parent Act for California is reprinted in full with explanatory comments at §§4.30, 4.31. Moreover, a sample surrogate mother-infertile couple contract is found at §4.32.

2. [§4.26] Ethical Considerations

Arrangements for surrogate mother agreements or contracts [see generally, §4.28] are typically made by attorneys. An issue to be aware of when drafting surrogate mother contracts centers on the ethical considerations for the participating attorney. The ethical issue may arise in the context of the requirement that an attorney shall not counsel or assist his client in conduct that the attorney knows to be illegal. See DR 7-102(a)(7). And since surrogate mother contracts have not yet received judicial or legislative approval, the issue of the contract's legality is unresolved.

In 1982 the Ethics Committee of the Association of the Bar of the City of New York was queried regarding the following factual situation: A law firm has been retained by a client to prepare a contract between the client and a third party. Under the terms of the proposed contract, the third party (a surrogate mother) would be artificially inseminated with the client's semen. If pregnancy and birth ensued, the surrogate mother would deliver the child to the client and his spouse, and would forfeit all her rights with respect to the child. The law firm advised the client that the contemplated contract may not be enforceable in the courts, but the client indicated his desire to proceed with the contract nonetheless. Specifically, the committee was asked whether it is ethically proper to prepare a contract in these circumstances. The committee, in opinion number 81-67, said that assuming the proposed contract is not illegal, no ethical rule prohibited a lawyer from preparing such an agreement. Moreover, the committee said:

> We may offer no opinion on the legality or enforceability of the contemplated contract for that is a question of law outside this committee's jurisdiction. It is, of course incumbent upon the inquiring law firm to determine whether the contract is illegal. If the law firm determines that it is illegal, then the lawyer must refuse to draft the contract. DR 7-102(a)(7) states that a lawyer shall not counsel or assist his client in conduct that the lawyer knows to be

illegal. If, however, the law firm concludes (as it apparently has) that the contract is merely voidable or unenforceable, then nothing in Cannon 7 or elsewhere in the code of professional responsibility prohibits the firm from drafting such a contract as long as the firm advises the client of the risks that the contract might not be enforced or may be voided by the other party.

We note that the law firm should advise the third party to seek separate counsel for it appears that the surrogate mother may have an actual, or potentially adverse interest to the firm's client.

3. [§4.27] Constitutional Considerations

The procedure of having a child by the method of surrogate motherhood [generally, see §4.25] is still unresolved in terms of its legality. The contract or agreement establishing the surrogate motherhood relationship with a couple unable to conceive a child may also be unenforceable. [Generally, see §4.29.] Nonetheless, there remains the issue of whether there exists a constitutional right to enter into a surrogate motherhood agreement or contract.

There has been a longstanding rule that individual states can determine their own domestic relations laws. Domestic relations is an area regarded as exclusively within the province of the states. *Sosna v Iowa*, 419 US 393, 95 SCt 553, 42 LE2d 532 (1975). However, with the recognition by the United States Supreme Court of a constitutional right to privacy, this may begin to change. An individual may make decisions relating to contraception, family relationships, and marriage without unjustified interference. See *Carey v Population Serv Internatl*, 431 US 678, 97 SCt 2010, 52 LE2d 675 (1977); *Roe v Wade*, 410 US 113, 93 SCt 705, 35 LE2d 147 (1973). And the right to privacy means the right of individual or married persons to be free from unwarranted governmental intrusion into matters so fundamentally affecting a person as the decision whether to bear or beget a child. *Planned Parenthood of Central Missouri v Danforth*, 428 US 52, 96 SCt 2831, 49 LE2d 788 (1976); *Eisenstadt v Baird*, 405 US 438, 92 SCt 1029, 31 LE2d 349 (1972).

One commentator has suggested that insofar as anti-black market statutes and equivalent judicial decisions invalidate surrogate motherhood contracts by which individuals effectuate their rights of procreation and familial self-determination, they appear to invade the protected realm of privacy in a direct way. The statutes are not invalid merely because they affect decision-making relative to procreation and the family. However, where a decision as fundamental as whether to bear or beget a child is involved, regulations imposing a burden on it may be justified only by compelling state interests, and must be narrowly drawn to express only those interests. The regulation must be no more restrictive than necessary to accomplish the purpose. Black, LEGAL PROBLEMS OF SURROGATE MOTHERHOOD, 16 New England LR 373 (1981).

However, it has been held in the context of a judicial review of a surrogate mother transaction that the right of privacy enunciated in *Carey*, above, does not prohibit state interference in a surrogate mother contractual arrangement. In *Doe v Attorney General*, 106 MiA 169, 307 NW2d 438 (1981), the court was asked to declare unconstitutional those sections of the Michigan Adoption Code which prohibit the exchange of money or other consideration in connection with adoption and related proceedings. The plaintiffs appealed from an order of a lower court which denied their motion for summary judgment and granted the defendant's own motion. It was alleged that Jane Doe had undergone a tubal ligation, rendering her biologically incapable of bearing children and that the Does wished to have a child biologically related to John Doe. Another party, Mary Roe, was employed as a secretary by John Doe. The complaint alleged that these parties contemplated and intended to enter into the following agreement: Jane Doe and John Doe would pay Mary Roe a sum of money in consideration for her promise to bear and deliver John Doe's child by means of artificial insemination; a licensed physician would conduct the artificial insemination process; prior to the delivery of the child, John Doe would file a notice of intent to claim paternity; at the time the child was born, John Doe would formally acknowledge the paternity of the child; Mary Roe would acknowledge that John Doe was the father of the child; and that Mary Roe would consent to the adoption of the child by John Doe and Jane Doe. The agreement also provided that the plaintiffs would pay to Mary Roe $5,000 plus medical expenses. In addition, Mary Roe would be covered by sick leave, pregnancy disability insurance, and medical insurance from her employment while she was off work having the child and recuperating from the delivery. The plaintiffs alleged, the court noted, that the disputed statutory provisions impermissibly infringed upon their constitutional right to privacy. The court noted that *Carey v Population Serv Internatl*, 431 US 678, 97 SCt 2010, 52 LE2d 675 (1977) held that the decision whether or not to bear or beget a child was among those protected by the constitutional right of privacy. However, the court did not view this right as a valid prohibition to state interference in the plaintiffs' contractual arrangement. The court said the statute in question did not directly prohibit John Doe and Mary Roe from having the child as planned. The statute instead precluded the plaintiffs from paying consideration in conjunction with their use of the state's adoption procedures. In effect, the court reasoned, the plaintiffs' contractual agreement disclosed a desire to use the adoption code to change the legal status of the child. The court did not perceive this goal as within the realm of fundamental interests protected by the right to privacy from reasonable governmental regulation.

Although surrogates are most often used by married couples, single persons who want to raise children have also sought these services. The rationale for limiting surrogate use to married couples may not withstand constitutional challenge in light of United States Supreme Court holdings that place the right of privacy in procreative matters with the individual. COMMENT, SURROGATE BIRTH, 67 Iowa LR 385 (1982). However, because the principle cases in this area have dealt with an individual's privacy rights only within the context of marriage [see *Carey v Population Serv Internatl*, 431 US 678, 97 SCt 2010, 52 LE2d 675 (1977); *Planned Parenthood of Central Missouri v Danforth*, 428 US 52, 96 SCt 2831, 49 LE2d 788 (1976); *Eisenstadt v Baird*, 405 US 438, 92 SCt 1029, 31 LE2d 349 (1972)], it remains unclear whether the reasoning of these decisions would apply to single persons. 67 Iowa LR at 388.

4. Contract Considerations

a. [§4.28] Generally

Contracts involving surrogate mother agreements have generally followed two patterns. First, some of the contracts have been in the form of memoranda or agreements between the two parties. These memoranda are usually short and simply set out the agreement between the two parties without going into detail. Second, the more popular type of contract appears to be those in which the agreements between the surrogate mother, and perhaps her husband, and the adopting father and wife are set out specifically and with much detail. For example, a more thorough contract might contain clauses addressing the following issues: the parties, their relationships, and their intents are specified; payment terms are established before insemination, and provision is made for the adopting couple to pay the attorney beforehand (fees are typically from $5,000 to $10,000 plus expenses), payments scheduled to include costs of the pregnancy as well as any medical complications arising for a limited period after the pregnancy, insurance to cover the death of the surrogate mother during the pregnancy, for her health and well-being for a period of six months after the pregnancy, and for the child should the inseminating father die before the child is born; a requirement that the surrogate mother and the inseminating father will go through medical and psychological tests before insemination; a provision that the surrogate mother and her husband will agree to terminate parental rights to the child after he or she is born; a provision that the surrogate mother shall not smoke, drink or take nonprescription drugs during the pendency of the pregnancy; a provision that the surrogate mother undergo an amniocentesis test during the pregnancy; a provision regarding abortion, when, and under what circumstances it would be performed; a provision for the parents to adopt the child after he or she is born, and in the alternative the right of the parents to bring an action for intentional infliction of emotional distress if the surrogate mother decides to keep the child after birth, reimbursement of the surrogate mother's attorney's fees; provisions for the protection of the anonymity of all parties; a provision that the surrogate mother's husband agrees not to assert that he is the child's legal father; a provision that a blood test be administered after the birth of the child to assure that the child was the inseminating father's offspring; a provision that the final fee to be paid to the surrogate mother is contingent upon final adoption by the parents. Generally, see Andrews, REMOVING THE STIGMA OF SURROGATE MOTHERHOOD, 4 Family Advocate 21 (1981); Handel and Sherwyn, SURROGATE PARENTING, Trial, April 1982, at 57. COMMENT, SURROGATE MOTHERS: THE LEGAL ISSUES, 7 American Journal of Law and Medicine 323 (1981). [For an example of a sample contract, which includes provisions for some of these items, see §4.32.]

If a surrogate mother contract is held legal and enforceable, practical difficulties in the enforcement of the contract may be present because of the unique features of the agreement. For example, if the biological father and his wife breached the contract by refusing to pay the agreed upon compensation, the surrogate mother could give the child up for adoption and bring suit against the couple for the compensation. However, if the surrogate mother breached the contract by refusing to submit to artificial insemination, the married couple could sue and seek the compensation already paid. The other alternative, specific performance, is available where damages are not an adequate remedy. But generally courts will not order specific performance of contracts for personal services because of the impracticality of assuring satisfactory performance. On the other hand, where the surrogate mother chooses to keep the child, thus attempting to prevent the married couple from obtaining the child, specific performance should be feasible since all that is needed is to order the surrogate mother to consent to the adoption and deliver the child to the custody of the other biological parent. See Black, LEGAL PROBLEMS OF SURROGATE MOTHERHOOD, 16 New England LR 373 (1981).

b. [§4.29] Policy and Statutory Considerations

There is no authority yet for the proposition that a contract providing for the hiring of a surrogate mother to carry the child of an infertile couple is a legal and binding agreement. [As to surrogate motherhood generally, see §4.25.] It has been suggested that in most states the contract providing for surrogate motherhood [generally, see §4.25] is probably void. Black, LEGAL

PROBLEMS OF SURROGATE MOTHERHOOD, 16 New England LR 373 (1981). This lack of authority is predicated on statutory and public policy considerations that militate against recognition of surrogate mother contracts. In general, contracts may be held void and or unenforceable under the general rule that the contract violates public policy or that the contract mandates performance of an illegal act. See, e.g., *International Dairy Queen Inc v Bank of Wadley*, 407 FSupp 1270 (MD Al 1976); *Board of Educ of Sch Dist No 68, DuPage Cty v Surety Developers, Inc*, 24 IlA3d 638, 321 NE2d 99 (1974).

The statutory and public policy objections to surrogate motherhood contracts [generally, see §4.28] have been based on statutes which make it a crime to make payments to a biological parent in connection with the adoption of his or her child. Black, LEGAL PROBLEMS OF SURROGATE MOTHERHOOD, 16 New England LR 373 (1981). If the payment the surrogate mother receives is simply a payment for her expenses in carrying the child to term, then it covers the cost of supplying a service. However, if the payment bears no relationship to costs of pregnancy, it begins to resemble a contract for the sale of a child. This type of contract has, historically, been prohibited. COMMENT, SURROGATE MOTHERS: THE LEGAL ISSUES, 7 American Journal of Law and Medicine 323 (1981). Examples of two illustrative statutes that might impede the surrogate motherhood process, in terms of initially seeking the surrogate mother and the subsequent contract between the surrogate mother and the infertile couple, are CAL CIV CODE §224p (West 1981), and CAL PEN CODE §273 (West 1970). Advertisements seeking surrogate mothers to bear children for infertile couples may constitute violations of state advertising for adoption statutes. For example, CAL CIV CODE §224p (West 1981) states that any person or organization, without holding a valid license or permit to place children, who advertises that he or she will place a child for adoption is guilty of a misdemeanor. In addition, some state laws prohibit the selling of babies. CAL PEN CODE §273 (1970) states that it is a misdemeanor for any person or agency to offer to pay money or to pay money to a parent for the placement for adoption, for the consent to an adoption, or for cooperation in the completion of an adoption of his child. It is a misdemeanor for any parent to obtain the financial benefits set forth in this statute with the intent to receive such financial benefits without completing the adoption or consenting to the adoption.

The statutory and public policy objections have been applied in a number of instances. For example, it was the opinion of the Attorney General of Kentucky, 7 FLR 2246 (1981), that any surrogate parenthood contract was illegal and unenforceable in Kentucky, because of three Kentucky statutes and a strong public policy against baby buying. The opinion cited KY REV STAT §199.500(5) which says that in no case shall an adoption be granted or consent for adoption be held valid if such consent for adoption is given prior to the fifth day after the birth of the child. However, the opinion asked the question whether, before the establishment of the surrogate arrangement, the couple can legally contract with the surrogate mother that for a stated consideration from the couple to the surrogate, the latter consents or will consent to the wife's adoption of the child. Inherent in the surrogate's promise is that she agrees to be artificially inseminated with the natural father's sperm and to carry the fetus to delivery. Prior to the birth, the opinion said, the surrogate mother cannot give legally binding consent for adoption because it would violate Ky Rev Stat §199.500(5). The purpose of this statute is to give the mother time after the birth of her child to consider whether to give the child up for adoption. But even if the contract was written to provide that the surrogate mother would give consent in the future, five days after the birth of the child, in the attorney general's opinion, the contract would still be illegal. It would not be enforced for reasons of public policy, for such a contract would be a subterfuge to get around the language of Ky Rev Stat §199.500(5). In addition, the opinion considered an alternative agreement in which the contract would be for the termination of parental rights by the surrogate mother and her husband. This agreement should be made between the natural father and the surrogate mother (and her husband if she is married). The surrogate mother and her husband would agree that on the fifth day after the birth or as soon thereafter as possible, they would institute proceedings to terminate their parental rights to the child. The attorney general noted that Ky Rev Stat §199.601(1) deals with parental filing of petitions for the voluntary termination of his or her parental rights. Under 199.601(2) no petition can be filed under this chapter prior to five days after birth. In the attorney general's opinion, the courts of Kentucky would not enforce a contract or find such a contract legal because of its intent to circumvent Ky Rev Stat §199.601(2) and the public policy behind the five-day waiting period. Although the attorney general said that either statute would be sufficient to declare the surrogate parenthood process illegal, he also said there was a strong legal prohibition against surrogate parenthood in Kentucky based on the strong public policy against the buying and selling of children. Pursuant to Ky Rev Stat §199.590(2) no person, agency or institution not licensed may charge a fee or accept remuneration for the procurement of any child for adoption purposes. The attorney general believed that this statute precluded not only the surrogate mothers from receiving payments for giving up children to adoption but also included all who are involved in the surrogate transaction, since each is involved in the procurement of a child for adoption purposes. Moreover, the attorney general said that even though there is no statutory equivalent to Ky Rev Stat §199.590(2) for termination of parental rights, there is the same public policy issue. It was the attorney general's belief that the courts of Kentucky would not allow persons to receive monetary consideration for the procurement of a child, regardless of whether it is referred to as an adoption proceeding or as a termination of parental rights.

And in *Syrkowski v Applewyard*, 8 FLR 2139 (1981), the court held that the Michigan Paternity Act was not intended and could not be used to establish the parental rights of a semen donor in a surrogate motherhood arrangement. Neither the law nor the public policy of Michigan permit the direct rendering of the judicial recognition and enforcement of surrogate mother agreements, the court said. The social wisdom and the legal recognition of such agreements are matters of legislative concern and not judicial preemption, the court said. In *Syrkowski* the plaintiff filed a complaint on June 19, 1981, under the Michigan Paternity Act alleging that the defendant, the surrogate mother, was pregnant with a child conceived by the plaintiff in March 1981. In July 1981, the surrogate mother-defendant admitted the allegations of the complaint, and asked the court for an appropriate order of filiation adjudging the plaintiff to be the natural and legal father of her child. Subsequently, the parties proposed a consent order of filiation which asked the court to declare that: first, the plaintiff was the natural father of the child; second, the plaintiff was awarded custody and was responsible for the care, support and education of the expected child; third, the expected child's birth certificate show that the plaintiff was the father; and fourth, the plaintiff may specify the child's surname. The attorney general, as an intervenor, argued that the child was presumed to be the legal child of the defendant and her husband. Moreover, the attorney general argued that the consideration paid by the plaintiff to the defendant for bearing the child and relinquishing custody violated public policy, and cited *Doe v Attorney General*, 106 MiA 169, 307 NW2d 438 (1981). The court said the issue in the case, whether the Paternity Act may be utilized as a procedural device to validate a contract for a surrogate parent arrangement, was an issue of first impression. The court noted the Paternity Act is silent regarding this, and therefore that it was obligated to ascertain the intent of the legislature. The Paternity Act was enacted to impose financial responsibility of illegitimate children upon those who fathered them and to protect the children from becoming a public charge, the court said. Pursuant to the act, the court said it had jurisdiction over paternity proceedings for the limited purpose of determining financial responsibility for a child born outside of marriage. The court said the plaintiff's petition asked it to recognize and endorse the terms of a surrogate parent arrangement. A careful reading of the act reveals that there was no legislative history or intent when the Paternity Act was enacted, or any time prior thereto, by which the legislature intended to apply the statute to the situation in this case, the court said. Furthermore, no amendment of the Act would alter the court's conclusion. Therefore, the court said, the legal and public policy considerations associated with the surrogate arrangements in general go beyond the scope of the Paternity Act and jurisdiction of the court. If Michigan is going to recognize these contracts, comprehensive legislation is needed to resolve the profound societal concerns relating to the rights, obligations, and interests of all parties affected by the arrangements, the court said.

However, at least one commentator has sought to distinguish anti-baby selling statutes from the surrogate motherhood process. Statutes that prohibit the selling of babies, such as CAL PEN CODE §273 (1970), serve a legitimate purpose in terms of forbidding the sale of infants as if they were chattels. By contrast, surrogate motherhood is significantly different from baby-buying and presents a situation never considered by the legislatures which enacted the current penal statutes. Furthermore, the policy reasons underlying the antipathy to payment for adoption suggest that they are inapplicable to surrogate motherhood. For example, in the typical baby-buying situation, the involuntarily pregnant mother gives birth to an illegitimate child in whom its biological father has no interest. The mother usually is financially unable to support the child even if she wishes to do so. The purchase of the baby by another party then ensues. In the surrogate situation, however, the factual situation is different. The infertile couple seeks a surrogate to carry the father's child, and the surrogate consciously chooses to bear the child. When the child is born, there is a home prepared for it consisting of the biological father and his wife. Black, LEGAL PROBLEMS OF SURROGATE MOTHERHOOD, 16 New England LR 373 (1981).

B. Sample Legislation

1. [§4.30] Form For Proposed Legislation

One of the major problems with surrogate mother [generally, see §4.25] agreements has been the lack of judicial or legislative approval, or guidelines, for the implementation and enforcement of the contract. See, e.g., *Syrkowski v Applewyard*, 8 FLR 2139 (Mi 1981). Because existing state laws do not provide for the legality and recognition of these contracts, a number of proposed surrogate mother statutes have been introduced. An illustrative example of such a proposed statute is California Assembly Bill No. 3771. The bill would provide a procedure for the approval of a petition incorporating a contract in which a woman agrees to be inseminated by the sperm of a man whose wife is unable to bear a child and to relinquish all legal rights to any child resulting from that insemination to the husband and wife, upon its birth, and for the enforcement of such a contract.

The proposed surrogate mother bill states as follows:

SECTION 1. Part 9 (commencing with Section 7500) is added to Division 4 of the Civil Code, to read:

PART 9. SURROGATE PARENT ACT

7500. This part shall be known and may be cited as the Surrogate Parent Act of 1982.

7501. In enacting this part, it is the intention of the Legislature to facilitate the ability of infertile couples to become parents through the employment of the services of a surrogate.

The Legislature finds and declares that surrogate contracts are in accord with sound social policy.

7502. As used in this act:

(a) "Infertile couple" means a husband who is capable of producing viable sperm and his wife who has been determined by a licensed physician to be incapable of conceiving or carrying a child to term without significant risk to her life or who has been unable to conceive for one year prior to the date of the execution of the contract.

(b) "Surrogate" means a woman who consents to be artificially inseminated by a man who is the husband of a woman described in subdivision (a) and to carry any child that she conceives by that man.

(c) "Surrogate contract" means an agreement between the infertile couple and the surrogate which determines the rights and obligations of each of the parties to the agreement, consistent with the provisions of this part.

7503. The department of the superior court to which proceedings under the Family Law Act (Part 5 (commencing with Section 4000) of Division 4) ordinarily are assigned shall have jurisdiction over all proceedings and actions pursuant to this part.

7504. The infertile couple and the surrogate shall be represented by separate counsel.

7505. (a) Upon the verified petition of an infertile couple and the surrogate, the court shall determine, based on affidavits or other documentary evidence, whether the requirements of this part have been satisfied.

(b) The petition shall include all of the following:

(1) The original executed copy of the contract.

(2) Evidence of the wife's infertility.

(3) Evidence of the medical evaluation of the husband and of the surrogate.

(4) Evidence that the infertile couple and the surrogate have retained separate legal counsel and that the opinion of counsel in each case is that his or her client's entry into the contract is voluntary and that the client understands the terms of the contract.

(5) Proof that the funds described in Section 7506 have been deposited in an escrow account or attorney trust account.

(6) Evidence that the surrogate is at least 18 years of age.

(7) Evidence of the marriage of the infertile couple.

(8) Evidence of the ability of the infertile couple to care for the child.

(c) The court shall approve the petition if it finds that the requirements of subdivision (b) have been met, a report recommending approval of the petition has been submitted by an agency approved by the court to conduct a home study of the infertile couple, and the court has reviewed any criminal record of either the husband or wife and found that the offense committed by that person should not affect his or her ability to function as a parent.

(d) A petition pursuant to this part shall be given calendar priority and shall be handled expeditiously.

7506. A contract approved pursuant to this part shall include, but shall not be limited to, all of the following provisions:

(a) That the surrogate agrees to relinquish all parental rights to, and the custody of, any child conceived as a result of the insemination to the infertile couple immediately after his or her birth, and to consent to the adoption of any such child by the wife.

(b) A requirement for medical evaluation of the surrogate and of the husband (in the case of the surrogate the medical evaluation shall include psychological screening).

(c) That responsibility for all medical expenses of the surrogate during pregnancy and a six-week postpartum period shall be paid in an agreed manner.

(d) The provision of term life and health insurance for the surrogate and infertile couple for such term and in such amounts as shall be determined by the parties to the contract.

(e) That reasonable monetary compensation shall be paid to the surrogate by the infertile couple in an agreed amount.

(f) That the amount of payment shall be placed in an escrow account or attorney trust account prior to the first insemination of the surrogate; however, a portion of the amount, as agreed by the parties, shall not be deposited until the child's birth.

(g) That legal and equitable remedies shall be available in the event of a breach of the surrogate contract by any of the parties.

(h) That the infertile couple agree to accept custody of, and parental responsibility for, any child conceived as a result of the insemination, immediately after his or her birth.

7507. As a part of its determination pursuant to Section 7505, the court shall review all information submitted by the parties to the proposed surrogate contract and may order the submission of such additional information as it deems necessary to insure the ability of the parties to comply with the terms of the surrogate contract.

7508. (a) Upon the court's approval of the petition, it shall retain jurisdiction in the matter until the entry of both a decree of adoption by the wife and a decree of paternity of the husband with regard to any child conceived pursuant to the contract. Notwithstanding any other provision of law, such a decree shall be entered within 45 days of the birth of the child. The infertile couple shall have the right to custody and control of the child prior to the entry of such a decree.

The fee established by Section 10619 of the Health and Safety Code shall be paid at the time of the entry of the decree of adoption.

(b) The husband shall be presumed to be the father of any child born to a woman who agrees to act as a surrogate pursuant to this part that was conceived during that period of time in which it was possible for her to have conceived as a result of insemination pursuant to a contract incorporated in a petition approved pursuant to this part. This presumption shall be a presumption affecting the burden of proof and may only be rebutted as specified in Section 606 of the Evidence Code, by clear and convincing evidence. A decree made pursuant to Section 7010 establishing a father and child relationship between the child and a man other than the husband shall be considered a rebuttal of this presumption.

7509. The surrogate shall not be inseminated prior to approval of a petition pursuant to this part.

7510. During the performance of the surrogate contract, the court may require such additional information from, testing of, and personal interviews with, the infertile couple and the surrogate as it deems necessary to insure compliance with the terms of the contract. All costs incurred in this connection shall be borne by the parties, as ordered by the court.

7511. Upon breach of a contract that is the subject of a petition approved pursuant to this part, the court may grant such legal and equitable relief as it deems appropriate, including specific performance.

7512. At the discretion of the supervising judge of the family law department, proceedings pursuant to this part, except for the procedures referred to in Section 7511, may be heard before an official of the family law department of the superior court designated by the court for this purpose.

7513. Subject to the power of the court to transfer actions and proceedings as provided in Title 4 (commencing with Section 392) of Part 2 of the Code of Civil Procedure, the county in which the contract is executed is the proper county for the filing of a petition pursuant to this part; and any proceeding in connection with that petition or the contract incorporated in any petition approved pursuant to this part.

7514. The presumption contained in Section 621 of the Evidence Code, and the presumptions contained in Sections 7004 and 7005, shall not be applicable to a child conceived by a woman who agrees to act as a surrogate pursuant to this part during that period of time in which it was possible for her to have conceived as a result of artificial insemination pursuant to a contract incorporated in a petition approved pursuant to this part.

7515. Payments made to a surrogate pursuant to subdivision (e) of Section 7506 shall be for the purpose of compensating her for her services and the making or the acceptance of such a payment shall not constitute a violation of Section 181 or 273 of the Penal Code.

7516. The court shall not approve the withdrawal of a consent to an adoption made in connection with a contract incorporated in a petition approved pursuant to this part unless it finds that extraordinary circumstances require that approval in order to protect the best interests of the child.

7517. The provisions of this part shall control over any other conflicting provision of law.

7518. In the event of a dispute as to the custody of a child conceived pursuant to a contract incorporated in a petition approved pursuant to this part, between the surrogate and the infertile couple, the provisions of the contract as to the custody of the child shall prevail over the provisions of Section 4600, unless the court finds that extraordinary circumstances require that the provisions of Section 4600 shall control.

SECTION 2. This act is an urgency statute necessary for the immediate preservation of the public peace, health, or safety within the meaning of Article IV of the Constitution and shall go into immediate effect. The facts constituting the necessity are:

In order that the provisions of this act shall be implemented to the maximum extent, it is necessary that it take effect at the earliest possible date.

2. [§4.31] Explanation of Proposed Legislation

Because of the novelty of and the recent developments in the process of surrogate motherhood [generally, see §4.25] many legal questions remain unresolved. In an effort to resolve some of these questions, proposed legislation has been introduced pertaining to the rights and responsibilities of the various parties in the surrogate motherhood process. One such proposal is California Assembly Bill No. 3771. The text of the bill appears at §4.30.

The bill was introduced in the California Assembly in April 1982. Its chief sponsor, Assemblyman Mike Roos, testified before committee hearings that the bill would provide a procedure for the execution and enforcement of a contract in which a woman agrees to be artificially inseminated with the sperm of a man whose wife is unable to bear a child, and relinquish all parental rights. Roos said the bill would protect those involved in two ways. First, it would provide regulations in the practice of surrogate parenting to protect the interest of all parties involved, and would provide legal recourse in the event the contract is broken. Second, it would remove the doubt as to the legality of the practice. Roos further explained that while surrogate parenting may not be the answer for everyone, there are many infertile couples with no alternatives to obtain an infant. He further stated that surrogate parenting is the parallel process to artificial insemination through sperm banks. In one case the male is infertile. In surrogate parenting the woman is infertile. In both cases one parent of the couple which keeps the child is a natural, biological parent, and the other is a step parent. This fact is important to distinguish both processes from regular adoptions. The fact that one parent is the biological parent of the child is not lost on the couple. This makes the process much more meaningful to a couple than a regular adoption.

The President of the Surrogate Parent Foundation, a California nonprofit organization formed to provide information to the public and to encourage new research in this area, testified that, from early 1981 to early 1982, the Foundation had received 20,000 requests for information. Moreover, he said with infertility on the increase and adoptable infants on the decrease, there is a need for an alternate method of childbearing.

The California Assembly Committee on Judiciary drafted a bill digest in which the major points of the bill were discussed. The digest stated that this bill would establish the Surrogate Parent Act to address situations in which a married couple and a woman enter into a contract for the woman to be artificially inseminated with the husband's sperm and to carry any child conceived to term, whereupon the child is to be given to the couple. The parties to a "surrogate contract" would be the "infertile couple" and the "surrogate", as defined. Each party would be represented by separate counsel.

The digest also stated that under the bill, a surrogate contract would have to include, but would not be limited to, all of the following provisions:

1. The surrogate's relinquishment of parental rights and custody immediately after the child's birth, and her consent to the wife's adoption of the child;
2. The infertile couple's acceptance of custody immediately after the child's birth;
3. Medical evaluation of the surrogate and the husband and psychological screening of the surrogate;
4. Responsibility for the surrogate's medical expenses during pregnancy and a six-week postpartum period;
5. Term life and health insurance for the parties;
6. Reasonable monetary compensation in an agreed amount to the surrogate, with placement of the money in an escrow or attorney trust account prior to the first insemination. However, a portion of the money would not be deposited until the child's birth;
7. That legal and equitable remedies would be available in the event of a breach of the contract.

The digest further stated that the bill would also require a court, upon the parties' petition, to determine whether they have complied with the provisions of the act. Supported by affidavits or other evidence, the petition would include, among other things, evidence that the wife is infertile, that the surrogate is at least 18 years of age, and that the couple is married and able to care for the child. A report recommending approval of the petition must be submitted by an agency approved by the court to conduct a home study of the infertile couple. The court would also review any criminal records of the husband and wife in order to determine whether a reported offense would affect their ability to function as parents. At any time, the court could order the submission of more information as it deemed necessary. Upon approval of the petition, the court would retain jurisdiction in the matter until entry of a decree of adoption by the wife and a decree of the husband's paternity, within 45 days of the birth of the child. Legal and equitable remedies, including specific performance, could be granted by the court, as it deemed appropriate, in case of breach of the contract.

C. [§4.32] Sample Contract Form

Although the legality and enforceability of surrogate motherhood contracts remain unanswered questions [generally, see §4.25], there have been surrogate mother contracts entered into. The contract itself is the integral part of the surrogate mother-infertile couple relationship since it provides the rights and responsibilities of the parties. Therefore, the contract must identify the crucial elements of the relationship and provide for the contingencies that may develop during the relationship.

The following contract is an example of a surrogate motherhood contract. The major purposes of the contract are to protect the confidentiality of the parties, advise the parties and protect them from the medical and emotional risks involved, and make appropriate use of expert opinion and guidance during the pendency of the surrogate mother-infertile couple agreement. In addition, attached to the contract is a sample medical statement to be given by the natural father. The statement identifies a number of serious diseases, and defines their respective meanings and symptoms. There is also attached a sample exhibit to the surrogate mother-infertile couple contract. The exhibit discusses a test called amniocentesis, which is used to detect congenital defects of the fetus.

II. SURROGATE MOTHER CONTRACT

AGREEMENT

THIS AGREEMENT is made this ______________ day of ________________________________, 1980, by and between ________________________________ (hereinafter referred to as "Husband") and ________________________________ (hereinafter referred to as "Natural Father").

RECITALS

THIS AGREEMENT is made with reference to the following facts:

(1) The Natural Father is a married individual over the age of eighteen (18) years who is desirous of entering into the following agreement.

(2) The Natural Father desires to have a child who is biologically related to him.

(3) The Surrogate and her Husband are a married couple each over the age of eighteen (18) years who are desirous of entering into the following agreements in consideration of the financial remuneration incident hereto.

NOW THEREFORE, in consideration of the mutual promises contained herein and with the intentions of being legally bound, hereby the parties agree as follows:

SECTION I. The Surrogate represents that she is capable of conceiving children, but agrees that she will not form or attempt to form a parent-child relationship with any child she may conceive pursuant to the provisions of this contract and shall freely and readily, in conformance with applicable statutory regulations, terminate all parental rights to said child pursuant to this agreement.

SECTION II. The Surrogate and her Husband have been married since ______________ and the Husband is in agreement with the purposes, intents, and provisions of this agreement and agrees that his wife, the Surrogate, shall be artificially inseminated pursuant to the provisions of this agreement. The Husband will not form a parent-child relationship with any child the Surrogate may conceive by artificial insemination as described herein and agrees to freely and readily terminate all parental rights to said child and acknowledges he will do all acts necessary to rebut the presumption of paternity (including blood testing) as provided under ________ __________, or any other similar statute or regulation in any other applicable state or country.

SECTION III. The Natural Father is hereby entering into a written contractual agreement with the Surrogate and her Husband, whereby the Surrogate shall be artificially inseminated, with the semen of the Natural Father, by ______________, M.D. The Surrogate, upon becoming pregnant, shall carry said embryo/fetus(s) (hereinafter referred to as "child") until delivery. Delivery shall occur in the state of ____________. The Surrogate and her Husband agree that they will on the fifth day after delivery of the child, or as soon thereafter as is medically possible, institute proceedings in ______________________ (city and state), to terminate their respective parental rights to said child and sign any and all necessary affidavits, documents, etc., in order to further the intent and purposes of this agreement. The Surrogate and her Husband agree to sign all necessary affidavits prior to the birth of the child in order to have the Natural Father's name placed on said child's birth certificate as the biological father purusant to ______________.

SECTION IV. The Natural Father and the Surrogate and her Husband recognize and acknowledge that the Attorney(s) for the Natural Father shall act as agent for the Natural Father in all matters pertaining to this agreement in order to maintain complete confidentiality.

SECTION V. The consideration for this agreement, in addition to other provisions contained herein, shall be as follows:

(a) $__________ shall be paid to the Surrogate and her Husband upon entry of the judgment fully terminating the parental rights of the Surrogate and her Husband as defined by the law in Kentucky to the child to be born pursuant to these provisions between the Surrogate and the Natural Father.

ALTERNATE PROVISION,

[*Section V(a)* The Natural Father shall not pay the Surrogate a fee of any kind pursuant to this agreement but shall pay the Surrogate's pregnancy and confinement expenses beginning on the date her pregnancy is verified and continuing for one (1) month subsequent to the contemplated birth. Said pregnancy and confinement expenses shall not exceed $_________ per month in addition to the following:____________________________.

(b) The consideration to be paid said Surrogate and her Huband, shall be deposited with the attorney for the Natural Father at the time of the signing of this agreement and held in escrow until completion of the duties and obligations of the Surrogate and her Husband as herein described.

(c) The Natural Father shall pay the expenses incurred by the Surrogate and her Husband pursuant to her pregnancy, more specifically defined as follows:

(1) All medical, hospitalization, and pharmaceutical, laboratory and therapy expenses incurred in the Surrogate's pregnancy, not covered or allowed by her present health and major medical insurance, including all extraordinary medical expenses, but excluding any expenses for emotional/mental conditions/problems related to said pregnancy, lost wages or other incidentals.

(2) The Natural Father shall not be responsible for any latent medical expenses occurring six (6) weeks subsequent to the birth of the child unless the medical problem/abnormality incident thereto was known prior to the expiration of said six (6) week period.

(3) The total cost of all paternity testing.

(4) The surrogate's travel expenses incurred pursuant to this agreement. These expenses shall be defined as follows:

1. Travel expenses incurred by automobile or cab to the inseminating physician's regular office not to exceed 18¢ per mile.

2. Travel expenses incurred by automobile or airplane during the Surrogate's trip to the hospital for delivery. Said expenses incident to the automobile travel shall not exceed 18c per mile. The expenses incurred pursuant to airline transportation shall not exceed the fair and reasonable value of said airline services.

3. Automobile travel expenses incurred by the Surrogate incident to her travel to and from any physician's office or medical facility for purposes of treatment or testing made necessary by or incident to the pregnancy at the rate of 18¢ per mile.

4. Single hotel accommodations not to exceed $40.00 per night incurred by the Surrogate during the time the Surrogate is in ____________________ (city and state), for purposes of inseminations by the inseminating physician or for three (3) days subsequent to the Surrogate's release from the hospital after her delivery of the child contemplated herein if the Surrogate's stay is required in order to terminate her parental rights.

5. Expenses incurred by the Surrogate for meals incurred during her travels to ________(city and state)________, for purposes of insemination and/or delivery not to exceed the following amounts:

(a) Breakfast . . . . $ 5.00
(b) Lunch 10.00
(c) Dinner 12.00

(5) The Natural Father shall not be responsible for any lost wages of the Surrogate or her Husband, child care expenses of the Surrogate's children, or any other expense not specifically enumerated herein.

SECTION VI. Immediately subsequent to the birth of the child, the Surrogate, the Natural Father, and the child shall undergo the following tests under the direction of a pathologist designated by ________________, M.D.:

(1) Blood Group
(2) Serum Proteins
(3) Red Cell Enzymes
(4) White Cell/H.L.A.*

*Note: The White Cell/H.L.A. test has been held admissible on the issue of paternity in the following states: Florida, California, New York, New Jersey, Massachusetts, Illinois, and Washington. Contra Utah. See 6 Fam. L. Rep. (BNA) 1173 (1980), for case citations.

In the event that the Natural Father is excluded by one (1) or more of the aforementioned tests, this contract shall be immediately terminated and all monies and/or all other consideration paid to the Surrogate and her Husband, or in their behalf, or expended to screen and/or investigate the Surrogate and/or her Husband in contemplation of this contract by the Natural Father shall be immediately returned by the Surrogate and her Husband to the Natural Father. In addition, the Surrogate and her Husband shall pay interest on said monies at the United States prime rate existing at the time said sum(s) were expended.

SECTION VII. The Natural Father shall pay the cost of a term life insurance policy payable to a named beneficiary of the Surrogate with a policy amount of $________ and said policy shall remain in effect for six (6) weeks subsequent to the birth of the child. In addition, the Natural Father shall make appropriate arrangements in his will for the support of the infant child should he die prior to the birth of said child and shall pay the cost of a term life insurance policy on his life payable in trust to said unborn child.

SECTION VIII. The Surrogate and her Husband understand and agree to assume all risks including the risk of death which are incident to conception, pregnancy, childbirth and postpartum complications.

SECTION IX. The Surrogate and her Husband hereby agree to undergo psychological/psychiatric evaluation by (1) Dr. ________ and (2) Dr. ________________, psychologist(s) designated by the Natural Father or an agent thereof. The Natural Father shall pay for the cost of said psychiatric and psychological reviews. The evaluations of said psychiatrist and psychologist shall be submitted to the Natural Father, absent any information which would tend to identify or allow identification of the Surrogate and her Husband. The Surrogate and her Husband shall sign prior to their evaluations, a medical release authorizing the Attorney for the Natural Father to secure the release of said psychiatric evaluations prior to said evaluation.

SECTION X. "Child" as referred to in this agreement shall include all children born simultaneously pursuant to the inseminations done pursuant to the terms and provisions of this agreement provided the tests enumerated in Section VI are completed and satisfactory as to each child.

SECTION XI. In the event that the child is miscarried prior to the fifth (5th) month of pregnancy, no compensation as enumerated in Section V(a) shall be paid to the Surrogate. However, the expenses enumerated in Section V(c) shall be paid or reimbursed to the Surrogate and her Husband in addition to any and all travel and incidental expenses incident hereto incurred by the Surrogate and/or her Husband. In the event the child is miscarried, dies, or is stillborn subsequent to the fourth (4th) month of pregnancy, the Surrogate shall receive $__________ in lieu of the compensation enumerated in Section V(a) only if the paternity testing enumerated in Section VI(6) is completed and satisfactory as to said child. In the event of a miscarriage or stillbirth as described above, this agreement shall terminate and neither the Surrogate nor the Natural Father will be under any further obligation under this agreement.

SECTION XII. The Surrogate and the Natural Father shall undergo a complete physical and genetic evaluation, under the direction and supervision of ______________________, M.D., to determine whether the physical health and well-being of each is satisfactory. Said physical examination shall include testing for venereal diseases, specifically including syphilis and gonorrhea. Said venereal disease testing shall be done prior to each insemination.

SECTION XIII. In the event that custody of the child is awarded to the Surrogate and/or her Husband or their family, or any individual or organization, not related to the Natural Father, by any court decision or otherwise, the Natural Father shall be indemnified by the Surrogate and/or her Husband, both jointly and severally, for any and all monies he is required to pay for child support or pregnancy related expenses pursuant to said court order and shall be entitled to immediate reimbursement from the Surrogate and her Husband for all monies and/or other consideration paid to the Surrogate pursuant to this agreement or expended on behalf of the Surrogate and/or her Husband.

SECTION XIV. The Natural Father agrees that he will not seek to learn the identity of the Surrogate and/or her Husband or their family, nor advise the child of said identity if known.

SECTION XV. The Surrogate and her Husband agree that they will not seek to learn the identity of the Natural Father of the child and will not attempt to contact same if their identity is learned.

SECTION XVI. In the event that pregnancy has not occurred within a reasonable time, in the opinion of the inseminating physician, ______________________, M.D., this agreement shall terminate by written notice from the Attorney for the Natural Father to the Surrogate and/or her Husband.

SECTION XVII. All parties hereto agree that they will not provide nor allow their agents to provide any information to the public, news media or any other individual or group which could lead to the disclosure of the identity of the parties hereto or the child.

SECTION XVIII. In the event the Surrogate and/or her Husband violate any of the provisions contained herein, this agreement may be immediately terminated at the option of the Natural Father without any further liability hereunder. In the event the Natural Father does terminate this agreement, the Natural Father shall be under no obligation to pay any monies to the Surrogate or reimburse any of her expenses or her Husband's expenses. In addition, the Surrogate and her Husband must reimburse the Natural Father for all monies expended on her behalf pursuant to this agreement.

SECTION XIX. The Surrogate and her Husband agree that they will provide no interviews of any kind whatsoever, either of a public or private nature, without the prior written consent of the Attorney for the Natural Father.

SECTION XX. The Surrogate agrees that she will not abort the child once conceived except, if in the opinion of the inseminating physician, such action is necessary for the physical health of the

Surrogate or the child has been determined by said physician to be physiologically abnormal. In the event of either of these two (2) contingencies, the Surrogate desires and agrees to have said abortion.

SECTION XXI. The Natural Father assumes the legal responsibility for any child who may possess congenital abnormalities and he has been previously advised of the risk of such abnormalities. (See attached Medical Statement of Natural Father).

SECTION XXII. In the event that the Natural Father predeceases the birth of the child, said child shall be placed in the custody of ____________________, for placement through a private adoption to a designated person upon consent of the appropriate social agency.

SECTION XXIII. The Surrogate and her Husband both agree that they will not seek to view the infant child born pursuant to this contract at any time, nor will the Surrogate and her Husband seek to view or meet with the Natural Father.

SECTION XXIV. The Surrogate further agrees to adhere to all medical instructions given to her by ____________________, M.D. as well as her independent obstetrician. The Surrogate also agrees not to smoke cigarettes, drink any alcoholic beverages, use any illegal drugs, non-prescription medications or prescribed medications without written consent from ________________________, M.D. The Surrogate agrees to follow a prenatal medical examination schedule to consist of no fewer visits than: one visit per month during the first seven months of pregnancy, two visits (each to occur at two week intervals) during the eighth month of pregnancy and four visits (each to occur at weekly intervals) during the ninth month of pregnancy. The Surrogate agrees to take all necessary steps to sign all necessary documents in order to have her medical records sent to the Attorney for the Natural Father on a monthly basis.

SECTION XXV. Each party acknowledges that he or she fully understands the agreement and its legal effect and that he or she is signing the same freely and voluntarily and that neither party has any reason to believe that the other(s) did not freely and voluntarily execute said agreement.

SECTION XXVI. In the event any of the provisions of this agreement are deemed to be invalid or unenforceable, the same shall be deemed severable from the remainder of this agreement and shall not cause the invalidity or unenforceability of the remainder of this agreement. If such provision shall be deemed invalid due to its scope or breadth, such provision shall be deemed valid to the extent of the scope of breadth permitted by law.

SECTION XXVII. This agreement may be executed in two (2) or more counterparts, each of which shall be an original but, all of which shall constitute one and the same instrument.

SECTION XXVIII. This agreement sets forth the entire agreement between the parties with regard to the subject matter hereof. All agreements, covenants, representations, and warranties, express and implied, oral and written, of the parties are contained herein. No other agreements, covenants, representations or warranties express or implied, oral or written, have been made by any party to the other(s) with respect to the subject matter of this agreement. All prior and contemporaneous conversations, negotiations, possible and alleged agreements and representations, covenants and warranties with respect to the subject matter hereof are waived, merged herein and superseded hereby. This is an integrated agreement.

SECTION XXIX. This agreement can be amended only by a written agreement signed by all parties hereto.

SECTION XXX. This agreement has been drafted, negotiated, executed and performed in ______________ (city and state), and shall be governed by, continued and enforced in accordance with the laws of the ______________ (state).

SECTION XXXI. No provision in this agreement is to be interpreted for or against any party because that party or that party's legal representative drafted the provisions.

____

Prepared by:

____

Attorney at Law

We, ______________ and ______________ recognize that there is a signature line on the attached page for signatures by the Natural Father and that in order to maintain confidentiality we will never see any signatures of said Natural Father, although it is our collective intention to enter into a binding legal obligation.

______________	______________
Surrogate	Date
______________	______________
Surrogate's Husband	Date
______________	______________
Attorney for Surrogate and her Husband	Date
______________	______________
Attorney for Natural Father	Date

STATE)
)
COUNTY)

The foregoing instrument was acknowledged before me this ____________ day of ____________________,
1980, by ____________________, ____________________,
____________________, and ____________________.

____

NOTARY PUBLIC
STATE AT LARGE

My Commission expires the _____ day of _________ , 19____.

I, ______________________________, recognize that there is a signature line on the attached page for signatures by the Surrogate and her Husband, and that in order to maintain confidentiality I will never see any signatures of said Surrogate and her Husband, although it is our collective intention to enter into a binding legal obligation.

____________________	____________________
Natural Father	Date
____________________	____________________
Attorney for Natural Father	Date
____________________	____________________
Attorney for Surrogate and her Husband	Date

STATE)
)
COUNTY)

The foregoing instrument was acknowledged before me this ____________ day of ____________________ , 19____,
by ____________________, ____________________ , and ____________________
____________________.

____

NOTARY PUBLIC
STATE AT LARGE

My Commission expires the ________ day of ________,
19____.

MEDICAL STATEMENT GIVEN BY NATURAL FATHER

I, ________________, Natural Father, hereby state that I am familiar with the following diseases and that no one in my family, to my knowledge, has ever experienced such diseases:

1. Tay-Sacs disease:

Tay-Sacs disease is primarily found in Jewish persons of east European descent and is characterized by a failure to thrive, hypertoxicity, progressive spastic paralysis, loss of vision and occurrence of blindness, usually with muscular degeneration and optic atrophy, convulsions, and mental deterioration.

2. Sickle-Cell Anemia:

This an hereditary disease that affects seven per cent to nine per cent of the United States black population. Homogenous carriers of the Sickle-Cell gene are characterized by the presence of crescent-shaped or sickle-shaped erythrocytes in peripheral blood; symptoms include those of leg ulcers, arthritic manifestations and acute attacks of pain.

3. Neurofibromatosis:

A familial condition, characterized by developmental changes in the nervous system, muscles, bones and skin, and marked superficially by the formation of multiple pedunculated soft tumors distributed over the entire body associated with areas of pigmentation.

4. Down's Syndrome:

Also known as Mongolism and Trisomy 21 Syndrome, is a syndrome of mental retardation associated with a variable constellation of abnormalities caused by representation of at least a critical portion of chromosome 21, three times instead of twice, in some or all cells; the abnormalities include retarded growth, hypoplastic face with short nose, prominent epicanthic skin folds, protruding lower lip, small round ears with prominent antihelix, fissured and thickened tongue, laxness of joint ligaments, pelvic dysplasia, broad hands and feet, stubby fingers, dry rough skin in older patients and abundant slack neck skin in newborn.

5. Polycystic Kidney Disease:

Characterized by numerous cysts of varying sizes scattered diffusely through the kidneys, sometimes resulting in organs that tend to resemble grape-like clusters of cysts.

6. Syphilis:

May result in deafness, blindness and mental retardation.

EXHIBIT

Amniocentesis is a test used by doctors to detect congenital defects of the fetus. It is usually performed between the sixteenth and twentieth week of pregnancy. Besides amniocentesis, there are other tests that may presently be employed or that will be available to the physician soon, to detect genetic defects of the fetus. They are: ultrasonography, radiography, setoscopy, maternal endocervical sampling, and maternal blood and urine sampling. The amniocentesis was first used in the 1930's, but it was not until about 1970 that the test was "commonly accepted in medical practice." The test is performed by removing a sample of amniotic fluid surrounding the fetus of the mother's placenta with a needle and syringe, and testing the fluid for chromosomal abnormalities. The test is useful in detecting a number of hereditary diseases, for example, Tay-Sacs disease and Downs' Syndrome, but will not detect Sickle-Cell Anemia, which is carried by seven per cent to nine per cent of the United States black population.

Amniocentesis is elective treatment and costs anywhere from $400 to $500. A doctor should recommend an amniocentesis only for certain circumstances, specifically if the mother developed Rubella during pregnancy. The mother's age at the time of conception may also require an amniocentesis. For an expectant mother between the age of 35 and 40 years, the chance of her child being born with Down's Syndrome is one in 280 . For the ages of 40 and above, the risk jumps to one in 50. Based on these statistics, most physicians in the United States offer amniocentesis to patients over 35 years of age. Many doctors consider the risks inherent in the test are not justified by the likelihood of detecting defects, especially for women under 40 years of age for whom the incident of defects is only one in 250 to 300. Statistics also indicate that in less than one per cent of the cases miscarriage may result because of the test.

[This sample surrogate mother contract, medical statement, and exhibit are reprinted, by permission, from Brophy, A SURROGATE MOTHER CONTRACT TO BEAR A CHILD, 20 Journal of Family Law 263 (1982).]

CHAPTER 5

Prenatal Stage: Established Law

I. ABORTION AND FETICIDE

I. ABORTION AND FETICIDE

A. Introduction

1. [§5.1] Early Criminal Abortion Law

Of the many, thorny constitutional issues confronting the United States Supreme Court over the past twenty-five years, one of the most volatile, if not insoluble, is the woman's right to an abortion. Although the legal concept of protecting the rights of the unborn child is of ancient origin, state regulation and restriction of abortion is surprisingly of relatively recent vintage. From early colonial times to approximately 1830, women in America enjoyed a common law freedom to terminate, at will, an unwanted pregnancy. In 1821, Connecticut became the first state to enact abortion legislation that related to a woman quick with child. Abortion before quickening was not made a crime in that state until 1860. Means, THE PHOENIX OF ABORTIONAL FREEDOM: IS A PENUMBRAL OR NINTH-AMENDMENT RIGHT TO ABORT TO RISE FROM THE NINETEENTH-CENTURY LEGISLATIVE ASHES OF FOURTEENTH CENTURY COMMON-LAW LIBERTY, 17 New York

Law Forum 335 (1971). State criminal abortion statutes supplanted the common law after the United States Civil War.

Historically, criminal abortion statutes in the United States were enacted and maintained for basically three reasons: (1) a social concern to discourage illicit sexual behavior; (2) a protection for the health and welfare of the expectant woman; and, (3) the state's duty to protect prenatal life.

Many 19th Century anti-abortion statutes used the "quickening" of the fetus as the demarcation point between the severity of criminal penalties. Most of these early laws dealt harshly with abortion after quickening but were lenient before quickening. Quickening can be defined as the first recognizable movement of the fetus in the womb, appearing usually from the 16th to the 18th week of pregnancy. Thus, an early New York law barred the destruction of the fetus. However, it made the destruction of an unquickened fetus only a misdemeanor, but that of a quickened fetus, second-degree manslaughter. Quickening is only one evidence of life, and is inconclusive. Science has proven that a fetus is capable of movement long before that movement is felt by the mother. Quickening has been described as nothing more than discernible movement of the unborn child. *Larkin v Cahalan*, 389 Mi 533, 208 NW2d 176 (1973).

As a result of this inexactness, the quickening distinction was eliminated from almost all state statutes. One lone exception is a Rhode Island criminal statute, G.L.R.I. §11-23-5, dealing with the willful killing of an unborn, quick child. The statutory definition of quick child, however, is closer to that of "viability", than the old definition of "quickening".

By the 1950's, most states had enacted strict laws banning abortion at any stage of gestation, unless done to preserve the life of the mother. However, about ten years later, some fourteen states adopted more liberal laws allowing abortions under certain specified circumstances, such as pregnancies caused by rape or incest. During this period, women's groups among others, continued to challenge both the traditional and the more liberal statutes as violating a woman's due process rights. The United States Supreme Court soon found itself confronted with the dilemma of choosing between the state's interest in the preservation of the life of the fetus, and the woman's right to terminate an unwanted pregnancy. Compounding this problem were the tremendous advances made in medicine that resulted in new abortion methods that increased the safety of abortions well into the second trimester of pregnancy.

It is within this social, political, and scientific milieu that the United States Supreme Court attempted to resolve the abortion conflict in two 1973 companion cases, *Roe v Wade*, 410 US 113, 93 SCt 705, 35 LE2d 147 (1973), and *Doe v Bolton*, 410 US 179, 93 SCt 739, 35 LE2d 201 (1973). [See §§5.2–5.4.]

2. Roe v Wade

a. [§5.2] Rights of Privacy

Any analysis of the constitutionality of modern state abortion statutes must concentrate on the seminal 1973 *Roe v Wade* decision, 410 US 113, 93 SCt 705, 35 LE2d 147. Recent abortion law has been shaped by this holding. Virtually all abortion statutes existing in 1973 were abrogated by *Wade* or its companion case *Doe v Bolton*, 410 US 179, 93 SCt 739, 35 LE2d 201 (1973). Subsequently enacted state laws have been framed to comply with the *Wade* and *Bolton* holdings.

The main issue resolved by the United States Supreme Court in *Wade* was whether a woman's decision to terminate her pregnancy is a fundamental right protected by the constitution. As a corollary to this issue, the court also defined the interest of the state to be weighed against a woman's right to privacy during each trimester of pregnancy.

The court in *Wade* grounded its decision on substantive due process under the Fourteenth Amendment. The test of constitutionality is whether a rational relationship exists between the statute and a valid legislative objective. However, in the case of a fundamental individual right, a more stringent standard is imposed. Where the statute burdens such a right, there must be a compelling state interest that outweighs the burden before the statute will be upheld.

In this case, the fundamental right in conflict with the state prohibition of abortion is the woman's right of privacy. Generally, the right of privacy is a non-enumerated right implicitly recognized in the Fourteenth Amendment concept of personal liberty and the limits on state action. Two different interests are involved: one, an individual interest in avoiding disclosure of personal matters; and another, an interest in preserving a woman's independence to make certain important personal decisions. *Whalen v Roe*, 429 US 589, 599–600, 97 SCt 869, 876, 51 LE2d 64 (1977) (right of the state to solicit doctors' drug prescriptions).

The woman's right of privacy yields to the interests of the state as the pregnancy nears term. The *Wade* decision, among other matters, describes the period when the state may regulate or even prohibit abortion in the protection of a fetal life. This time is not before the twenty-fourth week of gestation of the fetus, at which point the law recognizes that the fetus is presumably potentially capable of meaningful life outside the mother's womb. As a result, courts have recognized only 2 fetal periods: the period prior to viability, when a state may not regulate in the interest of the fetal life; and, the period after viability, when it may totally prohibit or regulate abortion as it sees fit, except where the life of the mother is threatened.

b. [§5.3] Analysis of Wade Decision

The Texas criminal abortion statute had been in effect for over one hundred years without substantial change. Under its provisions, it was a crime to procure or attempt to procure an abortion except where, in the opinion of a doctor, the life of the mother was threatened. At least twenty-seven states had similar statutes that would also be affected by the court's ruling.

The law was challenged by a class consisting of an unmarried and pregnant woman, a physician under indictment in a state court for violating the law, and a childless, married couple who alleged that their future parental plans were threatened by the restrictive law. The doctor and married couple were dismissed from the case on the issues of standing and justiciability.

The plaintiff advanced several arguments to bolster her claim that the Texas abortion law violated her constitutional right to terminate her pregnancy. This right existed either in the concept of personal liberty included in the due process clause of the Fourteenth Amendment, in the right of privacy that the court had previously recognized in as existing in the Bill of Rights or in its penumbras, or finally, among the rights reserved to its citizens by the Ninth Amendment.

The court rejected the Ninth Amendment argument, as well as the approach that the right of privacy existed from specific Bill of Rights provisions and their penumbras as applied to the states under the Fourteenth Amendment. However, the court found that a woman's abortion decision was among those rights of privacy protected under the Constitution. The Constitution, of course, does not specifically mention a right of privacy. The court had recognized, on a case-by-case basis rights of personal privacy or certain "zones of privacy." Only those personal rights that are fundamental or implicit in the concept of ordered liberty are included in the guaranty of personal privacy; these include marriage, procreation, conception, and education. The right of privacy was first recognized in *Griswold v Connecticut*, 381 US 479, 85 SCt 1678, 14 LE2d 510 (1965), a case involving the conviction of a doctor who provided information about contraception to married couples. But in that case, the court relied on the "penumbra of rights" argument. However, in the *Wade* case, it embraced the view that the right of privacy derives directly from the Fourteenth Amendment's concept of "liberty." This substantive due process approach led to the conclusion that the scope of privacy was broad enough to incorporate a decision to terminate a pregnancy.

The test of substantive due process is whether a real and substantial relationship exists between the law and a valid state objective. Where the law is a burden on fundamental individual rights, a "compelling state interest" must outweigh the infringements before the law is upheld.

Originally, Texas had three reasons for enacting the statute. The first, discouragement of sexual activity, was not propounded by the state in this case; second, medical dangers to the woman from the abortion procedures, may have been compelling when the law was first passed in 1870, but except for the late stage of pregnancy, was no longer a significant factor. The final reason, the protection of the unborn child was the most compelling of the three, and was the essential theme addressed by the court. Hardy, *Harris v McRae*, 31 Case Western LR 465 (1981).

A state may assert its interests in safeguarding the health of the mother, in maintaining medical standards, and in protecting the potential life of the child. A crucial issue resolved by the Court was at what point in the stage of the woman's pregnancy does the state's interest become compelling to sanction regulation of the factors that govern the abortion decision. *Wade*, 410 US 113, 154. The state's interest in preserving and protecting the health of the pregnant woman as well as the protection of the right of the potentiality of a human life grows substantially as the pregnancy approaches term.

Through an historical analysis of the Constitution and the Bill of Rights, the Court first determined that a fetus is not a person under the Fourteenth Amendment. Thus, its right to life is not constitutionally guaranteed. Basically then, the real confrontation was between the interest of the state and the woman's right of privacy.

Since abortions in the first twelve weeks of pregnancy are relatively safe, the abortion decision up until the end of the first trimester is left to the medical judgment of the woman and her attending physician. Only after the first twelve weeks does the state interest in safeguarding the woman's health justify involvement in the abortion decision. For stages after the end of the first trimester, the state may regulate the abortion procedures if they are reasonably related to the mother's health. Several examples of valid regulation of abortion include setting qualifications of those performing abortions, as well as licensing procedures, and requirements as to the site of the operation. For stages after the period of viability of the fetus, usually between the twenty-fourth and twenty-eighth weeks of pregnancy, the state's interest in the potentiality of human life becomes compelling. It may regulate, and even proscribe an abortion, except where it is necessary to preserve the life and health of the mother. (Viability is the point at which the fetus is presumed capable of life outside the mother's womb. See §§5.7–5.9.)

c. [§5.4] Doe v Bolton Decision

In a companion case to *Wade*, even a more liberal "second generation" abortion statute was struck down. The Georgia statute allowed abortions by physicians in cases where the pregnancy was induced by rape, endangered the life or health of the pregnant woman, or where the likelihood that the baby would be born with a permanent and irremediable mental or physical defect. Three procedural conditions, however, violated the patient's Fourteenth Amendment rights:

> (1) that the abortion be performed in a hospital accredited by the Joint Commission on Accreditation of Hospitals;
> (2) that the procedure be approved by the hospital abortion staff committee; and,
> (3) that the performing physician's judgment be confirmed by the independent examinations of the patient by two other licensed physicians.

The accreditation requirement was not based on differences reasonably related to the purposes of the act, i.e., the health and safety of the woman. The state failed to show that only a licensed hospital, rather than a clinic, satisfied these interests. Also, the state wrongfully included the first trimester of pregnancy within the scope of the regulation.

The injection of the hospital abortion committee within the abortion procedure was also unconstitutional. It unduly restricted the patient's rights that have already been medically established by her relationship with her personal physician. Finally, it was held that the two-doctor concurrence rule bore no rational relationship with a patient's needs and also unduly infringed upon the individual doctor's right to practice medicine. *Doe v Bolton*, 410 US 179, 93 SCt 739, 35 LE2d 201 (1973).

d. [§5.5] Conclusions

To summarize, the Supreme Court recognized that the right of privacy under the due process clause of the Fourteenth Amendment encompasses a woman's decision to terminate her pregnancy. A ban on abortions and the resultant birth of a child would have severe, detrimental effects both mentally and physically on the woman. Although the right of privacy was recognized, its scope is not unlimited or absolute. The state has a compelling right to safeguard health, maintain medical standards and protect potential life. These rights become more compelling as the pregnancy nears term.

To illustrate proper state action, the regulation of the advertising and sale of abortifacients is, within bounds, subject to the state police power. (An abortifacient is an instrument, medicine, drug, or any other substance or device known to cause fetal injury when employed in the usual and customary use for which it is manufactured, whether or not the fetus is known to exist when the substance or device is used.) The Michigan Supreme Court in interpreting *Wade* [§5.2] held that unlike another law that unconstitutionally characterized abortion as manslaughter whether performed by a doctor or layman, this provision specifically exempts "the written prescriptions of an established physician of the place where the sale is made." (MICH COMP LAWS ANN §750.15); *Larkin v Cahalan*, 389 Mi 533, 208 NW2d 176, 178 (1973).

The priority of protecting the woman's health and life over that of the fetus's remains unquestioned, regardless of the trimester involved. At least one commentator has proposed that the competing interests of the life of the expectant mother and the fetus, viable or otherwise, should be balanced on a case-by-case method. King, THE JURISDICTIONAL STATUS OF THE FETUS: A PROPOSAL FOR LEGAL PROTECTION OF THE UNBORN, 77 Michigan LR 1647, 1682–1683 (1979). However, this view has been rejected by other experts, as well as by the United States Supreme Court. See *United States v Vuitch*, 402 US 62, 91 SCt 1294, 28 LE2d 601 (1971) (District of Columbia abortion law (DC CODE ANN §22-201) declared unconstitutionally vague).

The *Wade* decision did not satisfy either women's groups who sought recognition of an absolute right to an abortion, or state governments that believed abortion should be controlled from the moment of conception. Because of this judicial accommodation, *Wade* is cited by virtually all abortion litigants whether by counsel representing a state attorney general or an abortion clinic, a municipal hospital refusing to perform abortions, or a civil right's group demanding abortion upon demand. A reference to *Wade* has become a staple in framing a legal argument in an attorney's brief.

With the passage of time, the actual impact of the *Wade* decision may have abated. This diluted influence may be traced to the shifting philosophy of the United States Supreme Court, or perhaps to the differing types of abortion cases, i.e., Medicaid, hospital zoning, brought before the Court. It is noteworthy that in a 1980 Medicaid funding abortion case, the majority opinion, in surveying *Wade*, described, but fails to acknowledge, the right of privacy. Rather, the majority recognizes that the "liberty" protected by due process includes not only those freedoms explicitly set forth in the first ten Amendments to the Constitution, but also a freedom of personal choice in certain matters of marriage and family life. This implicit right included the freedom of a woman to decide whether to terminate a pregnancy. The right protected is referred to under a rather nebulous phrase, "personal constitutional freedom", rather than a right of privacy as stated in *Wade*. *Harris v McRae*, 448 US 297, 100 SCt 2671, 2686, 65 LE2d 784 (1980).

Courts have employed this reasoning, along with the tri-parte sectioning of the pregnancy espoused in *Wade*, to resolve many of the issues arising from the abortion process. These issues include viability [see §§5.7–5.9], informed consent [§5.10], spousal [§5.14] or parental consent [§5.17], the rights of minors [§5.16], waiting periods [§5.20], recordkeeping [§5.27], hospital-required abortions [§5.30], zoning restrictions [§5.32], public funding of abortions [§5.35], and abortions by non-physicians [§5.34].

3. [§5.6] Judicial Interpretations of Wade

As a result of the impact of *Wade* and its progeny [§§5.2–5.6], two rationales have emerged among the federal circuits in ruling on the constitutionality of state abortion statutes, particularly in the first trimester. One line of reasoning will uphold this statute or regulation if it does not "unduly burden" the abortion decision. If the law unduly burdens the woman's right to an abortion, then it will be subject to strict scrutiny by the court; if not, then the state must merely meet the less stringent "rational relationship" test. *Maher v Roe*, 432 US 464, 97 SCt 2376, 53 LE2d 484 (1976); *Bellotti v Baird*, 428 US 132, 96 SCt 2357, 49 LE2d 844 (1976); *Women's Community Health Center, Inc v Cohen*, 477 FSupp 542 (D Me 1979). For example, a state statute requiring that the second trimester abortions be performed in a hospital was unconstitutional. (Mo Ann Stat §188.025). The law placed an undue burden on the pregnant woman since the most popular, as well as safest, abortion procedure was "D&E" (dilation and evacuation method), which was twice as expensive when performed in a hospital as opposed to an out-patient facility. The state did not meet its burden of establishing that the requirement was reasonably related to the protection of the woman's health, i.e., that non-hospitalized D & E could reasonably be considered more dangerous than hospital procedures. It also failed to show that the methods it claimed were safer than non-hospital D & E procedures were available to women in Missouri. *Planned Parenthood Assn of Kansas City v Ashcroft*, 664 F2d 687 (7th Cir 1981); first appeal, 655 F2d 848 (8th Cir 1981), cert granted, 102 SCt 2267 (1982).

A second line of reasoning initially determined whether the state regulation has a legally significant impact or consequence on the right to an abortion. If not, then no constitutional issue is raised. However, if the regulation interferes with the abortion decision to a sufficient degree, it must be supported by a legitimate and compelling state interest and be narrowly tailored to serve that interest. Unlike the first line of reasoning, the second does not apply the "unduly burdens" test at an early stage of the inquiry. If it is determined that a regulation is direct state interference with a protected activity, the regulation is subject to strict scrutiny by the court. Only at this stage in the balancing of the state's compelling interest against the method chosen to remedy the problem does the "unduly burdens" factor become significant. During the first trimester, the state has no compelling interest and no balancing is required. A regulation that has a legally significant impact on an abortion decision at this stage is invalid. Notwithstanding the fact that the regulation falls within a period that a state may have a compelling interest in the pregnancy, the regulation will fall if it unduly burdens the abortion decision.

For example, since a municipal ordinance that required a twenty four-hour waiting period between a woman's consent to an abortion and the actual operation had a legally significant impact or consequence on the abortion decision, it could not be applied to first trimester abortions. Although a state may have had some interest in postponing the abortion decision, such as the protection of the woman against unscrupulous doctors, the evidence did not support a compelling state interest served by the requirement. But, the state did have a compelling interest, the health of the mother, in regulating second trimester abortions. Thus, an ordinance requiring all abortions after the first trimester be performed in a hospital was upheld. The court noted that the plaintiff, an abortion clinic, did not rebut the formulation in *Wade* that the state's interest in protecting the maternal health is compelling after the first trimester. *Akron Center for Reproductive Health, Inc v City of Akron*, 651 F2d 1198, 1204, 1208 (6th Cir 1981), cert granted, 102 SCt 2266 (1981); *Margaret S v Edwards*, 488 FSupp 181, 192 (ED La 1980).

Courts have employed this reasoning, along with the tri-parte sectioning of the pregnancy period espoused in *Wade*, to resolve many of the issues arising from the abortion process. These issues include viability [see §§5.7–5.9], informed consent [§5.10], waiting period [§5.20], spousal [§5.14] or parental consent [§5.17], the rights of minors [§5.16], record-keeping [§5.27], and hospital-required abortions [§5.30].

4. Viability

a. [§5.7] Definitions

Viability is that stage of fetal development when the life of an unborn child may be continued indefinitely outside the womb either by natural or artificial life-supported systems. According to the *Wade* decision:

> For the stage subsequent to viability, the State in promoting its interests in the potentiality of human life may, if it chooses, regulate, and even proscribe, abortion except where it is necessary, in appropriate medical judgment, for the preservation of the life or health of the mother. 410 US at 164, 93 SCt at 732.

At that point, there must be a potentiality of "meaningful life", *id.*, at 163, 93 SCt at 732, and not just momentary survival. [For a discussion of *Wade*, see §§5.2, 5.3.]

According to the United States Supreme Court, it is not a legislative or judicial function to place viability, which essentially is a medical concept, at a specific point during gestation. The period of viability varies with each pregnancy and the determination of whether a particular fetus is viable is a matter of judgment by the attending physician. *Planned Parenthood of Central Missouri v Danforth*, 428 US 52, 96 SCt 2831, 49 LE2d 788 (1976).

For example, a South Carolina law (SC CODE 1962 §32-682 et seq.) prohibiting abortions after the twenty-fourth week of pregnancy violated the woman's right of privacy under the Fourteenth Amendment. The court held that the question of viability is to be decided on a case-by-case basis by the woman's attending physician; it is not a point in the pregnancy period arbitrarily chosen by the state legislature. *Floyd v Anders*, 440 FSupp 535 (DC SC 1977), vac, 440 US 445, 99 SCt 1200, 59 LE2d 442, reh den, 441 US 928, 99 SCt 2043, 60 LE2d 403 (1978). See also *Hodgson v Lawson*, 542 F2d 1350 (8th Cir 1976).

b. [§5.8] Factors Determining Viability

Theoretically, a fetus may be viable if a significant percentage of fetuses of a same weight and age survive childbirth. But, because of circumstances peculiar to a particular case, the fetus, in fact may not qualify. Only the woman's attending physician can determine with any certainty using subjective factors whether a particular fetus is viable. Courts have followed a course of minimum involvement in what can be characterized as inherently and primarily a medical decision. Due in part to the tremendous advances made in medicine and science, increased responsibility and discretion has been placed in the hands of the attending physician. Even if agreement is reached on the probability of the survival of the fetus outside the mother's womb, physicians may differ on the probabilities of survival of the fetus outside the mother's womb. Some in the medical profession even refuse to determine viability with any numerical probability. *Colautti v Franklin*, 439 US 379, 99 SCt 675, 58 LE2d 596 (1979).

A physician may judge whether a fetus is viable after weighing a number of factors including: the gestational age of the fetus derived from the reported menstrual history of the woman; fetal weight based upon an estimate of the size and condition of the uterus; the woman's general health and nutrition; the quality of available medical facilities; and other related factors.

Thus, those criminal abortion statutes that are vague as to the time of viability, may have a chilling effect on the willingness of doctors to perform abortions near the period of viability. What may be gleaned from the decisions beginning with *Wade* and continuing through *Colautti*, is that a criminal statute must be couched in terms clear enough to inform those to whom it applies of the conduct that is either required or forbidden. Also, laws must be explicit to prevent arbitrary and discriminatory enforcement. The vagueness of a statute that appears to intrude upon elemental constitutional liberties may curb and have a chilling effect on the exercise of those freedoms. For example, neither the state legislature nor the judiciary had the authority to declare any single factor as crucial in ascertaining whether a fetus is viable. The Pennsylvania abortion statute (35 PA STAT §6605(a)) that denied the attending doctor broad discretion in performing abortions, while also subjecting him or her to possible criminal prosecution for failing to adhere to the requirements of viability, was unconstitutionally void for vagueness. COMMENT, 52 Temp LQ 1240, 1242 (1979).

In *Colautti*, it was held that a provision of the Pennsylvania Abortion Control Act (35 PA STAT §6605(a)) failed to give an abortionist of ordinary intelligence fair notice that his contemplated conduct was forbidden. Section 6605(a) read:

> Every person who performs or induces an abortion shall prior thereto have made a determination based on his experience, judgment or professional competence that the fetus is not viable, and if the determination is that the fetus is viable or if there is sufficient reason to believe that the fetus *may be viable*, shall exercise that degree of professional skill, care and diligence to preserve the life and health of the fetus which such person would be required to exercise in order to preserve the life and health of any fetus intended to be born and not aborted and the abortion technique employed shall be that which would provide the best opportunity for the fetus to be aborted alive so long as a different technique would not be necessary in order to preserve the life or health of the mother. [Italics added.]

The duty of a physician to determine whether the fetus was viable or whether there was "sufficient reason to believe" that the fetus "may be viable" contained a double ambiguity. As a result, a doctor was denied the broad discretion necessary to determine the fetus's viability in light of all the circumstances. It was unclear whether the statute imposed a purely subjective standard or whether that standard consisted of a hybrid subjective/objective test. Secondly, it was uncertain whether the phrase in the statute "may be viable" simply referred to viability as that term had been defined in previous United States Supreme Court decisions, or to an undefined time prior to the stage of actual viability. *Colautti*, 439 US at 391, 99 SCt at 683.

However, whether a state may protect a fetus during the period that it is potentially able to survive is by no means resolved and is the subject of intense debate. In defending the Pennsylvania law against vagueness, Justice White emphasized in his dissent in *Colautti*, 439 US at 402, that viability is not the stage that the fetus actually is able, or actually has the ability, to survive outside the mother's womb with or without artificial aid. Rather it is at the point at which the fetus is *potentially* able to survive.

In line with the majority holding in *Colautti*, above, it was determined that the Minnesota abortion law impermissibly injected the concept of "potential viability" into the definition of viability: "Viable means able to live outside the womb even though artificial aid may be required. During the second half of gestation period a fetus shall be considered potentially viable." See MN STAT §145.411(2). The definition established a presumption that viability occurs at the end of the 20th week of pregnancy, in contravention of the 24th through the 28th week as espoused in *Wade*. *Hodgson v Lawson*, 542 F2d 1350, 1354 (8th Cir 1976). The term "potentially viable" also tainted other provisions of the Act that incorporated this definition by reference. *Hodgson*, 542 F2d at 1354.

c. [§5.9] Conclusions

Viability of the fetus is of paramount importance in abortion cases, as well as in cases involving feticide [see §§5.43–5.46]. Generally, a fetus reaches viability when it is capable of existence independent of the mother. This means that a fetus is deemed viable when it is able to survive the trauma of childbirth, although with an artificial aid, such as an incubator.

It is important to note that despite the statement in the majority opinion in *Wade* [see §5.3] placing viability between the 24th and 28th week of pregnancy, no general rule pinpointing the exact time of viability has been established. Whether a fetus is viable at a given point in the gestational period is a question of fact dependent upon the particular, medical circumstances of each case. As a result, the attending physician has been delegated broad discretion in deciding when a woman is entitled to an abortion. Before the fetus has reached viability, the physician, in consultation with the pregnant woman, may determine whether the pregnancy may be terminated. The state may not interfere with this decision unless the health or life of the woman is at stake.

B. Consent to Abortion

1. Informed Consent

a. [§5.10] Generally

Informed consent is a requirement imposed by state law that the attending physician communicate to his patients certain information about the impending abortion. The information may include, apart from the fact that in the doctor's best medical judgment the patient is pregnant, the number of weeks elapsed from the probable time of conception and the particular risks attendant with her pregnancy, and the abortion technique to be followed.

Most states adhere to the long-established common law requirement of informed consent for surgical operations in general. This broadly includes that the attending physician informed the patient of possible alternative treatments and the accompanying risks, including the alternative of no treatment at all.

Some commentators have suggested that although it differs from that of common law medical consent rule, the informed consent to an abortion does not rise to the level of a compelling state interest under the *Wade* decision. Clearly, an abortion involves considerations that do not arise in an ordinary medical operation, such as the potential anxiety to the patient caused by the destruction of the embryo. Therefore, the state may not impose an undue burden on the exercise of the right to choose abortion during the first or second trimester. Under this reasoning, it follows that if the informed consent requirement expands the common law disclosure requirement it must adhere to the more stringent standard of strict judicial scrutiny. COMMENT: THE MAINE ABORTION STATUTES OF 1979; TESTING THE CONSTITUTIONAL LIMITS, 32 Maine LR 315, 328 (1980).

A typical informed consent statute requires that the physician inform the woman that she is pregnant; of the number of weeks elapsed from the probable time of conception; of the particular risks attendant with her pregnancy and the abortion technique to be used; and, of alternatives to abortion, such as childbirth and adoption. See 22 ME REV STAT ANN §1598(2).

b. [§5.11] Disclosure v. Women's Rights

Problems have arisen in enforcing informed consent laws, particularly during the first trimester of the woman's pregnancy. In light of the *Wade* decision, many women have claimed that informed consent invades their right of privacy. The United States Supreme Court has ruled on the constitutionality of the series of state "informed consent" abortion statutes. A Missouri law [MO ANN STAT §188.020(2)] simply requiring a woman to certify in writing that her consent to the pending abortion was informed, as well as freely given, met constitutional muster. It was alleged that the law which mandated that a woman, prior to submitting to a first trimester abortion, certify in writing her informed and freely given consent to the procedure violated her right of privacy. Although no other law generally required a patient's prior written consent to surgery, it was determined that the decision to abort be made with full knowledge of its nature and its consequences. *Planned Parenthood of Central Missouri v Danforth*, 428 US 52, 96 SCt 2831, 49 LE2d 788 (1976).

Similarly, the informed consent provisions of the Pennsylvania Abortion Control Act were upheld. The law set forth certain elements of informed consent including statements of: (1) unforeseen, negative physical and psychological effects; (2) possible alternatives to abortion such as childbirth and adoption; and, (3) medical procedures to be followed. A group of plaintiffs, including doctors, a birth control organization and a pregnancy counseling service, did not establish that abortion had been singled out by the legislature for regulation, a factor considered in determining whether the regulation interfered with the abortion decision. Nor was there evidence that the provisions directly interfered with the decision. *Planned Parenthood Assn v Fitzpatrick*, 401 FSupp 554 (ED Pa 1975), summ affd sub nom, *Franklin v Fitzpatrick*, 428 US 901, 96 SCt 3202, 49 LE2d 1205 (1976). In accord, *Doe v Deschamps*, 461 FSupp 682 (DC Mt 1976) (Montana abortion law (R.C.M. §94-5-615(3)) constitutional).

An informed consent provision that encroaches upon a woman's consultation with her doctor may be constitutionally objectionable. Thus, a Missouri law [Mo Ann Stat §188.045 (1978)] requiring a physician to inform his patients that parental rights would terminate in the event that the abortion failed and that the child was born alive, was struck down. This irrelevant and extraneous consideration violated both the equal protection and due process clauses of the Fourteenth Amendment of the United States Constitution. This warning unconstitutionally singled out abortion from other surgical procedures and also invaded the unique and personal relationship between doctor and patient. *Freiman v Ashcroft*, 584 F2d 247 (9th Cir 1980), summ affd, 440 US 941 (1979).

The purpose of these informed consent provisions is to allay any unnatural fears of women who are about to undergo abortions. Those provisions that have the opposite psychological effect and actually increase apprehension or guilt are carefully examined by the courts. The Seventh Circuit Court of Appeals held that portion of the Illinois abortion law requiring a woman to be told by her physician, under threat of criminal penalty, the gestational age of the fetus and to view materials produced by the state of Illinois showing probable and anatomical and physiological features of the fetus unconstitutional. This requirement was punitive to the pregnant woman who elects an abortion because of serious genetic defects in the fetus or because her own health is endangered. It effectually compromised the physician's efforts to act in the best interest of his patient. Also, possible criminal penalties against a physician for failure to inform the pregnant woman of the possibility of organic pain to the fetus in cases where a reasonable medical certainty exists that the particular method of abortion will cause this pain was also struck down. It was undisputed during the trial that this information was medically meaningless, confusing and unjustified. *Charles v Carey*, 627 F2d 772 (7th Cir 1980).

In another case, the United States Court of Appeals, Eighth Circuit, divided the right of privacy into two components. One involved guarding against infringements of the patient-physician relationship necessary in the decision-making. The other protected the outcome of the decision from state interference. The first right is more fundamental than the second. A state requirement [MASS GEN LAWS Ch 112, §128] that a woman's written consent be obtained on a form did not intrude on the first protected right. Since all that was required of the patient was a signature on the form, the intrusion was *de minimis*. Also, the second right was not violated since the privacy of the decisional process was not unduly influenced by the single use of the form. Although most items on the disclosure form were permissible, one requiring a description of each stage in fetal development, was objectionable. The requirements burdened the woman's decision by presenting irrelevant and potentially prejudicial information. The information was not medically relevant, and indirectly, could cause great guilt and anxiety in the woman. The subtle coercion, although indirect, was coercion nonetheless. *Planned Parenthood League of Massachusetts v Bellotti*, 641 F2d 1006 (1st Cir 1981). See also *Womens Serv v Thone*, 636 F2d 206, 210 (8th Cir 1980), cert den, 452 US 911, 101 SCt 3043, 69 LE2d 414 (1981), (NEB REV STAT §28-326(8) (a) that required notice "of the reasonably possible medical and mental consequences resulting from an abortion, pregnancy, and childbirth", interfered with a woman's fundamental right to decide whether to terminate her pregnancy and failed the "strict scrutiny" test under a substantive due process analysis).

The information transmitted should aid the woman in arriving at a free, unburdened decision. However, a Rhode Island statute [RI GEN LAWS §23-4.7-2(4)] that mandated disclosure of fetal characteristics at various gestational stages was an unfair tactic of the state that unreasonably burdened a woman's right to an unfettered, objective choice. Also, by requiring the physician to perform a seemingly innocuous act, informing patients that this information was available from a health agency, the state intruded on the patient-physician relationship to the detriment of the woman's right to privacy. The doctor, in short, became an unwilling spokesman of the views of the state which had no compelling reason to force its philosophy of abortion on others. *Women's Medical Center of Providence, Inc v Roberts*, 530 FSupp 1136 (WD RI 1982).

In a case involving wholesale violations of the woman's right to privacy, the following Louisiana informed consent provisions [LSA-RS 40: 1299.35.6)] were struck down: (1) description of the fetus at the gestational point of development at the time the abortion is to be performed;

(2) assertion that the embryo is a human life from the moment of conception; (3) an irrebuttable presumption that viability occurs twenty-two weeks after conception; (4) a claim that the surgery can result in serious complications and result in severe emotional disturbances; and, (5) communication of required information dealing with natural and artificial birth control. The court found that the aforementioned requirements were either an interference in the patient-physician relationship, a violation of the woman's right to privacy, or not reasonably related to the purposes of informed consent. Specifically, the broad requirement that a woman be informed of the physical and mental consequences of abortion did not allow the physician discretion in basing a decision on the individual health of his patient. *Margaret S v Edwards*, 488 FSupp 181, 208-212 (ED La 1980).

An otherwise constitutionally-sound informed consent provision may fall when it is tainted by other burdensome provisions. An Arkansas implied consent law [ARK STAT ANN §41-2555] was struck down because it was not severable from other unconstitutional provisions of the law, including sections dealing with spousal and parental consent. *Smith v Bentley*, 493 FSupp 916 (ED Ar 1980).

In an unusual fact situation involving a comatose pregnant woman, a Pennsylvania trial court judge struck down a criminal statute [35 PA STAT §6603(a)] that barred an abortion (at least in the first trimester) without informed consent, unless the mother's life is in jeopardy. The mother of a pregnant woman, who remained hospitalized in a coma, sought a declaratory judgment authorizing her consent to an abortion for her daughter. The court ruled that limiting abortions to life-threatening situations violated the Fourteenth Amendment Due Process rights of a woman incompetent to give her informed consent. Under *Wade* [see §5.2], the physician's medical judgment should remain unfettered as to whether the abortion is in the best interest of the mother. Among the factors that a physician should weigh, as espoused in *Bolton* include physical, emotional, psychological, familial and age considerations affecting the patient, as well as the potentiality of life in the non-viable fetus. The last factor was not mentioned in *Bolton*, but was added to the list by the trial court in this case. *Pettit v Chester Cty Hosp*, 8 FLR 2728 (Pa 1982).

However, consent provisions should not be drawn so broadly that the information given may have a detrimental, physical or psychological effect on the woman. These provisions would clearly conflict with the woman's right of privacy, as well as her and her doctor's due process in equal protection rights under the Fourteenth Amendment.

c. [§5.12] Time Limit on Consent

On a collateral issue, a statutorily-imposed limit on the period during which a woman's consent to an abortion remains in effect has also been invalidated. This "cap" required a woman who failed to have her abortion within the specified time (7 days in Rhode Island, for example) for a second explanation on the possible dangers of the operation. Apart from escalating the cost of the abortion, there was no reason, rational or otherwise, for implementing this expiration period. Since the time period was not even rationally related to a legitimate state concern, it was declared unconstitutional. *Women's Medical Center of Providence v Roberts*, 530 FSupp 1136 (DC RI 1982).

d. [§5.13] Conclusion

A majority of courts have ruled that a legitimate state interest is served in insuring that a pregnant woman makes a fully-informed abortion decision. Requiring the physician to inform the woman that she is pregnant, of the probable number of weeks since conception, and that the risks associated with her pregnancy and the method of abortion to be used clearly furthers this interest. Other courts that have sustained similar informed consent provisions are as follows: *Wolfe v Schroering*, 541 F2d 523, 526 (6th Cir 1976); *Akron Center for Reproductive Health, Inc v City of Akron*, 651 F2d 1198 (6th Cir 1981), cert granted, 102 SCt 2266 (1982); *Doe v Deschamps*, 461 FSupp 682, 685–86 (DC Mt 1976); *Wynn v Scott*, 449 FSupp 1302, 1316–17 (ND Il 1978), affd sub nom, *Wynn v Carey*, 599 F2d 193, 194 (7th Cir 1979).

However, consent provisions should not be drawn so broadly that the information given has a detrimental physical or psychological effect on the woman. These provisions would clearly conflict with a woman's right of privacy as well as her and her doctor's due process and equal protection rights under the Fourteenth Amendment.

2. Spousal Consent

a. [§5.14] Generally

In the *Wade* and *Bolton* cases [see §§5.2–5.5], the United States Supreme Court postponed ruling on the question of whether the consent by the father as a prerequisite for an abortion was constitutional. In the interim, a number of jurisdictions, including Florida, Kentucky, and Pennsylvania struck down spousal consent statutes as an invasion of the woman's right to privacy.

The issue was finally resolved by the United States Supreme Court in *Planned Parenthood of Central Missouri v Danforth*, 428 US 52, 96 SCt

2831, 49 LE2d 788 (1976). A provision of a Missouri abortion law required the prior consent of the father during the first trimester of the pregnancy, "unless the abortion is certified by a licensed physician to be necessary in order to preserve the life of the mother." [See MO LAWS 1974, H.B. 1211, §3(3).] The state claimed that the husband possessed an interest comparable to his wife's in the growth and development of the fetus. Since the husband obviously had an integral role in the pregnancy, its termination could be effected by mutual consent with his wife. In response, the United States Supreme Court simply noted that since the state itself cannot regulate abortion during the first trimester, it is not empowered to delegate this authority to another party, in this case the other spouse. An abortion should ideally be a joint decision by both parties. In reality, however, if the spouses disagree, the wife, who physically bears the child, must make the ultimate decision. It would violate the woman's right of privacy to grant the husband a veto power over the abortion. Even if a state had the authority to delegate this power to the husband, it is unlikely that the action would further the interest of the state in protecting mutuality of decisions vital to the stability of the marriage relationship. *Planned Parenthood of Central Missouri v Danforth*, 428 US 52, 69, 96 SCt 2831, 49 LE2d 788 (1976). See also prior decisions *Wolfe v Schroering*, 541 F2d 523 (6th Cir 1976) (Kentucky law (KY REV STAT §311.740(2)) interferes with the woman's right to a second trimester abortion); *Doe v Rampton*, 366 FSupp 189, 193 (DC Ut 1973), vac and remd, 410 US 950, 93 SCt 1423, 35 LE2d 683 (1973) (Utah Consent provisions (UT CODE ANN 76-7-304) unconstitutional); *Doe v Deschamps*, 461 FSupp 682 (DC Mn 1976) (Montana law (RCM §94-5-616(2)) failed to provide method of notice to husband that would protect woman and physician from criminal liability.)

A related issue concerning spousal consent to abortion is whether a father has a duty to support a child even though the father has no right to decide that the child, while still a fetus, should be aborted and that the father offered to pay for the abortion. Where this issue was considered, it was held that to impose such a duty on the father does not deny the father due process or equal protection of the laws. The equal treatment the father sought could only be achieved by according the father the right to compel the mother of his child to procure an abortion, and this result is foreclosed by *Roe v Wade*, 410 US 113, 93 SCt 705, 35 LE2d 174 (1973). Moreover, a statutory presumption that a father should share in the duty of support, herein UNIFORM PARENTAGE ACT §19-6-101, et. seq., is not violative of the due process clause because the state has no reasonable alternative means of making the crucial determination that a nexus exists between conception and childbirth. See *In re S P B*, 9 FLR 2050 (Co 1982). See also, *Harris v State*, 356 So2d 623 (Al 1978); *Dorsey v English*, 390 A2d 1133 (Md 1978); *D W L v M J B L*, 601 SW2d 475 (Tx 1980).

b. [§5.15] Notice

Although citing the *Danforth* decision [see §5.14], the United States Court of Appeals, Fifth Circuit, upheld a Florida abortion statute [FLA STAT ANN §390.001(4)(b)]. This state law was distinguishable from the one struck down in *Danforth*, since it merely required notice to the husband of the impending abortion rather than actual consent. The possible intrusion into the woman's right of privacy was more than offset by another byproduct of the notice, namely, the preservation of marital integrity. The state had a substantial interest in insuring that the marriage was not damaged by one spouse secretly frustrating the other's desire for children. It was a minor concession to inform the husband that his wife was considering an abortion. The question of whether the husband was the actual father of the fetus was not controlling in this situation. The husband had an interest far beyond paternity, namely, whether the abortion had the potential of adversely affecting his spouse's future child-bearing ability. These two state interests, the maintenance of the marital relationship, and the protection of the husband's procreative potential in the marriage were sufficient to justify the burden on the woman's abortion decision. The state had a compelling interest in requiring this spousal notice, since without it, a husband may never realize why his desire for children was frustrated. However, the action was remanded to the trial court to determine whether a statute was drafted narrowly enough to pass constitutional scrutiny. It was a question of fact whether the state legislature acted properly despite its failure to limit the notice provision to abortions of jointly conceived children, and not for a married woman carrying the child of someone other than her husband. If it is concluded that proper abortion procedures may adversely affect a woman's future procreative ability, a state may require notice to the husband as to whether he is or is not the father of the fetus. *Scheinberg v Smith*, 659 F2d 476, reh den, 667 F2d 93 (1981).

3. Minors

a. [§5.16] Generally

It is well settled that the right to privacy, like many other constitutional rights, extends to minors. *Planned Parenthood of Central Missouri v Danforth*, 428 US 52, 96 SCt 2831, 49 LE2d 788 (1976); *T H v Jones*, 425 FSupp 873, 881 (Ut 1975), affd on other grds, 425 US 986, 96 SCt 2195, 48 LE2d 811 (1976). However, the state possesses broader powers to regulate the conduct of minors than of adults, particularly in cases where it is outside the child's ability to act in his or her own best interest. The breadth of state authority must be examined and viewed in light of the often competing interests of the minor and her parents.

b. [§5.17] Parental or Judicial Consent

A Missouri requirement (V.A.M.S. §188.0200(4)) that at least one parent consent to the abortion by an unmarried minor not more than twelve weeks pregnant violated the privacy rights of the minor. The state had claimed that the right to protect the welfare of minors was a compelling state interest. However, the United States Supreme Court disagreed, holding that the protection of the family unit and the maintenance of parental authority did not constitute a significant interest to justify state action against a minor who may possess the maturity to make the abortion decision. The state may not impose a blanket limitation requiring the consent of a parent before an abortion may be performed on an unmarried minor during the first trimester of the pregnancy. There was no evidence that a parental veto over the decision by the minor and her physician would strengthen the family unit. Nor would it improve parental authority where the minor and the parents are so greatly at odds over the efficacy of the abortion. Although the state may establish broad authority over minors as compared to adults, minors still possess constitutional rights. Parental interest in a possible abortion was offset by the right of privacy of a competent minor mature enough to have become pregnant. *Planned Parenthood of Central Missouri v Danforth*, 428 US 52, 96 SCt 2831, 49 LE2d 788 (1976).

Similarly, a Massachusetts regulation requiring parental consent before an abortion may be performed on an unmarried woman under the age of eighteen was also unconstitutional. No minor, irrespective of maturity or other personal traits, could undergo the operation without prior consent of both parents or a court judge. This absolute third-party veto infringed upon the privacy rights of the minor. It was recognized that the abortion decision differs from other decisions that a minor may make. The state must act carefully in the area of parental involvement to preserve constitutional rights in the unique personal nature of the abortion decision. If a state requires absolute parental or judicial consent, it must also create an alternative procedure for authorization of the abortion. The mere existence of the right to obtain judicial consent did not provide an effective path to relief. The minor must have the option to seek judicial consent without prior notification of the parents. The court may weigh the merits of the case determining whether the woman possesses the maturity and intelligence to make the decision. If, after due consideration, a court concludes that an abortion is in the best interests of the minor, then a court authorization may be granted without parental involvement. However, if the court deems it in the best interest of an immature minor to defer the decision until after parental consultation, the court may deny the request. The judge's determination should prevail, assuming the conclusion is supportable by the evidence. *Bellotti v Baird*, 443 US 622, 99 SCt 335, 61 LE2d 797, reh den, 100 SCt 185, 44 US 887, 63 LE2d 121 (1979).

A significant issue raised in other abortion cases, the denial of equal protection rights, was ignored by the majority in *Bellotti*. One commentator noted that several equal protection claims could have been addressed by the court. First, the state may not have maintained its neutrality regarding a pregnant woman's choice. The state may place a burden on those minors who opt to terminate their pregnancies, while not participating in the decision when the pregnancy is carried to term. Second, there may be no rational basis for the differing treatment of married minors, who are free to choose an abortion, and unmarried minors, who are not. One cannot assume that the former would make a more informed decision than the latter. Third, the Massachusetts law [MASS GEN LAWS ANN Ch 112, §12F] that codified a "mature minor" standard for all types of medical care specifically excludes abortion and sterilization. COMMENT: RESTRICTIONS ON ABORTION RIGHTS OF MINORS, 3 Harvard Women's LJ 119, 138–139.

In applying the *Bellotti* decision, the United States Court of Appeals struck down sections of the Florida abortion law [FLA STAT ANN §390.001(4)(a)], which mandated that courts base authorization on the minor's abortion on the best interest of the minor, irrespective of the maturity of the pregnant woman. The law, as enacted, could have barred the abortion of a minor found by the court to be mature and fully confident in making such a decision. *Scheinberg v Smith*, 659 F2d 476 (5th Cir 1981). In accord, *Women's Services v Thone*, 636 F2d 206, 210 (8th Cir 1980), cert den, 452 US 911 (1981) (parental consultation portion of NEB REV STAT §28-333 unconstitutional).

c. [§5.18] Parental Notice

A distinction has been drawn between laws that provide for parental consent for minors' abortions, and those laws that merely notify the parents of the minors' abortion decision. The state has a reasonable interest in protecting the minors by allowing for parental consultation in a decision that may have far-reaching implications. State action in promoting the life of an unborn child is rationally related to a legitimate governmental concern.

This rationale was drawn from a 1981 Supreme Court decision in which an unemancipated pregnant minor challenged the constitutionality of a Utah abortion law. In this case, the United States Supreme Court noted that the principal class of women involved in the *Bellotti* decision [see §5.17] consisted of unmarried minors who had an adequate capacity to give valid and informed consent to the abortion and who did not wish to notify their parents. Under the facts of this case, there was no basis to conclude that the appellant was either mature or emancipated. Since these traits had not been established, the appellant had no standing to challenge the constitutionality of a Utah abortion statute geared toward mature minors. Rather, the issue was whether the law [UTAH CODE ANN §76-7-304 (1978)] that required a doctor to "notify, if possible", the parents of a minor upon whom an abortion is to be performed was constitutional as applied to a minor child who: (1) resided with, and was dependent upon her parents; (2) was not emancipated by marriage or otherwise; and, (3) did not establish her maturity or her relationship with her parents. The law did not give either the parents or the judge a veto power over the minor's decision. When applied to immature and dependent pregnant minors, it served to protect the family integrity as well as the welfare of the adolescent. The significant state interest served was an opportunity for parents to provide necessary medical information to the physician, which can be so important when the patient is immature. *H L v Matheson*, 450 US 398, 101 SCt 1164, 67 LE2d 388 (1981).

The holding in *H L v Matheson* should be viewed in a limited context, however. As noted by Justice Marshall in his dissent, if a more precise pleading had been drafted, the appellant would have had the standing to challenge the overbreadth of the law, and probably would have succeeded in the action (*H L v Matheson*, Dissent, 101 SCt 1164, 1179 (1981)).

d. [§5.19] Waiting Period for Minors

The failure of the Utah parental notification statute [see §5.18] to provide for a mandatory waiting period after the attending physician notifies the parents was not unconstitutional. As has been recognized in earlier decisions, time can be of the essence in an abortion decision. The law was enacted to protect minors by enhancing the possibility that the parents may be consulted about the decision that could have traumatic and permanent consequences.

However, a number of states have enacted parental notification statutes containing brief but mandatory waiting periods. See also LA REV STAT ANN §40:1299.35.5 (1980 Supp) (twenty-four hours actual notice; seventy-two hours constructive notice except for court authorized abortions); MASS GEN LAWS ANN Ch. 12, §12S (1981 Supp) (twenty-four hours); ND GEN CODE §14-02.1-03 (24 hours); TENN CODE ANN §39-301 (1979 Supp) (2 days).

For a general discussion of the constitutionality of the waiting period, see §§5.20–5.22.

4. Waiting Periods

a. [§5.20] Generally

Another area of contention closely allied to informed consent [see §§5.10—5.13] is whether a mandatory waiting period, normally twenty-four to forty-eight hours, between the initial consultation with a physician and the actual abortion procedure, invades a woman's right of privacy. The state's purported interest in imposing the waiting period is to assure that the woman will arrive at that informed decision with time to reconsider all relevant information about possible consequences of the procedure. However, it has been successfully argued that there is no evidence that a waiting period heightens the awareness of the woman to make her consent more meaningful. To the contrary, it has been shown that even a brief waiting period may serve as a detriment to the health of the woman.

b. [§5.21] Invalidation of Waiting Periods

The most telling arguments against imposition of the waiting period are the potential enhancement of the medical risk, emotional distress, and increased financial cost of the abortion. Also, because of possible scheduling difficulties that may delay the operation from two days to a week, the waiting period may actually prevent the woman's decision from being implemented. The period has been termed too absolute. Its imposition is required despite the woman's maturity, psychological well-being or other relevant, subjective factors. *Women's Medical Center of Providence v Roberts*, 530 FSupp 1136 (D RI 1982).

Other federal jurisdictions have invalidated both forty-eight or twenty-four hour periods. In *Akron Center for Reproductive Health, Inc v City of Akron*, 651 F2d 1198 (6th Cir 1981), cert granted, 102 SCt 2266 (1982) (twenty-four hour period invalid); *Planned Parenthood League v Bellotti*, 641 F2d 1006 (1st Cir 1981), rev, 499 FSupp 215 (D Ma 1980) (twenty-four hour period invalid); *Planned Parenthood Assn of Kansas City, Missouri, Inc v Ashcroft*, 664 F2d 687 (8th Cir 1981), cert granted, 102 SCt 2267 (1982) (forty-eight hour period invalid); *Women's Serv v Thone*, 636 F2d 206 (8th Cir 1980); affd on reh, 690 F2d 667 (8th Cir 1982) (forty-eight hour period invalid); *Friendship Medical Health Center, Ltd v Chicago Bd of Health*, 505 F2d 1141 (7th Cir 1974) (twenty-four hour period invalid); *Margaret S v Edwards*, 488 FSupp 181 (ED La 1980) (twenty-four hour period invalid); and *Women's Community Health Center, Inc v Cohen*, 477 FSupp 542 (D Me 1979) (forty-eight hour period invalid).

A mandatory twenty-four hour waiting period in Illinois [ILL REV STAT Ch 38 §81-23.2(A) (1) (a)] was unconstitutionally burdensome, since it served no compelling state interest. The state had asserted that women contemplating abortions would be vulnerable to pressure by unscrupulous doctors and that the twenty-four hour cooling-off period insulated them from possible coercion. However, the court observed that a majority of women are capable of caring for themselves and that this waiting period would be more in the nature of an inconvenience and an added expense. *Charles v Carey*, 627 F2d 772 (7th Cir 1980). Previously, a 1977 Illinois law that applied only to minors under the age of eighteen was ruled unconstitutional as being a violation of the Equal Protection Clause of the Fourteenth Amendment. According to the court, the forty-eight hour waiting period was under-inclusive because it excluded married minors under its provisions and over-inclusive because it included mature, emancipated minors. *Wynn v Carey*, 599 F2d 193 (7th Cir 1979).

c. [§5.22] Validation of Waiting Periods

However, proponents of waiting periods have found an ally in state courts. Ironically, the Illinois Supreme Court upheld a village ordinance providing for a twenty-four hour period between the initial examination and determination of the pregnancy. It was not convinced that the state interest in assuring that abortion is voluntary and informed is not substantial and compelling. Because of the unique nature of the abortion decision, it was held that the twenty-four hour period did not impose an impermissible burden on women. *Village of Oak Lawn v Marcowitz*, 86 Il2d 406, 427 NE2d 36 (1981).

A twenty-four hour waiting period in Kentucky was sustained for similar reasons. Moreover, the appeals court, in reversing the trial court invalidation of the statute [K.R.S. §436.023] pointed to the imprecise line between abortion trimesters. A delay of merely twenty-four hours would not jeopardize an abortion by placing it in a more advanced trimester. *Wolfe v Schroering*, 541 F2d 523 (6th Cir 1976).

C. Physicians, Hospitals and Abortion Clinics

1. Standing

a. [§5.23] Generally

Most abortion cases are class actions comprised of an amalgam of parties including hospitals, out-patient clinics, women's groups, birth control organizations, and of course, pregnant women. Individual physicians who perform the abortion are often part of a class, but often sue individually on their own behalf. Although a doctor may not possess the intimate relationship with a case when compared to a pregnant woman, the attending physician does not lack standing to sue. The *Bolton* decision [see §5.4] resolved many procedural issues involved in standing as well as justiciable controversy. The United States Supreme Court noted:

> The physician is the one against whom these criminal statutes directly operate in the event he [or she] procures an abortion that does not meet the statutory exceptions and conditions. The physician-appellants, therefore, assert a sufficiently direct threat of personal detriment. They should not be required to wait and undergo a criminal prosecution as the sole means of relief. 410 US at 188.

Apart from facing incarceration, the physician has certain freedoms to pursue economic interests that may not be subject to arbitrary restraints. A staff doctor had standing to sue his hospital on behalf of patients who allegedly were deprived of constitutional rights because of the hospital's restrictive abortion policies, and on his own behalf because of personal economic and liberty interests. His interest in practicing medicine unfettered by arbitrary restraint was "inextricably bound up with the right to privacy of the patients seeking an abortion." *Greco v Orange Memorial Hosp Corp*, 513 F2d 873 (5th Cir 1975).

Imminent criminal prosecution is not a necessary element for standing in cases involving the abortion rights of indigent women. Ohio physicians who were part of a class that was also comprised of poor women had standing to challenge a state law that prohibited Medicaid payments for non-therapeutic abortions. The fact that the doctors were not threatened with criminal prosecutions "does not compel a different result." *Roe v Ferguson*, 515 F2d 279, 281 (6th Cir 1975); *Crossen v Breckenridge*, 446 F2d 833 (6th Cir 1971); *Nyberg v City of Virginia*, 495 F2d 1342 (8th Cir 1974).

b. [§5.24] Issues

Two separate questions of standing were identified by the United States Supreme Court in *Singleton v Wulff*, 428 US 106, 112, 96 SCt 2868, 2873, 49 LE2d 826 (1976):

> First, whether the plaintiff-respondents [doctors] allege 'injury in fact', that is, a sufficiently concrete interest in the outcome of their suit to make it a case or controversy subject to a federal court's Article III jurisdiction, and, second, whether as a prudential matter,

> the plaintiff-respondents are proper proponents of the particular legal rights on which they base their suit.

The *Singleton* case involved the right of physicians to challenge the constitutionality of a state law [MO REV STAT §208.152 (12)] excluding elective abortions from reimbursement under the Medicaid program. Undoubtedly, the physicians suffered monetary injury through the operation of the statute, thus satisfying the first requirement.

The issue of whether a doctor is a proper proponent of this action is more complex. Ordinarily, one may not assert the constitutional rights of third parties. See *Singleton*, citing *Barrows v Jackson*, 346 US 249, 73 SCt 1031, 97 LE2d 1586 (1953). Courts are hesitant to rule on the constitutional rights of third parties either because it is unnecessary or because the other parties are usually in a better position to assert their own rights. However, the Court looked to two factual elements to determine whether the rule should apply in this case. The first is the existence of a close relationship between the litigant and the third party. Here, the physician's assertion of the rights of the third party pregnant woman was based upon the close relationship between doctor and patient. The second factual element is the ability of the third party to assert her own rights. In abortion cases, there are several obstacles that may prevent a woman from asserting her own rights. She may be "chilled" from asserting her rights to protect the privacy of her decision from the publicity and notoriety of a public trial. Because of the brief period that a pregnant woman may assert her right to an abortion, another obstacle at least technically, is imminent mootness. For these reasons, it is generally appropriate for a physician to assert *jus tertii* against a government interference with the abortion decision. *Singleton*, 428 US at 117–118, 96 SCt at 2875–2876.

To exemplify this two-step inquiry in *Singleton*, above, a federal district court held that doctors had standing to challenge the constitutionality of the Arkansas criminal abortion law [AR STAT ANN §41-2551–2559]. Two of the provisions subjected the doctors and their assistants to criminal liability for attempting to perform or performing an abortion other than a "legal abortion", i.e., those performed in a state-licensed hospital. The state medical board was also authorized to revoke or suspend a physician's license if a physician committed an act falling within the definition of "unprofessional conduct", i.e., the procuring of a wrongful and criminal abortion. Thus, the risk of criminal prosecution, as well as the resultant disciplinary action, was sufficient to give doctors a stake in the outcome of the case. However, the physicians lacked standing to challenge a provision granting immunity from civil liability of persons refusing to perform abortions. The doctors were not within the zone of interests which the statute [AR REV STAT §41-2560] sought to protect. *Smith v Bentley*, 493 FSupp 916 (ED Ar 1980).

c. [§5.25] Limitations

The physician's standing to sue, although broad, is not absolute. Standing was one of the subordinate issues resolved by the United States Supreme Court in *Roe v Wade*, 410 US 113, 93 SCt 705, 35 LE2d 147 (1973) [see §5.3.] A doctor entered the case as a plaintiff-intervenor claiming that he had been prosecuted on several occasions for violating the Texas criminal abortion statute [TEX PEN CODE §§1191-1194, 1196]. At the time of the intervention, state criminal proceedings were pending against him. Without evidence of either state harassment or bad faith, a defendant in a pending state case cannot affirmatively challenge in federal court statutes under which the state is prosecuting him. On a peripheral issue, the Court noted that it did not consider whether the intervention would have been successful had the doctor sued on behalf of a class of similarly situated doctors. *Wade*, 410 US at 427, fn. 7.

Certain statutes apply only to women as prospective parents. Thus, a law requiring that a woman relinquish her parental rights to an infant that survives an abortion imposed no obligation of the attending physician. Nor can it be claimed that the statute posed a threat of injury to the physician. *Planned Parenthood of Central Missouri, Inc v Danforth*, 428 US 52, 62, 96 SCt 2831, 2838, 49 LE2d 788 (1976). See also *Hodgson v Lawson*, 542 F2d 1350, 1355 *n* 2 (8th Cir 1976). (Physician had no standing to challenge a state law (MINN STAT §145.415, subd 3) that provided for termination of parental rights if an abortion results in a live birth.)

Note that a similar law [UT CODE ANN §76-7-311] was invalidated because it provided for the termination rights without due process of law. In this case, however, the challenging party was a pregnant woman who obviously had standing to sue. *Doe v Rampton*, 366 FSupp 189, 193 (DC Ut 1973).

d. [§5.26] Abortion Clinics

The right of an abortion clinic to file actions on behalf of itself has also been viewed as analogous to a physicians' standing to sue, with one obvious limitation. There is some question whether these clinics have standing to assert their patients' claims. Due to their corporate character, the clinics are "another step removed" from the operation of the statute. The confidential relationship that exists between doctor and patient is more apparent than that between an abortion clinic and its client. *Margaret S v Edwards*, 488 FSupp 181, 188 (ED La 1980).

2. Recordkeeping

a. [§5.27] Generally

Under some state abortion laws, physicians, hospitals and other health care centers are required to maintain records irrespective of the stage of pregnancy of the woman. The state interest in recordkeeping derives from the extraction of only that information relevant to preserve maternal health. At first glance, it would seem that any state action in this area would infringe both on the woman's right of privacy and on her attending physician's right to form a medical judgment with respect to the termination of the pregnancy. However, the United States Supreme Court in *Danforth*, 428 US 52, 96 SCt 2831, 49 LE2d 788 (1976) held that these requirements under a Missouri statute [Mo Rev Stat §§188.050,-060 (Vern 1976)] did not conflict with its earlier holding in *Wade* [see §5.2].

Under the law, each hospital and attending physician is supplied with forms "the purpose and function of which shall be the preservation of maternal health and life by adding to the sum of medical knowledge through the compilation of relevant maternal health and life data into monitoring all abortions performed to assure that they are only done under and in accordance with the provisions of the law." (Mo Rev Stat §188.055(1)).

Although the state may not restrict or regulate the medical judgment of a physician during the first trimester of pregnancy, mere recordkeeping, if not abused, has no legally significant impact on the abortion decision or on the patient-physician relationship. However, it is clear that a state may not regulate abortion simply by the "sheer burden of recordkeeping detail." *Danforth*, 428 US at 80, 96 SCt at 2847. See also *Doe v Deschamps*, 461 FSupp 682 (DC Mt 1976) (Recordkeeping that was not performed in an unduly burdensome manner constitutional (RCM 94-5-619).)

Abuse arises when the information is not kept confidential. The added requirement of confidentiality preserves the constitutionality of the law. *Hodgson v Lawson*, 542 F2d 1350, 1357 (8th Cir 1976) (Recordkeeping requirement of Minn Stat §145.413(1) upheld); *Mobile Women's Medical Clinic, Inc v Board of Comm City of Mobile*, 426 FSupp 331 (DC Al 1977) (City ordinance constitutionally infirm because of lack of confidentiality.)

b. [§5.28] Specific Recordkeeping Provisions

The information gathered must serve a justifiable state interest, i.e., the health of all pregnant women, as well as preserving the confidentiality of the patient-physician relationship. In an Illinois federal district court decision, the following required material (Ill Rev Stat Ch. 38, ¶81-30 (1975)) was not characterized as "burdensome administrative detail", and passed constitutional scrutiny: a. identification of the facility where abortion was performed and date performed; b. the political subdivision in which the patient resides; c. patient's date of birth, race and marital status; d. number of prior pregnancies; e. date of last menstrual period; f. type of abortion procedure performed; and g. complications, if any.

However, another provision that required abortions performed after twenty weeks of gestation be recorded as a fetal death was struck down. The fetal death report, which included the name of the woman, was available upon request from interested third parties, including those with a personal or proprietary interest. The possible public disclosure of the woman's identity violated her right of privacy in two respects: (1) the damage to her reputation from the abortion; and, (2) the indirect adverse effect on her decision to undergo the abortion. *Wynn v Scott*, 449 FSupp 1302 (DC Il 1978), affd on other grds, 599 F2d 193 (7th Cir 1979), 439 US 8, 99 SCt 49, 58 LE2d 7 (1979).

Recordkeeping provisions under the Illinois Abortion Act were expanded in 1980. Apart from the information that was upheld in *Wynn*, above, the following data must be gathered by the physician: (1) the date the abortion was performed; (2) certification that the fetus was not viable or medical indications for any abortion performed when the fetus was viable; (3) medical indications for the use of saline amniocentesis; (4) medical indications for the nullification of any waiting period required under this Law; (5) the basis for any medical judgment that an emergency existed; (6) the basis for the clinical judgment that an abortion is necessary; (7) date of the medical consultation, the time it began and the time it ended; and (8) results of a pregnancy test performed on the woman before the abortion and the pathologist's test results. See ILL REV STAT Ch 38, ¶81-30.

In a similar case, a Michigan public health code regulation [M.A.C.R. 325.3847] that required a so-called free standing out-patient facility to file an "abortion report" with nineteen items to be filled in regarding each abortion procedure was valid. Confidentiality was maintained since the report excluded the name of the patient, which was later filled in by the attending physician. Collaterally, this regulation of certain facilities, including abortion clinics, did not violate the facilities' equal protection rights by impermissibly singling out abortion clinics for this treatment. There was no clear pattern of selective enforcement against abortion clinics as opposed to other out-patient facilities, from which to infer discrimination. *Birth Control Centers, Inc v Reizen*, 508 FSupp 1366 (ED Mi 1981).

Normally valid recordkeeping provisions have been voided where they could not be separated from other unconstitutional sections of an abortion statute. The entire Youngstown, Ohio, abortion ordinance, including its recordkeeping requirements, was declared unconstitutional for imposing burdensome medical and building code regulations on abortion clinics performing first trimester operations. The ordinance also imposed unconstitutional qualifications and controls on medical personnel who must maintain these records. For this reason, the court refused to rewrite the ordinance in order to preserve the constitutional provisions of the act. *Mahoning Women's Center v Hunter*, 610 F2d 456 (6th Cir 1979).

3. [§5.29] Prohibited Abortion Methods

To meet constitutional standards, state laws that proscribe various abortion methods must be necessary to preserve the life or health of the mother. A Missouri statute [Mo Stat Ann §188.050] prohibited the use of saline amniocentesis as an abortion technique after the first trimester. (At the time, *circa* 1974, about 70% to 80% of all post-first-trimester abortions in the United States were performed through this method.) The law describes saline amniocentesis as a method where amniotic fluid is removed and "saline or other fluid" is inserted into the amniotic sac. The state acknowledged that the use of this method was actually safer than childbirth. It justified the law by claiming that there were other, safer methods of abortion at this stage of the pregnancy, such as a prostaglandin injection.

The United States Supreme Court rejected this argument on four grounds, two of which deal with the infringement of the woman's right to an abortion. The state failed to recognize the utter predominance of the use of the saline amniocentesis method as an acceptable medical procedure around the country. Also, the state was apparently oblivious of the fact that these other abortion techniques had just passed through the experimental stage and were not readily available to the general public. Thirdly, the statute itself was poorly constructed. The prohibition of "saline and *other fluids*" would probably include the prostaglandin injection itself and other future, safer methods of abortion. Finally, the statute proscribed the use of saline, but did not ban more lethal techniques. The law infringed on the rights of the woman by forcing her and her physician to terminate the pregnancy by more dangerous methods, than the method prohibited. *Planned Parenthood of Central Missouri v Danforth*, 428 US 52, 75–79, 96 SCt 2831, 49 LE2d 788 (1976). See also *Wolfe v Schroering*, 541 F2d 523 (6th Cir 1976) affd 388 FSupp 631 (WD Ky 1974).

Because of the prevalence of the relatively safe dilation and evacuation (D&E) method, several circuits have determined that the state's interest in the health of the woman does not become compelling until the eighteenth week of pregnancy. The dilation and evacuation method was recognized as a medical advance, eliminating maternal health as a factor in the state interference during the early weeks (seventeenth and eighteenth week) of the second trimester. *Planned Parenthood Assn of Kansas City v Ashcroft*, 664 F2d 687 (8th Cir 1981), 483 FSupp 679 (1980), cert granted 102 SCt 2267 (1982).

4. Hospital-Required Abortions

a. [§5.30] Generally

The position of medical clinics and other non-hospital facilities performing abortions is that a female patient is as safe in their facility as in a hospital. States and municipalities have enacted laws and ordinances restricting abortions to accredited hospitals. Because of the *Wade* decision [see §§5.2, 5.3], most of these laws are framed so that only those abortions performed in the second trimester and beyond (when the state interest in the mother's health becomes compelling), are affected.

b. [§5.31] Illustrative Cases

Regulations promulgated by the Chicago Board of Health aimed at medical facilities offering abortions without regard to the trimester of pregnancy involved were unconstitutional. The regulations required, among other things, an affiliation agreement with a licensed Chicago hospital, the performance of various lab tests, and the presence of certain medical equipment to treat shock, cardiac arrest, and other emergencies. The unconstitutionality of the regulations were premised on the fundamental right of a woman to be free from government regulation affecting the abortion decision during the first trimester. *Friendship Medical Center, Ltd v Chicago Bd of Health*, 505 F2d 1141 (7th Cir 1976), cert den, 420 US 997, 95 SCt 1438, 43 LE2d 680 (1975).

Because of tremendous medical advances made since *Wade*, abortion clinics and physicians have claimed that this hospital requirement does not reasonably relate to the health of the woman. A relatively new technique called dilation and evacuation (D&E) is the safest method of abortion up until the eighteenth week of pregnancy, well into the second trimester, and may be performed as safely outside the hospital.

The mortality rates (per 100,000 cases) for post-first trimester abortion techniques for the years 1972 through 1977 are as follows: dilation and evacuation 8.3%; prostaglandins and other agents 10.8%; saline installation 15.5%; hysterectomy and hysterotomy 45.3%. Center for Disease Control, United States Dept. of Housing, Education, and Welfare, *Abortion Surveillance* 1977, Table 23.

In one case, this hospitalization requirement effectively rendered dilation and evacuation unavailable in Missouri, since allegedly only one state hospital permitted this method in the second trimester. Also, it was alleged hospitalized dilation and evacuations are more expensive than non-hospital dilation and evacuations. So it followed that this added financial burden substantially interfered with a woman's abortion decision. The appeals court found that non-hospitalized second trimester dilation and evacuation procedures were no more dangerous to maternal health than hospitalized procedures. The state law [Mo Ann Stat §188.025 (Vernon)] was unconstitutional since the requirement that all second trimester abortions be performed in a hospital was not reasonably related to maternal health. *Planned Parenthood Assn of Kansas City v Ashcroft*, 664 F2d 687 (8th Cir 1981), cert granted, 102 SCt 2267 (1982). Contra: *Hodgson v Lawson*, 542 F2d 1350, 1354 (8th Cir 1975) ("The requirement of (Minn Stat §145.412(3)(1)) that an abortion be performed in a hospital, which is not being challenged here, is an example of permissible state regulation subsequent to the first trimester"). In another case, a city ordinance placing medical and building code regulations on first trimester clinics imposed "heavy and unnecessary conditions on the performance of the operation." *Mahoning Women's Center v Hunter*, 610 F2d 456, 460 (6th Cir 1979). The Louisiana federal district court used a broader rationale in overturning a post-first trimester hospital restriction law that stated "no person shall perform or induce an abortion upon a pregnant woman subsequent to the end of the first trimester of her pregnancy, unless such abortion is performed in a hospital." La Rev Stat Ann §40:1299.35.3. Using the reasoning previously discussed, the court first concluded that restricting post-first trimester abortions to hospitals bore no rational relationship to the preservation of maternal health. However, it advanced this reasoning another step. Because the dilation and evacuation method is safer than childbirth until the eighteenth week of pregnancy, the state's interest in regulating abortion before this time is not "compelling." The court apparently broadened the restrictions on state actions first set forth in *Wade:* "If there is no *compelling* state interest until abortion threatens maternal health in the same degree as does childbirth, the state cannot impose regulations at a time — after the twelfth week and before the eighteenth week of pregnancy — when the abortion method used, dilation and evacuation, is far safer than childbirth. Thus, the state's interests in protecting maternal health does not become compelling until the eighteenth week of pregnancy." *Margaret S v Edwards*, 488 FSupp 181, 194–196 (ED La 1980).

However, a Cleveland municipal ordinance that prohibited the establishment of abortion clinics in certain retail areas of the city was constitutional. It did not burden either the abortion decision or the physician-patient relationship, since access to other abortion facilities remained in other areas of the city. [See also §5.32.] *West Side Women's*

Serv, Inc v Cleveland, 450 FSupp 796 (ND Oh 1978), affd mem, 582 F2d 1281 (6th Cir 1978), cert den, 439 US 983, 99 SCt 572, 58 LE2d 654 (1979).

5. Zoning Restrictions

a. [§5.32] Extent of State Police Power

The United States Supreme Court has consistently recognized zoning as a permissible exercise of a state's police power. One objective of its exercise is the protection of family values. Attempts have been made to protect these values through the passage of municipal ordinances regulating the location of abortion clinics within a community. As a result, these ordinances and the women's abortion rights recognized in *Wade* [see §5.3] have been at loggerheads.

Public sentiment against abortion, alone, cannot limit a woman's right to an abortion. The passage of zoning ordinances as a way of imposing its moral values against abortion has been viewed as an attempt by the state to invade a woman's right of privacy. Courts have differed as to what standard the state must follow in justifying its actions.

The Eighth Circuit Court of Appeal granted a preliminary injunction against a city that attempted to place special requirements on the location of abortion clinics. A 6-month moratorium had been imposed on the construction of separate abortion facilities, including out-patient clinics, until a study determining their impact could be made. The court found that restrictions on the construction of first trimester abortion clinics were an undue interference on the woman's right to an abortion. *Planned Parenthood of Minnesota v Citizens for Community Action*, 558 F2d 861 (8th Cir 1977). In accord *Framingham Clinic, Inc v Board of Selectmen*, 373 Ma 279, 367 NE2d 606 (1976) (Effect of the ordinance resulted in a total ban on first trimester abortions).

However, other circuits have employed the less stringent "rational basis" test in upholding zoning restrictions. For example, an injunction against enforcement of a Cleveland ordinance was denied, because the law only prohibited abortions in specified areas of the city, i.e., the retail business districts. Apparently, the city's motivation in enacting the ordinance was in response to public pressure against the visibility of these clinics in certain neighborhoods. In any event, the court also recognized the city's legitimate interest in advancing childbirth over abortion. The action was not detrimental to women's rights, since pregnant women were free to seek abortions at clinics in other areas of the city. *West Side Womens Serv, Inc v City of Cleveland*, 450 FSupp 796 (ND Oh 1978), affd mem, 582 F2d 1281 (6th Cir 1978), cert den, 439 US 983 (1978).

[§5.33] Injunctions

As can be ascertained from several of these decisions, the preliminary injunction has been an invaluable weapon in an abortion clinic's legal arsenal. Several elements must be established before an injunction may be granted: (1) The threat of an irreparable harm to the clinic; (2) The balancing of the prohibition to the threat of injury to the state or municipality if the injunction were granted; (3) The probability of success on the merits of the case; and, (4) The effect on the public interest in granting the injunction.

These four elements figured prominently in a Wisconsin federal district court decision. A court ordinance placed many severe limitations on the operation of proposed abortion clinics. Among them was a zoning requirement restricting clinics to areas designated for heavy industry. The court determined that since the clinic, which was located in a commercial area, had been leased and remodeled by the plaintiffs, the harm caused by the zoning requirement would be irreparable. Secondly, the threat of harm to the municipality was minimal when compared to the harm inflicted on the plaintiffs. Also, there was every evidence that the regulations were unconstitutionally burdensome, and that the plaintiffs would eventually succeed on the merits. Finally, if the ordinance was unconstitutional, the public interest would be served by adhering to the tenents of the United States Constitution. *Fox Valley Reproductive Health Center, Inc v Arft*, 446 FSupp 1072 (ED Wi 1978).

For purposes of granting an injunction, courts have held that an injury is "irreparable" only if it cannot be corrected through monetary remedies. *Speigel v City of Houston*, 636 F2d 997 (5th Cir 1981); *Parker v Dunlop*, 517 F2d 785 (5th Cir 1975). This is true when a woman's guarantee of privacy, a fundamental right under the Fourteenth Amendment, has been infringed upon. The fact that a woman's injury from being denied an abortion because of zoning restrictions may be minimal, particularly if abortions are readily available in other areas of the city, is not controlling. The presence of other abortion facilities "does not eliminate or render harmless the potential constitutional violation of a fundamental right." *Deerfield Medical Center v City of Deerfield Beach*, 661 F2d 328, 338 (5th Cir 1981).

6. [§5.34] Abortions by Non-Physicians

It is within the state police power to regulate and prohibit abortions by non-physicians regardless of the trimester of the pregnancy. The United States Supreme Court in *Connecticut v Menillo*, 423 US 9, 96 SCt 170, 46 LE2d 152 (1975) upheld a Connecticut criminal statute [CN GEN STAT REV

§53-29] that prohibited "any person" from attempting to perform an abortion. The Court drew a distinction from the *Wade* decision [see §5.2] that held a Texas law contravened a woman's right to a clinical abortion by medically competent personnel. The court did not hold the "Texas statutes unenforceable against a non-physician abortionist", as in this case. See also prior decisions: *People v Bricker*, 389 Mi 524, 208 NW2d 173 (1973) (Conviction of non-physician for conspiracy to commit an abortion affirmed under MICH COMP LAWS ANN §750.14); *May v State*, 254 Ar 194, 196, 492 SW2d 888 (1973); *Smith v Bentley*, 493 FSupp 916 (ED Ar 1980) (Although ARK STAT ANN §41-2553 cannot be constitutionally applied to physicians does not render the statute unconstitutional as applied to laymen); *State v Hultgren*, 295 Mi 299, 204 NW2d 197 (1973) (Contra: MN STAT §617.18 unenforceable against non-physician.); *Commonwealth v Jackson*, 454 Pa 429, 312 A2d 13 (1973) (18 PA STAT §§4718–4719 declared unconstitutional).

D. Medicaid

1. [§5.35] Generally; Social Security Act, Title XIX

Title XIX of the Social Security Act, 42 USC §1396, provides for the appropriation of federal funds to enable each state as far as practicable under the conditions to furnish medical assistance and rehabilitation services to low income individuals who are unable to meet the costs of necessary medical services. A state is not bound to participate in what is commonly referred to as the "Medicaid" program. However, if it participates, it must submit, and have approved, by the federal government, a state plan that satisfies various criteria. When the approved plan takes effect, a state may accept federal grants representing reimbursement for a portion of the expenditures incurred in providing specific medical services to eligible persons under the plan. No reimbursement is available for any amounts paid by a state to, or on behalf of, any ineligible individuals as defined by the Act.

One requirement of a participating state is agreement that it will provide financial assistance to specified needy persons in the following general areas of medical treatment: "1. in-patient hospital services; 2. Out-patient hospital services; 3. other laboratory and x-ray services; 4. skilled nursing facilities services, periodic screening and diagnosis of children, and family planning services, and 5. services of physicians." (42 USC §§1396a(a) (13) (B), 1396d(a) (1)—(5)).

Although a state is not forced to fund all these categories, the law does require that a state plan establish reasonable standards for determining the breadth of medical assistance consistent with the goals of Title XIX.

2. Funding of Abortions

a. [§5.36] Majority Rule

The United States Supreme Court, in two 1977 decisions, considered the issue of whether a state has an affirmative duty to subsidize abortions for indigent expectant mothers. In *Beal v Doe*, 432 US 438, 97 SCt 2366, 53 LE2d 464 (1977), the Court held that a Pennsylvania requirement of a certificate of medical necessity before a Medicaid abortion is funded neither contravened Title XIX nor denied indigent pregnant women their equal protection rights under the Fourteenth Amendment. The state is not obligated to fund the cost of all abortions permissible under state law. No language in Title XIX suggests that a state must fund every specified medical procedure, particularly an elective one. This exclusion is not unreasonable, since the state has a "valid and important interest in encouraging childbirth." *Beal*, 97 SCt at 445.

In a companion case to *Beal*, the Supreme Court reiterated that the scope of the right of privacy recognized in *Wade* does not include the right to Medicaid payments for first trimester abortions that are not medically necessary to preserve the health of the mother. A Connecticut welfare regulation granted Medicaid recipients payments for medical expenses incurred during childbirth, but not for non-therapeutic abortions. Two indigent women claimed that the regulation violated their equal protection guarantees of the Fourteenth Amendment through unequal subsidization of childbirth as opposed to abortion. The Court, however, drew a distinction between the state regulation in Connecticut, and the Texas law invalidated in *Wade* [see §5.2.] The regulation did not directly block a woman's access to an abortion — rather, it simply made childbirth a more attractive alternative economically. The state encouragement of an alternative activity is "consonant with legislative policy." Although a state may not impose unwarranted regulations directly interfering with access to abortions, it is not obliged to exercise its legislative power to remove pre-existing, non-governmental restrictions on a woman's access to abortions. *Maher v Roe*, 432 US 464, 97 SCt 2376, 53 LE2d 484 (1977).

b. [§5.37] Alternative Arguments

Justice Marshall's dissent in *Beal* [see §5.36] attacks the very foundation of the majority's treatment of the equal protection issue, the "outdated and intellectually disingenuous 'two tier' " analysis. He sees no difference between "laws that absolutely prevent exercise of the fundamental right of abortion and those that 'merely' make its exercise difficult," as in this case. The result is the same, a total prohibition of abortion for the indigent. Instead, in his view, three factors should be evaluated in an equal protection analysis: (1) the importance of the denied government benefits; (2) the character of the class; and, (3) the associated state interest. According to Marshall, the denial of benefits to a poor woman may result in the birth of an unwanted child, which contravenes the holding in *Wade* that a woman has a fundamental right to choose whether to bear a child. The state's interest in protecting the life of the fetus is insufficient to sanction interference with this right. If its interest does not justify several doctors' concurrence for an abortion as held in the *Bolton* decision, then the state cannot allow interference with the rights of a class of indigent women. *Beal v Doe*, 432 US 438, 459–461 (1977).

Although the Burger Court vehemently denied that *Wade* and its successors were being limited, it was clear that the line of reasoning in these cases was not being extended to its logical conclusion. This retrenchment of the Court is even more apparent in subsequent decisions. The Hyde Amendment to Title XIX that withholds funding of certain medically-necessary abortions did not impinge on the constitutional guarantees recognized in *Wade*. The Court reiterated that while the government may not encroach upon a woman's exercise of free choice in marriage and family matters, it is not obliged to remedy certain deficiencies, namely a woman's indigency. The woman is still left with the same range of choices in considering her abortion, even if Congress had not acted to subsidize certain medical procedures.

3. Hyde Amendment Ramifications

a. [§5.38] Generally

The Medicaid program was amended in 1976 to severely limit the reimbursement for the cost of abortions. The so-called Hyde Amendment has been attacked by various women's groups and various medical associations on the grounds that it violates the liberty and the equal protection guarantees of the Due Process Clause of the Fifth Amendment. The Amendment has undergone slight refinements over the years. Basically, all the Amendments to the program have banned federal funds for abortions, and vary only as to the exceptions to the rule.

The 1980 version of the Amendment states: "None of the funds provided by this joint resolution shall be used to perform abortions except when the life of the mother would be endangered if the fetus were carried to term; an exception to such medical procedure is necessary for the victims of rape or incest where such rape or incest has been reported promptly to a law enforcement agency or public health service." (Public Law No. 96-123, §109).

b. [§5.39] Harris v McRae Decision

In *Harris v McRae*, 448 US 297, 100 SCt 2671, 65 LE2d 784 (1980), the trial court had granted an injunction on behalf of a class of indigent pregnant women and others preventing enforcement of the Hyde Amendment. Allegedly, this form of the Amendment that relieved the states from funding unreimbursed, medically-necessary abortions violated the equal protection guarantees found in the Fifth Amendment Due Process Clause, as well as infringing on the Free Exercise of Religion Clause of the First Amendment.

Although federal reimbursement is available under Medicaid for essential medical services, the Hyde Amendment, which bans medically-necessary abortions from the program, does not violate equal protection rights under the Fifth Amendment. The classification neither invades a woman's constitutional rights or liberties nor rests on grounds wholly irrelevant to a governmental objective. Further, these women are not part of a "constitutionally suspect" class, since indigency is not a category entitled to strict scrutiny by the courts. So, the presumption of constitutionality remains.

In using the *Wade* rationale, the trial court in *Harris* had held that the restrictions on funding medically-necessary abortions from a program funding medically-necessary services generally, served no legal governmental interest. Thus, assuming *arguendo*, that indigency is not part of a "suspect" class, state action did not satisfy even the minimum rationality test required under the equal protection guarantees of the Fifth Amendment.

In reversing the trial court's decision, the United States Supreme Court first commented that Congress did not intend that a state unilaterally fund a health service under Medicaid. Title XIX does not require a state to pay for those medically-necessary abortions for which federal repayment is unavailable under the Hyde Amendment. The Hyde Amendment itself does not impinge upon the "liberty" protected by the Due Process Clause, since a woman's freedom of choice does not entitle her to financial resources to take advantage of the full range of protected choices. The restriction of her choice is not the product of the governmental non-action, but rather of her own indigency. A funding obligation would require Congress to pay for abortions even had it not enacted a Medicaid program to subsidize indigent persons.

In a companion case, a class of plaintiffs consisting of an indigent pregnant woman, a welfare organization and two physicians brought a civil rights action to enjoin enforcement of an Illinois law [ILL REV STAT Ch 23 §5-5] prohibiting state-paid abortions except in life-threatening situations. These funding requirements paralleled those of the Hyde Amendment. The federal district court concluded that both the state law and the Hyde

Amendment were unconstitutional for denying funding of medically-necessary abortions before the fetus is viable. The United States Supreme Court disagreed, ruling that the lower court lacked jurisdiction to void the Hyde Amendment, since the state statute and not the federal law had been challenged by the parties. The Illinois law was constitutional, with the court citing the rationale in *McRae* that upheld the validity of its federal counterpart, the Hyde Amendment. *Williams v Zbaraz*, 448 US 358, 100 SCt 2694, 65 LE2d 831 (1980).

c. [§5.40] Effect on Freedom of Religion

The Hyde Amendment does not run afoul of the establishment of religion clause of the First Amendment. It was argued that the Amendment illegally codified tenets of the Roman Catholic religion that prohibited abortion except when necessary to preserve the woman's life. However, the fact that the Amendment and certain religious doctrine are similar philosophically does not, standing alone, amount to a violation of the First Amendment. Also, the plaintiffs lacked standing to challenge the Hyde Amendment on the grounds that their free exercise of religion had been infringed upon. None of the parties were pregnant, indigent, or had religious convictions directing them to obtain an abortion. *Harris*, 448 US at 319, 100 SCt at 2689, 65 LE2d at 806.

The establishment argument was also raised by a pro-life advocate, with similar results. The United States Supreme Court denied certiorari and let stand a lower court denial of an injunction to prevent property taxes from being used to fund state-authorized abortions. It was alleged that state funding of sterilization, contraception, and abortion constituted an establishment of religion. *McKee v County of Ramsey*, 316 NW2d 555 (Mn SCt 1982).

4. [§5.41] Other Publicly-Funded Health Services

The rationale employed by the United States Supreme Court in *Maher* [see §5.36] to block Medicaid-funded abortions also extends to city-owned hospitals that provide publicly-financed hospital services. In *Poelker v Doe*, 432 US 519, 97 SCt 2391, 53 LE2d 528 (1977), a city, in a strict policy decision chose to provide municipally-funded hospital services for childbirth, but not for non-therapeutic abortions. An indigent woman brought a 42 USC §1983 civil rights action against the City of St. Louis citing the *Wade* and *Bolton* decisions as precedent. The argument was rejected under the reasoning set forth in *Maher*, above, i.e., the city has a rational interest in encouraging childbirth. The personal anti-abortion stand of the mayor of the city was irrelevant.

Although abortions may be available in private hospitals and clinics, left unanswered was the fate of indigent women living in rural areas where the public hospital is the only facility open to persons seeking abortion. As Justice Brennan noted in his dissent "if such a public hospital is closed to abortions, any woman 'rich or poor' will be seriously inconvenienced; and for women 'particularly poor women' the unavailability of abortions in the public hospital will be an insuperable obstacle." (*Poelker*, Dissent, Brennan 432 US 519, 524).

5. [§5.42] Conclusions

Even in light of favorable court decisions, the state is not entirely free in disrupting the abortion procedure in the case of indigent persons. A municipal hospital, which was the only licensed medical facility in the community, was enjoined from prohibiting its doctors from performing abortions on the premises, except in cases involving the life of the woman. The city government clearly overstepped its authority in this case. The United States Court of Appeals, Eighth Circuit found that previous United States Supreme Court decisions had merely upheld the denial of government funding of abortions. Here, the city tried to eliminate access to abortion services at the only hospital in town. The injunction by the federal district court simply required the city to allow staff doctors to perform abortions. It did not authorize free abortions, force the hiring of physicians who would perform abortions, or in any way, subsidize abortion services. A distinction may be drawn between this situation, and the unconstitutional requirement that a hospital spend public funds to hire doctors to perform abortions for indigent women. It is noteworthy that the state made no attempt to show any state interest in its regulation of its doctors. *Myberg v City of Virginia*, 667 F2d 754 (8th Cir 1982).

Clearly, a woman's fundamental freedom of choice does not entail a constitutional right to financial aid in subsidizing an abortion, even though her health may be adversely affected. State and federal regulations on the funding of abortions, both non-therapeutic and those medically necessary, do not violate the equal protection guarantees of the Fifth and Fourteenth Amendments. Financial need is not recognized as a "suspect class", and thus, the restrictions are not subject to strict scrutiny. The state action bears a rationale relationship to a legitimate state interest, i.e., protecting potential life by encouraging childbirth. Nor do these restrictions impinge upon due process rights since although a government may not impede a woman's exercise of her freedom of choice, it need not remove those not of its own creation.

The Medicaid cases from *Beal* through *Williams* demonstrate the difficulty in setting the parameters of a non-enumerated constitutional right. Historically, the content of a non-enumerated right is often subject to the philosophical and political bent of the court at the time a particular case is decided.

In contravening the spirit, if not the letter of the *Harris* decision, the New Jersey Supreme Court struck down a state Medicaid statute. The law [NJ STAT ANN §30:4D-6.1] which prohibited Medicaid funding for abortions except where necessary to preserve the woman's life violated the equal protection guarantees of the state constitution. (These equal protection provisions are more expansive than their federal constitution counterpart.) The law, which grants funds when life is at risk, but denies them when simply the health of the mother is endangered, wrongfully withheld equal protection guarantees to women entitled to necessary legal services under Medicaid. The state's compelling interest in preserving fetal life can never, at any point during the pregnancy, take priority over the life and health of the mother. However, the court noted that the state may pursue its interest in denying funding for non-therapeutic abortions, since neither the woman's life nor health was in jeopardy. *Right to Choose v Byrne*, 450 A2d 925 (NJ 1982).

E. Feticide

1. [§5.43] Introduction

Historically, homicide has been defined as the act of one human being taking the life of another. The English common law recognized that the fetus of a pregnant woman may be the victim of felonious homicide where the assailant would have been guilty of homicide had the mother died instead of the child. However, the act of felonious homicide contemplated only those victims born alive who had an existence independent of their mothers at the time of death. Absent statutory authority to the contrary, the act of homicide did not include causing the death of a fetus not born alive as a result of an assault on the mother.

Since the survival rate of fetuses near term is now so high, the present trend is to recognize viable fetuses as persons. Thus, a number of state jurisdictions have retreated from the old common law rule. This shift has been prompted, in part, by the tremendous advances made in science and medicine since World War II. Diseases can now be diagnosed by obstetricians while the fetus is still in its mother's womb. Because of these medical breakthroughs, fetuses, under certain circumstances, are recognized as entities within the parameters of the general term "person". State legislatures have amended their criminal homicide laws to include protection of viable fetuses.

This new understanding has reshaped the philosophy of some courts in this area. In 1982, the Kentucky Court of Appeals concluded that a long standing 1936 ruling that the birth of a child alive is an indispensable element in the prosecution of infanticide was no longer valid. The trial court had previously dismissed a murder indictment against the father who allegedly killed a seven-month-old fetus, ruling that the fetus itself was not a living human being at the time of the killing. However, this rationale was totally rejected on appeal. Since an unborn fetus has other guaranteed rights, such as an action for the wrongful death of a parent, there is no reason why the fetus should assume a lesser position simply because it is a homicide victim. The appeals courts stopped short of recognizing a seven-month-old fetus as a person. However, it agreed with the prosecution that the question of whether the deceased was a person at the time of the homicide, was a proper consideration for the jury. *Commonwealth v Hollis*, 8 FLR 2457 (Ky 1982).

As in the case of abortion [see §§5.7–5.9], fixing the point that the fetus becomes viable is important. In determining viability, expert testimony is pivotal. For example, in the opinion of one physician, testifying for the prosecution, an unborn child in its mother's womb twenty-eight to thirty weeks at the time of an assault was a viable fetus, assuming a normal delivery. It was noted that many fetuses born this prematurely survive and lead normal lives. See *Hollis*, above.

However, the period of viability is not fixed and may vary on a case-by-case basis. Under California law, the court must weigh expert medical testimony in resolving the issue of viability. In another feticide case, the defense claimed that since testimony established that the dead fetus was between 22 and 24 weeks old at the time of the assault, that as a matter of constitutional law, viability does not arise until at least the 24th week of gestation. [See *Wade*, §5.2.] But, the defense made no effort to refute prosecution evidence that the fetus was capable of independent existence outside the mother's womb. The holding in *Wade* did not prohibit medical evidence to the contrary or limit the definition of viability to a specific gestational time period. *People v Apodaca*, 76 CaA3d 479, 489–490, 142 CaR 830 (1978).

2. [§5.44] Statutory Construction

The threshold issue of whether the killing of a fetus should be recognized as felonious homicide centers on statutory construction. Did the legislature in defining and providing for the punishment of homicide, intend to include within the crime the killing of a fetus?

To illustrate, Louisiana's criminal code provides for the punishment of murder, but not for its definition. However, the code retains the old common law definition of murder as the felonious "killing of a human being." Thus, a descendant's assault on a pregnant woman causing the stillbirth of a child does not constitute murder. *State v Gyles*, 313 So2d 799 (La 1979).

In a case of first impression in New Jersey, it was held that the homicide and death by auto statutes [NJ STAT ANN 2C:11-2(a) and 2C:11-5(a)] do not expressly include a fetus. The prosecution had unsuccessfully argued that a fetus was within the protected class of the statute. However, the Penal Code of New Jersey fails to define the term "human being". Since the court was obligated to adhere to the strict rules of construction, the criminal complaint filed against the driver of a car alleging fetal homicide as the result of an automobile crash was dismissed. *In re A W S*, 182 NJ Super 278, 440 A2d 1144 (1981). Similarly, the Rhode Island Supreme Court held that since two other laws specifically referred to "unborn children", the fact that the vehicular-homicide statute did not mention "unborn children" supported the conclusion that the legislature did not intend to amend the common law meaning of the term "person." Under the Rhode Island common law, an unborn child had no status as a person. *State v Amaro*, 448 A2d 1257 (1982).

In *People v Guthrie*, 97 MiA 326, 293 NW2d 775 (1980), negligent homicide charges leveled against a driver in connection with an automobile accident in which a pregnant woman in the other car suffered a miscarriage, were dropped. Although the infant was scheduled for delivery within two days after the accident and was "ready for birth", the fetus was not recognized as a "person" within the meaning of the negligent homicide statute. Although the state legislature had passed laws dealing with assaultive abortion and manslaughter abortion, it did not act to amend the negligent homicide statute.

In another case, although a viable fetus is a person within the statutory definition of murder, the omission of the word "fetus" from the definition of manslaughter in California [CAL PEN CODE §197], precluded a manslaughter action against a man who attacked his pregnant, ex-wife, causing a miscarriage. *People v Apodoca*, 76 CaA3d 479, 142 CaR 830 (1978).

The language of the statute must be explicit in order to conform to constitutional standards. For example, the term "murderer" as defined by Illinois Criminal Code [IL REV STAT Ch 38 §9-1] is a person who kills an individual without lawful justification if in performing an act which caused the death he acts within certain mental states. The law was amended in 1977 to include human beings aborted alive. Its constitutionality was challenged by a class of physicians who claimed that the lack of a precise definition of the term "alive" left the doctors uncertain as to their duties toward the fetus. Although the Illinois Supreme Court has interpreted this section to apply only to fetuses that are born alive and subsequently expire, the Seventh Circuit Court of Appeals voided the statute because of vagueness. The meaning of the term "alive" contained many ambiguities. The court pointed out: "The meaning of the term 'alive' could include only the most minimal of life signs in a nonviable fetus or it could be limited to the capability of sustained survival." *Charles v Carey*, 627 F2d 772, 791 (7th Cir 1980).

3. [§5.45] Modern Trends — California

The evolution of criminal law toward recognition of feticide is best exemplified in the change in California law since 1970. Traditionally, California had adhered to the common law requirement of a live birth to support a felonious homicide indictment. For example, the common law requirement of birth as a *prima facie* element of murder was applied in a 1970 California appellate decision involving the destruction of a fully viable child carried by a woman in an advanced state of pregnancy. An unborn but viable fetus was not a human being under former CAL PEN CODE §187. According to the court, it was a formal established rule that in order to obtain a criminal conviction in the killing of a newly-born baby, the prosecution had to prove that the baby was born alive and had an independent and separate existence from its mother. *Keeler v Superior Court*, 2 Ca3d 619, 87 CaR 481, 470 P2d 617 (1970).

In partial response to the heinous nature of the assault by the defendant in *Keeler*, the California legislature amended its homicide law to recognize the death of a fetus as a crime punishable as murder under certain conditions. See CAL PEN CODE §187, which reads in pertinent part:

> a. Murder is the unlawful killing of a human being, or a fetus, with malice aforethought.
>
> b. This section shall not apply to any person who commits an act which results in the death of a fetus if any of the following apply:
>
> 1. The act complied with the Therapeutic Abortion Act, Chapter 11 (commencing with Section 25950) of Division 20 of the Health and Safety Code.
>
> 2. The act was committed by a holder of a physician's and surgeon's certificate, as defined in the Business and Professions Code, in a case where, to a medical certainty, the result of childbirth would be death of the mother of the fetus or where her death from

childbirth, although not medically certain, would be substantially certain or more likely than not.

3. The act was solicited, aided, abetted, or consented to by the mother of the fetus.

The recognition of the fetus under the homicide statute is qualified, however. For example, murder charges lodged against a man who allegedly kicked a pregnant woman in the stomach causing a miscarriage two weeks later were dismissed. The amended provision of the California law providing that the unlawful killing of a fetus with malice aforethought constituted murder is inapplicable in the case of a twelve-week-old fetus. Until the fetus is viable, §187 does not come into play. Viability is defined as the attainment of form and development of organs capable of living outside the uterus. Although the exact time of viability differs between fetuses, the court found that viability is usually placed between the 24th and 28th week of pregnancy. Consequently, the defendant could be prosecuted for assault on the pregnant woman, but not for the murder of the fetus. *People v Smith*, 59 CaA3d 751 (1976).

4. [§5.46] Feticide Statutes

Missouri is one of the few states that has enacted a separate feticide statute. The Missouri law [Mo Rev Stat §565.026] states that the willful killing of an unborn quick child caused by an injury inflicted on its mother is punishable as manslaughter if the attack would have been considered murder had it resulted in the death of the mother. For example, a feticide conviction was reversed without evidence that the defendant even struck the pregnant mother or that the alleged assault was malicious. "Malice" is an essential element of homicide that was not established in this case. *State v Harness*, 280 SW2d 11 (Mo 1955).

As stated earlier, most states have incorporated feticide into the criminal code provisions dealing with homicide. For example, Georgia's rarely invoked separate feticide statute was repealed in 1973. The state's homicide statute [Ga Code Ann §26-1191] refers only to the killing of a "human being" without mention of the term "fetus".

F. [§5.47] Survey of State Abortion Laws

Jurisdiction	Code Section	Statutory Definition of Illegal Abortion	Penalties	Requirement Regarding Legal Abortion Mother, Fetus	Requirements Regarding Health Care Provider, M.D.	Consent	Residency
AL	§13A-13-7	by drug, substance, instrument which induces abortion or miscarriage	fine $100 to $1,000 and imprisonment to 12 months	purpose to preserve life, health of mother			
AK	§18.16.010	knowingly doesn't meet standards for legal abortion	fine to $1,000 and/or imprisonment to five years	nonviable fetus	licensed M.D., approved health facility	of patient or guardian if patient less than 18	30 days before procedure
AZ	§13-3603	by drug, instrument with intent to procure miscarriage	imprisoned 2-5 years	necessary to preserve life of mother			
AR	§41-2551 to §41-2560	by drugs, medicine or any other means with intent to produce abortion, or premature delivery	fine to $1,000 and imprisoned 1-5 years	continuation of pregnancy would threaten life, health of mother; risk of child born with physical or mental defect or pregnancy result of rape, incest (reported to authorities within 7 days of occurrence)	licensed M.D.	written consent of mother; if minor, or incompetent, written consent of parents, husband or guardian	4 months before procedure unless emergency

Juris-diction	Code Section	Statutory Definition of Illegal Abortion	Penalties	Requirement Regarding Legal Abortion Mother, Fetus	Requirements Regarding Health Care Provider, M.D.	Consent	Residency
CA	Health and Safety Code §25950 to §25957; Penal Code §274-276	by drugs, medicine or instrument with intent to procure miscarriage	imprisonment	continuation of pregnancy would threaten life, health of mother or pregnancy result of rape or incest	approved health care facility, approval of medicare board		
CO	§18-6-101 to §18-6-105*	ends or causes to be ended pregnancy by any means other than justified medical termination	imprisonment 2-4 years and 1 year parole; if mother dies, imprisonment 8-12 years and 1 year parole	continuation of pregnancy likely to result in death or permanent physical or mental impairment of mother or child born with grave mental or physical retardation or within first 16 weeks of pregnancy and pregnancy result of sexual assault or incest	licensed hospital, licensed M.D. and certification of hospital board	mother; mother and father, if married; mother and parent/guardian if under 18 years	
CN	§53-29 to §53-31	by giving, administering, advising, causing to take or use instrument with	fine $1,000 and/or imprisonment to 5 years	preserve life of mother or unborn child			

Juris-diction	Code Section	Statutory Definition of Illegal Abortion	Penalties	Requirement Regarding Legal Abortion Mother, Fetus	Requirements Regarding Health Care Provider, M.D.	Consent	Residency
		intent to procure abortion or miscarriage					
DE	11 §651-654; 24 §1790-1794	by drugs or act done with intent to cause miscarriage including acts by mother	fine: established by court, and/or imprisoned to 10 years; mother: fine $1,000 and/or imprisoned to 2 years	continuation of pregnancy would result in death or injury to mother; mental and/or physical retardation of child or pregnancy result of rape, incest but must be performed within first 20 weeks	licensed M.D., national accredited hospital, approval of hospital review board	written consent of mother with full explanation, 24 hour waiting period following consent; if unmarried and under 18, consent of parent required	120 days before procedure unless employed in state or patient of state licensed M.D.
FL	§390.001 to §390.025; §707.02 and §797.03	termination of pregnancy during last trimester which does not meet requirements of legal abortion	fine to $5,000 and/or imprisoned to 5 years if mother dies; fine to $10,000 and/or imprisoned to 15 years	regulated only in last trimester, necessary to save life or preserve health of mother	2 licensed M.D.'s certifying necessity unless emergency, one sufficient; if 2 not available, licensed hospital	written informed consent of mother, if mentally incompetent, consent of guardian; if under 18 and unmarried written consent of parent or guardian or order of court; husband must be	

Jurisdiction	Code Section	Statutory Definition of Illegal Abortion	Penalties	Requirement Regarding Legal Abortion Mother, Fetus	Requirements Regarding Health Care Provider, M.D.	Consent	Residency
						given notice unless separated	
GA	§26-1201 to §26-1204	by administering medicine, drugs, substance or using instrument with intent to procure miscarriage or abortion	imprisoned 1-10 years	preserve life or health of mother	within first trimester: licensed M.D. and licensed hospital; within second trimester: M.D. and 2 consulting M.D.'s certify necessity of procedure		
HI	§453-16	failure to meet standards for legal abortion	fine to $1,000 and/or imprisoned to 5 years	nonviable fetus	licensed M.D., licensed hospital		90 days
ID	§18-603 to §18-615	provides, supplies, administers drug, substances to woman or uses instrument with intent to produce abortion	fine to $5,000 and/or imprisoned 2-5 years; mother, same fine, imprisoned 1-5 years		within first trimester: consultation between licensed M.D. and mother and determination by M.D. that abortion is "appropriate" considering various mental, physical,	mother and husband if she is married during any part of pregnancy	

Juris-diction	Code Section	Statutory Definition of Illegal Abortion	Penalties	Requirement Regarding Legal Abortion Mother, Fetus	Requirements Regarding Health Care Provider, M.D.	Consent	Residency
ID (cont.)					familial factors; within second trimester: same as within first except must be performed in licensed hospital; within third trimester: same as in second except requires consulting M.D. and procedure necessary to preserve life if mother or fetus would likely be unable to survive		
IL	Chapter 38 §81-21 to §81-55	use of any instrument, drug or any other device to terminate pregnancy with intent to cause fetal death that is not "necessary"	fine to $1,000 and/or imprisonment 3-7 years	if nonviable fetus and abortion not necessary to preserve mother's life: M.D. must certify nonviability if fetus viable, must be medically necessary to preserve, life, health of mother; M.D.	licensed M.D. determines abortion is "necessary"; after first trimester licensed hospital on in-patient basis with facilities if evidence of viability of fetus	voluntary informed consent of mother (guidelines in statute), mother certifies in writing she has received information from M.D.; parental consent required	24 hours following certification of informed consent; exception, unless medical emergency; if mother is a minor and unmarried, a

Jurisdiction	Code Section	Statutory Definition of Illegal Abortion	Penalties	Requirement Regarding Legal Abortion Mother, Fetus	Requirements Regarding Health Care Provider, M.D.	Consent	Residency
IL (cont.)				must certify this necessity		if mother is unemancipated minor, court can also issue consent but parents must receive notice of court hearing; parental and spousal consultation required between M.D. and parent/spouse before 24 hour waiting period; if spouse legally separated, no consultation required, exception, medical emergency	48 hour period
IN	§35-1-58.5-1 to §35-1-58. 5-7	failure to meet standards for legal abortion	fine to $10,000 and imprisoned; fixed term of 5 years plus to 3 years for aggravating circumstances;	after viability: procedure necessary to prevent impairment of life, health of mother	within first trimester: based upon professional judgment of attending, licensed M.D.; within second trimester: (be-	written consent of mother at least 24 hours after receiving consent form, not applicable if emergency; if unemancipated	

Juris-diction	Code Section	Statutory Definition of Illegal Abortion	Penalties	Requirement Regarding Legal Abortion Mother, Fetus	Requirements Regarding Health Care Provider, M.D.	Consent	Residency
IN (cont.)			minus to 3 years for mitigating circumstances		fore viability) same as first and licensed hospital; after viability: same as second trimester and reasons for procedure regarding mother certified by M.D. to hospital	minor notice must be given to parent or guardian at least 24 hours before procedure court can waive notice; not applicable in emergency	
IA	§707.7	intentionally terminates human pregnancy after end of second trimester	fine to $5,000 and imprisoned to 10 years; if fetus does not die, fine to $1,000 and imprisoned to 5 years	necessary to preserve the life or health of mother or fetus, after end of second trimester	licensed M.D., every effort made (not inconsistent with preserving life of mother) to preserve life of viable fetus		
KS	§21-3407 and §65-443 to §65-445	purposeful and unjustifiable termination of pregnancy that does not meet conditions of legal abortion	fine to $5,000 and/or imprisoned, indeterminate sentence, minimum of 1-3 years, maxi-	continuance would impair physical or mental health of mother or child would be born with physical or	licensed M.D., 3 M.D.'s certify in writing justifying circumstances, except in emergency		

Juris-diction	Code Section	Statutory Definition of Illegal Abortion	Penalties	Requirement Regarding Legal Abortion Mother, Fetus	Requirements Regarding Health Care Provider, M.D.	Consent	Residency
KS (cont.)			mum of 5-10 years	mental defects; pregnancy result of rape or incest or mother under 16 years	situations		
KY	§311.710 to §311.990; §436.023 and §436.026	failure to meet standards for legal abortion	if M.D. fails to counsel, fine to $500; failure to obtain informed consent from required parties, fine of $1,000 and/or imprisoned 1 year; other than licensed M.D. performs abortion, imprisoned 10-20 years; abortion performed after first trimester in violation of requirements for legal abortion, fine to $5,000 and/	after viability of fetus, necessary to preserve life or health of the mother	first trimester: upon advice of licensed M.D.; after first trimester, same as first trimester except must be in licensed hospital, exception when medical emergency; after viability, same as before except necessities regarding mother	written, informed consent with 24 hour waiting period of mother; after first trimester of husband if married woman; of parents/guardian if mother under 18 and unmarried; exception when medical emergency	

Jurisdiction	Code Section	Statutory Definition of Illegal Abortion	Penalties	Requirement Regarding Legal Abortion Mother, Fetus	Requirements Regarding Health Care Provider, M.D.	Consent	Residency
KY (cont.)			or imprisoned to 2 years; failure to adhere to 24 hour waiting period, fine to $1,000 and/or imprisoned to 1 year				
LA	14 §87-88	administration of drug, substance or use of instrument with intent of procuring premature delivery	imprisoned at hard labor 1-10 years	after viability or third trimester, necessary to preserve life, health of mother and/or fetus	after first trimester licensed M.D. must make judgment regarding advisability or necessity of abortion and procedure must be performed in licensed hospital		
ME	22 §1591-§1599	unlicensed person performs or assists in abortion; anyone performing abortion after viability unless necessary to pre-	fine to $1,000 and/or imprisoned to 1 year	necessary to life or health of mother	licensed M.D.	regarding unemancipated minor, notice must be given to one parent or guardian at least 24 hours before	

Juris-diction	Code Section	Statutory Definition of Illegal Abortion	Penalties	Requirement Regarding Legal Abortion Mother, Fetus	Requirements Regarding Health Care Provider, M.D.	Consent	Residency
ME (cont.)		serve life, health of mother				procedure, exception when medical emergency; informed consent of mother required, information given to mother at least 48 hours before procedure, except when medical emergency	
MD	Art 43 §137 to §139; HG §20-211 to §20-214	sells or gives any drug, substance or instrument for purpose of causing or inducing termination of human pregnancy or counsels for purpose of inducing abortion or assists in obtaining or performing abortion, exception when	fine to $5,000 for each offense and/or imprisoned to 3 years	continuation of pregnancy likely to result in death or impairment of physical or mental health of mother; fetus likely to be born with physical or mental retardation or pregnancy result of rape - also must be performed within first 26 weeks unless life of	licensed M.D., licensed hospital, approval of hospital board required	informed, written consent of mother required, except when medical emergency	

Jurisdiction	Code Section	Statutory Definition of Illegal Abortion	Penalties	Requirement Regarding Legal Abortion Mother, Fetus	Requirements Regarding Health Care Provider, M.D.	Consent	Residency
MD (cont.)		licensed M.D. in licensed hospital		mother threatened or fetus dead			
MA	C 112 §12J to §12U	failure to meet standards for legal abortion; violation of procedural standards such as informed consent, medical procedure required, etc.	imprisoned 1-5 years; fine $500 to $1,000 and/or imprisoned 3 months to 5 years	pregnancy of 24 weeks or more necessary to save life of mother or continuation will impose substantial risk of grave physical or mental impairment and no procedure can be used which destroys or injures fetus unless in M.D.'s judgment other available procedures would be greater risk to mother or future pregnancies	pregnancy less than 24 weeks: licensed M.D. and "necessary" in M.D.'s judgment under all attendant circumstances; pregnancy 24 weeks or more: licensed M.D., except when medical emergency; after 13th week: must be performed in licensed hospital	written, informed consent of mother required at least 24 hours before procedure; if mother is less than 18 years and unmarried, consent of parents/guardians or court also required, exception when medical emergency	
MI	§750.14 to §750.16	drug, substance or instrument employed with intent to procure miscarriage unless same is	fine to $2,000 and/or imprisonment to 4 years; if mother dies, fine to $7,500	necessary to preserve life of mother			

Jurisdiction	Code Section	Statutory Definition of Illegal Abortion	Penalties	Requirement Regarding Legal Abortion Mother, Fetus	Requirements Regarding Health Care Provider, M.D.	Consent	Residency
MI (cont.)		necessary to save mother's life	and/or imprisoned to 15 years				
MN	§145.411 to §145.423; §617.20 to §617.22	failure to meet standards for legal abortion; sale of manufacture of drug, substance or instrument intended for unlawful use in abortion procedure	fine to $5,000 and/or imprisoned to 5 years	after viability, necessary to preserve life, health of mother and procedure used will best assure live birth	licensed M.D., in hospital after first trimester; after viability, attending M.D. must certify that in his medical judgment procedure necessary	informed consent of mother	
MS	§97-3-3 to §97-3-5	failure to meet standards for legal abortion	imprisoned 1-10 years; if mother dies, imprisoned for life; regarding M.D. or nurse, license revoked	necessary to preserve mother's life; pregnancy result of rape	licensed M.D.; advice of 2 licensed M.D.'s required in writing		
MO	§188.015 to §188.075	failure to meet standards for legal abortion	fine to $1,000 and/or imprisoned to 1 year	after viability, necessary to life, health of mother; method used must be one most likely to preserve life, health of fetus	after viability, licensed M.D., must certify abortion necessary including medical indicators and method to be	informed, written consent of mother; if mother is less than 18 years, informed written consent of	

Jurisdiction	Code Section	Statutory Definition of Illegal Abortion	Penalties	Requirement Regarding Legal Abortion Mother, Fetus	Requirements Regarding Health Care Provider, M.D.	Consent	Residency
MO (cont.)				unless greater risk to mother	utilized with reasoning for decision; second M.D. must be in attendance to aid fetus	one parent/guardian required unless emancipated or court order; 48 hour waiting period following consent	
MT	§50-20-101 to §50-20-112	failure to meet standards for legal abortion; notice provision violations	fine to $1,000 and/or imprisoned to 5 years; fine to $500 and/or imprisoned to 6 months	after viability, necessary according to M.D. to preserve life or health of mother; procedure utilized must not negligently or intentionally endanger life of fetus unless to preserve mother's life	licensed M.D. after first 3 months of pregnancy, in licensed hospital; after viability, M.D. must certify in writing necessity of procedure including grounds for decision plus 2 other M.D.'s must confirm the decision, exception when necessary to preserve life of mother	informed consent of mother signed by her and M.D., exception when M.D. certifies necessary to preserve life of mother; if mother married, written notice of spouse; if mother under 18 years and unmarried, written notice of parent/guardian	

Jurisdiction	Code Section	Statutory Definition of Illegal Abortion	Penalties	Requirement Regarding Legal Abortion Mother, Fetus	Requirements Regarding Health Care Provider, M.D.	Consent	Residency
NB	§28-325 to §28-347	failure to meet standards for legal abortion including failure to use accepted medical procedure	fine to $10,000 and/or imprisoned to 5 years	after viability, necessary to preserve mother from imminent peril to life, health	licensed M.D.	provisions dealing with parental consultation (§28-333), informed consent (§28-326(8)), waiting periods (§28-327) and abortion reporting (§28-343) declared unconstitutional. *Women's Servs, PC v Thone,* 636 F2d 206 (8th Cir 1980), affd on reh (8th Cir 1982).	
NV	§200.220, §201.120 to §201.150 and §442.240 to §442.270	failure to meet standards for legal abortion	imprisoned 1-10 years and can be fined to $10,000	only within first 24 weeks unless abortion necessary to preserve life, health of mother	licensed M.D. must exercise "best clinical judgment" in determining whether to perform same; records of mother must contain facts	informed consent of mother - certified by M.D.; 24 hour waiting period, exception when medical emergency; if mother married, notice of husband is	

Juris-diction	Code Section	Statutory Definition of Illegal Abortion	Penalties	Requirement Regarding Legal Abortion Mother, Fetus	Requirements Regarding Health Care Provider, M.D.	Consent	Residency
NV (cont.)					M.D. based decision on	required at least 24 hours before procedure; if mother is under 18 years, unemancipated and unmarried, notice to parent/guardian required at least 24 hours before procedure	
NH	§585:12 to §585:14	willfully administers to mother substance or employs instrument with intent to procure abortion	fine to $1,000 and/or imprisoned to 1 year	if child is "quick" must be malformed, difficult or protracted labor, necessary to preserve life, or advised by 2 M.D.'s to be necessary			
		if child is "quick"	fine to $1,000 and/or imprisoned to 10 years				
		if mother dies	imprisoned to life				
NJ	(2A:87-1 et. seq. (Abortion) repealed effective September 1, 1979. No replacement statute enacted.)						

Juris-diction	Code Section	Statutory Definition of Illegal Abortion	Penalties	Requirement Regarding Legal Abortion Mother, Fetus	Requirements Regarding Health Care Provider, M.D.	Consent	Residency
NM	§30-5-1 to §30-5-3	failure to meet standards of justified termination	imprisoned to 18 months and/or fine to $5,000	continuation of pregnancy likely to result in death or impairment of health of mother or fetus likely to be physically or mentally retarded; or pregnancy result of rape or incest	licensed M.D. - licensed hospital, written certification of hospital board required	mother must "request" procedure; if under 18 years, the procedure must be requested by her and parent/guardian	
		if mother dies	imprisoned to 9 years and/or fine to $10,000				
NY	§125.05 to §125.55	failure to meet standards for legal abortion	imprisoned to 4 years	within first 24 weeks or necessary to preserve mother's life; if mother performs abortion, it must be on the advice of M.D.	licensed M.D.		
		if mother dies	imprisoned 1-15 years				
		and not within first 24 weeks;	imprisoned 8-25 years				

Juris-diction	Code Section	Statutory Definition of Illegal Abortion	Penalties	Requirement Regarding Legal Abortion Mother, Fetus	Requirements Regarding Health Care Provider, M.D.	Consent	Residency
NY (cont.)		if mother does not die	imprisoned to 7 years				
		and not within first 24 weeks;	fine to $1,000				
		if mother performs act and after 24 weeks	imprisoned to 1 year				
NC	§14-44 to §14-46	willfully administer to mother, prescribe, advise, procure substance or instrument with intent to destroy fetus	imprisoned to 10 years and/or fine	first 20 weeks of pregnancy, no medical requirements regarding mother, fetus after 20 weeks - must be substantial risk that continuance would threaten life, health of mother	licensed M.D., licensed hospital or clinic		
ND	§14-02, 1-01 to §14-02.1-12	non-licensed person performs procedure	fine $10,000 and/or imprisoned to 10 years	after viability, necessary to preserve life of mother or continuance would impair her physical or mental health	licensed M.D. using medical standards applicable; licensed hospital; required after first 12 weeks of pregnancy; M.D. must certify facts upon which he	informed consent of mother as certified by M.D.; required within 30 days to 48 hours before procedure; previability if mother is unemancipated	

Juris-diction	Code Section	Statutory Definition of Illegal Abortion	Penalties	Requirement Regarding Legal Abortion Mother, Fetus	Requirements Regarding Health Care Provider, M.D.	Consent	Residency
ND (cont.)					based decision of necessity, exception when medical emergency	minor, M.D. must inform both parents or guardian (same as mother) at least 24 hours before minor's consent; after viability, husband's written consent required or consent of parents/guardian if mother is less than 18 years and unmarried unless procedure necessary to preserve life, health of mother; court can authorize abortion on minor without parental consent	
		if licensed M.D. but doesn't conform to standards for legal abortion	fine $1,000 and/or imprisoned to 1 year				

Jurisdiction	Code Section	Statutory Definition of Illegal Abortion	Penalties	Requirement Regarding Legal Abortion Mother, Fetus	Requirements Regarding Health Care Provider, M.D.	Consent	Residency
OH	§2919.11 to §2919.14	failure to obtain informed consent	fine to $1,000 and/or imprisonment to 6 months			informed consent of mother; if mother is unmarried minor, parental informed consent also required	
		taking life of fetus, born alive or failing to provide reasonable medical attention to same	fine to $10,000 and imprisoned 4-25 years				
OK	63 §1-730 to §1-741; 21 §713-714-21 §861	non-licensed person performs abortion	imprisoned 1-3 years	after viability, necessary to preserve life, health of mother (viability presumed after 24th week)	licensed M.D.; approved hospital required after first trimester; M.D. must certify necessity of procedure after viability including factors considered; after viability, M.D. required		

Jurisdiction	Code Section	Statutory Definition of Illegal Abortion	Penalties	Requirement Regarding Legal Abortion Mother, Fetus	Requirements Regarding Health Care Provider, M.D.	Consent	Residency
OK (cont.)					for fetus, except when medical emergency		
		failure to meet standards for legal abortion	imprisoned 2-5 years				
		taking life of viable fetus unless necessary to preserve life, health of mother or failure to provide medical aid to fetus	imprisoned not less than 4 years				
OR	§435.405 to §435.990	failure to meet standards for legal abortion	fine to $5,000 and/or imprisonment to 15 years	substantial risk that continuance of pregnancy will impair physical, mental health of mother or child would be born with physical, mental defects; pregnancy result of rape or incest; no abortion per-	licensed M.D.; licensed hospital; 2 M.D.'s must certify circumstances that justify termination, except when medical emergency	written consent of mother; if mother is minor, unmarried, written consent of parent/guardian required; if mother married, written consent of husband required, except	

Jurisdiction	Code Section	Statutory Definition of Illegal Abortion	Penalties	Requirement Regarding Legal Abortion Mother, Fetus	Requirements Regarding Health Care Provider, M.D.	Consent	Residency
OR (cont.)				mitted after 150th day		when medical emergency	
		attempting self-abortion	imprisoned to 5 years				
PA	35 §6601 to §6608	failure to obtain informed consent	fine to $10,000 and/or imprisoned to 5 years	after viability, necessary to preserve life of mother	licensed M.D.; licensed hospital facility	written, informed consent of mother except when medical emergency; if mother married, spouse's consent required; if mother under 18 years and unmarried, parental/guardian consent required	
		killing of premature fetus	imprisoned for life				
		failure to meet standards for legal abortion	fine to $10,000 and/or imprisoned to 5 years				
RI	§23-4.7-1 to §23-4.7-6; 11-9-18	failure to obtain informed consent	fine to $500 and/or imprisoned to 1 year			informed, written consent at least 24 hours	

Jurisdiction	Code Section	Statutory Definition of Illegal Abortion	Penalties	Requirement Regarding Legal Abortion Mother, Fetus	Requirements Regarding Health Care Provider, M.D.	Consent	Residency
RI (cont.)						before procedure but not more than 7 days, except when medical emergency; if mother is minor, M.D. must exercise diligence in notifying parent/guardian	
		failure to provide for fetus born alive (unless necessary to preserve life of mother)	fine to $5,000 and/or imprisoned to 5 years				
		if fetus dies	imprisoned to 20 years				
SC	§44-41-10 to §44-41-80	failure to meet standards for legal abortion	fine to $5,000 and/or imprisonment 2-5 years	third trimester, necessary to preserve life or health of mother; if basis is mental health, must be so certified by consulting M.D.	first trimester, upon advice of licensed M.D.; second trimester, must be performed by licensed M.D. in licensed hospital; third	mother's written consent required if mother married and third trimester, husband's consent is required; if mother under 16 years and	

Juris-diction	Code Section	Statutory Definition of Illegal Abortion	Penalties	Requirement Regarding Legal Abortion Mother, Fetus	Requirements Regarding Health Care Provider, M.D.	Consent	Residency
SC (cont.)					trimester, second M.D.'s recommendation is required, facts and reasons supporting recommendation must be certified by both M.D.'s	unmarried, parental/guardian consent required except when medical emergency	
		self-abortion that does not meet standards for legal abortion	fine to $1,000 and/or imprisonment to 2 years				
SD	§22-17-5; §34-23A-1 to §34-23A-21	failure to meet standards for legal abortion	fine to $2,000 and/or imprisoned 2 years	after 24th week, necessary to preserve life, health of mother	first 12 weeks, licensed M.D., solely medical judgment; between 12th and 24th week, licensed M.D., licensed hospital; after 24th week, licensed M.D. and licensed hospital	written, informed consent of mother 24 hours before procedure; if mother is unmarried minor parent/guardian consent also required; if mother is married minor husband's consent required	

Juris-diction	Code Section	Statutory Definition of Illegal Abortion	Penalties	Requirement Regarding Legal Abortion Mother, Fetus	Requirements Regarding Health Care Provider, M.D.	Consent	Residency
SD (cont.)						except when medical emergency	
		failure of M.D. to obtain informed consent	fine $100 and/or imprisoned 30 days				
TN	§39-301 to §39-308	failure to meet standards for legal abortion include residency requirement	fine $5,000 and imprisoned 5-10 years	after viability, necessary to preserve life, health of mother	first 3 months, licensed M.D. upon his medical advice; after 3 months to viability, licensed M.D., licensed hospital; after viability, same as 3 months except M.D. must certify in writing to hospital that procedure was necessary	informed, written consent of mother; 2 day waiting period between M.D. giving mother information and consent except when medical emergency, but M.D. must still give information to mother; if mother less than 18 years and unemancipated minor, M.D. must inform parent/guardian 2 days prior to	mother must produce evidence she is bona fide resident of Tennessee to M.D. prior to procedure

Jurisdiction	Code Section	Statutory Definition of Illegal Abortion	Penalties	Requirement Regarding Legal Abortion Mother, Fetus	Requirements Regarding Health Care Provider, M.D.	Consent	Residency
TN (cont.)						procedure except when medical emergency	
		attempted criminal abortion	imprisoned 1-3 years				
		coerce or compel abortion	fine $500 to $1,000 and/or imprisoned 10 days to 11 months 29 days				
TX	§4512.1 to §4512.7	destroys the vitality or life of child in birth or before (which otherwise would have been born alive)	imprisoned 5 years to life				
UT	§76-7-301 to §76-7-324	failure to meet standards for legal abortion	fine to $10,000 and/or imprisoned 1-15 years	after viability, necessary to health, life of mother	licensed M.D.; after first 90 days, licensed hospital; M.D. must provide mother with information regarding abortion at least 24 hours before	notice, if possible, to parents/guardian if minor unmarried mother or husband if married; informed consent of mother required	

Juris-diction	Code Section	Statutory Definition of Illegal Abortion	Penalties	Requirement Regarding Legal Abortion Mother, Fetus	Requirements Regarding Health Care Provider, M.D.	Consent	Residency
UT (cont.)					procedure except when medical emergency		
		if coerce someone to have abortion	fine to $5,000 and/or imprisoned to 5 years				
VT	T. 13 §101 to §104	willfully administers, advises anything or any means with intent to procure miscarriage if mother dies	imprisoned 5-20 years	necessary to preserve mother's life			
		if mother does not die (mother not liable)	imprisoned 3-10 years				
VA	§18.2-71 to §18.2-76.2	failure to meet standards for legal abortion	imprisoned 2-10 years	first and second trimester, no restrictions; third trimester, continuation of pregnancy likely to result in death, physical or mental impairment of	anytime licensed M.D.; second and third trimester, licensed hospital; third trimester, attending M.D. and 2 consulting M.D.'s certify	informed, written consent of mother	

Juris-diction	Code Section	Statutory Definition of Illegal Abortion	Penalties	Requirement Regarding Legal Abortion Mother, Fetus	Requirements Regarding Health Care Provider, M.D.	Consent	Residency
VA (cont.)				mother	medical necessity; if necessary to save mother, no condition applies except licensed M.D.		
WA	§9.02.010 to §9.02.090	supply, advise use of any substance, use any instrument with intent to procure abortion	imprisoned, state penitentiary to 5 years or county jail to 1 year	necessary to preserve life of mother or fetus; not quick with child and within first 4 months, by M.D.	licensed M.D.; licensed hospital except when medical emergency	prior consent of mother; if married and cohabitating consent of husband; if unmarried, and less than 18 years, parental/ guardian consent	resident 90 days before procedure
		self-abortion	fine to $1,000 or imprisoned to 5 years				
WV	§61-2-8	administer substance or use means with intent to destroy unborn child or produce abortion	imprisoned 3-10 years	necessary to save life of mother or fetus			
		if mother dies	imprisoned 5 years to life				

Jurisdiction	Code Section	Statutory Definition of Illegal Abortion	Penalties	Requirement Regarding Legal Abortion Mother, Fetus	Requirements Regarding Health Care Provider, M.D.	Consent	Residency
WI	§940.04	intentionally destroys life of unborn child (other than mother)	fine to $5,000 and/or imprisoned to 3 years	necessary to save life of mother or advised by 2 consulting M.D.'s as necessary	licensed M.D., licensed maternity hospital except when medical emergency		
		intentionally destroys life or unborn child (other than mother) or causes death of mother during procedure	imprisoned to 15 years				
		mother intentionally destroys unborn child or consents to same	fine to $200 and/or imprisoned to 6 months				
		mother intentionally destroys life of unborn quick child or consents to same	imprisoned to 2 years				
WY	§35-6-101 to §35-6-115	any procedure after viability that is not "necessary", M.D. who intentionally terminates viabi-	imprisoned to 14 years	after viability, necessary to preserve health, life of mother	licensed M.D.		

Juris-diction	Code Section	Statutory Definition of Illegal Abortion	Penalties	Requirement Regarding Legal Abortion Mother, Fetus	Requirements Regarding Health Care Provider, M.D.	Consent	Residency
WY (cont.)		lity of unborn fetus during legal abortion					
		use of other than accepted medical procedures, other than licensed M.D. performs procedure	imprisoned 1-14 years				
DC	§22-201	by means of instrument, drug or whatever attempts to or procures abortion	imprisoned 1-10 years	necessary to preserve life or health of mother	under direction of licensed M.D.		
		if mother dies	imprisoned 20 years to life				
PR	§4010 to §4012	failure to meet standards for legal abortion	imprisoned 2-5 years	to preserve health, life of mother	"therapeutic prescription" by licensed M.D.		
		by mother	imprisoned 1-5 years				

*portions of Colorado's abortion law were declared unconstitutional by *People v Norton*, 181 Co 47, 507 P2d 862 (1973), although they have not been repealed

G. [§5.48] Abortion Medical Forms

The following forms relate to abortion in terms of a statement of need, a consent to the procedure, and an authorization to treat the condition created by a partial or recent abortion.

Statement of Need for Therapeutic Abortion

Date: ___1______, 19___2___ Time ___3___ o'clock ___4___m.

We find from observation and examination of ________5______ [name of patient] that she is pregnant and that she is suffering from the following ailment or condition: ___6_______________ [specify]. Further progress of her pregnancy would gravely endanger or imperil her life. Therefore, we are of the opinion that it is medically necessary to perform a therapeutic abortion on her.

[Signatures of at least three
duly licensed physicians]

Reprinted with permission of the American Medical Association.

Consent to Therapeutic Abortion

Date: ___1______, 19___2___ Time: ___3___ o'clock ___4___m.

1. I authorize and consent to the performance on ___5________ [me or name of patient] of a therapeutic abortion to be performed by or under the direction of Dr. ___6_______________ [treating physician].

2. I acknowledge that I have been informed by ___7__________ [Dr. ___8____________ or the following doctors: ___9_______________, M.D., ___10_______________, M.D., and ___11_______________, M.D.], that in ___12_______________ [his or her or their] opinion further progress of ___13_______________ [my pregnancy or the pregnancy of ___14_______________ (name of patient)] would gravely endanger or imperil ___15__________ [my life or the life of ___16__________], and that in ___17_______ ________ [his or her or their] opinion it is medically necessary to perform a therapeutic abortion.

3. I consent to the performance of operations and procedures in addition to or different from those now contemplated, whether or not arising from presently unforeseen conditions, which the above-named doctor or his associates or assistants may consider necessary or advisable in the course of the operation.

4. I consent to the administration of such anesthetics as may be considered necessary or advisable by the physician responsible for this service, with the exception of ___18_______________ [none or spinal anesthesia or as the case may be].

5. The nature and purpose of the operation, possible methods of treatment, the risks involved, the possible consequences, and the possibility of complications have been explained to me by Dr. ___19_______________ and by ___20_________________________.

6. I acknowledge that no guarantee or assurance has been given by anyone as to the results that may be obtained.

[Signature of patient or person
authorized to consent for patient]

[Attestation]

Reprinted with permisssion of the American Medical Association.

Authorization to Treat Condition of
Recent or Partial Abortion

Date: ___1_____, 19___2___Time: ___3___o'clock ___4___m.

I authorize Dr. ___5_______________ [treating physician] to treat me for the condition set forth in the following history: ___6_______________[set forth medical history relating to condition of recent or partial abortion]. This condition occurred prior to the time that I visited Dr. ___7_____________ for treatment.

[Signature]

[Attestation]

Reprinted with permission of the American Medical Association.

II. PRENATAL INJURY ACTIONS

A. Cause of Action for Personal Injury to Fetus

1. [§5.49] Generally

An unborn child can be injured through the tortious conduct of another person during the child's gestation. This medical fact has given rise to the legal consideration of whether unborn children can bring common law actions, after their live birth, for injuries they sustained while *in utero*. The RESTATEMENT OF TORTS originally stated that one who negligently caused harm to an unborn child was not liable to the child for the harm. However, in the most recent revision of the RESTATEMENT the previous rule was amended to provide that one who tortiously causes harm to an unborn child is subject to liability to the child for such harm if the child is born alive. See RESTATEMENT (SECOND) OF TORTS §869 (1977).

When the issue was first judicially considered it was held that prenatal injury actions were not actionable. *Dietrich v Inhabitants of Northampton*, 138 Ma 14 (1884). However, by the early 1970's the barriers to a right of action for injury inflicted in the prenatal stage had, where the issue had arisen, been removed. COMMENT, WRONGFUL BIRTH, THE EMERGING STATUS OF A NEW TORT, 8 St Mary's LJ 140 (1976). [For a more detailed discussion of the background of prenatal injury action, see §5.50.]

Moreover, there appears to be unanimous agreement among the states that there exists a right to bring a common law action for a prenatal injury. See, e.g., *White v Yup*, 85 Nv 527, 458 P2d 617 (1969); *Gay v Thompson*, 266 NC 394, 146 SE2d 425 (1966); *Evans v Olson*, 550 P2d 924 (Ok 1976). In some cases, the viability of the fetus at the time of the prenatal injury appears to be a prerequisite for a common law action to be maintained. See, e.g., *Wendt v Lillo*, 182 FSupp 56 (ND Ia 1960); *Woods v Lancet*, 303 NY 349, 102 NE2d 691 (1951); *Evans v Olson*, 550 P2d 924 (Ok 1976). However, there are other cases where a common law action for a prenatal injury can be maintained regardless of the viability of the fetus. See, e.g., *Hornbuckle v Plantation Pipe Line Co*, 212 Ga 504, 93 SE2d 727 (1956); *Renslow v Mennonite Hosp*, 67 Il2d 348, 10 Il Dec 484, 367 NE2d 1250 (1977); *Torigan v Waterton News Co*, 352 Ma 446, 225 NE2d 926 (1967); *Bennett v Hymers*, 101 NH 483, 147 A2d 108 (1958); *Smith v Brennan*, 31 NJ 353, 157 A2d 497 (1960); *Sinkler v Kneale*, 401 Pa 267, 164 A2d 93 (1960); *Sylvia v Gobeille*, 220 A2d 222 (RI 1966). And, in some cases the issue of the viability of the fetus is not directly addressed, but the right to bring a common law prenatal injury action is sustained. See, e.g., *Damasiewicz v Gorsuch*, 197 Md 417, 79 A2d 550 (1951); *Womack v Buchhorn*, 384 Mi 718, 187 NW2d 218 (1971); *Seattle-First Natl Bank v Rankin*, 59 Wa2d 288, 367 P2d 835 (1962). [As to a more detailed discussion of the issue of viability in the prenatal injury action context, see §5.51.]

Common law actions predicated on prenatal injuries have arisen from various factual settings including injuries received by an unborn child in an automobile accident [see, e.g., *Sinkler v Kneale*, 401 Pa 267, 164 A2d 93 (1960)], and medical malpractice [see, e.g., *Grodin v Grodin*, 301 NW2d 869 (Mi 1981); *Sylvia v Gobeille*, 101 RI 76, 220 A2d 222 (1966); *Seattle-First National Bank v Rankin*, 59 Wa2d 288, 367 P2d 835 (1962)].

In most instances, the prenatal injury action is brought against someone other than the child's parents. See, e.g., *Renslow v Mennonite Hosp*, 67 Il2d 348, 10 Il Dec 484, 367 NE2d 1250 (1977) (action against hospital and physician); *Sinkler v Kneale*, 401 Pa 267, 164 A2d 93 (1960) (action against driver of an automobile). However, an issue that has recently arisen is whether an infant may sue his or her parents for a prenatal injury caused by the parent. See NOTE, PARENTAL LIABILITY FOR PRENATAL INJURY, 14 Columbia Journal of Law and Social Problems 47 (1978); RECOVERY FOR

PRENATAL INJURIES: THE RIGHT OF A CHILD AGAINST ITS MOTHER, 10 Suffolk LR 582 (1976). For example, in *Curlender v Bio-Science Laboratories*, 106 Ca3d 811, 165 CaR 477 (1980), it was said in a case involving a wrongful life [as to wrongful life claims generally, see §§6.13-6.21] claim if a case arose where, despite due care by the medical profession in transmitting the necessary warnings concerning the possibility of the birth of a severely unhealthy child, the parents made a conscious choice to proceed with the pregnancy, with full knowledge that a seriously impaired infant would be born, that conscious choice would provide an intervening act of proximate cause to preclude liability insofar as defendants other than the parents were concerned. However, under such circumstances, the court found no sound public policy which should protect those parents from being answerable for the pain, suffering and misery which they would have wrought on their offspring.

In *Grodin v Grodin*, 102 MiA 396, 301 NW2d 869 (Mi 1980), the plaintiff-infant alleged that as a result of a physician's assurances that it was impossible for the infant's mother to become pregnant. The mother ingested a potentially harmful medication and only after consulting a different doctor who told her she was 7 or 8 months pregnant did the mother stop taking the medication. As a result of his mother's taking the drug, the plaintiff developed teeth that were brown and discolored, it was alleged. The complaint asserted that defendant-mother was negligent in her failure to seek proper prenatal care, for failure to request that the first physician perform a pregnancy test and in the failure to inform the first physician that she was taking the drug. The trial court granted the mother's motion for summary judgment basing the dismissal on a mother's immunity from suit for alleged negligence under an exception to the general abrogation of parent-child tort immunity provided by *Plumley v Klein*, 388 Mi 1, 199 NW2d 169 (1972). In *Plumley*, the court held that intrafamily tort immunity should be overruled, and that a child may maintain a lawsuit against his parent for injury suffered as a result of the alleged ordinary negligence of the parent. However, the court noted that there were two exceptions to the new rule of law: where the alleged negligent act involves an exercise of reasonable parental authority over the child; and where the alleged negligent act involves an exercise of reasonable parental discretion with respect to the provision of food, clothing, housing, medical and dental services and other care. The *Grodin* court noted that under its decision in *Womack*, it did not limit those who may be held liable for the negligently inflicted injury to an unborn child. Rather, the case referred only to wrongful conduct of another for which compensable damages are available, the court said. As a result, the litigating child's mother would bear the same liability for injurious, negligent, conduct as would a third person. A woman's decision to continue taking drugs during pregnancy is an exercise of her discretion, the court said. The focal question is whether the decision reached by a woman in a particular case was a reasonable exercise of parental discretion, the court said. The summary judgment of the trial court in this case precluded testimony on either the utility of the use of the drug for the maintenance of the mother's health, or the risk created for the plaintiff-infant, the court said. Therefore, the court reversed and remanded for a determination of the reasonableness of the alleged negligent conduct.

It should also be noted that prenatal injuries have also given rise to a number of emerging theories of recovery including wrongful birth [as to a more detailed discussion of wrongful birth, see §6.1], wrongful life [as to a more detailed discussion of wrongful life, see §6.13], and liability associated with the *in utero* exposure to diethylstilbestrol (DES) [as to a more detailed discussion of DES related actions, see §6.25].

2. [§5.50] Background

Originally, common law actions for prenatal injuries [generally, see §5.49] were not recognized. In 1884, Mr. Justice Holmes rendered the landmark decision, *Dietrich v Inhabitants of Northampton*, 138 Ma 14 (1884), which denied an action for the wrongful death of a child which did not survive its premature birth. In that case, it appeared that the infant's mother, while pregnant with the child, fell because of a highway defect and later suffered a miscarriage. Subsequently, in *Allaire v St Luke's Hosp*, 56 NE 638 (Il 1900), the *Dietrich* precedent was followed in a case that held that an action for injuries could not be maintained by a plaintiff who at the time of the injury was a prenatal infant with no separate legal existence. However, a dissent in the case urged that it was:

> sacrificing truth to a mere theoretical abstraction to say an injury was not to the child but wholly to the mother when the fetus was independently viable at the time of the injury. *Allaire*, at 641.

The dissent pointed out that it was demonstrable that:

> at a period of gestation in advance of . . . . parturition the foetus is capable of independent and separate life, and that though within the [mother's body] it is not merely a part of her body, for her body may die in all of its parts and the child remain alive and capable of maintaining life when separated from the dead body of the mother. *Allaire*, at 641.

The cases for the next 46 years after *Allaire* continued to deny recovery to the prenatally injured plaintiff. Nevertheless, in *Bonbrest v Kotz*, 65 FSupp

138 (D DC 1946), a court for the first time recognized a common law right of action for prenatal injuries. The *Bonbrest* decision relied on the *Allaire* dissent, and reasoned that an infant should be recognized as having a legal existence separate from its mother's at such time as it was capable of sustaining life separate from her. After *Bonbrest* there was, as one court described it, perhaps the most rapid reversal of a common law tradition as many courts held there was a common law right of action for personal injuries to a fetus. *Renslow v Mennonite Hosp*, 677 Il2d 348, 10 Il Dec 484, 367 NE2d 1250 (1977). And a legal commentator said that seldom in the law had there been such an overwhelming trend in such a relatively short period of time as there was in the trend towards allowing recovery for prenatal injuries to a viable infant. Keeton, CREATIVE CONTINUITY IN THE LAW OF TORTS, 75 Harvard LR 463 (1962).

For example, in *Woods v Lancet*, 303 NY 349, 102 NE2d 691, 695 (1951), the court said:

> To hold, as a matter of law, that no viable foetus has any separate existence which the law will recognize is for the law to deny a simple and easily demonstrable fact. This child, when injured, was in fact, alive and capable of being delivered and of remaining alive, separate from it's mother. We agree with the dissenting Justice below that 'To deny the infant relief in this case is not only a harsh result, but its effect is to do reverence to an outmoded, timeworn fiction not founded on fact and within common knowledge untrue and unjustified.'

And the court in *Smith v Brennan*, 31 NJ 353, 157 A2d 497, 503 (1960), said:

> And regardless of analogies to other areas of law, justice requires that the principle be recognized that a child has a legal right to begin life with a sound mind and body. If the wrongful conduct of another interferes with that right, and it can be established by competent proof that there is a causal connection between the wrongful interference and the harm sufferedby the child when born, damages for such harm should be recoverable by the child.

By 1982, the initial barriers to a right of action for injury inflicted prenatally had been removed in each jurisdiction where the question had arisen. COMMENT, WRONGFUL BIRTH, THE EMERGING STATUS OF A NEW TORT, 8 St. Mary's LJ 140 (1976).

3. [§5.51] Viability Requirement

It is generally recognized today that common law actions for prenatal injuries are maintainable. See, e.g., *Renslow v Mennonite Hosp*, 67 Il2d 348, 10 Il Dec 484, 367 NE2d 1250 (1977); COMMENT, WRONGFUL BIRTH, THE EMERGING STATUS OF A NEW TORT, 8 St. Mary's LJ 140 (1976). [As to prenatal injury actions generally, see §5.49.]

However, the issue of whether the fetus was viable when prenatally injured may be important depending on where the action is brought. In some cases, it has been held that the fetus must have been viable at the time of the injury in order for the common law injury action to be recognized. See, e.g., *Panagopoulous v Martin*, 295 FSupp 220 (DC WV 1969); *Hale v Manion*, 189 Ks 143, 368 P2d 1 (1962); *Woods v Lancet*, 303 NY 349, 102 NE2d 691 (1951); *Evans v Olson*, 550 P2d 924 (Ok 1976); *Leal v C C Pitts Sand & Gravel Inc*, 419 SW2d 820 (Tx 1967)].

But other cases have held that the issue of the unborn child's viability at the time of the injury has no bearing on whether the action is to be recognized. See, e.g., *Hornbuckle v Plantation Pipe Line Co*, 212 Ga 504, 93 SE2d 727 (1956); *Renslow v Mennonite Hosp*, 67 Il2d 348, 10 Il Dec 484, 367 NE2d 1250 (1977); *Bennett v Hymers*, 101 NH 483, 147 A2d 108 (1958); *Smith v Brennan*, 31 NJ 353, 157 A2d 497 (1960); *Sinkler v Kneale*, 401 Pa 267, 164 A2d 93 (1960); *Sylvia v Gobeille*, 220 A2d 222 (RI 1966).

The primary rationale for the classification of viability/non-viability has been that proving causation is difficult when the injury occurs in the early stages of pregnancy. Thus, in discussing limitations upon the recovery for pre-natal injuries, it has been stated:

> There is something to be said on both sides of this. Viability, of course, does not affect the question of the legal existence of the foetus, and therefore of the defendant's duty; and it is a most unsatisfactory criterion, since it is a relative matter, depending on the health of the mother and child and many other matters in addition to the stage of development. Certainly the infant may be no less injured; and all logic is in favor of ignoring the stage at which it occurs. But with our knowledge of embryology what it is, as we approach at the beginning of pregnancy medical knowledge, and therefore medical testimony and medical proof of causes, becomes increasingly unreliable and unsatisfactory, so that there is good reason for caution. This, however, goes to proof rather than principle; and if, as is undoubtedly the case there are injuries as to which reliable medical proof is possible, it makes no sense to deny recovery on any such arbitrary basis. Prosser, LAW OF TORTS (4th ed 1971) §55.

The cases holding that the fetus must have been viable at the time of the prenatal injury have relied on a number of theories. For example, there is authority for the proposition that the unborn child, if viable, is not part of its mother even though it is dependent on its mother for its sustenance. See *Bonbrest v Katz*, 65 FSupp 138 (D DC 1946). And a viable fetus has been held to be a person under a provision of a state constitution that guarantees a legal remedy to every person for an injury done to his land, goods or reputation. See *Williams v Marion Rapid Transit Inc*, 152 Oh 114, 87 NE2d 334 (1949).

However, the current trend would appear to allow a claim for a prenatal injury regardless of the unborn child's stage of development at the time of the injury. There have been various rationales cited for the holding that the issue of viability makes no difference in terms of the right to bring the action. The fetus, from the time of conception, becomes a separate organism and remains so throughout its life. The fact that the fetus may not live if its protection and nourishment are cut off earlier than the viable stage of its development is not to destroy its separability, but it is rather to describe conditions under which life will not continue. *Bennett v Hymers*, 101 NH 483, 147 A2d 108 (1958). The issue of whether an unborn child is viable at the time of a prenatal injury has little to do with the basic right to recover when the fetus is regarded as having an existence as a separate being from the moment of conception. *Sinkler v Kneale*, 401 Pa 267, 164 A2d 93 (1960). There is no sound reason for drawing a line at the moment of the fetal development when the child attains the capability of an independent existence. It is illogical to conclude that a claim for an injury inflicted before viability is any less meritorious than one sustained after viability. *Sylvia v Gobeille*, 101 RI 76, 220 A2d 222 (1966). Denial of claims for injuries to the previable fetus may indeed cut off some of the most meritorious claims, for there is medical authority that congenital structural defects caused by factors in the prenatal environment can be sustained only early in the previable stages. *Renslow v Mennonite Hosp*, 67 Il2d 348, 10 Il Dec 484, 367 NE2d 1250 (1977). And there is no real way of determining in a borderline case whether a fetus was viable at the time of injury, unless it is immediately born. Therefore, the viability rule is impossible for practical application. *Smith v Brennan*, 31 NJ 353, 157 A2d 497 (1960).

B. Cause of Action by Parents for Damages and Emotional Distress Arising From Prenatal Event or Injury

1. [§5.52] Harm Perceived; Child Born Healthy

In some instances, children have been born in a healthy condition following an untoward happening to the mother during the child's prenatal stage.

However, during the pendency of the pregnancy the happening, many times an injury to the mother, gives rise to emotional distress on the part of the parents relating to the eventual health of the as yet unborn child. [As to parental actions where the child is born in an unhealthy condition following a prenatal happening, see §5.53.]

Actions can be maintained for such injuries, and damages can be recovered. The plaintiff may perceive that the unborn child has been injured [see, e.g., *Oklahoma Furniture Mfg Co v Huff*, 414 SW2d 739 (Tx 1967)], or that the mother's injury will result in a miscarriage [see, e.g., *Lawrence v Tippens*, 53 MiA 461, 219 NW2d 787 (1974)]. For example, in *Oklahoma Mfg*, above, the plaintiff-mother was awarded $4,000 at trial for personal injuries arising from an auto accident. The plaintiff had been 6 months pregnant at the time of the injury. She alleged that after the accident her stomach hurt and that she experienced mental anguish as to the possibility of injury to the unborn child. The defendant argued, on appeal, that the award of damages to the mother was grossly excessive but the court believed that the judgment was not excessive. And in *Lawrence*, above, the plaintiff-mother alleged that she feared her child would be injured or subject to a miscarriage following a prenatal injury. On appeal the court said that damages are a question of fact which rest within the determinative powers of the trier of fact. See also, *Porter v Headings*, 527 P2d 403 (Or 1974).

2. [§5.53] Unhealthy Child Born

Claims for damages based on the parents' emotional distress associated with the birth of an unhealthy child, injured during the prenatal stage, have generally been denied. [As to damage recovery where the harm is perceived but the child is born in a healthy condition, see §5.52.] One court reasoned that recovery for such injury should not be allowed because there is no impact to the parents resulting from the birth of an unhealthy child following the ingestion of a drug during pregnancy. *Palo v Upjohn Co*, 310 So2d 30 (Fl 1975). Another court said that regardless of whether the parents suffered physical impact, they could not recover for their emotional distress in participating in the birth of an unhealthy child because to extend the perimeter of liability to a defendant, who allegedly negligently failed to properly serve a pregnant woman would lead to the drawing of artificial and arbitrary boundaries. See *Howard v Lecher*, 42 NY2d 109, 397 NYS2d 363, 366 NE2d 64 (1977). See also *Vaccaro v Squibb Corp*, 52 NY2d 809, 436 NYS2d 871, 418 NE2d 386 (1980). And where the plaintiff-father watched the delivery process, but had no way of knowing of the death of the fetus until after the fact, the court held that the shock caused by learning of the accident from others after its occurrence would not support a cause of action for emotional distress. *Justus v Atchison*, 19 Ca3d 564, 139 CaR 97, 565 P2d 122 (1977).

However, it was held a cause of action for emotional distress had been stated in *Austin v Regents of Univ of California*, 89 CaA2d 354, 152 CaR 420 (1979). In *Austin*, the plaintiff's wife was a patient of the defendants for the purpose of the delivery of a child. The wife died during the delivery procedure. After her death, the plaintiff-husband who was in the delivery room, was able to feel life in the as yet unborn child. He asked the attending physician and nurses to deliver the child, but they refused. The child died, and the plaintiff was able to ascertain the death by feeling the wife's body. The first cause of action sought to recover for the emotional distress resulting from the death of the child. The lower court held that there was no cause of action for emotional distress, but the appellate court disagreed. The elements of a cause of action for emotional distress were stated in *Dillon v Legg*, 68 Ca2d 728, 69 CaR 72 (1968), the court said. The essential elements of such a cause of action that the *Dillon* case stated, were: (1) that the plaintiff and the victim were closely related; (2) the plaintiff was present at the scene of the accident; and (3) the shock to the plaintiff resulted from the plaintiff's sensory perception of the injury to the victim. The trial court, the court noted, relied on *Justus*, above, and the court believed that that reliance was misplaced as to the first cause of action. In *Justus*, the court said, all the plaintiff claimed was that he was in the delivery room when the defendant improperly conducted a delivery. The court denied relief solely on the ground that, on the facts alleged, the plaintiff did not, and could not, have seen any allegedly negligent acts of delivery and that his distress arose only after the death when he was told of it by the defendant doctor, the court said. Here, however, the plaintiff alleged that he learned of the death by his own observation of the cessation of life in the fetus and that his shock and distress were occasioned by that sensory and contemporaneous realization of the death. Therefore, *Justus* was not applicable, the court reasoned. Since the presence of the other two elements required by Dillon, presence at the scene and relationship, were not disputed, it followed that the first cause of action did state triable cause of action.

C. Cause of Action for Wrongful Death of Fetus

1. [§5.54] Generally

The parents of an unborn child, who is injured in the prenatal stage and, because of the injury, is never born alive, may be able to maintain a cause of action in their capacities as surviving parents and sole beneficiaries for wrongful death. Wrongful death actions are statutory in nature and abrogate the common law rule that the death of a person may not be compensated by a civil court. See BLACK'S LAW DICTIONARY (West, 4th ed 1968).

A wrongful death statute is remedial in nature, designed to alleviate the harsh common law rule of no liability for the death of a person. The statute is designed to remedy an inequity in the common law, and to fill a void repugnant to general equitable principles. *Vaillancourt v Medical Center Hosp of Vermont*, 425 A2d 92 (Vt 1980). The essential thrust of a wrongful death statute is compensatory in purpose. *Moen v Hanson*, 85 Wa2d 597, 537 P2d 266 (1975). Wrongful death actions involving unborn children have arisen from various factual settings including prenatal injuries associated with medical malpractice including complications with the inducement of labor [see, e.g., *Presley v Newport Hosp*, 365 A2d 748 (RI 1976); *Vaillancourt v Medical Center Hosp of Vermont*, 425 A2d 92 (Vt 1980)], automobile accidents [see, e.g., *Hatala v Markiewicz*, 26 Cn 358, 224 A2d 406 (1966); *Hale v Manion*, 189 Ks 143, 368 P2d 1 (1962); *Danos v St Pierce*, 383 So2d 1030 (La 1980); *Fowler v Woodard*, 244 SC 608, 138 SE2d 42 (1964); *Hamby v McDaniel*, 559 SW2d 774 (Tn 1977); *Moen v Hanson*, 85 Wa2d 597, 537 P2d 266 (1975)], and the tortious death of the unborn child's mother [see, e.g., *Rainey v Horn*, 221 Ms 269, 72 So2d 434 (1954)].

Wrongful death statutes typically set forth a number of requirements for the existence of a right of action in wrongful death: (1) there must be a person who has died; (2) the person must have died of injuries resulting from a wrongful act, neglect, or default that would have conferred a right of action upon the person who has died, had that person survived; and (3) the act, neglect, or default that caused the fatal injury must have been performed by another. See, e.g., RI GEN LAWS §10-7-1. Generally, the plaintiff-parents are able to plead, and in some instances prove, the third requisite. However, the remaining issues are whether the fetus, which is never born alive, will be defined as a person within the meaning of the statute and whether the plaintiff can prove that the injury did in fact cause the unborn child's death.

In considering actions for the wrongful death of a fetus, some courts have addressed the problems of proving that the injury caused the unborn child's death, and whether the action should be dismissed because of the difficult problems of proof. The proof of a causal relationship between the injury *en ventre sa mere* and the damage which subsequently becomes apparent is difficult, but should not be the basis for rejecting the action. An injustice should not be denied because a wrong is not readily susceptible to proof. The burden of proof would have been almost insurmountable in the days of Blackstone and Holmes and probably greatly influenced their conceptions of the law. The physicians of today, however, have less trouble with the problem, and the right to bring an action is clearly distinguishable from the ability to prove the facts. *Hatala v Markiewicz*, 26 Cn 358, 224 A2d 406 (1966). And in light of modern medical technology, proof of the cause of an unborn child's death can be made by expert testimony. *Eich v Town of Gulf Shores*, 300 So2d 354 (Al 1974).

The second significant issue, the definition of the wronged person for purposes of the wrongful death statute is critical since if the fetus is not within the meaning of the statute, the action for the wrongful death of the fetus will not be recognized. See, e.g., *Justus v Atchison*, 19 Ca2d 564, 139 CaR 97, 565 P2d 122 (1977); *Weitl v Moes*, 311 NW2d 259 (Ia 1981). However, there are cases that hold a fetus to be a person in terms of a wrongful death statute regardless of viability. See, e.g., *Danos v St Pierce*, 383 So2d 1019 (La 1980); *Presley v Newport Hosp*, 365 A2d 748 (RI 1976). [As to a more detailed discussion of whether the definition of person in wrongful death statutes includes unborn children, see §5.55.]

A collateral issue to the definition of person in some wrongful death cases involves whether a fetus needs to be viable to be defined as a person for purposes of the wrongful death statute. There is a split of authority on this issue with some courts requiring that the fetus be viable at the time of the death causing injury to be considered a person [see, e.g., *Green v Smith*, 71 Il2d 501, 17 Il Dec 847, 377 NE2d 37 (1978); *Salazar v St Vincent Hosp*, 95 NM 150, 619 P2d 826 (1980)], while other courts holding that a live birth is necessary for the action to be maintained [see, e.g., *Endresz v Friedberg*, 24 NY2d 478, 301 NYS2d 65 (1969); *Scott v Copp*, 431 A2d 959 (Pa 1981)]. [As to a more detailed discussion of the requirements of viability or live birth in wrongful death actions involving unborn children, see §5.56 and §5.57.]

Damages in wrongful death involving unborn children are much the same as in other wrongful death actions. However, there is a split of authority on whether the pecuniary damages relating to the child's potential earnings can be determined with some courts holding they can be ascertained [see, e.g., *Rice v Rizk*, 453 SW2d 732 (Ky 1970)], while other courts have held they cannot [see, e.g., *Miller v Highland Ins Co*, 336 So2d 636 (Fl 1976)]. [As to a more detailed discussion of damages in wrongful death actions involving unborn children, see §5.58.]

2. [§5.55] Fetus As Person Under Wrongful Death Statute

In wrongful death statutes, one threshold requirement for the recognition of the action is the death of a person. See, e.g., CAL CIV PROC CODE §377 (West Supp 1982); ILL REV STAT Ch 70, ¶1 (1975); NC GEN STAT §28-173. This issue has critical significance in wrongful death actions brought by parents for the death of their fetus [generally, see §5.54] because the determination of whether the fetus is a person for purposes of the wrongful death statute can be determinative of the recognition of the action. If the fetus is defined as a person for purposes of the statute, the action will be recognized. See, e.g., *Presley v Newport Hosp*, 365 A2d 748 (RI 1976). However, if it is held that the fetus is not a person in terms of the statute, the action will be dismissed. See, e.g., *Justus v Atchison*, 19 Ca3d 564, 139 CaR 97, 565 P2d 122 (1977).

In some cases, it has been held that a fetus, regardless of viability at the time of the injury is a person for purposes of a wrongful death statute. For example, in *Presley v Newport Hosp*, 365 A2d 748 (RI 1976), the court held that the decedent-fetus, whether viable or nonviable, was a person within the meaning of the Rhode Island Wrongful Death Statute. The court was cognizant of the possible criticism that its holding would open the door to speculative, if not totally, meritless claims. But the court believed these difficulties were not peculiar to the field of prenatal torts, and that the mere difficulty of proving a fact was not a good reason for blocking all attempts to prove it. The legal right of a child to begin life with a sound mind and body should not be abridged by difficulties in proof of causation, the court believed. Recovery for prenatal injuries, like any injuries, whether they result in death, disability or temporary discomfort, is subject to the plaintiff's ability to establish by competent proof that there was a causal connection between the wrongful interference and the harm suffered, the court concluded.

And, in *Danos v St Pierre*, 383 So2d 1019 (La 1980), a concurring opinion stated that in terms of a statutory wrongful death action the word person should include an unborn child from the moment of fertilization and implantation. The opinion did not share the defendant's view that such a holding by the majority would open the floodwaters of litigation. The prime focus of litigation occurring as the result of the court's holding, the concurring opinion stated, will be for damages suffered by the parents for the wrongful killing of their unborn child.

Moreover, other courts have held that a fetus is a person under a wrongful death statute if the fetus is viable at the time of the injury. See, e.g., *Green v Smith*, 71 Il2d 501, 17 Il Dec 847, 377 NE2d 37 (1978); *Mone v Greyhound Lines Inc*, 331 NE2d 916 (Ma 1975); *Wallace v Wallace*, 421 A2d 134 (NH 1980); *Evans v Olson*, 550 P2d 924 (Ok 1976); *Moen v Hanson*, 85 Wa2d 597, 537 P2d 266 (1975); *Baldwin v Butcher*, 155 WV 431, 184 SE2d 428 (1971). For example, in *Green*, above, the court drew a clear distinction between a common law cause of action on behalf of a live-born infant for injuries suffered prior to its having become viable, and a statutory cause of action for the destruction of a fetus not yet viable. The extent of the loss incurred by a living child burdened with mental or physical defects resulting from a prenatal occurrence is not affected by whether the injuries were suffered prior to or after he or she became viable, the court reasoned. However, the wrongful death act provides for the recovery of the death of a person, and the court found no basis on which to hold that one can cause the death of a fetus not yet viable. Therefore, the court held that no cause of action exists for injuries and death of an unborn child unless at the time of the injury it had attained viability. [As to a more detailed discussion of the requirement of the viability of the fetus in wrongful death actions, see §5.56.]

However, other courts have held that a fetus is not a person within the meaning of a wrongful death statute, and thus a wrongful death action cannot be brought by the unborn child's parents or beneficiaries. See, e.g., *Justus v Atchison*, 19 Ca3d 564, 139 CaR 97, 565 P2d 122 (1977); *Stern v Miller*, 348 So2d 303 (Fl 1977); *Weitl v Moes*, 311 NW2d 259 (Ia 1981); *State ex rel Hardin v Sanders*, 538 SW2d 336 (Mo 1976); *Endresz v Friedberg*, 44 NY2d 478, 301 NYS2d 65 (1969); *Hamby v McDaniel*, 559 SW2d 774 (Tn 1977). Some courts have predicated such a holding on the belief that a fetus is not a person until there has been a live birth. See, e.g., *Justus v Atchison*, 19 Ca3d 564, 139 CaR 97, 565 P2d 122 (1977); *State ex rel Hardin v Sanders*, 538 SW2d 336 (Mo 1976). The ordinary meaning of the word person is a human being who has attained a recognized individual identity by being born alive. See, e.g., *Weitl v Moes*, 311 NW2d 259 (1981); *Cardwell v Welch*, 25 NC App 390, 213 SE2d 382, cert den 287 NC 464, 215 SE2d 623 (1975). And it has been held that even if, as science and theology suggest, the child begins a separate life from the moment of conception, except insofar as is necessary to protect the child's own rights, the law has never considered the unborn foetus as having a separate judicial existence or a legal personality or identity until the child is born. *Endresz v Friedberg*, 44 NY2d 478, 301 NYS2d 65 (1969). [As to a more detailed discussion of the live birth requirement and wrongful death actions, see §5.57]. Moreover, it was held in *Justus*, above, that it is not irrational for a legislature to refrain from providing a cause of action for the wrongful death to the parents of a stillborn fetus. The purpose of the wrongful death statute is to enable the heirs and certain specified dependents of a person wrongfully killed to recover compensation for the economic loss and deprivation of consortium as a result of the death, the court said. A fetus has no dependents and its only possible heirs are its parents, the court said. Moreover, the court noted that a fetus is evidently not a wage earner and its death therefore causes no appreciable economic loss to its survivors. And, in *Hamby v McDaniel*, 559 SW2d 774 (Tn 1977), the court believed that it was not appropriate or necessary to judicially determine when life begins because the creation of a wrongful death action is properly the business of the legislative branch of government, and expansion of its benefits to include viable fetus, fetus, and/or, embryo would likewise be within its exclusive province.

3. [§5.56] Viability Requirement

In wrongful death actions involving the death of unborn children [generally, see §5.54] some courts have held that if the fetus is injured while viable and then dies before being born alive, a wrongful death action will be recognized. See, e.g., *Simmons v Howard University*, 323 FSupp 529 (D DC 1971); *Eich v Town of Gulf Shores*, 300 So2d 354 (Al 1974); *Hatala v Markiewicz*, 26 Cn 358, 224 A2d 406 (1966); *Volk v Baldazo*, 8 FLR 2743 (Id 1982); *Green v Smith*, 71 Il2d 501, 17 Il Dec 847, 377 NE2d 37 (1978); *Britt v Sears*, 277 NE2d 20 (In 1972); *Hale v Manion*, 189 Ks 143, 368 P2d 1 (1962); *O'Neill v Morse*, 385 Mi 130, 188 NW2d 785 (1971); *Ramey v Horn*, 221 Ms 269, 72 So2d 434 (1954); *White v Yup*, 85 Nv 527, 458 P2d 617 (1969); *Poliquin v MacDonald*, 101 NH 104, 135 A2d 249 (1957); *Salazar v St Vincent Hosp*, 95 NM 150, 619 P2d 826 (1980); *Fowler v Woodward*, 244 SC 608, 138 SE2d 42 (1964); *Leal v C C Pitts Sand & Gravel Inc*, 419 SW2d 820 (Tx 1967); *Nelson v Peterson*, 542 P2d 1075 (Ut 1975); *Vaillancourt v Medical Center Hosp of Vermont*, 425 A2d 92 (Vt 1980); *Moen v Hanson*, 85 Wa2d 597, 537 P2d 266 (1975); *Kwaterski v State Farm Mutual Auto Ins Co*, 34 Wi2d 14, 148 NW2d 107 (1967).

Other courts, however, have held that a fetus, whether viable or not, is a person under a wrongful death statute [see, e.g., *Danos v St Pierre*, 383 So2d 1019 (La 1980); *Presley v Newport Hosp*, 365 A2d 748 (RI 1976)], or that a live birth is necessary before a wrongful death action can be brought by the heirs beneficiaries of a deceased fetus [see, e.g., *Endresz v Friedberg*, 24 NY2d 478, 301 NYS2d 65 (1969)]. [As to a more detailed discussion of the issue of a fetus as a person under a wrongful death statute, see §5.55; as to a more detailed discussion of the requirement of a live birth in order to maintain a wrongful death action for the death caused by prenatal injuries, see §5.57.]

The cases that hold the action recognizable if the fetus is viable at the time of the injury rely on a number of general theories. To deny recovery where the injury is so severe as to cause the death of a fetus subsequently stillborn, and to allow recovery where injury occurs during pregnancy and death results therefrom after a live birth, would only serve the tortfeasor by rewarding him for his severity in inflicting the injury. *Eich v Town of Gulf Shores*, 300 So2d 354 (Al 1974). Denial of recovery to an unborn child tortiously killed, on the arbitrary grounds that the child did not survive the tort long enough to be born alive, is illogical. Mental anguish and grief are experienced by parents whether or not a viable fetus survives to full term. *Moen v Hanson*, 85 Wa2d 597, 537 P2d 266 (1975). In a case where the unborn child was a full term baby at the time of its tortiously caused death it was held it is both just and logical to treat an unborn child who has been two hundred eighty days in gestation as having a legal being and legal personality distinct from that of its mother although it is enclosed in its mother's body and therefore dependent upon her breath for oxygen and upon her food for nourishment, and such a child is within the meaning of the statute which provides that a father may maintain an action for the death of a child. *Britt v Sears*, 277 NE2d 20 (In 1972).

Several courts have also specifically addressed the viability factor. For example, once the stage of viability is reached, the fetus is regarded as a legal person with a separate existence of its own. *Orange v State Farm Mutual Automobile Ins Co*, 443 SW2d 650 (Ky 1969). The unborn child, certainly after viability, is recognized as a distinct being capable of sustaining a legal wrong. *Fowler v Woodward*, 244 SC 608, 138 SE2d 42 (1964). An unborn child, after it reaches the prenatal age of viability when the destruction of life of its mother does not necessarily mean the end of its life also, and when, if separated from its mother would be so far a mature human being that it would live and grow mentally and physically, is a person. *Rainey v Horn*, 221 Ms 269, 72 So2d 434 (1954). And, although there is a split of authority upon the proper interpretation of the word person in a wrongful death statute, a viable fetus, though later stillborn, is within the meaning of person in a wrongful death statute. See, e.g., *Simmons v Howard University*, 323 FSupp 529 (D DC 1971); *Vaillancourt v Medical Center of Vermont*, 425 A2d 92 (Vt 1980); *Kwaterski v State Farm Mutual Auto Ins Co*, 34 Wi2d 14, 148 NW2d 107 (1967). Moreover, it has been held that the legislature, in enacting a wrongful death statute, did intend to provide a right of recovery for the wrongful death of a viable fetus. *Salazar v St Vincent Hosp*, 95 NM 150, 619 P2d 826 (1980).

4. [§5.57] Live Birth Requirement

In actions based on the wrongful death of an unborn child [generally, see §5.54] there is a split of authority on whether the fetus must first have been born alive, before its death, or whether a live birth is unnecessary to maintain a wrongful death action. Some cases have simply held that a fetus is a person in terms of a wrongful death statute. See, e.g., *Presley v Newport Hosp*, 365 A2d 748 (RI 1976). [As to a more detailed discussion of whether a fetus is a person for purposes of wrongful death statute, see §5.55.] And some cases have held that an unborn child, if viable, can be defined as a person for the purposes of wrongful death statutes. See, e.g., *Simmons v Howard University*, 323 FSupp 529 (D DC 1971); *Vaillancourt v Medical Center Hosp of Vermont*, 425 A2d 92 (Vt 1980); *Kwaterski v State Farm Auto Ins Co*, 34 Wi2d 14, 148 NW2d 107 (1967).

In these cases, the requirement of a live birth before the wrongful death action can be maintained has been rejected. Denial of recovery to an unborn child tortiously killed, on the arbitrary grounds that the child did not survive the tort long enough to be born alive is imminently illogical. *Moen v Hanson*, 85 Wa2d 597, 537 P2d 266 (1975). A rule fixing survival as the determinant rather than viability has the appeal of simplicity but would hardly aid justice. *Hatala v Markiewicz*, 26 Cn 358, 224 A2d 406 (1966). To deny recovery where the injury is so severe as to cause the death of a fetus subsequently stillborn, and to allow recovery where injury occurs during pregnancy and death results therefrom after a live birth, would only serve the tortfeasor by rewarding him for his severity in inflicting the injury. It would be bizarre to hold that the greater the harm inflicted the better the opportunity for exoneration of the defendant. Logic, fairness and justice compel recognition of an action for prenatal injuries causing death before a live birth. *Eich v Town of Gulf Shores*, 300 So2d 354 (Al 1974). The phenomenon of birth is not the beginning of life, but is merely a change in the form of life. The principle feature of that change is the fact of respiration. But the law does not regard the incidence of respiration as the sole determinative of life. If property interests of unborn persons are protected by the law, how much more solicitous should the law be of the first unalienable right of man, the right to life itself? If the mother can die and the fetus live, if the fetus dies and the mother lives, how can it be said that there is only one life? If tortious conduct can injure one and not the other, how can it be said that there is not a duty owing to each? A fetus having died within its mother's womb is dead, and it will not come alive when separated from her. A fetus living within the mother's womb is a living creature, and it will not die when separated from her unless the manner, the time or the circumstances of the separation constitute a fatal trauma. The fact of life is not to be denied. Neither is the wisdom of the public policy which regards unborn persons as being entitled to the protection of the law. *O'Neill v Morse*, 385 Mi 130, 188 NW2d 785 (1971).

There is neither reason nor logic in choosing live birth over viability for the purposes of interpreting the wrongful death statute. Conditioning a right of action on whether a fatally injured child is born dead or alive is not only an artificial and unreasonable demarcation, but is unjust as well. While a rule fixing survival as the determinant rather than viability has the appeal of simplicity, such a rule might aid the judiciary but hardly justice. *Mone v Greyhound Lines Inc*, 331 NE2d 916 (Ma 1975). See also, *Volk v Baldazo*, 8 FLR 2743 (Id 1982).

However, there is also authority that before a wrongful death action for an unborn child will be recognized there must be a live birth. Even if a child begins a separate life from the moment of conception, except insofar as is necessary to protect the child's own rights, the law has never considered the unborn fetus as having a separate judicial existence with a legal personality or identity until it sees the light of day. Translated into tort law, this means that there is but a conditional prospective liability created when an unborn child is injured through the wrongful act of the defendant, and such liability attaches only upon fulfillment of the condition that the child be born alive. Although it is arbitrary and illogical to draw the line at birth, with the result that the distributees of an injured fetus which survives birth by a few minutes may have a recovery while those of a stillborn fetus may not, such difficulties are always present where a line must be drawn. To make viability rather than birth a test would not remove the difficulty but merely relocate it and increase the problems of causation and damages. *Endresz v Friedberg*, 44 NY2d 478, 301 NYS2d 65 (1969). Requiring a live birth has the advantage of establishing to a legal certainty that there was a living person in existence, thereby bringing any survival or wrongful death action into conformity with other similar actions brought by persons or the representatives of persons who died as a result of wrongful or negligent injuries inflicted by another. *Scott v Copp*, 431 A2d 959 (Pa 1981). And, it is highly unlikely that the legislature which enacted the wrongful death statute intended to create a cause of action for the death of an unborn fetus. Had such an intention existed, it could easily have been clearly expressed. The greater probability is that by speaking of the death of a person and by creating a cause of action to be brought by the executor, administrator or collector of the decedent, the legislature was thinking solely in terms of and intended to create a cause of action only for the wrongful death of one who by live birth had attained a recognized individual identity so as to have become a person as that word is commonly understood. Practical considerations also favor this construction. It is true that the parents of an unborn child may suffer intense anguish if through the tortious act of another the child is stillborn. To say, however, that an action lies for the death if the child was viable at the time of its injury and death but that no action lies if the child was not yet capable of existing apart from its mother's womb does not solve but merely relocates the problem. From the moment of conception onward there must be some cut-off point and to place this at the moment of live birth has at least the merit of providing some degree of certainty to an otherwise speculative situation. *Cardwell v Welch*, 25 NC App 390, 213 SE2d 382, cert den, 287 NC 464, 215 SE2d 623 (1975). See also, *Hardin v Sanders*, 538 SW2d 336 (Mo 1976).

5. [§5.58] Damages

When a wrongful death action is brought by the heirs or beneficiaries of an unborn child [generally, see §5.54] an important issue centers on the recovery of damages. It has been held that although the extent of the damages may be difficult to prove, the cause of action for wrongful death may still be recognized. See, e.g., *Evans v Olson*, 550 P2d 924 (Ok 1976); *Fowler v Woodward*, 244 SC 608, 138 SE2d 42 (1964).

Damages may be awarded for the wrongful death of a viable fetus. See *White v Yup*, 85 Nv 527, 458 P2d 617 (1969). The death of a viable fetus should be considered as much a ground for damages as would a miscarriage. *Nelson v Peterson*, 542 P2d 1075 (Ut 1975).

One of the elements of damages that may be recoverable in wrongful death actions for the death of an unborn child is the net value to the parents of the child's prospective services. See, e.g., *Rice v Rizk*, 453 SW2d 732 (Ky 1970); *O'Neill v Morse*, 385 Mi 130, 188 NW2d 785 (1971). There is an inference that the child would have had some earning power, and in this lies the basis for recovery. *Rice*, above. Moreover, it has been held that there is no more speculation as to the probability of pecuniary loss with a stillborn than with a 5-year-old. *Evans v Olson*, 550 P2d 924 (Ok 1976). However, there is also authority that the element of damages associated with loss of services and support is not recoverable because, in the case of the wrongful death of an unborn child, there is no competent means of measuring the value of future services and support of the child. It would be impossible to prove by competent evidence the pecuniary value of future services and support of an unborn child. None of the usual indicia such as mental and physical capabilities, personality traits, aptitudes and training of the wrongfully killed are present. Evidences to the unborn child's probable net income available for distribution to the particular survivor, and the replacement value of the decedent's services to the survivor would be sheer speculation. There could be no competent evidences to the child's capabilities and potentialities. *Miller v Highlands Ins Co*, 336 So2d 636 (Fl 1976). See also *Gay v Thompson*, 266 NC 394, 146 SE2d 425 (1966).

In addition, the parents out-of-pocket medical expenses and funeral expenses have been held to be recoverable. *Miller v Highlands Ins Co*, 336 So2d 636 (Fl 1976).

Other elements of damages may be recoverable as well depending on the provision of the specific wrongful death statute. For example, where a wrongful death statute provided for recovery of elements of non-pecuniary loss it was held that in applying the statute elements such as the loss of society, association, companionship, comfort, affection of the decedent and the loss of acts of kindness which originate in the relationship between the decedent and the beneficiaries may be recovered. *White v Yup*, 85 Nv 527, 458 P2d 617 (1969).

In awarding damages in these cases, a trial judge may look to a number of factors to determine the extent of damages suffered by the parents. Some of the factors are: (1) the stage of pregnancy at which stillbirth occurs; (2) the medical history of the mother with respect to previous childbirth; (3) the number of children the couple presently has; (4) whether the mother used artificial means to induce pregnancy; (5) the probability of the pregnancy going to full term; (6) any prior history of miscarriage; (7) prenatal care of the stillborn child, and (8) prenatal preparation for the forthcoming child such as house additions, baby crib, and any other indicia of the degree of expectation exuded by the parents. *Danos v St Pierre*, 383 So2d 1019 (La 1980).

It has been argued that to permit recovery for the wrongful death of an unborn child while at the same time permitting recovery for prenatal losses would allow a double recovery. But one court has said that the character of the damages flowing from the respective claims is distinct and separate, and that therefore both claims should be allowed. *Moen v Hanson*, 85 Wa2d 597, 537 P2d 266 (1975).

D. [§5.59] Cause of Action by Parents for Death of a Fetus, Element of Parents' Damages

In conjunction with a wrongful death action brought by the heirs or beneficiaries of an unborn child [generally, see §5.54], the unborn child's parents may also bring a cause of action for their own damages suffered as a result of the death.

Generally, courts have held that such a cause of action for the parents' damages is appropriate where a cause of action for the wrongful death of the child has been denied. The mother or parents of the child can maintain an action for their injuries and include as an element of damages the suffering caused by the death of the child. *Scott v Kopp*, 431 A2d 959 (1981). The denial of the wrongful death claim for the unborn fetus does not affect the mother's claim for pain and anguish resulting from the miscarriage. *McKillip v Zimmerman*, 191 NW2d 706 (Ia 1971).

Birth is a major event in the development of a human being, but it is certainly not the beginning of an individual's life nor the beginning of his parent's love and concern. The mental pain and suffering of the parents of a stillborn child may be as great as that of parents whose child dies after birth. *Miller v Highlands Ins Co*, 336 So2d 636 (1976). However, recovery may be allowed for negligently causing emotional distress, not accompanied by physical impact, only when accompanied by substantial bodily injury or sickness, and subject to the limitation that the plaintiff has been within the zone of danger and is subject to a reasonable fear of immediate personal injury. Thus, in a case where the negligence causing the fetal death was not alleged to have threatened the personal safety of the plaintiff-husband, his recovery for emotional distress was precluded, but his wife's recovery was not precluded since she was necessarily within the zone of danger and subject to a reasonable fear for her own safety. *Vaillancourt v Medical Center Hosp of Vermont*, 425 A2d 92 (Vt 1980).

Moreover, the plaintiff-husband may recover for the loss of his wife's services and consortium in a case arising from the tortiously caused injury to his wife which also resulted in the death of the parents' unborn child. *Endresz v Friedberg*, 24 NY2d 478, 301 NYS2d 65 (1969).

It has also been recognized that in cases involving the wrongful death of an unborn child permitting a claim for the death of the fetus and permitting recovery for the wrongful death or injury to the mother would not result in a double recovery. The possibility of recovery by way of a separate claim for the death or injury of a mother carrying a fetus does not recognize and compensate for the mental anguish and suffering flowing from the death of the fetus. The character of the damages pertaining to the respective claims are distinct and separate, just as they are in the event of the tortious loss of a postnatal child and its mother. *Moen v Hanson*, 85 Wa2d 597, 537 P2d 266 (1975).

III. MISCELLANEOUS RIGHTS AND ENTITLEMENTS OF FETUS

A. [§5.60] Fetus as Person Under 42 USC §1983 and Fourteenth Amendment

Although live born children are considered persons for the purposes of the law, this is not necessarily the case in terms of a fetus in the prenatal stage of development. The issue of whether a fetus is a person has arisen most often in judicial consideration of civil rights actions brought pursuant to 42 USC §1983 and the Fourteenth Amendment to the United States Constitution.

Under 42 USC §1983, a right of action exists against any person acting under color of state law who subjects "any citizen of the United States or other person" to a deprivation of the rights secured by the United States Constitution or federal laws. The statute was enacted in accordance with the Fourteenth Amendment. Since the landmark *Roe v Wade*, 410 US 113, 93 SCt 705, 35 LE2d 147 (1973), decision [see below for more discussion of *Wade*], which struck down a Texas criminal anti-abortion statute courts in general have not recognized unborn children as persons.

For example, a mother brought a federal civil rights action, pursuant to 42 USC §1983, on behalf of herself and her child against a police officer for allegedly assaulting her while she was pregnant. It was claimed that the infant received prenatal injuries in the intentional attack. Since the unborn child was not deemed a person under the Fourteenth Amendment at the time of the injury, it followed that the unborn child could not pursue a right of action under §1983. The legislative history of a civil rights action gave no indication that the scope of coverage should be extended to the unborn. *Harman v Daniels*, 525 FSupp 798 (WD Va 1981); *Poole v Endsley*, 371 FSupp 1379 (ND Fl 1974).

Recently, however, one jurisdiction has made a significant departure from this majority rule. The Connecticut Federal District court recognized that a baby born with severe head injuries, allegedly the result of an attack by policemen on his mother while she was five and one-half months pregnant, had a civil rights action against the officers. The viable fetus was a "person" within the parameters of the Civil Rights Act, notwithstanding other federal court rulings to the contrary. The court reasoned that firmly entrenched rules have expanded the legal rights of the viable fetus in many situations, including damages for wrongful death, murder and vehicular homicide. Thus, there was no reason not to extend these rights to this federal tort action. *Douglas v Hartford*, 542 FSupp 1267 (DC Cn 1982).

The landmark United States Supreme Court case regarding whether a fetus is a person for purposes of the Fourteenth Amendment to the United States Constitution is *Roe v Wade*, 410 US 113, 93 SCt 705, 35 LE2d 147 (1973). The Court said the Constitution does not define person in so many words. Section 1 of the Fourteenth Amendment contains three references to "person." The first, in defining "citizens," speaks of "persons born or naturalized in the United States." The word also appears both in the due process clause and in the equal protection clause, the Court said. In addition, the Court said that the word person is used in numerous other places in the Constitution, but it noted that in nearly all these instances, the use of the word is such that it has application only postnatally. None indicates, the Court said, with any assurance, that it has any possible prenatal application. All of this, the Court said, together with its observation that throughout the major portion of the 19th Century prevailing legal abortion practices were far freer than they were in 1973, persuaded the court that the word "person" as used in the Fourteenth Amendment, does not include the unborn. But the mere fact that a fetus is not constitutionally entitled as a "person" to claim certain remedies or rights in no way prevents Congress from extending protection to unborn children by appropriate legislation. *Harman v Daniels*, 525 FSupp 798 (WD Va 1981).

B. [§5.61] Right of Fetus to Medical Services or Treatment

During the prenatal period of gestation it is possible that the fetus may require medical care in order to prevent injury or disease. In the past, medical treatment of the fetus, during the prenatal stage of development, has been restricted to management of the maternal environment and the mother in an effort to treat the fetus. However, today sophisticated medical treatment of unborn children is becoming more widely accepted with the development of improved diagnostic techniques such as ultrasonographic visualization and amniocentensis. These techniques allow diagnosis of some fetal anomalies that may be amenable to treatment during the prenatal stage. Fetal growth and development, and the general health of the fetus, may be aided by these prenatal treatments, thus allowing the fetus to be born safely and in a healthier condition. See Clewell, et. al., A SURGICAL APPROACH TO THE TREATMENT OF FETAL HYDROCEPHALUS, 306 New England Journal of Medicine 1320 (1982).

As a general rule, cases involving medical treatment for unborn children are heard in court because of a mother's unwillingness to submit to a medical procedure, regardless of the mother's reasons, and the possibility that the lack of medical care will hurt or injure the unborn child. In these instances a third party, typically the health care provider, will seek a court order requiring the mother to submit to the procedure. See, e.g., *Jefferson v Griffin Spalding County Hosp Auth*, 274 SE2d 457 (Ga 1981); *Raleigh Fitkin-Paul Morgan Memorial Hosp v Anderson*, 42 NJ 421, 201 A2d 537, cert den, 377 US 985, 84 SCt 1894, 12 LE2d 1032 (1964). The types of medical care to a fetus that have been involved in judicial consideration have included a request by a county hospital to perform a caesarean section on an unwilling mother [see *Jefferson*, above] and a request by a hospital to administer a blood transfusion to a mother who refused to undergo such treatment [see *Raleigh Fitkin*, above].

The primary issue that arises in this context is whether the court can or will order an unwilling mother to undergo a medical procedure, to aid the health of the unborn child. A number of cases have considered this issue, and have held that the judicial intervention and orders approving the medical procedure are appropriate under certain circumstances. For example, in *Raleigh Fitkin-Paul Morgan Memorial Hosp v Anderson*, 42 NJ 421, 201 A2d 537 (1964), cert den, 377 US 985, 84 SCt 1894, 12 LE2d 1032 (1964), the plaintiff-hospital brought an action in the superior court seeking authority to administer blood transfusions to the defendant-mother in the event that such transfusion should be necessary to save her life and the life of her unborn child. At the time of the case the pregnancy was beyond the thirty-second week. The defendant had notified the hospital that she did not wish blood transfusions for the reason that they would be contrary to her religious conviction as a Jehovah's Witness. The evidence established a probability that at some point in the pregnancy the defendant would hemorrhage severely and that both she and the unborn child would die unless a blood transfusion was administered. The trial court held that the judiciary could not intervene in the case of an adult or with respect to an unborn child. Because of the emergency, the Supreme Court of New Jersey directed the immediate argument of the hospital's appeal. At the argument, the court was advised that the defendant left the hospital on the day before the argument against the advice of the attending physician and the hospital. The court said it was doubtful whether the hospital had a remaining interest but the parties requested the court to determine the issues since it was likely that the matter would arise again at the instance of an interested party. The court noted that in *State v Perricone*, 37 NJ 463, 181 A2d 751 (1962), it held that the state's concern for the welfare of an infant justified blood transfusions notwithstanding the objection of its parents who were also Jehovah's Witnesses, and in *Smith v Brennan*, 31 NJ 353, 157 A2d 497

(1960), the court held that a child could sue for injuries negligently inflicted prenatally. The court was satisfied that the unborn child is entitled to the law's protection and that an appropriate order should be made to ensure necessary blood transfusions to the mother. And in *Jefferson v Griffin Spalding Cty Memorial Hosp*, 274 SE2d 457 (Ga 1981), the court affirmed the trial court's orders that authorized the plaintiff-hospital to administer to the defendant-mother all medical procedures deemed necessary by the attending physician to preserve the life of the defendant's unborn child. However, the authority provided by the court order was only effective if the defendant-mother voluntarily sought admission to the plaintiff's hospital for the emergency delivery of the child. In addition, the order granted the state department of human resources and the county's department of family and children services the authority to make all decisions, including giving consent to surgical delivery, concerning the birth of the unborn child. In *Jefferson*, the county hospital authority petitioned a superior court, as a court of equity, for an order authorizing it to perform a caesarean section and any necessary blood transfusions upon the defendant, an out-patient resident of the hospital, in the event she presented herself to the hospital for delivery of her unborn child. The superior court conducted an emergency hearing and drafted an order indicating the following: the defendant was in her thirty-ninth week of pregnancy; she had presented herself to the county hospital for prenatal care; the examining physician had found and the defendant had been advised that she had a complete placenta previa; that the afterbirth was between the baby and the birth canal; that it was virtually impossible that this condition would correct itself prior to delivery; and that it was a ninety-nine per cent certainty that the child could not survive natural childbirth. The chances of the defendant surviving vaginal delivery were not better than fifty per cent. The examining physician believed that a delivery by caesarean section prior to labor beginning would have an almost one hundred per cent chance of preserving the life of the child, along with the defendant. On the basis of religious beliefs, the defendant had advised the hospital that she did not need surgical removal of the child and would not submit to it. Further, she refused a blood transfusion. The hospital was required by its own policies to treat any patient seeking emergency treatment. It sought the authority of the superior court to administer medical treatment to the defendant to save the life of the mother and her unborn child.

In addition, some medical researchers have suggested that an "advocate" should be appointed to represent the interests of the unborn child when medical treatment involving an unborn child is considered. The researchers said:

> . . . [A]ny proposed fetal treatment really involves two patients: the fetus and the mother. Whereas parents may consent to allow the

fetus to be treated through the mother's body, who can give consent for the fetus? We believe that it is appropriately the parents themselves who bear this responsibility, but we also believe that it is best if a separate advocate can be identified for the fetus. This person not only seeks the best treatment for the fetus but also protects it from unwarranted or unnecessary assaults. Being separate from the fetus and the parents, the advocate can more objectively view the entire situation and the potential interventions. In some cases, the advocate may recommend no intervention and thus relieve potential parental guilt. Finally, since the advocate stands between the fetus and the physicians who are called on to render potential treatment, he or she can give an unbiased informed consent. Although such a system seems cumbersome, this approach is warranted until the real risks and outcomes of fetal treatments are known. . . . [Reprinted with permission from Clewell, et. al., A SURGICAL APPROACH TO THE TREATMENT OF FETAL HYDROCEPHALUS, 306 New England Journal of Medicine 1320 (1982).]

C. [§5.62] Fetus as a Dependent Child Under Aid to Families With Dependent Children Program

The purpose of the federal Aid to Families with Dependent Children Program (AFDC) is to encourage the care of dependent children in their own homes or in those of relatives in order to stabilize the family unit. See 42 USC §§601 et. seq. Federal funds are channeled to those states that have, by option, implemented an approved plan for aid and services to indigent families with children. A state receiving federal assistance under the AFDC program is not obligated to offer welfare benefits to pregnant women on behalf of their unborn children. Under the provisions of the federal law, the comprehensive definition of "dependent child" does not encompass unborn children.

A pregnant woman brought a class action against state welfare officials in Iowa claiming that the denial of benefits to unborn children clashed with eligibility standards under the Social Security Act (42 USC §606(a)). Section 406(a) of the Act defines the term "dependent child" as a needy child under 18 years of age who has been deprived of parental support or care because of the death, continued absence or incapacitation of the parent, and who lives with certain designated relatives. The United States Supreme Court held that Congress used "child" to designate an individual already born with an existence apart from its mother. The Court's conclusion was based on the proposition that the statutory language in the Act should be given its ordinary meaning absent persuasive reasons to the contrary. The failure of the legislature to explicitly provide for pregnant women strongly intimated that Congress had no desire to include the unborn within the protection of the Act. *Burns v Alcala*, 420 US 575, 95 SCt 1180, 43 LE2d 469 (1975).

In a subsequent decision, a pregnant woman claimed that her Fourteenth Amendment equal protection rights were violated since, as a prospective mother, she was barred from receiving AFDC payments that were granted mothers of unborn children. (These constitutional arguments were mentioned in *Burns*, but since they had not been briefed and argued, were remanded to the trial court for further consideration.) However, the government established to the court's satisfaction that there was a rational basis for their actions, i.e., administrative convenience in the operation of the state's welfare system. The needs of a born child are more readily discernible than those of the unborn. Also, aid to pregnant women might result in fraud where the recipient later decides to undergo an abortion. The state was not required to explain its policies in terms of a compelling state interest, since the right to welfare was not a suspect class that would be the object of close judicial scrutiny. Rather, the court instead looked for evidence of a "rationale basis" consistent with the requirements of the United States Constitution. *Green v Stanton*, 451 FSupp 567 (ND In 1978).

In another post-*Burns* decision, a group of pregnant women filed a class action in North Carolina challenging their denial of AFDC eligibility, diverting the issue to three other areas to circumvent the adverse *Burns* holding. However, the plaintiffs failed to show that the denial of eligibility was either: (1) racially discriminatory, since a disproportionate percentage of blacks were welfare recipients; (2) an invasion of the pregnant women's right to privacy; and, (3) a violation of the Equal Protection Clause of the Fourteenth Amendment. No evidence of racial bias against a class of unwed mothers was shown. The state had a non-racial rational justification for refusing to expand AFDC, namely, the preservation of the fiscal integrity of the state. The violation of the right to privacy argument was meritless, since the state policy only remotely and tenuously interfered with the woman's choice of bearing a healthy child and terminating her pregnancy by abortion. Finally, no equal protection rights were infringed upon. The purpose of the AFDC program is to aid eligible family units. The differences between a family unit and a pregnant individual with no other children were sufficient to remove the case from an equal protection analysis. The needs of the two groups are different, and justify different remedies. Since the state chose to deal with the problem of prenatal nutrition and medical care through other state programs, its judgment was rational and not invidious. *Taylor v Hill*, 420 FSupp 1020 (WD NC 1976), cert den, 430 US 961, 97 SCt 1639, 52 LE2d 352 (1976).

Although not obligated, several states have voluntarily chosen to include the unborn within the coverage of the AFDC program. California is among those states. The terms "needy child" or "children" under its state welfare law, include the unborn, although the payments provided were smaller than that allocated to other family members. A regulation promulgated by the California Department of Social Welfare looked to state and federal law authorizing grant reductions in welfare payments by the amount of non-exempt income or resources available to the recipient. Thus, the value to the fetus of resources furnished by the mother in the form of reduced needs for food, clothing, and shelter, was viewed as non-exempt income. Accordingly, the size of the grant of the AFDC payments was reduced by this non-exempt income. The California Supreme Court ruled otherwise, holding that the mother's body does not constitute a resource of the fetus that may be deducted from the assistance grant otherwise payable to the mother upon pregnancy. The state welfare department overstepped its authority in excluding or reducing the grant to unborn children. Because of the firmly-entrenched legislative policy to provide aid on behalf of the unborn, this child was entitled to be treated as any other person for purposes of imputing AFDC aid. *California Welfare Rights Organization v Brian*, 520 P2d 970, 113 CaR 154 (1974). A state county board challenge of this federal regulation permitting states the option to require payments to needy pregnant women was rejected due, in part, to lack of standing on the part of the board. *Plumas Cty Bd of Supervisors v Califano*, 594 F2d 756 (9th Cir 1979).

The inclusion of the unborn within AFDC eligibility requirements has spawned other problems, too. In New York, a woman in her fourth month of pregnancy may qualify for AFDC aid for her unborn child. A class consisting of pregnant women sued the state food stamp program to protect the inclusion of their AFDC allowances for unborn children in determining the amount of their food stamp benefits. The added AFDC allowances resulted in reduced benefits. The pregnant women's argument that those payments were actually to third-party beneficiaries, which then would not be included in income, was rejected. Since a federal law required inclusion of AFDC grants in setting food stamp benefits and since the New York allowances for unborn children are AFDC grants, they must be included as income. *McCoy v Bergland*, 519 FSupp 796 (ND NY 1981).

D. [§5.63] Appointment of Guardian on Behalf of Fetus

In some instances a court may be requested to appoint a guardian to represent the interests of an unborn child. There is precedent for the proposition that a court can appoint a guardian for an unborn child. See, e.g., *Hatch v Riggs Natl Bank*, 361 F2d 559 (DC DC 1966); *Wainwright v*

Moore, 374 So2d 586 (Fl 1979); *Gunnell v Palmer*, 370 Il 206, 18 NE2d 202 (1938).

It is not uncommon in cases involving trusts for the court to appoint a guardian ad litem for an unborn or unascertained beneficiary for purposes of consent to modification or revocation of a trust. See *Hatch*, above. Providing for the appointment of a competent disinterested person as a trustee to protect the interest of persons not in being provides the same protections to unborn persons as traditional doctrines of equitable representation. See *Gunnell*, above. See also, *In re Will of Silver*, 72 Misc 2d 963, 340 NYS2d 335 (1973) (guardians ad litem may be appointed for unborns either under Surrogate's Court Procedure Act 711 or the inherent authority of the court).

In other instances, specifically where medical treatment is contemplated for an unborn child, it has been suggested that appointment of an advocate to represent the interests of the unborn child would be appropriate. See Clewell, et. al., A SURGICAL APPROACH TO THE TREATMENT OF FETAL HYDROCEPHALUS, 306 New England Journal of Medicine 1320 (1982). [As to a more detailed discussion of the preceding medical journal article and the issue of the appointment of an advocate in medical situations, see §5.61.]

Moreover, in one case, *Jefferson v Griffin Spalding Cty Memorial Hosp*, 274 SE2d 457 (Ga 1981), the court affirmed a trial court order that granted temporary custody of an unborn child to the state department of human resources and a county department of family and children services. In this case, the defendant-mother was unwilling to submit to medical procedures which would, possibly, save the life of her unborn child. The court said the department would have authority to make all decisions, including giving consent to surgical delivery if necessary, appertaining to the birth of the child. The order said temporary custody would terminate when the child was born or until the child died. [As to the unborn child's right to medical treatment in *Jefferson*, see §5.61.]

E. [§5.64] Posthumous Child's Right to Social Security Benefits

One purpose of the Social Security Act is to provide support to children who have lost either the actual support of an insured parent or the anticipated support which that parent would have been expected to give had his death not intervened. *Jiminez v Weinberger*, 417 US 628, 634, 94 SCt 2496, 41 LE2d 363 (1974). Thus, a posthumously born illegitimate child was entitled to his late father's social security survivor of benefits. The claimant had been denied benefits on the ground that a child's eligibility was based upon the father's regular and continuous support of the child. However, the appeals court reversed, observing that this test would prevent almost all posthumous children from qualifying. Support for an unborn child cannot be gauged on this basis. Rather, the test is whether the support by the father for the unborn child was commensurate with the needs of the child at the time of the father's death. Contributions made to the mother for food, medical care and other living expenses although indirect, are considered "support" for purposes of the Social Security Act. *Adams v Weinberger*, 521 F2d 656 (2d Cir 1975). See also, *Wagner v Finch*, 413 F2d 267 (5th Cir 1969); *Moreno v Richardson*, 484 F2d 899 (9th Cir 1973).

F. [§5.65] Posthumous Child's Right to Worker's Compensation Benefits

The rights of afterborn children of a deceased worker, i.e., those born after the compensated injury and before the injury-related death, are determined by the controlling state worker's compensation statutes. These laws, relating to, or affecting the status of the rights of the children of a deceased employee as dependents are ordinarily interpreted as including those born after the occurrence of the injury or death of the employee. Of paramount importance in the allocation of these benefits is the state law's definition of the terms "dependent" and/or "beneficiary." In some states, afterborn children are specifically mentioned as beneficiaries, at least when the mother was pregnant at the time of injury. However, where payment of compensation to dependents was contingent on the employee's earnings for support at the time of the accident, afterborn children have been denied compensation. *State ex rel Meaney v State Industrial Accident Comm*, 115 Or 484, 237 P 680 (1925); *Hatton Brown & Co v Holbrook*, 159 Va 224, 165 SE 403 (1932).

However, a child not conceived at the time of the injury was not considered a statutory dependent of the employee at the time of the injury, and as a result, was not entitled to death benefits. This rule even extends to death benefits to a worker's son who was almost 9 years old at his father's death. Because the injury occurred over ten years before, the afterborn son was denied death benefits. The issue of dependency was irrevocably fixed as of the date of the injury. *Ezell v Industrial Comm*, 23 Az Ct Ap 448, 533 P 1185 (1975). This reasoning was analogous to the rule holding that a widow not married to an employee at the time of his injury could not receive subsequent death benefits. See ARIZ REV STAT ANN §§23-1046(A) and 23-1046(A) (3). Similarly, a death benefit was paid to a deceased worker's parents, rather than to his posthumous illegitimate child. The crucial issue was not whether, at the time of his death, the father had an obligation to support the unborn child, but whether the unborn child fell within any of the several classifications of "dependency" within the Wisconsin Worker's

Compensation Act. At the time of the injury, the child could not be considered a "member of the family or a spouse, or a divorced spouse who has not remarried, or lineal descendant or ancestor, or brother or sister of the deceased employee." Although posthumously born, the respondent argued that on the date of the injury his father had an obligation to support him. The state supreme court disagreed and said that the respondent was not alive on the date of the injury. His future existence was obviously contingent on his being born alive. Until that occurrence there was no obligation to support because there was no being to be supported. *Larson v Wisconsin Dept of Industry*, 76 Wi2d 595, 252 NW2d 33, 45 (1977).

In contrast, the Alaska workers' compensation law (ALASKA STAT 23.30.265(4)) specifically recognizes the recovery right of a posthumous child, even though the father may have been unaware of the pregnancy at the time of his death. But Alaska adhered to the old English common law rule that a child en ventre sa mere is considered in existence if it is for the child's benefit. *S L W v Alaska Workmen's Compensation Bd*, 490 P2d 42 (Ak 1971). Likewise, a child conceived and born between the time of a welder's disabling heart attack and subsequent death was entitled to worker's compensation death benefits under New Jersey law. The term "dependency" by statute included those dependent upon the worker at the time of his death. *Close v Kordulak Bros*, 44 NJ 589, 210 A2d 753 (1965). See also, *Brown v Workmen's Compensation Appeal Bd*, 342 A2d 134 (Pa 1975).

A beneficiary need not be completely dependent to recover. Many state laws allow partial dependency for payment of benefits. It is difficult to calculate the benefits to a posthumous child under the worker's compensation formula providing for payments to one only partially dependent upon the decedent. Since there is no method of determining contributions for the support of the unborn, the statutory minimum has been awarded. *Fontenot v Annelida Acres, Inc*, 302 So2d 690, 697 (La 1974).

The right to workmen's compensation benefits also extends to unacknowledged, illegitimate afterborn children. A Louisiana law that excluded them from the class of "children" and relegated them to a lesser status of "other dependents" violated the Equal Protection Clause of the Fourteenth Amendment. The United States Supreme Court determined that the statutory classification did not bear a rational relationship to a legitimate state purpose. *Weber v Aetna Casualty & Surety Co*, 406 US 164, 92 SCt 1400, 31 LE2d 768 (1972).

CHAPTER 6

Prenatal Stage: Emerging Theories of Liability

I. WRONGFUL BIRTH

A. In General

1. [§6.1] Definition

Genetic counselors and physicians now, in some instances, have the ability to detect disorders and defects in unborn children because of recent significant advances in medical technology and genetic study. Therefore, in these instances, the parents of an unborn, and perhaps unconceived, child may have information prior to the child's birth or conception regarding the prospective health of the child. With this information available the parents are allowed the opportunity to make decisions about whether to utilize contraceptives, or to terminate a pregnancy if conception has previously taken place, if it appears that an unhealthy child will be born. Because of the advances in medical practice and genetic study, and the ensuing allegations of negligence in advising parents regarding the chances of healthy unborn or unconceived children, courts and legislatures have begun to address these allegations and the cause of action that embodies the allegations and is referred to as wrongful birth. [As to a more detailed discussion of the background of wrongful birth actions, see §6.2.]

Wrongful birth lawsuits are brought by the parents of a deformed or diseased child. The parents assert that they would have avoided conception or terminated the pregnancy had they been properly advised of the risk of giving birth to a potentially defective child. In essence the parents claim that the physician's, or genetic counselor's, negligence deprived them of the opportunity to make an informed decision about whether to have the child. COMMENT, TORTS—WRONGFUL BIRTH AND WRONGFUL LIFE, 8 Hofstra LR 257 (1979). The types of damages the parents seek include the expenses of caring for the child and for their own pain and suffering. See COMMENT, "WRONGFUL LIFE": THE RIGHT NOT TO BE BORN, 54 Tulane LR 480 (1980). Moreover, it has been said that the allowance of a parental cause of action for special damages in a wrongful birth case is consistent with established principles of damages. See *Turpin v Sortini*, 174 CaR 128, 119 CaA2d 690 (1981), rev on other grds, 31 CaA3d 220, 182 CaR 337, 643 P2d 954 (1982). It has been suggested that a claim for wrongful birth is not a new and distinct cause of action, but rather that the injury can be redressed through conventional tort principles. In *Phillips v United States*, 508 FSupp 544 (D SC 1981), the court said the increasing importance of medical procedures such as amniocentesis and their entry into the mainstream of accepted medical practices, as well as the sensitivity of the interests and issues involved, dictate that the plaintiffs' rights be afforded some protection, and that the most appropriate mechanism for this protection is the ancient, yet vital and constantly evolving doctrine of negligence.

Lawsuits brought by, or in behalf of, the deformed or diseased infant and arising from similar factual settings are referred to, by contrast, as wrongful life actions. It should be noted that in wrongful life actions the damages sought are those associated with the direct pain and suffering of the child, not the child's parents. See Peters and Peters, WRONGFUL LIFE: RECOGNIZING THE DEFECTIVE CHILD'S RIGHT TO A CAUSE OF ACTION, 18 Duquesne LR 857 (1980). [As to a more detailed discussion of wrongful life actions, see §6.13.] In many instances both wrongful birth and wrongful life actions are brought together or simultaneously because of injuries arising from the same factual setting. See, e.g., *Phillips v United States*, 508 FSupp

537 (D SC 1980); *Phillips v United States*, 508 FSupp 544 (D SC 1980); *Berman v Allan*, 80 NJ 421, 404 A2d 8 (1979).

Moreoever, wrongful birth cases should be distinguished from wrongful conception and wrongful pregnancy cases. Wrongful birth cases involve the birth of a planned, but unhealthy child who is born because of the defendant's alleged negligence in failing to properly or accurately advise the child's parents of the possibility that the child will be unhealthy, and thus denies the parents of the opportunity to make an informed decision about whether to conceive the child or whether to continue a pregnancy if conception has occurred. In wrongful conception cases, however, the parents argue that but for the negligence of the defendant the child would never have been conceived, or in wrongful pregnancy cases that the pregnancy would not have been continued, and the unplanned child would never have been born. See 54 Tulane LR 480. Therefore, wrongful pregnancy and wrongful conception actions involve a healthy, but unwanted child while wrongful birth actions involved planned children who are born in a diseased or deformed condition. See Rogers, WRONGFUL LIFE AND WRONGFUL BIRTH: MEDICAL MALPRACTICE IN GENETIC COUNSELING AND PRENATAL TESTING, 33 South Carolina LR 713 (1982). [As to a more detailed discussion of wrongful conception and wrongful pregnancy actions, see §3.8.]

Typically, wrongful birth claims arise from postconception negligence by a physician or genetic counselor. For example, wrongful birth actions have been recognized in cases involving the alleged negligent failure to advise the parents regarding the risks of pregnancy, and the possible birth of a deformed child, to an older woman [see *Becker v Schwartz*, 46 NY2d 401, 386 NE2d 807, 413 NYS2d 895 (1978)], the failure to inform a patient of the availability of amniocentesis [see *Berman v Allan*, 80 NJ 421, 404 A2d 8 (1979)], negligence in the performance of an amniocentesis [see *Gildiner v Thomas Jefferson University Hosp*, 451 FSupp 692 (ED Pa 1978)], negligent genetic counseling [see *Phillips v United States*, 508 FSupp 544 (D SC 1981)], failure to diagnose and/or warn of an inheritable disease [see *Moores v Lucas*, 405 So2d 1022 (Fl 1981)], failure to diagnose or advise the patient regarding rubella [see *Robak v United States*, 658 F2d 471 (7th Cir 1981); *Jacobs v Theimer*, 519 SW2d 846 (Tx 1975); *Dumer v St Michael's Hosp*, 69 Wi2d 766, 233 NW2d 372 (1975)], and negligence in failing to diagnose a hereditary disease in an earlier born child [see *Schroeder v Perkel*, 87 NJ 53, 432 A2d 834 (1981)].

2. [§6.2] Background

The first case to significantly address the issue of the right to maintain an action for wrongful birth [as to a definition of wrongful birth, see §6.1] was

Gleitman v Cosgrove, 49 NJ 22, 227 A2d 689 (1967). In *Gleitman*, the court refused to recognize as a valid cause of action a claim for wrongful birth put forth by the parents of an unhealthy infant. The wrongful birth prayer for relief was based on the allegation that had the physician treating the plaintiff-mother during her pregnancy followed standard medical practice, an abortion would have been procured and the child would never have come into existence. The court relied on two primary reasons for rejecting the wrongful birth cause of action. First, the court said in order to determine the parents' compensatory damages it would have to evaluate the denial to them of the intangible, immeasurable, and complex human benefits of motherhood and fatherhood and weigh these against the alleged emotional and monetary injuries. The court believed that such a weighing is impossible to perform. Second, the court concluded that substantial policy reasons precluded judicial allowance of the opportunity to take an embryonic life.

Subsequently, however, the courts that addressed the damages related and public policy objections to the recognition of wrongful birth actions disagreed with the rationale of the *Gleitman* decision [see, e.g., *Gildiner v Thomas Jefferson University Hosp*, 451 FSupp 692 (ED Pa 1978); *Phillips v United States*, 508 FSupp 544 (D SC 1981)], and even the court that decided *Gleitman* later questioned its decision and recognized a cause of action for wrongful birth in *Berman v Allan*, 80 NJ 421, 404 A2d 8 (1979). In reviewing its earlier decision, the *Berman* court said in light of the changes in the law which had occurred since *Gleitman* was decided, the policy reasons relating to preventing abortions can no longer stand in the way of judicial recognition of a cause of action founded on wrongful birth. The court noted that the United States Supreme Court's ruling in *Roe v Wade*, 410 US 113, 93 SCt 705, 35 LE2d 174 (1973), established that a woman possesses the constitutional right to decide whether her fetus should be aborted, at least during the first trimester of pregnancy. Therefore, the *Berman* court said public policy now supports, rather than militates against, the proposition that a woman not be impermissibly denied a meaningful opportunity to reach that decision. Moreover, the court said as in all other cases of tortious injury, a physician whose negligence has deprived a mother of this opportunity should be required to make amends for the damage which the physician has proximately caused. Any other ruling, the court reasoned, would in effect immunize from liability those in the medical field providing inadequate guidance to persons who would choose to exercise their constitutional right to abort fetuses which, if born, would suffer from genetic defects. In addition, the court said although the measure of damages was troublesome, to deny the plaintiff-parents redress for their injuries merely because damage cannot be measured with precise exactitude would constitute a perversion of fundamental principles of justice.

In addition, another court has said that a cause of action for damages arising from the denial of an opportunity to obtain an abortion is not contrary to public policy. The defendants in *Gildiner v Thomas Jefferson University Hosp*, 451 FSupp 692 (ED Pa 1978), argued that the recognition of a cause of action for damages arising from a denial of an opportunity to obtain an abortion could induce physicians to recommend the abortion of all marginally defective fetuses. However, the court believed that public policy actually supports the recognition of a cause of action for damages arising from negligence in the performance of testing for Tay-Sachs disease. The court believed that the value of genetic testing programs is based on the opportunity of parents to abort afflicted fetuses within appropriate time limitations. Society has an interest, the court reasoned, in insuring that genetic testing is properly performed and interpreted, and the failure to properly perform or interpret an amniocentesis could cause either the abortion of a healthy fetus, or the unwanted birth of a child afflicted with Tay-Sachs disease. Either of these occurrences would be contrary to public policy, the court said. The recognition of a cause of action for negligence in the performance of genetic testing would encourage the accurate performance of such testing by penalizing physicians who fail to observe customary standards of good medical practice, the court concluded. And in *Phillips v United States*, 508 FSupp 544 (D SC 1981), a case involving the birth of an unhealthy infant, the court said the plaintiff-parents' wrongful birth claim falls within the traditional boundaries of negligence, and that the essential elements of duty, breach, proximate cause, and damages are undeniably present. The court believed that the increasing importance of medical procedures such as amniocentesis and their entry into the mainstream of accepted medical practices, as well as the extreme sensitivity of these issues and interests involved, dictate that the plaintiff-parents' rights be afforded some protection. The most appropriate mechanism for this protection, the court reasoned, is the ancient, yet vital and constantly evolving doctrine of negligence. The court said that the plaintiffs' wrongful birth claim does not state a new and distinct cause of action, but rather their injury can be redressed through conventional tort principles, and thus the resolution of these issues does not infringe on a legislative prerogative since the determination of the common law doctrine of negligence is within the province of the judiciary.

Moreover, it has been recognized that the recovery of damages by the parents in wrongful birth cases is appropriate. [As to damages generally in wrongful birth actions, see §6.7.] It has been held that costs for care and treatment of children with Down's Syndrome born as a consequence of physicians' tortious conduct are recoverable [see *Becker v Schwartz*, 46 NY2d 401, 386 NE2d 807, 413 NYS2d 895 (1978)] and that parents may recover for the emotional pain caused by a child born with Tay-Sachs disease which was not properly diagnosed by a physician's amniocentesis report [see *Gildiner v Thomas Jefferson University Hosp*, 451 FSupp 692 (ED Pa 1978)].

The issue of whether to recognize wrongful birth actions has also received legislative attention. The measures that have been enacted thus far have sought to limit or proscribe, the recognition of actions based on wrongful birth. For example, 1982 MINN LAWS, Ch. 521, is an act relating to tort actions involving wrongful birth allegations. The act states that no person shall maintain a cause of action or receive an award of damages on the claim that but for the negligence of another, a child would have been aborted. In addition, SD CODIFIED LAWS ANN §21-55-2 (Smith 1981 Supp) states that there shall be no cause of action or award of damages on behalf of any person based on the claim that but for the negligence of another, a person should not have been permitted to have been born alive. [As to a more detailed discussion of the statutory response to wrongful birth actions, see §6.3.]

For further background on wrongful birth actions, and issues arising in wrongful birth actions, see the following medical and law journal articles: Capron, TORT LIABILITY IN GENETIC COUNSELING, 79 Columbia Law Review 618 (1979); Chapman, WHAT ARE YOUR ODDS IN THE PRENATAL GAMBLE, Legal Aspects of Medical Practice 31 (1979); Feinman, GETTING ALONG WITH THE GENETIC GENIE, Legal Aspects of Medical Practice 38 (1979); Friedman, LEGAL IMPLICATIONS OF AMNIOCENTESIS, 123 University of Pennsylvania LR 92 (1974); Goodner, PRENATAL GENETIC DIAGNOSIS: PRESENT AND FUTURE, 19 Clinical Obstetrics and Gynecology 965 (1976); Kass and Shaw, THE RISK OF BIRTH DEFECTS: JACOBS v. THEIMER AND PARENTS' RIGHT TO KNOW, 2 American Journal of Law and Medicine 213 (1977); Milunsky and Reilly, THE "NEW" GENETICS: EMERGING MEDICOLEGAL ISSUES IN THE PRENATAL DIAGNOSIS OF HEREDITARY DISORDERS, 1 American Journal of Law and Medicine 71, 76 (1975); Nadler and Gerbie, PRESENT STATUS OF AMNIOCENTESIS IN UTERINE DIAGNOSIS OF GENETIC DEFECTS, 38 Obstetrics and Gynecology 789 (1971); Reilly, GENETIC COUNSELING AND THE LAW, 12 Houston LR 640 (1975); Saul et al., AMNIOCENTESIS AND PRENATAL DIAGNOSIS IN SOUTH CAROLINA: A COLLABORATIVE REPORT FOR THE YEARS 1976 TO 1979, 76 Journal of South Carolina Medicine 387 (1980); Shaw, GENETICALLY DEFECTIVE CHILDREN: EMERGING LEGAL CONSIDERATIONS, 3 American Journal of Law and Medicine 333 (1977); FATHER AND MOTHER KNOW BEST: DEFINING THE LIABILITY OF PHYSICIANS FOR INADEQUATE GENETIC COUNSELING, 87 Yale Law Journal 1488 (1978); GENETICALLY DEFECTIVE CHILDREN: EMERGING LEGAL CONSIDERATIONS, 5 American Journal of Law and Medicine 333 (1977); WRONGFUL BIRTH DAMAGES: MANDATE AND MISHANDLING BY JUDICIAL FIAT, 13 Valparaiso LR 127 (1978); WRONGFUL BIRTH: JUDICIAL RETICENCE WITH AN EMERGING TORT: THE NEGLIGENT PERFORMANCE OF GENETIC COUNSELING, 6 University of Dayton LR 115 (1981); WRONGFUL LIFE AND WRONGFUL BIRTH CAUSES OF ACTION – SUGGESTIONS FOR A CONSISTENT ANALYSIS, 63 Marquette LR 611 (1980); National Registry for

Amniocentesis Study Group, MIDTRIMESTER AMNIOCENTESIS FOR PRENATAL DIAGNOSIS: SAFETY AND ACCURACY, 236 Journal of the American Medical Association 1471 (1976).

3. [§6.3] Statutory Limitation or Denial of Cause of Action

In addition to the judicial response to wrongful birth actions [generally see §6.4-§6.11] there has also been recent legislative action in a few states. The purpose of these statutory enactments has been to proscribe the recognition of a cause of action for wrongful birth. The following statutes have been enacted to resolve the issue of the recognition of a cause of action for wrongful birth in the negative:

> 1982 MINN LAWS, Ch. 521
> Subd. 2 [Wrongful Birth Action Prohibited] No person shall maintain a cause of action or receive an award of damages on the claim that but for the negligent conduct of another, a child would have been aborted.
> SD CODIFIED LAWS ANN
> 21-55-2. Action or damages for birth of another prohibited. There shall be no cause of action or award of damages on behalf of any person based on the claim that, but for the conduct of another, a person would not have been permitted to have been born alive.
> Source: SL 1981, ch 172, §2.
> 21-55-3. Consideration of failure to prevent live birth restricted in actions. The failure or the refusal of any person to prevent the live birth of a person is not a defense in any action.
> Source: SL 1981, ch 173, §3.
> 21-55-4. Limited effect of chapter. The provisions of this chapter do not prohibit a cause of action or the awarding of damages, except as specifically provided in this chapter, by or on behalf of any person based on the claim that a person is liable for injury caused by such person's willful acts or caused by such person's want of ordinary care or skill.
> Source: SL 1981, ch 172, §4.

B. Elements of Cause of Action

1. [§6.4] Generally

In wrongful birth [as to a definition of wrongful birth, see §6.1] actions based on tort it is necessary to plead and establish the elements of duty [as to a more detailed discussion of duty in wrongful birth actions, see §6.5], breach, proximate cause [as to a more detailed discussion of proximate cause in wrongful birth actions, see §6.6], and damages. See *Phillips v United States*, 508 FSupp 544 (D SC 1981). The duty element may include the duty of a physician to inquire whether a woman, who appeared to have a rubella-like rash, was pregnant [see *Dumer v St Michael's Hosp*, 69 Wi2d 766, 233 NW2d 372 (1975)], or the duty to advise parents of a previously born infant that that infant had an hereditary disease so that the parents could make an informed decision whether to have future children. See *Schroeder v Perkel*, 87 NJ 53, 432 A2d 834 (1981). In addition, it has been held that proximate cause will be established if it can be established that had the parents been fully informed about the possibility of birth of an unhealthy infant they would have terminated the pregnancy. That showing would be essential for a causal connection between the defendant's failure to inform and the plaintiffs' damages. See *Jacobs v Theimer*, 519 SW2d 846 (Tx 1975). The element of actionable injury, meaning direct rather than indirect injury, has been held to exist in a wrongful birth case where an erroneous disease report deprived the plaintiff-mother, and derivatively her husband, of the opportunity to accept or reject her continued pregnancy and the birth of a fatally defective child. See *Naccash v Burger*, 290 SE2d 825 (Va 1982).

2. [§6.5] Duty

In a tort action based on wrongful birth [as to a definition of wrongful birth, see §6.1] it is necessary to plead and prove the essential elements of a traditional negligence action which are duty, breach, proximate cause [as to a more detailed discussion of the proximate cause element in a wrongful birth action, see §6.6], and damages. See *Phillips v United States*, 508 FSupp 544 (D SC 1981). Essential to a recognition of a cause of action for wrongful birth is the existence of a duty owed to the plaintiff-parents. See *Naccash v Burger*, 290 SE2d 825 (Va 1982). In the context of wrongful birth actions, it has been held that a physician has a duty to inquire whether a woman, who appeared to have a rubella-like rash, was pregnant [see *Dumer v St Michael's Hosp*, 69 Wi2d 766, 233 NW2d 372 (1975)], that a physician's duty may extend beyond the interests of an infant-patient, who he negligently diagnosed as not having an hereditary ailment, to members of the patient's family who were adversely affected by the birth of another unhealthy child [see *Schroeder v Perkel*, 87 NJ 53, 432 A2d 834 (1981)], and that a physician has a duty to disclose his or her diagnosis and inform a mother of the risks involved in continuing her pregnancy [see *Eisbrenner v Stanley*, 106 MiA 357, 308 NW2d 290 (1981)].

In *Dumer*, the plaintiff-mother sought treatment for an upper body rash. She suggested to the defendant-physician that she thought her condition was rubella. However, the physician negligently diagnosed her condition as an allergic reaction and discharged her. At this time the plaintiff had been pregnant for about one month. Later a child afflicted with rubella-syndrome was born to the plaintiff-mother. The plaintiffs, the mother and her parents, alleged that as a result of the negligent diagnosis by the defendants and their failure to advise the mother of the possible effects of rubella on the fetus and of the possibility of abortion, the infant was not aborted, to the financial injury of the parents. The court concluded that the defendant-physician was negligent in not diagnosing the mother's condition as rubella. Moreover, the court concluded that the physician had a duty to inquire as to whether the mother was pregnant and, if she was, to inform her of the probable effects of rubella on the fetus, including its irreversible nature. In *Schroeder*, the plaintiff-parents alleged that the negligent failure of the defendants to diagnose cystic fibrosis, an hereditary disease, in their first child deprived them of an informed choice whether to have a second child. A second child was born, and this child was also afflicted with the disease. The defendants contended that the first child was their patient, and that their duty was to her, not her parents, and thus if the defendants had no duty to the plaintiff-parents the defendants could not be liable for depriving the parents of the decision not to have another child. However, the court disagreed and said the contention of the defendant-physicians took a myopic view of the responsibility of a physician treating a child with a genetically transferable disease such as cystic fibrosis. The scope of the duty in negligence, except as limited by policy considerations, is coextensive with the reasonable foreseeability of the consequences of a negligent act, the court said. The foreseeability of injury to members of a family other than one immediately injured by the wrongdoing of another must be viewed in light of the legal relationships among family members, the court reasoned. A family is woven of the fibers of life and if one strand is damaged, the entire structure may suffer, the court said, and thus the filaments of life, although individually spun, create a web of interconnected legal interests. Moreover, the court believed the foreseeability of harm to parents from an injury to a child flows not only from the bonds between parent and child, but also from the responsibility of the parents to provide medical care for their children. And in *Naccash v Burger*, 290 SE2d 825 (Va 1982), the plaintiffs alleged that the defendants had negligently failed to discover that the fetus carried by the plaintiff-mother was afflicted with an incurable genetic disorder, and thus the plaintiffs had decided to forego an abortion and carry the child to term. Subsequently, an unhealthy child was born. The court said when the plaintiffs presented themselves for genetic testing they were owed the duty of reasonable care in the handling of the blood withdrawn for the tests, and this duty encompassed the obligation to provide the plaintiffs with accurate information concerning the condition of their unborn child so they could make an informed decision regarding abortion. However, it has been held that a doctor is not negligent in failing to advise a woman carrying a potentially diseased fetus of the availability of an abortion because the doctor does not have a legal duty to so advise the woman where there is no question as to the life or health of the mother. Whether the woman should seek and submit to an abortion is in the first instance a moral decision of the parents uninfluenced by the physician. See *Dumer v St Michael's Hosp*, 69 Wi2d 766, 233 NW2d 372 (1975).

3. [§6.6] Proximate Cause

It is necessary to plead and prove the essential elements of a traditional negligence action in a tort action based on wrongful birth. [As to a definition of wrongful birth, see §6.1]. These elements include proximate cause as well as duty [as to a more detailed discussion of the element of duty in a wrongful birth context, see §6.5], breach, and damage. See *Phillips v United States* 508 FSupp 544 (D SC 1981). Essentially the plaintiff-parents argue not that the defendant's negligence caused the injury to the resulting unhealthy infant, but that the negligence was the proximate cause of the plaintiffs' inability to make an informed decision whether to have the child. COMMENT, TORTS WRONGFUL BIRTH AND WRONGFUL LIFE, 8 Hofstra LR 257 (1979). Moreover, the plaintiffs must prove that the pregnancy would have been ended in order to establish proximate cause since that showing would be essential for a causal connection between the defendant's failure to inform, or diagnose, and the plaintiffs' damages. See *Jacobs v Theimer*, 519 SW2d 846 (Tx 1975).

The defendants, in some wrongful birth cases, contend that no proximate cause exists because irrevocable injury to the fetus has already taken place before the negligent acts are committed. But courts have disagreed and held that a negligent act need not be the sole cause of the injury complained of in order to be a proximate cause of that injury, and if the defendant had not breached its duty to the plaintiff-mother she would have obtained an abortion and therefore the defendant's negligence was a proximate cause of the injury. For example, in *Robak v United States*, 658 F2d 471 (7th Cir 1981), an unhealthy infant was born to the plaintiffs following the negligent performance of an amniocentesis test on the mother which indicated that the plaintiff-mother did not suffer rubella during the pregnancy with the infant. Subsequently an accurate performance of the test which indicated rubella was completed, but the plaintiff-mother was not advised of the result. The court noted that once the plaintiff-mother was infected by the rubella virus the harm to the fetus had already been done. But, the court said, a negligent act need not be the sole cause of the injury to meet the proximate cause requirement. Moreover, the cause of action was not based on the injuries to the fetus but on the defendant's failure to diagnose the plaintiff-mother's rubella and inform her of the consequences, the court said. If the defendant had not breached its duty to the plaintiff-mother, she would have had a legal abortion that would have saved the plaintiffs the damages they incurred, the court said. Thus, the defendant's negligence was, the court concluded, a proximate cause of their injuries. In *Gildiner v Thomas Jefferson University Hosp*, 451 FSupp 692 (ED Pa 1978), it was alleged that the plaintiff-parents were assured after the performance of an amniocentesis that their child would not have Tay-Sachs disease, but that subsequently the infant was born afflicted with the disease. The court held that the relevant causal relationship was that between the defendant's negligence in performing or interpreting the amniocentesis and the subsequent birth of the child. The complaint stated a sufficient causal relationship between the alleged negligence of the defendants and the failure of the plaintiffs to obtain an abortion to defeat a motion for judgment on the pleadings based on a lack of proximate cause, the court said. And in *Eisbrenner v Stanley* 106 Mi 351, 308 NW2d 209 (1981), an infant was born in a severely deformed condition after the defendant-physician had allegedly negligently failed to diagnose rubella in the plaintiff-mother during the pregnancy. The defendant argued the element of proximate cause was missing because his alleged negligence did not cause the child's abnormalities and no treatment existed which could have prevented the abnormalities. But the court disagreed and said the defendant's argument misconstrued the plaintiffs' theory because the parents claimed that because the defendant breached his duty to render proper medical treatment, they were deprived of information which would have led them to terminate the pregnancy at a stage where abortion was legal. From the parents point of view, the child was born and lived as a result of the defendant's negligence, and the court therefore believed that the plaintiffs properly alleged proximate cause.

C. Damages

1. [§6.7] Generally

Elements of damages sought in wrongful birth [as to a definition of wrongful birth actions, see §6.1] cases have typically been costs for the care and treatment of the child [generally, see §6.8] and damages for the plaintiff-parents' emotional suffering and distress [generally, see §6.10]. Recovery for damages associated with the care and treatment of the unhealthy infant has been held to be recoverable in wrongful birth actions. See, e.g., *Becker v Schwartz*, 46 NY2d 401, 386 NE2d 807, 413 NYS2d 895 (1978); *Schroeder v Perkel*, 87 NJ 53, 432 A2d 834 (1981); *Jacobs v Theimer*, 519 SW2d 846 (Tx 1975). However, there is disagreement among the courts regarding the ability to recover damages associated with the plaintiff-parents' emotional distress in giving birth to an unhealthy child. It has been held that such a recovery of damages is an appropriate measure of the harm suffered by the plaintiff-parents deriving from the plaintiff-mother's loss of the right to abort the fetus. See *Berman v Allan*, 80 NJ 421, 404 A2d 8 (1979). But it has also been held that such a damages award is too speculative because of the difficulty in measuring emotional loss, and thus recovery for emotional distress should be denied. See *Jacobs v Theimer*, 519 SW2d 846 (Tx 1975). In one instance, where recovery was allowed both for the costs of care and treatment and emotional distress the benefit rule was applied in measuring the damages suffered. In *Eisbrenner v Stanley*, 106 MiA 351, 308 NW2d 290 (1981), the court held that the benefit rule should be applied in mitigation of damages in a wrongful birth action brought by the plaintiff-parents. The court cited its earlier decision in *Troppi v Scarf*, 31 MiA 240, 187 NW2d 511, leave den, 385 Mi 753 (1971), a wrongful pregnancy case, in which the court had applied the RESTATEMENT (SECOND) OF TORTS §920 (1977), the benefit rule. In *Troppi*, the court indicated that the damages awarded should be determined under the benefit rule, whereby any benefit to the plaintiff resulting from the defendant's tortious conduct would be considered in mitigation of damages. The *Troppi* decision supported the allowance of damages for mental distress in the present case, the *Eisbrenner* court said, and it said that the benefit rule should be applied in similar future cases.

2. [§6.8] Care and Treatment

In wrongful birth [as to a definition of wrongful birth, see §6.1] actions one of the types of damages that has been sought and recovered by the plaintiff-parents relates to the cost of caring for and treating the unhealthy infant [as to other damages sought by the plaintiff-parents, see §6.7]. Damages for the cost of caring for and treating the infant have been held to be within methods of proof by which courts are accustomed to determine awards in personal injury cases. See *Jacobs v Theimer*, 519 SW2d 846 (Tx 1975). The pecuniary expenses sought by the plaintiff-parents for the expenses they bear for care and treatment are ascertainable. Calculation of pecuniary damages necessary to make the plaintiff-parents whole in relation to these expenditures requires nothing extraordinary. See *Becker v Schwartz*, 46 NY2d 406, 386 NE2d 807, 413 NYS2d 895 (1978). Moreover, the awarding of this type of damages is not against public policy because it is impossible to justify a policy which at once would deprive parents of information by which they could elect to terminate a pregnancy likely to produce an infant with a defective body, a policy which would require that a deficient embryo be carried to full gestation until the infant is born, but would then deny recovery from the tortfeasor of the cost of treating and caring for the defects of the child. See *Jacobs*, above. In limiting damage recovery to those expenses actually attributable to the infant's affliction a windfall is not being conferred on the plaintiff-parents, one court has said. In *Schroeder v Perkel*, 87 NJ 53, 432 A2d 834 (1981), the court said although the plaintiff-parents might derive some pleasure from their infant, that pleasure would be derived in spite of, rather than because of, the infant's affliction, and that the plaintiff-parents would receive no compensating pleasure from incurring the extraordinary expenses on behalf of their infant. And the *Schroeder* court noted that although the infant actually had the primary obligation to pay for his own medical expenses, a wrong should not go unrequited and an entire family left to suffer because of this technicality. One of the types of care and treatment items that is recoverable is past and future medical expenses. See *Gildiner v Thomas Jefferson University Hosp*, 451 FSupp 692 (ED Pa 1978); *Moores v Lucas*, 405 So2d 1022 (Fl 1981); *Eisbrenner v Stanley*, 106 MiA 357, 308 NW2d 209 (1981); *Schroeder v Perkel*, 87 NJ 53, 432 A2d 834 (1981); *Dumer v St Michael's Hosp*, 69 Wi2d 766, 233 NW2d 372 (1975). In *Schroeder*, the court said it would be unreasonable to compel parents to bear the expense of medical treatment required by the infant and to allow the wrongdoer to go free. Other types of care and treatment expenses that have been held to be recoverable have included the cost of residential education and care during the infant's minority, the cost of a qualified companion, the cost of maintaining the infant for the infant's adult life [see *Robak v United States*, 658 F2d 471 (7th Cir 1981)], and the cost of daily therapy for the infant [see *Schroeder v Perkel*, 87 NJ 53, 432 NY2d 834 (1981)].

The damages for the care and treatment of an infant in a wrongful birth action may be limited to expenses which the plaintiff-parents have reasonably and necessarily suffered, and will to a reasonable medical certainty suffer in the future by reason of the additional medical, hospital and supportive expenses occasioned by the deformities of the infant as contrasted to a normal, healthy child. See *Dumer v St Michael's Hosp*, 69 Wi2d 766, 233 NW2d 372 (1975). Moreover, the expenses relating to the care and treatment of the child must not be reduced by the costs of raising a normal child since the plaintiff-parents would not have had to bear them but for the defendant's negligence. See *Robak v United States*, 658 F2d 471 (7th Cir 1981). [As to the application of these general damages principles relating to care and treatment in specific wrongful birth cases, see §6.9.]

3. [§6.9] —Illustrative Cases

The following cases are illustrative of the general principles relating to recovery of damages in wrongful birth cases for costs of the care and treatment of the infants. [Generally, see §6.8.] In these cases recovery was permitted:

In *Robak v United States*, 658 F2d 471 (7th Cir 1981), the court held as recoverable the cost of maintaining a rubella afflicted infant for her adult life because, the court said, she would never be self-supporting. In *Robak*, the plaintiff-parents brought a medical malpractice action against the United States pursuant to the Federal Tort Claims Act alleging that a military clinic negligently failed to diagnose the plaintiff-mother's rubella and to inform the parents of its possible consequences to the fetus. At the conclusion of the trial, the trial court ruled in favor of the plaintiffs and later awarded $900,000 in damages to the plaintiffs, $450,000 to each of the plaintiff-parents. The court divided the recovery between the parents reasoning that both parents are equally and separately liable under the law for the child's maintenance during her minority and impaired adulthood. In affirming the right of the plaintiff-parents to recover damages for maintenance costs, the court noted that the plaintiffs had shown damages of at least $900,000. The court noted that the trial court had awarded the damages for the special costs the plaintiffs would incur in maintaining their rubella syndrome child. However, the court noted that the district court had reduced these damages by an unspecified amount for what the district court considered to be the cost of raising and supporting a normal child. The court disagreed with that holding. This action for wrongful birth is not based upon the injuries to the child, the court said. If it was, the court reasoned, then no recovery at all would be possible, for those injuries occurred as soon as the plaintiff-mother contracted rubella, before the negligent acts of the clinic staff. Rather, the court said, the action was based on the negligent failure by the staff to diagnose the rubella and inform the plaintiff-mother of it. If they had not breached their duty, Mrs. Robak would have obtained an abortion, the court said. The child's birth, and all expenses resulting therefrom, were thus the proximate result of the defendants' negligence. These expenditures must include the costs of raising a normal child, for the Robaks would not have had to bear them but for the defendants' negligence, the court said. These costs included past expenses, the cost of residential education and care to age 21, discounted to present value, the cost of a qualified companion, skilled in sign language and experienced in dealing with emotionally disturbed persons, for the remainder of the child's adult life, or comparable institutional care, and the cost of maintaining her for her adult life, since she would never be self-supporting, the court concluded.

In *Schroeder v Perkel*, 87 NJ 53, 432 A2d 834 (1981), the court said that the normal measure of damages for the commission of a tort is all damages proximately caused by the injury. However, the application of that standard has perplexed courts where the tort results in the birth of an afflicted child, the court noted. The court cited an earlier decision, *Berman v*

Allan, 80 NJ 421, 404 A2d 8 (1979), in which it had denied recovery for the ordinary costs of raising and educating a child who was born in a diseased condition. The court noted that in the *Berman* case the child had been born with Down's Syndrome, and the parents sought recovery for the ordinary costs of raising and educating their child. The damages sought by Mr. and Mrs. Schroeder, by contrast, were the medical, hospital, and pharmaceutical expenses needed for their son's survival. The court said that these kinds of expenses, regularly measured by the courts, included the prescription of enzymes and antibiotics, check-ups every one or two months, and hospitalization, which typically occurs only in emergencies or towards the end of the life of the victim. The court noted that the parents also intended to seek recovery for the cost of daily therapy for their son. The cost of such therapy was recoverable, the court noted, but added that at the trial the plaintiffs must prove the probability not only of the need and cost of therapy, but that it would be rendered by someone other than themselves. By limiting damages to those expenses that were actually attributable to the affliction, the court said it was not conferring a windfall on Mr. and Mrs. Schroeder. Although they may derive some pleasure from their son, that pleasure would be derived in spite of, rather than because of, his affliction. Mr. and Mrs. Schroeder would receive no compensating pleasure from incurring extraordinary medical expenses on behalf of their son, the court said. In *Schroeder*, the plaintiff-parents of two children born with cystic fibrosis brought action on behalf of themselves against the defendant-physicians who treated the first-born child and allegedly negligently failed to diagnose her condition in time to prevent the second pregnancy or to timely abort it.

In *Becker v Schwartz*, 46 NY2d 401, 413 NYS2d 895, 386 NE2d 807 (1978), the court held that the pecuniary expenses for the care and treatment of impaired infants sought as damages by the plaintiff-parents were ascertainable. The *Becker* decision consolidated two lower court decisions, *Becker v Schwartz*, 60 AD2d 587, 400 NYS2d 119 (1977), and *Park v Chessin*, 60 AD2d 80, 400 NYS2d 110 (1977), in which the plaintiff-parents of impaired infants alleged actions based on negligence against the defendant-physicians for failing to inform the parents accurately of risks involved in the respective pregnancies, resulting in the parents' decisions to conceive or not to terminate the pregnancy. The court believed the plaintiff-parents' causes of action, founded essentially upon a theory of negligence or medical malpractice, did allege ascertainable damages: the pecuniary expense which they had borne and in *Becker* continued to bear, for the care and treatment of their infants. Assuming the validity of the plaintiffs' allegations, the court said in traditional tort language that but for the defendants' breach of their duty to advise the plaintiffs, the latter would not have been required to assume these obligations. Calculation of damages necessary to make the plaintiffs whole in relation to these expenditures requires nothing extraordinary, the court said. However, the court said, there was no occasion, in passing on the sufficiency of the complaints to state a cause of action, to determine with particularity what items of expense or loss could be properly taken into account in computation of the damages recoverable.

In *Jacobs v Theimer*, 519 SW2d 846 (Tx 1975), the court said the economic burden related to the physical defects of the plaintiff-parents' child created expenses which are within the methods of proof by which the courts are accustomed to determine awards of personal injury cases. The plaintiff-parents had alleged that the defendant-physician had misdiagnosed Mrs. Jacobs' rubella condition, and that subsequently a rubella afflicted child was born to the plaintiffs. In addition, the court said no public policy obstacle should be interposed between the plaintiff-parents and their recovery. The court said it was impossible to justify a policy which at once would deprive parents of information by which they could elect to terminate a pregnancy likely to produce a child with a defective body, a policy which in effect would require that the deficient embryo be carried to full gestation until the deficient child is born, and then would deny recovery from the tortfeasor of the cost of treating and caring for the defects of the child. However, the court said that recovery would be limited to expenses reasonably necessary for the care and treatment of the child's physical impairment due to Mrs. Jacobs having contracted rubella. The court said it did not have before it further issues upon the measure of damages such as the period of time for which future expenses are recoverable or the offsetting costs of legal abortion and therefore those issues were not addressed.

In *Dumer v St Michael's Hosp*, 69 Wi2d 766, 233 NW2d 372 (1975), the court held that damages would be recoverable for the losses the plaintiff-parents had sustained because of the deformity and defects of the child who was born following the allegedly negligent diagnosis by the defendant-physicians of the plaintiff-mother's condition of rubella and their corresponding failure to advise the plaintiff-mother of the possible effects of rubella on the fetus and of the possibility of abortion. However, the court said that the damages must be limited to those expenses which the plaintiff-parents had reasonably and necessarily suffered, and would to a reasonable medical certainty suffer in the future by reason of the additional medical, hospital, and supportive expenses occasioned by the deformities of the child as contrasted to a normal, healthy child.

4. [§6.10] Emotional Distress

In wrongful birth [as to a definition of wrongful birth, see §6.1] actions one of the types of damages that has been sought by the plaintiff-parents has related to the emotional distress suffered by them. [As to other damages recoverable in wrongful birth actions by the plaintiff-parents, see §6.7.] Some courts have allowed recovery of damages related to emotional distress [see, e.g., *Eisbrenner v Stanley*, 106 MiA 351, 308 NW2d 209 (1981); *Berman v Allan*, 80 NJ 421, 404 A2d 8 (1979); *Naccash v Burger*, 290 SE2d 825 (Va 1982)] while others have rejected the inclusion of damages for emotional distress in wrongful birth actions [see, e.g., *Moores v Lucas*, 405 So2d 1022 (Fl 1981); *Becker v Schwartz*, 46 NY2d 401, 386 NE2d 807, 413 NYS2d 895 (1978)].

Where recovery for the emotional distress suffered by the parents has been allowed it has been said that the monetary equivalent of this distress is an appropriate measure of the harm suffered by the plaintiff-parents deriving from the plaintiff-mother's loss of the right to abort the fetus. Moreover, placing a monetary value upon emotional suffering of the plaintiff-parents is not an impossible task. Mental and emotional distress is just as real as physical pain, and its valuation is no more difficult. See *Berman v Allan*, 80 NJ 421, 404 A2d 8 (1979). Moreover, it has been noted that although emotional damages are not recoverable unless they result directly from tortiously caused physical injury there are exceptions to the general rule. However, where there is no suggestion that the plaintiff-parents' emotional distress was feigned or that their claim was fraudulent to go ahead and apply the general rule would constitute a perversion of fundamental principles of justice. See *Naccash v Burger*, 290 SE2d 825 (Va 1982).

However, recovery for emotional distress in wrongful birth cases has not been universal. Such a damages award may be too speculative because of the difficulty in determining the pluses and minuses of parental mind and emotion. See *Jacobs v Theimer*, 519 SW2d 846 (Tx 1975). And regardless of an infant's abnormality parents may still experience a love for the infant that even an abnormality cannot dampen. See *Becker v Schwartz*, 46 NY2d 401, 413 NYS2d 895, 386 NE2d 807 (1978). Moreover, the claim for the plaintiff-parents emotional distress has been denied based on the impact doctrine which provides that where no impact has taken place to the plaintiffs no recovery can be granted to them for physical injury resulting from emotional distress caused by negligent conduct. See *Moores v Lucas*, 405 So2d 1022 (Fl 1981). [As to application of these general damages principles relating to emotional distress in specific wrongful birth cases, see §6.11.]

5. [§6.11] —Illustrative Cases

The following cases are illustrative of the general principles relating to recovery of damages in wrongful birth cases for emotional suffering and distress. [Generally, see §6.10.] In these cases recovery was permitted:

In *Eisbrenner v Stanley*, 106 MiA 351, 308 NW2d 209 (1981), the court held that damages were properly recoverable for mental distress in a wrongful birth action. In *Eisbrenner* the plaintiff-parents brought a medical malpractice action against the defendant-physician following the birth of their severely deformed child. The plaintiffs alleged that their child was born in a severely deformed state because the child's mother contracted rubella during pregnancy, and that the defendant-physician negligently failed to diagnose the plaintiff-mother's rubella or advise the parents of the possible consequences on the health of the fetus. The court, however, indicated that any damages awarded in the case, including damages for emotional distress, should be determined under the benefit rule, whereby any benefit to the plaintiff resulting from the defendant's tortious conduct is considered in mitigation of damages. In the future, the court said, the allowance of damages for mental distress would be appropriate and the benefits rule should be applied.

In *Berman v Allan*, 80 NJ 421, 404 A2d 8 (1979), the plaintiff-parents brought a medical malpractice action against the defendant-physicians. The plaintiff-parents alleged that the defendant-physicians deviated from accepted medical standards by failing to inform the plaintiff-mother during her pregnancy of the existence of a procedure known as amniocentesis. Subsequently, the plaintiff-mother gave birth to a child who was afflicted with Down's Syndrome. The court held that should the plaintiffs' allegations of negligence be proven at trial, they were entitled to be recompensed for the mental and emotional anguish they had suffered and would continue to suffer on account of their child's condition. In failing to inform the plaintiff-mother of the availability of amniocentesis, the defendant-physician directly deprived her and, derivatively, her husband of the option to accept or reject a parental relationship with the child and thus caused them to experience mental and emotional anguish upon their realization that they had given birth to a child afflicted with Down's Syndrome. The court said that the monetary equivalent of this distress was an appropriate measure of the harm suffered by the parents deriving from the plaintiff-mother's loss of her right to abort the fetus. The court said that placing a monetary value upon the emotional suffering that the plaintiff-parents had and would continue to experience was not an impossible task for the trier of fact. The court noted that mental and emotional distress was just as real as physical pain, and that its valuation was not more difficult. Moreover, the court said that to deny the plaintiff-parents redress for their injuries merely because damages cannot be measured with precise exactitude would constitute a perversion of fundamental principles of justice.

In *Naccash v Burger*, 290 SE2d 825 (Va 1982) the court said that as a general rule damages for emotional distress are not recoverable unless they directly result from tortiously caused physical injury. However, the court noted that there are exceptions to this general rule. For example, the court said in *Hughes v Moore*, 214 Va 27, 197 SE2d 214 (1973), it held that where the claim is for emotional distress and physical injury resulting therefrom, recovery is permissible notwithstanding the lack of physical impact, providing there is shown by clear and convincing evidence an unbroken chain of causal connection between the negligent act, the emotional disturbance, and the physical injury. And in *Womack v Eldridge*, 215 Va 338, 210 SE2d 145 (1974), the court held that emotional distress resulting directly from a nontactile tort may be compensable, provided four elements are shown: (1) that the tort is intentional or reckless; (2) that the tortfeasor's conduct is outrageous and intolerable; (3) that the wrongful conduct and emotional distress are causally connected; and (4) that the emotional distress is severe. The defendant in *Naccash* contended that the plaintiff-parents had not brought their claim for emotional damages within the rationale of either *Hughes* or *Womack*. The defendant argued that the plaintiffs had proven neither physical injury resulting from emotional distress nor emotional distress resulting from intentional or reckless conduct. Therefore, the defendant maintained, the parents' entire claim rested on their witnessing the birth, suffering, and the death of their child, and that any injury to the parents was indirect rather than direct. The court believed, however, that the circumstances of this case justified another exception to the general rule that damages for emotional distress are not allowable unless they result directly from tortiously caused physical injury. The restrictions upon recovery imposed by the provisos in *Hughes* and *Womack* were designed to discourage spurious claims asserted by chance witnesses to physical torts involving others, the court said. The considerations prompting imposition of the limitations do not exist here; no one suggests that the plaintiffs' emotional distress was feigned or that their claim was fraudulent, the court said. Indeed, to apply the restrictions here, or to refuse to recognize an exception to the general rule, would constitute a perversion of fundamental principles of justice. Furthermore, the court believed it would be wholly unrealistic to say that the plaintiff-parents were mere witnesses to the consequences of the tortious conduct involved in this case. In the court's view, the parents' emotional distress was no less a direct result of wrongful conduct than the distress endured by the plaintiffs in *Hughes* or in *Womack*; the evidence showed an unbroken chain of causal connection directly linking the erroneous Tay-Sachs report, the deprivation of the parents' opportunity to accept or reject the continuance of the plaintiff-mother's pregnancy, and the emotional distress the parents suffered following the birth of their fatally defective child.

In the following case recovery for damages related to emotional distress was denied:

In *Becker v Schwartz*, 46 NY2d 401, 413 NYS2d 895, 386 NE2d 807 (1978), the court held that the plaintiff-parents could not recover for psychic or emotional harm alleged to have occurred as a consequence of the birth of their infant in an impaired state. The plaintiff-parents had alleged that the defendant-physicians had been negligent in failing to inform the parents accurately of risks involved in pregnancy. Subsequently, the infants were born in diseased conditions. After stating that the plaintiff-parents could recover pecuniary damages suffered as a consequence of the births, the court stated that that did not mean that the plaintiffs could recover for psychic or emotional harm alleged to have occurred as a consequence of the birth of their infants. The recovery of damages for such injuries must of necessity be circumscribed the court said. The court cited its earlier decision in *Howard v Lecher*, 42 NY2d 109, 397 NYS2d 363, 366 NE2d 64 (1977), regarding its determination that a wrongful birth action which sought damages only for mental distress and emotional disturbance failed to state a cause of action. The court said that while it was sympathetic to the plight of the parents, it declined for policy reasons to sanction the recovery of damages for their psychic or emotional harm occasioned by the birth and gradual death of their child. To have permitted recovery in *Howard*, the court observed, would have inevitably led to the drawing of artificial and arbitrary boundaries. To be sure, the court said, parents of a deformed infant will suffer the anguish that only parents can experience upon the birth of a child in an impaired state. However, notwithstanding the birth of a child afflicted with an abnormality, and certainly dependent upon the extent of the affliction, parents may yet experience a love that even an abnormality cannot fully dampen, the court said. To assess damages for emotional harm endured by the parents of such a child would, in all fairness, require consideration of this factor in mitigation of the parents' emotional injuries, the court believed. Unlike the plaintiff-parents' causes of action for pecuniary loss in the instant cases, which were held recoverable, calculation of damages for the plaintiffs' emotional injuries remains too speculative to permit recovery notwithstanding the breach of a duty flowing from the defendants to themselves, the court said. The cognizability of the plaintiff-parents' actions for emotional harm is a question best left for legislative address, the court concluded.

D. [§6.12] Sample Complaint

A complaint instituting a cause of action for wrongful birth [as to a definition of wrongful birth, see §6.1] needs to allege that an unhealthy infant has been born due to the negligence of the defendant. Moreover, the complaint needs to state that damages were suffered by the plaintiff-parents and that no infant would have been born had the defendant not been negligent in some manner. The following sample complaint suggests one way a cause of action for wrongful birth may be initiated. This action is brought pursuant to the Federal Tort Claims Act for negligence on the part of military medical providers.

COMPLAINT

Plaintiffs, complaining of the Defendant, allege:

I.

This action is brought under the Federal Tort Claims Act, and this matter is within the jurisdiction of this honorable Court.

II.

On ________________, Counsel for the Plaintiffs submitted a claim for the damages described herein on Standard Form to the District Legal Office, ____. This claim was for the amount of the prayer herein, and said claim has never been denied. More than six months have elapsed since that claim was submitted.

III.

On ________________, Plaintiffs' son, ________________, was born at the ____. All of the prenatal care and counseling for Plaintiff [mother] was provided by employees of Defendant, United States of America, acting within the scope and course of their employment at the ____. Plaintiff [father] is the father of the child.

IV.

When [infant] was born, it was discovered that he had a severe disorder known as Down's syndrome, commonly known as mongolism, as well as cardiac problems.

V.

Plaintiffs are certain that if the employees of the Defendant had exercised appropriate and reasonable medical care for [mother] including amniocentesis and genetic counseling, the child would not have been born and had to suffer the serious effects of Down's syndrome, also known as mongolism, and the subnormal and anguishing existence which he has to live, with the resulting damage to Plaintiffs.

VI.

As a direct and proximate result of the aforesaid, Plaintiffs' son is profoundly retarded and lives a life of misery, of pain, lack of accomplishment, anguish, inability to function normally, and inability to enjoy life at home or in any sort of employment and Plaintiffs have been damaged thereby in the sum of ____ Dollars.

WHEREFORE, Plaintiffs pray for judgment against the Defendant in the sum of ________________ Dollars plus the costs and disbursements of this action.

____

[Name of Attorney]

[Date]

II. WRONGFUL LIFE

A. In General

1. [§6.13] Definition

In recent years developments in medical technology and genetic study have permitted physicians to predict the possible occurrence of birth defects in unborn children. When this information is available to the parents before the conception or birth of a child, they are allowed the option of utilizing contraceptive methods or terminating the pregnancy with an abortion if there exists the potential of preventing the conception or birth of a defective or diseased child. It has been as a result of the advances in medical technology and genetic study that courts and legislatures have begun to address the issues raised by claims based on a physician's failure to detect or to disclose the possibility that a defective or diseased child will be born. [As to a more detailed discussion of the background of wrongful life actions, see §6.14.]

Lawsuits based on behalf of or in the name of the child, and predicated on such physician failures, have been termed wrongful life actions. See Peters and Peters, WRONGFUL LIFE: RECOGNIZING THE DEFECTIVE CHILD'S RIGHT TO A CAUSE OF ACTION, 18 Duquesne LR 859 (1980). Therefore, a cause of action for wrongful life has been defined as consisting of an allegation by the child that the physician's negligence, his failure to adequately inform the parents of the risk of the child's diseased or defective birth, has caused the birth of the child. The child does not, by contrast, allege that the physician's negligence caused the child's deformity. Instead, the child claims that but for the inadequate, and in some cases inaccurate, advice, the child would not have been born and thus subjected to the pain and suffering attributable to the deformity. See COMMENT, "WRONGFUL LIFE": THE RIGHT NOT TO BE BORN, 54 Tulane LR 480 (1980). The essential postulate of a wrongful life claim has been defined as the right of a child to be born as a whole, functional human being. See *Park v Chessin*, 60 AD2d 81, 400 NYS2d 110 (1977), modified on this point in *Becker v Schwartz*, 46 NY2d 401, 413 NYS2d 895, 386 NE2d 807 (1978) where the court said there was no precedent for the lower court's recognition of the fundamental right of a child to be born as a whole, functional human being.

It is important to note in considering the scope of a wrongful life action that this cause of action is only brought by, or in the name of, the diseased or defective child. An action brought by the child's parents for their injuries associated with the birth of the child is a separate and distinct cause of action. See Peters and Peters, *above*. The cause of action brought by the parents for their injuries resulting from the birth of the child is referred to as one for wrongful birth. In these actions the parents allege that they were precluded from making an informed decision about whether to have the child because the physician failed to inform them of the possibility the child would be conceived and/or born in a diseased or defective state. See COMMENT: BERMAN V. ALLAN, 8 Hofstra LR 257 (1979). [As to a more detailed discussion of wrongful birth actions, see §§6.1–6.12.] Because of the factual similarity in wrongful life and wrongful birth cases, in many instances the causes of action are brought simultaneously by the respective plaintiffs, the parents and the child. See, e.g., *Phillips v United States*, 508 FSupp 537 (D SC 1980); *Phillips v United States*, 508 FSupp 544 (D SC 1981); *Berman v Allan*, 80 NJ 421, 404 A2d 8 (1979).

It should also be noted that wrongful life cases are distinguishable from wrongful conception or wrongful pregnancy cases. Wrongful life cases involve the birth of a planned, but unhealthy, child who is born because of the defendant's alleged negligence in failing to advise the child's parents of the possibility that the child will be unhealthy. In these situations the parents allege that the defendant's negligence prevented them from having the opportunity to make an informed judgment regarding whether to have the child. By contrast, wrongful conception or wrongful pregnancy cases involve the birth of an unplanned, and sometimes unhealthy, child. In wrongful conception cases, the parents argue that but for the negligence of the defendant the child would never have been conceived, or in wrongful pregnancy that the pregnancy would have been terminated, and the unplanned child would never have been born. See COMMENT, "WRONGFUL LIFE": THE RIGHT NOT TO BE BORN, 54 Tulane LR 480 (1980). In other words, the *sine qua non* of wrongful conception or wrongful pregnancy cases is the unplanned, as contrasted to uninformed, nature of the child's birth. See Rogers, WRONGFUL LIFE AND WRONGFUL BIRTH: MEDICAL MALPRACTICE IN GENETIC COUNSELING AND PRENATAL TESTING, 33 South Carolina LR 713 (1982). [As to a more detailed discussion of wrongful conception and wrongful pregnancy actions, see §§3.8–3.51.]

In addition, some cases have been referred to as wrongful life actions, but actually involve not a diseased or defective infant but rather an infant who is born illegitimately. In these cases the infant-plaintiff asserts that the damages flowed from the stigma of bastardy. See, e.g., *Zepeda v Zepeda*, 41

11A2d 240, 190 NE2d 849 (1963), cert den, 379 US 945, 85 SCt 444, 13 LE2d 545 (1964); *Williams v State,* 18 NY2d 481, 276 NYS2d 885, 223 NE2d 343 (1966). Despite the frequent use of wrongful life to describe these claims they are not most commonly referred to as dissatisfied life claims. See Rogers, WRONGFUL LIFE AND WRONGFUL BIRTH: MEDICAL MALPRACTICE IN GENETIC COUNSELING AND PRENATAL TESTING, 33 South Carolina LR 713 (1982); COMMENT, "WRONGFUL LIFE": THE RIGHT NOT TO BE BORN, 54 Tulane LR 480 (1980). [As to a more detailed discussion of dissatisfied life actions, see §§6.22–6.24.]

For the most part wrongful life claims are based on post conception negligence by a physician. For example, some wrongful life cases have involved Down's syndrome. The plaintiff-infant alleges that after the diagnosis of pregnancy the physician failed to inform the prospective parents of the increased chances that the resulting child would be born in a diseased or defective state because of advanced maternal age or family history [see, e.g., *Phillips v United States*, 508 FSupp 537 (D SC 1980); *Berman v Allan*, 80 NJ 421, 404 A2d 8 (1979); *Karlsons v Guerinot*, 57 AD2d 73, 394 NYS2d 933 (1977)], and failed to advise the parents about testing procedures. However, some wrongful life actions have arisen from the alleged negligent failure to accurately perform genetic screening test on potential parents [see, e.g., *Curlender v Bio-Science Laboratories*, 106 CaA3d 811, 165 CaR 477 (1980)], or accurately tell the parents of the hereditary, and thus transmittable, nature of disorders discovered in previously born children [see *Park v Chessin*, 60 AD2d 80, 400 NYS2d 110 (1977), modified sub nom, *Becker v Schwartz*, 46 NY2d 401, 413 NYS2d 895, 386 NE2d 807 (1978)]. See Rogers, WRONGFUL LIFE AND WRONGFUL BIRTH: MEDICAL MALPRACTICE IN GENETIC COUNSELING AND PRENATAL TESTING, 33 South Carolina LR 713 (1982). And a physician's alleged negligent failure to diagnose rubella in a pregnant woman who subsequently gives birth to a deformed child has served as the basis of wrongful life claims. See, e.g., *Eisbrenner v Stanley*, 106 MiA 357, 308 NW2d 209 (1981).

In the typical wrongful life factual setting, the cause of action is asserted against a defendant who is a physician or genetic counselor. However, it has been suggested that public policy may not protect parents from being liable for the pain, suffering and misery which results to a child if the child is born after the prospective parents are warned that the child might be born in an unhealthy condition. If the parents made the conscious choice to proceed with the pregnancy, with full knowledge that a seriously impaired infant would be born, that choice would provide an intervening act of proximate cause to preclude liability insofar as defendants other than the parents were concerned. See *Curlender v Bio-Science Laboratories*, 106 CaA3d 811, 165 CaR 477 (1980).

2. [§6.14] Background

The terms wrongful life [as to a definition of wrongful life, see §6.13] first appeared in 1963 in the Illinois appellate court opinion of *Zepeda v Zepeda*, 41 IlA2d 240, 190 NE2d 849 (1963), cert den, 379 US 945, 85 SCt 444, 13 LE2d 545 (1964). In *Zepeda*, the court denied recovery to an infant-plaintiff who claimed that his defendant-father had injured him by causing him to be born illegitimately. The court declined to equate an illegitimate birth with the type of injury deemed actionable at law in American jurisprudence. The court reasoned that recognition of the plaintiff-infant's claim would mean creation of a new tort, a cause of action for wrongful life. The court believed that the legal implications of such a tort would be vast, and the social impact staggering. If the new litigation was confined just to illegitimates it would be formidable, the court said. The *Zepeda* decision represented an initial attempt by American courts to define the perimeter of the wrongful life cause of action. The *Zepeda* holding was followed in *Williams v State*, 18 NY2d 481, 276 NYS2d 885, 223 NE2d 343 (1966). In *Williams*, the plaintiff-infant's mentally deficient mother was raped while in a state mental institution, under circumstances giving rise to the claim that the rape had been the proximate result of the institution's negligence with the plaintiff-infant's illegitimate birth a consequence. The court observed that being born under one set of circumstances rather than another, or to one pair of parents rather than another, is not a suable wrong that is cognizable at law, and therefore the action was dismissed. The *Williams* decision has often been cited along with the *Zepeda* as being the initial cases in the area of wrongful life. These cases, now however, are more properly termed ones for dissatisfied life rather than wrongful life. [As to a more complete discussion of claims based on dissatisfied life, see §6.22.]

A major, and much cited, opinion considering a claim for damages by an impaired infant-plaintiff is *Gleitman v Cosgrove*, 49 NJ 22, 227 A2d 689 (1967). The plaintiffs, which included Mr. and Mrs. Gleitman and their infant, brought a malpractice suit against Mrs. Gleitman's physician for damages because the Gleitman child had been born with serious impairments of sight, speech, and hearing. Mrs. Gleitman contracted rubella during the first trimester of her pregnancy. The defendant-physician was aware of this fact, but failed to inform Mrs. Gleitman of any potentially harmful consequences to her child. Mrs. Gleitman, by contrast, was assured by the defendant-physician that such consequences would not occur, although it was common medical knowledge that rubella, contracted during early pregnancy, often caused the types of defects suffered by the child. The majority of the court barred recovery on two grounds: first, the court felt it would be impossible to compute damages, and second, the court thought the recognition of such a cause of action would violate public policy. The court described the plaintiff-infant's cause of action as requiring the infant to say not that he should have been born without defects but that he should not have been born at all. In the language of tort law, the court noted, the infant's position was that but for the negligence of the defendants he would not have been born to suffer from an impaired body. In other words, the child claimed that the conduct of the defendant-physicians prevented his mother from obtaining an abortion which could have avoided his existence, and that his very life is wrongful. In addition, Chief Justice Weintraub, who dissented on another issue, said ultimately the child's complaint was that he would be better off not to have been born. Man, who knows nothing of death or nothingness, cannot possibly know whether that is so, he said and added, to recognize a right not to be born is to enter an area in which no one could find his way. A different view was expressed by a dissenting opinion in *Gleitman*. It was stated by the dissenter that the majority permits a wrong with serious consequential injury to go wholly unredressed. That provides no deterrent to professional irresponsibility and is neither just nor compatible with expanding principles of tort liability.

A later case also denied recognition of a cause of action for wrongful life. In *Dumer v St Michael's Hosp*, 69 Wi2d 766, 233 NW2d 372 (1975), a cause of action was brought on behalf of an infant-plaintiff for injuries caused by rubella suffered by the infant's mother during the first trimester of the mother's pregnancy. The infant was born with deformities because her mother had rubella during pregnancy. The infant, through her guardian *ad litem* alleged that as a result of the negligence of the defendants in negligently diagnosing the rubella and their failure to advise the mother of the dangers of rubella the resulting infant was not aborted and was allowed to be born into a wrongful life. The court said the major obstacle to the claim of the infant-plaintiff was a determination of damages. The *Dumer* court cited with approval the *Gleitman* rationale and concluded that the damages claimed by the infant-plaintiff could not be measured by any standards recognized by law. Therefore the court concluded that the complaint of the infant did not state a cause of action.

Since the *Gleitman* and *Dumer* decisions most courts have refused to recognize wrongful life claims. See, e.g., *Smith v United States*, 392 FSupp 654 (ND Oh 1975); *Gildiner v Thomas Jefferson University Hosp*, 451 FSupp 692 (ED Pa 1978); *Phillips v United States*, 508 FSupp 537 (D SC 1980); *Berman v Allan*, 80 NJ 421, 404 A2d 8 (1979); *Becker v Schwartz*, 46 NY2d 410, 413 NYS2d 895, 386 NE2d 807 (1978); *Karlsons v Guerinot*, 57 AD2d 73, 394 NYS2d 933 (1977).

However, three courts, one supreme court and two middle level appellate courts, have recognized the cause of action of wrongful life. In *Turpin v Sortini*, 182 CaR 337 (1982), the California Supreme Court concluded that while an infant-plaintiff in a wrongful life action may not recover general damages for being born impaired as opposed to not being born at all, the child may recover special damages for the extraordinary expenses necessary to treat the hereditary ailment. The plaintiff-infant alleged that the defendant, a licensed professional specializing in the diagnosis and treatment of speech and hearing defects, negligently examined, tested, and evaluated the infant's sister and incorrectly advised the sister's pediatrician that her hearing was within normal limits when, in reality, she was deaf as a result of a hereditary ailment. Before learning of their daughter's ailment, the infant's parents, in reliance on the defendant's diagnosis, conceived another child, the infant-plaintiff. The infant alleged that had the parents known of the hereditary nature of the ailment, they would not have conceived the child. The infant-plaintiff was subsequently born with the same total deafness that afflicted her sister. The infant-plaintiff sought, in part, general damages for being deprived of the fundamental right of a child to be born as a whole, functional human being without total deafness. The court described the gist of the plaintiff's claim as that she suffered harm or damage as a result of the defendants' negligent performance of their professional tasks, and that, as a consequence, she is entitled to recover under generally applicable common law tort principles. The court believed that it was reasonably foreseeable that the infant's parents and their offspring would be directly affected by the defendant's negligent failure to discover that the infant's prior born sister suffered from an hereditary ailment and the court noted that the defendants did not contend that they owed no duty to the parents or the infant-plaintiff. Instead, the court noted, the defendants contended that the infant suffered no legally cognizable injury or rationally ascertainable damages as a result of their alleged negligence. However, the court believed that it was hard to see how an award of damages to a severely handicapped or suffering child would disavow the value of life or in any way suggest that the child is not entitled to the full measure of legal and nonlegal rights and privileges accorded to all members of society. Moreover, the court did not think it was accurate to suggest that the state's public policy establishes, as a matter of law, that under all circumstances impaired life is preferable to nonlife. Regarding the issue of recovery of damages the court held that although the plaintiff's claim for special damages could be awarded, those for general damages could not be. The court denied recovery for general damages because it would be impossible to determine whether the plaintiff suffered an injury in being born impaired rather than in not being born, and even if that determination could be made, it would be impossible to assess general damages in a nonspeculative manner. But the special damages for teaching, training, and learning equipment were deemed recoverable by the court because these damages were both certain and measurable. Moreover, the court said a defendant's negligence in failing to diagnose an hereditary ailment places a significant medical and financial burden on the whole family unit. And in *Curlender v Bio-Science Laboratories*, 106 CaA3d 811, 165 CaR 477 (1980), overruled on another issue in *Turpin*, above, a middle level appellate court held that there existed a duty owed by a medical laboratory engaged in genetic testing to parents and their as yet unborn children to use ordinary care in the administration of available tests for the purpose of providing information concerning potential genetic defects in the unborn. The public policy considerations with respect to the individuals involved and to society as a whole dictate recognition of such a duty, the court said. In *Curlender*, the infant-plaintiff was afflicted with Tay-Sachs disease. The principal defendant in Curlender was a medical laboratory which allegedly had been negligent in performing blood tests which the infant's parents had undergone for the purpose of determining if their offspring were likely to suffer from Tay-Sachs disease.

The only other decisions recognizing the cause of action for wrongful life are *Park v Chessin*, 60 AD2d 80, 400 NYS2d 110 (1977), and *Becker v Schwartz*, 60 AD2d 587, 400 NYS2d 119 (1977). *Park* and *Becker* were decided by the same appellate court. Both decisions were modified regarding the wrongful life holding in *Becker v Schwartz*, 46 NY2d 401, 413 NYS2d 895, 386 NE2d 807 (1978). In *Becker*, it was alleged that throughout Mrs. Becker's pregnancy she was never advised by the defendant-physicians of the increased risk of Down's Syndrome in children born to women over 35 years of age. Nor were they advised, the action alleged, of the availability of an amniocentesis test to determine whether the fetus carried by Mrs. Becker would be born afflicted with Down's Syndrome. In the companion case of *Park v Chessin*, Mrs. Park gave birth to a baby who, afflicted with polycystic kidney disease, died five hours after birth. Concerned with the possible reoccurrence of this disease in a child conceived in the future, Mrs. Park and her husband consulted the defendants, the obstetricians who treated Mrs. Park during her first pregnancy to determine the likelihood of this contingency recurring. In response to the Parks' inquiry the defendants were alleged to have informed the Parks that inasmuch as polycystic kidney disease was not hereditary, the chances of their conceiving a second child afflicted with this disease were practically nil. Based on this information the Parks alleged that they exercised a conscious choice to seek conception of a second child. As a result Mrs. Park became pregnant and gave birth to a child who similarly suffered from polycystic kidney disease. Unlike the first child, however, the second child lived for two and one-half years before death was caused by the disease. Alleging that contrary to the defendants' advice polycystic kidney disease is an inherited condition, and that had the Parks been correctly informed of the true risk of recurrence of the disease in a second child, they would not have conceived the child, the plaintiffs brought actions including one for wrongful life. The court believed the conduct by the defendants, if the allegations were proven, represented a wrong which is cognizable at law. Since the plaintiff-wife was the patient of the defendants, and the one to whom a duty of professional medical care was directly owed, it was inconceivable to the court that the defendants were not aware of the risk of danger that false advice would pose. The plaintiffs were entitled to be protected against this foreseeable wrong, the court said. Moreover, the court noted that cases are not decided in a vacuum, but rather must keep pace with social and technological changes. The court said prospective parents have the right, within certain statutory and case law limitations, not to have a child. The breach of this right may be said to be tortious to the fundamental right of a child to be born as a whole, functional human being. Therefore, it was concluded that the action for wrongful life, and the accompanying request for recovery on behalf of the infant for injuries and conscious pain and suffering caused by the defendants' negligence should be permitted to stand.

In addition, a number of legislatures have considered wrongful life causes of action and have enacted measures limiting, or proscribing, actions brought by, or on behalf of, plaintiff-infants for injuries arising in wrongful life settings. For example, 1982 MINN LAW, Ch. 52, is an act relating to tort actions based on wrongful life. The act provides for the prohibition of tort actions, and states that no person shall maintain a cause of action or receive an award of damages on behalf of himself or herself based on the claim that but for the negligent conduct of another, he or she would have been aborted. And SD CODIFIED LAWS ANN §21-55-1 (1981) states, in part, that there shall be no cause of action or award of damages on behalf of any person based on the claim that, but for the conduct of another, the person would not have been permitted to have been born alive. [As to a more complete discussion of the statutory reaction to wrongful life actions, see §6.20.]

It should be noted that in many cases in which wrongful life claims have been rejected by the court, claims brought by the parents for their injuries arising from the same factual setting have given rise to recognized actions for wrongful birth. See, e.g., *Gildiner v Thomas Jefferson University Hosp*, 451 FSupp 692 (ED Pa 1978); *Moores v Lucas*, 405 So2d 1022 (Fl 1981); *Berman v Allan*, 80 NJ 421, 404 A2d 8 (1979); *Becker v Schwartz*, 46 NY2d 401, 413 NYS2d 895, 386 NE2d 807 (1978); *Dumer v St Michael's Hosp*, 69 Wi2d 766, 233 NW2d 372 (1975).

B. Recognition of Cause of Action

1. [§6.15] Generally

The primary issue in actions brought on behalf of, or by, infant-plaintiffs for wrongful life [as to a definition of wrongful life, see §6.13] is whether the cause of action will be recognized. Generally actions involving wrongful life claims have not received judicial [see, e.g., *Smith v United States*, 392 FSupp 654 (ND Oh 1975); *Gildiner v Thomas Jefferson University Hosp*,

451 FSupp 692 (ED Pa 1978); *Phillips v United States*, 508 FSupp 537 (D SC 1980); *Dumer v St Michael's Hosp*, 69 Wi2d 766, 233 NW2d 372 (1975)] or legislative [see, e.g., 1982 MINN LAWS, Ch. 521; SD CODIFIED LAWS ANN §21-55 (1981)] approval, but this is not always the case [see, e.g., *Turpin v Sortini*, 182 CaR 337 (1982); *Curlender v Bio-Science Laboratories*, 106 CaA3d 811 (1980)].

One rationale that has served as the basis for rejection of the wrongful life action has been that the cause of action is not legally cognizable based on public policy considerations. The preciousness and sanctity of human life militate against the recognition of this cause of action. While scientific and technological advances, together with the changes in moral attitudes that often accompany such advances, may eventually provide a new perspective from which to analyze such causes of action, public policy discourages recognition at this time. See *Phillips v United States*, 508 FSupp 537 (D SC 1980). Moreover, in asserting a cause of action for wrongful life an infant maintains that he would be better off not to have been born. Therefore, the choice is not between being born with health or being born without it, but rather the choice is between a worldly existence and none at all. To recognize a right not to be born is to enter an area in which no one could find his or her way. See *Gleitman v Cosgrove*, 49 NJ 22, 227 A2d 689 (1967) [C. J. Weintraub dissenting in part]. See also, *Moores v Lucas*, 405 So2d 1022 (Fl 1981).

In considering whether a cause of action should be recognized for wrongful life, another issue that has been raised has been whether the infant-plaintiff has suffered a legally cognizable injury. If the court determines that the infant's disease or affliction is not an injury legally cognizable at law, then the action may be dismissed due to a lack of an injury on which to base a cause of action. See, e.g., *Becker v Schwartz*, 46 NY2d 401, 413 NYS2d 895, 386 NE2d 807 (1978); *Karlsons v Guerinot*, 57 AD2d 73, 394 NYS2d 933 (1977). However, there is authority for the proposition that an infant bringing a wrongful life action has suffered a legally cognizable injury. See *Turpin v Sortini*, 182 CaR 337 (1982). [As to a more detailed discussion of the legal cognizability of injuries in wrongful life actions, see §6.16.]

In addition, general damage considerations have been relied on to hold that a cause of action for wrongful life is not recognizable. For example, in a tort action the normal measure of damages is to provide compensation for the plaintiff to put him or her in the same position they were before the negligence on the part of the defendant. However, it has been suggested a court cannot weigh the value of life with impairments against the nonexistence of life itself because the comparison is logically impossible to make. See *Gleitman v Cosgrove*, 49 NJ 22, 227 A2d 689 (1967). And it has been held that an infant-plaintiff in a wrongful life setting does not suffer damage that is cognizable at law. Life, whether experienced with or without major physical handicaps, is more precious than nonlife, it has been said. See *Berman v Allan*, 80 NJ 421, 404 A2d 8 (1979). However, where it was held that damages were recoverable in a wrongful life action the damages were limited to special, as opposed to general, damages because the special damages could be reasonably calculated and measured. See *Turpin v Sortini*, 182 CaR 337 (1982). [As to a more detailed discussion of damage considerations in wrongful life actions, see §6.17.]

Even though most of the courts that have considered wrongful life actions have rejected them [see, e.g., *Becker v Schwartz*, 46 NY2d 401, 413 NYS2d 895, 386 NE2d 807 (1978)], there are cases in which the cause of action has been recognized. For example, in *Turpin v Sortini*, 182 CaR 337 (1982), the court found that the tort concept of foreseeability was present and in *Curlender v Bio-Science Laboratories*, 106 CaA3d 811, 165 CaR 477 (1980), the concept of duty to the infant-plaintiff was held to exist in a wrongful life setting. [As to a more detailed discussion of cases in which a cause of action was held stated in a wrongful life action, see §6.19.]

In addition to the judicial response to wrongful life actions, there have also been statutes enacted to address the issue. These statutes, which are of recent enactment, have prohibited or limited the right to bring causes of action for wrongful life. See, e.g., 1982 MINN LAWS, Ch. 521; SD CODIFIED LAWS ANN §21-55 (1981). [For a more complete discussion of these statutes, see §6.20.]

2. [§6.16] Existence of Legally Cognizable Injury

One of the principle issues in wrongful life [as to a definition of wrongful life, see §6.13] actions centers on whether the infant-plaintiff has suffered a legally cognizable injury by being born. If no legally cognizable injury has been suffered by the infant, then the cause of action may be rejected, thus leaving the infant-plaintiff with no remedy. See, e.g., *Becker v Schwartz*, 46 NY2d 401, 413 NYS2d 895, 386 NE2d 807 (1978); *Karlsons v Guerinot*, 57 AD2d 73, 394 NYS2d 933 (1977). But where it is determined that a legally cognizable injury has been suffered, the plaintiff-infant may be allowed to pursue the cause of action. See *Turpin v Sortini*, 182 CaR 337 (1982).

One reason that a court refused to recognize that the infant suffered an injury cognizable at law in a wrongful life case was based on the lack of precedent. There is no precedent for the belief that a child has a fundamental right to be born as a whole, functional human being. *Becker v Schwartz*, 46 NY2d 401, 413 NYS2d 895, 386 NE2d 807 (1978). Moreover, recognition of the infant's cause of action would necessitate a finding that she was injured by the defendants' conduct, and that she had been placed in a worse position than she would have been in had the defendants not been negligent. Thus, the threshold question here is not whether life is less preferable than death, but rather whether it is less preferable than the utter void of nonexistence. Such a decision, by the very nature of the concepts sought to be compared and their far-reaching implications is beyond the scope of judicial decision-making and must await legislative action. See *Karlsons v Guerinot*, 57 AD2d 73, 394 NYS2d 933 (1977). And whether it is better never to have been born at all than to have been born with even gross deformities is a mystery more properly left to the philosophers and the theologians. The law can assert no competence to resolve the issue, particularly in view of the very nearly uniform high value which the law and society has placed on human life, rather than its absence. Moreover, the implications of recognizing a cause of action for wrongful life are staggering. Would claims be honored, assuming the breach of an identifiable duty, for less than a perfect birth, and by what standard or by whom would perfection be defined? See *Becker*, at 900.

However, one court has found that the infant in wrongful life cases does suffer a legally cognizable injury. The injury in a wrongful life case has been described as not the particular defect with which a plaintiff is afflicted, but the birth of the plaintiff with such a defect. See *Curlender v Bio-Science Laboratories*, 106 CaA3d 811, 165 CaR 477 (1980). For example, one court said although it was easy to understand decisions which hold that the plaintiff has suffered no injury cognizable at law, it questioned whether these considerations alone provide a sound basis for rejecting the child's tort action. It is difficult to see how an award of damages to a severely handicapped or suffering child would disavow the value of life or in any way suggest that the child is not entitled to the full measure of legal and nonlegal rights and privileges accorded to all members of society. Moreover, while society and the legal system unquestionably place the highest value on human life, it is not accurate to suggest that public policy establishes, as a matter of law, that under all circumstances impaired life is preferable to nonlife. In the wrongful life context the unborn child cannot personally make any choice as to the relative value of life or death. As the wrongful birth [as to a more complete discussion of wrongful birth, see §§6.1–6.12] decisions recognize, when a doctor or other medical care provider negligently fails to diagnose an hereditary problem, parents are deprived of the opportunity to make an informed and meaningful decision whether to conceive and bear a handicapped child. Although in deciding whether to bear such a child parents may properly take into account their own interests, parents also presumptively consider the interests of their future child. Thus, when a defendant negligently fails to diagnose an hereditary ailment, he harms the potential child as well as the parents by depriving the parents of information which may be necessary to determine whether it is in the child's own interest to be born with defects or not to be born at all. Thus, it cannot be asserted in every instance that there would be a societal consensus that life is preferable to never having been born at all. *Turpin v Sortini*, 182 CaR 337 (1982). See also *Curlender v Bio-Science Laboratories*, 106 CaA3d 811, 165 CaR 477 (1980).

3. [§6.17] Damage Considerations

There are a variety of damage related issues that arise in the context of the recognition of wrongful life [generally, see §6.13] actions. For example, the proposition that since damages in a tort action are compensatory in nature, the existence of such damages is grounded in the premise that but for the negligence of the defendant, the plaintiff would be in a better position than he is [see, e.g., *Karlsons v Guerinot*, 57 AD2d 73, 394 NYS2d 933 (1977)] has received consideration by courts in terms of whether the cause of action should be recognized. However, some courts have asked, can it be determined whether the plaintiff-infant would be in a better position if he or she was not born? A court cannot weigh the value of life with impairments against the nonexistence of life itself. By asserting that he should not have been born, an infant-plaintiff makes it logically impossible for a court to measure the alleged damages because of the impossibility of making the comparison required by compensatory remedies. See, e.g., *Gleitman v Cosgrove*, 49 NJ 22, 227 A2d 689 (1967); *Dumer v St Michael's Hosp*, 69 Wi2d 766, 233 NW2d 372 (1975). And, in the case of a claim predicated on wrongful life, a computation comparing the condition the plaintiff would have been in, had the defendant not been negligent, with the plaintiff's impaired condition as a result of the negligence would require the trier of fact to measure the difference in value between life in an impaired condition and the utter void of nonexistence. Such an endeavor is literally impossible. See *Berman v Allan*, 80 NJ 421, 404 A2d 8 (1979).

Moreover, damage recovery should not be based on speculation. An infant's claim for damages in a wrongful life action assumes the infant suffered a detriment by being born defective instead of being aborted, but such a comparison is not possible to make and juries should not be allowed to speculate on the child's damages. Recognition of the infant's cause of action would turn the courts into forums for pure gambling events, since damage awards could range from zero to millions of dollars based on essentially the same evidence. It would make as much sense to award damages based on a throw of the dice. See *Eisbrenner v Stanley*, 106 MiA 351, 308 NW2d 209 (1981).

Another damages related consideration involved in the recognition of the cause of action is whether there exists any damage suffered by that infant-plaintiff that is cognizable at law. The issue is whether by being brought into the world the infant has suffered cognizable damage. The existence of damages is an essential element of any action in tort, and, absent such damages, no suit will lie. See, e.g., *Karlsons v Guerinot*, 57 AD2d 73, 394 NYS2d 933 (1977). In one instance it was held that the child had failed to state an actionable claim for relief because the child had not suffered any damage cognizable at law by being brought into existence. Life, whether experienced with or without a major physical handicap, is more precious than nonlife. Each person suffers from some ailments or defects, whether major or minor, which make impossible participation in all the activities the world has to offer. But lives are not thereby rendered less precious than those of others whose defects are less pervasive or less severe. See, e.g., *Gildiner v Thomas Jefferson University Hosp*, 451 FSupp 692 (ED Pa 1978); *Berman v Allan*, 80 NJ 421, 404 A2d 8 (1979). In addition, policy considerations have been relied on when holding that the complaint on behalf of the infant-plaintiff is not actionable because the conduct complained of does not give rise to damages cognizable at law. The rationale for these policy considerations is that it is basic to the human condition to seek life and hold onto it however heavily burdened it may be. The right to life is inalienable. A court cannot say what defects should prevent an embryo from being allowed life such that denial of the opportunity to terminate the existence of a defective child can support a cause of action. There are examples of famous persons who have had great achievement despite physical defects. A child need not be perfect to have a worthwhile life. See *Gleitman v Cosgrove*, 49 NJ 22, 227 A2d 689 (1967).

Finally, there is authority that special damages for extraordinary expenses involved with caring for an impaired child can be awarded in a wrongful life case, but that general damages will not be awarded. While it seems doubtful that a child's claim for general damages should properly be denied on the rationale that the value of impaired life, as a matter of law always exceeds the value of nonlife, with respect to the child's claim for pain and suffering or other general damages, recovery should be denied because it is impossible to determine in any rationale or reasoned fashion whether the plaintiff-infant has suffered an injury in being born impaired rather than in not being born, and even if it were possible to overcome the difficulty in making the determination, it would be impossible to assess general damages in any fair, and nonspeculative manner. The practical problems associated with the general damages in wrongful life actions are exacerbated when it comes to the matter of arriving at an appropriate award. Although the valuation of pain and suffering or emotional distress in terms of dollars and cents is unquestionably difficult in an ordinary personal injury action, jurors at least have some frame of reference in their own general experience to appreciate what the plaintiff has lost, normal life without pain and suffering. In a wrongful life action, that is not the case for what the plaintiff has lost is not life without pain and suffering but rather the unknowable status of never having been born. In this context, a rational, nonspeculative determination of a specific monetary award in accordance with normal tort principles is outside the realm of human competence. The difficulty is ascertaining or measuring an appropriate award of general damages in this type of case is also reflected in application of the benefit doctrine in tort damages. RESTATEMENT (SECOND) OF TORTS §920 provides that when a defendant's tortious conduct has harmed the plaintiff, but in doing so has also conferred a benefit on the plaintiff, the value of the benefit conferred is considered in mitigation of damages. In requesting general damages in a wrongful life case, the plaintiff seeks monetary compensation for the pain and suffering he or she will endure because of his or her hereditary affliction. Under the benefit doctrine, however, such damages must be offset by the benefits incidentally conferred by the defendant's conduct to the interest of the plaintiff that was harmed. With respect to general damages, the harmed interest is the child's general physical, emotional, and psychological well-being, and in considering the benefit to this interest which the defendant's negligence has conferred, it must be recognized that as an incident of the defendant's negligence the plaintiff has in fact obtained a physical existence with the capacity both to receive and give love and pleasure as well as to experience pain and suffering. Because of the incalculable nature of both elements this harm-benefit equation, it reasoned, a nonarbitrary award of general damage is not obtainable. However, there is a qualitative difference between the difficulties faced by a jury in assessing general damages in a normal personal injury or wrongful death action, and the task before a jury in assessing general damages in wrongful life cases. A defendant's negligence in failing to diagnose an hereditary ailment places a significant medical and financial burden on the family unit. Unlike the child's claim for general damages, the damage involved in the claim for specialized teaching and training equipment is both certain and readily measurable. See *Turpin v Sortini*, 182 CaR 337 (1982).

A compilation of illustrative cases that address the various damage related considerations that have arisen in wrongful life cases appears at §6.18.

4. [§6.18] —Illustrative Cases

A courts ruling on damage considerations [generally, see §6.17] may sometimes bar or limit, recovery in a wrongful life [generally, see §6.13] context. For example, the following cases are illustrative of damage principles relating to the difficulty in ascertaining and measuring damages in a wrongful life case. In these cases the courts unanimously hold that the damages were not measurable:

In *Gleitman v Cosgrove*, 49 NJ 22, 227 A2d 689 (1967), the infant-plaintiff was born with birth defects due to exposure to rubella during her mother's pregnancy. The infant's parents consulted the defendant-physician who advised the mother she was two months pregnant. She told the doctor she had recently had German Measles. The physician told her this would have no effect upon the child to be born. The plaintiffs, who included the infant and infant's parents, claimed that because of the advice of the doctor the parents were denied the opportunity to terminate the life of the child in its embryonic state. The majority opinion in *Gleitman* in considering the claim of the infant-plaintiff stated that the infant, pursuant to its complaint, was required to say not that he should have been born without defects but that he should not have been born at all. The court described the infant's cause in tort law as saying that but for the negligence of the defendants, he would not have been born to suffer with an impaired body. The court noted that the normal measure of damages in tort actions is compensatory, and that these damages are measured by comparing the condition the plaintiff would have been in, had the defendants not been negligent, with the plaintiff's impaired condition as a result of the negligence. The infant-plaintiff would have the court measure the difference between his life with defects against the utter void of nonexistence, the court said, but it is impossible to make such a determination. The court believed that it could not weigh the value of life with impairments against the nonexistence of life itself. By asserting that he should not have been born, the infant-plaintiff made it logically impossible for a court to measure his alleged damages because of the impossibility of making the comparison required by compensatory remedies, the court concluded. And in *Berman v Allan*, 80 NJ 421, 404 A2d 8 (1979), suit was brought on behalf of the infant-plaintiff for medical malpractice. Mrs. Berman had become pregnant in her late 30's, a circumstance involving a substantial risk that the child would be born with Down's Syndrome, one of the major characteristics of which is mental retardation. The child, when born, was so afflicted. Amniocentesis, by that time a well-established technique for discerning birth defects *in utero* had not been suggested to the Bermans. The *Berman* court rejected the concept that the infant-plaintiff possessed an independent cause of action, and referring to the difficulty of measuring damages in such a case, the court declared that the primary purpose of tort law is that of compensating plaintiffs for the injuries they have suffered wrongfully at the hands of others. As such, damages are ordinarily computed by comparing the condition the plaintiff would have been in, had the defendants not been negligent, with the plaintiff's impaired condition as a result of the negligence, the court said. In the case of a claim predicated upon wrongful life, such a computation would require the trier of fact to measure the difference in value between life in an impaired condition and the utter void of nonexistence. Such an endeavor, the court believed, is literally impossible.

Another consideration that has received judicial attention in terms of damages and the ability to maintain wrongful life actions relates to whether the infant-plaintiff suffered damage by its birth that is cognizable at law. The following cases indicate how this issue has been addressed and resolve it in the negative:

In *Berman v Allan*, 80 NJ 421, 404 A2d 8 (1979) [see above for facts], the court concluded that the infant-plaintiff had failed to state an actionable claim for relief because she had not suffered any damage cognizable at law by being brought into existence. One of the most deeply held beliefs of society is that life, whether experienced with or without a major physical handicap, is more precious than nonlife, the court said. The court referred to several manifestations of this belief including the federal constitution, which characterizes life as one of three fundamental rights of which no person can be deprived without due process of law, the New Jersey State Constitution, which proclaims that the enjoying and defending of life is a natural right, and the Declaration of Independence, which states that the primacy of person's unalienable right to life is a self-evident truth. No-where in these documents is there to be found an indication that the lives of persons suffering from physical handicaps are to be less cherished than those of non-handicapped human beings, the court said. Moreover, the court noted that no person is perfect and each person suffers from some ailments or defects, whether major or minor, which make impossible participation in all the activities the world has to offer. Lives are not thereby rendered less precious than those of others whose defects are less pervasive or less severe, the court said. The court said it recognized that as a mongoloid child, the infant-plaintiff's abilities would be more circumscribed than those of normal, healthy children and that she, unlike them, would experience a great deal of physical and emotional pain and anguish. However, the court could not say that she would have been better off had she never been brought into the world. Notwithstanding her affliction with Down's Syndrome, the infant, by virtue of her birth, would be able to love and be loved and to experience happiness and pleasure, emotions which are truly the essence of life and which are far more valuable than the suffering she may endure. To rule otherwise, the court said, would require it to disavow the basic assumption upon which society is based. Accordingly, the court held that the infant-plaintiff had failed to state a valid cause of action founded upon wrongful life. And in *Gleitman v Cosgrove*, 49 NJ 22, 227 A2d 689 (1967) [see above for facts], the court held that the count of the complaint on behalf of the infant-plaintiff was not actionable because the conduct complained of, even if true, did not give rise to damages cognizable at law. It is basic to the human condition to seek life and hold on to it however heavily burdened, the court said. If the infant-plaintiff could have been asked as to whether his life should be snuffed out before his full term of gestation could run its course, the court believed he would almost surely choose life with defects as against no life at all. The right to life is unalienable in society, the court said. A court cannot say what defects should prevent an embryo from being allowed life such that denial of the opportunity to terminate the existence of a defective child in embryo can support a cause for action, the court said. Examples of famous persons who have had great achievement despite physical defects come readily to mind, the court said. The court reasoned that a child need not be perfect to have a worthwhile life.

However, damage recovery in wrongful life actions has not been universally denied. The following case provides an example of how the one court which allowed recovery handled the respective issues of general damages and special damages:

In *Turpin v Sortini*, 182 CaR 337 (1982), the infant-plaintiff's parents, acting on the advice of their pediatrician, brought their first, and at that time their only, daughter, to a rehabilitation center for the evaluation of a possible hearing defect. The child was examined and tested, and allegedly the infant's parents were incorrectly advised that her hearing was within normal limits when, in reality, she was deaf as a result of an hereditary ailment. Relying on the defendant's diagnosis, the parents conceived a second child, the infant-plaintiff. The complaint averred that had the parents known of the first child's hereditary deafness they would not have conceived the second child. The second child was born and suffered from the same total deafness as her earlier born sister. A cause of action for wrongful life was brought on behalf of the infant-plaintiff and sought general damages for the deprivation of the fundamental right of a child to be born as a whole, functional human being without total deafness and special damages for the extraordinary expenses for specialized teaching, training, and hearing equipment which she would incur during her lifetime as a result of her hearing impairment. The court believed that with respect to the child's claim for pain and suffering or other general damages recovery should be denied because it is simply impossible to determine in any rational or reasonable fashion whether the plaintiff had in fact suffered an injury in being born impaired rather than not being born, and even if it were possible to overcome that determination, it would be impossible to assess general damages in any fair, nonspeculative manner. The court believed that there was a profound qualitative difference between the difficulties faced by a jury in assessing general damages in a normal personal injury or wrongful death action, and the task before a jury in assessing general damages in a wrongful life case. The court said the practical problems involved would be exacerbated when it came to the matter of arriving at an appropriate award of damages. In fixing damages in a tort case, the jury generally compares the condition the plaintiff would have been in but for the tort, the court said, with the position the plaintiff is now in, compensating the plaintiff for what has been lost as a result of the wrong. Although the evaluation of pain and suffering or emotional distress in terms of dollars and cents is unquestionably difficult in an ordinary personal injury action, jurors at least have some frame of reference in their own general experience to appreciate what the plaintiff has lost, normal life without pain and suffering, the court said. In a wrongful life action, however, that simply is not the case, for what the plaintiff has lost is not life without pain and suffering but rather the unknowable status of never having been born, the court said. In this context, the court reasoned, a rational amount speculative determination of a specific monetary award in accordance with normal tort principles appears to be outside the realm of human competence. Moreover, the court said the difficulty in ascertaining or measuring an appropriate award of general damages in this type of case is also reflected in the application of the benefit doctrine in tort damages. RESTATEMENT (SECOND) OF TORTS §920 provides that when the defendant's tortious conduct has caused harm to the plaintiff and in doing so has conferred a special benefit to the interest of the plaintiff that was harmed, the value of the benefit conferred is considered in mitigation of damages, to the extent that this is equitable, the court said. In requesting general damages in a wrongful life case, the court noted, the plaintiff seeks monetary compensation for the pain and suffering he or she will endure because of his or her hereditary affliction. Under §920's benefit doctrine, however, such damages must be offset by the benefits incidentally conferred by the defendant's conduct to the interest of the plaintiff that was harmed, the court said. With respect to general damages, the court said, the harmed interest is the child's general physical, emotional, and psychological well-being, and in considering the benefit to this interest which the defendant's negligence has conferred, it must be recognized that as an incident of the defendant's negligence, the plaintiff has in fact obtained a physical existence with the capacity to receive and give love and pleasure as well as to experience pain and suffering. Because of the incalculable nature of both elements of this harm-benefit equation, the court believed that a reasoned, nonarbitrary award of general damages simply was not obtainable. A monetary award of general damages, as opposed to the claim for medical expenses, cannot in any meaningful sense compensate the plaintiff for the loss of the opportunity not to be born, the court said. Although the court determined that the infant-plaintiff's claim for general damages would not be recognized, the court concluded that the infant's claim for the extraordinary expenses for specialized teaching, training and hearing equipment that she will incur during her lifetime because of her deafness stood on a different footing. Realistically, the court said, a defendant's negligence in failing to diagnose an hereditary ailment places a significant medical and financial burden on the whole family unit. Unlike the child's claim for general damages, the damage here is both certain and readily measurable, the court believed. Furthermore, the court said that in many cases these expenses would be vital not only to the child's well-being but to his or her very survival. If, as alleged, the defendant's negligence was in fact a proximate cause of the child's present and continuing need for such special, extraordinary medical care and training, the court believed that it was consistent with basic liability principles to hold the defendants liable for the cost of such care, whether the expense was to be borne by the parents or by the child. Moreover, the court said that permitting the infant-plaintiff to recover the extraordinary, additional medical expenses that are occasioned by the hereditary ailment is also consistent with the established perimeters of the general tort benefit doctrine. In this case the harm for which the plaintiff sought compensation was an economic loss, the extraordinary, out-of-pocket expenses that she would have to bear because of her hereditary ailment, the court said. Unlike the claim for general damages, the defendants' negligence had conferred no incidental, offsetting benefit to this interest of the plaintiff, and accordingly, assessment of the special damages should pose no unusual or insoluble problems, the court concluded.

5. [§6.19] Cause of Action Stated

A cause of action for wrongful life [as to a definition of wrongful life actions, see §6.13] brought by or on behalf of an infant-plaintiff has been recognized in a limited number of cases. See *Turpin v Sortini*, 182 CaR 337 (1982); *Curlender v Bio-Science Laboratories*, 106 CaA3d 811, 165 CaR 477 (1980); *Park v Chessin*, 60 AD2d 80, 400 NYS2d 110 (1977), modified on this issue, *Becker v Schwartz*, 46 NY2d 401, 413 NYS2d 895, 386 NE2d 807 (1978). As a prelude to the recognition of the cause of action, it has been noted that an infant in a wrongful life action does suffer a legally cognizable injury. [As to a more detailed discussion of the existence of a legally cognizable injury in wrongful life actions, see §6.16.] In *Turpin v Sortini*, 182 CaR 337 (1982), the court said it is questionable whether considerations based on the supposed disavowal of the sanctity and value of less than perfect human life provide, standing alone, a sound basis for the rejection of a wrongful life tort action. In *Turpin*, the infant-plaintiff's parents brought their first, and at that time their only, daughter to a licensed professional specializing in the diagnosis and treatment of speech and hearing defects. The complaint alleged that the defendant negligently examined, tested, and evaluated this daughter, and incorrectly advised the parents that the daughter's hearing was within normal limits, when in reality the daughter was deaf. In reliance on this information, the parents conceived the infant-plaintiff. The complaint further stated that had the parents known of the hereditary deafness they would not have conceived the plaintiff. The plaintiff was born and was afflicted with the same deafness as her older sister. It is difficult to see how an award of damages to a severely handicapped or suffering child would disavow the value of life or in any way suggest that the child is not entitled to the full measure of legal and nonlegal rights and privileges accorded to all members of society, the court said. Moreover, the court did not believe that it is accurate to suggest that public policy establishes, as a matter of law, that under all circumstances impaired life is preferable to nonlife. Therefore the court concluded that it could not assert with confidence that in every situation there is a societal consensus that life is preferable to never having been born at all. And in *Curlender v Bio-Science Laboratories*, 106 CaA3d 811, 165 CaR 477 (1980), the court said the circumstance that the birth and injury came hand-in-hand should not bar recovery. The reality of the wrongful life concept is that such a plaintiff both exists and suffers, due to the negligence of others, the court said. It is neither necessary nor just to retreat into meditation on the mysteries of life, the court continued. The court said it was not concerned with the fact that had the defendants not been negligent, the plaintiff might not have come into existence at all because the certainty of genetic impairment is no longer a mystery.

Moreover, it has been recognized that a duty can run from the defendant-physician to a plaintiff-infant in the typical wrongful life situation. In *Curlender v Bio-Science Laboratories*, 106 CaA3d 811, 165 CaR 477 (1980), the court said it had no difficulty in ascertaining and finding the existence of a duty owed by medical laboratories engaged in genetic testing to parents and their as yet unborn children to use ordinary care in administration of available tests for the purpose of providing information concerning potential genetic defects in the unborn. In *Curlender*, the plaintiff-infant brought a wrongful life action against the defendant's medical laboratory. The laboratory had allegedly been negligent in performing blood tests which the infant's parents had undergone for the specific purpose of determining if their offspring were likely to suffer from Tay-Sachs disease. Relying on the laboratory's finding that their offspring would not be afflicted with Tay-Sachs, the infant's parents sought her conception, and subsequently the infant was born afflicted with the disease. The court said the public policy considerations with respect to the individuals involved and society as a whole dictated recognition of a duty of ordinary care, and therefore the court found no bar to a holding that the defendant owed a duty to the infant-plaintiff and that the duty was breached.

In addition, courts have held that the results of the defendant's negligence were foreseeable, thus satisfying the requirement that an injury be foreseeable to be actionable. In *Park v Chessin*, 60 AD2d 80, 400 NYS2d 110 (1977), modified on this issue, *Becker v Schwartz*, 46 NY2d 401, 413 NYS2d 895, 386 NE2d 807 (1978), the court said if the infant-plaintiff's allegations were proven, the defendants were negligent in giving inaccurate medical advice or in failing to ascertain the correct state of medical knowledge to so advise the infant's parents or both. In *Park*, the infant-plaintiff was conceived and born after the infant's parents were informed that the infant would not suffer polycystic kidney disease, a disease an earlier born child had suffered. The defendants allegedly informed the plaintiffs the disease was not hereditary in nature, and based on this information, the infant was conceived. Subsequently, the infant was born and was afflicted with the disease. The court said while for one to be held liable in negligence he or she need not foresee novel or extraordinary consequences, it is enough that he or she is aware of the risk of danger. The court said that since the infant's mother was the patient of the defendant-physicians, and the one to whom a duty of professional care was directly owed, it was inconceivable to conclude that the defendants were not aware of the risk of danger that false advice would pose. The act of giving the wrong genetic-medical advice to the plaintiff's parents, who would foreseeably rely on the defendants' superior knowledge, was an act in regard to the plaintiff's parents with possibilities of danger so many and apparent as to entitle the plaintiff and his parents to be protected against the doing of it though the harm was unintentional, the court said. And in *Turpin v Sortini*, 182 CaR 337 (1982), [see above for facts], the court held it was reasonably foreseeable that the plaintiff-infant's parents and their potential offspring would be directly affected by the defendants' negligent failure to discover that the plaintiff-infant's older sister suffered from an hereditary ailment that was also suffered by the infant. The court noted that this foreseeability existed even though the plaintiff's mother, and not the plaintiff herself, was the defendants' immediate patient.

6. [§6.20] Statutory Limitation or Denial of Cause of Action

In addition to the judicial reaction to wrongful life actions [generally see §6.15–§6.19] there has also been recent legislative reaction in a small number of states. The purpose of these statutes, thus far, has been to limit or deny the cause of action for wrongful life brought by, or on behalf of, an infant-plaintiff. See, e.g., 1982 MINN LAWS, Ch. 521, SD CODIFIED LAWS ANN §21-55 (1981). Moreover, legislation has been introduced in recent years in several states including Alabama, Indiana, New Jersey, Oklahoma and Rhode Island that would bar a cause of action for wrongful life.

The following statutes illustrate two statutory approaches to resolving the issue of the recognition of a cause of action for wrongful life. Both statutes deny the right to bring a wrongful life action. One of the statutes was enacted by South Dakota in 1981:

SD CODIFIED LAWS ANN, §21-55

ACTIONS FOR WRONGFUL LIFE PROHIBITED

21-55-1. Action or damages for conception or birth prohibited — "Conception" defined. There shall be no cause of action or award of damages on behalf of any person based on the claim of that person that, but for the conduct of another, he would not have been conceived or, once conceived, would not have been permitted to have been born alive. The term "conception," as used in this section, means the fertilization of a human ovum by a human sperm, which occurs when the sperm has penetrated the cell membrane of the ovum.

Source: SL 1981, ch 172, §1

21-55-3. Consideration of failure to prevent live birth restricted in actions. The failure or the refusal of any person to prevent the live birth of a person may not be considered in awarding damages or in imposing a penalty in any action. The failure or the refusal of any person to prevent the live birth of a person is not a defense in any action.

Source: SL 1981, ch 172, §3.

21-55-4. Limited effect of chapter. The provisions of this chapter do not prohibit a cause of action or the awarding of damages, except as specifically provided in this chapter, by or on behalf of any person based on the claim that a person is liable for injury caused by such person's willful acts or caused by such person's want of ordinary care or skill.

Source: SL 1981, ch 173, §4

Minnesota's Legislature enacted a measure in 1982 to prohibit tort actions for wrongful life. The Minnesota enactment states:

1982 MINN LAWS, Ch. 521

Section 1. [145.424] [PROHIBITION OF TORT ACTIONS.]

Subdivision 1. [WRONGFUL LIFE ACTION PROHIBITED.] No person shall maintain a cause of action or receive an award of damages on behalf of himself based on the claim that but for the negligent conduct of another, he would have been aborted. . . .

Subdivision 3. [FAILURE OR REFUSAL TO PREVENT A LIVE BIRTH.] Nothing in this section shall be construed to preclude a cause of action for intentional or negligent malpractice or any other action arising in tort based on the failure of a contraceptive method or sterilization procedure or on a claim that, but for the negligent conduct of another, tests or treatment would have been provided or would have been provided properly which would have made possible the prevention, cure, or amelioration of any disease, defect, deficiency, or handicap; provided, however, that abortion shall not have been deemed to prevent, cure, or ameliorate any disease, defect, deficiency, or handicap. The failure or refusal of any person to perform or have an abortion shall not be a defense in any action, nor shall that failure or refusal be considered in awarding damages or in imposing penalty in any action.

C. [§6.21] Example Complaints

The exact contents of a pleading initiating a cause of action for wrongful life [as to a definition of wrongful life, see §6.13] will vary depending on the facts of the case. However, the following example complaints from wrongful life cases indicate how a wrongful life pleading may be drafted.

For example, in *Turpin v Sortini*, 182 CaR 337 (1982), an action for wrongful life was brought by an infant-plaintiff for the defendants' negligence relating to the failure to advise the infant's parents of the hereditary nature of an ailment that had afflicted the infant's prior born sister, and subsequently afflicted the plaintiff. The reprinted portion of the complaint includes pertinent allegations made by the wrongful life-plaintiff's sister so as to provide background regarding how the wrongful life action developed. The pleading stated as follows:

> Comes now the plaintiff, HOPE TURPIN [the sister of the plaintiff who alleged the wrongful life action] through her guardian ad litem, JAMES TURPIN, and alleges as follows:
>
> FIRST CAUSE OF ACTION
>
> 1. That the true names and capacities, whether individual, corporate, associate or otherwise, of defendants named herein as DOES I through X are unknown to plaintiff, who therefore sues said defendants by such fictitious names, and plaintiff will amend this Complaint to show their true names and capacities when the same have been ascertained.
>
> 2. That at all times herein mentioned, each of the defendants above named was the agent, servant or employee of each of the other defendants, and was at all times herein mentioned acting within the course and scope of said agency and employment.
>
> 3. That at all times herein mentioned, ADAM J. SORTINI was, and now is, a licensed professional individual specializing in the diagnosis and treatment of speech and hearing defects and was practicing his profession in the County of Fresno, State of California.
>
> 4. That at all times herein mentioned, defendant, ADAM J. SORTINI, was the agent, employee and manager of the defendant,

LEON S. PETERS REHABILITATION CENTER, which, upon information and belief, is and was a business entity organized and existing by virtue of the laws of the State of California and was and is in the business of providing diagnosis and treatment of speech and hearing defects in the County of Fresno, State of California.

5. That at all times herein mentioned defendant, FRESNO COMMUNITY HOSPITAL was and is a corporation organized and existing by virtue of the laws of the State of California and was and is in the business of providing health care services in the County of Fresno, State of California.

6. That at all times herein mentioned, defendants DOE I through DOE X, inclusive, were and are speech and hearing diagnosticians and therapists and were and are the agents, servants, and employees of the defendants, and each of them, and at all times herein mentioned, were acting within the course and scope of their agency and employment.

7. That plaintiff HOPE TURPIN is a two year old minor child of plaintiffs JAMES TURPIN and DONNA WRENN TURPIN.

8. That on or about September 24, 1976, plaintiff, HOPE TURPIN, became a patient of the defendants, and each of them, and came under the care and attention of defendants for the purpose of receiving a hearing evaluation because of the concern of the minor plaintiff's parents and her pediatrician that she suffered from a hearing defect.

9. That at said time and place the defendants, and each of them, so negligently and carelessly took a history, examined, tested, and evaluated the minor plaintiff so that an advisement was made to her pediatrician by the defendants that her hearing was within normal limits; that in reality the minor plaintiff was stone deaf and this condition remained undiagnosed until Oct. 15, 1977, when she was re-evaluated by other speech and hearing specialists. . . .

SECOND CAUSE OF ACTION

As and for a Second Cause of Action, plaintiff, JOY TURPIN, by and through her guardian ad litem, JAMES TURPIN, alleges:

11. That plaintiff, JOY TURPIN, realleges and incorporates herein by reference the allegations set forth in Paragraphs 1 through 9 of the First Cause of Action as though set forth at length herein.

12. That JOY TURPIN is an eleven month old minor.

13. That on August 23, 1977, plaintiff, JOY TURPIN, was born with the similar total deafness abnormality with which her sister, HOPE TURPIN, had been afflicted; that this deafness is hereditary in origin and once JOY TURPIN was conceived there was a

reasonable degree of medical probability that she would, in fact, be born with the similar deafness abnormality.

14. That relying on the negligent and careless evaluation by the defendants, and each of them, of their daughter, HOPE TURPIN, as aforesaid, and in the belief that HOPE TURPIN's hearing was within normal limits and not suspecting that she suffered from any hereditary abnormality, JAMES TURPIN and DONNA WRENN TURPIN conceived JOY TURPIN; had they been apprised of the true facts, to wit, that HOPE TURPIN was deaf, they would not have conceived JOY TURPIN.

15. That because of the hereditary nature of this total deafness abnormality, the defendants, and each of them, were aware of the risk of giving incorrect opinions and evaluations because it was foreseeable that parents, such as JAMES TURPIN and DONNA WRENN TURPIN, would rely on such opinions and evaluations in deciding whether or not to conceive other children.

16. That as a direct and proximate result of the negligence and carelessness of the defendants, and each of them, as aforesaid, the minor plaintiff, JOY TURPIN, was deprived of the fundamental right of a child to be born as a whole, functional human being without total deafness, all to her general damages.

17. That as a further direct and proximate cause of the negligence and carelessness of the defendants, as aforesaid, the plaintiff, JOY TURPIN, will incur during her lifetime extraordinary expenses for specialized teaching, training and hearing equipment, in an amount presently unknown. Plaintiff prays leave to amend this Complaint when the total amount may be reasonably and foreseeably ascertained.

WHEREFORE, plaintiff, JOY TURPIN, prays for judgment as hereinafter set forth. . . .

2. General damages on behalf of JOY TURPIN according to proof;

3. Special damages on behalf of JOY TURPIN according to proof; . . .

8. For such other and further relief as to this Court may seem just and proper. . . .

And in *Phillips v United States*, 508 FSupp 537 (D SC 1980), an action for wrongful life was brought based on the defendants' alleged negligent failure to provide adequate genetic counseling and to perform an amniocentesis. The complaint stated as follows:

Plaintiff, complaining of the Defendant, alleges:

I.

This action is brought under the Federal Tort Claims Act, and this matter is within the jurisdiction of this honorable Court.

II.

On September 11, 1978, Counsel for the Plaintiff submitted a claim for the damages described herein on Standard Form 95 to the District Legal Office, U. S. Naval Base, Charleston, South Carolina. This claim was for the amount of the prayer herein, and said claim has never been denied. More than six months have elapsed since that claim was submitted.

III.

On September 23, 1977, Plaintiff was born at the Naval Regional Medical Center, U.S. Naval Base, Charleston, South Carolina. All of the prenatal care and counseling for Plaintiff's mother, Kathleen D. Phillips, was provided by employees of Defendant, United States of America, acting within the scope and course of their employment at the Naval Regional Medical Center.

IV.

When Plaintiff was born, it was discovered that he had a severe disorder known as Down's syndrome, commonly known as mongolism, as well as cardiac problems. At the time of his birth, Plaintiff had a disorder known as Patent Ductus Arteriosis, but this was not diagnosed until Plaintiff was taken to the Medical University of South Carolina in June of 1978, whereupon immediate surgery was performed in an attempt to correct this heart defect.

V.

Plaintiff is informed and believes that if the employees of the Defendant had exercised appropriate and reasonable medical care for Plaintiff's mother, including amniocentesis and genetic counseling, he would not have been born and had to suffer the serious effects of Down's syndrome, also known as mongolism, the grave difficulties with the Patent Ductus Arteriosis and the subsequent surgery, and the subnormal and anguishing existence which he has to live.

VI.

As a direct and proximate result of the aforesaid, Plaintiff is profoundly retarded and lives a life of misery, of pain, lack of accomplishment, anguish, inability to function normally, inability to enjoy life at home or in any sort of employment and he is informed and believes that this will continue for the rest of his life.

Accordingly, Plaintiff has been injured and damaged in the sum of Five Million ($5,000,000.00) Dollars.

WHEREFORE, Plaintiff prays for judgment against the Defendant in the sum of Five Million ($5,000,000.00) Dollars plus the costs and disbursements of this action. . . .

III. DISSATISFIED LIFE: ILLEGITIMACY

A. [§6.22] Definition

The cause of action loosely denominated as dissatisfied life has developed slowly over the past two decades, but there has been general judicial agreement in refusing to recognize it [see §6.23 regarding policy considerations]. The cause is based on the birth of an illegitimate child, and is brought in the name of the child against the defendant for damages [as to the basis of damages in dissatisfied life actions, see §6.24] related to the child's status as an illegitimate or bastard. See, e.g., *Zepeda v Zepeda*, 41 IlA2d 240, 190 NE2d 849 (1963), cert den, 379 US 945, 85 SCt 444, 13 LE2d 545 (1964); *Slaweck v Stroh*, 62 Wi2d 295, 215 NW2d 9 (1974).

In these actions the plaintiff-infant argues that various damages flow from the stigma of illegitimacy or bastardy. In most cases, dissatisfied life claims are brought against the plaintiff-infant's putative father [see, e.g., *Pinkney v Pinkney*, 198 So2d 52 (Fl 1967); *Slaweck v Stroh*, 62 Wi2d 295, 215 NW2d 9 (1974)], but in some cases they have been brought against third parties [see *Williams v State*, 18 NY2d 481, 223 NE2d 343, 276 NYS2d 885 (1966)]. See Rogers, WRONGFUL LIFE AND WRONGFUL BIRTH: MEDICAL MALPRACTICE IN GENETIC COUNSELING AND PRENATAL TESTING, 33 South Carolina LR 713 (1982).

Nonetheless judicial recognition of this cause of action has yet to be granted in any state. The courts that have considered a cause of action in dissatisfied life cases have uniformly rejected it. See, e.g., *Stills v Gratton*, 55 CaA2d 698, 127 CaR 652 (1976); *Pinkney v Pinkney*, 198 So2d 52 (Fl 1967); *Zepeda v Zepeda*, 41 IlA2d 240, 190 NE2d 849 (1963), cert den, 379 US 945, 85 SCt 444, 13 LE2d 545 (1964); *Williams v State*, 18 NY2d 481, 276 NYS2d 885, 223 NE2d 343 (1966); *Slaweck v Stroh*, 62 Wi2d 295, 215 NW2d 9 (1974). See also Wolff and Cirillo, THE BASTARD'S CAUSE OF ACTION: A STATUTORY CAUSE OF ACTION FOR ILLEGITIMATE CHILDREN, 19 Journal of Family Law 463 (1981).

By contrast, paternity proceedings are usually based on the plaintiff's desire to have the paternity of the child adjudicated in a legal proceeding, and to compel the father to contribute to the infant's support. See, e.g., *Lawrence v Boyd*, 207 Ks 776, 486 P2d 1394 (1971).

It should be noted that actions for dissatisfied life have been described as actions for wrongful life [as to a detailed definition of wrongful life actions, see §6.13] in some instances [see, e.g., *Zepeda v Zepeda*, 41 IlA2d 240, 190 NE2d 849 (1963), cert den, 379 US 945, 85 SCt 444, 13 LE2d 545 (1964).] However, now these cases are more commonly referred to as dissatisfied life cases. "WRONGFUL LIFE": THE RIGHT NOT TO BE BORN, 54 Tulane LR 480 (1980). Wrongful life cases are distinguishable since they involve actions brought by unhealthy infants for damages predicated on the negligent action of the defendants. They allege that but for the negligence of the defendant they would not have been born and made to suffer in their unhealthy condition. See, e.g., *Gildiner v Thomas Jefferson University Hosp*, 451 FSupp 692 (ED Pa 1978); *Becker v Schwartz*, 46 NY2d 401, 386 NE2d 807, 413 NYS2d 895 (1978).

B. [§6.23] Policy Considerations

Policy considerations have, in some dissatisfied life [as to the definition of dissatisfied life actions, see §6.22] cases, led to the rejection of the cause of action. The underlying theory has been that because of the magnitude of a decision to recognize a cause of action for dissatisfied life, the policy decision regarding recognition should be entrusted to the legislature. For example, the *Zepeda v Zepeda*, 41 IlA2d 240, 190 NE2d 849 (1963), cert den, 379 US 945, 85 SCt 444, 13 LE2d 545 (1964), the court said that although the wrong committed was a tort, lawmaking while inherent in the judicial process, should not be indulged in where the result would be as sweeping as in this case. The court said the interest of society is so involved, the action needed to redress the tort could be so far reaching, that the policy of the state should be declared by the legislature. The court noted that recognition of the infant-plaintiff's claim would be the creation of a new tort the legal complications of which would be vast, the social impact staggering. If the new litigation were confined just to illegitimates it would be formidable, the court said. That the doors of litigation would be opened wider might make the court proceed cautiously in approving a new action, but it would not deter it the court said. But it was not the suits of the illegitimates which gave the court the most concern. What disturbed the court most was the nature of the new action and the related suits which would be encouraged. Encouragement would extend to all others born into the world under conditions they might regard as adverse, the court said. One might seek damages for being born of a certain color, another because of race, one for being born with a hereditary disease, another for inheriting unfortunate family characteristics, one for being born into a large and destitute family, another because a parent had an unsavory reputation, the court reasoned. The court also reasoned that if such a legal action were to be recognized it should be preceded by a thorough study of the consequences. Changing economic, social or political conditions, or scientific advancements, produce new problems which are constantly thrust upon the courts, the court noted. These problems often require the remolding of the law, the extension of old remedies, or the creation of new and instant remedies, but no recent development is presented by this case which demands an immediate remedy to keep abreast of progress, the court believed. In *Slaweck v Stroh*, 62 Wi2d 295, 215 NW2d 9 (1974), the court cited the *Zepeda* decision, and concluded that while it was probably not powerless to recognize this tort as a valid cause of action, it believed that the creation and recognition of this type of cause of action would have vast social ramifications and the creation of such a cause is the type of public policy decision that should be made by the people of Wisconsin through their elected legislative representatives. And in *Williams v State*, 18 NY2d 481, 276 NYS2d 885, 223 NE2d 343 (1966), the court said because no such claim had ever before been accepted by a court was not an unscalable barrier. However, to uphold the cause of action would be to say that being born out of wedlock in itself gives a right to damages, the court said. The impossibility of entertaining this suit, the court said, stemmed not so much from the difficulty of measuring the alleged damages as from the absence from legal concepts of any such idea as a wrong to a later born child caused by a woman bearing an out-of-wedlock infant. The policy and social reasons against providing compensation for the plaintiff-infant are at least as strong as those which may be thought to favor it, the court said.

C. [§6.24] Nature of Injury and Basis of Damages Sought

Issues involving the nature of the injury and the basis of damages sought have typically arisen in dissatisfied life [as to a definition of dissatisfied life, see §6.22] actions. One of the initial issues regarding the injury question relates to whether an action for dissatisfied life alleges an injury that will be recognized.

It has been suggested that it would be specious to argue that the burden of illegitimacy is a less compensable injury than many physical ailments or defects because it may not in fact be true that an illegitimate child is doomed to a life of hardship and social stigma. See *Turpin v Sortini*, 174 CaR 128 (1981). And in *Zepeda v Zepeda*, 41 IlA2d 240, 190 NE2d 849 (1963), cert den, 379 US 945, 85 SCt 444, 13 LE2d 545 (1964), the court said the wrong committed against the plaintiff-infant was a tort even though the court refused to recognize the cause of action for dissatisfied life. Children born illegitimate have suffered an injury, and if legitimation does not take place the injury is continuous, the court said. If legitimation cannot take place, the injury is irreparable, the court said. Moreover, the court reasoned that the injury is not as tangible as a physical defect but it is as real. This is acknowledged, the court believed, by the state itself since the statutory provisions that a child's illegitimacy must be suppressed, in certain public records, is an admission of the hardships that can be caused by its disclosure. How often during his life does an illegitimate try to conceal his parentage and how often does he wince in shame when it is revealed, the court asked. Public opinion may, the court believed, bring about more laws ameliorating further his or her legal status, but laws cannot temper the cruelty of those who hurl the epithet "bastard" nor ease the bitterness in the child who bears it, knowing it to be true. An illegitimate's very birth places him or her under a disability, the court said. However, in *Williams v State*, 18 NY2d 481, 276 NYS2d 885, 233 NE2d 343 (1976), the court said the impossibility of entertaining a suit for dissatisfied life comes not so much from the difficulty in measuring the alleged damages as from the absence from legal concepts of any such idea as a wrong to a child born out of wedlock. Being born under one set of circumstances rather than another or to one pair of parents rather than another is not a suable wrong that is cognizable in court, the court said. To uphold the plaintiff-infant's claim would be to say that being born out-of-wedlock in itself gives a right to damages and that the damages include compensation for the supposed or possible disadvantages of an illegitimate birth, the court reasoned. The court concluded that the closest reach of New York law in these cases is to paternity proceedings and that is accomplished by statute. And in *Pinkney v Pinkney*, 198 So2d 52 (Fl 1967), the court said that although the plaintiff-infant may have to bear the unfair burden of illegitimacy as have many other children of shame and sorrow, the law knows no cure for it. If for policy or social reasons compensation is to be provided to those suffering the plight of the plaintiff-infant, other than for simple support as provided by statute, such provision must be made by the legislature, the court said.

The types of injuries that have been claimed by plaintiff-infants in dissatisfied life actions have centered on the perceived lower status of illegitimate persons. For example, in *Zepeda v Zepeda*, 41 IlA2d 240, 190 NE2d 849 (1963), cert den, 379 US 945, 85 SCt 444, 13 LE2d 545 (1964), the plaintiff-infant in a dissatisfied life action asserted that he had been injured in his person, property, and reputation by being born as an adulterine bastard. More specifically, the plaintiff-infant attempted to define his injuries as falling within the coverage of mental suffering and defamation. Considering the alleged mental suffering injury, the court said, to some persons, the shame of being an adulterine bastard might cause genuine and severe emotional distress as that resulting from other serious provocation. However, in the absence of proper and adequate averments, the court said, it must hold that the complaint stated no action in tort. Likewise, the court rejected the injury theory predicated on defamation since there was no allegation by the infant-plaintiff of publication to third persons. Finally the court considered, but rejected, the infant's contention of being deprived of the normal home that might have been his and or equality with legitimate children that might have been. A legitimate child has the natural right to be wanted, loved, and cared for, the court believed. He also has an interest in preserving his family life and he may protect this interest against outside disturbance, the court said. However, the court noted that a legitimate child cannot maintain an action against his own parents for lack of affection, for failure to provide a pleasant home, for disrupting the family life or for being responsible for a divorce which cannot be broken up at home. An illegitimate child cannot be given rights superior to those of a legitimate child, and the plaintiff has no cause of action on this account, the court said. And in *Slaweck v Stroh*, 62 Wi2d 295, 215 NW2d 9 (1974), the plaintiff-infant alleged that as a result of her illegitimate birth she suffered and would continue to suffer mental pain, anguish, and humiliation and embarrassment.

The basis for damages in dissatisfied life actions have varied with the individual actions. For example, one claimant sought damage recovery for the infant's deprivation of property rights, deprivation of a normal childhood and home life, deprivation of proper parental care, support and rearing, and the burden of bearing the stigma of illegitimacy. See *Williams v State*, 18 NY2d 481, 276 NYS2d 885, 223 NE2d 343 (1966).

IV. DIETHYLSTILBESTROL (DES) RELATED LIABILITY

A. In General

1. [§6.25] Definition

Diethylstilbestrol (DES) is a non-steroid estrogen used as a substitute for the natural estrogenic hormones. Blakiston, GOULD MEDICAL DICTIONARY (McGraw-Hill 4th ed 1979). It is capable of providing all the therapeutic and pharmacologic reactions caused by natural estrogens. PHYSICIANS' DESK REFERENCE (36th ed 1982).

DES was first approved by the Federal Drug Administration in 1947 for use in complications, primarily miscarriage, in pregnancy. COMMENT, DES AND A PROPOSED THEORY OF ENTERPRISE LIABILITY, 46 Fordham LR 963 (1978). DES was ingested by several million women between 1945 and 1971 to treat complications in pregnancy. It has also been suggested that DES was prescribed to produce a healthier baby. DES was an unpatented, fungible commodity and therefore could be filled with any of numerous generic brands of the drug. It has been estimated that hundreds of companies manufactured and marketed the drug under numerous brand names. In 1971, it was reported that there was a high incidence of a rare cancer, clear cell adenocarcinoma, in daughters of women who had ingested DES during their pregnancies. These daughters had been exposed to the drug *in utero*. See COMMENT, DIETHYLSTILBESTROL: EXTENSION OF FEDERAL CLASS ACTION PROCEDURE TO GENERIC DRUG LITIGATION, 14 University of San Francisco LR 461 (1980). Moreover, in the same year the Food and Drug Administration, contraindicating DES for use by pregnant women, effectively banned its use to prevent miscarriages because of its danger and ineffectiveness. See NOTE, DES AND A PROPOSED THEORY OF ENTERPRISE LIABILITY, 46 Fordham LR 963 (1978). [As to a more detailed discussion of the background of DES related cases, see §6.26.]

In recent years there has developed an increasing number of lawsuits brought by DES daughters for injuries allegedly attributable to the ingestion of DES by their mothers during the daughters' pregnancy. See, e.g., *Payton v Abbott Labs*, 512 FSupp 1031 (D Ma 1981); *Sindell v Abbott Laboratories*, 26 Ca3d 607, 163 CaR 132, 607 P2d 924, cert den, 449 US 912 (1980); *Abel v Eli Lilly & Co*, 94 MiA 59, 289 NW2d 20 (1980); *Ferrigno v Eli Lilly & Co*, 175 NJ Super 551, 420 A2d 1305 (1980); *Bichler v Eli Lilly & Co*, 55 NY2d 571 (NY 1982). In these cases, plaintiffs have encountered numerous impediments including establishing a duty to the fetus, statute of limitations issues [as to issues relating to statute of limitations in the DES context, see §6.38], and questions arising from cause in fact and the identity of the manufacturer [as to cause in fact and manufacturer identity generally, see §6.29].

DES is still marketed in the United States for a wide variety of purposes including the treatment of women for menopausal disturbances, senile vaginitis, and the relief of breast engorgement during lactation suppression. Men may be treated with DES for prostate cancer. Moreover, DES is one ingredient of the morning after pill to prevent pregnancy. See NOTE, DES AND A PROPOSED THEORY OF ENTERPRISE LIABILITY, 46 Fordham LR 963 (1978).

2. [§6.26] Background

Diethylstilbestrol (DES) [as to a definition of DES, see §6.25], a synthetic estrogen, was first synthesized by scientists in Britain in 1938. Its use represented a significant advance over other natural estrogens since DES was cheaper and could be administered orally. See NOTE, DES AND A PROPOSED THEORY OF ENTERPRISE LIABILITY, 46 Fordham LR 963 (1978).

It was believed by some researchers during the 1940's that DES might prevent spontaneous abortion caused by such complications as diabetes, premature birth, late pregnancy toxemia, and history of miscarriage. One group of researchers speculated that DES was capable of producing healthier babies. Early research suggested that DES produced toxic effects when given in large doses to animals used in experiments. However, the drug was approved by the American Medical Association's Council on Pharmacy and Chemistry following a finding that the toxic effects were apparently eliminated when the dosages of DES were reduced. See COMMENT, DIETHYLSTILBESTROL: EXTENSION OF FEDERAL CLASS ACTION PROCEDURES TO GENERIC DRUG LITIGATION, 14 University of San Francisco LR 461 (1980).

In 1941 the Food and Drug Administration (FDA) approved new drug applications for DES following research by a group of United States drug manufacturers led by Eli Lilly and Company. The FDA's approval provided that DES could be used to treat certain female disorders believed to stem from low levels of the estrogen hormone. Subsequently, in 1946, the makers of DES received FDA approval to market the drug as a miscarriage preventative. The FDA, in 1952, declared that DES was no longer to be considered a new drug, and found that DES was to be regarded as generally safe. In 1971 the FDA reversed its earlier decision and required DES manufacturers to label the drug as contraindicated for use in the prevention of miscarriages. One significant reason for the FDA's action was consideration of studies which showed a link between the use of DES by pregnant women and a rare form of cancer in their daughters. In response to this discovery, more than 1,000 suits have been filed against drug manufacturers on behalf of the daughters who allege that they have contracted cancer because of their contact with DES while *in utero*. See Robinson, MULTIPLE CAUSATION IN TORT LAW: REFLECTIONS ON THE DES CASES, 68 Virginia LR 713 (1982).

Generally, vaginal cancer in young women was practically unknown until the late 1960's. Before 1966 only three cases of clear cell adenocarcinoma of the vagina in young women were reported. However, eight young women in the Boston area were treated for the disease between 1966 and 1969. Therefore, a case study was begun to consider what facts might be associated with the sudden rise in the occurrence of this disease, once though to be almost unknown in young women. The result of the study demonstrated a highly significant association between mothers who ingested DES during pregnancy and the subsequent development of adenocarcinoma of the vagina in their daughters. Later studies confirmed the results of the initial study. See Abrahams and Musgrave, THE DES LABYRINTH, 33 South Carolina LR 663 (1982).

Estimates of the development of clear cell adenocarcinoma have ranged from a high of one in 250 to a low of one in 10,000. 46 Fordham LR at 965. Moreover, it has been suggested that the risk of vaginal adenocarcinoma is 100 times greater among daughters of women who ingested DES during pregnancy. Abrahams and Musgrave, at 697. In addition, women exposed *in utero* to DES are also known to suffer other abnormalities including adenosis, which is a possible precancerous condition. 46 Fordham LR at 968. Adenosis has been reported in 30 per cent to 90 per cent of postpubertal women whose mothers received DES or a closely related substance during pregnancy. See 40 FED REG 32, 773 (1975). Other studies have suggested that as women who were exposed *in utero* to DES grow older, DES-related cancer will occur with more frequency because of the rarity of vaginal cancer among young women. See, e.g., Herbst, Poskamzer, Robboy, Friedlander, and Scully, PRENATAL EXPOSURE TO STILBESTROL, 292 New England Journal of Medicine 334 (1975).

Statistical evidence has not been able to demonstrate a clear cause and effect relationship between a woman's exposure to DES *in utero* and the later development of clear cell adenocarcinoma. Abrahams and Musgrave, at 698. The causation of cancer in these cases could, in an absolute sense, only be proven by an understanding of the biological process whereby the introduction of a substance into the body would create a tumor. However, in the case of DES, this is not yet understandable. 46 Fordham LR at 965. Commentators have suggested that the evidence demonstrates a high statistical relationship between the development of cancer in female offspring and the offspring's mother's ingestion of DES during pregnancy, and that together with DES studies conducted on laboratory animals and the rarity of this disease before DES was marketed can lead reasonable persons to the conclusion that it is more probable than not that the DES ingestion resulted in the subsequent development of clear cell adenocarcinoma in daughters of the mothers. Abrahams and Musgrave at 701.

In one case, *Bichler v Eli Lilly & Co*, 55 NY2d 471 (NY 1982), a jury verdict for the DES-plaintiff was affirmed. The court did not disturb the jury's findings, and concluded the jury could infer closely parallel conduct among manufacturers of DES. [As to a discussion of the causation in fact theory the court applied, alternative liability, see §6.32.] The jury approved the following written interrogatories in support of their verdict:

> (1) Was DES reasonably safe in the treatment of accidents of pregnancy when it was ingested by plaintiff's mother in 1953?
> No.
>
> (2) Was DES a proximate cause of plaintiff's cancer?
> Yes.
>
> (3) In 1953 when plaintiff's mother ingested DES, should the defendant, as a reasonably prudent drug manufacturer, have foreseen that DES might cause cancer in the offspring of pregnant women who took it?
> Yes.

(4) Foreseeing that DES might cause cancer in the offspring of pregnant women who took it, would a reasonably prudent drug manufacturer test it on pregnant mice before marketing it?

Yes.

(5) If DES had been tested on pregnant mice, would the tests have shown that DES causes cancer in their offspring?

Yes.

(6) Would a reasonably prudent drug manufacturer have marketed DES for use in treating accidents of pregnancy at the time it was ingested by plaintiff's mother, if it had known that DES causes cancer in the offspring of pregnant mice?

No.

(7) Did defendant and other drug manufacturers act in concert with each other in testing and marketing of DES for use in treating accidents of pregnancy?

Yes.

The PHYSICIANS' DESK REFERENCE (36th ed 1982) includes the following warning in its definition and description of DES:

> 2. ESTROGEN SHOULD NOT BE USED DURING PREGNANCY - The use of female sex hormones, both estrogens and progestrogens, during early pregnancy may affect the offspring. It has been reported that females exposed *in utero* to diethylstilbestrol, a nonsteroidal estrogen, may have an increased risk of developing later in life a rare form of vaginal or cervical cancer. This risk has been estimated to be 0.14 to 1.4 per 1,000 exposures. Furthermore, from 30 to 90 percent of such exposed women have been found to have vaginal adenosis and epithelial changes of the vagina and cervix. Although these changes are histologically benign, it is not known whether they are precursors of malignancy.... In the past, female sex hormones have been used to treat threatened or habitual abortion; however, their efficacy was never conclusively proved or disproved. . . . If diethylstilbestrol is administered during pregnancy, or if the patient becomes pregnant while taking this drug, she should be apprised of the potential risks to the fetus and of the advisability of pregnancy continuation.

Another issue that has been considered in DES-related litigation has been whether a class action made up of DES-plaintiffs will be recognized. In one instance the certification of a class of DES-plaintiffs was not recognized under a state class action statute in *Morrissy v Eli Lilly & Co*, 76 IlA3d 753,

394 NE2d 1369 (1979), while in another instance a class of plaintiffs was conditionally certified under the federal class action statute in *Payton v Abbott Labs*, 83 FRD 382 (D Ma 1979). In *Morrissy*, the court held that the proposed class action involving DES plaintiffs could not be sustained because individual determinations of proximate cause would be required which would predominate over common questions of law and fact. The court considered the requirements of ILL ANN STAT Ch 110, §57.2 (Smith Hurd 1980) which states in part there must be questions of fact or law common to the class which predominate over any questions affecting only individual members. Included among the individual determinations of proximate cause, the court said, were whether the product was properly prescribed for the mother's then existing medical condition, the dosage of DES prescribed, the amount of DES actually ingested, the point during the pregnancy at which DES was started and ended, the heredity and genetic history and background of the patient and incidences of cancer or other disorders suspected, the patient's exposure to known carcinogenic agents in the environment, and the personal habits of the individual subjects.

However, in *Payton* the court found, pursuant to FED R CIV P Rule 23, that common questions of law and fact predominated over questions affecting individual members of the plaintiff class, and that a class action was superior to other available methods for the fair and efficient adjudication of the controversy. Mass marketing of potent drugs is a modern phenomenon, the court said. Traditional models of litigation, pitting one plaintiff against one defendant, were not designed to, and cannot, deal with the potential for injury to numerous and geographically dispersed persons that mass marketing presents, the court reasoned. The courts are faced with the choice of adapting traditional methods to the recurrent phenomenon of widespread drug litigation or leaving large numbers of people without a practical means of redress, the court said. In the court's opinion, certification of the litigation under Rule 23(b)(3) offered the best means to adapt an established and tested structure to a modern phenomenon. [Generally, see COMMENT, DIETHYLSTILBESTROL: EXTENSION OF FEDERAL CLASS ACTION PROCEDURES TO GENERIC DRUG LITIGATION, 14 University of San Francisco LR 461 (1980).]

In response to the DES controversy, one state has enacted a statute aimed at locating, monitoring, and establishing special programs for DES daughters. In 1978, the New York Legislature enacted NY PUB HEALTH LAW §2500-c, which deals with special programs with respect to DES. In part the statute says:

Special programs with respect to diethylstilbestrol

1. For the purpose of identifying persons who have been exposed to the potential hazards and afflictions of diethylstilbestrol, and for the purpose of educating the public concerning the

> symptoms and prevention of associated malignancies, the commissioner shall establish, promote and maintain a public information campaign on diethylstilbestrol. Such campaign shall be conducted throughout the state and shall include but not be limited to a concerted effort at reaching those persons or the offspring of persons who have been exposed to diethylstilbestrol in order to encourage them to seek medical care for the prevention or treatment of any malignant condition.
>
> 2. (a) The commissioner shall designate and enter into contracts with providers of health care for the purpose of establishing regional screening programs for diethylstilbestrol exposed persons. . . .
>
> 3. Each provider of health care that enters into a contract as provided for in this section shall conduct a training program in conjunction with the department for purposes of instructing physicians, physician assistants and nurses within the respective health systems agency in the detection, diagnosis, treatment and prevention of diethylstilbestrol exposed persons.
>
> 4. The bureau of cancer control within the health department shall establish and maintain a registry of women who took diethylstilbestrol during pregnancy and their offspring who were exposed to diethylstilbestrol prenatally for the purpose of follow-up care and treatment of long term problems associated with diethylstilbestrol exposure. Enrollment in the registry shall be upon a voluntary basis. . . .
>
> Effective Date. Section effective Aug. 7, 1978, pursuant to L.1978, c. 715, §4.

In conjunction with the enactment of the DES statute the New York Legislature made the following findings:

> The effective identification, screening, diagnosis, care and treatment of persons who have taken diethylstilbestrol, commonly referred to as DES, or who have been exposed to DES prenatally is of paramount public importance.
>
> Between 1940 and 1970, DES a synthetic estrogen-type hormone, was extensively administered to pregnant women threatened with miscarriage. Subsequently, a causal association was found between DES and an unusual type of cervical and vaginal cancer in the female offspring of those who took the drug during pregnancy. As a result of these findings, the use of DES during pregnancy has been discontinued, however, it is estimated that at least one hundred thousand persons in New York state were exposed prenatally. The

> vast majority of these persons are unaware of their exposure and have not been adequately screened for any malignant condition.
>
> This problem in cancer control is likely to grow significantly over the next few years as exposed female offspring reach reproductive age, the time when abnormalities become apparent. The situation is compounded by the relative newness of the studies associating DES with cancer. Thus, many physicians are not yet familiar with screening and treatment techniques or with the implications of the most recent research results.
>
> It is, therefore, imperative that both a program for identification, screening, diagnosis, care and treatment of DES-exposed persons and a professional education program for physicians be established so that exposed persons may benefit from the best possible diagnostic procedure and treatment.

The following law journal articles discuss the background and development of DES related actions: Abrahams and Musgrave, THE DES LABYRINTH, 33 South Carolina LR 663 (1982); Robinson, MULTIPLE CAUSATION IN TORT LAW: REFLECTIONS ON THE DES CASES, 68 Virginia LR 713 (1982); COMMENT, BEYOND ENTERPRISE LIABILITY IN DES CASES -SINDELL, 14 Indiana Law Review 695 (1981); COMMENT, DES AND A PROPOSED THEORY OF ENTERPRISE LIABILITY, 46 Fordham LR 963 (1978); A REMEDY FOR THE "DES DAUGHTERS": PRODUCTS LIABILITY WITHOUT THE IDENTIFICATION REQUIREMENT, 42 University of Pittsburgh LR 669 (1981); DES CASES AND THE MOVE TOWARD NEW TORT REMEDIES, 49 University of Missouri at Kansas City LR 245 (1981); MARKET SHARE LIABILITY: A NEW METHOD OF RECOVERY FOR DES LITIGANTS, 30 Catholic University LR 551 (1981); MARKET SHARE LIABILITY: AN ANSWER TO THE DES CAUSATION PROBLEM, 94 Harvard LR 668 (1981). The following medical articles discuss DES in terms of medical issues: Dunn and Green, CYSTS OF THE EPIDIDYMIS, CANCER OF THE CERVIX, GRANULAR CELL MYOBLASTOMA, AND OTHER LESIONS AFTER ESTROGEN INJECTION IN NEW BORN MICE, 31 Journal of National Cancer Institute 425 (1963); Fu, Robboy and Prat, NUCLEAR DNA STUDY OF VAGINAL AND CERVICAL SQUAMOUS CELL ABNORMALITIES IN DES EXPOSED PROGENY, 52 Journal of Obstetrics and Gynecology 129 (1978); Greenwald, Barlow, Nasca and Burnett, VAGINAL CANCER AFTER MATERNAL TREATMENT WITH SYNTHETIC ESTROGENS, 285 New England Journal of Medicine 878 (1971); Herbst, Ulfelder and Poskanzer, ADENOCARCINOMA OF THE VAGINA, 384 New England Journal of Medicine 878 (1971); McLachlon, Newbold and Bullock, LONG-TERM EFFECTS ON THE FEMALE MOUSE GENITAL TRACT ASSOCIATED WITH PRENATAL EXPOSURE TO DIETHYLSTILBESTROL, 40 Cancer Research 3988 (1980); Poskanzer and Herbst, EPIDEMIOLOGY OF VAGINAL ADENOSIS AND ADENOCARCINOMA ASSOCIATED WITH EXPOSURE TO STILBESTROL IN UTERO, 39 Cancer 1892 (1977);

Ulfelder, THE STILBESTROL-ADENOSIS-CARCINOMA SYNDROME, 38 Cancer 426 (1976).

3. [§6.27] Causes of Action Alleged

In cases that have been brought based on injury allegedly caused by *in utero* exposure to diethylstilbestrol (DES) [as to a definition of DES, see §6.25], plaintiffs have generally relied on three causes of action theories: strict liability [see, e.g., *Bichler v Eli Lilly & Co*, 55 NY2d 571 (NY 1982)], negligence [see, e.g., *Ferrigno v Eli Lilly & Co*, 175 NJ Super 551, 420 A2d 1305 (1980)], and breach of implied warranty [see, e.g., *Ferrigno*, above]. However, regardless of the plaintiff's cause of action, the plaintiff must:

1) demonstrate a duty to her while she was a fetus;
2) successfully argue that the statute of limitations did not run;
3) answer the cause-in-fact issue — who made the pills her mother ingested;
4) prove legal causation by means of statistical proof rather than the easier to observe cause and effect;
5) prove damages, including the physical trauma involved and the value of the potential future problems she will face.

See Abrahams and Musgrave, THE DES LABYRINTH, 33 South Carolina LR 663 (1982).

The most significant issue in the initial DES cases has centered on whether the plaintiff can identify the specific manufacturer of the injury causing DES. This issue is important because, as a general rule, a plaintiff in a products liability case must prove that the defendant-manufacturer actually produced the injury causing product. Prosser, HANDBOOK OF THE LAW OF TORTS, §103 (4th ed. 1971). Several DES cases have been resolved in the defendant's favor based on the plaintiff's inability to specifically identify the defendant. See, e.g., *Pipon v Burroughs-Wellcome Co*, 532 FSupp 637 (D NJ 1982); *Barros v E R Squibb & Sons*, No. 75-1226 (ED Pa 1978); *Gray v United States*, 445 FSupp 337 (SD Tx 1978).

In *Gray*, for example, the plaintiff brought a civil damage suit against a drug company, Eli Lilly and Company, and the United States. The plaintiff alleged that she had been harmed by DES taken by her mother during the plaintiff's period of gestation. The court said that in essence this was a products liability case. Lilly contended that the plaintiff had failed to identify it as the particular manufacturer of the drug which caused her injury. The court said that is a fundamental principle of products liability law that a plaintiff must prove, as an essential element of the case, that a defendant-manufacturer actually made the particular product which caused the injury. The court said it was apparent that the plaintiff was unable to identify Lilly as the particular manufacturer of the DES taken by her mother. In 1953 and 1954 there were at least 100 separate companies offering to sell some form of DES. The plaintiff could not of her own knowledge identify which of these companies manufactured the drug taken by her pregnant mother, the court said. Moreover, the plaintiff's mother testified that she could not identify what brand of DES she took, nor could she remember the shape, color, or dosage of the DES ingested. Therefore, the court granted Lilly's motion for summary judgment.

However, this problem area, which comes under the causation in fact element of a DES action, does not always lead to the dismissal of the action. In some cases, courts have chosen to apply substitutes to the manufacturer identity issue, and thus the plaintiff has been allowed to pursue the action without being required to specifically identify the manufacturer. The types of substitutes that have been considered have been alternative liability [see, e.g., *Ferrigno v Eli Lilly & Co*, 175 NJ Super 551, 420 A2d 1305 (1980); generally, see §6.32], concert of action [see, e.g., *Payton v Abbott Labs*, 521 FSupp 1031 (D Ma 1981); generally, see §6.30], enterprise liability [see, e.g., *Namm v Charles E Frosst & Co*, 178 NJ Super 19, 427 A2d 1121 (1981); generally, see §6.34], and market share liability [see *Sindell v Abbott Laboratories*, 26 Ca3d 588, 163 CaR 132, 607 P2d 924, cert den, 449 US 912 (1980); generally, see §6.36]. The cause-in-fact manufacturer identity issue is discussed in more detail in §6.29.

Another principle issue in DES cases is whether the plaintiff can prove legal causation between the plaintiff's injury and the ingestion of DES. There have been suggestions that DES and the development of vaginal clear cell adenocarcinoma are linked [see, e.g., Abrahams and Musgrave, THE DES LABYRINTH, 33 South Carolina LR 663 (1982); Herbst, Poskanzer, Robboy, Friedlander and Scully, PRENATAL EXPOSURE TO STILBESTROL, 292 New England Journal of Medicine 334 (1975)], but only one case has addressed this issue. In *Bichler v Eli Lilly & Co*, 55 NY2d 571 (NY 1982), the court affirmed a jury verdict for the DES-plaintiff, and did not disturb the jury's findings that DES was a proximate cause of the plaintiff's injury. [As to the interrogatories the jury answered in *Bichler* upon which liability was predicated, see §6.26.]

Other causes of action alleged by plaintiffs in DES cases have been aiding and abetting [see *Payton v Abbott Labs*, 512 FSupp 1031 (D Ma 1981)], civil conspiracy, [see *Ryan v Eli Lilly & Co*, 514 FSupp 1004 (D SC 1981)], joint venture [see *Payton v Abbott Labs*, 512 FSupp 1031 (D Ma 1981)], and battery [see *Mink v University of Chicago*, 460 FSupp 713 (ND Il 1978)].

4. [§6.28] Damages Sought and Awarded

The damages sought in cases involving actions based on the *in utero* exposure to diethylstilbestrol (DES) [as to a definition of DES, see §6.25] are much the same, and in some instances identical, to the damages sought in other products liability actions. For example, DES-plaintiffs have sought compensatory damages for personal injury [see, e.g., *Sindell v Abbott Laboratories*, 26 CaA3d 588, 163 CaR 132, 607 P2d 924, cert den, 449 US 912 (1980); *Bichler v Eli Lilly & Co*, 55 NY2d 571 (NY 1982)], as well as punitive damages [see, e.g., *Bichler*, above]. Moreover, equitable relief has been sought by a DES-plaintiff requesting a court order that the DES-defendants warn physicians and others of the danger of DES and the necessity of performing certain tests to determine the presence of disease caused by the drug, and that free clinics be established in California to perform such tests. See *Sindell*, above.

Damage awards in DES cases have not received much appellate judicial review since in most DES cases the causation-in-fact element of the action [as to a more detailed discussion of this element in DES cases, see generally §6.29] has thus far predominated over the damages issue. However, a jury award of $500,000 to a DES-plaintiff was affirmed in one action. See *Bichler v Eli Lilly & Co*, 55 NY2d 571 (NY 1982). In another DES action, *Axler v E R Squibb & Sons, Inc*, Sept. term 1978, No. 2888 (Common Pleas Court of Philadelphia County), a plaintiff won a $1.75 million jury verdict for damages stemming from her *in utero* exposure to DES. See DES USER'S DAUGHTER GETS $1.75 MILLION AWARD, The National Law Journal, April 12, 1982, p. 11. DES-plaintiffs also recovered damages by means of a settlement in *Mink v University of Chicago*, 77-C-1431 (ND Il). In *Mink*, the plaintiffs were three women who unwittingly took part in a medical experiment involving DES. The plaintiffs did not claim that they had been injured, but rather argued that they had suffered mental distress because of the health problems their daughters might potentially face. In the settlement, the women received $250,000 for their emotional suffering, and it was provided that the defendant-university would provide free medical treatment to DES exposed women who contract clear cell adenocarcinoma of the vagina or cervix. See EXPERIMENTAL DES USERS PAID $225,000 IN SETTLEMENT, The National Law Journal, March 15, 1982, p. 3. [As to a detailed discussion of damages in products liability cases, see Sherman, PRODUCTS LIABILITY FOR THE GENERAL PRACTITIONER, (Shepard's/ McGraw-Hill 1981).]

B. Causation-In-Fact: Manufacturer Identity

1. [§6.29] Generally

After a diethylstilbestrol (DES) [as to a definition of DES, see §6.25] plaintiff has established a duty to the unborn fetus [generally, see §5.49], an injury, proximate cause, and has brought the action within the time period of the statute of limitations [as to limitation on actions in DES cases, see §6.38], the DES plaintiff must address the issue that is perhaps the most significant issue in DES actions — the identification of the proper DES manufacturer. This is referred to as the causation-in-fact, as distinguished from the legal causation [as to a more detailed discussion of legal causation, see §6.26] portion of the DES action. Abrahams and Musgrave, THE DES LABYRINTH, 33 South Carolina LR 663 (1982). This issue is important since, under general rules applicable in products liability actions, the plaintiff must show a causal connection between the defendant-manufacturer and the product. See *Ryan v Eli Lilly & Co*, 514 FSupp 1004 (D SC 1981).

In considering the causation-in-fact issue it is important to know how the drug was developed and marketed. DES is a generic name for the drug was manufactured by several hundred companies and marketed under numerous brand names. COMMENT, DIETHYLSTILBESTROL: EXTENSION OF FEDERAL CLASS ACTION PROCEDURES TO GENERIC DRUG LITIGATION, 14 University San Francisco LR 461 (1980). There existed common chemical standards, generic marketing techniques, and uniform labeling and product literature in the development of DES. Abrahams and Musgrave at 675. The DES industry was led by 12 manufacturers in the attempt to secure Food and Drug Administration (FDA) approval to market DES. Initially, applications to market DES were rejected. Subsequently, however, the 12 manufacturers, including Eli Lilly and Company, were convened at the request of the FDA. The manufacturers agreed to cooperate in the approval process. Thereafter, these 12 worked through a voluntarily formed committee known as the "Small Committee," which consisted of representatives of four of the manufacturers and was chaired by Lilly. The Small Committee pooled all clinical data pertaining to DES for submission to the FDA. Lilly's literature became the model for the literature used as the package insert. Although the subsequent FDA approval was limited to use for several conditions, none of which was related to pregnancy, there was evidence that Lilly was even then contemplating use of DES for toxemia in pregnancy.

In 1947, Lilly and other drug companies filed supplemental applications with the FDA for permission to market DES for treatment of certain complications of pregnancy involving early termination of pregnancy or death of the fetus. See *Bichler v Eli Lilly & Co*, 79 AD2d 317, 436 NYS2d 625 (1981). It has been estimated that Lilly and five or six other manufacturers accounted for 90 per cent of the DES market. COMMENT, DES AND A PROPOSED THEORY OF ENTERPRISE LIABILITY, 46 Fordham LR 963 (1978). And in one case, expert testimony suggested that Lilly was the largest producer of DES with a 45 per cent share of the market. *Bichler*, above.

The identification of the defendant is a critical issue since it involves a necessary component of the cause-in-fact requirement of a negligence action. See Abrahams and Musgrave, THE DES LABYRINTH, 33 South Carolina LR 663 (1982). Where the identity of the drug company that manufactured the DES which caused the plaintiff's injuries is known, these lawsuits can be prosecuted within well established principles of products liability as those principles have been adapted to the manufacturing and marketing of prescription drugs. See *Bichler v Eli Lilly & Co*, 55 NY2d 571 (NY 1982). However, because of the destruction of many doctors' records as a result of the time lapse between the time DES was ingested, the manifestation of the injury, and the initiation of the action, many DES plaintiffs have not been able to identify the specific manufacturer of the DES which allegedly caused the injury. See COMMENT, DES AND A PROPOSED THEORY OF ENTERPRISE LIABILITY, 46 Fordham LR 963 (1978). The result, as described by one court, is that DES plaintiffs face a dilemma: they have, if their claim is upheld, been injured by parallel conduct of a group of pharmaceutical manufacturers. But the practical impossibility for most victims of pinpointing the manufacturer directly responsible for their particular injury threatens to bar any recovery. *Bichler*, above.

Because of the fungible nature of DES, and because many litigants may be unable to identify the manufacturer of the DES, traditional theories of products liability law have tended to offer an inadequate basis for compensation to DES-plaintiffs. See NOTE, MARKET SHARE LIABILITY: A NEW METHOD OF RECOVERY FOR DES LITIGANTS, 30 Catholic University LR 551 (1981). Therefore, DES plaintiffs have had to rely on other methods for satisfying the cause-in-fact element. If the plaintiff fails to gain judicial acceptance of one of these substitute methods her suit will be lost even before it can be considered whether she was injured by the defendant's negligence. See *Barros v E R Squibb & Sons*, Inc, No. 75-1226 (ED Pa 1978); Abrahams and Musgrave, at 675. Moreover, it has been said regarding these substitute methods for proving cause-in-fact, products liability law cannot be expected to stand still where innocent victims face inordinately difficult problems of proof. *Bichler*, above. Thus, courts as well as commentators have proposed means which permit recovery by prenatally exposed DES-plaintiffs. The proposals involve the application of already accepted tort principles of concert of action and alternative liability to the unusual DES fact pattern as well as resort to more novel theories of enterprise and market share liability.

The first of these substitutes, concert of action [generally, see §6.30] has two main elements. First, the plaintiff must establish that the defendant and the other manufacturers had an agreement to perform the tortious act or achieve the particular result. Second, the plaintiff must prove that the defendant's own conduct was tortious. See *Payton v Abbott Labs*, 512 FSupp 1031 (D Ma 1981). The concert of action theory derives from a criminal law concept. See *Ryan v Eli Lilly & Co*, 514 FSupp 1004 (D SC 1981). The concert of action theory has received both judicial rejection [see, e.g., *Payton v Abbott Labs*, 512 FSupp 1031 (D Ma 1981)] and acceptance [see *Abel v Eli Lilly & Co*, 94 MiA 59, 289 NW2d 20 (1980)] in the context of DES actions.

The theory of alternative liability [generally, see §6.32] has also been used as a means of satisfying causation-in-fact. This theory involves independent acts by two or more tortfeasors, all of whom have acted wrongfully, but only one of whom has injured the plaintiff. Because it is impossible to determine which defendant was responsible for the plaintiff's injury joint and several liability is imposed on the defendants. See *Abel v Eli Lilly & Co*, 94 MiA 59, 289 NW2d 20 (1980). Some courts have approved the application of this theory to DES cases [see, e.g., *Ferrigno v Eli Lilly & Co*, 175 NJ Super 551, 420 A2d 1305 (1980)], while others have prevented its application [see, e.g., *Ryan v Eli Lilly & Co*, 514 FSupp 1004 (D SC 1981)] in DES cases.

The theory of enterprise liability [generally, see §6.34] has also been considered as a substitute to specifically identifying the defendant. Enterprise liability focuses on industry-wide conduct, but does not require a tacit agreement. See Abrahams and Musgrave, THE DES LABYRINTH, 33 South Carolina LR 663 (1982). In enterprise liability, the plaintiff is required to establish that the plaintiff is not at fault for the inability to define the causative agent, that the defendants owed a duty to the plaintiff, and that there existed an insufficient industry-wide standard of safety as to the manufacture of the product. See COMMENT, DES AND A PROPOSED THEORY OF ENTERPRISE LIABILITY, 46 Fordham LR 963 (1978). This theory has yet to receive judicial acceptance in a DES case. Abrahams and Musgrave, THE DES LABYRINTH, 33 South Carolina LR 663 (1982).

Finally, the theory of market share liability has been asserted as a way to satisfy the causation-in-fact element of the action. In market share liability, the plaintiff joins those defendants who have manufactured a substantial share of the market. Then the burden of proof is shifted to the defendants to prove their innocence. See COMMENT, MARKET SHARE LIABILITY FOR DEFECTIVE PRODUCTS: AN ILL-ADVISED REMEDY FOR THE PROBLEM OF IDENTIFICATION, 76 Northwestern University LR 300 (1981). The concept of market share liability in DES actions has been accepted in one instance [see *Sindell v Abbott Laboratories*, 26 Ca3d 588, 163 CaR 132, 607 P2d 924, cert den, 449 US 912 (1980)] and rejected in another [see *Mizell v Eli Lilly & Co*, 526 FSupp 589 (D SC 1981)].

2. [§6.30] Concert of Action

One of the substitute means by which a plaintiff in an action predicated on a mother's ingestion of diethylstilbestrol (DES) [as to a definition of DES, see

§6.25] and subsequent injury to the fetus can meet the cause-in-fact requirement of a negligence action is through the theory of concert of action. This approach is made necessary because in many instances the DES-plaintiff is not able to specifically identify the manufacturer who made the DES the plaintiff's mother ingested. [As to a more detailed discussion of the background of DES actions, see §6.26.] It has been suggested that the purpose of the concert of action concept is not so much to solve problems of identification of the defendant as to deter anti-social behavior. See *Lyons v Premo Pharmaceutical Labs, Inc*, 170 NJ Super 183, 406 A2d 185 (1979). RESTATEMENT (SECOND) OF TORTS §876 sets out the following definition of concert of action:

> For harm resulting to a third person from the tortious conduct of another, one is subject to liability if he (a) does a tortious act in concert with the other or pursuant to a common design with him, or (b) knows that the other's conduct constitutes a breach of duty and gives substantial assistance or encouragement to the other so to conduct himself, or (c) gives substantial assistance to the other in accomplishing a tortious result and his own conduct, separately considered, constitutes a breach of duty to the third person.

With respect to this doctrine, Prosser has stated that:

> [T]he original meaning of a joint tort was that of vicarious liability for concerted action. . . . All those who, in pursuance of a common plan, a design to commit a tortious act, actively take part in it, or further it by cooperation or request, or who lend aid or encouragement to the wrongdoer, or ratify and adopt his acts done for their benefit, are equally liable with him. Prosser, HANDBOOK OF THE LAW OF TORTS §46 (4th ed 1971).

Therefore, there are two main elements of the concert of action theory. First, the plaintiff must establish that the defendant and the others have an agreement to perform the tortious act or achieve the particular result. The plaintiff need not prove the existence of an agreement by direct evidence. Rather, an agreement can be inferred from conduct of the parties suggesting that they had an implied meeting of minds. And second, the plaintiff must prove that the defendant's own conduct was tortious. This does not mean that the defendant's conduct must cause or be a substantial factor in causing the plaintiff's injury. Rather, this element requires only that the defendants have acted negligently or in an intentionally tortious manner. See *Payton v Abbott Labs*, 512 FSupp 1031 (D Ma 1981).

The concert of action theory derives from a criminal law concept, aiding and abetting. Concert has been found in such conduct as group assault and battery, illegal highway racing, and conversion and trespass by related corporations. See *Ryan v Eli Lilly & Co*, 514 FSupp 1004 (D SC 1981).

An injured plaintiff may pursue any one joint tortfeasor on a concert of action theory. Such tortfeasor may, in turn seek contribution from others who acted in concert with him. The clearest example of concert of action liability is the drag race. Where two drivers agree to race and one collides with and injures a third party, the other driver is fully responsible for the third party's injury even though there was no contact between that driver's car and the injured person. See *Bichler v Eli Lilly & Co*, 55 NY2d 57 (NY 1982). Therefore, even if the defendant caused no harm itself, the defendant will be liable for the harm caused by his fellow manufacturers because all acted jointly. See *Abel v Eli Lilly & Co*, 94 MiA 59, 289 NW2d 20 (1980).

It has been held in a DES case that the existence of pharmaceutical trade associations, the practice of drug companies sending representatives to scientific conferences, and the fact that some defendants sold DES to competitors does not support an inference of agreement. There is nothing inherently wrong with membership in an industry-wide trade association, with participating in scientific conferences, or with selling products to a competitor in an arms-length transaction, the court said in *Payton*, above. And another court has suggested that application of the concept of concert of action in a DES case would expand the doctrine far beyond its intended scope and would render virtually any manufacturer liable for the defective products of an entire industry, even if it could be demonstrated that the product which caused the injury was not made by the defendant. See *Sindell v Abbott Laboratories*, 26 Ca3d 607, 163 CaR 132, 607 P2d 924, cert den, 449 US 912 (1980). But there is authority that the concert of action concept can be applied in a DES case. See *Bichler v Eli Lilly & Co*, 55 NY2d 571 (NY 1982). [As to specific cases illustrative of the general principles of concert of action as applied in DES cases, see §6.31.]

3. [§6.31] —Illustrative Cases

The following cases are illustrative of the general principles related to the concert of action [generally, see §6.30] theory in a diethylstilbestrol (DES) [as to a definition of DES, see §6.25] context where the courts hold the theory was not applicable:

In *Payton v Abbott Labs*, 512 FSupp 1031 (D Ma 1981), the court held that there was no evidence that the defendants agreed not to test DES properly for its use as a miscarriage preventative or not to warn of its carcinogenic dangers. Therefore, the court said the plaintiffs failed to meet their burden of establishing an issue of fact under the concert of action theory. The plaintiffs argued that the drug companies that marketed DES tortiously agreed not to test the drug properly to determine its safety and efficacy as a miscarriage preventative and not to warn of the carcinogenic danger which DES posed to the fetus. The plaintiffs acknowledged that there was no direct evidence of an agreement not to test DES properly or to warn of its carcinogenic effects. They asserted, however, that such an agreement could be inferred from the consciously parallel behavior of the drug companies, in particular the fact that all the companies failed to test DES on pregnant laboratory animals, that all failed to warn of the carcinogenic danger which DES posed to the fetus, and that all marketed the drug in spite of compelling evidence that it was not effective to prevent miscarriages. The court said that parallel conduct by itself cannot prove agreement, but noted that the plaintiffs also argued that other factors, including evidence of actual collaboration among companies regarding DES in 1939-1941, and evidence of the opportunity to collaborate, taken in conjunction with the parallel behavior gave rise to a reasonable inference that the companies had an agreement. The plaintiffs argued that the defendants' collaborative activity regarding DES in 1939 through 1941 raised a strong inference that such collaboration continued into the future, and included an agreement about testing and warnings. Such an inference, however, does not flow naturally from the facts established in the record, the court said. The 1941 collaboration was confined to the activities of the "Small Committee", the sole purpose of which was to collect and organize clinical data that had already been accumulated by the individual drug companies filing new drug applications (NDA). The scope of this collaboration was extremely limited, the court said. The committee did not decide what type of testing was to be performed, it did not regulate the volume of testing, and indeed, it had no impact whatsoever on the scientific content of the clinical data submitted to the Food and Drug Administration, the court said. The court did not see how a broad scaled agreement not to test properly or warn could reasonably be inferred from such a limited cooperative effort. Another factor that the plaintiffs relied on in establishing inference of agreement was that the drug companies had ample opportunity to collaborate and plan such an agreement. In particular, the plaintiffs pointed to three facts, the existence of pharmaceutical trade associations, the practice of drug companies sending representatives to scientific conferences, and the fact that some of the defendants sold DES to competitors, as evidence that the drug companies were often in contact with one another regarding DES. These facts did not, however, support an inference of agreement, the court said. There was nothing inherently wrong with membership in an industry-wide trade association, with participating in scientific conferences, or with selling products to a competitor in an arms-length transaction. Indeed, these practices are probably common to most industries, the court said. Therefore, the court concluded that there was no evidence that the defendants agreed not to test DES properly for its use as a miscarriage preventative or not to warn of its carcinogenic dangers, and held that the plaintiffs failed to meet their burden of establishing an issue of fact under the concert of action theory.

In *Ryan v Eli Lilly & Co*, 514 FSupp 1004 (D SC 1981), the plaintiff alleged that she developed a precancerous condition as a result of her prenatal exposure to DES taken by her mother during 1952 and 1953. The plaintiff was born May 1, 1953. Prior to that time her mother had ingested DES obtained by a prescription from her doctor to prevent possible miscarriage. The plaintiff alleged that the DES ingested by her mother was manufactured by Eli Lilly and Company or by E. R. Squibb and Sons. In addition to Lilly and Squibb, the plaintiff joined five other drug manufacturers as party defendants, alleging a conspiracy in their production of synthetic estrogens. The matter came before the court upon the defendants' joint motion for summary judgment. In response to the defendants' motion, the plaintiff alleged four new theories which included concert of action. The court said the concert of action theory had been applied in both North and South Carolina, but each case involved an extremely narrow fact pattern. Like civil conspiracy, the concert of action theory derives from a criminal law concept, aiding and abetting, and renders jointly and severally liable all who intentionally participate in an unlawful activity that proximately caused the plaintiff's injuries, the court noted. Although concert of action does not require for its application a conspiracy among the parties to engage in particular conduct, mere common plan, design, or even express agreement is not enough for liability itself, the court said. There must be acts of a tortious character in carrying it into execution, the court said. In a product liability action against drug manufacturers, a plaintiff seeking to base a complaint on a concert of action theory would have to prove in addition to a parallel course of conduct among defendants, evidence of some agreement, express or tacit, or a common plan among manufacturers not to test adequately or not to warn of dangers that were known, and this the plaintiff cannot do, the court concluded.

In *Sindell v Abbott Laboratories*, 26 Ca3d 607, 163 CaR 132, 607 P2d 924, cert den, 449 US 912 (1980), the plaintiff brought an action against 11 drug companies and Does one through 100 on behalf of herself and other women similarly situated. The complaint alleged that the defendants were in the business of manufacturing, promoting, and marketing DES, and that during the period the defendants marketed DES, they knew or should have known that it was a carcinogenic substance, that there was a grave danger it would cause cancer in the daughters of mothers who ingested it, and that it was ineffective to prevent miscarriage. The court noted that under federal law prior to 1962, a new drug was defined as one not generally recognized as safe. Such a substance could be marketed only if a new drug application had been filed with the Food and Drug Administration and had become effective, the court noted. If the agency determined that a product was no longer a new drug, it could be manufactured by any drug company without submitting an application to the agency, the court said. According to defendants, 123 new drug applications for DES had been approved by 1952, and in that year DES was declared not to be a new drug, thus allowing any manufacturer to produce it without prior testing and without submitting a new drug application to the Food and Drug Administration. The plaintiff contended that her complaint stated a cause of action under these principles. She alleged that the defendants' wrongful conduct was the result of planned and concerted action, express and implied agreements, collaboration in, reliance upon, acquiescence in and ratification, exploitation and adoption of each other's testing, marketing methods, lack of warnings and other acts or omissions and that acting individually and in concert, defendants promoted, approved, authorized, acquiesced in, and reaped profits from sales of DES. These allegations, the plaintiff claimed, stated a tacit understanding among the defendants to commit a tortious act against her. In the court's view, however, the charges were insufficient to allege a cause of action under the rules for concerted action. The gravamen of the charge of concert is that defendants failed to adequately test the drug or to give sufficient warning of its dangers and that they relied upon the tests performed by one another and took advantage of each others' promotional and marketing techniques, the court noted. These allegations did not amount to a charge that there was a tacit understanding or a common plan among the defendants to fail to conduct adequate tests or give sufficient warnings, and that they substantially aided and encouraged one another in these omissions, the court believed. The complaint charged also that defendants produced DES from a common and mutually agreed upon formula, allowing pharmacists to treat the drug as a fungible commodity and to fill prescriptions from whatever brand of DES they had on hand at the time. It was difficult for the court to understand how these allegations could form the basis of a cause of action for wrongful conduct by defendants, acting in concert. The formula for DES is a scientific constant, the court noted. It is set forth in the UNITED STATES PHARMACOPOEIA, and any manufacturer producing that drug must utilize the formula set forth in that compendium, the court said. What the complaint appears to charge, the court believed, is the defendants engaged in parallel or imitative conduct in that they relied upon each others' testing and promotion methods. But such conduct describes a common practice in industry: a producer avails himself of the experience and methods of others making the same or similar products, the court said. Application of the concept of concert of action to this situation would expand the doctrine far beyond its intended scope and would render virtually any manufacturer liable for the defective products of an entire industry, even if it could be demonstrated that the product which caused the injury was not made by the defendant, the court concluded.

In *Lyons v Premo Pharmaceutical Labs, Inc*, 170 NJ Super 183, 406 A2d 185 (1979), the deceased's mother ingested DES in 1956 to prevent spontaneous abortion. Subsequently the plaintiff was born. In 1973, the deceased discovered she had clear cell adenocarcinoma of the cervix, and subsequently death ensued. The deceased's administrator brought an action against various DES manufacturers alleging that the DES had resulted in the death. The court, in considering the concert of action theory, noted that in 1940 American drug manufacturers began seeking FDA permission to produce and market the drug. The FDA requested that the applications be consolidated. The court noted that applications in the early 1940's sought authorization to manufacture and distribute DES for four purposes: the treatment of postmenopausal symptoms; senile vaginitis; gonorrheal vaginitis in the prepubertal girls; and suppression of lactation. In 1947, in order to benefit from all this interest and activity, many drug companies filed additional applications requesting authorization to market DES in larger dosages to treat pregnancy problems. The court believed the plaintiffs tried to ignore all distinctions between the 1940 and 1947 applications to market drugs with DES. It should be remembered that the use of DES to combat abortions, which is the only issue here, resulted from the 1947 applications, the court said. It was true, as plaintiffs argued, that the companies made reference in their 1947 applications to those of 1940; however, it must be borne in mind that it is not the safety of DES which is being questioned; it is only its ingestion by pregnant women which has been declared unsafe, and the 1940 applications did not contemplate that use, the court said. There was nothing anti-social about placing DES on the market for its pre-1947 purposes, the court believed. It can hardly be said, therefore, that the drug companies' conduct in seeking approval for the drug in 1940 should be classified as tortious, the court said. The plaintiffs failed to show that the drug company defendants were in any way responsible for the particular product which caused the deceased's death, the court concluded.

The following cases are illustrative of the general principles related to the concert of action theory in a DES context where the courts' held the theory could be applied:

In *Abel v Eli Lilly & Co*, 94 MiA 59, 289 NW2d 20 (1980), the defendants argued that permitting the plaintiffs to proceed to trial on their concert of action theory was without precedent and was tantamount to imposing liability on an innocent manufacturer for the actions of his fellow manufacturers. The court said this argument misperceived the nature of the plaintiffs' claim. It is well established that if two or more persons engage negligently in a concerted activity, and as a result the plaintiff is injured, all are liable even though only one directly caused the injury, the court said. Liability is posed on all because all have joined in breaching their duty of care to the plaintiff, and he or she was injured as a result of that breach, the court added. The plaintiffs in their complaint alleged that the defendants acted in concert to produce and market ineffective and dangerous products, without adequate testing and without adequate warnings. These allegations were sufficient to state a cause of action, and summary judgment in favor of the defendants as to the concerted activity claim was improper, the court said. Moreover, the court said, the concert of action claim is a true joint tort, and once the fact of a tortfeasor's liability is established, its extent is clear: the tortfeasor is jointly and severally liable for the entire amount of the damages, although the joint tortfeasor may be entitled to contribution from fellow tortfeasors. Although a joint tortfeasor may, and usually does, dispute the fact of liability, the joint tortfeasor may not dispute the extent thereof, the court said. The joint tortfeasor may seek to show that only the tortfeasor's co-defendant, and not the tortfeasor, acted wrongfully, but the tortfeasor may not seek to show that the fellow tortfeasor caused all or the greater portion of the damage and should therefore pay a greater share, the court said. Therefore, even if the defendant causes no harm itself, the court concluded, it is liable for the harm caused by its fellows because all acted jointly.

In *Bichler v Eli Lilly & Co*, 55 NY2d 571 (NY 1982), the court reviewed the trial court's instructions to the jury in a DES case in which the plaintiff won a $500,000 jury verdict. The plaintiff alleged she contracted cancer at age 17 because of her prenatal exposure to DES. Because the trial court submitted two theories of concerted action on which Lilly's liability for plaintiff's injuries could be premised, concerted action by agreement and concerted action by substantial assistance, and the court did not know which theory was accepted by the jury, it evaluated the sufficiency of the evidence to support recovery under either. As the court read the trial court's instructions on concerted action by agreement, the jury was permitted to infer from evidence of consciously parallel behavior that an implied agreement existed between Lilly and other drug companies to market DES for problems of human pregnancy without first conducting tests with DES upon pregnant mice. No "direct evidence" or "plus factor" is required, the court said, and consciously parallel conduct by itself was enough. Similarly, the trial court's charge on concerted action by substantial assistance required the jury to find only that Lilly's failure to test DES on pregnant mice before marketing the drug for use by pregnant women substantially aided or encouraged other DES manufacturers to do the same. No express agreement was required, the court said. Nor was it necessary for the jury to find that Lilly itself was responsible for the manufacture of the DES tablets taken by plaintiff's mother, the court noted. Review of the evidence solely on the basis of events beginning in 1947, showed that it was sufficient to support jury findings of both conscious parallelism and substantial assistance or encouragement under the jury instructions to which no exception was taken. The court said the record showed that eight companies filed new drug applications (NDA) to market DES for problems of pregnancy between April 1947 and October 1948. Lilly's application was the second of these, filed only two weeks after the leader. Each of the eight applications relied substantially on the same studies of three research teams that were reported between 1941 and 1947, the court said. Each requested approval to market 25 milligram tablets, a dosage five times more powerful than the maximum five milligram tablets approved in 1941. For the jury to infer that this closely parallel conduct was conscious or that Lilly's participation in this first wave of DES pregnancy-related NDA filings substantially encouraged the other 140 companies which were engaged in manufacturing and marketing DES for the same purpose by 1953 was within the realm of the fact-finding function, the court believed.

4. [§6.32] Alternative Liability

One of the most difficult issues in cases alleging injury caused by *in utero* exposure to diethylstilbestrol (DES) [as to a definition of DES, see §6.25] is that of identifying the specific manufacturer. This is generally necessary so as to satisfy the cause-in-fact requirement in a negligence action. COMMENT, DES AND A PROPOSED THEORY OF ENTERPRISE LIABILITY, 47 Fordham LR 963 (1978). One substitute to specifically identifying the defendant in meeting this issue is by the concept of alternative liability. [As to other methods of addressing the manufacturers' identity issue, see §6.29.]

Alternative liability involves not a joint tort, but rather independent acts by two or more tortfeasors, all of whom have acted wrongfully, but only one of whom has injured the plaintiff. Joint and several liability is imposed, not because all are responsible for the damage, but because it is impossible to tell which one is responsible. Rather than deny the innocent plaintiff recovery because the plaintiff cannot prove which of two or more wrongdoers caused the injury, liability is imposed jointly on all wrongdoers. In cases of alternative liability, a defendant is free to absolve himself or herself of blame and cast the entire burden on his or her fellows, even if it be shown that he or she acted wrongfully, but the defendant must bear the burden of proving that his or her wrongful act was not the cause of the plaintiff's injury. See *Abel v Eli Lilly & Co*, 94 MiA 59, 289 NW2d 20 (1980).

The leading alternative liability case has been referred to as *Summers v Tice*, 33 Ca2d 80, 199 P2d 1 (1948). In *Summers*, the plaintiff was injured when two hunters negligently shot in his direction. It could not be determined which of them had fired the shot which actually caused the injury to the plaintiff's eye, but both defendants were nevertheless held jointly and severally liable for the whole of the damages. The court reasoned that both were wrongdoers, both were negligent toward the plaintiff, and that it would be unfair to require the plaintiff to isolate the defendant responsible, because if the one pointed out were to escape liability, the other might also, and the plaintiff-victim would be denied remedy. In these circumstances, the court held, the burden of proof is shifted to the defendants to absolve themselves. Under these circumstances a defendant is in a better position to offer evidence to determine whether he or she or another defendant caused the injury, the court reasoned. The rule formulated in *Summers* has been embodied in the RESTATEMENT (SECOND) OF TORTS §433B which states: where the conduct of two or more actors is tortious, and it is proved that harm has been caused to the plaintiff by only one of them, but there is uncertainty as to which one has caused it, the burden is upon each such actor to prove that he or she has not caused the harm.

Where the plaintiff establishes the specific manufacturer of the DES, she is no longer able to rely on the alternative liability theory since it requires the plaintiff to be ignorant of the source of her injury. See *Lyons v Premo Pharmaceutical Labs, Inc*, 170 NJ Super 183, 406 A2d 185 (1979).

5. [§6.33] —Illustrative Cases

In the following cases, the general principles applicable to cases seeking the application of the theory of alternative liability [generally, see §6.32] in a diethylstilbestrol (DES) context are discussed. The courts hold in these cases that the theory of alternative liability should not be applied:

In *Ryan v Eli Lilly & Co*, 514 FSupp 1004 (D SC 1981), the court said the plaintiff's reliance on alternative liability was misplaced. The court noted that the concept provides an exception to one of the most basic tenets of tort law, proof of proximate cause. Whether a South Carolina court would accept the theory of alternative liability is a moot question, the court said, because before it can be applied to permit the burden of proof to be shifted to the defendants, the plaintiff must demonstrate that the party that caused the harm is named as a defendant. Specifically, the court said, the plaintiff must produce evidence that one of the defendants' products was taken by her mother and caused her injuries. A suit against seven of 188 manufacturers must fail on this theory, the court said.

In *Sindell v Abbott Laboratories*, 26 Ca3d 588, 163 CaR 132, 607 P2d 924, cert den, 449 US 912 (1980), the court believed that the concept of alternative liability, as previously applied, could not relieve the plaintiff of the burden of proving the identity of the manufacturer which made the DES that allegedly caused the plaintiff's injury. The defendants asserted that the principles of alternative liability were inapplicable because as a predicate to applying alternative liability the defendants must have greater access to information regarding the injury than the plaintiff, whereas in this case the plaintiff had better access to the information. The court believed that in this case, as in the leading alternative liability case of *Summers v Tice*, 33 Ca2d

80, 199 P2d 1 (1948) [as to a more detailed description of the *Summers* case, see §6.32], the circumstances of the injury appeared to render identification of the manufacturer of the drug ingested by plaintiff's mother impossible by either plaintiff or defendants, and it could not reasonably be said that one was in a better position than the other to make the identification. Because many years elapsed between the time the drug was taken and the manifestation of plaintiff's injuries she, and many other daughters of mothers who took DES, are unable to make such identification. Certainly there can be no implication that the plaintiff is at fault in failing to do so —the event occurred while plaintiff was *in utero*, a generation ago, the court said. On the other hand, it cannot be said with assurance that defendants have the means to make the identification, the court said. In this connection, the defendants pointed out that drug manufacturers ordinarily have no direct contact with the patients who take a drug prescribed by their doctors, the court noted. The defendants sell to wholesalers, who in turn supply the product to physicians and pharmacies. Manufacturers do not maintain records of the persons who take the drugs they produce, and the selection of the medication is made by the physician rather than the manufacturer, the court said. Nor did the court conclude that the absence of evidence on this subject was due to the fault of defendants. While it was alleged that they produced a defective product with delayed effects and without adequate warning, the difficulty or impossibility of identification resulted primarily from the passage of time rather than from their allegedly negligent acts of failing to provide adequate warnings, the court reasoned. The court observed that while the defendants did not have means superior to plaintiff to identify the maker of the precise drug taken by her mother, they might in some instances be able to prove that they did not manufacture the injury-causing substance. In the present case, the court said one of the original defendants was dismissed from the action upon proof that it did not manufacture DES until after the plaintiff was born. Thus, the court concluded that the fact that defendants did not have greater access to information which might establish the identity of the manufacturer of the DES which injured plaintiff did not per se prevent application of the *Summers* rule. There was an important difference between *Summers* and *Sindell* the court believed. In *Summers*, all the parties who were or could have been responsible for the harm to the plaintiff were joined as defendants, whereas in *Sindell* there were about 200 drug companies which made DES, any of which might have manufactured the injury-producing drug. Therefore, the court concluded that the rule, as previously applied, could not relieve the plaintiff of proving the identity of the manufacturer which made the drug causing her injuries.

In *Namm v Charles E Frosst & Co*, 178 NJ Super 19, 427 A2d 1121 (1981), the court rejected on principle the theory of alternative liability in a DES case. The application of the principle of alternative liability to any one or all of the 44 defendants herein would impose liability without fault on any one who manufactured a product manufactured by others as well, the court said. It would result in the taking of the property of all the named defendants in order to pay for harm which may have been caused by only one of the defendants, or even by one who is not a party to the lawsuit, who is unknown to the defendants, over whom they have no control or even any meaningful contact. In addition, the court said there was a more cogent reason for its refusal to adopt the theory of alternative liability. In order to apply the theory traditional concepts and basic principles would of necessity be either distorted or abandoned altogether, the court said. An intermediate appellate court should not take such action, the court concluded.

In *Lyons v Premo Pharmaceutical Laboratories, Inc*, 170 NJ Super 183, 406 A2d 185 (1979), the plaintiffs argued on appeal that the trial court judge erred in granting summary judgment for the drug companies. The court said that the application of alternative liability to the present case could be rejected immediately since once the plaintiff succeeded in establishing that Premo manufactured the particular brand of DES ingested, the plaintiff was arguably unable to rely on the alternative liability theory since it requires that a plaintiff be ignorant of the source of his or her injury. The court said the theory applies to a situation in which the plaintiff is unable to determine either which one of a number of potential tortfeasors is actually liable for his injury or the share of each for joint liability. Such a radical shifting of burdens from a plaintiff to a defendant is not undertaken lightly, but is necessitated only by strong policy which favors recovery by innocently injured plaintiffs who could not otherwise recover because they could not identify the source of their injuries, the court reasoned. Here, the court noted, not only had the plaintiffs identified the sources of their injury, but they had achieved a settlement with them.

However, in these cases the courts hold the concept of alternative liability could properly be applied in a DES setting:

In *Abel v Eli Lilly & Co*, 94 MiA 59, 289 NW2d 20 (1980), the court said that the alternative liability theory involves not a joint tort, but rather independent acts by two or more tortfeasors, all of whom have acted wrongfully, but only one of whom has injured the plaintiff. Joint several liability is imposed, not because all are responsible for the damage, but because it is impossible to tell which one is responsible, the court noted. Rather than deny the innocent plaintiff recovery because the plaintiff cannot prove which of two or more wrongdoers caused the injury, joint liability is imposed on all wrongdoers, the court said. In cases of alternative liability, a defendant is free to absolve itself of blame and cast the entire burden on the others, even if it be shown that the defendant acted wrongfully, but the defendant must bear the burden of proving that its wrongful act was not the cause of the plaintiff's injury, the court noted.

Although no cases directly on point were noted by the court, the shifting of the burden of disproving causation once the defendant's wrongful conduct has been established appears in other contexts in Michigan law, the court said. For example, in *Maddux v Donaldson*, 362 Mi 425, 108 NW2d 33 (1961), which involved successive automobile collisions, the court held that where the plaintiff was unable to prove what portion of the damages were caused by each collision because of the circumstances of the accident, the burden of uncertainty should fall on the wrongdoers, who would be jointly and severally liable for all the plaintiff's damages. The court in *Maddux* held that if injustice is inevitable, the burden should fall on the wrongdoer rather than on the innocent plaintiff, and the *Abel* court agreed with that reasoning.

In *Ferrigno v Eli Lilly & Co*, 175 NJ Super 551, 420 A2d 1305 (1980), the court applied the alternative liability theory to a case brought by eight female offspring for personal injuries they allegedly sustained because each of their mothers took DES during pregnancy. Initially, the court said in New Jersey there is a strong policy favoring recovery by innocently injured plaintiffs who could not otherwise recover because they cannot identify the source of their injuries. That policy becomes even more compelling when an innocent plaintiff is paired off against allegedly culpable defendants, the court said. The possibility that one wrongdoer can escape liability altogether while another tortfeasor may be compelled to pay more than its actual share of damages has long been tolerated, the court said. Under the so-called "single indivisible injury" rule applied to chain collisions of automobiles which crash in rapid succession to produce a single end result, it is impossible to establish what damages are separately caused by each party's collision or even whether a particular crash participant caused any damage at all, the court said. Yet, a defendant will be held jointly and separately responsible if the defendant is unable to exculpate itself, the court said. The court listed five reasons for accepting the application of alternative liability: the defendants were members of a group in which every member was potentially at fault; the defendants owed a special duty to the plaintiffs; the plaintiffs were totally innocent; the plaintiffs' injuries were not foreseeable to them; and DES, by its nature, did not give any clues of its ill effects until a generation after its use, long after any records that any consumer might keep were reasonably discarded. Under the alternative liability theory to be applied in these cases, the court said, there are many ways a defendant may exculpate itself including to identify the actual manufacturer, prove that it never manufactured or sold the generic drug involved in a particular case, show it did not manufacture DES until after the plaintiff was born, show that it never manufactured or marketed a synthetic estrogen for the purpose of preventing miscarriages, show that none of the synthetic estrogen it manufactured or marketed could have reached the outlet where the plaintiff mother purchased it, or show that it never manufactured the drug in the size, shape, color or with the labeling of that which the plaintiff mother ingested. Moreover, those defendants who are not able to exculpate themselves will not be left totally without a remedy, the court noted. If more than one fails to exculpate itself and liability attaches, those who remain will be jointly or severally liable in tort for the same injury. Consequently, any unexculpated defendant will be able to recover contribution from any other joint tortfeasor for any excess over its pro rata share paid in satisfaction of a judgment, the court said.

6. [§6.34] Enterprise Liability

Oftentimes in cases involving injuries allegedly caused by *in utero* exposure to diethylstilbestrol (DES) [as to a definition of DES, see §6.25] the plaintiff encounters a fact situation wherein it is impossible to specifically identify the defendant. [As to a more detailed discussion regarding the background of DES cases, see §6.26.] The identification of the defendant is important since it constitutes a portion of the cause-in-fact element the plaintiff must meet. See COMMENT, DES AND A PROPOSED THEORY OF ENTERPRISE LIABILITY, 46 Fordham LR 963 (1978).

One of the substitutes for specifically identifying the defendant is provided by the concept of enterprise liability. Enterprise liability has also been referred to as industry-wide liability. See *Sindell v Abbott Laboratories*, 26 Ca3d 588, 163 CaR 132, 607 P2d 924, cert den, 449 US 912 (1980). This concept has been described as a synthesis of two other substitutes for specific identification, concerted action [generally, see §6.30] and alternative liability [generally, see §6.32]. Enterprise liability focuses on industry-wide conduct, but does not require a tacit agreement. The defendant is also allowed, under enterprise liability, to exculpate itself after the burden has been shifted to it, but does not require that all potential wrongdoers be joined. See Abrahams and Musgrave, THE DES LABYRINTH, 33 South Carolina LR 663 (1982).

Enterprise liability requires the plaintiff to meet the following elements: the plaintiff is not at fault for his lack of ability to identify the causative agent; the defendants manufactured a generically similar product; this product's defect caused the plaintiff's injury; the plaintiff was a member of a class to whom the defendant owed a duty; there exists clear and convincing evidence that the plaintiff's injury was caused by the product of one, or some, of the defendants; an insufficient industry-wide standard of safety as to the manufacture of the product existed; the requirements of the cause of action alleged are met by all the defendant-tortfeasors. Once these elements are satisfied by the plaintiff's proof, the causation burden of proof shifts to the defendants. Each defendant can exculpate itself only by showing that its product could not have been the one which injured the plaintiff. Any or all of the elements of the plaintiff's case may also be disproved by the defendant. See 46 Fordham LR, at 681. This theory has yet to receive judicial approval in a DES case. Abrahams and Musgrave, at 681.

Moreover, in one case, the court considering application of the theory in a DES case, said the expansive notion of vicarious liability represented by the enterprise liability concept would render every manufacturer an insurer not only of the safety of its own products, but of all generically similar products made by others, and is repugnant to the most basic tenets of tort law. See *Ryan v Eli Lilly & Co*, 514 FSupp 1004 (D SC 1981). And it was stated in another case that adoption of this theory would, of necessity, result in total abandonment of the well-settled principle that manufacturers are only responsible for damages caused by defective products upon proof that the product was defective and that the defect arose while the product was in the control of the defendant. See *Namm v Charles E Frosst & Co*, 178 NJ Super 19, 427 A2d 1121 (1981).

7. [§6.35] —Illustrative Cases

The following cases are illustrative of the general principles applicable to actions seeking to apply the concept of enterprise liability [generally, see §6.34] in a diethylstilbestrol (DES) context. These cases reject the application of enterprise liability in DES cases:

In *Sindell v Abbott Laboratories*, 26 Ca3d 588, 163 CaR 132, 607 P2d 924, cert den, 449 US 912 (1980), the plaintiff brought an action against 11 drug companies and Does one through 100 on behalf of herself and other women similarly situated. She alleged that her mother, and the mothers of the other women, had taken DES during pregnancy, and that the ingestion of DES may cause cancerous vaginal and cervical growths in the daughters exposed to it before birth. One of the causes of action alleged by the plaintiff relied on the concept of enterprise liability. The court noted that this theory was suggested in *Hall v E I duPont de Nemours & Co, Inc*, 345 FSupp 353 (ED NY 1972), in which the plaintiffs were 13 children injured by the explosion of blasting caps in 12 separate incidents which occurred in 10 different states between 1955 and 1959. The defendants were six blasting cap manufacturers, comprising virtually the entire blasting cap industry in the United States, and their trade association. There were, however, a number of Canadian blasting cap manufacturers which could have supplied the caps. The gravamen of the complaint was that the practice of the industry of omitting a warning on individual blasting caps and of failing to take other safety measures created an unreasonable risk of harm, resulting in the plaintiffs' injuries. The complaint did not identify a particular manufacturer of a cap which caused a particular injury. The court reasoned in *Hall* that there was evidence that the defendants, acting independently, had adhered to an industry-wide standard with regard to the safety features of blasting caps, that they had in effect delegated some functions of safety investigation and design, such as labeling, to their trade association, and that there was industry-wide cooperation in the manufacturing and design of the blasting caps. In these circumstances, the evidence supported a conclusion that all the defendants jointly controlled the risk. Thus, if the plaintiffs could establish by a preponderance of the evidence that the caps were manufactured by one of the defendants, the burden of proof as to causation would shift to all the defendants. The *Hall* court noted that this theory of liability applied to industries composed of a small number of units, and that what would be fair and reasonable with regard to an industry of five to 10 producers, might be manifestly unreasonable if applied to a decentralized industry composed of countless small producers. In *Sindell*, the plaintiff attempted to state a cause of action under the rationale of *Hall*. She alleged joint enterprise and collaboration among the defendants in the production, marketing, promotion, and testing of DES, and concerted promulgation and adherence to industry-wide testing, safety, warning, and efficacy standards for the drug. The court noted that it had concluded that the allegations that the defendants relied upon one another's testing and promotion methods did not state a cause of action for concerted conduct to commit a tortious act. Under the theory of industry-wide liability, however, each manufacturer could be liable for all injuries caused by DES by virtue of adherence to an industry-wide standard of safety, the court said. However, the court said it would decline to apply this theory in the present case. At least 200 manufacturers produced DES, but in *Hall*, only six manufacturers represented the entire blasting cap industry in the United States, the court noted. Moreover, in *Hall*, the court said, the conclusion that the defendants jointly controlled the risk was based upon allegations that they had delegated some functions relating to a trade association, but there were no such allegations in *Sindell*. Equally important, the drug industry is closely regulated by the Food and Drug Administration, which actively controls the testing and manufacture of drugs and the method by which they are marketed, including the contents of warning labels. To a considerable degree therefore, the court said, the standards followed by drug manufacturers are suggested or compelled by the government. Adherence to those standards cannot, of course, absolve a manufacturer of liability to which it would otherwise be subject, the court said. But since the government played such a pervasive role in formulating the criteria for the testing and marketing of drugs, it would be unfair to impose upon a manufacturer liability for injuries resulting from the use of a drug which it did not supply simply because it followed the standards of the industry, the court concluded.

In *Namm v Charles E Frosst & Co*, 178 NJ Super 19, 427 A2d 1121 (1981), the plaintiffs appealed from a summary judgment dismissing their complaint against approximately 44 drug manufacturing and distributing companies. The plaintiffs argued that liability should be imposed upon the defendants collectively because the acceptance of DES by the medical profession and the unsuspecting public was the consequence of accumulative effort by all who entered the market as manufacturers and of immense promotion and advertising to which the defendants' contributed. The plaintiffs conceded in the trial court and at least tacitly before the appellate court, the court noted, that this theory is contrary to the established law of New Jersey, but claimed that the traditional requirement of manufacturer identification in the product liability case should be discarded here because each defendant participated in an industry enterprise and a pervasive and cumulative market effort. This theory, referred to a enterprise liability or industry-wide liability, if adopted, would impose liability upon each member of an industry who manufactures or produces a product which causes injury or harm to a consumer, the court said. The share of liability of each member of the industry would be measured by reference to that defendant's share of the market for the product, the court said. The court said adoption of this legal theory, would, of necessity, result in total abandonment of the well-settled principle that manufacturers are only responsible for damages caused by defective products upon proof that the product was defective and that the defect arose while the product was in the control of the defendant. The traditional methods of assessing and apportioning damages among defendants would also, of necessity, have to be abandoned and new ones fashioned, the court said. Extensive policy shifts of this magnitude should not be initiated by an intermediate appellate court, the court said. The appropriate tribunal to accomplish such drastic change is either the supreme court or the legislature. Therefore, the court rejected the theory of enterprise liability on both principle and precedent.

8. [§6.36] Market Share Liability

A difficult issue in cases alleging injury based on *in utero* exposure to diethylstilbestrol (DES) [as to a definition of DES, see §6.25] is that of specifying the particular drug manufacturer that made and marketed the DES that was ingested [as to a more detailed discussion regarding the background of DES actions, see §6.26]. This issue is significant since it directly relates to proving the cause-in-fact element of the action. COMMENT, DES AND A PROPOSED THEORY OF ENTERPRISE LIABILITY, 46 Fordham LR 963 (1978).

One method of meeting the cause-in-fact issue without specifically identifying the manufacturer of the DES is through application of a concept referred to as market share liability. [As to a discussion of other substitutes for identifying the specific manufacturers, see §§6.30–6.35.]

The theory of market share liability, which applies to generic items, does away with the traditional prerequisite of identifying the manufacturer of the injury causing product. Rather, the plaintiff needs to allege that the specific defendant cannot be identified, and then joins those defendants who have manufactured a substantial share of the market. At this point, the burden of proof is shifted to the defendants to prove their innocence. Unnamed defendants may be brought into the action by the named defendants. In addition, the named defendants may seek contribution from unnamed defendants. If the plaintiff is successful in proving that liability exists, apportionment of damages among the defendants is made based on each of the defendant's share of the product market. See COMMENT, MARKET SHARE LIABILITY FOR DEFECTIVE PRODUCTS: AN ILL-ADVISED REMEDY FOR THE PROBLEM OF IDENTIFICATION, 76 Northwestern University LR 300 (1981). It has been suggested that the market share liability shared by the defendants will approximate each defendant's responsibility for the injuries caused by its own product. If a defendant can prove it did not produce the specific product that harmed the plaintiff, the defendant will avoid liability. See *Sindell v Abbott Laboratories*, 26 Ca3d 588, 163 CaR 132, 607 P2d 924, cert den, 449 US 912 (1980).

The concept of liability predicated on a defendant's share of the product market has been accepted in a DES case. See *Sindell v Abbott Laboratories*, 26 Ca3d 588, 163 CaR 132, 607 P2d 924, cert den, 449 US 912 (1980). However, in another DES case it was said that the market share liability theory represents a radical departure from the body of products liability law. See *Mizell v Eli Lilly & Co*, 527 FSupp 589 (D SC 1981).

9. [§6.37] —Illustrative Cases

The following cases are illustrative of the general principles of market share liability [generally, see §6.36] as applied in diethylstilbestrol (DES) cases. The following case accepts the application of market share liability in a DES case:

In *Sindell v Abbott Laboratories*, 26 Ca3d 588, 163 CaR 132, 607 P2d 924, cert den, 449 US 912 (1980), the court approved the use of the market share liability concept in a DES case. The court noted that if it was confined to the theory of alternative liability or concert of action, it would be constrained to hold that the judgment in favor of the defendant must be sustained. The court noted that if it required that the plaintiff identify the manufacturer which supplied the DES used by her mother or that all DES manufacturers be joined in the action, she would effectively be precluded from any recovery. As the defendants candidly admitted, the court noted, there is little likelihood that all the manufacturers who made DES at the time in question are still in business and that they are subject to the jurisdiction of the California courts. However, the court said, there were forceful arguments in favor of holding that the plaintiff had a cause of action. In the contemporary complex industrialized society of the United States, advances in science and technology create fungible goods which may harm consumers and which cannot be traced to any specific producer, the court said. The response of the courts can be either to adhere rigidly to prior doctrine, deny recovery to those injured by such products, or to fashion remedies to meet these changing needs, the court believed. The most persuasive reason for finding that the plaintiff had stated a cause of action is that as between an innocent plaintiff and a negligent defendant, the latter should bear the cost of the injury, the court said. Here the plaintiff is not at fault in failing to provide evidence of causation, and although the absence of such evidence is not attributable to the defendants either, their conduct and marketing a drug the effects of which are delayed for many years played a significant factor in creating the unavailability of proof, the court said. From a broader policy standpoint, the defendants are better able to bear the cost of injury resulting from the manufacture of a defective product, the court reasoned. The court held it to be reasonable in the present context to measure the likelihood that any of the defendants supplied the product which allegedly injured the plaintiff by the percentage which the DES sold by each of them for the purpose of preventing miscarriage bears to the entire production of the drug sold by all for that purpose. The plaintiff asserted that in her brief that Eli Lilly and Company and five or six other companies produced 90 per cent of the DES marketed. If at trial this was established to be the fact, then there is a corresponding likelihood that this comparative handful of producers manufactured the DES which caused the plaintiff's injuries, and only a ten per cent likelihood that the offending producer would escape liability, the court said. If the plaintiff joined in the action the manufacturers of a substantial share of the DES which her mother might have taken, the injustice of shifting the burden of proof to the defendants to demonstrate that they could not have made the substance which injured the plaintiff would be significantly diminished, the court believed. The presence in the action of a substantial share of the appropriate market also provides a ready means to apportion damages among the defendants, the court reasoned. Each defendant will be held liable for the proportion of the judgment represented by its share of that market unless it demonstrates that it could not have made the product which caused the plaintiff's injuries. Once the plaintiff has met her burden of joining the required defendants, the defendant in turn may cross complain against other DES manufacturers, not joined in the action, which the defendant can allege might have supplied the injury-causing product, the court said. Some minor discrepancy in the correlation between market share and liability is inevitable, and therefore, the court said, a defendant may be held liable for a somewhat different percentage of the damage than its share of the market would justify. Just as a jury cannot be expected to determine the precise relationship between fault and liability in applying the doctrine of comparative fault, the difficulty of proportioning damages among the defendant producers in exact relation to their market share does not seriously militate against the rule, the court said. The defendants urged that it would be unfair and contrary to public policy to hold them liable for the plaintiff's injuries in the absence of proof that one of them supplied the drug responsible for the damage. Most of their arguments, however, are based on the assumption that one manufacturer would be held responsible for the products of another or for those of all other manufacturers if the plaintiff ultimately prevails, the court said. But under the rule the court adopted, each manufacturer's liability for an injury would be approximately equivalent to the damages caused by the DES it manufactured.

However, in these cases the court rejected the proposed application of market share liability in a DES case:

In *Mizell v Eli Lilly & Co*, 526 FSupp 589 (D SC 1981), it was the opinion of the court that the application of the *Sindell* market share liability theory would violate the public policy. The court declined to apply the *Sindell* rationale because the court said the market share liability theory represents a radical departure from the body of products liability law that has been developed in South Carolina. By removing the traditional requirement that the plaintiff identify the responsible manufacturer, the doctrine destroys the nexus between production of a defective item and the plaintiff's injury, the court said. As a result, the court said, liability is placed on defendants bearing no responsibility for the defective product.

And, in *Ryan v Eli Lilly & Co*, 514 FSupp 1004 (D SC 1981), the court said the market share theory did not apply to this case. The plaintiff had neither alleged nor offered any evidence that the defendants before the court accounted for a substantial share of the relevant DES market, the court said. Thus, even if the theory of market share liability could be reconciled with the plainly contrary law of the only state interested in this controversy, South Carolina, the plaintiff had offered no basis for its application. The court said the California court's market share theory of liability in *Sindell* represented a rejection of over 100 years of tort law which required that before tort liability was imposed a matching of the defendants' conduct and plaintiff's injury was absolutely essential. The courts of both Carolinas, however, the court said, still adhere to this fundamental principle. The unequivocal law of South Carolina is the plaintiff in a negligence action has not only the burden of proving negligence but also the burden of proving that the injury or damage was caused by the actionable conduct of the particular defendant, the court said.

C. Limitation on Actions

1. [§6.38] Generally

Limitation issues are, in some instances, significant in actions involving cases alleging injury because of *in utero* exposure to diethylstilbestrol (DES) [as to a definition of DES, see §6.25] since they may be dispositive of the case. In many DES cases, the plaintiff does not know of the wrongful act since the plaintiff was not yet born. Moreover, in DES cases it is generally a number of years before the injury manifests itself. Abrahams and Musgrave, THE DES LABYRINTH, 33 South Carolina LR 663 (1982). Therefore an important question that arises is when does the statute of limitations begin to run. Generally, the running statute of limitations has been measured from the time of the injury or from the time the injury should have been discovered. This latter concept, known as the discovery rule, has been considered in the context of a number of DES related actions. It has been held that where a plaintiff becomes aware of her cancerous condition and the possibility that it is DES-related, but does not have certain knowledge of causation, the statute will not be prevented from running. See *Dawson v Eli Lilly & Co*, 543 FSupp 1330 (D DC 1982).

Moreover, where the plaintiff does not exercise due diligence in discovering the injury, and the possible connection with DES, the statute will run from the time the plaintiff should have discovered the injury and the connection to DES. See *O'Brien v Eli Lilly & Co*, 668 F2d 704 (3d Cir 1982). [As to a more detailed discussion of the application of the discovery rule in DES cases, see §6.39.]

Another method of determining the date an action accrues is based on the date the allegedly injurious product was delivered. However, in one instance, this method was held to be unconstitutional in a DES case. In *Diamond v E R Squibb & Sons, Inc*, 397 So2d 671 (1981), the plaintiffs alleged that in 1955 and 1956 the plaintiff-mother had ingested DES, and that the unborn fetus was exposed *in utero* to the drug. The plaintiffs alleged that subsequently they became aware of a possible connection between DES and the subsequent development of cancer in females exposed *in utero* to DES. The defendant moved for summary judgment based on a date of delivery statute that prohibited the initiation of a products liability action unless it was brought within 12 years after the date of delivery of the product to its original purchaser regardless of the date the defect in the product was or should have been discovered. The court held that the statute operated to bar the cause of action before it ever accrued so that no judicial forum would be available to the plaintiff. Therefore the court concluded that the statute would be in violation of the Florida Constitution's guaranty of access to the courts.

The accrual of a cause of action in a DES case may be held to be tolled if the defendants fraudulently conceal the circumstances behind the initial ingestion of DES. In *Mink v University of Chicago*, 460 FSupp 713 (ND Il 1978), the plaintiff brought an action against the University of Chicago and Eli Lilly and Company on behalf of themselves and some 1,000 women who were given DES between September 1950 and November 1952. The drug was administered to the plaintiffs during their prenatal care at the university's hospital as part of a study to determine the value of DES in preventing miscarriages. However, the women were not told that the pills administered to them were DES, nor were they told they were part of an experiment. The plaintiffs' complaint sought recovery in three causes of action, including that the defendants had committed a series of batteries on the plaintiffs by conducting a medical experiment on them without their knowledge or consent. The University of Chicago argued that any actionable claims should be barred by laches or the statute of limitations. However, the court said since the plaintiffs were unaware of the facts giving rise to their battery cause of action until late 1975 or 1976, it could not be said that they were guilty of laches in filing. The court noted that the running of the limitations period may be tolled if the defendants fraudulently concealed the cause of action from the plaintiffs. Generally, this tolling provision requires more than mere silence on the part of the defendant, the court said. Some affirmative act of concealment is contemplated, the court continued. However, the court noted that some courts had held that in some circumstances the requirement may be relaxed. The plaintiffs in this action alleged that the defendants intentionally and fraudulently concealed the circumstances of the experiment from 1950 until the present period, the court noted. This allegation demonstrated intentional concealment of known facts which in the court's opinion exceeded mere silence and approached affirmative action. Therefore, the court rejected the university's contention that the action should be barred as a matter of law.

2. [§6.39] Discovery Rule: Date of Accrual

The discovery rule as it relates to the accrual of the statute of limitations provides that the cause of action accrues not when the injury first occurs but when the plaintiff discovers, or by the exercise of due diligence, should have discovered the facts giving rise to the plaintiff's claim. See *Dawson v Eli Lilly & Co*, 543 FSupp 1330 (D DC 1982). The discovery rule as applied to a drug products liability action is that the statute of limitations begins to run from the time the plaintiff learns, or in the exercise of due diligence could have learned, that the plaintiff's injuries were not simply misfortune, but resulted from an undisclosed defect in the defendant's product. See *Grigsby v Sterling Drug Inc*, 428 FSupp 242 (D DC 1975), affd, 543 F2d 417 (DC Cir 1976), cert den, 431 US 967 (1977).

The plaintiff does not need to have a clear and certain knowledge of a causal relationship before the statute begins to run. For example, in *Dawson v Eli Lilly & Co*, 543 FSupp 1330 (D DC 1982), the plaintiff did not make such a claim, the court said, and the plaintiff did not claim to have received any information that tended to dispute the relationship between diethylstilbestrol (DES) and her condition at any time. If the statute of limitations did not begin to run merely because a plaintiff who knew of a possible causal relationship and did not rely on any representations to the contrary did not have certain knowledge of causation, no claim where causation could be disputed would ever accrue, the court reasoned. The plaintiff contended that her knowledge of the possible connection between DES and her injuries was not sufficient to determine as a matter of law that she had discovered the causal relationship more than three years before she brought this suit, but the court said it had found no case which holds that a plaintiff must have clear and certain knowledge of a causal relationship before the statute begins to run. Further, a defendant's continuing denial of the causal relationship has been found to delay the accrual of the cause of action only where the plaintiff claims to have relied on that denial, as where a patient relies upon her doctor's advice or a consumer relies upon a drug manufacturer's representations as to safety, the court added. The record presented supports the conclusion that, as a matter of law, the plaintiff discovered the connection between DES and her injuries sometime in 1973, and that the disability of her minority for statute of limitations purposes was removed in 1976, when she reached 21 years of age, the court said.

3. [§6.40] —Illustrative Cases

The following cases are illustrative of the general principles of the discovery rule [generally, see §6.39] as applied to cases involving diethylstilbestrol (DES) claims:

In *O'Brien v Eli Lilly & Co*, 668 F2d 704 (3d Cir 1982), the plaintiff's mother had ingested DES while pregnant with the plaintiff in 1956. Subsequently, the plaintiff developed cancer. In 1971 the plaintiff was hospitalized and a cancerous tumor was removed from her vagina. However, the plaintiff's parents asked that the plaintiff not be told the tumor was malignant, and so she was not so informed. Before a doctor's appointment in 1976, the plaintiff read an article in a magazine about DES. The plaintiff was aware at this time that her mother had suffered a miscarriage before the plaintiff was born. In a deposition the plaintiff said there were significant similarities between her past condition and that described in the DES article. Later the plaintiff said she asked her mother whether DES had been ingested during the plaintiff's pregnancy and that her mother denied taking the drug. In 1979, the plaintiff discovered that her mother had taken DES. The question for decision in this appeal from a summary judgment in favor of four defendant pharmaceutical manufacturers in a diversity action was whether the district court properly applied the Pennsylvania discovery rule which modified the personal injury statute of limitations. The district court had determined that, if she had exercised due diligence, the plaintiff reasonably could have discovered in February 1976 that her mother had taken DES during her 1956 pregnancy and that the drug arguably caused the plaintiff's subsequent cancer. However, the plaintiff did not file her complaint until December 31, 1979. Accordingly, the district court concluded that the suit was barred by the two-year statute of limitations. The plaintiff contended that whether she possessed the knowledge necessary in 1976 to start the running of the statute was a jury question. However, on appeal, the court found no genuine issue of material fact and affirmed the grant of summary judgment. The court said the principle of the Pennsylvania discovery rule is not a plaintiff's actual acquisition of knowledge but whether the knowledge was known or common through the exercise of diligence, and was knowable to the plaintiff. The court agreed with the district court that, as a matter of law, the crucial knowledge was knowable to the plaintiff in 1976 and could have been obtained through the exercise of due diligence. Therefore, the district court's conclusion that the action was barred by the statute of limitations was affirmed.

In *Thomas v Ferndale Laboratories, Inc*, 97 MiA 718, 296 NW2d 160 (1980), the defendant appealed an order denying a motion for accelerated judgment based on the expiration of the statute of limitations. The court noted that in the mid-1950's the plaintiff's mother consumed the drug DES during pregnancy. On May 5, 1956, the plaintiff was born. In 1972, the plaintiff's mother became aware of the potential harm to the offspring of women who had taken DES. During that same year, the plaintiff began medical treatment for the identification of possible DES related injuries. In 1973, the plaintiff contacted a physician for further medical treatment. The results of a test showed the presence of certain growths. After an additional examination, the physician informed the plaintiff of an adenosis condition which was caused by DES. At this time, the plaintiff became aware of her cause of action and the parties stipulated to this fact. On May 7, 1974, the plaintiff filed a suit naming Eli Lilly and Company and the physician as defendants. On September 9, 1974, the physician advised the plaintiff that Ferndale Laboratories had manufactured and distributed the DES taken by the plaintiff's mother. The plaintiffs suit against Eli Lilly and Company and the physician was dismissed for no progress on February 10, 1975. The plaintiff filed a complaint against Ferndale Laboratories based on negligence and breach of warranty on May 23, 1977. In its answer, the defendant raised the affirmative defense of the expiration of the statute of limitations. In a deposition taken on January 3, 1978, the plaintiff admitted that she was aware of her injuries and their DES causation in 1973. Ferndale Laboratories moved for accelerated judgment on the ground that the statutory limitation period had elapsed. The circuit judge denied the motion and ruled that the limitation period did not begin to run until September 1974 when the plaintiff became aware of the identity of the drug manufacturer. The defendant's motion for rehearing was denied. The court said that the sole issue on appeal was could the running of the statute of limitations be delayed until the plaintiff became aware of the identity of the alleged tortfeasor, when that knowledge was ascertained after the date that all of the elements of the cause of action occurred. The court answered the question in the negative and concluded that the trial court erred in denying the motion for accelerated judgment. The court said the accrual date of the plaintiff's cause of action was not delayed until she became aware of the identity of the specific defendant-tortfeasor that might ultimately be liable for her injuries.

D. [§6.41] Example Complaint

The following complaint was filed in the case of *Bichler v Eli Lilly & Co*, 55 NY2d 571 (NY 1982), an action brought by a plaintiff allegedly injured by *in utero* exposure to diethylstilbestrol (DES). [As to a definition of DES, see §6.25.] In *Bichler*, the plaintiff brought actions against the hospital where the DES was administered to her mother, the attending physician, and the defendant-drug manufacturer. In the plaintiff's cause of action against the drug manufacturer, she alleged the theories of negligence, breach of warranty, and strict liability. [For a more detailed discussion of the substantive holding in *Bichler*, see §6.26; for a more detailed discussion of the cause-in-fact theory applied in Bichler, alternative liability, see §6.32.] In addition, the plaintiff's father brought a cause of action for his expenses in caring for the plaintiff. The *Bichler* complaint stated as follows:

Plaintiffs, complaining of the defendants . . . respectfully allege:

FOR A FIRST CAUSE OF ACTION ON BEHALF OF INFANT PLAINTIFF JOYCE BICHLER, AGAINST DEFENDANTS, BRONX LEBANON HOSPITAL CENTER and ABRAHAM FLEISCHER:

1. Upon information and belief, at all the times hereinafter mentioned, defendant, BRONX LEBANON HOSPITAL CENTER, was and still is a domestic corporation, duly organized and

existing under and by virtue of the laws of the State of New York hereinafter referred to as Defendant Hospital.

2. Upon information and belief, at all the times hereinafter mentioned, defendant hospital owned hospital premise located at 1276 Fulton Avenue, in the Borough of Bronx, City of New York.

3. Upon information and belief, at all the times hereinafter mentioned, defendant hospital, its agents, servants, and/or employees, operated, maintained, managed and were in control of the said hospital and held itself out as a hospital duly qualified and capable of rendering adequate medical care, treatment, obstetrical attention and surgery to the public, and for such purposes, hired doctors, nurses, anesthetists, attendants and other personnel.

4. Upon information and belief, at all the times hereinafter mentioned, defendant, ABRAHAM FLEISCHER, was a physician duly licensed to practice medicine in the State of New York.

5. That the defendant, ABRAHAM FLEISCHER, held himself out as duly qualified to render proper and adequate medical services to members of the general public, including infant plaintiff's mother, DOROTHY BICHLER, and infant plaintiff JOYCE BICHLER.

6. That on or about the 19th day of January, 1954, and prior and subsequent thereto, infant plaintiff herein and infant plaintiff's said mother came under the care and treatment of defendant hospital.

7. That prior and subsequent thereto, infant plaintiff herein and infant plaintiff's mother, DOROTHY BICHLER, came under the care and treatment of defendant, ABRAHAM FLEISCHER.

8. That the medical care, diagnosis, treatment, obstetrical care, discharge and aftercare rendered by the defendants to the infant plaintiff herein and her mother, DOROTHY BICHLER, were performed in a negligent, careless manner and constituted professional negligence resulting in severe permanent personal injuries to infant plaintiff herein.

9. That the defendant hospital was careless in its employment and supervision of doctors, nurses and paramedical help at the hospital and failed to render or perform proper medical care, diagnosis, treatment, obstetrical care, discharge aftercare and, in addition, failed to discover and treat the conditions of the infant plaintiff and her mother, DOROTHY BICHLER caused by acts of the defendant physicians.

10. That by reason of the foregoing, infant plaintiff, JOYCE BICHLER, sustained grievous and permanent personal injuries; became sick, sore, lame and disabled; suffered mental anguish;

injury to her nervous system; was confined to hospital, bed and home for a lengthy period of time and may, in the future, be so confined; was incapacitated from attending to her usual duties and may, in the future, be so incapacitated; and infant plaintiff was otherwise damaged.

11. That by reason of the foregoing, infant plaintiff, JOYCE BICHLER, has been damaged in an amount not to exceed the sum of Five Million ($5,000,000) Dollars.

FOR A SECOND CAUSE OF ACTION AGAINST DEFENDANTS, BRONX LEBANON HOSPITAL CENTER and ABRAHAM FLEISCHER:

12. Plaintiffs repeat, reiterate and reallege each and every allegation contained in the paragraphs of this complaint numbered "1" through "10" both inclusive, with the same force and effect as if herein more fully at length set forth.

13. That the defendants herein named failed to advise or inform the plaintiffs and infant plaintiff's mother, DOROTHY BICHLER, of the dangers in the medical, obstetrical and other treatment and the drugs and medication given by the defendants to the infant plaintiff, JOYCE BICHLER, and her mother, DOROTHY BICHLER, that the defendants failed to receive their informed consent thereto and the defendants herein were otherwise negligent in the premises.

14. That by reason of the foregoing, plaintiffs have been damaged in an amount not to exceed the sum of Five Million ($5,000,000) Dollars.

FOR A THIRD CAUSE OF ACTION ON BEHALF OF INFANT PLAINTIFF, JOYCE BICHLER, AGAINST DEFENDANT, ELI LILLY & CO.:

15. That at all the times herein mentioned, defendant, ELI LILLY & CO., was a foreign corporation, duly authorized to do business in the State of New York.

16. That at all the times herein mentioned, this defendant manufactured and produced a drug known as "Diethylstilbestrol".

17. That at all the times herein mentioned, this defendant sold and distributed said drug "Diethylstilbestrol" under the said trade name.

18. That in or about the month of July, 1953, and subsequent thereto, infant plaintiff's mother, DOROTHY BICHLER, ingested the said drug "Diethylstilbestrol" during her pregnancy with infant plaintiff herein.

19. That as a result of the ingestion of the aforesaid drug by infant plaintiff's mother, DOROTHY BICHLER, during her aforesaid pregnancy, infant plaintiff herein, JOYCE BICHLER, was rendered seriously, grievously and permanently injured; she was required and will require extensive hospital and other medical care and attention; she was and is incapacitated from attending to her usual duties; and this infant plaintiff has been otherwise damaged.

20. That the negligence of the defendant, ELI LILLY & CO., its servants, agents and/or employees, consisted of manufacturing, selling and distributing the aforesaid drug "Diethylstilbestrol", without making proper and sufficient tests to determine the dangers and contraindications thereof; in negligently failing to adequately warn the public and the medical profession of the dangers and contraindications and side effects inherent in the use of the aforesaid drug; in failing to properly inspect the aforesaid drug; in negligently advertising and recommending the use of the aforesaid drug without sufficient knowledge as to its dangerous propensities; in negligently representing that the aforesaid drug was safe for use for therapeutic purposes, when in fact, said drug was unsafe for use; that said defendant had not conducted a sufficient testing program to determine whether or not the aforesaid drug was safe for use; that defendant herein knew or, in the exercise of reasonable diligence, should have known that said drug was unsafe and unfit for use by reasons of the dangerous effects, contraindications, and dangers to a fetus during the pregnancy of its mother; and said defendant was otherwise negligent and careless in the premises.

21. That by reason of the foregoing, infant plaintiff, JOYCE BICHLER, has been damaged in an amount not to exceed the sum of Five Million ($5,000,000) Dollars.

FOR A FOURTH CAUSE OF ACTION
AGAINST DEFENDANT, ELI LILLY & CO.

22. Plaintiffs repeat, reiterate and reallege each and every allegation contained in the paragraphs of this complaint numbered "15" through "20" both inclusive, with the same force and effect as if herein more fully at length set forth.

23. That this defendant represented and warranted that the aforesaid drug sold under the trade name of "Diethylstilbestrol"

was safe and fit for use as a therapeutic drug, was of merchantable quality and did not produce any side effects dangerous to life and limb.

24. That, in fact, the aforesaid representations and warranties were false and untrue in that the aforesaid drug was not safe or fit for use as a therapeutic drug, was not of merchantable quality and, in fact, did produce serious side effects, was contraindicated and was otherwise dangerous and unsafe.

25. That as a result of the aforementioned breach of warranties on the part of this defendant, and breach of its representations, plaintiffs have been damaged in an amount not to exceed the sum of Five Million ($5,000,000) Dollars.

FOR A FIFTH CAUSE OF ACTION
AGAINST DEFENDANT, ELI LILLY & CO.

26. Plaintiffs repeat, reiterate and reallege each and every allegation contained in the paragraphs of this complaint numbered "15" through "24" both inclusive, with the same force and effect as if more fully at length set forth herein.

27. That by reason of the foregoing, this defendant has violated statutes, codes, laws, ordinances and is liable to plaintiffs herein by reason of such statutory violations.

28. That by reason of the foregoing, plaintiffs have been damaged in an amount not to exceed the sum of Five Million ($5,000,000) Dollars.

FOR A SIXTH CAUSE OF ACTION
AGAINST DEFENDANT, ELI LILLY & CO.

29. Plaintiffs repeat, reiterate and reallege each and every allegation contained in the paragraphs of this complaint numbered "15" through "27" both inclusive, with the same force and effect as if more fully at length set forth herein.

30. That by reason of the foregoing, this defendant is liable to plaintiffs herein under the Doctrine of Strict Liability.

31. That by reason of the foregoing, plaintiffs have been damaged in an amount not to exceed the sum of Five Million ($5,000,000) Dollars.

FOR A SEVENTH CAUSE OF ACTION ON
BEHALF OF PLAINTIFF, MAX BICHLER:

32. Plaintiff repeats, reiterates and realleges each and every allegation contained in the paragraphs of this complaint numbered

"1" through "30", both inclusive, with the same force and effect as if herein more fully at length set forth.

33. That at all the times herein mentioned, infant plaintiff, JOYCE BICHLER, was the daughter of this plaintiff and as such daughter, resided with plaintiff and plaintiff was responsible for her support and maintenance; and this plaintiff was entitled to her services, companionship and society.

34. That by reason of the foregoing, this plaintiff has incurred expenses and obligations for hospitalization, physician's services, nursing, and medicines and, in addition, this plaintiff has been deprived of the services, companionship and society of his said daughter and was otherwise damaged.

35. That by reason of the foregoing, this plaintiff has been damaged in an amount not to exceed the sum of One Million ($1,000,000) Dollars.

WHEREFORE, plaintiffs demand judgment against the defendants, IN THE FIRST CAUSE OF ACTION, in an amount not to exceed the sum of Five Million ($5,000,000) Dollars; IN THE SECOND CAUSE OF ACTION, in an amount not to exceed the sum of Five Million ($5,000,000) Dollars; IN THE THIRD CAUSE OF ACTION in an amount not to exceed the sum of Five Million ($5,000,000) Dollars; IN THE FOURTH CAUSE OF ACTION, in an amount not to exceed the sum of Five Million ($5,000,000) Dollars; IN THE FIFTH CAUSE OF ACTION, in an amount not to exceed the sum of Five Million ($5,000,000) Dollars; IN THE SIXTH CAUSE OF ACTION, in an amount not to exceed the sum of Five Million ($5,000,000) Dollars; and IN THE SEVENTH CAUSE OF ACTION, in an amount not to exceed the sum of One Million ($1,000,000) Dollars; all together with the costs and disbursements of this action.

[Name of Attorney]

[Date]

Medical Glossary

Abdomen: The large, inferior cavity of the trunk, extending from the brim of the pelvis to the diaphragm, bounded in front and at the sides by the lower ribs and abdominal muscles and behind by the vertebral column and the posas and quadratus lumborum muscles.

Abortifacient: A drug or agent inducing abortion.

Abortion: The spontaneous or artificially induced expulsion of an embryo or fetus before it is viable. The premature expelled product of conception.

Acute: Sharp; severe. Having a rapid onset, a short course, and pronounced symptoms.

Adenocarcinoma: In histologic classification, a carcinoma in which the anaplastic parenchymal cells form glands.

Adenosis: Development of an excessive number of glandular elements without tumor formation. Any glandular disease, especially of the lymph nodes.

Afterbirth: The placenta and membranes expelled from the uterus following the birth of the child.

Aliquot: In quantitative chemistry and pharmacy, a definite known fraction of a larger sample, used to facilitate analysis.

Amniocentesis: Puncture of the intrauterine amniotic sac through the abdominal wall with a trochar and cannula to obtain a sample of amniotic fluid; used in prenatal diagnosis of certain chromosomal disorders, such as Down's Syndrome, and many hereditary metabolic diseases, and to study fetal maturation in late pregnancy.

Amnion: The innermost of the fetal membranes forming a fluid-filled sac for the protection of the embryo. Its thin, translucent wall is composed of an inner layer of ectoderm and an outer layer of mesoderm continuous with the embryonic somatopleure at the unbilicus. After the second month of development, it obliterates the extraembryonic coelom, forms a sheath about the umbilical cord, and fuses loosely with the chrionic mesoderm.

Amniotic: Of or pertaining to the amnion.

Anesthesiologist: A physician who specializes in anesthesiology.

Anesthesiology: The art and science of administering local and general anesthetics to produce the various types of anesthesia.

Anesthetic: A drug that produces local or general loss of sensibility.

Antibiotic: Of or pertaining to the products of certain organisms (as penicillin) used against infections caused by other organisms.

Antibody: One of a class of substances, natural or induced by exposure to an antigen, which have the capacity to react with specific or closely related antigens. In the serum, they occur within the immunoglobulins.

Aorta: The large vessel arising from the left ventricle and distributing, by its branches, arterial blood to every part of the body. It ends by bifurcating into the common iliacs at the fourth lumbar vertebra. The portion extending from the heart to the third thoracic vertebra is divided into an ascending, an arch, or transverse part, and a descending part. The thoracic portion extends to the diaphragm; the abdominal, to the bifurcation.

Appendectomy: Excision of the vermiform appendix.

Appendix: Vermiform Appendix, an appendage.

Artery: A vessel conveying blood away from the heart. It is composed of three coats: the intima (interna), the media, and the adventitia (externa). In comparison to veins, arteries have a thick wall and small lumen.

Aspiration: The withdrawal by suction of fluids or gases from a cavity, as with an aspirator.

Atrophy: An acquired local reduction in the size of a cell, tissue, organ, or region of the body, which may be physiologic or pathologic. To undergo such reduction.

Azoospermia: Absence of live spermatozoa in the semen.

Birth: In viviparious species, the offspring's emergence from the womb of the mother.

Birth Control: Any means used to help control reproduction, such as methods of facilitating, timing, or preventing conception, sexual abstinence or alternatives, abortion, sterilization, and artificial insemination.

Bladder: A hollow organ which serves as a reservoir for urine or bile, as the urinary bladder or gallbladder.

Blastocyst: The modified mammalian blastula consisting of trophoblast, inner cell mass, and blastocoele.

Blastula: A spherical mass consisting of a central cavity surrounded by a single layer of cells produced by the cleavage of the ovum; frequently modified by the presence of yolk.

Carcinogen: Any agent or substance which produces cancer, accelerates the development of cancer, or acts upon a population to change its total frequency of cancer in terms of numbers of tumors or distribution by site and age.

Castration: The excision of one or both testes or ovaries; taken as evidence of hypersecretion of follicle-stimulating or luteinizing hormone or both.

Cerebral Thrombosis: Thrombosis occurring in a cerebral blood vessel. Cerebral infarction secondary to thrombotic occlusion of a cerebral blood vessel.

Cerebrovascular Accident: A symptom complex resulting from cerebral hemorrhage or from embolism or thrombosis of the cerebral vessels, characterized by alterations in consciousness, seizures, and development of focal neurologic deficits.

Cesarean-Caesarean Section: Delivery of the fetus through an abdominal and uterine incision.

Chromosome: Any one of the separate, deeply staining bodies, commonly rod-, J- (or L-), or V-shaped, which arise from the nuclear network during mitosis and meiosis. They carry the hereditary factors (genes), and are present in constant number in each species. In humans, there are 46 in each cell, except in the mature ovum and sperm where the number is halved. A complete set of 23 is inherited from each parent.

Chronic: Long continued; or long duration or frequent recurrence.

Circumcision: The removal of foreskin; excision of the prepuce.

Coarctation: Narrowing or stricture of a vessel, as the aorta, or of a canal.

Conception: The fertilization of the ovum by the spermatozoon, occurring in the female usually about the twelfth to fifteenth day after the first day of menstrual flow.

Conceptus: That which is conceived; an embryo or fetus.

Condom: A sheath of thin rubber, plastic, or skin worn over the penis during copulation for preventing conception or infection.

Congenital: Existing before or at birth, though not necessarily detected at that time.

Conjugal: Of or pertaining to marriage or to husband and wife.

Consanguinity: The relationship arising from common close ancestors; blood relationships. In breeding, consanguineous mating.

Contraception: Prevention of conception, as a means of birth control.

Contraceptive: Preventing or tending to prevent conception. An agent which prevents conception, such as medicated jelly in the vagina, a condom, a cervical pessary or diaphragm, or a systematically acting steroid that inhibits ovulation.

Cystic Fibrosis of the Pancreas: A generalized heritable disease of unknown etiology, associated with dysfunction of exocrine and eccrine glands, observed chiefly in infants, children, and adolescents; manifested mainly by elevated sweat electrolyte concentration, absence of pancreatic enzymes with the clinical appearance of the celiac syndrome, and evidence of chronic lung disease.

Cystocele: Herniation of the urinary bladder into the vagina.

Cystoscope: An instrument used in diagnosis and treatment of lesions of the urinary bladder, ureter, and kidney. It consists of an outer sheath bearing the lighting system, a well-fitted obturator, space for the visual system, and room for the passage of ureteral catheters and operative devices to be used under visual control.

Cystoscopy: The procedure of using the cystoscope.

Deaf-Mute: A person who lacks the sense of hearing and the ability to speak.

Diagnosis: The art or the act of determining the nature of a patient's disease. A conclusion reached in the identification of a patient's disease.

Down's Syndrome: A syndrome of congenital defects, especially mental retardation, typical facies responsible for the older descriptive term mongoloid idiocy, or mongolism, and cytogenetic abnormality consisting of trisomy 21 or its equivalent in the form of an unbalanced translocation.

Ectopic Gestation: Extrauterine gestation.

Endometrium: The mucous membrane lining the uterus.

Estrogen: Any substance possessing the biologic activity of estrus-producing hormones, either occurring naturally or prepared synthetically.

Eugenics: The applied science concerned with improving the genetic constitution of populations, and specifically, of human populations. Positive eugenics involves selection for undesirable types; negative eugenics involves selection against undesirable types.

Extrauterine: Outside the uterus.

Extrauterine Gestation: Development of the fertilized ovum outside the uterine cavity.

Fallopian Tube: Uterine tube, the oviduct in mammals.

Feeble-Minded: Mentally deficient or retarded.

Ferning: The formation of a crystallized fern pattern in dried mucus from the uterine cervix before ovulation, resulting from estrogen stimulation. Pregnancy and progestational changes prevent ferning; in pregnancy ferning indicates the presence of amniotic fluid in the vagina following premature rupture of membranes.

Fetus-Foetus: The unborn offspring of viviparious mammals in the later stages of development; in human beings, from about the beginning of the ninth week after fertilization.

Fibroid Tumor: Fibroma.

Fibroma: A benign tumor composed principally of fibrous connective tissue.

Genetic: Pertaining to or having reference to origin, mode of production, or development. Produced by genes.

Genital: Of or pertaining to the organs of generation or to reproduction.

Gestation: Pregnancy.

Gonorrhoea: A venereal disease caused by Neisseria gonorrhoea, characterized by mucupurulent inflammation of the mucosa of the genital tract; may produce septicemia with involvement of synovial tissues and serosal surfaces, causing arthritis, endocarditis, or meningitis.

Gynecologist: A physician who practices gynecology.

Gynecology: The science of the disease of women, especially those affecting the sexual organs.

Hemolysis: The destruction of red blood cells and the resultant escape of hemoglobin.

Hemophilia: An X-linked recessive hereditary bleeding disorder caused by factor VIII or factor IX deficiency and characterized clinically by hemarthrosis, hematomas, ecchymoses, gastrointestinal and genitourinary bleeding and excessive traumatic bleeding.

Hemorrhage: An escape of blood from the vessels, either by diapedesis through intact capillary walls or by flow through ruptured walls; bleeding.

Hereditary: Of or pertaining to inheritance; inborn; inherited.

Hormone: A specific chemical product of an organ or of certain cells of an organ, transported by the blood or other body fluids, and having a specific regulatory effect upon cells remote from its origin.

Huntington's Chorea: A dominantly heritable disorder of the central nervous system characterized by the onset, usually in adult life, of progressive choreoathetosis, emotional disturbances, and dementia.

Hydrocephalus: Distention of the cerebral ventricles with cerebrospinal fluid due to obstruction of the flow of spinal fluid within the ventricular system or in the subarachnoid space, preventing its absorption.

Hyperbilirubinemia: A severe and prolonged physiologic jaundice, sometimes seen in a premature newborn.

Hypertension: Excessive tension or pressure, especially that exerted by bodily fluids such as blood or aqueous humor. Specifically, high blood pressure.

Hypertrophic: Pertaining to or characterized by hypertrophy.

Hysterectomy: Total or partial surgical removal of the uterus.

Hysterosalpingography: Radiographic examination of the uterus and oviducts after injection of a radiopaque substance into their cavities.

Hysterotomy: Cesarean section, incision of the uterus.

Imbecile: A person afflicted with imbecility.

Imbecility: An intermediate grade of mental deficiency in which the subject's mental age is between 3 and 7 years with an intelligence quotient between 20 and 45.

Impotence: Inability in the male to perform the sexual act, most frequently for psychologic reasons. By extension, lack of sexual vigor or of power generally.

Incontinence: Inability to control the natural evacuations, as the feces or the urine; specifically, involuntary evacuation due to organic causes.

Inflammation: The reaction of the tissues to injury, characterized clinically by heat, swelling, redness, pain, and loss of function, pathologically, by vasoconstriction followed by vasodilatation, stasis, hyperemia, accumulation of leukocytes, exudation of fluid, and deposition of fibrin; and according to some authorities, the processes of repair, the production of new capillaries and fibroblasts, organization, and cicatrization.

Infusion: The slow injection of a solution into a vein or into subcutaneous or other tissue of the body, from which it is absorbed into the bloodstream.

Intrauterine Contraceptive Device (IUD): Any mechanical device placed in the uterine cavity to prevent implantation or growth of the embryo.

In Vitro: In glass; referring to a process or reaction carried out in a culture dish or test tube.

Jaundice: Yellowness of the skin, mucous membranes, and secretions; due to hyperbilirubinemia.

Karyo-Type: The total of characteristics, including number, form, and size, or chromosomes and their grouping in a cell nucleus. It is characteristic of an individual, race, species, genus, or larger grouping.

Labor: The series of processes, especially the coordinated, periodic uterine contractions, whereby the fetus is expelled in parturition.

Laparoscopy: Peritoneoscopy.

Laparotomy: An incision through the abdominal wall; the operation of cutting into the abdominal cavity through the loin or flank.

Malignant: Endangering health or life. Specifically, characterizing the progressive growth of certain tumors which if not checked by treatment, spread to distant sites terminating in death.

Menstrual Cycle: The periodically recurring series of changes in the uterus, ovaries, and accessory sexual structures associated with menstruation and the intermenstrual periods in primates.

Menstruation: A periodic discharge of a sanguineous fluid from the uterus, occurring during the period of a woman's sexual maturity from puberty to the menopause stage.

Miscarriage: Expulsion of the fetus before it is viable.

Mongoloid: Having physical characteristics associated with Down's Syndrome.

Multiple Sclerosis: A common disease of young adults, characterized clinically by episodes of focal disorder of the optic nerves, spinal cord, and brain, which remit to a varying extent and recur over a period of many years; and pathologically by the presence of numerous, scattered, sharply defined demyelinative lesions (plaques) in the white matter of the central nervous system.

Myasthenia Gravis: A disorder, characterized by a fluctuant weakness of certain voluntary skeletal muscles, particularly those innervated by the bulbar nuclei, affecting women twice as often as men, and sometimes associated with hyperthyroidism or, in the older age group, with carcinoma, as well as with thymic hyperplasia or with thymic tumor.

Neisseria Gonorrhoeae: The bacterium that causes gonorrhea; the type of species of its genus.

Neonatal: Pertaining to a newborn infant.

Neurofibromatosis: A hereditary disease characterized by presence of neurofibromas in the skin or along the course of peripheral nerves.

Obstetrician: One who practices obstetrics.

Obstetrics: The branch of medicine concerning the care of women and their offspring during pregnancy and parturition, with continued care of the women during the puerperium.

Occlusion: A closing or shutting up, the state of being closed or shut.

Oligospermia: Scarcity of spermatozoa in the semen; specifically, less than 20 million per ml.

Oligozoospermia: Oligospermia.

Oral Contraceptive: Any medication taken by mouth that inhibits fertility in a woman as long as the medication is continued.

Osteopathy: A school of healing which teaches that the body is a vital mechanical organism whose structural and functional integrity are coordinate and interdependent, the abnormality of either constituting disease. Its major effort in treatment is in manipulation, but medicine, surgery, and the specialities are also utilized.

Ova: Plural of ovum.

Ovary: One of a pair of glandular organs which contains and releases ova. It consists of a fibrous framework or stroma, in which are embedded the ovarian follicles, and is surrounded by a serous covering derived from the peritoneum.

Ovum: A female germ cell; an egg cell; a cell capable of developing into a new member of the same species. The human ovum is a large, spheroidal cell containing a large mass of cytoplasm and a large nucleus (germinal vesicle), within which is a nucleolus (germinal spot).

Pelvis: The bony ring formed by the two hipbones and the sacrum and coccyx.

Peritoneoscopy: The method of examining the peritoneal cavity by means of a peritoneoscope.

Placenta: The organ on the wall of the uterus to which the embryo is attached by the umbilical cord. Developed from the chorion of the embryo and the decidua basalis of the uterus, it performs the functions of nutrition, respiration, and excretion, as well as secretion of estrogen, progesterone, and other hormones. At term the average human placenta weighs about one sixth as much as the fetus, and is about 2 cm thick at its center and 15 cm in diameter.

Placenta Previa: A placenta superimposed upon and about the os uteri internum, which may produce serious hemorrhage before or during labor.

Plasmodium Falciparum: The species of Plasmodium that is the etiologic agent of falciparum malaria.

Polycystic Kidney Disease: Hereditary bilateral cysts distributed throughout the renal parenchyma, resulting in markedly enlarged kidneys and progressive renal failure.

Postoperative: Occurring after an operation; following closely upon an operation.

Prenatal: Existing or occurring before birth.

Procreate: To beget.

Prophylactic: Any agent or device that prevents or helps to prevent the development of disease.

Prostaglandin: One of several physiologically potent compounds, of unbiquitous occurrence, that has a unique structure containing 20 carbon atoms and are formed from essential fatty acids, and with activities affecting the nervous system, circulation, female reproductive organs, and metabolism. The highest concentration of prostaglandins has been found in normal human semen.

Prostate: The organ surrounding the neck of the urinary bladder and beginning of the urethra in the male (prostatic urethra). It consists of two lateral lobes, an anterior and a posterior lobe, and a middle lobe, and is composed of muscular and glandular tissue; a distinct capsule surrounds it. It is the largest auxiliary gland of the male reproductive system and its secretions comprise approximately 40% of the semen.

Prostatitis: Inflammation of the prostrate gland.

Radiograph: A photograph made on a sensitive film by projection of x-rays through a part of the body.

Radiography: The practice or act of making radiographs.

Rectocele: Protrusion or herniation of the rectum into the vagina.

Resection: The operation of cutting out, as the removal of a section or segment of an organ.

Retardate: A person with mental retardation.

Retardation: Slow mental or physical functioning, specifically, mental retardation.

Rubella: An acute benign viral contagious disease of children and young adults characterized by fever, a pale pink rash, and posterior cervical lymphadenitis. Associated with fetal abnormalities when maternal infection occurs in early pregnancy.

Salpingectomy: Excision of a uterine tube.

Salpingoophorectomy: Excision of a uterine tube and an ovary.

Sedative: Any drug that can be used to calm anxious and disturbed patients and to produce drowsiness.

Sensitization: The coating of cells with antibody so that they may be agglutinated, or lysed if complement is added. The process of becoming reactive or hypersensitive, especially to pollens, serums, and other antigens.

Septic Abortion: An abortion complicated by acute infection of the endometrium.

Sickle Cell Anemia: A chronic hemolytic and thrombotic disorder in which hypoxia causes the erythrocytes to assume a sickled shape; it occurs in persons (usually blacks) homozygous for sickle cell hemoglobin.

Sickle Cell Trait: The heterozygous genetic constitution in which there is one gene for normal adult hemoglobin and one for sickle cell hemoglobin. Usually no clinical disease is present, and in malarious areas children with the trait are relatively resistant to the more severe forms of Plasmodium Falciparum infection, possibly because infected cells are selectively sickled and eliminated from the circulation.

Somatic: Bodily, corporeal.

Spermatic Cord: The cord extending from the testis to the deep inguinal ring and consisting of the ductus deferens, the vessels and nerves of the testis and of the epididymis and the accompanying connective tissue.

Spermatozoa: Plural of spermatozoon.

Spermatozoon: The mature male germ cell.

Spinnbarkeit: The ability of cervical mucus to form a thin, continuous thread; usually occurs shortly before ovulation.

Spontaneous Abortion: Unexpected premature expulsion of the product of conception before the 20th completed week of gestation.

Sterile: Not fertile; not capable of reproducing.

Sterility: Total inability to reproduce.

Sterilize: To render sterile or free from live microorganisms.

Stroke: Cerebrovascular accident.

Symptom: A phenomenon of physical or mental disorder or disturbance which leads to complaints on the part of the patient; usually a subjective state, such as headache or pain, in contrast to an objective sign such as papilledema.

Syphilitic: Of, pertaining to, or affected with syphilis. A person affected with syphilis.

Tay-Sachs Disease: A form of G_m2 gangliosidosis which begins during the first 3 to 6 months of age and is characterized by an abnormal startle reaction, axial hypotonia leading to spasticity, and, in most cases, cherry red spots in the retinas; death occurs at 3 to 5 years. The disease results from a deficiency of, or defect in, the enzyme hexosaminidase.

Testicle: A testis: especially, the scrotal testis of larger animals.

Therapeutic: Pertaining to therapy or to therapeutics.

Toxemia: A condition in which the blood contains poisonous products, either those produced by the body cells or those resulting from microorganisms.

Transfusion: The introduction into a blood vessel of blood, saline solution, or other liquid.

Translocation: The displacement of part or all of one chromosome to another.

Transurethral: Via the urethra.

Tubal Ligation: The operation of tying, especially arteries, veins, ducts, or tubes, with some form of knotted ligature in the uterus.

Tubectomy: Salpingectomy; excision of a tube, specifically a uterine tube.

Tumor: Any abnormal mass resulting from the excessive multiplication of cells, a swelling.

Unsex: To remove the testes in male, or the ovaries in female, animals.

Ureter: Either of the long, narrow tubes conveying the urine from the pelvis of each kidney to the urinary bladder.

Urethra: The canal through which urine is discharged, extending from the neck of the urinary bladder to the external urethral orifice, divided in the male into the prostatic portion, the membranous portion, and the spongy or penile portion, and 8 to 9 inches long. In the female, it is about 1½ inches long.

Urinary: Of or pertaining to urine; pertaining to, part of, in, or associated with the urinary system.

Uterus: The womb; the organ or gestation which receives and holds the fertilized ovum during the development of the fetus, and becomes the principal agent in its expulsion during parturition.

Vagina: The musculomembranous canal from the vulvar opening to the cervix of the uterus.

Vaginal: Pertaining to or affecting the vagina.

Vas Deferens: Ductus deferens, the portion of the excretory duct system of the testis which runs from the epididymal duct to the ejaculatory duct.

Vasectomy: Surgical division or resection of the ductus deferens; used to produce male sterility for birth control.

Viable: Capable of living; likely to live.

Womb: Uterus.

X-Ray: Any electromagnetic radiation having a wavelength in the approximate range of 0.1 to 100 angstroms, usually produced by bombarding a metal target with fast electrons in a highly evacuated tube and that has a spectrum characteristic of the target metal. X-rays penetrate various thicknesses of solids, strongly ionize tissues, affect photographic plates, and cause certain substances to fluoresce.

[The terms and definitions in this glossary are derived from Blakiston, GOULD MEDICAL DICTIONARY (McGraw-Hill 4th ed 1979).]

Table of Cases

A

B

C

D

E

F

G

H

I

J

K

L

M

N

O

O'Neill v Morse, 385 Mi 130, 188 NW2d 785 (1971): §5.56, §5.57, §5.58

Ooft v City of New York, 104 Misc 2d 879, 429 NYS2d 376 (1980): §2.36

Orange v State Farm Mutual Automobile Ins Co, 443 SW2d 650 (Ky 1969): §5.56

Oresman v G D Searle & Co, 321 FSupp 449 (D RI 1971): §2.28

Orford v Orford, 58 D.L.R. 251 (1921): §4.2

Ortho Pharmaceutical Corp v Chapman, 388 NE2d 541 (In 1979): §2.32, §2.33

P

P v Portadin, 178 NJ Super 465, 432 A2d 556 (1981): §3.27, §3.28, §3.31, §3.34, §3.36, §3.37, §3.39, §3.40, §3.41, §3.42

Padin v Fordham Hosp, 392 FSupp 447 (SD NY 1975): §2.21

Palo v Upjohn Co, 310 So2d 30 (Fl 1975): §5.53

Panagopoulous v Martin, 295 FSupp 220 (D WV 1969): §5.51

Park v Chessin, 60 AD2d 80, 400 NYS2d 110 (1977): §6.9, §6.13, §6.14, §6.19

Parker v Dunlop, 517 F2d 785 (5th Cir 1975): §5.33

Payton v Abbott Labs, 83 FRD 382 (D Ma 1979): §6.26

Payton v Abbott Labs, 512 FSupp 1031 (D Ma 1981): §6.25, §6.27, §6.29, §6.30, §6.31

Pearson v Boines, 367 A2d 653 (De 1976), affd, 386 A2d 651 (De 1978): §2.14, §2.15

Pearson v Boines, 386 A2d 651 (De 1978): §2.17

People v Apodaca, 76 CaA3d 479, 142 CaR 830 (1978): §5.43, §5.44

People v Bricker, 389 Mi 524, 208 NW2d 173 (1973): §5.34

People v Guthrie, 97 MiA 326, 293 NW2d 775 (1980): §5.44

People v Smith, 59 CaA3d 751 (1976): §5.45

People v Sorensen, 66 CaR 7, 437 P2d 495 (1968): §4.1, §4.2, §4.5

Peters v Gelb, 303 A2d 685 (De 1974), affd, 314 A2d 901 (De 1974): §3.22

Petro v McCullough, 385 NE2d 1195 (In 1979): §2.6, §2.7

Pettit v Chester Cty Hosp, 8 FLR 2728 (Pa 1982): §5.11

Pharmaceutical Manufacturers Assn v Food & Drug Admin, 484 FSupp 1179 (D De 1980): §2.32

Phillips v United States, 508 FSupp 537 (D SC 1980): §6.1, §6.13, §6.14, §6.15, §6.21

Phillips v United States, 508 FSupp 544 (D SC 1981): §6.1, §6.2, §6.4, §6.5, §6.6

Pierce v DeGracia, 103 IlA3d 511, 59 Il Dec 267, 431 NE2d 768 (1982): §3.9, §3.27, §3.28, §3.40, §3.43, §3.46, §3.47

Pierce v Piver, 45 NC App 111, 262 SE2d 320 (1980): §3.13

Pierce v Smith, 301 So2d 805 (Fl 1974): §2.14, §2.15

Pierson v Ray, 386 US 547, 87 SCt 1213, 18 LE2d 288 (1967): §2.27

Pinkney v Pinkney, 198 So2d 52 (Fl 1967): §6.22, §6.24

Pipon v Burroughs-Wellcome Co, 532 FSupp 637 (D NJ 1982): §6.27

Planned Parenthood Assn v Fitzpatrick, 401 FSupp 554 (ED Pa 1975), summ affd sub nom, *Franklin v Fitzpatrick*, 428 US 901, 96 SCt 3202, 49 LE2d 1205 (1976): §5.11

Planned Parenthood Assn of Kansas City v Ashcroft, 664 F2d 687 (8th

R

S

T

U

V

W

Y

Z

Index

A

B

C

D

E

F

G

H

I

J

L

M

N

P

R

S

T

U

V

W

Z

Handling Pregnancy & Birth Cases

FEBRUARY, 1989 SUPPLEMENT

Family Law Series

Insert in the pocket at the back of the bound book. Discard issue dated February, 1988.

Prepared by Publisher's Editorial Staff

Shepard's/McGraw-Hill, Inc.
P.O. Box 1235
Colorado Springs, CO 80901

ISBN 0-07-056745X

HPB1

CHAPTER 2

Preconception Stage: Established Law

I. SURGICAL STERILIZATION

A. In General

2. [§2.2] Background and Constitutionality

Article I, Section 1 of the California Constitution protects the right of a woman to choose whether or not to bear a child and thus to control her social role and personal destiny. Since the right to elect sterilization as a method of contraception is generally available to adult women, a restriction must be justified by a compelling state interest under either Article I, Section 1, or under the equal protection guarantee of Article I, Section 7 of the Constitution. Under an equal protection analysis, it must be determined whether the state has a compelling interest in restricting access to sterilization for incompetent, developmentally disabled adults and, if so, whether banning all such sterilization is necessary to accomplish the state purpose. Similarly, in assessing any restriction on the exercise of a fundamental constitutional right, it must be determined whether the state has a compelling interest that is within the police power of the state in regulating the subject, whether the regulation is necessary to accomplish the purpose, and if the restriction is narrowly drawn. A conservator is permitted to exercise his or her own judgment as to the best interests of the conservatee in matters of birth control, except in the case of the election of sterilization as a means of preventing conception. It was determined that Section 2356, Subdivision (d) of the Probate Code, which prevents the sterilization of a ward or conservatee, was unconstitutionally overbroad and could not be invoked to deny the probate court the authority to grant a conservator the power to consent to sterilization in those cases in which no less intrusive method of contraception was available to a severely retarded conservatee. *Conservatorship of Valerie N*, 40 Ca3d 143, 219 CaR 387, 707 P2d 760 (1985).

STERILIZATION TECHNOLOGY AND DECISIONMAKING: RETHINKING THE INCOMPETENT'S RIGHTS, 2 J Contemp Health L & Pol'y 275 (1986).

B. Liability for Surgical Sterilization

2. Negligence

a. [§2.14] Generally

An action may be maintained for medical negligence or malpractice in the performance of an unsuccessful vasectomy upon a husband and in the sperm testing and advice which follows that results in the pregnancy of the wife. The court noted that the failure to recognize a cause of action against a physician who negligently performed a surgical sterilization procedure would be a grant of absolute immunity to a physician whose negligence resulted in injury to a patient. A physician who assumes responsibility for a sterilization procedure at the request of a patient assumes a professional duty to render appropriate service, including testing and advice regarding the procedure and exercising the same standard of care applicable to other members of the medical profession in the community. However, a physician is not required to guarantee the success of the procedure. Failure of the physician to achieve success does not automatically indicate negligence. He or she is only required to exercise the required standard of care during the surgery and in later attempting to verify the success or failure of the procedure and to appropriately advise the patient. A physician performing this type of operation is held to the standard of care required of all members of the same school of medicine in the community in which they practice. Such a physician is answerable only if negligence in the performance of the services is established by proof. The court held that the birth of a normal, healthy child is not a legal wrong for which damages may be recovered. However, damages which are the direct, natural, and probable result of the wrongful act are recoverable. Those damages may include the expense of the unsuccessful operation, the physical pain and suffering of the patient in connection with the surgery, the cost of prenatal care, delivery, and subsequent sterilization surgery, the physical pain and suffering in connection with the pregnancy, childbirth, and sterilization thereafter, and the loss of consortium at the time of the sterilization operation, during the latter stages of pregnancy, and during a reasonable recovery period thereafter. *Johnston v Elkins*, 241 Ks 407, 736 P2d 935 (1987).

A woman who became pregnant after a failed bilateral tubal ligation was denied recovery on the basis that the Voluntary Sterilization

Act [OCGA §31-20-1 et seq] barred recovery, where the woman failed to produce any affidavits or counter-affidavits to rebut the affidavits submitted by the defendant and his expert witness affirming that he exercised that degree of care and skill ordinarily exercised and possessed by the medical profession generally. It was uncontroverted that there was no negligence in the performance of the operation and the sterilization procedure was performed in full compliance with the Act. Therefore, the woman's claim, whether based on contract or some other negligence, fell within the scope of the Act, and the trial court correctly granted summary judgment in favor of the defendant. *Cummings v Dudley*, 180 GaA 545, 349 SE2d 543 (1986).

b. [§2.15] Illustrative Cases

Where a sterilization operation was negligently and mistakenly performed on the plaintiff, she was not permitted to recover for loss of offspring because damages would be too speculative to be compensable. However, she would be permitted recovery of pain and suffering, whether physical or emotional, including emotional upset attending the breach of duty. *Rosini v Cunanan*, 132 Misc2d 246, 503 NYS2d 969 (1986), later proceeding, 130 AD2d 956, 516 NYS2d 146 (1987).

D. Sterilization of Incompetent Persons

1. [§2.22] Generally

A statutory prohibition against a court ordering the sterilization of an incompetent person does not apply where the purpose of the proposed sterilization is to treat a life endangering disease rather than to prevent the person from bearing children. *Butte Cty Public Guardian v Superior Ct*, 8 FLR 2717 (Ca 1982).

MINN STAT §252A.13, subd. 4 (1982), which creates a judicial procedure for determining whether sterilization is in the best interests of a ward of the state, does not violate the due process clause of the United States Constitution if the standard of proof required is clear and convincing evidence. Clear and convincing evidence is constitutionally required because the governmental imposition of a surgical procedure that terminates the capacity to bear or beget children is a substantial intrusion in the area of a fundamental right. There are important societal as well as important personal interests on both sides of the equation, and the decision must be carefully made because it is irreversible. In order to assure that abuses do not occur, and to screen out those individuals who should not be sterilized, clear and convincing evidence is required. On the record in this case, the state failed to meet its burden of showing by clear and convincing evidence that sterilization was in a mentally retarded person's best interest. The statute requires consideration of the medical risks of sterilization and alternative methods of contraception. Hence, sterilization is a last resort means of contraception. The best interest standard, therefore, requires, at a minimum, a showing that the woman was likely to engage in sexual intercourse. Because she required 24-hour supervision, her "vulnerability to being seduced" was not a valid factor in making that decision. *Matter of Welfare of Hillstrom*, 363 NW2d 871 (MnA 1985).

2. [§2.23] Consent and Authorization

Prior judicial approval is required before a guardian may consent to the administering of extraordinary medical treatment, such as a sterilization operation, to an incompetent person. *Matter of Terwilliger*, 304 Pa Super 553, 450 A2d 1376 (Pa 1982). But a family court's order authorizing the natural parents of a retarded child to proceed with sterilization of their child was affirmed where an extensive hearing revealed that it was highly unlikely that the child would ever improve. *Brode v Brode*, 278 SC 457, 298 SE2d 443 (1982).

3. [§2.24] Jurisdiction of the Court

The jurisdiction to hear a matter involving a court authorization to have a person declared incompetent and to have the person's guardian appointed for the purpose of consenting to the person's sterilization was not restricted solely to the orphan's court, but could have been pursued in another "appropriate" division of the court of common pleas. Although a court appointed guardian is vested with the care and management of the person under legal disability, the appointee, being an officer of the court, is always under the court's control and is subject to its directions as to the person of the ward. Prior judicial approval is required before a guardian may consent to administering or withholding of proposed extraordinary medical treatment. Therefore, there is no reason why the orphan's court's inherent parens patriae jurisdiction should not apply to a petition for sterilization of an incompetent. *Matter of Terwilliger*, 304 Pa Super 553, 450 A2d 1376 (Pa 1982).

The family court properly assumed jurisdiction of an action seeking authorization by the natural parents of a retarded child to proceed with sterilization of their daughter. The provisions of S. C. CODE §20-7-400.A (Cum. Supp. 1981) grant exclusive original jurisdiction to family courts in matters concerning any child whose "behavior" or "condition" could "injure or endanger his welfare." The same section empowers the family court to provide "for the treatment . . . of a mentally defective or mentally disordered or emotionally disturbed child." *Brode v Brode*, 278 SC 457, 298 SE2d 443 (1982).

A specific enabling statute is not required to authorize the sterilization of an incompetent person. Therefore, a juvenile court had jurisdiction to authorize the sterilization of an incompetent child since the court had before it clear and convincing evidence that the medical procedure was in the best interest of the child. In this case the child was a 12 year old female with an IQ of 46. She suffered from moderate mental retardation, autism, and dyspraxia. The evidence established that she was self destructive and, unless restrained, was capable of inflicting substantial harm to herself and her environment. Furthermore, there was expert testimony by a former head of a department of neurosurgery and a case worker for a county department of public welfare that if the child were to become pregnant it would threaten her life. Under these circumstances, the court held that the sterilization operation would be authorized. *P S v W S*, 452 NE2d 969 (In 1983).

NC GEN STAT §35-43 expressly authorizes a judge to enter an order of sterilization based upon either of two grounds. The statute, which involves the sterilization of persons mentally ill and mentally retarded, provides that the first ground is if the person would probably be unable to care for a child or children. The second ground is if the person would be likely, unless sterilized, to procreate a child or children which probably would have serious physical, mental, or nervous diseases or deficiencies. In order for a sterilization to be based on either ground, there must be a finding that the mentally ill or mentally retarded person was sexually active. *Matter of Truesdell*, 313 NC 421, 329 SE2d 630 (1985).

4. [§2.25] Standards for Authorization

The following standards are to be applied by the trial court in considering the petition for sterilization of a person who is otherwise unable to give intelligent or knowledgeable consent to such a procedure: (1) possibility that the incompetent or disabled person could become pregnant; (2) possibility that the incompetent person would experience trauma or psychological damage if she became pregnant or gave birth as considered with the possibility of trauma or psychological damage resulting from sterilization; (3) the likelihood that the individual would voluntarily engage in sexual activities or be placed in situations where sexual activities might be imposed upon her; (4) the inability of the incompetent person to understand reproduction or contraception and the likelihood of permanence of that inability; (5) feasibility and medical advisability of less drastic means of contraception both at the present time and in the foreseeable future; (6) the advisability of sterilization at the time of the application as opposed to such a procedure at some future date; (7) the ability of the incompetent person to care for a child with the possibility that the incompetent person may at some future date be able to marry and, with a spouse, care for a child; (8) evidence scientific or medical advances may occur within the foreseeable future which might make possible improvement of the individual's condition or alternatives in less drastic sterilization procedures; (9) demonstration that the proponents of the sterilization are seeking it in good faith and that their primary interest is for the best interest of the incompetent person rather than for their own or the public's convenience. Using these standards the court granted an order permitting the sterilization of an incompetent person. It was established that the person was presumably fertile and capable of bearing a child, that psychological trauma could result if she became pregnant and gave birth to a child, that the person was becoming aware of boys and there existed the possibility that she would participate in sexual activities or in view of her mental retardation that sexual activities could be imposed upon her, that in view of the person's mental retardation it would be unlikely that she would understand the technics related to contraception and, that in view of the fact that her mental retardation would remain, there would be a likely permanence of that inability, that the person would not be competent to care for a child, and that the parents of the child, who sought the petition, were concerned with the best interests of the child, were seeking the application in good faith, and were not doing so for their own benefit or as related to public convenience. *Application of Nilsson*, 122 Misc2d 458, 471 NYS2d 439 (1983).

Because sterilization necessarily results in the permanent termination of the intensely personal right of procreation, the trial judge must take the greatest care to ensure that the incompetent's rights are jealously guarded. Initially, the court should consider only the best interests of the incompetent person, not the interests or convenience of the individual's parents, the guardian, or of society. Moreover, the court must demand from the advocates of the proposed operation proof by clear and convincing evidence that sterilization is in the best interest of the incompetent. Upon the filing of the petition with the court, the judge shall first appoint an independent guardian ad litem, who will vigorously defend the interests of the incompetent at a full judicial hearing. Second, the trial judge must find that the individual lacks capacity to make a decision about sterilization and that the incapacity is not likely to change in the foreseeable future. Third, the person for whom sterilization is requested must be proven capable of reproduction. These guidelines are not intended to be an exhaustive list of the factors which the court should consider before ruling on a petition for sterilization. Rather, they constitute minimal requirements that need to be examined to protect the constitutional rights of the incompetent person. The need for additional inquiries and the weight to be given to each factor will vary with the particular facts and circumstances of each case. *Matter of Terwilliger*, 304 Pa Super 553, 450 A2d 1376 (Pa 1982).

The seriousness of an individual's interest at stake in a state initiated sterilization proceeding is such that due process requires "clear and convincing evidence" to exist for a court to authorize the sterilization of an individual. *Motes v Hall Cty Dept of Family & Children Services*, 251 Ga 373, 306 SE2d 260 (1983).

The duty of determining whether sterilization is in a retarded person's best interest falls on the court, and not on the person's parents or guardian. This is because the constitutional right of reproductive autonomy is a right personal to the individual. In the exercise of that right, the interests of the parents of a retarded person cannot be presumed to be identical to those of the child. Thus, a judicial determination is necessary to insure that the child's personal right is protected. In addition, it must be proved by clear and convincing evidence that sterilization is in the best interest of the person being considered for sterilization. The court shall find that sterilization is in the best interest of the person being considered for sterilization if it is shown by clear and convincing evidence that (1) methods of contraception less drastic than sterilization have proven to be unworkable or inappropriate for the person, and (2) sterilization is necessary to preserve the physical or mental health of the person. In this case, the district court could not reasonably have concluded that the retarded person's procreative capability was highly probable where the petition for sterilization was accompanied only by the statement of two psychologists, neither of whom was identified in the record as a physician. One reported that according to the retarded person's physician, the person was physiologically capable of procreation. The other psychologist did not mention the subject. The person's physician testified at the hearing that he agreed with the question that the person was a physically, sexually mature person. The physician's response was ambiguous at best and could easily be interpreted to mean only that the person was capable of sexual activity. Thus, the court concluded that the petition for sterilization was improperly granted and the judgment in favor of the sterilization was vacated. *In re Debra B*, 495 A2d 781 (Me 1985) [construing 34-B MRSA §§7001 et seq].

The petitioner in an action to have a mentally retarded or mentally ill person sterilized pursuant to NC GEN STAT §35-43 must prove by clear, strong, and convincing evidence that there is a substantial likelihood that the person will voluntarily or otherwise engage in sexual activity likely to cause impregnation before the district court judge may enter an order authorizing the sterilization procedure. Furthermore, when the state petitions the court for a compulsory sterilization, some minimal best interest standards are constitutionally required. The petitioner must establish that the person would be likely, unless sterilized, to procreate a child or children which probably would have serious physical, mental, or nervous diseases or deficiencies. In this case, there were no findings to support the possibility of trauma to the mentally ill person. Additionally, there was insufficient evidence to support a finding that the person was substantially likely to engage in sexual activity likely to cause impregnation. Instead, the facts indicated that the occasions for the person's heterosexual contact were severely limited because she was closely supervised. However, the court noted that the person might be exposed in the future to more social interaction. If and when she is not as closely supervised and should increased heterosexual social interaction develop, such evidence may be sufficient to sustain a finding that she is substantially likely to engage in sexual activity which is likely to cause impregnation, the court said. In life-threatening or emergency situations where sterilization is medically necessary, a petition could be granted absent a showing of the required factors, the court said. However, in this case, there was insufficient evidence to prove that the person was in imminent danger for her life or that her health was severely jeopardized if a hysterectomy was not immediately performed. *Matter of Truesdell*, 313 NC 421, 329 SE2d 630 (1985).

5. [§2.26] Survey of State Incompetent Persons' Sterilization Statutes

The Georgia statutory scheme that provides for the involuntary sterilization of certain mentally incompetent persons [O.C.G.A. §31-

20-3] is unconstitutional because it denies those persons the right to procreate. *Motes v Hall Cty Dept of Family & Children Services*, 251 Ga 373, 306 SE2d 260 (1983).

II. CONTRACEPTION

A. [§2.28] In General

In an action seeking equitable relief consisting of a worldwide recall of an intrauterine device known as the Dalkon Shield, it was held that no private right of action can be implied under the Federal Food, Drug & Cosmetic Act. Moreover, there is no basis under state law for the requested equitable relief. The plaintiffs sought to have the defendant A. H. Robins Company indemnify former users for the cost of removal, conduct an identification and notification campaign for present users, and in those cases where the user then opted for removal, require Robins to pay the costs. The plaintiffs characterized the desired relief as amounting to a worldwide recall of the Dalkon Shield. *National Women's Health Network v A H Robins Co*, 545 FSupp 1177 (D Ma 1982).

A jury finding that ingestion of a birth control pill by the plaintiff resulted in acute kidney failure was affirmed based on substantial, competent evidence. The three specialists who were called to testify by the plaintiff all concluded that the plaintiff's ingestion of an oral contraceptive resulted in the plaintiff's irreversible kidney failure. Moreover, the record indicated that the proof of medical causation was detailed, logical, and based upon scientific studies. *Wooderson v Ortho Pharmaceutical Corp*, 235 Ks 387, 681 P2d 1038 (1984) cert den 105 SCt 365.

A nonsuit in favor of the manufacturer of an oral contraceptive was affirmed where the plaintiff was unable to meet the test of proximate cause with regard to the allegedly injury-causing oral contraceptive. The plaintiff alleged that she developed a precancerous condition after ingesting the manufacturer's oral contraceptive. The only evidence the plaintiff introduced relating to the causal connection between the oral contraceptive and the plaintiff's precancerous condition was described by the court as being the highly conjectural and ambiguous testimony of the plaintiff's two experts that the ingestion of the drug may have had some effect on the development or progression of the disease. The law is well settled that in a personal injury action, causation must be proven within a reasonable medical probability based upon competent expert testimony. Mere possibility alone is insufficient to establish a prima facie case. There can be many possible causes which can produce an injury or disease. A possible cause only becomes probable when, in the absence of other reasonable causal explanations, it becomes more likely than not that the injury was a result of its action. The fact that a determination of causation is difficult to establish cannot, however, provide a plaintiff with an excuse to dispense with the introduction of some reasonably reliable evidence proving this essential element of the case. The court said that the only reasonable inference which could be drawn from the evidence was that the proximate cause of the plaintiff's condition remained unknown and unproved. Specialists in both gynecology and pharmacology admitted that the causal connection between the ingestion of the oral contraceptive and the plaintiff's condition was something less than a 50-50 possibility. On the issue of whether the drug accelerated the normal progression of the disease, the testimony was equally as uncertain and speculative. In this case, the plaintiff had developed carcinoma in situ of the cervix after having ingested the manufacturer's oral contraceptive. The plaintiff also contended that because the manufacturer purportedly violated certain federal regulations in conducting its premarketing clinical studies of the oral contraceptive, the burden of proof with respect to causation should have been shifted to the defense. However, the court disagreed. The court was unpersuaded by the plaintiff's contention that the defendant's failure to comply with federal regulations made it impossible for her to prove causation. Nor would the court, as the plaintiff inferentially suggested, presume that had the defendant conducted the clinical studies the plaintiff contended should have been done, those studies would have established that the defendant's product caused cancer. *Jones v Ortho Pharmaceutical Corp*, 209 CaR 456, 163 CaA3d 396 (1985).

The plaintiffs in a product liability action against a manufacturer of an intrauterine device alleging that the device caused injuries such as pelvic inflammatory disease, ectopic pregnancy, and perforation of the uterus face a difficult burden of proof. Evidence or absolute scientific certainty may be impossible for either plaintiffs or defendant to obtain in a product liability case of this nature, because it is difficult to isolate one of a variety of factors which may have caused an injury. Proof of causation must be presented in scientific and medical terms which may be misinterpreted in a legal setting. For example, reliable evidence of a strong association between a product and an injury may lead a reasonable juror to conclude that a causal relationship is more probable than not, even though the expert witness never mentioned causation and only testified to an association. Nevertheless, when presenting evidence of an association, just as with any other expert testimony, there must be some basis beyond mere theory and speculation for the opinion. If the use of epidemiological evidence does enhance the integrity of the fact-finding process, it will be helpful to all parties and, if possible, should be used. The evidentiary inquiry is whether reliable scientific evidence, which is based upon sound methodology, has been presented, and whether through that evidence, plaintiffs arguably have satisfied their burden of proof. The scientific evidence need not prove an absolute certainty of causation, but must be sufficient to support a finding of reasonable probability of causation. *Marder v G D Searle & Co*, 630 FSupp 1087 (D Md 1986), affd without op, *Wheelahan v G D Searle & Co*, 814 F2d 655 (4th Cir 1987).

B. Liability of Manufacturer or Seller of Contraceptive

1. Breach of Warranty

a. [§2.29] Generally

A purchaser of an intrauterine device, which subsequently injured the buyer, gave adequate notice of a prospective breach of warranty claim by giving notice to the immediate seller of the intrauterine device, the buyer's physician. There was sufficient evidence establishing that the woman gave notice to the physician of the defective character of the Dalkon shield and that this notice came to the attention of the physician within the meaning of Co Rev Stat §4-1-201(26) when the woman presented herself to the physician in a life-threatening condition which arose while she was pregnant and still was using the intrauterine device. In addition, there was sufficient evidence to support a reasonable conclusion by the jury that the manufacturer's representations concerning the superiority, effectiveness, and safety of the shield formed an essential part of the woman's decision to have that device inserted in her body and to continue using it as safe and effective method of contraception. It is not necessary for an express warranty that the seller use formal words such as warrant or guarantee or that the seller have a specific intention to make a warranty, but a statement purporting to be merely the seller's opinion or commendation of the goods does not create a warranty. Whether a particular statement constitutes an express warranty is generally an issue of fact. With regard to this issue, the jury found that the woman's physician's statements to her that the shield was a superior intrauterine device, safer than the birth control pill, and 98.9% effective in preventing pregnancy, did constitute an express warranty. Moreover, there was sufficient evidence in the case to justify the submission of both warranty claims, breaches of implied warranty of fitness for a particular purpose and implied warranty of merchantability, to the jury. The physician's usual practice in advising patients about contraception was to inform them about the effectiveness of the pill and also to warn them about the possible adverse consequences of its use. The physician followed this procedure with the woman when she visited his office. The woman rejected the pill as a contraceptive method because of her apprehensions over its safety and the serious health problems associated with it. It was at this point, according to the woman, that the physician recommended the shield because it was safer and almost as effective as the pill. The woman, relying on the physician's recommendation, chose the shield because she believed it would be safer than other forms of contraception and would be almost as effective as the pill in preventing pregnancy. This evidence was sufficient to support the woman's claim that she selected the shield not only to prevent pregnancy, the ordinary purpose for which an IUD is selected, but also for the particular purpose of providing her with a safe contraceptive device that averted such hazards as stroke, vascular clotting, and other harmful effects on the body. There can be no question that the manufacturer knew or had reason to know of the special or particular safety features attributed to its product. Under these circumstances, the submission to the jury of the dual implied warranties of fitness for a particular purpose and merchantability was justified. As a result of the jury's findings, the woman was awarded $600,000 in compensatory damages for the damage caused by the intrauterine device (the suffering of a septic abortion and a subsequently performed hysterectomy) and $6.2 million in punitive damages which was affirmed in favor of the woman. The manufacturer argued that the trial court erred in permitting the jury to consider punitive damages in connection with a products liability claim based on §402A of the Restatement (Second) of Torts. The purpose of a strict liability claim under §402A is compensation for actual damages. A punitive damages claim, in contrast, is calculated to punish wrongful conduct and to deter a repetition of that conduct. If punitive damages are predictably certain, they become just another item in the cost of doing business, much like other production costs, and thereby induce a reluctance on the part of the manufacturer to sacrifice profit by removing a correctible device. The court held, therefore, that punitive damages were recoverable in connection with a strict liability claim founded on §402A. *Palmer v A H Robins*, 684 P2d 187 (Co 1984).

2. [§2.31] Defective Design

Summary judgment in favor of the manufacturer of a birth control pill was affirmed where the plaintiff did not allege that the drug which she took contained any contaminants and no allegation was made concerning the nature of the defect present in the birth control pill although the plaintiff did contend that the drug was defective in design, composition, formulation or manufacture so that it was unreasonably dangerous in its normal use. Although drugs and medications must be carefully administered and cautiously consumed, they are not so inherently dangerous that the manufacturer is held to guarantee that no harm will come to those who use such products. Since the birth control pills taken by the plaintiff were not contaminated or defectively manufactured, they cannot be considered as unreasonably dangerous, if properly used. *Cobb v Syntex Laboratories, Inc*, 444 So2d 203 (La 1983).

3. Defective Warning

a. [§2.32] Duty to Warn

A manufacturer of a pharmaceutical product has a duty to warn the medical profession, not the patient, of any risks inherent in the use of the product which the manufacturer knows or should know to exist. A manufacturer has a continuing duty to inspect and test its product during the course of manufacture and to warn the medical profession of any side effects associated with the product's use. Therefore, a judgment in favor of the plaintiff was reversed in a case where the plaintiff contracted pelvic inflammatory disease in connection with her use of the Lippes Loop IUD, since the manufacturer of the IUD sent revised warning literature to the plaintiff's doctor who failed to inform her of the new warning information. *Beyette v Ortho Pharmaceutical Corp*, 823 F2d 990 (6th Cir Mi 1987).

The manufacturer of a birth control pill has a duty to give timely and adequate warnings to the medical profession of any dangerous side effects produced by its drugs of which it knows, or has reason to know. By contrast, the law is not that a drug manufacturer is not bound to provide warnings until the occurrence of side effects is so frequent and the evidence of causation so clear cut that the drug maker is convinced that the drug contributes to such side effects. During the times relevant to this lawsuit, the label which accompanied the birth control pill, when purchased by the patient, instructed the patient not to take the drugs without her doctor's continued supervision. It warned that the drug could cause side effects, but it did not elaborate upon those side effects except to say that the most serious known side effect was abnormal blood clotting. The warnings that the manufacturer sent to the physician did not include any possible association between the use of the birth control pill and renal failure. Expert testimony and the plaintiff's exhibits disclosed that there was an abundance of published information in medical journals, prior to and during the years when the plaintiff was taking the oral contraceptive, which linked its use with acute renal failure. Therefore, the manufacturer had a duty to warn the prescribing physician, and a jury verdict in favor of the plaintiff on this issue was affirmed. *Wooderson v Ortho Pharmaceutical Corp* 235 Ks 387, 681 P2d 1038 cert den 105 SCt 365 (1984).

The manufacturer of a prescription drug has the obligation to inform the prescribing physician of any potential adverse side effects or risks from the drug's use. The manufacturer has no duty to warn the consumer directly of any risks or contraindications associated with the drug. The manufacturer of the drug has fulfilled its obligation when it has informed the prescribing and treating physicians of the risks of harm from the drug so that they may intelligently decide on its use and advise the patient. *Cobb v Syntex Laboratories, Inc*, 444 So2d 203 (La 1983).

In a case involving whether the manufacturer of an intrauterine contraceptive device has a duty to directly warn the ultimate consumer, it was held that the duty of a manufacturer to warn of possible side effects is satisfied if an adequate warning is given to the prescribing physician. In the absence of FDA regulations to the contrary, the manufacturer has no obligation to warn a consumer if the prescribing physician has been adequately warned of any adverse side effects. The manufacturer's duty is to warn the physician, who acts as a learned intermediary between the manufacturer and the consumer, because the physician is in the best position to evaluate the patient's needs, assess the benefits and risks of a particular therapy, and to supervise its use. *McKee v Moore*, 649 P2d 21 (Ok 1982).

A manufacturer of birth control pills owes a duty to the consumer to warn of the dangers inherent in the use of the pill. The rule in jurisdictions that have addressed the question of the extent of a manufacturer's duty to warn in cases involving prescription drugs is that the prescribing physician acts as a learned intermediary between the manufacturer and the patient, and the duty of the ethical drug manufacturer is to warn the doctor, rather than the patient, although the manufacturer is directly liable to the patient for a breach of such duty. Oral contraceptives, however, bear peculiar characteristics which warrant the imposition of a common law duty on the manufacturer to warn users directly of associated risks. Whereas a patient's involvement in decision-making concerning use of a prescription is typically minimal or non-existent, the healthy, young consumer of oral contraceptives is usually actively involved in the decision to use the pill as opposed to other birth control products, and the prescribing physician is relegated to a relatively passive role. Furthermore, the physician prescribing the pill, as a matter of course, examines the patient once before prescribing an oral contraceptive and only annually thereafter. Thus, the patient may only seldom have the opportunity to explore her questions and concerns about the medication with the prescribing physician. The oral contraceptive thus stands apart from other prescription drugs in light of the heightened participation of patients in decisions relating to the use of the pill, the substantial risks associated with the product's use, the feasibility of direct warnings by the manufacturer to the user, the limited participation by the physician, and the possibility that oral communications between physicians and consumers may be insufficient or too scanty standing alone to fully apprise consumers of the product's dangers at the time the initial selection of a contraceptive method is made. Thus, the manufacturer of oral contraceptives is not justified in relying on warnings to the medical profession to satisfy its common law duty to warn. The manufacturer's duty is to provide the consumer written warnings conveying reasonable notice of the nature, gravity, and likelihood of known or knowable side effects, and advising the consumer to seek fuller explanation from the prescribing physician or other doctor of any such information of concern to the consumer. *MacDonald v Ortho Pharmaceutical Corp*, 394 Ma 131, 475 NE2d 65 (1985), cert den, *Ortho Pharmaceutical Corp v MacDonald*, 106 SCt 250, 88 LE2d 258 (1985).

A jury finding that a manufacturer had a duty to warn that certain patients might be susceptible to blood clotting disorders from the ingestion of an oral contraceptive and that the manufacturer should have warned that women with blood type A who took birth control pills had a three times greater risk of developing blood clotting disorders than similarly situated women with blood type O were questions for the jury and were affirmed on appeal. The plaintiff, the court said, presented evidence which tended to show that the manufacturer had a duty to make these warnings and breached that duty. Therefore, a jury verdict rendered against the manufacturer for the death of a 20-year-old woman who ingested birth control pills in the amount of $2,275,000 was affirmed. *May v Parke, Davis & Co*, 142 MiA 404, 370 NW2d 371 (1985).

The manufacturer of an oral contraceptive has a duty to warn the user of possible side effects. The reasoning behind the rule of the learned intermediary—the reliance placed by the patient on the physician and interference with that relationship—simply does not hold up when the drug involved is an oral contraceptive. A patient does not rely on the physician to nearly the same degree when it comes to choosing a method of contraception as in a decision regarding a therapeutic drug. In contrast to the general physician-patient relationship with regard to the prescribing of a drug, when a woman takes an oral contraceptive as a means of birth control, supervision is minimal. The woman generally sees the physician only once a year, and even then, a visit is not necessarily required when all that is needed is a refill. Therefore, there is little opportunity for the physician to notice and avert any problems resulting from the use of the oral contraceptive. Another policy behind the learned intermediary rule, the avoidance of instilling unnecessary fear in a patient who may not understand a warning and who may, as a result, object to the use of the drug and thereby jeopardize his or her life, appears to have little application with regard to an oral contraceptive. A woman obviously has a number of options open as to methods of birth control. The more information the woman is supplied with directly, the easier it is to ensure that informed choice is made among the available options. Finally, as to those cases which have justified the learned intermediary rule because of difficulty of direct user/manufacturer communication, the Food and Drug Administration is (FDA) regulations mandating package inserts in the booklet have established the means for direct warning. The defendant's arguments that the FDA's regulations have also mandated the substantive contact of these warnings has not been established. The FDA has set a minimum; more in the way of warnings may be required as a matter of state law. Not only is the rule establishing a duty to warn the user of oral contraceptives directly the more reasoned rule of law, the court said, but it was satisfied that it would be the rule of law that the Michigan Supreme Court would most likely adopt. *Odgers v Ortho Pharmaceutical Corp* 609 FSupp 867 (ED Mi 1985) [Mi law]. See also *Stephens v G D Searle & Co*, 602 FSupp 379 (ED Mi 1985) [the manufacturer of a prescription oral contraceptive has a duty under Michigan law to warn users directly of the risks and potential side effects of the drug when used for contraceptive purposes.]

A manufacturer of a prescription drug has a duty to warn the medical profession of any risks inherent in the use of the drug which the manufacturer knows or should know exist. If warnings or instructions are required, the information provided must be adequate, accurate, and effective. Determination of whether this duty has been breached in the context of a negligence claim necessitates that the warnings given be examined as to their reasonableness under the circumstances. Whether referred to "the specific standard of care," or simply as "the reasonableness of the defendant's conduct," the issue is for the jury, unless all reasonable persons would agree or where there is some overriding legislative policy to the contrary. The adequacy of a warning and the reasonableness of a failure to warn are questions of fact. Thus, where there were questions of fact with regard to whether the manufacturer of an oral contraceptive had adequately warned that ingestion of the oral contraceptive might result in the formation of blood clots, it was error for the trial court to direct a verdict in favor of the manufacturer. *Taylor v Wyeth Laboratories*, 362 NW2d 293 (MiA 1984).

A manufacturer who has actual or constructive knowledge that use of its product entails non-obvious, foreseeable dangers has a duty to warn users of its product of these dangers. This duty, which arises at the time of sale and delivery, is to exercise reasonable care in warning users of the product of such dangers. In this action, the plaintiffs, a deformed child and the child's parents, brought an action against the maker of a spermicide alleging that the spermicide had caused a deformity suffered by a child. The plaintiffs satisfied each of the elements of the defective warning theory. The court found that the defendant had actual or constructive knowledge that the product might cause an increased risk of birth defects because various studies suggesting this risk were available to the defendant well before the mother first obtained the product in 1980. Based on credible expert testimony presented by the plaintiffs, the court also found that the defendant's failure to warn fell beneath the standard of ordinary care required under the circumstances. Finally, the court found that the defendant's failure to warn proximately caused the birth defects in the child. *Wells v Ortho Pharmaceutical Corp*, 615 FSupp 262 (ND Ga 1985), affd, mod in part, remd, 788 F2d 741 (11th Cir 1986), reh den, en banc 795 F2d 89 (11th Cir 1986), cert den, 107 SCt 437, 93 LE2d 386 (1986).

Cause of Action Against Drug Manufacturer for Failure to Warn of Side Effects Associated With Prescription Drug, 3 Shepard's Causes of Action 815 (1983).

b. [§2.33] Adequacy of Warning

Warnings concerning risks of the use of a birth control pill were adequate where the plaintiff's physicians were sufficiently warned by the manufacturer of side effects and risks of a birth control pill. The manufacturer of the drug fulfilled its obligation when it informed the prescribing and treating physicians of the risks of harm from the drug so that they could intelligently decide on its use and advise the patient. Both of the plaintiff's physicians stated in affidavits that they received and reviewed the material supplied by the manufacturer and that they considered the warnings adequate. *Cobb v Syntex Laboratories, Inc*, 444 So2d 203 (La 1983).

A manufacturer's failure to warn of the association between the use of its product and the development of acute renal failure was established as a cause in fact of the plaintiff's injury where there was an abundance of evidence that the early diagnosis of acute renal failure and malignant hypertension is extremely important. There was evidence indicating that a lower dosage birth control pill might have prevented the plaintiff's kidney problems, and even if the higher dosage of estrogen contained in the birth control pill was given, the plaintiff's attending physician, if warned of the possibility of kidney problems, might have made an earlier diagnosis which, according to expert testimony, might have averted the plaintiff's injuries. The duty to warn extended throughout the time that the plaintiff was taking the oral contraceptive. No warnings were given by the manufacturer during that period of time, and thus the physicians were not informed to be on the alert for symptoms of kidney problems. The question of whether this failure to warn was a cause of the plaintiff's injury was properly submitted to the jury. *Wooderson v Ortho Pharmaceutical Corp*, 235 Ks 387, 681 P2d 1038 (1984) cert den 105 SCt 365.

A manufacturer of an oral contraceptive breached its duty to warn the consumer of the contraceptive side effects where there was evidence that the manufacturer did not inform the user of the potential dangers of using the contraceptive. The manufacturer contended initially that its warnings complied with Food and Drug Administration's (FDA) labeling requirements, and that those requirements preempt or define the bounds of the common law duty to warn. The court disagreed. The regulatory history of the FDA requirements belies any objective to cloak them with preemptive effect. Although the common law duty to warn is to a large degree coextensive with the regulatory duties imposed by the FDA, in instances where a trier of fact could reasonably conclude that a manufacturer's compliance with FDA labeling requirements or guidelines did not adequately apprise oral contraceptive users of inherent risks, the manufacturer should not be shielded from liability by such compliance. The common law duty to warn necessitates a warning comprehensible to the average user which conveys a fair indication of the nature and extent of the danger to the mind of a reasonably prudent person. Whether a particular warning measures up to the standard is almost always an issue to be resolved by a jury. The manufacturer argued in this case that reasonable minds could not differ as to whether the plaintiff was adequately informed of the risk of the injury she sustained by Ortho's warning that the oral contraceptives could cause "abnormal blood clotting which can be fatal" and further warning of the incremental likelihood of hospitalization or death due to blood clotting in "vital organs, such as the brain." The court disagreed. The fact finder may find a warning to be unreasonable, hence inadequate, in its factual content, its expression of the facts, or the method or form in which it is conveyed. The adequacy of such warnings is measured not only by what is stated, but also by the manner in which it is stated. The court could not say that the jury's decision that the warning was inadequate was so unreasonable as to require the opposite conclusion as a matter of law. The jury may well have concluded, in light of their common experience and the plaintiff's testimony, that the absence of a reference to "stroke" in the warning unduly minimized the warning's impact or failed to make the nature of the risk reasonably comprehensible to the average consumer. Similarly, the jury may have concluded that there are fates worse than death, such as the permanent disablement suffered by the plaintiff, and that the mention of the risk of death did not, therefore, suffice to apprise an average consumer of the material risks of oral contraceptive use. *MacDonald v Ortho Pharmaceutical Corp*, 394 Ma 131, 475 NE2d 65 (1985), cert den, *Ortho Pharmaceutical Corp v MacDonald*, 106 SCt 250, 88 LE2d 258 (1985).

C. [§2.35] Liability of Physician

A motion for partial summary judgment in favor of a physician was granted as to a plaintiff's claims involving an intrauterine device and the doctrine of res ipsa loquitur. In this case, the intrauterine device was placed in the woman, but subsequently, she asked the physician to remove it. The plaintiff alleged that during the procedure the plaintiff's uterus was perforated and that as a result of this, the plaintiff was injured. The court held that the intrauterine device was not a foreign object unintentionally left within the body of the patient following surgery because in this case, the intrauterine device was present in the plaintiff's body before the procedure commenced [construing 18 De Code §6853]. The court noted that the second consideration was whether the object was unintentionally left within the person's body following surgery. This connotes that the health care provider must have not intended to leave the object in the patient's body. The complaint alleged that the physician attempted to remove the IUD two times but failed. The clear meaning of this allegation is that the physician was aware of the need to remove the intrauterine device but was unable to do so. There was no allegation that the physician was unaware that he had not removed the IUD or that he unintentionally permitted it to remain. Therefore, the court concluded that the res ipsa loquitur allegations did not satisfy 18 De Code §6853. *Lacy v G D Searle*, 484 A2d 527 (De Super 1984).

D. [§2.36] Limitation on Actions

A statute of limitations in a malpractice action was not tolled by the "foreign object" exception where the only negligence, if any, of the defendant-physicians was that they did not discover or diagnose the presence of an intrauterine device after a normal delivery. The statutory exception for a foreign object applies to cases where something never intended to be inserted at all or something only temporarily utilized was negligently permitted to remain in a patient's body, such as a clamp or sponge following surgery, and not to an object which had been deliberately implanted there, such as an intrauterine contraceptive device. To hold under the circumstances of this case that the physicians negligently left the intrauterine device in the plaintiff's body is not within the meaning of the exception. The physicians did not place the device into the plaintiff's uterus, its presence was known to the plaintiff, and it was not inadvertently inserted. Moreover, the statutory exception was intended to apply to cases where the defendant health care provider was in some way responsible for the initial presence of the foreign object complained of. *Hall v Ervin*, 642 SW2d 724 (Tn 1982).

The statute of limitations for personal injury caused by the malfunctioning of a contraceptive device implanted or inserted into the body runs from the date of the injury resulting from the malfunction, not necessarily from the date of implantation or insertion. Therefore, in an action alleging that the plaintiff was injured by an infection caused by an intrauterine device, the limitations period began to run when the bacteria which caused the infection entered the plaintiff's uterus. *Lindsey v A H Robins Co*, 91 AD2d 150, 458 NYS2d 602 (1983), affd, *Martin v Edwards Laboratories*, 60 NY2d 417, 469 NYS2d 923, 457 NE2d 1150 (1983).

The date from which the statute of limitations ran in a case involving an intrauterine device which allegedly caused an infection in the plaintiff was when the the infection occurred. Hospital records which indicated that the injury to the plaintiff took place sometime in

November 1978 were sufficient to defeat the defendant's motion to dismiss the complaint based upon the statute of limitations. However, because it could not be said as a matter of law that the infection process began earlier than November 1978, the court found an issue of fact had been sufficiently raised which required a trial of this action. *Davis v A H Robins Co*, 99 AD2d 342, 473 NYS2d 182 (1984).

A cause of action against the manufacturer of an intrauterine device begins to run not when the plaintiff learns that she is ill, but when she learns, or reasonably could have learned, the cause of her illness. Therefore, summary judgment in favor of the defendant was vacated where although the plaintiff discovered she was ill in 1974, she did not know the cause of her illness until 1982 when she discovered that the intrauterine device was responsible and sued the manufacturer. Thus, it was concluded that if the plaintiff was correct in asserting that she did not know, nor should reasonably have known of the cause of her illness more than two years before suit, her claim was not barred by Texas law. *Mann v A H Robins Co*, 741 F2d 79 (5th Cir 1984).

A tort claim accrues on the date the injury is discovered, or with reasonable diligence should be discovered, whichever occurs first. Thus, where a plaintiff's claim accrued on June 26, 1978, and her complaint was filed on June 24, 1981, the action was filed within a three year statute of limitations period. In 1974 an intrauterine device had been inserted into the plaintiff. Subsequently, she became ill. She saw a physician on June 13, 1978, and was told that it was unlikely she had pelvic inflammatory disease, which could have been caused by the intrauterine device. The record revealed that on June 16, 1978, she had been asymptomatic. Sometime thereafter the symptoms returned. On June 26, 1978, the plaintiff went to see another physician who finally diagnosed her condition as pelvic inflammatory disease. Under these circumstances, the court said that the plaintiff should not have discovered her injury any earlier than June 26, 1978. She could not be expected to personally diagnose her condition or consult with a physician more frequently than she did. Therefore, the court concluded, that the action was not time-barred. *Hansen v A H Robins, Inc*, 113 Wi2d 550, 335 NW2d 578 (1983).

The definition of "foreign objects" in the context of ID Code §5-219(4) does not include devices deliberately placed in the body with the patient's knowledge and consent. Thus, an IUD placed in a woman was not a foreign object with regard to the malpractice statute of limitations. However, if the IUD's continued presence in the body becomes medically contraindicated, the IUD then would become a foreign object within the statute. The statute establishes a general statute of limitation which runs for two years from the time of the occurrence, act or omission of the malpractice without regard to when it was discovered. If the foreign object exception applies, however, the cause of action can be brought either within two years of the date of occurrence or within one year of the date of discovery of the malpractice by the plaintiff. Applying the statute to the facts of this case, the plaintiffs were required to commence their cause of action either within two years of the occurrence, act or omission complained of, or within one year of the discovery date. The "condition or matter complained of" has been construed to mean the condition which ultimately is alleged to constitute the malpractice or negligence of the doctor, in this instance, the leaving of a foreign object in the plaintiff's body. The action accrues when the foreign object is left in the patient's body. Thus, in this action, the physician's failure to remove the IUD during the plaintiff's tubal ligation on April 28, 1977, established the time of the occurrence, act or omission complained of. However, the date of accrual under the discovery rule was February 21, 1979, the day the IUD was discovered and removed. Thus, the plaintiffs did not have to commence their cause of action within two years from the omission complained of, that is, by April 28, 1979. Their action was not barred until February 21, 1980, one year after the IUD was discovered. However, since the suit was not commenced until May 2, 1980, the plaintiffs' cause of action was barred. On March 29, 1976, the plaintiff had the defendant insert an IUD. Shortly after this, the plaintiff began to experience pain and developed infections. As a result, the plaintiffs decided the IUD should be removed. On April 28, 1977, the defendant performed a laparoscopic tubal ligation and reported that he had also removed the IUD. However, the pain and the infections continued unabated. In November of 1978, the defendant recommended that the plaintiff have a hysterectomy. A second doctor was consulted in February 1979. The second doctor discovered that the IUD had never been removed. On February 21, 1979, the second physician removed the IUD and performed a hysterectomy. The date of the commencement of this action was May 2, 1980. Because of the court's findings with regard to the statute of limitations, the action was time-barred. *Ogle v De Sano*, 693 P2d 1074 (IdA 1984).

CHAPTER 3

Preconception Stage: Emerging Theories of Liability

I. PRECONCEPTION TORTS

A. In General

1. [§3.1] Generally; Definitions

A duty may extend to persons not yet conceived at the time of a negligent act or omission. Such a duty is limited, however, by the element of foreseeability. *Harbeson v Parke-Davis*, 98 Wa2d 460, 656 P2d 483 (1983) later proceeding 746 F2d 517 (9th Cir 1984).

PUSHING THE *Feres* DOCTRINE A GENERATION TOO FAR: RECOVERY FOR GENETIC DAMAGE TO CHILDREN OF SERVICE MEMBERS 32 Am U LR 1039 (1983).

NOTE, STEP BACKWARD FOR THE INFANT PLAINTIFF IN PRECONCEPTION TORT ACTIONS: *Albala v City of New York,* 15 Conn LR 161 (1982).

Collins, AN OVERVIEW AND ANALYSIS: PRENATAL TORTS, PRECONCEPTION TORTS, WRONGFUL LIFE, WRONGFUL DEATH, AND WRONGFUL BIRTH: TIME FOR A NEW FRAMEWORK, 21 J Family L 677 (1983-1984).

B. Bases of Liability

1. [§3.4] Medical Malpractice

The plaintiffs filed suit against the infirmary and the doctor, who had been treating the wife, alleging that the defendants had been negligent in failing to treat the abruptio placenta prior to the premature delivery of the infant and that the defendant's actions or inactions had caused the infant's death. A jury verdict in favor of the plaintiffs was reversed by the court, except for a small award to the wife for her pain and suffering during a delay in the doctor's attending to her, because the plaintiffs failed to prove that any act or omission by the doctor resulted in the wrongful death of the infant. There was no showing that had the doctor attended to the plaintiff sooner, it was more probable that this death would have been prevented. *Coleman v Touro Infirmary of New Orleans*, 506 So2d 571 (LaA 1987), cert den, 507 So2d 1247 (1987), writ den, 507 So2d 1248 (1987).

2. [§3.5] Products Liability

Plaintiffs, parents of a deformed child, brought a products liability action on behalf of their infant daughter and the mother individually against the manufacturer of a spermicide believed to have caused the multiple birth defects suffered by the infant. The central issues which emerged were whether the spermicide manufactured and marketed by the defendant and used by the plaintiff before the infant's conception proximately caused the birth defects, and whether the defendant negligently failed to warn the plaintiff mother that an increased risk of birth defects accompanied the use of its product. In this type of case, the plaintiffs' evidence must show to a reasonable degree of medical certainty that the defendant's product was responsible. The plaintiffs will not be able to recover if there is only a bare possibility that the product caused the birth defects or if there are other theories of causation which are equally plausible. The plaintiffs' ultimate burden, however, is not to produce an unassailable scientific study which proves that spermicides have caused birth defects in animals or members of a large group, but rather to show from all the evidence presented, to a reasonable degree of medical certainty, that the spermicide caused some or all of the birth defects. After assessing the credibility of all witnesses, including the experts' background, training, experience, and familiarity with the circumstances of the particular case, as well as the rationality and internal consistency of each expert's testimony in light of all the evidence, the plaintiffs were able to prevail because they had carried their burden of proving that the spermicide proximately caused some, but not all, of the birth defects and that the defendant had been negligent in failing to warn the plaintiffs of this danger. *Wells v Ortho Pharmaceutical Corp*, 615 FSupp 262 (ND Ga 1985), affd, mod in part, remd, 788 F2d 741 (11th Cir 1986), reh den, 795 F2d 89 (11th Cir 1986), cert den, 55 USLW 3335 (1986).

B. Bases of Liability

3. [§3.6] Radiation Injuries; Federal Tort Claims Act

A holding that a claim against the United States for radiation injuries that allegedly subsequently manifested themselves as defects in a father's children was not barred by the *Feres* doctrine in *Hinke v United States*, 524 FSupp 277 (ED Pa 1981) was reversed in *Hinke v United States*, 715 F2d 96 (3d Cir 1983). In holding that the *Feres* doctrine applied, and thus that the plaintiffs' complaint failed to state a claim upon which relief could be granted, the court said that in addition to barring injuries suffered by military personnel incident to active duty military service, the doctrine extends to service-related suits when the injury to a civilian has its genesis in the injury suffered by the military personnel incident to military service.

A plaintiff's action for damages under the Federal Tort Claims Act and the Constitution for genetic injuries caused by her father's exposure to radiation while he was on active duty in the United States Army was barred under the *Feres* doctrine. In barring the action the court noted that rarely does the law burden a child with the consequences of actions attributed to the parents. Nevertheless, the Supreme Court has construed the Federal Tort Claims Act to subordinate the interests of children of service personnel to the exigencies of military discipline. Where the case concerns an injury sustained by a soldier while on duty, the effect of the action upon military discipline is identical whether the suit was brought by the soldier directly or by a third party. The litigation would take virtually the identical form in either case, and an issue would be the degree of fault, if any, on the part of the government's agents and the effect upon the serviceman's safety. The trial would, in either case, involve second guessing military orders, and would often require members of the Armed Services to testify in court as to each other's decisions and actions. Therefore, the *Feres* doctrine subordinates the interests of children of service personnel to the exigencies of military discipline. Consequently, the court concluded, the claims of the child were barred. *Mondelli v United States*, 711 F2d 567 (3d Cir 1983) cert den 465 US 1021 (1984).

II. WRONGFUL CONCEPTION AND WRONGFUL PREGNANCY

A. In General

1. [§3.8] Definitions: Wrongful Conception and Wrongful Pregnancy

Wrongful pregnancy or wrongful conception actions are brought by the parents of a child whose conception or birth was due to the negligence of a physician in performing a sterilization or abortion. *Fulton-DeKalb Hospital Authority v Graves*, 252 Ga 441, 314 SE2d 653 (1984).

Wrongful pregnancy or wrongful conception describes an action brought by the parents of a healthy, but unplanned, child against a physician who negligently performed a sterilization or abortion. *Nanke v Napier*, 346 NW2d 520 (Ia 1984).

An action for wrongful conception or wrongful pregnancy is generally brought by parents of a healthy, but unplanned, child against a physician or other health care provider for negligently performing a sterilization procedure or an abortion, or against a pharmacist or pharmaceutical manufacturer for negligently filling a contraceptive prescription. This action is to be distinguished from one for wrongful birth, which is generally brought by parents of an impaired child who claim that but for the negligence of the physician or other health care provider they would not have conceived or would have terminated the pregnancy. A third action, for wrongful life, is generally brought by or on behalf of the impaired child. *Jackson v Bumgardner*, 71 NC App 107, 321 SE2d 541 (NC App 1984), rev gtd, app dis 312 NC 797, 325 SE2d 486 (1985).

Weisberg, MISCONCEPTION OF WRONGFUL CONCEPTION, 16 Trial Law Q 36 (1984).

2. [§3.9] Background

A good source of statistical information about the success and failure rates of various types of contraceptives including sterilization operations, condoms, oral contraceptives, intrauterine devices, and spermicidal foams, is found in Hatcher, CONTRACEPTIVE TECHNOLOGY 1982-83.

An action for wrongful pregnancy is recognizable. *James G v Caserta*, 332 SE2d 872 (WV 1985).

Cause of Action Against Physician for Wrongful Conception or Wrongful Pregnancy, 3 Shepard's Causes of Action 83 (1983).

B. Tort Actions Considered

1. [§3.10] Public Policy Considerations

The birth of a normal unwanted child is not a wrong; it is an event which, of itself, is not a legally compensable, injurious consequence, even if the birth is partially attributable to the negligent conduct of someone purporting to be able to prevent the eventuality of childbirth. *Szekeres v Robinson*, 715 P2d 1076 (Nv 1986).

2. [§3.11] Malpractice Considerations

In recognizing a cause of action for wrongful pregnancy, Indiana decided to follow the course of action of other states which have addressed the issue and recognized that some damages would flow from the unwanted pregnancy caused by the negligent performance of a sterilization procedure and/or follow-up. This cause of action is indistinguishable from any other medical negligence action. The plaintiff must allege and will have to establish the existence of the three elements of the cause of action: (1) the duty on the part of the defendant; (2) a failure to perform that duty; and (3) damages or injuries proximately resulting to the plaintiff as a result of that failure. *Garrison v Foy*, 486 NE2d 5 (InA 1985).

An action for wrongful pregnancy or wrongful conception may be maintained in Virginia. Non-recognition of such a cause of action would leave a void in the area of recovery for medical malpractice and dilute the standard of professional conduct and expertise in the area of family planning. Under traditional tort principles, it is clear that a physician who performs an abortion or sterilization procedure owes a legal duty to the patient. Where the patient can establish failure to perform the procedure with reasonable care and damages proximately resulting from breach of the duty, she is entitled to recover as in any other malpractice action. *Miller v Johnson*, 231 Va 177, 343 SE2d 301 (1986).

An action for wrongful pregnancy or wrongful conception should be recognized in Georgia. Such an action is no more than a species of malpractice which allows recovery from a tortfeasor in the presence of an injury caused by intentional or negligent conduct. *Fulton-DeKalb Hospital Authority v Graves*, 252 Ga 441, 314 SE2d 653 (1984).

There is a cause of action in tort based upon traditional medical malpractice principles for negligence in the performance of a sterilization procedure. *Jones v Malinowski*, 299 Md 257, 473 A2d 429 (1984).

If medical procedures are undertaken to avoid the conception or birth of a defective child, a health care provider has a duty to perform these procedures with due care. This duty includes, therefore, the requirement that a health care provider who undertakes to perform an abortion use reasonable care in doing so. Recognition of the duty will deter medical malpractice. *Harbeson v Parke-Davis*, 98 Wa2d 460, 656 P2d 483 (1983) later proceeding 746 F2d 517 (9th Cir 1984).

An action against physicians who allegedly negligently performed an abortion procedure on the plaintiff was a conventional action for malpractice, in which damages are recoverable. *Mears v Alhadeff*, 88 AD2d 827, 451 NYS2d 133 (1982).

An action for wrongful conception has strong support in the law. It is not a new cause of action but merely a descriptive label for a form of malpractice. As a form of malpractice, wrongful conception gives rise to compensatory damages that are measurable. *Miller v DuHart*, 637 SW2d 183 (Mo 1982).

An action for wrongful pregnancy or wrongful conception is no more than a species of malpractice and should be recognized. *Blash v Glisson*, 173 GaA 104, 325 SE2d 607 (1984).

The complaint stated a recognizable claim for medical malpractice as to the plaintiff-wife, where the injury complained of was the defendant's improper failure to replace an intrauterine device resulting in the wife's pregnancy and subsequent birth of a healthy child. Whatever a woman's reason for desiring to avoid pregnancy, when a physician undertakes to provide medical care or advice to her for that purpose, he or she must provide the professional services in that case, just as in the rendering of professional services in any instance, according to the established professional standards. The complaint alleged that the plaintiff consulted with the defendant in his professional capacity for medical treatment for uterine bleeding, that the defendant undertook to treat her by performing operations on two separate occasions, and that the defendant promised that her intrauterine device would be replaced if it became necessary to remove it during the operations. These facts were sufficient to establish that the plaintiff-wife was the defendant's patient and that he therefore owed her a legal duty. The complaint alleged that the defendant completely failed to replace the IUD and further failed to warn the plaintiff wife of this omission, despite the fact that he knew she relied on it for the prevention of pregnancy, had other children, did not want to become pregnant, and would suffer economic hardship if she did become pregnant. The complaint also alleged that the defendant breached his duty to her to exercise reasonable care and diligence in the application of his knowledge and skill in treating her. The plaintiff wife was thus left unprotected against pregnancy and unaware of her loss of protection. As a result, she became pregnant and suffered the very result that she had specifically sought defendant's professional assistance to avoid. The plaintiff had therefore alleged sufficient facts to show the existence of a duty, breach of that duty, and damages resulting from the breach. *Jackson v Bumgardner*, 318 NC 172, 347 SE2d 743 (1986).

3. a. [§3.13] Unsuccessful Sterilization or Contraception

Plaintiff brought a medical malpractice action against the defendant hospitals because she became pregnant with her fifth child approximately 11 months after elective surgical sterilization by tubal ligation. The sole basis for the malpractice action was the plaintiff's allegation that the defendants failed to inform her that there was a one per cent chance of failure of tubal ligation to prevent future pregnancies. She alleged that had she known the failure rate of one per cent she would not have undergone that procedure. Judgment in favor of the plaintiff was reversed because the court concluded that the plaintiff failed to meet her burden of proof on the issue of proximate cause. It was not enough for the plaintiff to subjectively assert at trial that had she known the tubal ligation was only 99 per cent effective, she would have chosen instead the 90 per cent effective birth control pills that made her sick. It was incumbent upon the plaintiff to prove by objective evidence that a reasonable person in possession of the omitted information would have rejected the treatment. The only inference from the objective evidence was that a reasonable person in the plaintiff's position would not have refused the tubal ligation under the circumstances. Moreover, it was a demonstrable, irrefutable conclusion from the undisputed facts that after her last daughter was born and she was now well aware of the risk of failure, the plaintiff still elected to have another tubal ligation four months prior to filing the action. *Marshall v Univ of Chicago Hospitals & Clinics*, 165 IlAp3d 754, 117 Il Dec 389, 520 NE2d 740 (1987).

The plaintiffs claimed that the defendant physician negligently performed a bilateral tubal ligation on the plaintiff wife and failed to inform her that the operation had been improperly performed. Consequently, she became pregnant and gave birth to a child with a birth defect. The court held that clearly, under the circumstances, the doctor owed a duty to the plaintiffs to exercise the degree of care ordinarily exercised by surgeons performing such operations in that specialty. Moreover, if he was aware of the failure of the operation, he owed a duty to inform them that the object of sterilization had not been attained. Furthermore, there is now general agreement that a doctor who negligently fails directly to prevent the conception or birth of an unwanted child, as by negligently performing a sterilization or abortion procedure, or by failing to diagnose or inform the parents that the child might be born with a birth defect because of a disease or genetic condition, breaches his duty of care owed to the parents. However, the defendant doctor did not owe a duty to protect the child from the risk of albinism because it is hard to predict. Moreover, when the physician knows or should know of the existence of an unreasonable risk that a child will be born with a birth defect, he owes a duty to the unconceived child as well as its parents to exercise reasonable care in warning the potential parents and in assisting them to avoid the conception of a deformed child. They held that logic and sound policy require recognition of a legal duty to a child not yet conceived but foreseeably harmed by the negligent delivery of health care services to the child's parents. *Pitre v Opelousas General Hosp*, 530 So2d 1151 (La 1988).

In *Garrison v Foy*, 486 NE2d 5 (In App 1985), the plaintiff had a vasectomy performed by the defendant. Approximately two weeks later, the defendant performed a test on the plaintiff's sperm sample and informed the plaintiff that he was sterile. Approximately a year and a half later, the plaintiff mother gave birth to a child who was suffering from various deformities. The court approached the case as any other medical negligence action. The possible damages which may be recovered are limited to those directly caused by the unsuccessful sterilization and resultant pregnancy, and do not include costs of raising the child nor exceptional expenses associated with the child's defect.

A wrongful conception action based on the alleged negligent performance of a vasectomy states a valid cause of action. *Weintraub v Brown*, 98 AD2d 339, 470 NYS2d 634 (1983).

The law is clear that the parents of an unplanned child have a cause of action sounding in negligence against a physician for performing a negligent vasectomy or sterilization which results in the birth of an unwanted child. *Ramey v Fassoulas*, 414 So2d 198 (Fl 1982), affd, 450 So2d 822 (Fl 1984). But where the evidence with regard to whether a sterilization operation had been performed properly was essentially equal, a trial court finding that a sterilization operation was properly performed in favor of the defendant-physician was affirmed. To prove negligence, the plaintiff attempted to show, via an operation report filed by the defendant-physician and the testimony of two medical experts, that neither her right nor left fallopian tube was properly ligated in accordance with the procedures described by the defendant-physician. However, the defendant's expert testified that the tissue removed from the plaintiff and sent to the pathology lab indicated that the sterilization operation had been properly performed. Moreover, the defendant's expert testified that even if a tubal ligation sterilization is properly performed, it is always possible for the ligation to fail so that the patient might conceive a child in the future. *McNeal v United States*, 689 F2d 1200 (4th Cir 1982).

A cause of action for damages was stated where physicians in a mental health facility failed to make contraceptive care available to an incompetent woman and subsequently she became pregnant and gave birth to an unplanned child. However, it was noted, the plaintiff would need to show that had contraceptive care been available she would have taken advantage of it and that it would have been effective. In *Foy v Greenblott*, 141 CaA3d 1, 190 CaR 84 (1983), an incompetent mental patient was placed in a mental health facility for care and treatment. While in the facility she became pregnant and gave birth to a child.

No rational basis exists for distinguishing between temporary and permanent methods of birth control for the purpose of determining whether a complaint states a claim for wrongful conception or wrongful pregnancy. The United States Supreme Court has recognized that a woman has the right to plan the size of her family. This right is not dependent upon the choice or the means of birth control. There is no compelling reason to limit a patient's right to non-negligent health care to situations in which the patient chooses sterilization over the surgical insertion of an intrauterine device. This action is simply a species of malpractice which allows recovery from a tortfeasor in the presence of an injury caused by intentional or negligent conduct. An avoidable pregnancy resulting from negligent medical care is a recognizable injury. Thus, a plaintiff's assertion that a physician failed to maintain in place or to insert an intrauterine device stated a claim for medical malpractice. *Jackson v Bumgardner*, 71 NC App 107, 321 SE2d 541 (NC App 1984), rev gtd, app dis, 312 NC 797, 325 SE2d 486 (1985).

CAUSE OF ACTION AGAINST PHARMACIST OR DRUGGIST FOR INJURY OR DEATH FROM USE OF DRUG OR MEDICINE, 1 Shepard's Causes of Action 153 (1983).

Mills, POSTVASECTOMY PREGNANCY: IS NONCOMPLIANCE A DEFENSE, 10 Legal Aspects of Medical Practice 5 (May 1982).

Strausberg, THE FAILED TUBAL LIGATION, 21 Trial 30 (May 1985).

b. [§3.14] Misdiagnosis or Failure to Diagnose Pregnancy

Where there was an allegation that a plaintiff's physicians failed to diagnose her pregnancy, and thus an unplanned child was born, it was held that the plaintiff would need to show either that she would have consented to an abortion or, if she lacked capacity to consent, that her conservator would have been able to make to a court the type of extraordinarily strong showing which would permit the court to authorize this surgery. In this case the plaintiff was an incompetent mental patient who became pregnant and gave birth to a child while she was in a mental health facility. *Foy v Greenblott*, 141 CaA3d 1, 190 CaR 84 (1983).

c. [§3.15] Unsuccessful Abortion

A wrongful conception action may be brought against a physician who negligently performs an abortion which results in an unwanted child being born. *Jean-Charles v Planned Parenthood Association*, 99 AD2d 542, 471 NYS2d 622 (1984).

A malpractice cause of action based on the negligent performance of an abortion which results in the birth of an unplanned child is viable. *Delaney v Krafte*, 98 AD2d 128, 470 NYS2d 936 (1984).

The parents of an unplanned child have a cause of action sounding in negligence against a physician who performs a negligent abortion which results in the birth of an unwanted child. *Mears v Alhadeff*, 88 AD2d 827, 451 NYS2d 133 (1982).

4. [§3.16] Proximate Cause

Where the plaintiffs' medical expert's testimony was equivocal with regard to whether the plaintiff was already pregnant at the time the defendant performed a sterilization operation on her, the court held that the plaintiffs did not meet their burden to show causation with a reasonable degree of medical certainty. In this case the plaintiff's medical expert testified that conception could have occurred right around the time of the sterilization operation. *Stewart v Bepko*, 576 FSupp 182 (D DC 1983), affd 735 F2d 617 (DC Cir 1984).

7. [§3.19] —Illustrative Cases

The plaintiffs determined they did not wish to have any more children and, on the basis of information given to them by physicians, determined that the husband should have a vasectomy. The plaintiffs went to the public health service to sign a consent form. Prior to signing the form, they met with a physician to discuss the operation. The court found that the physician informed the plaintiffs that the operation should be considered permanent. His warning focused almost exclusively on the irreversibility of the procedure and was intended to ensure that the husband was prepared psychologically to accept permanent sterility. The physician further told the plaintiffs to continue practicing birth control after the operation until a test confirmed that the husband had a zero sperm count. However, the court found that the physician did not inform the plaintiffs, who had no previous reliable knowledge about such matters, that a vasectomy could fail to sterilize a man permanently and that consequently there was a possibility of pregnancy associated with this method of birth control. After the operation, the husband returned to the public health service and was told that his sperm count was zero. A little over a year later, the wife became pregnant. A sperm count on the husband at that time indicated that he was capable of fathering a child. The wife gave birth to a child with multiple physical and mental defects which required extensive and frequent hospitalization, surgery, and other medical care which continued until her death. The court found, based on the evidence, that the failure of the husband's vasectomy to render him permanently sterile resulted from recanalization. Recanalization, although a rare occurrence, was well-known by the medical community at that time. However, the plaintiff was not informed of the possibility by either the counseling physician or the surgeon. The consent form signed by the plaintiffs did not mention failure due to recanalization and, in fact, stressed the permanency and irreversibility of the sterility achieved by vasectomy. Finally, the plaintiff's belief that technical surgical error was the only type of failure associated with the vasectomy was reinforced by the public health service employee who informed him that his sperm count was zero. The court noted that the ultimate harm to which the plaintiffs were exposed was the possibility that the wife would become pregnant. With regard to the consequences resulting from the pregnancy, both plaintiffs testified that another child would endanger the family's financial security. There was no evidence to suggest that pregnancy posed a risk to the woman's health or that the resulting child would be abnormal. Regarding the likelihood of recanalization, expert testimony showed that the failure rate of vasectomy due to recanalization is between .08 per cent and .36 per cent of all patients. Additionally, one article cited by defendant's expert indicated that recanalization is even more infrequent after post-operative zero sperm count, occurring in only .04 per cent of patients. An unrevealed risk that should have been made known must materialize, since otherwise the omission is legally without consequence. A plaintiff must show that had the proper information been provided, neither he nor a reasonable person in similar circumstances would have undergone the procedure. In this case, even assuming that the risk of recanalization was material, the plaintiffs did not prove by a preponderance of the evidence that had the risk of recanalization been disclosed, a reasonable person in similar circumstances would have declined the procedure. Therefore, judgment was entered for the defendant. *Ostergard v United States*, 677 FSupp 1259 (D Ma 1987).

C. Contract Actions Considered

1. [§3.22] Generally

If a physician or someone else is found to have contracted to prevent a pregnancy from occurring, it was within the contemplation of the contracting parties that failure to carry out the process in the manner promised would result in an award at least of the costs of medical, surgical, and hospital care associated with the failed surgery. *Szekeres v Robinson*, 715 P2d 1076 (Nv 1986).

2. Necessity of Express Warranty

a. [§3.23] Generally; Burden of Proof

A breach of warranty theory in a wrongful pregnancy action did not state a viable claim because a breach of contract claim arising out of the rendering of medical services will be held legally sufficient only when it is based upon an express promise to provide a cure or to accomplish some definite result. In the complaint, however, the plaintiff alleged an undertaking on the physicians' part to perform an abortion procedure, but she did not allege an express promise to achieve that result. Rather, the plaintiff specifically stated in the complaint that the representation made by the defendant physicians that they would abort her pregnancy was implicit or implied. Accordingly, the plaintiff failed to adequately support her cause of action sounding in breach of contract. *Delaney v Krafte*, 98 AD2d 128, 470 NYS2d 936 (1984).

D. Damages

1. In General

a. [§3.27] Background; Policy Considerations

The state of Tennessee limited a defendant's liability in an action for wrongful pregnancy based on a failed tubal ligation on the ground that the state imposes, by statute, the responsibility for the support of children upon the parents, thereby relieving the defendant of liability for the support of the plaintiff's healthy child. Considering not only the extensive statutory law regarding the obligation to support, but in light of both the common law obligation to support and the court's restricted role in declaring public policy, shifting the common law and statutory obligation from the parents to the defendant in such cases necessarily had to be left to legislative action. The plaintiff has a remedy for the tort, but recovery is limited to the injuries suffered by the woman and proximately caused by the defendants. A plaintiff's claim for punitive damages may be asserted in the same manner as in any ordinary tort action. *Smith v Gore*, 728 SW2d 738 (Tn 1987).

BY WHAT MEASURE?: THE ISSUE OF DAMAGES FOR WRONGFUL PREGNANCY, 16 NC Cent LJ 59 (1986).

DAMAGES: RECOVERY OF DAMAGES IN ACTIONS FOR WRONGFUL BIRTH, WRONGFUL LIFE AND WRONGFUL CONCEPTION, 23 Washburn L Journal 309 (1984).

b. [§3.28] Elements, Generally

Punitive damages may be recoverable in an appropriate case alleging wrongful conception. *Johnson v Terry*, 9 FLR 2375 (Wi 1983).

A damages item relating to the interruption of the mother's education and employment may be recoverable in a wrongful pregnancy action. *Mears v Alhadeff*, 88 AD2d 827, 451 NYS2d 133 (1982).

PHYSICIAN'S NEGLIGENCE GIVING RISE TO THE BIRTH OF A HEALTHY BUT UNPLANNED CHILD: A SUMMARY OF DAMAGES RECOVERABLE BY THE PARENTS, 17 U Richmond L R 403.

c. [§3.29] Mitigation

Parents should not be forced to mitigate damages by choosing abortion or adoption, and the parents failure to do either may not be considered as an offset in determining damages. The rules requiring mitigation of damages require only that reasonable measures be taken. The decision not to conceive a child is quite different from the decision to abort or put the child up for adoption once it has been conceived. If parents are confronted in such a situation with the choices which they consider to be unenviable alternatives, they should not be precluded from recovering damages because they select the most desirable of these choices. *Univ of Arizona v Superior Court*, 136 Az 579, 667 P2d 1294 (1983), later proceeding, *Univ of Arizona v Pima County*, 150 Az 184, 722 P2d 352 (1986), later proceeding, *Lindsey v Dempsey*, 153 Az 230, 735 P2d 840 (1987).

A wrongful conception or wrongful pregnancy action presents issues that are particularly unsuited for the traditional adversarial process of a negligence action in a court of law. One issue is the application of the avoidable consequences doctrine. The avoidable consequences doctrine is that one injured by the tort of another is not entitled to recover damages for any harm that the person could have avoided by the use of reasonable effort. Applying the doctrine to a wrongful conception case would mean that a plaintiff could recover for damages only if the plaintiff could demonstrate that he or she could not have reasonably avoided the consequences of the physician's negligence, the birth of a healthy child. One obvious way of avoiding the consequences of a negligently performed surgical sterilization would be to avoid the resultant parenthood by abortion; and another method would be to place the child for adoption. The application of the avoidable consequences doctrine, the rule of law established in negligence cases, implicates controversial and emotionally charged issues and illustrates the unique concerns wrongful pregnancy and wrongful conception actions raise. The application of the avoidable consequences doctrine to a negligence action of this sort illustrates not only that there are grave moral issues in the litigation of a wrongful pregnancy or wrongful conception action but also necessarily probe into a parent's beliefs about abortion, adoption, and the value of a child's companionship. *Flowers v District of Columbia*, 478 A2d 1073 (DC 1984).

There was no error in a jury instruction which instructed the jury that, in calculating damages, it was not to consider that the plaintiff refused to submit to an abortion or that the plaintiff and her husband declined to place the child for adoption. As a matter of law, neither course of action would be reasonable and consequently is not required. The best interest of the child, and the natural instincts of the parent, make it unreasonable to require parents to submit the child in the womb to abortion, or the child after it is born to adoption. *Jones v Malinowski*, 299 Md 257, 473 A2d 429 (1984).

A plaintiff in a wrongful pregnancy action did not have an obligation to mitigate damages upon learning that she was pregnant by submitting to an abortion. By the time the plaintiff learned that her pregnancy had not been terminated by an earlier abortion operation, her circumstances had changed. Well into the second trimester of her pregnancy, the plaintiff arguably faced a greater risk to her health in trying to abort a second time. Furthermore, while the plaintiff had a right to have an abortion at this time, this right may not be automatically converted into an obligation to have one. The plaintiff's decision not to have a second abortion should not affect the issue of the defendants' liability. *Delaney v Krafte*, 98 AD2d 128, 470 NYS2d 936 (1984).

Sayre, Abortion or Adoption: A Rational Application of the Avoidable Consequences Rule to the Computation of Wrongful Conception Damages, 12 W St U L Rev 781 (1985).

Wrongful Birth: The Avoidance of Consequences in Mitigation of Damages, 53 Fordham L Rev 1107 (1985).

2. Parents' Injury or Loss

a. [§3.31] Generally

Under traditional tort principles, the proper measure of damages in a wrongful pregnancy action, where the child is born reasonably sound and healthy, is that which is the reasonable and proximate consequence of the breach of duty. The mother, therefore, may recover damages for medical expenses, pain and suffering, and lost wages for a reasonable period directly resulting from the negligently performed abortion, the continuing pregnancy, and the ensuing childbirth. The mother is also entitled, under the general rule, to recover damages for emotional distress causally resulting from the tortiously caused physical injury. *Miller v Johnson*, 231 Va 177, 343 SE2d 301 (1986).

A father shares a mother's right to seek damages for the negligent wrongful conception or pregnancy because he is directly affected emotionally and financially by the birth of the unplanned child and he shares the legal obligation to provide for the child's care and support. Thus, plaintiff-husband has standing to bring a wrongful pregnancy action. *Jackson v Bumgardner*, 71 NC App 107, 321 SE2d 541 (NC App 1984), rev gtd, app dis 312 NC 797, 325 SE2d 486 (1985).

b. [§3.32] Emotional Distress

Recovery may be had in a wrongful conception or wrongful pregnancy action for emotional distress but only to the extent that it resulted from the actual or anticipated physical pain and suffering associated with the pregnancy and delivery. *Anderson v Wiener*, 100 AD2d 919, 474 NYS2d 801 (1984).

Damages for mental distress in a wrongful conception action are recoverable but only to the extent that the distress resulted from the actual or anticipated physical pain and suffering associated with the pregnancy and delivery. *Jean-Charles v Planned Parenthood Association*, 99 AD2d 542, 471 NYS2d 622 (1984).

In a wrongful pregnancy action, a plaintiff may not recover damages allegedly incurred as a result of the psychological trauma of having to raise an illegitimate child and of being forced to apply for public assistance. *Delaney v Krafte*, 98 AD2d 128, 470 NYS2d 936 (1984).

The mother in a wrongful pregnancy action can recover for emotional distress resulting from the actual or anticipated physical pain and suffering associated with the pregnancy and delivery. *Weintraub v Brown*, 98 AD2d 339, 470 NYS2d 634 (1983).

d. [§3.34] Pain and Suffering

Damages may be recovered for a pain and suffering claim brought in a wrongful conception or wrongful pregnancy action. *Fulton-DeKalb Hospital Authority v Graves*, 252 Ga 441, 314 SE2d 653 (1984).

Recovery may be had in a wrongful conception action for damages related to pain and suffering. *Jean-Charles v Planned Parenthood Association*, 99 AD2d 542, 471 NYS2d 622 (1984).

A plaintiff in a wrongful pregnancy action can recover damages for physical pain and suffering resulting from the unanticipated pregnancy. *Weintraub v Brown*, 98 AD2d 339, 470 NYS2d 634 (1983).

Damages associated with the pain and suffering of an unplanned pregnancy and delivery may be recovered. *McKernan v Aasheim*, 102 Wa2d 411, 687 P2d 850 (1984).

The mother of an unplanned child may recover damages for her pain and suffering during pregnancy and childbirth without regard to the benefits of child raising. *Hartke v McKelway*, 707 F2d 1544 (DC Cir 1983), cert den, 104 SCt 425 (1983).

If the plaintiff sustains the burden of proving either the negligent performance of a sterilization operation, or the breach of an express or implied warranty in the performance of the operation, the plaintiff is entitled to compensation for pain and suffering incurred during the prenatal through post-natal periods. *Mason v Western Pennsylvania Hosp*, 499 Pa 484, 453 A2d 974 (Pa 1982).

As a form of malpractice, wrongful conception gives rise to compensatory damages such as the mother's pain and suffering during the pregnancy and delivery. *Miller v DuHart*, 637 SW2d 183 (Mo 1982).

Damages with regard to pain and suffering are recoverable in a wrongful conception case. *Johnson v Terry*, 9 FLR 2375 (Wi 1983).

The physical and mental pain suffered by the wife as a result of an unplanned pregnancy and subsequent childbirth and as a result of undergoing two sterilization operations are compensable in a wrongful pregnancy action. *James G v Caserta*, 332 SE2d 872 (WV 1985).

Damages associated with pain and suffering may be recovered. *Blash v Glisson*, 173 GaA 104, 325 SE2d 607 (1984).

e. [§3.35] —Illustrative Cases

A woman received an award of $75,000 for the physical problems, pain, and considerable discomfort she experienced during her pregnancy which resulted after a failed sterilization operation. The record also indicated that her normal household, work, and social activities were curtailed and restricted because of her physical problems. In addition, her testimony established with a fair degree of probability a basis for the assessment of loss of income because of her physical problems. *Clay v Broadsky*, 148 IlA3d 63, 101 Il Dec 701, 499 NE2d 68 (1986).

f. [§3.36] Lost Wages or Income

Damages may be recovered in a wrongful conception or wrongful pregnancy action for lost wages. *Fulton-DeKalb Hospital Authority v Graves*, 252 Ga 441, 314 SE2d 653 (1984).

In a wrongful conception action there may be no recovery for future lost wages resulting from the mother's inability to carry on a job by reason of her obligation to raise the unplanned child. *Jean-Charles v Planned Parenthood Association*, 99 AD2d 542, 471 NYS2d 622 (1984).

If the plaintiff sustains the burden of proving the performance of a negligent sterilization operation, or the breach of an express or implied warranty in the performance of the sterilization operation, the plaintiff is entitled to recover lost wages related to prenatal care, delivery, and post-natal care. *Mason v Western Pennsylvania Hosp*, 499 Pa 484, 453 A2d 974 (Pa 1982).

Lost wages are recoverable as one element of damages in a wrongful conception case. *Johnson v Terry*, 9 FLR 2375 (Wi 1983).

Lost wages are recoverable in a wrongful pregnancy action. *James G v Caserta*, 332 SE2d 872 (WV 1985).

Lost wages may be recovered. *Blash v Glisson*, 173 GaA 104, 325 SE2d 607 (1984).

g. [§3.37] Loss of Consortium

Recovery may be allowed for damages for loss of consortium in a wrongful conception or wrongful pregnancy action. *Fulton-DeKalb Hospital Authority v Graves*, 252 Ga 441, 314 SE2d 653 (1984).

As a form of malpractice, wrongful conception gives rise to recovery for compensatory damages such as loss of consortium. *Miller v DuHart*, 637 SW2d 183 (Mo 1982).

Damages are recoverable by the father in a wrongful pregnancy action for the loss of his wife's services and consortium. *Weintraub v Brown*, 98 AD2d 339, 470 NYS2d 634 (1983).

Damages involving the loss of consortium may be recovered in a wrongful pregnancy or wrongful conception action. *McKernan v Aasheim*, 102 Wa2d 411, 687 P2d 850 (1984).

Recovery for loss of consortium is appropriate in a wrongful pregnancy action. *James G v Caserta*, 332 SE2d 872 (WV 1985).

Damages for loss of consortium may be recovered in a wrongful conception or wrongful pregnancy action. *Blash v Glisson*, 173 GaA 104, 325 SE2d 607 (1984).

i. [§3.39] Medical Expenses

A claim for certain damages may arise out of the negligent performance of sterilization operations. Because the petition in this case alleged negligence and actual, ordinary damages arising out of the negligence, i.e., $2,000 in medical expenses incurred as a result of the unplanned pregnancy, the court held that the petition adequately stated a claim for which relief could be granted. *Goforth v Porter Medical Associates, Inc*, 755 P2d 678 (Ok 1988).

A husband was awarded $8,000 compensation after his wife became pregnant and gave birth following an unsuccessful sterilization operation. Evidence established that he had incurred medical bills totaling $2,668.51, which resulted from his wife's pregnancy and subsequent delivery. There was also testimony that due to the physical problems the wife encountered, household help was required for up to 19 months. *Clay v Broadsky*, 148 IlA3d 63, 101 Il Dec 701, 499 NE2d 68 (1986).

In a wrongful conception case, the plaintiff wife may recover expenses associated with her pregnancy. *Jackson v Bumgardner*, 318 NC 172, 347 SE2d 743 (1986).

Plaintiff's petition alleged that the defendant doctor negligently inserted an IUD, and as a result the plaintiff-wife gave birth to an unplanned, but healthy child. The allegations of the petition, if proven, would allow the plaintiff-wife to recover for her own injuries and expenses. *Yasar v Cohen*, 483 So2d 1099 (LaA 1986).

In a case where a physician or someone else contracted to prevent a pregnancy from occurring, failure to carry out the process in the manner promised may result in an award of the costs of medical, surgical, and hospital care associated with the failed surgery. *Szekeres v Robinson*, 715 P2d 1076 (Nv 1986).

Medical expenses associated with the unsuccessful medical procedure which led to conception or pregnancy and the costs of delivery are recoverable in a wrongful conception or wrongful pregnancy action. *Fulton-DeKalb Hospital Authority v Graves*, 252 Ga 441, 314 SE2d 653 (1984).

The mother of an unplanned child may recover damages for her medical expenses associated with pregnancy and childbirth without regard to the benefits of child raising. *Hartke v McKelway*, 707 F2d 1544 (DC Cir 1983), cert den, 104 SCt 425 (1983).

If the plaintiff is able to prove that a sterilization operation was negligently performed or constituted the breach of an express or implied warranty, the plaintiff is entitled to recover all medical expenses related to prenatal care, delivery, and postnatal care. *Mason v Western Pennsylvania Hosp*, 499 Pa 484, 453 A2d 974 (1982).

Medical expenses are recoverable in a wrongful conception action. *Jean-Charles v Planned Parenthood Association*, 99 AD2d 542, 471 NYS2d 622 (1984).

Damages are recoverable in a wrongful pregnancy action for the medical expenses for the care and treatment of the mother during pregnancy and delivery of the baby. *Weintraub v Brown*, 98 AD2d 339, 470 NYS2d 634 (1983).

Medical and surgical costs, including the costs and expenses of prenatal and postnatal care, are incidental to an unsuccessful sterilization operation, and thus are recoverable. *Nolan v Merecki*, 88 AD2d 1021, 451 NYS2d 915 (1982).

As a form of malpractice, wrongful conception gives rise to recovery for compensatory damages such as prenatal and postnatal medical expenses. *Miller v DuHart*, 637 SW2d 183 (Mo 1982).

Expenses associated with a failed sterilization operation and the subsequent birth of a child may be recovered. *McKernan v Aasheim*, 102 Wa2d 411, 687 P2d 850 (1984).

Hospital and medical expenses are recoverable where an unplanned child is born as the result of an improperly performed vasectomy. *Johnson v Terry*, 9 FLR 2375 (Wi 1983).

In a wrongful pregnancy action, any medical and hospital expenses incurred as a result of a physician's negligence, including the costs of the initial unsuccessful sterilization operation, prenatal care, childbirth, postnatal care, and a second sterilization operation, if obtained, are recoverable. *James G v Caserta*, 332 SE2d 872 (WV 1985).

Expenses for the unsuccessful medical procedure which lead to conception or pregnancy may be recovered. And the costs of delivery may be recovered. *Blash v Glisson*, 173 GaA 104, 325 SE2d 607 (1984).

3. Child Rearing Expenses

a. [§3.40] Elements, Generally

In a wrongful conception action, the plaintiff parents may not recover the costs of rearing their child. *Jackson v Bumgardner*, 318 NC 172, 347 SE2d 743 (1986).

Hampton, The Continuing Debate Over Recoverability of The Costs of Child-Rearing in "Wrongful Conception" Cases: Searching for Appropriate Judicial Guidelines, 20 Fam LQ 45 (1986).

Recovery of Child Rearing Expenses in Wrongful Birth Cases: A Motivational Analysis, 32 Emory L Journal 1167 (1983).

b. [§3.41] Policy and Other Considerations Against Award

In answering certified questions, the Supreme Court of Oklahoma combined two cases in which the female plaintiffs had sought to be sterilized through medical procedures. The plaintiffs in both cases contended that these procedures were negligently performed, and, as a result of the negligence, neither was truly sterilized. Both women subsequently became pregnant and both gave birth to healthy female children. One element of the damages for which both sets of plaintiffs sought recovery is the cost of rearing the children born to them following the attempted sterilizations. The first two questions presented concern whether this element of damages is recoverable in the jurisdiction and whether, if recoverable, the costs of rearing are to be offset by the benefits to the parents from the birth of the child. The court adopted the majority rule for the jurisdiction. In a medical malpractice action for negligent sterilization, the projected cost of rearing a normal, healthy child to majority may not be recovered. As a matter of public policy, the birth of a normal and healthy child does not constitute a legal harm for which damages are recoverable. The birth of a normal, healthy child may be one of the consequences of a negligently performed sterilization, but the court held that it is not a legal wrong for which damages should or may be awarded. Since the answer to the first question was negative, the court did not specifically address the second question. Moreover, the court found that since the plaintiff parents in a medical malpractice action for negligent sterilization suffer no legally cognizable harm as a result of the life of the unplanned child, they are under no legal obligation to dispose of that life. Further, the concept of disposal of that life would be, as a matter of law, unreasonable as an action in mitigation of damages in this context. *Morris v Sanchez*, 746 P2d 184 (Ok 1987); *Goforth v Porter Medical Associates, Inc*, 755 P2d 678 (Ok 1988).

The issue of whether a plaintiff may recover the cost of rearing a healthy but unplanned child is a matter better left to legislative action rather than to judicial fiat. *Flowers v District of Columbia*, 478 A2d 1073 (DCA 1984).

The cost of raising a child cannot be recovered in a wrongful conception or wrongful pregnancy action. The soundness of a rule denying recovery for the cost of raising a child lies in that, given the values of society, a parent cannot be said to have suffered an injury in the birth of a child. *Fulton-DeKalb Hosp Auth v Graves*, 252 Ga 441, 314 SE2d 653 (1984).

The parent of a normal, healthy child may not maintain an action to recover the expenses of rearing that child from a physician whose alleged negligence in performing a therapeutic abortion permitted the birth of the child. Public policy dictates that a parent cannot be said to have been damaged or injured by the rearing of a normal, healthy child because the invaluable benefits of parenthood outweigh the mere monetary burdens as a matter of law. *Nanke v Napier*, 346 NW2d 520 (Ia 1984).

In a medical malpractice action the parents of an unwanted but otherwise healthy and normal child may not recover the ordinary costs of raising that child as damages resulting from the defendant's negligence in the performance of a surgical birth control procedure. *Morse v Soffer*, 101 AD2d 856, 476 NYS2d 170 (1984).

A cause of action seeking recovery of the ordinary costs of raising a healthy child does not state a legally cognizable claim. *Jean-Charles v Planned Parenthood Assn*, 99 AD2d 542, 471 NYS2d 622 (1984).

A plaintiff in a wrongful pregnancy action may not recover for the expenses occasioned by raising a normal, healthy child. Such damages have been consistently disallowed on the grounds that they are too speculative and that they are impossible to calculate when counterbalanced by the intangible and complex benefits of parenthood. *Delaney v Krafte*, 98 AD2d 128, 470 NYS2d 936 (1984).

Ordinary child rearing costs should be denied in wrongful pregnancy actions. As a matter of public policy the birth of an unwanted but otherwise healthy and normal child does not constitute an injury to the child's parents and is, therefore, not compensable in a medical malpractice action. To hold otherwise would be incompatible with contemporary views concerning the birth of a normal and healthy child. A rule, the primary effect of which is to increase the parents' disparagement by denial of the value of their child's life, should not be adopted. While cases should not be adjudicated on the basis of emotion, sentiment, or personal preferences, a proper respect for the value of life does not run counter to this ruling. *Weintraub v Brown*, 98 AD2d 339, 470 NYS2d 634 (1983).

It is a fundamental principle of Anglo-American tort law that an act contrary to law, which does not result in legal harm, is not actionable and does not give rise to any claim or cause. Liability for negligent conduct exists only when it proximately causes legal harm to a fully protected interest of another. In order to accord the plaintiffs a cause of action for the recovery of the ordinary costs of raising a healthy, normal child arising from the alleged wrongful conception, the plaintiffs must show not only a breach of the defendant's obligation, but also injury to themselves in the sense of damage recognized by law. The birth of a healthy child, as a matter of public policy, does not constitute a cognizable legal harm for which an action in tort will lie. The law and mankind have placed a very nearly uniform high value upon human life. In view of society's acknowledgment of the sanctity of life, it cannot be said, as a matter of public policy, that the birth of a healthy child constitutes a harm cognizable at law. The moral, social, and emotional advantages arising from the birth of a healthy child are to be preferred to the protection of purely economic interests. To hold that the birth of a healthy child represents a legal harm would be to engage in the improper task of recasting the immutable, intrinsic value of human life according to the financial burden thus imposed upon the parents. Thus, the birth of a healthy child, as but one consequence of the defendant's tortious conduct, does not constitute a harm cognizable at law. *O'Toole v Greenberg*, 64 NY2d 427, 488 NYS2d 143, 477 NE2d 445 (1985).

Where a healthy, normal child is born after an unsuccessful sterilization operation, the parents of the child may not recover damages in a wrongful conception or wrongful pregnancy action for the cost of rearing and educating the unplanned child. A child is more than an economic liability. A child may provide its parents with love, companionship, a sense of achievement, and a limited form of immortality. Thus, when a parent comes before a court alleging that he or she was damaged by the unplanned birth of a child, the only logical method of determining whether such damage has occurred would be to weigh child rearing costs against the benefits of parenthood. However, this approach should not be applied. Damages may not be recovered unless they are established with reasonable certainty. Uncertainty as to the fact of damages is a ground for denying liability. It is impossible to establish with reasonable certainty whether the birth of a healthy, normal child damaged its parents. Perhaps the costs of rearing and educating the child could be determined through use of actuarial tables or similar economic information. But whether these costs are outweighed by the emotional benefits which will be conferred by that child cannot be calculated. Furthermore, under a benefits approach, the parents would be obliged to prove their child was more trouble than it was worth. Moreover, even if the benefits approach were not applied, and parents were allowed to sue for the full cost of rearing their unplanned child, the simple fact that the parents saw fit to allege their child as a damage to them would carry with it the possibility of emotional harm to the child. Thus to permit recovery of child rearing costs would violate public policy. *McKernan v Aasheim*, 102 Wa2d 411, 687 P2d 850 (1984).

Parents cannot recover damages based on the costs of raising a healthy but unexpected child from a physician following an unsuccessful sterilization procedure. The parents of a normal, healthy child whom they now love have not suffered any injury or damage. The benefits conferred by the child's existence clearly outweigh any economic burden involved. The claimed injury is far too speculative and remote to be reasonably connected to the alleged negligence. Recovery for such damages is contrary to public policy. That a child can be considered as an injury offends fundamental concepts attached to human life. There is no reason to allow the parents to recover for the costs of raising a child and then place an unreasonable financial burden on the physician for a misdiagnosis of pregnancy or possible negligence in performing a sterilization. The parents would retain the benefit of having the child while seeking to place the enormous expenses of his or her raising on the physician. *Schork v Huber*, 648 SW2d 861 (Ky 1983).

To permit recovery of the cost of raising a healthy child until it reaches the age of majority would be against public policy. To allow such damages would mean that the parents are allowed to retain such benefits as the fun, joy, and affection of raising the child, while the defendant is burdened with all of the bills. *McNeal v United States*, 689 F2d 1200 (4th Cir 1982) [action brought under Federal Tort Claims Act; Virginia law applied].

The financial and emotional costs of raising a healthy child are not compensable. The benefits of joy, companionship, and affection which a normal, healthy child can provide must be deemed as a matter of law to outweigh the costs of raising that child. To allow such damages would be against public policy. *Mason v Western Pennsylvania Hosp*, 499 Pa 484, 453 A2d 974 (1982).

The benefit of having a child cannot be equated with or diminished by the economic burden of rearing that child. Allowing the parents to recover the cost of rearing a child constitutes a windfall to the parents and an unreasonable financial burden on physicians and the result is to inflict a penalty on the physician that is out of all proportion to the amount of his or her culpability. *Hickman v Myers*, 632 SW2d 869 writ ref n.r.e. (Tx 1982).

Damages resulting from the expenses of rearing a healthy child are not recoverable because they are subject to an objection that they would be based merely on speculation. *Sutkin v Beck*, 629 SW2d 131 writ ref n.r.e. (Tx 1982).

Parents are not entitled to damages for past and future expenses for the care and upbringing of an unplanned child against a tortfeasor physician who negligently performs a vasectomy unless the child is born with substantial physical or mental defects, in which event, the parents are entitled to recover the special medical and educational expenses, apart from the normal rearing costs, associated with raising such a child to majority. *Ramey v Fassoulas*, 414 So2d 198 (Fl 1982), affd, 450 So2d 822 (Fl 1984).

It is clear that public policy commands the development and the preservation of family relations. To permit parents in effect to transfer the costs of rearing a child would run counter to that policy. Permitting recovery would require the parents to demonstrate not only that they did not want the child but that the child had been of minimal value or benefit to them. They would have to show that the child was an uncherished, unwanted burden so as to minimize the offset to which the defendant would be entitled. The adoption of the rule allowing recovery would thus engender the unseemly spectacle of parents disparaging the value of their children or the degree of their affection for them in open court. Thus, public policy does not permit the recovery of child rearing expenses. *Cockrum v Baumgartner*, 95 Il2d 193, 69 Il Dec 168, 447 NE2d 385 (1983), cert den, *Raja v Michael Reese Hosp*, 104 SCt 149 (1983).

The keystone of any analysis about whether a rule of law should be changed is whether there is a societal need for the change. While holding a physician liable for the costs of rearing an unplanned child because of the physician's negligence would certainly act as a serious deterrent against poor medical practice, there is ample exposure of a physician in the direct expenses of the birth of an unplanned child. These expenses are hospital and medical expenses, pain and suffering, and lost wages. In addition, in an appropriate case, punitive damages against a physician might be appropriate. Thus, there is no need to expand the parameters of liability to include the costs of rearing a normal, healthy child. *Johnson v Terry*, 9 FLR 2375 (Wi 1983).

In a medical malpractice action for negligent sterilization, the projected cost of rearing a normal, healthy child may not be recovered. As a matter of public policy, the birth of a normal and healthy child does not constitute a legal harm from which damages are recoverable. The birth of a normal, healthy child may be one of the consequences of a negligently performed sterilization, but it is not a legal wrong for which damages should or may be awarded. *Byrd v Wesley Medical Center*, 237 Ks 215, 699 P2d 459 (1985).

The main problem with awarding damages for ordinary child-rearing expenses in a wrongful pregnancy action is in attempting to project the future emotional and other benefits that might be derived from having the healthy child. As a consequence, the cost of child-rearing expenses should be declined because the damages are too speculative. To form a legal basis for recovery of future permanent consequences of the negligent infliction of a personal injury, it must appear with reasonable certainty that such consequences will result from the injury; contingent or merely possible future injurious effects are too remote and speculative to support a lawful recovery. Thus, the ordinary costs of raising a healthy child cannot be recovered in a wrongful pregnancy action. *James G v Caserta*, 332 SE2d 872 (WV 1985).

d. [§3.43] Policy and Other Considerations Favoring Award

In a tort action for negligence the plaintiff may recover not only for the consequences which have actually and naturally resulted from the tort, but also for those which may certainly or reasonably and probably result therefrom as proximate consequences. Therefore, the trier of fact should be permitted to consider awarding damages to parents in a wrongful conception or wrongful pregnancy action for child rearing costs to the age of the child's majority, offset by the benefits derived by the parents from that child's aid, society, and comfort. In wrongful conception or wrongful pregnancy actions the parents seek damages, not because they do not love and want to keep the unplanned child, but because the direct, foreseeable, and natural consequences of the physician's negligence has forced upon them burdens which they saw and had a right to avoid by submitting to sterilization. In this regard, the assessment of damages associated with the healthy child's birth, if any, should focus upon the specific interest of the parents that were actually impaired by the physician's negligence, i.e., was the sterilization sought for reasons that were (a) genetic—to prevent the birth of a defective child, or (b) therapeutic—to prevent harm to the mother's health or (c) economic—to avoid the additional expense of raising a child. Child rearing costs are neither too unquantifiable nor too speculative to deny the recovery. The computation of such costs requires a routine calculation of reasonably foreseeable expenses that will be incurred by the parents to maintain, support, and educate the child to majority age. *Jones v Malinowski*, 299 Md 257, 473 A2d 429 (1984).

Child rearing costs may be recovered if the child rearing constitutes an injury to the parents of an unplanned child. Thus, where the mother of an unplanned child, once the extraordinary dangers of childbirth for her were passed, shared the general view that having a child would, on balance, be a positive experience, it was held that the jury could not rationally have found that the birth of the child was an injury to the plaintiff. *Hartke v McKelway*, 707 F2d 1544 (DC Cir 1983), cert den, 104 SCt 425 (1983).

A decision allowing recovery of child rearing expenses, *Cockrum v Baumgartner*, 99 IlA3d 271, 425 NE2d 968 (1981), was reversed in *Cockrum v Baumgartner*, 95 Il2d 193, 69 Il Dec 168, 447 NE2d 385 (1983), cert den, *Raja v Michael Reese Hosp*, 104 SCt 149 (1983).

Some costs of child rearing can be recovered in a wrongful conception action if the child is born with substantial physical or mental defects. In that event, the parents would be entitled to recovery for the special medical and educational expenses, apart from the normal rearing costs, associated with raising such a child to majority. *Ramey v Fassoulas*, 414 So2d 198 (Fl 1982), affd, 450 So2d 822 (Fl 1984).

f. [§3.45] —Illustrative Cases

A decision holding as recoverable child rearing expenses, *Cockrum v Baumgartner*, 99 IlA3d 271, 425 NE2d 968 (1981), was reversed in *Cockrum v Baumgartner*, 95 Il2d 193, 69 Il Dec 168, 447 NE2d 385 (1983), cert den, *Raja v Michael Reese Hosp*, 104 SCt 149 (1983).

g. [§3.46] Benefit Rule; Reduction of Recovery

The benefits of child rearing may be offset against the expenses thereof, but not against the expenses and pain associated with an unplanned pregnancy itself. The latter expenses and pain are more clearly separable from the benefits of raising a child than are the expenses of raising the child. More important, if the benefits of child rearing were offset against all damages, it might result that the defendant would pay no damages whatsoever, which would not provide any disincentive to negligence. *Hartke v McKelway*, 707 F2d 1544 (DC Cir 1983), cert den, 104 SCt 425 (1983).

Parents of an unplanned child may recover the costs of rearing and educating the child as offset by the pecuniary and other benefits which the parents will receive from their relationship with the child. A jury verdict based on knowledge of all relevant circumstances is a better reflection of whether the real damage exists in each case than can be obtained from the use of any abstract, iron-clad rule which would apply regardless of the circumstances of the particular case. The danger of permitting an award of damages where no real injury exists is minimized by giving weight and consideration in each case to the plaintiffs' reasons for submitting to sterilization procedures. Such evidence is perhaps the most relevant information on the question of whether the subsequent birth of a child actually constitutes damage to the parents. The parents' preconception calculation of the reasons for preventing procreation is untainted by bitterness, greed, or sense of duty to the child and is perhaps the most telling evidence of whether or to what extent the birth of the child actually injured the parents. The inherent good sense of the jury is the best safeguard to "runaway" verdicts and unfounded speculation in the award of damages, provided that the jury is allowed to consider the issues in realistic terms. Through application of the benefit rule the courts give recognition to the philosophy that the costs and benefits associated with the introduction of an unplanned child to the family will vary depending upon the circumstances of the parents. By recognizing these circumstances, the benefit rule encourages and entrusts the trier of fact with the responsibility of weighing and considering all of the factors associated with the birth of the unplanned child in a given wrongful pregnancy case. *Univ of Arizona v Superior Court*, 136 Az 579, 667 P2d 1294 (1983), later proceeding, *Univ of Arizona v Pima County*, 150 Az 184, 722 P2d 352 (1986), later proceeding, *Lindsey v Dempsey*, 153 Az 230, 735 P2d 840 (1987).

The application of the benefit rule to a wrongful conception or wrongful pregnancy action would necessarily put at issue before the jury the dollar value to the plaintiff of a child and require testimony and evidence on both economic and other advantages and disadvantages of having the child. Thus, a parent seeking to recover for an unplanned child would be strongly tempted to denigrate the child's value to the extent possible in order to obtain as large a recovery as possible. Thus, damages are not recoverable for the cost of raising a child. *Flowers v District of Columbia*, 478 A2d 1073 (DCA 1984).

The benefits rule approach to allowing child rearing expenses is awkward and unacceptable. If it was applied the parents would need to demonstrate not only that they did not want the child but that the child had been of minimal value or benefit to them. In addition they would have to show that the child remained an uncherished, unwanted burden so as to minimize the offset to which the defendant would be entitled. The adoption of the benefits rule under this circumstance would engender the unseemly spectacle of parents disparaging the value of their child or the degree of their affection for him or her. *Nanke v Napier*, 346 NW2d 520 (Ia 1984).

Child rearing costs, as offset by benefits received to the parents from the birth of the child, are recoverable. Calculating child rearing costs is neither too unquantifiable nor too speculative to deny their recovery. The primary area of complexity with respect to the damage calculations in wrongful pregnancy and wrongful conception cases focuses on the benefits rule which requires the jury to mitigate economic damages by weighing them against the worth of the child's companionship, comfort, and aid to the parents. The jury must assess these benefits in light of the circumstances of the particular case under consideration, taking into account, among other things, family size and income, age of the parents and other relevant factors in determining the extent to which the birth of the child represents a benefit to the parents. *Jones v Malinowski*, 299 Md 257, 473 A2d 429 (1984).

4. [§3.48] Siblings' Losses

No basis in law exists for an action by siblings for damages for the birth of an additional child to their family. Although children may expect their mother's society, comfort, protection, and financial support, they have no vested right to a particular share of it. Before damages can be awarded, the siblings are required to demonstrate the existence of a duty, the breach of which may be considered the proximate cause of the injuries claimed. It would be unreasonable to find that a physician owes a duty to the siblings of an unplanned child to prevent the birth of the unplanned child, or that the breach of that duty results in the loss of their share of their mother's society, comfort, care, protection, and financial support. No duty owed them has been breached. No fundamental right has been violated. There is no correlation between a wrongful conception action and the damages sought by the unplanned child's siblings. *Miller v DuHart*, 637 SW2d 183 (Mo 1982).

The siblings of an unplanned child may not recover damages for the birth of an unexpected brother or sister. *Blash v Glisson*, 173 GaA 104, 325 SE2d 607 (1984).

E. Limitations; Discovery Rule Applied

1. [§3.49] Generally

Where a sterilization procedure was performed by the defendant on July 19, 1978, and on September 28, 1978, the defendant advised the plaintiff that she was 13 to 14 weeks pregnant, and by the plaintiff's own admission she knew of her pregnancy on October 6, 1978, the statute of limitations expired where the limitations period was three years and the complaint was not filed until October 15, 1981. The plaintiff was unsuccessful in attempting to escape the bar of the statute of limitations on two theories. First, the plaintiff argued that the cause of action did not arise until the child was born. However, the court said the cause of action was complete when the plaintiff knew that she had conceived notwithstanding the sterilization procedure. Second, the plaintiff argued that she did not know until 1981 that the sterilization procedure antedated her pregnancy. However, the court said that such an argument was unpersuasive because it appeared that the pregnancy antedated the procedure. Here the most that could be said in the plaintiff's favor, the court said, was that she discovered only after the statute of limitations had run what, in the exercise of due diligence, she should have discovered earlier. For these reasons, the court concluded that there was no genuine issue as to material fact and that the defendant was entitled to judgment as a matter of law. *Stewart v Bepko*, 576 FSupp 182 (DDC 1983) [applying DC Code Ann §12-301(8)], affd 735 F2d 617 (DC Cir 1984).

In a wrongful conception action it was held that the statute of limitations began to run when the injury that the parents suffered occurred. That injury took place at the point of conception. Thus, the court refused to adopt the discovery rule in this malpractice action. *Miller v DuHart*, 637 SW2d 183 (Mo 1982).

A wrongful conception action was time-barred where the sterilization in question took place on or about October 10, 1980, but the petition was not filed until August 18, 1983. The patient and her husband had two years from the date of the act complained of to bring suit and because they did not, the action was barred by the statute of limitations. *Sanders v H Nouri*, 688 SW2d 24 (MoA 1985) [construing Mo Rev Stat §516.105 (1978).]

CHAPTER 4

Conception Stage

I. ARTIFICIAL INSEMINATION

A. In General

1. [§4.1] Definition; Overview

Lorio, In Vitro Fertilization and Embryo Transfer: Fertile Areas for Litigation, 35 Southwestern LJ 973 (1982).

In Vitro Fertilization: Hope for Childless Couples Breeds Legal Exposure for Physicians, 17 U Richmond LR 311 (1983).

Legal Aspects of New Reproductive Technologies, 6 Whittier L Rev 783 (1984).

Lorio, Alternative Means of Reproduction: Virgin Territory for Legislation, 44 La L Rev 1641 (1984).

1. [§4.2] Background

Andrews, The Stork Market: The Law of the New Reproductive Technologies, ABA Journal 50 (Aug 1984).

Smith, Sexuality, Privacy and the New Biology, 67 Marquette LR 263 (1984).

Wadlington, Artificial Conception: The Challenge for Family Law, 69 Va LR 65 (1983).

B. Rights and Obligations of Particular Parties

1. Relations Between Husband and Wife

c. [§4.5] Husband's Rights and Obligations

When a husband consents to heterologous insemination of his wife, that consent is presumed to continue through the time the wife becomes pregnant unless the husband establishes by clear and convincing evidence that such consent has been withdrawn. Moreover, a husband who orally consents to the treating physician that his wife be heterologously inseminated for the purpose of producing a child is estopped to deny that he is the father of the child. Rather, he impliedly agrees to support the child and act as his father. Thus, a husband was held to have a duty to support a child conceived by heterologous insemination with oral consent but without written consent even though the artificial insemination statute, KAN STAT ANN §§23-128, 129, and 130 require the written consent of the husband before a child born as the result of heterologous insemination can be considered the same as a naturally conceived child of the husband. *R S v R S*, 9 KsA 39, 670 P2d 923 (1983).

3. [§4.8] Unmarried Female Rights and Obligations

An Oklahoma Attorney General's opinion has stated that the artificial insemination of an unmarried woman is prohibited by statute. A fundamental rule for construction of a statute is to ascertain the intent of the legislature by a consideration of the statute's language. As the artificial insemination statute [OKLA STAT tit. 10, §§551, et seq.] makes no provision for permitting an unmarried woman to be artificially inseminated, it follows that the legislature intended to prohibit such a possibility. The specific language of OKLA STAT tit. 10, §552 demonstrates the legislature's intention to protect a child from illegitimacy. This section provides that a child born as a result of heterologous artificial insemination is not merely presumed to be the legitimate child of the consenting husband and wife, but rather shall be considered at law to be their naturally conceived child. Oklahoma Attorney General's Opinion, 9 FLR 2761 (Ok 1983).

MOTHER KNOWS BEST: CONSTITUTIONAL PERSPECTIVE ON SINGLE MOTHERHOOD BY CHOICE, 1984 S Ill ULJ 329 (1984).

REPRODUCTIVE TECHNOLOGY AND THE PROCREATION RIGHTS OF THE UNMARRIED, 98 Harv L Rev 669 (1985).

4. [§4.9] Status of Child; Legitimacy

EQUAL PROTECTION FOR ILLEGITIMATE CHILDREN CONCEIVED BY ARTIFICIAL INSEMINATION, 21 San Diego L Rev 1061 (1984).

D. Legislative Considerations

1. [§4.17] Statutory Survey

ARTIFICIAL CONCEPTION: A LEGISLATIVE PROPOSAL, 5 Cardozo L Rev 713 (1984).

3. [§4.19] Model Legislation

ARTIFICIAL CONCEPTION: A LEGISLATIVE PROPOSAL, 5 Cardozo L Rev 713 (1984).

II. IN VITRO FERTILIZATION

A. In General

2. [§4.21] Background

Andrews, THE STORK MARKET: THE LAW OF THE NEW REPRODUCTIVE TECHNOLOGIES, ABA Journal 50 (Aug 1984).

Wadlington, ARTIFICIAL CONCEPTION: THE CHALLENGE FOR FAMILY LAW, 69 Va LR 465 (1983).

SOCIAL VALUES IN A BRAVE NEW WORLD: TOWARD A PUBLIC POLICY REGARDING EMBRYO STATUS AND IN VITRO FERTILIZATION, 29 St Louis U LJ 817 (1985).

III. SURROGATE MOTHERHOOD

A. In General

1. [§4.25] Definition and Background

Legislation to legalize and establish legal requirements for surrogate mother contracts was considered during the 1983 legislative session in a number of states including the following: Minnesota [9 FLR 2323]; New Jersey [9 FLR 2695]; Rhode Island [9 FLR 2398]; and South Carolina [9 FLR 2338].

Coleman, SURROGATE MOTHERHOOD: ANALYSIS OF THE PROBLEMS AND SUGGESTIONS FOR SOLUTIONS, 50 Tenn LR 71 (1982).

Feldman, WOMBS FOR RENT: SURROGATE MOTHERS AND SEMEN DONORS, 10 Legal Aspects of Medical Practice 8 (May 1982).

Graham, Surrogate Gestation and the Protection of Choice, 22 Santa Clara LR 291 (1982).

Maule, Federal Tax Consequences of Surrogate Motherhood, 60 Taxes 656 (Sept 1982).

Mawdsley, Surrogate Parenthood: A Need for Legislative Direction, 71 Il Bar J 412 (1983).

Rushevsky, Legal Recognition of Surrogate Gestation, 7 Women's Rights L Reporter 107 (1982).

Andrews, The Stork Market: The Law of the New Reproductive Technologies, ABA Journal 50 (Aug 1984).

Smith, The Razor's Edge of Human Bonding: Artificial Fathers and Surrogate Mothers, 5 Western New England LR 639 (1983).

Townsend, Surrogate Mother Agreements: Contemporary Legal Aspects of a Biblication Notion, 16 U Richmond LR 467 (1982).

Wadlington, Artificial Conception: The Challenge for Family Law, 69 Va LR 465 (1983).

The Surrogate Child: Legal Issues and Implications for the Future, 7 Journal Juvenile L 80 (1983).

An Incomplete Picture: The Debate About Surrogate Motherhood, 8 Harv Women's LJ 231 (1985).

Cohen, Surrogate Mothers: Whose Baby Is It?, 10 Am JL & Med 243 (1984).

Handel, Surrogate Parenting, In Vitro Insemination and Embryo Transplantation, 6 Whittier L Rev 783 (1984).

Surrogate Motherhood: Contractual Issues and Remedies Under Legislative Proposals, 23 Washburn LJ 601 (1984).

2. [§4.26] Ethical Considerations

The Supreme Court of New Jersey in *In re Baby M*, 109 NJ 396, 537 A2d 1227 (1988), was asked to determine the validity of a "surrogacy contract." The court invalidated the surrogacy contract because it conflicted with the law and public policy of the state. The court found the payment to a "surrogate" mother illegal, perhaps criminal, and potentially degrading to women. The court noted, however, that there was no offense to New Jersey laws where a woman voluntarily and without payment agrees to act as a "surrogate" mother, provided that she is not subject to a binding agreement to surrender her child. Moreover, the court's ruling did not preclude the legislature from altering the current statutory scheme, within constitutional limits, so as to permit surrogacy contracts.

They further held that New Jersey law prohibits paying or accepting money in connection with any placement of a child for adoption

[NJSA 9:3-54a]. Excepted are fees of an approved agency and certain expenses in connection with childbirth [NJSA 9:3-54b]. The natural father knew he was paying for the adoption of a child; the surrogate knew she was accepting money so that a child might be adopted; and the Infertility Center knew that it was being paid for assisting in the adoption of a child. The actions of all three worked to frustrate the goals of the statute. Baby selling potentially results in the exploitation of all parties involved. Conversely, adoption statutes seek to further humanitarian goals, foremost among them the best interests of the child. Moreover, the termination of the surrogate's parental rights called for by the surrogacy contract at issue failed to comply with the stringent requirements of New Jersey law. The law, recognizing the finality of any termination of parental rights, provides for such termination only where there has been a voluntary surrender of a child to an approved agency or to the Division of Youth and Family Services, accompanied by a formal document acknowledging termination of parental rights, or where there has been a showing of parental abandonment or unfitness. In this case, a termination of parental rights was obtained not by proving the statutory prerequisites, but by claiming the benefit of contractual provisions. A contractual agreement to abandon one's parental rights or not to contest a termination action will not be enforced in the courts.

The surrogacy contract's invalidity resulting from its conflict with statutory provisions is further underlined when its goals and means are measured against New Jersey's public policy. The contract's basic premise, that the natural parents can decide in advance of birth which one is to have custody of the child, bears no relationship to the settled law that the child's best interests shall determine custody. The surrogacy contract guarantees permanent separation of the child from one of its natural parents. The state policy, however, has long been that, to the extent possible, children should remain with and be brought up by both of their natural parents. Moreover, the surrogacy contract violates the policy of the state that the rights of natural parents are equal concerning their child, the father's right no greater than the mother's. The parent and child relationship extends equally to every child and to every parent, regardless of the marital status of the parents.

Under the contract, the natural mother is irrevocably committed before she knows the strength of her bond with her child. She never makes a totally voluntary, informed decision, for quite clearly any decision prior to the baby's birth is, in the most important sense, uninformed, and any decision made after that, compelled by a preexisting contractual commitment, the threat of a lawsuit, and the inducement of a $10,000 payment, is less than totally voluntary. Although the interest of the natural father and adoptive mother is certainly the predominant interest, even they are left with less than public policy requires. They know little about the natural mother, her genetic makeup, and her psychological and medical history. Moreover, not even a superficial attempt is made to determine their awareness of their responsibilities as parents. Worst of all, however, is the contract's total disregard of the best interests of the child. There is not the slightest suggestion that any inquiry will be made at any time to determine the fitness of the natural father and his wife as custodial parents, of the natural father's wife as an adoptive parent, their superiority to the surrogate, or the effect on the child of not living with her natural mother. In the scheme contemplated by the surrogacy contract in this case, a middle man, propelled by profit, promotes the sale. Whatever idealism may have motivated any of the participants, the profit motive predominates, permeates, and ultimately governs the transaction. The court noted that in America we decided long ago that merely because conduct purchased by money is "voluntary" does not make it good or beyond regulation and prohibition. The surrogacy contract is based on principles that are directly contrary to the objectives of state laws. In New Jersey, the surrogate mother's agreement to sell her child is void. *In re Baby M*, 109 NJ 396, 537 A2d 1227 (1988).

Flickinger, Surrogate Motherhood: The Attorney's Legal and Ethical Dilemma, 11 Capital Univ LR 593 (1982).

3. [§4.27] Constitutional Considerations

A constitutional challenge to the California Surrogate Parenting Statute [Ca Civ Code §7005(d)] was rejected where the plaintiffs, who were attorneys who represented parties involved in surrogate parenting arrangements, were held to lack standing to attack the constitutionality of the statute. The plaintiffs, as individuals, did not allege that they or either of them were, or planned to be, a party to a surrogate parenting agreement, the court said. The plaintiffs merely alleged that they, as attorneys, represented more than 100 couples who were parties to such arrangements. Therefore, the court said, the complaint stated a cause of action in someone, but not in the plaintiffs. *Sherwyn & Handel v California State Dept of Social Services*, 12 FLR 1010 (CaA 1985).

4. Contract Considerations

b. [§4.29] Policy and Statutory Considerations

The Supreme Court of New Jersey invalidated surrogacy contracts because they conflict with the law and public policy of the state. The surrogacy contract conflicts with: (1) laws prohibiting the use of money in connection with adoptions [NJSA 9:3-54a]; (2) laws requiring proof of parental unfitness or abandonment before termination of parental rights is ordered or adoption is granted [NJSA 9:2-16, 17; 9:3-41; 30:4C-23]; and (3) laws that make surrender of custody and consent to adoption irrevocable in private placement adoptions [NJSA 9:3-41a; 30:4C-23]. Moreover, the surrogacy contract's invalidity results from direct conflict with New Jersey public policy. The contract's basic premise, that the natural parents can decide in advance of birth which one is to have custody of the child, bears no relationship to the settled law that the child's best interests shall determine custody. The contract guarantees permanent separation of the child from one of its natural parents. The state policy, however, has been that, to the extent possible, children should remain with and be brought up by both natural parents. Further, the surrogacy contract violates the policy of the state that the rights of natural parents are equal concerning their child, the father's right being no greater than the mother's. The court also noted that whatever idealism may have motivated any of the participants, the profit motive predominates, permeates, and ultimately governs the transaction. In sum, the harmful consequences of the surrogacy arrangement appeared to the court to be palpable. In New Jersey, the surrogate mother's agreement to sell her child is void. *In re Baby M*, 109 NJ 396, 537 A2d 1227 (1988).

A circuit court has subject-matter jurisdiction over a biological father's Paternity Act request for an order of filiation declaring the father's paternity when the biological father and mother have entered into a surrogate parenting agreement. The trial court and the court of appeals held that the circuit court lacked jurisdiction because this action was beyond the scope and purpose of the Paternity Act. The plaintiff, the child's biological father, was married but that marriage had not produced any children. The defendant, the surrogate mother, was also married. However, the plaintiff artificially inseminated the defendant. The defendant agreed to bear the plaintiff's child in return for the plaintiff's promise to pay the defendant $10,000 over and above all medical and confinement expenses. The litigation began five months before the child's birth. The plaintiff's complaint for filiation relied on the Paternity Act, particularly subsections 4(b) and (f): "(b) Proceedings in pursuance of this Act may be instituted during the pregnancy of the mother . . . (f) The father or putative father of a child so born out of wedlock may file the complaint in the circuit court of the county in which such child or mother resides or is found, praying for the entry of the order of filiation . . . The court, following the hearing, shall enter the order of filiation which shall have the same effect, be subject to the same provisions and enforced in the same manner as an order of filiation would be if entered on complaint of the mother." [Mi Cod Laws §722.714; Mi Stat Ann §25.494.] The defendant answered the complaint by admitting all of the plaintiff's allegations and joining in the request for relief. Subsequently, the attorney general intervened and alleged that the circuit court lacked subject-matter jurisdiction. The attorney general argued that the court had jurisdiction only over actions involving a "child born out of wedlock," and that the child was not born out of wedlock since at least two statutes establish the presumption that a child born to an artificially inseminated married woman is treated for all purposes as her husband's child. The attorney general also relied on a second statutory provision that provided if a child is born or conceived during a marriage, both spouses are presumed to be the natural parents of the child for all purposes of intestate succession. [Mi Cod Laws §700.11(2); Mi Stat Ann §27.5111(2).] On appeal, the court said that the plaintiff sought only an order of filiation formally stating something that no one seriously disputed, that the plaintiff was the biological father of the child. The court expressed no opinion about the plaintiff's entitlement to any other relief in the future. The court concluded that the circuit court had subject-matter jurisdiction over an action to identify the father of a child born out of wedlock. Any other conclusion requires an impossibly restrictive and unnecessary interpretation of the statutory language, the court said. *Syrkowski v Appleyard*, 11 FLR 1159 (Mi 1985).

A statutory prohibition against the purchase and sale of babies for adoption prohibits surrogate parent arrangements. The contracts and procedures of an organization established to promote surrogate parent arrangements seeks to financially benefit the organization from the contractual creation of human life and its subsequent transfer for what must be considered adoptive purposes. Recent legislative developments, judicially noticed to interpret pre-existing public policy, and a realistic, rational view of the parties and the nature of surrogate parenting lead to the conclusion that the activities and procedures of the organization violated Ky Rev Stat 199.590(2) as it existed prior to its revision by the 1984 legislature. *Kentucky ex rel Armstrong v Surrogate Parenting Assn*, 11 FLR 1359 (KyA 1985).

A termination of parental responsibilities motion was denied to a surrogate mother and her husband in *In re Baby Girl*, 9 FLR 2348 (Ky 1983). The surrogate mother alleged that she was artificially inseminated with the semen of a man not her husband, and that she and her husband wished to terminate their parental rights in and to the child, transfer the custody of the child to the alleged biological father, and have him adjudged the natural father with authority to take the child into full custody as his own natural child. At the outset, it appeared to the court that the parties were seeking a legal determination far beyond the scope permitted by the termination act [Ky Rev Stat §199.600]. The termination act is not a paternity act and it contains no provision under which a court may adjudge paternity of a child as sought in this action, the court said. A child born in wedlock is presumed to be the legitimate child of the husband and wife. There is a long line of cases setting forth the requirement of clear and compelling proof to show that a child born to a husband and wife is an illegitimate child of a third person. The mere affidavit as to artificial insemination without other positive proof of nonaccess and blood grouping is not sufficient to assume and adjudge the donor to be the natural and biological father of the child, the court said. Even if it could be established that the donor was the natural and biological father of the child, the court said a proceeding under the termination act would not be the appropriate action. The termination statute was enacted for the purpose of providing a procedure by which a birth-parent may terminate his or her parental rights and place custody of the child with a licensed child placing agency for adoption.

The Oklahoma Attorney General has stated in an official opinion that a surrogate gestation contract which provides for payment of compensation beyond statutory limitations in order to effect the adoption of a child is illegal under the Oklahoma Trafficking in Children Statute [Ok Stat tit. 21, §866]. The opinion stated that pursuant to the statute a person shall not accept any compensation for any kinds of services in connection with the adoption of a child from the person wishing to adopt. Moreover, the opinion stated that it is possible under Ok Stat tit. 10, §§551 et seq., the artificial insemination statute, that a married couple could agree to have the wife artificially inseminated with the sperm of a third party who wants to adopt the child conceived from such procedure. However, the surrogate or her husband would be prohibited by the trafficking in children statute from receiving compensation other than medical and reasonable attorney's fees, the opinion stated. That one of the prospective adopted parents would also be a biological parent does not alter the fact that a surrogate agreement interjects compensation into an adoption proceeding beyond those expenses specifically excepted by statute, the court concluded. Oklahoma Attorney General's Opinion, 9 FLR 2761 (Ok 1983).

CHAPTER 5

Prenatal Stage: Established Law

I. ABORTION AND FETICIDE

A. Introduction

2. Roe v Wade

a. [§5.2] Rights of Privacy

The right of privacy is based on a long recognized and essential element of personal liberty the court stated in *Akron v Akron Center for Reproductive Health*, 462 US 416, 103 SCt 2481, 76 LE2d 687 (1983). In *Akron* the Court reaffirmed its earlier abortion holding in *Roe v Wade*, 410 US 113, 93 SCt 705, 35 LE2d 147 (1973).

b. [§5.3] Analysis of Wade Decision

In *Akron v Akron Center for Reproductive Health*, 462 US 416, 103 SCt 2481, 76 LE2d 687 (1983), the Court reaffirmed *Roe v Wade*, 410 US 113, 93 SCt 705, 35 LE2d 147 (1973).

d. [§5.5] Conclusions

Rust, The Abortion Cases, 72 ABA J 50 (1986).

The Trimester Approach: How Long Can The Legal Fiction Last? 35 Mercer LR 891 (1984).

3. [§5.6] Judicial Interpretations of *Wade*

A county regulation requiring pregnant inmates to obtain a court-ordered release unquestionably had a significant impact on and impermissibly burdened a woman's right to choose an abortion and, therefore, was unconstitutional under the United States Constitution. *Monmouth County Correctional Institution Inmates v Lanzaro*, 643 FSupp 1217 (D NJ 1986).

The federal district court issued a preliminary injunction enjoining the enforcement of an ordinance, which provides that aborted human fetal remains must be interred, deposited in a vault or tomb, cremated, or otherwise disposed of in a manner approved by the Commissioner of Health or the state. The court found that the *Wade* decision provided for abortion free of interference by the state. The term "free of interference" includes freedom from excessive intervention, harassment, or any other means whereby the state would seek to discourage the individual's freedom of choice. Although the city asserted that it was concerned with the sanitary disposal of fetuses, the court found that there was neither a comparable ordinance regarding other human tissue disposal, nor any evidence that fetal tissue represented a greater health hazard. In the absence of such evidence, it was apparent that the ordinance was intended to interfere with or discourage abortions. Therefore, the ordinance was found to be an interference and accordingly void. *Planned Parenthood Assn v Cincinnati*, 635 FSupp 469 (SD Oh 1986), affd, 822 F2d 1390 (6th Cir 1987).

b. [§5.8] Factors Determining Viability

The state may not dictate that a physician make a "finding" of gestational age in order to determine viability. Moreover, the state cannot dictate that tests be performed to determine whether or not the fetus is viable. Therefore, the court struck down that portion of a statute which required a physician to perform or cause to be performed medical examinations and tests as necessary to make a finding of the gestational age, weight, and lung maturity of the fetus. The state failed to demonstrate that either of these requisites were narrowly tailored to further the state's interest in either maternal health or the life of the fetus when imposed at a point when the woman is 20 to 24 weeks pregnant. Further, amniocentesis imposes additional significant health risks for both the pregnant woman and the fetus. Even where the state exercises its compelling interest in a viable fetus, it may not require action that imposes an increased risk to the woman's health. *Reproductive Health Services v Webster*, 662 FSupp 407 (WD Mo 1987), affd in part, revd in part on other grnds 851 F2d 1071 (8th Cir 1988).

4. Viability

c. [§5.9] Conclusions

Section 3210(b) of the Pennsylvania Abortion Control Act sets forth two independent requirements for a postviability abortion. First, it demands the exercise of that degree of care which such person would be required to exercise in order to preserve the life and health of any unborn child intended to be born and not aborted. Second, the abortion technique employed must be that which would provide the best opportunity for the unborn child to be aborted alive, unless in the physician's good faith judgment, that technique would present a significantly greater medical risk to the life or health of the pregnant woman. An intentional, knowing, or reckless violation of this standard is a felony of the third degree. This section is unconstitutional because it requires a tradeoff between the woman's health and fetal survival, and fails to require that maternal health be the physician's paramount consideration. Section 3210(c), which requires that a second physician be present during an abortion performed when viability is possible, and that that physician must take immediate control of the child and provide immediate medical care for the child, taking all reasonable steps necessary to preserve the child's life and health, is unconstitutional because it failed to provide a medical-emergency exception. *Thornburgh v American College of Obstetricians & Gynecologists*, 106 SCt 2169, 90 LE2d 779 (1986).

A statute which defined viability as that stage of fetal development when, in the medical judgment of the attending physician based on the particular facts of the case, there is a reasonable likelihood of sustained survival of the fetus outside the womb, with or without artificial support was constitutional. *Charles v Carey*, 579 FSupp 464 (ND Il 1983) affd in part and revd in part 749 F2d 452 (7th Cir 1984), app dis, *Diamond v Charles*, 106 SCt 1697, 90 LE2d 48 (1986).

GENETIC SCREENING, EUGENIC ABORTION, AND *Roe v Wade*: HOW VIABLE IS ROE'S VIABILITY STANDARD? 50 Brooklyn LR 113 (1983).

B. Consent to Abortion

1. Informed Consent

a. [§5.10] Generally

The states are not free, under the guise of protecting maternal health or potential life, to intimidate women into continuing pregnancies. *Thornburgh v American College of Obstetricians & Gynecologists*, 106 SCt 2169, 90 LE2d 779 (1986).

In a very unusual case, the Court of Appeals held that a woman had a cause of action against genetic counselors for harm she suffered after undergoing an unnecessary abortion based on the defendant's erroneous information to her. While the plaintiff was in the first trimester of her pregnancy, she was referred to the defendants for genetic counseling to determine whether medication taken in a supposedly improper dosage during the first month of her pregnancy would have an effect on the fetus. The defendants advised that her baby would be born with the congenital birth defect of microcephaly or an anencephaly. Based on this advice, she submitted to an abortion, believing it would be justified under the extraordinary circumstances presented to her by the defendants. After the abortion was performed, she learned that the advice the defendants had given her was erroneous and that the abortion was unnecessary. The court held that the plaintiff's mental anguish and depression were the direct result of the defendants' breach of duty to her in giving her erroneous advice, on which she affirmatively acted in deciding to have the abortion. The emotional distress for which she sought recovery did not derive from what happened to the fetus; it derived from the psychological injury directly caused by her agreeing to an act which, as the jury found, was contrary to her firmly held beliefs. The defendants' breach of duty was the precipitating and proximate cause of that injury. The court found that under these unusual circumstances, where there was a breach of duty owed by the defendants to the plaintiff, the breach of that duty resulting directly in emotional harm was actionable. *Martinez v Long Island Jewish Hillside Medical Center*, 70 NY2d 697, 518 NYS2d 955, 512 NE2d 538 (1987), on remd, 133 AD2d 264, 519 NYS2d 53 (1987).

The court invalidated a provision in a statute which required that the attending physician certify in writing that he or she had apprised the pregnant woman of certain facts before an abortion could be performed. The required information included a statement as to whether the woman was or was not pregnant according to the best medical judgment of the physician. The United States Supreme Court had invalidated a similar provision, holding that there was no state interest in requiring that a physician performing an abortion, or for that matter any physician, personally counsel the patient in absence of a request. This provision is also constitutionally flawed in other respects. The statute mandates that the physician must present this information to each and every patient, regardless of the medical advisability of presenting it in any particular case. Some physicians, in the exercise of their best medical judgment, would choose to respect the woman's evaluation of her emotional status and not foist upon her specific information which she does not wish to hear. The requirement deprives the woman seeking an abortion of the right to consult with her physician and rely on his or her discretion and professional judgment. *Reproductive Health Services v Webster*, 662 FSupp 407 (WD Mo 1987), affd in part revd in part on other grnds 851 F2d 1071 (8th Cir 1988).

The Fifth Circuit struck down as unconstitutional a statute which required the attending physician, within 24 hours after performing an abortion, to inform the woman that she could choose to have the fetus cremated, buried, or disposed of as waste tissue. *Margaret S v Edwards*, 794 F2d 994 (5th Cir La 1986).

An ordinance which provided that a woman must be orally informed by her physician of the status of her pregnancy, the development of her fetus, the date of possible viability, the physical and emotional complications that may result from an abortion, and the availability of agencies to provide her with assistance and information with respect to birth control, adoption, and childbirth, was held to be unconstitutional in *Akron v Akron Center for Reproductive Health*, 462 US 416, 103 SCt 2481, 76 LE2d 687 (1983). First, the Court noted, much of the information required was designed not to inform the woman in order to obtain the woman's consent but rather to persuade her to withhold it altogether. An additional, and equally decisive objection to the ordinance was its intrusion upon the discretion of the pregnant woman's physician, the court stated. An ordinance may require that a physician makes certain that his or her patient understands the physical and emotional implications of having an abortion, the Court said. But this ordinance went far beyond merely describing the general subject matter relevant to informed consent. By insisting upon recitation of a lengthy and inflexible list of information, the ordinance unreasonably placed obstacles in the path of the doctor upon whom the woman is entitled to rely for advice in connection with her decision, the Court said.

b. [§5.11] Disclosure v Women's Rights

A requirement that the woman give what is truly a voluntary and informed consent, as a general proposition, is proper and is not unconstitutional. But the state may not require the delivery of information designed to influence the woman's informed choice between abortion or childbirth. Therefore, §§3205 and 3208 of the Pennsylvania Abortion Control Act are unconstitutional because they are an attempt to wedge the Commonwealth's message discouraging abortion into the privacy of the informed-consent dialogue between the woman and her physician. The mandated description of fetal characteristics at two-week intervals, no matter how objective, is overinclusive. This is not medical information that is always relevant to the woman's decision and would serve only to confuse and punish her and heighten her anxiety, contrary to accepted medical practice. Further, the requirement that the woman be advised that medical assistance benefits may be available and that the father is responsible for financial assistance in the support of the child similarly is a poorly disguised element of discouragement for the abortion decision. Much of this would be nonmedical information beyond the physician's area of medical expertise and, for many patients, would be irrelevant and inappropriate. For a patient with a life-threatening pregnancy, the information, in its very rendition, may be cruel as well as destructive of the physician-patient relationship. The requirement that the woman be informed by the physician of the detriment of physical and psychological effects and of all particular medical risks compound the problem of medical attendance, increase the patient's anxiety, and intrude upon the physician's exercise of proper professional judgment. This type of compelled information is the antithesis of informed consent. *Thornburgh v American College of Obstetricians & Gynecologists*, 106 SCt 2169, 90 LE2d 779 (1986).

c. [§5.12] Time Limit on Consent

An ordinance which prohibited a physician from performing an abortion until 24 hours after the pregnant woman signed a consent form was held to be unconstitutional in *Akron v Akron Center for Reproductive Health*, 462 US 416, 103 SCt 2481, 76 LE2d 687 (1983). The Court found there was no evidence suggesting that the abortion procedure would be performed more safely, nor was it convinced that the state's legitimate concern that the woman's decision be informed is reasonably served by requiring a 24 hour delay as a matter of course. The decision whether to proceed with an abortion is one as to which it is important to afford the physician adequate discretion in the exercise of his or her medical judgment. In accordance with the ethical standards of the profession, a physician will advise the patient to defer the abortion when he or she thinks this will be beneficial to the patient, but if a woman, after appropriate counseling, is prepared to give her written informed consent and proceed with the abortion, a state may not demand that she delay the effectuation of that decision.

2. Spousal Consent

a. [§5.14] Generally

The petitioner filed an application with the Supreme Court to enter an order enjoining his estranged wife from obtaining an abortion of their unborn child. The application was denied. The court noted that at the time conception occurred, the father was separated from his wife of six months, and upon leaving the defendant he became reunited with his first wife. Further, the mother testified she was physically, emotionally, and economically unwilling to bear the child. The court waived the testimony and held that it was apparent that although the plaintiff expressed a legitimate and apparently sincere interest in the unborn fetus, his interest would not be sufficient to outweigh the constitutionally protected right of the defendant to abort her child. It would appear from the *Danforth* decision that in order to require the mother to carry a child to term against her wishes, the father must demonstrate clear and compelling reasons justifying such an action. In this case, the father failed to do so. The court noted that, among other facts, the evidence disclosed that the parties were not married, that there was no suggestion they would ever reunite, that the plaintiff is able to father other children and in fact has other children, and that the plaintiff has shown substantial instability in his marital and romantic life. A court held that even if the *Danforth* decision permitted the court to balance the interests of the father of the unborn child against those of the mother, in this particular case the balancing is in favor of the mother. *Doe v Smith*, 108 SCt 2136, 100 LE2d 909 (1988).

The Ninth and the Fourteenth Amendments to the Constitution yield a privacy right to a woman with regard to whether to have an abortion, and there is no authority that a father's right to defend his unborn child is paramount at least during the first trimester of pregnancy. Therefore, a husband who sought an injunction to restrain his wife from having an abortion, was constitutionally prohibited from enjoining the abortion of the wife. *Coleman v Coleman*, 57 MdA 755, 471 A2d 1115 (1984).

b. [§5.15] Notice

Husband Notification for Abortion in Utah: A Patronizing Problem, 1986 Utah L Rev 609 (1986).

3. Minors

a. [§5.16] Generally

A statute which provided that a mature minor must go to a court to avoid a notification of the minor's parents that the minor was having an abortion was constitutional. In addition a statutory provision that notice under the statute should be waived by the juvenile court if the court found that the minor was mature enough to make an abortion decision independently or that notification would not be in the minor's best interests was also constitutional. However, a provision that the juvenile court must rule on a petition for waiver within 48 hours of the filing of the petition and specified no procedures for appellate review of an adverse decision was not constitutional. The court noted that a waiver statute must assure expeditious consideration of appeals. If the statute had specified the procedure for appeals or at least directed the Indiana Supreme Court to promulgate rules governing expedited appeals, the court said, that provision would have been constitutional. *Indiana Planned Parenthood v Pearson,* 716 F2d 1127 (7th Cir 1983) [interpreting IN CODE ANN §35-1-58.5-2.5].

Green, PARENTS, JUDGES, AND A MINOR'S ABORTION DECISION: THIRD PARTY PARTICIPATION AND THE EVOLUTION OF A JUDICIAL ALTERNATIVE, 17 Akron LR 87 (1983).

b. [§5.17] Parental or Judicial Consent

Act No. 87-286, Acts of Alabama 1987, went into effect on September 23, 1987. The Act, *inter alia,* provides that an unemancipated minor must receive the consent of one parent prior to obtaining an abortion. The Act also provides that, under certain circumstances, a waiver of parental consent may be granted to a minor by the trial courts of the state. Specifically, the Act provides that consent shall be waived if the court finds either: that the minor is mature and well-informed enough to make the abortion decision on her own, or that the performance of the abortion would be in the best interest of the minor [§4(6) (a)(b), 1987 Ala Acts 87-286]. In overturning the trial court's denial of the waiver to a minor, the appellate court noted that at the hearing the minor appeared fully aware of the nature of the proceedings in which she was the only witness. She testified to her reasons for wanting the abortion without the consent of either parent. The record showed a family that was less than stable, thereby contributing to a situation in which the minor was apprehensive of the potential effect of seeking consent from either parent. Her answers both to the counsel and court, under difficult circumstances, reflected a young woman who had given considerable thought to both the means and effects of obtaining an abortion. Her personal life reflected an extraordinary degree of self-reliance, resilience, and foresight regarding how best her interests would be served by obtaining the abortion without parental consent. Specifically, the testimony revealed that the minor was within a month of her 18th birthday. She lives by herself a majority of the time and holds down a full-time job. She went through the 12th grade, but did not graduate from high school. She planned to take the GED as soon as she turned 18. She testified that she had thought of her alternatives, either of keeping the baby or giving it up for adoption. She further stated that she had thought of her future and long-range goals. Additionally, her testimony revealed that she was on good terms with her mother but had chosen not to discuss the abortion question with her, because her abusive step-father would find out and that would cause problems for her mother. The appellate court noted that some courts have seriously considered evidence of the decision to seek the waiver of parental consent is in itself an indicia of maturity. Nevertheless, the trial judge concluded that the minor was immature and that it would not be in her best interest to obtain the abortion. The appellate court held that his determinations were conclusory only and provided no specific findings regarding upon what facts, if any, he based his judgment. Therefore, he did not comply with the statute's requirement that legal conclusions be supported with specific findings [§7, 1987 Ala Acts 87-286]. Moreover, the appellate court could neither discern from the trial court's judgment nor from the record any ground upon which the trial court's conclusion could rest. The court concluded that this minor met the criteria for maturity under the statute. Therefore, the trial judge was plainly and palpably wrong and abused his discretion by denying the minor's request for a waiver of parental consent to obtain an abortion. The law is clear that a waiver may be granted if the minor is mature and well-informed. Clearly, the evidence presented showed that the minor was mature and well-informed enough to make the decision to have the abortion. *In re Anonymous*, 515 So2d 1254 (Al 1987).

After conducting a hearing under G.L.c. 112 §12S, a Superior Court judge declined to authorize an abortion of a 16-year-old minor's pregnancy. The Appeals Court of Massachusetts vacated the order of denial and authorized the performance of the required abortion. The appellate court was concerned first with the conduct of the hearing. After asking the minor some of the questions suggested in Standing Order No. 12-80 of the Superior Court, the judge refused the persistent requests of the minor's counsel to ask the minor questions.

Section 12S provides for the appointment of counsel for a minor seeking to exercise rights under the statute. The right to counsel conferred by the statute carries with it the concomitant right to have counsel present evidence on behalf of the minor's petition through questioning of the minor and otherwise. Counsel also has the right to argue on behalf of the minor. In the case of a hearing to obtain consent to an abortion pursuant to §12S, the Superior Court judge understandably strives to minimize the intimidating effect the proceeding is likely to have on the minor. The judge, therefore, may wish to play the primary role in questioning the applicant. It is open to the judge to invite counsel to suggest questions to be put by the judge. Nothing in the nature of the proceedings under §12S, however, precludes the right of a minor to have relevant questions asked by her own counsel. Counsel for the applicant, with foreknowledge of the case, may be able to draw out salient information which the judge's questioning will miss. The appellate court also focused on the interests of the minor. A transcript of the hearing shows that the minor's counsel sought to elicit testimony from the minor about her medical history and was not permitted to do so. Yet the minor's medical condition had a decisive bearing on the second test imposed by the statute, whether the best interests of the child warranted an abortion. The minor suffered from a cardiac defect which on three occasions had been the focus of surgery. She was receiving medication which involved a risk of birth defects. Curtailment of that medication would produce serious risks to her health. Although the minor mentioned that she had heart trouble, the judge neither followed up that testimony nor permitted the minor's lawyer to ask questions which would have allowed the minor to elaborate on her medical condition. The court further noted that this was not the minor's first pregnancy. She already had a child at home and there had been an intervening pregnancy which was terminated under circumstances not clear in the record. That account, as well as the idea that the minor's choice was strongly influenced by the biological father, persuaded the hearing judge that the minor was immature and incapable of giving informed consent to the abortion. Having so concluded, however, it was error for the judge not to proceed, although requested by counsel to do so, to the best interests test. The appellate court determined that the health risks to the minor in carrying to term were such as to require a finding that the performance of the abortion was in her best interests. *Matter of Moe*, 26 MaA 915, 523 NE2d 794 (1988).

An ordinance may not make a blanket determination that all minors under the age of 15 are too immature to make an informed decision about the performance of an abortion or that an abortion may never be in the minor's best interest without parental approval, the Court stated in *Akron v Akron Center for Reproductive Health*, 462 US 416, 103 SCt 2481, 76 LE2d 687 (1983). The state must provide an alternative procedure whereby a pregnant minor may demonstrate that she is sufficiently mature to make the abortion decision herself or that, despite her immaturity, an abortion would be in her best interest.

In *Planned Parenthood Assn v Ashcroft*, 462 US 476, 103 SCt 2517, 76 LE2d 733 (1983), the Court upheld a Missouri statute [Mo Rev Stat §188.028.2] regarding parental consent and abortions. The statute provided in relevant part: "(4) In the decree, the court shall for good cause: (a) Grant the petition for majority rights for the purpose of consenting to the abortion; or (b) Find the abortion to be in the best interest of the minor and give judicial consent to the abortion, setting forth the grounds or so finding; or (c) Deny the petition, setting forth the grounds on which the petition is denied." The Court held that this statutory provision was a satisfactory alternative procedure whereby a pregnant minor might demonstrate that she was sufficiently mature to make the decision to have an abortion herself or that, despite her immaturity, an abortion would be in her best interests. The Court approved the eighth circuit court of appeals' reasoning that a court could not deny a petition "for good cause" unless it first found, after having received the required evidence, that the minor was not mature enough to make her own decision. Therefore, the Court upheld the constitutionality of the state's parental and judicial consent statutory provision.

After a hearing, a judge of the superior court found that a pregnant minor was mature and capable of giving informed consent to an abortion pursuant to a decision reached in consultation with her physician in accordance with applicable law. The order stated that the abortion could be performed without the consent of either of her parents. At the behest of her parents, a single justice of the appellate court stayed the order of the superior court judge and ordered that the matter be remanded to the superior court for a further hearing, which afforded counsel for the parents the opportunity to present evidence on the merits and for a determination as to whether the parents had standing to assert any rights in such a proceeding. The full appellate court found that there was no occasion for the single justice to stay the initial order of the superior court judge or to require that the judge afford the parents the right to participate in the proceedings. *In re Moe*, 23 MaA 902, 498 NE2d 1358 (1986).

A mandatory parental notice provision in an abortion statute is unconstitutional. *Charles v Carey*, 579 FSupp 464 (ND Il 1983) affd in part and revd in part 749 F2d 452 (7th Cir 1984), app dis, *Diamond v Charles*, 106 SCt 1697, 90 LE2d 48 (1986).

The states have broader authority to regulate the abortion decisions of minor women than of adult women. However, states cannot require parental consent for minors to obtain abortions without also providing an alternative procedure for authorizations of these abortions. A pregnant minor is entitled in such a proceeding to show either that she is mature enough and well-informed enough to make her abortion decision in consultation with her physician, independently of her parents' wishes, or that even if she is not able to make this decision independently, the desired abortion would be in her best interests. The procedure must ensure that the provision requiring parental consent does not in fact amount to the absolute and possibly arbitrary veto of an abortion decision. It should be noted, however, that the Constitution is not violated by statutes requiring parental notice to the parents of immature, dependent minors seeking abortions. Section 2151.85(C) of Ohio H.B. 319 mandates that the determinations of whether a minor is sufficiently mature and well enough informed to make her abortion decision without notification, and whether notification would not be in her best interest must be demonstrated by clear and convincing evidence for the juvenile court to issue an order authorizing the abortion to proceed without parental notification. This requirement is unconstitutional because the U.S. Supreme Court held that due process required that heightened burdens of clear and convincing evidence be placed upon the state when it acted to deprive individuals of a liberty interest. In this bill, the state attempts to place the same burden on individuals seeking to exercise a liberty interest rather than on itself. *Akron Center for Reproductive Health v Rosen*, 633 FSupp 1123 (ND Oh 1986), affd *Akron Center for Reproductive Health v Slaby*, 854 F2d 852 (6th Cir 1988).

The federal district court reaffirmed the facial constitutionality of Mo Rev Stat §188.028. The court noted that in accordance with the Supreme Court's ruling that Missouri had promulgated a rule of court demanding an expedited appeal of cases under the statute. *C L G v Webster*, 616 FSupp 1182 (WD Mo 1985).

A state's interest in protecting immature minors will sustain a requirement of a consent substitute, either parental or judicial. It is clear, however, that the state must provide an alternative procedure whereby a pregnant minor may demonstrate that she is sufficiently mature to make the abortion decision herself or that, despite her immaturity, an abortion would be in her best interest. *Glick v McKay*, 616 FSupp 322 (D Nv 1985).

A pregnant 14-year-old petitioned the court for waiver of parental consent to abortion. Her petition was denied on the grounds that she did not have sufficient maturity to make the decision independently and that the evidence was conflicting as to stage of pregnancy. The evidence indicated that the pregnancy could be at a term anywhere from 18 to 23 weeks, crucial with regard to the question of the viability of the fetus and the attendant hazards to the petitioner if an abortion was to be performed. *Re T H*, 484 NE2d 568 (In 1985).

MINORS' RIGHT OF PRIVACY: ACCESS TO ABORTIONS WITHOUT PARENTAL NOTIFICATION, 9 J Juv L 101 (1985).

c. [§5.18] Parental Notice

The plaintiffs, providers of abortions and abortion-related services, filed a class action seeking relief against the recently enacted Georgia Parental Notification Act [Ga Off'l Code Ann §§15-11-5 and 15-11-110 et seq] which requires an unemancipated, unmarried minor to notify one parent of her intention to terminate her pregnancy or to bypass the parental notification requirement and petition the juvenile court for waiver of that requirement. The plaintiffs contend that the Act is an unconstitutional restriction on the right to abortion because it will severely impede their minor patients' access to abortion services. The plaintiffs sought preliminary injunctive relief to stop the function of the Act, asserting that the Act is unconstitutional on its face and would be unconstitutionally applied if allowed to be put into practice. Moreover, the plaintiffs sought declaratory and permanent injunctive relief on the ground that the Act unduly restricts the right to privacy and due process and equal protection of the laws. The court held that that state has a significant interest in promoting parental consultation with a minor before her decision to have an abortion. On the other hand, however, a mature minor, or an immature minor in whose best interest it is to have an abortion, has a constitutional right to have an abortion without notifying her parents. The Supreme Court has not specifically ruled on the constitutionality of a parental notification statute, as opposed to a parental consent statute. While the Supreme Court has not specifically ruled on the necessity of a judicial alternative to a "notification" statute, the *Akron* decision instructs that the Court contemplated such a requirement. In its recitation of the law on minors' abortion rights, the Court said that "state and parental interests must give way to the constitutional right of a mature minor, or of an immature minor, whose best interests are contrary to parental involvement." The district court noted that courts recognizing, as a practical matter, that a notification requirement will have the same detrimental effect on a minor having an abortion as a consent statute have also rejected any suggestion that the standards of such a judicial bypass should be less stringent where notice laws are involved. Therefore, the state of Georgia must provide a judicial alternative to parental notification. The Act requires verification of notification. This may be accomplished by having the minor's parent or guardian accompany her to the abortion facility or furnish an affidavit that he or she is the minor's parent or guardian. Otherwise, the minor must find another adult to accompany her to the facility and furnish an affidavit to the effect that a parent or legal guardian of the minor has been notified. The court held that requiring the minor or her nonobjecting parent to involve an outsider to the nuclear family unit in seeking an abortion for the minor imposes a substantial and unnecessary burden upon the minor's rights. This requirement breaches the other branch of the right of privacy recognized by the Supreme Court in *Whalen v Roe*, 429 US 589, 97 SCt 869, 51 LE2d 64 (1977), the interest in avoiding disclosure of personal matters. The burden of verification increases when the minor's parents object to the abortion. In this instance, the minor is faced with locating an adult who, knowing that her parents object to the abortion, will nevertheless accompany her to the abortion clinic. The requirement unduly burdens the minor's rights. Under the Georgia statute, no matter how thoroughly discussed and well-considered the decision to terminate a pregnancy may be, a family acting in good faith compliance with the statute may not be able to implement that decision without unnecessary, costly, and medically dangerous delay and expense. *Planned Parenthood v Harris*, 670 FSupp 971 (ND Ga 1987), later proceeding 691 FSupp 1419 (1988).

If the state chooses to enact a law requiring parental involvement, it must provide an alternative procedure for the minor to seek a waiver of the requirement from a judge or a neutral third party. Such an alternative is mandatory because there are few situations in which denying a minor the right to make an important decision will have consequences so grave and indelible. The constitutional requirements for the alternative procedure are as follows:

(1) The minor must have access to the alternative procedure without first consulting her parents.

(2) If the court or other neutral tribunal finds the minor to be mature enough to consent to the abortion in consultation with her physician without parental involvement, it must waive the parental consent requirement and allow the minor to obtain an abortion on her consent.

(3) If the court finds the minor immature, it must nevertheless authorize the abortion without parental consent if the abortion would be in the minor's best interest.

(4) The proceedings must be anonymous and sufficiently expedited to give the minor woman an effective opportunity to exercise her constitutional rights.

The district court found that the requirement of the use of minor's name and social security number and the lack of specific provisions for confidential recordkeeping failed to assure constitutionally adequate anonymity. The Act provides that the waiver of the minor's petition must be granted if the "unemancipated minor" is mature and well-informed enough to make intelligently the abortion decision on her own. In order for this section to pass constitutional muster, the court read the language of the statute to encompass the standard that the unemancipated minor is mature and well-informed enough to make intelligently the abortion decision in consultation with her physician, but without the participation of her parents. The court held that the plaintiffs met the requirements for granting a preliminary injunction and granted the plaintiffs' requested injunctive relief enjoining the implementation of the Georgia Parental Notification Act. *Planned Parenthood v Harris*, 670 FSupp 971 (ND Ga 1987), later proceeding 691 FSupp 1419 (1988).

The U.S. District Court for Minnesota held unconstitutional a statute which required minors to notify both parents of their desire to obtain an abortion without providing an alternative access to the courts to obtain consent. A state regulation that burdens an individual's right to decide to terminate her pregnancy by substantially limiting her access to the means of effectuating that decision is subject to strict judicial scrutiny. The Supreme Court, however, has long recognized that a state has somewhat broader authority to regulate the activities of children than of adults. The difference between abortion statutes which regulate adults and those which regulate only minors is that the latter may be justified by significant state interest that is not present in the case of an adult. A state's interest in protecting immature minors will sustain the requirement of consent, either parental or judicial. But even the state's interest in encouraging parental involvement in their minor children's decision to have an abortion must give way to the constitutional right of a mature or an immature minor whose best interests are contrary to parental involvement. MINN STAT §144.343(2)-(7) requires minors either to notify their parents of their desire to obtain an abortion or to obtain the judicial waiver of this requirement. The statute does not require parental consent or waiver of parental consent. The court found that it is parental involvement that an emancipated or mature minor must have the opportunity to avoid without regard to whether that involvement takes the form of notification or consent. Subdivision 2 of §144.343 prohibits performing an abortion on an unemancipated minor or upon a woman for whom a guardian or conservator has been appointed because of a finding of incompetency, until at least 48 hours after written notice of the pending operation has been delivered to the minor's parents or guardian or conservator. States choosing to encourage parental involvement in their minor child's decision to have an abortion must provide an alternative procedure through which a minor may demonstrate that she is mature enough to make her own decision or that the abortion is in her best interest. The unique nature and consequences of the abortion decision make it inappropriate to give a third party an absolute and possibly arbitrary veto over the decision of a physician and his or her patient to terminate the patient's pregnancy, regardless of the reason for withholding the consent. Therefore, the court concluded that it had to permanently enjoin the defendants from enforcing Minn Stat §144.343(2) as unmodified by Subdivision 6. In view of the evidence, the court found that Minn Stat §144.343(2)-(7) had no greater beneficial effect on immature minors than it did upon mature minors and minors whose best interests were not served by notification. In view of this, the court found as a matter of fact that the statute failed to serve the state's asserted interest in fostering intra-family communication and protecting pregnant minors. However, the court found that the judicial bypass procedure, created by Minn Stat §144.343(6) as presently executed by the Minnesota courts and other offices that participate in the bypass proceedings, complies with the procedural requirements set forth by the Supreme Court. Therefore, the court rejected the plaintiff's challenge to the Minnesota notification/bypass requirement as a whole. Subdivision 3 of §144.343 identifies the individuals entitled to notification as both parents of the pregnant woman if they are both living, one parent of the woman if only one is living or if the second cannot be located through reasonably diligent efforts, or the guardian or conservator if the pregnant woman has one. The court found that this requirement placed a significant burden upon pregnant minors who do not live with both parents. Particularly in these cases, notification of an abusive or even disinterested, absent parent has the effect of reintroducing that parent's destructive or unhelpful participation into the family at a time of acute stress. Similarly, the two-parent notification requirement places a significant obstacle in the path of minors in two-parent homes who voluntarily have consulted with one parent but not with the other out of fear of psychological, sexual, or physical abuse toward either the minor or the notified parent. The United States Supreme Court has concluded that the requirement of obtaining both parents' consent does not unconstitutionally burden a minor's right to seek an abortion, at least when the parents are together and the pregnant minor is living at home. However, the Minnesota district court concluded that a regulation requiring notification of both parents, even when the nuclear family unit has either broken apart or never formed, is not reasonably designed to further the state's interest in protecting pregnant minors. Therefore, the court enjoined the defendants from enforcing the two-parent notification requirement. *Hodgson v Minnesota*, 648 FSupp 456 (D Mn 1986), affd, 827 F2d 1191 (8th Cir Mn 1987).

The United States District Court for Utah refused to enjoin the application of a Utah statute which requires a physician to notify the parents of a minor seeking an abortion. The statute was construed by the Utah Supreme Court to mandate notice where feasible to parents of all minors seeking abortions. However, on appeal, the United States Supreme Court fashioned the issue to clarify that it made no ruling with respect to whether notice must be given where the individual seeking an abortion is "mature." Therefore, it was held that the state has a legitimate interest in requiring notice to a minor's parents, and the privacy interest of the minor does not supersede that interest, at least as applied to minors who are not mature. The Supreme Court did not explicitly define "maturity" in the context of a state law requiring parental consent or notice of a decision to perform an abortion on a minor. However, it was noted that during the formative years of childhood and adolescence, minors often lack the experience, perspective, and judgment to recognize and avoid choices that could be detrimental to them. The court, in determining maturity in the abortion decision context, considered factors such as sufficient experience and perspective to make a realistic, independent, and informed judgment regarding one's best interests, including demonstrated understanding of immediate and long-term consequences. The minor in this case did not reach that level of maturity or mature decision making in the court's opinion, and therefore the case was dismissed. *H B v Wilkinson*, 639 FSupp 952 (D Ut 1986).

Ohio H.B. 319 violates the due process clause of the Fourteenth Amendment to the Constitution. One section of the bill required the physician to give 24 hours' actual notice of the pending abortion to one of the minor woman's parents, guardian, or custodian. While the state's interest is minimal, this provision unduly burdens a minor woman's right to choose an abortion. *Akron Center for Reproductive Health v Rosen*, 633 FSupp 1123 (ND Oh 1986) affd *Akron Center for Reproductive Health v Slaby*, 854 F2d 852 (6th Cir 1988).

d. [§5.19] Waiting Period for Minors

A statutory provision providing a mandatory 24-hour waiting period between actual notice and the performance of an abortion was unconstitutional, but a 48-hour waiting period for constructive notice by certified mail was constitutional. The court said that although the state does have an interest in encouraging parental involvement in the abortion decision, it was not persuaded that this interest outweighs the severe burden the statute as written places upon the minor's abortion right. Notification itself in most cases should lead to parental consultation without the state's additional help because minors are particularly susceptible to parental wishes, the court said. By contrast, the court upheld the constitutionality of the 48-hour constructive notice provision to the extent that it allowed a delay in the performance of the abortion to effectuate notice. The court noted that the abortion may proceed if, after 48 hours, the parent has not responded to notification. If a parent does not respond before 48 hours, additional delay may not be required by the state. *Indiana Planned Parenthood v Pearson*, 716 F2d 1127 (7th Cir 1983).

4. Waiting Periods

b. [§5.21] Invalidation of Waiting Periods

Minn Stat §144.343(2) prohibits performing an abortion on an unemancipated minor until at least 48 hours after written notice of the pending operation has been delivered to the minor's parents. The court held that the waiting period must effectuate actual consultation without unduly burdening the opportunity of pregnant minors to obtain an abortion. Therefore, in view of the logistical obstacles facing Minnesota women who live in counties without a regular provider of abortion services, the court found that a 48-hour waiting period is excessively long. Under the conditions existing in Minnesota at present, the court enjoined the defendants from enforcing the 48-hour waiting period imposed. *Hodgson v Minnesota*, 648 FSupp 756 (D Mn 1986), affd, 827 F2d 1191 (8th Cir Mn 1987).

C. Physicians, Hospitals and Abortion Clinics

1. Standing

a. [§5.23] Generally

A physician who performs abortions, and facilities at which abortions are performed, have standing to assert the due process rights of their patients and their own rights as well. *Akron Center for Reproductive Health v Rosen*, 633 FSupp 1123 (ND Oh 1986) affd *Akron Center for Reproductive Health v Slaby*, 854 F2d 852 (6th Cir 1988).

A physician has standing to assert both his or her own rights and those of the female patients to challenge the constitutionality of a statute preventing a physician from performing an abortion on an unemancipated minor without first notifying parents or receiving court authorization to perform the abortion. *Glick v McKay*, 616 FSupp 322 (D Nv 1985).

2. Recordkeeping

b. [§5.28] Specific Recordkeeping Provisions

Sections 3214(a) and (h), and 3211(a) of the Pennsylvania Abortion Control Act are unconstitutional because they require, among other things, that the physician report the performing and referring physician's information as to the woman's residence, age, race, marital status, number of prior pregnancies, the basis for any judgment that a medical emergency existed and for any determination of nonviability, and the method of payment for the abortion. These sections provided that the reports would not be deemed public records, but would be available for public inspection and copying in a form that would not lead to disclosure of the identity of any person filing a report. Such reporting requirements raise the specter of public exposure and harassment of women who choose to exercise their personal, intensely private right with their physician to end a pregnancy. Thus, they pose an unacceptable danger of deterring the exercise of that right and, therefore, are invalid. The court also struck down §3211(a) which required the physician, after the first trimester, to report the basis for his determination that a child was not viable. *Thornburgh v American College of Obstetricians & Gynecologists*, 106 SCt 2169, 90 LE2d 779 (1986).

A provision in an abortion statute which required the doctor performing the abortion to describe, on a form provided by the state, the basis of his or her best clinical judgment that the abortion was necessary was unconstitutional. Although there was no constitutional difficulty in requiring a physician to certify that the abortion was medically necessary, to insist that a doctor describe the basis for that clinical judgment unnecessarily interfered with both the confidentiality of the woman's abortion decision and the physician-patient consultation. *Charles v Carey*, 579 FSupp 464 (ND Il 1983) affd in part and revd in part 749 F2d 452 (7th Cir 1984), app dis, *Diamond v Charles*, 106 SCt 1697, 90 LE2d 48 (1986).

4. Hospital-Required Abortions

a. [§5.30] Generally

Pursuant to the provisions of G.L.c 112 §12S, a minor sought the consent of the court to obtain an abortion without the consent of or notice to either of her parents. The judge found that the petitioner was mature and capable of giving informed consent and concluded that she could give consent to undergo an abortion pursuant to a decision reached in consultation with her physician, without the consent of either of her parents. Since the petitioner was beyond the 13th week of pregnancy, the judge thought that G.L.c 112 §12Q required that the abortion be performed only in a hospital duly authorized to provide facilities for general surgery. He found that the clinic to which the petitioner wished to go was not such a hospital and expressly limited the authorization granted the petitioner to an abortion to be performed in a hospital duly authorized to perform general surgery. In overturning the court's decision, the appellate court acknowledged the decision of the United States Supreme Court in *Akron v Akron Center for Reproductive Health Inc*, which struck down a city ordinance which purported to require that second trimester abortions be performed only in a hospital. Therefore, the court held that a judge who finds that a minor is sufficiently mature to decide for herself whether to undergo an abortion is without any authority to limit his approval of the abortion by conditioning that it be performed only in a hospital authorized to perform general surgery. *Matter of Moe*, 25 MaA 931, 517 NE2d 170 (1987).

The plaintiffs, a class of all duly licensed physicians and surgeons performing or desiring to perform pregnancy terminations in Illinois, and a class of all women in the state of Illinois of childbearing age who desire or may desire an abortion at some time in the future, sought declaratory and injunctive relief to the effect that three Illinois statutes and their regulations violate the constitutional right to privacy as established in *Roe* and subsequent Supreme Court cases. Section 16(1) of the Medical Practice Act (MPA), 111 Ill Rev Stat ¶4433(1), allows for revocation or suspension of the license of any physician who performs an "elective abortion" in any place other than a licensed Ambulatory Surgical Treatment Center (ASTC), a hospital, or facility run by the state or federal government. The Ambulatory Surgical Treatment Center Act, 111 1/2 Ill Rev Stat ¶¶157-8.1 et seq (ASTCA), provides for the licensure of all ASTCs, which it defines as any place devoted primarily to the performance of surgical procedures or any facility in which a medical or surgical procedure is utilized to terminate a pregnancy, irrespective of whether the facility is devoted primarily to this purpose. In addition, the plaintiffs challenged those sections of the Health Facilities Plannning Act, 111 1/2 Ill Rev Stat ¶¶1151 et seq (HFPA), which require anyone seeking to open an ASTC to obtain a certificate of need for the facility from the Department of Public Health after a public hearing and 120-day review period. The bulk of the plaintiffs' specific challenges, however, were directed at the ASTCA, its regulations, and their application via the MPA, to physicians desiring to perform first and early second trimester abortions. Section 6.1 of the ASTCA requires any corporation operating an ASTC devoted primarily to providing facilities for abortion to have on its board of directors a physician who is licensed to practice medicine in all of its branches and is actively engaged in the practice of medicine at the ASTC. The Act also provides for licensing fees and requires that a licensed facility be under the supervision of one or more physicians having admitting and surgical privileges in an Illinois hospital, requires statements regarding the ownership and financial condition of the facility, requires Department approval of construction or alteration to the facility, and provides for quarterly inspection of the facilities. The remedial sections of the Act provide an array of enforcement mechanisms. The Seventh Circuit was asked to consider whether the requirements of the statutory and regulatory scheme violate the right to privacy and to abortion as established in *Roe* and its progeny. Where first trimester abortions are involved, not only must the impact of the challenged regulation be insignificant in terms of the woman's exercise of her right, but the regulation must also be justified by important state health objectives. Thus, the medical necessity standard is the correct one to apply in determining the validity of a statute or regulation. The court found that the physical plant requirements of the regulations required ASTCs to be the functional equivalent of small hospitals and that these requirements may be medically detrimental. Moreover, the court refused to ignore the fact that the ASTCA was enacted primarily with abortion clinics in mind and only applied to out-patient surgical clinics generally in an effort to save the statute from unconstitutionality. The State could not, merely by applying the expedient and conclusory label "surgery" to a medical procedure, apply requirements which would be necessary to major surgical procedures in the abortion context where it would be wholly inappropriate. The district court found, and the appellate court agreed, that the regulations substantially burden the effectuation of the decision to have an abortion. Specifically, the regulations raised the cost of abortions, by $25 to $40, for abortions performed at one of the plaintiff's clinics, and, more importantly, they would limit the availability of abortions in that, unless the regulations were enjoined, the clinic would close for lack of a suitable location that could be renovated to comply with them. Additionally, the district court found that the regulations prevented an individual plaintiff from offering abortion services at her clinic because the cost of compliance was prohibitive. The court acknowledged that although the financial per-patient cost of compliance might not seem overwhelming, it is not the only burden that must be considered. The lack of availability of abortions caused by the up-front cost and difficulty of obtaining a complying facility is at least as real, and possibly more burdensome, to women seeking abortions. Futhermore, there was testimony of the psychological burdens which would result from having to undergo an abortion in a hospital-like facility when the more psychologically comforting setting of a doctor's office would serve just as well from a medical standpoint. These burdens are not *de minimis*. Therefore, they must be justified by important state health objectives. The court held that the state's attempt to regulate experienced, and therefore safer, physicians more heavily than the occasional abortion provider appears to lack even a reasonable basis. Purely as a matter of the plain language of the statutory and regulatory scheme, once the licensing requirement falls, the remainder of the requirements fall with it. The specific substantive requirements are not applicable to abortions per se, but rather to ASTCs. In the alternative, however, the court analyzed those specific substantive aspects of the regulations focused on at trial which rendered the scheme unconstitutional as a whole. The abortion-specific subpart of the regulations were of particular concern to the court. Many of the requirements set forth in that subpart seem clearly contrary to either prior Supreme Court precedent or Seventh Circuit cases. In particular, §205.730(a) (2) requires the physician who is to perform the abortion to also perform a pregnancy test on the patient, regardless whether such testing had previously been done by another physician. The Seventh Circuit previously invalidated a similar "same doctor" requirement in an Illinois statute. The requirement in this regulation is, if anything, more burdensome and less justified than the one invalidated previously. The counseling requirements, too, suffer from constitutional defects. Section 205.730(b) (3) attempts to prescribe the precise content of counseling in mandatory terms applicable to all cases. Moreover, (2) (D) requires that counselors have no financial interest in the patient's decision. The court found it impossible to read this provision in such a way that it does not, at least in some cases, preclude the performing physician from providing the counseling. This is fundamentally at odds with the emphasis placed on the physician-patient relationship by *Roe* and its progeny. Thus, the requirement that counseling be conducted by one who has no financial interest in the patient's decision was held unconstitutional. Likewise, the physical plant equipment and staffing requirements are totally unjustified from a medical standpoint. The testimony regarding many of the physical plant requirements makes clear they have no medical justification whatsoever when applied to first and early second trimester abortions of the type involved in this case. The court had little trouble concluding that these requirements, which impose a substantial burden and are not justified by health objectives, are unconstitutional. Further, the "certificate of need" proceeding requirement of the Health Facilities Planning Act was also held to be unconstitutional. *Ragsdale v Turnock*, 841 F2d 1358 (7th Cir 1988).

The plaintiffs brought an action for declaratory and injunctive relief in which they challenged the constitutionality of §188.080, RSMo (1986). This section provides in pertinent part that a physician who performs an abortion, and who does not have surgical privileges at a hospital which offers obstetrical or gynecological care, is guilty of a class B felony. The plaintiffs contended that the section impermissibly burdens a woman's right to privacy guaranteed under the First, Fourth, Fifth, Ninth, and Fourteenth Amendments of the Constitution, denies women their due process and equal protection rights, and is unconstitutionally vague. The District Court found the section to be constitutional and entered judgment in favor of the defendants. The court found that an abortion performed in the first or second trimester of pregnancy may give rise to complications which necessitate prompt hospital care. These complications arise in approximately 0.3 per cent to 0.2 per cent of all first and second trimester abortions. Testimony indicated that it was accepted medical practice in Missouri for a physician who performs first or second trimester abortions to have surgical privileges at a hospital which provides obstetrical or gynecological care. This practice ensures that the physician will have the authority to admit a patient in a hospital whose facilities and resources are familiar to him or her. It also ensures that the patient will have immediate access to secondary or tertiary care. However, it is also the custom in Missouri for hospitals to provide emergency care even if the patient's physician is without surgical privileges at the hospital. The court noted that it is not the accepted medical practice for a physician who performs first or second trimester abortions to rely exclusively on such a custom. If the physician does, a patient may be denied the care of the treating physician who is most familiar with her condition. The patient may also fail to receive the same level of diagnostic acumen as she would from her treating physician if the physicians on duty in the emergency room, or even the physicians on call at the hospital, do not have the same expertise in obstetrics or gynecology. The *Standards for Obstetrics and Gynecological Services*, Sixth Edition, promulgated by the American College of Obstetrics and Gynecology, are substantially similar to the accepted medical practice in Missouri. Given the mandate of *Roe* and its progeny, the court could uphold the section only if it found it had "no significant impact" on a woman's right to an abortion, defined in *Roe* to include both the abortion decision and its effectuation, and that such a section was justified by an "important state health objective." The court, based on its findings of fact, found that the section met these requirements and did not violate a woman's right to privacy within the meaning of *Roe*. The plaintiffs further contended that the section violates their due process rights because the state is impermissibly delegating to a hospital the power to regulate abortions. However, the court noted that the *Roe* analysis is predicated upon the assumption that the abortion procedure is performed by medically competent personnel under conditions ensuring maximum safety for the woman. *Roe* notes that a state can proscribe any abortion performed by a physician who is not currently licensed to practice medicine in that state. The delegation of authority to a state licensing board to license a physician is different only in degree, not kind, from the delegation of authority to a public hospital to grant surgical privileges. Accordingly, the court found that the section does not constitute an unlawful ordination of power within the meaning of the Fourteenth Amendment. The court also found that the section did not violate the equal protection rights of a physician without surgical privileges at a hospital. The court noted that the Eighth Circuit has held that where the state regulates abortion beyond its regulation of similar surgical procedures, the differences in treatment must be shown to be necessitated by the particular characteristics of the abortion procedure. The court found that the defendants made such a showing and, therefore, the section did not violate equal protection rights. *Women's Health Center Inc v Webster*, 681 FSupp 1385 (ED Mo 1988).

In *Akron v Akron Center for Reproductive Health*, 462 US 416, 103 SCt 2481, 76 LE2d 687 (1983), the Court held that an ordinance that required all second trimester and beyond abortions to be performed in a hospital was unconstitutional. By preventing the performance of dilation and evacuation abortions in an appropriate nonhospital setting, the city imposed a heavy, and unnecessary, burden on women's access to a relatively inexpensive, otherwise accessible, and safe abortion procedure. The ordinance has the effect of inhibiting the vast majority of abortions after the first 12 weeks, and therefore unreasonably infringes upon a woman's constitutional right to obtain an abortion. The Court's rationale was based, in part, on the fact that present medical knowledge no longer requires the performance of all second trimester abortions in a hospital.

A statute which required that all abortions after 12 weeks of pregnancy be performed in a hospital was held unconstitutional in *Planned Parenthood Assn v Ashcroft*, 462 US 476, 103 SCt 2517, 76 LE2d 733 (1983). The Court relied on its holding in *Akron v Akron Center for Reproductive Health*, 462 US 416, 103 SCt 2481, 76 LE2d 687 (1983), in arriving at its decision.

In *Simopoulos v Virginia*, 462 US 506, 103 SCt 2532, 76 LE2d 755 (1983), the Court upheld a Virginia statute [Va Code §18.2-73 (1982)] which stated that a second trimester abortion must be performed in a hospital licensed by the Virginia State Department of Health. The Court noted that the abortion statute did not define the term hospital, but rather that the term was defined in another portion of the statutes [Va Code §32.1-123.1] to include "out-patient . . . hospitals." Thus, the Court noted, under Virginia law, a second trimester abortion may be performed in an out-patient surgical hospital provided that facility has been licensed as a "hospital" by the state. Virginia's requirements that second trimester abortions be performed in licensed clinics is not an unreasonable means of furthering the state's compelling interest in protecting a woman's health and safety. The Court noted that Virginia's second trimester hospitalization requirement differed from those at issue in *Akron v Akron Center for Reproductive Health*, 462 US 416, 103 SCt 2481, 76 LE2d 687 (1983), and *Planned Parenthood Assn v Ashcroft*, 462 US 476, 103 SCt 2517, 76 LE2d 733 (1983). In those cases the Court recognized that at least during the early weeks of the second trimester, dilation and evacuation abortions might be performed as safely in an out-patient hospital as in a full service hospital. However, the Court noted, an ordinance in *Akron* and a statute in *Planned Parenthood* mandated that all second trimester abortions be performed in general, acute care hospitals. In contrast, the Court reasoned, the Virginia statutes and regulations did not require that second trimester abortions be performed exclusively in full service hospitals. Rather, under Virginia's hospitalization requirement, out-patient surgical hospitals might qualify for licensing as "hospitals" in which second trimester abortions might lawfully be performed.

Mo Stats §188.025 provides that every abortion performed at or subsequent to the first 16 weeks' gestational age must be performed in a hospital. The standard for evaluating the constitutionality of laws which regulate the performance of abortions after the first trimester is well settled. The United States Supreme Court held that a state regulation which substantially impacts on a woman's access to abortion prior to the viability of the fetus will be upheld only to the extent that the regulation reasonably relates to the preservation and protection of maternal health. The state may not adopt abortion regulations that depart from accepted medical practice. The health regulation imposed by the state must be legitimately related to the objective the state seeks to accomplish. Further, the state must make a reasonable effort to limit the regulation to that specific time during and after the second trimester when the health interest will be furthered. The state has the burden of proving a health justification. The Supreme Court held that a hospitalization requirement for all second trimester abortions was unconstitutional because such a requirement unreasonably infringes on a woman's constitutional right to obtain an abortion. However, the Court did not draw a line to indicate at what point in the second trimester a state may require that abortions be performed in a hospital setting. This determination depends on the impact of the regulation and its reasonableness, that is, whether it departs from acceptable medical practice. A hospitalization requirement clearly places a significant obstacle in the path of a woman seeking an abortion. The Supreme Court determined that the increased cost of hospitalization and the fact that second trimester abortions were rarely performed in area hospitals combined to significantly limit a woman's ability to obtain an abortion. If forced to travel to find available facilities a woman would incur not only financial expense, but also additional health risks. It is evident that hospitalization significantly increases the cost of an abortion; moreover, the availability of hospital services for abortions is limited in Missouri. Therefore, increased financial burden and restricted availability of hospital-based abortion services create a substantial interference with and impose a direct burden on a woman's decision to have an abortion. Because the Court concluded that §188.205 significantly impacts on abortion rights, the state was required to show that the 16-week hospitalization requirement reasonably relates to the state's interest in maternal health. In order to meet this burden, the state had to show that non-hospitalized abortions at 16 weeks' or greater gestational age can be considered more dangerous than hospitalized abortion procedures at an identical stage of pregnancy. The defendants failed to establish that the potential for uterine bleeding necessitates that abortions be performed in a hospital. This complication is evidently best controlled by contraction of the uterine musculature with drugs and massage. The data presented at trial suggested that it rarely becomes necessary to transfer a patient to a hospital for treatment. Nor was there proof that the incidence of infection was diminished when post-16-week abortions were performed in hospitals rather than in free-standing clinics.

Rather, there was evidence that nosocomial infections, those acquired in a hospital setting, tend to be more resistant to antibiotic therapy. The defendants provided evidence that the mortality rate for D & E abortions increases significantly after 16 weeks' gestation, but there was no indication that hospitalization would result in a lower morbidity or mortality rate. The state failed to meet its burden of proof on this issue. Because §188.025 significantly impacts on a woman's access to abortion and the state failed to prove that the 16-week hospitalization requirement reasonably relates to the state's interest in maternal health, this provision was held invalid. *Reproductive Health Services v Webster*, 662 FSupp 407 (WD Mo 1987), affd in part revd in part on other grnds 851 F2d 1071 (8th Cir 1988).

D. Medicaid

4. [§5.41] Other Publicly Funded Health Services

The federal district court concluded that under the New Jersey state constitution and New Jersey law, a county must provide funding for all requested inmate abortions which are medically necessary, i.e., all those necessary to protect the life or health of the mother. In considering whether the county was financially obligated to assume the full cost of its inmates' elective as well as medically necessary abortions, the court noted that inmates are totally dependent on the penal institution to meet their medical needs. This supposed dependency derives not only from their physical confinement, but from the unavailability of other outside resources such as gainful employment or Medicaid coverage while they are incarcerated. Their ability to pay for abortions, even given the fact of possible release, is diminished accordingly. This financial obstacle, imposed upon them by their status as inmates, substantially restricts their ability to exercise their right to choose to terminate their pregnancies. Therefore, the court concluded that the county was financially obligated to assume the full cost of its inmates' elective as well as medically necessary abortions, since these abortions are simply one type of medical treatment to which inmates are legally and equitably entitled. *Monmouth County Correctional Institution Inmates v Lanzaro*, 643 FSupp 1217 (D NJ 1986).

5. [§5.42] Conclusions

The sections of Missouri law which prohibited the expenditure of public funds, actions of public employees, and use of public facilities for the purpose of performing or assisting an abortion, and encouraging or counseling a woman to have an abortion if it is not necessary to save her life [Mo Rev Stat §§188.205, 188.210, 188.215] were determined to be unconstitutionally vague. Moreover, the court concluded that the prohibitions on speech set forth in these sections imposed a significant barrier to a woman's right to consult with her physician and exercise her freedom of choice. *Reproductive Health Services v Webster*, 662 FSupp 407 (WD Mo 1987), affd in part revd in part on other grnds 851 F2d 1071 (8th Cir 1988).

E. Feticide

2. [§5.44] Statutory Construction

A defendant was convicted of violating Minn Stat §145.412, Subdivision 1 (1986), which makes it unlawful to willfully perform an abortion unless the abortion is performed by a physician licensed to practice medicine in a hospital or abortion facility, if the abortion is performed after the first trimester in a manner consistent with the lawful rules promulgated by the state and commissioner of health and with the consent of the woman submitting to the abortion after a full explanation of the procedure. The defendant had beaten and kicked the victim in the abdomen knowing that she was eight months pregnant. The court found that the phrase "willfully perform an abortion" does not denote specific intent as an element of the crime. The court found that the most common definition of the word "willfully," as used in a penal statute, is something done with bad purpose or evil intent. The court further found that the term "abortion" as defined by the statute includes an act, procedure, or use of any instrument, medicine, or drug which is supplied or prescribed for or administered to a pregnant woman which results in the termination of the pregnancy, was broad enough to include an assault committed upon a pregnant woman. Moreover, the statute proscribes an act which results in termination of pregnancy, rather than one which is designed to produce a termination of pregnancy. *State v Wickstrom*, 405 NW2d 1 (MnA 1987).

II. PRENATAL INJURY ACTIONS

A. Cause of Action for Personal Injury to Fetus

1. [§5.49] Generally

The plaintiff, an infant born prematurely and with severe brain damage, brought an action against various medical personnel involved in her birth for the injuries she suffered as a result of their negligence. The jury verdict awarding the child $2.5 million for damages she suffered was affirmed on appeal. *Ensor v Wilson*, 519 So2d 1244 (Al 1987).

The plaintiff appellee brought suit against the defendant physician for brain damage and injury to his left clavicle sustained during the birth process. Although the hospital provided the equipment necessary for determining, prior to delivery, the relation of the width of the mother's pelvic opening to the size of the baby's head, and although the defendant knew how to use the equipment, he did not do so. During the plaintiff's labor the defendant did not use electronic fetal monitoring that was available. In delivering the plaintiff, the defendant used a forceps on the baby's head. He used the forceps again to pull the plaintiff through the birth canal. It was even the defendant's opinion that the plaintiff could have been delivered without the use of forceps if his mother had labored for another hour or two. The plaintiff's expert testified that the plaintiff's mother's pelvic opening was inadequate for a normal size baby to pass through. It was the expert's opinion that the use of forceps could have been avoided if the defendant had followed the standard medical practice and determined the size of the mother's pelvic opening and the size of the baby's head prior to delivery. Moreover, it was his opinion that the defendant's use of forceps, combining rotation and extraction through the pelvis, resulted in damage both to the baby's head and the baby's shoulder girdle. The defendant himself acknowledged that it would be injudicious to use forceps to deliver a baby through a pelvic opening which was too small to admit passage of the baby's head. The defendant agreed that the injudicious use of forceps could cause the injuries that the plaintiff suffered. The defendant also testified that forceps would not have been necessary if the mother had been allowed to continue labor for another hour or two. Based on this testimony alone, it could be inferred that the defendant's use of forceps was "injudicious," resulting in the injuries to the clavicle and brain damage suffered by the plaintiff. Based on this evidence, the jury awarded $100,000 in damages to the plaintiff for the prenatal injury he sustained. *Forrestal v Magendantz*, 848 F2d 303 (1st Cir 1988).

The infant plaintiff was awarded $1,500,000 for pain and suffering, $740,000 for lost earning capacity, and $35,000 for lost services for injuries he sustained prior to birth. The evidence indicated that he suffered permanent debilitating injury, including a reduced ability to become educated, to care for himself, or to sustain himself economically. He is retarded, has epilepsy, and requires special education and therapy. The infant plaintiff was born in obvious distress after only 31 weeks of gestation, weighing about three pounds. His mother had engaged one of the defendants, an obstetrician, after another defendant had for several months failed to diagnose that she was pregnant. During the pregnancy, the mother had complained of staining and elevated blood pressure. She had several episodes of bleeding which were severe enough to cause her to be taken to the hospital emergency room. The day of the infant's birth, the mother was taken by ambulance to the hospital. For an hour or more, one of the defendants received reports from the labor room nurses who were monitoring the mother. A loss of the fetal heartbeat was reported some 31 minutes before the infant's delivery by Caesarean section. In the delivery room, the infant required resuscitation; his APGAR score was 1 at one minute after birth, 5 at five minutes, and 4 at 10 minutes. He was transferred to another hospital where a tracheotomy was performed to help him breathe. He was tube fed for about six months, after which he spent 14 months at another medical center. *Kavanaugh v Nussbaum*, 71 NY2d 535, 528 NYS2d 8, 523 NE2d 284 (1988).

An award of $1,275,000 was made to an infant who had suffered a skull fracture and brain damage as a result of a physician's failure to promptly take the baby by Caesarean section and his use of forceps to the skull of the baby to force a normal birth. The evidence showed that the defendant physician had fractured the infant's skull and as a result the child developed cerebral palsy, seizure disorder, blindness, deafness, and mental retardation. The evidence showed that the child would live into adulthood, possibly beyond age 50, and would need 24-hour care, physical and occupational therapy, sophisticated ancillary personal attention, a long-term care program, and special equipment. *Low v United States*, 795 F2d 466 (5th Cir Tx 1986).

An infant suffered permanent brain damage, a form of cerebral palsy that involves all four extremities and a seizure disorder, as a result of a failure to treat her mother for a condition known as *abruptio placentae* prior to the infant's birth. The infant was permitted to recover an award of $1,000,000 for her pain and suffering and mental anguish. She will also be permitted to recover for her pecuniary loss, the amount to be determined on remand. *Trevino v United States*, 804 F2d 1512 (9th Cir Wa 1986), cert den, 108 SCt 70 (1987).

An infant was awarded damages based on testimony that the defendant obstetricians were negligent in failing to perform a Caesarean section earlier in the mother's labor, and that the hospital staff departed from proper medical standards of care in not monitoring the fetal heartbeat at least every 15 minutes. The experts testified with a reasonable degree of medical certainty that it was probable that the fetus suffered hypoxia during labor and that as a result of this negligence, the plaintiff suffered severe and permanent personal injuries. *Ledogar v Giordano*, 122 AD2d 834, 505 NYS2d 899 (1986).

While foreseeability of future injury alone does not establish the existence of a duty owing to an unborn infant by its mother's physicians, it is beyond dispute that in the case of negligence resulting in prenatal injuries, both the mother and the child in utero may each be directly injured and/or each owed a duty, independent of the other. Therefore, encompassed within the independent duty flowing between doctor and infant in utero is the obligation of the physician to obtain informed consent from the parent when a medical treatment may affect the infant. The infant plaintiff's cause of action is independent from his or her mother's. Since the failure to disclose the alternatives and reasonably foreseeable risks and benefits of treatment and diagnostic procedures may result in direct physical injury to the fetus alone, as opposed to the mother, it is vital that the cause of action belong to the infant, born alive, as well as the mother. To deny an independent cause of action to the infant is to deny any recovery for direct physical injury, for the mother cannot recover in her own right for the infant's injuries. While it is true that the law is not required to provide relief for every injury suffered, it has not yet denied recovery for actual physical injuries sustained as a direct and foreseeable result of a party's wrongful act. The only problem to be encountered is one of proof. It is enough that the infant plaintiff bears the burden of proving the lack of informed consent, presumably through the testimony of the mother among others. The choice or decision regarding medical treatment is the mother's, but it must be made with knowledge of the risks to her unborn child. To the latter, an independent duty of disclosure, via the mother, is owed by the physician. *Hughson v St Francis Hosp of Port Jervis*, 92 AD2d 131, 459 NYS2d 814 (1983).

A cause of actions lies for the wrongful death of a child born alive who dies as a result of injuries sustained while the child was a fetus. *Group Health Assn v Blumenthal*, 295 Md 104, 453 A2d 1198 (1983).

One who tortiously causes harm to an unborn child is subject to liability to the child for the harm if the child is born alive. *Hopkins v McBane*, 359 NW2d 862 (ND 1984).

An injured child has a right to an independent cause of action against a physician for in utero injuries stemming from the physician's failure to obtain an informed consent only upon birth. Thus, where a woman gave birth to a stillborn child, the cause of action for lack of informed consent related only to the stillborn's mother. *Khan v Hip Hosp*, 127 Misc2d 1063, 487 NYS2d 700 (NY SCt 1985).

3. [§5.51] Viability Requirement

A tort action may be maintained to recover damages for prenatal injuries negligently inflicted if the injured child is born alive. Under the terms of CA CIV CODE §29, birth is a condition precedent to the accrual of legal rights. Birth fixes the beginning of the child's rights; it is this condition precedent which must occur before legally cognizable rights accrue to an unborn child. *Wilson v Kaiser Foundation Hosps*, 141 CaA3d 891, 190 CaR 649 (1983).

B. Cause of Action by Parents for Damages and Emotional Distress Arising From Prenatal Event or Injury

2. [§5.53] Unhealthy Child Born

The plaintiffs claimed that the defendant, acting by and through its attending obstetrician, failed to exercise a proper degree of care in the treatment of the mother during labor and delivery of her baby, and that as a consequence the baby was born with a devastated brain. The child is a helpless individual, significantly delayed developmentally, and unable to see; she will never be able to walk, talk, feed, or take care of herself in any way. For all the various items of damage, the plaintiffs were awarded $11,037,964. The damages included home care, residential care, noneconomic losses, and economic losses. The Rhode Island Supreme Court determined that bystander emotional distress claims are not compensable absent some physical symptomology. *Reilly v United States*, 665 FSupp 976 (D RI 1987), later proceeding 538 A2d 155 (RI 1988), ctfd ques ans, 547 A2d 894 (1988).

The infant plaintiff suffered prenatal injury caused by the defendant's negligent response to the baby's shoulder dyscotia. The child's shoulder was lodged against the mother's pubic bone and the doctor pulled on the baby with such force as to tear the brachial nerves. The child was awarded $175,000 for loss of earning capacity, $150,000 general damages, $8,266 for future medical expenses, and the mother was awarded $25,000 for her mental anguish. *Jackson v Huang*, 514 So2d 727 (LaA 1987), cert den 518 So2d 1050 (1988), later proceeding, 519 So2d 119 (1988).

The parents of an infant who suffered permanent brain damage as a result of the failure to treat the mother for a condition known as *abruptio placentae* were permitted to recover a total of $100,000 for the loss of love and companionship and injury to the parent-child relationship. *Trevino v United States*, 804 F2d 1512 (9th Cir Wa 1986), cert den, 108 SCt 70 (1987).

A father was permitted to recover for his emotional distress suffered as a result of the outrageous conduct of the physician in playing "Russian roulette" when he failed to promptly attend to the birth of the father's infant, the result of which was severe and permanent physical and mental disabilities to the infant. There was sufficient evidence to conclude that the conduct of the defendant was so extreme and outrageous as to permit recovery. Even the defendant's own expert witness agreed that the defendant's conduct could be termed egregious. The evidence clearly showed that the father was present at the hospital, that he was aware of difficulty with the delivery, that he knew the defendant failed to attend the labor and delivery, that he witnessed efforts to resuscitate the infant and the infant's poor physical condition when she was taken from the delivery room, and he witnessed the condition of his wife on her exit from the delivery room. *Boyd v Bulala*, 647 FSupp 781 (WD Va 1986), reconsideration den, slip op (1987).

The duty of the physician not to negligently injure a child during the birth process is owed to the father as well as to the mother and, therefore, both the father and mother have a cause of action against a physician for negligent injury to a child during the birth process. *Skorlich v East Jefferson General Hosp*, 478 So2d 916 (LaA 1985).

A mother forms a sufficiently close relationship with her fetus during pregnancy so that its stillbirth will foreseeably cause her severe emotional distress. Where the stillbirth results from medical malpractice rather than from natural and unavoidable causes the loss is all the more "poignant" and should be legally redressable. Thus, the emotional distress arising from the sensory impact of the death of the child is compensable as part of the mother's cause of action for malpractice to herself. The sensory perception of the fetus' death and the emotional distress which it causes are aspects of the mother's cause of action for personal injuries which enhance her measure of damages. *Johnson v Superior Court*, 123 CaA3d 1002, 177 CaR 63 (1981).

C. Cause of Action for Wrongful Death of Fetus

1. [§5.54] Generally

In recognizing a wrongful death action for the death of a viable fetus, the court held that an administrator's action brought for wrongful death of a viable fetus must be joined with any claims based on the same acts of alleged negligence brought by the parents in their own right. *DiDonato v Wortman*, 320 NC 423, 358 SE2d 489 (1987).

A child born dead cannot maintain an action at common law for injuries received while in its mother's womb, and consequently, the personal representative could not maintain an action under a wrongful death statute limiting such actions to those which, if death had not ensued, would have entitled the party injured to maintain an action and recover damages. *Smith v Columbus Community Hosp Inc*, 222 Nb 776, 387 NW2d 490 (1986).

In an action for the wrongful death of a fetus the attending physician is under a duty to know the status and well-being of his patient. He is responsible for knowing when fetal abnormalities are occurring and to be with his patient as soon as possible after they begin. In this case he should have been in contact with the hospital or, at least, have assured that hospital personnel would be in contact with him regarding the status of the patient. The fetal tracings showed a baby in distress, which should have been delivered by Caesarean section. The defendant's status made him the only person who could have surgically intervened to deliver the baby. This evidence was sufficient to allow the jury to conclude that the defendant had a duty to report to the hospital, assess the mother and fetus in light of the monitor tracing, and safely deliver the baby. The evidence was sufficient to allow for the conclusion that the defendant's failure to do so resulted in the death of the fetus. *Crooks v Williams*, 508 A2d 912 (DCA 1986).

A wrongful death action against a physician may be brought by the estate of a stillborn fetus. However, the fetus must have been viable at the time the allegedly wrongful act took place. A viable fetus is an independent person with the right to be free of prenatal injury. If a viable fetus is a person at the time of the injury, then the fetus is a person when he dies of those injuries, and it can make no difference in liability under the wrongful death and survival statutes whether the fetus dies of the injuries just prior to or just after the birth. To hold otherwise would perpetuate the injustice the statutes were intended to prevent—that an injury would be inflicted for which no remedy existed and a tortfeasor would escape liability by inflicting injury so severe that death resulted. *Greater Southeast Community Hosp v Williams*, 482 A2d 394 (DCA 1984).

2. [§5.55] Fetus as Person Under Wrongful Death Statute

The plaintiffs brought a cause of action for the wrongful death of their stillborn fetus caused by the defendant's malpractice. The appellate court held that the law in Florida is well settled that a wrongful death claim does not lie for the wrongful death of a fetus, regardless of viability, under §768.19, Fla Stat (1983), because a fetus is not a "person" under the statute. Moreover, the court rejected the claim for negligent infliction of mental distress through medical malpractice because it was, in essence, a claim for the wrongful death of the fetus and the plaintiff's mental suffering associated therewith. Nor could the plaintiffs recover for their mental suffering since that claim, like the negligent infliction of emotional distress claim, was determined to be a thinly disguised claim for the wrongful death of the fetus. *Abdelaziz v AMISUB of Florida, Inc*, 515 So2d 269 (Fl 1987), rev den, 525 So2d 876 (1988).

The North Carolina Supreme Court has held that the word "person" in the Wrongful Death Act includes a viable fetus *en ventre sa mere*. In so doing, it has overruled decisions which are inconsistent with the holding. *DiDonato v Wortman*, 320 NC 423, 358 SE2d 489 (1987).

The South Dakota wrongful death statute [SDCL 21-5-1], as it existed prior to the 1984 amendment, provided a cause of action for the death of a viable, unborn child. The 1984 amendment specifically stated that a viable unborn child was a person within the meaning of the wrongful death statute. *Re Certification of Question of Law from United States District Court*, 387 NW2d 42 (SD 1986).

The Wrongful Death Act provides recovery for damages arising from an injury that causes an individual's death. The words "individual" or "person" have not been construed to include an unborn fetus. A fetus has no cause of action for injury until subsequent live birth. Under the clear language of the statute, there is no cause of action for death where there would be no cause of action for injuries. Therefore, since there is no cause of action for injuries to a living fetus, there can be no cause of action for the death of a fetus. *Witty v American General Capital Distributors Inc*, 727 SW2d 503 (Tx 1987).

In reversing prior holdings, the Pennsylvania Supreme Court extended to the estate of a child born dead the right to institute a survival and wrongful death action for death-dealing injuries suffered while *en ventra sa mere*. A child *en ventra sa mere* is a separate individual from the moment of conception. Live birth is no longer a limiting prerequisite to the maintenance of an action. The child's wrongful death is a separate injury from that of the mother's. The child's wrongful death is compensable in damages and the child's estate is the proper party to seek recovery for the decedent child's funeral and medical expenses and pecuniary losses under the Wrongful Death Statute and for the loss of earning power less the costs of maintenance and for the decedent's pain and suffering under the Survival Statute. *Amadio v Levin*, 509 Pa 199, 501 A2d 1085 (1985).

A viable fetus is a person for purposes of the wrongful death statute. Conditioning a right of action on whether a fatally injured child was born dead or alive is not only an artificial and unreasonable demarcation, but is unjust as well. *Commonwealth v Cass*, 392 Ma 799, 467 NE2d 1324 (1984).

A decision in *State ex rel Hardin v Sanders*, 538 SW2d 336 (Mo 1976), which denied recovery for the death of a viable but unborn child, was overruled in *O'Grady v Brown*, 654 SW2d 904 (Mo 1983). The decision to overrule *Hardin* was based on a legislative change in the state's wrongful death statute. Formerly, recovery could be had under Mo Rev §§537.080–537.100, only where damages would fairly and justly compensate the plaintiff. Subsequently, the language of the wrongful death statute was changed so as to provide compensation for the loss of the companionship, comfort, instruction, guidance, counsel, and support of the one who would have been alive but for the defendants' wrong. Mo Rev Stat §537.090. Permitting the plaintiff to maintain a wrongful death action for the death of a viable fetus would, therefore, be consistent with the broad purpose for which the statute was passed. To hold otherwise would frustrate the remedial purpose for which the statute was intended, the court said.

There is no cause of action for the wrongful death of an unborn or stillborn child. Recognition of such an action must await legislative action. *Kuhnke v Fisher*, 683 P2d 916 (Mt 1984), later app, 740 P2d 625 (1987).

A fetus is not a person within the meaning of a wrongful death statute. *Wilson v Kaiser Foundation Hosps*, 141 CaA3d 891, 190 CaR 649 (1983); *Dunn v Rose Way*, 333 NW2d 830 (Ia 1983); *Raymond v Bartsch*, 84 AD2d 60, 447 NYS2d 32 (1981).

Absent a clear and definitive demonstration of legislative intent to the contrary, the word "person" in the wrongful death statute [Az Rev Stat §12-611 et seq] encompasses a stillborn, viable fetus. The overall legislative policy of compensation and protection for a fetus militates in favor of construing the wrongful death statute to give parents a remedy when their viable child is negligently killed. It is more sensible to permit recovery by the survivors of a viable fetus than to impose an artificial cutoff by permitting recovery if the injured child survives or is born alive and then dies, but prohibiting recovery for anyone if the viable child fails to survive through the moment of delivery. Such a narrow construction of "person" would not only deny compensation to the survivors, but would also run contrary to the apparent legislative objective of providing protection for the fetus. *Summerfield v Superior Court*, 144 Az 467, 698 P2d 712 (Az 1985).

The wrongful death statute, ND Cen Code §32-21-01, is a remedial statute whose purpose is to provide a right of action against one whose tortious conduct causes the death of another. The statute authorizes a wrongful death action against one whose tortious conduct caused the death of a viable unborn child. *Hopkins v McBane*, 359 NW2d 862 (ND 1984).

3. [§5.56] Viability Requirement

There is a cause of action in North Carolina for the wrongful death of a viable fetus. In this case the plaintiff wife suffered from hypertension, a known risk factor in causing growth retardation in fetuses. The defendant doctor was aware of the plaintiff's hypertension but did nothing to warn her of the risks it posed to her baby; nor did he properly treat the hypertension or advise the plaintiff on ways to control it. Approximately seven months into her pregnancy, the plaintiff began experiencing abdominal pain so severe she want to the hospital where a test was administered. The results of the test were relayed to the defendant, who misinterpreted the results and ordered that the plaintiff simply be sent home with medication for the pain. On other occasions, the plaintiff saw the defendant on account of her severe abdominal pain. The defendant continued to misinterpret the results of tests given at those times. Only after the plaintiff told the defendant that she no longer felt any fetal movement were more tests ordered. These tests confirmed that the approximately 34-week-old fetus was dead. The complaint alleged that the death of the stillborn child was the proximate result of the defendant's negligence in failing to properly treat the plaintiff's hypertension, his failure to properly advise her of ways to control her hypertension, his misreading of the non-stress tests, and his failure to order more complete tests to ascertain the cause of the episodes of extreme pain. These allegations were clearly sufficient to make out a claim for the negligent obstetrical care of the plaintiff and her baby by the defendant. Therefore, the estate of the stillborn baby could pursue a cause of action for the injuries suffered by the fetus caused by the negligence of the physician. *Ledford v Martin*, 87 NC App 88, 359 SE2d 505 (1987), rev den, 321 NC 473, 365 SE2d 1 (1988).

At the time the trial court dismissed this wrongful death claim, the courts of North Carolina held that a stillborn fetus was not a "person" whose personal representative could sue for the fetus's wrongful death. However, since that time, the Supreme Court has held that the language of the wrongful death statute, its legislative history, and recognition of the statute's broadly remedial objectives permitted an action to recover for the destruction of a viable fetus *en ventre sa mere*. The appellate court held that although this action was begun before the Supreme Court's determination, there was no reason why the Court's holding should not be applied retroactively to this case. The purview of the wrongful death remedy only extends to the death of a viable fetus. A viable fetus is, by definition, capable of life independent of its mother. A viable fetus is genetically complete and can be taxonomically distinguished from nonhuman life forms. Although there is apparently no clear medical consensus as to the specific gestational age at which this capability is currently achieved, a gestational range of 20 to 26 weeks has been suggested. The determination of a fetus's viability is a question of fact. In addition to alleging the death of a viable fetus, the plaintiffs must allege facts showing the defendants breached a duty to the fetus such that the decedent could have maintained an action for negligence or some other misconduct if he had survived. The court noted that a portion of the defendants' negligence necessarily occurred after fetal viability was achieved, since the defendants' failure to treat the diabetic condition of the mother continued until the fetus had reached 40 weeks of gestational age. The plaintiffs had therefore sufficiently alleged that the defendants breached the duty owed their fetus after it had become viable. Given the apparent state of current medical capability and the ongoing nature of the defendants' failure to treat the mother's diabetes, the plaintiffs' pleadings disclosed no facts which would, as a matter of law, prohibit their proving that the defendants breached a duty of care to their fetus. Therefore, the court reversed the summary dismissal of the plaintiffs' wrongful death claim. *Johnson v Ruark Obstetrics & Gynecology Associates*, 89 NC App 154, 365 SE2d 909 (1988), rev gtd, 322 NC 606, 370 SE2d 246 (1988).

In order to bring a wrongful death action for the death of a fetus, the fetus must have been viable at the time of the injury. *Summerfield v Superior Court* 144 Az 467, 698 P2d 712 (Az 1985) [construing Az Rev Stat §12-611 et seq.].

A child must be born alive to be recognized as a "person" within the meaning of G.S. 28 A-18-2. *DiDonato v Wortman*, 80 NC App 117, 341 SE2d 58 (1986).

A cause of action may be brought against a tortfeasor for the wrongful death of an unborn child as long as the child was viable at the time of death. *Hopkins v McBane*, 359 NW2d 862 (ND 1984) [construing ND CEN CODE §32-21-01.]

4. [§5.57] Live Birth Requirement

Live birth is required for a child to have a cause of action for prenatal injuries. Similarly, where there has been no live birth, the clear, unambiguous language of the Wrongful Death Act precludes recovery for the death of a fetus. *Witty v American General Capital Distributors Inc*, 727 SW2d 503 (Tx 1987).

It is not necessary for a fetus to be born alive in order to bring a wrongful death action for the death of the fetus. It is more sensible to permit recovery by the survivors of a viable fetus than to impose an artificial cutoff by permitting recovery if the injured child survives or is born alive and then dies, but prohibiting recovery for anyone if the viable child fails to survive through the moment of delivery. *Summerfield v Superior Court*, 144 Az 467, 698 P2d 712 (Az 1985) [construing AZ REV STAT §12-611 et seq.].

5. [§5.58] Damages

Lost income damages, normally available under the Wrongful Death Act, cannot be recovered in an action for the wrongful death of a stillborn child. However, damages for the pain and suffering of a decedent fetus are recoverable if they can be reasonably established. Medical and funeral expenses as well as punitive and nominal damages are just as susceptible to proof as in any other tort case and will be allowed where appropriate. *DiDonato v Wortman*, 320 NC 423, 358 SE2d 489 (1987).

A jury verdict of $125,000 in a wrongful death action involving an unborn child was affirmed on appeal. The court noted that while the statutory scheme in the wrongful death statute provides compensation to the next of kin for pecuniary loss as a result of a wrongful death, it is extremely difficult to provide satisfactory evidence directed to the issues of earning power and probable contribution to the parents, in the case of an infant or young child. Therefore, the court noted, that there is a rebuttable presumption of pecuniary loss, which is usually accompanied by some supporting evidence. The court said that while it may have awarded a considerably smaller sum, it found the question properly to have been for the jury, and it would not disturb the jury's award. *Jones v Karraker*, 109 IlA3d 363, 64 Il Dec 868, 440 NE2d 420 (1982), affd, 98 Il2d 487, 75 Il Dec 233, 457 NE2d 23 (1983).

D. [§5.59] Cause of Action by Parents for Death of a Fetus, Element of Parents' Damages

The plaintiffs sought recovery for the wrongful death of their stillborn child, the pain and suffering of the plaintiff wife, and the loss of the wife's consortium for the plaintiff husband. The court held that the mental suffering of the wife was clearly a foreseeable consequence of the obstetrical care. A fetus is connected to its mother in the most intimate of ways. Further, the plaintiff's mental suffering was not remote since she suffered physical injury in enduring severe abdominal pain and in having to undergo surgery. The abdominal pain and surgery were sufficient to constitute the "physical injury" required to support a claim for the negligent infliction of mental suffering. The plaintiff set forth facts sufficient to support a claim for mental anguish suffered by the plaintiff wife as a proximate result of the defendant's negligent obstetrical care. Additionally, the plaintiff husband has an actionable claim for loss of consortium. Loss of consortium damages are recognized in North Carolina as ancillary to a claim for personal injury brought by the spouse of the person seeking loss of consortium damages. *Ledford v Martin*, 87 NC App 88, 359 SE2d 505 (1987), rev den, 321 NC 473, 365 SE2d 1 (1988).

In their individual capacities, both parents claimed damages arising from the emotional distress of enduring the labor with the knowledge that their unborn child was dead, the delivery of a dead child, and the mental distress resulting from the dramatic circumstances surrounding the stillbirth of their child. The court noted that while the prohibition against recovery for the distress of another is no longer absolute, the trial judge may nevertheless be required to weigh public policy limitations on negligence liability where the plaintiff's injuries are arguably too remote as a matter of law. As to the "physical injury" requirement for negligently inflicted emotional distress, a physical "injury" is not required in North Carolina where, coincident in time or place with the occurrence producing the mental stress, some actual physical impact is caused to the plaintiff. However, absent some impact, the emotional distress claimant must manifest some resulting physical injury. Treating the mother's allegations as true, the court noted that she suffered not one, but two, physical injuries as a result of the defendants' failure to treat her diabetes. First, her own incipient diabetes remained untreated for over nine months. Second, the fetus attached to her body died of malnutrition arising from the defendant's failure to treat her diabetes. Under these circumstances, the physical injury to the fetus was also a physical injury to the mother which gave rise to her individual action for mental anguish. Therefore, the trial court erroneously dismissed the mother's claim for mental anguish arising from the death of the fetus. Moreover, the court held that the father should be permitted to introduce evidence that his mental distress resulted in the necessary physical injury. The court also noted that the father's damages were not, as a matter of law, so removed in time or location from the injuries to his wife and child that recovery should be barred as a matter of public policy. Nor would it be too highly extraordinary that the defendants' causing the fetus's death would in turn cause the father's emotional distress; on the contrary, this would seem to be the ordinary result of such negligence. Moreover, the court could not say, as a matter of law, that allowing the father's claim for emotional distress for the death of the child would place a burden on physicians any less reasonable than that already imposed with respect to the physician's treatment of the mother, nor should there be an increased possibility of fraudulent claims given the clearly traumatic circumstances of the case. The plaintiffs also sought to recover certain increased medical expenses as well as funeral bills. Such damages may only be recovered by the administrator of the fetal estate pursuant to an action under §28A-18-2. Both parents also claimed all costs associated with medical care and lost wages during the entire term of a full-term pregnancy which resulted in fetal death *in utero*. Insofar as such costs and lost wages exceed the administrator's possible recovery under the wrongful death statute, such damages are compensable only in connection with the mother's, rather than the father's, injuries, since the father's emotional injuries only arose at the end of the pregnancy. However, since the mother herself was injured by the defendant's failure to treat her diabetes, the court could not say as a matter of law that she had not stated a claim for damages apart from her emotional distress arising from the death of her child. The court, therefore, held that the mother should be allowed to prove she incurred these other damages throughout her pregnancy as a result of defendants' acts and omissions. The trial court erroneously dismissed the administrator's wrongful death claim, as well as the parents' claims for negligently inflicted emotional distress, and the mother's claim for other damages. *Johnson v Ruark Obstetrics & Gynecology Associates*, 89 NC App 154, 365 SE2d 909 (1988), rev gtd, 322 NC 606, 370 SE2d 246 (1988).

Injury to an unborn child constitutes injury to the mother, and she may recover for such injury and mental suffering associated with a stillbirth. She is not entitled, however, to damages ordinarily recoverable in a wrongful death action. For example, a mother may not recover for anticipated loss of the child's society, companionship, comfort, or guidance. She may not be compensated for an expected loss of income of the child or for services, protection, care, or assistance expected to be provided by the child had he or she lived. An award of $750,000 in compensatory damages was held to be not excessive where the jury could have concluded from the proof that the plaintiff suffered mental anguish in many ways. For example, she was permitted to lie conscious in a hospital for nearly two hours knowing that the heartbeat of her unborn child was diminishing steadily. She was bound to have been aware that her unborn child was in danger of dying, and yet her physician who lived minutes from the hospital failed to appear and care for her and the fetus. She undoubtedly knew that her own condition was extremely grave. She was forced to deliver spontaneously and unattended a dead child. Furthermore, the plaintiff was pregnant with a male child, which, as the evidence showed, she and her husband had eagerly anticipated. During her pregnancy, her toxemia was permitted to worsen to an extreme degree. According to the evidence, her labor while in the hospital was tumultuous because of the untreated toxemia. It was clear from the evidence that the plaintiff suffered severe emotional distress. *Modaber v Kelley*, 232 Va 60, 348 SE2d 233 (1986).

The plaintiffs lost their fetus as a result of a complete hysterectomy which was performed on the wife after a serum pregnancy test was administered and the results of this test were negligently and erroneously reported as negative. However, the plaintiffs' claim was barred by the statute of limitations where the plaintiffs were informed within a few days after surgery that the wife had been pregnant and that as a result of the operation she lost the fetus, but the plaintiffs did not even request hospital records for three years subsequent to the operation. *Price v United States*, 775 F2d 1491 (11th Cir Fl 1985).

The plaintiff, whose fetus was killed as a result of an injury in the employment setting, could not recover under a common-law claim for mental anguish suffered as a result of the loss of her fetus because this claim was barred under the Worker's Compensation Act. *Witty v American General Capital Distributors Inc*, 727 SW2d 503 (Tx 1987).

Absent independent physical injury, a plaintiff may not recover for emotional and psychic harm as a result of a stillbirth. Further, a plaintiff may not recover for her labor pains, since they are incident to childbirth and unrelated to the stillbirth. *Wittrock v Maimonides*

Medical Center-Maimonides Hosp, 501 NYS2d 684 (App Div 1986), later proceeding, 119 AD2d 747, 501 NYS2d 764 (1986).

III. MISCELLANEOUS RIGHTS AND ENTITLEMENTS OF FETUS

A. [§5.60] Fetus as Person Under 42 USC §1983 and Fourteenth Amendment

FETAL RIGHTS: DEFINING "PERSON" UNDER 42 USC §1983, 1983 Univ Il LR 347.

THE FETUS UNDER SECTION 1983: STILL STRUGGLING FOR RECOGNITION, 34 Syracuse LR 1029 (1983).

D. [§5.63] Appointment of Guardian on Behalf of Fetus

The mother controls the fetus until viability occurs. That control is a constitutional right. If the mother is incompetent, control must be exercised through a guardian. However, the appointment of a guardian for the fetus prior to its viability is improper. Further, a fetus is not a person and, therefore, where the law provides for civil commitment procedures and authorizes the appointment of a guardian ad litem and attorney for a "minor," there is no reference to a fetus. The court may appoint a guardian ad litem for an infant or alleged incompetent person on its own motion. However, this precludes the appointment of a guardian for a fetus in light of the court's determination that a fetus is not a person. *Re D K*, 204 NJ Super 205, 497 A2d 1298 (1985).

The appointment of a guardian ad litem for an unborn child was appropriate where the alleged father of the unborn child had died and his estate was pending in a surrogate court. It may be generally concluded that a fetus does not have a legal personality or identity until it is born alive, the court said. However, historically, the law has indulged in the fiction that for the purpose of inheritance or other devolution of property, an unborn child, while not a person, has certain legal rights, contingent upon being born alive which are entitled to protection. It was noted that the letters of guardianship, would terminate in the absence of a live birth. *Matter of Thomas*, 118 Misc2d 456, 460 NYS2d 716 (1983).

CHAPTER 6

Prenatal Stage: Emerging Theories of Liability

New Section in This Topic:

[§6.36.1] Market-Share Alternate Liability

I. WRONGFUL BIRTH

A. In General

1. [§6.1] Definition

Wrongful birth is a cause of action brought by the family of an infant which seeks to impose liability on a defendant for damages and expenses incurred by the parents of a child born with birth defects when, but for the negligence of the defendant, the child would not have been conceived or carried to term. Its premise is that but for the negligence of the defendant, the child would not have been born. In this type of action the parents of the child assert that the physician's negligence precluded their making an informed decision about whether to have a child, and that they would have avoided conception or terminated the pregnancy had they been properly advised of the risk of congenital impairment. Recovery is sought for the expenses of caring for the disabled child, and for the pain and suffering of the parents. *Blake v Cruz*, 698 P2d 315, 10 FLR 1660 (Id 1984).

The term wrongful birth describes a cause of action brought by parents when negligent medical treatment deprives them of the option to terminate a pregnancy to avoid the birth of a defective child. *Procanik By Procanik v Cillo*, 97 NJ 339, 478 A2d 755 (1984), on remd, 206 NJ Super 270, 502 A2d 94 (1985).

A wrongful birth action is an action brought by parents against a physician who failed to inform the parents of the increased possibility that the mother would give birth to a child suffering from birth defects thereby precluding an informed decision by the parents about whether to have the child. *Harbeson v Parke-Davis*, 98 Wa2d 460, 656 P2d 483 (1983) later proceeding 746 F2d 517 (9th Cir 1984).

Collins, AN OVERVIEW AND ANALYSIS: PRENATAL TORTS, PRECONCEPTION TORTS, WRONGFUL LIFE, WRONGFUL DEATH, AND WRONGFUL BIRTH: TIME FOR A NEW FRAMEWORK 21 J Family L 677 (1983-1984).

2. [§6.2] Background

The plaintiff parents alleged that they were tortiously injured because the mother was deprived of the option of making an informed and meaningful decision either to abort the already existing and defective fetus, a decision which, at least during the first trimester of pregnancy, is not subject to state interference, or to give birth to a potentially defective child. In this case of first impression in Illinois, the Supreme Court determined that an action for wrongful birth of a genetically or congenitally defective child may be maintained by the parents of the child. *Siemieniec v Lutheran General Hosp*, 117 Il2d 230, 111 Il Dec 302, 512 NE2d 691 (1987).

The Supreme Court of Utah held that assuming, but not deciding, that should Utah jurisprudence recognize an action for wrongful birth, the cause of action would accrue upon the birth of the child not prior to the birth. *Payne v Myers*, 743 P2d 186 (1987).

A parental claim for wrongful birth states a cause of action sounding in negligence or medical malpractice. *Phillips v United States*, 566 FSupp 1 (D SC 1981), later proceeding, 575 FSupp 1309 (D SC 1983).

Even though a father has no legally enforceable right to either compel or prevent an abortion, he has a right to participate in the decision. Thus, he shares the mother's right to seek damages for the negligent wrongful birth of a child because the father shares the legal obligation to provide for the child's care and support. The father's right is not dependent upon the mother's cause of action but is his individually. *DiNatale v Lieberman*, 409 So2d 512 (Fl 1982).

A wrongful birth action conforms to the structure of tort principles. Recognition of wrongful birth claims is a logical and necessary development of tort law. *Harbeson v Parke-Davis*, 98 Wa2d 460, 656 P2d 483 (1983) later proceeding 746 F2d 517 (9th Cir 1984).

New Hampshire now recognizes a cause of action for wrongful birth. The wrongful birth cause of action is unique. Although it involves an allegation of medical malpractice, it is not a claim arising from physical injury. It is instead based on a negligent invasion of the parental right to decide whether to avoid the birth of a child with congenital defects. When parents are denied this opportunity to make this decision, important personal rights may be impaired, including an interest in avoiding special expenses necessitated by the condition of a child born with defects, an interest in preventing the sorrow and anguish that may befall the parents of such a child, and an interest in preserving personal autonomy, which may include the making of informed reproductive choices. *Smith v Cote*, 128 NH 231, 513 A2d 341 (1986).

A cause of action for wrongful birth should be recognized. The failure of a physician to discover a birth defect and to advise the parents of its consequences will give rise to a cause of action on their behalf for the extraordinary expenses incurred as a result of the child being born with a birth defect. In this situation, the negligence based on a duty owed to furnish reasonable medical care and to advise the parents of the possibility of birth defects can be demonstrated. *James G v Caserta*, 332 SE2d 872 (WV 1985).

Donovan, WRONGFUL BIRTH AND WRONGFUL LIFE: QUESTIONS OF PUBLIC POLICY, 28 Loyola LR 77 (1982).

Zaslow, WRONGFUL CONCEPTION, WRONGFUL BIRTH, AND WRONGFUL LIFE: THE PARAMETERS OF LIABILITY, 10 Legal Aspects of Medical Practice 4 (May 1982).

DAMAGES: RECOVERY OF DAMAGES IN ACTIONS FOR WRONGFUL BIRTH, WRONGFUL LIFE AND WRONGFUL CONCEPTION, 23 Washburn L Journal 309 (1984).

WASHINGTON RECOGNIZES WRONGFUL BIRTH AND WRONGFUL LIFE—A CRITICAL ANALYSIS—*Harbeson v Parke-Davis, Inc*, 656 P2d 489 (Wash), 58 Wash LR 649 (1983).

WRONGFUL BIRTH: WHO OWES WHAT TO WHOM AND WHY?, 40 Washington & Lee LR 123.

CAUSE OF ACTION FOR WRONGFUL BIRTH OR WRONGFUL LIFE, 7 Shepard's Causes of Action 589 (1985).

Snyderman, WRONGFUL LIFE AND WRONGFUL BIRTH CLAIMS: JUDICIAL RECOGNITION AND ACCEPTANCE, 32 Med Trial Tech Q 15 (1985).

WRONGFUL LIFE AND WRONGFUL BIRTH: THE CURRENT STATUS OF NEGLIGENT GENETIC COUNSELING, 3 Cooley L Rev 175 (1985).

3. [§6.3] Statutory Limitation or Denial of Cause of Action

During the course of the plaintiff's prenatal care, the defendant physician discovered the fetus was suffering from hydrocephalus, a condition which results from backing up of cerebrospinal fluid into the brain ventricles. This condition usually produces retarded brain development. The plaintiff gave birth to a child who was born with virtually no brain. Mother and child sued the doctor, alleging the doctor was negligent in failing to disclose material information concerning abortion as an alternative course of treatment. The patient argued that she told the doctor she could not raise an abnormal child and that had the doctor informed her of abortion as an available alternative, she would have chosen that course of treatment. The doctor argued, and the Supreme Court agreed, that when the doctor first discovered the hydrocephalus, the fetus was viable and thus abortion was not an available alternative. Therefore, the doctor had no duty to disclose information about an alternative treatment not legally available to the patient. Moreover, the doctor's duty to inform his patient of material risks and alternative treatments is judged by the patient's need to know. As a defense, a physician may plead and prove that a patient knew of the risks or alternatives, or show that an emergency existed to prevent consent from being given. The patient could not recover in this case because the record of the proceedings clearly showed she knew that abortion was an alternative treatment. The patient had consulted the doctor during a previous pregnancy where she sought an abortion although she later decided against that option. Further, the doctor had no duty to inform her that abortion, although prohibited in Oklahoma at her stage of pregnancy, was available in other states. *Spencer v Seikel*, 742 P2d 1126 (Ok 1987).

Section 188.130, RSMo 1968, precludes wrongful life and wrongful birth actions. The effective date of this statute was August 13, 1986. Moreover, the Missouri Supreme Court held that neither of these causes of action would have been recognized in 1983, some three years prior to the adoption of the statute. The court focused on the difficulty, if not impossibility, of assessing damages in a wrongful life action. The court denied recovery on the wrongful birth action based on the lack of a causal connection between the defendant's alleged negligence and the plaintiff's injury. The heart of the problem in these cases is that the physician cannot be said to have caused the defect. The disorder is genetic and not the result of any injury negligently inflicted by the doctor. In addition, it is incurable and was incurable from the moment of conception. Thus the doctor's negligent failure to detect it during prenatal examination cannot be considered a cause of the condition by analogy to those cases in which a doctor has failed to make a timely diagnosis of a curable disease. The child's handicap is an inexorable result of conception and birth. *Wilson v Kuenzi*, 751 SW2d 741 (Mo 1988), cert den, 57 USLW 3259 (1988).

Despite a strong trend among jurisdictions to recognize a cause of action for wrongful birth, the court refused to recognize such a cause of action in the absence of a clear mandate by the legislature. *Azzolino v Dingfelder*, 315 NC 103, 337 SE2d 528 (1985), cert den 107 SCt 131, 93 LE2d 75 (1986).

MINN STAT §145.424, prohibiting the maintenance of a wrongful birth action was determined to be constitutional. *Hickman v Group Health Plan Inc*, 396 NW2d 10 (Mn 1986).

A wrongful birth action sounds in professional negligence and is governed by the medical malpractice statute of limitations. A malpractice cause of action accrues in accordance with the provisions of the medical malpractice statute [MI STAT ANN §27A.5838] which provides that the two-year limitation period runs from the date of the last treatment for a matter out of which the claim arose or six months from the date when the malpractice was or should have been discovered, whichever is later. Thus, where the last day of treatment for the plaintiff-mother relative to determining whether she was a carrier of sickle cell anemia was 1967, the unhealthy child was born in 1971 and was diagnosed as suffering from sickle cell anemia, but the action was not brought until 1979, the court held that the plaintiff-mother should have discovered that her physician had failed to predict the sickle cell anemia in or about 1971. *Dorlin v Providence Hosp*, 118 MiA 831, 325 NW2d 600 (1982).

UTAH CODE ANN §§78-11-24 and 78-11-25 prohibit the bringing of an action for wrongful birth.

WRONGFUL BIRTH AND WRONGFUL LIFE: ANALYSIS OF THE CAUSES OF ACTION AND THE IMPACT OF UTAH'S STATUTORY BREAKWATER, 1984 Utah L Rev 833 (1984).

B. Elements of Cause of Action

1. [§6.4] Generally

In reversing the lower court's dismissal of a wrongful birth claim, the appellate court held that the mother was entitled to maintain an action for wrongful birth to recover extraordinary medical and other health care expenses to be incurred as a result of the child's mental and physical abnormalities. In construing the complaint in the light most favorable to the plaintiff, the court assumed as true that at the time of the pregnancy, the defendant failed to properly counsel the plaintiff regarding the advisability of performing an amniocentesis; this failure to recommend amniocentesis constituted a departure from acceptable medical practice; had the defendant recommended an amniocentesis, the plaintiff would have submitted to the procedure; the results of an amniocentesis would have indicated that the child, if born, would be afflicted with Down's Syndrome; and upon being notified of this fact, the plaintiff would have terminated the pregnancy. Thus, under standard principles of tort law, the plaintiff met her burden to establish the elements of a negligence action against the physician. *Haymon v Wilkerson*, 535 A2d 880 (DCA 1987).

In a case of first impression, the New Hampshire Supreme Court recognized a cause of action for wrongful birth. *Smith v Cote*, 128 NH 231, 513 A2d 341 (1986).

This is a case of first impression in North Carolina premised on pre-conception negligence resulting in the birth of a defective child. The plaintiffs were given incorrect information regarding a chromosome abnormality based on a negligent and incorrect analysis of genetic tests completed on a child of the plaintiffs who had died of multiple birth defects. The plaintiffs were informed that based on the results of genetic tests showing no chromosomal deficiencies in the child that died, the plaintiffs' chances of having a normal child were similar to those of other couples in the general population. Further, because of the incorrect reading of the genetic tests, neither of the plaintiffs were tested for abnormal genetic traits or other chromosomal variances. As a result, the plaintiffs conceived a child who was born with multiple birth defects and who was shown to have a chromosomal abnormality. Upon reexamination of the initial genetic tests, it was shown that the child who died had also suffered from the same chromosomal abnormality that the plaintiffs' living child now suffers from. In this case of first impression in North Carolina, the federal court held that a cause of action for wrongful birth exists in North Carolina when a health care provider negligently provides counseling and information which induces a couple to conceive a defective child. *Gallagher v Duke Univ*, 638 FSupp 979 (MD NC 1986).

The injury in a wrongful birth claim is the birth of the child. This is the inevitable consequence of recognizing the parents' right to avoid the birth of a defective child. *Blake v Cruz*, 698 P2d 315 (Id 1984).

The parents of a birth defective child have a cause of action for wrongful birth. *Goldberg v Ruskin*, 128 IlA3d 1029, 84 Il Dec 1, 471 NE2d 530 (1984), affd in part, 113 Il2d 482, 101 Il Dec 818, 499 NE2d 406 (1986).

The recognition that the birth of a defective child is an actionable injury flows from the parents' right to avoid the birth of such a child. However, the real question as to injury is not the existence of the injury, but the extent of that injury. *Harbeson v Parke-Davis*, 98 Wa2d 460, 656 P2d 483 (1983) later proceeding 746 F2d 517 (9th Cir 1984).

2. [§6.5] Duty

The plaintiffs alleged that their child suffers from birth defects caused by the failure of the defendant physician to diagnose an illness of the mother in the first trimester of pregnancy, thereby depriving the parents of the option of aborting the unborn child. Until now, the Michigan court has not directly faced the wrongful birth issue. The court determined that the issue was whether physicians have a duty to ascertain and advise parents of information necessary for the parents to exercise the options provided by *Roe*, whatever the physician personally believes. If a physician breaches the appropriate duty under the facts of a case, and it can be established that the parents would have avoided or terminated the pregnancy, the necessary causal connection is established. The parents should recover for their extraordinary medical expenses and the extraordinary costs of raising the child, as well as for the emotional harm they have suffered. As long as abortion remains an option allowed by law, the physician owes a duty to furnish patients with adequate information for them to be able to decide whether to choose that course of action. *Proffitt v Bartolo*, 162 MiA 35, 412 NW2d 232 (1987), app den, 430 Mi 860 (1988).

If a plaintiff establishes that a physician-patient relationship with respect to her pregnancy existed between the defendants and her, it follows that the defendants assumed a duty to use reasonable care in attending and treating her. The plaintiff contracted rubella early in her pregnancy and while she was under the defendants' care, the defendants negligently failed to test for and discover in a timely manner her exposure to the disease. Moreover, the defendants negligently failed to advise the plaintiff of the potential for birth defects in a fetus exposed to rubella, thereby depriving her of the knowledge necessary to make an informed decision as to whether to give birth to a potentially impaired child. The due care standard may have required the defendants to ensure that the plaintiff had the opportunity to make an informed decision regarding the procreative options available to her. It is a question of fact whether this standard required the defendants, at an appropriate stage of the plaintiff's pregnancy, to test for, diagnose, and disclose her exposure to rubella. The standard is defined by reference to the standards and recommended practices and procedures of the medical profession, the training, experience, and professed degree of skill of the average medical practitioner, and all other relevant circumstances. If the applicable standard of care required the defendants to test for and diagnose the rubella infection in a timely manner and to inform the plaintiff of the possible effects of the virus on the child's health and the defendants fail to fulfill this obligation, then the defendants breached their duty of due care. *Smith v Cote*, 128 NH 231, 513 A2d 341 (1986).

In *Phillips v United States*, 566 FSupp 1 (D SC 1981), later proceeding, 575 FSupp 1309 (D SC 1983), the court rendered findings of fact and conclusions of law with regard to *Phillips v United States*, 508 FSupp 522 (D SC 1981). In the later decision the court noted that while the two most important indicia of increased fetal risk of Down's Syndrome are advanced maternal age and prior afflicted children, a positive family history of Down's Syndrome does constitute "a serious and important risk factor," and the appearance of that risk factor necessitates further genetic counseling. Thus, where the mother's physicians knew of the occurrence of Down's Syndrome in the mother's family, the failure of her physicians to provide adequate genetic counseling and prenatal testing in light of the positive family history of Down's Syndrome constituted a breach of the applicable standard of obstetrical care, which precluded an informed parental decision about whether to avoid the birth of a severely afflicted child.

An attending physician is under a duty, when treating a middle aged woman, to test for Down's Syndrome and to advise the parents of the results of that test, leaving to the parents the decision whether to seek an abortion or permit the fetus to develop to the point of delivery. *Call v Kezirian*, 135 CaA3d 189, 185 CaR 103 (1982).

Parents have a right to prevent the conception or birth of children suffering defects. Physicians owe a duty to parents to preserve that right. Physicians may breach this duty either by failure to impart material information or by negligent performance of a procedure to prevent the birth of a defective child. The parents' right to prevent the birth of a defective child and the correlative duty flowing from that right is the basis of the wrongful birth action. *Harbeson v Parke-Davis*, 98 Wa2d 460, 656 P2d 483 (1983) later proceeding 746 F2d 517 (9th Cir 1984).

The failure of a physician to discover a birth defect and to advise the parents of its consequences gives rise to a cause of action on their behalf for the extraordinary expenses incurred as a result of the child being born with such a birth defect. In this situation, the negligence based on a duty owed to furnish reasonable medical care and to advise the parents of the possibility of birth defects can be demonstrated. *James G v Caserta*, 332 SE2d 872 (WV 1985).

3. [§6.6] Proximate Cause

A plaintiff can establish causation in a wrongful birth suit if the plaintiff can show that but for the defendants' negligent failure to inform her of the risks of bearing a child with birth defects, she would have obtained an abortion. Naturally, establishment of causation will depend on proof of a counterfactual, i.e., that had the plaintiff been properly informed, she would have chosen to terminate the pregnancy. This circumstance, however, does not entail inability to establish that proof; it is present in every informed consent case involving a subjective standard of causation. *Smith v Cote*, 128 NH 231, 513 A2d 341 (1986).

A proximate cause relationship between a breach of the applicable standard of obstetrical care and the birth of a severely afflicted child was held to exist where physicians failed to provide adequate genetic counseling and prenatal testing in light of the plaintiff-mother's positive family history of Down's Syndrome. *Phillips v United States*, 566 FSupp 1 (D SC 1981), later proceeding, 575 FSupp 1309 (D SC 1983).

The element of proximate cause in a wrongful birth action does not present an obstacle to the wrongful birth analysis, assuming that the parents allege and show that, but for the physician's negligence, they would have terminated the pregnancy or avoided conception, and therefore no child would have been born. *Blake v Cruz*, 698 P2d 315 (Id 1984).

Proximate cause must be established by, first, a showing that the breach of duty was a cause in fact of the injury, and, second, a showing that as a matter of law liability should attach. Cause in fact can be established by proving that but for the breach of duty, the injury would not have occurred. As a matter of law in wrongful birth cases, if cause in fact is established, the element of proximate cause is satisfied. *Harbeson v Parke-Davis*, 98 Wa2d 460, 656 P2d 483 (1983) later proceeding 746 F2d 517 (9th Cir 1984).

C. Damages

1. [§6.7] Generally

If a physician breaches the duty to ascertain and advise parents of information necessary for the parents to exercise the options provided by *Roe*, and it can be established that the parents would have avoided or terminated the pregnancy, the parents should recover for their extraordinary medical expenses and the extraordinary costs of raising the child, as well as the emotional harm they have suffered. *Proffitt v Bartolo*, 162 MiA 35, 412 NW2d 232 (1987), app den, 430 Mi 860 (1988).

In a wrongful birth action, the parents, upon proper proof, may recover for the expenses incurred during pregnancy and delivery, the mother's pain and suffering, the father's loss of consortium, service, and society, and their emotional and mental distress associated with the birth of an unplanned and unwanted child, and the unexpected restriction upon their freedom to plan their family. The parents may not, however, recover for the special expenses regarding the child's deformity or for emotional and mental distress associated with the child's deformity. Moreover, the plaintiffs could not recover for the economic costs of rearing an unplanned and unwanted child, expenses of the change in family status, including extra money to compensate for the fact that the mother must spread her society, comfort, care, protection, and support over a larger group, or money to replenish the "family exchequer" so that the child would not deprive the other family members. These are the ordinary vicissitudes that befall any family with the birth of a healthy, normal child. Unfortunately, the child in this case may represent a greater burden than a healthy child, but the burden is the result of the child's albinism which the court determined was not a legal consequence of the defendant's conduct. Therefore, proof of the ordinary economic impact of an additional child would not constitute proof of loss to the parents or family. *Pitre v Opelousas General Hosp*, 530 So2d 1151 (La 1988).

A $970,000 settlement in a wrongful birth action was arrived at in *Graham v Pima Cty*, Pima Cty Super Ct, No 190297 (Jan 18, 1983) 26 American Trial Lawyers Assoc L Rep 284 (Aug 1983).

DAMAGES FOR WRONGFUL BIRTH AND WRONGFUL LIFE IN ILLINOIS, Loyola U Chi LJ 799 (1984).

Scheid, BENEFITS VS BURDENS: THE LIMITATION OF DAMAGES IN WRONGFUL BIRTH, 23 J Fam L 57 (1984-1985).

WRONGFUL BIRTH: THE AVOIDANCE OF CONSEQUENCES DOCTRINE IN MITIGATION OF DAMAGES, 53 Fordham L Rev 1107 (1985).

2. [§6.8] Care and Treatment

The Illinois Supreme Court recognized for the first time an action for the wrongful birth of a genetically or congenitally defective child. The court aligned itself with the majority of jurisdictions which limit the parents' recovery of damages to extraordinary expenses, i.e., medical, hospital, institutional, educational, and otherwise, which are necessary to properly manage and treat the genetic or congenital disorder. *Siemieniec v Lutheran General Hosp*, 117 Il2d 230, 111 Il Dec 302, 512 NE2d 691 (1987).

In seeking to recover the extraordinary and other health care expenses proximately caused by her physician's negligence in this wrongful birth case, the plaintiff sought damages that were proportionate to the defendant's wrongful conduct. By limiting damages to those expenses that were actually attributable to the affliction, the court was not conferring a windfall on the plaintiff. Although the plaintiff may derive pleasure from her daughter, that pleasure will be derived in spite of, rather than because of, her affliction. The plaintiff will receive no compensating pleasure from incurring extraordinary medical expenses on behalf of her daughter. Permitting the recovery of extraordinary expenses avoids the speculative damages issue of concern to most courts. Furthermore, allowing recovery for the negligent deprivation of a woman's right to decide whether to terminate her pregnancy is consistent with the District of Columbia's public policy that physicians should be liable for losses proximately caused by their negligence. The hold otherwise would, in effect, immunize from liability the physician providing inadequate guidance to persons who would choose to exercise their constitutional right to terminate a pregnancy where the child, if born, would suffer from genetic defects. The extraordinary medical expenses attributable to the plaintiff's daughter's physical and mental abnormalities are part of the plaintiff's loss caused by the deprivation of her right to decide whether to terminate her pregnancy. If the plaintiff proves at trial that the defendant deprived her of the parental right to choose whether to avoid the birth of a child afflicted with Down's Syndrome, the defendant can be held liable for the extraordinary medical and other expenses attributable to the care of that child. *Haymon v Wilkerson*, 535 A2d 880 (DCA 1987).

In most jurisdictions, the parents may recover only the extraordinary medical and educational costs attributable to the birth defects. Although the extraordinary costs rule departs from traditional principles of tort damages, it is neither illogical nor unprecedented. The rule represents an application in a tort context of the expectancy rule of damages employed in breach of contract cases. Wrongful birth plaintiffs typically desire a child from the outset. It is the defendant's duty to help them achieve this goal. When the plaintiffs' expectations are frustrated by the defendant's negligence, the extraordinary costs rule merely attempts to put the plaintiffs in the position they expected to be in with the defendant's help. Under this view of the problem ordinary child-rearing costs are analogous to a price the plaintiffs were willing to pay in order to achieve an expected result. According to contract principles, plaintiffs may not have a return in damages of the price and also receive what was to be obtained for the price. Expectancy damages are recoverable in other types of tort cases. The extraordinary costs rule ensures that the parents of a deformed child will recover the medical and educational costs attributed to the child's impairment. At the same time, it establishes a necessary and clearly defined boundary to liability in this area. Because New Hampshire requires parents to support their disabled adult offspring, the parents may recover extraordinary costs incurred both before and after their child attains majority. Recovery may also include compensation for extraordinary maternal care. This may include such parental obligations and duties as feeding, bathing, and exercising the impaired child. A parent may recover for his or her ministrations to his or her child to the extent that such ministrations are made necessary by the child's condition; clearly exceed those ordinarily rendered by parents of a normal child; and are reasonably susceptible to evaluation. Further, to the extent that the parents' emotional distress results in tangible pecuniary losses, such as medical expenses or counseling fees, such losses are recoverable. *Smith v Cote*, 128 NH 231, 513 A2d 341 (1986).

The plaintiff in a wrongful birth action could not recover the costs of the extraordinary expenses which the plaintiff might incur for the continued support and special care of his son, born with thalassemia major, after the child reaches the age of 21. Under New York law, the parent has no legal obligation to continue the support of a child after reaching the age of majority, notwithstanding the plaintiff's assertion of a moral obligation to do so in this case. The plaintiff may be compensated only in the amount that represents his legally cognizable injury, namely the increased financial obligation arising from the extraordinary medical treatment rendered the child during minority. *Bani-Esraili v Lerman*, 69 NY2d 807, 513 NYS2d 382, 505 NE2d 947 (1987).

In a wrongful birth action if a parent can prove that the child will require extraordinary care in the future, then the parent is entitled to recover damages for those extraordinary expenses. *DiNatale v Lieberman*, 409 So2d 512 (Fl 1982).

In a wrongful birth action damages can be recovered to compensate the parents for the costs of the child's medical and hospital care. In addition expenses for the support and maintenance of the child beyond the age of majority are recoverable to the extent such expenses can be reasonably established through competent evidence at trial. Any economic award will be placed in trust for the use and benefit of the child. *Blake v Cruz*, 698 P2d 315 (Id 1984).

Plaintiffs in a wrongful birth action are entitled to damages for all of the extraordinary expenses necessitated by their child's condition. However, the defendant is not liable for all of the expenses incident to raising the child, whether or not those expenses are directly attributable to the child's condition. Thus, under the circumstances of this case, the plaintiff's recovered the following: $124,669 for the reasonable value of care, food, clothing, housing and other necessary items from the child's birth to age 4.4 years; $450,202 for the child's care until he reaches age 18.42 which must be reduced by the cost of raising a normal child until the same age which cost was calculated to be $62,500. Thus, the net allowable economic loss from birth to age 18.4 is $512,371. In addition, the plaintiffs recovered the present value of the element of damages relating to the child's prospective stay in a nursing home from age 18.42 until his 40th birthday of $771,394. Thus, the total economic damages from the child's birth to his life expectancy of 40 years is $1,283,765. *Phillips v United States*, 575 FSupp 1309 (D SC 1983) [South Carolina law].

In a wrongful birth action recovery may include the hospital and medical expenses attributable to the child's birth and to its defective condition. *Harbeson v Parke-Davis*, 98 Wa2d 460, 656 P2d 483 (1983) later proceeding 746 F2d 517 (9th Cir 1984).

In a wrongful birth action, the parents may recover for the extraordinary expenses incurred as a result of the child being born with a birth defect. These extraordinary costs may be recovered not only for the child's minority, but also after the child reaches the age of majority if the child is unable to support himself or herself because of physical or emotional disabilities. *James G v Caserta*, 332 SE2d 872 (WV 1985).

4. [§6.10] Emotional Distress

Damages for emotional distress were initially recoverable in a wrongful birth action in the amount of $500,000. The child's mother testified that she experienced great anguish as a result of her child's condition. She testified that the child's condition had caused marital stress, that she gave up all her social activity, became nervous, and was not able to live a normal life because of the special care required by her son. The court noted that it is also necessary in computing damages for emotional distress that the benefits received by the plaintiffs be calculated in determining a final amount of damages. Under this rule in calculating the plaintiffs' damages, any benefits they derive from the defendant's negligence may properly be offset against the detriments which flow from that conduct in accordance with traditional tort principles. Because the benefits at issue in this case were essentially emotional in nature, the principle applies to the parents' mental suffering and emotional distress. The court found that the benefits flowing from the child's birth despite his condition amounted to 50 percent of the damages for the plaintiffs' mental anguish and emotional distress. Accordingly, the damages attributable to the plaintiffs' emotional distress were reduced to $250,000. *Phillips v United States*, 575 FSupp 1309 (D SC 1983) [South Carolina law].

To the extent that a parent's emotional distress results in tangible pecuniary losses, such as medical expenses and counseling fees, such losses are recoverable. However, parents cannot recover solely for the emotional distress that arises from the birth of a defective child. *Smith v Cote*, 128 NH 231, 513 A2d 341 (1986).

In determining damages for emotional injury in a wrongful birth action, countervailing emotional benefits attributable to the birth of the child should be considered and the award adjusted accordingly. *Blake v Cruz*, 698 P2d 315 (Id 1984).

In a wrongful birth action the parents may recover for emotional injury caused by the birth of the defective child. In considering damages for emotional injury, the jury should be entitled to consider the countervailing emotional benefits attributable to the birth of the child. *Harbeson v Parke-Davis*, 98 Wa2d 460, 656 P2d 483 (1983) later proceeding 746 F2d 517 (9th Cir 1984).

II. WRONGFUL LIFE

A. In General

1. [§6.13] Definition

Wrongful life actions are suits brought by an impaired child in which the child alleges that, but for the defendant doctor's negligent advice to or treatment of the parents, the child would not have been born. The essence of the child's claim is that the defendants wrongfully deprived the parents of information which would have prevented the child's birth. In a wrongful life action, as in any negligence action, the defendant must owe the plaintiff a legal duty, the defendant must breach that duty, and the breach must be a proximate cause of the plaintiff's harm. In wrongful life, the theory is that the physician had a duty adequately to inform the parents, who are acting on behalf of the unborn child, of the probability that the child would be born impaired, and that had the parents been so informed, they would have avoided conception. *Continental Casualty Co v Empire Casualty Co*, 713 P2d 384 (CoA 1985).

In general, in an action for wrongful life, a child who has been born with a disease or other disorder asserts that he or she would not have been born had the physician or other health care professional in question informed his or her parents that the particular ailment might occur. Essential to such an action is the assertion that the parents would not have conceived the child or would have aborted the pregnancy if they had been given the information. *Goldberg v Ruskin*, 113 Il2d 482, 101 Il Dec 818, 499 NE2d 406 (1986).

The term wrongful life refers to a cause of action brought by or on behalf of a defective child who claims that but for the defendant doctor's negligent advice to or treatment of its parents, the child would not have been born. *Procanik By Procanik v Cillo*, 97 NJ 339, 478 A2d 755 (1984), on remd, 206 NJ Super 270, 502 A2d 94 (1985).

Wrongful life is the child's equivalent of the parents' wrongful birth action. *Harbeson v Parke-Davis*, 98 Wa2d 460, 656 P2d 483 (1983).

The underlying theory for a wrongful life action is that a physician or other health care provider failed to discover a birth defect and to advise the parents so that they could intelligently decide whether to forebear having the child or, after the mother has become pregnant, to consider the termination of the pregnancy. *James G v Caserta*, 332 SE2d 872 (WV 1985).

Collins, An Overview and Analysis: Prenatal Torts, Preconception Torts, Wrongful Life, Wrongful Death, and Wrongful Birth: Time for a New Framework, 21 J Family L 677 (1983-1984).

Harbeson v Parke-Davis, Inc: A Major Step Forward in the Evolution of Wrongful Life, 10 J Contemporary Law 203 (1984).

2. [§6.14] Background

Whereas wrongful birth actions have apparently been accepted by all jurisdictions to have considered the issue, wrongful life actions have been received with little favor. *Harbeson v Parke-Davis*, 98 Wa2d 460, 656 P2d 483 (1983) later proceeding 746 F2d 517 (9th Cir 1984).

A child born with physical or mental defects does not have a cause of action against anyone on account of his or her having been born. *DiNatale v Lieberman*, 409 So2d 512 (Fl 1982).

One of the underlying premises in this area of the law is that a birth defect is not curable while the child is in the fetal stage. Consequently, the physician is not being charged with the failure to cure the birth defect, but rather with the failure to give the parents information about it so that an informed choice could be made. This duty to inform does not extend to the unborn child as it is the parents' decision to risk conception or to terminate a pregnancy. Therefore, a claim for wrongful life does not exist in the absence of any statute giving rise to such a cause of action. *James G v Caserta*, 332 SE2d 872 (WV 1985).

The basic rule of tort compensation is that the plaintiff is to be put in the position that he or she would have been in absent the defendant's negligence. In a personal injury case, that standard requires a comparison of the condition that the plaintiff would have been in without the negligence with the plaintiff's actual condition as a result of the defendant's negligence. In this, as in all wrongful life cases, however, there is no allegation that but for the defendant's negligence the child would have had a healthy, unimpaired life. Instead, the claim is that without the doctor's negligence the plaintiff never would have been born. Thus, the cause of action unavoidably involves the relative benefits of an impaired life as opposed to no life at all. All courts, even the ones recognizing a cause of action for wrongful life, have admitted that this calculation is impossible. This holding is not based on a mere difficulty in assessing a dollar amount of damages. It has long been held that imprecision of damages is not a bar to recovery. But this is not just a case in which the damages evade precise measurement. Here, it is impossible to rationally decide whether the plaintiff has been damaged at all. Thus, there is no cause of action for wrongful life. *Nelson v Krusen*, 678 SW2d 918 (Tx 1984), reh ovrld.

Goldstein and Hirsh, WRONGFUL LIFE, 28 Medical Trial Technique Quarterly 279 (1982).

Gray, THE "WRONGFUL LIFE" DILEMMA: COURTS STRUGGLE WITH SUITS BY PARENTS—AND CHILDREN—WHO CLAIM GENETIC DISORDERS SHOULD HAVE BEEN DIAGNOSED, 2 California Lawyer 52 (Sept 1982).

Zaslow, WRONGFUL CONCEPTION, WRONGFUL BIRTH, AND WRONGFUL LIFE: THE PARAMETERS OF LIABILITY, 10 Legal Aspects of Medical Practice 4 (May 1982).

CAUSE OF ACTION FOR WRONGFUL BIRTH OR WRONGFUL LIFE, 7 Shepard's Causes of Action 589 (1985).

Nelson v Krusen: TEXAS DENIES "WRONGFUL LIFE" CLAIM, 37 Baylor L Rev 513 (1985).

WRONGFUL LIFE AND WRONGFUL BIRTH: THE CURRENT STATUS OF NEGLIGENT GENETIC COUNSELING, 3 Cooley L Rev 175 (1985).

B. Recognition of Cause of Action

1. [§6.15] Generally

In an action alleging wrongful life brought against the federal government pursuant to the Federal Tort Claims Act an issue was raised with regard to whether the action was barred by the *Feres* doctrine. The infant's mother was a member of the Air Force when she discovered that she was pregnant. The physician who treated the mother never requested her medical records from an Air Force base where she had earlier served even though the physician administered two rubella tests that indicated that the mother had been exposed to rubella at some point in the past. The mother was discharged from the Air Force because of her pregnancy and subsequently gave birth to the infant-plaintiff who suffered from severe congenital defects. The mother said that if she had known about the probable rubella diagnosis and the effect of rubella on an unborn child, she would have aborted the fetus she was carrying. The court noted that under the *Feres* doctrine actions against the federal government are precluded if maintenance of the action would serve to undermine military discipline. The court stated that if it must second guess the judgment of military officers in assessing their treatment of a member of the armed services, the claim will be deemed to have a disruptive effect on discipline and will be dismissed. In *Scales* the court stated that whether the physician's treatment of the mother constituted negligence with respect to the child could not be determined without requiring the court to second guess military judgment. This second guessing would be inconsistent with the concern for military discipline that underlies the *Feres* doctrine the court said. Therefore, the court dismissed the claim as barred by *Feres* and noted that it was not addressing, in any way, whether the child had presented a supportable legal theory. *Scales v United States*, 685 F2d 970 (5th Cir 1982), reh den, 691 F2d 502 (5th Cir 1982), cert den, 103 SCt 1772, 76 LE2d 344 (1983).

There is no cause of action on behalf of a birth defective child for wrongful life. *Goldberg v Ruskin*, 128 IlA3d 1029, 84 Il Dec 1, 471 NE2d 530 (1984), affd, in part, 113 Il2d 482, 101 Il Dec 818, 499 NE2d 406 (1986).

There is no cause of action on behalf of an infant for wrongful life. *Alquijay v St Luke's-Roosevelt Hospital Center*, 99 AD2d 704, 472 NYS2d 2 (1984), affd, 63 NY2d 978, 483 NYS2d 994, 473 NE2d 244 (1984).

A child afflicted with Tay-Sachs disease may not maintain a wrongful life action to recover damages against laboratories and physicians who failed to determine prenatally that the child was or probably would be so afflicted in sufficient time to prevent his birth. There is no precedent that holds that a child has a fundamental right to be born as a whole, functional human being. In addition it is impossible to determine damages. Finally, there are policy reasons against allowing tort damages for failing or refusing to take an embryonic life. Placing the child in a position he or she would have occupied had the defendants not committed the alleged wrongful act, whether it be a tort or breach of contract, is impractical, for to do so would render the child nonexistent. *Rubin By Rubin v Hamot Medical Center*, 478 A2d 869 (Pa Super 1984), app gtd, 498 A2d 868 (1985).

A duty may extend to persons not yet conceived at the time of a negligent act or omission. Such a duty is limited, however, like any other duty by the element of foreseeability. In most wrongful life cases, it should not be difficult to establish foreseeability. For example, where the parents inform a physician of their intention to have further children, it is foreseeable that these future children may be endangered if the physicians fail to take reasonable steps to determine whether the mother's ingestion of a drug will harm the future children. Imposition of the duty will foster a societal objective of accurate genetic counseling and prenatal testing, and will discourage malpractice. In addition, recognition of the duty will provide more comprehensive and consistent compensation for those injured by such malpractice than would be available if the duty were confined only to the parents. This duty will be breached by failure to observe the appropriate standard of care. *Harbeson v Parke-Davis*, 98 Wa2d 460, 656 P2d 483 (1983) later proceeding 746 F2d 517 (9th Cir 1984).

Donovan, WRONGFUL BIRTH AND WRONGFUL LIFE: QUESTIONS OF PUBLIC POLICY, 28 Loyola LR 77 (1982).

BETTER OFF NEVER BORN?, 72 ABA J 46 (1986).

THE TREND TOWARD JUDICIAL RECOGNITION OF WRONGFUL LIFE: A DISSENTING VIEW, 31 UCLA LR 77 (1983).

GENETIC COUNSELING AND MEDICAL MALPRACTICE: RECOGNIZING A CAUSE OF ACTION FOR WRONGFUL LIFE, 8 Thurgood Marshall L Rev 154 (1982).

2. [§6.16] Existence of Legally Cognizable Injury

The plaintiffs alleged that the defendant's negligent performance of a bilateral tubal ligation on the mother and failure to warn the parents that the operation had been improperly performed caused their child to be born with albinism. Although the court concluded provisionally that under the facts alleged in the petition, the doctor did not owe a duty to protect the child from the risk of albinism, they rejected the defendant's arguments calling for a categorical denial of any duty on the part of the physician to protect an unconceived child from being born with a birth defect. When a physican knows, or should know, of the existence of an unreasonable risk that a child will be born with a birth defect, he owes a duty to the unconceived child as well as to the parents to exercise reasonable care in warning the potential parents and in assisting them to avoid the conception of the deformed child. However, in this case, the court's study of some of the literature on albinism indicated that it cannot easily be predicted or foreseen by a treating physician. The plaintiff's petition did not contain any allegation that the defendant physican knew, or should have known, of the risk of this abnormality. The policy considerations affecting tort law did not impel the recognition of a duty when the doctor had no reason to suspect that the danger existed and did not have reasonable means of detecting its potentiality. However, the court did hold that in the event that the court's appreciation of the nature of the birth defect or of the precautions available to the medical profession was in error, the child's petition would be dismissed provisionally with leave to amend the petition within 30 days of the finality of the decision. *Pitre v Opelousas General Hosp*, 530 So2d 1151 (La 1988).

Basic to culture is the precept that life is precious. Laws have as their driving force the purpose of protecting, preserving, and improving the quality of human existence. To recognize wrongful life as a tort would do violence to that purpose and contradicts the belief that life is precious. The fact that a wrongful life plaintiff will live in a severely disabled condition is unquestionably a tragedy; nevertheless, life whether experienced with or without major physical handicap is more precious than nonlife. Thus, a plaintiff who brings a wrongful life action has suffered no legally cognizable wrong by being born, and therefore has no cause of action. *Blake v Cruz*, 698 P2d 315 (Id 1984).

One of the major obstacles to a claim for wrongful life is the impossibility of determining whether the child has suffered an injury in being born impaired rather than not being born. *Goldberg v Ruskin*, 128 IlA3d 1029, 84 Il Dec 1, 471 NE2d 530 (1984), affd, in part, 113 Il2d 482, 101 Il Dec 818, 499 NE2d 406 (1986).

The life of an infant plaintiff who is born in an impaired state and brings a wrongful life action does not constitute an injury to the infant. *Alquijay v St Luke's-Roosevelt Hospital Center*, 99 AD2d 704, 472 NYS2d 2 (1984), affd, 63 NY2d 978, 483 NYS2d 994, 473 NE2d 244 (1984).

In rejecting a cause of action for wrongful life, the Supreme Court of North Carolina concluded that life, even with severe defects, cannot be an injury in the legal sense. *Azzolino v Dingfelder*, 315 NC 103, 337 SE2d 528 (1985), cert den 107 SCt 131, 93 LE2d 75 (1986).

THE TREATMENT OF INJURY IN WRONGFUL LIFE CLAIMS, 20 Colum JL & Soc Probs 145 (1986).

3. [§6.17] Damage Considerations

The weight of authority refuses to permit a child to recover general damages in an action for wrongful life. The nearly universal rejection by the courts of a child's recovery of general damages for wrongful life is based for the most part on the value of life and the inherent difficulty of ascertaining a cognizable injury for which damages may be meaningfully awarded. However, the plaintiffs sought to find support for their action in the developing view that special damages may be recovered by a child in an action for wrongful life. The damages allowed in those cases have been based on the past and future medical expenses and other special costs resulting from the child's disease or condition. The Illinois court held that a child may not recover, in an action for wrongful life, damages for pain and suffering associated with the disease or condition that underlies the action. *Goldberg v Ruskin*, 113 Il2d 482, 101 Il Dec 818, 499 NE2d 406 (1986).

Even if it were held that wrongful life was a legally cognizable injury, the impossibility of measuring damages would preclude recognition of the cause of action. *Blake v Cruz*, 698 P2d 315 (Id 1984).

A child may recover in a wrongful life action for special damages for extraordinary medical expenses incurred during infancy, and the child may recover those expenses expected to be incurred during his majority. However, the child may not recover for pain and suffering and for a diminished childhood. In regard to the latter element of damage there is a philosophical problem of finding that a defective life is worth less than no life. Sound reasons exist not to recognize a claim for general damages. The infant plaintiff never had a chance of being born as a normal, healthy child. For him, the only options were nonexistence or an impaired life. There is no rational way to measure nonexistence or to compare nonexistence with the pain and suffering of the child's impaired existence. It is too speculative to permit an infant plaintiff to recover for emotional distress caused by birth defects when that plaintiff claims he would be better off if he had not been born. Even more problematic is the evaluation of a claim for diminished childhood. The essential proof in such a claim is that the doctor's negligence deprived the parents of the knowledge of the condition of the fetus. The deprivation of that information precluded the choice of terminating the pregnancy by abortion and left the parents unprepared for the birth of a defective child, a birth that caused them emotional harm. The argument proceeds that the parents are less able to love and care for the child, who thereby suffers as an impaired child. That sort of claim is flawed in those instances in which the parents assert not that the information would have prepared them for the birth of the defective child, but that they would have used the information to prevent that birth. Furthermore, the claim for diminished childhood may not be readily divisible from that suffered by the child's parents. The award of the cost of the extraordinary medical care to the child or the parents, when combined with the right of the parents to assert a claim for their own emotional distress, comes closer to filling the objectives of the tort system. *Procanik By Procanik v Cillo*, 97 NJ 339, 478 A2d 755 (1984), on remd, 206 NJ Super 270, 502 A2d 94 (1985).

In a wrongful life action, damages for extraordinary expenses for specialized teaching and training and special equipment that an unhealthy infant will need because of her defect are recoverable. *Call v Kezirian*, 135 CaA3d 189, 185 CaR 103 (1982).

General damages are recoverable in a wrongful life action. They are capable of being established with reasonable certainty, and thus are not beyond computation. For example, the costs associated with extraordinary expenses for a child's medical care and special training are calculable and are subject to being measured with reasonable certainty. However, special damages are not recoverable in a wrongful life action because they cannot be established with reasonable certainty. *Harbeson v Parke-Davis*, 98 Wa2d 460, 656 P2d 483 (1983) later proceeding 746 F2d 517 (9th Cir 1984).

The inherent difficulty in assessing damages, both special and general, was the rationale for denying a child's cause of action for wrongful life in *Strohmaier v Associates in Obstetrics & Gynecology*, 122 MiA 116, 332 NW2d 432 (1982). The court noted that the plaintiff's damages, general and special, consisted of the difference between his life with defects and no life at all. The plaintiff's economic liabilities, like the daily pain and suffering he must endure, are a part and parcel of his life with birth defects, the court said. The court could not view those economic losses apart from the incalculable benefit of life conferred upon the child by the events after his birth. Consequently, the court concluded that the plaintiff's special damages were as unrecognizable as any general damages for pain and suffering.

Likewise a child's claim for wrongful life was not recognized because the assessment of damages would be too speculative and impossible to make. *Dorlin v Providence Hosp*, 118 MiA 831, 325 NW2d 600 (1982); *Nelson v Krusen*, 635 SW2d 582 (Tx 1982).

A settlement of $380,000 for a wrongful life action was arrived at in *Graham v Pima Cty*, Pima Cty Super Ct, No 190297 (Jan 18, 1983) 26 American Trial Lawyers Assoc L Rep 284 (Aug 1983).

A child's claim for loss of earnings in a wrongful life action was not granted where the court said there was no loss of earning capacity caused by the doctor negligently permitting the child to be born with a genetic defect that precluded earning a living. One cannot lose what one never had. The child never had a wage-earning capacity that was taken away by the conduct of the doctor and cannot, therefore, claim compensation for its loss. The child's inability to earn wages is attributable to the child's genes and, for the present at least, it is meaningless to speak of a doctor altering or ameliorating this circumstance. *Andalon v Superior Court*, 162 CaA3d 600, 208 CaR 899 (1984).

DAMAGES: RECOVERY OF DAMAGES IN ACTIONS FOR WRONGFUL BIRTH, WRONGFUL LIFE AND WRONGFUL CONCEPTION, 23 Washburn L Journal 309 (1984).

5. [§6.19] Cause of Action Stated

A defendant's motion to dismiss a cause of action for wrongful life was denied where it was held that damages were calculable and recognition of the action would not violate public policy. *Woodruf v Hoffman*, 27 American Trial Lawyers Assoc L Rep 6 (Cn Super 1983).

An infant plaintiff may recover in a wrongful life action as special damages the extraordinary medical expenses attributable to his affliction, but the infant may not recover general damages for emotional distress or for an impaired childhood. The threshold problem in the past has been the assertion by infant plaintiffs not that they should not have been born without defects, but that they should not have been born at all. However, with the recognition of the parents' right to recover in a wrongful birth action, it is necessary to recognize the child's right to recover in a wrongful life action. Law is more than an exercise in logic, and logical analysis, although essential to a system of ordered justice, should not become an instrument of injustice. Whatever logic inheres in permitting parents to recover for the cost of extraordinary medical care incurred by a birth defective child, but in denying the child's own right to recover those expenses, must yield to the inherent injustice of that result. The right to recover the often crushing burden of extraordinary expenses caused by an act of medical malpractice should not depend on the wholly fortuitous circumstance of whether the parents are available to sue. Thus, the child's claim states a viable cause of action. *Procanik by Procanik v Cillo*, 97 NJ 339, 478 A2d 755 (1984), on remd, 206 NJ Super 270, 502 A2d 94 (1985).

A child may maintain an action for wrongful life in order to recover the extraordinary expenses to be incurred during the child's lifetime, as a result of the child's congenital defect. It would be illogical to permit only parents, not the child, to recover for the cost of the child's own medical care. The child's need for medical care and other special costs related to his or her defect will not disappear when the child attains majority. In many cases the burden of those expenses will fall on the child's parents or the state. Rather than allowing this to occur by refusing to recognize the cause of action, the burden of those costs should be placed on the party whose negligence was in fact a proximate cause of the child's continuing need for such special medical care and training. *Harbeson v Parke-Davis*, 98 Wa2d 460, 656 P2d 483 (1983).

WRONGFUL LIFE: A FINALLY RECOGNIZED TORT, 8 Journal Juvenile L 127 (1984).

WASHINGTON RECOGNIZES WRONGFUL BIRTH AND WRONGFUL LIFE—A CRITICAL ANALYSIS— *Harbeson v Parke-Davis, Inc*, 656 P2d 489 (Wash), 58 Wash LR 649 (1983).

6. [§6.20] Statutory Limitation or Denial of Cause of Action

The Illinois courts refused to recognize a cause of action for wrongful life. They held that because no right not to be born, even into a life of hardship, has ever been recognized in the judicial system of the state, the plaintiff infant suffered no legally cognizable injury by being brought into existence afflicted with hemophilia. Moreover, the infant's claim for relief for the extraordinary medical expenses which he expects to incur during his majority is not actionable because the negligent conduct complained of, even if true, does not give rise to an injury cognizable at law. In addition to the apparent absence of any legally cognizable injury, public policy considerations precluded the court from allowing the infant to recover damages for the extraordinary medical expenses incurred as a result of being born with a congenital or genetic disorder. To recognize that the infant had a fundamental right not to be born would undermine the legislatively expressed policy favoring childbirth over abortion. *Siemieniec v Lutheran General Hosp*, 117 Il2d 230, 111 Il Dec 302, 512 NE2d 691 (1987).

In rejecting a wrongful life claim, the court noted that by deciding that the physician has no responsibility to the child to pay for his or her extraordinary expenses in an action brought on behalf of the child, they would be shifting that responsibility, in many cases, to the state which will have to care for the child, and adult if the child lives, far into the future in the more aggravated cases where other funds are unavailable. The net economic effect of the holding may be that when the physician fails to give proper information to the parents, all of the people of the state pay the price. The court then invited the legislature to resolve the conflicting economic and moral interests. *Proffitt v Bartolo*, 162 MiA 35, 412 NW2d 232 (1987), app den, 430 Mi 860 (1988).

New Hampshire does not recognize a cause of action for wrongful life. *Smith v Cote*, 128 NH 231, 513 A2d 341 (1986).

A child suffering from multiple birth defects had no cause of action for wrongful life against a physician who negligently counseled her parents prior to her conception because the negligent physician owed no duty to an unconceived child. *Gallagher v Duke Univ*, 638 FSupp 979 (MD NC 1986).

Minn Stat §145.424, which prohibits the maintenance of an action for wrongful life, was determined to be constitutional. *Hickman v Group Health Plan Inc*, 396 NW2d 10 (Mn 1986).

A child born deformed and diseased as a result of the failure of physicians to inform its parents of the possibility of a diseased birth may not recover in its own right for being born diseased. The court recognized that in the case of a hereditary disease, the "injury" is not a harm that is inflicted on one person or entity by the negligence of another. The condition about which the plaintiff complains, a diseased life, was not inflicted on the plaintiff by any person, but by the plaintiff's own genetic constitution. Therefore, it could not be said that the plaintiff suffered a legal injury. *Ellis v Sherman*, 512 Pa 14, 515 A2d 1327 (1986).

A cause of action for wrongful life is not recognized in Kansas. *Bruggeman v Schimke*, 239 Ks 245, 718 P2d 635 (1986).

Where the plaintiff in a wrongful life action is a minor, it is not the knowledge of the injury or lack thereof by the minor, but the knowledge or lack thereof by the minor's parents which determines the time of the accrual of a cause of action. When the plaintiff has notice or information of circumstances to put a reasonable person on inquiry or has the opportunity to obtain knowledge from sources open to his investigation, the statute begins to run. The statute of limitations in Ca Civ Code §29 for prenatal malpractice is subject to being tolled where the parents' failed to discover, and in the exercise of due diligence should not have discovered, the negligent cause of an injury. Thus, the suit is not barred if parents can show delayed discovery, because the statute in a medical malpractice case runs from the discovery date, or from the date when, in the exercise of reasonable diligence, the plaintiff should have discovered the wrongful act. When there is a belated discovery of a physician's possible malpractice in a wrongful life action the issue of whether the plaintiff exercised reasonable diligence in discovering the malpractice is a question of fact and where there is a professional relationship, the degree of diligence in ferreting out the negligence for the purpose of the statute of limitations is diminished. In this case, the court held that an intelligent person would not necessarily know the birth of a Down's Syndrome child could be predicted by performing an amniocentesis, without specialized knowledge about that particular medical test. Thus, the court concluded, the statute of limitations would not begin to run until the child's parents had such specialized knowledge. Whether the child's parents should have realized the child's condition could have been predicted by amniocentesis was a question of fact, the court said. *Call v Kezirian*, 135 CaA3d 189, 185 CaR 103 (1982).

UTAH CODE ANN §§78-11-24 and 78-11-25 prohibit the bringing of an action for wrongful life.

IV. DIETHYLSTILBESTROL (DES) RELATED LIABILITY

A. In General

2. [§6.26] Background

DES identification and education programs have been established in a number of states. The programs seek to identify persons exposed to DES and encourage them to seek medical care for early detection of DES ailments. See, e.g., CA HEALTH & SAFETY CODE §349 et seq; MA ANN LAWS ch 111, §§4K, 4L.

At least one state has enacted legislation that provides that no policy of health insurance may be denied or canceled by the insurer solely because the mother of the insured used drugs containing DES prior to the insured's birth. See OR REV STAT §743.125.

A recent medical journal article suggests that there may be a relationship between a mother's ingestion of DES during pregnancy and the subsequent development in a prenatally exposed son of a form of testicular cancer. The article states that the medical community should be aware of the possibility of an association between a male's exposure to DES and the development of testicular cancer. Conley, Sant, Ucci, Mitcheson, SEMINOMA AND EPIDIDYMAL CYSTS IN A YOUNG MAN WITH KNOWN DIETHYLSTILBESTROL EXPOSURE IN UTERO, 249 Journal of the American Medical Association 1325 (1983).

Part of the identification problem for the DES plaintiff is that during the period between 1947 and 1971 DES was manufactured and distributed mostly as a generic drug. Pharmacists many times did not know who manufactured the DES they purchased because the chain of distribution went from manufacturer to wholesaler to pharmacist in its generic form, and records of the particular manufacturer were not kept or were destroyed. *McElhaney v Eli Lilly & Co*, 564 FSupp 265 (D SD 1983), later proceeding, 575 FSupp 228 (D SD 1983) affd 739 F2d 340 (8th Cir 1984).

Levine, "Gilding the Lilly": A Des Update, 20 Trial 18 (Dec 1984).

3. [§6.27] Causes of Action Alleged

The plaintiffs in this litigation are the daughters of women who were given DES during their pregnancies to prevent miscarriage. The plaintiffs claim that the drug was unsafe for use in preventing miscarriage and resulted in severe injury to them. The plaintiffs claim that the defendants knew that the drug contained a cancer-causing substance, yet failed to warn users or their physicians of these dangerous characteristics. The plaintiffs sought to hold the defendants liable on theories of strict liability, breach of express and implied warranty, fraud, and negligence. The California Supreme Court held that a drug manufacturer's liability for a defectively designed drug should not be measured by the standards of strict liability. Moreover, because of the public interest in the development, availability, and reasonable price of drugs, the appropriate test for determining responsibility is the test stated in Comment K [Restatement (Second) of Torts 402A] which addresses the question of unavoidably unsafe products. For the same public policy reasons, the court disapproved an earlier holding that only those prescriptions found to be unavoidably dangerous should be measured by the Comment K standard and that strict liability should apply to drugs that do not meet that description. The court held that a manufacturer is not strictly liable for injuries caused by a prescription drug so long as the drug was properly prepared and accompanied by warnings of its dangerous propensities that were either known or reasonably scientifically knowable at the time of distribution. *Brown v Superior Court*, 44 Ca3d 1049, 245 CaR 412, 751 P2d 470 (1988).

A plaintiff was allowed to maintain a strict products liability action against the manufacturer of DES in a diversity of jurisdiction action where the court held that Tennessee law, which recognizes strict liability actions, would be applied rather than North Carolina law, which does not recognize strict liability actions. The plaintiff's mother was a domiciliary and resident of North Carolina during the time she was pregnant with the plaintiff. The mother's doctor prescribed treatment with DES as a means of preventing spontaneous abortion. That treatment and the plaintiff's birth occurred in North Carolina. At the time of her birth no one diagnosed the plaintiff as having a DES related injury. Rather, the injury, an incompetent cervix, apparently developed at a later date when the plaintiff was living in Tennessee. The court noted that generally the courts of Tennessee require that the substantive law of the place where the tort occurred be applied. However, the court noted that there is a public policy exception to this rule where the law of the jurisdiction where the tort occurred is against good morals or natural justice, or for some other reason, its enforcement would be prejudicial to the general interests of the forum's citizens. The court further noted that the underlying concern of RESTATEMENT (SECOND) OF TORTS §402A is to fairly allocate risk and social cost. A large national corporation doing business in all states does not make its marketing decisions on the basis of whether a state has or has not adopted strict products liability, the court said. Product liability insurance, or self-insurance reserves, are for protection of the consumer, and financial protection of the company, generally, and are not dependent upon whether a consumer may live, become pregnant, have a baby, or the injury become manifest. On the other hand, the court said, Tennessee had strong public policy reasons for protecting its citizens against ingestion of dangerous prescription drugs and also for allocating the social cost of resulting injuries where the consumer was a resident of the state at the time of the manifestation of the injury. For these reasons, the court said, the motion for summary judgment brought by the manufacturer was denied. *Trahan v E R Squibb & Sons, Inc*, 567 FSupp 505 (MD Tn 1983) [Tennessee law].

A manufacturer of DES had no duty to warn of adverse side effects of DES of which the manufacturer was unaware when it, in 1949, sold the product as a prescription drug. The plaintiff had brought a strict products liability action against the manufacturer, but the court said that absent any proof by the plaintiff that the manufacturer was, in 1949, aware or that it should have been aware of the DES side effects, the plaintiff, as a matter of law, was barred from recovery against the manufacturer. The court noted that under RESTATEMENT (SECOND) OF TORTS §402A comments j and k, the manufacturer owed a duty to warn of potential adverse side effects of which it knew or reasonable should have known at the time the plaintiff's mother ingested the drug. However, the court said that to hold the manufacturer liable for failure to warn of a danger of which it would be impossible to know based on the present state of human knowledge would make the manufacturer the virtual insurer of the product. The plaintiff contended that the manufacturer had the burden of proof on the issue of whether the manufacturer knew or should have known in 1949 that ingestion of DES might result in conditions such as those complained of by the plaintiff. However, the court said that in a strict liability case under §402A the burden is placed on the plaintiff to prove that the product was defective at the time it left the manufacturer's control. *McElhaney v Eli Lilly & Co,* 575 FSupp 228 (D SD 1983) affd 739 F2d 340 (8th Cir 1984).

As between the plaintiff, who was probably not at fault, and the defendants, who may have provided the DES which caused the injury, the interests of justice and fundamental fairness demand that the latter bear the cost of injury. Although the defendants in this case may not have acted in concert under the concert of action theory, all participated in either gaining approval of DES for use in pregnancy or in producing or marketing DES in subsequent years. Each defendant contributed to the risk of injury to the public and, consequently, the risk of injury to the individual plaintiffs. The plaintiff needs to commence suit against only one defendant and allege the following elements: that the plaintiff's mother took DES; that DES caused the plaintiff's subsequent injury; that the defendant produced or marketed the type of DES taken by the plaintiff's mother; and that the defendant's conduct in producing or marketing the DES constituted a breach of a legally recognized duty to the plaintiff. In the situation where the plaintiff cannot allege and prove what type of DES the mother took, as to the third element the plaintiff need only allege and prove that the defendant drug company produced or marketed DES for use in preventing miscarriages during pregnancy. At the trial the plaintiff will have to prove each of these elements to the satisfaction of the trier of fact. However, the plaintiff need not prove that a defendant produced or marketed the precise DES taken by the plaintiff's mother. Rather, the plaintiff need only establish by a preponderance of the evidence that a defendant produced or marketed the type of the DES taken by the plaintiff's mother; the plaintiff need not allege or prove any facts related to the time or geographic distribution of the subject DES. Under a negligence theory, the plaintiff must prove that the defendant drug company had a duty of care and breached that duty of care when it produced or marketed DES. The plaintiff may also proceed under a theory of strict products liability. In order to prevail on this theory, the plaintiff must prove (1) that the DES was defective when it left the possession or control of the drug company; (2) that it was unreasonably dangerous to the user or consumer; (3) that the defect was a cause of the plaintiff's injuries or damages; (4) that the drug company engaged in the business of producing or marketing DES or, that this was not an isolated or infrequent transaction not related to the principle business of the drug company; and (5) that the product was one which the company expected to reach the user or consumer without substantial change in the condition in which it was sold. Once the plaintiff has proven a prima facie case under either cause of action, the burden of proof shifts to the defendant to prove by a preponderance of the evidence that it did not produce or market the subject DES either during the time period the plaintiff was exposed to DES or in the relevant geographical market area in which the plaintiff's mother acquired the DES. *Collins v Eli-Lilly Co*, 116 Wi2d 166, 342 NW2d 37 (1984), cert den, 105 SCt 107 (1984).

In *Bichler v Willing*, 58 AD2d 331, 397 NYS2d 57 (1977), a DES-plaintiff's action based on negligence or breach of expressed warranty against the dispensing pharmacist was rejected. The court said that in view of the absence of any showing of a difference between the DES chosen by the druggist and the other available brands, the pharmacist's choice of the particular brand of DES ingested by the plaintiff's mother could not be classified as negligence.

Where the plaintiff alleged that a DES manufacturer had failed to adequately and properly place warning labels on its product, and thus violated the Food, Drug and Cosmetic Act [21 USC §301, et seq.] by misbranding the drug, it was held that there is no private cause of action under the Food, Drug and Cosmetic Act. *Keil v Eli Lilly & Co*, 490 FSupp 479 (ED Mi 1980).

4. [§6.28] Damages Sought and Awarded

Recovery may not be awarded in a DES case for the mental distress suffered by mothers who ingested DES with regard to fear and concern as to their children's current and possible future medical problems. It does not follow that if recovery for pain and suffering is an element of damages recovery would be necessarily allowed for a cause of action solely based on anxiety and dread without the need for a showing of some type of symptom. Tort damages are awarded in order to compensate an individual for injuries sustained. To allow this suit to go forward, the court said, based on nothing more than the hypothesis that pain and suffering is an element of recovery in a proper case would not be proper. In addition, it does not appear that the Rhode Island Supreme Court would join a new trend permitting recovery for careless infliction of emotional strain notwithstanding the absence of corresponding physical manifestations thereof. *Plummer v Abbott Laboratories*, 568 FSupp 920 (D RI 1983) [Rhode Island law].

Punitive damages were not recoverable in a DES action where the plaintiff sued multiple defendants and stated that she could not prove which defendant actually caused her injuries. Punitive damages are designed to punish a wrongdoer and to serve as a deterrent. The concept of punitive damages embodies a rule for individualized punishment of a wrongdoer whose conduct toward the plaintiff is particularly outrageous. Implicit in this concept is the notion that, where punishment is to be exacted, it must be certain that the specific wrongdoer being punished actually caused the plaintiff's injuries. *Collins v Eli Lilly Co*, 116 Wi2d 166, 342 NW2d 37 (1984), cert den, 105 SCt 107 (1984).

TORT LAW—EMOTIONAL DISTRESS AND WRONGFUL LIFE IN DES LITIGATION: INJURY WITHOUT REMEDY—*Payton v Abbott Laboratories*, 437 NE2d 171 (Mass), 6 W New Eng LR 1039 (1984).

B. Causation-In-Fact: Manufacturer Identity

1. [§6.29] Generally

Because of the difficulty of direct proof of manufacturer identity, a plaintiff may prove the identity by inference. In *Payton v Abbott Laboratories*, 780 F2d 147 (1st Cir Ma 1985), plaintiff presented evidence that the pharmacy at which plaintiff's mother purchased the DES, in all probability, filled her prescription with defendant's drugs. The plaintiff established that the pharmacy had a policy not to keep supplies of 25-mg. DES in stock because there was little call for it. It also had a policy to order only drugs manufactured by the defendant or another drug company. It would have been uneconomical and contrary to pharmacy policy to purchase the DES from the other drug company because that company only marketed the product in bottles of 1000, whereas the defendant's drugs came in bottles of 100. Further, the pharmacist testified that he had never seen a bottle of 25-mg. DES made by the other drug company in the store. Based on this evidence, it could be inferred that the DES prescription was filled by DES manufactured by the defendant.

In *McMahon v Eli Lilly & Co*, 774 F2d 830 (7th Cir Il 1985), plaintiffs were able to demonstrate that the DES ingested by plaintiff's mother was manufactured by Lilly, based on the testimony of the individual who purchased DES for the pharmacy during the time when plaintiff's mother purchased the drug from that store. He testified that the only brand he recalled purchasing was the Lilly brand. Plaintiffs also placed in evidence the affidavit of the pharmaceutical buyer for the wholesaler with which the pharmacy did business. He testified that the only DES sold by the wholesaler to any pharmacy in that area was manufactured by Lilly. As with other elements of proof in a civil action, product identification need only be established by a preponderance of the evidence.

In *McElhaney v Eli Lilly & Co*, 564 FSupp 265 (D SD 1983), later proceeding, 575 FSupp 228 (D SD 1983) affd 739 F2d 340 (8th Cir 1984), the court adopted RESTATEMENT (SECOND) OF TORTS §433B(3) regarding the burden of proof in a DES case in which the plaintiff could not identify the DES manufacturer. In essence, the rule provides that the burden of proof is upon actors whose conduct has been tortious to prove that harm caused to the plaintiff was not caused by a specific actor. In adopting the rule the court said the rule does not relieve the plaintiff of proving DES caused her injury or lessen the burden as to any other element necessary under negligence, or strict liability theories. It does, however, remove from the plaintiff the burden of identifying the source of the DES which allegedly injured her and would shift to each defendant, the burden of proving it was not the source of the DES to which the plaintiff was exposed, the court stated. The §433B burden of proof rule may not produce perfect results in all cases, the court said, but it represents a reasonable application of the rationale which supports strict liability, given the unusual nature of the facts and circumstances in a case involving DES.

A plaintiffs' motion for partial summary judgment against a drug company on several issues relating to DES, invoking offensive collateral estoppel, was denied in *Wetheril v Univ of Chicago*, 548 FSupp 66 (ND Il 1982). The plaintiffs had claimed that certain issues were determined adversely to Lilly in a prior prenatal DES exposure suit [*Bichler v Eli Lilly & Co*, 55 NY2d 571, 450 NYS2d 776, 436 NE2d 182 (1982)], that determination of those issues was necessary to the resolution of *Bichler* in favor of the plaintiff there, and that those issues were identical to several controlling issues raised by the plaintiffs. The plaintiffs sought to estop Lilly from relitigating the issues. However, the court denied the plaintiffs' motion for partial summary judgment. First, the court said that the plaintiff submitted to the court neither the pleadings nor the trial record nor the actual record of the judgment in *Bichler*, but instead tendered only a copy of the opinion of the New York Court of Appeals affirming the jury verdict. Absence of the *Bichler* trial record foreclosed accurate discernment of just what facts were fairly established at the trial or just what facts were necessary to the resolution in favor of the Bichler plaintiff, the court said.

Moreover, the court said that even if it knew the facts fairly determining *Bichler*, it could not discern from the New York court's opinion alone how those facts related to the issues actually controlling that case. Without the pleadings that framed the *Bichler* issues, the court said, the controlling issues could only be guessed at. Finally, the court said the plaintiffs had not met their burden of establishing the identity between the issues supposedly determined in *Bichler* and those controlling in this case. For example, the court noted that *Bichler's* concerted action theory of liability was irrelevant to this action since Lilly was the identified source of the DES that allegedly injured the plaintiffs. And the court stated that although *Bichler* was also apparently decided on a theory of wrongful marketing and failure to test, the plaintiffs had not shown how such a theory was even relevant to Illinois products liability law.

A plaintiff in a product liability action must ordinarily prove that a manufacturer-defendant produced the product that allegedly caused the injury. *Morton v Abbott Laboratories*, 538 FSupp 593 (MD Fl 1982) [Florida law].

Roberts and Royster, DES AND THE IDENTIFICATION PROBLEM, 16 Akron LR 447 (1983).

CAUSE OF ACTION AGAINST DRUG MANUFACTUER FOR FAILURE TO WARN OF SIDE EFFECTS ASSOCIATED WITH PRESCRIPTION DRUG, 3 Shepard's Causes of Action 815 (1983).

TORTS—PLAINTIFF, INJURED AS A RESULT OF HER MOTHER'S USE OF THE DRUG DIETHYLSTILBESTROL, IS ENTITLED TO A REMEDY AT LAW FOR HER INJURIES AND NEED COMMENCE SUIT AGAINST ONLY ONE DRUG MANUFACTURER, *Collins v Eli Lilly*, 342 NW2d 37 (Wis), 23 J Fam L 148 (1984-1985).

2. [§6.30] Concert of Action

A cause of action for concerted action cannot be established in Pennsylvania if the plaintiff is unable to identify the person who acted in concert with the wrongdoer, or who gave assistance or encouragement. The concern that a manufacturer would become liable for defects in its competitor's products is shared by an overwhelming majority of jurisdictions which have considered the concerted action theory. These courts have uniformly refused to apply the theory in DES cases. Pennsylvania has elected to follow the majority and refuses to apply the theory in DES cases. *Burnside v Abbott Laboratories*, 505 A2d 973 (Pa Super 1985).

A concert of action theory may be used as the basis for liability in a DES case. This theory, although not developed to ease the plaintiff's traditional burden of proof of causation, may have that effect. If the plaintiff can establish that all defendants acted tortiously pursuant to a common design, they will all be held liable for the entire result. In order to withstand a motion for summary judgment based on a failure to state a cause of action, a plaintiff need only allege that the defendants were jointly engaged in tortious activity as a result of which the plaintiff was harmed. In this case the plaintiffs alleged that the defendants acted together in negligently manufacturing and promoting drugs which were ineffective and dangerous, were inadequately tested, and were distributed without sufficient warnings. These allegations were sufficient to withstand summary judgment. *Abel v Eli Lilly & Co*, 418 Mi 311, 343 NW2d 164 (1984), cert den, 105 SCt 123 (1984).

Concert of action rests on the principal that those who, in the pursuance of a common plan or design to commit a tortious act, actively take part in it, or further it by cooperation or request, or who lend aid or encouragement to the wrongdoer, or ratify and adopt acts done for their benefit, are equally liable with the wrongdoer. Express agreement is not necessary, and all that is required is that there be a tacit understanding. Even assuming that the defendants acted tortiously towards the plaintiff, the plaintiff, under concert of action must also prove that there was agreement or, at the least, a tacit understanding among the defendants. In this case, the gravamen of the charge of concert of action was that the defendants failed to adequately test DES or to give sufficient warning of its dangers and that they relied upon the tests performed by one another and took advantage of each others promotional and marketing techniques. Such allegations do not support the theory that the defendant tacitly agreed to produce and market DES without adequately testing the drug or warning of its potential dangers. Although there was a substantial amount of parallel action by the defendants in producing and marketing DES for use in pregnancy, this does not rise to the level of acting in concert. Furthermore, the conceptual basis of the concert of action theory makes it inapplicable to DES cases. Concert of action generally is applied to situations in which, unlike this DES case, a particular defendant is already identified as having caused the plaintiff's harm, and the plaintiff desires to extend liability to those acting in league with that defendant. The theory rarely has been used to help defendants avoid the identification requirement. *Collins v Ely Lilly & Co*, 116 Wi2d 166, 342 NW2d 37 (1984), cert den, 105 SCt 107 (1984).

The concert of action theory should be rejected as a basis of liability in DES cases. Although in this case there was a substantial amount of parallel activity by the defendant manufacturers of DES, this did not rise to the level of concerted action. *Martin v Abbott Laboratories*, 102 Wa2d 581, 689 P2d 368 (1984).

3. [§6.31] —Illustrative Cases

DES manufacturers did not act in concert in the manufacturing and marketing of DES. Their filings with the Food and Drug Administration did not represent a concerted tortious conduct. In 1940, several companies filed wholly separate applications with the FDA to market DES. By these applications, the manufacturer sought to market DES for purposes unrelated to pregnancy. The FDA rejected these several applications, requiring the companies to coordinate a single "master" filing of clinical data. The manufacturers then formed a "small committee" to assemble the data into a master clinical file, and this file was submitted to the FDA in 1941. Thereafter, the several companies each resubmitted their applications. The master filing was not concerted tortious conduct for two reasons. First, the act of filing a unified compilation was done at the request of the FDA. Second, the master filing related to the marketing of DES for purposes other than those for which it has been shown or alleged to be dangerous. It was not until several years later, in 1947, that the drug manufacturers began applying to the FDA for permission to sell DES for pregnancy-related purposes, and these filings were made completely independently. *Morton v Abbott Laboratories*, 538 FSupp 593 (MD Fl 1982).

The application of theory of concert of action in a DES case would extend the theory beyond its intended purpose. Moreover application of the theory would be unfair in a DES case because it would apply joint and several liability to all defendants, some of whom could not have caused the injury. *Martin v Abbott Laboratories*, 26 American Trial Lawyers Assoc L Rep 127 (Wa 1982).

4. [§6.32] Alternative Liability

The theory of alternative liability will be applied in those DES cases in which all the defendants have acted tortiously, but only one unidentifiable defendant caused the plaintiff's injury. If a plaintiff brings all the possible defendants into court and establishes the other elements of the underlying cause of action, the court should equitably shift the burden of causation in fact to the defendants. If the defendants are unable to exonerate themselves, joint and several liability results. In this case, some of the plaintiffs alleged sufficient facts to withstand summary judgment on the causation issue. The plaintiffs, who numbered 180, alleged that all the defendants, which numbered 16, acted negligently in manufacturing and promoting DES despite scientific research indicating that DES was likely to cause cancer. The plaintiffs also stated that all the manufacturers who promoted DES for use during pregnancy in Michigan during the time period 1947-1964 were before the court. Difficulties arose, however, in that not all the plaintiffs alleged that they were unable to identify the manufacturer of the product that their mothers ingested, the court said. The rationale for the adoption of alternative liability is to shift the proof requirement for to do otherwise would leave an innocent plaintiff remediless, the court said. Where the plaintiffs are able to indentify the causation in fact of their injury, traditional tort remedies must be used to secure relief. However, pleading practices permit the ascertion of inconsistent claims. Even in this situation, where proof of one claim would defeat the existence of another, the plaintiff is allowed to present both claims. Once the plaintiffs prove the identity of the manufacturer of the DES product ingested, the option of alternative liability is no longer available to them. In this case 113 plaintiffs had alleged that they were unable to identify the manufacturer of the product which harmed them. These plaintiffs explained their failure to name a specific manufacturer by citing legislation requiring pharmacists to maintain prescription drug records for only five years, and the defendants' use of generic marketing schemes to promote the product. These pleadings constituted sufficient allegations to withstand summary judgment. The 70 plaintiffs who alleged that they were able to identify the manufacturer of the product which harmed them could bring forth their proofs at trial. If they were unable to establish the required identification, they also had the option of pursuing the alternative liability theory. *Abel v Eli Lilly Co*, 418 Mi 311, 343 NW2d 164 (1984), cert den, 105 SCt 123 (1984).

The alternative liability theory does not present a viable theory for DES cases. First, the alternative liability theory is, in part, premised on the assumption that defendants will be in a far better position than the plaintiff to offer evidence to determine which one caused the injury. In this case, both the plaintiff and the defendants have problems with access to information about DES production and marketing. Second, the alternative liability theory formulation contemplates that all negligent defendants will be joined in the suit. Thus, the court can be sure that at least one of the defendants was directly responsible for the plaintiff's harm. In a DES case, however, there may be hundreds of defendants that may be liable, and, therefore, the probability that any one defendant caused the plaintiff's harm may be small. Moreover, it may be impossible to identify all DES producers or marketers because of the fluid nature of the market over the years DES was produced or marketed for use in pregnancy. Third, the alternative liability formula does not, in its pure form, provide a fair way to apportion damages among the defendants. Under the alternative liability theory, defendants that produced or marketed small amounts of DES and those that produced or marketed large amounts would be equally liable. *Collins v Eli Lilly & Co*, 116 Wi2d 166, 342 NW2d 37 (1984), cert den, 105 SCt 107 (1984).

Strict application of alternate liability does not present a viable theory for DES cases. The alternate liability theory formulation contemplates that all tortious defendants will be joined in the suit. Thus, the court can be sure that at least one of the defendants was directly responsible for the plaintiff's harm. However, the alternate liability formula does not, in its pure form, provide a fair way to apportion damages among the defendants. Under the alternate liability theory, defendants that produced or marketed small amounts of DES and those that produced or marketed large amounts would be equally liable. *Martin v Abbott Laboratories*, 102 Wa2d 581, 689 P2d 368 (1984).

5. [§6.33] —Illustrative Cases

In a case of first impression in Washington, a court held that alternate liability may be applied where the plaintiff was unable to prove which DES manufacturer made the DES ingested by her mother. The court adopted the theory of alternate liability as stated in RESTATEMENT (SECOND) OF TORTS §433B. The theory creates a rebuttable presumption of liability against DES manufacturers and shifts the burden to each manufacturer to prove that it did not manufacture the drug which eventually caused the plaintiff's injury. *Martin v Abbott Laboratories*, 26 American Trial Lawyers Assoc L Rep 127 (Wa 1982).

The theory of alternative liability cannot apply in a DES case where the plaintiffs, by their own admission, cannot show that one of the defendants caused the injury. *Morton v Abbott Laboratories*, 538 FSupp 593 (MD Fl 1982).

6. [§6.34] Enterprise Liability

Pennsylvania has rejected the concept of enterprise liability in connection with DES cases. *Burnside v Abbott Laboratories*, 505 A2d 973 (Pa Super 1985).

The theory of enterprise liability was rejected where there were hundreds of potential defendant drug companies. The assumption that the defendants jointly controlled the risk of injury is necessarily weak given the fact that so many drug companies entered and left the DES marketplace from 1947 to 1971. Furthermore, the drug industry operates under the control of the Food and Drug Administration, which sets the standards and conditions the drug industry must meet to produce and market a particular drug. It is less clear in DES cases than in the leading enterprise liability case, *Hall v E I DuPont de Nemours & Co*, 345 FSupp 353 (ED NY 1972), that the defendant drug companies were each violating a standard of safety, whether federally imposed or industry imposed, in producing and marketing DES for use in pregnancy. *Collins v Ely Lilly & Co*, 116 Wi2d 166, 342 NW2d 37 (1984), cert den, 105 SCt 107 (1984).

The theory of enterprise or industry-wide liability is grounded on the premise that losses to society created or caused by an enterprise or, more simply, by an activity, ought to be borne by that enterprise or activity. Enterprise liability holds the defendants liable for sharing in industry-wide misconduct. The law of torts does not include a theory of liability which would allow an entire industry to be held strictly liable for an injury caused by a defective product. Thus, the theory of enterprise liability may not be used to establish liability in a DES case. *Martin v Abbott Laboratories*, 102 Wa2d 581, 689 P2d 368 (1984).

7. [§6.35] —Illustrative Cases

The concept of enterprise, or industry-wide, liability has no application in a DES case. In the case which suggested such a theory, *Hall v DuPont de Nemours & Co*, 345 FSupp 353 (ED NY 1972), there were six manufacturers in the industry. However, in this DES case there were 149. Moreover, in this case there was no industry-wide delegation of safety functions to a drug manufacturers' trade association. Thus, the concept of enterprise liability cannot support liability in this DES case. *Morton v Abbott Laboratories*, 538 FSupp 593 (MD Fl 1982).

8. [§6.36] Market Share Liability

A plaintiff who proceeds on a market share theory may not prosecute a cause of action for fraud or breach of warranty. Further, the court held that the imposition of joint liability on defendants in a market share action would be inconsistent with its own rationale. Any defendant could be held responsible for the entire judgment even though its market share may have been comparatively insignificant. Liability would, in the first instance, be measured not by the likelihood of responsibility for the plaintiff's injuries, but by the financial ability of the defendant to undertake payment of the entire judgment or a large portion of it. A defendant who paid a larger percentage of the judgment than warranted by its market share would have the burden of seeking indemnity from other defendants and it would bear the loss if producers of DES that might have been held liable in the action were not amenable to suit, or if a codefendant was bankrupt. In short, the imposition of joint liability among defendants in a market share action would frustrate *Sindell's* goal of achieving a balance between the interests of DES plaintiffs and manufacturers of the drug. *Brown v Superior Court*, 44 Ca3d 1049, 245 CaR 412, 751 P2d 470 (1988).

Although the market share liability theory appears to be fundamentally fair in shifting the burden of proof to the defendants, the theory should not be adopted for apportioning damages. The market share liability theory does not constitute the most desirable course to follow in DES cases because the theory is limited in practical applicability. There is great practical difficulty in defining and proving market share. It appears that many drug companies simply do not have records available from which a fact finder could determine how much DES a given defendant produced or marketed, or when and where the DES was produced and marketed. Even assuming that some drug companies have records, the fact finder still may not be able to compose an accurate assessment of the total market of which those companies were a part. Thus, defining the market and apportioning market share would appear to be a nearly impossible task if it is to be done fairly and accurately in order to approximate the probability that a defendant caused the plaintiff's injuries. Further, there would be a waste of judicial resources inherent in a second trial to determine market share of various defendants. *Collins v Eli Lilly Co*, 116 Wi2d 166, 342 NW2d 37 (1984), cert den, 105 SCt 107 (1984).

Although the market share theory is conceptionally attractive, it would be inappropriate to apply it in a DES case due to its inherent distortion of liability. It is evident that the definition of "substantial market share" directly affects the degree to which the defendant's liability is distorted. The lower the percentage of the market that is required to be joined, the higher will be the resulting distortion. *Martin v Abbott Laboratories*, 102 Wa2d 581, 689 P2d 368 (1984).

Miller, MARKET SHARE LIABILITY IN DRUG CASES, 41 J Mo B 359 (1985).

The Application of a Due Diligence Requirement to Market Share Theory in Des Litigation, 19 U Mich JL Ref 771 (1986).

[§6.36.1] Market-Share Alternate Liability

The crux of the problem in DES cases is that the plaintiff cannot identify the drug company that she alleges caused her injury. Thus, there is a conflict between the familiar principle that a tortfeasor may be held liable only for damage that it has caused, and the sense of justice which urges that the victims of a tragedy should not be denied compensation because of the impossibility of identifying the individual manufacturer of generic drugs if their manufacture and distribution were otherwise culpable. Thus, a modification of the alternate liability theory somewhat along the lines of the market share theory is warranted. Because certain manufacturers and distributors produced or marketed an allegedly defective drug for accidents of pregnancy, those manufacturers and distributors all contributed to the risk of injury, even though they may not have contributed to the actual injury of a given plaintiff. Although the defendants in this case did not act in concert under the concert of action theory, all participated in either gaining approval of DES for use in pregnancy or in producing or marketing DES in subsequent years. Each defendant contributed to the risk of injury to the public and, consequently, the risk of injury to individual plaintiffs. Thus, each defendant shares a degree of culpability in producing or marketing DES. Moreover, as between the injured plaintiff and the possibly responsible drug company, the drug company is in a better position to absorb the cost of the injury. The drug company can either insure itself against liability, absorb the damage award, or pass the cost along to the consuming public as a cost of doing business. It is better to have drug companies or consumers share the cost of the injury than to place the burden solely on the innocent plaintiff. Thus, the plaintiff need commence suit against only one defendant and allege the following elements: that the plaintiff's mother took DES; that DES caused the plaintiff's subsequent injury; that the defendant produced or marketed the type of DES taken by the plaintiff's mother; and that the defendant's conduct in producing or marketing the DES constituted a breach of a legally recognized duty to the plaintiff. The plaintiff need not prove that a defendant produced or marketed the precise DES taken by the plaintiff's mother. Rather, the plaintiff need only establish by a preponderance of the evidence that a defendant produced or marketed the type (for example, dosage, color, shape, markings, size, or other identifiable characteristics) of DES taken by the plaintiff's mother. The plaintiff need not allege or prove any facts related to the time or geographic distribution of the subject DES. While the type of DES ingested by the mother should be within the domain of her knowledge, facts relating to time and distribution should be particularly within the domain of knowledge of the DES manufacturers and distributors. A particular defendant's potential liability under this theory is proportional to the probability that it caused the plaintiff's injury. Individual defendants are entitled to exculpate themselves from liability by establishing that they did not produce or market the particular type of DES taken by the plaintiff's mother, that they did not market the DES in the geographic market area where the plaintiff's mother obtained the drug, or that it did not distribute DES in the time period of the plaintiff's mother's ingestion of the drug. The defendants that are unable to exculpate themselves from potential liability are designated members of the plaintiff's DES market. These defendants are entitled to rebut the presumption to have had equal shares of the market and thereby may reduce their potential liability by establishing their respective market share of DES in the plaintiff's particular geographic market. To the extent that other defendants fail to establish their actual market share, their presumed market share is adjusted so that 100% of the market is accounted for. *Martin v Abbott Laboratories*, 102 Wa2d 581, 689 P2d 368 (1984).

WASHINGTON ADOPTS MARKET SHARE LIABILITY FOR DES PRODUCERS—*Martin v Abbott Laboratories*, 689 P2d 368 (Wa), 60 Wash LR 543 (1985).

[§6.37] —Illustrative Cases

In *McCormack v Abbott Laboratories*, 617 FSupp 1521 (D Ma 1985), the court held that a plaintiff who cannot meet the traditional identification requirement may avail herself of a market-share theory of liability by alleging the following elements: (1) that the plaintiff's mother ingested DES during the pregnancy which resulted in the plaintiff's birth; (2) that DES caused the plaintiff's subsequent injuries; (3) that the defendant or defendants produced or marketed the type of DES taken by the plaintiff's mother; and (4) that the defendant or defendants acted negligently in producing or marketing the DES. The plaintiff must prove each of these elements by a preponderance of the evidence. The plaintiff need not allege or prove that a defendant produced or marketed the particular DES that caused her subsequent injuries. However, the plaintiff must establish that a defendant produced or marketed the type of DES, as distinguished by color, shape, size, or markings, ingested by the plaintiff's mother. Individual defendants may exculpate themselves from liability by proving by a preponderance of the evidence that they did not produce or market the particular type of DES taken by the plaintiff's mother, or that they did not market DES in the relevant geographic market area, or that they did not distribute the drug during the time period of the plaintiff's mother's pregnancy. Defendants who are unable to establish that the DES they produced or marketed could not have been ingested by the plaintiff's mother will become part of the DES market as narrowed and defined on a case-by-case basis, by the specificity of the evidence as to the geographic market area, the time of ingestion, and physical characteristics of the subject DES. Such defendants are presumed initially to have equal shares of the market. However, defendants may rebut this presumption by establishing by a preponderance of the evidence their individual market share of DES in the plaintiff's particular geographic market, during the time period in question. Defendants who fail to prove an actual market share will be liable equally for the remaining market. On the other hand, where all defendants successfully establish a reduced actual market share, the portion of the judgment representing the remaining unclaimed share of the market may not be recovered by the plaintiff.

The theory of market share liability was held to apply in a DES case where the plaintiff alleged that a manufacturer shared a portion of the DES miscarriage preventative market although the manufacturer claimed that its DES was marketed only for treatment of prostate cancer in males. *Miles v Superior Court*, 133 CaA3d 587, 184 CaR 98 (1982). The plaintiff had alleged that the defendant knew, or should have known, that its drug was being used as a miscarriage preventative and did nothing to prevent such use and by acquiescing in such use claimed for itself a share of the market. Miles, the manufacturer in question, moved for summary judgment on the ground that its DES was not marketed for female use, but the court denied the motion. The court noted that the plaintiff's allegation was not countered in the defendant's motion for summary judgment. To limit liability solely on the declaration of the defendant that it did not produce the drug for the purpose for which it was used misses the point of the plaintiff's allegations, the court said. The manufacturer's conduct, if true, is actionable under the logic and spirit of *Sindell v Abbott Laboratories*, 26 Ca3d 588, 163 CaR 132, 607 P2d 924, cert den, 449 US 912 (1980), the court concluded.

There is no indication that the decisions of the courts of Florida would allow a market share liability theory. Thus, it is necessary for the plaintiff to allege and prove which manufacturer of DES made the drug which subsequently injured the plaintiff. *Morton v Abbott Laboratories*, 538 FSupp 593 (MD Fl 1982) [Florida law].

C. Limitation on Actions

1. [§6.38] Generally

A plaintiff should have been allowed to amend her complaint in an action for damages against manufacturers of DES even though the amendment might have led to the running of the five-year mandatory dismissal provisions of the code of civil procedure with regard to bringing the action to trial. The matter had been originally set for trial on December 11, 1979, which was within the five-year statute of limitations. Thereafter, a motion for continuance was granted to and including June 1, 1980, pending a decision by the supreme court in *Sindell v Abbott Laboratories*, another DES case. On March 20, 1980, the supreme court issued its opinion in *Sindell*, and held that a plaintiff may recover even if she is unable to identify the manufacturer of the DES consumed by her mother. At the time of the *Sindell* decision, the plaintiff had not established, and could not establish, which of the named defendants had produced the drug ingested by her mother. On April 4, 1980, the plaintiff filed a motion seeking to amend her complaint to include a fifth cause of action, alleging a claim incorporating the theory of recovery propounded by the *Sindell* court. When the motion came on for hearing on April 11, 1980, the court stated that the plaintiff could amend her complaint as requested on the condition that the at-issue memorandum be strickened to enable the defendants to conduct discovery. Recognizing that the five-year statute of limitations would compel dismissal of the action within two months, the plaintiff withdrew her motion to amend the complaint, and proceeded to trial without the advantage of having stated a *Sindell* cause of action. At trial, a verdict was rendered for the defendant manufacturers. The court noted that under the statutory provision in question the plaintiff had a responsibility to have the case tried within the limitations period unless the plaintiff could not have been reasonably expected to bring the action to trial within the limitations period. Here, the court said, under the circumstances present the plaintiff could not have been reasonably expected to amend her complaint at any earlier time. She subsequently filed to amend her complaint within days after the supreme court decision was rendered and before it had become final, the court noted. The magnitude of this decision was such that the granting of her motion should have been considered paramount to the limitations of the statute. Having concluded that the failure of the plaintiff to amend her complaint earlier was due to circumstances beyond her control, the court held that the trial court should have authorized the amendment of the complaint and tolled the provisions of the statute. *Mertan v E R Squibb & Sons, Inc*, 141 CaA3d 511, 190 CaR 349 (1983) [applying CA CODE CIVIL PRACTICE §583, subdivision (b)] op withdrawn by court.

Kensinger v Abbott Laboratories [217 Cal Rptr 313]: DES AND THE STATUTE OF LIMITATIONS, 17 Pac LJ 1531 (1986).

2. [§6.39] Discovery Rule: Date of Accrual

In a DES case the statute of limitations did not accrue until the plaintiff had the opportunity, after making reasonably diligent efforts, to identify the manufacturer of the drug in question, since the identity of the alleged tort feasor was a critical fact or essential element in the cause of action. Thus, the defendant's motion to dismiss was denied. In this case the plaintiff became aware of her alleged injuries and that the generic drug DES was involved in January 1973. Despite diligent efforts, she did not discover until August 1979 which of the several DES manufacturers selling the drug had actually manufactured and sold the drug her mother consumed. The case was subsequently filed on February 8, 1980, within the time period of the statute of limitations. In a products liability case such as this where the critical factor in bringing a DES claim is the identity of the drug manufacturer, and where it is well recognized that such identity is an extremely difficult, if not often impossible task, and where a plaintiff has made reasonable diligent efforts to identify the tort feasor, it cannot be said that all of the elements of the cause of action are present until the identity of the tort feasor is established, the court said. Equitable principals underlie the statutes of limitation. These statutes allow a plaintiff a day in court, but also protect a defendant from having to deal with cases in which the search for truth may be seriously impaired by the loss of evidence, whether by death or disappearance of witnesses, fading memories, disappearance of documents, or otherwise. Delaying the accrual of a personal injury cause of action is an equitable question which compels balancing the plaintiff's right to seek redress for injury incurred against the defendant's reasonable expectation of the duration of its exposure to liability, as well as possible prejudice to the defendant due to delay. Here the balance is in the plaintiff's favor, the court said. *Yustick v Ely Lilly & Co*, 573 FSupp 1558 (ED Mi 1983) [applying MI COMP LAWS ANN §600.5805(9).]

The Massachusetts statute of limitations governing negligence actions provides that tort actions could be brought only within three years after the cause of action accrues. The discovery rule applies to determine when the action accrues. The discovery rule provides that a cause of action does not accrue within the meaning of the statute of limitations until the plaintiff knows or reasonably should have known if he or she has been injured as a result of the conduct of the defendant. The rule requires cognizance of the injury and its cause before the limitation period is deemed to commence running. Implicit is the duty on the plaintiff to exercise reasonable diligence in ascertaining the operative facts and whether the injury is legally compensable. Additionally, under the rule, the plaintiff bears the burden of proving such facts as to take the case outside the impact of the three-year statute of limitation. A cause of action accrues when the plaintiff has knowledge of both the injury and its likely cause or has sufficient facts available so that he or she reasonably should discover the probable causal relationship between the injury and the conduct of the defendant. The plaintiff was diagnosed as suffering from a form of vaginal cancer in July of 1973. At that time, her treating physician informed her parents that the cancer was probably linked to *in utero* exposure to DES. The plaintiff's medical records and doctor's reports prepared between 1973 and 1979 contained references to the causal connection between *in utero* exposure to DES and the plaintiff's vaginal cancer. However, the plaintiff alleged that she did not learn that her mother had taken DES until her mother told her in July of 1980. Before that time, the plaintiff never attempted to determine the cause of her cancer or inspect her medical records. The court denied the defendant's motion for summary judgment based on a bar by the statute of limitations. The court recognized that for statute of limitations purposes, a diagnosis of cancer is quite different from an injury sustained in an automobile accident. The development of cancer will not constitute, in many situations, the happening of an event likely to put the plaintiff on notice of the invasion of legal rights, particularly where the injury suffered by the plaintiff was allegedly caused by a drug ingested by her mother 21 years before the plaintiff learned of her cancer. While it was conceded that the plaintiff could have discovered the cause of her cancer in 1973 by asking her family or doctors or examining her medical records, the crucial question was whether, under all the circumstances, she reasonably should have discovered the cause prior to July of 1980. Resolution of such a question requires a determination of the reasonableness of the plaintiff's conduct and raises genuine factual issues as to when the plaintiff's cause of action accrued within the meaning of the statute. *Errichiello v Eli Lilly & Co*, 618 FSupp 484 (D Ma 1985).

Partial summary judgment was granted in favor of a plaintiff on the limitations issue where in April 1981 the plaintiff was diagnosed as having clear cell adenocarcinoma and the plaintiff filed her lawsuit against the manufacturer in April 1982. The statute in question required that a tort action be brought within two years of the time it occurred, but that it should not be deemed to have accrued until the act giving rise to the cause of action first caused substantial injury, or, if the fact of injury was not reasonably ascertainable until sometime after the initial act, then the period of limitation should not commence until the act of injury became reasonably ascertainable to the injured party, but in no event should the period be extended more than 10 years beyond the time of the act giving rise to the cause of action. The manufacturer had argued that its allegedly wrongful conduct, selling DES without adequately testing it for harmful effects, occurred more than 30 years ago and that the statutory extension of limitation period when the fact of injury is not reasonably ascertainable was rendered inoperative by the final 10 year cutoff clause of the statute. The court said the validity of this premise was doubtful. If the statute was construed as the manufacturer argued, the court said, it would be grossly unfair, even irrational, since it would give a blamelessly ignorant plaintiff 10 years to discover an injury that is immediate, but only two years to discover an injury that comes into existence long after its cause. Therefore, the court rejected this argument. In addition, the manufacturer had argued that the plaintiff suffered substantial injury for purposes of the lawsuit no later than in 1979 when she underwent a hysterectomy. The court said it was willing to grant that the plaintiff's 1979 pain, in the abstract, might be deemed substantial injury. However, the court noted that the plaintiff was not suing for those old injuries, but rather that she was suing for her clear cell adenocarcinoma which is an entirely separate and distinct disease. In addition, the court said that the plaintiff had an option to waive tort recovery for her adenosis-related injuries and sue for the more serious carcinoma. The court reasoned, in part, that concern for judicial economy influenced its decision. Upon diagnosis of an initial illness, the injured party may not need or desire judicial relief. Other sources, such as private insurance, may provide adequate recompense for the initial ailment. However, if the person is told that another, more serious disease may manifest itself later on, and that a remedy in court will be barred unless an anticipatory action is filed currently, there will be a powerful incentive to go to court, for the consequences of a wait and see approach to the commencement of the litigation may be too severe to risk. *Colby v E R Squibb & Sons, Inc*, 589 FSupp 714 (D Ks 1984) [applying Ks Stat Ann §60-513(b).]

The date of accrual of a plaintiff's cause of action involving her mother's ingestion of DES which subsequently caused harm to the plaintiff was the date the plaintiff's vaginal cancer was first discovered. *Cavanaugh v Abbott Laboratories*, 496 A2d 154 (Vt 1985).

Table of Cases

A

B

C

D

E

F

G

H

I

J

K

L

M

N

O

P

R

S

T

U

W

Y

Z